Marc J. Wolenik
Damian Sinay

Microsoft® Dynamics CRM 4.0

UNLEASHED

800 East 96th Street, Indianapolis, Indiana 46240 USA

Microsoft® Dynamics CRM Unleashed

ISBN-13: 978-0-672-32970-8
ISBN-10: 0-672-32970-0

Library of Congress Cataloging-in-Publication Data

Wolenik, Marc J.
Microsoft Dynamics CRM unleashed / Marc J. Wolenik, Damian Sinay.
p. cm.
ISBN 0-672-32970-0
1. Customer relations—Management—Computer programs. 2. Management information systems. I. Sinay, Damian. II. Title.
HF5415.5.W635 2008
658.8'12028553—dc22

2008005518

Printed in the United States of America

Third Printing: June 2009

Trademarks

Warning and Disclaimer

Bulk Sales

Sams Publishing offers excellent discounts on this book when ordered in quantity for bulk purchases or special sales. For more information, please contact

U.S. Corporate and Government Sales
1-800-382-3419
corpsales@pearsontechgroup.com

For sales outside the United States, please contact

International Sales
international@pearsoned.com

Associate Publisher
Greg Wiegand

Acquisitions Editor
Loretta Yates

Development Editor
Kevin Howard

Technical Editor
John Straumann

Managing Editor
Gina Kanouse

Project Editor
Anne Goebel

Copy Editor
Krista Hansing Editorial Services, Inc.

Indexer
Erika Millen

Proofreader
San Dee Phillips

Publishing Coordinator
Cindy Teeters

Book Designer
Gary Adair

Compositor
Nonie Ratcliff

This Book Is Safari Enabled

Contents at a Glance

Table of Contents

About the Authors

Marc J. Wolenik, MCP, PMP, and MBS CRM certified professional, is the founder and CEO of Webfortis, a consulting company based in northern California. Webfortis specializes in solutions around Dynamics CRM and is a Microsoft Gold Certified Partner. His relationship with Microsoft gives him advance information about the changes coming in the new version of the product, and his experience with customers gives him insight into what sort of questions and problems new users of Dynamics CRM customarily face. He has extensive experience with CRM implementation, integration, and migration for companies of all sizes and is heavily involved in vertical solutions around the Dynamics platform. Marc can be reached at marc@webfortis.com.

Damian Sinay, MCP, MCSD, MCAD for .NET, MCTS in SQL Server 2005, and MBS CRM certified professional, is a partner of Webfortis, a Microsoft Gold Certified Partner consulting company in northern California. Damian is currently the development manager and a senior .NET developer. He has extensive experience working with all related technologies that make up Dynamics CRM, having worked on projects involving extremely complex customizations, integrations, and implementations for Dynamics CRM customers.

Acknowledgments

I'd like to personally thank the CRM project team at Microsoft (Menno, Mark, Stefan, and John, to name a few). They provided valuable help and resources, and continually impress me with their professionalism and dedication. Additionally, I'd be remiss without acknowledging both Nicole and Adam, as without their support, the long nights and early mornings would not have been possible.

—Marc

I want to especially thank Marc for all the patience he had and for his help while working on the book, as well as to the entire Webfortis development team for all their effort on our projects. Finally, I want to dedicate this book to my life partner, Paula, who first introduced me to writing, something that, without her influence, I would never have thought about pursuing.

—Damian

We Want to Hear from You!

As the reader of this book, *you* are our most important critic and commentator. We value your opinion and want to know what we're doing right, what we could do better, what areas you'd like to see us publish in, and any other words of wisdom you're willing to pass our way.

As an associate publisher for Sams, I welcome your comments. You can email or write me directly to let me know what you did or didn't like about this book—as well as what we can do to make our books better.

Please note that I cannot help you with technical problems related to the topic of this book. We do have a User Services group, however, where I will forward specific technical questions related to the book.

When you write, please be sure to include this book's title and authors, as well as your name, email address, and phone number. I will carefully review your comments and share them with the authors and editors who worked on the book.

Email: feedback@samspublishing.com

Mail: Greg Wiegand
Associate Publisher
Sams Publishing
800 East 96th Street
Indianapolis, IN 46240 USA

Reader Services

Visit our website and register this book at informit.com/title/9780672329708 for convenient access to any updates, downloads, or errata that might be available for this book.

Introduction

When Microsoft Business Solutions (MBS) released Customer Relationship Management (CRM) Version 1.0 in early 2003, it was the start of something big.

Today the MBS division has been renamed to Dynamics and features some of the most robust applications in the Microsoft arsenal.

In addition to CRM, the Dynamics division has acquired a rich set of offerings and now includes Axapta (AX), Great Plains (GP), Navision (NAV), and Solomon (SL), as well as several other business-management and enterprise resource planning (ERP) solutions.

Utilizing the unifying force of Microsoft has enabled these previously disparate applications to work together and empower users and organizations of all sizes.

As a result of this consolidation, Microsoft Dynamics CRM has definitely improved, and its current form leaves its predecessors in the dust. With its vastly improved performance, architecture, and multitenancy capabilities, Microsoft Dynamics CRM delivers on the promise from Microsoft to "work the way you do."

Microsoft Dynamics CRM leverages several Microsoft technologies:

- Windows Server/Small Business Server (SBS)
- SQL Server
- SQL Server Reporting Services (SSRS)
- Exchange (optionally)
- Internet Information System (IIS)
- Outlook
- Internet Explorer
- .NET Framework 2.0 and 3.0

Therefore, Microsoft Dynamics CRM is not actually one application, like Microsoft Excel or Microsoft Word. Rather, it is the integration of some or all of these applications into a business solution that delivers a powerful product that is fully customizable, extensible, scalable, and simple to use and administer.

Microsoft Dynamics CRM is available in three options:

- CRM Online
- On Premise
- Partner Hosted

CRM Live was changed to CRM Online in Q2 of 2008 While some of the material in this book references the original version of CRM Online (i.e. CRM Live), it should still be applicabl.

Chapter 3, "The Evolution of Microsoft Dynamics CRM 4.0," explains these options in greater detail, but for now, CRM Online is the Microsoft SaaS service; On Premise is when your organization owns Microsoft Dynamics CRM in-house; and Partner Hosted is the use of Microsoft Dynamics CRM in the same SaaS model as CRM Online, but with different options (per partner) for security, access, and other integrated solutions.

In this book, we show you how to get the most from your CRM system. We will delve into how Microsoft Dynamics CRM works, explain why you should set up certain features, and explore advanced configuration and customization options.

Microsoft Dynamics CRM has the potential to change how you work. Let us show you how.

CHAPTER 1

New Features of Microsoft Dynamics CRM

IN THIS CHAPTER

- Interface
- Lookup and Smart Find
- Report Wizard
- Multitenancy
- Multilanguage
- Multicurrency
- Resource Center
- E-mail Smart Tracking
- E-mail Routing
- MRU
- Exporting
- CRM Clients
- Mail Merge
- Data Migration
- Duplicate Detection
- Relationships
- Programming
- CRM Online
- Bulk Record Deletion
- Workflow

If you have picked up this book for the first time and are wondering what might be new or so great about Microsoft Dynamics CRM 4.0, this chapter is for you. Even if you are very familiar with Microsoft CRM 3.0, this chapter highlights many of the new features that come out of the box with Microsoft Dynamics CRM 4.0.

If you have never worked with Microsoft Dynamics CRM or any CRM before, you may want to skip this chapter as it touches on many improvements made to the previous version of Microsoft CRM.

Several of these features are detailed further in separate chapters throughout the book, but we figured it might make sense to consolidate the information here for easy reference.

Interface

The Microsoft Dynamics CRM interface has been redesigned to include a more modern look and feel. It also includes the Microsoft Dynamics CRM Jewel Button in the upper-left corner common to Microsoft Office 2007, which is useful when working within Microsoft Dynamics CRM (see Figure 1.1).

The Business Required and Business Recommended fields no longer appear in blue or red text; instead, Business Required fields have a red asterisk notation next to them (see the `Last Name` field in Figure 1.1), and Business Recommended fields have a blue plus next to them (see the `First Name` field in Figure 1.1).

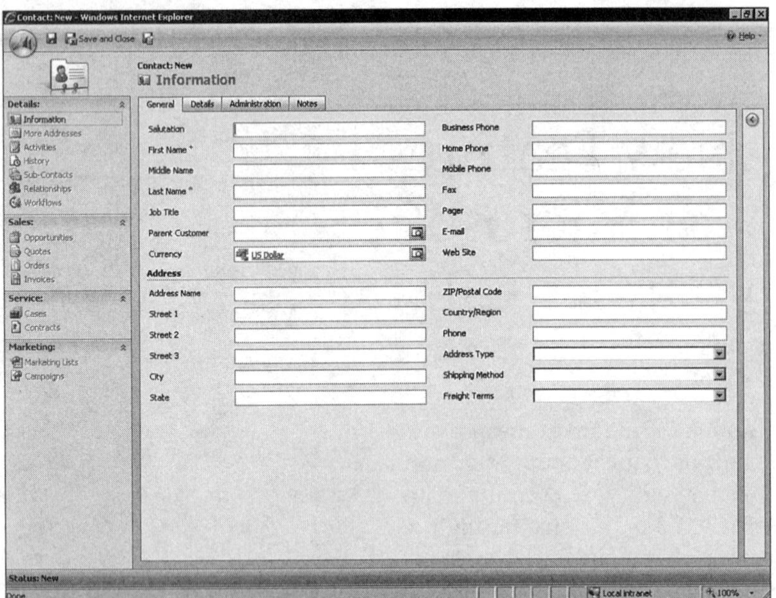

FIGURE 1.1 New Contact form in Microsoft Dynamics CRM 4.0.

Additionally, in a fashion similar to "link to e-mail," you now have the option to copy the location of the page (or record) and send it to other users via e-mail. This allows users to click on the link and be taken directly to the area that they are referring (assuming, of course, that they have the necessary permissions). You can perform this action either by right-clicking the page or record and selecting either Copy Shortcut or Send Shortcut, or by selecting the same options from the More Actions drop-down menu (see Figure 1.2).

Refer to the section "Actions" in Chapter 7, "Common Functions," for more information about this feature.

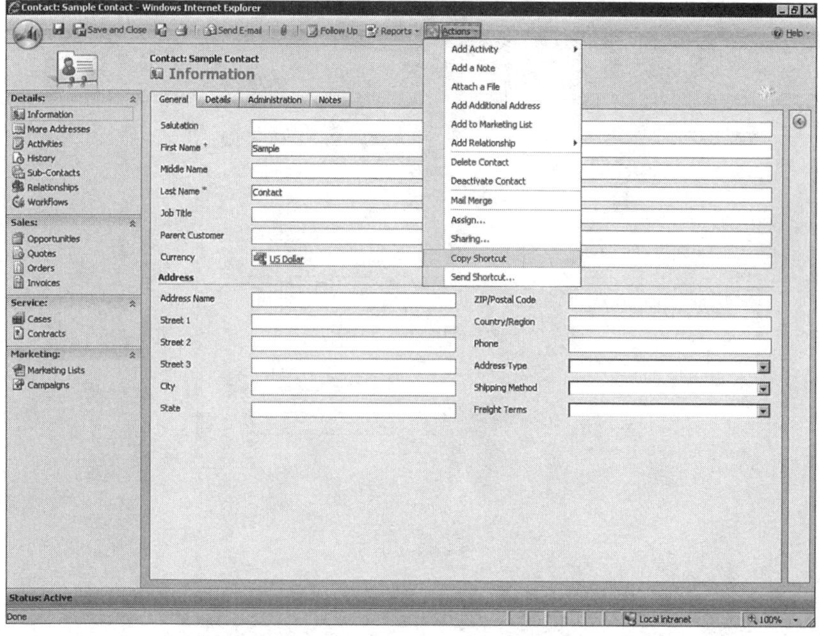

FIGURE 1.2 Copy Shortcut from the Contacts form in Microsoft Dynamics CRM 4.0.

Lookup and Smart Find

Lookup fields retain their functionality and have a new feature: You can now enter and edit text directly in the lookup field cells (see the `Parent Customer` field in Figure 1.4).

After you enter your partial information, you can press Ctrl+K to have the system attempt to perform a match on the entered data. Alternatively, when you lose focus of that field (that is, when you go to another field), the system automatically attempts to reconcile what was entered. If the system finds a match, it shows this with blue underlined text; red underlining with an x indicates no match (see Figure 1.3). If the system finds a partial match, you have the option to select a value as a drop-down list of all the matches appears, allowing you to quickly and easily select the appropriate value that matches any partial entry (see Figure 1.4).

NOTE

Smart Find is on by default; however, it can be turned off on a field level basis by setting the required value on Field Properties by selecting "Turn off automatic resolution" within the form customization properties.

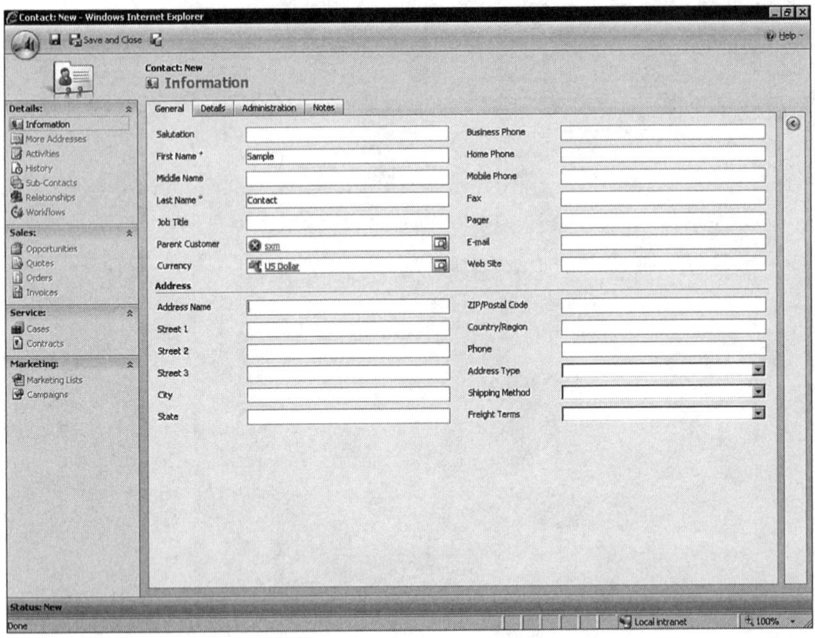

FIGURE 1.3 Partial entry in `Parent Customer` of the `New Contact` form.

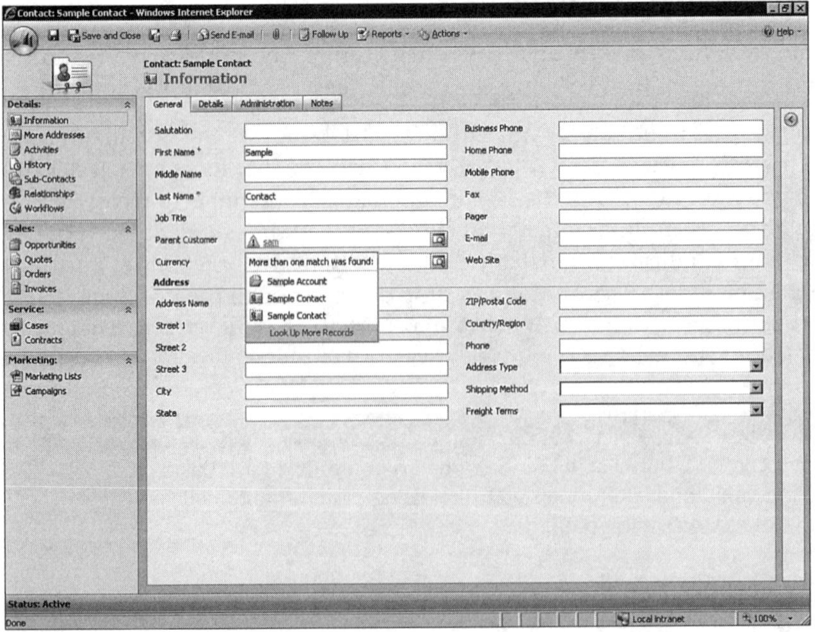

FIGURE 1.4 Smart Find in the `Parent Customer` field of the New Contact form.

Report Wizard

The Report Wizard is an extremely powerful addition that helps users create reports quickly and easily in a format you can easily use. New to Microsoft Dynamics CRM, the reports are not just advanced find queries, but actual reports in SQL Server Reporting Services Report Definition Language (RDL) format.

This feature previously required either installation of a third-party component or extensive knowledge of Visual Studio to design and build the reports.

Refer to Chapter 13, "Reporting," for more information about the Report Wizard.

Multitenancy

One of the most sought-after features in Microsoft CRM is the capability to house more than one organization. In previous versions, each organization required a dedicated server. With Microsoft Dynamics CRM, multiple organizations can reside on a single installation. This provides vast benefits to Service Provider (SP) companies that need to host multiple organizations. Additionally, with this option, organizations can derive huge benefits in the architecture due to the insular nature of organizations within Microsoft Dynamics CRM, as Business Units might be insufficient for their needs.

Chapter 17, "Forms Authentication," further explains the new features of multitenancy.

Multilanguage

Microsoft Dynamics is expected to have more than 22 languages at or shortly after its final ship date. The language offerings are available via Multilingual User Interface (MUI) Packs that the administrator can install and set up. When implemented, the application displays the language the Microsoft Dynamics CRM user has selected, and can be specific to the user. (See Chapter 14, "Settings and Configuration," for help installing the MUI Packs).

NOTE

The MUI Packs must be installed separately, and the application interface displays the **users** selected language. It is important to note that the displayed language is based not on the users' computer language setting or browser setting, but on their Microsoft Dynamics CRM language settings.

To select a different language, select Tools, Options from the drop-down list. The last tab on the options page is Languages. From there, you can see the languages that the administrator has installed and made available. Although you can select different languages for the user interface language and the help language, when you select the user interface language, the help language defaults to your selection. Additionally, you cannot change the base language. Note that if a selected language cannot make a translation, it falls back to the base language which is set at the time of installation. Figure 1.5 displays the user interface with German selected.

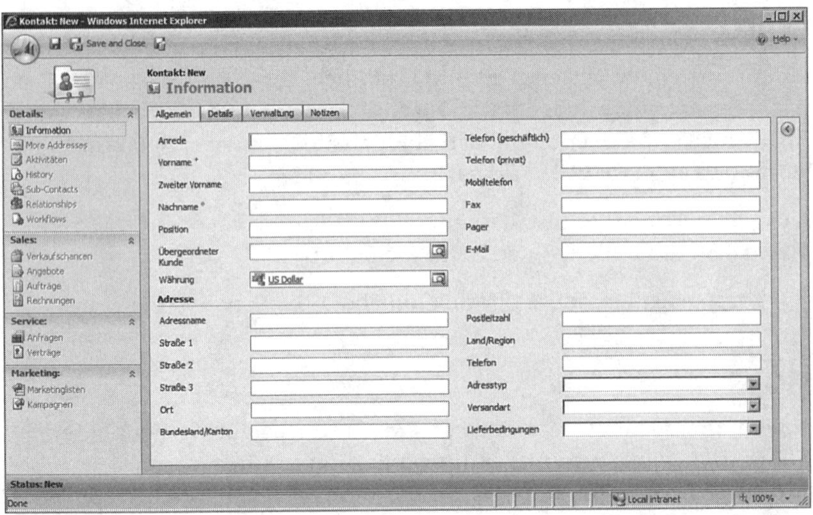

FIGURE 1.5 German Language Contact user interface selected.

NOTE

Unlike the user interface labels, the base data is not translated—regardless of the language selected.

The Multilanguage feature has native support for right-to-left languages and automatically switches the left navigation (or the near navigation) to the right side when a right-to-left language is installed, such as Arabic or Hebrew.

Multicurrency

Multicurrency is now completely supported in Microsoft Dynamics CRM. You can select different default base currencies for Entities, and you can select different currencies easily and manage their exchange rates, as long as an administrator has added them and set them as Active (see Chapter 14 to do this). Otherwise, you're limited to whatever currencies are available (if any are available, other than the base).

TIP

Unfortunately, the exchange rate system in Microsoft Dynamics CRM is static and, once set, must be manually adjusted. (See Chapter 14 for examples on how to update the exchange rate.) However, you can easily change this so it's updated automatically via a Web Service. (See Chapter 22, "Web Services," for examples on how to work with Microsoft Dynamics CRM Web Services.)

NOTE

When the base currency for an organization is set, it is fixed and cannot be changed. If you need to change the base currency, you must set up Microsoft Dynamics CRM again.

Resource Center

In addition to online help (which is still available on most pages by selecting Help from the upper-right corner of the application), the Resource Center can be used to display information about new or advanced features, as well as display resource communities for Microsoft Dynamics CRM and related information. By default, the Resource Center points to Microsoft; however, you can change it to display information from any source, such as an internal website. For more information about working with the Resource Center, refer to Chapter 7.

TIP

If your organization does not need the Resource Center, you can remove this button and/or interface entirely.

E-mail Smart Tracking

Unlike previous versions of Microsoft Dynamics CRM, a tracking token is no longer required to be inserted into the e-mail message subject line. Instead, a complex proprietary matching technique is employed that looks at the `From`, `To`, `Subject`, and `CC` fields in the e-mail to match and record in Microsoft Dynamics CRM.

NOTE

The tracking token is optional, but you can still use it if you'd like.

Because of the matching technique described earlier, it is possible to not have 100% tracking. This is because of a variety of reasons, such as users changing the `Subject` or forwarding the e-mail. If this is a concern to your organization, you might want to turn on the tracking token. Refer to Chapter 14 for more information about working with e-mail settings and the tracking token.

E-mail Routing

Although support exists for both Exchange 2003 and Exchange 2007, Exchange is no longer required to route e-mail. Instead, e-mail can be routed using any of the following:

- Exchange
- Post Office Protocol 3 (POP3)

- Simple Mail Transport Protocol (SMTP)
- Outlook
- Forward mailboxes

Refer to Chapter 4, "Requirements for CRM 4.0," for more information about the e-mail requirements, and Chapter 15, "E-mail Configuration," for more information about setting up and/or using any of the e-mail options previously described.

MRU

Most Recent Used (MRU) lists are now an integrated part of Microsoft Dynamics CRM. When setting Regarding (for an e-mail) or Set Parent (for a Contact) in Outlook, the most recently used items applicable (up to seven) are displayed.

Additionally, the five most commonly used are displayed, which provides for quick and easy reference when tracking items in Microsoft Dynamics CRM.

Exporting

When exporting records from Microsoft Dynamics CRM into Microsoft Excel, users have the option to create Dynamic PivotTables and worksheets (see Figure 1.6). Additionally, a new feature is the capability to roll back (delete) a set of imported records easily.

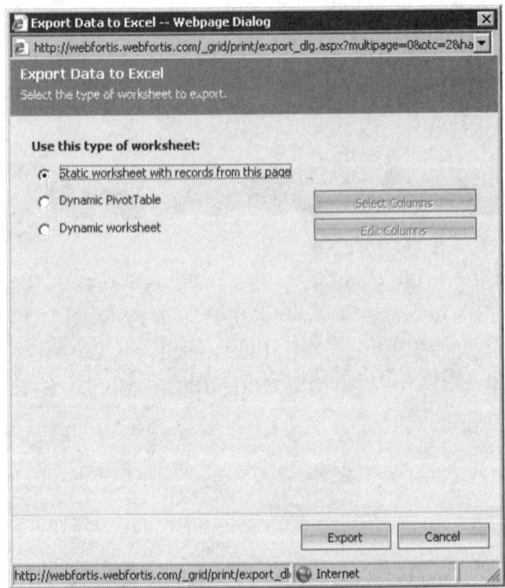

FIGURE 1.6 Exporting records.

CRM Clients

The user experience has been greatly improved to provide for a more robust and quicker experience. Additionally, offline SDK support for the laptop client provides for a much richer environment for development options. (Previous versions of Microsoft Dynamics CRM did not support certain customizations when using the Offline Outlook client.)

Furthermore, the Outlook client now has all the features that were previously available only in the Internet Explorer client. This includes all the Microsoft Dynamics CRM Settings options, providing a dramatically improved setup, better performance, and richer feature set.

Some of the new features found in the Outlook client that did not previously exist include:

- Tasks, appointments, faxes, phone calls, letters, and Contacts are now synchronized. (Previous versions did not support phone calls, faxes, or letter synchronization.)
- Synchronization can be performed without going offline, and a background synchronization process does partial synchronization all the time, speeding synchronization as it is already partially done.
- Mail merge functionality has improved.
- The `Regarding` field now appears in the Microsoft Dynamics CRM pane of the Outlook item.
- Tasks can be closed in Outlook and are then closed in Microsoft Dynamics CRM.
- Items can be easily "untracked" if you decide you don't want them tracked in Microsoft Dynamics CRM.
- Multiple e-mails (up to 20) can be promoted to Microsoft Dynamics CRM at one time.
- As stated in the previous section, smart tracking has replaced the e-mail tracking token.

In addition to all these, Microsoft Dynamics CRM Office client diagnostics have been added with wizards to troubleshoot synchronization problems. The diagnostics run more than 40 tests on the Outlook client to check problems, including system diagnostics, connections, synchronization history, and the URL, to make sure they are correct. If the diagnostics can fix a problem, they will make the fix for you. Additionally, you can turn off different checks if you want to localize issues, and you can add tracing to all the client checks. As a final measure, you can create a support file that includes all system information and environmental variables captured for diagnostics and have it sent to Microsoft or your internal IT department for troubleshooting.

Mail Merge

Mail merge functionality now exists in both Internet Explorer and the Outlook client, and you can create and save Word templates within Microsoft Dynamics CRM.

Data Migration

Data Migration was completely rewritten for Microsoft Dynamics CRM, and the Data Migration Framework (DMF) has been replaced by the Data Migration Manager. Data Migration now supports custom entities and operates in an asynchronous manner, displaying its status as it is working. Errors are displayed quickly and you're able to easily drill down on them to determine the problem.

Refer to Chapter 6, "Data Migration and Conversion," for more information about Data Migration.

Duplicate Detection

Built-in support for duplicate detection now exists. Duplicate detection rules can be set on virtually any attribute of any entity and provide warnings when attempting to create a duplicate value.

Refer to Chapter 20, "Workflow Development," for more information about duplicate detection.

Relationships

Entity relationship (not to be confused with customer relationship) has been significantly improved. Previous versions supported only one-to-many and many-to-one relationships. Many-to-many relationships are now supported as well. This gives the user much more flexibility when working with the application. For example, a user (or Account or Contact, and so on) can be associated with an Account multiple times (as a Tier 1 support manager, a Tier 2 support manager, and so on) and vice-versa, meaning that the account can also be related to more than one contact (a contact who works for more than one company).

Additionally, relationships that are self-referential have been added, which allows entities to relate directly to themselves. This is helpful if you need to reference parent/child relationships and want to reference the parent as the source of children.

Programming

With a new software development kit (SDK) that supports offline customizations, a unified event model, and richer metadata application programming interfaces (APIs), extending functionality of Microsoft Dynamics CRM has become much easier. Additionally, you can now add entities and attributes programmatically through the metadata Web Service. Finally, the deployment of custom workflows and plug-ins can be done through Web services and don't require the CRM server to be restarted.

Refer to Chapters 16–24 for more information about programming with Microsoft CRM.

CRM Online

A completely new model for Microsoft is CRM Online. CRM Online is a hosted service provided by Microsoft that gives full-featured functionality of Microsoft Dynamics CRM to users on a per user, per month basis.

This option provides users with the ability to quickly and easily get up and running with Microsoft Dynamics CRM, with the proven backing of Microsoft as their hosting partner.

Bulk Record Deletion

The ability to quickly and easily delete records via the new Bulk Record Deletion has been added. Migrated data can be easily rolled back when using this tool, allowing for easy testing and cleanup of migrated data.

Workflow

Probably the most powerful feature of Microsoft Dynamics CRM, Workflow programming has been moved from the server as a separated application and integrated directly into the Microsoft Dynamics CRM client. It is based on Windows Workflow Foundation (WWF) that is part of .NET 3.0 and can be developed directly with Visual Studio 2005.

Additionally, Workflow functionality now includes record attributes change events for **any** attribute and the ability to easily add steps and conditions.

Refer to Chapter 20 for more information about working with Workflow.

Summary

We have listed only some of the most important new changes to Microsoft Dynamics CRM in this chapter. Although there are too many to list in one chapter, we have attempted to callout and/or indicate in other chapters where a feature is new or significantly improved from previous versions.

As you can easily see from this chapter, considerable effort has gone into this version of Microsoft Dynamics CRM. From replacing the Data Migration Framework completely, to redesigning the interface to make it easier and faster, Microsoft Dynamics CRM 4.0 has many new features.

CHAPTER 2

Why Businesses Need a CRM System

IN THIS CHAPTER

- Managing Your Business, Customers, and Resources
- People Versus Resource Management
- CRM Versus ERP
- Historical Data and Legal Requirements
- Real-Time/All-the-Time Need for Data
- Lead/Opportunity Management
- Marketing
- Challenges of CRM

As we move beyond a world of data "on-demand" to one where data can provide us with forecasts and complex analysis, our expectations of information that is "necessary" to do business has changed.

No longer can a customer be told to wait while the accounting department searches for previous invoices or orders. Nor can salespeople be expected to schedule appointments without having access to their delivery and/or route schedules. Now we require the capability not only to access data at any time, but also to have advanced insight into what the data means.

Additionally, marketing efforts are more complex than ever. Internet marketing and e-commerce require a high level of technical sophistication as well as the capability to read and trend various efforts. This places a premium on campaigns that are easy to develop, maintain, and track.

Finally, for customer service, departments within the same organization, as well as different representatives within the same department, need to know about contact history. Who hasn't called a company for a service-related issue, when the call accidentally dropped, only to call back and have a different representative resume where the call left off. Your representative better know the contact history in real time, because customers can easily note the difference between companies that solve problems using a CRM system as described and those that don't. Customers might not know whether a company is using a CRM system, but they do know about quality of service received.

Businesses need a CRM system to handle all of these things without having to go to different places and involve different departments. The goal of any CRM should be to quickly, easily, and efficiently manage communication with your customers (whether they're current, future, or past customers), employees, and business partners. This includes historical communication, trending data, and associative information.

Managing Your Business, Customers, and Resources

As communication between you and your customers increases, the mechanisms for retrieving the history of communications needs to be more powerful and, at the same time, easier to use. The business model of a dedicated sales representative handling all contact with customers is no longer valid. Regulatory, contractual, and other legal issues, are also reasons why communication needs to be tracked. As such, most companies need a centralized form of communication management.

Communication also has many different aspects and usually includes some form of the following:

- Phone calls
- Faxes
- E-mails
- Regular mail (letters)
- Meetings and/or appointments

Without a centralized management system such as a CRM, companies have no way to track and record all these different forms of communication. Instead, the items are completed and recorded in different systems (calendaring for meetings, outbox for e-mail, photocopy/saved document for a letter, and so on) or, worse, hopefully remembered when needed.

Additionally, internal resource management and visibility is more important than ever. With most business, labor division is divided into logic groups (see Figure 2.1), and management needs the ability to control and report on each division.

Finally, very few, if any, businesses today don't have either a website or e-mail. Certainly, if you're reading this book, it is assumed that you do. Because you send e-mail, you need a mechanism for tracking sent e-mail. Reviewing the sent items in any e-mail programs is a great way to do so. By sorting on the `To` field in the Sent folder, you can see the entire e-mail communication history for each person. However, as we discuss more in the next chapter on Business Contact Manager (BCM), this method involves several limitations. For example, imagine that we have a business contract with a large company (Company XYZ) and that we want to view all e-mail correspondence related to every contact we've had with that company. We would need to know each person and then search within our sent items for each person. It would be great if we could just create an Account named Company XYZ and have all e-mail correspondence for each contact roll up to the company level of Company XYZ automatically. That way, when we needed to check for anything sent to that company, we would see every piece of e-mail sent to every individual who is in some way related to that company. A CRM solution offers this type of ready rollup.

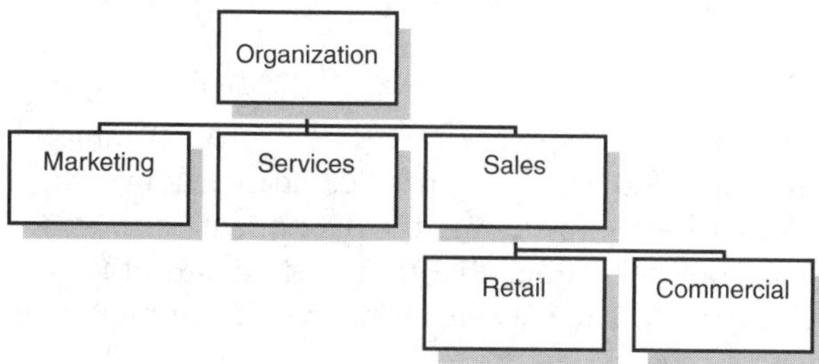

FIGURE 2.1 Business divisions.

People Versus Resource Management

Managing centralized schedules is one thing, but the capability to also manage the resources necessary for those schedules ties into a business's capability to be ready on all fronts.

A good example of this is an automotive repair shop. The shop needs to have people on hand who not only know how to do the repair, but who also are available to do the repair (and are not working on another repair at the same time). Compound that with the fact that the shop has only three service bays in which to perform the repairs, and this creates a need for a management tool to ensure the following:

- When a customer makes an appointment, you have the resources necessary to complete the job.
- The people with the required skills are available to perform them at the time you want to schedule the job.
- The shop has available room to perform the work.

You can easily see how having all this information in one place and in an easy-to-use manner would facilitate effective management.

Not every CRM system has these capabilities, but they should be required of every CRM solution, and Microsoft Dynamics CRM delivers this from its Service Scheduling interface.

CRM Versus ERP

Whereas an enterprise resource planning (ERP) system may be able to function as a CRM system, a CRM cannot likely function as an ERP system.

Some non-Microsoft ERP systems on the market today include these:

- SAP
- PeopleSoft
- Oracle

The goal of a true ERP system is to unify most or all aspects of a business into a common backbone system. Obviously, at the core of any ERP is a centralized database from which all data is derived. However, several different ways of accessing the data might exist, and users might be using different systems and/or applications that ultimately tie into the main system (and might not even be aware of it). The reasons for having this unified system are apparent enough, but some downsides do exist:

- **One system and, thus, one way of doing business**—The ERP requires data to be processed and entered (or saved) in the prescribed format. Deviation requires complex customizations and/or business process changes.
- **Cost**—The sheer cost of licensing, integration, and customization associated with an ERP makes it prohibitive except for the largest organizations.
- **Too many options**—In an attempt to be everything to everybody, an ERP might have a huge number of features that make it cumbersome to use.
- **Incapability to quickly adapt to new processes and procedures**—In conjunction with the first point, it is crucial to be able to quickly incorporate new ideas and/or processes that might have positive effects on a company's sales, growth, or revenue.

  Incorporating streamlined processes into a sales process or developing a new interface that enables customers to access their sales history in ways they couldn't do before requires rework that might takes weeks or months and that might not be budgeted for.

When considering a CRM system versus an ERP system, it is important to recognize the above points as well as consider the fact that while a CRM can do a lot of things, at its core, it is designed to manage customer relations. It is for this reason that this book will address everything that Microsoft Dynamics CRM does but will not address things that it may not do. An example of this might be maintaining a General Ledger or Chart of Accounts (functions of an accounting system). Another thing to consider is the CRM functionality that might be promised, or built into another system. Our experience has led us to believe that systems that promise CRM type functionality tend to include only minimal CRM functionality, and much of it appears as an afterthought. In the last chapter of this book (Chapter 27, "Other Microsoft Dynamics Products"), we discuss a few of the other ERP systems in the Microsoft Dynamics family and their relationship to CRM.

Historical Data and Legal Requirements

Records management involves a complex and varying set of requirements, depending on your business industry, degree of secrecy, and audit requirements. Because business is done by e-mail these days, there are many reasons to maintain complete and full business records.

Although every business undoubtedly has differing requirements, a good example of this is current requirements in place for financial services firms. Rules such as the National Assoication of Securities Dealers (NASD) Conduct Rule 3010/3110 require that financial security firms establish written procedures for the review of incoming and outgoing written and electronic correspondence (e-mail). Additionally, they must be able to produce evidence of implementation and execution of these procedures or risk sanctions and possibly more severe punitive actions.

Although the implementation of a CRM system may not address every requirement that exists, it can certainly be expected to be a valuable resource to that end.

Real-Time/All-the-Time Need for Data

Businesses need access to data without having to wait. Salespeople need to be able to quickly tell prospective clients about material costs and delivery dates associated with an order. Instead of saying, "I'll send that to you in an e-mail when I have it all together," salespeople need to be able to say, "I'll have that in just a minute." Otherwise, clients will have already called a competitor, who likely will be able to tell them what they want to know while on the phone.

The ability to empower salespeople with trending and forecasting based on their customers' previous transactions is no longer an optional or nice-to-have consideration. It is required, and businesses that fail to anticipate the demands of their current and future clients risk falling behind to their competitors who are able to outsell, based on knowing what their customers will want and providing it to them now.

Additional requirements include the ability for clients to self-manage or the ability to provide customers with answers without having to contact your organization. A perfect example of this is a rich and thorough knowledge base that is exposed to the public for searching that they can use to resolve their problems without having to contact you. Additional tools frequently delivered to clients include sales history, trouble-ticket generation, and management, as well as dynamic real-time order processing.

When implementing a CRM solution, it is important to consider how the proposed system will address all of these needs and demands.

Lead/Opportunity Management

A typical sales process involves creating Leads (potential customers), converting Leads to Opportunities (sales opportunities), and, finally, making a sale.

As anyone in the business world knows, Leads have a delicate nature and a finite life span. We want to encourage their growth and conversion, while not taking them for granted. Thus, we want to be able to tailor marketing material specifically to the Leads or prospective customers and, at the same time, be sure they don't receive either information that they aren't entitled to or products that they aren't interested in.

For this reason, we generally don't want to mix Leads and Opportunities with other customers. We do, however, want to establish them within the CRM system for easy conversion, contact history, and management by other individuals or groups within the organization.

Opportunities are generally related to existing customers. Because it is usually much easier to sell a new service to existing customers than to a new Lead, knowing your current customers' needs (and sales history) will make it easier to improve sales of new services.

It is important, then, for these reasons that Leads are segregated and considered as separate when thinking about a CRM system.

Marketing

One of the most requested features of any CRM is marketing capabilities. Marketing is the component that is most closely tied with Lead and Opportunity generation and conversion, as well as selling new or enhanced services to existing customers. When you think about working with your CRM, marketing should be an area that ties to all other aspects.

It is also important to consider marketing as not just a sales tool. Although the goal of most companies is to sell products and services, not every marketing effort is directly related to that end. Consider company sponsorship at various events, as well as e-mails, to customers announcing the addition of a new VP of Development and/or offices at a company. The sponsorship and announcement e-mails are not made to influence direct sales; however, they should be considered marketing, as their goal is to make your organization better known, seen as more responsible, or as having better or necessary resources to better service customers.

Of course, when it comes to sales, marketing efforts should also be quantifiable and allow for easy exposure as to the effectiveness of the marketing effort. Consider the idea of creating a spring sale event whose goal is to clear winter inventory from your shelves. With a proper marketing effort, you would be able to specifically target customers who have a strong buying indication for such a sale (because they responded to previous marketing efforts, for example). Alternatively, you might want to tailor your marketing specifically to customers whose previous buying patterns do *not* indicate that they would participate in such an event, by offering them a strong incentive to do so (something you wouldn't have to offer for the first group of people).

The final piece should be the ability to see what marketing has been done and to which customers. It would be just as irresponsible to send marketing material to customers who have specifically requested not to receive any, as it would be to not reach out to regular customers that haven't done business in the last 60 days.

Challenges of CRM

The biggest challenge of any CRM system is user adoption. Without adequate adoption of the system, usage will be minimal and data will not be reliable. As part of that challenge, three other challenges arise:

- Business challenge
- Management challenge
- IT challenge

The business challenge is successful user adoption of the system. This includes users accepting the system as a core business application that all members of the organization can rely on for reliable data. Strong user adoption is usually brought on by ease of use, training, and management support.

It is not enough to just issue a new business policy from management that requires using CRM as part of a business process. Instead, management needs to fully support its use. To do this, management should ensure that necessary work is done both before and after implementation to support necessary business processes, customizations, and other requirements that make adoption easier. Management also needs to *use* the CRM system, to be aware of how users are using the data and making contact with customers.

Some of the issues associated with the IT challenge that should be addressed involve the architecture of the system (including scalability and fault tolerance), the extensibility of the system, and the availability of both tools and people with the skills to support a system. User adoption in Microsoft Dynamics CRM is easy because users can use it within the Outlook client, an application familiar to most users, so the learning curve is short.

Summary

As you can see, a customer relationship management system is more than just a buzzword. It is a powerful tool that, when used correctly, can propel and facilitate relationships among businesses, employees, and customers.

There is a lot to consider when evaluating CRM systems and functionality; however, it is readily apparent that businesses that fail to provide themselves, their staff, and their customers with the tools that a CRM system provides will have a much more difficult time providing the level of service that customers are growing to expect.

CHAPTER 3

The Evolution of Microsoft Dynamics CRM 4.0

IN THIS CHAPTER

- BCM
- Version 1.0
- Version 1.2
- Version 3.0
- Current (4.0)
- What Dynamics Means to Microsoft

That Microsoft Dynamics CRM is arguably one of the easiest-to-use CRM applications on the market should come as no surprise to anyone. Combined with the need for most businesses to have a CRM solution and the market dominance of Windows (and, specifically, Outlook), this gives Microsoft a significant edge on integration and ease of use.

Although Microsoft Dynamics CRM is designed around Outlook, initial versions suffered problems with installation and compatibility/functionality. Thus, the road to Microsoft Dynamics CRM 4.0 was not without some difficulties.

This chapter explains the history of Microsoft Dynamics CRM 4.0 and offers an insight into Microsoft's goals with CRM. Additionally, for users considering Microsoft Dynamics CRM 4.0 who might be using a previous version of Microsoft CRM or Microsoft Business Contact Manager, this chapter provides reasons as to the benefits of upgrading to Microsoft Dynamics CRM 4.0.

BCM

Microsoft introduced Business Contact Manager (BCM) with Office 2003 as a tool for the small business owner to manage contacts and accounts in ways similar to a full-blown CRM system.

BCM shares many similar features with CRM. As you can see from Figure 3.1, BCM offers the capability to track accounts and contacts, as well as the capability to manage opportunities and to create and manage product and service item lists.

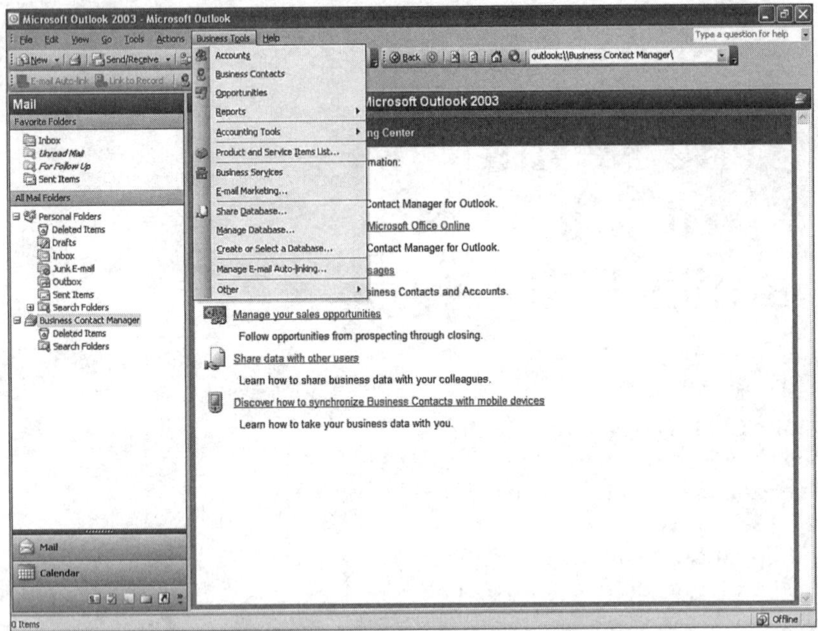

FIGURE 3.1 Business Contact Manager.

However, the area where BCM really comes up short is its inability to integrate Workflow for the automation of routine and/or necessary tasks.

Some other weaknesses of BCM include these:

- Outlook is required. BCM is considered an Outlook plug-in, so if you're interested in just the BCM components, or if you have objections to working with Outlook, you're out of luck. (While Microsoft Dynamics CRM 4.0 is also an Outlook plug-in, it *also* is available [with full functionality] via the Internet Explorer client.)
- No Remote Access is enabled. This is a problem if you need ready access to your BCM data via your web-enabled e-mail interface (such as Outlook Web Access).
- Data mining is limited. It lacks many of the easy-to-use "find" features in Microsoft Dynamics CRM 4.0 that give users information on demand.

Note, however, that our goal is not to sell BCM short in this context. Many businesses start with BCM and migrate to Dynamics CRM as their needs increase. However, BCM clearly lacks the capability to extend full-featured CRM functionality across an entire organization.

Refer to Chapter 6, "Data Migration and Conversion," for more information related to BCM and migration to CRM from BCM.

Version 1.0

In early 2003, Microsoft Business Solutions CRM hit the U.S. market. Its market adoption was not significant (certainly when compared with other products in the Microsoft product line) because it was cumbersome to use and set up, had technical problems and limitations, and required customizations for almost every installation. Additionally, although it integrated with Outlook, it did not perform as expected.

Version 1.1 was slated for release later in 2003 with more international language support (Version 1.0 was released with English only), but it was upgraded and re-released as Version 1.2.

Version 1.2

By the end of 2003, Microsoft Business Solutions released the next version of CRM, Version 1.2. It increased its language offerings (up to nine, including International English, U.S. English, French, Italian, German, Danish, Dutch, Spanish, and Brazilian Portuguese), and it offered a number of service and product enhancements, including a somewhat easier setup and more reporting options.

Unfortunately, even with the changes, it suffered from usage and setup problems that made it less than ideal from a user and system administrator's perspective. Microsoft realized that it needed to step up development efforts on the CRM platform for its next release and devoted many more resources toward the next version.

Version 3.0

Version 2.0 was originally slated for the first quarter of 2004. However, an overhaul of the reporting engine (it was moved from Crystal Enterprise to SQL Server Reporting Services [SRS]) and a major user interface redesign allowed Microsoft to skip directly to Version 3.0 in mid-2005. Additional offerings included support for 23 languages and a more intuitive setup process.

To address the continued problematic setup with CRM, Version 3.0 included a better version of an environmental diagnostics wizard, which did a "precheck" of most of the required settings and systems, alerting the user about problems before the system continued. (Previous versions of the diagnostic wizard overlooked several key issues, resulting in failed and/or aborted installations.)

Microsoft Service Providers (MSPs) began to offer CRM 3.0 as a service shortly after its release as service providers could license it on a monthly basis. However, because of the way Microsoft CRM 3.0 works with organizations and Active Directory, this option required a dedicated server instance for each version of CRM. As a result, the monthly price associated with Microsoft CRM for even a few users was high.

In late 2005, Microsoft released SQL Server 2005, which was of great benefit to Microsoft CRM primarily because of the enhancements it brought to reporting services. Users with SQL Server 2005 could now leverage a SQL Server Reporting Services (SRS) application that was substantially easier to set up, configure, and maintain. In addition, they enjoyed the benefits of SQL Server 2005 (greater scaling, sizing, and administration).

At about the same time, the Microsoft Business Solutions division was undergoing the rename to Dynamics, and the new release (combined with its suite of other enterprise accounting packages) allowed Microsoft to showcase all Dynamics offerings under one division.

By the fourth quarter of 2007, Microsoft Dynamics CRM 3.0 was readily accepted by users and companies with more than 500,000 users. There were many add-ons and tools for download/purchase to extend its functionality, and there are many forums, blogs, and newsgroups related to the product that make for helpful deployment, troubleshooting, and extending functionality.

Current (4.0)

When Microsoft announced the release of Microsoft Dynamics CRM 4.0 in January 2008, it promised customers the "power of choice." Microsoft has delivered on that promise by providing a host of new services and features to Microsoft CRM 4.0.

Although some of the new features of Microsoft Dynamics CRM are outlined in Chapter 1, "New Features of Microsoft Dynamics CRM," the following represent some of the core improvements:

- **Multitenancy**—Multiple organizations can exist within a single CRM implementation.
- **Report Creation Wizard**—Unlike previous versions of CRM that required use of Visual Studio to build and manage reports, you can design, create, and deploy reports from within the CRM system via the Report Creation Wizard.
- **Different server roles**—From a scaling standpoint, the capability to have different servers performing different functions results in dramatically higher performance. The different roles are listed here:
    - **Application server role**—Provides Microsoft CRM 4.0 web user interface and services.
    - **Platform server role**—Provides services such as the Workflow and Bulk E-mail services (asynchronous services) to separate computers.
    - **Specific server roles**—Individual services such as HelpServer or WebService can be deployed individually or grouped on one or multiple servers to increase performance. (See Chapter 5, "Setting Up CRM 4.0," for more information related to server roles.)
- **Microsoft Dynamics CRM 4.0 Connector for SQL SRS**—This resolves a common authentication problem when trying to access and run reports in previous versions of Microsoft CRM, referred to as "the Kerberos double-hop authentication issue."
- **Multilingual User Interface (MUI)**—MUI Packs let users display the Microsoft CRM

4.0 user interfaces in different languages than the base language. Additionally, users can display Help in a language that differs from either the base language and the language displayed in the Microsoft Dynamics CRM 4.0 user interface.

- **Multicurrency**—Multiple currencies are now supported for transaction-based records.
- **Resource Center**—Both users and administrators can use the Resource Center as a location where they can share and use information related to Microsoft CRM 4.0 (see Figure 3.2).

FIGURE 3.2 Microsoft CRM 4.0 Resource Center.

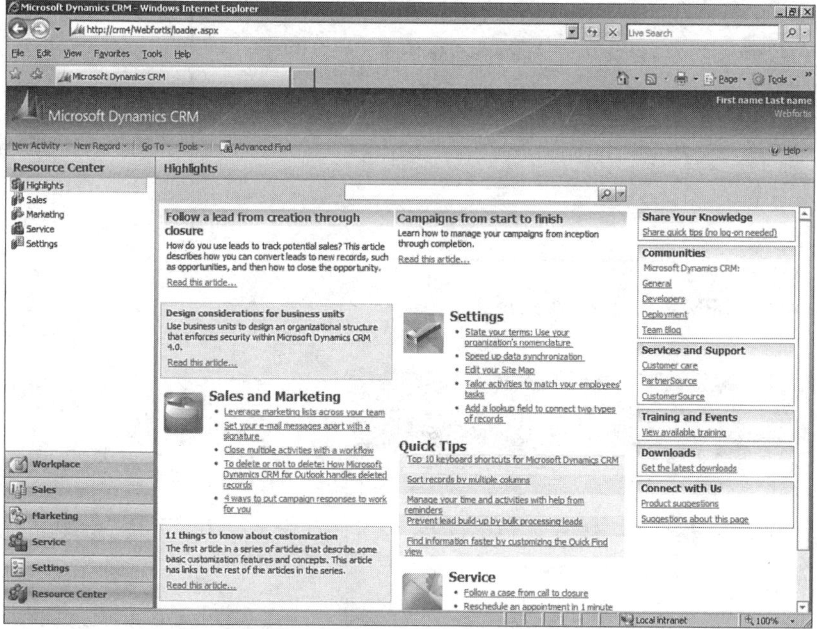

- **The Data Migration Manager** (see Figure 3.3) enables users to easily perform migrations previously reserved for system integrators and/or system implementers.
- **Workflow** (see Figure 3.4) has been dramatically redesigned to allow access to the Workflow tool from the CRM interface instead of having a separate application that the user would need to access to create and manage Workflow.
- Finally, the **E-mail Router** has been upgraded and provides seamless integration with the latest version of Exchange and its 64-bit requirements. Additionally, Exchange is no longer a required component to enable CRM e-mail functionality.

FIGURE 3.3 Microsoft CRM 4.0 Data Migration Manager.

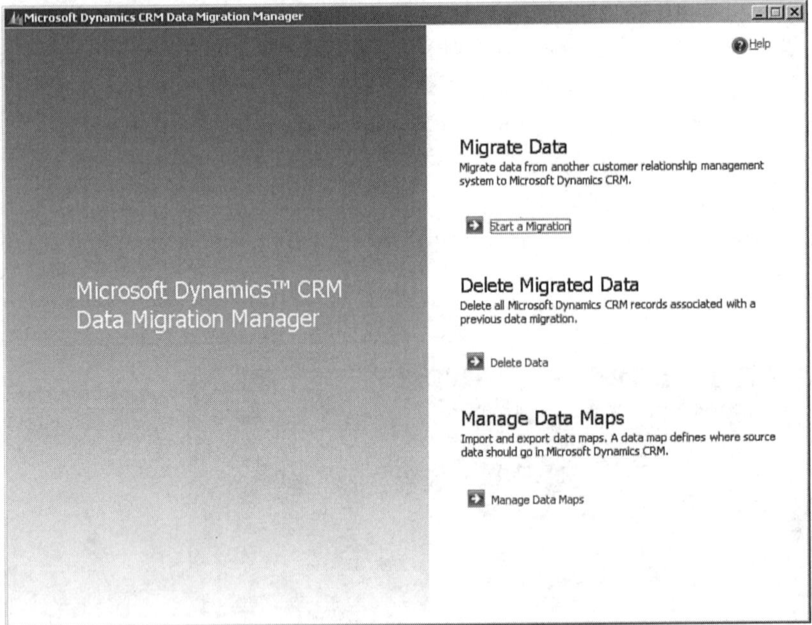

FIGURE 3.4 Microsoft CRM 4.0 workflow screen.

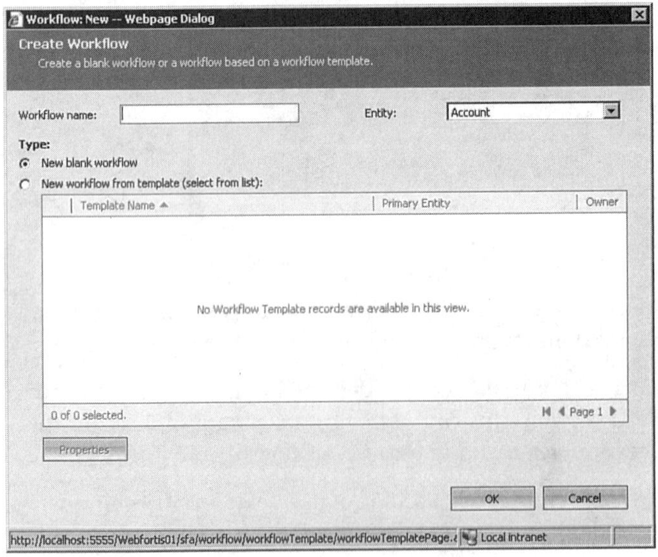

With the release of Microsoft CRM 4.0, Microsoft has given customers an assortment of choices regarding which platform to use and how they want to work with Microsoft CRM 4.0. This is important because Microsoft CRM leverages existing Microsoft architecture and integrates easily into it. Users who have existing Microsoft Windows servers and related technology will (in most cases) be able to easily add Microsoft CRM 4.0 into their systems.

However, if there is little or no existing Microsoft infrastructure, adding Microsoft CRM 4.0 requires adding services and components such as Active Directory, SQL Server, SQL Reporting Services (SRS) and Internet Information Services (IIS). *All* of these must be installed, running, and configured before running Microsoft CRM 4.0 (see Chapter 4, "Requirements for CRM 4.0").

Microsoft recognizes that some companies don't have the necessary infrastructure for Microsoft Dynamics CRM 4.0 and have directly addressed that issue by offering a number of new ways to use Microsoft Dynamics CRM 4.0.

Microsoft Dynamics CRM Online (previously CRM Live)

NOTE

Information for the Microsoft Dynamics CRM Online service included in this chapter is prerelease information and valid at the time of press. Be sure to check the Microsoft Dynamics CRM Online website for updated information.

Microsoft Dynamics CRM Online is shown in Figure 3.5. This is a monthly service from Microsoft that grants access to Microsoft CRM 4.0 from Microsoft servers.

FIGURE 3.5 Microsoft Dynamics CRM Online.

With this option, Microsoft Dynamics CRM Online uses a similar business model as one of Microsoft's fiercest competitors in the CRM market, Salesforce.com. As with Salesforce.com, Microsoft is offering the CRM service as a SaaS, or Software as a Service. The customer has no software to buy or servers to worry about because Microsoft is managing the customer relationship software. The customer simply accesses the data from Microsoft-provisioned servers via a secure login and has the fully functional CRM 4.0 interfaces to work with. The client requirements for using the Microsoft Dynamics CRM Online service are the same as the client requirements for the On Premise version, with the addition of a Windows Live ID.

The CRM Online option is currently offered in two different ways:

- Professional Edition
- Professional Plus Edition

Professional Edition offers the complete online sales, service, and marketing business suite with point-and-click system and workflow customization options.

Professional Plus Edition includes all the options in Professional Edition, with additional system customization and integration options, as well as offline data access and synchronization options not available in Professional Edition.

Although final pricing has yet to be determined, both options will likely offer pricing based on a per user/per month model with 12- and 24-month contracts and different support options available. The support is based on online and telephone support with varying response times (up to 24 hours for Professional Edition and 8 hours for the Professional Plus Edition). Note that there is also a mechanism set up for a business critical support problem, such as the server being down and users unable to log in. Upon contract completion, users can renew their contract or go to a month-to-month option. Other contract specifics follow:

- The billing is monthly, based on the date of initial signup on a 30-day cycle.
- New/additional users can be added any time, and the cost will be prorated based on the date of addition.
- Although users can be changed with no charge, canceling a user will result in a cancelation fee. Canceling a user will not, however, cancel the CRM Online subscription.
- Users can start with the Professional Edition, then upgrade to the Professional Plus Edition.
- Users can start with the Live version, and then migrate to the On Premise version.

Additional features of CRM Online include an unlimited number of users (at a per user cost, of course), a free 30-day trial, credit card payments, and support in both English and French.

To sign up for Microsoft Dynamics CRM Online, users can sign up online, via the 800 number, within retails stores, and via a partner referral. Note that Partner referrals are not the same as Partner Hosted also discussed in this chapter. Rather, it is a method whereby Microsoft partners refer customers to the Microsoft Dynamics CRM Online service and usually provide customization services and support (outside of the included Microsoft Dynamics CRM Online support options).

Microsoft Dynamics CRM Online can be reached at the CRM Online website located at http://
crm.dynamics.com/.

When considering Live, here are some of the pros and cons:

Pros:

- It's backed by Microsoft. Customers can feel secure knowing that Microsoft is dedicating the most state-of-the-art technology for the infrastructure and that it's using advanced monitoring tools to ensure maximum uptime. Additionally, Microsoft handles all security updates, so there's never any need to worry about whether your data can be compromised because of the failure to install a necessary update.
- Pricing and security provide excellent proof of concept when considering Microsoft CRM 4.0 as your CRM. Instead of investing capital in testing and evaluating systems, prospective businesses and users can test Microsoft CRM 4.0 through Live access. They can then easily migrate their data to On Premise servers and continue to use the same interfaces when they commit to Microsoft CRM 4.0 as their CRM system. Because the interfaces, access, and data are the same, they can perform the transition very easily. Microsoft supports these transitions as migrations and waives the cancellation fee related to the Live service.

Cons:

- Data storage is limited, and Microsoft Dynamics CRM clients are based on the selected package. With the Professional Edition, users have 5GB of data storage and 20GB with the Professional Plus Edition. These are relatively large numbers, however, so unless your organization has a huge amount of data and users, either should be acceptable. Additional storage can be purchased if necessary.
- Workflow has customization restrictions depending on the version. The Professional Edition limits you to 100 custom entities and 200 custom attributes, whereas Professional Plus Edition has double that limit: 200 custom entities and 400 custom attributes. Additionally, you are limited to a combined total of 100 workflow processes in Professional and 200 in Professional Plus. (Workflow processes are workflows [custom], assignment-based rules, notification rules, and stage-based processes.)
- Live has code restrictions. Viewed by most as a con, both versions of Live are served and managed by Microsoft, and there is a limit to the system customization and integration that a customer can perform. Microsoft will not let errant code run on servers because it could adversely affect the performance of other customers. So although functionality is limited to what Microsoft delivers, you can be sure that

other users on the system will not affect your capability to use Microsoft CRM 4.0. However, customers might want to extend functionality beyond what CRM Online allows them to do; Chapter 16, "Configuration and Customization Tools," explains several of these further. The On Premise edition is available for this reason.

If you do go with CRM Online and later cancel your subscription, be sure to take advantage of its backup service offered at the time of cancellation, as all data is deleted 90 days after the cancellation date. (You can technically resume your service within 90 days of cancellation; however, it is better to be safe when working with your data, just in case.) Backing up your CRM Online data will allow you to store it locally for later deployments and/or internal reasons.

On Premise

On Premise is the version of CRM that customers purchase, (without recurrent licensing costs), and, usually, although not always, host from their servers. Although a customer's servers can be located anywhere, the idea is that they will be located at one of the locations' premises, hence the term On Premise (or, in Microsoft parlance, On Prem).

Microsoft On Premise CRM is available in the following versions:

- **Workgroup**—This version is limited to five or fewer users. It can be installed on Microsoft Windows Small Business Server 2003 R2 Premium Edition, any of the supported Microsoft Windows Server 2003 editions, or Microsoft Windows Server 2008. This version is limited to a single organization and a single server computer.
- **Professional**—Similar to the CRM Online Professional version in functionality, the On Premise version does not have the same user limit. This version is limited to a single organization, but it can be installed on more then one computer.
- **Enterprise**—This version has no user limit. Additional features include support for multiple organizations, multiple server instances, and role-based service installation.

TIP

Microsoft has a 90-day trial for these versions available on the Microsoft website. You can install the trial version and then upgrade without losing any data.

As its name implies, you host the CRM at your location, or premise. Because you own the software, you control what you want it to do, how it is accessed, and how it interacts within your corporate infrastructure. As with the previous version of CRM, you have complete access for any kind of system customization and/or integration. This includes both supported and unsupported customizations (see Chapter 19, "Customizing Entities").

Partner Hosted

The third option to using Microsoft Dynamics CRM 4.0 is Partner Hosted. The Partner Hosted option enables Microsoft partners to deliver Microsoft Dynamics CRM 4.0 over the Web, similar to CRM Online (that is, as SaaS). However, the partner, not Microsoft, sets pricing and access. Additionally, no relationship exists between the customer and Microsoft; the relationship is between the customer and the partner.

For a number of reasons, users might prefer the Partner Hosted option over the CRM Online services:

- Specific industry and/or regional solutions not offered from and/or by Microsoft. This is the biggest reason for organizations to consider Partner Hosted solutions for Microsoft CRM 4.0. Microsoft tends to think in broad terms when it comes to service solutions, and in a number of vertical areas, partners are better suited at providing solutions. Verticals can include healthcare (with specific security requirements governing who can view what data), manufacturing (integrated systems might be offered as part of the service offering), or industries such as not-for-profit organizations.
- Customization options that the Partner Hosted service provides that the CRM Online services doesn't, such as support for plug-ins.
- Varied pricing and cancellation options.
- Whereas Microsoft Dynamics CRM Online is only available in the U.S. and Canada, Partner Hosted services are available in other countries and languages.

Of course, the following issues should be considered when evaluating the Partner Hosted solution:

- Reliability can vary. Because the CRM system is accessed from the partner service provider, if the partner loses connectivity to the Internet (because of power failure, because their Internet or servers go down, or, worse, because they go out of business), you don't have access to your CRM data. Obviously, the same can be said of the CRM Online service, but the CRM Online service is managed by Microsoft and has a robust architecture to protect against failure.
- Pricing irregularities that might not be obvious when signing up. Other well-known CRM service companies offer what appears to be great pricing, but when you realize that you want and/or need access to advanced features (which you didn't think you would need when you signed up), the price increases significantly.
- You don't "own" your data. Although this isn't entirely true, it might be. Because your data is hosted on the partner's infrastructure rather than your own, you merely access it. This can create a host of concerns for potential customers that mostly center on security questions.

We're not saying that you shouldn't use or trust the Partner Hosted solutions, but be sure to check any potential service provider when considering this solution. Partners should have a very clear policy that addresses these issues so that you don't have any doubts about their reliability, pricing, or security.

What Dynamics Means to Microsoft

Under the Dynamics division, Microsoft aligns its development efforts toward a common direction and goal set. In Chapter 27, "Other Microsoft Dynamics Products," we discuss integration options between the applications. Furthermore, Microsoft has indicated that it will one day have a single product from the Dynamics division: Dynamics. It will feature everything in one product and give the customer the benefit of a single integrated application with a common platform.

When CRM Version 1.2 was released, the Microsoft Business Solutions division had only three solutions: CRM, Axapta, and Navision. As of publication of this book, it has the following:

- Customer Relationship Management (CRM)
- Axapta (AX)
- Navision (NAV)
- Great Plains (GP)
- Solomon (SL)
- Retail Management Systems (RMS)
- Point of Sale

The Dynamics division enables customers to leverage the familiar Office and Windows platform that they already have and are comfortable with by delivering enterprise applications that work with them.

For a complete and current list of products that are covered under the Dynamics division, visit www.microsoft.com/dynamics/. When visiting the Dynamics website, two links are available to customers or partners:

- CustomerSource
- PartnerSource

CustomerSource is available to current customers and provides a wealth of information to customers. Some of the resources there include these:

- Knowledge Base articles
- Support communities
- Dynamics application training

PartnerSource is the resource for Microsoft partners that is involved with Dynamics support, sales, and customizations, and they must have different skills and certifications than a regular Microsoft partner to access this area. The PartnerSource area has the same resources as CustomerSource (listed previously), as well as tools for managing Dynamics customers.

Summary

As should be apparent, Microsoft has fully supported Microsoft CRM to become the mature product that Version 4.0 is. Additionally, although Microsoft CRM is part of the Dynamics division (and receives all the benefits from that, including CustomerSource and PartnerSource), the CRM application development budget actually resides internally within Microsoft under the same umbrella as Microsoft's flagship product, Microsoft Office. Because of that, Dynamics CRM can not only leverage Office integration and interoperability, but it also can utilize the resources dedicated for Office development to make it a truly great product.

CHAPTER 4

Requirements for CRM 4.0

IN THIS CHAPTER

- Server
- Database
- E-mail Router
- Other
- Client
- Upgrading
- Licensing

Microsoft Dynamics CRM 4.0 is an application that leverages other Microsoft technology. As previously stated, most businesses usually have some, if not all, of the technology required for Microsoft Dynamics CRM 4.0, and Microsoft readily admits that if you're not already on the Microsoft platform, the adoption of Microsoft Dynamics CRM for On Premise can be steep.

The On Premise version of Microsoft Dynamics CRM is the version that requires the most amount of infrastructure. This is simply because you're dedicating server resources (if not several servers) to hosting the Microsoft Dynamics CRM application. The other versions (CRM Online and Partner Hosted) require only Outlook and/or Internet Explorer. This chapter deals with the requirements associated for both the On Premise and the CRM Online and Partner Hosted requirements, but you should read this only if you're considering an On Premise installation; otherwise, you can skip to the "Client" section of this chapter.

Server

You can deploy Microsoft Dynamics CRM several different ways when considering an On Premise deployment. These include choosing single- versus multiple-server deployment and determining which version of Microsoft Dynamics CRM to run (see Chapter 5, "Setting Up CRM 4.0," for more information about single- versus multiple-server deployment).

The operating system requirements for the Microsoft Dynamics CRM 4.0 Server are as follows:

- Windows Server 2008 (formerly Longhorn Server).
- Windows Server 2003, Standard Edition, with SP2.

- Windows Server 2003, Enterprise Edition, with SP2.
- Windows Server 2003, Datacenter Edition, with SP2.
- Windows Server 2003, Web Edition, with SP2.
- Windows Server 2003 64x Standard Edition, with SP2.
- Windows Server 2003 64x Enterprise Edition, with SP2.
- Windows Server 2003 64x Datacenter Edition, with SP2.
- Windows Server 2003, Small Business Edition, Standard with SP1.
- Windows Server 2003, Small Business Edition, Premium with SP1.
- Microsoft Windows 2000 Server versions (and previous) are not supported for installing a Microsoft Dynamics CRM Server.

Windows Server 2003 Small Business Edition (SBS) deserves some special attention because of the design advantages and constraints associated with it.

Two editions are available for SBS:

- Standard
- Premium

The Standard version of SBS comes with the following services and features:

- Windows Server 2003 operating system
- Exchange Server 2003 SP2
- Office Outlook 2003
- Windows Server Update Services (WSUS)
- Windows SharePoint Services
- Shared Fax Services

The Premium version of SBS comes with everything the Standard version has and includes the following:

- SQL Server 2005 Workgroup Edition
- Microsoft Internet and Security Acceleration (ISA) Server 2004
- Office FrontPage 2003

The Small Business Servers have had a large impact on smaller businesses because their pricing, when compared to a dedicated Windows Server and the features associated with them (Microsoft Exchange, SQL Server, and so on), is usually quite competitive. However, some limitations arise when considering a Small Business Server:

- It has a 75-user limitation.
- It must function as the domain controller.
- It has a four-processor maximum and a limitation of 4GB of RAM.
- Multiple Small Business Servers cannot reside on the same network.

Additionally, although not required, it is highly recommended to upgrade your Small Business Server with the R2 service release. Released in August 2006, it includes a number of performance and reporting enhancements to SBS, as well as to SQL Server 2005 Workgroup edition. Previous (non-R2) versions of SBS will work if they have at least SP 1 and SQL Server 2005, but you should seriously consider upgrading to the R2 release because it provides considerably better performance and security features to the SBS platform. For more information about R2 and how to upgrade, visit www.microsoft.com/windowsserver2003/sbs/r2/default.mspx#3.

For the previous reasons, Small Business Servers perform very well in small business environments. However, for larger organizations and/or organizations that need to be scalable, Small Business Servers might not be the best choice; dedicated Windows Servers are preferred in these cases.

Whichever server you decide to go with from the previous list, it will have Active Directory included.

Active Directory is a Microsoft service that provides authentication and authorization for Windows-based users, computers, and services in a centralized location. It is a necessary component for access into Microsoft CRM 4.0. The advantage of leveraging Active Directory is that, through a single system sign-on process, application access can be granted without requiring multiple sign-ons. The easiest way to think of this is that when users log on to the Windows network, they are essentially logging on to not only the network, but also to all network resources, including printers, file shares, and applications that they have access to.

Active Directory works by organizing network objects hierarchically.

A forest is the top level of Active Directory. Forests contain domains, and domains contain Organizational Units (OUs) (see Figure 4.1).

All Active Directory forest modes (Windows 2000, Windows 2003 interim, and Windows 2003 forest mode) are supported for Microsoft CRM 4.0. However, when installing to a Windows Server 2003 that is a domain member or domain controller in a domain, one of the following Active Directory service modes must be running:

- Windows 2000 Native
- Windows Server 2003 Native
- Windows Server 2003 Interim
- All Windows Server 2008 modes

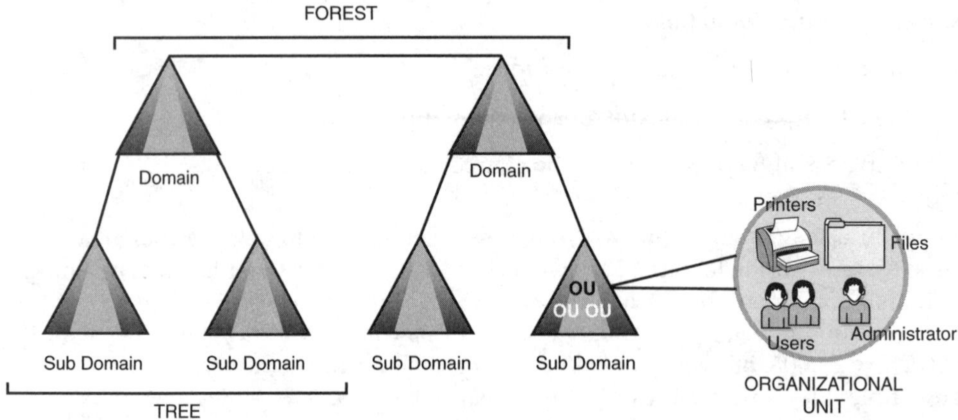

FIGURE 4.1 Graphical display of Active Directory forest, domain, and Organizational Unit.

Other Active Directory requirements include these:

- On a server-separated install (in which the CRM SQL Server database is on another computer), the Active Directory domain must contain both the Microsoft CRM 4.0 and the SQL Server computer.
- The computer that is running Microsoft CRM 4.0 must be on the same domain that has the accounts used to run Microsoft CRM 4.0.
- A single OU must house all the Microsoft CRM 4.0 security groups (UserGroup, PrivUserGroup, SQLAccessGroup, ReportingGroup, PrivReportingGroup). Note, however, that the OU does not have to be in the same domain as the computer running Microsoft CRM 4.0.
- A one-way trust must exist (in which the user domain trusts the Microsoft CRM 4.0 domain) when accessing Microsoft CRM 4.0 from another domain.

For more information about Active Directory, trusts, and domains, go to www.microsoft.com/technet/prodtechnol/windows2000serv/technologies/activedirectory/default.mspx.

Active Directory is an integral part of Microsoft Dynamics CRM. From the beginning of Microsoft CRM (starting with the earliest versions), Active Directory was the centralized location for user management and security into the system. When users first attempt to log into the network, they are validating who they are against the information in Active Directory. When on the network, Microsoft CRM uses another internal security mechanism to determine record access. This division of security is known as *Authentication* and *Authorization.*

Authentication (or who the user is) is the process by which a user is verified, by providing credentials. In the case of Active Directory, the credentials consist of a username, password, and Windows domain name. In the Windows and Microsoft CRM model, authentication is determined when a user logs on to the network. When a user attempts to access Microsoft CRM, he is not prompted for credentials because he has already been verified (see Figure 4.2).

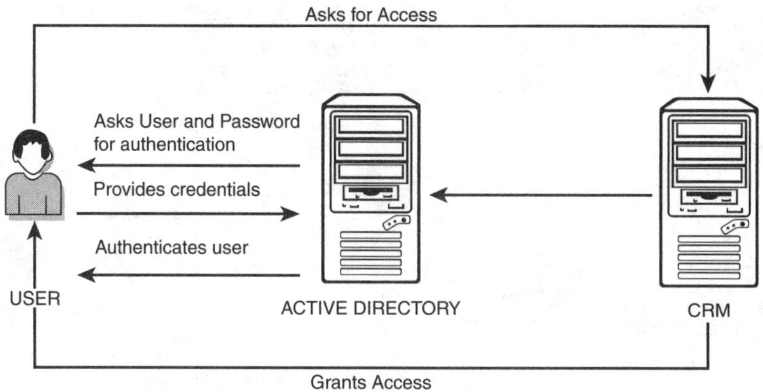

FIGURE 4.2 Active Directory and Microsoft CRM authentication.

Authorization (or what the user can do) is the process by which users are granted the rights to certain resources based on what security levels and permissions they have. For example, a network administrator might have full access rights to the entire system, whereas a secretary might have very limited access rights.

Further, the previous example is specific to the network rights that users have; however, whatever Microsoft Dynamics CRM rights they might have are completely independent of their network rights. As such, the secretary previously mentioned, who has very limited access rights, might be a full Microsoft CRM Administrator and able to do virtually anything in the CRM system, while the network administrator might have read-only rights.

If it sounds confusing, it may be easier to think of it like this:

- Users need to be valid network users to be given access to Microsoft Dynamics CRM 4.0.
- After granted access to Microsoft CRM 4.0, users need to be given a security role to determine what level of access they have to work within Microsoft CRM 4.0.
- There is no inherent correlation between network permissions and Microsoft CRM 4.0 permissions.

To explain further, just because users can log on to the network does not necessarily mean they have the rights or the capability to log on to Microsoft CRM 4.0. The reason for this is that although Active Directory controls network and network resource access, users must *also* be set up in Microsoft CRM 4.0 as valid users.

For example, if you had 85 people in your organization, but only the CEO has been set up in the Microsoft CRM 4.0 as a valid user, only the CEO would be able to access Microsoft CRM 4.0; other users would encounter the error shown in Figure 4.3.

The number of valid Microsoft CRM 4.0 users that you can have is established by the version of Microsoft CRM 4.0 that you purchase, as well as the particular licensing used (see the "Licensing" section of this chapter).

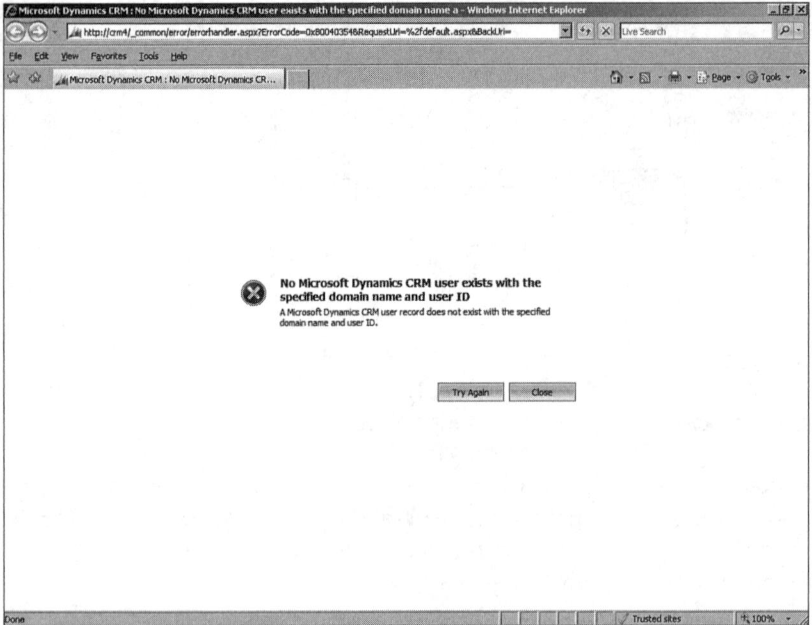

FIGURE 4.3 A valid network user but not added to Microsoft CRM.

The authorization process is further broken down within Microsoft Dynamics CRM 4.0 as outlined in Chapter 14, "Settings and Configuration."

Database

Microsoft SQL Server is the only supported database for Microsoft CRM 4.0.

Microsoft CRM 4.0 supports the following versions of Microsoft SQL Server:

- Microsoft SQL Server 2005, Workgroup Edition, with SP2
- Microsoft SQL Server 2005, Standard Edition, with SP2
- Microsoft SQL Server 2005, Enterprise Edition, with SP2
- Microsoft SQL Server 2005, Enterprise Edition, x64 with SP2
- Microsoft SQL Server 2005, Standard Edition, x64 with SP2

All versions of SQL Server prior to SQL Server 2005, as well as Express versions of SQL Server 2005, are not supported with Microsoft CRM 4.0. SQL Server 2008 is supported for CRM 4.0; however, at press time, specifications were unavailable.

Additionally, Microsoft CRM 4.0 supports a named instance of SQL Server when adding or creating organization databases, and both SQL Server Agent and SQL Server Full Text Indexing must be installed and running before you attempt to install Microsoft CRM 4.0.

SQL Server authentication can be set to either Mixed or Windows. (Microsoft CRM 4.0 uses Windows authentication, and it is the Microsoft preferred method.)

Microsoft has the following requirements and recommendations for SQL Server when attempting a Microsoft CRM 4.0 installation:

- SQL Server Agent must be started. You can configure this service to automatically start when the computer is started.
- The SQL Server service must be started. You can configure this service to automatically start when the computer is started.
- The service account that SQL Server uses to log on to the network must be either a local system account or a domain administrator account. Installation of Microsoft Dynamics CRM Server will fail if the SQL Server service account is the local administrator.
- The SQL Server Reporting Services service must be started. You must configure this service to automatically start when the computer is started.

Reporting Services

The following versions of Microsoft SQL Server Reporting Services (SRS) are supported with Microsoft CRM 4.0:

- Microsoft SQL Server 2005, Workgroup Edition, with SP2
- Microsoft SQL Server 2005, Standard Edition, with SP2
- Microsoft SQL Server 2005, Enterprise Edition, with SP2
- Microsoft SQL Server 2005, Enterprise Edition, x64 with SP2
- Microsoft SQL Server 2005, Standard Edition, x64 with SP2

As with SQL Server, versions prior to SQL Server Reporting Services 2005 are not supported with Microsoft CRM 4.0.

Previous versions of Microsoft CRM had a problem with multiple-server deployment and authentication with SQL Server Reporting Services and CRM. This issue was referred to as the Kerberos double-hop problem, and it had to do with the default NTLM authentication scheme that Windows Server operating systems use. The workaround was a tricky deployment of trusts and delegation that had to be done correctly to resolve.

Thankfully, Microsoft released the Reporting Services Connector, a required software service component that connects Microsoft CRM 4.0 to SQL Server Reporting Services and eliminates the Kerberos double-hop authentication problem.

The connector is not required to be installed separately for non-Internet Facing Deployments (IFD); however, it has these specific requirements:

- The connector setup must be run *after* the CRM is set up.
- The connector can be set up only on a computer that has SQL Server Reporting Services installed.

Note that failure to install the connector results in an incapability to use or view the Microsoft CRM 4.0 reports.

The installation process of the connector is explained further in Chapter 5.

E-mail Router

The Microsoft CRM E-mail Router is a combination of components that enable Microsoft CRM to automatically track inbound and outbound e-mail messages:

- The E-mail Router component
- The Rule Deployment Manager component

The E-mail Configuration Manager is installed when the E-mail Router component is installed. It is used to configure the Microsoft CRM 4.0 e-mail messages via the E-mail Router.

The Rule Deployment Manager determines how Microsoft CRM e-mail messages are routed.

With Microsoft CRM 4.0, Microsoft Exchange is no longer a required application of the Microsoft CRM infrastructure. Although it is technically "required" as part of previous versions of Microsoft CRM, you could always have operated Microsoft CRM without Microsoft Exchange Server by using any Simple Mail Transfer Protocol (SMTP) server to send e-mail; however, you lose the capability to track messages automatically. Now, by using the Microsoft CRM 4.0 E-mail Router, full support is offered for SMTP servers *as well as* Post Office Protocol (POP3) services. It is important to note, however, that the POP3 e-mail server *must* be capable of supporting e-mail messages that are sent as attachments to other e-mail messages. In addition, when installing the E-mail Router to connect to the POP3, the RFC 1939 standard is supported; for the SMTP server, the RFC 2821 and 2822 standards are supported (for more information about the various RFC standards, visit http://tools.ietf.org/html/).

Of course, Microsoft Exchange is still fully supported with the E-mail Router.

The following versions of Microsoft Exchange are supported with the Microsoft CRM 4.0 E-mail Router:

- Exchange 2003, Enterprise Edition, with SP2
- Exchange 2003, Standard Edition, with SP2

- Exchange Server 2007, Enterprise Edition
- Exchange Server 2007, Standard Edition

Note that Exchange Server 2007 is supported only in 64 bits, and the Microsoft CRM E-mail Router is not supported for Microsoft Exchange 2000 and versions prior to this.

Additional considerations when deploying the Microsoft CRM E-mail Router include these:

- The .NET 3.0 Framework must be installed on the computer that is running Microsoft Exchange and where the E-mail Router will be installed.
- Windows Server 2003 or Windows Server 2008 is required for the Microsoft CRM E-mail Router.
- The Microsoft Exchange Server Messaging API (MAPI) client runtime libraries must be installed on the Windows Server.

The setup and installation of the e-mail router is fully explained in Chapter 15, "E-mail Configuration."

Other

The following requirements are necessary before you attempt to install Microsoft CRM 4.0:

- .NET Framework (2.0 and 3.0)
- ASP.NET
- Internet Information Services (IIS) 6.0 or 7.0
- Microsoft Windows Indexing Service, set to start automatically
- SMTP service
- MDAC 2.81
- MMC 3.0 (required to run Deployment Manager)
- IIS Admin service
- World Wide Web Publishing service

Client

You can access Microsoft CRM 4.0 in two different ways: by using Microsoft Office Outlook or by using Microsoft Internet Explorer.

Microsoft CRM Client for Internet Explorer

When using the Microsoft CRM Client for Internet Explorer, only Internet Explorer is required. This is an ideal situation in many situations:

- Remote and/or offsite access is necessary.
- Support staff doesn't necessarily need Office.
- A thin client solution is desired.

Note that only Microsoft Internet Explorer can be used as a Microsoft CRM Client, and other browsers, such as Firefox and Opera, are not supported. (Although not supported, it *is* possible to use browsers other than Internet Explorer as a Microsoft CRM client if you enable their IE compatibility functions. Because of the mixed results and lack of support from Microsoft, however, we don't recommend this.)

The following versions of Internet Explorer are required:

- Internet Explorer 6 with SP1
- Internet Explorer 7

When using the Microsoft CRM Client for Internet Explorer, the following operating systems are supported:

- Windows Vista
- Windows XP Professional with SP 2
- Windows XP Home Edition with SP 2
- Windows XP Tablet PC Edition with SP 2
- Windows 2000 Professional with SP 4

Microsoft CRM Office Client for Outlook

With Outlook, the Microsoft CRM 4.0 client is installed directly into Outlook and can be accessed by simply navigating to the Microsoft CRM node (see Figure 4.4).

The Microsoft CRM Outlook client comes in two versions (both are in the same installer), and the Microsoft Dynamics CRM Online client is in a separate installer/download:

- CRM for Outlook
- CRM for Outlook with Offline Access

Although both features are similar, the Laptop client has the capability to go "offline" and enables users to work with CRM data while not connected to the Microsoft CRM server. The offline capabilities are available by clicking the Go Offline button on the Microsoft CRM Outlook toolbar (see Figure 4.5).

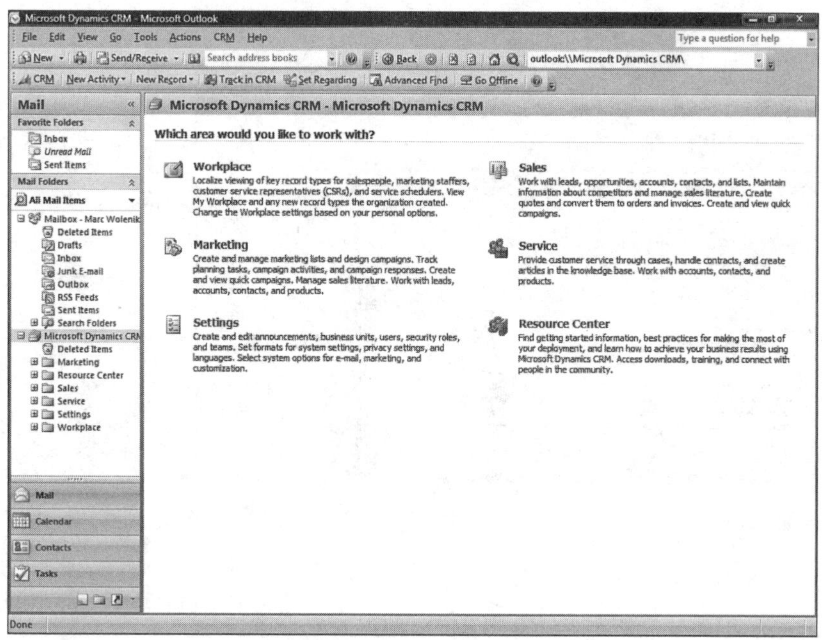

FIGURE 4.4 Microsoft Outlook with Microsoft CRM.

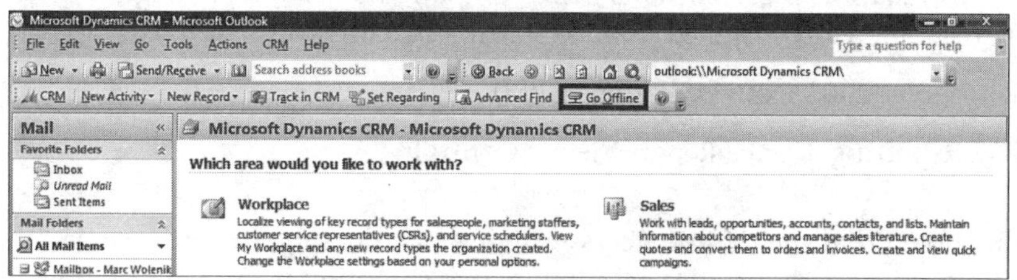

FIGURE 4.5 Microsoft Outlook with Microsoft CRM Laptop client while online.

When users have completed their offline tasks and return to the Microsoft CRM 4.0 Server, they can click the Go Online button (see Figure 4.5), and a synchronization process checks for updated data on both the Microsoft CRM server and the Microsoft CRM Outlook client (see Figure 4.6).

Additionally, a major difference between the two clients is that the Laptop client version uses a version of the Microsoft CRM interface that is local to the Laptop client and is delivered to the user via an internal web server (when in offline mode). Most users will never notice a difference, but this can have major impacts on customizations because the User Interface pages delivered from the Microsoft CRM server are not sent to the client—only the data is.

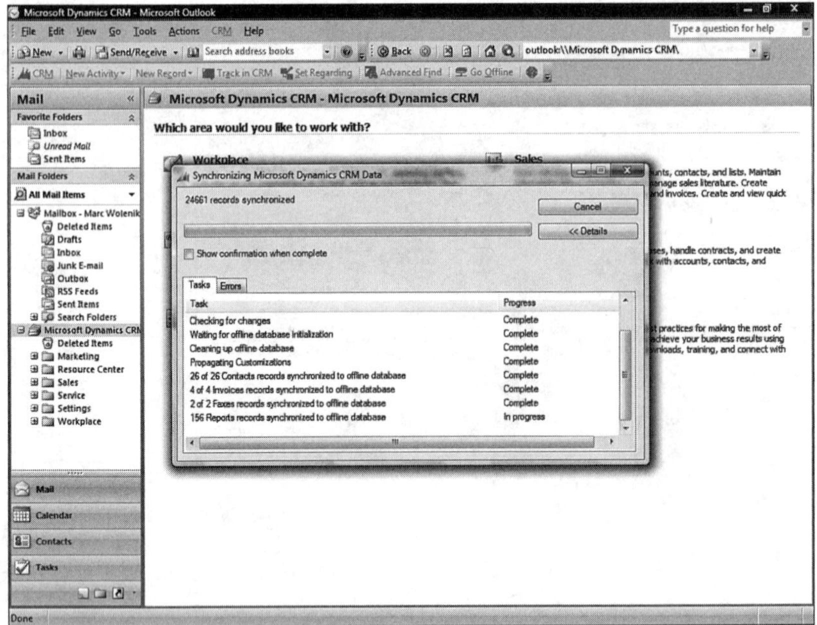

FIGURE 4.6 Microsoft Outlook with Microsoft CRM Laptop client Synchronizing to go offline.

The Outlook Client Installation wizard installs these components when installing the Laptop client only (if not already installed prior to starting installation):

- Microsoft SQL Server 2005 Express Edition (CRM)
- Microsoft SQL Reporting Service Report Viewer Control

Finally, it should be noted that the Offline Access Client mode does *not* require installation on a laptop. If you choose to install the Offline Access Client mode on your desktop, it will have the same functionality as the Desktop client, but it will install the required components outlined earlier. There are not too many reasons for doing this, however, other then testing and development purposes, as it is unlikely that you'll be taking your desktop offline.

For more information related to the differences in clients, refer to Chapter 16, "Configuration and Customization Tools."

Regardless of which Microsoft CRM Client is used, the following operating systems are required for the Microsoft CRM Office client for Outlook:

- Windows Vista
- Windows XP Professional with Service Pack 2 (SP 2)

- Windows XP Professional x64 Edition
- Windows XP Tablet PC Edition with Service Pack 2 (SP 2)

The Microsoft CRM Office clients for Outlook are both 32-bit-based applications, so they must run in the Windows on Windows (WOW) system when the operating system is either Windows Vista x64 or Windows XP Professional x64 Edition.

Note that XP Media Center is not a supported operating system for the Microsoft CRM Office client for Outlook.

Additionally, the following components must be installed (and running) before you attempt a Microsoft CRM Office client for Outlook installation:

- Internet Explorer 6 with SP1 or Internet Explorer 7
- Microsoft Office 2003 with SP2 or Microsoft Office 2007 system
- Indexing Service (must be installed and running)
- Windows Installer (MSI) 3.1

The following components are required. However, the installer automatically installs them as part of the installation process:

- SQL 2005 Express Edition with SP1 (Offline Access Client mode only)
- .NET Framework 3.0

Finally, the Outlook client (either version) cannot be installed on the same server that has Exchange 2003 on it.

Upgrading

When upgrading to Microsoft Dynamics CRM 4.0 from 3.0, there is a wizard that will perform the upgrade. Refer to Chapter 5 for more information about performing upgrades.

Licensing

With the different versions now available for Microsoft CRM 4.0, customers have greater choice for licensing.

The licensing model for Microsoft CRM 4.0 has been changed to use only one license key for the version, the server and Client Access Licenses (CALs). This is a significant improvement over earlier versions which required separate licenses for each.

The Microsoft CRM versions, supported operating systems, and licensing are broken down as follows:

Microsoft CRM Version	Supported Operating Systems	Users	Organizations	Computers
Workgroup Edition	• Microsoft Windows Server 2008 • Microsoft Windows Server 2003 (any of the previously listed supported versions) • Microsoft Windows Small Business Server 2003 R2 Enterprise Edition	Five or fewer	Single organization	Single computer
Professional Edition	Any of the previously listed supported operating systems	No user limit	Single organization	Multiple computers
Enterprise Edition	Any of the previously listed supported operating	No user limit	Multiple organizations	Multiple computers

To manage licenses in Microsoft CRM 4.0, the Deployment Manager is used on the server. From the Deployment Manager, you can view and upgrade licenses (see Figure 4.7).

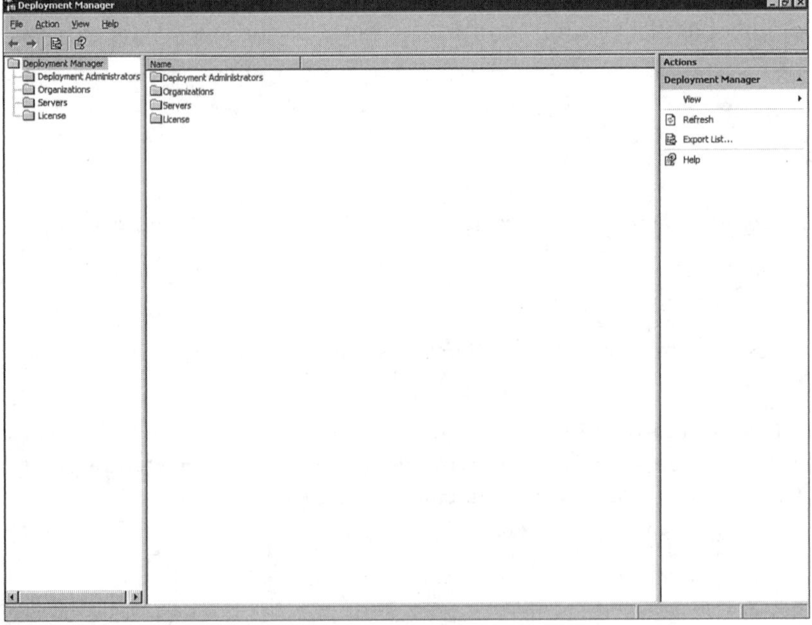

FIGURE 4.7 Microsoft Dynamics CRM Deployment Manager.

Microsoft CRM 4.0 uses *named* licenses (or user CALs) as well as Machine licenses (or device CALs) as its licensing model. Named licenses require that every user who accesses the Microsoft CRM 4.0 must have a license. If that user leaves the company or no longer needs to use the CRM, the license can be transferred to another individual; however, the previous individual then no longer has access to Microsoft CRM 4.0. Machine licenses allow a single computer to be licensed to Microsoft CRM 4.0, and multiple users can use the same machine provided they aren't accessing it simultaneously. This is a significant improvement with regard to licensing when you consider call centers or similar organizations that operate around the clock. Named and Machine CALs can be mixed in a deployment.

Two different kinds of Microsoft CALs are available with Microsoft CRM 4.0:

- **Full**—Full system functionality is granted to a user with this type of license. These users have full system access and full permission to modify records, limited only by whatever security role and privileges might be set for them.
- **Limited-use**—This CAL is a read-only CAL and comes in two options: Administrative or Read-only. With this license, users have the ability to view all areas and records in Microsoft CRM 4.0. However, they cannot make any changes. The Administrative version gives users the ability to modify records only in the Settings area.

Note that the licensing differences apply only when Microsoft CRM 4.0 is accessed via the web client. To use the Outlook client, you *must* have the Full CAL.

Microsoft makes CRM licensing available in the following different ways:

- Retail
- Volume

You can purchase retail licensing from any vendor that sells software.

Volume licensing is a method by which Microsoft makes licenses available based on the following criteria:

- Size of the purchasing organization
- Type of licensing desired
- Licensing term desired
- Payment options

When purchasing licenses through volume licensing, customers also can add Software Assurance (SA). SA enables customers to upgrade their software if Microsoft releases a newer version within a certain timeframe. Customers then can purchase software and not worry about it being obsolete and/or having to repurchase again when a new version comes out.

Volume licensing is broken down into the following four methods:

- **Open License**—Organizations that Microsoft considers small or midsized (usually with fewer than 250 computers) have the option to purchase licensing and receive benefits such as discounts, Software Assurance (mentioned previously), and easy deployment and management. The only restrictions on open licensing are that a minimum of five licenses must be purchased at a time, and payment is expected at the time of the transaction.

  These specific licensing options are available with Open License:

  - Open Value
  - Open Business
  - Open Volume

  Each option has different advantages, depending largely on your business needs. To learn more about these options, go to www.microsoft.com/licensing/programs/open/overview.mspx.

- **Select License**—Organizations have the option to create a payment plan and are given discounts based on the amount of software ordered. Generally, the Select License option is reserved for organizations that have more than 250 computers.

- **Enterprise Agreement**—Enterprise Agreement licensing is similar to the Select License option, but there are more significant discounts (usually reserved for larger orders).

- **Enterprise Subscription Agreement**—This is a subscription-based model similar to the Enterprise Agreement option. However, because the software is not purchased, it offers discounts at a greater rate. Again, this option is usually reserved for organizations with more than 250 computers.

Although you can purchase the Microsoft CRM 4.0 licenses via retail methods, we recommend purchasing licensing through volume licensing rather than retail if possible.

If you are a developer or an ISV, or if you are interested in enhancing or working with some of the features of Microsoft CRM 4.0, you might want to consider acquiring an MSDN license, which includes a copy of CRM for development purposes. You can find more information about the MSDN program at www.microsoft.com/msdn.

Upgrading

Existing Microsoft Dynamics CRM 3.0 customers who would like to upgrade to 4.0 can select whether they want to convert their named/user CALs to either a User or Device CAL. Additionally, customers that have Microsoft Dynamics 3.0 Professional Edition can upgrade their server and external connector licenses to Microsoft Dynamics CRM 4.0 Professional version.

The upgrade path for Microsoft Dynamics CRM 3.0 Small Business Edition is unavailable at time of press, so be sure to check the Microsoft website for more information at www.microsoft.com/dynamics.

External Connector Licensing

A special license known as the External Connector License is required when you want to work directly with the data contained in your Microsoft Dynamics CRM database for any purpose. This is common when organizations want to extend functionality of Case creation to their external customer facing websites, for example. In this scenario, a user could go to the organizations website, log in, and create a Case directly in the website. The information would then be processed within Microsoft Dynamics CRM as a new Case and assigned to either a support queue or user. Because this type of functionality requires us to touch Microsoft Dynamics CRM data, we need one of two licenses:

- External Connector (Full)
- External Connector (Read-Only)

As its name implies, the full connector allows you to do whatever you want with the database, including reading, writing, or deleting. The read-only connector allows you to only display information from the database and not update it in any fashion. The latter would be helpful if you wanted to share information with your organization or external partners relating to Microsoft Dynamics CRM data, such as upcoming sales and/or caseloads.

Either of these licenses are available with the Professional or Enterprise Edition; however, neither is available with the Workgroup edition. If you are working with the Workgroup edition and wish to use a connector for whatever reason, you must upgrade to either Professional or Enterprise.

Windows Users

Note that Microsoft Windows has separate CAL requirements and, hence, can place restrictions on Microsoft CRM users. A good example of this is the 75-user limit on Windows Small Business Servers. The Professional Edition of Microsoft CRM 4.0 supports an unlimited number of users, but each user must be listed in Active Directory. Active Directory in SBS supports only 75 users, so you can have only 75 users in Microsoft CRM 4.0.

Carefully consider this when planning the infrastructure.

Summary

There are several different configuration options for both the Microsoft Dynamics CRM server and its clients.

When working with an On Premise version of Microsoft Dynamics CRM, be sure that all the components listed previously are installed and correctly configured.

Finally, the related licensing options have been greatly improved, as well as the ability for customers to upgrade.

CHAPTER 5

Setting Up CRM 4.0

IN THIS CHAPTER

With the exception of the "Microsoft Dynamics CRM Clients" and "Microsoft Dynamics CRM Online Setup" sections, virtually everything in this chapter applies to the On Premise setup.

Single- Versus Multiple-Server Deployment

You can deploy Microsoft Dynamics CRM across multiple servers or on a single server. Although the method of deployment depends on your system requirements and server availability, some restrictions govern which version you can deploy and how you can do so.

Single-Server Deployment

Unlike the previous version of Microsoft Dynamics CRM, both Microsoft Windows Small Business Server (SBS) 2003 Enterprise Edition R2 and Microsoft Windows Server 2003 editions support a single-server deployment. However, the Workgroup Edition version can *only* be deployed and run on a single server configuration.

In a single-server deployment, a single server performs all of these functions:

- Domain controller
- Microsoft Dynamics CRM Server
- SQL Server 2005
- SQL Server Reporting Server (SRS)
- Microsoft Exchange Server 2003 (optional)

It is important to consider these when planning the deployment because the resource requirements for any one of these can be extensive. Thus, we recommend considering a multiple-server deployment whenever you might be using the server for more than just Microsoft Dynamics CRM.

Refer to Chapter 4, "Requirements for CRM 4.0," when considering a SBS deployment because the early versions of SBS came with SQL Server 2000, which is unsupported for Microsoft Dynamics CRM 4.0.

Multiple-Server Deployments

Both the Professional and the Enterprise versions of Microsoft CRM can be spread across multiple servers during deployment (and later, if necessary). Multiple servers offer these benefits:

- Scalability
- Performance
- Server resource allocation and control
- Shortened disaster recovery time
- Server roles

Server roles provide the capability to deploy specific services and components to different computers for scaling and performance benefits. You can select two predefined server role groupings when installing Microsoft Dynamics CRM under the Custom Setup process (by default, both server role groupings are installed with a Typical install), as shown in Figure 5.1.

- The Application Server role provides the Microsoft Dynamics CRM web user interface and services.
- The Platform Server role provides the asynchronous services, such as the Workflow and Bulk E-mail services.

Alternatively, you can install any one or more of these specific server roles when using Microsoft CRM Dynamics Enterprise Edition via the command line:

- **Application Server**—Provides the necessary components and Web Services needed to run the web application server that is used to connect users to Microsoft Dynamics CRM data
- **WebService**—Installs the components needed to run the Microsoft Dynamics CRM platform

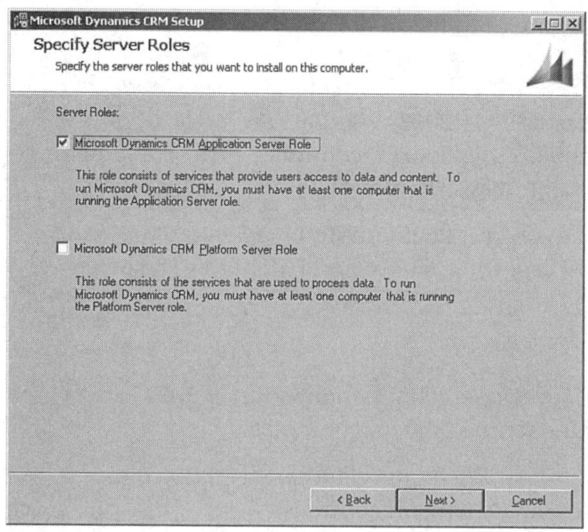

FIGURE 5.1 Role grouping options during Custom setup.

- **Microsoft Dynamics CRM Processing Asynchronous Service**—Processes queued asynchronous events, including these:
    - Workflow
    - Data import
    - Bulk e-mail
- **DeploymentService**—Installs the components required to manage the deployment by using the methods described in the Software Development Kit (SDK), such as creating an organization or removing a Deployment Administrator role from a user
- **DiscoveryService**—Installs the components required for users to find the organization that they are a member of in a multitenant deployment
- **Microsoft Dynamics CRM SDK Server**—Provides the components needed to run applications that use the methods described in the SDK
- **HelpServer**—Provides the components needed to make Microsoft Dynamics CRM Help available to users

Note that no role exists specifically for Workflow services. Instead, you must deploy the Microsoft Dynamics CRM Processing Asynchronous Service because this service handles Workflow.

Another consideration related to multiple-server deployments is the Microsoft CRM LAN topology. The topology should include the Microsoft Dynamics CRM Server as well as both Active Directory and SQL Server on the same LAN, primarily because of the large amount of network traffic that they create and use. Failure to have a permanent high-speed network connection between any of these computers can seriously affect performance and possibly cause data corruption.

Microsoft recommends using a topology similar to this:

- **Team topology (two servers)**
  - Computer 1: Running Windows Server 2008, Windows Server 2003, or Windows 2000 Server as a functioning domain controller. If the computer is running Windows Server 2003, it may also run Microsoft Exchange 2003.
  - Computer 2: Running Windows Server 2008 or Windows Server 2003, SQL Server 2005, SQL Server 2005 Reporting Services, and Microsoft Dynamics CRM Server.
- **Division topology (five servers)**
  - Computer 1: Running Windows Server 2008, Windows Server 2003, or Windows 2000 Server as a functioning domain controller
  - Computer 2: Running Windows Server 2008, Windows Server 2003, or Windows 2000 Server as a secondary domain controller

  - Computer 3: Running Windows Server 2008 or Windows Server 2003 and Microsoft Dynamics CRM Server
  - Computer 4: Running Windows Server 2008 or Windows Server 2003, Microsoft SQL Server 2005, and SQL Server 2005 Reporting Services
  - Computer 5: Running Windows Server 2008 or Windows Server 2003, Microsoft Exchange Server, and the E-mail Router
- **Multiforest and multidomain Active Directory topology**

For very large user bases that span multiple domains and, in some cases, forests, the following configuration is supported:

- **Forest A: Parent Domain**
  - Computer 1: Running Windows Server 2008, Windows Server 2003, or Windows 2000 Server as a functioning domain controller
  - Computer 2: Running Windows Server 2008, Windows Server 2003, or Windows 2000 Server as a secondary domain controller
  - Computer 3: Running Windows Server 2008 or Windows Server 2003 and Microsoft Dynamics CRM Server
  - Computer 4: Running Windows Server 2008 or Windows Server 2003 and Microsoft SQL Server 2005
  - Computer 5: Running Windows Server 2008 or Windows Server 2003 and SQL Server 2005 Reporting Services
  - Computer 6: Running Windows Server 2008 or Windows Server 2003, Microsoft Exchange Server, and the Microsoft Dynamics CRM E-mail Router

- **Forest A: Child Domain**
  - Computer 7: Running Windows Server 2008, Windows Server 2003, or Windows 2000 Server as a functioning domain controller
  - Computer 8: Running Windows Server 2008, Windows Server 2003, or Windows 2000 Server as a secondary domain controller
  - Computer 9: Running Windows Server 2008 or Windows Server 2003 and Microsoft Exchange Server
- **Forest B: Parent Domain**
  - Computer 10: Running Windows Server 2008, Windows Server 2003, or Windows 2000 Server as a functioning domain controller
  - Computer 11: Running Windows Server 2008, Windows Server 2003, or Windows 2000 Server as a secondary domain controller
  - Computer 12: Running Windows Server 2008 or Windows Server 2003 and Microsoft Exchange Server

Setup Process

When installing Microsoft Dynamics CRM for the first time, it is a good idea to confirm that all the requirements for Microsoft Dynamics CRM listed in Chapter 4 are configured properly, are running, and have the most updated service packs.

Additionally, you must have the following as part of the Microsoft CRM Dynamics Server setup process:

1. Microsoft CRM license code
2. Desired Microsoft Dynamics CRM server type (application, platform, or both)
3. Organization name
4. Organization friendly name
5. Desired base currency
6. Location/port of the Microsoft Dynamics CRM website
7. Location of Microsoft SQL Server
8. Location of SQL Server Reporting Services Report Server
9. E-mail Router server name (optional)

It is not necessary to have the Microsoft Dynamics CRM server set up to install the Microsoft CRM Dynamics Outlook clients; however, you cannot configure the clients with the Microsoft Dynamics CRM server until the server is set up.

Microsoft Dynamics CRM Server Setup

When setting up Microsoft Dynamics CRM, it is recommended to set up the server first and then the e-mail router. Although you *can* install the E-mail Router before you install Microsoft Dynamics CRM, it is recommended that you first install Microsoft Dynamics CRM, because the service accounts that are necessary to run the E-mail Router service are automatically added when you specify the incoming e-mail server during the setup process.

Follow these steps to complete the Microsoft Dynamics CRM installation:

1. Start the setup process by launching the `setupserver.exe` file from the root directory. The setup screen appears (see Figure 5.2), and you are given the option to download updated installation files.

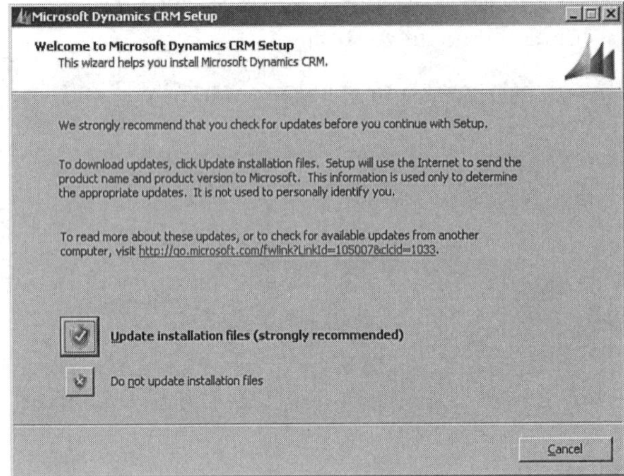

FIGURE 5.2 Microsoft Dynamics CRM setup screen.

Although you can update Microsoft Dynamics CRM after you've installed it, it is recommended that you check for updates from Microsoft at this point in the setup. They then are automatically downloaded, to ensure that your installation goes smoothly. Click Next to continue.

2. Enter your license code (see Figure 5.3). When you have finished entering your license code, a message appears with your license status summary; it should match your license agreement from Microsoft. Click Next to continue.
3. Accept the license agreement and click "I Accept" to continue.
4. The installer then performs a system check to see if required components necessary for the installation to continue are installed (see Figure 5.4). If you are not missing any components necessary for the installer to continue, you will not see this screen.

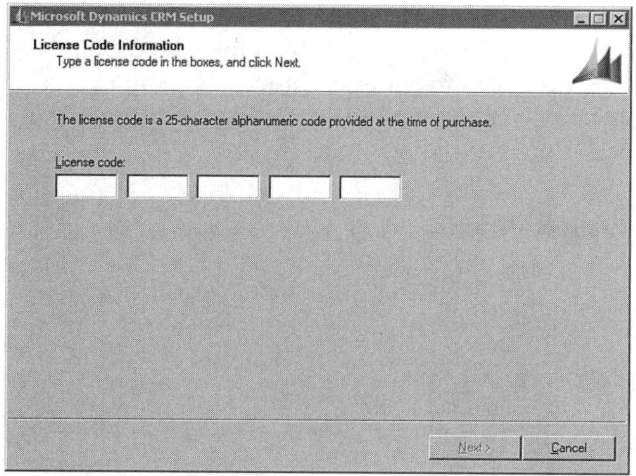

FIGURE 5.3 Microsoft Dynamics CRM license code prompt.

NOTE

This check is for the installer only. If you are missing or have misconfigured required Microsoft Dynamics CRM components such as SQL Server Reporting Services, you will be able to continue from this screen; however, you will receive an error when the installer performs a system requirements check as the last step.

Missing installer components will be installed for you when you click Install. After setup confirms that all required components are installed, click Next to continue.

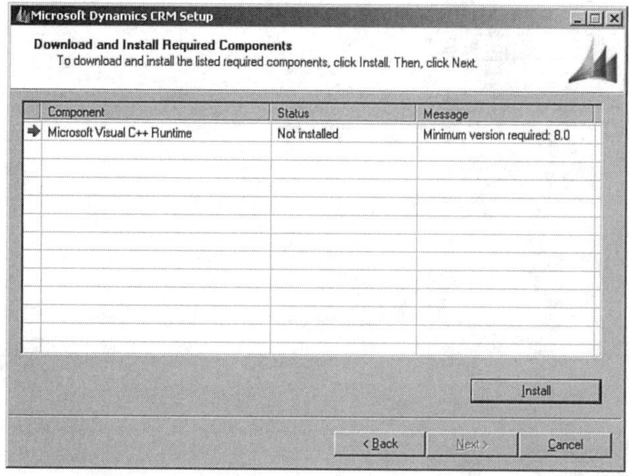

FIGURE 5.4 Microsoft Dynamics CRM Installer check for missing components.

5. You must specify the setup type on the next screen (see Figure 5.5). You have the option to install different server roles (mentioned previously in this chapter). If you select Typical, both server roles are installed. If you select Custom, you can choose which (or both) server roles you would like to set up (see Figure 5.6). For this installation, select a Typical installation. Click Next to continue.

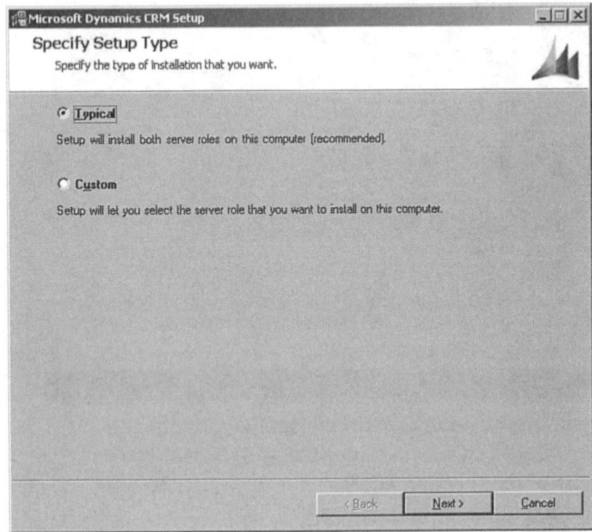

FIGURE 5.5 Microsoft Dynamics CRM Installer setup type screen.

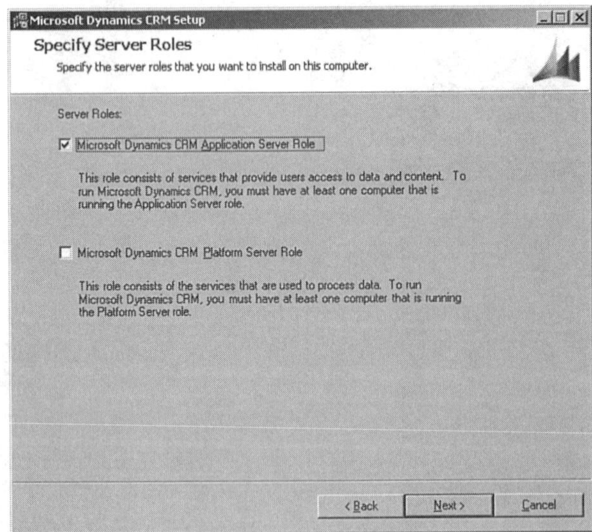

FIGURE 5.6 Microsoft Dynamics CRM Installer with the predefined server roles options displayed.

Note that if you want to install any of the specific server roles (not the predefined server role groupings) such as HelpServer or WebService, you cannot select them from here as they must be installed via a command-line installation only.

6. Select the SQL Server that will be used for Microsoft Dynamics CRM (see Figure 5.7). By default, no SQL Servers are listed. However, clicking the Refresh option next to the drop-down shows SQL Servers identified on the network.

   Additionally, by default, the database option is Create New Databases. If you already have an existing Microsoft Dynamics CRM database, you can select Connect to Existing Databases, and setup will use that database during setup.

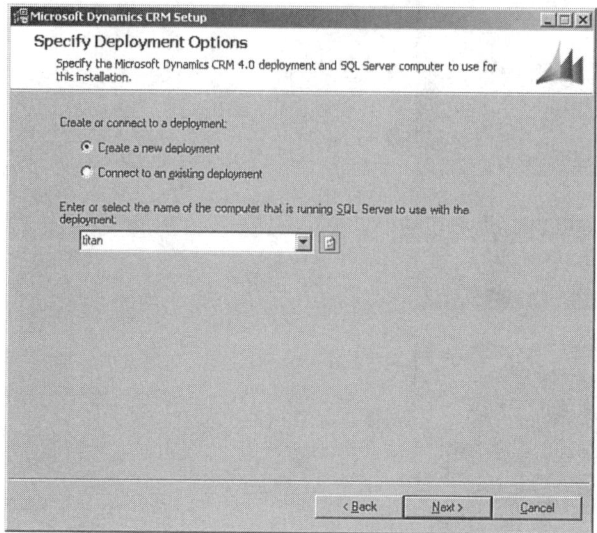

FIGURE 5.7 Microsoft Dynamics CRM Select SQL Server setup.

The Display name is the "long name" or descriptive name of your organization. (It has a 250-character limit.) The Name is the name of your organization. (It has a 30-character limit) (see Figure 5.8).

Select the ISO currency code from the pop-up after selecting Browse (see Figure 5.9). This information is necessary for Microsoft Dynamics CRM to create an organizational database (something that does not happen during a custom installation and must be set up in the deployment manager after installation). Click Next to continue.

7. Select whether you want to participate in the Customer Experience Improvement Program (CEIP), and select Next to continue.

   Select the installation location. Click Next to continue.

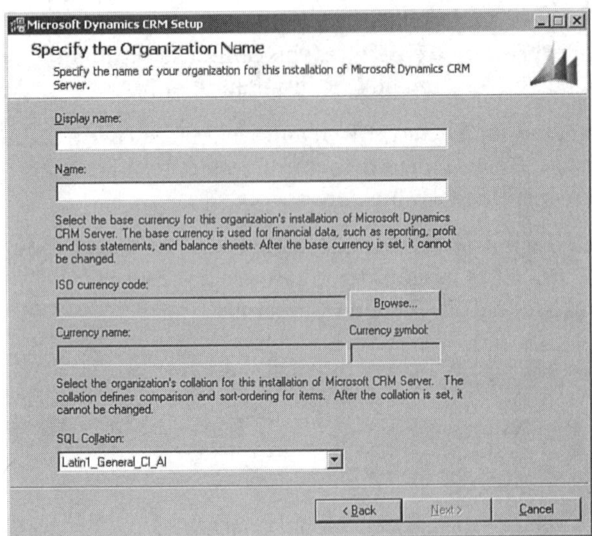

FIGURE 5.8 Microsoft Dynamics CRM organization information.

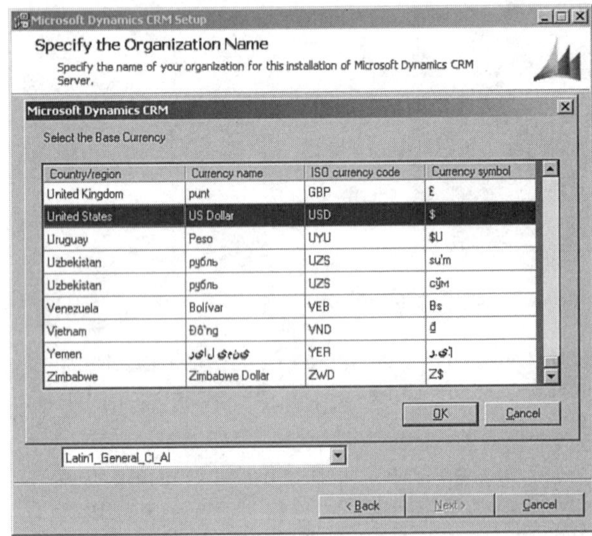

FIGURE 5.9 Microsoft Dynamics CRM ISO selection screen.

8. Select the installation directory. Select the website where you want Microsoft Dynamics CRM to be installed (see Figure 5.10).

   By default, the application is loaded onto the default website using server bindings (port) 80. However, if Create new Web site is selected (see Figure 5.11), the website is created using server bindings on the port you enter in the text box (by default, it is 5555). The difference is whether you want to dedicate your port 80 for Microsoft Dynamics CRM exclusive use; other web applications then will not be able to use that port.

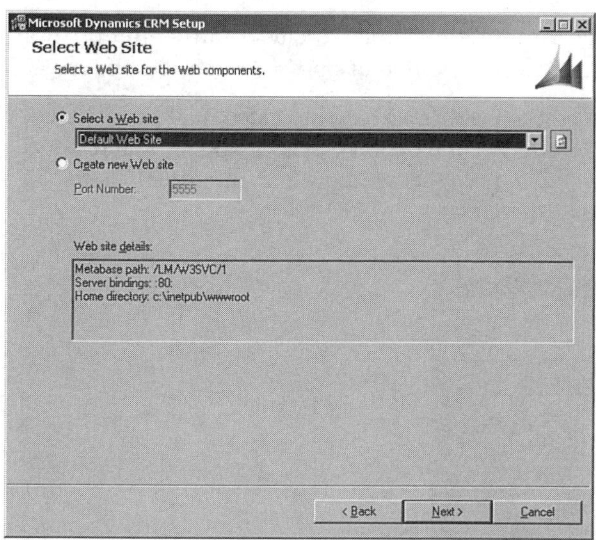

FIGURE 5.10 Microsoft Dynamics CRM website selection for installation.

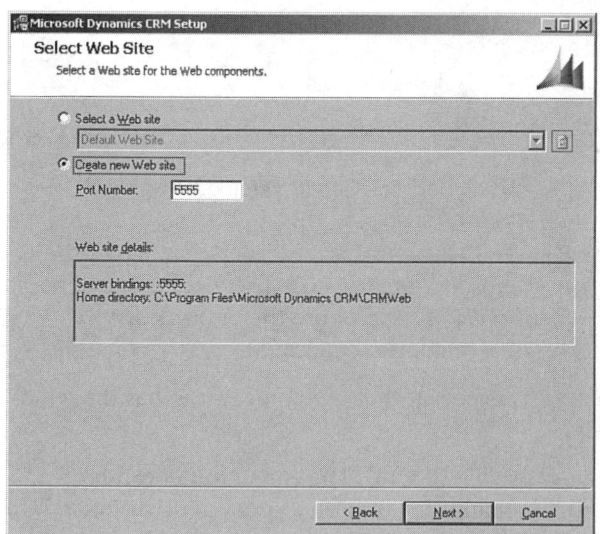

FIGURE 5.11 Microsoft Dynamics CRM new website selected. Notice that server binding is selected instead of 80.

5

Because port 80 is the default port for web traffic, carefully consider your options when selecting this setting. If you're unsure or you have other web-based applications that you are running (or would like to run from this server), we recommend you select the Create New Web site option.

Chapter 16, "Configuration and Customization Tools," includes further information about the default website setup and how the different port settings affect the server.

9. Enter the Reporting Services Server (see Figure 5.12). As indicated, make sure that you specify the Report Server URL and not the Report Manager URL. If you're unsure of the difference, you can open a browser window and enter the URL to verify that it is not the Report Manager URL.

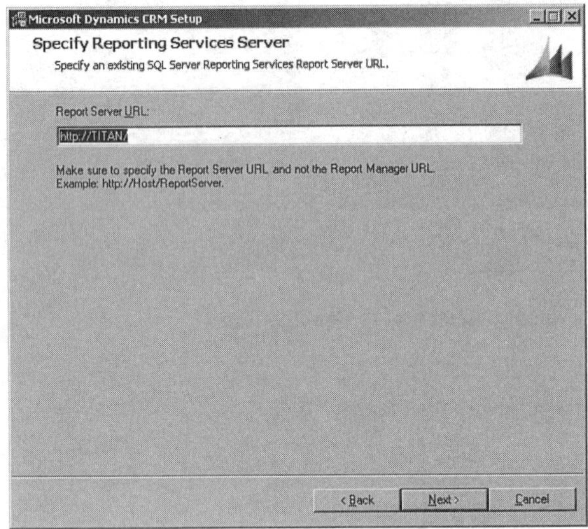

FIGURE 5.12 Microsoft Dynamics CRM Reporting Services Server setup.

10. Select the Organization Unit (see Figures 5.12 and 5.13), and click Next to continue. Specify the security account for the Microsoft Dynamics CRM services that will be installed. By default, Microsoft Dynamics CRM services use the network service account, but you can change this to use a domain user account.

    Be sure that if you select a domain user account, that the domain user has the requisite permissions (listed previously).

11. Enter the e-mail router server name (see Figure 5.13). The e-mail router can be installed on a server with Microsoft Exchange 2003 or on a computer that has a connection to an Exchange server. Additionally, because Exchange is not required, you can install the E-mail Router on any POP3-compliant e-mail server.

    Note that if you are installing the E-mail Router on a computer that previously had the Microsoft CRM 3.0 Router installed on it, you must manually remove the Microsoft CRM 3.0 Router before installing the Microsoft Dynamics CRM E-mail Router.

If you elect to install the E-mail Router later, leave the field blank and click Next.

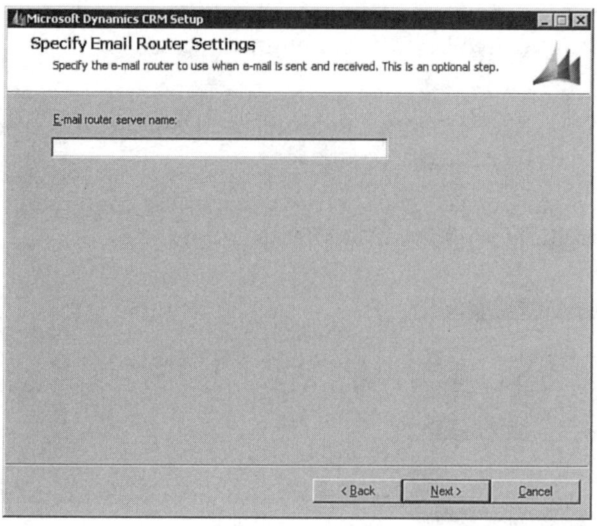

FIGURE 5.13 Microsoft Dynamics CRM E-mail Router setup.

12. Setup alerts you that you need to add the incoming Exchange Server to the Microsoft CRM PrivUserGroup when the E-mail Router setup is completed (see Figure 5.14). (PrivUserGroup is a security group created during the Microsoft CRM server setup process.) Click OK to continue.

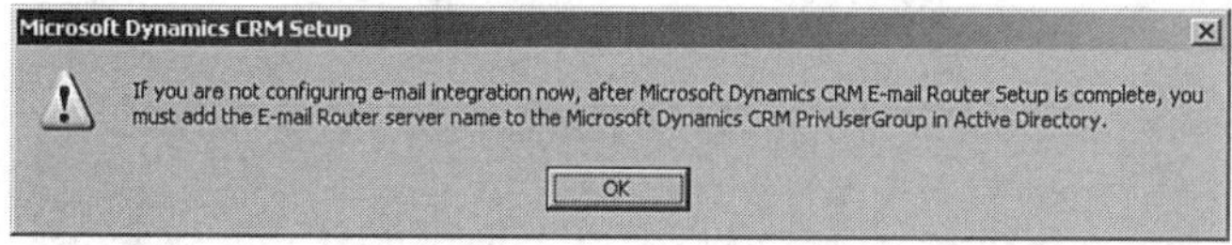

FIGURE 5.14 Microsoft Dynamics CRM E-mail Router setup reminder.

For more information on how the E-mail Router works, see Chapter 15, "E-mail Configuration."

13. The last step of the setup involves the system requirements (see Figure 5.15). This is where the proper installation, configuration, and status of each of the following is confirmed:

- **Microsoft Windows Operating System**—Version and service pack status. Additional checks include pending restart status.
- **Microsoft CRM Server User Input**—License, organization, and ISO specification.

- **Internet Information Services (IIS)**—Version and accessibility.
- **Microsoft SQL Server**—Version and service pack status.
- **Microsoft SQL Server Reporting Services**—Version and service pack status. Also checks the specified URL entered because part of the setup can be resolved to the Report Server.
- **Active Directory**—Whether Active Directory is accessible and whether the specified security account has the necessary permissions.

If any errors arise with these components, you must correct them before continuing with the installation. When everything is resolved, click Next to continue.

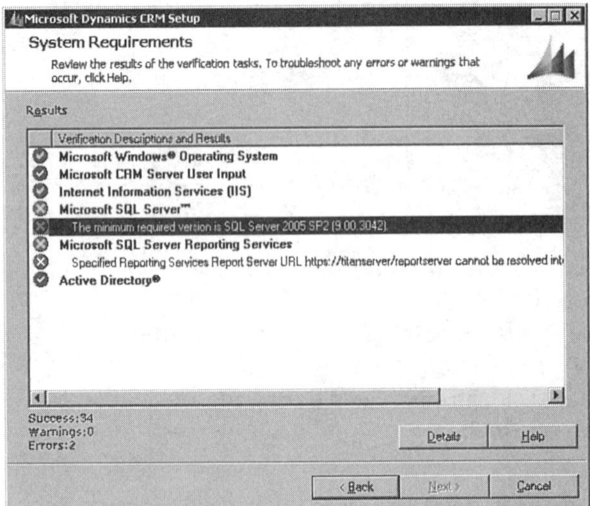

FIGURE 5.15 Microsoft Dynamics CRM system requirements verification.

When you have completed the Microsoft Dynamics CRM setup, you will be able to access the application by opening your browser and navigating to the URL you selected previously. Usually, this is http://localhost or http://localhost:5555, depending on the bindings selected.

Additional Steps

After the server is set up, there are a few other tasks that either need to be completed for full functionality or are recommended, depending on the type of server install you've selected.

Microsoft Dynamics CRM Data Connector (for IFD Installations)

The Microsoft Dynamics CRM Data Connector is required for Microsoft Dynamics CRM reporting and by default, the Microsoft Dynamics CRM Data Connector is installed as part of the Microsoft Dynamics CRM installation process when performing a non-IFD installation. However, unlike the E-mail Router, Microsoft Dynamics CRM Server setup must be completed before you install the Microsoft Dynamics CRM Data Connector as part of an IFD installation. Additionally, installation must be done on the computer that has the Microsoft SQL Server Reporting Services (SRS) that you will use for your installation of Microsoft Dynamics CRM.

To install the Microsoft Dynamics CRM Data Connector, follow these steps:

1. Navigate to the setup files on your Microsoft CRM Server CD/DVD.
2. Locate the directory from the root called `srsdataconnector` and launch the application `setupsrsdataconnector.exe`.
3. The Microsoft Dynamics CRM Data Connector Setup Wizard prompts you to download installation files (see Figure 5.16). Click the Update Installation Files (recommended) option.

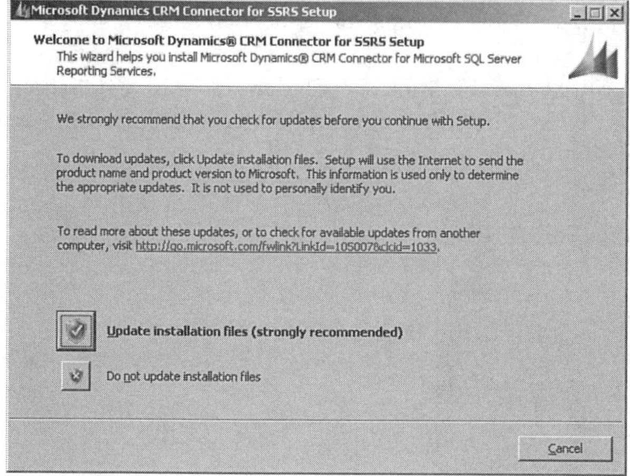

FIGURE 5.16 Microsoft Dynamics CRM Data Connector Setup Wizard check for updated files.

4. Accept the Microsoft Dynamics CRM Data Connector license agreement and click I Accept to continue.
5. The installer then performs a system check to see if required components necessary for the installation to continue are installed (see Figure 5.17). If you are not missing any components necessary for the installer to continue, you will not see this screen.

   Install any missing components by clicking Install; setup will not continue until they are installed. Click Next to continue after all components are installed.

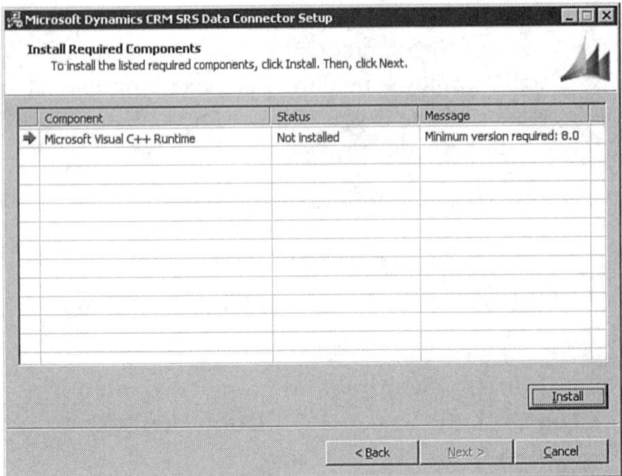

FIGURE 5.17 Microsoft Dynamics CRM Data Connector missing components check.

6. Specify the name of the computer that has the Microsoft Dynamics CRM SQL Server configuration database (see Figure 5.18). The configuration database for Microsoft Dynamics CRM is named `MSCRM_CONFIG`.

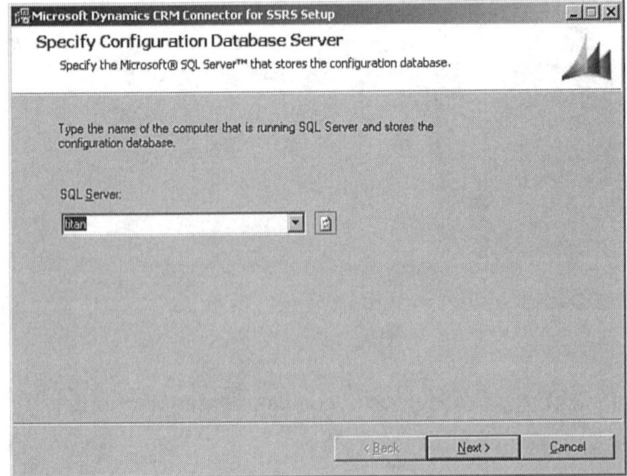

FIGURE 5.18 Microsoft Dynamics CRM Data Connector database configuration screen.

7. System requirements are verified and, if necessary, must be corrected before you continue the setup process. When all requirements are met, click Next to continue.

8. The setup summary screen appears. You can make any corrections at this time by clicking Back. Click Install to continue.

9. The installer then installs the Microsoft Dynamics CRM Data Connector and, when completed, displays a completion screen (see Figure 5.19). Click Finish to complete the installation.

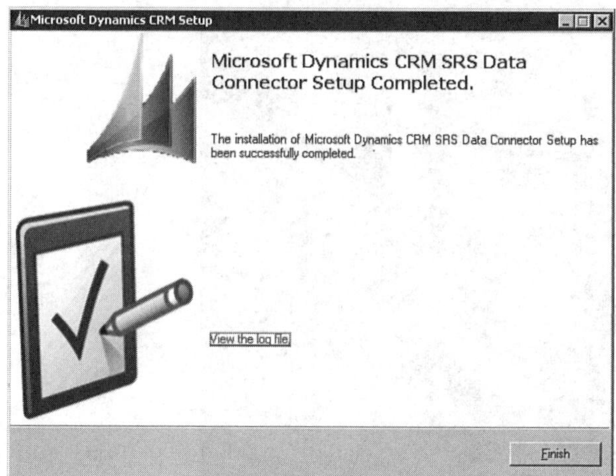

FIGURE 5.19 Microsoft Dynamics CRM Data Connector completion.

Registration Wizard

Microsoft Dynamics CRM must be registered after it is installed. You will continue to receive reminders that it hasn't been registered until you do so.

To register your system, navigate to Start, All Programs, Microsoft Dynamics CRM, Registration Wizard (see Figure 5.20).

Follow the steps on the Registration Wizard to complete your registration.

Deployment Manager

To create new organizations, manage your licenses and database, you will need to use the Deployment Manager. The Deployment Manager is found on the CRM server by going to Start, Programs, Microsoft Dynamics CRM, and selecting Deployment Manager (see Figure 5.21).

You must be a member of the Deployment Administrators group, otherwise you will receive an error when you try to launch it. By default, the user who performs the installation of Microsoft Dynamics CRM will be added to this group.

With the Deployment Manager, you can manage other members of the Deployment Administrators group, and set up/manage organizations, your servers, and licenses (see Figure 5.21).

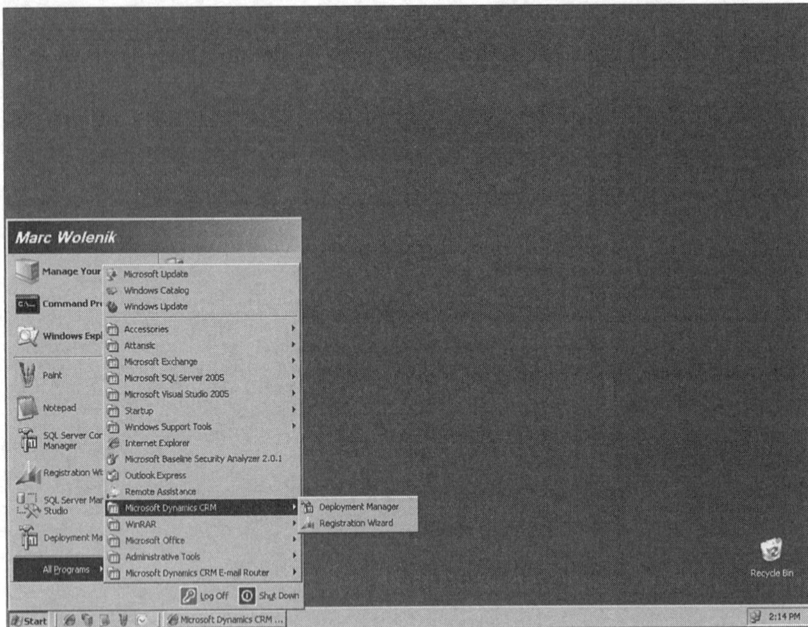

FIGURE 5.20 Location of the Registration Wizard.

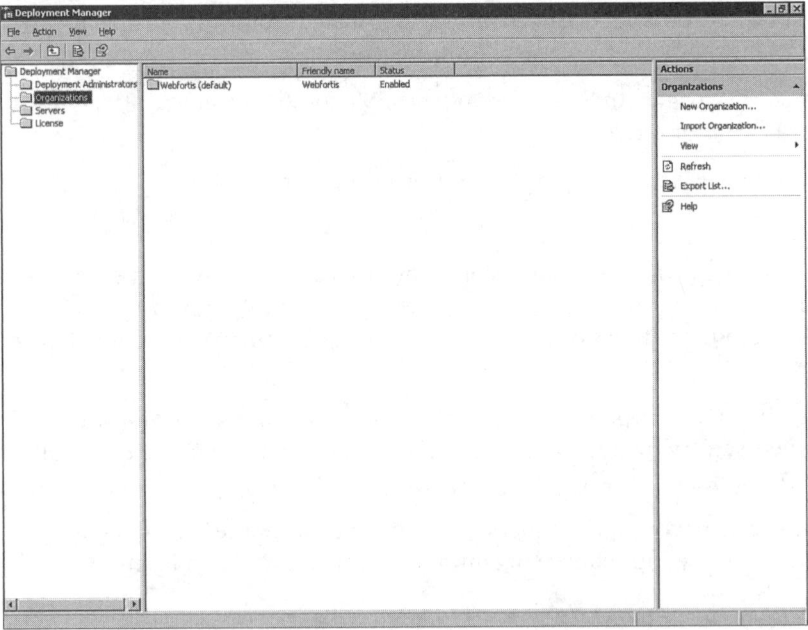

FIGURE 5.21 Deployment Manager.

To add users to the Deployment Administrators group, they must be added through the Deployment Manager. Users can be added by right-clicking the Deployment Administrators node and selecting New Deployment Administrator.

To provision a new organization, follow these steps (you must have a Microsoft Dynamics CRM version that supports multiple organizations to add new organizations to your system):

1. Right-click Organizations, and select New Organization.
2. Complete the required fields in the New Organization Wizard by entering the Display Name, Name, and selecting a currency by selecting the Browse button and then selecting a currency from the displayed currency options. When you're ready to continue, your form should look similar to Figure 5.22. Select Next to continue.

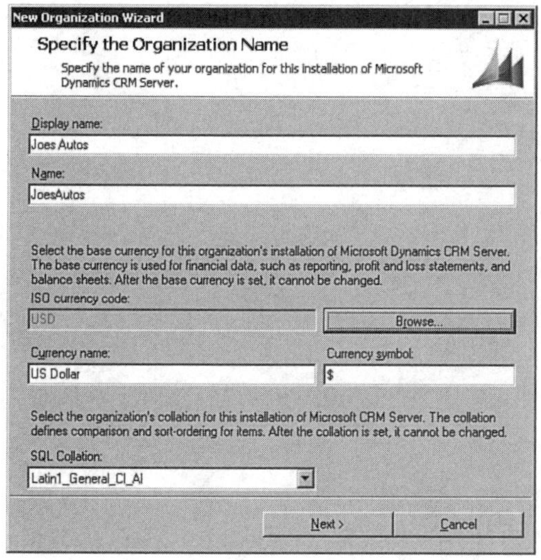

FIGURE 5.22 New Organization Wizard.

3. Select whether you'd like to participate in the Customer Experience Improvement Program, and select Next to continue.
4. Enter the location of your SQL Server (see Figure 5.23). Select Next to continue.
5. Enter the URL for your Report Server (see Figure 5.24). Select Next to continue.
6. The system will perform a Systems Requirements check on the organization information, SQL Server, and reporting services information entered. If there are any problems (such as an incorrect reporting server URL), they will be indicated and must be corrected prior to continuing by selecting Back or Cancel. Select Next to continue.

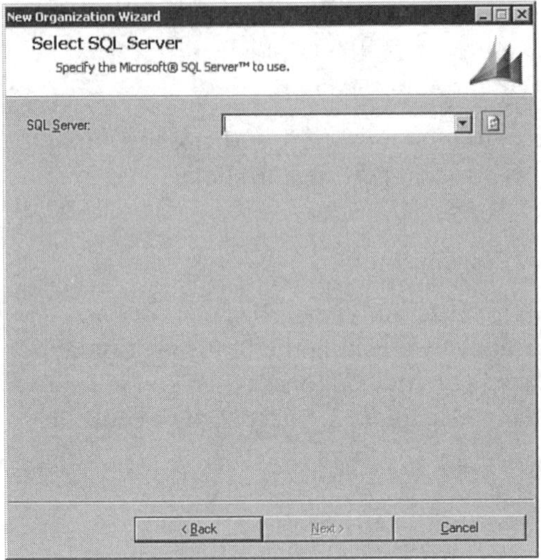

FIGURE 5.23 New Organization Wizard—Select SQL Server.

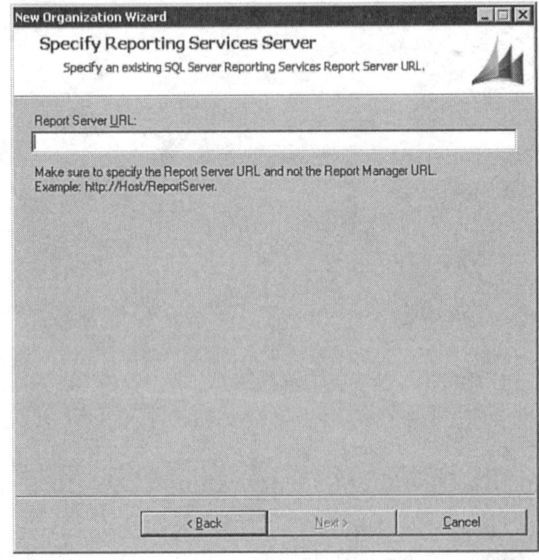

FIGURE 5.24 New Organization Wizard—Enter Report Server URL.

7. The entered information will be presented for a final review. If any corrections need to be made, you can select Back and make them. Select Create to create the organization.

8. The system will provision the new organization, and when complete, return a confirmation that the new organization has been created. It can then be managed in the Deployment Manager (see Figure 5.25).

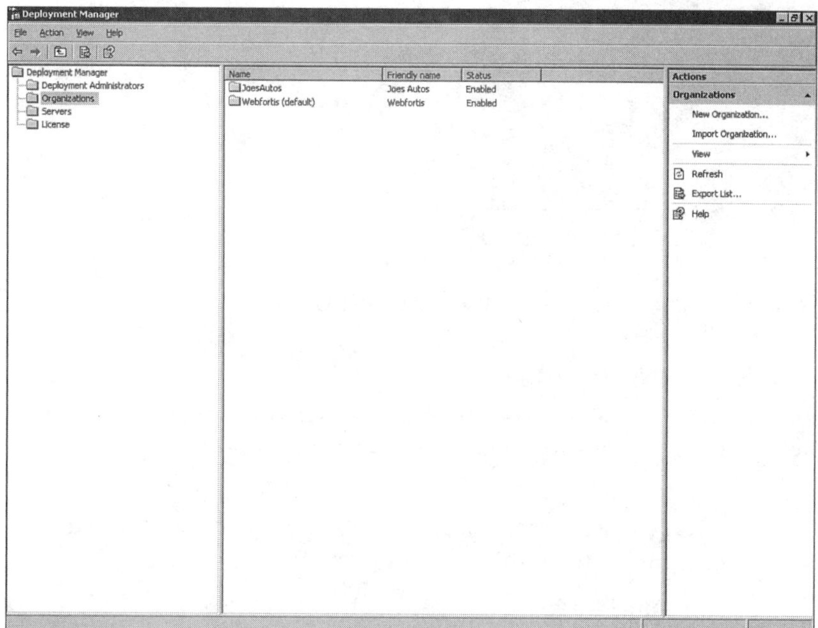

FIGURE 5.25 Deployment Manager with new organization.

Additional options that can be performed within the organization node are the ability to delete, edit, or disable/enable an existing organization. It is important to note that an organization must first be disabled prior to being deleted. Additionally, a deleted organization has its organization information deleted only from the configuration database—the organization database remains and must be removed manually by using SQL tools.

The edit options allow you to easily change an organization name, the SQL Server, and/or the SRS Server. This is usually done when a database is moved to a new server.

The Server option displays information about the server, Microsoft Dynamics CRM version, and the role, whereas the License option displays information relevant to the Microsoft Dynamics version and users. If you double-click the displayed license, you will get a summary of the licenses used (see Figure 5.26).

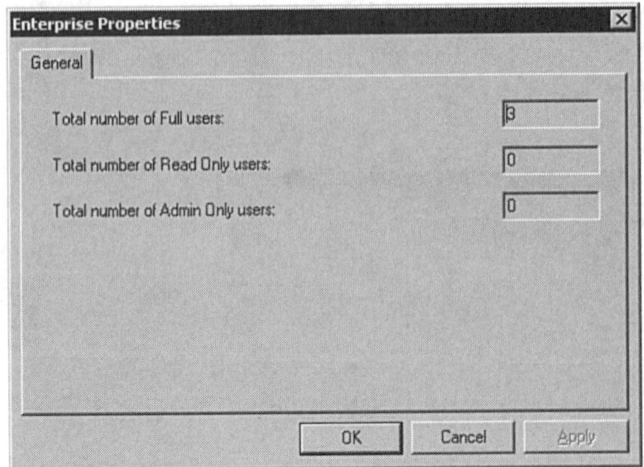

FIGURE 5.26 Deployment Manager displaying licensing information.

Microsoft Dynamics CRM Clients

With a fully functional Internet Explorer–based interface as well as the Microsoft Dynamics CRM Outlook Client, users can choose how they want to work with Microsoft Dynamics CRM.

Regardless of which client you choose to work with, the CRM website must be added as a trusted site on the client computers. To do this, follow these steps:

1. Navigate to the Control Panel by going to Start, Control Panel.
2. Launch Internet Options.
3. Select the Security tab.
4. Click Trusted Sites; then click the Sites button.
5. On the Trusted Sites dialog page, enter the URL to your CRM website. Be sure to include the http:// or https:// if your server uses secure (SSL) connection. Uncheck Require Server Verification (https:) for all sites in this zone if you are not running your CRM over a secure (SSL) connection.
6. Click Close and OK to close the Internet Options dialog page.

You are now set to install or configure one of the Microsoft CRM clients.

Internet Explorer

When accessing Microsoft Dynamics CRM from Internet Explorer, users merely have to enter the URL for their Microsoft CRM installation. A default installation URL consists of http://<servername>:5555 or http://<servername>, where `<servername>` is the name of the CRM server. When users are authenticated on the same network, Microsoft Dynamics CRM loads in the browser automatically. If users are connecting to the Microsoft CRM Server via the Internet, they receive a Microsoft Windows authentication request consisting of user-name and password after they request use of the application by default; however, you can also set this to use forms (IFD) or passport authentication. (Refer to Chapter 17, "Forms

Authentication," for more information about how to access the CRM server when IFD is enabled.)

With this version of Microsoft Dynamics CRM, the application is set by default to not run in application mode, and it loads as a tabbed page in Internet Explorer 7 (see Figure 5.27).

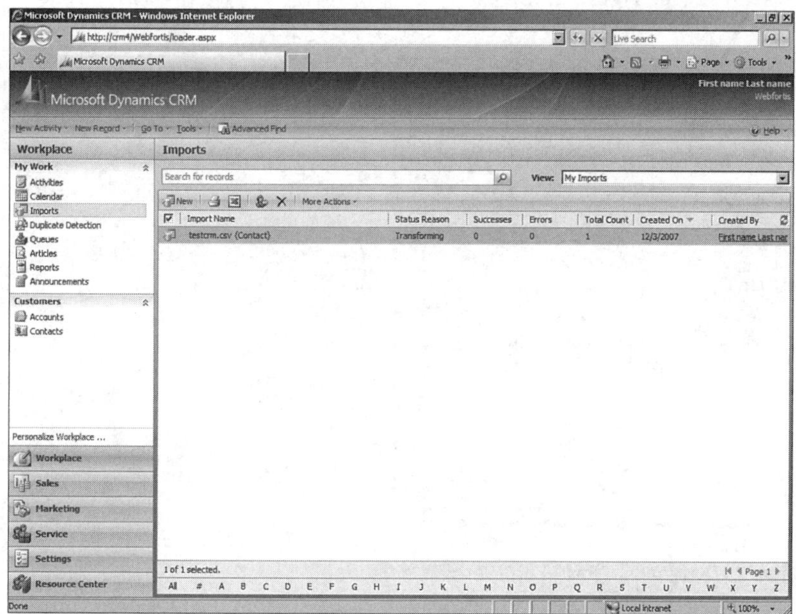

FIGURE 5.27 Microsoft Dynamics CRM tabbed browsing interface.

Application mode hides the URL address information in the Internet Explorer window, and, when used, it acts more like a Windows application. If you want to use application mode, be sure users don't have a pop-up blocker installed, or they will have trouble opening the CRM web application.

Outlook Client

The Outlook client is available in two different modes:

- CRM for Outlook
- CRM for Outlook with Offline Access

As explained in Chapter 4, the versions are essentially the same (the Laptop version has offline support), and only one installation package exists for both.

An important addition to Microsoft Dynamics CRM with regard to the Outlook client is that it is now broken down into two steps:

- Installation
- Configuration

Installation To install either version of the Outlook Client, start the client setup application found on the Microsoft Dynamics CRM setup disks and follow these steps:

1. Start the client installation by launching the setup application setupclient.exe.
2. Select the client version you want to install (either Online or Offline Access) and click Next to continue (see Figure 5.28).

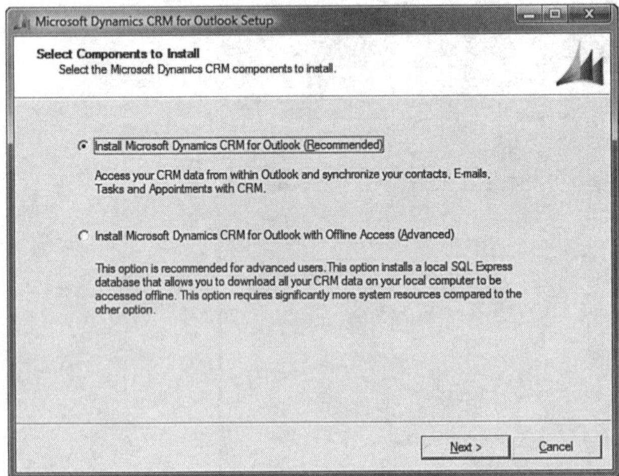

FIGURE 5.28 Microsoft Dynamics CRM client version selection.

3. The license terms from Microsoft are displayed. You must accept the license agreement to continue. After you do so, click I Accept to continue.
4. The installer performs a system check to see if required components necessary for the installation to continue are installed. If you are not missing any components necessary for the installer to continue, you will not see this screen.

   Install any missing components by clicking Install; setup will not continue until they are installed. Click Next to continue when all components are installed.
5. Select the installation location. Click Next to continue.
6. System requirements are verified. If any are found lacking, you must correct them before continuing the setup process (see Figure 5.29). When all requirements are met, click Next to continue.
7. The program will install and when setup is completed, you will see a completed confirmation (see Figure 5.30 below).

As noted in Chapter 4, you must have a Full user access license (CAL) to be able to use the Outlook client. Read-Only and Administrative CALs will not function with the Outlook client.

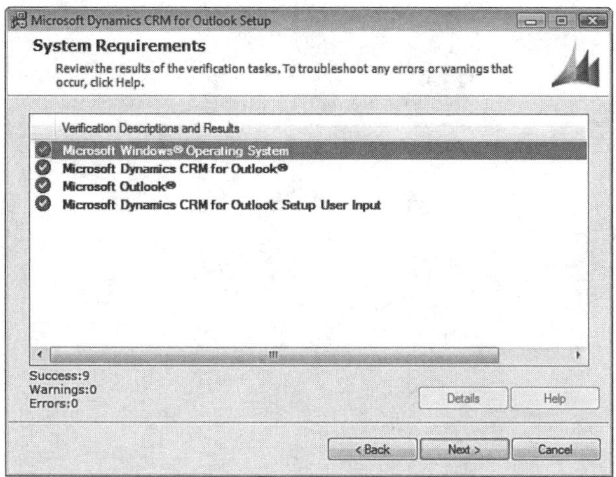

FIGURE 5.29 Microsoft Dynamics CRM Outlook client system requirements.

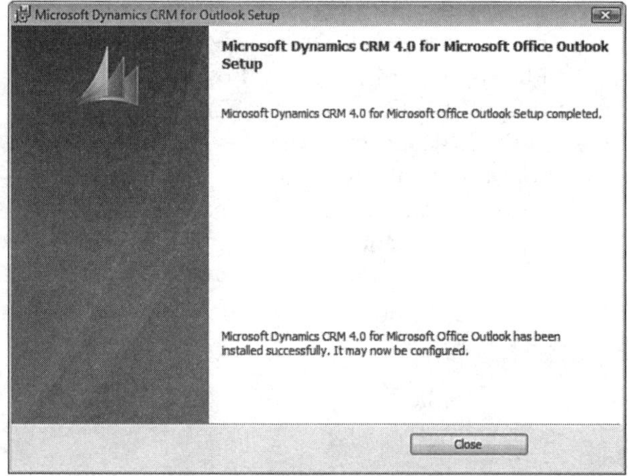

FIGURE 5.30 Microsoft Dynamics CRM Outlook client system setup confirmation.

Configuration After the Outlook client has been installed on to your system, it must be configured. To configure the Outlook client, follow these steps (note that Outlook must be closed before running the configuration, or you will get an alert to close it):

1. Navigate to Start, All Programs, Microsoft Dynamics CRM, and select Configuration Wizard. The Configuration Wizard will start. Select Next to continue.

2. Select where your Microsoft Dynamics Server is located. If you are using your server or an On Premise server without IFD enabled, select My Company; otherwise, select the second option for On Premise with IFD enabled or Hosted Partners (which typically used IFD) (see Figure 5.31).

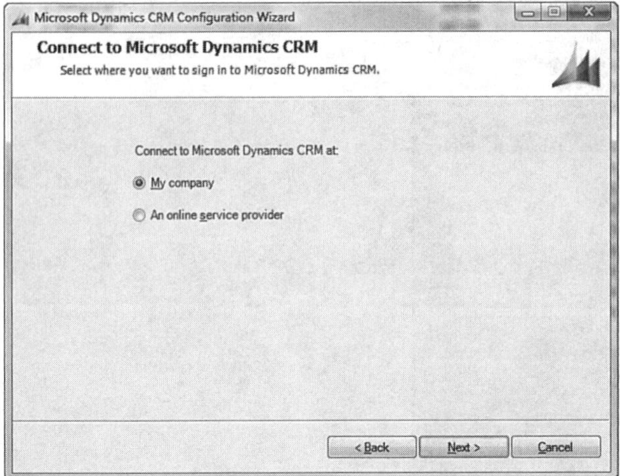

FIGURE 5.31 Microsoft Dynamics CRM Outlook client wizard.

3. Regardless of which option you select in step 2, your next step is to enter the server information. For On Premise installations, this is usually http://<servername> or http://<servername>:5555. For either Microsoft CRM Online or hosted servers, enter the URL information that you received from them (see Figure 5.32). Note that you will only see Figure 5.32 if you selected the first option in the previous step (My Company). If you selected the second option in the previous step, then you will only need to enter the URL to the CRM server. Additionally, the machine must be joined to the domain where the CRM server is installed, and you must be a valid CRM user or the setup won't let you continue.

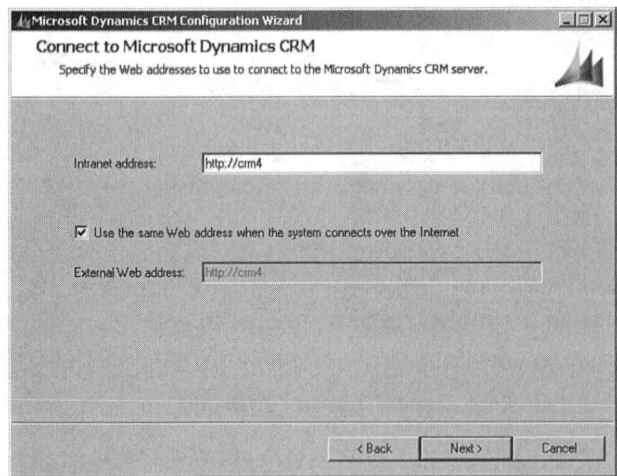

FIGURE 5.32 Microsoft Dynamics CRM Outlook client wizard.

4. If the CRM server address you entered has more than one organization, you will be asked to choose one organization in this step (see Figure 5.33). If your server contains only one organization, this step will be skipped. Select Next to continue.

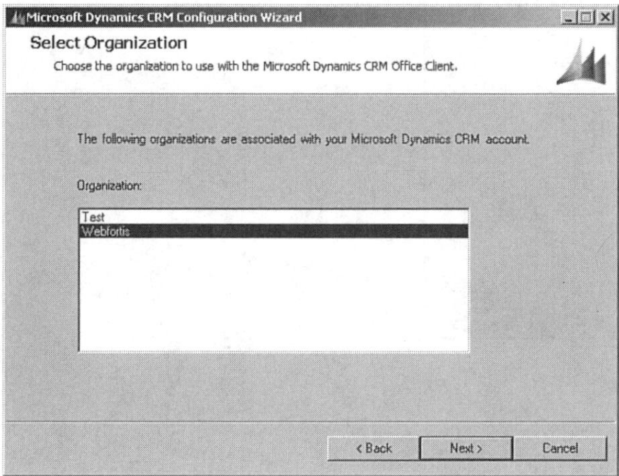

FIGURE 5.33 Selecting organization.

5. Select whether you would like to participate in the Customer Feedback Program, then select Next to continue. The setup will validate all the system requirements (see Figure 5.34). Select Next to continue.

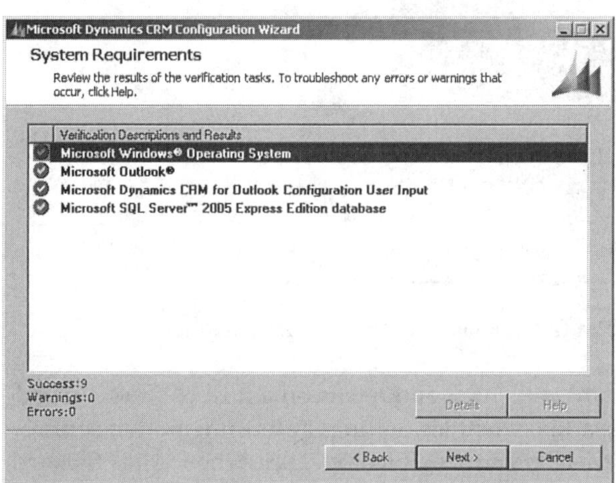

FIGURE 5.34 System Requirements validation.

6. The setup will configure the Outlook client for the selected organization. When the setup finishes, it will show the configuration complete dialog box (see Figure 5.35).

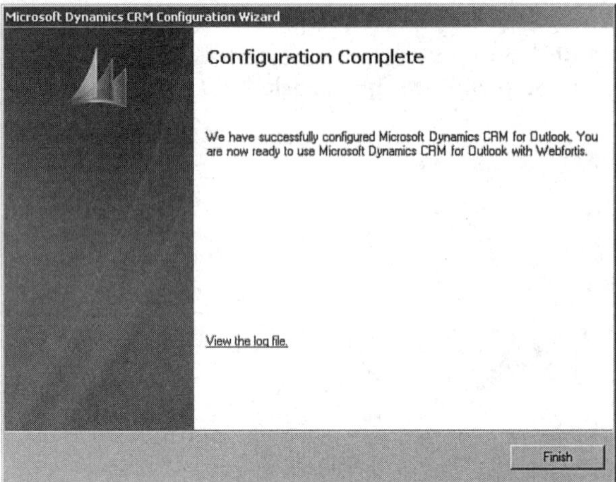

FIGURE 5.35 Configuration complete.

Outlook Diagnostics

When the Microsoft Dynamics CRM Outlook client is installed, it also installs the Outlook Diagnostics Wizard. This is a great tool that can be used to help troubleshoot problems with the CRM client. To launch the wizard, go to Start, All Programs, Microsoft CRM, and select Diagnostics. The wizard will open, allowing you run diagnostics (see Figure 5.36).

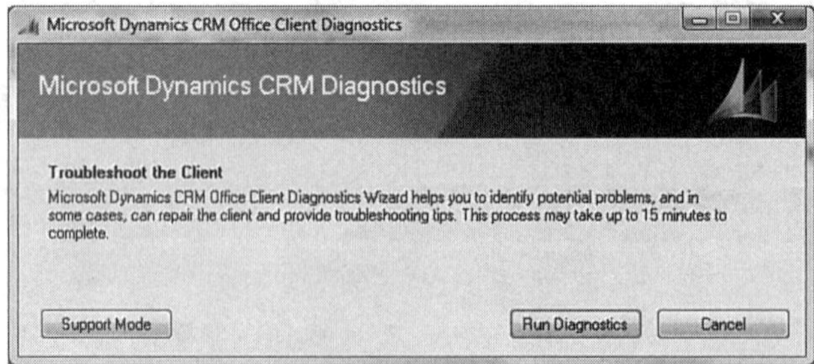

FIGURE 5.36 Microsoft Dynamics CRM Outlook client system setup confirmation.

If you select Run Diagnostics, the wizard will check and report on a host of issues, including internet connectivity, CRM access and credentials, settings and configuration settings on the client machine, and whether there are any required updates. When it has finished, it will report on the results with recommendations, as well as the option to perform the fixes if it is able to do so automatically.

If you select Support Mode, you can select which of the above checks it should run, whether certain synchronization should be turned on or off for the diagnostics, as well as generate support files for advanced troubleshooting.

Microsoft Dynamics CRM Online Setup

The setup for Microsoft Dynamics CRM Online is wizard-driven and consists of two steps:

- Account and billing setup
- Organization setup

The account and billing setup consists of signing up in one of the four methods outlined in Chapter 3, "The Evolution of Microsoft Dynamics CRM 4.0"—online, via telephone, in a retail store, or through a partner referral. When signing up online, follow these steps:

1. Navigate to http://crm.dynamics.com and select the Join Now or Sign Up option.
2. Select the Microsoft Dynamics CRM Online version and any other options available.
3. Associate your Windows Live ID with the account. (If you don't have one, you're prompted to get one at this point in time.)
4. Enter your information and any partner referral information, if applicable.
5. Accept the Terms of Service and enter credit card billing information.
6. You'll receive an e-mail thereafter confirming your purchase, access instructions, and other information related to your account. The access instructions include a link to organization setup.

To perform the organization setup, follow the access instructions received after account signup. The first time users log into their account, they will receive a welcome screen allowing them to perform the configuration process or invite someone else to perform the configurations. Because the person who performs the configurations is automatically an administrator, he can perform any function within the system.

As part of the organization configuration process, a wizard prompts for users the preferred base currency, allows you to import data into the system, and prompts for business goals that prompt for further/continued setup of different areas in the system for the organization prior to initial use. After this setup has been completed, the system is available for use by your users.

Upgrading from Previous Versions

The only supported upgrade to Microsoft CRM 4.0 is an upgrade from Microsoft 3.0. If you're running a version of Microsoft CRM prior to 3.0 (i.e. 1.0 or 1.2), you must first upgrade to 3.0 and then to 4.0. Additionally, there is no support for Microsoft Dynamics 3.0 Mobile, and it should be uninstalled prior to attempting an upgrade.

Note that upgrading Microsoft CRM 1.0 or 1.2 to Microsoft 3.0 is beyond the scope of this book.

Considerations when upgrading:

- **Customizations**—The upgrade process attempts to upgrade all published customizations automatically, but all unpublished customizations will be lost. Make sure that all customized forms are fully published before you upgrade. Furthermore, an entity might not be upgraded if it is missing required fields. (Be sure to check the setup log file if you encounter this.)
- **Reports**—Special effort has been made to ensure that reports are upgraded and to make them compatible with the new Microsoft CRM Data Connector. A new view added to the Reports entity, called Microsoft Dynamics 3.0 Reports, has been created to support the existing Microsoft CRM 3.0 reports. If you have modified any of the reports, they will not upgrade properly, as there are known problems when trying to upgrade reports that have been modified to use either stored procedures or expressions for linking. Additionally, reports that rely on Microsoft CRM 3.0 workflow will not upgrade.
- **Ownership issues**—Reports are given organization ownership and are available to all users.
- **Workflow**—Due to the changes in how Microsoft Dynamics CRM works with Workflow, previous Workflows must be part of the migration process. (They cannot be imported.) The upgrade process attempts to upgrade all previous Workflows; however, you should carefully examine upgraded Workflows after migration to ensure that they don't fail and that they perform as expected.

Although Microsoft Dynamics CRM 4.0 supports an "in-place" upgrade, the following steps are recommended as part of the upgrade process:

1. Back up the existing Microsoft CRM 3.0 database. This includes both the SQL Server CRM database and the metadatabase for CRM. The database names are formatted as <organizationname>_MSCRM and <organizationname>_METABASE.
2. Back up all reports, including any custom and modified reports from the existing Microsoft Dynamics CRM application. This can be done easily using the tool called `DownloadReports.exe` which is usually located in the C:\Program Files\Microsoft CRM\Reports folder of the CRM 3.0 Server installation path.
3. Export and back up all customizations from the Microsoft CRM 3.0 application. This needs to be done from the CRM web interface by going to Settings, Customizations, Export Customizations.

When you have completed and verified these steps, follow the steps previously outlined in this chapter under "Microsoft Dynamics CRM Server Setup" to upgrade the Microsoft

CRM 3.0 server to a Microsoft Dynamics CRM server. After the installer completes its system check (step 5) and installs any missing components, it automatically recognizes that Microsoft CRM 3.0 is installed (see Figure 5.37). Click Next to continue.

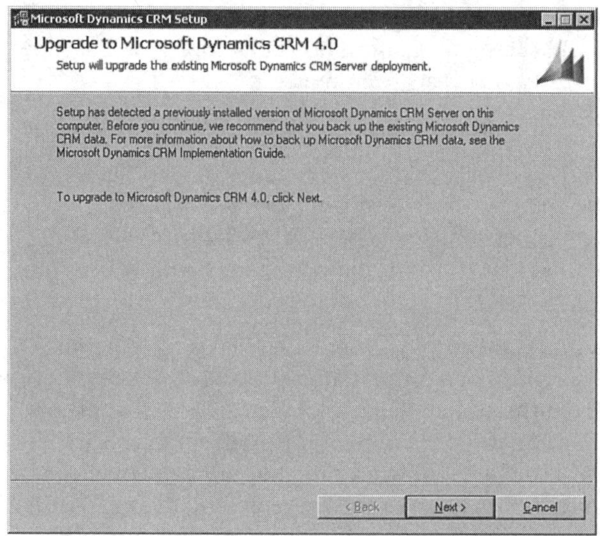

FIGURE 5.37 Microsoft Dynamics CRM/Microsoft CRM 3.0 upgrade notification.

By default, Microsoft CRM 3.0 is upgraded with both Application and Platform server roles as part of the upgrade.

Complete the remaining steps outlined. When the installation finishes, you are prompted to restart your computer.

If you encounter any issues not mentioned here, check the setup log that is created when the server installation completes.

Setting Up Your Business in Microsoft Dynamics CRM

Regardless of which version and platform of Microsoft Dynamics CRM you're working with, after you complete setting up your system, you need to configure your business. Microsoft Dynamics CRM is extremely flexible and can be made to work with virtually any business. When working with Microsoft Dynamics CRM Online, the wizard walks you through many of the setup steps; however, there are still many things that can be configured, and it is helpful to know about the options if you want to change the configurations. If you're not using Microsoft Dynamics CRM Online, you need to perform these settings.

The following list represents some of the things that need to be configured. For a complete list of all settings and configuration options, as well as more information related to everything below, refer to Chapter 14, "Settings and Configuration."

- **Organizations**—When considering working with your organization, you'll want to consider the hierarchy of your organization, as well as how it is structured. Within Microsoft Dynamics CRM, there are options to break out your organization by business unit, territories, and sites. When thinking about how to configure your organization, it is helpful to spend some time preparing how it should be structured within the Microsoft Dynamics CRM framework, both how it is now, as well as how you believe it will be in six months to two years from now.
- **Business Units**—Business units are important and can be used by even the smallest organizations to easily control access and divide records.

  Because business units cannot be changed or deleted when created (they can, however, be disabled) and when business units are changed, all security roles for users must be reassigned, it is a good idea to think about how they will work within your organization.
- **Users**—Because Microsoft Dynamics CRM employs user-based licensing, determining who will need access to the system is very important, because it will affect not only the cost, but also how users in the system will work together. For example, if only customer service people are using the system, then it is unlikely that you'll be using the leads functionality, because that is mostly a function of salespeople. Another example is when you have both customer service representatives and salespeople in the system but not your marketing staff; then Microsoft Dynamics CRM marketing functionality will likely be underutilized.

  It is a good idea to outline who needs to use the system immediately, as well as anticipated users, so you can plan for both growth and other licensing requirements. We have found that initial estimates of users are usually light, because the system is so powerful and easy to use that when users see it, they want to work with it. With the new licensing options for Microsoft Dynamics CRM, this isn't as prohibitive as it was in earlier versions.

  Although users are established in the system, they can be deactivated, and other users can use the license. Note that this practice is not recommended for routine use and should only be used when users leave the company or no longer need access to the Microsoft Dynamics CRM system. Managing users is easy, and unlike previous versions, the ability to quickly and easily add one or multiple users to the system is now available directly from the application interface by navigating to Settings, Administration, and selecting New from the Users option.

  If you are working with Microsoft Dynamics CRM Online, you have the option to create users when you first perform your system setup via the Setup Wizard. Additionally, and only available with Microsoft Dynamics CRM Online, you have the option to send invitations to the newly added users via their entered e-mail addresses. If you select this option, the users are sent an e-mail that explains how to access Microsoft Dynamics CRM Online.
- **Customers**—Microsoft Dynamics CRM defines customers in two ways, Accounts and Contacts. These entities can be easily renamed if your organization requires it

(for example, Companies and Customers instead of Accounts and Contacts). Working with customers is explained fully in Chapter 8, "Working with Customers;" however, it is important to consider the account and contacts structure when migrating from other CRM applications, because other systems may use a different hierarchy, and data will need to be migrated using this structure. If this is your case, consider referential accounts and contacts where accounts have a parent–child relationship (for example, there might be an account called Joe's Auto that has two subaccounts called Joe's Auto—Retail and Joe's Auto—Commercial, and contacts that report directly to either of these, but none to the master parent account of Joe's Auto), or work with business units instead.

Additionally, while both accounts and contacts are considered customers, you will likely have a mix of records contained within these records. For example, your account records might have supplier and/or vendor records, as well as their contact information.

- **Roles**—Microsoft Dynamics CRM is role-based, and every user must have a valid role to work within the system. This is outlined in Chapters 4 and 14; however, it is important to recognize the difference in roles that might exist between a user on the network and Microsoft Dynamics CRM.

  The roles that come by default with Microsoft Dynamics CRM are well defined; however, be sure to review the permissions carefully when utilizing them. The most common cause of users having problems working within their system is related to their permissions. Additionally, be sure whichever role you set for your users has the level of control that you expect.

- **Queues and Teams**—Queues and teams are a powerful way of setting up your system to ensure that both record load is leveled and records can be shared when required.

- **E-mail**—When setting up e-mail with Microsoft Dynamics CRM, there is a host of new options that easily extend functionality, regardless of what you're using for your e-mail server.

  Also, be sure to carefully check your settings for e-mail tracking. Occasionally, users will set the tracking of e-mails to All for their mailbox, and later find that their personal messages are appearing in Microsoft Dynamics CRM. We generally recommend setting the All option for dedicated mailboxes, such as support@yourdomain.com or sales@yourdomain.com.

Summary

Within this chapter, we reviewed how to set up Microsoft Dynamics CRM, with consideration given to both the architecture as well as the business for both On Premise and Microsoft Dynamics CRM Online. It is important to realize that these can be related or unique processes, and an understanding of what options are available can dictate a successful or failed implementation.

CHAPTER 6

Data Migration and Conversion

IN THIS CHAPTER

If you were setting up Microsoft Dynamics CRM for a new company, you might not need to import any data into the system. If that is your case, you could completely skip this chapter. However, in most cases, customers want to move their current CRM records from other applications or customer relationship management systems, and importing data into Microsoft Dynamics CRM used to be a real challenge.

This version of Microsoft Dynamics CRM has improved the difficult task of importing data from other systems significantly. You can import external data in Microsoft Dynamics CRM in two ways:

- The Import Wizard
- The Data Migration Manager

NOTE

There might be some cases where importing data is more complex than explained in this chapter. In those cases, we recommend developing either a custom application or the utilization of a third-party migration tool (refer to Chapter 25, "Migrating Data from Other Systems to Microsoft Dynamics CRM").

The Import Wizard Tool

The Import Wizard tool is the easiest and most user-friendly way to import data into Microsoft Dynamics CRM. Any Microsoft Dynamics CRM user can do it, and it doesn't require administrative permissions by default. This option can be disabled in the core records permissions by modifying the Data Import option from the Settings, Administration, Security Roles interface (see Chapter 14, "Settings and Configuration," for more details about how to change and set CRM permissions). In addition, this tool is embedded directly within Microsoft Dynamics CRM, so no other application needs to be installed or used. The Import Wizard is available from either the Outlook client or the Internet Explorer client.

To run the Import Wizard, the data to be imported must be in a CSV (Comma Separated Values) file. Although the fields in the CSV file can be in any order, the header names are helpful in avoiding the creation of a Data Map. (Data Maps are explained later in this chapter.)

Before you import any data, you might have to create a mapping. This is a new feature for Microsoft Dynamics CRM and greatly improves the entities that we can import data for. Previous versions allowed you to import data for only the following entities:

- Account
- Contact
- Lead
- Campaign Response

With Microsoft Dynamics CRM 4.0, you can import data for every entity in the system, including custom entities you might have created.

Data Management Interface

The Import Wizard is accessed from the new Data Management interface. To navigate to the Data Management interface, select Settings, Data Management (or choose Data Management from Go To and Settings from the top menu) (see Figure 6.1).

The interface has the following tools related to the data import function (see Figure 6.2):

- Duplication Detection Settings
- Duplicate Detection Rules
- Duplicate Detection Jobs
- Bulk Record Deletion
- Data Maps
- Imports

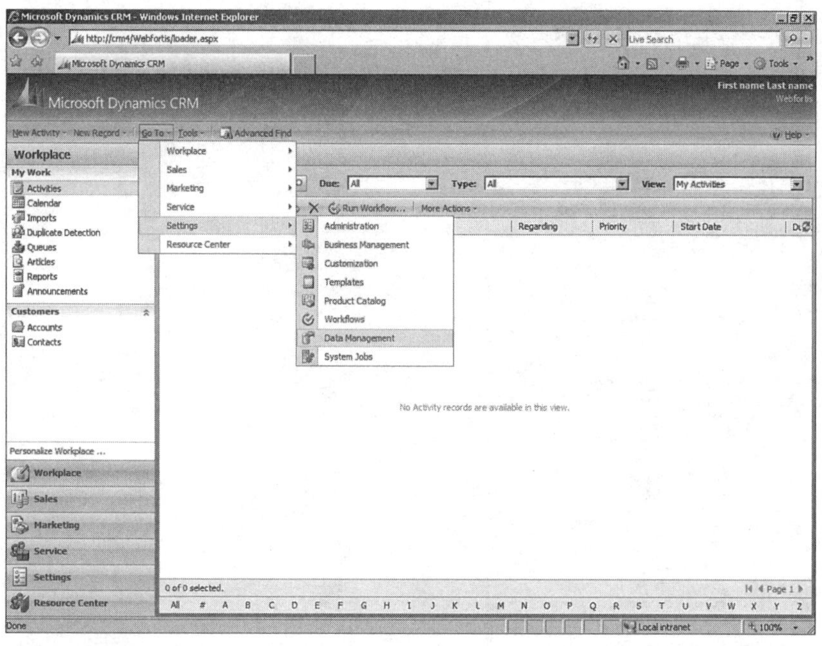

FIGURE 6.1 The new Data Management interface.

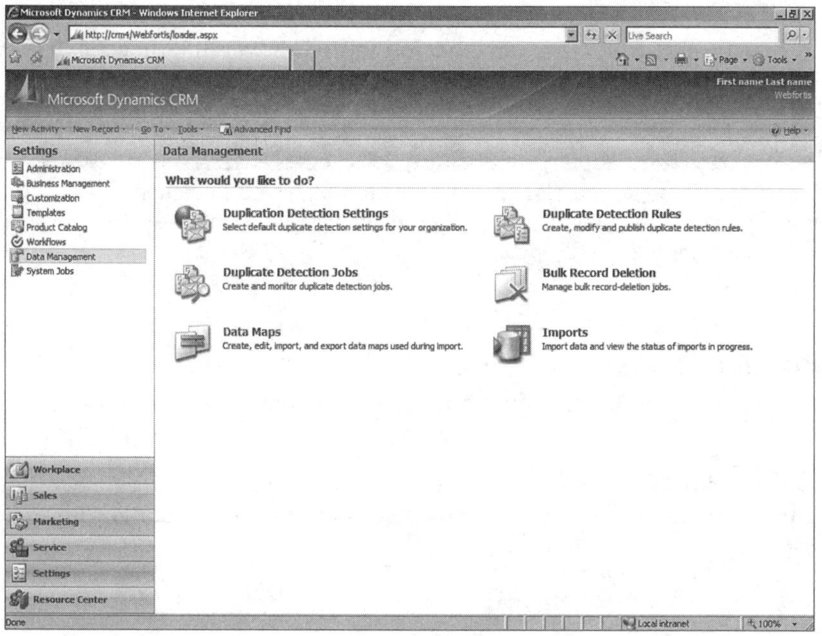

FIGURE 6.2 The Data Management options.

Duplication Detection Settings

Duplicate detection is a new feature that can prevent duplicate data in the system. From this dialog box, you can enable, disable, or configure this feature (see Figure 6.3).

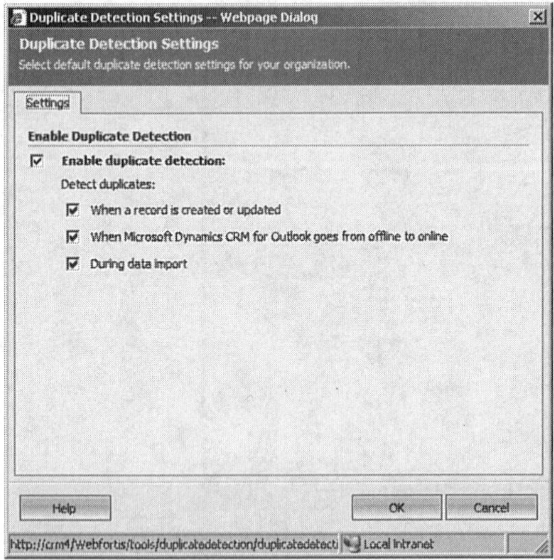

FIGURE 6.3 Duplicate Detection Settings.

These settings apply to the entire organization, and you can select whether they apply to data import.

NOTE

If you disable Duplicate Detection, you also unpublish all the Duplicate Detection Rules. You then must enable the rules manually after re-enabling the Duplicate Detection feature if you want them to be published.

Duplicate Detection Rules

From here you can set up rules to prevent duplicate records in your organization (see Figure 6.4).

Some rules are created and published by default; however, you can create other rules manually. For example, you might want to prevent users from creating Accounts with the same name or phone numbers.

Duplicate Detection Jobs

This interface allows you to create jobs to detect duplicate records for any entity in the system that has a Duplicate Detection Rule.

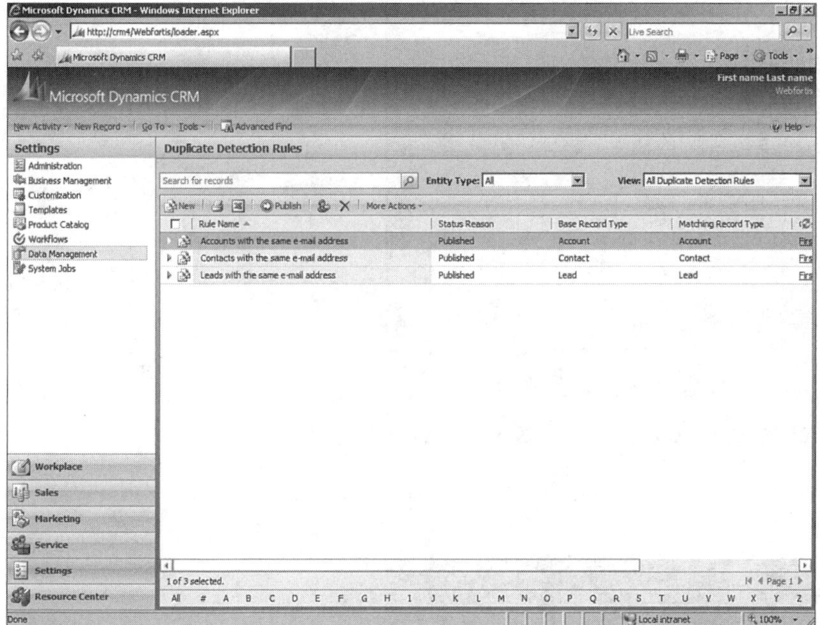

FIGURE 6.4 Duplicate Detection Rules interface.

NOTE

You can set up Duplicate Detection Jobs by creating Duplicate Detection Rules for the other entities and then publishing them. Note that you may need to wait about 5 minutes until the rule is available to run.

To create a new Duplicate Detection Job, follow these steps:

1. Select New and a new wizard will be open, as shown in Figure 6.5.
2. Click the Next button to continue and select the entity where you want to check for duplicated records. Select the entity to run the job on. Notice that only entities that have a rule will be available (see Figure 6.6). You can also select an existing View or create a new one to filter the columns you want to check.

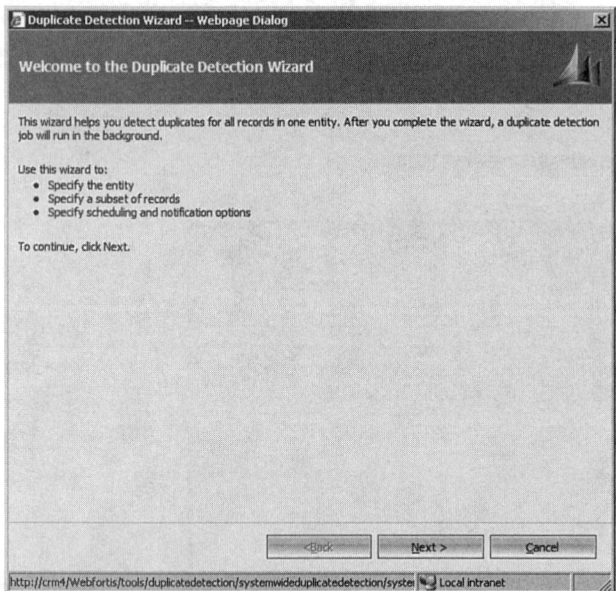

FIGURE 6.5 Welcome to the Duplicate Detection Wizard.

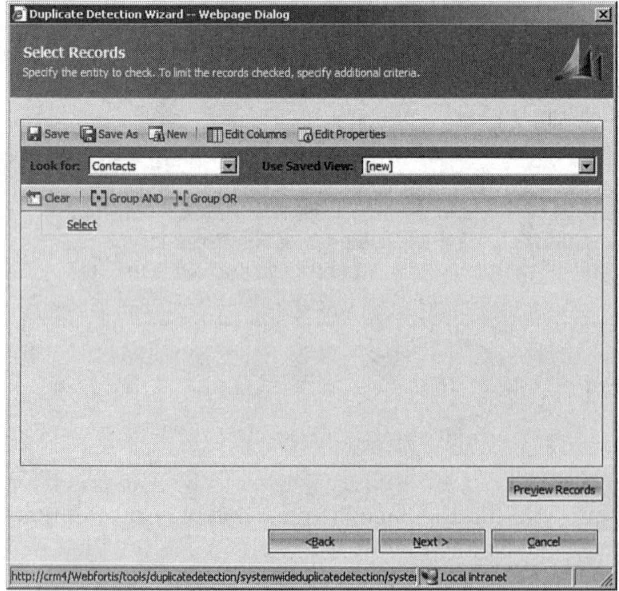

FIGURE 6.6 Select Records.

3. Click the Preview Records button to check the records and fields from the selected view (see Figure 6.7).

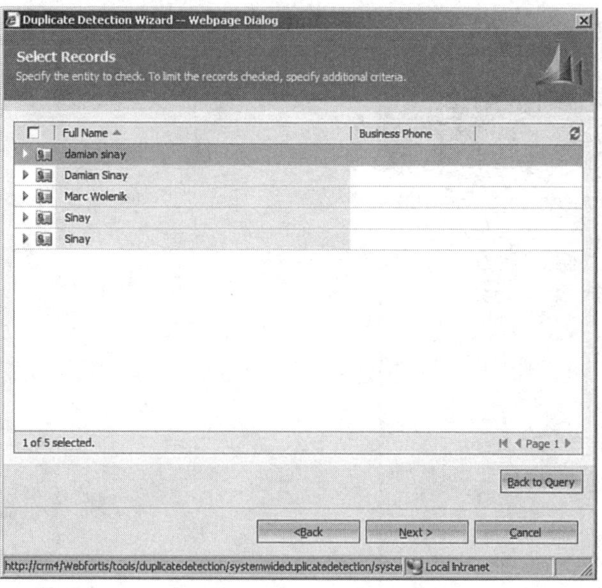

FIGURE 6.7 Previewing records.

4. Click the Next button and enter a name for this Job. You can also configure when you want to have this job run with the ability to automate this process to be scheduled every X number of days. Also, you can set the Users who will be notified when the job finishes (see Figure 6.8). Click Next to continue.

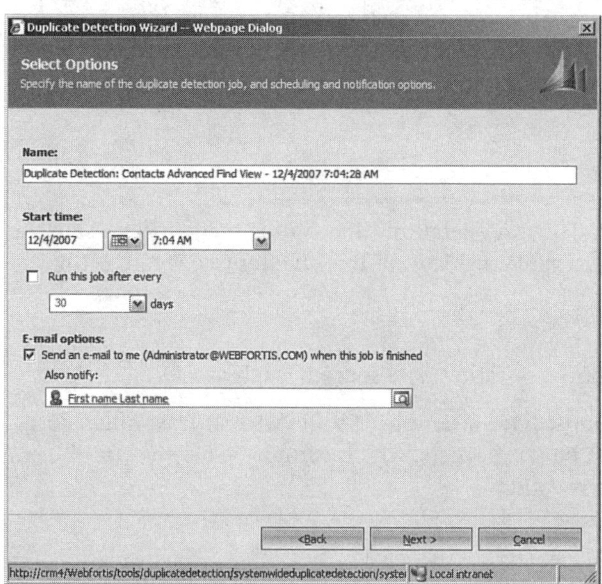

FIGURE 6.8 Selection options.

5. Click the Finish button to create and save this job (see Figure 6.9).

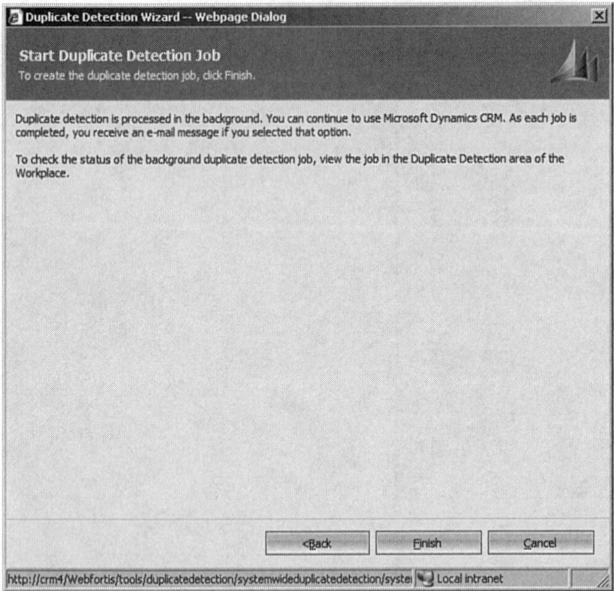

FIGURE 6.9 Start Duplicate Detection Job.

NOTE

If you didn't select a recurrence for the job, then you won't be able to modify the Duplicate Detection Jobs after it finishes. You will have to create a new job if you want to rerun the detection manually.

Bulk Record Deletion

This interface is used to monitor bulk deletion operations that can be made when using the Data Migration Manager application, as explained later in this chapter (see Figure 6.10).

Data Maps

Data Maps let you create mappings based on other data sources (such as CSV).

To create a new Data Mapping, you must have a sample CSV file with at least one record on it. Additionally, the first row must be the headers, which cannot be empty. For example, the following CSV data file is valid:

```
Full Name,Last Name,Parent Customer,Business Phone
Damian Sinay, Sinay,,
```

Notice in the preceding example that blank values in the data columns are acceptable.

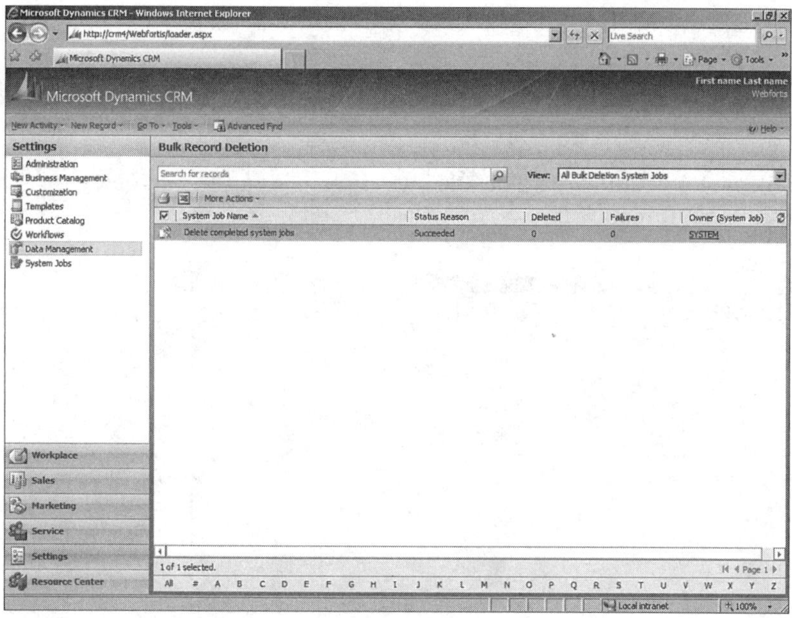

FIGURE 6.10 Bulk Record Deletion interface.

The Data Map interface shows the active Data Maps created by the user logged in by default. To see **all** active Data Maps, change the view to Active Data Maps (see Figure 6.11).

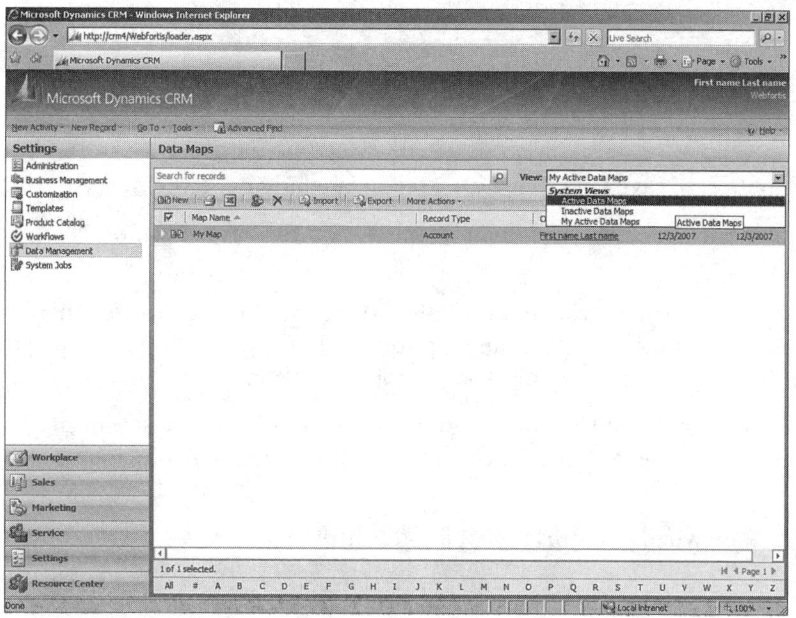

FIGURE 6.11 The Active Data Maps view showing all views.

To create a new Data Map, follow these steps:

1. Click New and then enter a name for the new Data Map (for example, Maximizer Data Map). Then select the entity you want to use on this mapping. For this example, choose Account (see Figure 6.12).

   The description enables you to write a detailed description about the mapping in the text box, but it is not required.

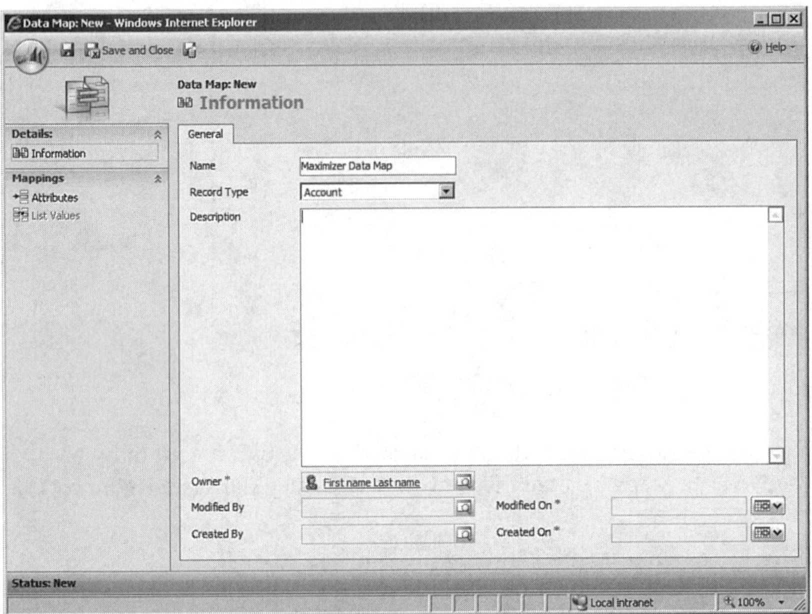

FIGURE 6.12 Creating a new Data Map.

2. Click the Save button to save your new Data Map before moving to the next step.
3. Select the Attributes option, which is under Mappings on the left navigation bar (see Figure 6.12).
4. Click the Load Sample Data button and find the CSV file by clicking Browse. Then click OK to load the sample data. You can map the columns by selecting Unmapped Attributes on the right and clicking the Map button (see Figure 6.13).
5. If your CSV file contains records with properties that are picklist types, you must go to the List Values section and map the picklist option values manually (see Figure 6.14).
6. Click Save and Close when you finish mapping the attributes.

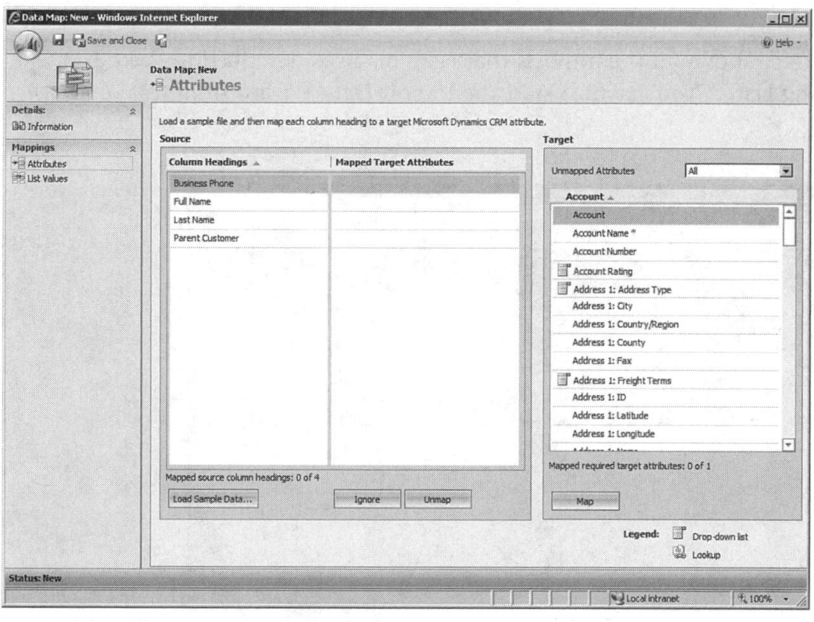

FIGURE 6.13 Mapping attributes.

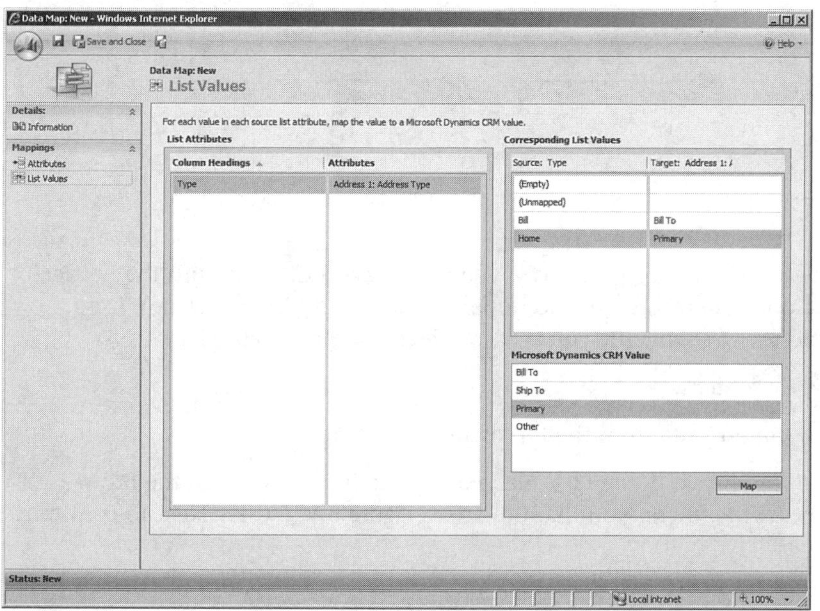

FIGURE 6.14 Mapping list values.

Imports

The Imports interface shows all the imports that were made as described in the next section, "Importing Data." You can also start the Import Data Wizard from this interface (see Figure 6.15).

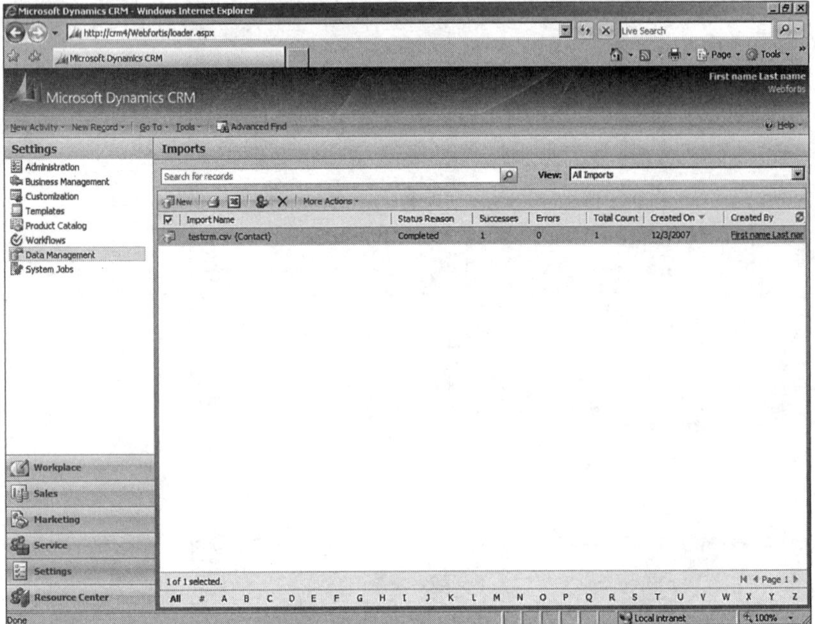

FIGURE 6.15 Imports.

Importing Data

As with the Data Maps explained previously, you must have a CSV file with the header labels and at least one data record on it to import data with the Import Data Wizard. Ideally, you should use the same file you used when creating the Data Map.

To import, follow these steps:

1. Go to Tools, Import Data from the top menu (see Figure 6.16).
2. Enter the full local path of the CSV file you want to import, or click the Browse button to locate the file on your hard disk (see Figure 6.17). Click Next to continue.

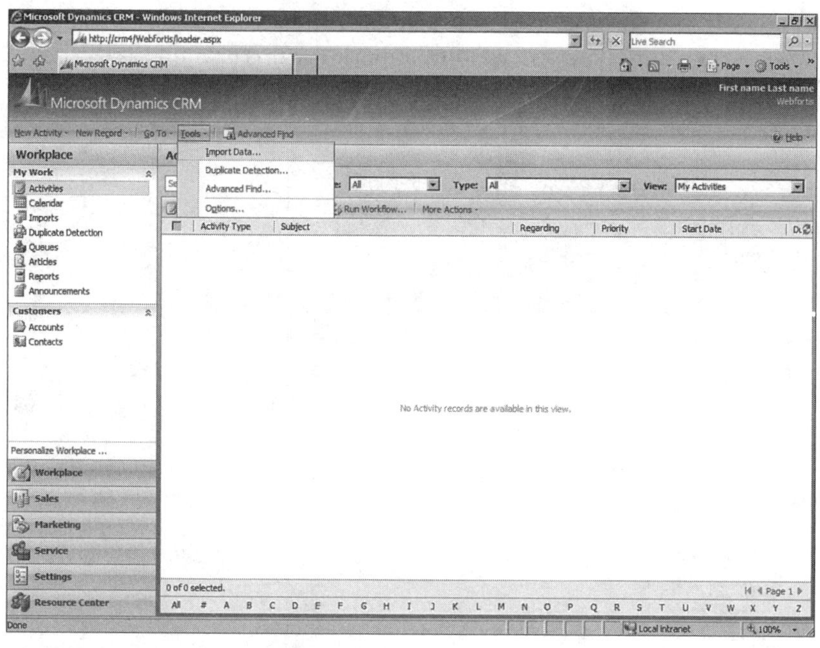

FIGURE 6.16 Import Data menu option.

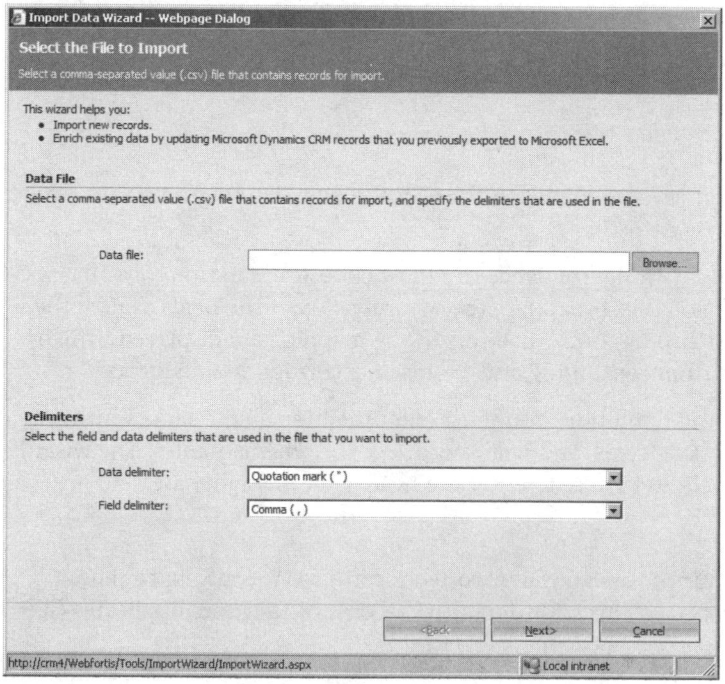

Import Data Wizard -- Webpage Dialog

Select the File to Import

Select a comma-separated value (.csv) file that contains records for import.

This wizard helps you:

- Import new records.
- Enrich existing data by updating Microsoft Dynamics CRM records that you previously exported to Microsoft Excel.

Data File

Select a comma-separated value (.csv) file that contains records for import, and specify the delimiters that are used in the file.

Data file: Browse...

Delimiters

Select the field and data delimiters that are used in the file that you want to import.

Data delimiter: Quotation mark (")

Field delimiter: Comma (,)

<Back Next> Cancel

http://crm4/Webfortis/Tools/ImportWizard/ImportWizard.aspx Local intranet

FIGURE 6.17 Selecting the file to import.

3. Record Type shows all the entities that the loaded file can be related to (see Figure 6.18). Select the entity type you want to import. For this example, select the Contact entity.

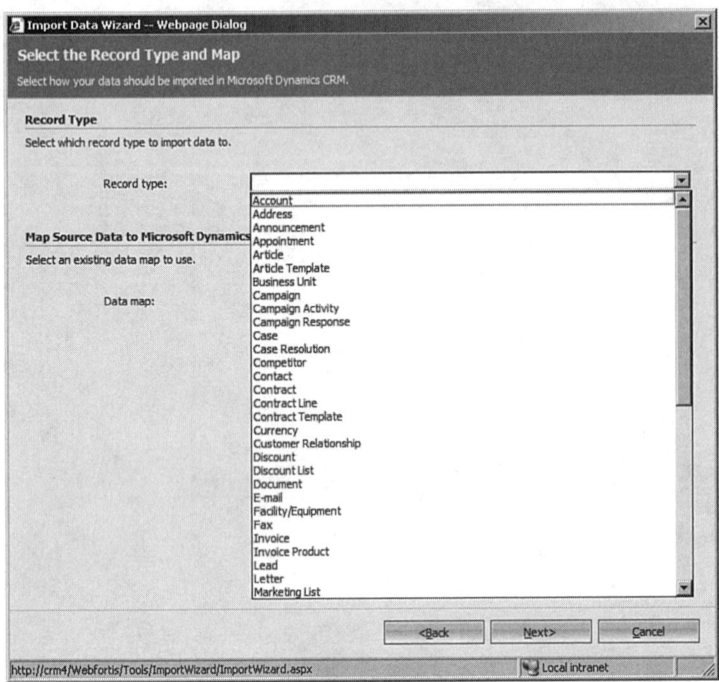

FIGURE 6.18 Selecting the entity type.

4. Depending on the names of the fields in the CSV file, the Map might be automatically resolved, as in Figure 6.19.

   If the Map is not automatically resolved, you must choose a Map from one that was created before. After you select the Map, the wizard validates the fields against the CSV file you are trying to import. Any errors in the mapping are displayed, which prevents the import from continuing and avoids data corruption and errors.

   For automatic mapping resolution, you must enter the headers the same way as they are displayed in the forms, and you cannot use the schema names. The wizard is case-sensitive as well, so be sure to enter the headers in the right case.

   Click Next to continue.

5. Select the user you want to assign the imported records to. You also have the option to tell the wizard to check for duplicates records or to ignore duplicates (see Figure 6.20).

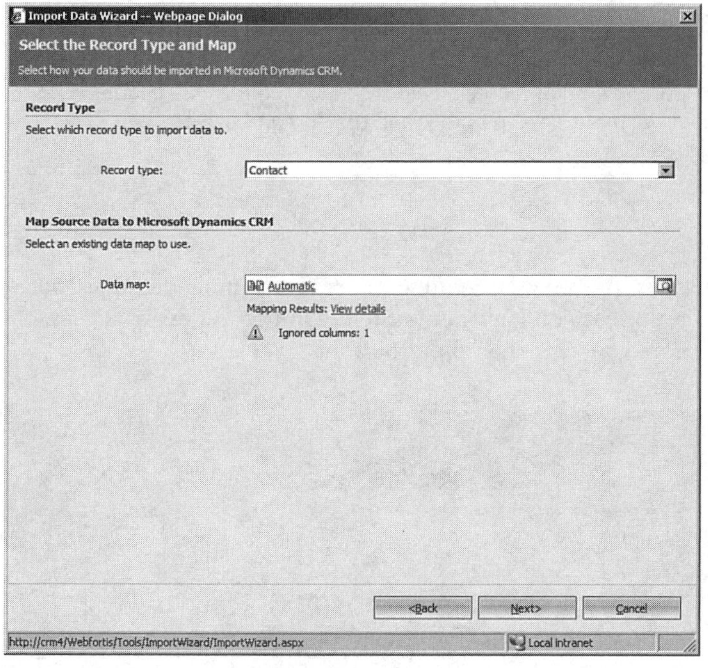

FIGURE 6.19 Automatic mapping resolved.

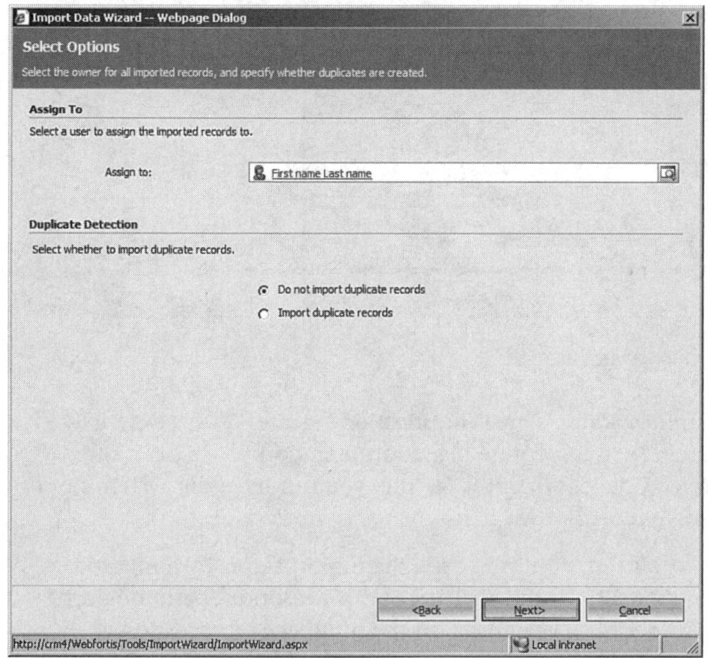

FIGURE 6.20 Assigning the imported records to a user.

NOTE

If the dataset you are importing needs to be assigned to different users, you might want to consider using the Data Migration Manager, as described later in this chapter. Alternatively, the dataset can be imported separately, and the correct user can be assigned for each import.

Click Next to continue.

6. Enter a name for the import process (see Figure 6.21). It is recommended that you use a friendly name here so that you later can locate the import set easily. Review the summary details before you click the Import button.

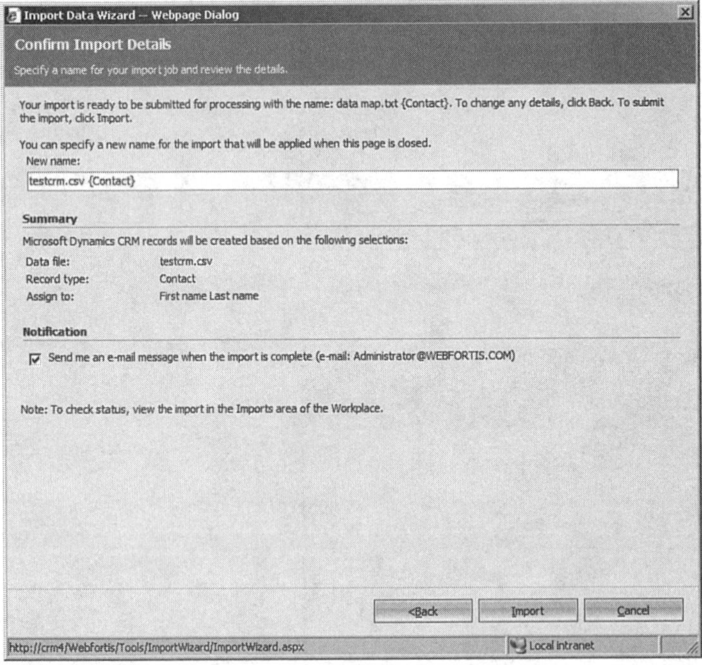

FIGURE 6.21 Import Summary review screen.

The Import Data Wizard has added a great notification feature. This is especially helpful because CSV files are usually quite big, and the import process can often take several minutes to complete. With this feature, you can have the system notify you via e-mail when the import process is complete.

After clicking the Import button, you can check the import status by going to the Imports option (see Figure 6.22). Notice that the Status Reason property might be different when you first check it. Depending on the number of records to be imported, this process might take some time to complete. The process is done asynchronously, so you can continue to select the refresh icon to see the current status.

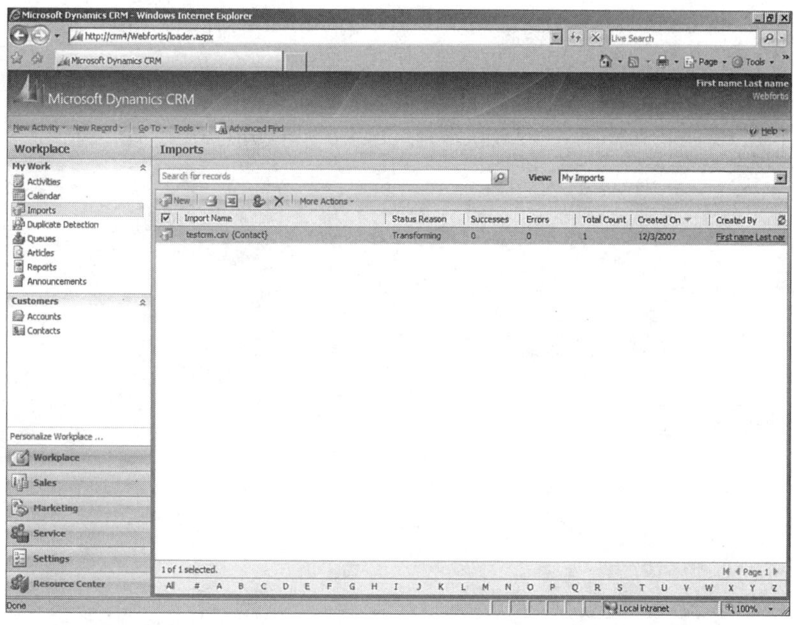

FIGURE 6.22 Imports status.

7. When the import process completes, you see the Status Reason of the import change to Completed (see Figure 6.23).

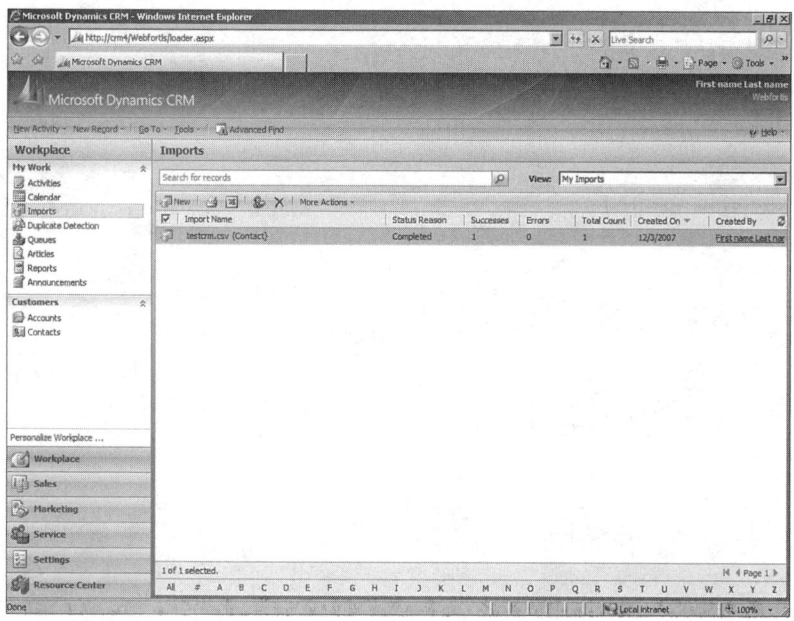

FIGURE 6.23 Imports status completed.

If you choose the option to be notified, you receive an e-mail with the import result status and a link to access the Imports interface.

8. If you double-click the import row and click the Contacts Created option (inside the Details section on the left side of the window, as shown in Figure 6.24), you see all the contacts that were imported.

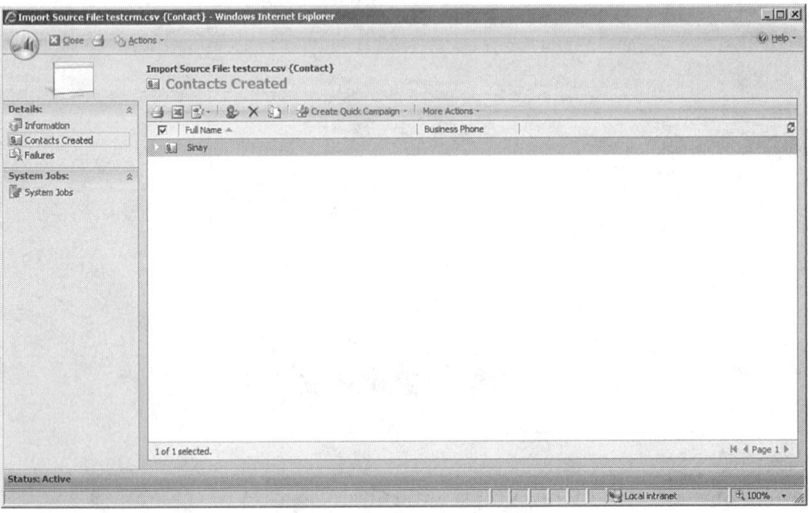

FIGURE 6.24 Reviewing imported contacts.

Exporting and Importing Data Maps

You can export or import the Data Maps for local backup purposes or to move mappings from one CRM organization or system to another.

Exporting a Data Map

To export a Data Map, go to Settings, Data Management, Data Maps. Click the Export button (see Figure 6.25).

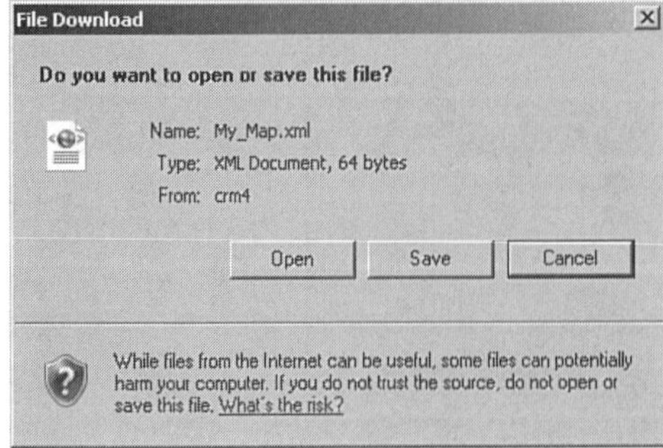

FIGURE 6.25 Exporting a Data Map.

NOTE

If the Data Map contains spaces, they will be replaced by the '_' char in the filename when exporting.

The Data Map is exported as an XML file. This is an example of a sample XML file of a Data Map:

```
<Map Name="Contacts Map" Source="" Id="03f688a4-6c4d-44a0-872b-2b2f8638aa1d">
    <Description>Custom Map</Description>
    <EntityMaps>
        <EntityMap TargetEntityName="contact" SourceEntityName="">
            <AttributeMaps>
                <AttributeMap Id="c9b96fde-c1f9-46a7-99b9-4b7307a130ed">
                    <SourceAttributeName>First Name</SourceAttributeName>
                    <TargetAttributeName>firstname</TargetAttributeName>
                    <ProcessCode>Process</ProcessCode>
                </AttributeMap>
                <AttributeMap Id="1d558a3c-1112-4251-b0a0-548d151196de">
                    <SourceAttributeName>Last Name</SourceAttributeName>
                    <TargetAttributeName>lastname</TargetAttributeName>
                    <ProcessCode>Process</ProcessCode>
                </AttributeMap>
                <AttributeMap Id="853d68b3-c193-4eea-bd8a-c7b01908a0d0">
                    <SourceAttributeName>Salutation</SourceAttributeName>
                    <TargetAttributeName>salutation</TargetAttributeName>
                    <ProcessCode>Process</ProcessCode>
                </AttributeMap>
            </AttributeMaps>
        </EntityMap>
    </EntityMaps>
</Map>
```

Importing a Data Map

To import a Data Map, go to Settings, Data Management, Data Maps. Click the Import button (see Figure 6.26).

Enter the full local path of your XML Data Map file or click Browse to locate the file on your hard disk. Click OK to continue. Enter a new name for the Data Map to be imported (see Figure 6.27).

After you click Continue, the Data Map is imported.

You can import the Data Maps exported from this interface in the Data Migration Manager, discussed in the next section.

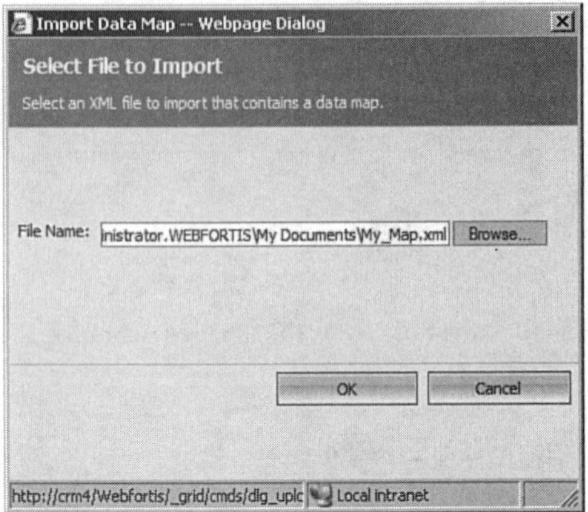

FIGURE 6.26 Importing a Data Map.

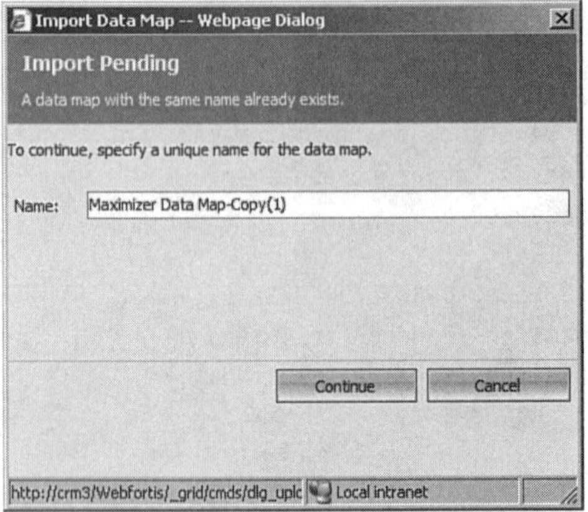

FIGURE 6.27 Naming the Data Map before importing.

The Data Migration Manager

The Data Migration Manager is an upgraded version of what was previously called the Data Migration Framework (DMF) in Microsoft CRM 3.0. Microsoft has greatly improved this tool and the process of data migration. Some of the new features include the capability to delete previously migrated data and create custom entities from unmapped data files.

Installing the Data Migration Manager

This tool is not installed on the server by default when Microsoft Dynamics CRM is set up. Rather it is located on the Microsoft Dynamics CRM setup disk in the DMWizard folder or can be downloaded from the Microsoft.com website. The reason it is not included as part of the standard installation is because it might not be necessary, and you might want to install it on a machine other then where the Microsoft Dynamics CRM Server is installed.

1. When executing the `setupdmclient.exe` file, the license terms from Microsoft appear (see Figure 6.28). You must accept the license agreement to continue. Click I Accept to continue.

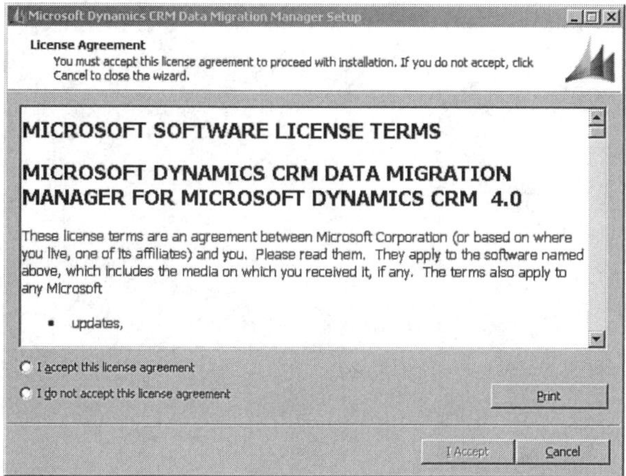

FIGURE 6.28 Microsoft Dynamics CRM license agreement.

2. The Data Migration Wizard needs a SQL Server 2005 database to work, so you need to connect to an existing SQL Server 2005. Alternatively, the wizard can install SQL Server 2005 Express Edition for you (see Figure 6.29). We recommend selecting the same database instance as the one that the Microsoft Dynamics CRM installation is using, if possible. (If you will be using this tool on a Microsoft Dynamics Live CRM account or a hosted solution, you will need to use a different database.)

   After selecting the database option, click Next to continue.

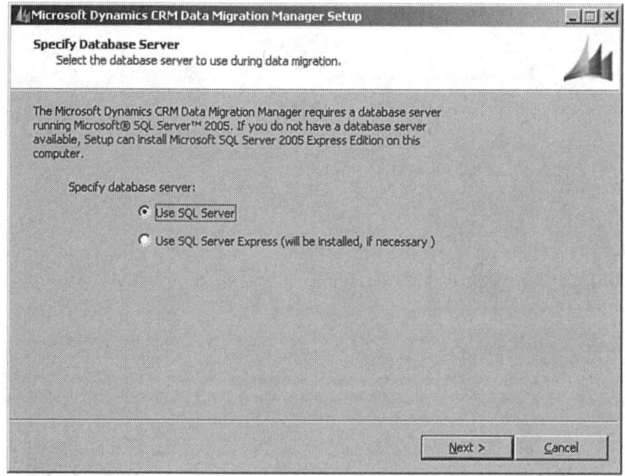

FIGURE 6.29 Specifying the database server.

3. The installer then performs a system check to see if required components necessary for the installation to continue are installed (see Figure 6.30). If you are not missing any components necessary for the installer to continue, you will not see this screen.

   Missing installer components will be installed for you when you click Install. After setup confirms that all required components are installed, click Next to continue.

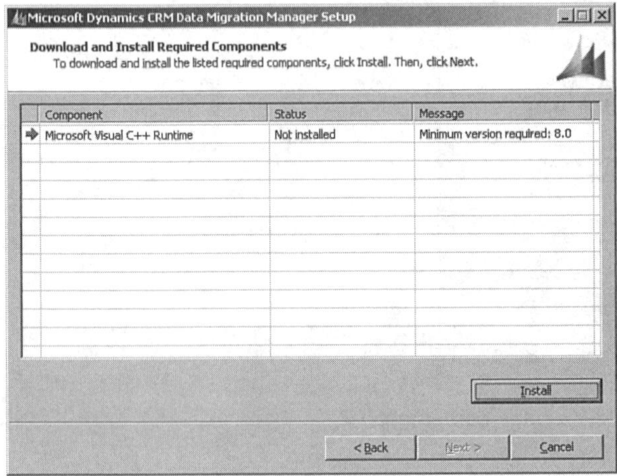

FIGURE 6.30 Installing required components.

4. Select the installation directory, and click the Next button (see Figure 6.31).

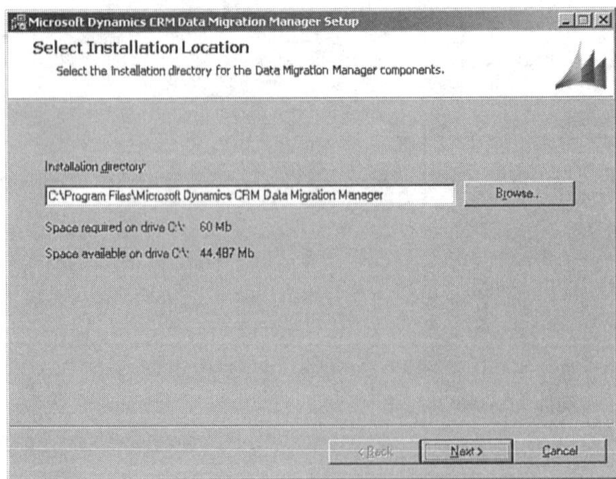

FIGURE 6.31 Select Installation Location.

5. The setup will validate all the system requirements and will show any errors found on the next step. If everything is validated, click Next to continue (see Figure 6.32).

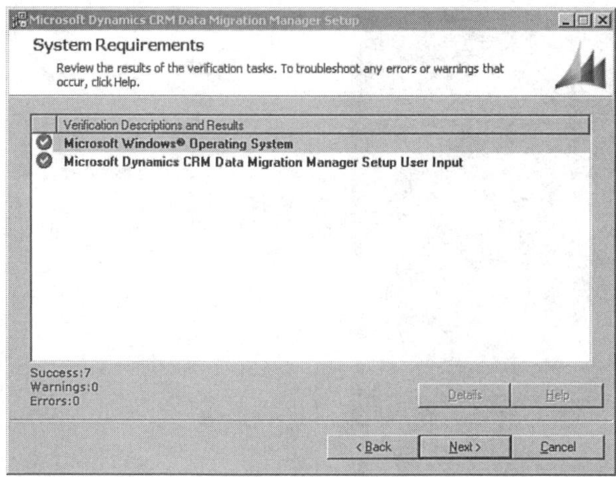

FIGURE 6.32 System Requirements.

6. When the installation finishes, it will show the screen in Figure 6.33. Click Close to continue.

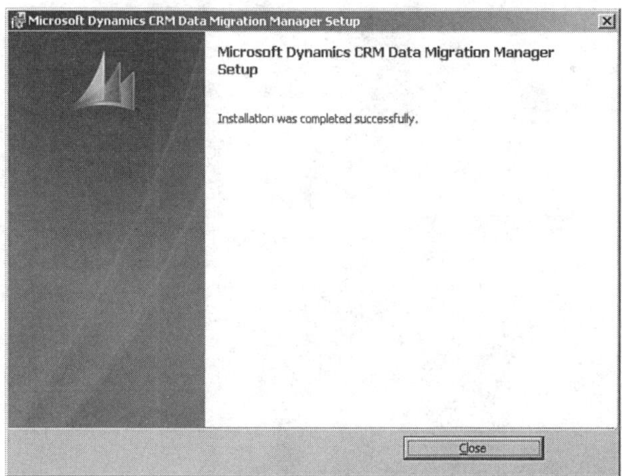

FIGURE 6.33 Installation completed.

7. The setup will install the Microsoft Dynamics CRM Data Migration Manager in the Microsoft Dynamics CRM program groups that can be found by going to Start, All Programs, as shown in Figure 6.34.

   The Data Migration Manager installs and uses a Windows service called Microsoft CRM Asynchronous Processing Service (client) that needs to be running. The user credentials set to this service are the ones that are used when you start the Microsoft Dynamics CRM Data Migration Manager application and sign in. The screen in Figure 6.35 appears. You must sign in to configure the installation.

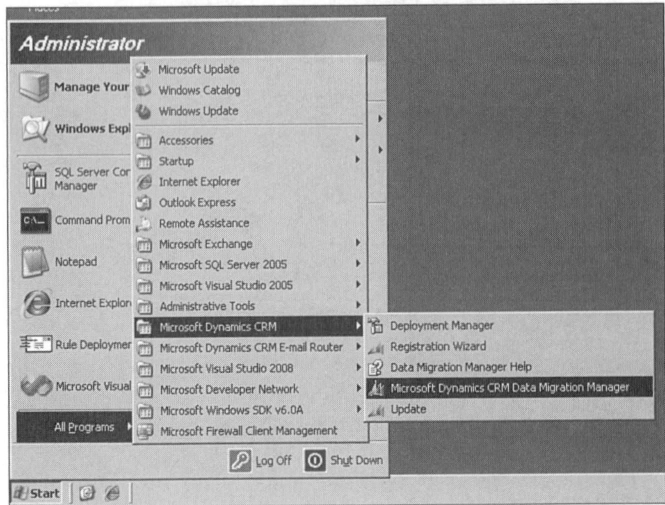

FIGURE 6.34 Microsoft Dynamics CRM Data Migration Manager.

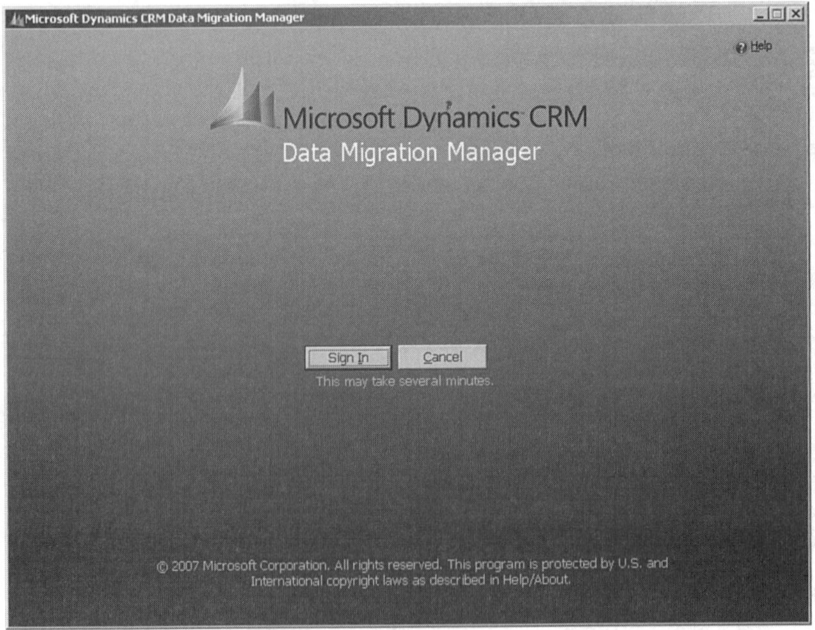

FIGURE 6.35 Data Migration Manager sign-in.

8. After signing in, you will see a welcome dialog (see Figure 6.36). Click Next to continue.

NOTE

If you installed the Data Migration Manager on a client computer where you also installed the Microsoft CRM client for Outlook, you will need to close Outlook before clicking Sign In.

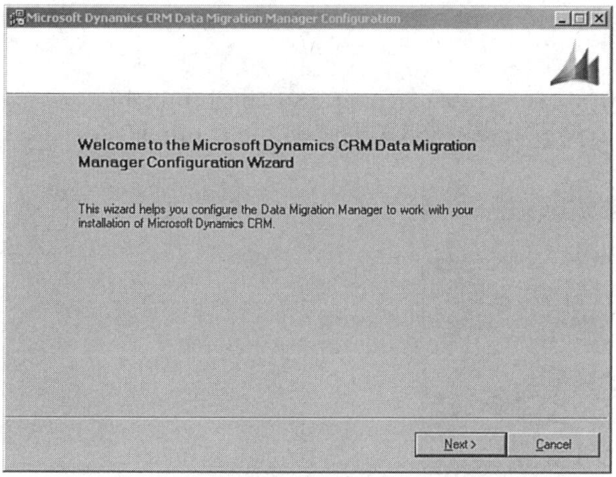

FIGURE 6.36 Data Migration Manager welcome.

9. You need to specify the installation type of your CRM organization (see Figure 6.37). As you know, Microsoft Dynamics CRM can be installed as On Premise, on a hosted server provided by a CRM partner, or with Microsoft Dynamics Live servers.

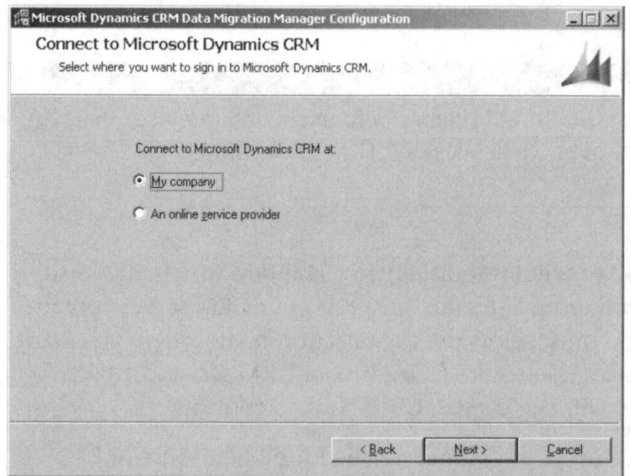

FIGURE 6.37 Selecting the CRM installation mode.

NOTE

The Data Migration version that comes with the CRM CD only works with On Premise or Hosted CRM versions. To use the Data Migration Manager on CRM Online, you must download and install a different setup from the Microsoft.com website.

For this example, select the first option using the On Premise CRM server. Click Next to continue.

10. Enter the URL of the Microsoft CRM server (see Figure 6.38). This is usually http://<servername> or http://<servername>:5555. Click Next to continue.

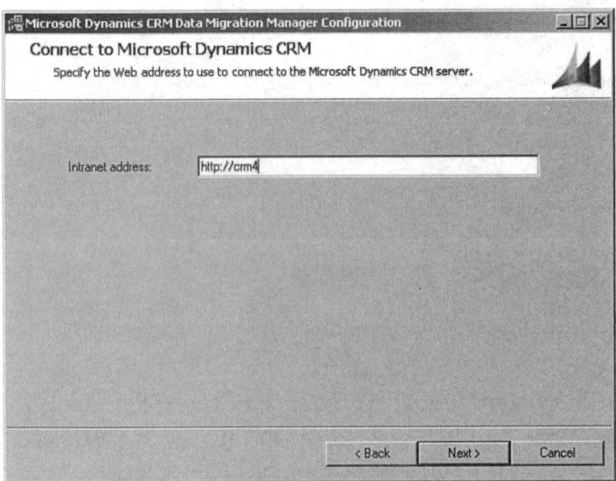

FIGURE 6.38 Entering the CRM internal URL.

NOTE

When you click Next, the configuration wizard will validate your username (the user that you are currently logged in as); if it is not a valid Microsoft Dynamics CRM user, it won't allow you to continue.

11. Because Microsoft Dynamics CRM includes multitenancy abilities, which allows support for more than one organization on the same server, if your CRM server contains more than one organization, you must select the organization name where you want to use the Data Migration Manager (see Figure 6.39). If your CRM server contains only one Organization, this step will be skipped. Click Next to continue.

12. Setup installs a Windows service on your computer called the Microsoft CRM Asynchronous Processing Service (client). This service needs a valid CRM User with a System Administrator security role to run, and it will use the user you are currently logged in as to configure it. You must enter only your password for the service on this screen (see Figure 6.40). Click Next to continue.

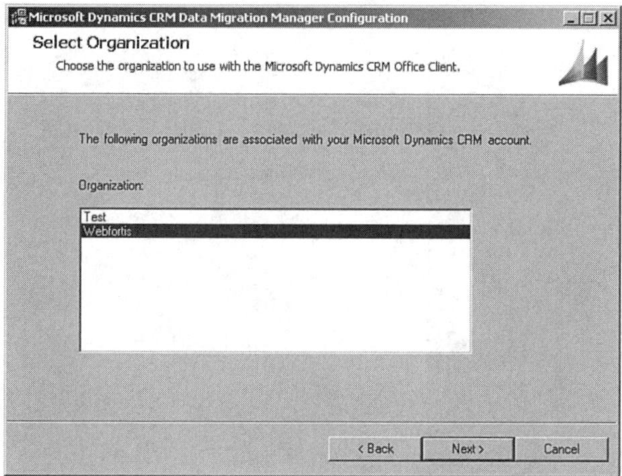

FIGURE 6.39 Select the organization name.

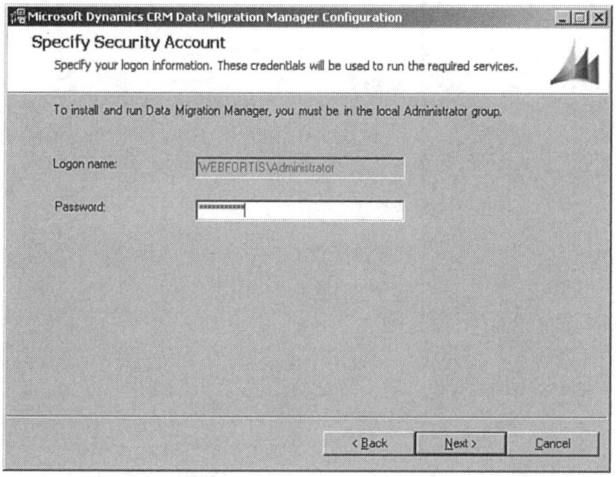

FIGURE 6.40 Configuring a Windows user for the Data Migration Manager Service.

13. Enter the server name where the Microsoft SQL Server 2005 is installed (see Figure 6.41). Click Next to continue. Notice that the Setup will validate the SQL server name and connection when you click Next and will show an error if the SQL server name can't be reached or if it was misspelled.
14. Check whether you want to participate in the Customer Experience Improvement Program (CEIP) (see Figure 6.42). Click Next to continue.

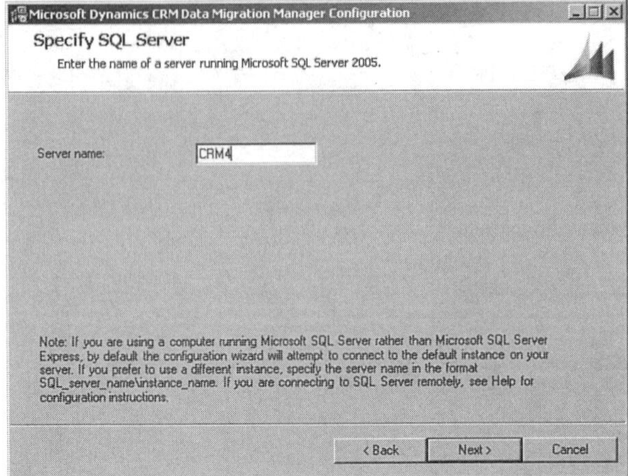

FIGURE 6.41 Configuring SQL Server 2005 server name.

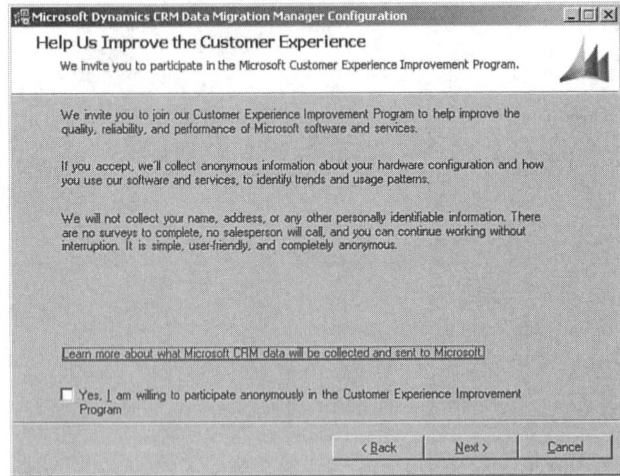

FIGURE 6.42 Microsoft CRM Customer Experience Improvement Program (CEIP).

15. Setup verifies that the machine and the system meet the minimum requirements before starting the installation (see Figure 6.43). If any errors arise with the components required, you need to correct them before you continue with the installation. Click Next to continue. Notice that this process may take several minutes because it will prepare the migration database.

16. When the Data Migration Manager configuration finishes successfully, it will show the start screen, as shown in Figure 6.44.

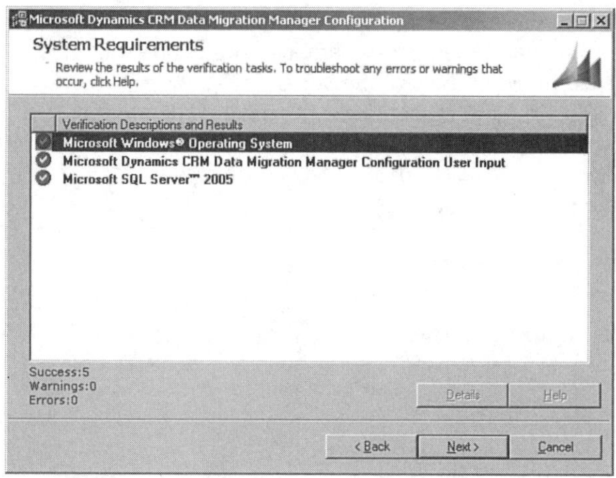

FIGURE 6.43 System requirements verification.

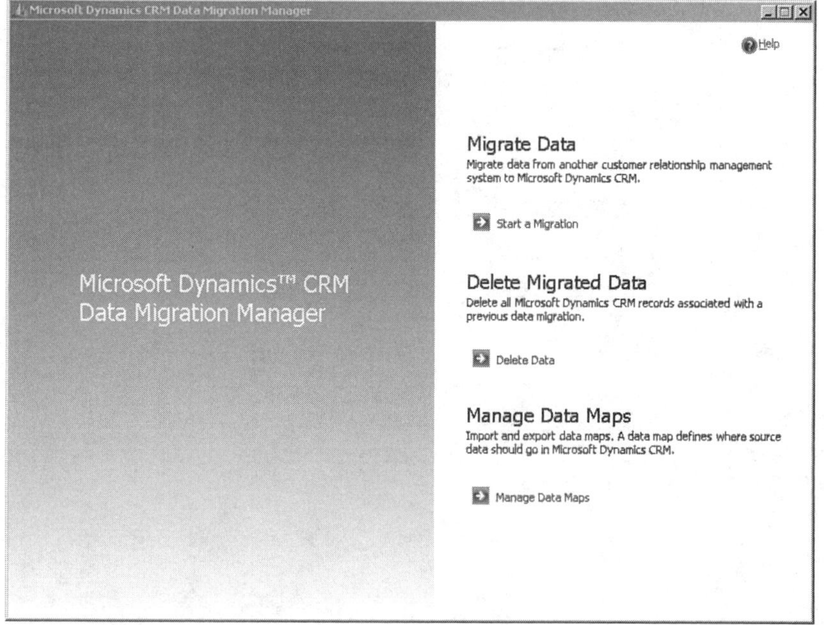

FIGURE 6.44 Data Migration Manager start page.

NOTE

When installed and configured, the Data Migration Manager can be used only for the organization you selected upon the initial configuration. If you want to use this tool for more than one organization, you will have to install it either on another machine or completely uninstall it and reinstall it again for the other organization. Before reinstalling the application, you will have to manually delete the database or rename it if you are willing to use the same instance name of the SQL Server, because the setup will try to create a new one, and it will fail if the database already exists. To delete the database, you must do so manually using SQL Server Tools. The database that needs to be deleted is the one with the name MSCRM_MIGRATION, and you must also rename the mdf and ldf files associated with the database.

Using the Data Migration Manager

The Data Migration Manager has three main functions:

- Migrate data
- Delete migrated data
- Manage Data Maps

Migrate Data

With this option, you can perform the following functions (see Figure 6.45):

- Create a new migration from an existing Data Map
- Create a new, blank migration
- Create a new migration based on a previous migration

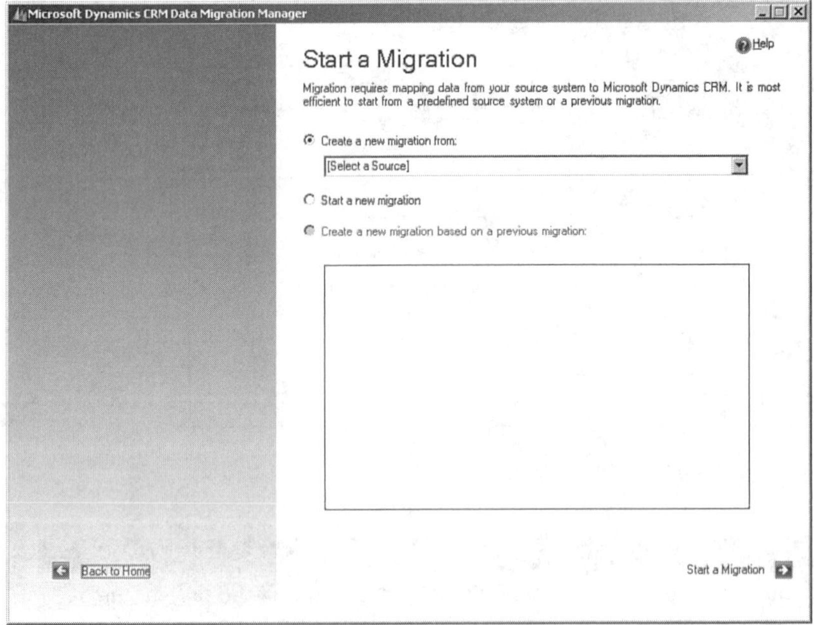

FIGURE 6.45 Migrate data options.

Create a New Migration from an Existing Data Map With this option, you can use the drop-down list to select from one of the existing Data Map files that come out of the box with the Data Migration Manager. The Data Migration Manager comes with prebuilt data-mapping files for the following applications:

- SalesForce.com
- Microsoft Office Outlook 2007 with Business Contact Manager:
- Microsoft Office Outlook 2003 with Business Contact Manager
- ACT! 6

This book illustrates how to migrate data from Microsoft Office Outlook 2007 with Business Contact Manager:

1. Select Microsoft Office Outlook 2007 with Business Contact Manager and click Start a Migration.
2. The wizard has two options: Express mode (recommended) and Standard mode (see Figure 6.46). Select the Express mode, and click Next to continue.

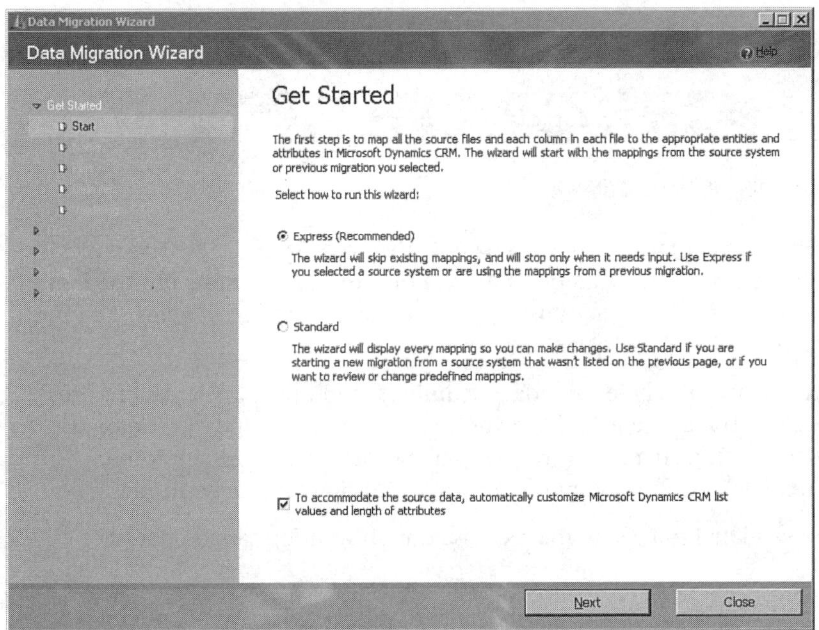

FIGURE 6.46 Migrating data from Microsoft Office Outlook 2007 with Business Contact Manager.

3. For either of these modes, you must provide a name for the data migration. It is recommended that you enter a friendly name so that you can easily find and reuse it for future migrations (see Figure 6.47). Enter a name and click Next to continue.

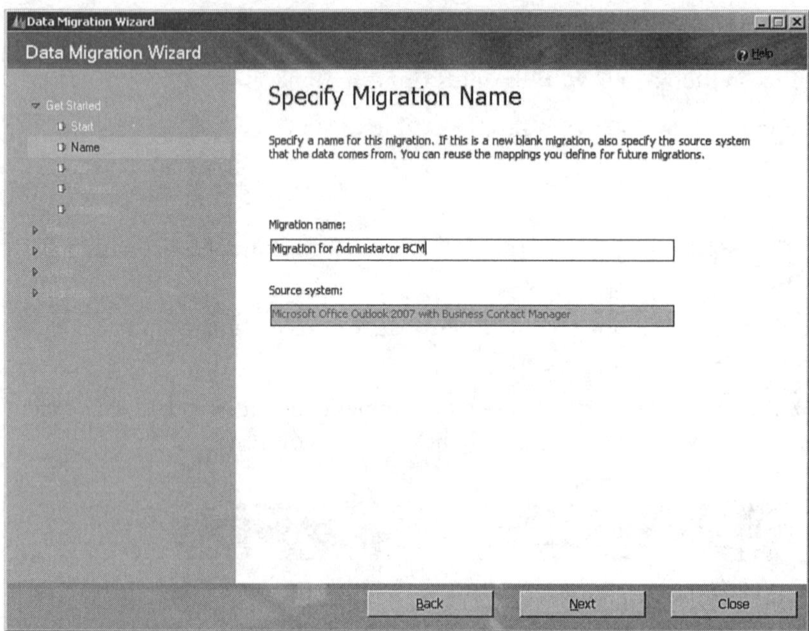

FIGURE 6.47 Naming the data migration.

4. Select the files that contain the data to be migrated (see Figure 6.48). These files must be CSV files. You can add more than one file at the same time, but the files must be in the same format and must contain the same number of fields. Add the files by clicking Add and then Next to continue.

5. Verify and/or change the fields and data delimiters, and preview the data records (see Figure 6.49). The available fields delimiter options are Comma (,), Colon (:), Semicolon (;), and Tab character (\t); the available data delimiters are None, Quotation mark ("), and Single quotation mark ('). Click Next to continue.

6. The files are validated to be sure the records contain well-formatted data (see Figure 6.50).

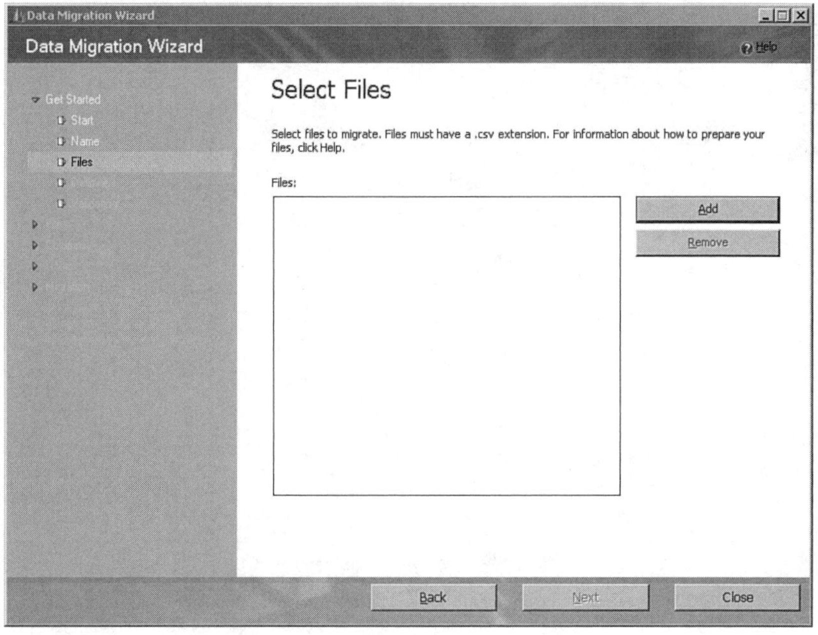

FIGURE 6.48 Selecting files for data migration.

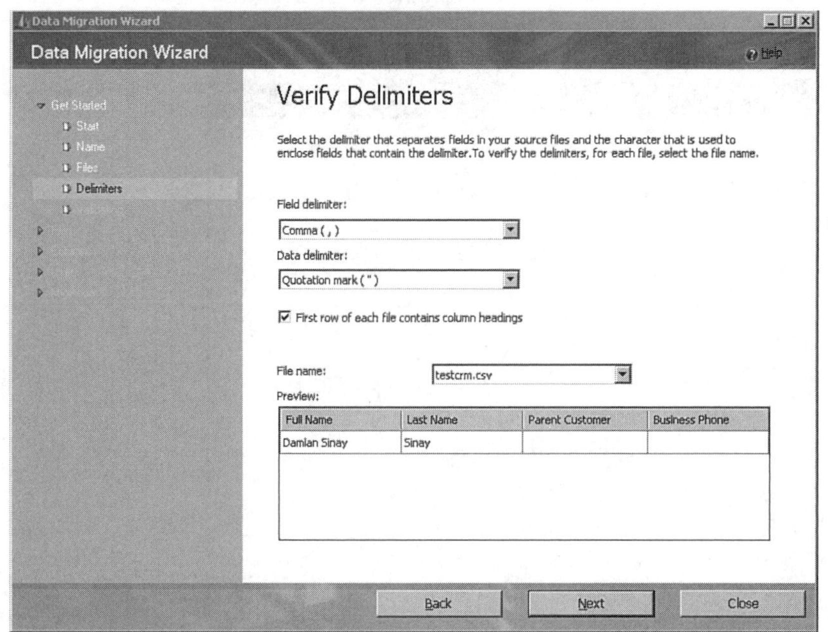

FIGURE 6.49 Verifying delimiters.

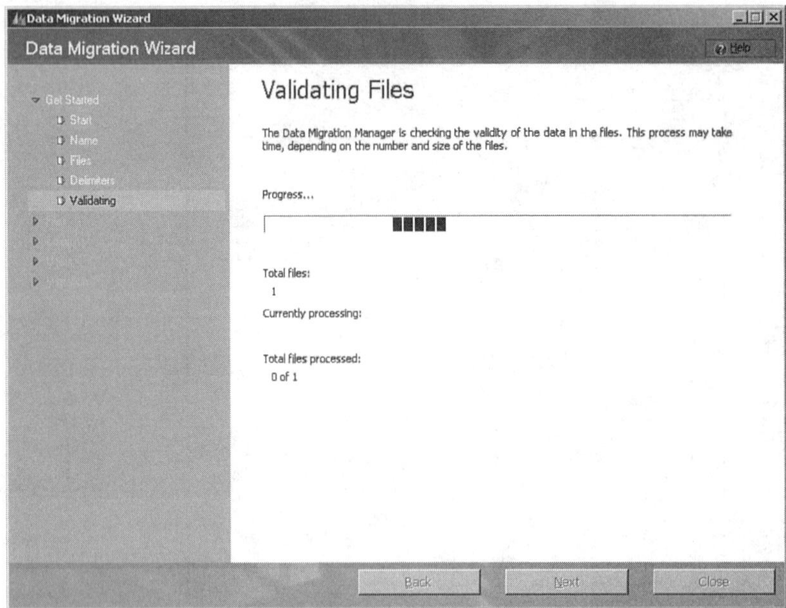

FIGURE 6.50 Validating files.

7. The results display when the validation is completed (see Figure 6.51).

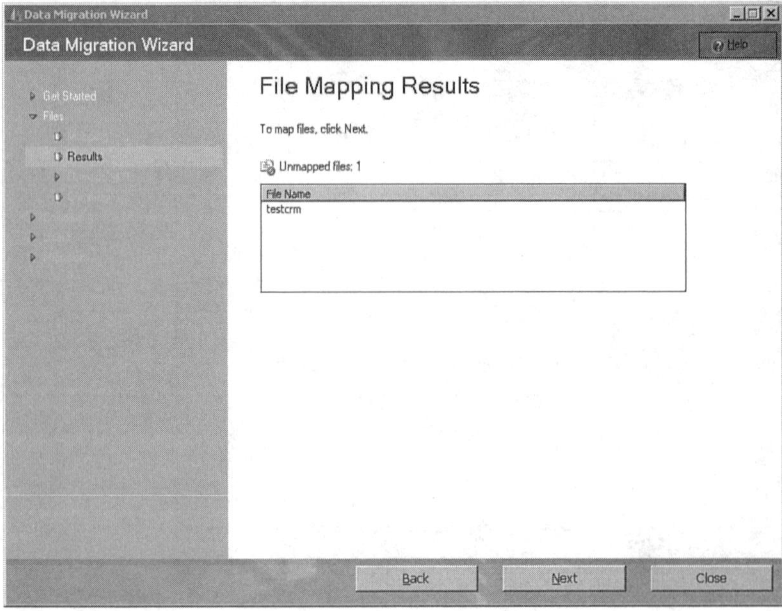

FIGURE 6.51 Unmapped file sample result.

If the file contains any error, you have the option to create a custom CRM entity based on the data of the unmapped file (see Figure 6.52). This is a very useful feature and an easier way to create custom entities when you are moving data from another system that you might want to integrate in Microsoft Dynamics CRM.

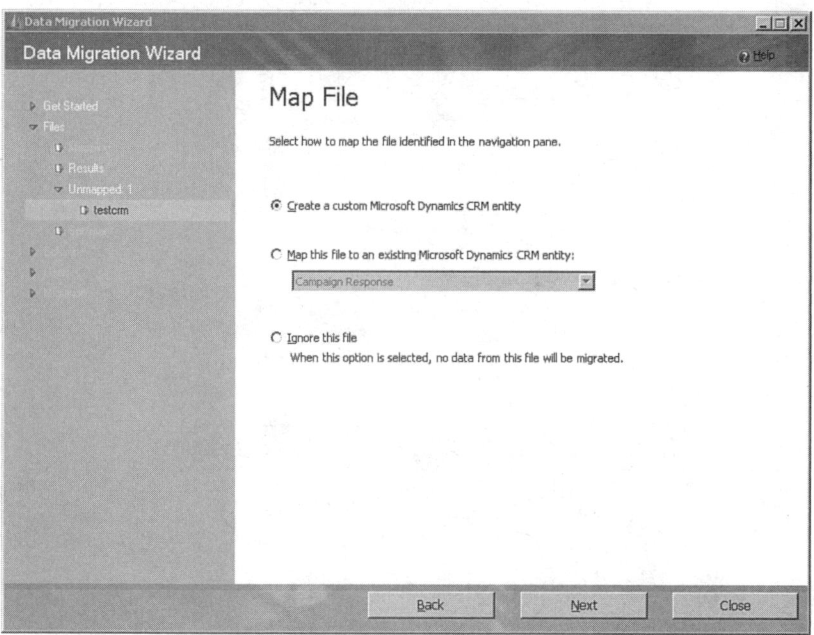

FIGURE 6.52 Creating a custom entity based on an unmapped file.

8. Enter the entity name, plural name, primary attribute, ownership (user or organization), and owner column the same way you did when you created the custom entity from the Customizations section of the Microsoft CRM web interface (see Figure 6.53).
9. You must define the new attributes' field types, or you can choose to not migrate data on the missing data columns (see Figure 6.54).

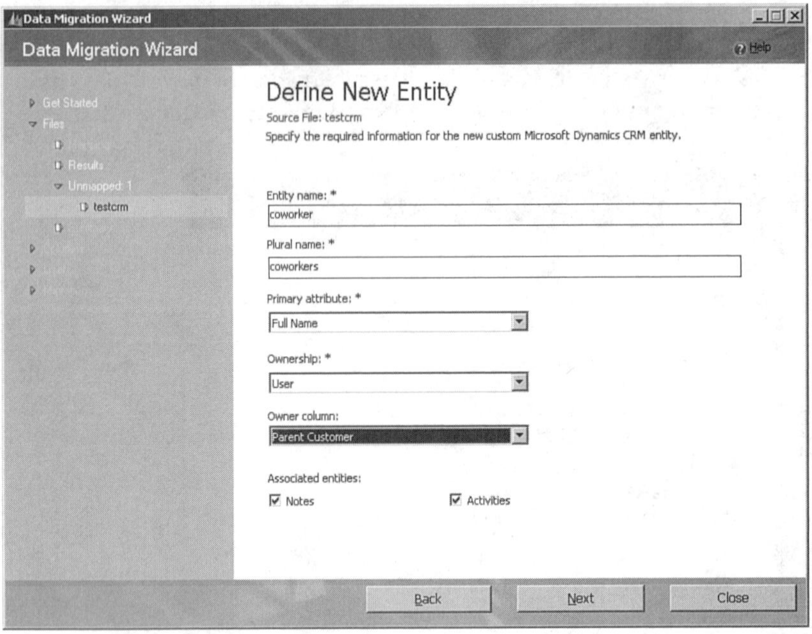

FIGURE 6.53 Defining the new entity.

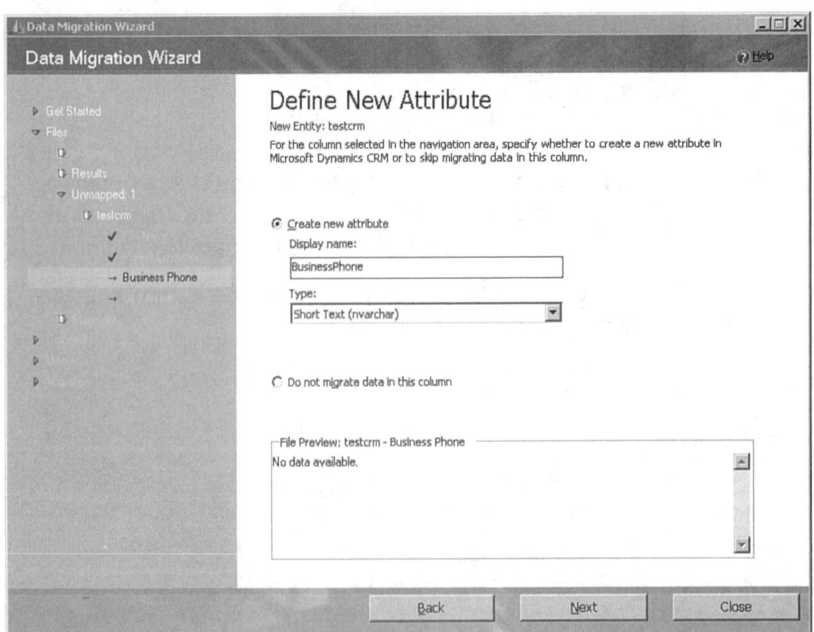

FIGURE 6.54 Defining new attributes.

10. If you selected to create a new attribute, you have the option to specify the format in the next screen, shown in Figure 6.55. Click Next to continue.

NOTE

Steps 9 and 10 can be repeated several times depending on the unmapped fields in the files you added that need to be defined.

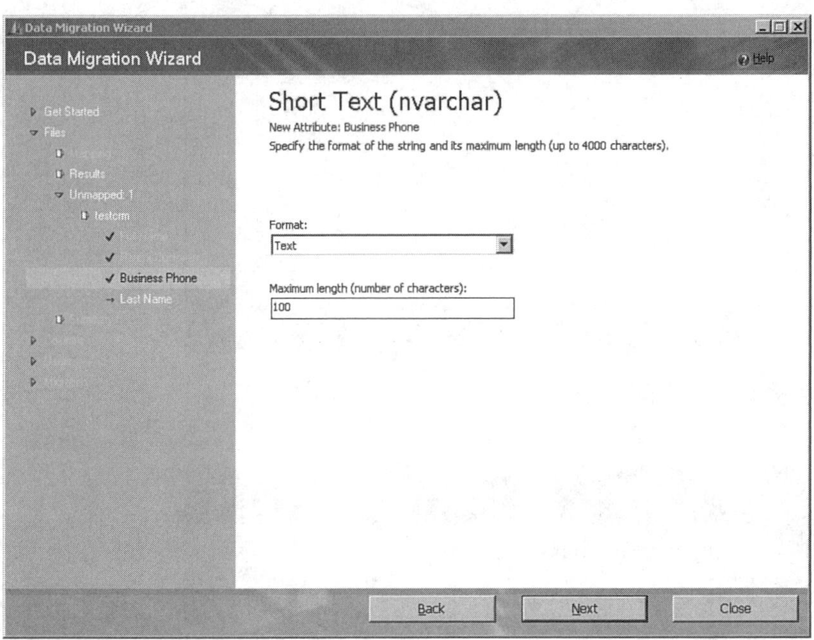

FIGURE 6.55 Defining new attribute format.

11. After you define all the new attributes with their formats, you see the file summary screen (see Figure 6.56). Click Next to continue.

12. If you defined columns, you see the Column Summary step (see Figure 6.57). Click Next to continue.

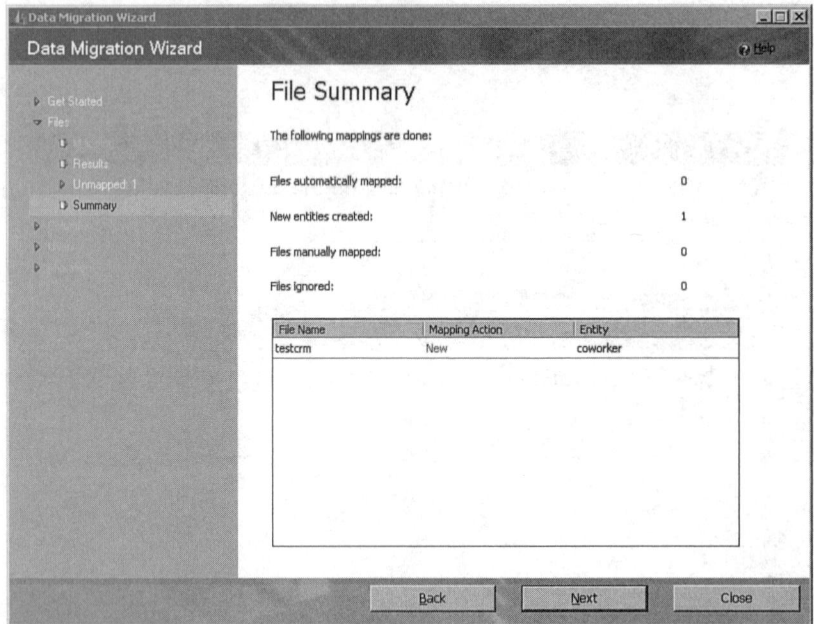

FIGURE 6.56 File summary step.

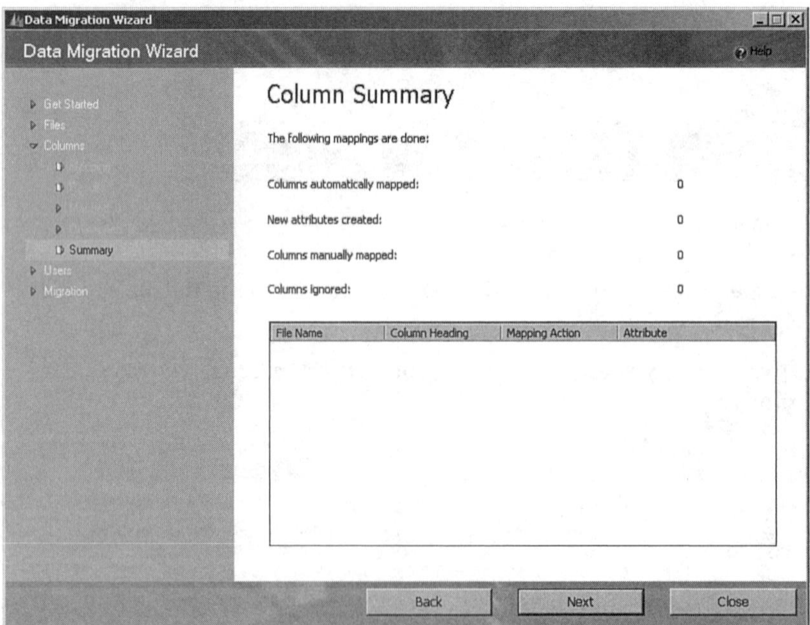

FIGURE 6.57 Column summary step.

13. A warning dialog box will tell you that all the records to be migrated will be assigned to the current user who is running the Data Migration Wizard (see Figure 6.58). Click Next to continue.

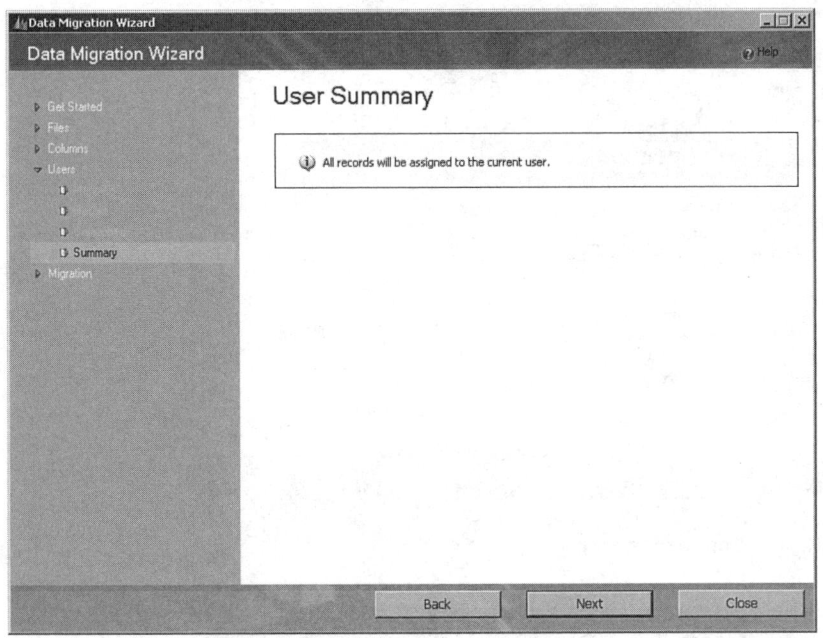

FIGURE 6.58 User summary step.

14. The final step is the Review Summaries where you have the last and global image for reviewing the data (see Figure 6.59). Click Next to continue.

15. Now you are ready to start the data migration (see Figure 6.60). Click Migrate Data.

NOTE

This process might take a long time to complete depending on the number of records you are migrating.

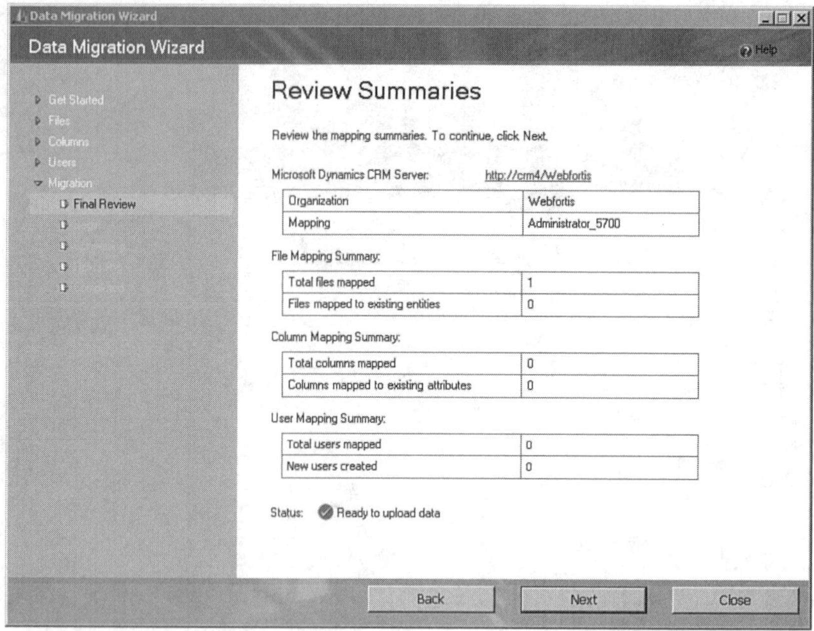

FIGURE 6.59 Review Summaries step.

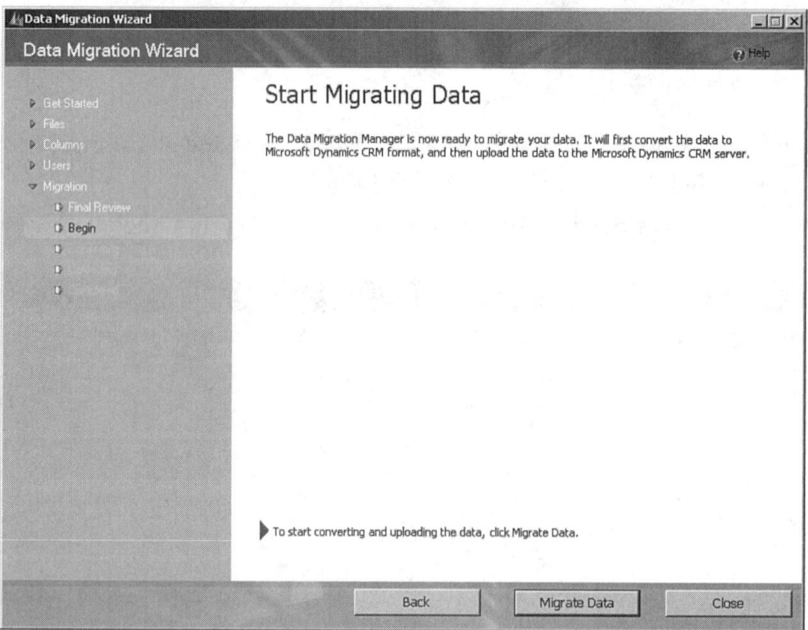

FIGURE 6.60 Start migrating data step.

16. The new entity is created and published, and the data is imported (see Figure 6.61).

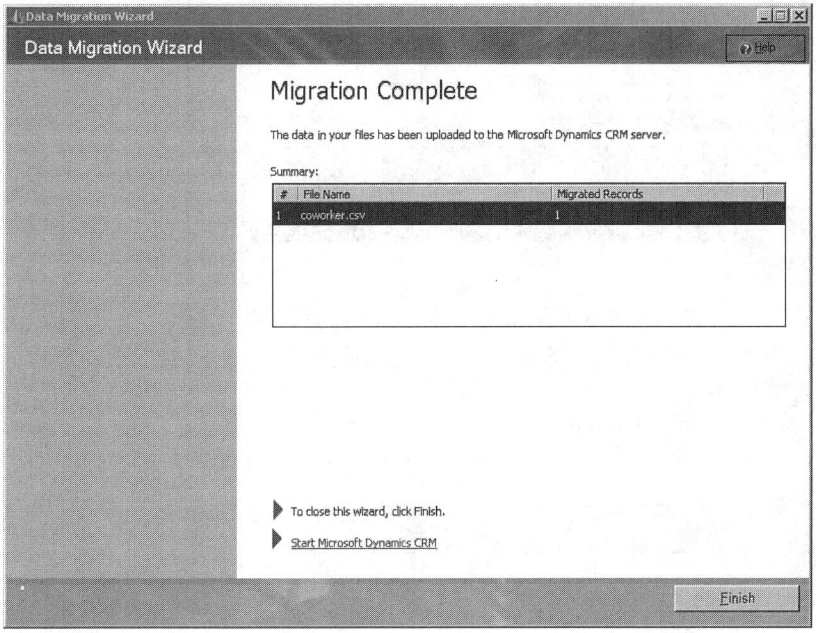

FIGURE 6.61 Migration complete step.

When selecting the option to create a new entity, be sure the entity you are going to create doesn't exist in the CRM Server. If the data migration fails, you will see the error details in the next step, as shown in Figure 6.62. This screen also has the ability to export the errors to a CSV file for better analysis and correction. Depending on the errors, you will have no choice but to close the wizard and start again.

Note that the new entity is published. After running this wizard, all users can see and use this new entity, without requiring additional steps.

You can find the new entity created under the Extensions section in the workplace (see Figure 6.63).

Create a New, Blank Migration This option is basically the same as the option described previously with the only difference that you will have to create and define a new Data Map from scratch because it doesn't use any predefined Data Map for the data validation. This option is useful if you need to migrate data from a system that is not listed in the options available on the Create a New Migration form.

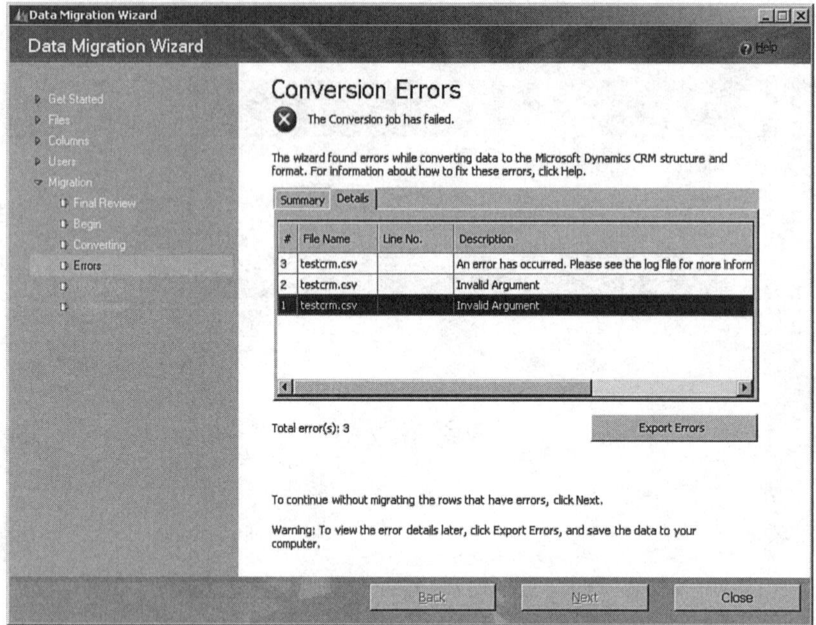

FIGURE 6.62 Error details.

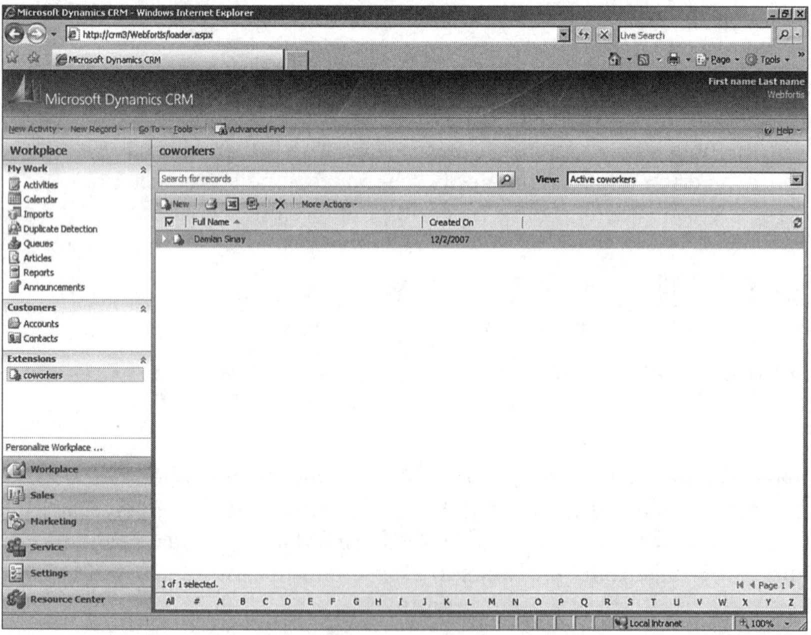

FIGURE 6.63 New entity created under Extensions.

Create a New Migration Based on a Previous Migration After you migrated the records using the methods described previously, you will have the ability to reuse the settings to process other similar files without having to set the columns mappings again. This option is useful if you want to test with a migration with just a few records and you need to make changes to the column mappings before doing the real migration with all the necessary records. As shown in Figure 6.64, when you select this option, the list shown in the previous migrations is enabled so you can select one of them.

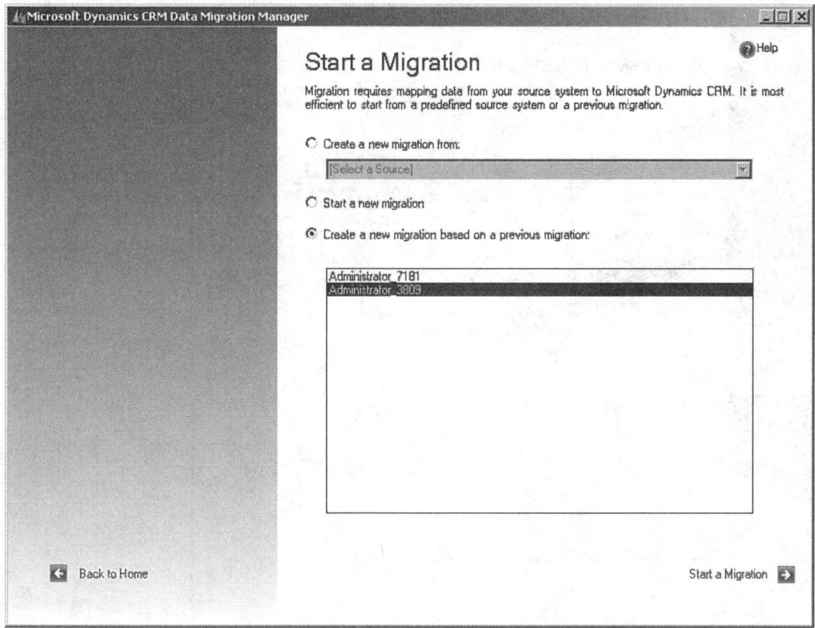

FIGURE 6.64 Creating a New Migration Based on a Previous Migration.

After selecting a previous migration and clicking Start a migration on the right-bottom of the dialog box, you will start the same wizard with the steps described on the Create a New Migration Form. You will have the ability to make any modifications to the columns mapping, or just click the Next button several times if you don't need to make any changes. You must select new files when using this option as previously migrated files are not stored.

NOTE

Custom Data Maps that are imported will be available in the option Create a New Migration based on a previous migration.

Delete Migrated Data

If you are not happy with the migrated data and you need to make some modifications in the Data Map, you can use this option to delete the migrated data.

To delete migrated data, follow these steps:

1. Selecting this option displays a list with all the migrations that were performed on the server (see Figure 6.65).

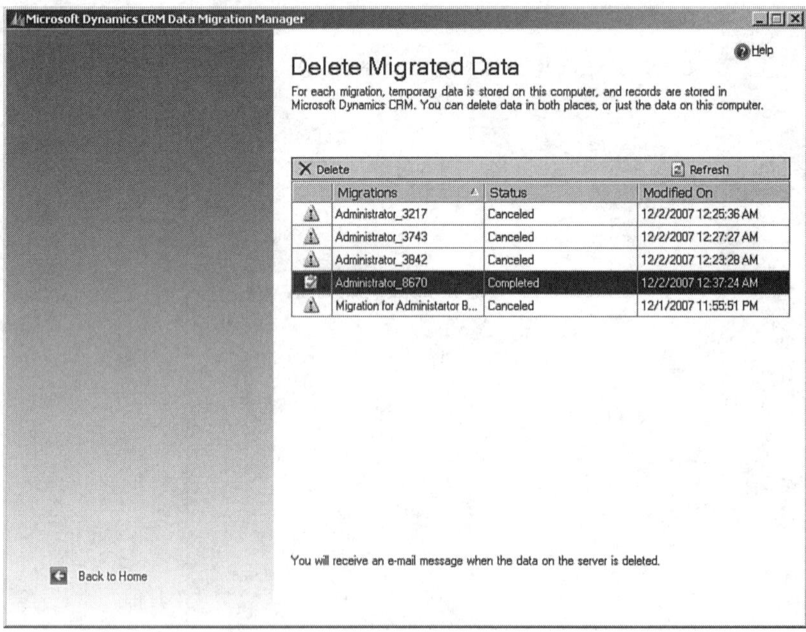

FIGURE 6.65 Selecting the migration data to be deleted.

2. Select the migration you want to delete (as shown in Figure 6.66), and click the Delete button with an X icon to continue.

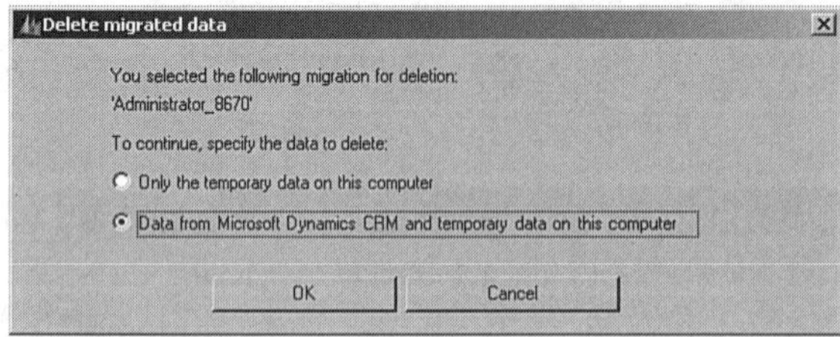

FIGURE 6.66 Choosing whether to delete the temporary data or the CRM data.

Manage Data Maps

The Data Migration Manager comes with four prebuilt data-mapping files for ACT! 6, Microsoft Office Outlook 2003 with Business Contact Manager, Microsoft Office Outlook 2007 with Business Contact Manager, and SalesForce.com (see Figure 6.67).

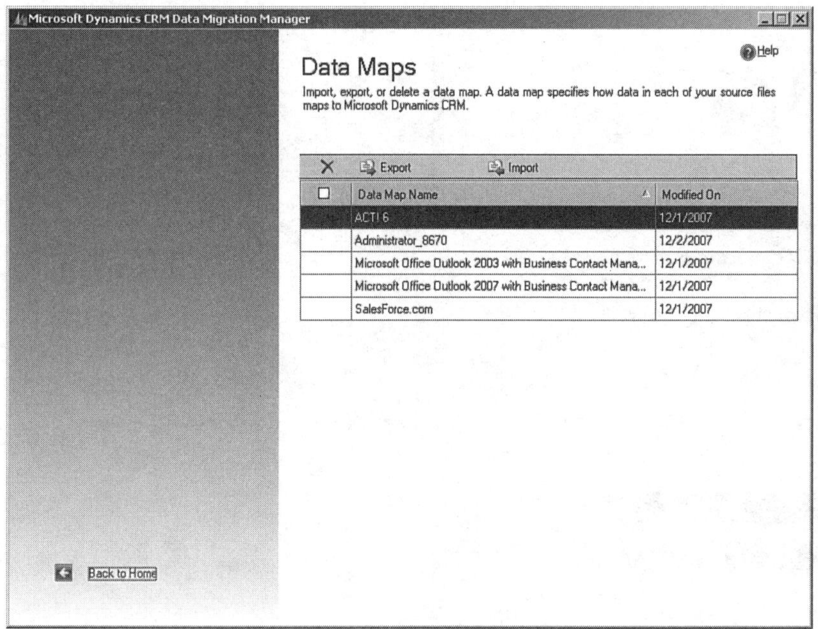

FIGURE 6.67 Data Maps.

Notice that you will also see the Data Maps you might have created when migrating data, as described earlier.

From this interface, you perform the following operations:

- Delete
- Export
- Import

Delete

The Data Map is deleted permanently.

Export

This exports the Data Map to an XML format file (see Figure 6.68). It is useful to export the current Data Map to files for backups and also to use as the base for other customized Data Map files. You also can import the exported Data Map files in the Microsoft Dynamics CRM system for use by the Import Wizard tool.

FIGURE 6.68 Exporting a Data Map.

Import

This function imports an XML file to the Data Migration Manager (see Figure 6.69).

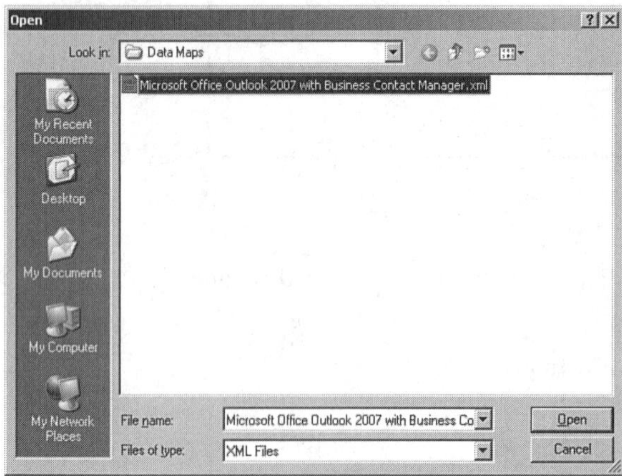

FIGURE 6.69 Importing a Data Map.

> **NOTE**
>
> Custom Data Maps that are imported will be available in the option Create a New Migration based on a previous migration.

Summary

This chapter illustrated how to migrate and import external data into the Microsoft Dynamics CRM system using either the Import Wizard or the Data Migration Manager Client application. It also explained how to monitor the imports and bulk deletions operations and what kind of data we can migrate with these applications that are only CSV files. The chapter explained what kind of permissions the user must have to run the applications to import data and how to prevent users from performing data migrations.

This chapter also explained the creation, export, and import of Data Maps for reuse on other systems and within other organizations.

CHAPTER 7

Common Functions

IN THIS CHAPTER

- Actions
- Activities
- History
- Notes
- Attachments
- Run Workflow
- Advanced Find
- Form Assistant
- Record Merge
- Send Direct E-mail
- Resource Center

Microsoft Dynamics CRM has a number of common features. By "common," we mean that, when working with most of the entities, they have the same functionality included in this chapter.

As an example, Accounts, Contacts, Leads, Opportunities, and Cases all have functionality on their main form that includes the following:

- Actions
- Activities
- History
- Notes
- Attachments
- Workflows

Because they are so similar (regardless of which entity you're working with), we have grouped these functions in this chapter to consolidate the description of their functionality.

The Resource Center is included with this chapter because all users of the application use it in the same manner.

NOTE

The Actions, Notes, and Attachments options are not available on the form until the record form has been saved. The record form does not need to be saved and closed—it just needs to be saved, and an expanded toolbar will appear. As an example of what we're describing, look in Figure 7.1 below the new Account form.

After the record form is saved (which, of course, requires entering the Business Required fields—in this case, the `Account Name` field), the icon options for Actions, Notes, and Attachments appear (along with the other advanced options), enabling you to perform these actions on the record (see Figure 7.2).

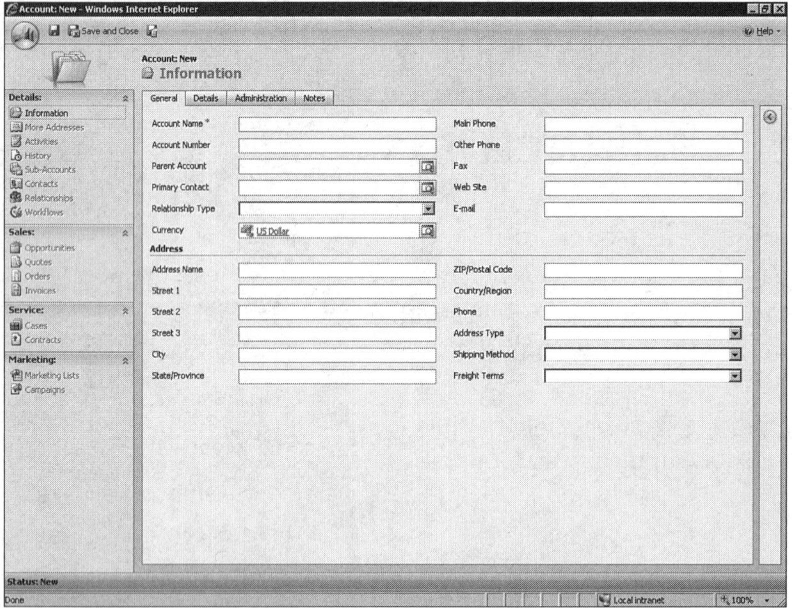

FIGURE 7.1 New Account form in Microsoft Dynamics CRM prior to save—notice the lack of options on the toolbar.

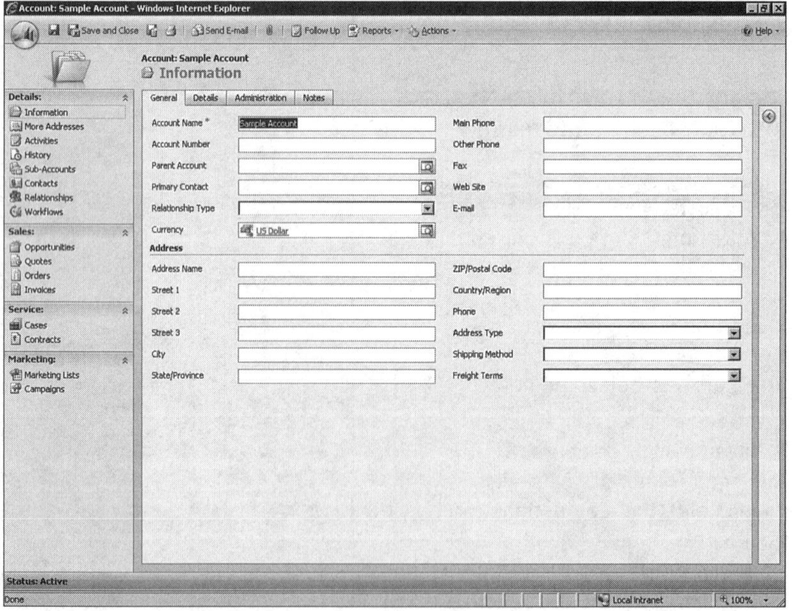

FIGURE 7.2 Save Account form in Microsoft Dynamic CRM after save—notice the toolbar options that have appeared.

Actions

The Actions icon (presented with a small hand on a star) has a drop-down menu that enables you to easily perform a number of Actions on a record without having to navigate to the near navigation. It often reduces the total number of clicks to accomplish something. The following Actions are available to Accounts, Contacts, Opportunities, and Leads. Although each Entity has Actions specific to it that are not listed, these are the most common:

- Add Activity
- Add a Note
- Attach a File
- Add Additional Address (Accounts and Contacts)
- Add to Marketing List (Accounts, Contacts, and Opportunities)
- Add Relationship (Accounts, Contacts, and Opportunities)
- Delete Record
- Deactivate Record (or Activate Record, if it is deactivated)
- Mail Merge (Accounts, Contacts, and Leads)
- Assign
- Sharing
- Copy Shortcut
- Send Shortcut

Most of the options available in the Actions drop-down menu are available elsewhere on the form and, in fact, are merely shortcuts. (For example, Add Additional Address has the same functionality as if you went to More Addresses and selected New Address.) Additionally, the Copy Shortcut and Send Shortcut options from the Actions drop-down menu should not be confused with the Copy Shortcut and Send Shortcut options from the More Actions when working with subrecords (explained later in this chapter).

Add Activity

Add Activity enables you to quickly add a new Activity to the main entity you're working with. When selecting this option, it has the same effect as selecting Activities from the near navigation and selecting New.

For a complete list of the available Activities, see the "Activities" section later in this chapter.

Add a Note

Add a Note opens the note dialog box with Regarding set to the entity you're working with by default (see Figure 7.3).

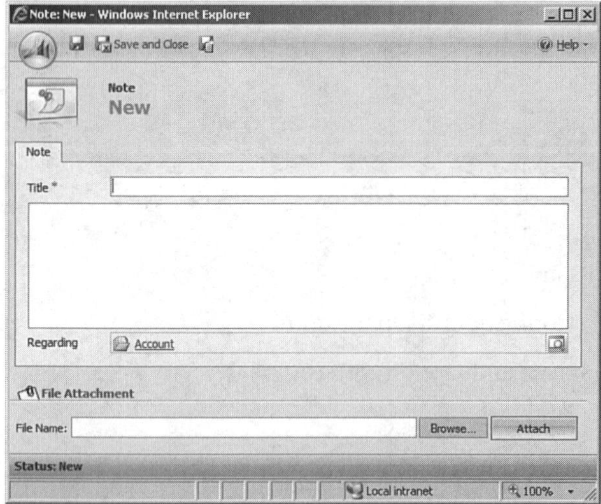

FIGURE 7.3 Add new note dialog box.

> **TIP**
>
> When working with the Add a Note option, you have the capability to enter the title of the note, as well as upload a file from the same form. This is helpful because the main Notes tab allows you to enter only the note, not the title. (See the "Notes" section later in this chapter.)

Attach a File

Attach a File opens the attachment dialog box, enabling you to upload a file to the entity you're working with. The uploaded file appears within the Notes tab section. Any file type can be uploaded and then opened by clicking the file within the Notes section (see Figure 7.4).

> **TIP**
>
> Previously, there was a 4MB limitation when uploading files. If you wanted to change this limitation, you had to perform a series of Registry edits. This version of Microsoft Dynamics CRM has increased the limitation to 5MB, and you can easily set and change this by navigating to the Systems Settings section of the Settings section.

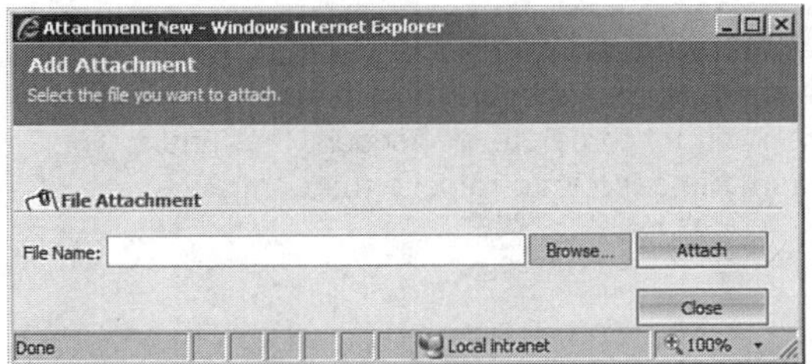

FIGURE 7.4 Add attachment.

Add Additional Address

Add Additional Address has the same functionality as selecting More Addresses from the near navigation and selecting New.

Add to Marketing List

Add to Marketing List enables you to quickly add the entity to an existing Marketing List. As explained in Chapter 11, "Working with Marketing," Marketing Lists are specific to Accounts, Contacts, or Leads. If you are working with Accounts and have only Marketing Lists for Contacts, you will be unable to add the Account to the existing Marketing List. However, you can create a new Marketing List for Accounts after you select Add to Marketing List that consists of only the Account you're working with. (You can manage the Marketing List further either by opening it under Marketing Lists on the Account page or by navigating to Marketing and selecting Marketing Lists there.)

Add Relationship

Unlike the near navigation option of Relationships, which enables you to create only a Customer Relationship, you can easily associate the entity with an Opportunity relationship. For more information about relationships, refer to Chapter 8, "Working with Customers."

Delete <Entity Name> (Account, Contact, etc.)

Delete <Entity Name> enables you to completely delete the record. Use this option with caution and carefully consider whether you want to delete or deactivate a record (see the next section). The reason for this is that when an Entity such as an Account is deleted, all records associated with the account are deleted and features such as reporting on the record are no longer available.

NOTE

In some circumstances, you aren't allowed to delete an entity and you receive a warning message. An example of this is when you try to delete an Account that has a Contract associated with it. Your only option in this case is to remove the Contract association or deactivate the record.

Deleting an Account has the following actions:

- Contacts associated with the Account are deleted.
- Activities associated with the Account are deleted.
- Opportunities associated with the Account are deleted.
- Subaccounts associated with the Account are not deleted but are removed from the Account.
- The Account is deleted and no longer available to report on.

Deleting a Contact has the following actions:

- Activities associated with the Contact are deleted.
- Opportunities associated with the Contact are deleted.
- Cases associated with the Contact are deleted.
- Subcontacts associated with the Contact are not deleted but are removed from the Contact.
- The Contact is deleted and no longer available to report on.

Deleting a Lead has the following actions:

- The Lead is deleted and no longer available to report on.

Deleting an Opportunity has the following actions:

- The Opportunity is deleted and no longer available to report on.

TIP

Even though you might have chosen Delete from the Actions menu, a warning should appear alerting you that you are about to perform the requested action. Furthermore, when you are deleting Accounts or Contacts, an option to merely deactivate is presented on the warning pop-up menu (see Figure 7.5).

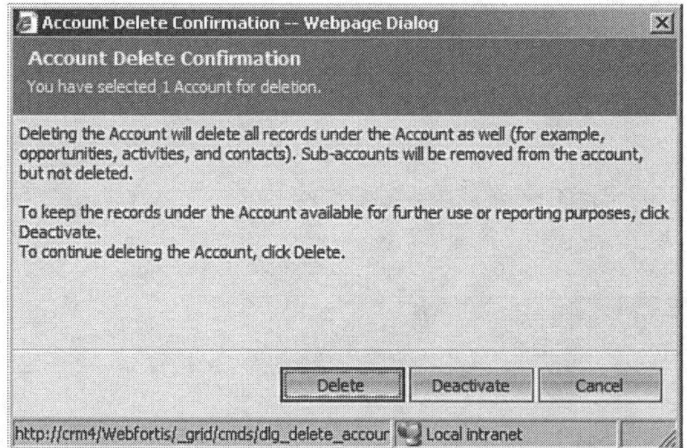

FIGURE 7.5 Confirm record deletion dialog box.

Deactivate Record

Deactivate Record (or Activate Record, if it is deactivated) enables you to set the status of the record. This is the preferred method (rather than deleting) when working with older records because reporting visibility remains along with historical information. Also, when a record is deactivated, the associated records are kept as active as opposed to when it is deleted and the associated records are deleted. This is an important distinction, as it is possible to deactivate an Account and still have active Contacts that are associated with the Account that must be manually deactivated as well.

TIP

The status of a record is always shown in the bottom lower-left corner of the main entity form.

Mail Merge

Mail Merge (Accounts, Contacts, and Leads) is a new option available on both the Internet Explorer client and the Outlook client. Previously, this option was available only on the Outlook client.

Mail Merge is a powerful and easy-to-use feature that enables you to perform the following as part of its wizard steps:

- Select the records you want to use for the Mail Merge.
- Create Activity records for the records, reflecting the Mail Merge contact.
- Assign the Activity records to another user.
- Create a new quick campaign for the Mail Merge records.
- Use an existing template or create a new template based on the document type.

To access Mail Merge, select either the Mail Merge option from the Actions menu drop-down (when available) or the Mail Merge icon located on the toolbar directly above the records you're working with (see Figure 7.6).

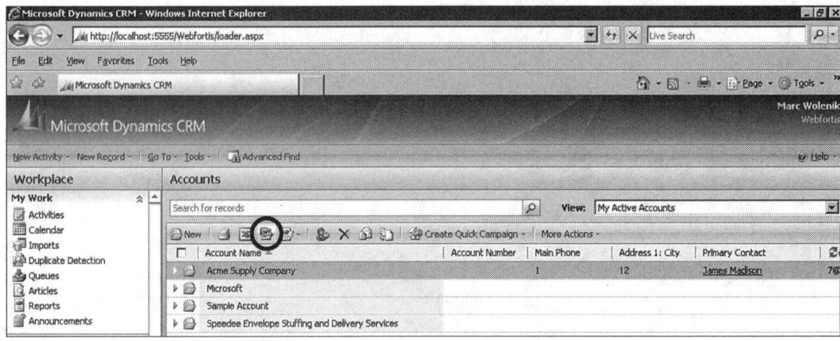

FIGURE 7.6 Mail Merge icon.

When working with the Mail Merge function, a pop-up window called Microsoft Dynamics CRM Mail Merge for Microsoft Office Word presents the available options (see Figure 7.7).

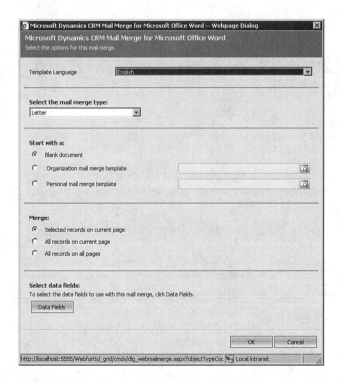

Microsoft Dynamics CRM Mail Merge for Microsoft Office Word -- Webpage Dialog

Microsoft Dynamics CRM Mail Merge for Microsoft Office Word
Select the options for this mail merge.

Template Language: English

Select the mail merge type: Letter

Start with a:
- Blank document
- Organization mail merge template
- Personal mail merge template

Merge:
- Selected records on current page
- All records on current page
- All records on all pages

Select data fields:
To select the data fields to use with this mail merge, click Data Fields.

Data Fields

OK Cancel

http://localhost:5555/Webfortis/_grid/cmds/dlg_webmailmerge.aspx?objectTypeCoc Local intranet

FIGURE 7.7 Microsoft Dynamics CRM Mail Merge for Microsoft Office Word.

By default, the base language is selected for the Template Language. However, you can change it to any of the languages your administrator has made available (refer to Chapter 14, "Settings and Configuration," for more information about language options). Notice there is no drop-down menu if no MUIs have been installed.

Selecting the Mail Merge type defaults Microsoft Word to the correct page layout, and you have the option to work with either existing templates or create new blank one. Existing documents are available on either a personal or an organizational level. However, you can easily create a new template if none exists and set the access level (personal or organizational) manually.

Additional options include record merge options and the capability to select specific data fields.

For the following example on how to use Mail Merge, assume that you have no existing Mail Merge templates (either personal or organizational) and that you will create a new letter to send to all active Accounts announcing the relocation of your main offices to a new address.

NOTE

Options are limited on the Mail Merge dialog to only the following:

- Selected Records on Current Page
- All Records on Current Page
- All Records on All Pages

You could easily select a subset of these records by either performing a simple search on the main page and then selecting a merge from there using the last option (All Records on All Pages), or performing an Advanced Find and working with the results of that to create the Mail Merge (see "Advanced Find" later in this chapter for more information about working with Advanced Find).

Additionally, these options are explained as follows:

- **Selected Records on Current Page**—If you have selected one or more records on the page, only the highlighted (or selected) records will be used for the Mail Merge.

TIP

To select multiple records on a page, hold down either the Ctrl or Shift key while making your selections. As with most Windows applications, Ctrl can be used to select individual nonsequential records, whereas Shift selects a range of records. With this technique, you can select only the records you want. Also, this technique works on filtered views just as well. If you have selected records and then change the page, you will lose the previously selected records.

- **All Records on Current Page**—Remember that Microsoft Dynamics CRM displays only the first 50 records per page, by default. If you have more records, you must navigate to the next page to see the records. As such, this option sends only to the records you have on this current page.

  Typically, this is the best option when you have entered a value in the `Search` field and returned a subset of existing records. A good example of this is if you have multiple Contacts named Bob Smith and you want to send an e-mail to every Bob: You could enter `Bob` in the text search and, with the results displayed, select Mail Merge and then All Records on Current Page. The Mail Merge would create records for only the selected Bob records—assuming that they all fit on the existing page.

TIP

You can change this setting of 50 records by navigating to Options and selecting a different value for the number of CRM records to display (see Figure 7.8).

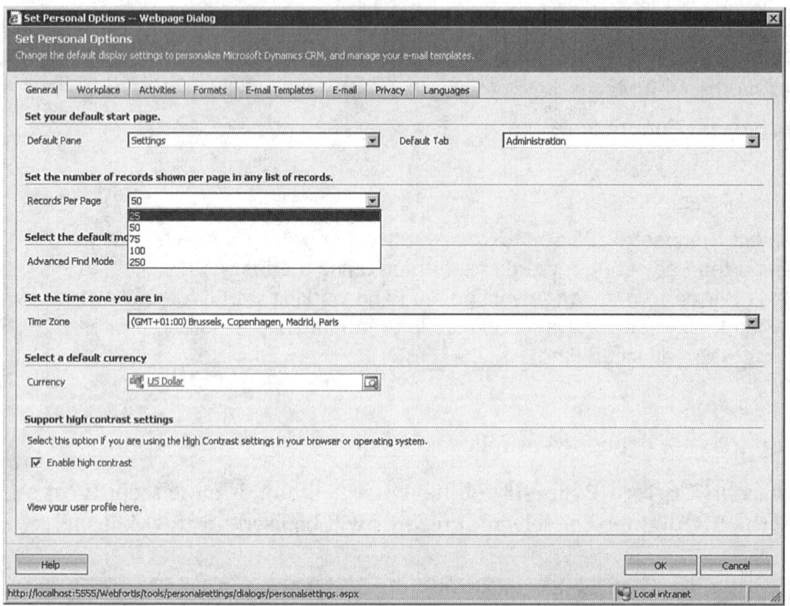

FIGURE 7.8 Microsoft Dynamics CRM options page showing 50 records as the default.

- **All Records on All Pages**—Selects every record you have for that Entity, regardless of whether it is displayed on the current page.

  As with the previous example, if you did a search for Contacts that started with `Bob` and you had 400 different Bob type Contacts, you would need to select this option so that you would send to more than just the first 50 (or whatever value you selected for your records to display) Bob Contacts.

TIP

Advanced Find has significantly more options and thus enables users to perform a much more complicated underlying record query. In this example, if you wanted to find all Accounts (not just active or inactive), you would use Advanced Find and remove any filter for account status, to return all Accounts. When you need more than just matching search results or the views predefined in the views, rely on Advanced Find.

Follow these steps to create a mail merge (While you can use either the Web client, or the Outlook client, the Outlook client offers some features that the Web client doesn't. See the last step of this example for more information):

1. Select Account Entity and the View type from the drop-down list.

2. *Important:* Select the View type as Active Accounts from the View drop-down, as shown in Figure 7.9.

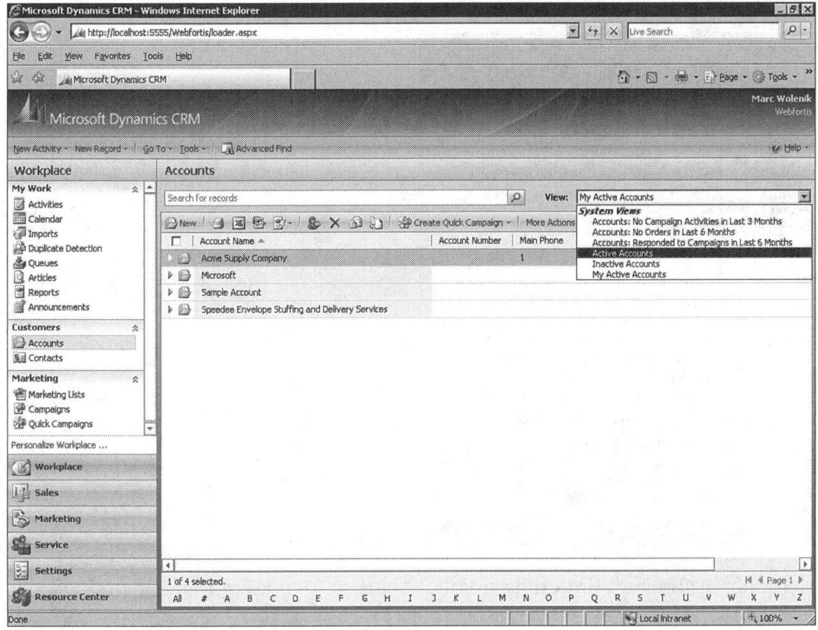

FIGURE 7.9 Microsoft Dynamics CRM Accounts View drop-down list.

By selecting the view, you are adding what is essentially a "prefilter" on the available records. If you had selected a different view type, the records available by default on this mail merge would be different (for example, if you had been working with the default view of My Active Accounts).

3. Select the Mail Merge icon. The Mail Merge pop-up menu appears (see Figures 7.6 and 7.7).

4. Leave Template Language as its default English, and leave the Mail Merge type as its default of Letter. Because you'll be creating a new document as part of this sample, leave the Start with A setting as its default of Blank Document as well.

5. Because you want to send this letter to all your Accounts, select the Merge option of All Records on All Pages.

6. By default, the most commonly used fields for an Entity are selected as its data fields; however, by selecting the Data Fields button, you can easily select or change the columns that you want to have available for Mail Merge.

TIP

Entity relationships are available within the data fields and are easily recognizable by the parenthesis (see Figure 7.10). This is extremely helpful if you need to add records associated with existing relationships (such as data from the Contact Entity, in which you have the relationship of Primary Contact to Account).

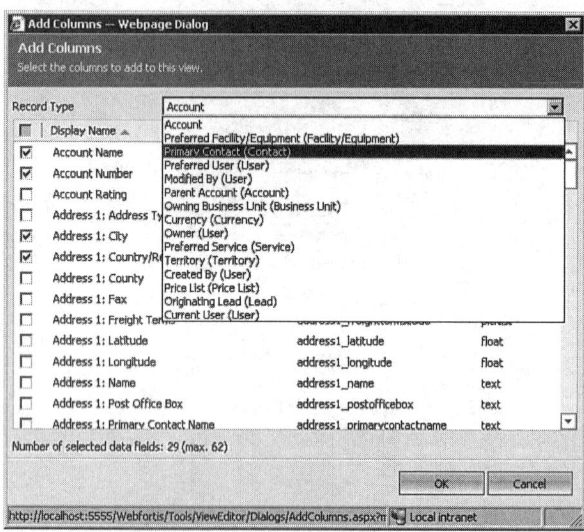

FIGURE 7.10 Microsoft Dynamics CRM Entity Relationships in Mail Merge.

Leave the defaults, and select OK to close the Data Fields window; then select OK to continue.

7. Microsoft Word automatically starts with the selected Mail Merge type format (Letter, Envelope, Fax, or Label), and the Mail Merge Wizard displays the list of recipients that will be used in the merge. By default, all records are selected; however, if you want to exclude one or more, you can uncheck the selection here. From here you can also add sorting and filtering options (see Figure 7.11).

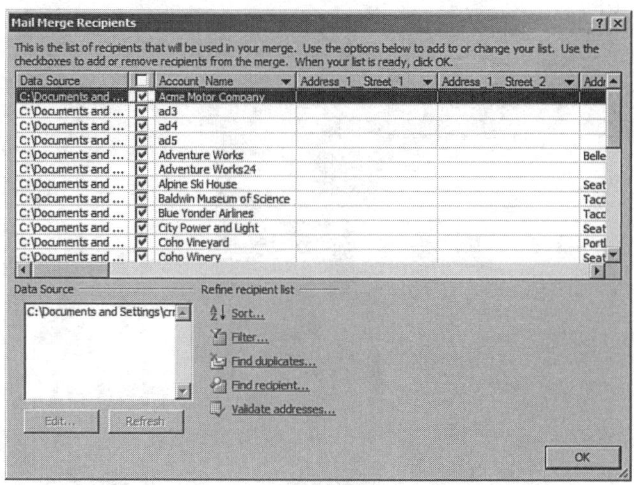

FIGURE 7.11 Microsoft Word Mail Merge Wizard select recipients.

Click OK to continue.

8. You may be presented with a dialog box asking if you want to Open or save this file. Select Open to continue.

9. To use the Mail Merge feature, macros need to be enabled. If you have already enabled macros, you can skip this step; otherwise, select Options near the security warning and then Enable this content to continue the mail merge (see Figure 7.12).

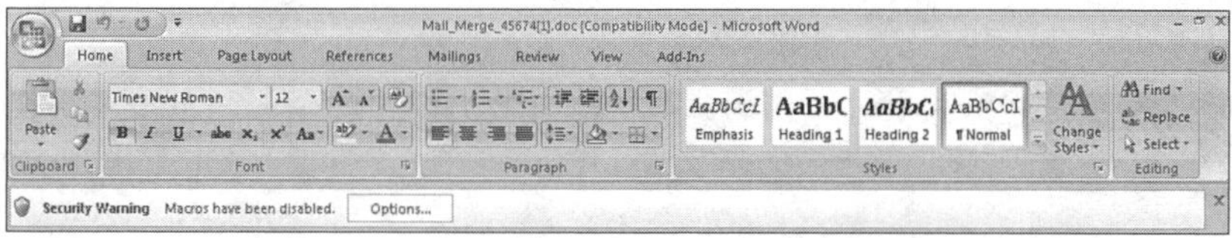

FIGURE 7.12 Enable macros in Microsoft Word.

After you've enabled macros, select either the Add-Ins or CRM option from the top tab; then click the CRM icon to continue with the mail merge.

10. Working within Microsoft Word, you now have the option to follow the Mail Merge Wizard, located in the lower-right corner of the new document, where it reads Step 1 of 4 (see Figure 7.13).

Click Next: Write Your Letter to continue.

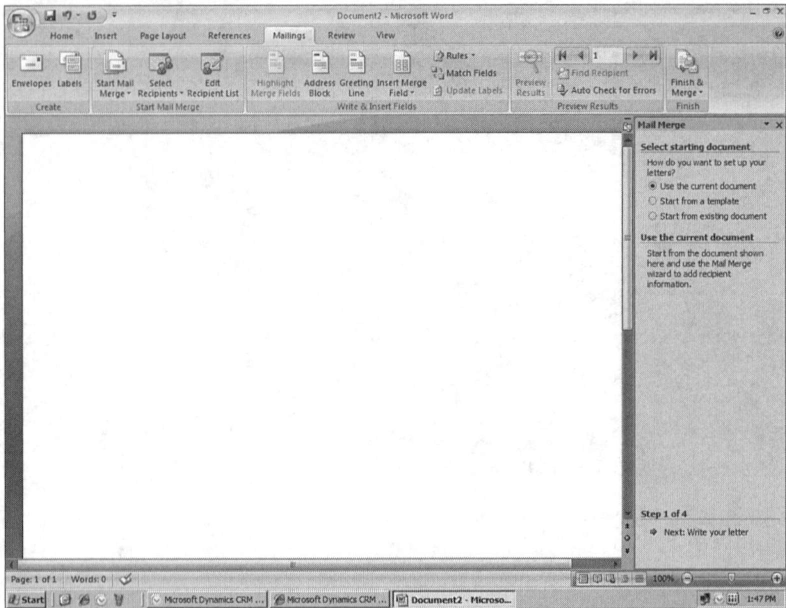

FIGURE 7.13 Microsoft Word Mail Merge Wizard (lower-right corner).

11. Following the Mail Merge Wizard, you can compose your letter and enter your data fields as appropriate (see Figure 7.14).

    Click Next: Preview Your Letters to Continue to continue.

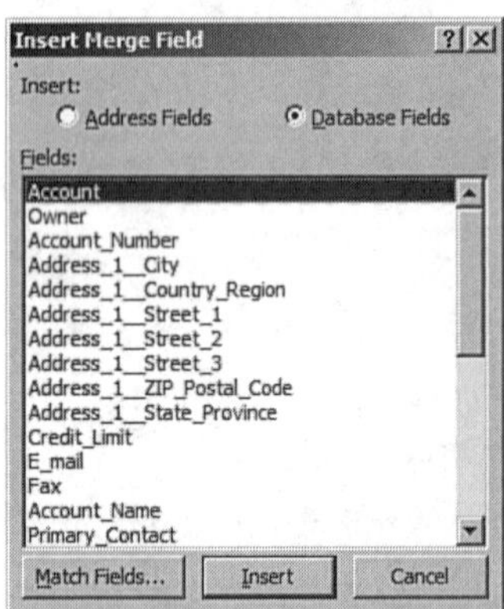

FIGURE 7.14 Microsoft Word Mail Merge letter composed with data fields added.

12. Completing the steps in the Mail Merge Wizard enables you to preview the records and make any changes or exclusions you might need to make at this point (see Figure 7.15).

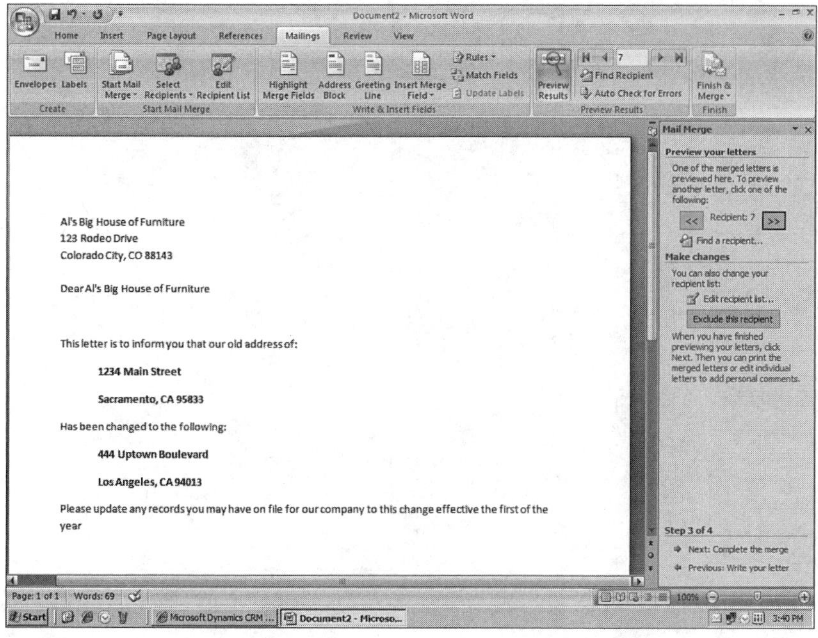

FIGURE 7.15 Microsoft Word Mail Merge letter preview.

Click Next: Complete the Merge to continue.

13. In the last step of the Mail Merge Wizard (Step 4 of 4), you are presented with three options:

    - Print
    - Edit Individual Letters
    - Upload Template to CRM (when using the Outlook client)

    Upload Template to CRM is available only when using the Outlook client. If you want to work with this document again, select Upload Template to CRM. Click Yes when asked whether you want to create a new mail merge template; the Microsoft Dynamics CRM Mail Merge Template opens, enabling you to name, assign, and save the template for future use.

    See Chapter 14 for working with templates.

    When selecting either Print or Edit Individual letters, the merge job completes and you are presented with the option Create Activities for the Mail Merge (see Figure 7.16). Again, this option is only available when working with the Outlook client.

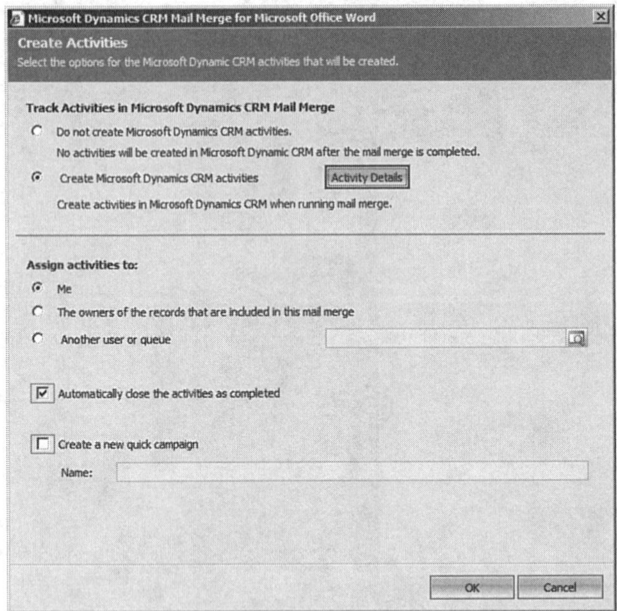

FIGURE 7.16 Microsoft Word Mail Merge Create Activities options.

Track Activities for the Mail Merge

By default, no Activities are created in Microsoft Dynamics CRM after the mail merge is completed. Because you want to track that you sent this letter to your active Accounts only, you will change the default setting and ask that Activities be created after the mail merge is completed. Although it is not necessary to select the Activity Details button, you can easily view and change what the Activity will look like when it has been completed (see Figure 7.17).

> **NOTE**
>
> When viewing the Activity Details in Figure 7.17, notice that you cannot change several fields: `Sender`, `Recipient`, `Address`, `Direction`, `Regarding`, and `Owner`. These are set by default as part of the Mail Merge function. You can change the `Subject` (which defaults to the standard CRM Activity type and date/time/user stamp), the description (message), the `Duration`, the `Due` date, `Priority`, `Category`, and `Subcategory`. In the example, you'll leave the defaults.

Assign Activities

Because you are creating Activity records, you have the option to change the Activity assignment (see Figure 7.16). By default, the owner of the Activity is the user who completed the mail merge; however, because the records might belong to different owners, you can set the ownership to the owners of the record that were included in the mail merge. Alternatively, if you wanted to manually assign them to another user entirely (say an administrative assistant who is responsible for managing the outgoing correspondence for example), we could change the setting to Another User or Queue.

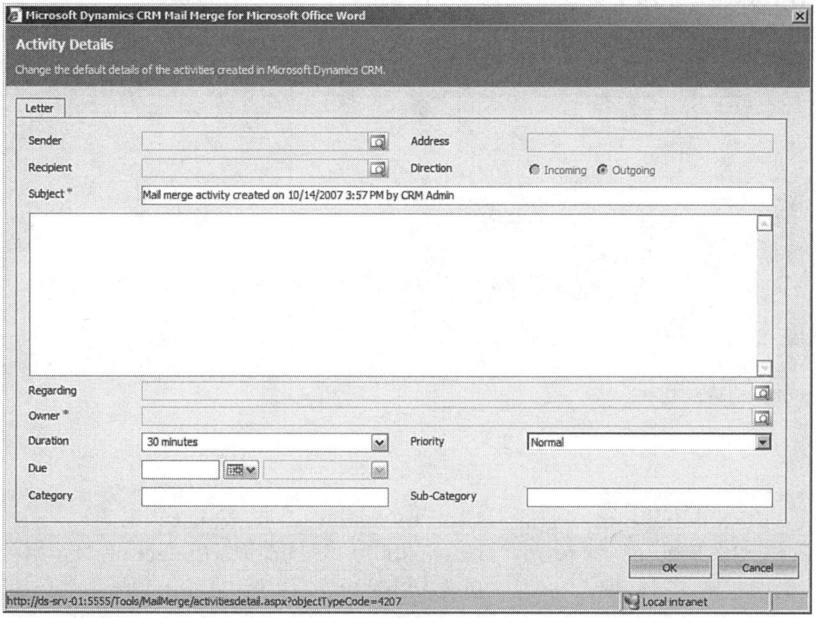

FIGURE 7.17 Microsoft Word Mail Merge Activity Details.

If you chose to keep the records open for follow-up, be sure to change the default selection for Automatically Close the Activities as Completed.

Finally, the option Create a New Quick Campaign enables you to quickly and easily manage the Mail Merge as a campaign and, therefore, track responses.

For more information about quick campaigns, refer to Chapter 11.

Depending on the size of your mail merge, you might experience a delay while Microsoft Word is preparing the merge and while Microsoft Dynamics CRM 4.0 creates the Activity records, assigns them accordingly, closes them (if applicable), and adds them to a new quick campaign.

You can easily view the Activities in the History (if you selected them to be closed) or in the Activities tab of the affected Contacts.

Assign

Assign enables you to set record ownership by selecting a new user or queue within the system, depending on the Entity type. For example, an Account can be assigned only to another user. An Activity, on the other hand, can be assigned to either a user or a queue, as shown in Figure 7.18 (for more information about working with queues, refer to Chapter 14).

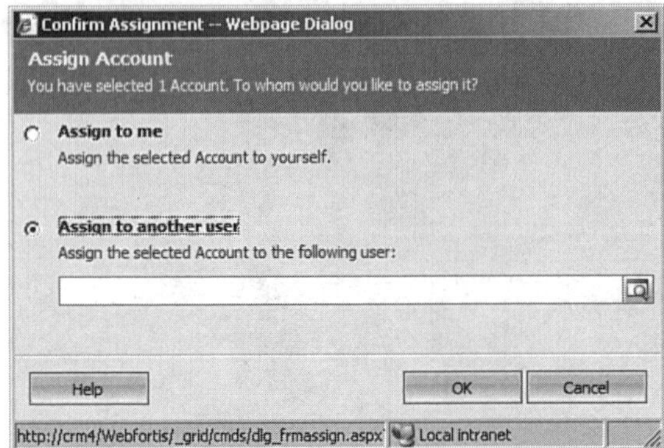

FIGURE 7.18 Assign dialog box.

Sharing

As its name implies, the Sharing option enables you to share the record with other Microsoft Dynamics CRM 4.0 users or teams. The capability to perform the act of sharing is set with the security roles for a user (see Chapter 14 for more information about security roles). When you share a record with another user, the other user inherits the security settings on the associated records of the record.

The following is the list of records that can be shared:

- Accounts
- Contacts
- Cases
- Campaigns
- Invoices
- Quotes
- Orders
- Reports
- Opportunities
- Marketing Lists
- Leads
- Contracts

When sharing, select the user or team and then toggle the permissions you want to give (see Figure 7.19).

Copy Shortcut and Send Shortcut

Copy Shortcut and Send Shortcut are new options available with Microsoft Dynamics CRM. Do not confuse them with Copy Shortcut and Send Shortcut from the More Actions option located at the top of the Quickview. Although both provide the capability to quickly and easily create shortcuts directly to the record, when you select from the

Actions drop-down, the main record you're working with (Account, Contact, and so on) will be selected instead of the specific associative records (if chosen from the Quickview menu option—that is, Contacts associated with the Account or History for the Account). For this reason, you might get the error message shown in Figure 7.20 when you select Copy Shortcut from the Quickview menu but fail to select any associative records (to avoid this error, select one or more records and then try again).

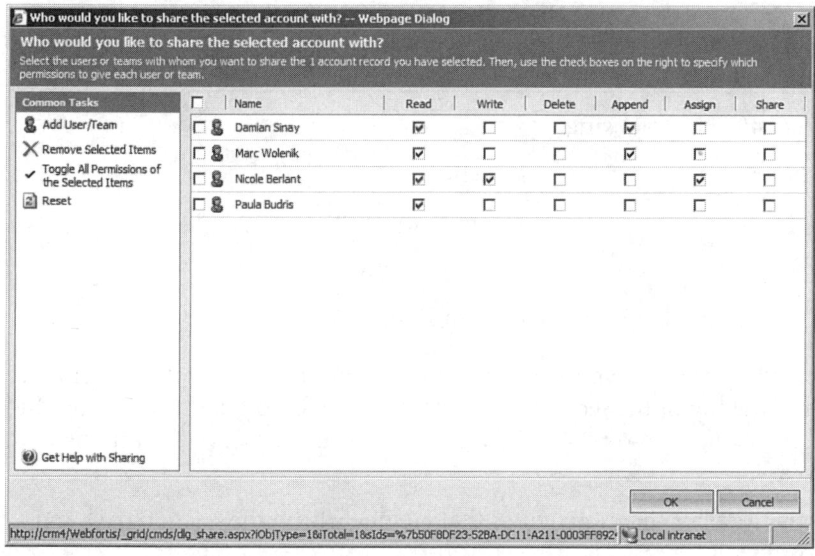

FIGURE 7.19 Microsoft Dynamics CRM share permissions form.

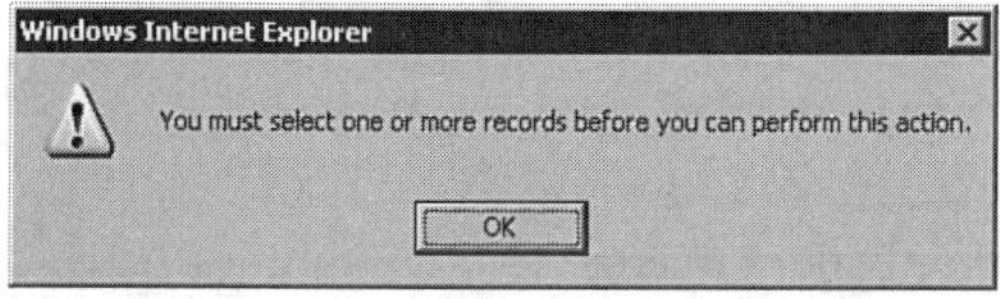

FIGURE 7.20 Copy Shortcut chosen from the Quickview, but without any subrecords selected.

TIP

The capability to send the shortcut to another user does not preclude that user's appropriate security role to view the record. So even if you have the capability to view a record, the user you're sending it to might not and would then receive an error page when attempting to access the link you send.

Activities

Think of Activities as how work gets assigned. For example, if you have an Account that requires a follow-up Phone Call, you would open the Account, create a new Activity with type equal to Phone Call, and assign it to yourself (or another user). Quite commonly, employees who use Microsoft Dynamics CRM come into the office in the morning and, after checking their e-mails, check their pending Activities.

As with all Entities that have Activities, the Activities display nonclosed actions applicable to the Entity. When an Activity becomes closed, it is not visible here; you can find it in the History (see the next section).

An Activity can consist of the following:

- Task
- Fax
- Phone Call
- E-mail
- Letter
- Appointment
- Service Activity
- Campaign Response

Additionally, within the Activities, you have the option to run manual Workflow via Run Workflow, located at the top of the section. The option to run a Workflow is based on the entity you're working with, so to run Workflow manually, you must have at least one Workflow created for it.

By default, the Activities filter shows Activities that are due within the next 30 days and filters on This Record Only.

NOTE

An Activity that does not have a due date shows in all filter views until a date is assigned to it.

Unlike previous versions where activities could only be converted to opportunities, activities can now be converted to leads and cases as well.

Finally, when working with Activities, you are limited to only the Activities that come with Microsoft Dynamics CRM, and you cannot create one as you could with a custom entity. So if have a specific Activity that is not in the previous list (Task, Fax, Phone Call, and so on), you must change your business process to accommodate these Activity types only.

For more information about using Activities, see Chapter 9, "Working with the Workplace."

History

Think of History as where all work (or Activities) that has been closed or completed resides, along with e-mail correspondence. Similarly, when you send an e-mail from CRM or from Outlook and select the Track in CRM option, this is where you find the history of that e-mail.

As with the Activities section, you have the option to run manual Workflow via Run Workflow, located at the top of the screen. The History shows the last 30 days and filters on This Record Only.

For more information about using the History, see Chapter 9.

Notes

The `Notes` field enables you to enter notes about the Entity free form. Generally, if you have standardized data about an Entity (for example, favorite restaurant) and you want to record similar information across the Entities (such as for all Accounts or Contacts), it is a better idea to add a new field to the Entity interface via customization rather then enter the data here. There are a couple of reasons for this however, it is usually a better idea to standardize the entry (via a drop-down box of restaurants, for example) and have a common location that you can control entry to.

To enter a note, navigate to the Notes tab (generally, the last tab) on the main Information tab, and select Click Here to Add a New Note. By default, the title of the note is Note Created on *<date/time>* by *<user>*. To change the title, save the Note either by selecting Save from the top menu options or by merely clicking somewhere else on the form (this automatically saves any entered date); then double-click the Note icon to open the Note form, where you can make changes to the title of the Note as well as the Note contents.

TIP

If you need to make a quick change or add a new note quickly, we recommend not opening the Note form—just enter it on the Notes tab by clicking where it says Click Here to Add a New Note. If you need to make a Note with a title or upload something, select the Add a Note option from the Actions drop-down, described earlier in this section.

Additional Notes considerations are the capability to easily see when a note was entered and by whom, as well as when a note was edited and by whom (see Figure 7.21).

TIP

Notes do not support either rich text or HTML. If you need to have content such as this, consider uploading an attachment instead.

FIGURE 7.21 Account Notes entry screen.

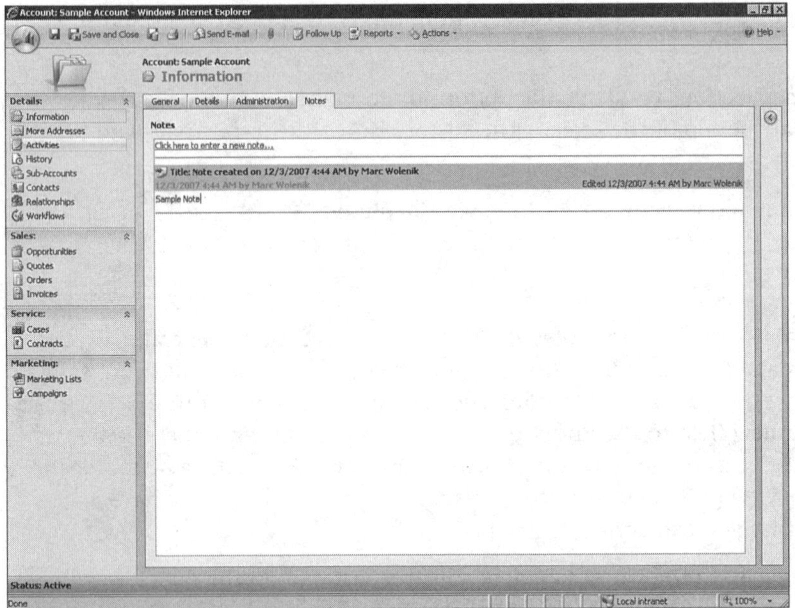

Attachments

When you upload a document to the Account entity, it is placed in the Notes section with the same audit information mentioned previously.

NOTE

As mentioned previously in this chapter, you cannot upload anything to a newly created Entity until it is saved first (see Figure 7.22). After it is saved, the Paper Clip icon appears (as well as the other advanced options), enabling you to perform the actions on the record (see Figure 7.21).

Attachments are stored in the CRM database. After you've uploaded them, you can view them by selecting them from the Notes.

TIP

When viewing attachments, the location of the file can sometimes be misleading. The reason for this is that, when you are viewing an attachment, its location is your C:\ drive. We have had many calls from concerned clients saying that they were sure they had uploaded files from their C:\ drive, only to view them and, when viewing the properties, find they were on the C:\ drive also. The explanation is simple: When you view a file from the CRM, it downloads the file for viewing to your Temporary Internet Settings folder (usually located on your C:\ drive). So when you're viewing an uploaded file, you're really viewing a local *copy* of the file.

FIGURE 7.22 Account screen prior to saving. Notice the lack of the Paper Clip icon (allowing you to upload) present in Figure 7.21.

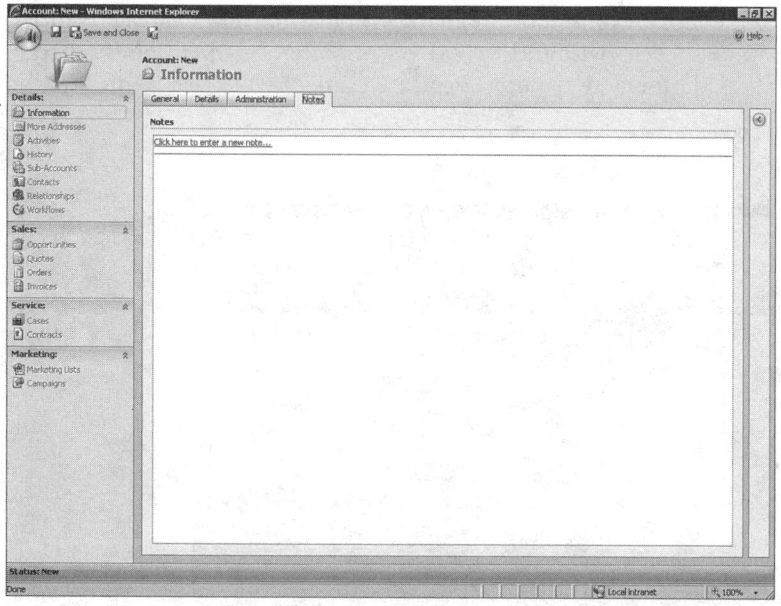

NOTE

To make edits to an uploaded file, you must first download it, edit it, and then reupload it. Microsoft Dynamics CRM does not have the capability to handle versioning or online document editing. If this is a requirement that you might have, we suggest that you look at an integrated Microsoft Dynamics CRM and Microsoft Office SharePoint Server (MOSS) solution.

Run Workflow

When located as part of the Quickview, the Run Workflow option enables you to quickly and easily run a workflow that has been marked as Run on Demand.

By default, the Workflows are entity dependent, so there will not be an option to Run Workflow if you have not created at least one workflow for the entity you're working with.

TIP

If you need to run a workflow and are unsure from where to run it, you can always navigate to the Settings and Workflow page to check its attributes and manually run it, if necessary. When checking, you might notice that no workflow exists for the Activity Entity; each Activity is a separate option for Workflow (such as E-mail and Appointment). These items all are available from the Activity Run Workflow.

For more information about Workflow, refer to Chapter 20, "Workflow Development."

Advanced Find

In our opinion, one of the most helpful tools in giving visibility to CRM data is Advanced Find. It enables users to query deep within the CRM system, often creating significantly powerful queries that would otherwise require a dedicated support staff (see Figure 7.23).

FIGURE 7.23 Advanced Find.

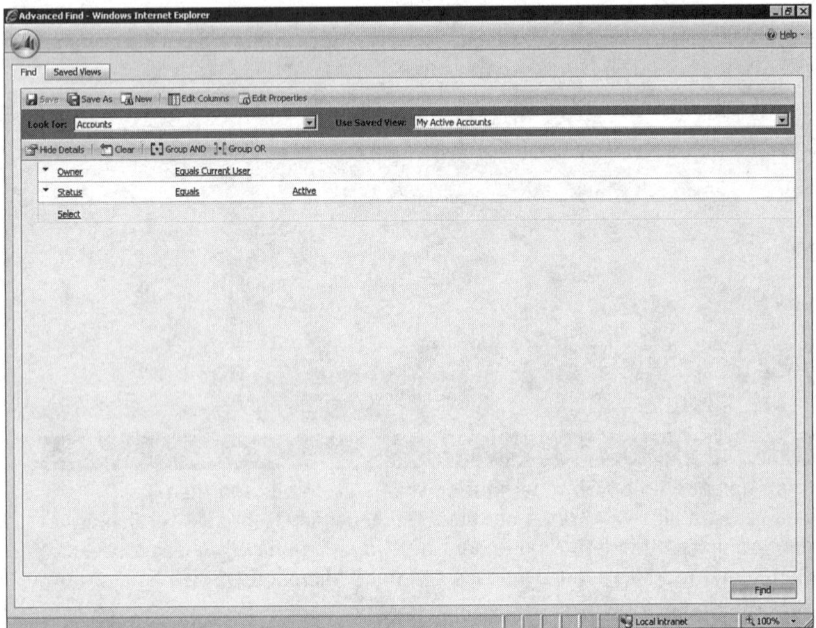

With Advanced Find, users can easily query on the following:

- All system Entities, such as Accounts and Contacts, as well as, Notes
- System objects, such as Workflows, Templates, Roles, and System Jobs
- Related Entity Attributes

Additionally, when working with Advanced Find, users can perform a variety of actions to get the data they want, including this:

- Selecting specific columns
- Selecting the sort column and sort order
- Adding grouping options
- Modifying a system view (but not overwriting it)
- Saving Advanced Find as a view that can be quickly run when working with that Entity later

- Exporting the results to Excel
- Performing a mail merge
- Performing duplicate detection on the resulting records
- Merging records
- Sending direct e-mail to the resulting records
- Reporting on the records
- Printing the records
- Assigning the records to another user
- Activating or deactivating
- Creating a Quick Campaign on the resulting records

When working with Advanced Find, the first step is to select the main Entity you want to work with. Choose the Entity or system object from the drop-down where it says Look For.

After you have selected the Entity, any associated system views are available for you to select in the Use Saved View drop-down.

TIP

Although you can modify a system view, you cannot overwrite it. However, you can save it as a user view that will be available as a view for the entity you're working with, found after the system views.

Figure 7.24 illustrates the system views for the Account Entity, as well as a new view that we created to show all Accounts.

The view that you're seeing on Advanced Find is the same view that is available when working with the Accounts Entity within Microsoft CRM (see Figure 7.25).

This is a nice feature because it enables you to create custom views into the data through Advanced Find that you can save and run quickly while working with the Entity directly (without having to go back to Advanced Find).

When working with Advanced Find, there are several components to it. These are discussed next.

FIGURE 7.24 Advanced Find Saved views.

FIGURE 7.25 Accounts view.

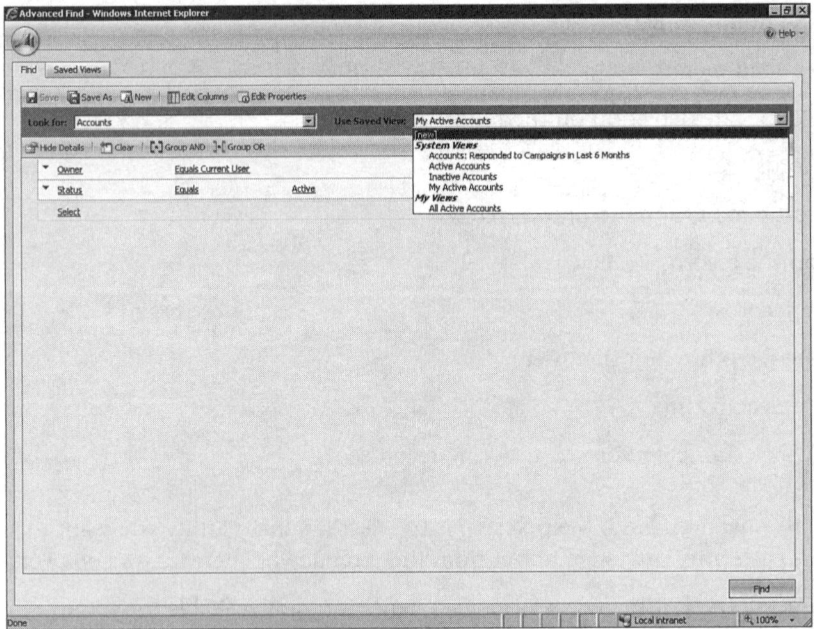

Find and Saved Views Tabs

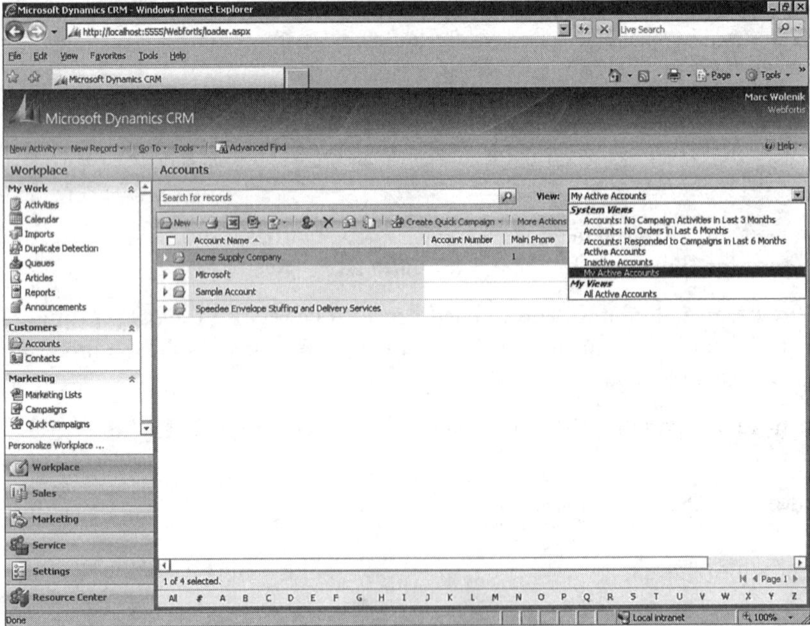

All the functionality for searching is located on the Find tab. The Saved Views tab, as its name implies, is where you will find the views listed as My Views from Use Save View (see

Figure 7.26).

FIGURE 7.26 A saved view located under My Views in Advanced Find.

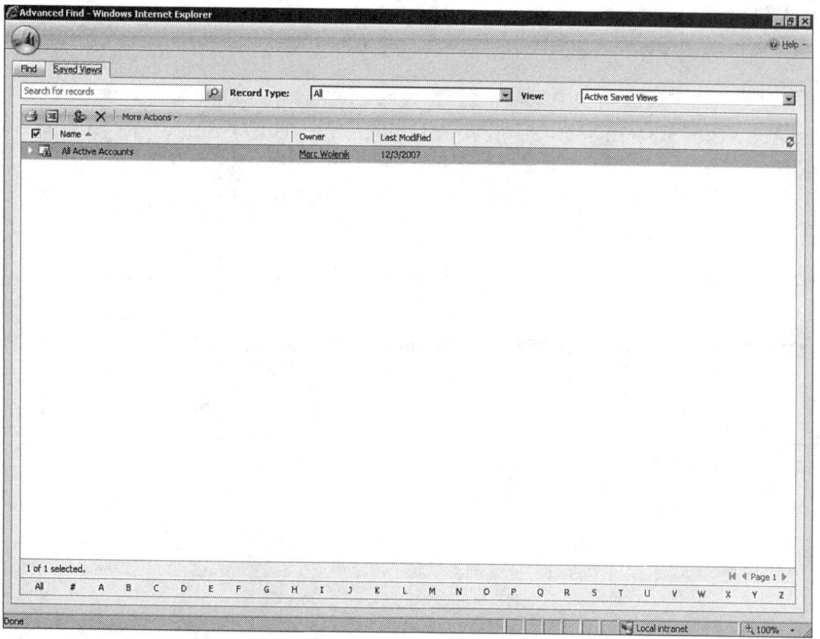

The Toolbar Options

The navigation options in the toolbar of the Find tab feature the following:

- Save
- Save As
- New
- Edit Columns
- Edit Properties

If you choose to work with an existing view, the view you select is displayed in detail on the form, enabling you to review with the logic.

As you'll see in the following example, Edit Columns enables you to select the columns from the underlying query that you would like to have returned on the view. The Change Properties link enables you to easily change the name and add a description, if desired.

TIP

By default, when working with an existing system view, Save is disabled, preventing you from making changes to it. However, you can choose to use Save As and save it under a different name.

Advanced Find Details

When working with queries in Advanced Find, you can look at the criteria in two ways: Detail mode and Simple mode.

When viewing the Accounts System view of Accounts: Responded to Campaigns in Last 6 Months, both Figures 7.27 and 7.28 show the same view. However, Figure 7.27 is in Simple mode and Figure 7.28 is in Detail mode. (Notice the menu option displayed that says either Show Details or Hide Details.)

FIGURE 7.27 Accounts System view of Accounts: Responded to Campaigns in Last 6

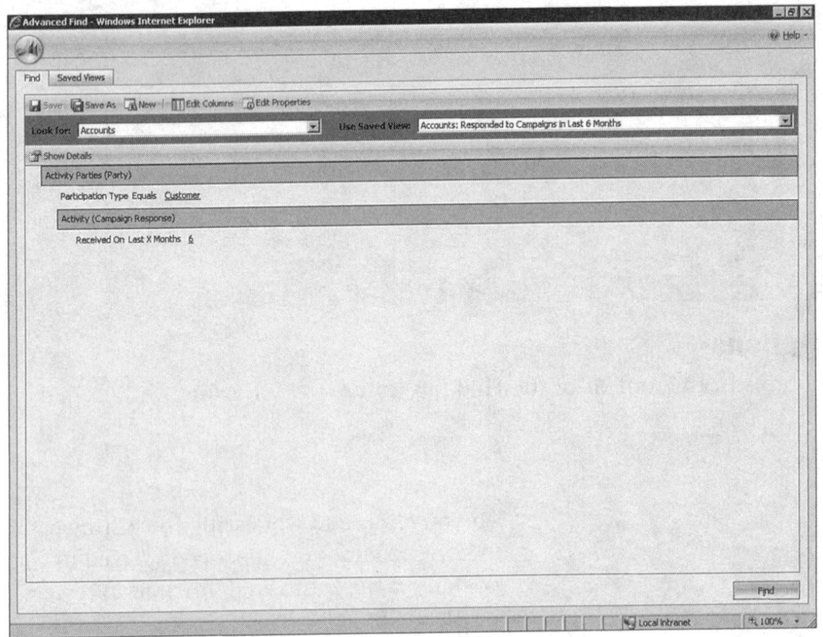

Months in Simple mode.

FIGURE 7.28 Accounts System view of Accounts: Responded to Campaigns in Last 6

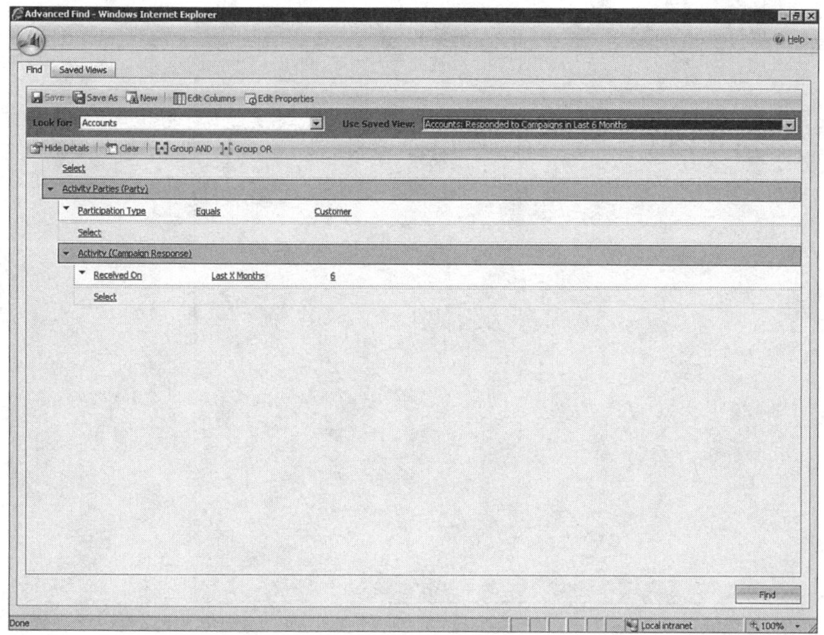

Months in Detail mode.

You can find and set the default settings for Advanced Find mode in the Personal Options form.

When working in Details mode, you are further presented with the option to add an And clause or an Or clause to our query.

As an example of how the And and Or clauses work, let's query on Account names:

1. Open Advanced Find and select Account as the Entity. Be sure that the Use Saved View is selected to New.

2. Working in Detail mode (be sure the Advanced Find says Hide Details directly below the text Look for:), mouse over the word Select (which will expand), and select Account Name and Begins With, using the letter a.

3. Adding another row, select the same criteria, but this time use the letter b. This query should look similar to Figure 7.29.

   If you were to run this query as it stands, you would have no records returned because it is looking for all records that have an Account name starting with a and b. It uses Boolean and logic, so results will only be returned if the account name starts with both a and b. Since Account Names can only start with one letter, we'll never see results.

FIGURE 7.29 Advanced Find with two select clauses.

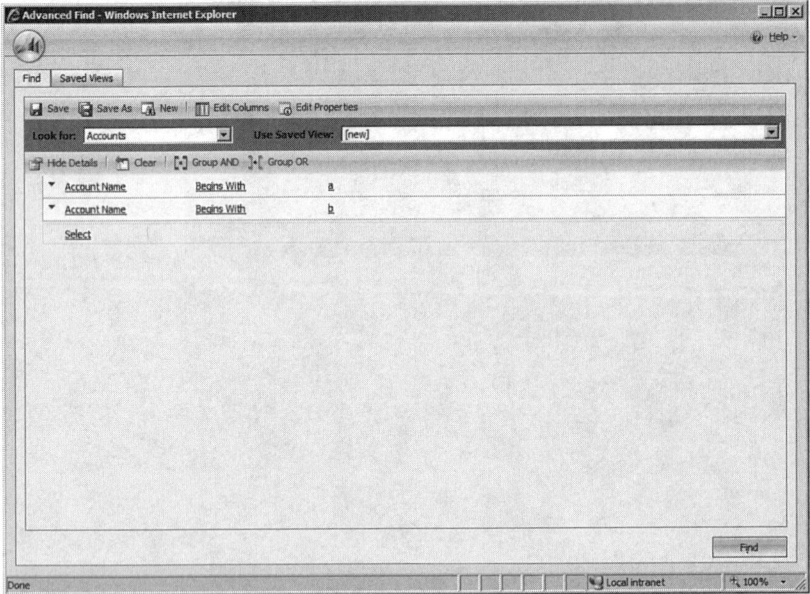

4. Select each row as illustrated in Figure 7.30.

FIGURE 7.30 Selecting rows in Advanced Find.

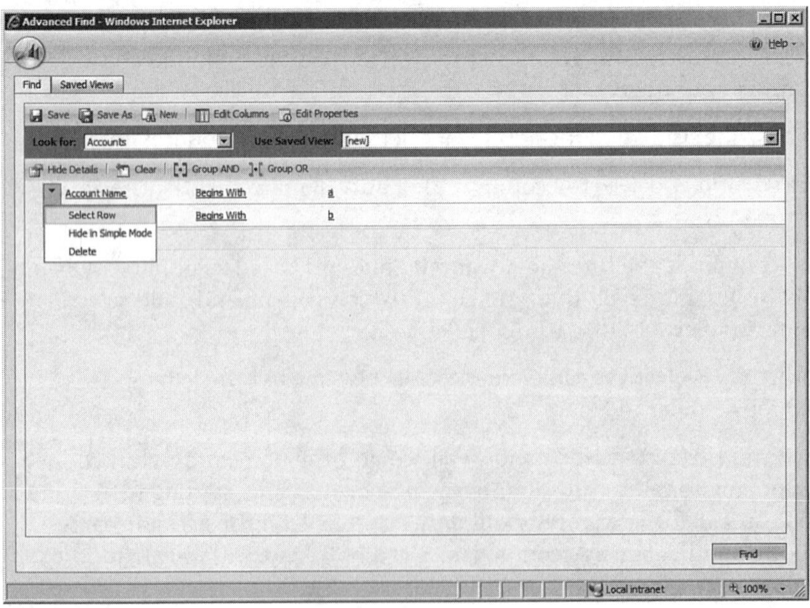

5. Now select the Group Or option. The two selected rows are grouped with an OR next to them (see Figure 7.31).

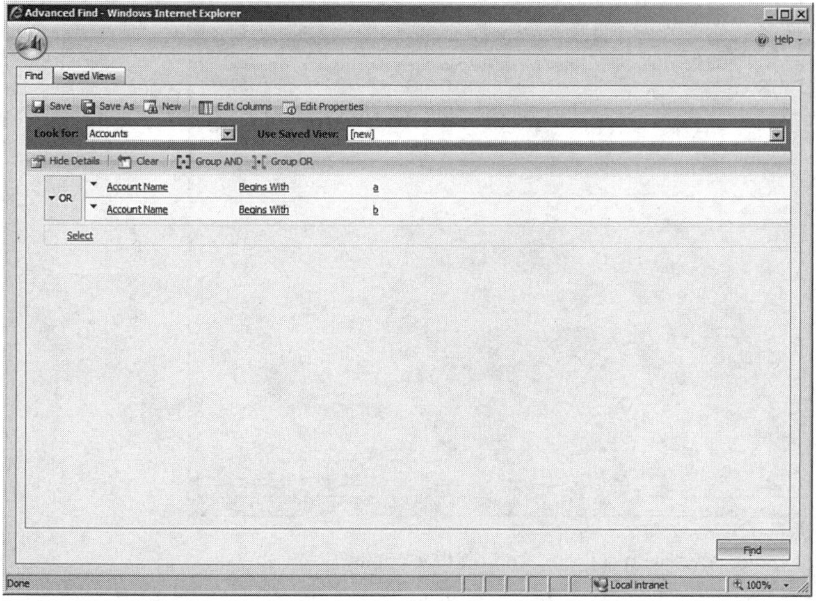

FIGURE 7.31 Selected rows with a group OR applied.

Running the query now returns all Account records in which the Account name begins with either a or b.

The Grouping options can be applied multilevel, grouping And or Or clauses by selecting different criteria. In Figure 7.32, multiple And and Or clauses have been applied to selectively return desired records.

Advanced Find Example

As previously mentioned, the Advanced Find feature is incredibly powerful. The following example demonstrates how to perform a popular find: returning all the Contacts that have had an Account created in the last 10 days so you can send a welcome mail.

1. Open Advanced Find. Advanced Find is always located on the main navigation screen on the web client and as part of the CRM toolbar within Outlook (see Figure 7.33).

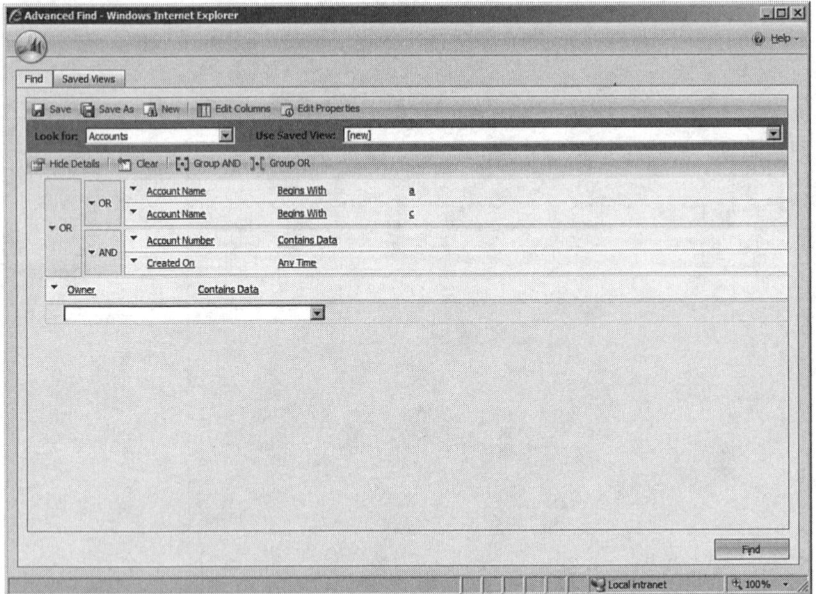

FIGURE 7.32 Selected rows with a group And and Or applied.

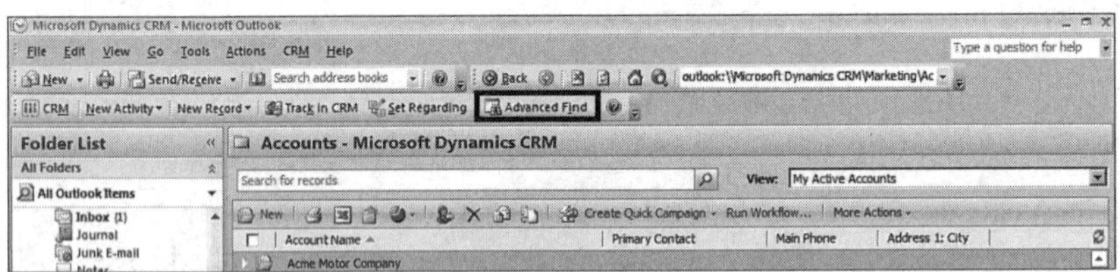

FIGURE 7.33 Advanced Find on the CRM Outlook toolbar.

2. By default, Advanced Find automatically selects the Entity that you're working with as its default Look For. If you were not working with Contacts when you started the Advanced Find, change the Look For to Contacts.

   Because you're going to be sending a piece of mail, you need to edit the columns to make sure that you're returning the right columns for your mailer. Select Edit Columns from the top toolbar and the Edit Columns dialog box is displayed (see Figure 7.34).

3. By default, when working with Contacts, only the full name and business phone are returned. Because you're going to be working with Mail, you need to select Add Columns located on the right navigation pane of the dialog box. Select the columns you want to have added to the results, and click OK to continue (see Figure 7.35).

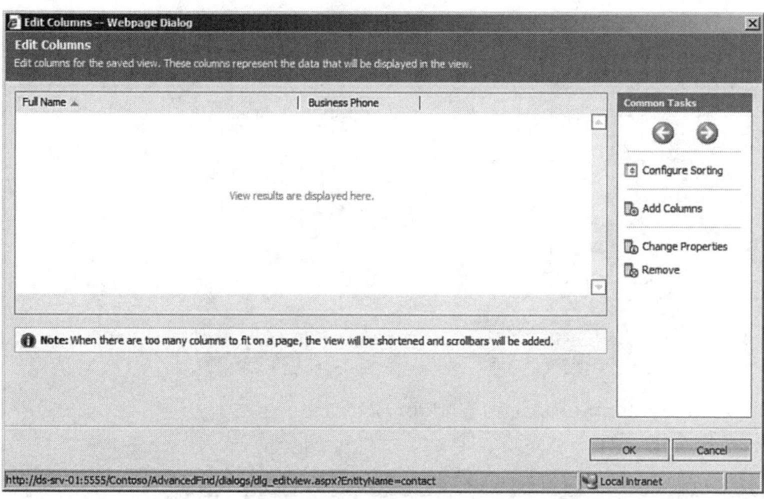

FIGURE 7.34 Edit Columns on Advanced Find for Contacts.

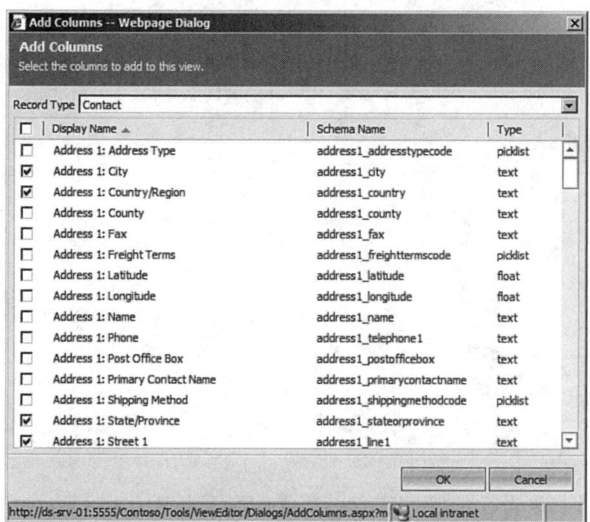

FIGURE 7.35 Selecting columns from Advanced Find for Contacts.

4. From here you can configure the sort order of the returned records by selecting Configure Sorting (see Figure 7.36). Click OK twice to continue.

5. You need to add the criteria now to your Find because you have selected only the Contacts and the fields you want returned. If you were to run your query now, you would return every Contact, not just those that are associated with an Account created 10 days ago. To add this logic, mouse over the Select option; it changes to a drop-down (see Figure 7.37).

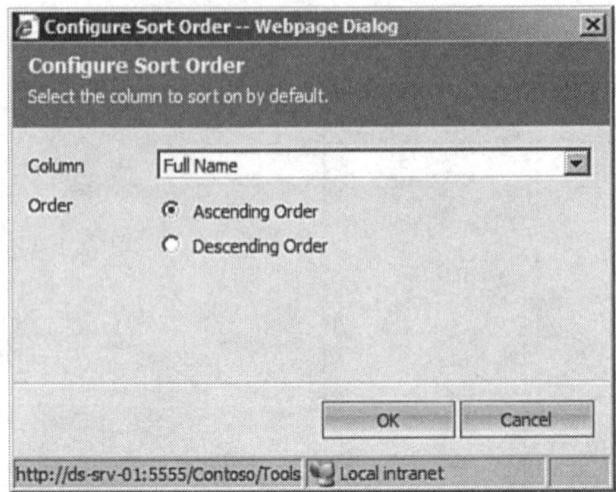

FIGURE 7.36 Selecting sorting from Advanced Find for Contacts.

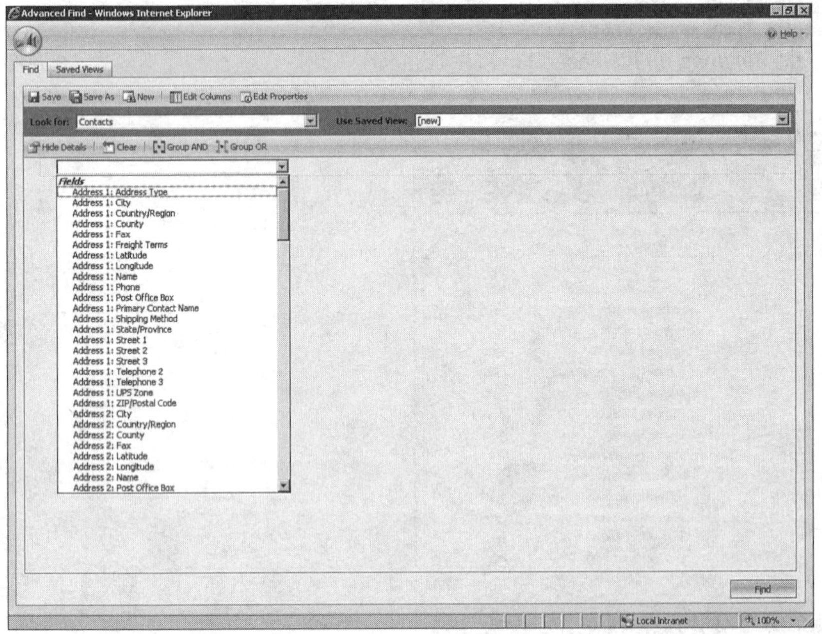

FIGURE 7.37 Selecting Fields and Related from Advanced Find.

TIP

Notice that, in the drop-down, these are the same fields you saw when you added fields to your query. However, selecting them here does not add them as a column to the returned records; selecting them here only enables you to add a filter on them.

6. Scrolling down the drop-down, you'll notice that the available fields to apply a filter to are broken into two sections:

   - Fields
   - Related

   Fields are the base fields for the entity you're working with—in this case, the fields for the Contact entity. Notice that every field applicable to the Contact entity is listed there, along with any custom fields you might have added.

   Related enables you to select related entities to the primary entity you're working with—in this case, the entities related to the Contact entity. Again, every relationship to the Contact entity should be listed there, along with any custom ones added.

TIP

The Related section shows you the relation and then the entity in parenthesis. If you're unsure of what entity the relation ties to, check the value in parenthesis listed right after the relation.

Select the Parent Customer (Account) from the Related section (see Figure 7.38).

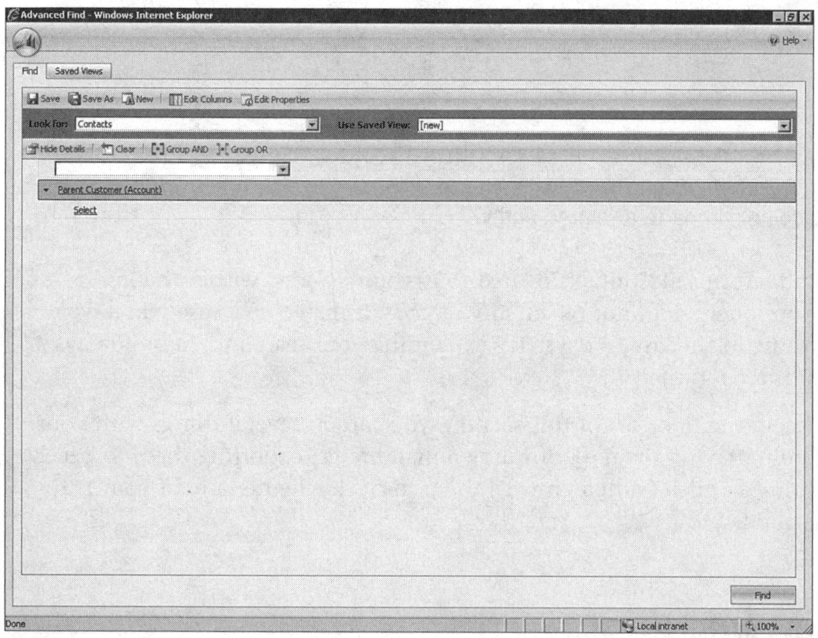

FIGURE 7.38 Parent Customer (Account) selected on Advanced Find.

Now that you have the relation established on your Advanced Find, you need to add the last bit of logic, Accounts added within the last 10 days.

7. Mouse over the Select under Parent Customer (Account), and select Created On. Notice that the fields displayed are of the base entity Account—this is because you're now working and able to query on the fields for the related entity. Change the option to Last x Days and enter **10** as the value (see Figure 7.39).

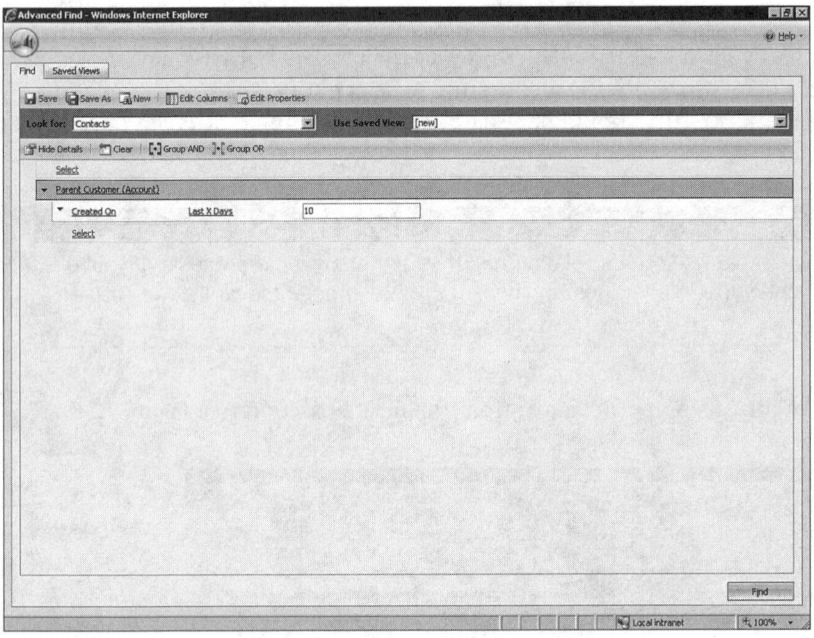

FIGURE 7.39 Adding criteria to a related entity.

Selecting Find returns all Contacts related to Accounts added within the last 10 days. If your query does not return any records, it may be because you have not adding anything in the last 10 days. Try expanding your search to 20 or 30 days or until results are returned.

As mentioned in the first part of this section, you can do several things with your results, including saving them, performing a mail merge, exporting them to Excel, or even creating a Quick Campaign with them to track whether any of your mail has been responded to.

Form Assistant

The Form Assistant is ubiquitous throughout the application and can always be found on the right side of any form you're working with. If you open a new Contact, you'll see it on the right side of the form (see Figure 7.40). Note that your data will likely differ from the information displayed in Figure 7.40, as it will be applicable to your organization.

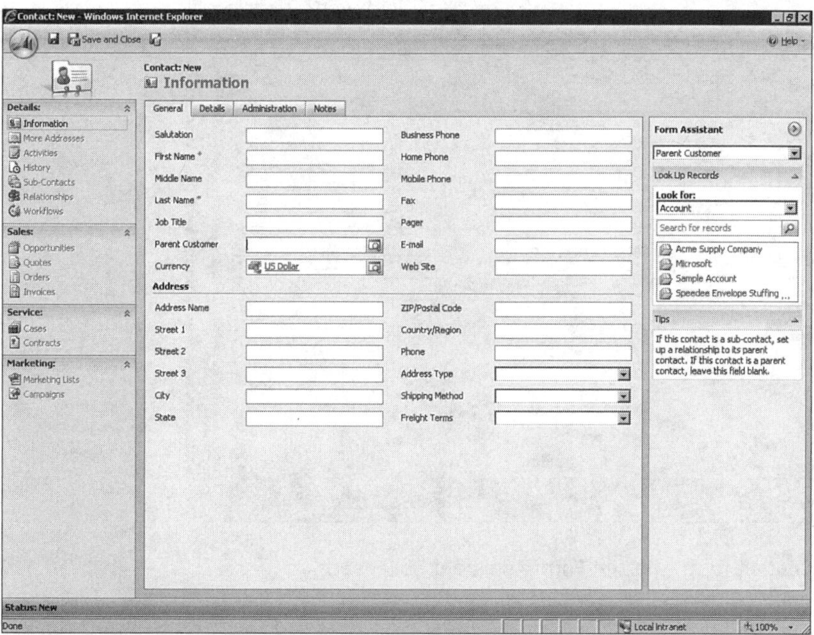

FIGURE 7.40 Contact form with the Form Assistant expanded.

If you don't see the Form Assistant, it might be collapsed (see Figure 7.41). You can expand it either by selecting the left arrow in the upper-right corner of the form or by pressing Ctrl+Shift+F. This is a very helpful resource and can aid in quick entry of data that requires lookup fields.

The Form Assistant has the capability to select an entry for virtually every field on the page that has a lookup field associated with it, without having to open the lookup pop-up window. Additionally, it enables you to populate all lookup fields on a page without having to tab to each. Finally, it has the same search functionality built in and can quickly locate records when searched.

NOTE

For all the great and easy-to-use features that the Form Assistant provides, it does have some limitations. You do not have the ability to view properties of prospective records, and you can't do a Quick Add of the entity, as you can when working with the full pop-up lookup.

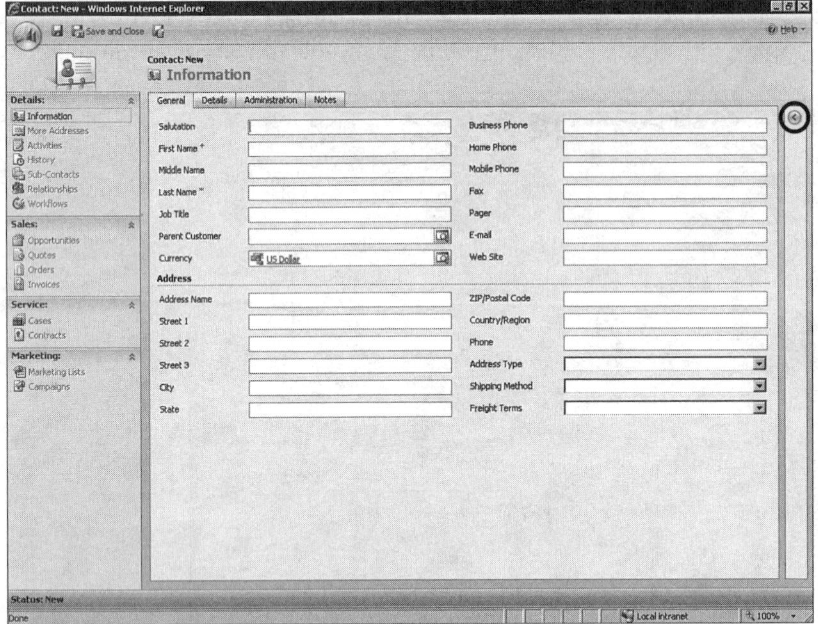

FIGURE 7.41 Contact form with the Form Assistant collapsed.

Record Merge

When working with records, it is possible that you need to merge two records into one record. This might be because a customer consolidated or shut down offices or locations, or because you found a duplicate record in the system.

This functionality is included in the toolbar by selecting the Merge icon, as shown in the Web client in Figure 7.42.

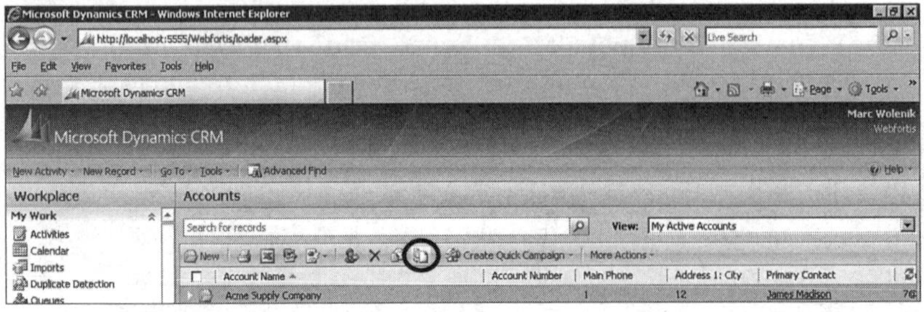

FIGURE 7.42 Merge icon.

When you select to merge two records, the records are displayed on the Merge Records interface allowing you to select which one has the master data (see Figure 7.43). By selecting the fields you want to keep from each section, you tell the system which record it should have after the merge. The other data in the field is discarded.

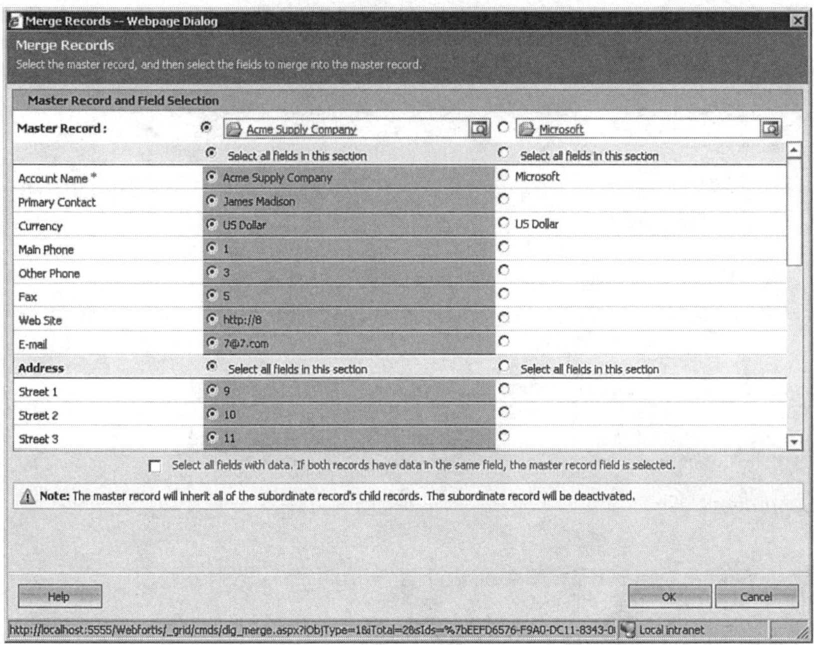

FIGURE 7.43 Merge Records dialog box.

When the merge is complete, the selected records are kept, and the subordinate record is deactivated. If the subordinate record had associations to Contacts (in the case of Accounts), the new Master record now has the Contacts.

Fields that aren't listed in Figure 7.43, such as Notes, are merged into one record.

Send Direct E-mail

The option to quickly and easily send a direct e-mail exists for most entities in the system. Found on the toolbar next to Mail Merge (see Figure 7.44), it allows you to send an e-mail directly from CRM to one or more selected records.

Note that until the e-mail router is configured, this option will not work unless you open the Outlook client.

The e-mail can consist of either a global or specific to the entity template (see Figure 7.45).

7

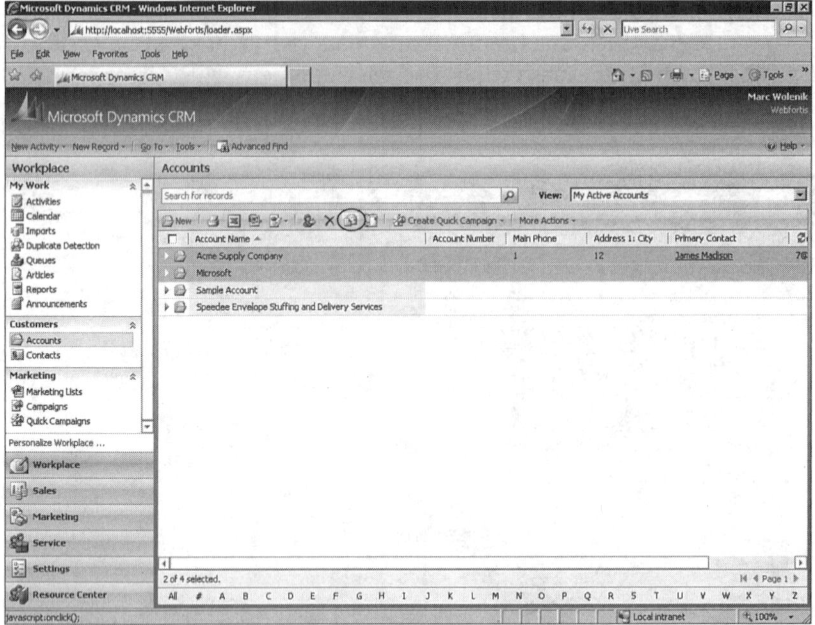

FIGURE 7.44 Send direct e-mail option.

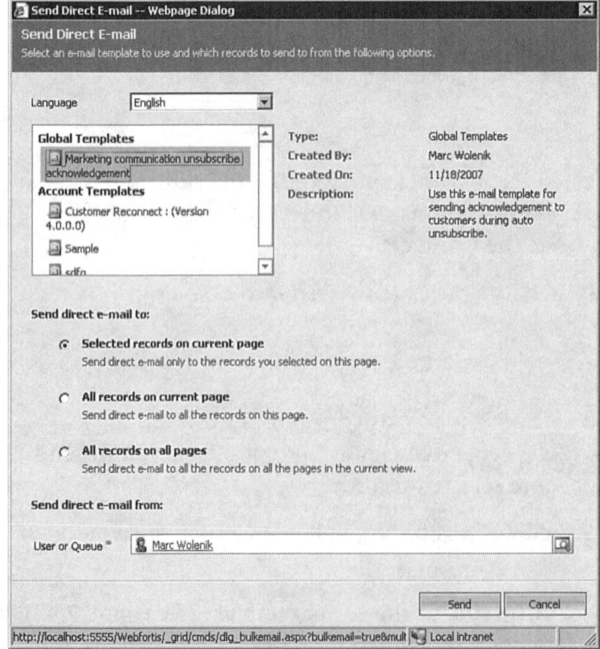

FIGURE 7.45 E-mail templates.

Resource Center

The Resource Center is a new addition to Microsoft Dynamics CRM that, by default, connects to Microsoft for updated content. The content on the Resource Center includes the following:

- Microsoft Dynamics Communities and Blogs
- Learning and Training Resources
- Articles related to Microsoft Dynamics

The Resource Center is located by navigating to the last option in the near navigation (see Figure 7.46).

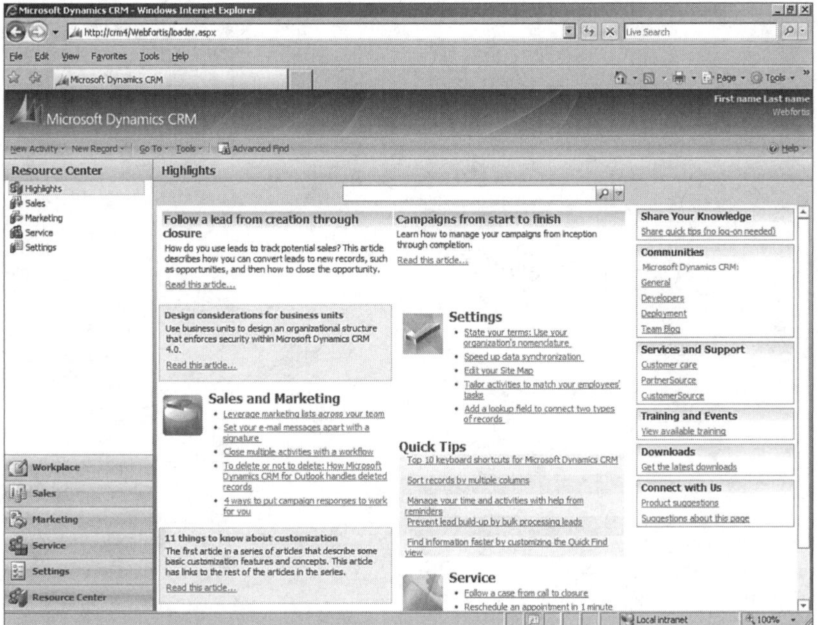

FIGURE 7.46 The Resource Center.

When working with the Resource Center, it should be noted that the content is delivered dynamically from Microsoft.com and might or might not be relevant to your particular situation. You can remove the Resource Center from the application by modifying the site map, or you can change what the users see when accessing the Resource Center (see Chapter 19, “Customizing Entities,” for more information on working with the site map). An example of the latter might be to change the Resource Center to point to an internal intranet site that displays company information.

Summary

We have looked at a number of features that are similar throughout the application and not specific to any one Entity.

When working with the various features of Microsoft Dynamics CRM, such as Advanced Find or Mail Merge, it is important to understand that the system is incredibly flexible. Any customizations and modifications that have been made to the system are available to be queried. This provides for a powerful tool when searching and creating a set of records dynamically.

Although there are some differences in functionality depending on where you're accessing them from, these features are common throughout the application.

CHAPTER 8
Working with Customers

IN THIS CHAPTER

- Accounts
- Contacts

When working with Customers, you'll become very familiar with two Entities: Accounts and Contacts. Both can contain records that Microsoft Dynamics considers Customers. In fact, when associating records to Customers (as on the Contact form where it says Parent Customer), you select either an Account or a Contact value. As such, consider Customers in Microsoft Dynamics CRM to be equal to either of these Entities.

NOTE

It is sometimes helpful to rename Accounts to Companies, and Contacts to Customers—something that can easily be done by editing its display name under Settings and Customization. Refer to Chapter 19, "Customizing Entities."

Additionally, it is important to remember that, when using Microsoft Dynamics CRM, Leads are unqualified, potential customers and, therefore, are not required to have an association to an existing Contact or Account record. Opportunities, however, must reference an existing Customer (that is, an Account or a Contact). Therefore, when thinking about how you want to work with your customers, you should also consider your sales process and how you want to associate records as part of it.

Accounts

In general terms, users should consider Accounts as businesses or organizations. Some Accounts have many contacts associated with them (such as a normal customer that has two dozen employees whom you have contact with on some level); other Accounts have no contacts associated with them (the Internal Revenue Service might be a good example of this).

The Account Entity can be used not only for businesses you sell to, but also for vendors you purchase from, again tracking contacts that work for the vendor.

Finally, while not generally common, another use for Accounts is to track Competitors. This situation arises if you have a lot of information about Competitors (such as individual employee data) or if the existing Competitor Entity (found in the Sales area) in Microsoft Dynamics CRM is not sufficient enough for your needs.

You can find the most common usage types for Accounts in the Relationship Type drop-down list:

- Competitor
- Consultant
- Customer
- Investor
- Partner
- Influencer
- Press
- Prospect
- Reseller
- Supplier
- Vendor
- Other

NOTE

Generally, we don't recommend using Accounts to track Competitors. We recommend augmenting the Competitors Entity with customizations, as necessary, and using it instead. The reason for this is that, when you close Opportunities in Microsoft Dynamics CRM, you have the option to tie lost opportunities to *only* the Competitors Entity (and not other Accounts or Contacts). Therefore, you effectively lose visibility into Competitors win/loss metrics relating to your opportunities when you don't use the Competitors Entity.

Because of the amount of time spent by most users working with Customers, we have taken extra effort in this chapter to explain most, if not all, the fields on the Account and Contact forms.

Details, Information

The Details tab is by default the first tab that receives focus when the form is opened. (Although this can be changed with some scripting applied.) As such, users frequently ask for customizations consisting of simply moving fields from other tabs to this tab for ease of use. Although this is acceptable, the division of fields is logical and should be considered when rearranging the layout.

General Tab

When working with Accounts, only two fields are required by default: `Account Name` and `Owner`. (However, you can easily customize the form to make other fields required if your business needs require it.) The `Account Name` field is limited to 160 characters and, by default, can be the same value as an existing Account name. Because the `Account Name` is the first field shown on the default quick find view (see Figure 8.1), it is important to be descriptive here.

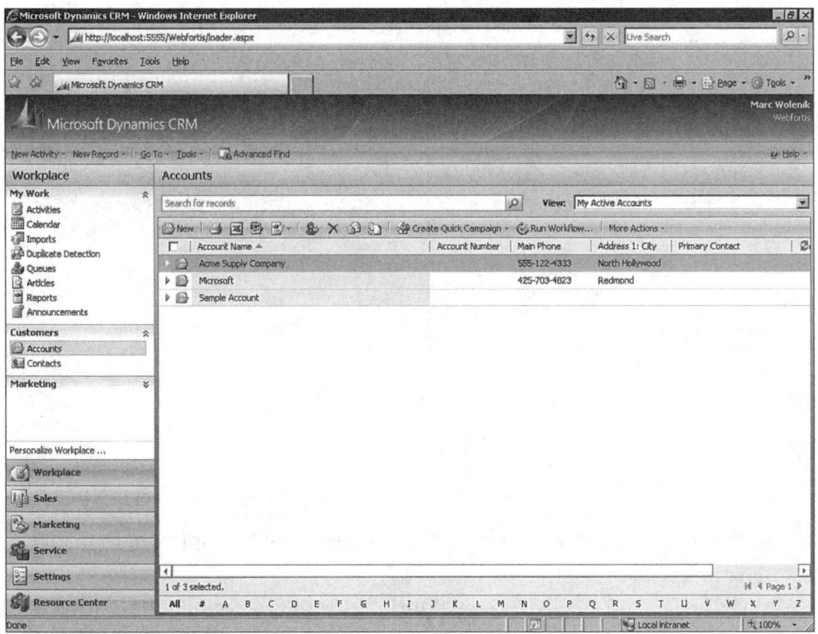

FIGURE 8.1 Accounts in Microsoft Dynamics CRM.

TIP

Because the `Account Name` field has no built-in functionality to avoid duplicates, be sure to add a Duplicate Detection Rule on `Account Name` if you have concerns about duplicates here (see Chapter 20, "Workflow Development," for more information about Duplicate Detection Rules). An example of duplicate detection is shown in Figure 8.2.

By default, the Owner (located on the Administration tab) is set to the user who created the record; however, you can change this to select another user in the system.

TIP

Be sure that the User has permissions to view the record. If not, you will receive a security warning prompt indicating that the user doesn't have the necessary security permissions to access the record, and you will be unable to assign it to him.

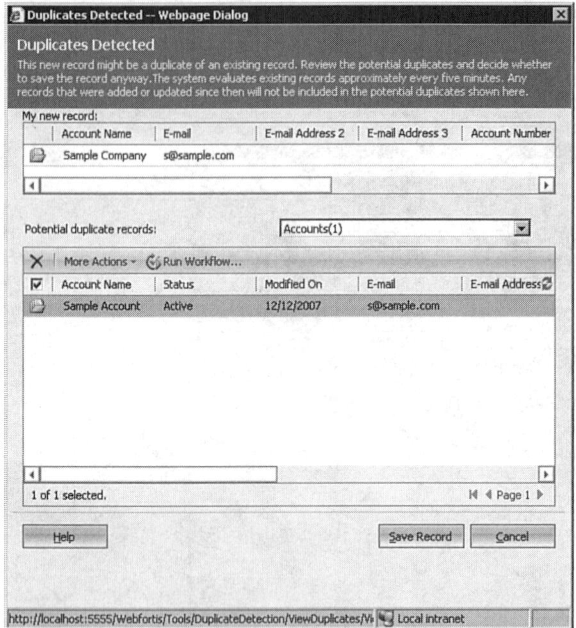

FIGURE 8.2 Duplicate Detection example when entering a duplicate Account name.

To add a new Account, select New and the new Account form opens (see Figure 8.3).

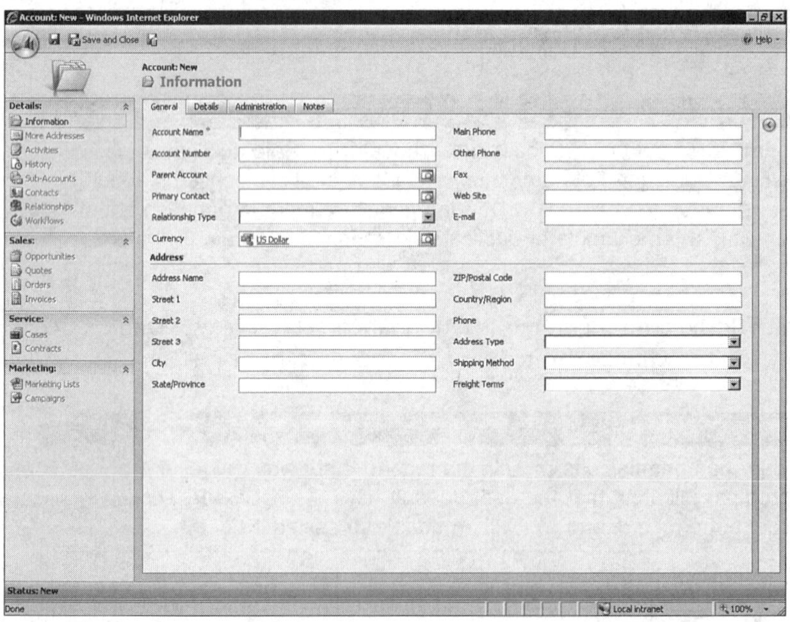

FIGURE 8.3 Create New Account interface.

Besides the two required fields previously indicated, the following comprise the list of fields that can be used:

- `Account Number`—This free-form entry field can be used to enter any number or alphanumeric combination. This field can be tied to existing ERP, Accounting, or other systems for quick-and-easy reference. Again, as noted earlier with the `Account Name`, duplicate entries are not checked on this field by default; therefore, it is possible to enter the same Account Number unless you have a Duplicate Detection Rule running here as well.
- `Parent Account`—The `Parent Account` field is used when the Account rolls up to another Account. An example of this is a Customer that has several different business units that report to a corporate Entity.
- `Primary Contact`—The `Primary Account` field ties the Contact record. This is not a required association, but the Primary Contact is shown on the Account Quickview by default and can make similar Accounts easier to identify and work with.
- `Currency`—The `Currency` field enables users to select the primary currency that this Entity deals with. You must select a currency option here to work with other attributes of the form (such as the `Annual Revenue` field on the Details tab). The currency options shown are only those that the system administrator has set within the system (for more information about currency, check Chapter 14, "Settings and Configuration").

NOTE

It is important that the `Currency` field is populated when working with imported records, because it will not populate by default when importing records and you will receive an error when trying to add values to any `Currency` value field.

- `Main Phone`, `Other Phone`, and `Fax`—These free-form entry fields accept any alphanumeric value. Because any value is accepted here, you might want to enforce entry standards by using scripting. For more information about working with scripts, see Chapter 19.
- `Website`—The `Website` field accepts any value and automatically formats it as a URL by prepending the entered value with `http://`. (If the entered value already has `http://`, it uses the entered value.) Users can double-click the entered value to go directly to the website which opens in a new window.
- `Email`—The `Email` field accepts an address for any domain. However, a check is done to be sure that it is properly formatted as an e-mail address. This is a very important field because the system prompts you with errors if you try to send an e-mail to the Account and this value is missing (see Figure 8.4).

Additional considerations around the `E-mail` field are duplicate detection jobs. By default, Microsoft Dynamics CRM comes with three duplicate detection jobs (found in Settings,

Data Management, Duplicate Detection Rules). By default, these jobs look at the e-mail addresses of Accounts, Contacts, and Leads, so if you enter a duplicate e-mail, you will be warned, as shown in Figure 8.2. (See Chapter 20 for more information about Duplicate Detection Rules.)

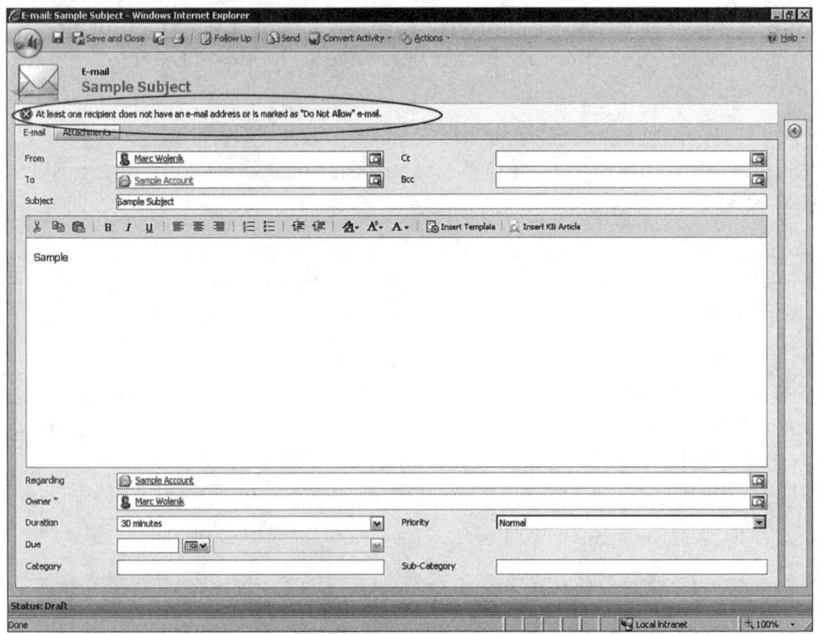

FIGURE 8.4 Error message when creating an E-mail Activity task for an Account that does not have an e-mail address.

The remaining fields on the General tab consist of address information. These fields are also available in the More Addresses option on the left navigation if an Account has multiple addresses.

Details Tab

Options on the Details tab (shown in Figure 8.5) follow:

- `Territory`—If you have set up your CRM to use Territories, you can select one of them here. For more information on setting up Territories, refer to Chapter 14.
- `Annual Revenue`—The `Annual Revenue` field is a free-form field that requires you to enter the base currency for the Account on the General tab. If you have selected a currency and entered a value here, and then try to change the currency, you will receive an error message that you must remove the entered value before setting the currency again.

Other options on the Details tab include Category, Industry, Ownership, No. of Employees, Ticker Symbol, and Description; these are fairly self-explanatory. The SIC Code is the Standard Industrial Classification code used to specify what industry this Account belongs to. You can find more information about SIC codes and the code values at www.sec.gov/info/edgar/siccodes.htm.

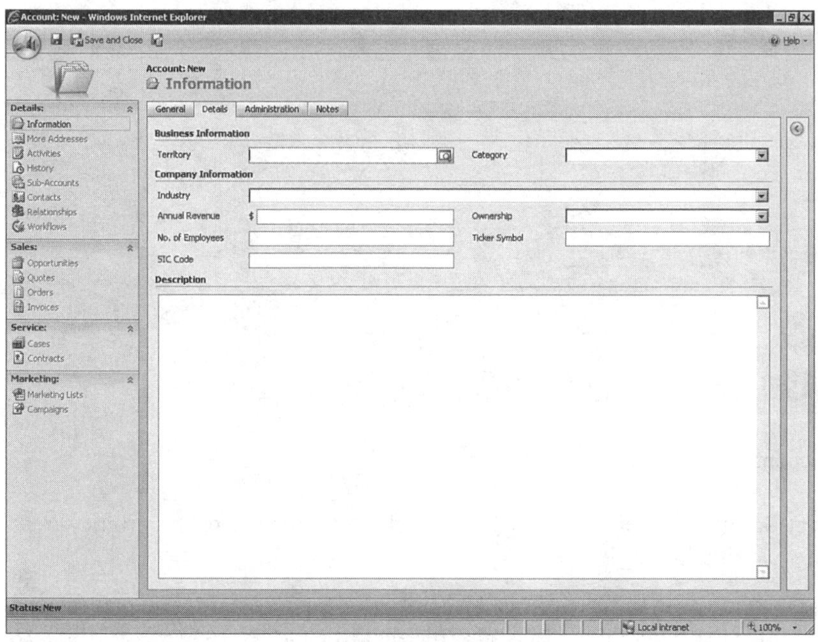

FIGURE 8.5 Account Creation Details tab.

Administration Tab

Options on the Administration tab (shown in Figure 8.6) follow:

- `Owner`—As stated earlier, the `Owner` field is automatically populated when the record is created. However, you can change this if the new owner user has the necessary permissions.
- `Originating Lead`—This field is populated only when an Account is converted from an originating Lead and cannot be changed. If the Account is not converted from a Lead, this field is blank.

NOTE

If the Account has been converted from a Lead and the Lead is deleted, the Lead information remains; however, it will generate an error when selected. This does not happen if the Lead has been deactivated, so be sure to delete Leads with caution.

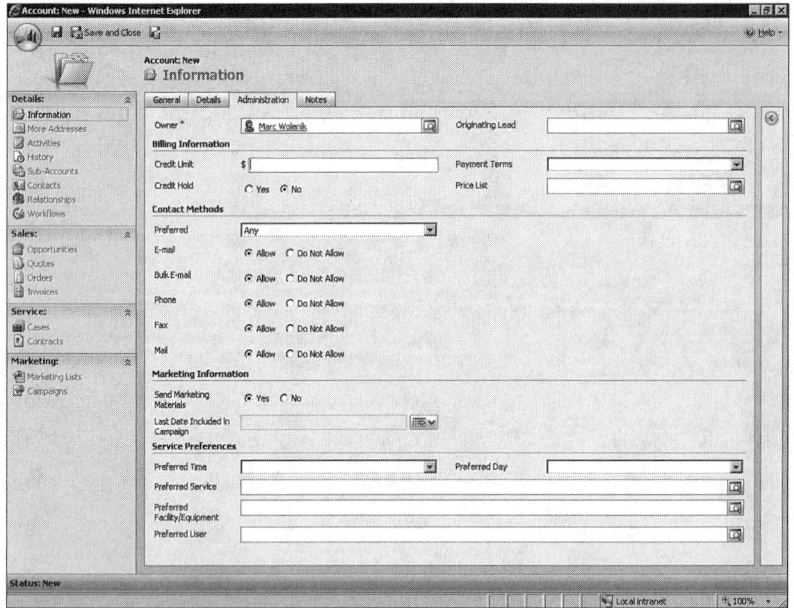

FIGURE 8.6 Account Creation Administration tab.

- ▶ `Credit Limit`—Similar to the `Annual Revenue` field, you must select a currency value to enter a value here.
- ▶ `Price List`—When using different Price Lists for your organization, you can select the preferred Price list here. Price Lists are explained in Chapter 14.
- ▶ `Credit Hold` and `Payment Terms`—You can select these fields when setting up the Account, and you can change them during the Account's life. (If you are thinking about integrating CRM into an existing ERP or other accounting system, the fields in the Billing Information section get special attention.)
- ▶ `Contact Methods`—When selecting the Contact Methods, the system defaults all values to Allow. It is extremely helpful to have each of these options when doing bulk activities such as e-mail campaigns because you can exclude Accounts that do not want to be contacted by this method. Additionally, if you have selected Do Not Allow for the e-mail, you will receive the warning error message when trying to send the Account an e-mail from CRM (see Figure 8.3).

NOTE

Although the system prevents you from sending an e-mail from CRM to an Account that has Do Not Allow set for e-mail, nothing prevents users from sending e-mail to an Account directly from Outlook.

- `Marketing Information`—Similarly to the `Contact Methods` field, you can set whether the Account should receive marketing information. Additionally, you have the option to view the date that the Account was last included in a campaign.
- `Service Preferences`—If the Account has any kind of service preferences (see Chapter 12, "Working with Service"), you can record that here. This is especially helpful in recording preferences for quick look up by Account.

Finally, when working with the Administration tab and the related Billing Information, you can manipulate and hook this data to external accounting and ERP systems. Microsoft Dynamics has announced that there will be a connector between GP; however, as of the date of publication for this book, it was unavailable and its features are not covered here.

Notes Tab

Refer to Chapter 7, "Common Functions," for information about Notes (shown in Figure 8.7).

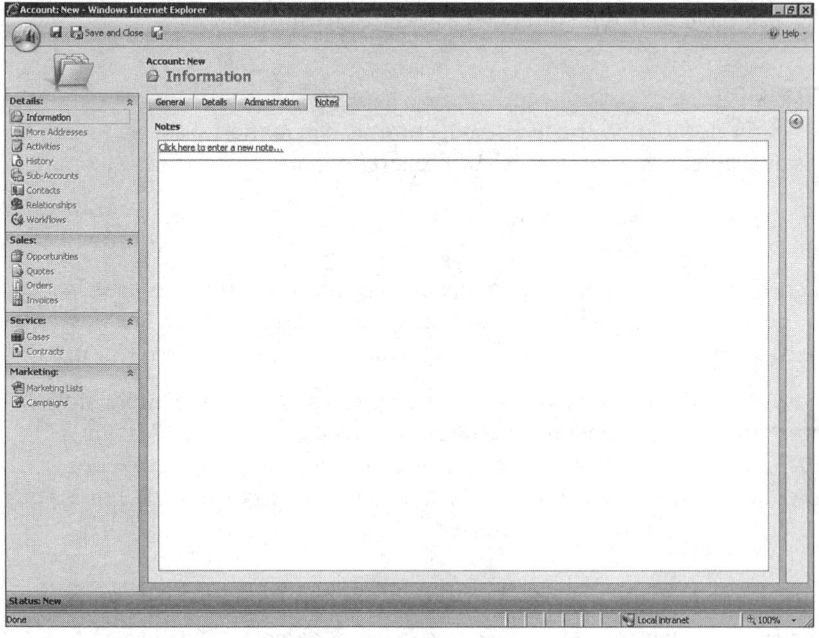

FIGURE 8.7 Account Creation Notes tab.

Contacts

Contacts are individuals that either are Customers or are in some way related to an Account. Although they aren't required to have a relationship with an Account, they often do. An example of a Contact without a relationship to an Account is someone like the mailman, whom you want to keep in the system so that all the employees can get information about him such as his name or birth date (everyone should wish the mailman happy birthday), but there might not be reason to have the United States Post Office as an Account just for the mailman.

When creating/adding new Contacts to the system, there are generally easy methods:

- Navigating to the Contacts form and selecting New
- Creating a new Contact from the Accounts form by selecting Contacts and New Contact

The first method allows you to select the Parent Customer (if applicable), while the second method prepopulates that information for you. (In addition to the Parent Customer, the address information and currency information is populated from the Account that spawned the new Contact form, and is therefore the recommended method.)

It is important to understand that when working with Contacts, they inherit Account information *only* if they are propagated from the Account. This is important because different Accounts may have different currencies associated with them.

Details, Information

The Information section (located on the near navigation) is where most users will work. There are four tabs available: General, Details, Administration, and Notes. These tabs are explained below.

General Tab

By default, Contacts have two required fields. One, on the Information tab, is `Last Name`; the other, one on the Administration tab, is `Owner`. The `First Name` field is a Business Recommended field, so we always recommend using it whenever possible (see Figure 8.8).

`Parent Customer` is a very important field: By populating it, you create a relationship between the Contact and the Customer. As discussed in the earlier section, "Accounts," if you enter a value in this field (either an Account or a Contact), the Contact you're working with shows up as either a Subcontact (if you enter a Contact Customer) or a Contact (if you enter an Account Customer) related to that entry.

TIP

As indicated, the Parent Customer can be either an Account or a Contact. This has an interesting effect on the Outlook client the displays this field as the Company. If you select a Contact, Outlook displays that person as the Company (refer to Figure 8.10).

As mentioned, in addition to `Parent Customer`, you should populate the other fields on this form (`Salutation`, `Middle Name`, `Job Title`, `Street 1`, `Street 2`, `Street 3`, `City`, `State/Province`, `Business Phone`, `Home Phone`, `Mobile Phone`, `Fax`, `Email`, `Zip/Postal`

`Code`, and `Country/Region`) as necessary, as they will all correlate to a Contact in Microsoft Outlook. The only exception to this is `Pager` and `Phone`.

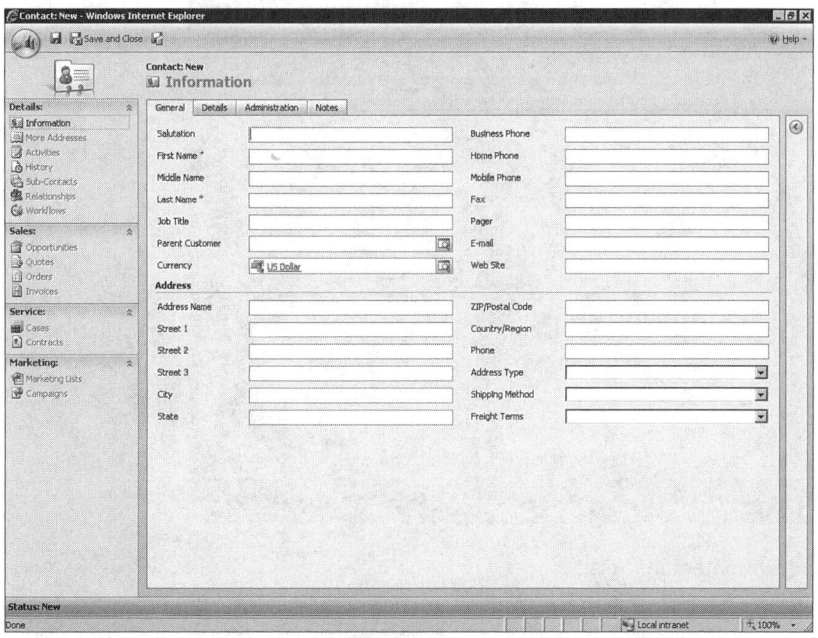

FIGURE 8.8 Creating a new Contact interface.

TIP

Do not confuse `Phone` with either `Business Phone`, `Home Phone`, or `Mobile Phone`—all of which are transferred to the Outlook Contact form (and vice versa). `Phone` does not appear in the Outlook Contact form, as shown in Figure 8.10. Use this field as an extra field for the `Phone` entry (or do not use it at all). This is important because, when using the Contacts from Outlook to synchronize to a mobile device, you will not have it available unless it is one of the previous mapped fields.

Refer to Figures 8.9 and 8.10 for an example of a Contact in CRM and its corresponding fields in the Outlook client. Notice that values in `Page` and `Phone`, in particular, do not reflect the Outlook Contact form. Also notice that the Parent Customer of the Contact named Frank Sinatra is the Company.

`Currency` has the same properties as `Currency` in Accounts. (See the section preceding this one for more details.)

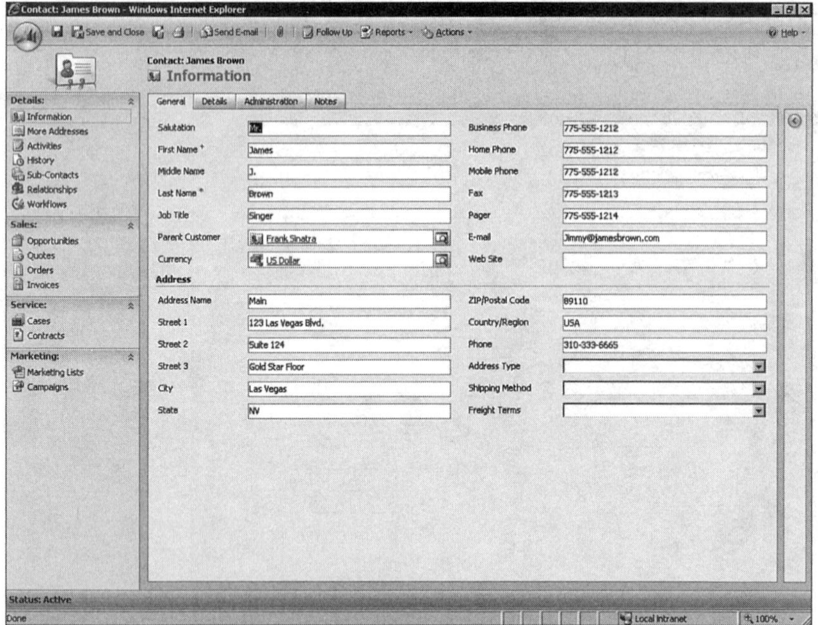

FIGURE 8.9 Sample Contact in CRM.

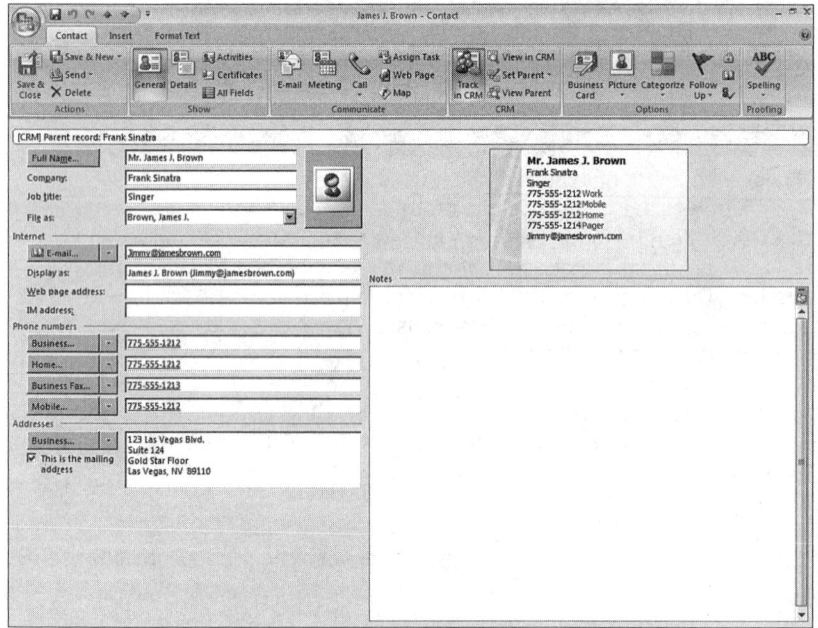

FIGURE 8.10 Sample Contact in Outlook.

Details Tab

This is the most overlooked tab in the Contacts form, but it has great value. The `Professional Information` fields are invaluable when trying to develop organizational information, and the `Personal Information` fields are of great benefit when you need to know salient details about the Contact. The `Description` field is used for general information relevant to the contact that isn't likely to change (see Figure 8.11).

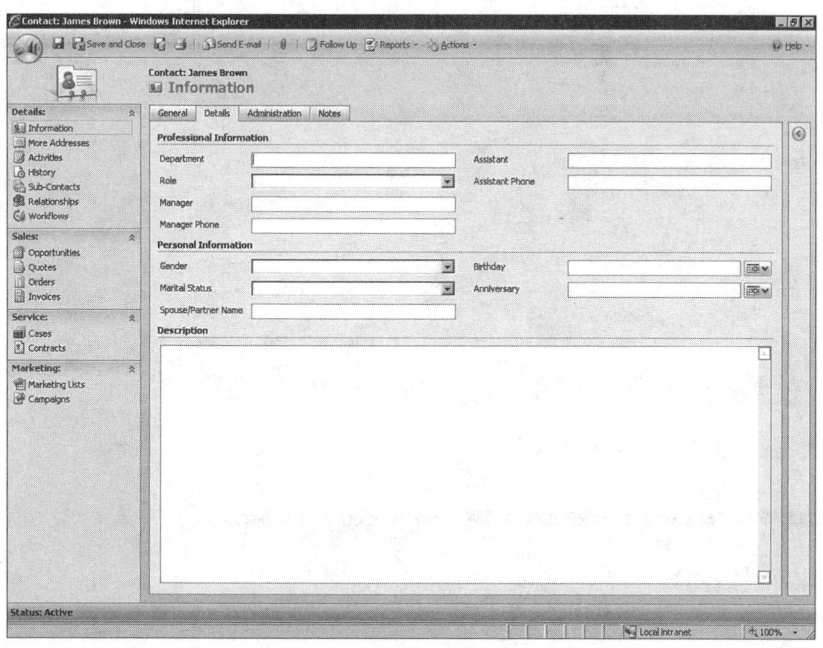

FIGURE 8.11 Contacts Details tab.

> **TIP**
>
> The `Birthday` field is a great excuse for customer contact. Who wouldn't like to receive a call, e-mail, or small gift from a vendor on her birthday?

8

Administration Tab

See the earlier section, "Accounts," for more information on the Administration tab, shown in Figure 8.12.

Notes Tab

See the earlier section, "Accounts," for more information on the Notes tab, shown in Figure 8.13.

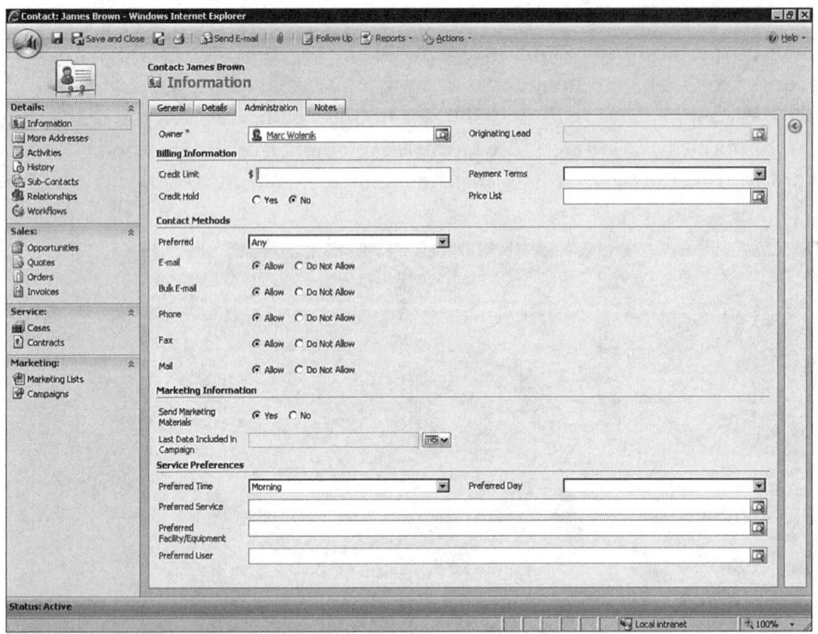

FIGURE 8.12 Contacts Administration tab.

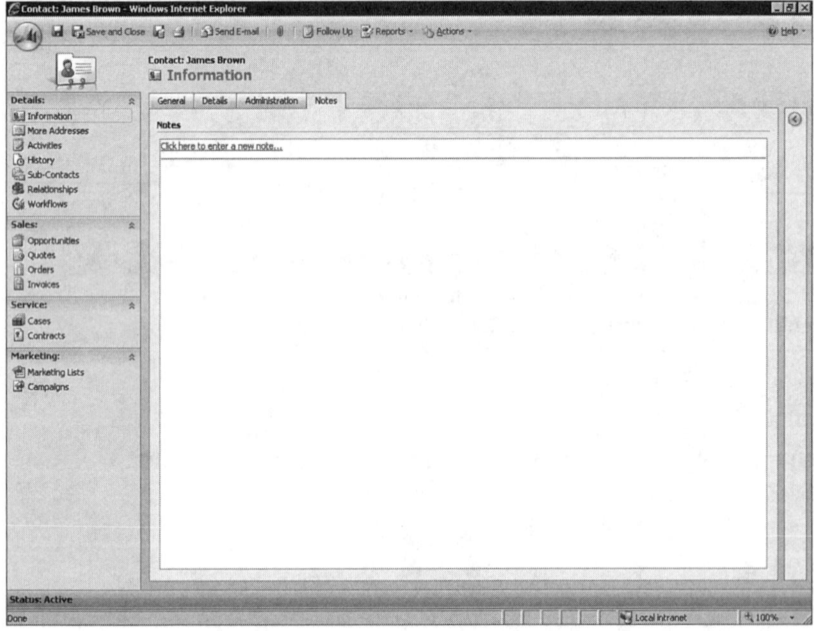

FIGURE 8.13 Contacts Notes tab.

General Information for Either Accounts or Contacts

The following information applies to either the Accounts or the Contacts Entities forms:

As with many of the Entities in the system, some options are available only after the record is saved. (It doesn't need to be closed—just saved.) These options are available for the Account/Contact Entity prior to saving (and completing Business Required fields):

- New (Lead, Opportunity, Account, and so on from the QuickButton)
- Save
- Save and Close
- Save and New
- Close

If you attempt to close the record after you have already started to enter data, you will receive a warning prompt if Business Required fields are blank (in the case of Accounts, `Account Name` and `Owner`; in the case of Contacts, `Last Name` and `Owner`).

These options are available after saving:

- All options listed previously
- Form Properties (from the QuickButton)
- Print (from both the QuickButton and the top menu)
- Send E-mail
- Attach a File
- Follow Up
- Reports
- Run Workflow (if there is a workflow associated with the entity)
- Actions

Refer to Chapter 7 for more information on these options.

So if you're wondering how to send an e-mail or upload a document to an Account/Contact because there doesn't appear to be any way to do that, be sure you've saved the record first. (Refer to Chapter 7 for more information about this functionality.)

Follow Up

Using Follow Up is an easy way to create a new Activity for the Account/Contact by using the Form Assistant.

For more information about the Form Assistant, refer to Chapter 7.

8

Reports

By default, the Account Entity has the following reports associated with it:

- Account Overview
- Account Summary
- Products by Account

The Contact Entity has this report:

- Products by Contact

When any of these are selected, the selected report is opened and the Account/Contact you're working with is displayed by default.

Refer to Chapter 13, "Reporting," for more information about reports.

Run Workflow

This enables you to run any manual Workflow that is available to run On Demand. This button is only available if the Account or Contact has an existing workflow associated with it.

Refer to Chapter 20 for more information on Workflow.

Actions

Refer to Chapter 7 for information on Actions.

Details, More Addresses

More Addresses (shown in Figure 8.14) is generally used when an Account/Contact has multiple locations. This can include different departments within an organization at a different organization, different shipping addresses, or different primary addresses. The `Address Name` field (not the `Address Type` field) should differentiate them because it is displayed on the Quickview form.

Details, Activities

Refer to Chapter 7 for information on Activities.

Details, History

Refer to Chapter 7 for information on History.

Details, Subaccounts/Subcontacts

The Subaccounts/Subcontacts section is an easy way to view associated Accounts/Contacts (see Figure 8.15). Any Account/Contact that has the Account/Contact you're working with listed as its Parent Account for Accounts and Parent Customer for Contacts appears here. Additionally, if you select the option New Account within the Subaccount, or New Contact within the Subcontact, you can quickly create a new Account/Contact that inherits several attributes of the Account/Contact you're working with, such as currency and Parent Account or Parent Customer.

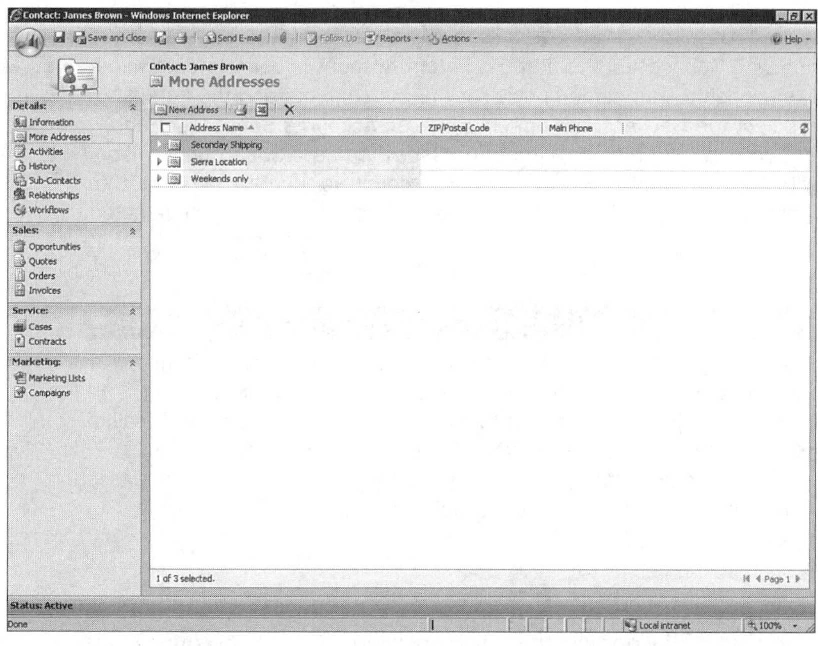

FIGURE 8.14 Contacts More Addresses.

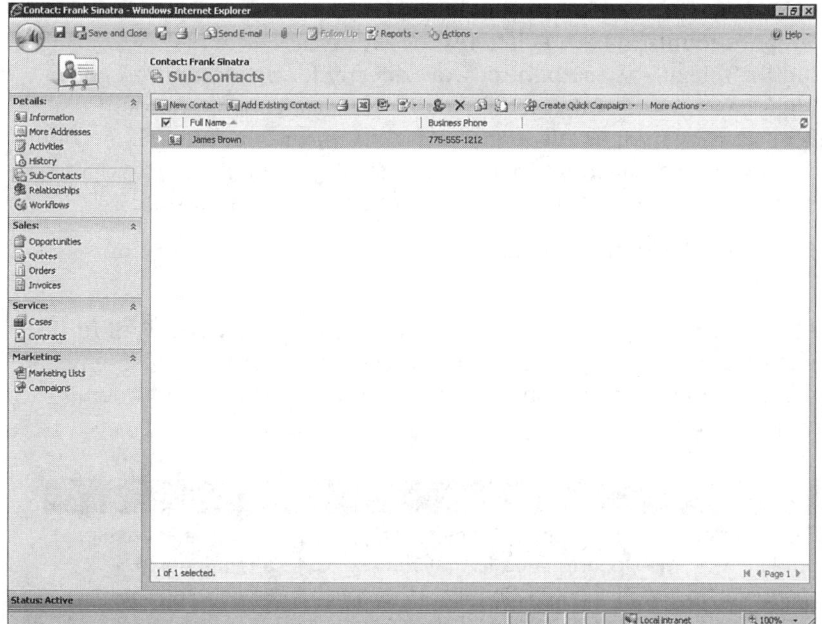

FIGURE 8.15 Contacts Subcontacts.

TIP

The key to working with Subaccounts is that the Parent Account is used to determine the Subaccount relationship. The same is true for the Subcontacts and the Parent Customer. If you select the New Account option within an Accounts Subaccount and change the Parent Account, the record will not be associated as a Subaccount. Also, if you're working with Accounts and select an existing Account as a Parent Account, the Account you're working with then shows as a Subaccount of the Account you selected.

NOTE

The nesting level is only one deep. So if you have Account 1 and make Account 2 a Subaccount (by selecting Account 1 as the Parent Account), you will see Account 2 as the Subaccount for Account 1. However, if you add a new Subaccount to Account 2, called Account 3, you will not see Account 1 when you look at Subaccounts for Account 1. This is because you see only the Accounts (that is, direct Subaccounts) that have the Account you're working with listed as Parent Accounts as Subaccounts.

Details, Contacts

The Contacts section shows all Contacts that are associated with this Account/Contact.

For more information on Contacts, refer to the "Contacts" section in this chapter.

Details, Relationships

It is quite common for Accounts to have Relationships with other Accounts or Contacts that don't fit within the role of a Subaccount or work directly for the Account. A good example of this might be an Account that manufactures ice cream and an Account that produces milk. Although they have no hierarchal relationship, without the milk Account, the ice cream Account can't manufacturer ice cream. As such, you would add a Relationship between the two Accounts here to record this type of relationship.

You can create relationships between either an Account or Contacts using this form (see Figure 8.16).

When adding the Relationship, you must select the Account or Contact you want to relate. If you have created Relationship Roles, you can select them here as well as enter a further description related to the Relationship (for more information about setting up Relationship Roles, see Chapter 14).

NOTE

You can select from Customers (Accounts or Contacts) only when creating relationships. However, when working with the Opportunities form, you can create a relationship between the Opportunity and an Account or Contact. (The option to easily associate a relationship between the Account you're working with and an Opportunity is available via the top Actions menu, but that relationship is visible only on the Opportunity Entity.)

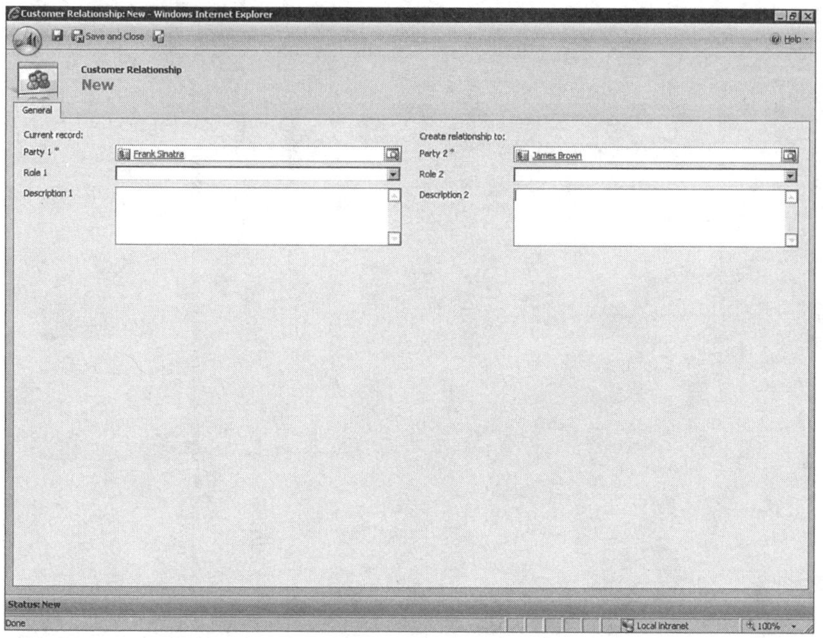

FIGURE 8.16 Relationships.

Relationships are a great way to record relations of a nonbusiness nature, such as friendships, family and relatives, and other nonbusiness organizations. They provide a quick-and-easy way to view relationships with an Account that are nonhierarchal in nature.

TIP

When working with Advanced Find, be sure to not use the Attribute `Relationship Type` when attempting to query on existing relationships. The `Relationship Type` Attribute relates to the drop-down option found on the General tab of the Account form. Instead, be sure to select Related Customer Relationships (either Party 1 or Party 2) and select either Role 1 or Role 2.

Details, Workflows

Any Workflow that has been run or is currently running that affects the Account you're working with is displayed here (see Figure 8.17). You can Cancel, Resume, Postpone, or Pause Workflows from More Actions located at the top of the Quickview.

Additionally, you can open any Workflow listed here to see further information about it, such as what the Workflow was responsible for, when it started, and when it completed.

Refer to Chapter 20 for more information about how Workflows work.

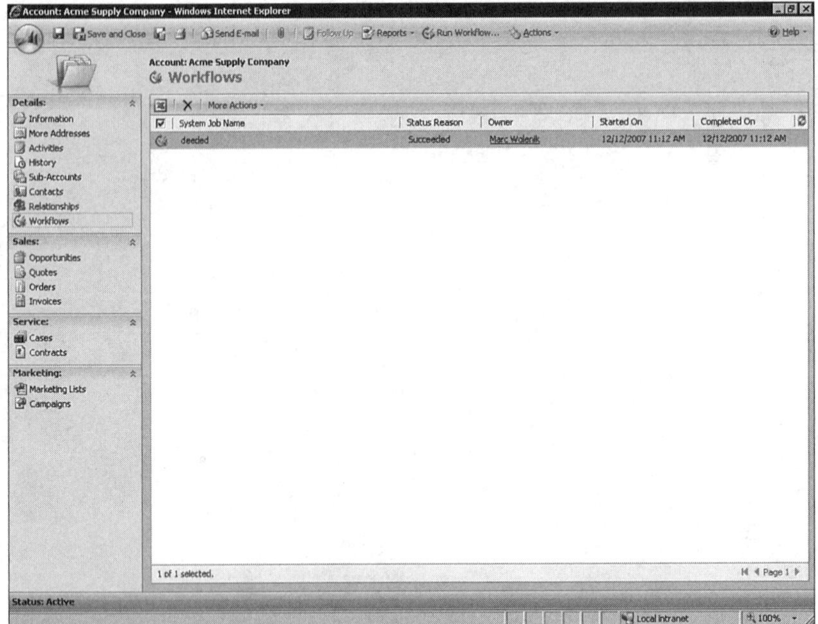

FIGURE 8.17 Account Workflows interface.

Summary

This chapter reviewed that a Customer is an Account or a Contact when working with Microsoft Dynamics CRM. It also discussed how to use the Accounts and Contact Entities in depth.

When working with Accounts and Contacts, understanding how they work and relate is an important concept when working with your Customers.

CHAPTER 9

Working with the Workplace

IN THIS CHAPTER

- Activities
- Calendar
- Imports
- Duplicate Detection
- Queues
- Articles
- Reports
- Announcements
- Exporting Data
- Personalize Workplace

The Workplace, as it's referred to in Microsoft Dynamics CRM, is where most end users will spend a lot of their time. It is important to understand the various features that make up the Workplace, as well as how to customize it for your needs.

You can customize the Workplace to include Sales, Marketing, Service, and Scheduling (see Figure 9.1). However, this chapter covers only the core components; other chapters discuss those other modules specifically. Additionally, while Customers, Accounts, and Contacts are included in the Workplace, refer to Chapter 8, "Working with Customers," for information on working with them.

TIP

By default, the only items in the My Workplace area are My Work and Customers. To add or remove the other modules mentioned earlier (Sales, Marketing, and so on), review the last section in this chapter, "Personalize Workplace."

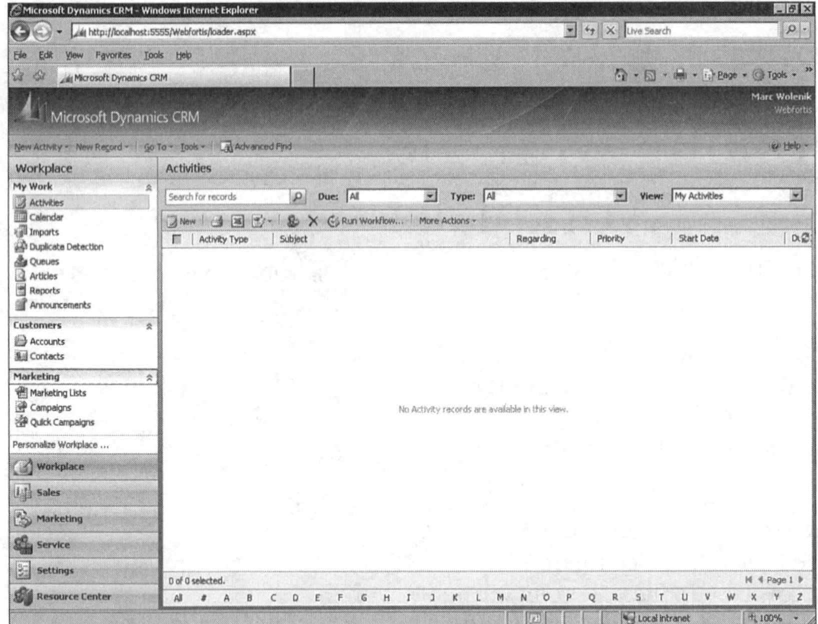

FIGURE 9.1 My Workplace (with Marketing added to it).

Activities

Work gets assigned, completed, and reported on through Activities. Combined with Queues (explained further in this chapter), Activity management offers a good reflection of the status of work in an organization.

An Activity can consist of the following:

- Task
- Fax
- Phone Call
- E-mail
- Letter
- Appointment
- Service Activity
- Campaign Response

When you select the New button to create a new Activity, you will be prompted to select the type of the Activity (see Figure 9.2).

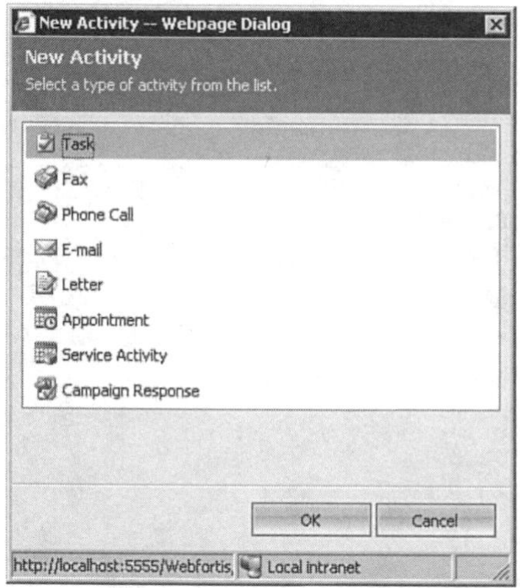

FIGURE 9.2 Activities list.

After an Activity is created, it can be assigned to another User or Queue, as long as they have the necessary permissions.

TIP

When an Activity record is assigned to another User, the `Owner` attribute immediately updates to the newly assigned User. When a record is assigned to a Queue, the `Owner` attribute does not change until a Queue User accepts it; then the `Owner` attribute updates with the User who accepted the record. To accept an Activity that is in a Queue, do not open the Activity. Rather, find the Accept button that is on the top of the tree view where the queues are listed and select it. That will also move the Activity record from its shared queue to your In Progress Queue.

NOTE

Unfortunately, you cannot change or add to Activities. However, you can customize them. For example, you might want to have not just Phone Call, but Incoming Phone Call, Outgoing Phone Call, Lead Call, Support Call, and so on. You would need to add a custom attribute directly to the Phone entity to account for that, rather than including those as Activity types. (If you check the Phone Call Activity, you will see that Incoming and Outgoing are already there.)

You should consider some other important properties when working with Activities:

- Regardless of whether you set the `Duration` and `Due` dates (the fields you use to set the date when the Activity is or should be performed), Appointment and Service Activities are the only Activities that show up on the Microsoft CRM Calendar. For more information about the Microsoft CRM Calendar, see the "Calendar" section later in this chapter.

- After you close an Activity, you cannot edit or reopen it (with the exception of Campaign Responses). Table 9.1 outlines what you can do to an Activity (besides deleting it) that has been marked as closed.

TABLE 9.1 Actions Available on Closed Activities

Activity	Actions Available After It Has Been Closed
E-mail	Forward, Repy To, Convert to Opportunity, Case, or Lead
Task	No further action
Phone Call	No further action
Fax	No further action
Letter	No further action
Appointment	No further action
Campaign Response	Copied or Reactivated

- You cannot convert an Activity to another Activity type. If this is necessary, you must delete the first Activity or mark it as complete, and then create a new Activity of the correct type.
- Reminders (similar to Outlook pop-up reminders) are not available using either version of the CRM clients. However, you can set reminders in Outlook by setting a reminder for an appointment and then saving the appointment as a Microsoft CRM Activity by selecting Track in CRM for the entered appointment. In doing so, you promote the Activity to Microsoft Dynamics CRM, and a reminder is set in Outlook. Activities created in CRM are synchronized with the Outlook client, but reminders are not set for them; be sure to set all Appointments directly in Outlook and promote to CRM if your business requires reminders.
- CRM reminders are very easy to implement by using the Follow Up Form Assistant after you have saved the Activity and before you have closed it. The Form Assistant enables Users to quickly create a new Task of any type with the required fields displayed and `Regarding` set to the same value as the record you're working with (see Figure 9.3).
- You cannot schedule recurrent Activities in Microsoft Dynamics CRM.
- Although you cannot edit more than one Activity at a time, you can create an Activity for more than one record at a time. For example, if you wanted to be sure to send holiday cards to every active Account, you would not want to have to create the Activity for every Account. Fortunately, you can create a Quick Campaign and set this Task as the Campaign Activity.

  To create a Quick Campaign, open the Advanced Find and select the records you want to set the Activities on. Then select Create Quick Campaign to open the wizard. For more information on creating Quick Campaigns, refer to Chapter 11, "Working with Marketing."

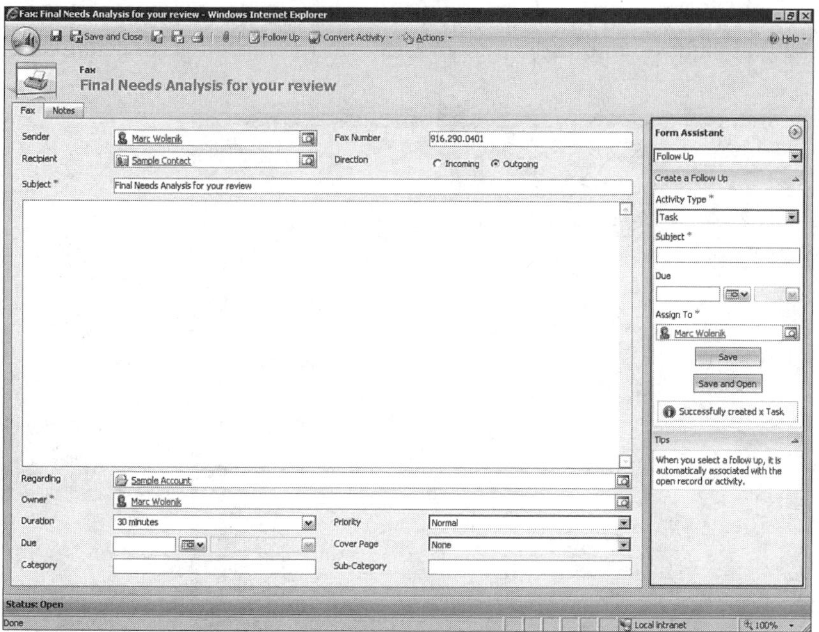

FIGURE 9.3 Follow Up Form Assistant on a Fax Activity.

- Before closing but after saving Fax, Appointment, Phone Call, Task, E-mail, and Letter Activities, you can convert these to an Opportunity or a Case by selecting Convert Activity from the Actions drop-down menu. You can convert Campaign Response Activities into a new Lead, an existing Lead, or a new Quote, Order, or Opportunity record for an existing customer.
- Duration time entered for Activities is converted to hours when the duration exceeds 1 hour. The displayed value shows the rounded hour total, but the actual value (in minutes) is stored in the database and is used for total billing time when working on cases.

TIP

Although it seems contrary, the `Category` and `Subcategory` fields have no correlation with either Categories in Outlook or Subjects in CRM. They are free-form entry fields that are often used by Users that can incorporate business logic (such as setting the `Category` equal to Billable, for example).

Task

Task Activities (see Figure 9.4) are those that have some kind of action that doesn't fall within the other categories. The Task Activity will be the one most commonly used when the work doesn't fit neatly within the existing Activity types (Appointment, Phone, and so on). As such, the Task Activity is considered the catchall Activity.

An example of a Task Activity might be the preparation of a document or a reminder to yourself to put your golf clubs in your car before you leave in the morning, for example.

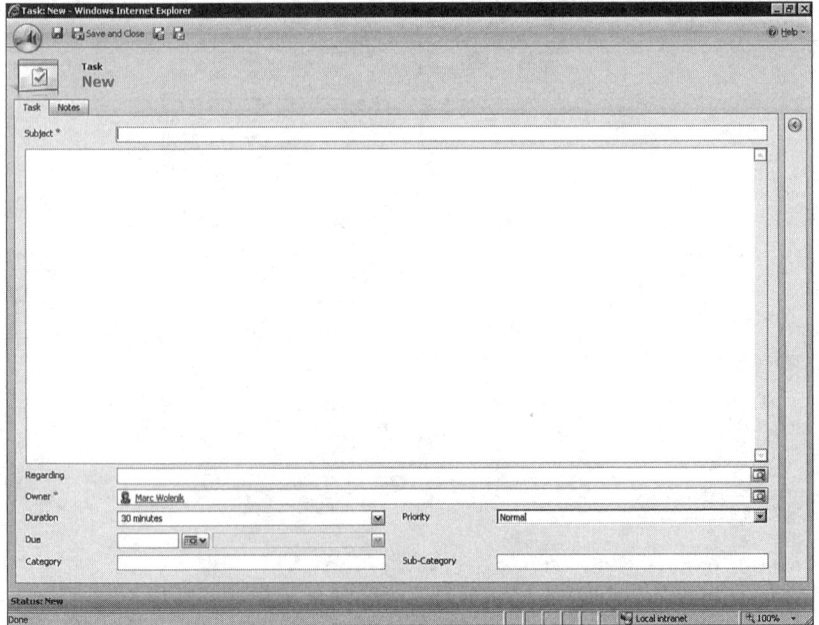

FIGURE 9.4 Task Activity.

When working with the new Task Activity form, `Subject` and `Owner` are the only required fields in creating a Task. The area directly below the `Subject` field is generally reserved for details related to the Subject, but you can include those details on the Notes tab if you prefer. The `Regarding` field is not required by default; however, if you don't complete this field, the Task will not be part of a record's history. This is acceptable if you're creating Tasks for yourself, such as when preparing a document. However, if the preparation of a document Task is for an existing customer, Lead, or other entity, you'll want to enter that information so that the document preparation record becomes part of the related record.

The `Regarding` field can be related to any of the following entities:

- Account
- Campaign
- Invoice
- Lead
- Opportunity
- Case
- Contact
- Contract
- Order
- Quote
- Any custom entity that has the Activities relationship check box set

NOTE

It is important to remember that you can easily change the Regarding field after setting it. However, if you do not set the Regarding field when the Task is created, it will not be associated with an existing record's history. This is generally acceptable when you are creating Tasks that have no correlation to a Customer or similar entity, such as overhead or internally related issues. Usually, it is a good idea to get into the practice of associating Activities with existing entities so that the Task history is available when working with the entity.

Tasks are synchronized with Outlook, allowing Task Activities to be created and managed within either application. Additionally, you can create Task Activities directly within Outlook, which can be promoted to Microsoft Dynamics CRM. Because you can synchronize your mobile device with Tasks in Outlook, you close a Task Activity directly within Microsoft Dynamics CRM, Microsoft Outlook, or your mobile device.

Fax

Fax Activities (see Figure 9.5) are those related to either incoming or outgoing Faxes. Fax Activities are designed to have the actual Fax attached to the Notes section of the Activity; they are not used to actually send Faxes by default.

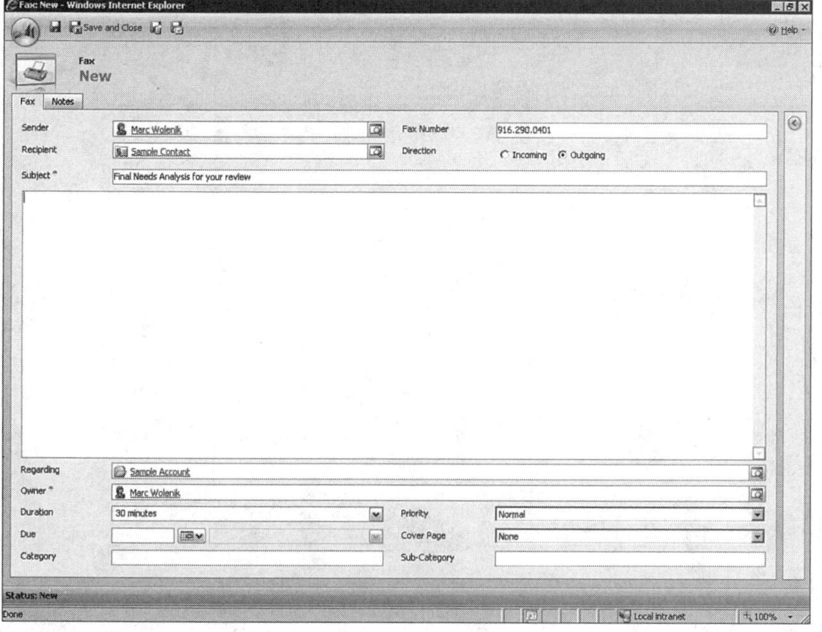

FIGURE 9.5 Fax Activity.

TIP

Although no included functionality covers sending or receiving Faxes directly from Microsoft CRM, previous versions offered several options. These included the Business Data Lookup snap-in, to look up and view Microsoft CRM Data directly in Word, Excel, or Outlook. With this functionality, data from CRM could be added directly to the Word document and saved directly within CRM as an Activity. Additionally, when working with a Small Business Server (SBS) and Microsoft Dynamics CRM Small Business Edition, a Microsoft CRM Fax Router Service added both routing logic and send and receive functionality to Fax Activities by adding a Send button to the Fax Activity Actions drop-down menu.

It is unknown at press time whether this functionality will be included and with which versions of Microsoft Dynamics CRM.

Phone Call

Similarly to Faxes, Phone Call Activities are Phone Calls either sent or received (see Figure 9.6). It is good practice to be sure to have all staff enter this information routinely so that it is available to all CRM Users when viewing the Customer record.

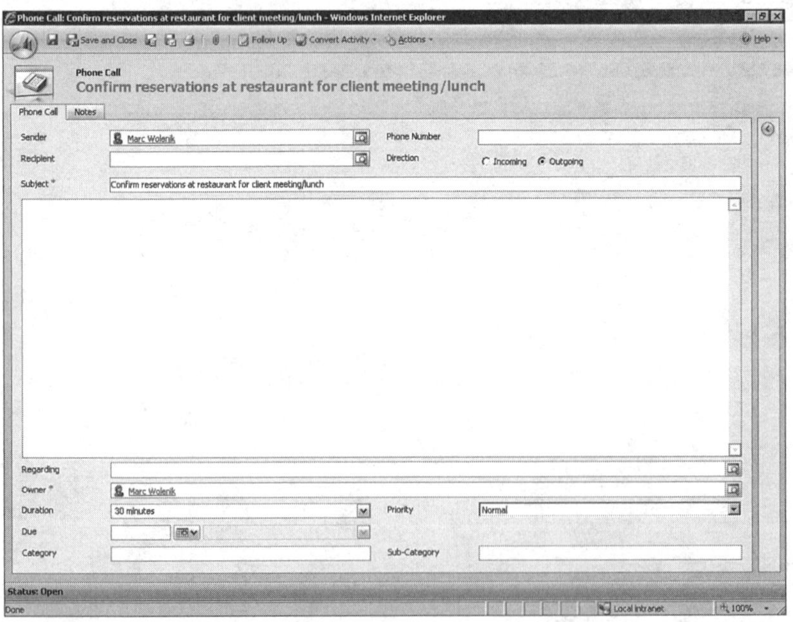

FIGURE 9.6 Phone Call Activity.

TIP

Microsoft Dynamics CRM can be extended to TAPI-compliant phone systems to perform a wide number of functions, including automatically dialing the number reflected on a record. TAPI stands for Telephony Application Program Interface. It provides a programming interface for applications with your phone system. The scope of this custom functionality and integration exceeds this book; several third-party components offer this type of functionality, and it can be integrated with some programming.

E-mail

E-mail Activities are Activity records that indicate either an incoming or an outgoing E-mail. Similar to Faxes, they don't necessarily indicate an actual E-mail; rather, they indicate an E-mail Activity that has occurred (e-mail has been sent) or will occur (E-mail Activity should be sent on the due date).

E-mail Activities create a record whereby the E-mail is sent to the Account, Contact, Lead, Queue, or User listed in the `To`, `Cc`, or `Bcc` fields. The Subject of the E-mail Activity is the Subject of the E-mail, and the Text is the Body of the E-mail. Any attachments to the E-mail Activity are included.

After an E-mail Activity has been sent (via the Send button at the top of the E-mail Activity), it is automatically closed and available on the History tab. Figure 9.7 shows an unsent E-mail.

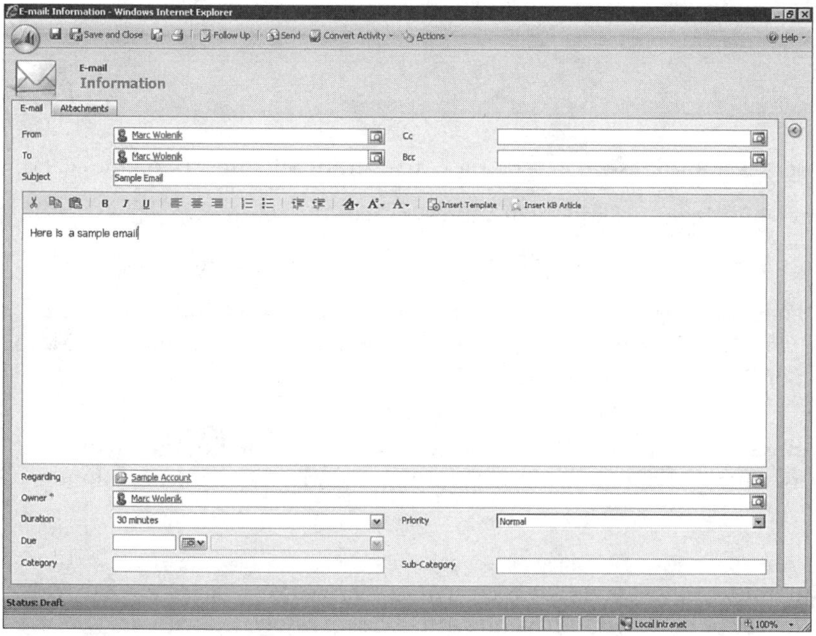

FIGURE 9.7 E-mail Activity.

Figure 9.8 shows the received E-mail. Notice the Microsoft Dynamics CRM token of CRM:0001013 in the subject line of the received E-mail in Figure 9.8. The optional CRM token is used for tracking purposes and is automatically added to CRM E-mails. For configuration options as well as tracking options other than with the tracking token, refer to Chapter 14, "Settings and Configuration."

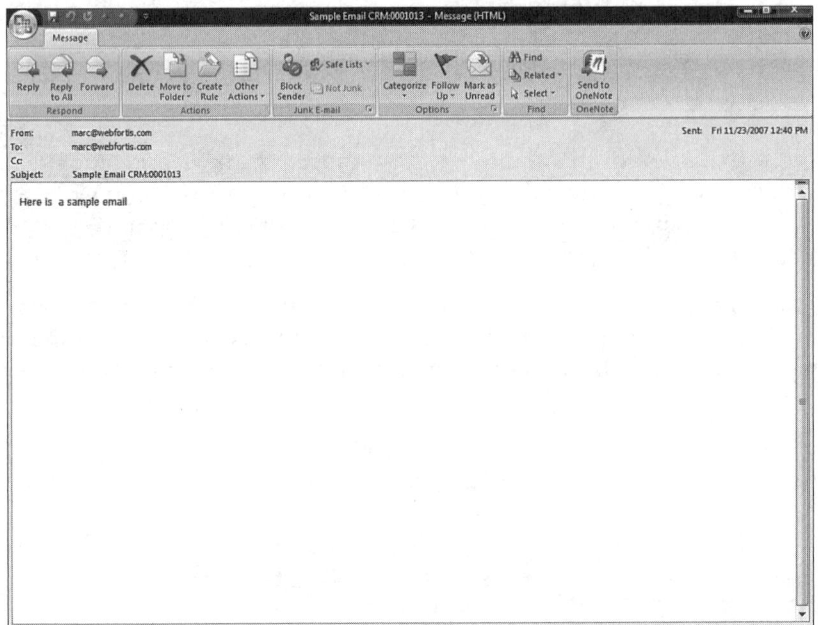

FIGURE 9.8 Received E-mail.

You should consider several things when sending E-mails from Microsoft Dynamics CRM:

- The recipients must have a valid E-mail address as part of their record.
- The recipients must have Allow E-mail set to Allowed on their Contact methods.
- Microsoft Dynamics CRM must be set up and configured to send E-mails from the application. Chapter 15, "E-mail Configuration," gives more information on how to set up Microsoft Dynamics CRM to work with E-mails.

If any of these settings are not correct, you might receive a yellow alert on the Activity, warning that the e-mail could not be sent and requiring investigation and correction.

Letter

Letter Activities indicate when a Letter has been sent or received (see Figure 9.9). As with Faxes, the Letter Activity is designed to have the actual Letter associated with it.

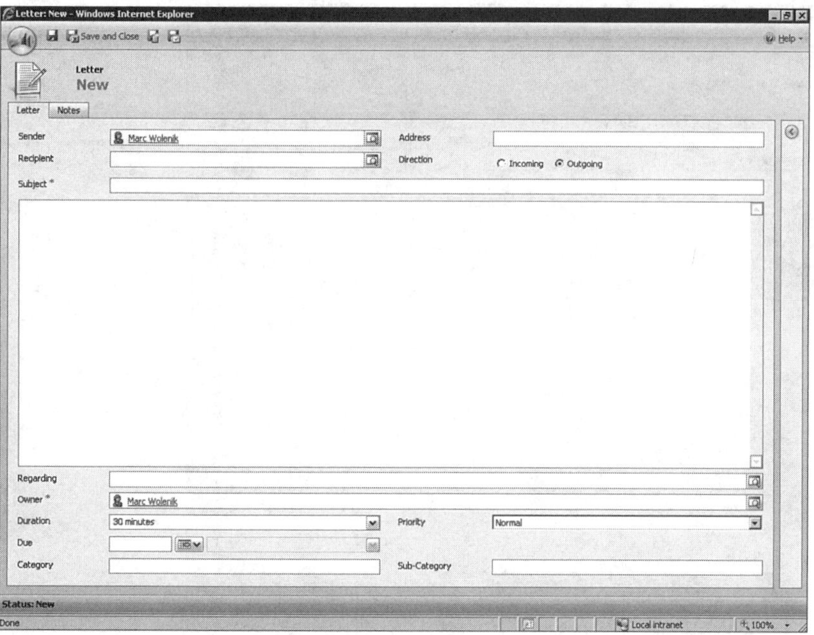

FIGURE 9.9 Letter Activity.

If you want to create a Letter using mail merge, you can create the Letter and then automatically set Activities associated with the merge.

For more information on working with mail merge, refer to Chapter 7, "Common Functions."

Appointment

You can use an Appointment Activity to schedule Users for appointment-type activities (see Figure 9.10).

Both the `Required` and `Optional` fields allow multiple records consisting of Accounts, Business Units, Contacts, Facility/Equipment, Lead, Team, or Users.

TIP

To rapidly enter information in the `Required` or `Optional` fields, enter the names separated with a semicolon. The system attempts to resolve the entered information automatically; where it is unable to do so, it displays a warning enabling you to either select from the quick-find (with multiple matches) or create a new entry (see Figure 9.11).

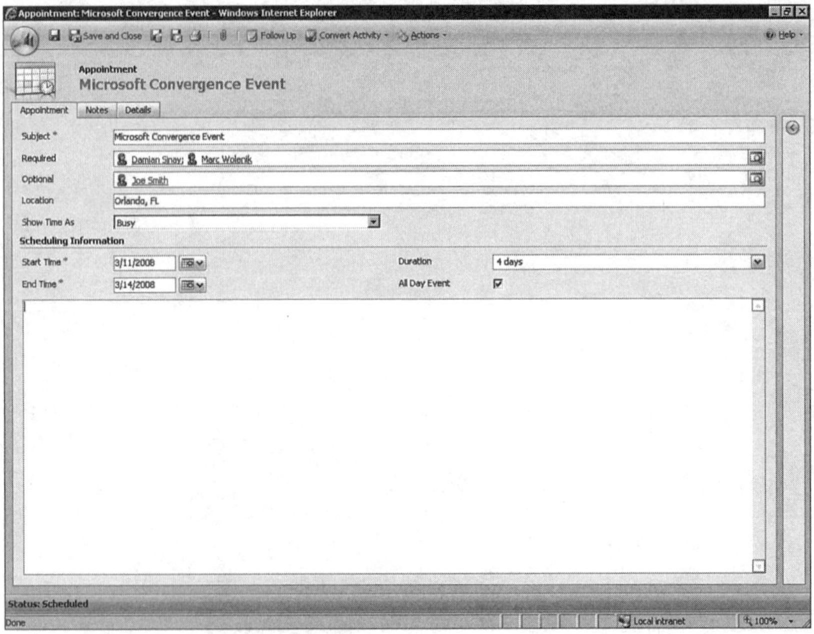

FIGURE 9.10 Appointment Activity.

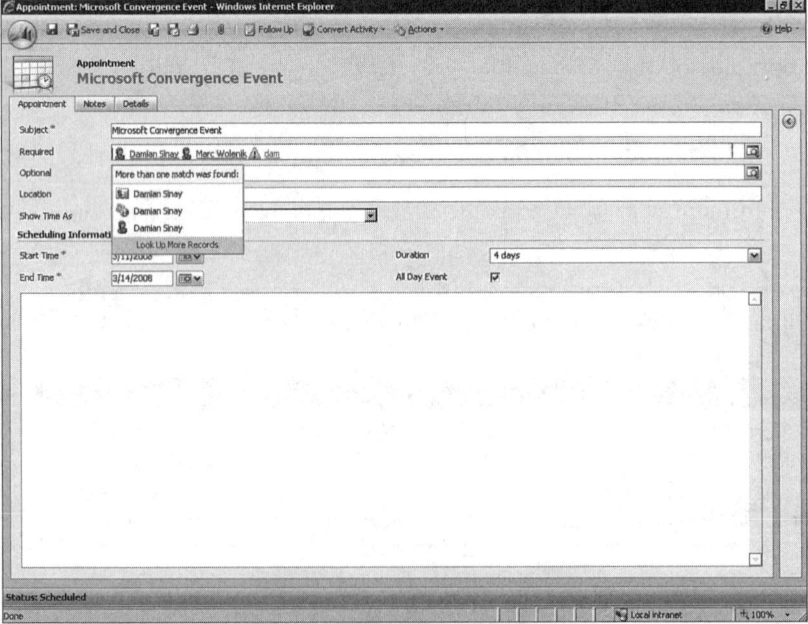

FIGURE 9.11 Appointment Activity warning.

Appointments created in Outlook that have been promoted to CRM via Track in CRM are visible in the Activities pane as an Appointment Activity and also appear on the Service Calendar. The same is true for Appointments created in CRM: When synchronized with Outlook, they appear on the User's Outlook calendar. Additionally, Users who have been added to the Appointment as either Required or Optional have the Appointment Activity show up on their calendar (see Figure 9.12).

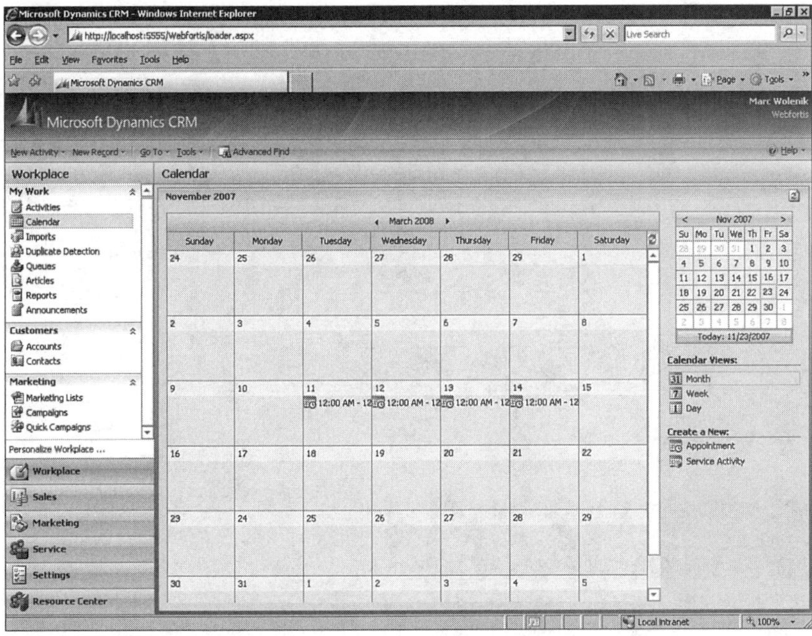

FIGURE 9.12 Appointment Activity on the calendar.

NOTE

Appointment Activities whose start date and/or due date have passed do not become completed by default. They must be manually set as completed either before or after the date has passed.

Service Activity

As with Appointments, Service Activities are scheduled on the Microsoft Dynamics CRM Calendar. Service Activity Activities require a Subject and a Service (see Figure 9.13).

Failure to add any Resources creates a scheduling alert notifying you, "No resources have been selected for this activity" (see Figure 9.14).

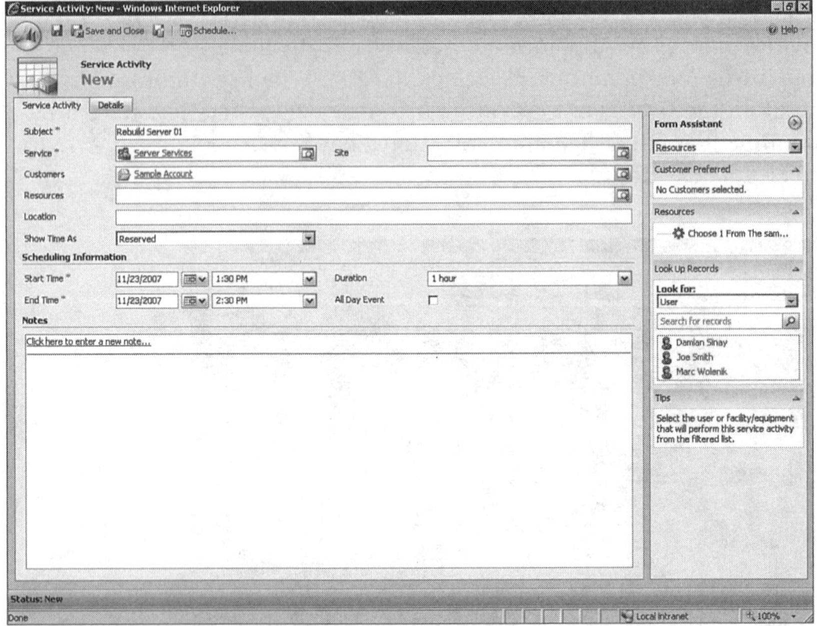

FIGURE 9.13 Service Activity.

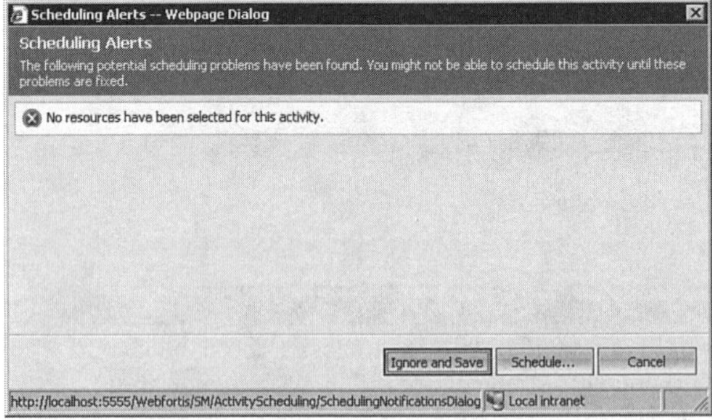

FIGURE 9.14 Scheduling Alert.

You can ignore and schedule the Activity by selecting Ignore and Save. However, selecting Schedule enables you to create the Service Schedule Activity (see Figure 9.15).

For more information on working with Service Scheduling, refer to Chapter 12, "Working with Service."

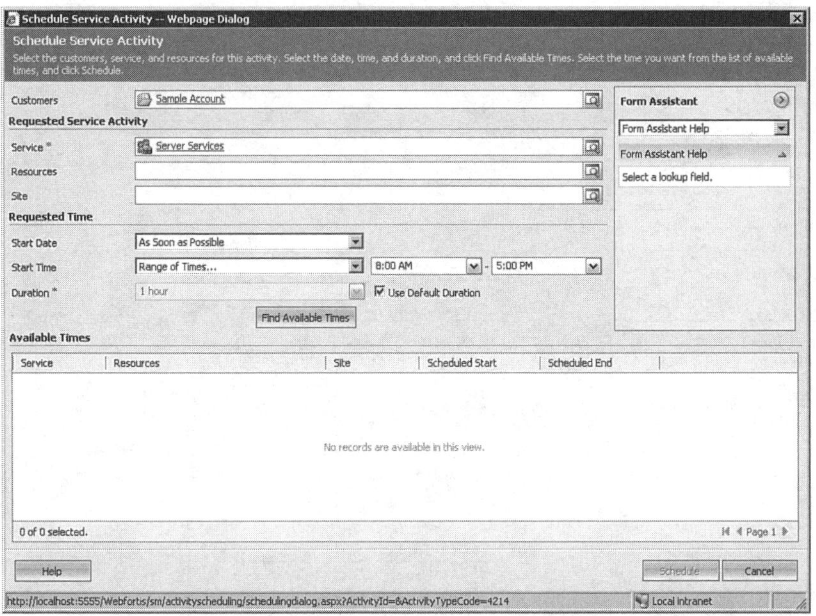

FIGURE 9.15 Scheduling Alert.

TIP

Reminders are not sent automatically to either customers or resources for service activities, but you can have reminders sent automatically by creating workflow to do just that. Refer to Chapter 20, "Workflow Development," for more information on working with workflow.

Campaign Response

The Campaign Response Activity is a record indicating a response received in response to a Campaign. The Campaign Response Activity found in My Workplace is the same type found on the Marketing tab, under Campaigns, Campaign Responses. Both require the `Parent Campaign` and `Subject` fields and include other information fields specific to Campaigns (see Figure 9.16).

Chapter 11 contains information about Campaigns and related Marketing efforts; however, it is helpful to know that Campaign Response Activities are sort of an Activity hybrid specific to Campaigns: They can consist of an E-mail, Phone Call, Fax, Letter, or Appointment—they even have an Others designation for word of mouth, for example.

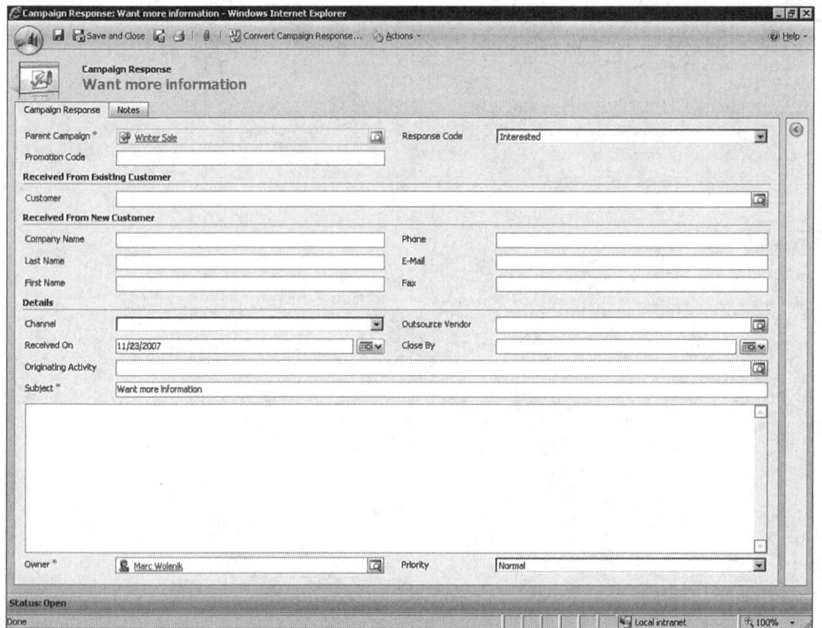

FIGURE 9.16 Campaign Response Activity.

Calendar

The calendar is used to display information related to any Appointments or Service Activities that have been scheduled for you (see Figure 9.17).

The calendar displays the current day by default. (You can change that setting by adjusting the default calendar view in personal options, explained later in this chapter.) By selecting the options from the far navigation, you can change the view to months or weeks. Additional options enable you to create a new Appointment or Service Activity with the selected day entered as the default Start time for the Activity. Finally, the far navigation also displays a mini calendar that you can use to quickly navigate to a specific month, week, or date.

TIP

Navigating to a specific month, week, or day on the mini calendar does not move the main calendar until you have selected a day on the mini calendar.

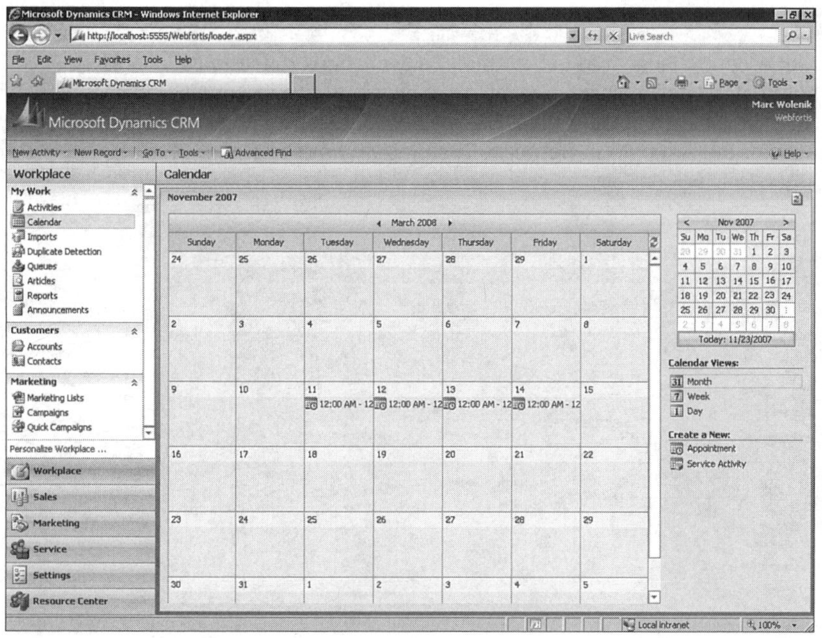

FIGURE 9.17 Calendar.

Imports

Imports enables you to import data directly into Microsoft Dynamics CRM.

Imports can be used to import data directly into the system. This would happen for a variety of reasons, such as data migration. Refer to Chapter 6, "Data Migration and Conversion," for more examples and a more exhaustive look at the Data Migration Wizard when considering data migration from other CRM systems.

There are other more common uses, for example, if you returned from a convention and you wanted to upload all the new contact data you collected while you were there. To do this, navigate to Imports, select New, and follow the wizard steps for importing a CSV file.

TIP

The Import Wizard that is found in Tools, Import Data is the same Import Wizard that is launched by going to Imports and selecting New.

In our example, we assume we have two Contact records in Excel format with header values of `First Name`, `Last Name`, and `Full Name`. Because we have the minimally required fields for a Contact of `First Name` and `Last Name`, the import will accept the job. You can, however, add additional fields if you like. We need to save the Excel document in CSV format and then you're ready to import the data by going to Imports.

TIP

Not every field will accept changes. In our example, any changes made to `Full Name` will not be accepted, and you'll receive a warning during the re-import process about this field. You can check which fields are eligible for manipulation by checking the Requirement Level for the Attribute in Settings, Customizations (see Figure 9.18). Attributes with Read-Only will not accept changes.

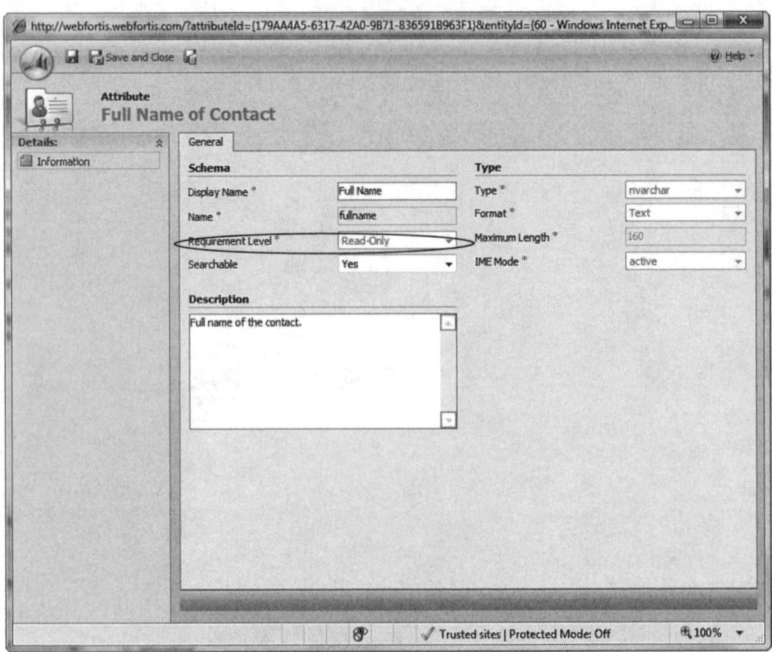

FIGURE 9.18 Full Name Attribute values.

1. Select New to display the Import Data Wizard from the Imports area (see Figure 9.19). Enter the file by selecting Browse and navigating to the file. Select Next to continue.

2. Select the Record type from the drop-down menu. In our case, it is Contact. After the Record type is selected, the file is parsed and a recommended Data map is set if available (see Figure 9.20). If the data can't be parsed or the mapping isn't recognized, you're prompted to create a new Data map. Notice on our example that we have one ignored column. This is because the import will ignore the `Full Name` attribute as discussed earlier. Select Next to continue.

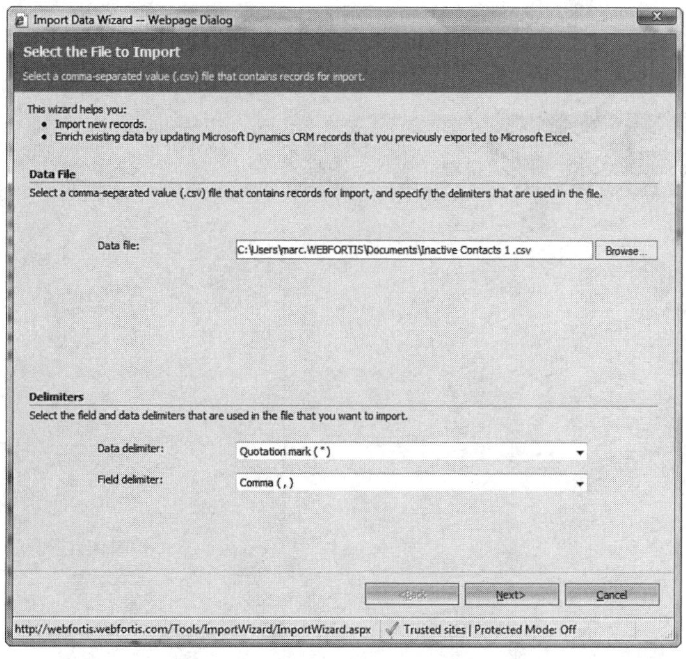

FIGURE 9.19 Import Data Wizard—Select the File to Import.

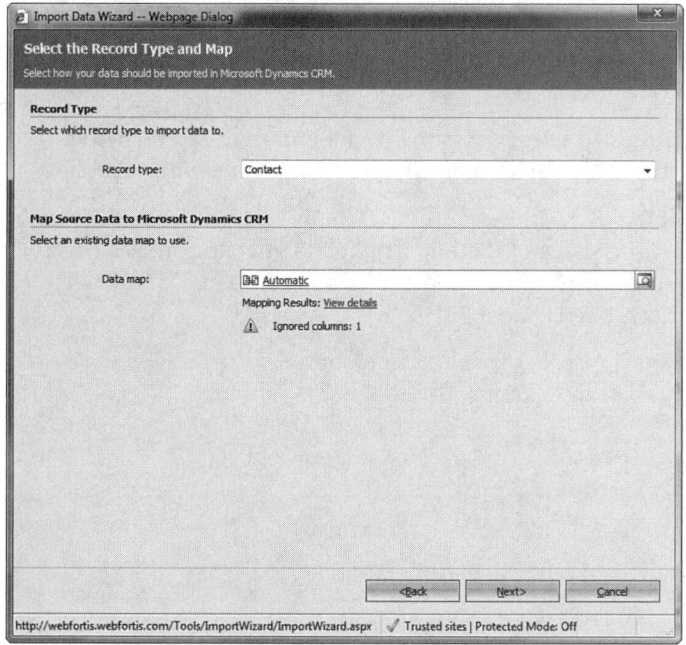

FIGURE 9.20 Import Data Wizard—Select the Record Type and Map.

3. Select whom the records should be assigned to and whether to import duplicate records (see Figure 9.21). Select Next to continue.

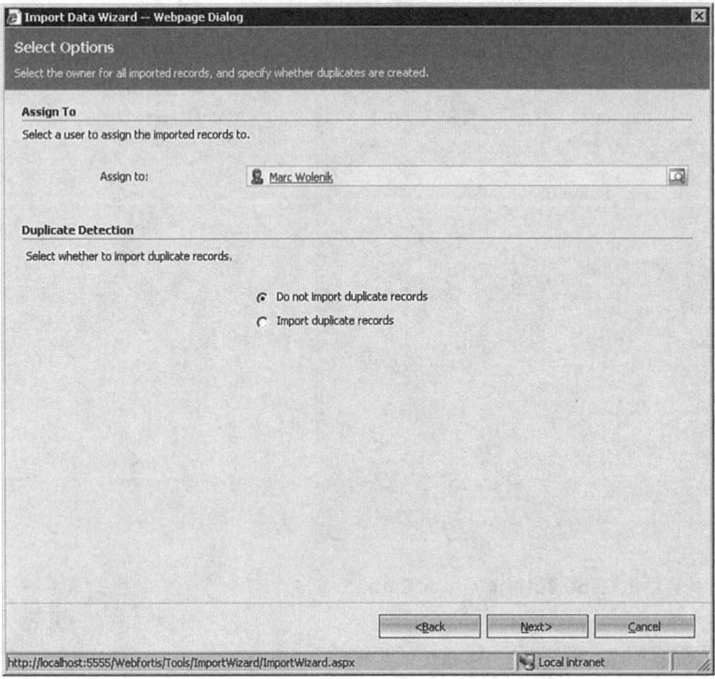

FIGURE 9.21 Import Data Wizard—Assign records and select duplicate option.

4. The final step of the import is to select the name of the import and set whether to send an E-mail when the import is completed. Select Import to continue (see Figure 9.22).

5. The Imports screen shows the status of the import under Status Reason. Selecting the refresh icon updates the status of the import. When completed, Completed displays as the Status Reason (see Figure 9.23).

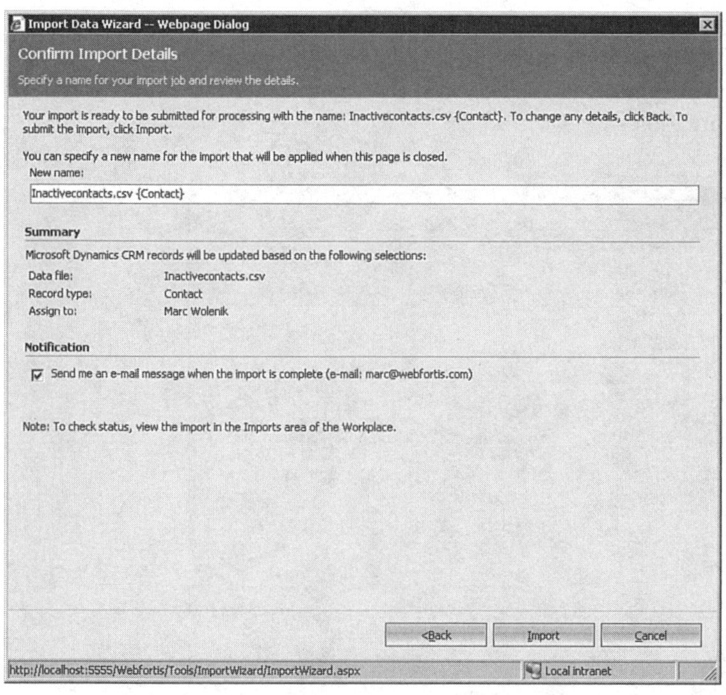

FIGURE 9.22 Import Data Wizard—Confirm Import Details.

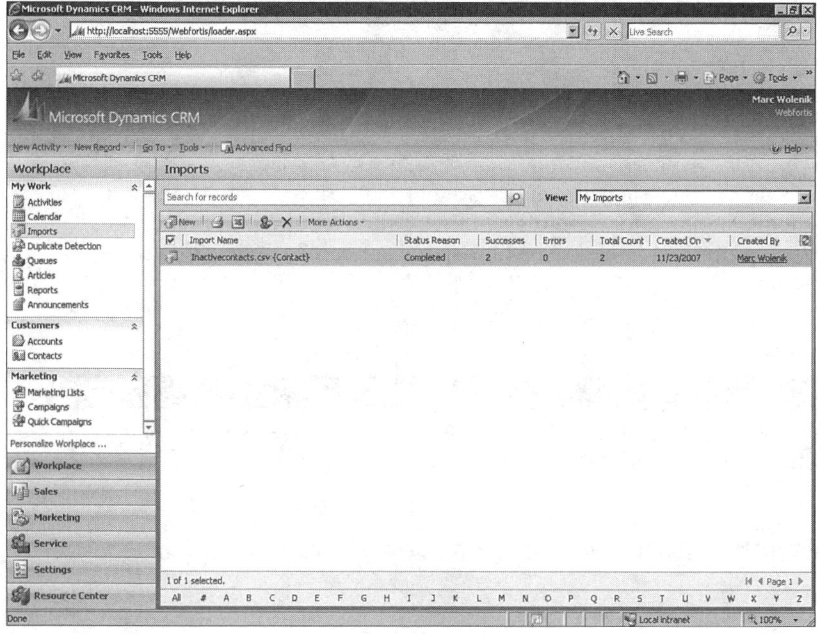

FIGURE 9.23 Imports screen—completed import.

6. Opening the Imports record displays information related to the import, as well as the actual Contacts updated and any failures in detail (see Figure 9.24). Any upload failures can be exported exclusively and then re-imported without having to re-import the entire job again.

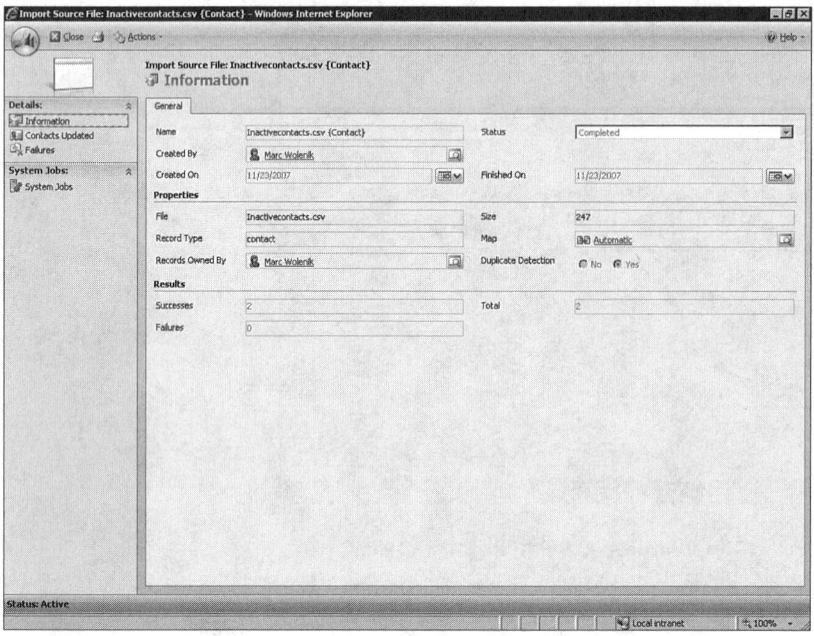

FIGURE 9.24 Import details.

TIP

For the previous example, you will notice three System Jobs. These system jobs are created when records are imported, and they go through the status of Submitted to Parsing (parsing), Transforming to Importing (transforming), and finally Importing to Completed (importing).

TIP

Imports are technically System Jobs, with the Owner set as the User. You can find them in the System Jobs section of the Settings area.

For additional information about working with importing data, refer to Chapter 6.

Duplicate Detection

Duplicate Detection is a great new feature with this version of Microsoft Dynamics CRM. Previously, duplicates often riddled a system, requiring complex workflows or regular purging of data. Now the system can be set to control duplicates, and Users can choose whether to accept the data.

To create a duplicate detection job, you must enable Duplicate Detection in Settings, Data Management, and at least one rule for Duplicate Detection must exist for the selected record type (Account, Contact, or Lead). By default, three rules exist: one for Accounts, one for Contacts, and one for Leads with the same E-mail address (see Figure 9.25). These rules are applied when working with Duplicate Detection in the My Workplace area. New rules added here also apply to any new Duplicate Detection jobs that will be run on a per entity basis.

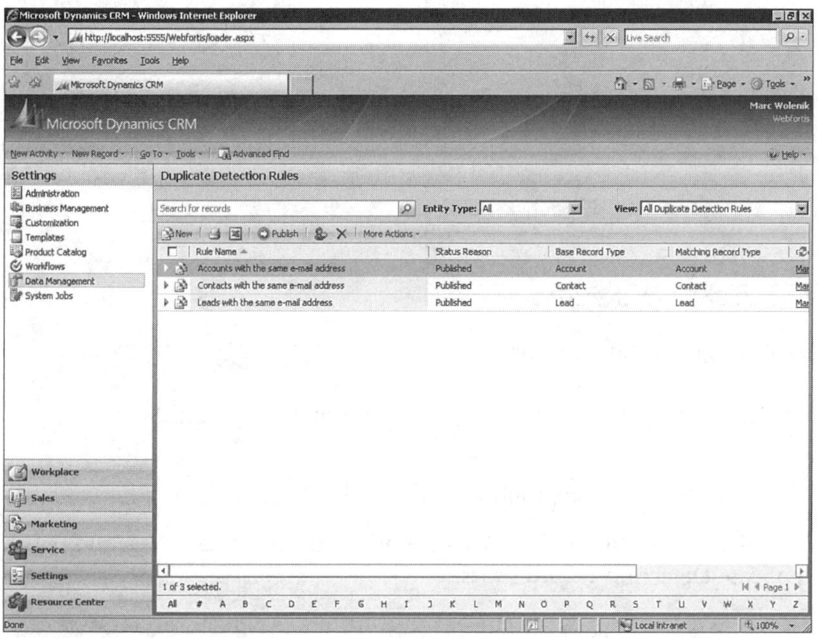

FIGURE 9.25 Duplicate Detection Rules from Settings, Data Management.

The Duplicate Detection Settings in this section also control whether Duplicate Detection is enabled when records are created or updated, when Outlook goes offline to online, and during data import.

To create more rules and to work with the other Data Management options, refer to Chapter 20.

Although the rules check for duplicates, it may still be possible to create duplicates within the system. This is because, when adding records to Microsoft Dynamics CRM, the codes used for the detection of duplicates, or match codes, are updated only every 5 minutes.

Therefore, it is possible to enter a duplicate record right after creating a rule, and the rules will appear to not work. However, if you wait 5 minutes and then attempt to add a record, you should see an alert similar to the one shown in Figure 9.26.

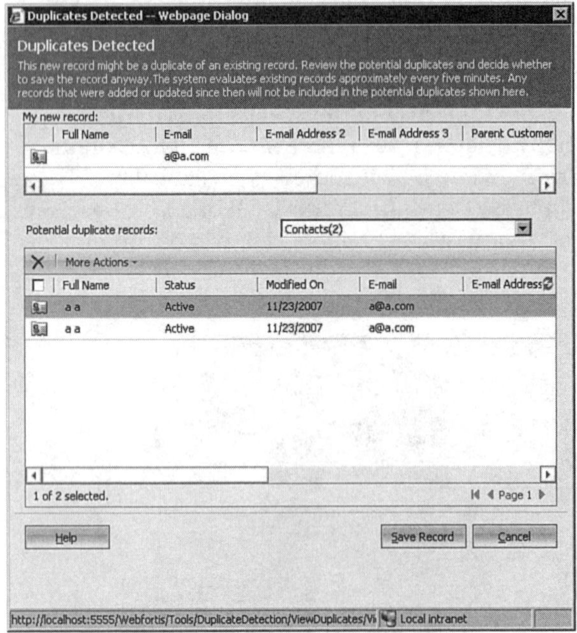

FIGURE 9.26 Duplicates Detected dialog box.

For this reason, you might want to run Duplicate Detection manually from My Workplace.

To create a new Duplicate Detection job, follow these steps:

1. Navigate to Duplicate Detection in My Work found in the Workplace area and select New. The Duplicate Detection wizard starts.

2. After the welcome screen appears, select Next to continue. A screen similar to the Advanced Find appears, but unless you've created Duplicate Detection rules to work on other entities, it is limited to Accounts, Contacts, or Leads by default, as those entities have rules associated with them by default (see Figure 9.27). You can apply any kind of advanced criteria to the selected entity, or you can leave it blank (with no criteria) to check all records. Our example in Figure 9.27 checks all Contact records created within the last 2 hours only.

   If desired, you can preview the records to ensure that the selected criteria will actually examine the records you want to check by selecting Preview Records. Click Next to continue.

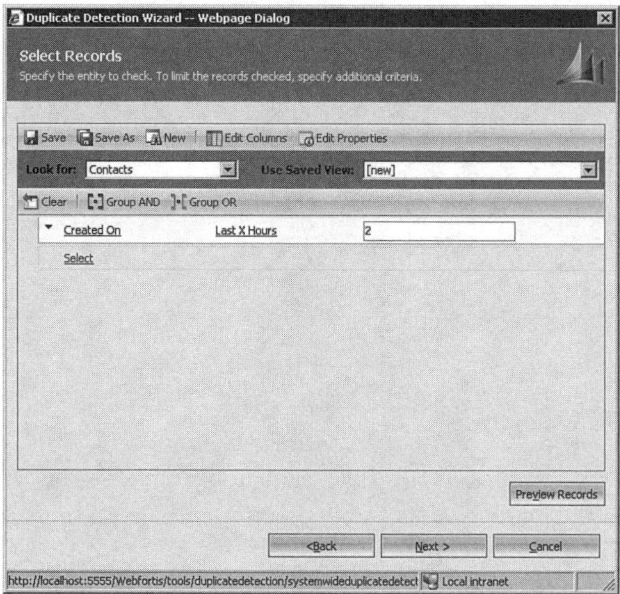

FIGURE 9.27 Duplicate Detection Find.

TIP

You can launch Duplicate Detection directly from an Advanced Find by selecting Detect Duplicates from the More Actions drop-down menu.

TIP

By default, all records of the selected entity are chosen, including deactivated records. You can easily set this within the Duplicate Detection Find to check for only records in which Status is equal to `Active`.

3. The Select Options are displayed with naming options, as well as the Start Time and whether the job should be scheduled for recurrence (see Figure 9.28). The E-mail options enable you to have an E-mail sent to you as well as other selected Users when the job is completed. Click Next to continue and then Finish to complete the Duplicate Detection job.

4. The job is now scheduled and, if selected for immediate running, starts running. The Status Reason displays the status of the job; you can refresh this by clicking the refresh icon. (Depending on the quantity of records in the system, this process may take a long time to complete.) When completed, the Status Reason will display Succeeded or Failed (see Figure 9.29). You can double-click the record to check the status.

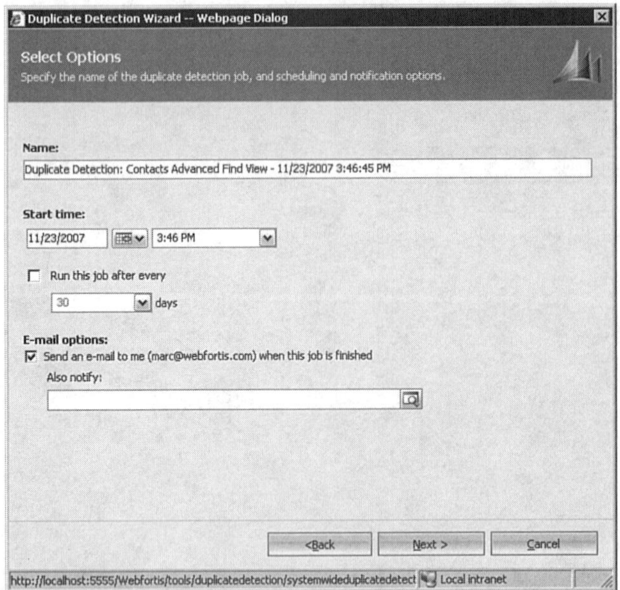

FIGURE 9.28 Duplicates Detected Select Options.

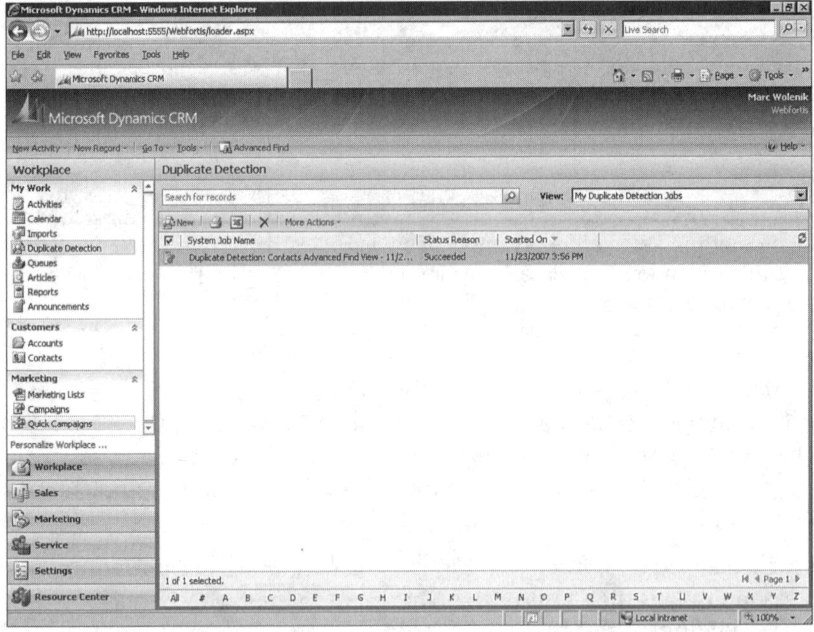

FIGURE 9.29 Duplicate Detection jobs.

5. Opening the Duplicate Detection job displays general information about the job. The View Duplicates option from the near navigation displays any duplicates that were found as part of the job (see Figure 9.30).

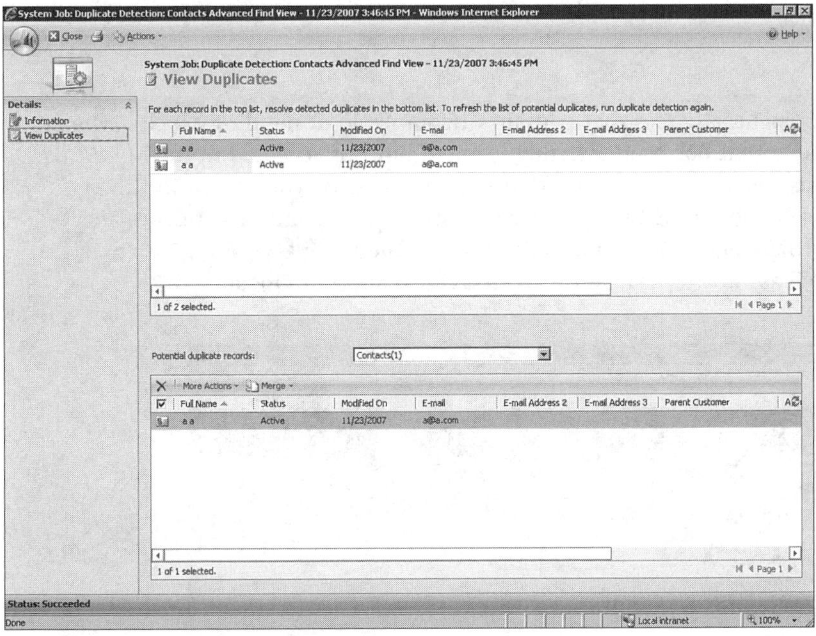

FIGURE 9.30 Duplicates found on the Duplicate Detection job.

6. To correct any duplicates, select the options from the menu bar above the bottom list. You have these options for dealing with a duplicate record:

- Deleting the record.
- Editing, deactivating, or activating the record from the More Actions drop-down menu. Because you can edit only an active record, you might need to activate the record.
- Merge the records either Automatically or by selecting the Master record from the Merge drop-down menu.

TIP

Only completed or canceled Duplicate Detection jobs can be deleted. If you want to delete a job that is pending, cancel it and then delete it.

TIP

Similarly to Duplicate Detection jobs, Imports are technically System Jobs, with the Owner set as the User. Imports are found in the System Jobs section of the Settings area.

Queues

You can think of Queues as areas that contain uncompleted or pending articles. They can contain any Activity that has been assigned to them but not accepted in the My Work, Assigned queue, as well as any Activities that you're currently working on in the My Work, In Progress queue. These two queues are system queues; any new queues are displayed below them. Figure 9.31 shows the system Queues of My Work, Assigned, and In Progress, as well as another Queue we created called Support Queue.

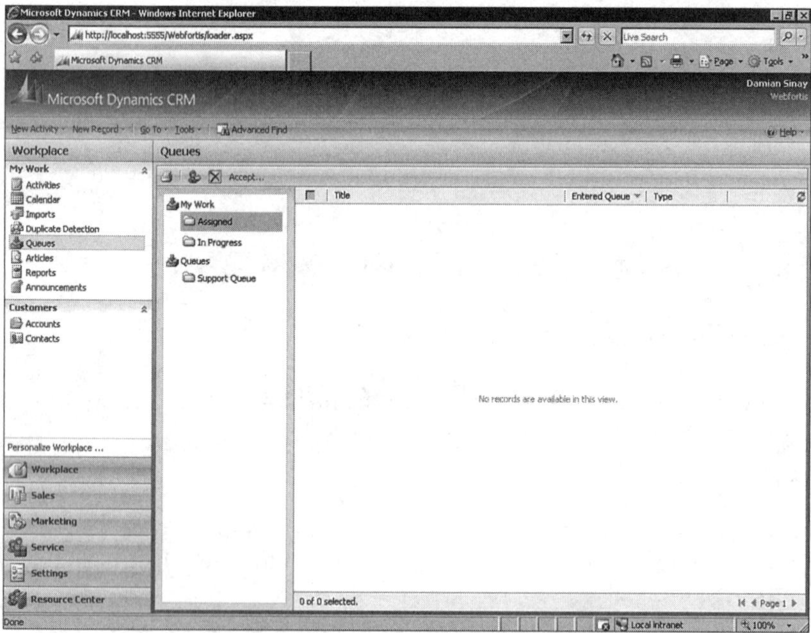

FIGURE 9.31 Queues.

For more information about Queues, refer to Chapter 14.

Articles

Articles enable Users to quickly and easily search the company's Knowledge Base. The Knowledge Base is set up and maintained in the Service area and can contain information, such as product specifications, company procedures, and common solutions to customer and employee problems, or anything that you want to make available to Users.

Figure 9.32 shows an example Knowledge Base Article that exists in our sample Microsoft Dynamics CRM system.

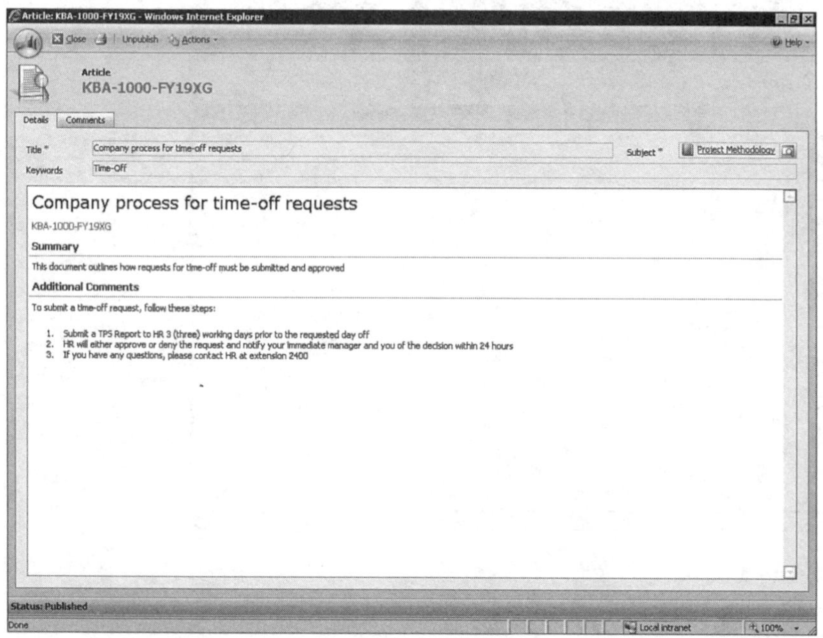

FIGURE 9.32 Knowledge Base Article.

Using this Knowledge Base Article as our example, we can use the Articles tab to search for it among the many Knowledge Base Articles that might exist.

Using the search features from the drop-down menu, we can select the criteria and where to search for Articles (see Figure 9.33). Options include searching using the exact text entered or similar text via Use Like Words. The later option includes a pseudoheuristic search that matches words with their corresponding tenses. For example, a search for *submit* would match *submitting*, *submits*, and *submitted*.

After you find an Article, you can view, print, or E-mail it.

9

NOTE

If an Article doesn't appear in the Articles area, the system might not have indexed it yet. Normally, it takes up to 15 minutes for Articles to be approved and made available in the Articles area.

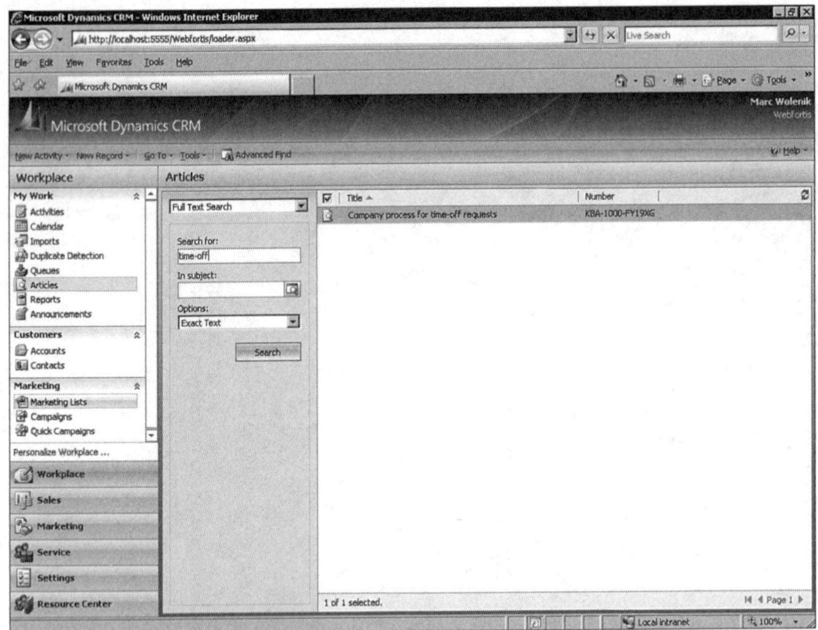

FIGURE 9.33 Found Article.

TIP

Only approved Knowledge Base Articles are available in the Articles area. To search for unapproved Articles, you must navigate directly to the Knowledge Base in Service.

For more information about creating and working with the Knowledge Base, refer to Chapter 12.

Reports

The Reports area is where you will run, manage, and create Microsoft Dynamics CRM reports.

For more information on working with Reports, refer to Chapter 13, "Reporting."

Announcements

Announcements displays any unexpired announcements that the system administrator has set in the Settings area. These can include any general company information or industry-specific news that you want to share with your Users (see Figure 9.34).

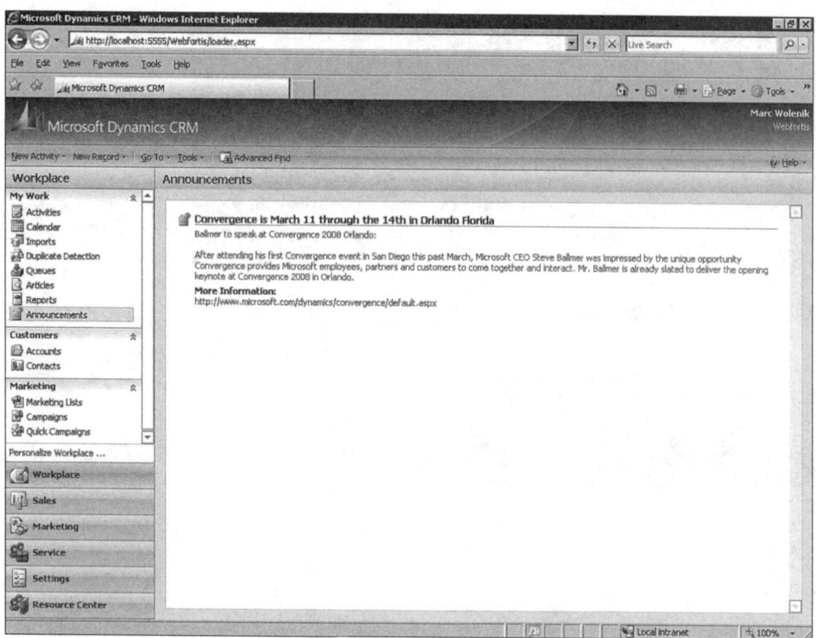

FIGURE 9.34 Announcements.

For more information about working with Announcements, refer to Chapter 14.

Exporting Data

Virtually every area of Microsoft Dynamics CRM has the ability to export to Excel. In addition to being able to export using the Advanced Find, you can select the Excel icon within Microsoft Dynamics CRM (see Figure 9.35).

Exporting data allows you to perform advanced manipulation and reporting within the familiar interface of Excel.

To export data from an entity, follow these steps:

1. Navigate to the entity that contains the records you want to export. In this example, you'll export all Inactive Contacts. To do this, navigate to Contacts; then select Inactive Contacts from the drop-down view. Select the Excel icon to display the Export Data to Excel dialog box (see Figure 9.36).
2. The Export to Data to Excel dialog box has three options:
    - Static Worksheet with Records from This Page—This option will export the records on the page, with only the columns that are visible on the view from the page. By default, the Inactive Contacts only have Full Name, Parent Customer, and Business Phone, so those will be the only fields exported. You can modify your view and additional columns by going to Settings, Customize and adding columns to the view, if necessary.

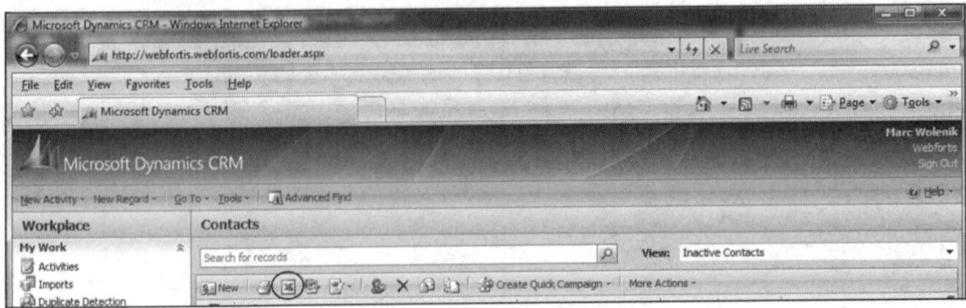

FIGURE 9.35 Excel icon in Contacts.

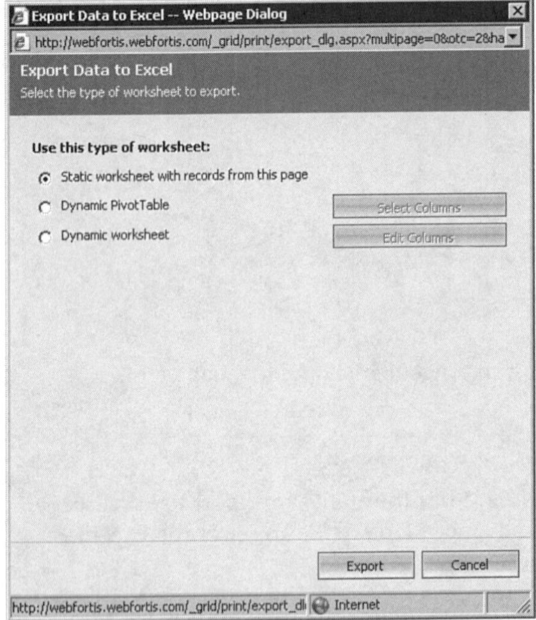

FIGURE 9.36 Export Data to Excel dialog box.

- Dynamic Pivot Table—When selected, the Select Columns button becomes enabled, allowing you to optionally add additional columns to the export (see Figure 9.37). After you're finished adding columns, you can export the data by selecting Export, and Excel will open in Pivot Table design mode allowing you to drag and drop to create Pivot Tables. This option is generally used to manipulate and report on data from Microsoft Dynamics CRM.
- Dynamic Worksheet—Selecting this option will allow you to add new columns (as described in the first option, static worksheet); however, the columns are only added for the purpose of export and do not change the underlying view (see Figure 9.38).

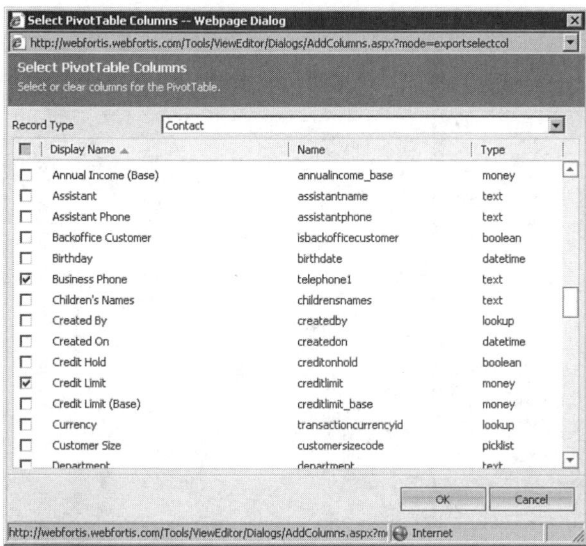

FIGURE 9.37 Select columns to export.

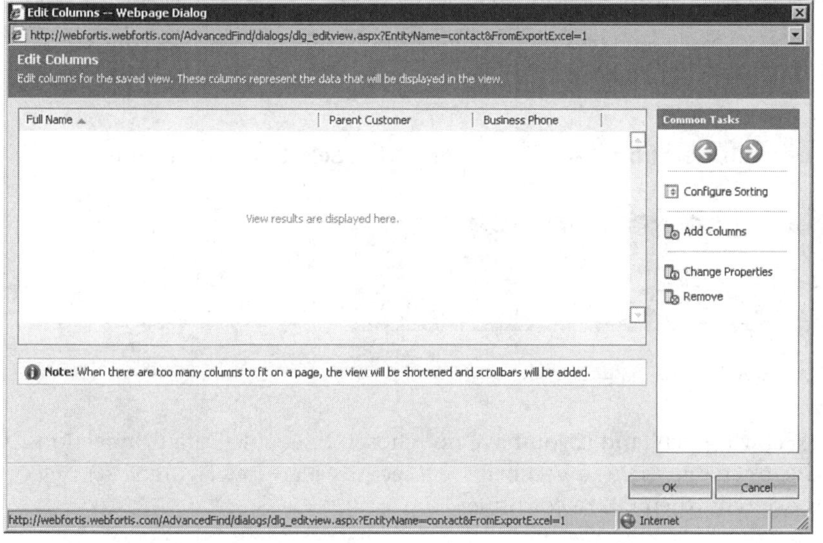

FIGURE 9.38 Select columns to add for export.

For our example, we'll select the Dynamic Worksheet option, and add three columns consisting of `First Name`, `Last Name`, and `Credit Limit` (see Figure 9.39). Select OK twice; then Export to export the data to Excel.

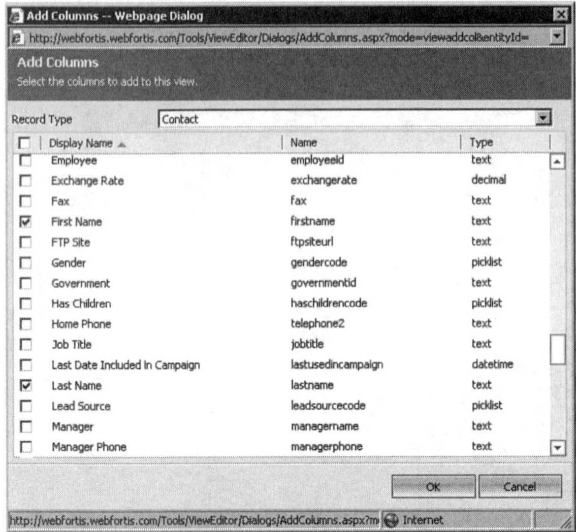

FIGURE 9.39 Select columns to edit for export.

TIP

Both the Dynamic Pivot Table and the Dynamic Worksheet require Microsoft Dynamics CRM for Outlook installed to view exported data.

3. You may receive an alert from Excel (see Figure 9.40). Select Yes to continue.

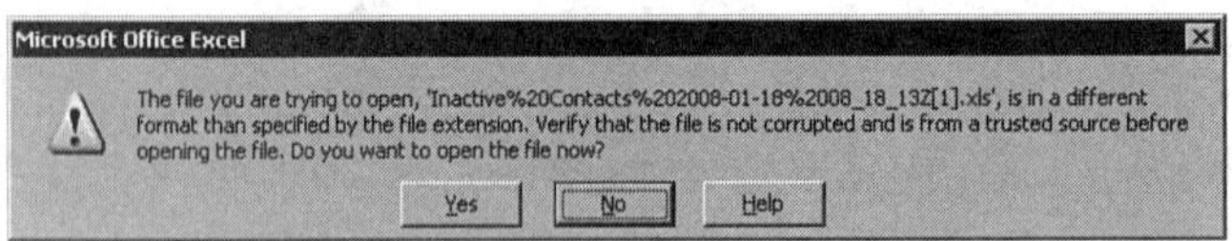

FIGURE 9.40 Microsoft Office Excel warning alert.

4. Microsoft Excel will open, and if you have not chosen to enable Data Connections, you may have to enable them or you will see a security alert (see Figure 9.41). Select Enable This Content, then OK to continue.

5. When the content downloads, it is displayed in Excel, as shown in Figure 9.42.

TIP

Notice in Figure 9.42 that the Data tab is selected and there is an option to Refresh from CRM. Microsoft Excel will refresh automatically from CRM when it re-opens; however, if you want to reflect changes made to your data without closing and re-opening, you can select this option. Additionally, it is important to remember that this is only one-way. Changes made to your data in Excel will *not* be pushed up to CRM. Rather, they must be re-imported following the steps outlined here.

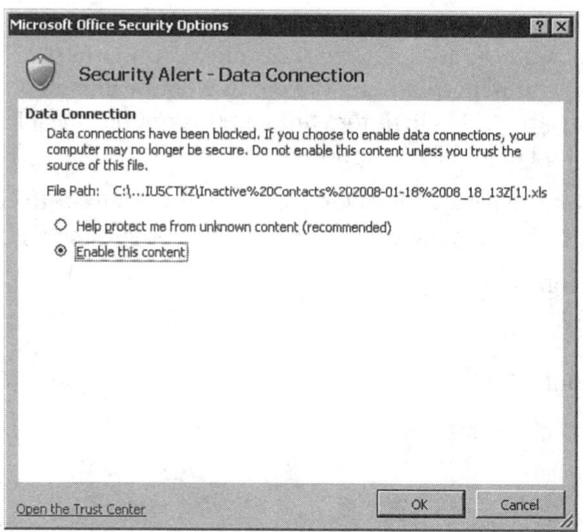

FIGURE 9.41 Microsoft Office Excel data connection security warning alert.

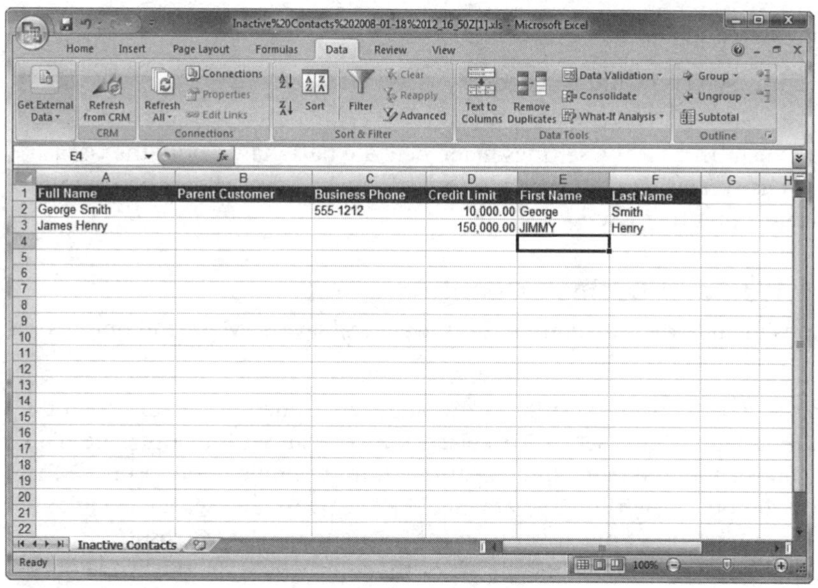

FIGURE 9.42 Microsoft Office Excel with CRM Data.

Personalize Workplace

One of the most powerful aspects of the Workplace is that you can personalize or customize it. To customize it, either select Options from the Tools drop-down menu (using either clients) or select the Personalize Workplace link found on the near navigation (using the Web client). Notice that you need to select the Tools menu option in the CRM toolbar, not the similarly named menu item on Internet Explorer when working with the Web client. When working with the CRM client for Outlook, this option is available by selecting CRM from the top menu bar and then Options.

You will encounter a few differences with the Personalize Workspace when working with the Outlook client versus the Web client. We have indicated the differences accordingly.

The options to personalize include the following:

- General (both Web and Outlook clients)
- Synchronization (Outlook client only)
- Workplace (both Web and Outlook clients)
- Activities (Web client only)
- Formats (Web client only)
- E-mail Templates (both Web and Outlook clients)
- E-mail (both Web and Outlook clients)
- Privacy (both Web and Outlook clients)
- Languages (both Web and Outlook clients)

It is important to remember that the settings made here are personal to only the User profile making the changes. When set, they are applied to whichever client the User uses and will have no affect on other Users.

General (Both Web and Outlook Clients)

The General options include the capability to set the general layout, view, and options (see Figure 9.43).

Default Pane refers to which area receives the focus and is expanded by default when the system is started. By default, this is set to Workplace, but you can set it to any pane. This is very helpful if you work in the marketing department, for example—you can have that area selected when you open Microsoft Dynamics CRM. We personally set the default pane to Settings because we do so much work on the configuration of Microsoft Dynamics CRM. Similarly, you can set Default tab or the node where the start page opens (Web client only).

Select Which Forms to Use enables you to set whether to use Microsoft Dynamics CRM forms for the indicated items or use the native Outlook forms. Because Microsoft Dynamics CRM is so closely integrated with Outlook, either form works, provided that the Outlook forms are promoted to CRM (Outlook client only).

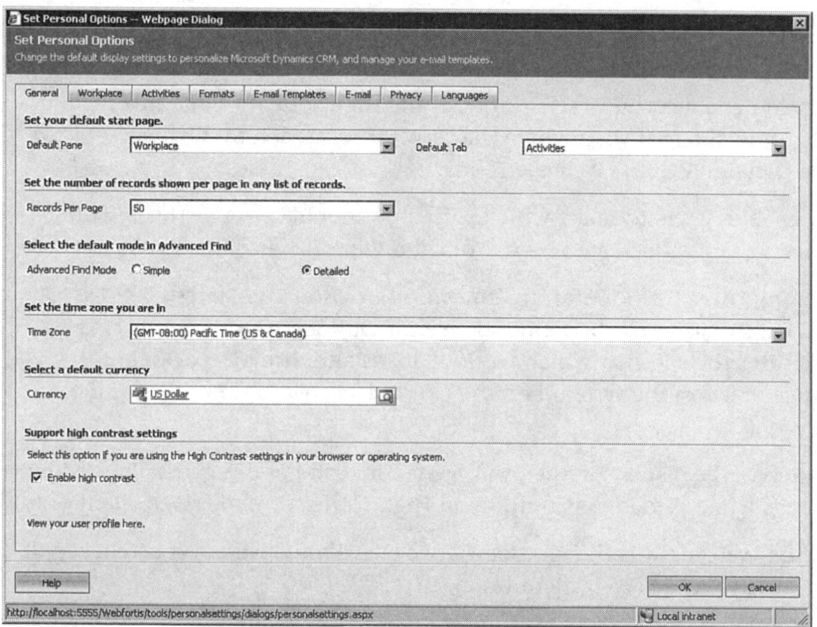

FIGURE 9.43 Personal Options, General (Web client).

TIP

Customizations to Microsoft Dynamics CRM forms are not available if you select to work with the Outlook forms. An example of this might be adding a new field to the Contact record that tracks the `Industry` of the Contact. This field will not be on the Outlook form.

Number of Records Displayed Per Page is a global setting (for your User only) that sets the maximum number or rows, or records, to display on any list of records. The maximum is 250. If you frequently work with large record sets, you might want to set it to the maximum for less paging requirements (both Web and Outlook clients).

TIP

We've noticed in our testing that the larger the number you select for rows, the longer it takes for the page to load. This is because more records need to load on a given page, thereby slowing the load time. Additionally, there is no easy way to change this number to greater than 250.

Default Mode for Advanced Find is the option to select between Simple and Detailed. Simple mode doesn't display the query/filter options; Detailed mode shows and lets you modify the query/filter options. Note that, regardless of the setting here, you can select either mode when working with the Advanced Find by selecting Hide Details or Show Details on the form manually (both Web and Outlook client).

The Time Zone option enables you to select and set the time zone for your area/region. Note that this might be different than where the server is located, and it can affect how you use Microsoft Dynamics CRM (Web client only).

Default Currency enables Users to select which Currency should be set as the default Currency when new records are created (Both Web and Outlook clients).

Setting the option Improve Outlook Startup Time and Microsoft Dynamics CRM Display Speed allows Outlook to run in the background, even if Outlook is not loaded. This option greatly increases the speed at which Outlook loads and displays pages, but it does have a resource draw on the system because Outlook is always running (Outlook client only).

High Contrast improves the display of Microsoft Dynamics CRM and is generally used by vision-impaired Users while Windows is running in High Contrast mode (Web client only).

At the bottom of the Web client is the link View Your User Profile Here. When clicked, it takes Users to view their profile (Web client only).

Synchronization (Outlook Client Only)

To modify how Outlook synchronizes with Microsoft Dynamics CRM, you make changes here (see Figure 9.44).

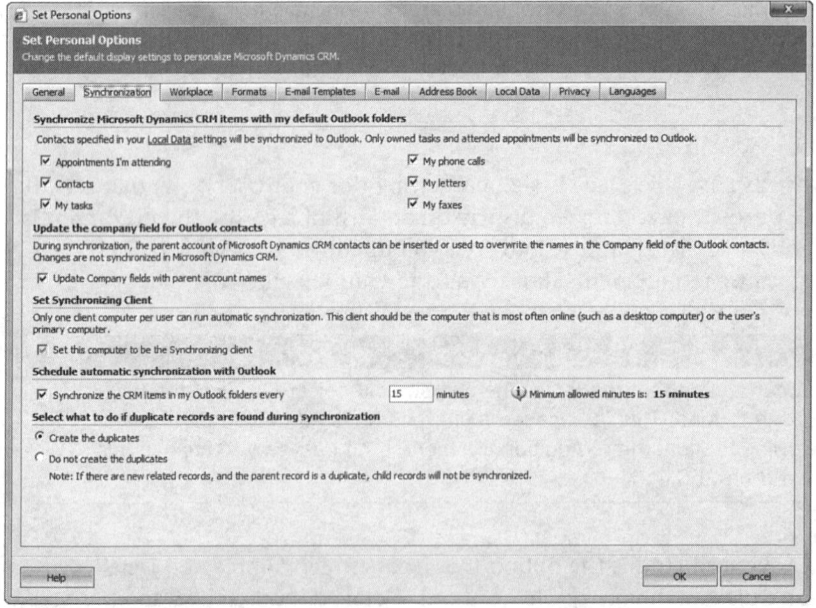

FIGURE 9.44 Personal Options, Synchronization (Outlook client).

Outlook can synchronize any Task, Phone Call, Letter, or Fax that you are the owner of, as well as Appointments for which you're listed as an attendee. Contacts are a little trickier: Only the Contacts that you've specified in the Local Data settings are synchronized. You can navigate to the Local Data settings by clicking Local Data or by navigating to CRM, Modify Local Data Groups from the Outlook client.

By default, Local Data synchronizes only Contacts for which you are listed as the owner. This prevents problems when organizations have a huge number of Contacts from all of them synchronizing with Outlook. However, if you want to have every Contact in the organization, or if you want to have all of your Contacts as well as all the Contacts your employees own, you can dynamically set that value here. Figure 9.45 shows the option available from Outlook that can be accessed by going to CRM from the top menu and selecting Modify Local Data Groups.

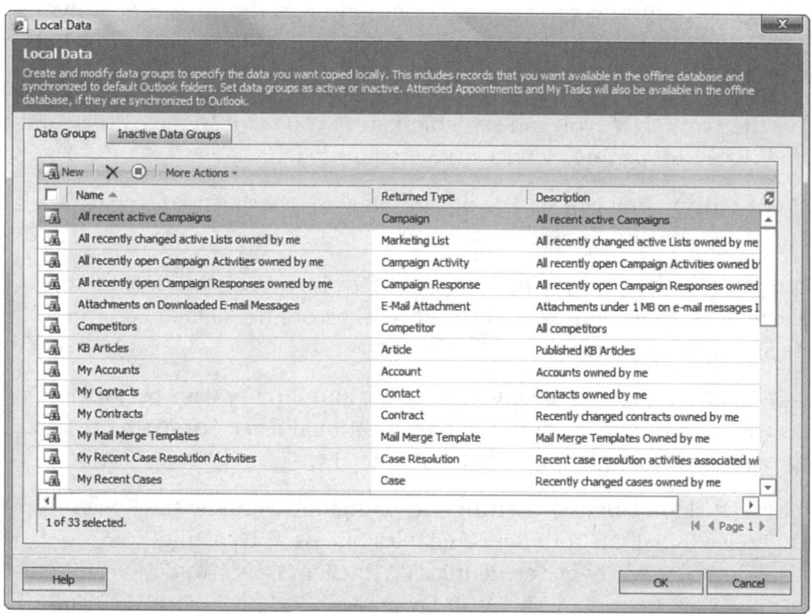

FIGURE 9.45 Local Data Groups as accessed from the CRM client for Outlook.

TIP

Remember that although it might seem like a great idea to have every Contact in the organization in your Outlook, your handheld phone/pocket PC device probably synchronizes with Outlook. If that is the case and you attempt to synchronize 25,000 Contacts with your handheld, you might quickly run out of memory or have an unmanageable device.

Updating the `Company` field is a new option with this version of Microsoft Dynamics CRM, as previous versions required a workaround to display it. It is highly recommended that you have this checked because it displays the parent Account name in the `Company` field.

NOTE

Unlike other fields, the Company synchronization is one-way. Changes to this field are pushed down from CRM to Outlook, but they are not pushed from Outlook to CRM.

When setting the synchronizing client, it is necessary to consider changing this option only if you have more than one computer. If so, consider which computer you will use most often, and set that computer as the primary client. If you use more than one computer with the Outlook client, Microsoft Dynamics might prompt you to set this.

Synchronization with CRM occurs every 15 minutes or as often as the automatic synchronization is set. This is optional: You can set synchronization manually by going to CRM, Synchronize with CRM.

Workplace—Within the Workplace, you can set which areas you want to have quick-and-easy access to, such as Sales, Marketing, Service, or Scheduling.

Activities (Web Client Only)—You can set the default view for the calendar to day, week, or month, and you also can set the default work hours.

Formats (Web Client Only)—Here you select the format for how you want information such as numbers, currencies, time, and dates: You can select from the defaults or customize these specifically to your region.

E-mail Templates—E-mail Templates enable you to create and modify your personal E-mail templates, as well as promote them to the Organizational level. For more information about working with E-mail templates, refer to Chapter 14.

E-mail (Both Web and Outlook Clients)—Setting the configuration Allow the E-mail Router to Send and Receive E-mail on Your Behalf enables Microsoft Dynamics CRM to send E-mails directly from CRM with your credentials (Web client only). You also can determine how E-mail messages are tracked in Microsoft Dynamics CRM here (both Web and Outlook client). For more information about both of these options, refer to Chapter 15.

Privacy (Both Web and Outlook Clients)—The Privacy option checks to see how to send error information to Microsoft related to problems with Microsoft Dynamics CRM.

Languages (Both Web and Outlook Clients)—With the Languages setting, you can set the User Interface and Help language. The only options available are those that the system administrator has installed and made active. However, Users can customize their Microsoft Dynamics CRM experience based on their preferred language.

NOTE

The Base language is set when Microsoft Dynamics CRM is first loaded and cannot be changed. Additionally, setting the language here changes only the way the Microsoft Dynamics interface is displayed. Data contained within the system will not change.

For more information on working with languages, refer to Chapter 14.

Summary

The Workplace is where Users will spend most of their time managing Activities and customers. It is very customizable, and there are several options that allow you to extend the functionality related to customers, calendar, and tasks directly to mobile devices through Outlook.

The Activities are how work gets assigned, managed, and completed. This chapter explained how to work not just with Activities, but also how to assign them to Users and Queues. Activities are used to drive tasks, as well as many reports that rely on Activities (the Neglected Accounts report, for example) and should be used to record every customer contact.

Duplicate Detection, as well as how to work with data that can be exported and imported, showed how easy it is to work with data both in and out of the CRM Application. It is important to remember that when working with Dynamic data in Excel, it will be refreshed from the underlying data source, and you might open a spreadsheet that doesn't contain data (or has new data) other than you originally were working with.

CHAPTER 10

Working with Sales

IN THIS CHAPTER

- ▶ Leads
- ▶ Opportunities
- ▶ Competitors
- ▶ Products
- ▶ Quotes, Orders, and Invoices

The Sales area in Microsoft Dynamics CRM is where you work with current and prospective customers. Here you manage Leads and Opportunities, and where the only workflow other than Knowledge Base approval is included with Microsoft Dynamics CRM by default. The workflow is presented via the Lead conversion process when a User selects Convert Lead from the top menu. The Lead is either qualified and converted to a customer, or disqualified and deactivated.

Other sections in the Sales area, such as Accounts, Contacts, are explained in Chapter 8, "Working with Customers"; Marketing Lists, Sales Literature, and Quick Campaigns are included in Chapter 11, "Working with Marketing," and are not covered in this chapter.

Leads

Leads are not customers but rather potential customers. This is an important distinction because it provides a needed level of separation when working with your customer base. As explained later in this chapter, Leads are converted to customers when they become qualified. If they are disqualified, they remain as an inactive Lead.

Using Leads properly can provide rich insight into your organization on several levels. Because Leads are not yet qualified (they are potential customers who haven't yet met internal criteria to be converted to customers), they should be considered the customer entry point into the CRM system. Although it is certainly possible that you will be adding Accounts and Contacts directly into Microsoft Dynamics CRM, entering Leads enables you to manage what new customers might be interested in your products, how your salespeople are cultivating their new customer base, and what kind of criteria is being used to convert Leads to customers.

As mentioned earlier, Leads are also used for specific marketing efforts. Any growing business usually aims to add new customers, and the capability to create marketing efforts tailored to interested customers is much more efficient than preparing marketing for everyone.

When creating a Lead, you must specify the Topic (or what the Lead pertains to—this can be the specific product or service specific to the Lead), the Last Name, and the Company Name (see Figure 10.1). These fields are used when the Lead is qualified and converted to either Account, Contact, or Opportunity.

To create a new Lead, navigate to Sales, Leads and select New.

Figure 10.1 shows a new Lead entered and saved.

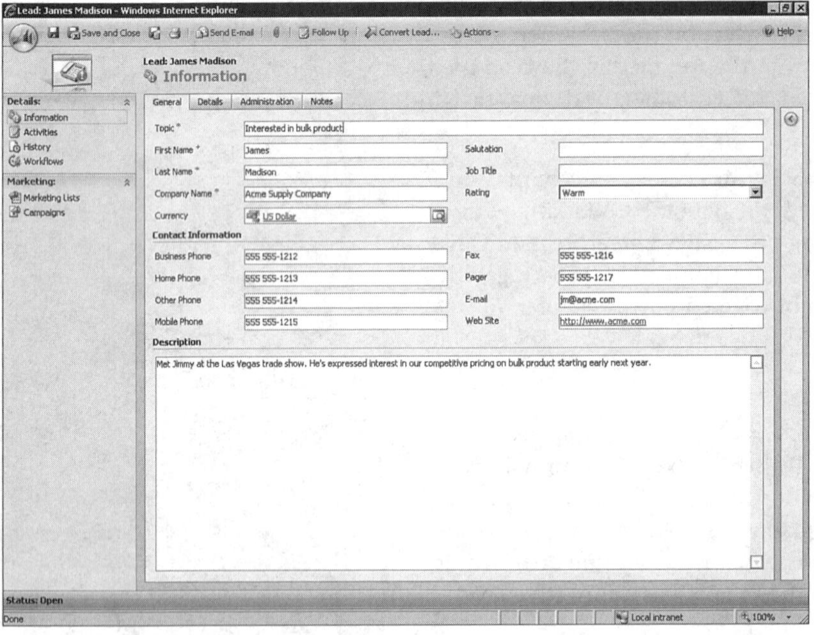

FIGURE 10.1 New Lead, General tab.

Notice that there is no lookup for, or association with, any existing data in the CRM system (other than Currency). This is because the Lead is a new record and is not related to any existing record. If you're creating a Lead and want to associate it with an existing customer, you probably want to work with Opportunities, explained in the next section. Notice also that, when working with Leads, you cannot include potential sales information anywhere other than the notes and Description fields. This is because Leads are considered potential customers, not potential sales. This is an important distinction: Potential sales information should be captured with an Opportunity, not a Lead.

Although the remaining fields on the form and tabs are not required, it is helpful to populate them; the information entered and saved automatically carries over to the converted Account, Contact, and Opportunity records when they have been qualified.

Most of the information on the General tab is self-explanatory, with the exception of Rating. This is a self-assessment of the Lead itself and can be Cold, Warm, or Hot. When used properly, it can drive Workflow events, such as a callback by the sales manager within 1 day if the Lead is hot, or within 5 days if the Lead is Cold, for example.

The Details tab includes address and company information similar to that found on the Account and Contact forms (see Figure 10.2).

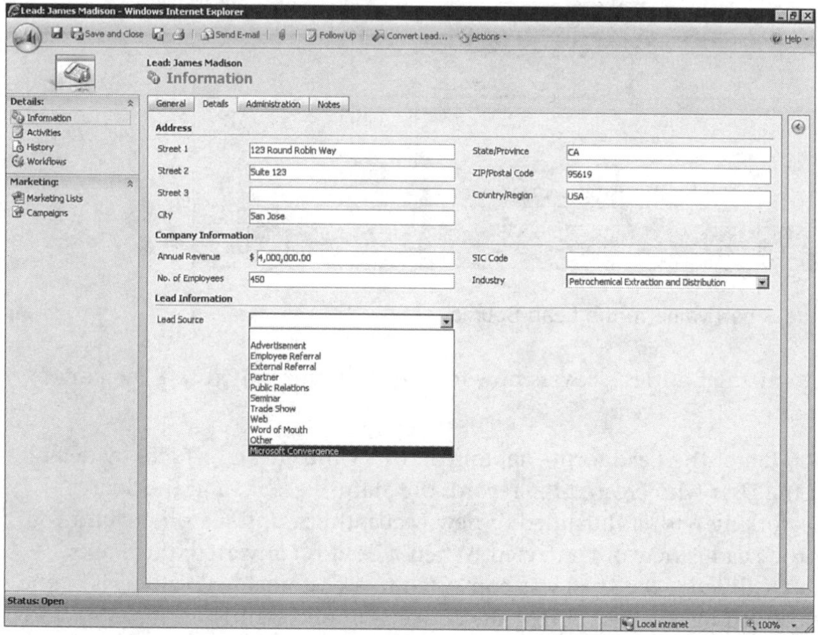

FIGURE 10.2 New Lead, Details tab with the Lead Source drop-down list expanded.

The Lead Source drop-down list (as shown in Figure 10.2) offers a great way of running reverse metrics on a trade show or seminar. You can easily add to this drop-down list by customizing the `leadsourcecode` attribute and adding specific events that your company might sponsor or attend. Figure 10.3 shows the customization options for this field and the addition of a new event called Microsoft Convergence, which is shown in the drop-down list in Figure 10.2. To make this customization, navigate to Settings, Customization, and select the Lead form; then select the Source of Lead attribute to modify.

Using this information, you can easily determine who was contacted and at which event by querying on this field.

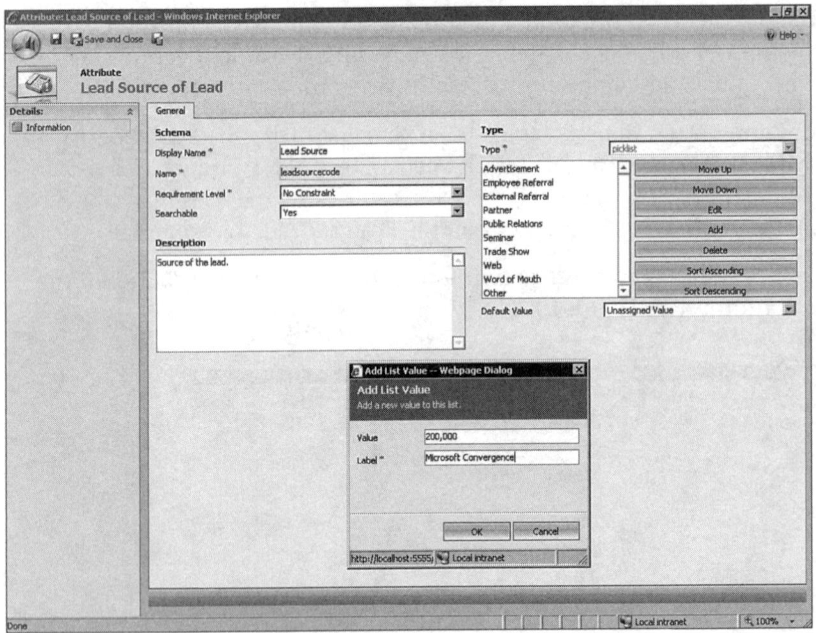

FIGURE 10.3 Add a new value to the Lead Source.

Chapter 19, "Customizing Entities," covers how to fully customize Microsoft Dynamics CRM entities.

The Administration tab of the Lead form enables you to set the Owner, which, by default, is populated with the User who created the record, the Status Reason, and the Source Campaign. When working with unqualified or new Leads, the Status Reason enables you to select whether the Lead is new or contacted. When a Lead is converted, the Status Reason changes to Qualified if the Lead was converted to a customer, or it changes to the reason it was disqualified (as selected during the conversion process). The Source Campaign enables you to tie the Lead to any Campaign generated from Microsoft Dynamics CRM.

The Contact Methods and Marketing Information are the same as found on the Account and Contact forms (see Figure 10.4).

The options at the top of a Lead (after it is saved) include the capabilities to send E-mail, add an attachment, create a follow-up Task, or convert the Lead. More actions from the drop-down list and the options on the near navigation include the capability to add an Activity and to view the history related to the Lead, as well as any Workflow triggered from or by this Lead. With the exception of Convert Lead, all of these options are covered in Chapter 7, "Common Functions," and Chapter 11. The next section explains Lead conversion.

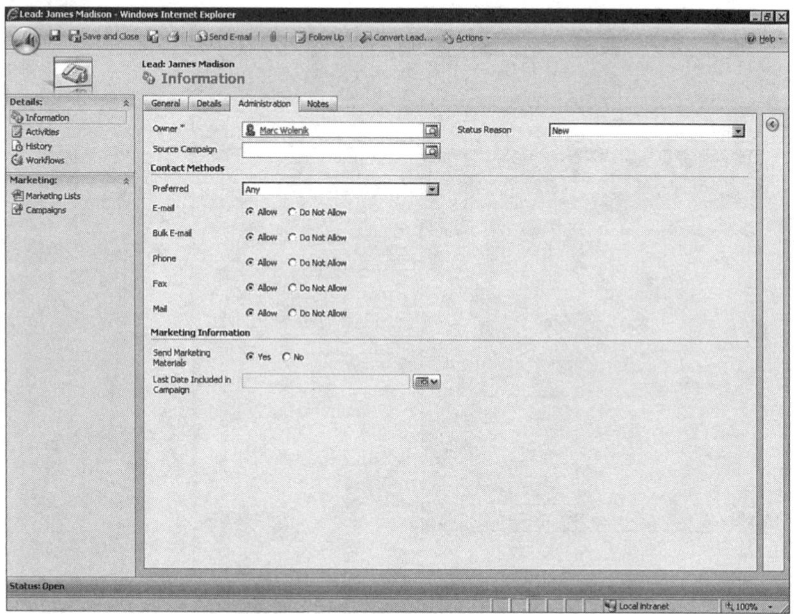

FIGURE 10.4 New Lead, Administration tab.

Converting Leads

As mentioned at the beginning of this chapter, the only Sales Force Automation (SFA) included by default in Microsoft Dynamics CRM is in Lead conversion. All other SFA is customizable by creating specific Microsoft Dynamics CRM Workflow.

Leads are converted to customers when they have met internal qualifications and become customers. Internal qualifications can be anything from a Lead indicating that he is ready to buy, to a background/credit check and line of credit approval prepared by your accounting department. Additionally, Leads are converted to disqualified customers (and removed as active Leads) through the conversion processes for a variety of reasons, such as Lead disinterest or an inability to contact.

To convert a Lead, select the Convert Lead option from the top menu bar. The Convert Lead form opens, as shown in Figure 10.5.

Lead conversion in Microsoft Dynamics CRM enables you to quickly create the necessary customer records in Microsoft Dynamics CRM by automatically creating an Account, a Contact, or an Opportunity automatically from the existing information on the Lead. When a Lead is converted (either qualified or disqualified), the original Lead record status is changed to indicate the new status of the Lead, and the Lead is closed. When a Lead is closed, no further edits can be made to it unless it is reactivated. You can reactivate any closed Lead by opening the closed Lead and selecting Reactivate Lead from the Actions drop-down list (see Figure 10.6). Any activities will remain with the Lead regardless of whether it is active or deactivated.

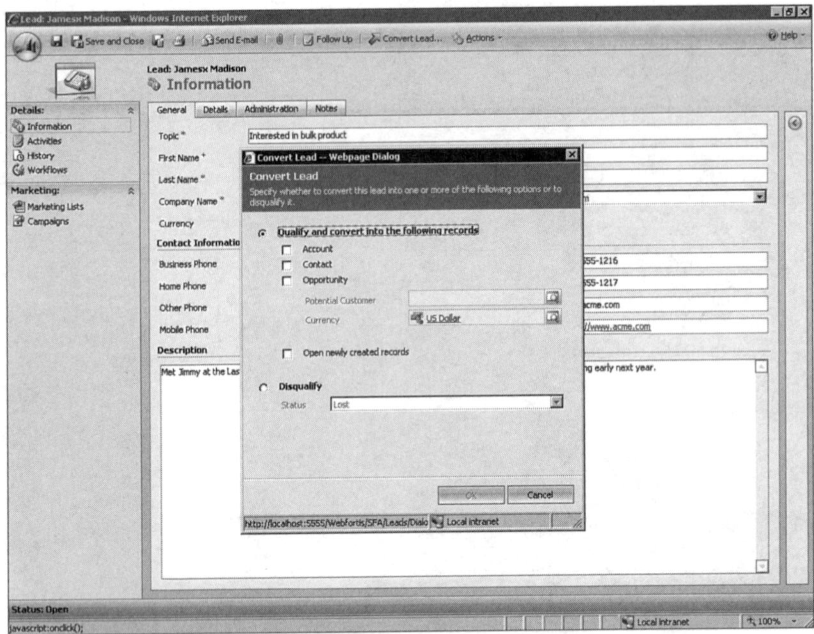

FIGURE 10.5 Convert Lead dialog box.

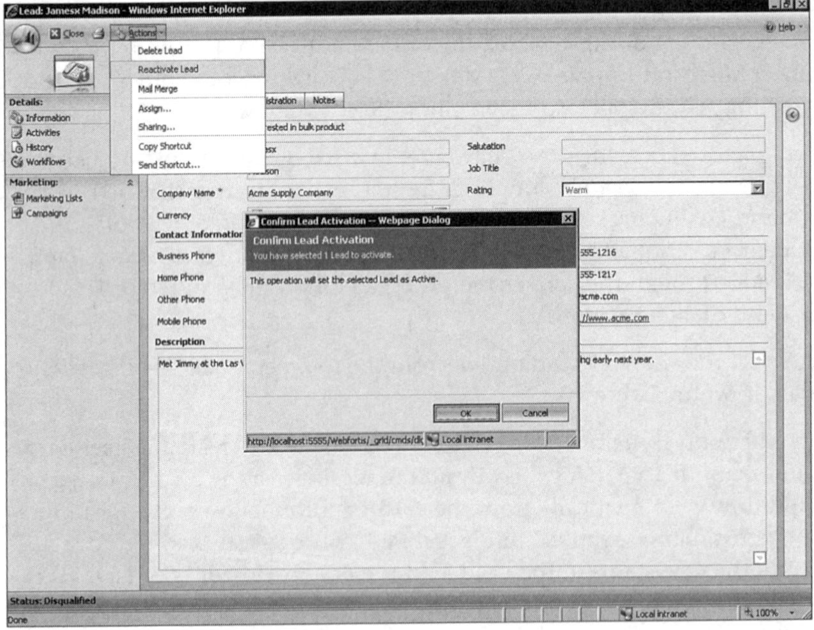

FIGURE 10.6 Lead activation.

NOTE

It is important to know that when a Lead is reactivated for whatever reason, any qualified records that might have been generated (such as Accounts, Contacts, or Opportunities) continue to exist. You can end up creating duplicate records if you frequently reactivate closed Leads.

If the Lead fails to qualify, select Disqualify (as shown in Figure 10.5). Select from the drop-down options listed in the Status and click OK. This closes the Lead and sets its status to whatever value was selected.

If the Lead has qualified, select Qualify and select whether to convert the Lead record into a new Account, Contact, or Opportunity record. It is possible to convert the Lead directly to one or all of the options. The effects of either of the options are as follows:

- If Account is selected, regardless of the other options, a new Account record is created, with the value entered for Company Name in the Lead record as the Account Name. The Lead address, details, and administration information also transfer to the new Account record, but the notes do not, because it is assumed that the notes are Lead notes, not Account notes. (You can, however, still check the original Lead notes by opening it and checking the notes there.) The Originating Lead field on the Administration tab of the Account associates to the Lead (see Figure 10.7).

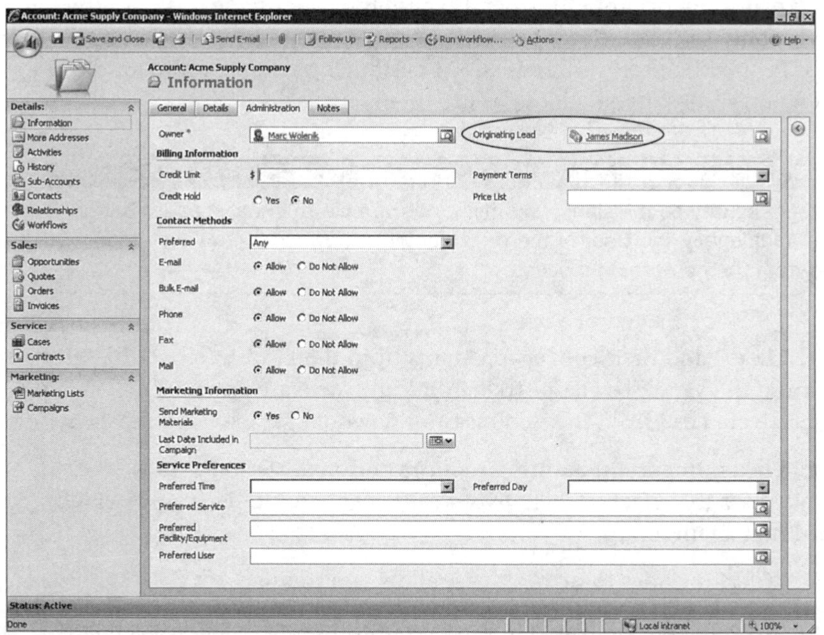

FIGURE 10.7 Originating Lead field on the Account Administration tab.

- If Contact is selected, regardless of the other options, a new Contact record is created, with the values entered for First Name and Last Name as the Contact information. The Lead address and administration information also transfer to the new Contact record, but similar to creating an Account, the notes do not. The Originating Lead field on the Administration tab of the Contact associates to the Lead (similar to Figure 10.7).
- If both Account and Contact are selected, the Account record will have the Contact record as the Primary Contact field, and the Contact record will have the Account record in the Parent Customer field.
- If Opportunity is selected and either Account or Contact is selected, a new Opportunity is created (along with the selected Account and Contact records). However, if Opportunity is selected and neither Account nor Contact is selected, you must associate the Lead with an existing customer. If the Lead is associated with an existing customer, the Lead information stays with the Lead record. The Originating Lead and the Source Campaign fields on the Administration tab of the Opportunity will associate with the Lead. The Lead notes will not transfer to the Opportunity record.
- The option to open and work with any of these selected records immediately upon conversion and creation is available by selecting Open Newly Created Records.

The next section explains opportunities further, because they are the next step in the sales process. If you select only to create either an Account or a Contact from the Lead, the customer will exist in the Microsoft Dynamics CRM customer base but will require you to manually create Opportunities if you choose to use them.

NOTE

Depending on your security permissions, you might not be able to qualify Leads that you do not own. Additionally, the User of the originating Lead owns all newly created records created from the conversion process.

You can view closed Leads and their conversion status from the Leads interface by selecting Closed Leads from the view (see Figure 10.8). You can reactivate any Lead by opening it and selecting Reactivate Lead from the Actions drop-down list, as explained earlier.

Closed Leads should be an important auditing tool of your organization because these Leads can be analyzed for the effectiveness of your sales team and to determine which Campaigns created how many Leads.

Microsoft Dynamics CRM includes these tools that allow you to query on their status:

- Two reports, the Lead Source Effectiveness report and the Neglected Leads report, found in the Report section of My Work.
- Capability to view closed Leads from Lead view.

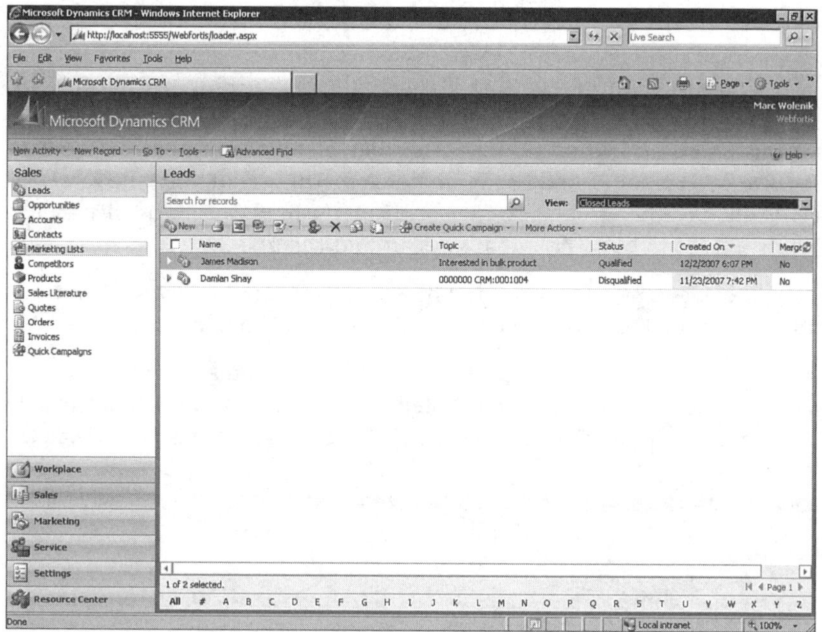

FIGURE 10.8 View closed Leads.

- More complex queries using Advanced Find to determine conversion dates, as well as Opportunities and customer records, or associations with existing customer records.

Finally, you can now convert Leads in groups, if required, instead of having to do it one by one. To convert multiple Leads, you must add them to a Marketing list as Marketing List Members and then select Convert Lead from the More Actions drop-down list.

For information about working with Marketing Lists, refer to Chapter 11.

Opportunities

Just as a Lead can ultimately lead to a customer, an Opportunity is considered a potential sale to a customer. For this reason, Opportunity records must associate with existing customer records. Also, although it is not a required part of a sales process, Opportunities provide insight into potentially upcoming sales and, when used in conjunction with the Sales Pipeline report, can forecast revenue by date, probability, and potential revenue.

Opportunities tie closely to Quotes, Orders, and Invoices because they use the base information found on the originating Opportunity when they are being created. Additionally, Opportunities are commonly created from Leads and contain the base information from the originating Lead.

Opportunities are created when "an opportunity" to make a sale is found for an existing customer. Whereas Opportunities require the existence of a customer record, you can easily create a new Account or Contact record to associate the Opportunity with if the customer is new. By doing this, however, you skip the step of creating Leads and then converting Leads to customers and Opportunities. This may be how your business works. Perhaps your sales cycle is very quick, and Leads are not something that you cultivate. However, if you generally have potential customers, consider using Leads to qualify them and then using Opportunities to build potential sales around them.

For this example, you'll create a new Opportunity; however, you could easily work with an Opportunity that was created as part of the conversion process from a Lead.

To create a new Opportunity, navigate to Opportunities in the Sales area and select New. The required fields for an Opportunity are Topic, Potential Customer, and Currency (see Figure 10.9). The Potential Customer field can be any existing active Account or Contact.

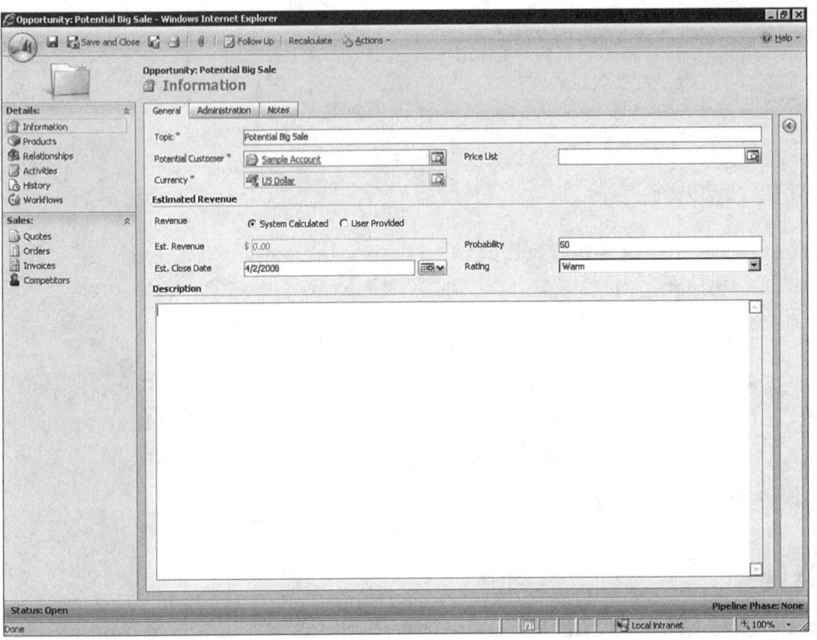

FIGURE 10.9 New Opportunity form.

Although the Price List is not required, you cannot add any products to the Opportunity until you have selected one. Probability is a field designed to contain a number between 1 and 100 to represent the probability of a close. This example uses a probability of 50—that is, a 50% chance that we'll be able to convert this Opportunity into a sale—and a forecasted value of 50% of the estimated revenue. The probability is a free-form field that is used for forecasting purposes and frequently adjusted by Workflow automatically. The Estimated Close Date indicates the date that the Opportunity might be converted to a sale, which is necessary for forecasting when considering sales. Failure to enter the

Estimated Close Date prevents the Opportunity from appearing on the Sales Pipeline report. The Rating indicates the overall rating of the Opportunity; you can change this in the customization screen to include ratings that might fit your organization better.

The Estimated Revenue section defaults to System Calculated and, when first created, has a total value of $0. When products are added to the Opportunity, the estimate revenue adjusts accordingly. Alternatively, you can select User Provided and enter any value into the Estimated Revenue text box. If User Provided is selected, however, adding products and clicking Recalculate will have no effect on the Estimated Revenue.

The Administration tab contains record ownership information, originating Lead, Status, and Source Campaign (see Figure 10.10). The Source Campaign information is populated only when a Lead has this information and is converted to an Opportunity; when you change the Opportunity record, you cannot edit the Originating Lead and the Source Campaign information.

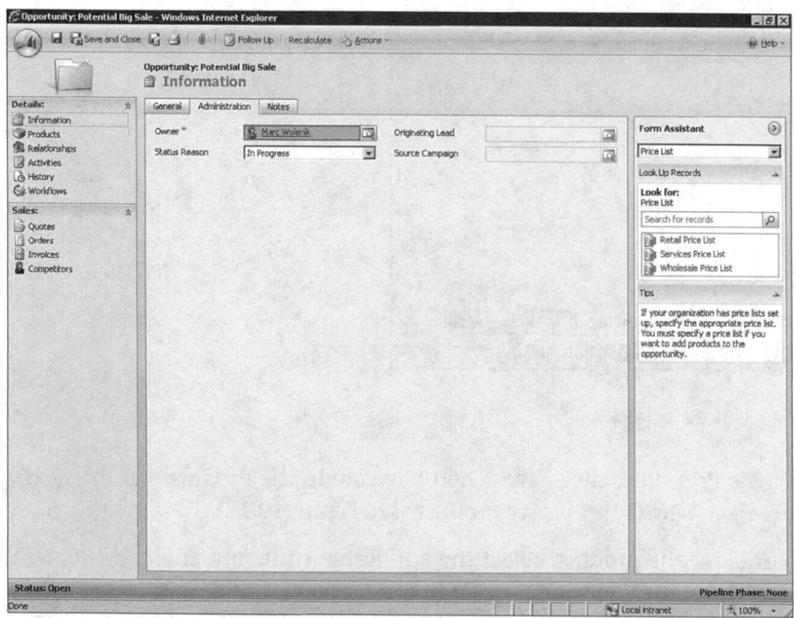

FIGURE 10.10 New Opportunity, Administration tab.

The options at the top of an Opportunity (after it is saved) include the capability to add an attachment, create a follow-up Task, recalculate the Opportunity, or choose more actions from the drop-down list. With the exception of Recalculate, all of these options are covered either in Chapter 7 or later in this chapter.

To create a complete Opportunity, including adding products, follow these steps:

1. Select New from the Sales, Opportunity area.
2. Complete the Topic, Potential Customer and Currency selection.

3. Select whether the Opportunity Estimated Revenue should be calculated by the system or User. Because you'll have the system calculate the estimated revenue for this example, leave the Revenue as System Calculated.

4. Enter the Probability, Estimated Close Date, and Rating. Before you can add products, you must also select the Price List (see Figure 10.11).

   For information on constructing your Price Lists, refer to the "Product Catalog" section in Chapter 14, "Settings and Configuration."

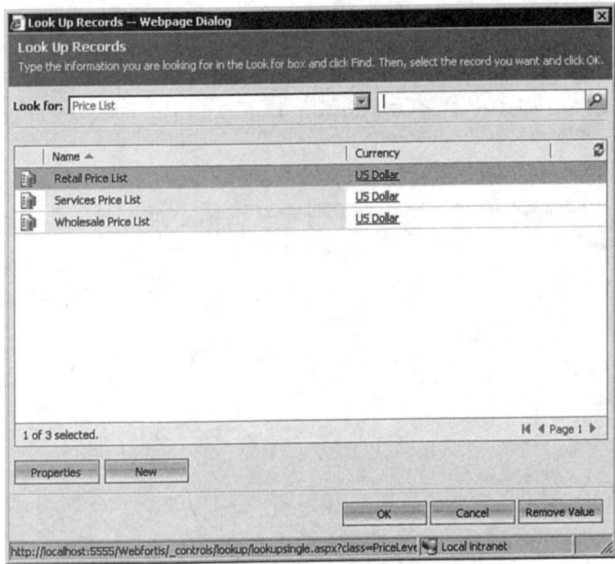

FIGURE 10.11 Price List selection.

   After you select the Price List, click Save. Then navigate to the Products on the near navigation and select New Opportunity Product (see Figure 10.12).

5. Either look up or enter the product, select the applicable Unit, and enter the quantity as well as any discount you want to give (if any). You can click Save to view the information before closing the form, or Save and Close to view the information on the quick view (see Figure 10.12). In the example, we've added a quantity of 250 products and set a price of $10 per unit; because we didn't include any discount, the extended amount is $2,500 (see Figure 10.13).

NOTE

If you want to edit the quantity or discounts, you must double-click the product line, not the underlined name of the product. If you select the product name, the product details screen opens.

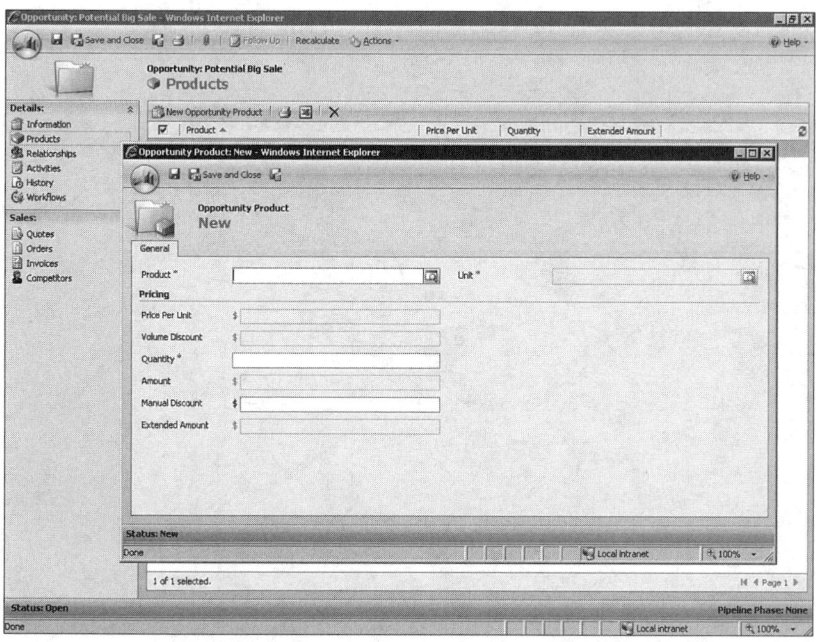

FIGURE 10.12 New Opportunity Product dialog box—Add new product.

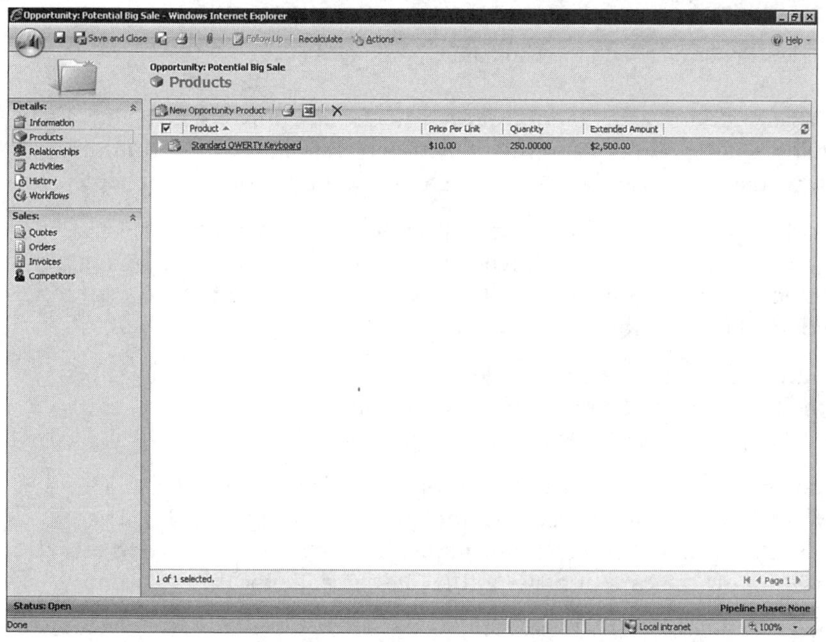

FIGURE 10.13 New Opportunity Product dialog box.

10

6. Navigating back to the main or Information screen, you should now see the Estimated Revenue at $2,500 (see Figure 10.14).

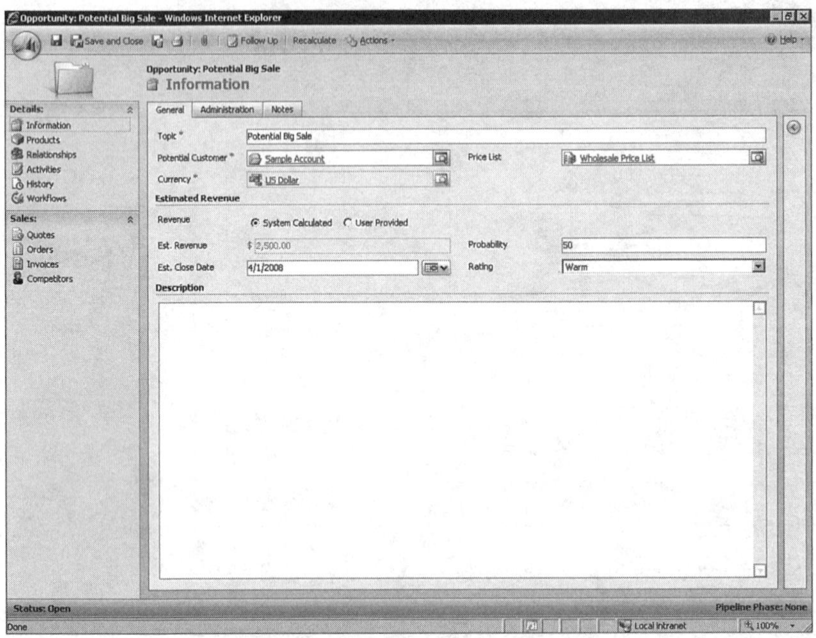

FIGURE 10.14 New Opportunity with the Estimated Revenue calculated.

Remember that, when working with Opportunities, you can add only products that are in your product catalog. Quotes, Orders, and Invoices (which associate to Opportunities) allow for write-in products and are covered in the Quotes section later in this chapter.

The handy Recalculate option enables you to easily recalculate the estimated revenue without having to save and close, and then reopen the form when adjusting pricing for products. A common use of this is when you are building an Opportunity and want to change the underlying Price List for it.

When working with Opportunities, you can add both Relationships and Competitors associated with the Opportunity. Chapter 8 explains relationships; Competitors are explained in the "Competitors" section later in this chapter.

Another important tool when working with Opportunities is the Pipeline Phase. This is found in the lower-right corner of the Opportunity (as shown in Figure 10.14). The Pipeline Phase was referred to as the Step Name in previous versions of CRM and uses the attribute `stepname` to show the current phase in the sales pipeline for the opportunity.

TIP

If you used the default sales process for Opportunities in CRM 3.0, you may ask why these labels have been changed. The answer is that in Microsoft Dynamics CRM 4.0, more than one workflow can perform updates to Opportunities. This is unlike previous versions that automatically displayed the current stage of the default sales process workflow job. Because more than one workflow can update this field, any update to it must be done programmatically within the workflow.

Finally, for users of previous versions of CRM, the Sales Stage has been renamed Process Code. (If you performed a new installation instead of an upgrade, you may not see this option, as it was retained for backward-compatibility only.) While the Process Code continues to function as a tool that can represent the current state of a manual sales process for an opportunity, Microsoft has recommended using workflow instead.

NOTE

Because previous versions of CRM only had stages for opportunity sales processes, it is important to understand the distinction between the stages and workflow steps.

Stages are collections of steps that must be labeled with a descriptive label (shown as the current status when viewing the workflow). Steps are the workflow items that operate within predefined stages. Both can be used extensively when working with the Opportunity entity to manage sales processes.

Refer to Chapter 20, "Workflow Development," for more information about working with workflows.

Closing Opportunities

Before you close an Opportunity, you can associate Quotes, Orders, and Invoices with it. When the Opportunity has been realized (by either winning or losing the business), you must close it. Closing Opportunities helps you effectively manage forecasted sales.

To close an Opportunity, select Close Opportunity from the Actions drop-down list. When closing an Opportunity, you are prompted for information about why you are doing so (see Figure 10.15).

When an Opportunity is closed, it is either Won or Lost. Selecting the status as Won when closing an Opportunity indicates that the revenue associated with the Opportunity has been realized and that the business has been closed (or will be on the date indicated). When you select Lost, you indicate that the Opportunity is no longer viable; either it has been lost to a Competitor or the customer is no longer interested.

TIP

You cannot close an Opportunity (as either Won or Lost) if active or draft Quotes are associated with it. To close the Opportunity, you must first close the active or draft Quotes.

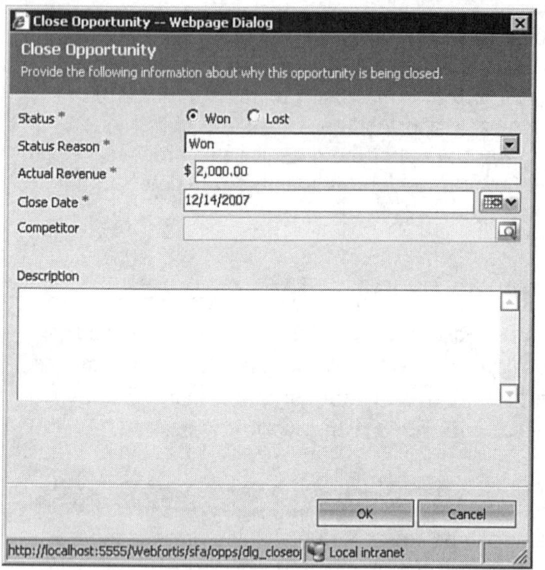

FIGURE 10.15 Close Opportunity dialog box.

After you close the Opportunity, it can no longer have new Quotes, Orders, and Invoices associated with it unless it is reopened. You can easily reopen an Opportunity by selecting Reopen Opportunity from the Actions drop-down list (see Figure 10.16).

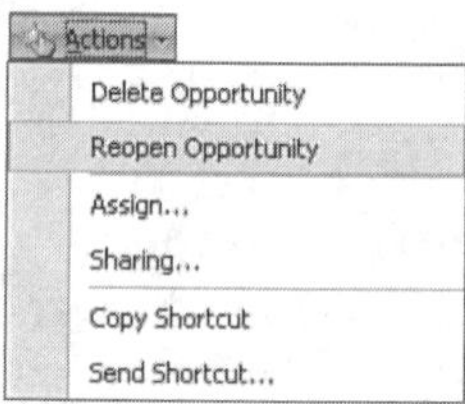

FIGURE 10.16 Reopen Opportunity option.

TIP

Closing an Opportunity does not affect the Probability Rating of the Opportunity. Depending on your situation, this might be fine, but you might end up closing Opportunities with a 0 Probability Rating as Won. Based on your business needs, you might want to consider adding a custom workflow that updates the Probability Rating to 0 if you close the Opportunity as Lost, and 100 if you close the Opportunity as a Win.

If you reopen a closed Opportunity, all related sales processes for the Opportunity are cleared.

Competitors

Managing your Competitors is just as important as managing your Customers. The more you know about your competition, the better you'll be able to compete.

Microsoft Dynamics CRM can track Competitors associated with your Opportunities and Sales Literature, which provides rich information to your sales force when working with either of these records. Additionally, as previously explained in the "Opportunities" section in this chapter, closed Opportunities that are lost can be associated with Competitors. Doing so provides the underlying data for the default Competitor Win Loss report.

TIP

Although the functionality for working with Competitors exists within the Sales module of Microsoft Dynamics CRM, Competitors apply only to Opportunities and Sales Literature, not Leads. If you're were interested in tracking Competitors against your Leads, you must extend the functionality of Microsoft Dynamics CRM by adding a relationship for Leads and Competitors.

The Competitor record is considered a high-level overview of the Competitor's company, related analysis, and associated products (see Figure 10.17).

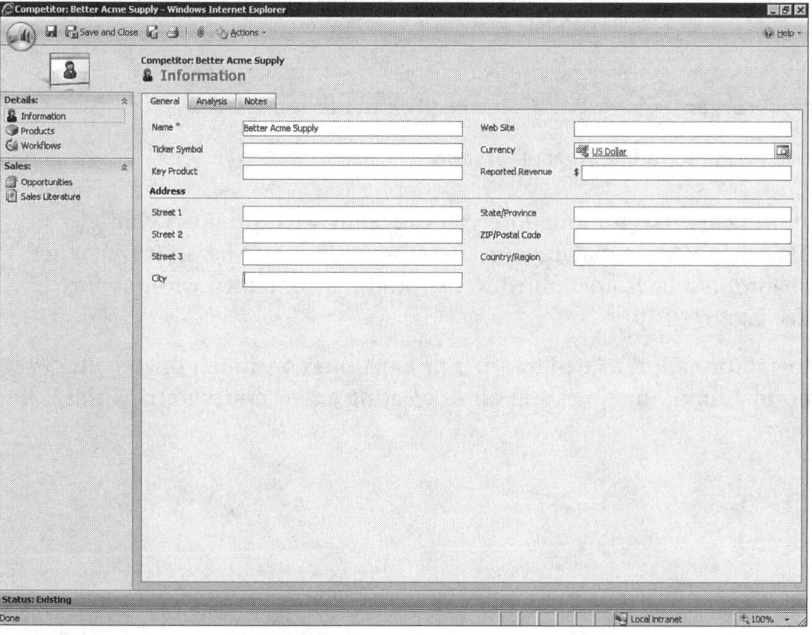

FIGURE 10.17 Competitor form.

When working with Competitor records, you can easily add key information about the Competitor on the General tab (see Figure 10.17) and include overview information as well as strengths, weaknesses, opportunities, and threats (SWOT) on the Analysis tab (see Figure 10.18).

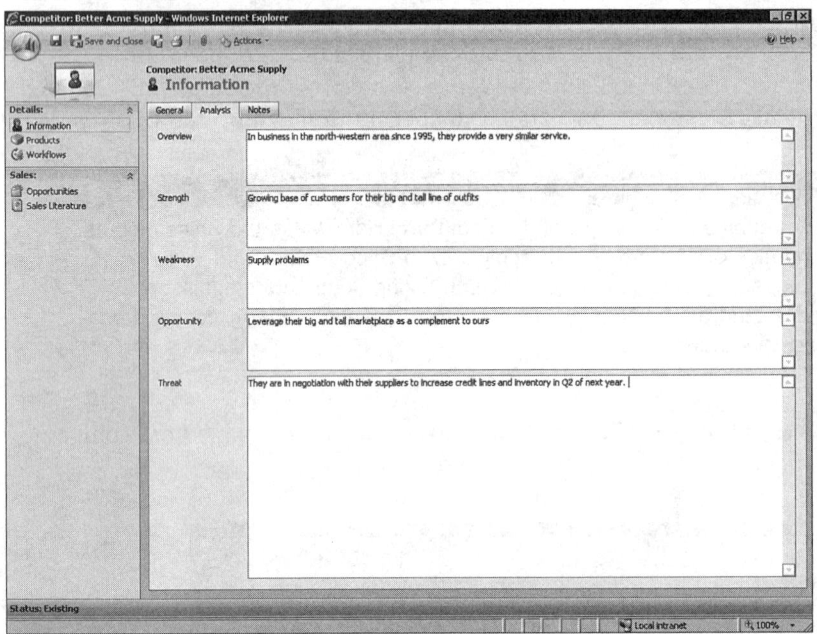

FIGURE 10.18 Analysis tab of the Competitor form.

In addition to capturing analysis information, you can show what products your Competitor is selling that directly match yours. Because of the way Microsoft Dynamics CRM works, Competitor Products are limited to the products contained within your product catalog (see Figure 10.19).

If you want to show information related to other product lines or similar ones, consider including that information in the notes section or creating a new entity to track this information.

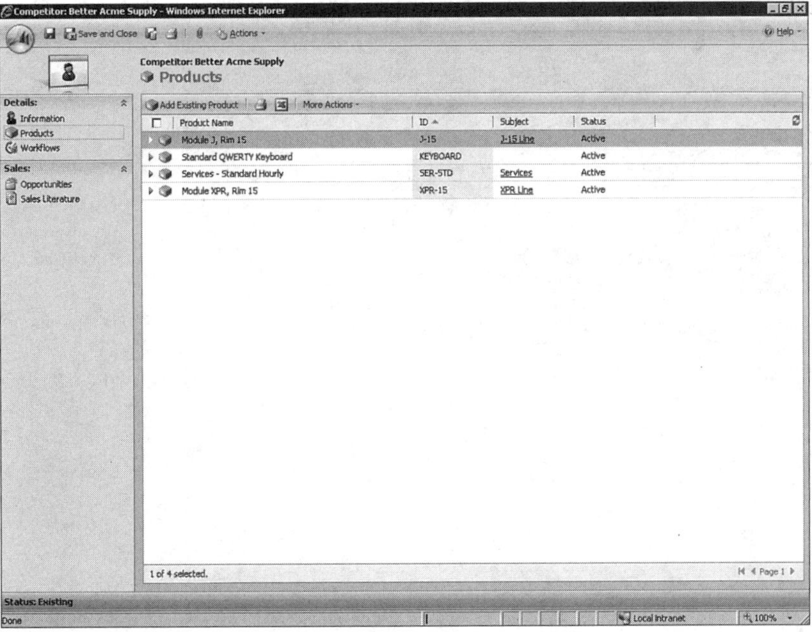

FIGURE 10.19 Competitor Products.

Products

Products in the Sales area are unique, in that, unlike the Products option that is available in the Settings, Product Catalog area, this area does not allow you to create or add new products. (Although you can edit existing products provided you have the necessary permissions.) Although it has this limitation, salespeople can still fully browse the products contained within the Product Lists. Products are, therefore, protected from salespeople attempting to add products on their Product Lists—unless, of course, they have permissions to edit the Product List directly (by going to Settings).

In Figure 10.20, notice that the Product List appears the same as the Product List in the Settings area, but there is no capability to add or delete.

See Chapter 14 for more information about working with Products.

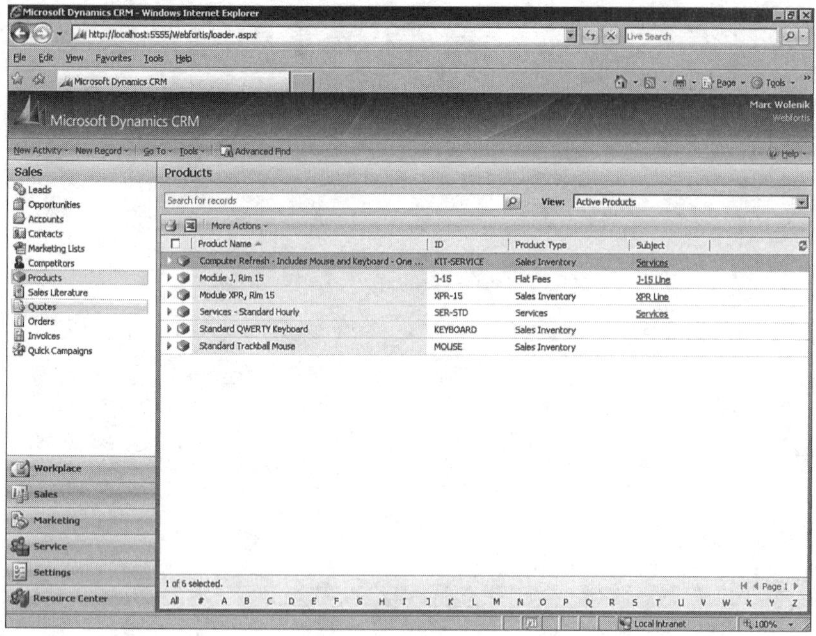

FIGURE 10.20 Product List from the Sales area.

Quotes, Orders, and Invoices

Microsoft Dynamics CRM includes functionality for working with Quotes, Orders, and Invoices. They are defined as follows:

- **Quote**—A proposed offer for products or services for an existing customer. The Quote can include specific payment, a discount, and delivery terms.
- **Order**—An accepted Quote.
- **Invoice**—A billed Order.

Additional features apply to these entities:

- Multiple pricing lists/models
- Line item discounting based on volume, customer type, or manual overrides
- Quote-level discounting

TIP

It is important to understand how Quote, Orders, and Invoices work with Microsoft Dynamics products, particularly product inventory. Although Microsoft Dynamics CRM has the functionality to create Orders, Quotes, and Invoices, it is not designed to be a stock-control application. If you want to affect inventory levels (quantity on hand, for instance), you must do this either with custom workflows or by integrating an accounting/ERP system. That system should also be used to handle additional calculations such as sales tax and value added tax (VAT).

See Chapter 27, "Other Microsoft Dynamics Products," for a list of other Dynamics products that can be integrated and used to manage this information.

Quotes

As the name implies, a Quote in Microsoft Dynamics CRM is an offer to sell your products or services for a certain price. When working with a Quote from an associated Opportunity, you can generate the Quote using some, all, or none of the product items on the Opportunity. This provides the flexibility to create Quotes based on a number of criteria, such as mixed product-delivery dates, other optional products (referred to as write-in products), and discounts.

Several common scenarios and status arise when working with Quotes and existing Opportunities. A common example is an Opportunity that might be realized within the next 3 months for $25,000. During this time period, you might prepare a Quote and submit it to the customer for review. The customer might decide to move forward with the Quote and agree to the sale. You would complete the sales process and close the Opportunity as Won. Another scenario might be a 12-month Opportunity with multiple sales activities associated with it—in this example, it could be product sales every 30 days. Instead of creating 12 Opportunities, you could create 1 Opportunity for the total amount and then create 12 associated Quotes (and Orders and Invoices). This is a little tricky from a forecasting perspective, however, because your realized/earned dollars will be represented on the Invoices, and your estimated revenue will be consistent with a single close date.

Quotes do not need to have an associated Opportunity to them; however, there are some advantages to working with them when there is an Opportunity.

- Quotes can easily get product information from the Opportunity.
- When a Quote is spawned from an Opportunity directly (by selecting Quote from the Opportunity record rather than selecting Quote from the Sales area), the Quote information is autopopulated with the underlying customer information.
- Although it might not apply to your organization, business rules can be enforced if you require Quotes to have an active/open Opportunity.

As with Orders and Invoices, you can create a Quote by selecting Quotes from the Sales area and selecting New (see Figure 10.21).

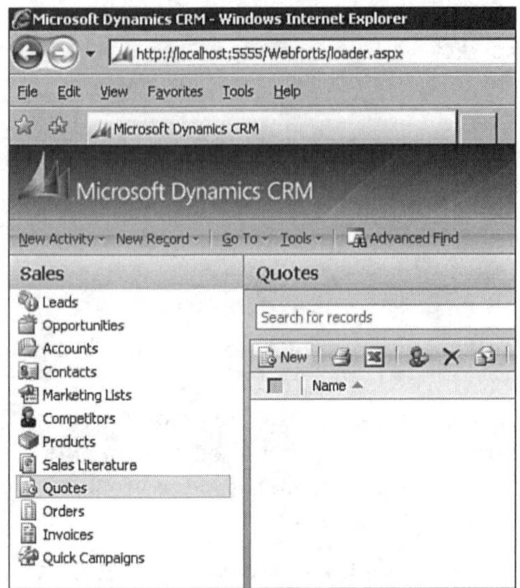

FIGURE 10.21 New Quote option.

When working with Quotes, it is important to understand their status options:

- Draft
- Active
- Won
- Closed

Figure 10.22 illustrates how a Quote correlates to an existing customer and Products/Price Lists (required), and Opportunities (optional), and also shows the status options.

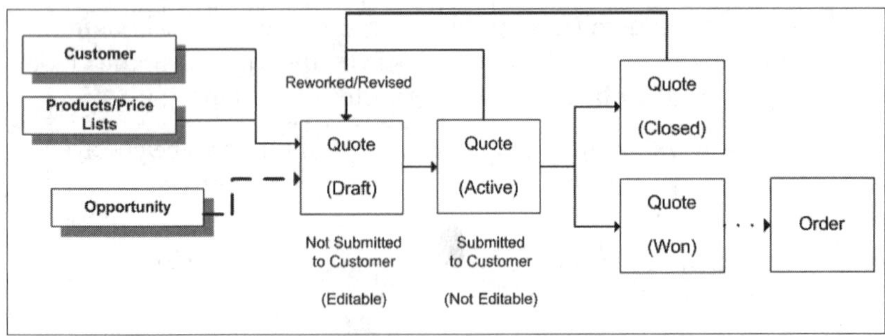

FIGURE 10.22 Quote lifecycle.

A Quote likely will be revised many times, and Microsoft Dynamics CRM has built-in functionality via the Draft and Active status for this.

Draft Status

When a Quote is in Draft status, it has been created but generally not ready to be submitted to customers. This is the only time Quotes can be completely modified with products added or removed, and discounts applied as well as deleted (see Figure 10.23).

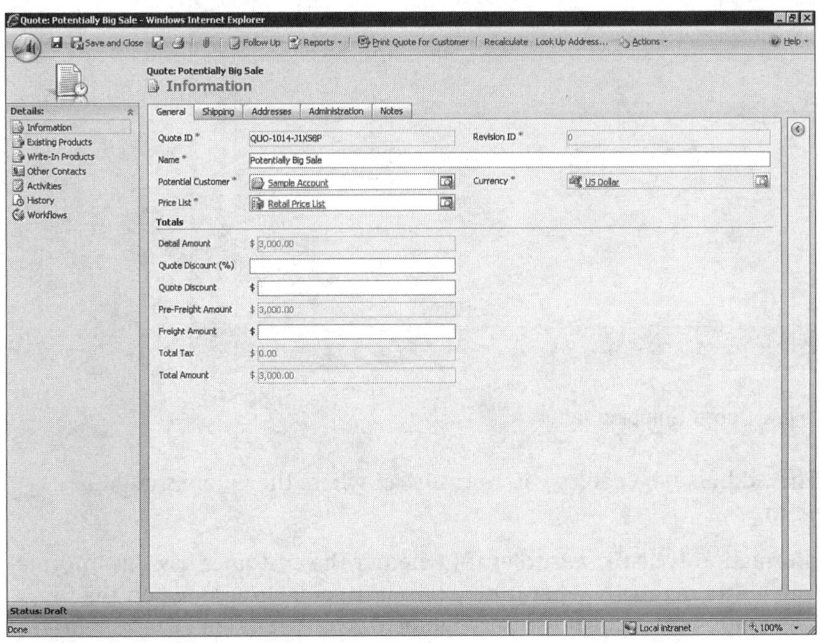

FIGURE 10.23 New Quote in Draft status.

General Tab After the Quote is created, it automatically sets the Quote ID using the auto-numbering set up by the system administrator. You can change this by configuring Auto-Numbering in the Settings area (refer to Chapter 14 for more information about working with this option). The Revision ID is automatically established and set as 0 when first created. If the Quote is revised, it will go from Active to Draft status and the Revision ID will automatically increase. You can modify the name of the Quote, but it is the same as the Opportunity that spawned it and blank if it is not associated with an Opportunity. The potential customer, Currency, and Price List must be selected and are also the same as the Opportunity that spawned it; with the exception of Currency (which defaults to the base Currency), these are blank if there is no associated Opportunity.

Shipping Tab The Shipping tab has effective dates that you can select to set for how long the Quote is valid for and to set delivery and due dates. Additionally, you can select the shipping method, payment, and freight terms (see Figure 10.24).

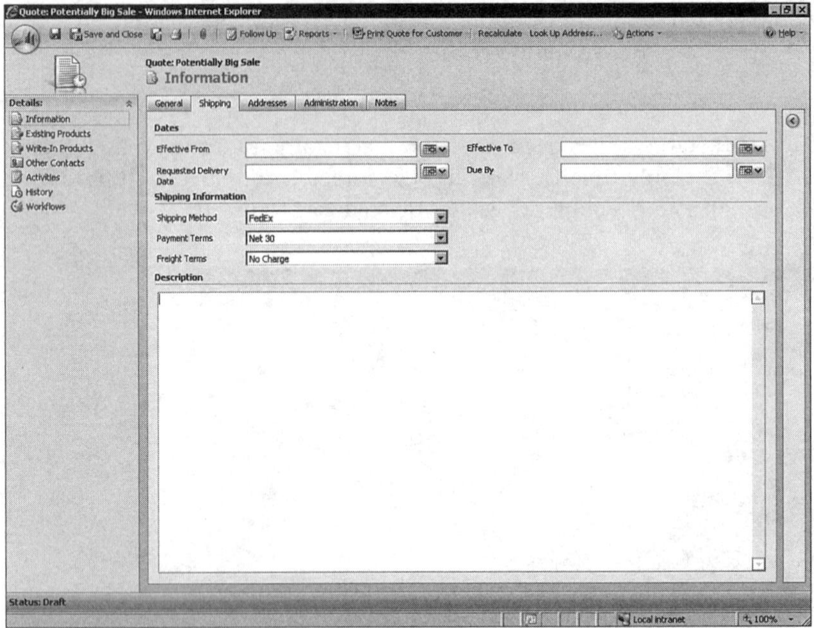

FIGURE 10.24 New Quote Shipping tab.

Addresses Tab The Address tab enables you to easily set where the Quote should be billed and shipped to.

By default, this information is blank, regardless of whether the customer has this information on file. You can either manually enter it here or select Look Up Address on the top menu bar or on the Actions drop-down list (see Figure 10.25).

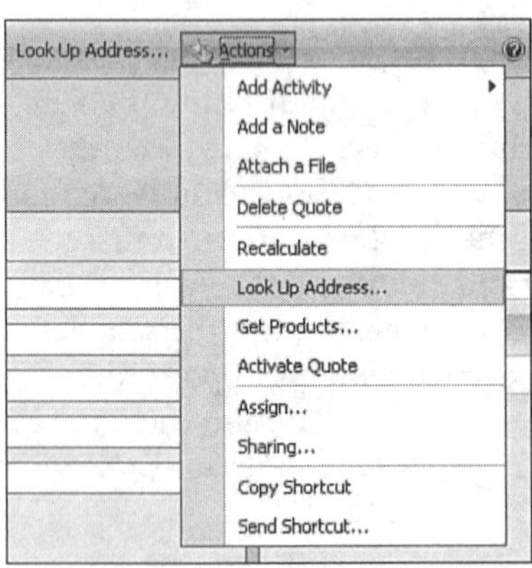

FIGURE 10.25 Look Up Address options.

If you select Look Up Address, the dialog box shown in Figure 10.26 appears.

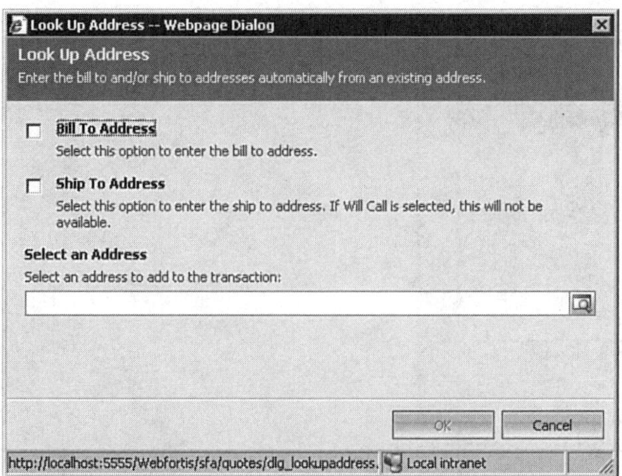

FIGURE 10.26 Look Up Address dialog box.

From this dialog box, you can select to autopopulate either the Bill To Address or the Ship To Address information with address information from customer records. When you select the lookup option, you can see the addresses that you have on file, listed by Address Name (see Figure 10.27).

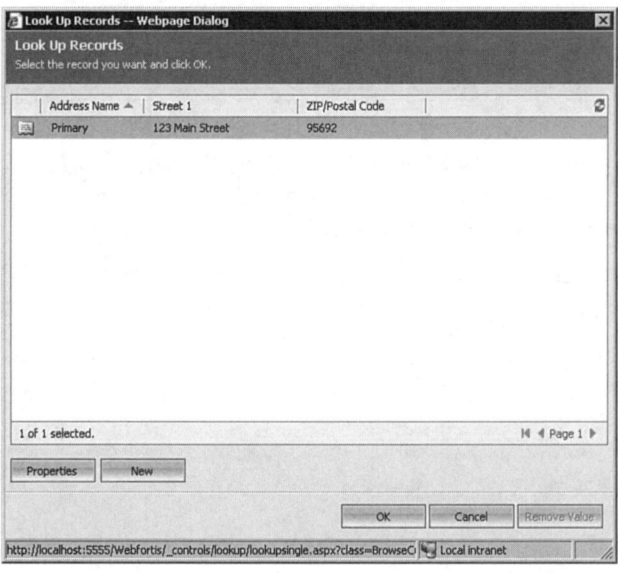

FIGURE 10.27 Look Up Records dialog box, select addresses.

This example has only one address on file for the customer, but we select it as the address for both the Bill To and Ship To addresses (see Figure 10.28).

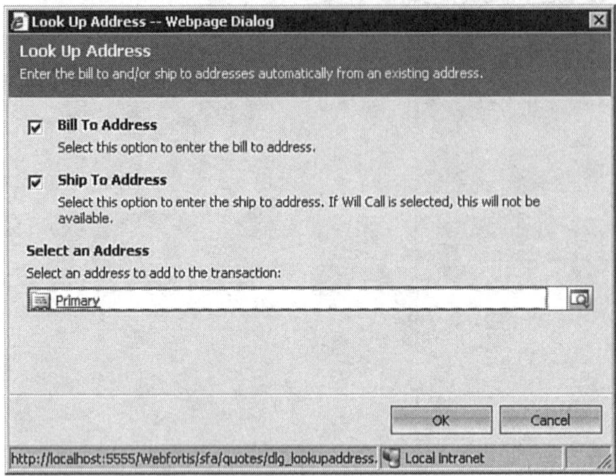

FIGURE 10.28 Look Up Address dialog box selected.

After you select this, click OK, The address information then is populated on the Addresses tab.

TIP

The Look Up Address option overwrites *any* existing address information entered. If you want to edit or add information related to the addresses, be sure to perform the lookup first and then edit it.

If the Quote will be picked up, you can select Will Call to lock and disable the Ship To Address information (see Figure 10.29). Additionally, if you select Will Call and then select Look Up Address, you cannot select a Ship To Address.

Administration Tab The Administration tab includes ownership information, the status reason, and the underlying Opportunity and Source Campaign, if applicable (see Figure 10.30).

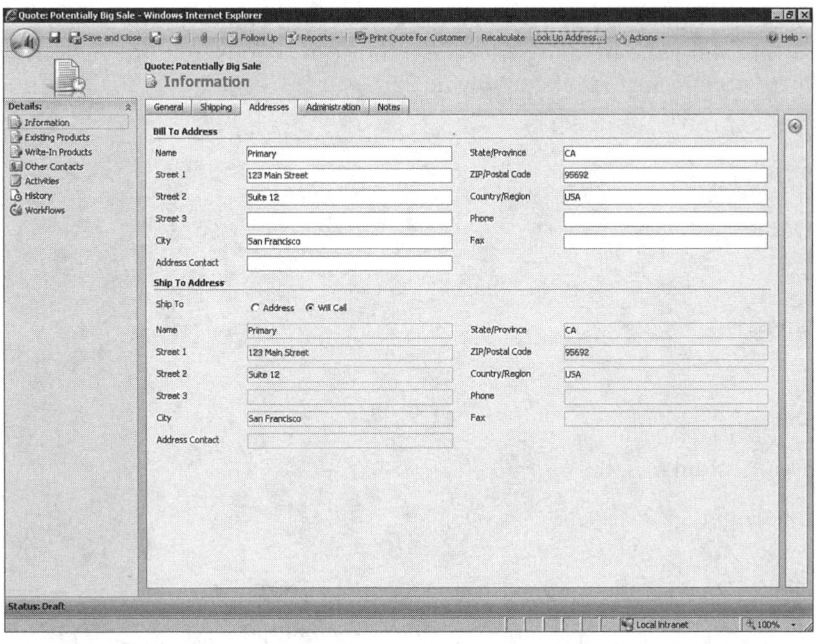

FIGURE 10.29 Completed address information with Ship To selected as Will Call.

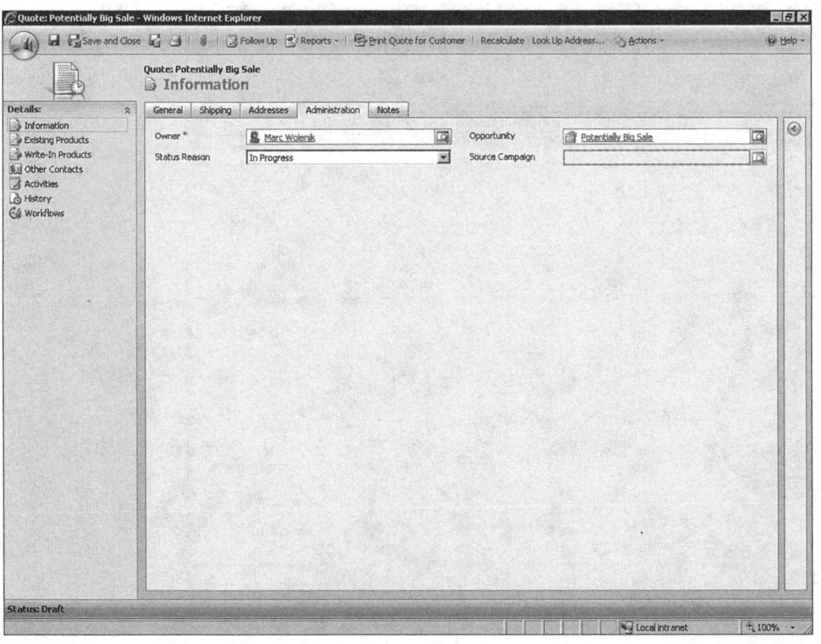

FIGURE 10.30 Administration tab.

When in Draft status, the Quote has a large amount of flexibility. Options exist to add products (both existing and write-in) and perform a number of actions from the Actions drop-down list. These options include the following:

- Add Existing Products
- Add Write-In Products
- Delete the Quote
- Recalculate
- Look Up Address
- Get Products
- Activate Quote
- Print Quote for Customer
- Run the Quote Report

Add Existing Products You can add products to the Quote in several ways:

- If the Quote is spawned from an Opportunity, the products are automatically listed on the Existing Products tab (see Figure 10.31).

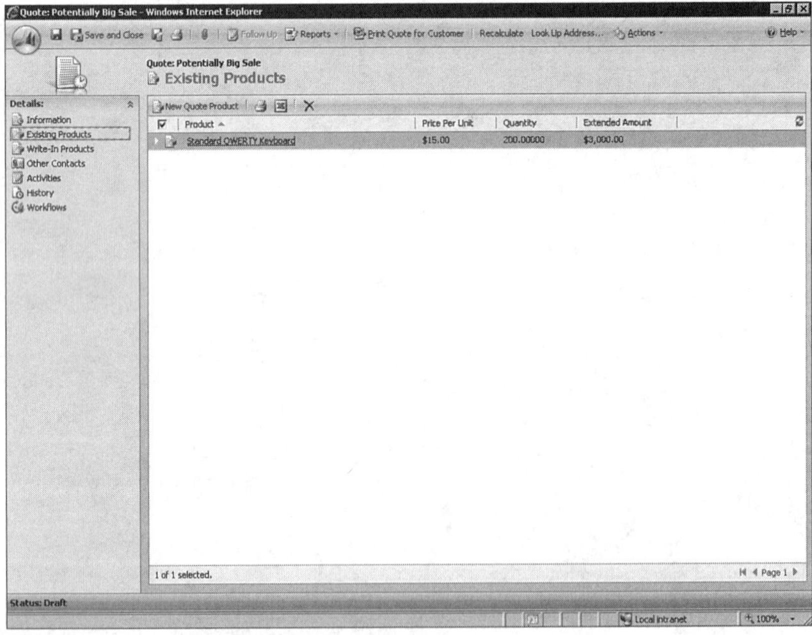

FIGURE 10.31 Products added automatically to a Quote.

- You can add an existing product to the Quote, regardless of whether the product is on the underlying Opportunity, by selecting New Quote Product from the Existing Products tab (see Figure 10.32).

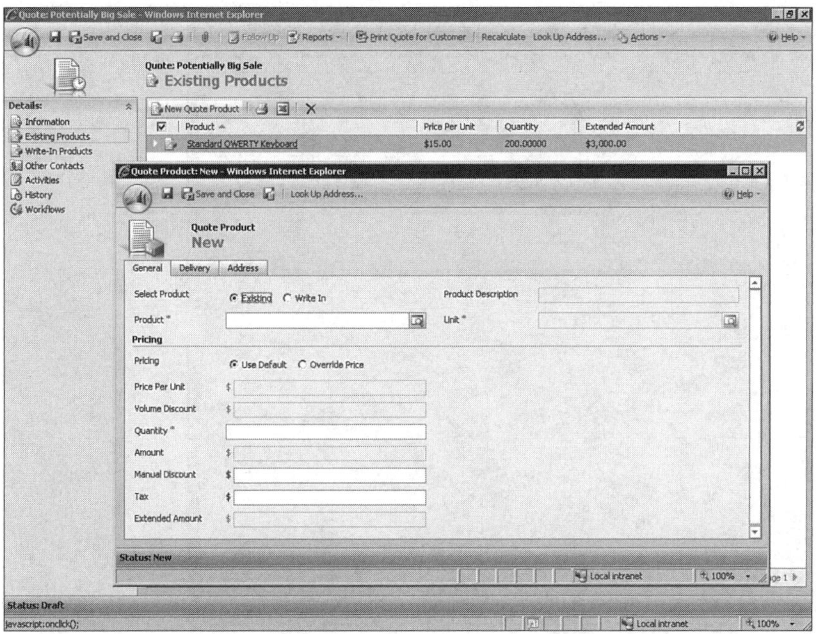

FIGURE 10.32 Products added by selecting New Quote Product.

- Select Get Products from the Actions drop-down list (see Figure 10.33). This option automatically adds the product list from any existing Opportunity.

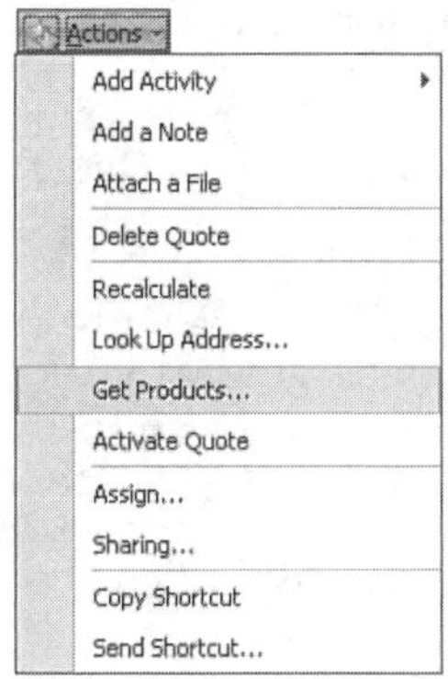

FIGURE 10.33 Products added by selecting Get Products.

Add Write-In Products If your product catalog doesn't have the product, you can manually create it on-the-fly by selecting Write-In Products and then New Quote Product. The Quote Product screen opens and defaults to Write In (see Figure 10.34).

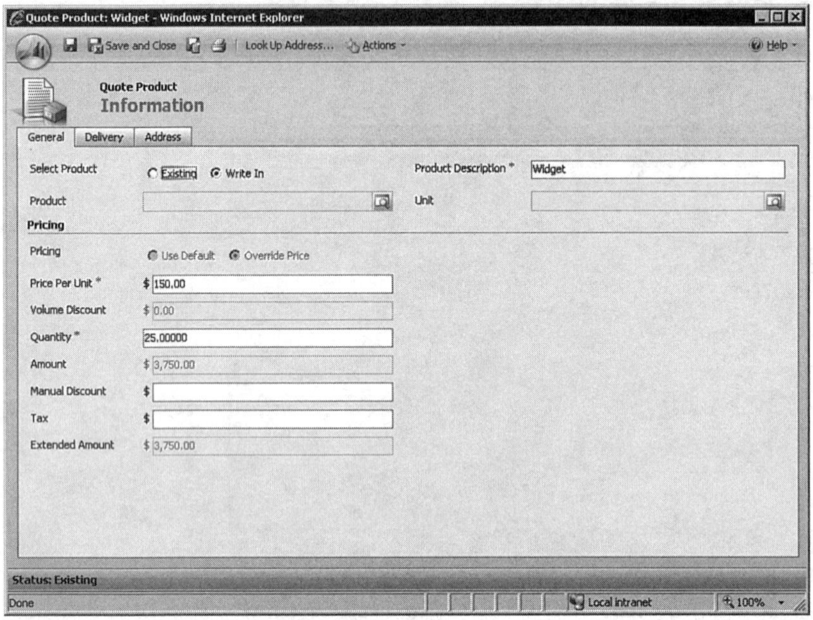

FIGURE 10.34 Quote Product screen.

From this screen, you can add virtually anything, completing the necessary fields. When you select Save or Save and Close, the entered product appears on the Write-In Products screen (see Figure 10.35).

The Quote reflects the new total, including this information. (You might need to select Recalculate to adjust the totals after you modify the products.)

Delete the Quote The Quote can be deleted only when in Draft status. To delete a Quote, select Delete from the Actions drop-down list or from the top menu bar.

Recalculate As explained previously, the Recalculate option enables you to update the Totals and other amounts on the Quote when you modify the Quote (see Figure 10.36). This is helpful because, without this functionality, you would have to save, close, and reopen the Quote in order to have it recalculate.

Look Up Address The Look Up Address functionality was explained previously when working with the Addresses tab of the Quote.

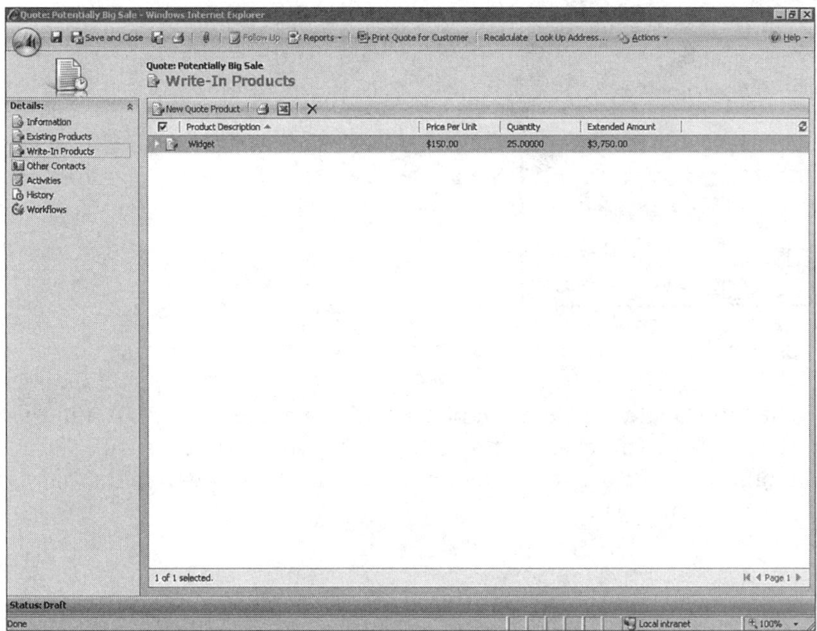

FIGURE 10.35 Write-In Products tab.

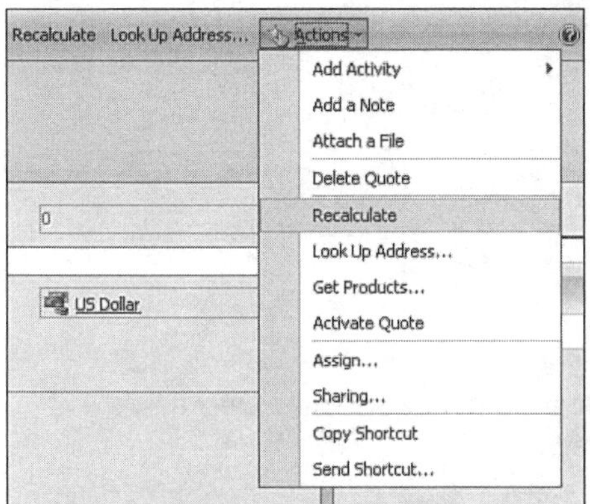

FIGURE 10.36 Recalculate option.

Get Products Get Products enables you to add products from existing Opportunities (see Figure 10.37).

Note that the Get Products option enables you to get the products on any existing Opportunity, as well as the existing Opportunity that might have spawned the Quote. Therefore, it is possible to duplicate the Product List on the Existing Products if you have already populated it.

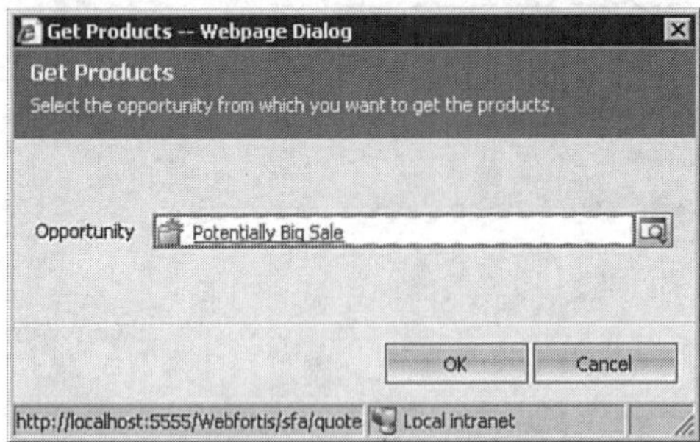

FIGURE 10.37 Get Products dialog box.

Activate Quote When the Quote has been completed and you are ready to send it to the customer, you must activate it. This changes the status of the Quote to Active and prevents further modifications. To activate a Quote, select Activate Quote from the Actions drop-down list (see Figure 10.38).

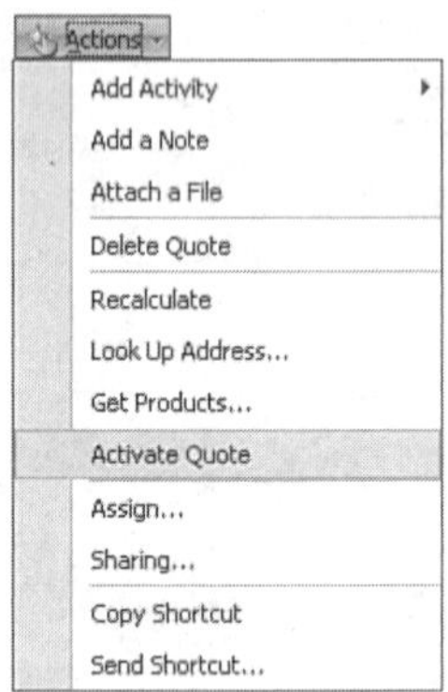

FIGURE 10.38 Activate Quote.

When the Quote is Active, it must be revised to be modified. Revising a Quote is explained further in the upcoming section "Active Status."

Print Quote for Customer You can print the Quote for the customer at any point in time by selecting the Print Quote for Customer option from the top menu bar (see Figure 10.39).

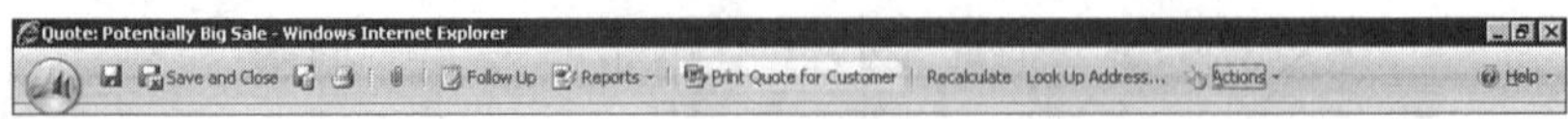

FIGURE 10.39 Print Quote for Customer.

When this option is selected, a mail merge is started that enables you to merge data fields from the Quote into a Microsoft Word document (see Figure 10.40).

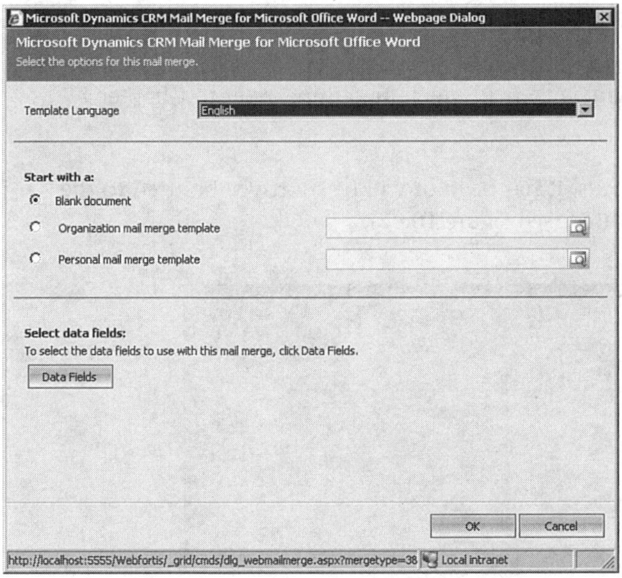

Microsoft Dynamics CRM Mail Merge for Microsoft Office Word -- Webpage Dialog
Microsoft Dynamics CRM Mail Merge for Microsoft Office Word
Select the options for this mail merge.
Template Language English
Start with a:
Blank document
Organization mail merge template
Personal mail merge template
Select data fields:
To select the data fields to use with this mail merge, click Data Fields.
Data Fields
OK Cancel

FIGURE 10.40 Print Quote for Customer—Mail Merge.

The mail merge enables you to select a template language and merge to either a blank document or an organizational or personal template, as well as select the data fields. By default, Microsoft Dynamics CRM comes with an organizational template for Quotes called Quote for Customer (see Figure 10.41).

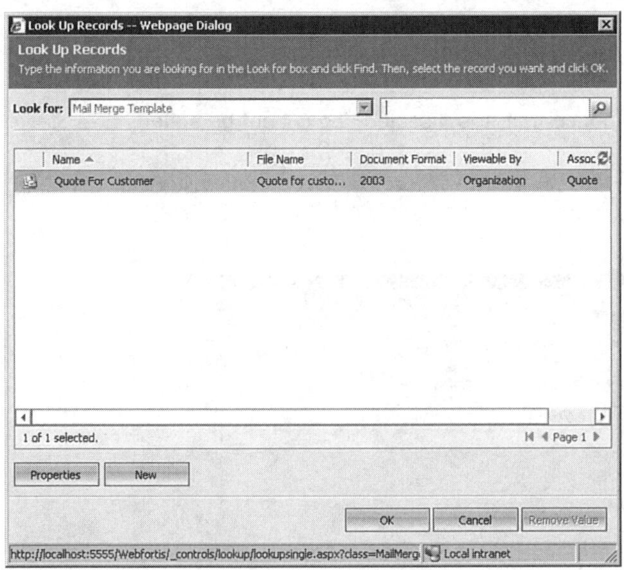

FIGURE 10.41 Mail Merge Template for Quotes.

If you select this option, be sure you have customized it for your organizational layout requirements.

For more information about working with mail merge functions, refer to Chapter 7.

Active Status

When a Quote moves to Active status, it has been or will be shortly submitted to the customer and therefore can't be edited (see Figure 10.42).

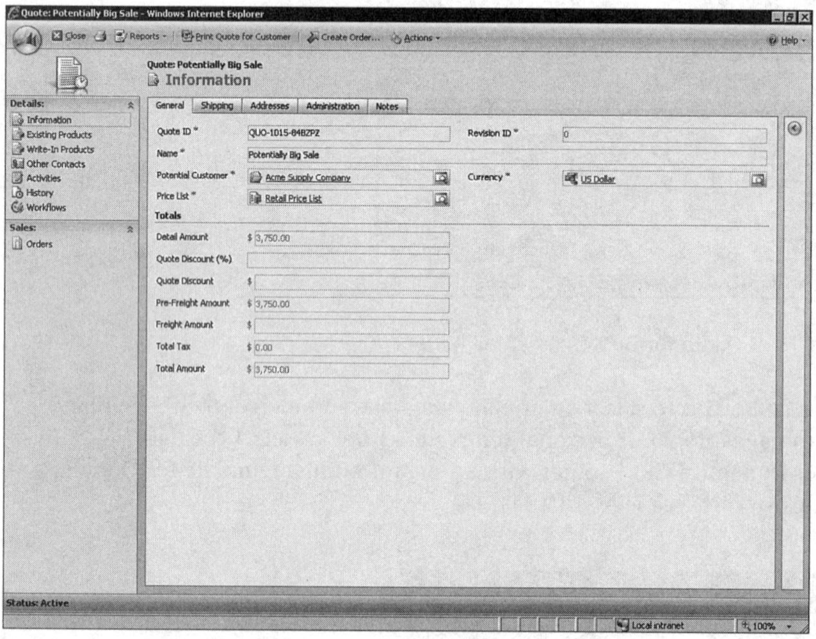

FIGURE 10.42 An Active Quote—notice that it is disabled and cannot be edited.

If modifications are necessary, you can revise the Quote by selecting Revise from the Actions drop-down list (see Figure 10.43).

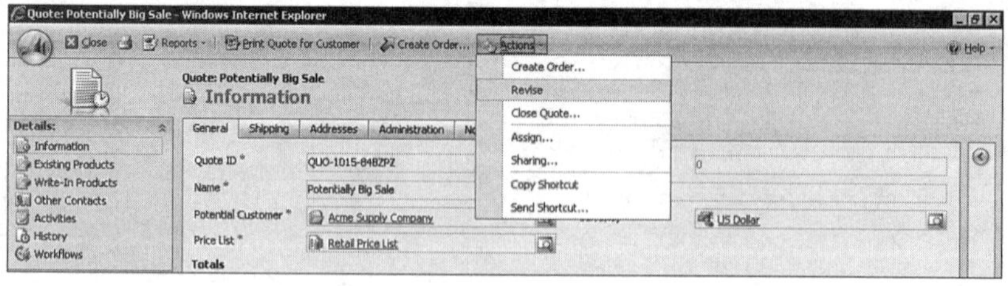

FIGURE 10.43 Revising a Quote.

Revising a Quote closes the existing Quote and opens a new Quote with a status of Draft, and assigns a new Revision ID. The Quote ID remains the same, however.

At this point, the Quote can be either revised, closed, or Won—converted to an Order. To convert a Quote to an Order, either select Create Order from the top menu or select Create Order from the Actions drop-down list (see Figure 10.44).

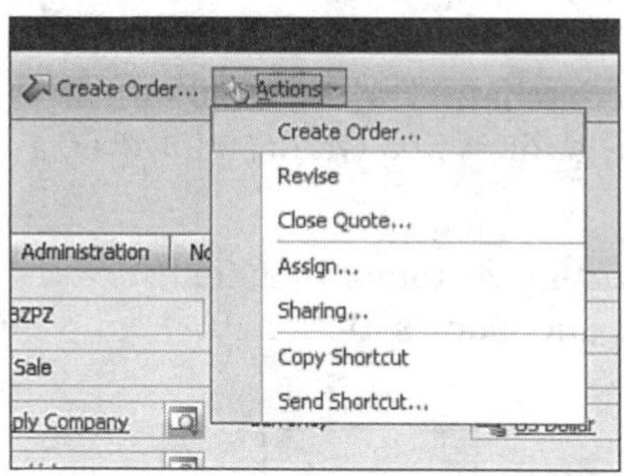

FIGURE 10.44 Converting a Quote to an Order.

Selecting Create Order opens the Create Order dialog form (see Figure 10.45).

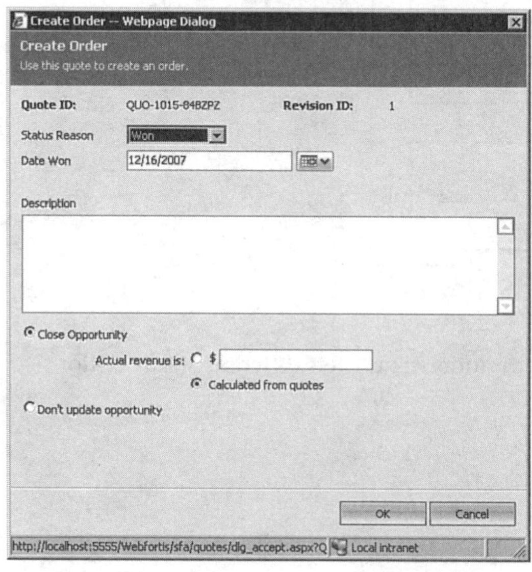

FIGURE 10.45 Converting a Quote to an Order—Updating the Status.

The dialog form enables you to select the date the Order was Won and to calculate the revenue or enter it manually; you also can close the related Opportunity. After you select OK, the status of the Quote changes to Won and the corresponding Order opens.

Won/Closed Status

A Quote that is in Won status generally has an Order associated with it, but you can select Create Order and create another Order, if necessary.

Quotes that are in Closed status can be revised and reactivated for approval or made active.

Orders

An Order is created when a customer is ready to make a purchase. The customer either has accepted the Quote or is ready to make a purchase regardless of a Quote. (However, a Quote is not required to create an Order.)

Figure 10.46 illustrates how an Order correlates to an existing customer (required), Products/Price Lists (required), Opportunities (optional), and Quotes (optional).

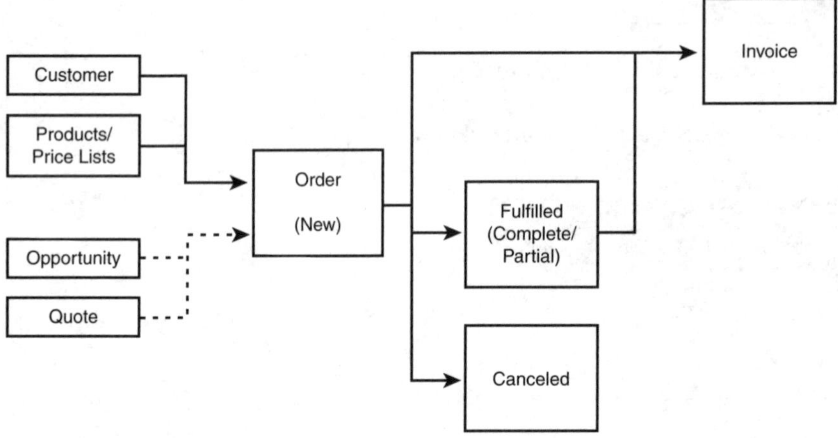

FIGURE 10.46 Order lifecycle.

When working with Orders, it is important to understand their different status options:

- Active
- Fulfilled
- Cancelled

An Active Order can be deleted, canceled, and edited (see Figure 10.47). Editing an Active Order includes updating products associated with the Order, as well as discount, shipping, and address information. The tab options for Shipping, Addresses, Administration, and notes are similar to those defined in Quotes.

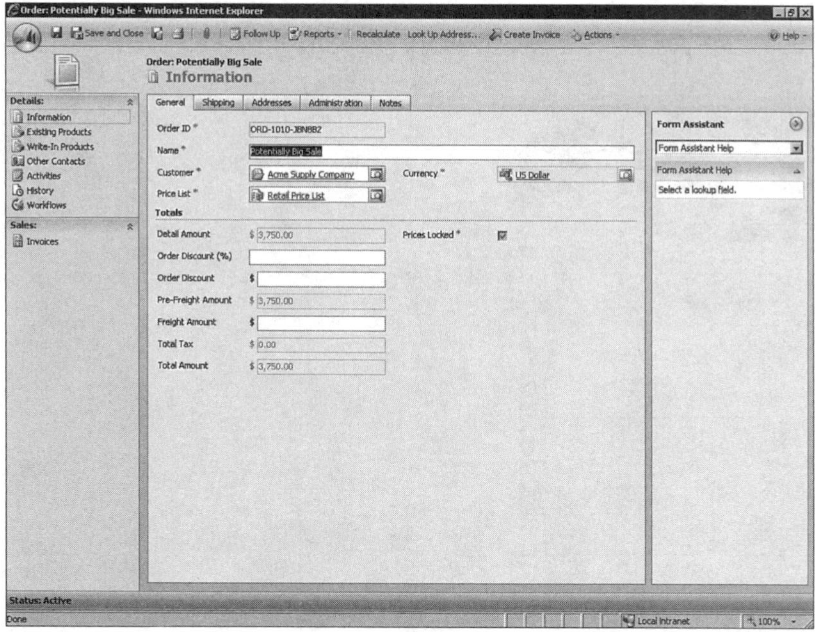

FIGURE 10.47 Active Order.

An Order that has been Fulfilled has had its products shipped or delivered. To fulfill an Order, select Fulfill Order from the Actions drop-down (see Figure 10.48).

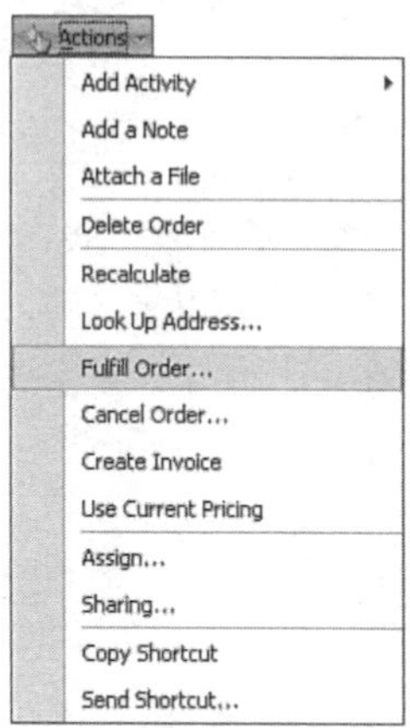

FIGURE 10.48 Fulfill Order option.

The Fulfill Order dialog box then opens (see Figure 10.49).

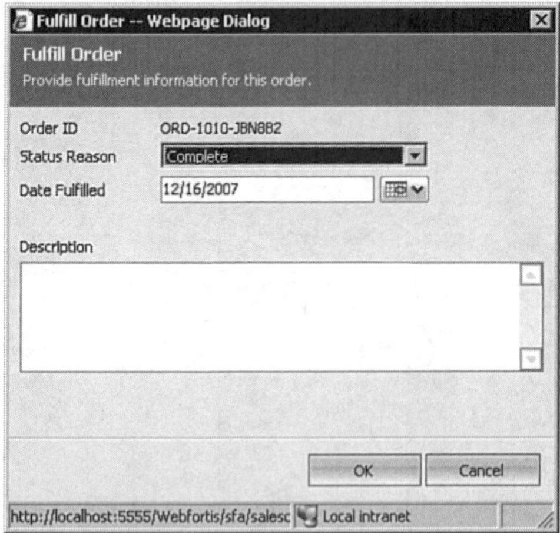

FIGURE 10.49 Fulfill Order dialog box.

This dialog box enables you to indicate that the order has been shipped.

NOTE

When selecting how to fulfill the Order, you should know that you can't edit the Order after you select any option. This includes selecting Partial Fulfillment.

You can select whether the Order should use current pricing or whether to lock the pricing. This is a helpful option when there are price fluctuations and the Order might remain unfulfilled for a period of time. By default, the prices are locked, but you can change that by selecting Use Current Pricing from the Actions drop-down list (see Figure 10.50).

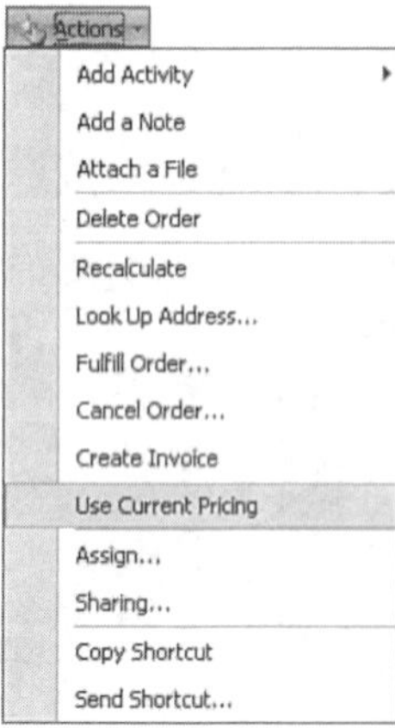

FIGURE 10.50 Fulfill Order dialog box.

Finally, you can create an Invoice from an Order by selecting Create Invoice from the top menu bar or from the Actions drop-down list (see Figure 10.51). When you create an Invoice from an Order, the Order remains in Active status until it is fulfilled.

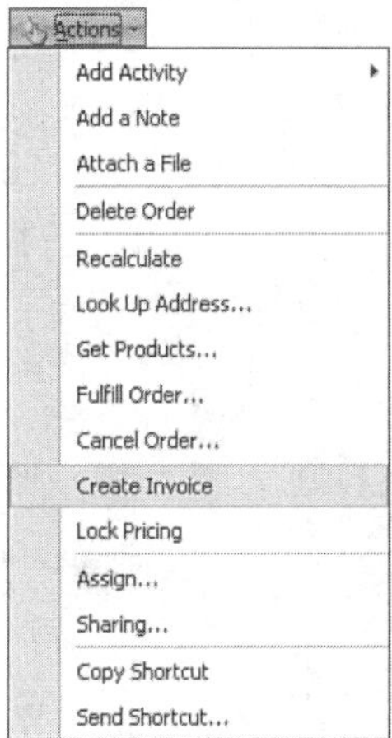

FIGURE 10.51 Create Invoice.

Invoices

When the terms of the sale have been completed, the sale is recorded using an Invoice.

When working with Invoices, it is important to understand their different status options:

- Active
- Closed

Figure 10.52 illustrates how an Invoice correlates to an existing customer (required), Products/Price Lists (required), Opportunities (optional), and Quotes (optional).

An Invoice is very similar to an Order, in that you can perform the following actions:

- You can add new products from your product catalog.
- You cannot add new write-in products.
- You can perform various functions on the Invoice, including selecting whether to use current or locked pricing and recalculate accordingly.

Figure 10.53 illustrates an active Invoice. The tab options for Shipping, Addresses, Administration, and Notes are similar to those defined in Quotes.

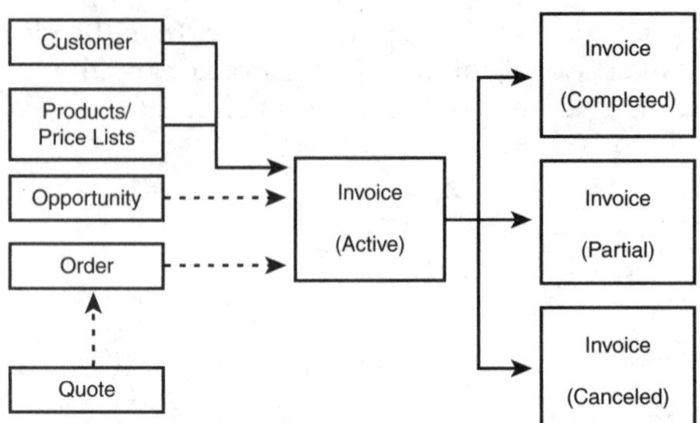

FIGURE 10.52 Invoice lifecycle.

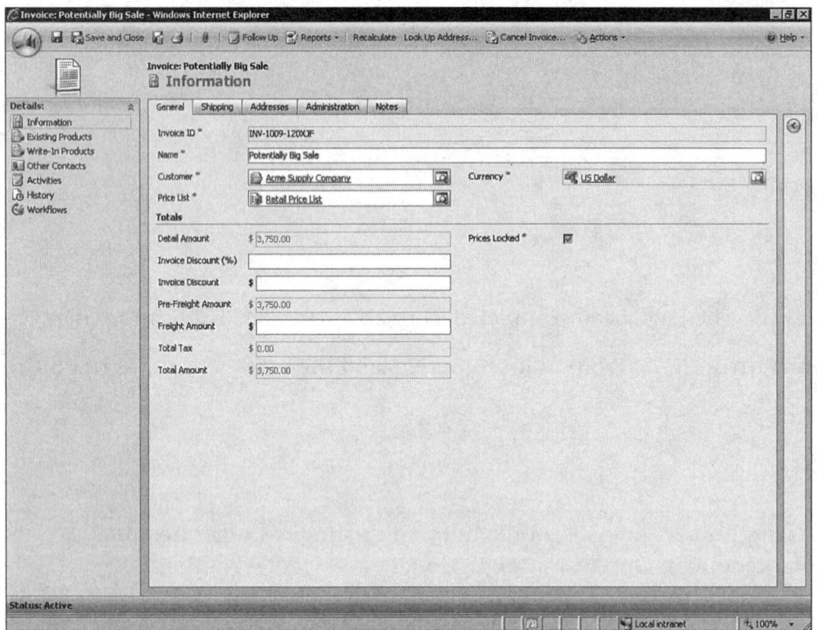

FIGURE 10.53 An Active Invoice.

As with Orders fulfillment, if you mark an Invoice as Paid, you have the option to select Partial or Complete (see Figure 10.54).

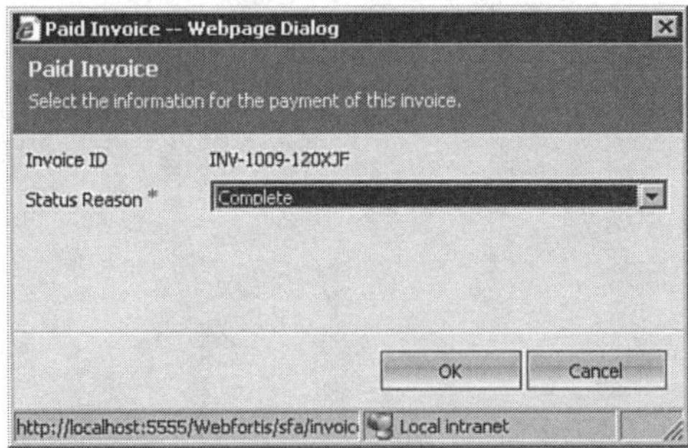

FIGURE 10.54 Marking an Invoice as Paid.

Regardless of your selection, after you mark an invoice as Paid or Partial, you cannot edit it.

Extending Functionality

When working with a back-end accounting or ERP system, you might often create and manage Orders in Microsoft Dynamics CRM and have them posted (when approved) in the back-end/ERP system. Doing so can enforce more complex business rules (such as VAT calculations), and the back-end/ERP posting process should be responsible for creating an Invoice record in Microsoft Dynamics CRM so that sales staff can see the process status without having to navigate to their ERP system.

Extending functionally of the Sales Quotes, Orders, and Invoices to specific back-end/ERP systems exceeds the scope of this book.

Summary

This chapter illustrated how to work with the Sales area of Microsoft Dynamics CRM. The most important aspects to remember in this chapter are that Leads are separated from your regular customer base and that you can convert them to Accounts, Contacts, or Opportunities using the included Sales Force Automation (SFA).

Additionally, this chapter explained how to manage and use Opportunities. Finally, we thoroughly examined Quotes, Orders, and Invoice functionality, and we reviewed their integration options with regard to back-end accounting systems. Because Microsoft Dynamics CRM is not designed to be a stock control, accounting, or invoicing system, we recommend reviewing Chapter 27 if you have one of these needs.

CHAPTER 11

Working with Marketing

IN THIS CHAPTER

- Marketing Lists
- Campaigns
- Sales Literature
- Quick Campaigns

A powerful feature that sets Microsoft Dynamics CRM ahead of its competitors is its capability to build, manage, track, and report on the effectiveness of marketing efforts. When thinking about marketing, consider how you currently market. Do you want to send the same sales literature to potential customers as you would to existing customers? Probably not. Therefore, when you're considering creating a marketing campaign (Microsoft Dynamics CRM refers to any kind of targeted marketing effort as a Campaign, with differences between a Quick Campaign and Campaign [explained later in this chapter]), consider your audience.

Typically, marketing efforts designed to appeal to existing customers include incentives to buy more, reestablish buying after a lapse, or appeal to customers to purchase from you in other ways. Marketing efforts designed around potential customers are usually very different, in that generally you want to appeal to them to start purchasing from you.

Thousands of books and companies specialize in how to market to potential and existing customers. We're by no means attempting to explain how best to market for your organization. Instead, we're explaining in depth the Marketing features Microsoft Dynamics CRM provides so that when you want to market your organization, products, or personnel, you will have a solid understanding of how Microsoft Dynamics CRM can do so.

This chapter reviews the items specific to marketing found on the Marketing tab, such as Marketing Lists, Campaigns, Sales Literature, and Quick Campaigns, as well as other areas within the application that touch on marketing.

For information about the other aspects of the Marketing tabs, such as Leads or Products, refer to Chapter 10, "Working with Sales." For information about Accounts and Contacts, refer to Chapter 8, "Working with Customers."

Marketing Lists

Marketing Lists are great tools for managing marketing efforts. You can use Marketing Lists to create a list of members that will receive the marketing material. The members can be comprised of either existing customers (Accounts or Contacts) or potential customers (Leads). There is no way to prepare a single Marketing List for both existing and potential customers, so if you need to do so, consider creating two or more Marketing Lists.

After they're created, you can directly market to Marketing Lists via a Mail Merge, a Quick Campaign, or a Campaign.

TIP

After you have created a Marketing List, you cannot change its base entity assignment (for example, from an Account Marketing List to a Leads Marketing List). You must create a new Marketing List if you need to use a different base entity.

To create a new Marketing List, navigate to the Marketing area, and then select Marketing Lists, New.

As shown in Figure 11.1, we've created a new Marketing List by completing the `Name` and `Member Type` fields of the Marketing List and saving the list. Note that the only Member Types allowed are Account, Contact, or Lead.

Other attributes on the Marketing List include the Source, which can be any free form value, the Currency and Cost, and whether new members can be added to the list by selecting whether the list is Locked. Additionally, notice in the lower-left corner the Status of the Marketing List. By default, new Marketing Lists are active, but you can easily deactivate them when necessary by selecting Deactivate from the More Actions drop-down menu.

TIP

Be sure not to lock the Marketing List by selecting the Locked radio option (as shown in Figure 11.1) before you've added the members to it. You will be unable to perform any additions or subtractions to the membership if it is locked. (Of course, you can always unlock a Marketing List if you need to by opening the Marketing List and changing the Locked option.)

To add members to the Marketing List, select Marketing List Members from the near navigation, and select Manage Members from the top quick-view menu (see Figure 11.2). As with many of the forms in Microsoft Dynamics CRM, the Marketing List must first be saved before members can be added.

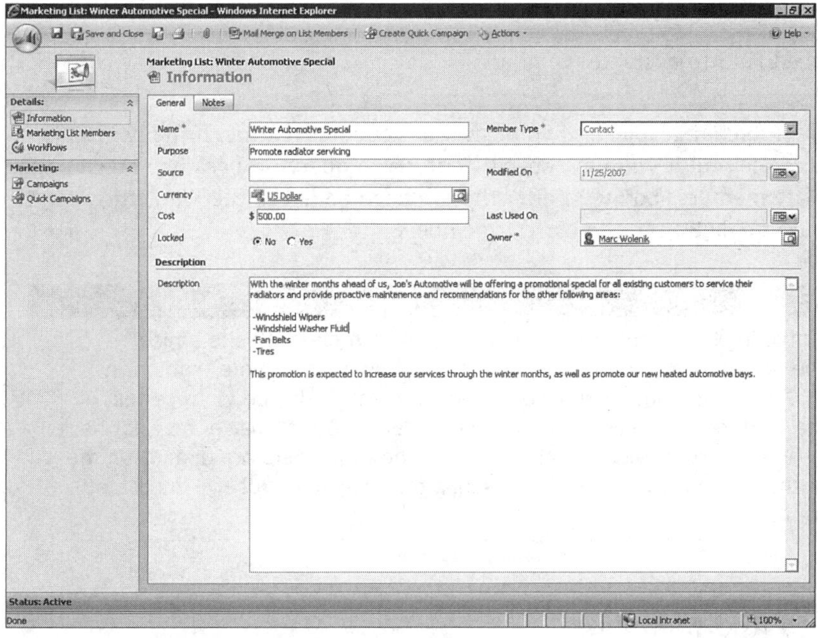

FIGURE 11.1 New Marketing List for existing customers (Contacts).

FIGURE 11.2 Manage Members display.

When adding members, you have four different options:

- Use Lookup to add members
- Use Advanced Find to add members

- Use Advanced Find to remove members
- Use Advanced Find to evaluate members

These options are interchangeable, and you can use them at any time, if the list has not been locked. This is helpful if you have specific criteria to query on because you can add, remove, or evaluate members before or after they've been added to the Marketing List, to ensure that you are marketing to the correct members.

NOTE

Members of Marketing Lists cannot be added to more than once. This is a nice feature because sometimes you need to use the previous options more than once. For example, you might use Advanced Find to find all members located in a certain geographic area, and then use Lookup to add more members that may or may not be in the geographic area you previously selected. If the new members are already on the Marketing List, they will appear only once, ensuring that they don't receive duplicated marketing material.

Use Lookup to Add Members

Using Lookup to add members displays the Look Up Records dialog box for the base entity of the Marketing List (in this case, Contacts) and enables you to search and add quickly and easily by selecting active records and adding them to the right-pane navigation (see Figure 11.3). Be sure to select the magnifying glass icon to see all available records.

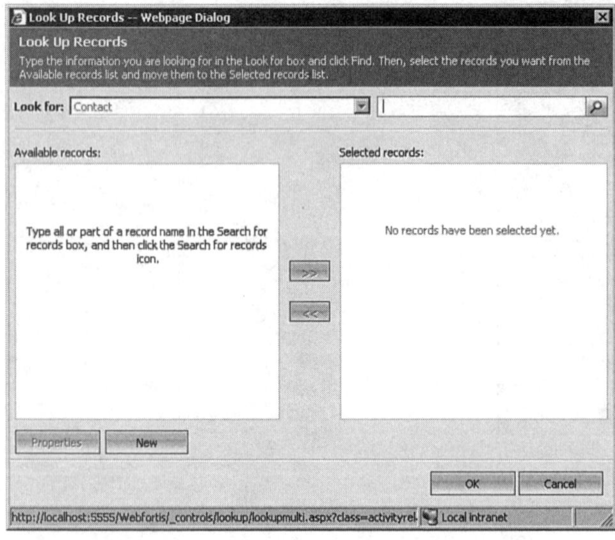

FIGURE 11.3 Look Up Records dialog box.

Use Advanced Find to Add Members

Using Advanced Find enables you to add complex criteria to ensure that you find only the specific members you want to market to.

In the following example, we've created a query using Advanced Find to add only active Contacts that have been created in the last 2 months and that we own (see Figure 11.4). It is important to note that Advanced Find will be blank until you create your query.

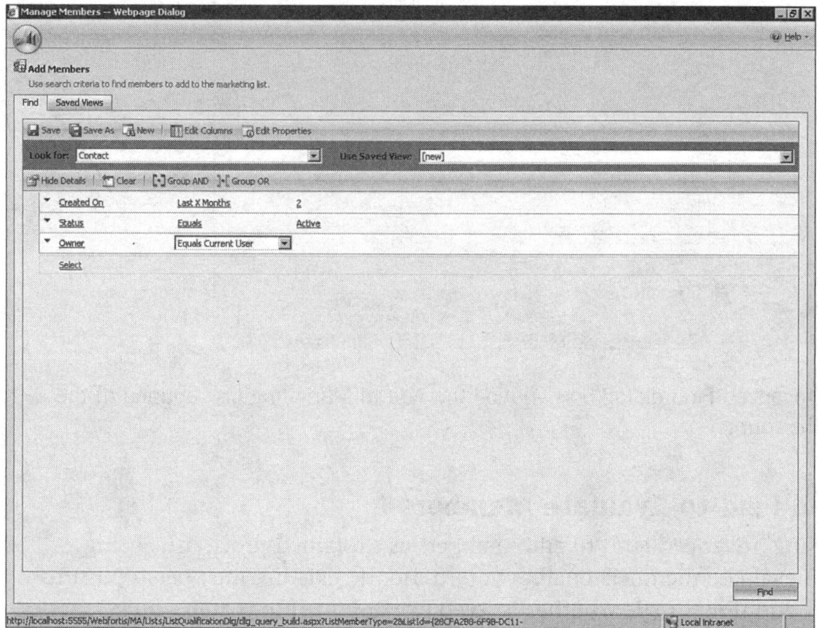

FIGURE 11.4 Advanced Find dialog box.

You can easily adjust this query to include Contacts that have not placed an order with you in *x* number of months, have *x* number of sales with you over the last *x* number of months, or any similar criteria using the Advanced Find features. Refer to Chapter 7, "Common Functions," for more information about working with Advanced Find.

After you've prepared your query, select the Find button to view members that match your query logic. You have the option to select individual members from the results (by selecting individual members using either the Ctrl or Shift keys), or to simply add all members returned by the search to the Marketing List by making the appropriate selection from the radio buttons on the lower-left side and selecting Add to Marketing List (see Figure 11.5).

Use Advanced Find to Remove Members

Similar to using Advanced Find to add members, you can use the Advanced Find to remove members. This method enables you to add complex query logic via Advanced Find and remove any members that match your entered criteria.

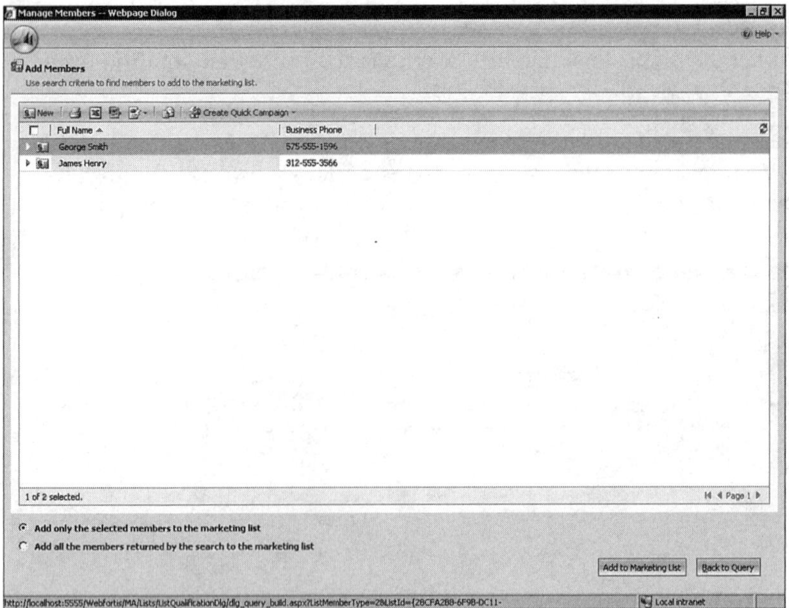

FIGURE 11.5 Advanced Find dialog box—notice the Add to Marketing List options at the lower-left side of the form.

Use Advanced Find to Evaluate Members

Also similar to using Advanced Find to add members as explained previously, using Advanced Find to evaluate members enables you to use the existing membership list to evaluate with any additional logic whether to keep existing members after you've applied the new logic.

When the Marketing List has the desired members to it, you can lock it to prevent any further modifications to the membership.

Other Marketing List Features

Once you have created Marketing Lists, you can perform several functions with them. You can use them interchangeably on multiple Campaigns or Quick Campaigns. You can merge them (provided the base entity of each is the same—for example, both lists are Accounts, Contacts, or Leads) by going to the More Actions drop-down menu and selecting Copy To. You can easily see where and which Campaigns or Quick Campaign have been used by opening any Marketing List and selecting Campaign or Quick Campaign from the near navigation.

Campaigns

Campaigns are structured events that enable you to create and manage targeted marketing efforts. Campaigns differ from Quick Campaigns in that Campaigns can work with multiple marketing lists (Quick Campaigns can only work with single marketing lists), can have complex activity distribution (Quick Campaigns can only have a single activity type), and can have complex planning and management information. However, both Campaigns and Quick Campaigns can receive campaign responses. The actual marketing effort can be virtually anything—a new product announcement, company exposure at a popular event, or even an effort to convert previous customers to buy products again.

Campaigns allow for the structured creation of Tasks related to planning the Campaign, Activities specific to the Campaign, and metrics related to the responses received from a Campaign.

In this section, you create a Campaign example that involves some simple Tasks and Activities to illustrate how a Campaign might work. Obviously, when creating a Campaign for your organization, you want to consider your specific needs related to Tasks and Activities, but using the examples provided can give you a solid foundation for working with Campaigns.

TIP

Campaigns in Microsoft Dynamics CRM are designed to define, create, task, and track Marketing efforts from beginning to end. They can have multiple Tasks and Activities associated with them, and they allow for a large amount of structure. Consider using a Quick Campaign (explained later) if your organization won't benefit from the structure Campaigns provide.

When working with new Campaigns, you have two options: a new Campaign or a new Campaign Template. A Campaign Template is used when you anticipate needing to use the Campaign and its related Tasks and Activities again.

When working with Campaigns and Campaign Templates, you can easily manage which one to work with by viewing the Template Status on the quickview (see Figure 11.6).

Campaign Templates differ from Campaigns in that they must be converted to Campaigns (from the Actions drop-down menu) to be used to record Campaign Responses against.

You can copy the Campaign Templates as a Campaign or as a Template from the Actions drop-down menu when opened (see Figure 11.7). The Campaign Template generally won't include any scheduling data because it a reusable template, and that information is generally populated only when an actual Campaign is planned.

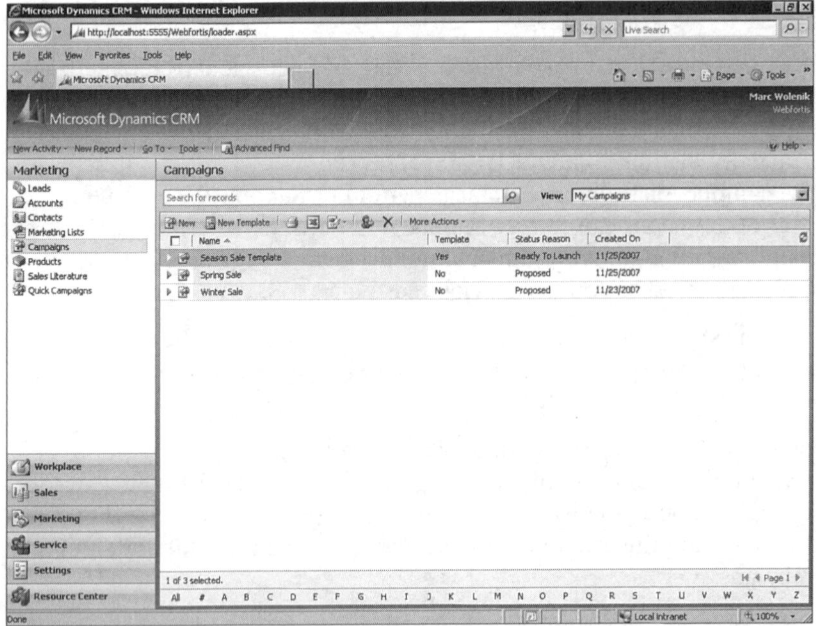

FIGURE 11.6 Campaigns quickview.

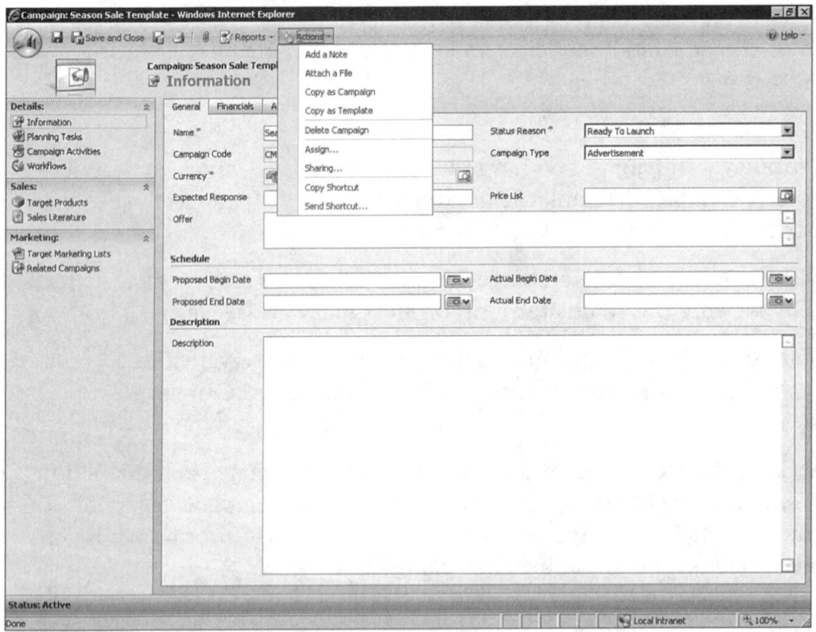

FIGURE 11.7 Campaign Template options.

To create a new Campaign, follow these steps:

1. Navigate to Campaigns in the Marketing area and select New. For this example, you'll create a Campaign without using a Template and start on the General tab. As with most entities in CRM, the top menu and the near navigation are disabled until you save the Campaign, at which time you can work with these objects, as shown in Figure 11.8.

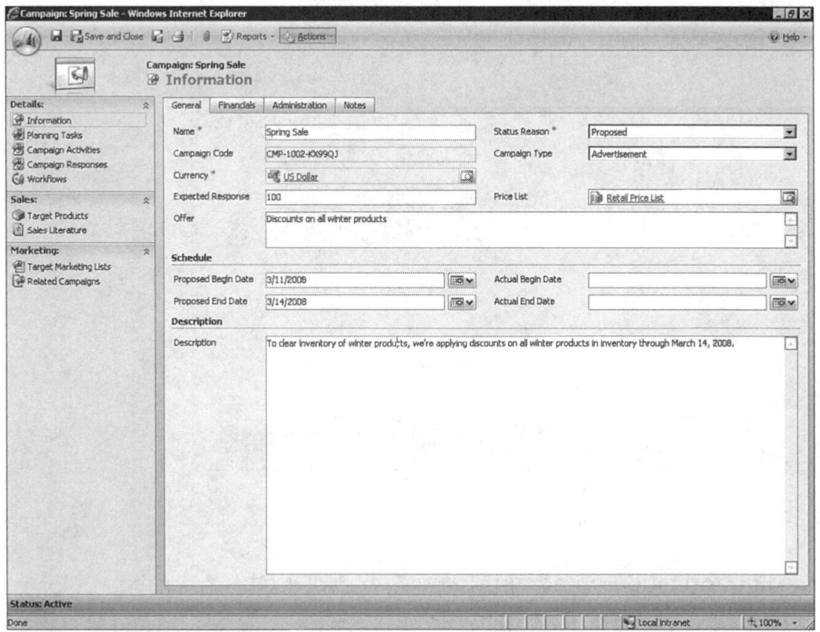

FIGURE 11.8 New Campaign.

Enter a descriptive Name of the Campaign, and select the Status Reason for the Campaign. Because you're creating a new Campaign, leave it at the default of Proposed. You can enter a Campaign Code or have the system assign an automatic Campaign Code to your Campaign by leaving it blank; however, after the Campaign has been saved, you cannot edit this field. Selecting a Campaign Type tells others the type of Campaign that it is. By default, Currency is the system base Currency, and the Expected Response defaults to 100 responses. Although it is not required, selecting a Price List enables you to compare the cost versus revenue generated from the Campaign. The Offer is used to explain the detail of the Campaign.

Enter the Schedule information and Description, if desired.

2. Select the Financials tab and enter the Budget Allocated, Miscellaneous Costs, and the Estimated Revenue for the Campaign (see Figure 11.9). The Total Cost of Campaign calculates automatically and, because you have no Activities yet, equals the Miscellaneous costs only. When we add costs to the Campaign by adding

Campaign Activities, costs will automatically be shown here. (You may have to save, close, and re-open the form prior to seeing the costs reflected.)

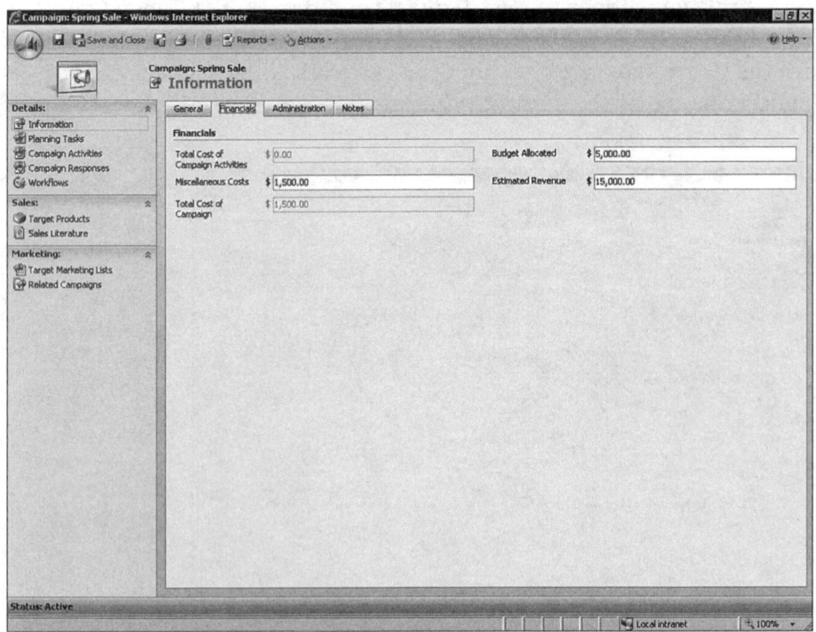

FIGURE 11.9 New Campaign, Financials.

You can add/edit information on Administration and Notes tabs, if desired.

Now that you've created the basic framework for the Campaign, you need to add any Planning Tasks associated with the Campaign. The Campaign must be saved prior to being able to add any Planning Tasks to the Campaign.

3. Planning Tasks are simply Task Activities, with the `Regarding` field set to the Campaign. Navigate to the Planning Tasks and select New to create a Planning Task (see Figure 11.10).

   As with any Activity, after you have created it, you can assign it to another User or queue. It will appear as an Activity in the assigned User's My Work and will have associated follow-up Tasks or Activities assigned to the User if added.

   For this Campaign, you'll have only one Activity. Normally, however, a Campaign has several Planning Tasks. If the Campaign will be reused, the Planning Tasks likely will be common to the Campaign; it might make sense to convert the Campaign to a Campaign Template from the More Actions drop-down menu when you finish adding the necessary Planning Tasks to the Campaign.

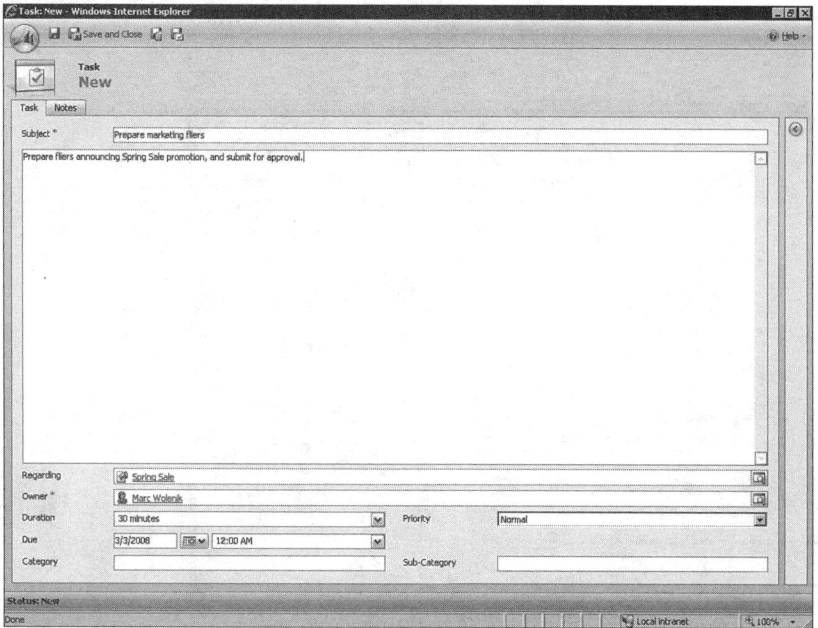

FIGURE 11.10 New Campaign, Planning Tasks.

You have only one Task, so you add a Campaign Activity next.

1. Campaign Activities are different than common Activities and are specific to the Campaign. To add Campaign Activities, navigate to Campaign Activity and select New (see Figure 11.11).

   Select the Channel or method of marketing specific to this Activity, the Type of Activity, and the Campaign Activity Subject. The Channel directly correlates to the distribution of the Activity, as explained shortly. The Owner, by default, is the User creating the Campaign Activity. However, you can change that by clicking the Lookup button and assigning the Campaign Activity to another User. To assign the Activity to a queue, the Activity needs to be created and Assign needs to be selected Menu from the Actions drop-down menu, which allows assignment of the Activity to a queue. Select any Outsource Vendors that might be used with this particular Task, and enter the Scheduled Start and End dates and any Budget Allocated. The Anti-Spam setting excludes members from receiving any marketing material by preventing the Activity from being Distributed to the member for the number of days entered.

   Campaign Activities must be assigned to Marketing List members by being Distributed to the members of the associated Marketing Lists. Distribution simply means assigning the specified Activity to the owner of the member in the Marketing List. Before Distribution of Campaign Activities, you must set which Marketing Lists to use as part of this Campaign.

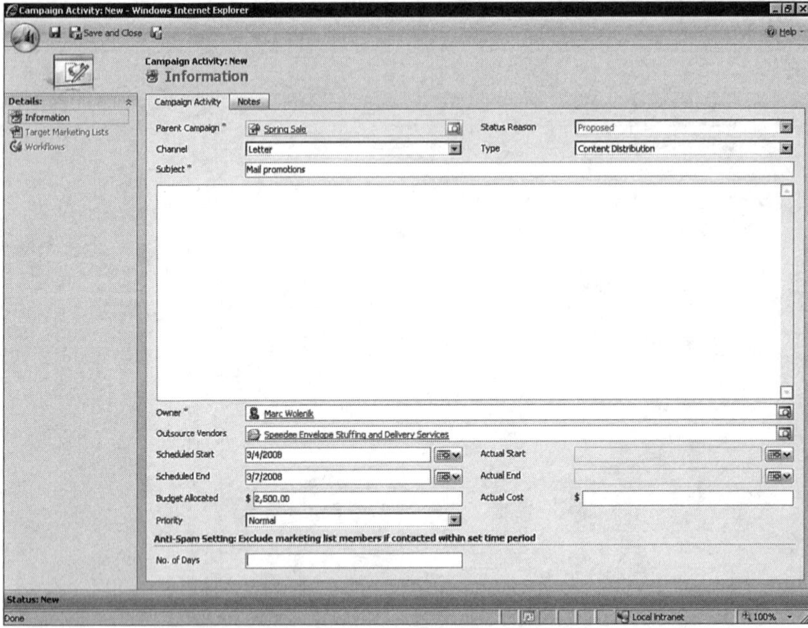

FIGURE 11.11 New Campaign, Campaign Activity.

2. To add Marketing Lists, navigate to the near navigation on the Campaign form and select Target Marketing Lists; then Add (see Figure 11.12).

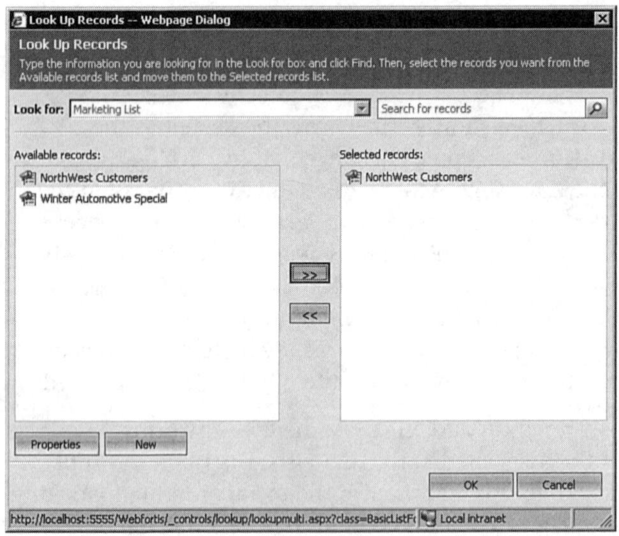

FIGURE 11.12 New Campaign, Add Marketing List.

From here, you can easily add any existing Marketing Lists or create a new one. After you select one, you are prompted whether to include the Marketing List in any undistributed Campaign Activities (see Figure 11.13).

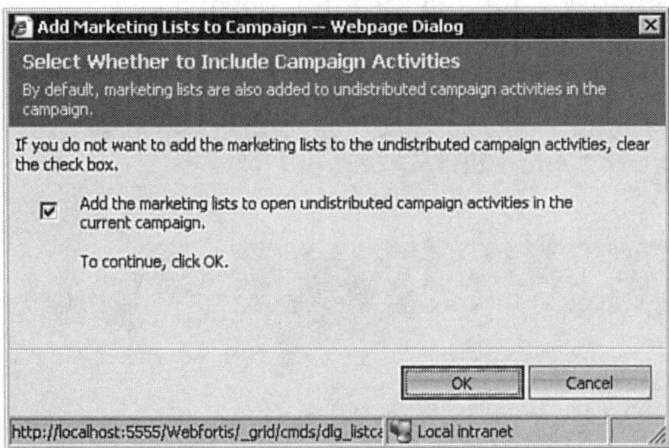

FIGURE 11.13 Add Marketing Lists to Campaign dialog.

Because you have already started a Campaign Activity in this example, leave the option checked. The selected Marketing List automatically associates with your Campaign Activity (see Figure 11.14).

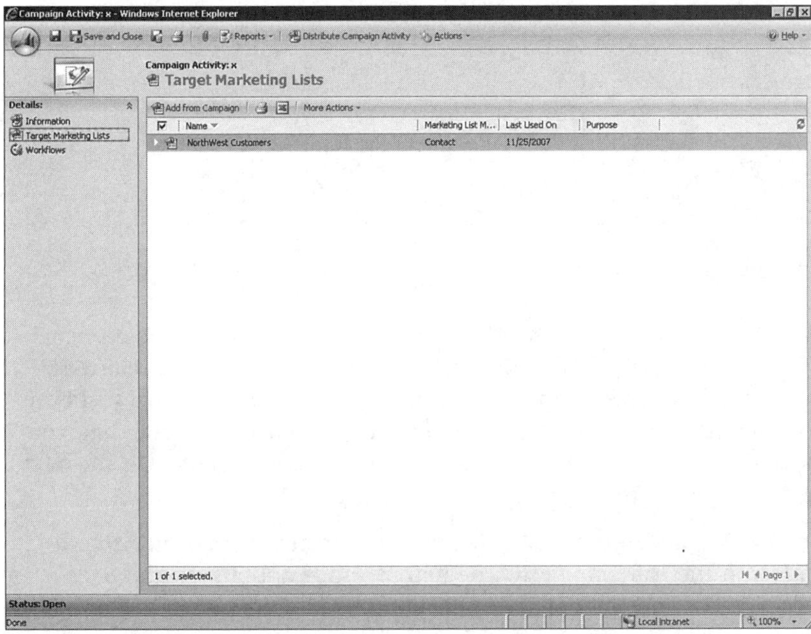

FIGURE 11.14 Campaign Activity Marketing List.

3. Now that you've created the Campaign Activity and associated a Marketing List, you can Distribute the Campaign Activities from the top menu bar. To do this, navigate to the Information tab (on the near navigation) of the Campaign Activity, and select the appropriate Channel of the Activity. For our example, we've selected Letter; however, you can select any of the options in the Channel drop-down menu. After you select Save, you can select Distribute Campaign Activity from the top menu bar. (You'll be prompted to save the Campaign Activity if you change or set the Channel and then try to select Distribute Campaign Activity prior to saving). The Create New Letter dialog box will appear, as shown in Figure 11.15.

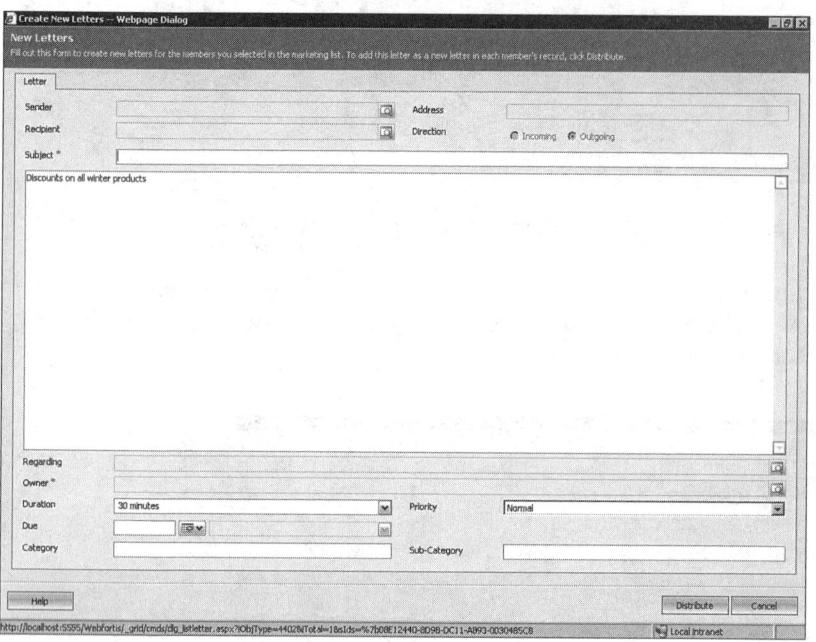

FIGURE 11.15 Distribute Campaign Activity.

Depending on the Channel type selected for the Campaign, a dialog box opens enabling you to enter the requisite information. In this example, we've selected to send a Letter, so the form asks for the Subject of the Letter. If the channel had been e-mail, you would have seen an e-mail dialog box; if it had been a Phone Call, you would have seen a Phone Call dialog box; and so on. Select Distribute. On the next screen, select the owner of the Activity.

4. The Activities are assigned to the designated owners and appear as open Activities for each member in the Marketing List. The Activity node options expand to include Letters Created and Failures after distribution, enabling you to review and examine successes and failures of the distribution (see Figure 11.16).

   Notice also that the Status Reason for the Campaign Activity changes from Proposed to Completed upon distribution.

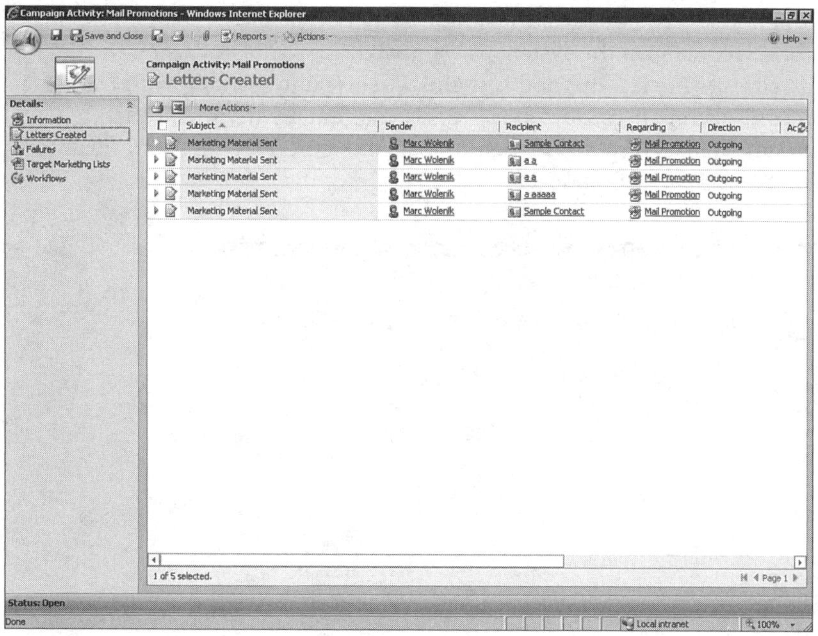

FIGURE 11.16 Letters creation.

Be sure to complete the Actual Cost Amount of the Campaign Activity when completed because that information rolls up to the total Campaign cost on the Campaign Financials Tab.

NOTE

When working with Mail Merge Campaign Activities, be sure that the selected Marketing Lists are all the same base entity (Contacts, Accounts, or Leads exclusively); otherwise, the merge will fail. If you need to create a Mail Merge Campaign Activity for mixed entities, create separate Campaign Activities for each entity.

5. The last part of Campaigns is the Campaign Responses. As the name indicates, Campaign Responses are responses that your organization receives in response to a Campaign. They are very useful in determining the effectiveness of Campaigns and can indicate many things, such as geographic trending, responsiveness to Campaign particulars such as discounts and other incentives, and how well your target audience is receiving the Campaigns. It is important to note that Campaign Responses are responses received from potential customers in response to your Campaign, not automated responses sent to your customers as part of your Campaign. You can automatically convert Campaign Activities to Campaign Responses or you can manually create them.

   In addition to manually creating a Campaign Response by selecting New on the Campaign Response tab located on the near navigation of the Campaign, you can create Campaign Responses by selecting a new Activity type of Campaign Response or by importing records into the system as Campaign Responses by using the Import Data Wizard. This last method is useful when you're working with a large number of records offline because you can easily manipulate them and then tie them to the Campaign as responses when uploaded. Figure 11.17 shows a newly added and saved Campaign Response.

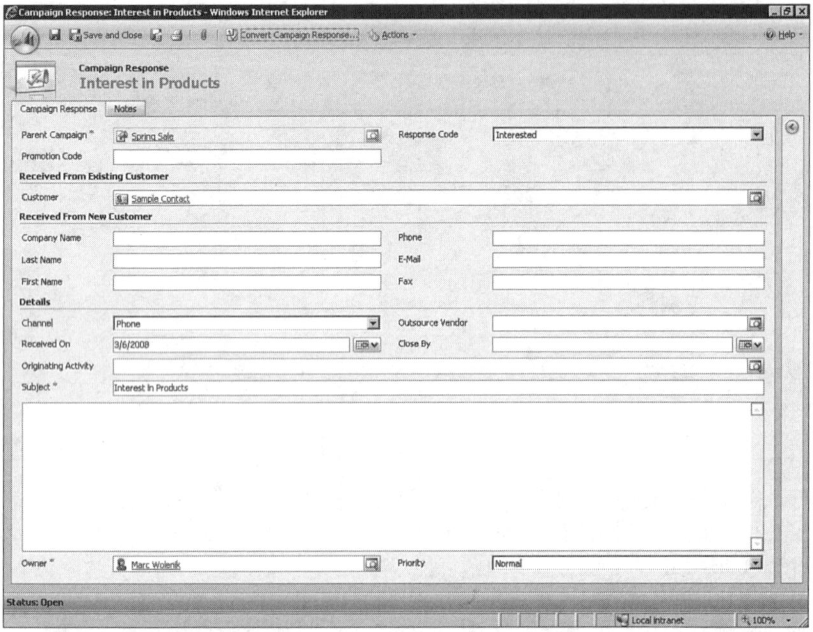

FIGURE 11.17 Campaign Response.

The last method for creating a Campaign Response is via e-mail responses if e-mail tracking has been enabled in settings. When an e-mail is sent in response to a Campaign, the incoming e-mail can be automatically created as a Campaign Response.

When a Campaign Response has been entered and saved, you can select Convert Campaign Response (located in the top menu bar of Figure 11.17). When selected, this will allow you to close the response and convert the record as follows:

- Convert into a new Lead
- Convert an existing Lead into a new Account or Contact
- Create a new Quote, Order, or Opportunity for an existing customer
- Simply close the response and mark it as completed or canceled

As a final note, it is important to realize that while the Campaign Response functionality previously described is applicable to Campaigns and Quick Campaigns, the three Campaign reports available in the Reports area (Campaign Activity Status, Campaign Comparison, and Campaign Performance) are applicable only to Campaigns by default. These reports are powerful and display Campaign information in a manner that is easy-to-understand and useful for determining metrics on Campaigns. We recommend frequently reviewing both of them when building Campaigns as well as viewing the status of executed Campaigns.

Sales Literature

Found in the Marketing area, Sales Literature is documentation about your products designed to be used by your sales force to gain deeper knowledge about your products and can be given to customers to drive sales. Additionally, Sales Literature can provide specific instructions on how to use a given product or services, as well as identify Competitors.

To create a new piece of Sales Literature, first select New (see Figure 11.18).

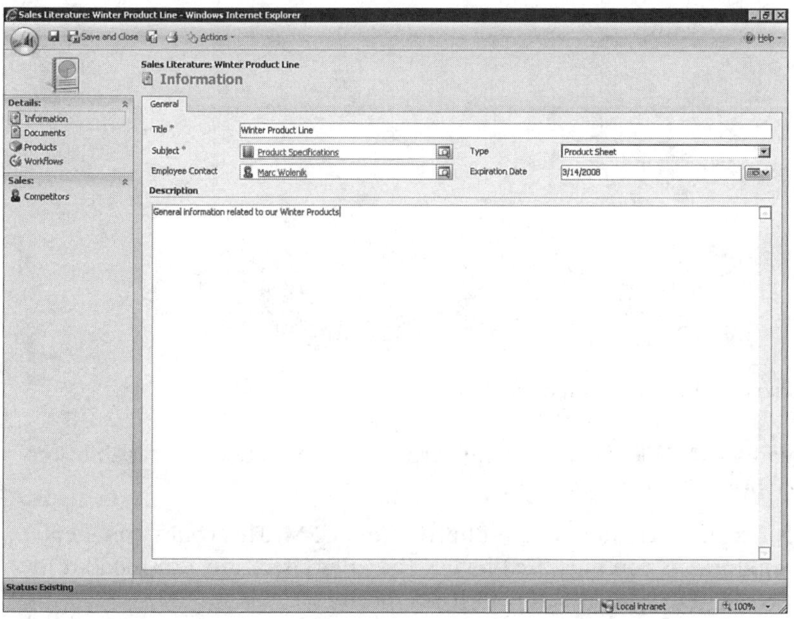

FIGURE 11.18 Sales Literature.

Enter the Title of the literature and the Subject from your corresponding Subject Tree (for more information about working with Subjects, refer to Chapter 14, "Settings and Configuration"). Additional optional information includes Employee Contact, Type, Expiration Date, and Description.

NOTE

While the Expiration Date field has no functionality other than to tell the salesperson when it expires, it would be easy to add another custom View to the Sales Literature interface that shows only current or nonexpired Sales Literature.

Sales Literature can have as many pieces of documentation as desired. To create a new Sales Literature document, select Documents, New (see Figure 11.19).

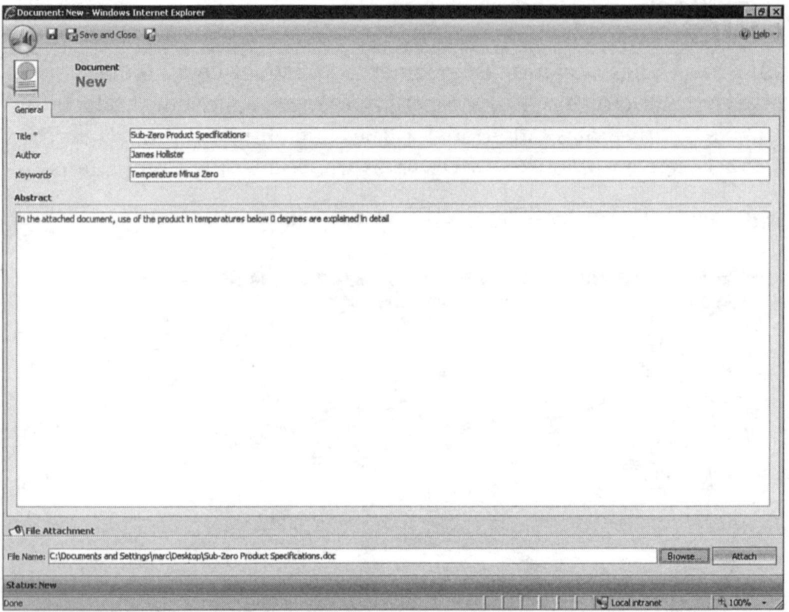

FIGURE 11.19 Sales Literature, Documents.

Additional functionality available when working with Sales Literature is the capability to add Products and identify Competitors.

Unfortunately, Sales Literature cannot be sent directly from CRM. This could present a challenge to your workforce as you must first review the Sales Literature, download it to your system, and then send it as an attachment if you need to.

Quick Campaigns

A Quick Campaign is a simplified version of a Campaign: Unlike Campaigns, which can contain many Activities, Quick Campaigns have one Activity. The capability to create a Quick Campaign is easy, using a wizard that you can launch from Advanced Find or directly from the Account, Contact, or Lead forms.

When discussing Quick Campaigns, we must consider two aspects: their creation and status. We review both in this section.

Creating Quick Campaigns

As indicated, creating Quick Campaigns is easy. To launch a Quick Campaign, click the button Create Quick Campaign from either the Contact, Account, or Lead forms. For this example, you'll launch a Quick Campaign from Advanced Find using the Contacts entity.

1. Open Advanced Find and select Contacts as the base entity. You'll do a targeted Quick Campaign for all your Contacts in the State of California (see Figure 11.20). Select Find to continue.

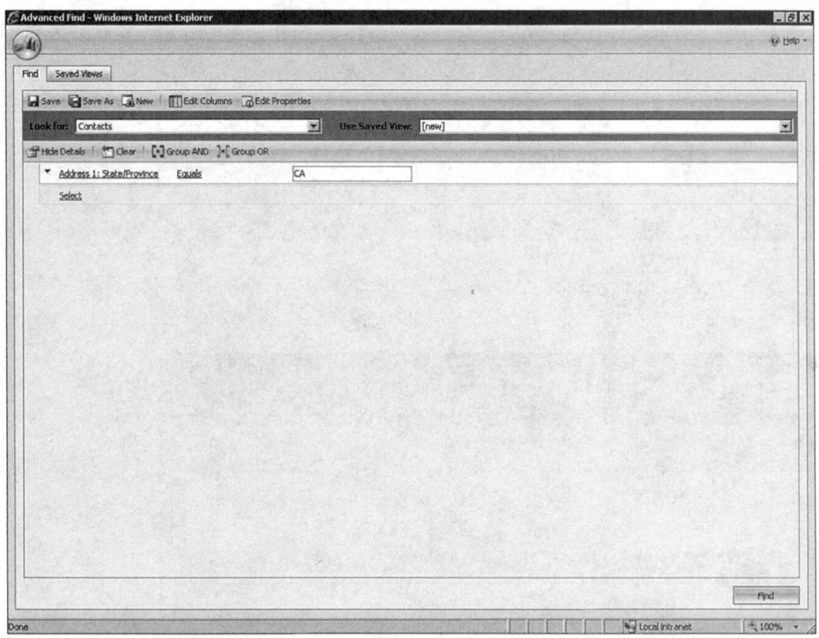

FIGURE 11.20 Advanced Find for Contacts in California.

2. From the results screen, select Create Quick Campaign and select the option indicated (see Figure 11.21). In this example, select All Records on All Pages. The Quick Campaign Wizard starts and welcomes you. Click Next to continue.

3. Enter the name of the Campaign and click Next to continue. Select the Activity Type of the Quick Campaign, as well as who will own the Activities (see Figure 11.22). If the Activity type selected is an e-mail (as in our example), the system can automatically send the e-mails and close the Activities, if selected. Otherwise, the Activities will belong to the selected owners as pending and will require action by them to close them out.

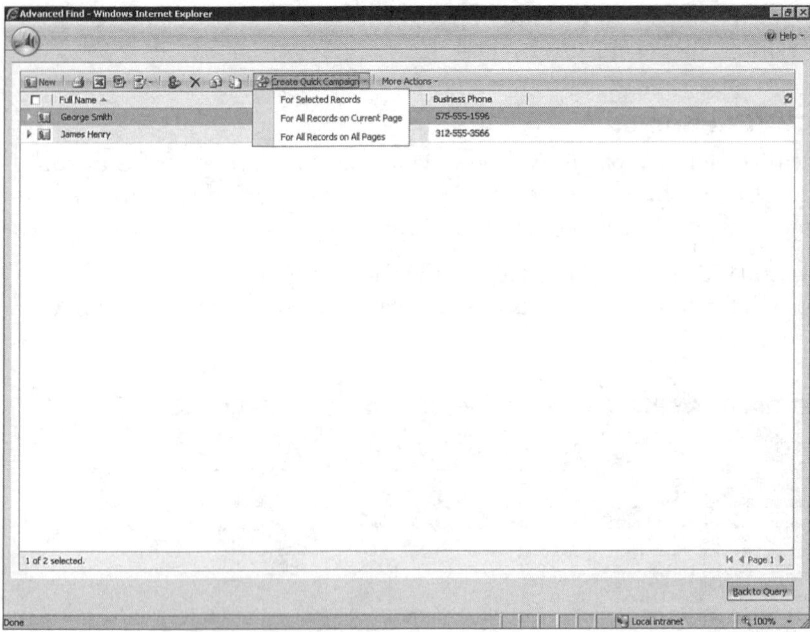

FIGURE 11.21 Advanced Find results.

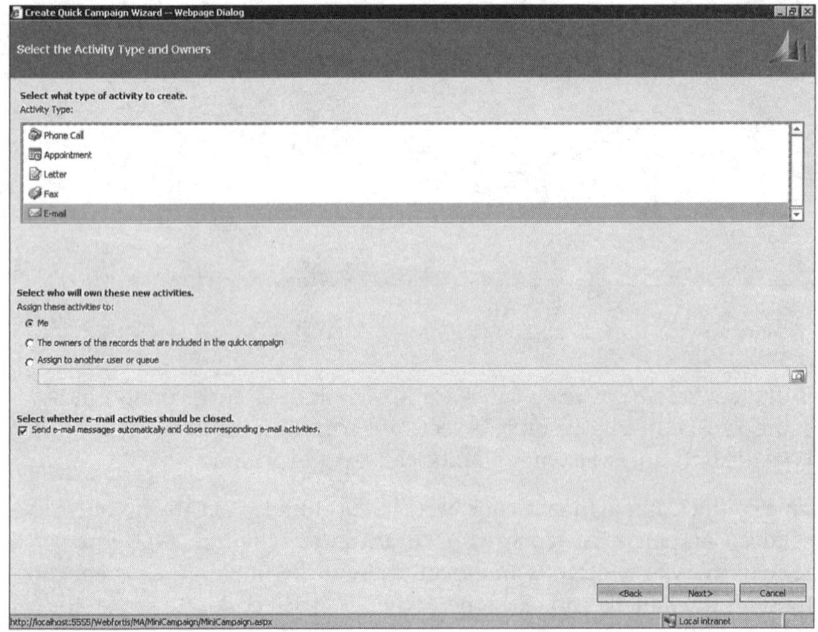

FIGURE 11.22 Activity Type.

4. Because you've selected e-mail, we're prompted to enter the e-mail information shown in Figure 11.23. If you had selected another Activity, you would be prompted to complete the appropriate fields for that Activity. Our example is a simple e-mail, which has the downside of limited customization. If we were to use the Channel option of Letter via Mail Merge, we could personalize the letter fully as well as include additional data fields. Click Next to continue and then Create to create the Quick Campaign.

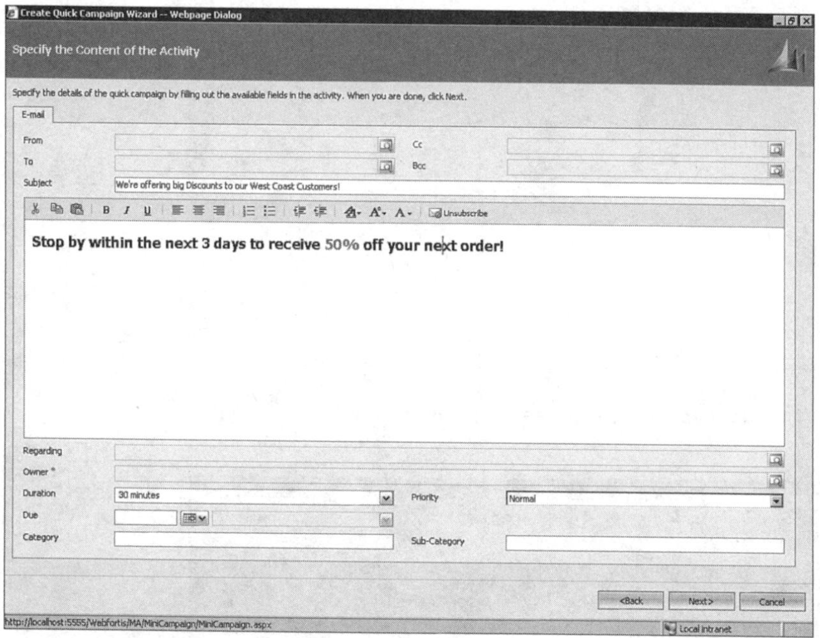

FIGURE 11.23 E-mail Activity Type.

NOTE

To use the Unsubscribe option, select some text in the body of the e-mail by highlighting, and click the Unsubscribe button (for example, add and select the following text: To stop receiving our e-mails, click here). This will format the selected text as a link that Users can click to set their preferences to not allow marketing materials.

5. The wizard completes and the Activity is created. It waits in the person's Activities to complete unless it was an e-mail (in which case the e-mail goes out directly) (see Figure 11.24).

Status of Quick Campaigns

Although you can't launch Quick Campaigns directly from the Quick Campaign node of the Marketing area, you can monitor their status from there (see Figure 11.25).

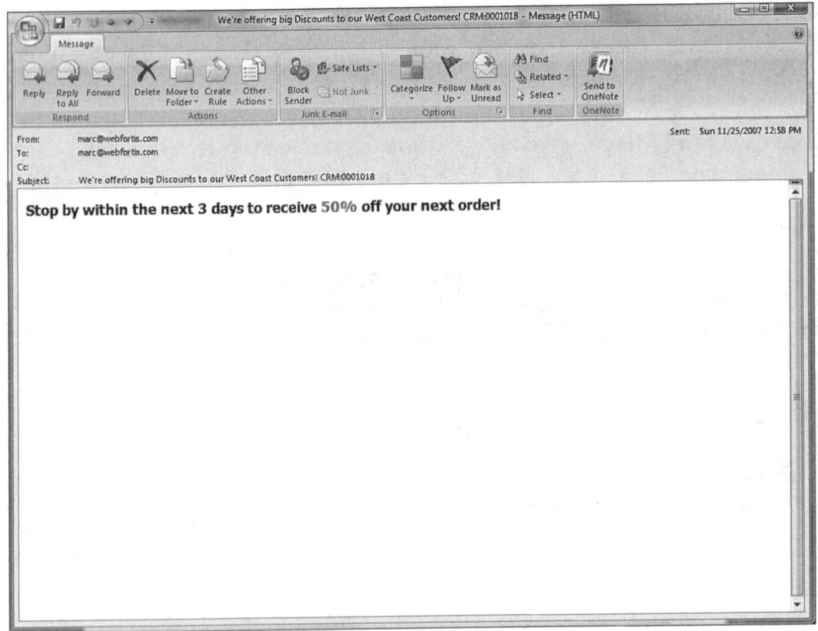

FIGURE 11.24 E-mail received in response to a Quick Campaign.

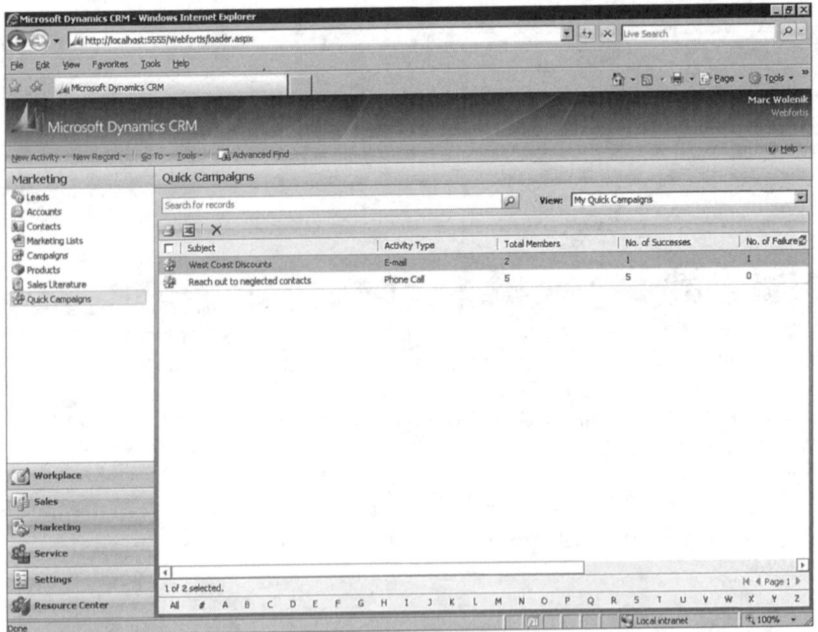

FIGURE 11.25 Marketing, Quick Campaigns.

Open a Quick Campaign by double-clicking it to bring up information about the success and failure of the Quick Campaign (see Figure 11.26).

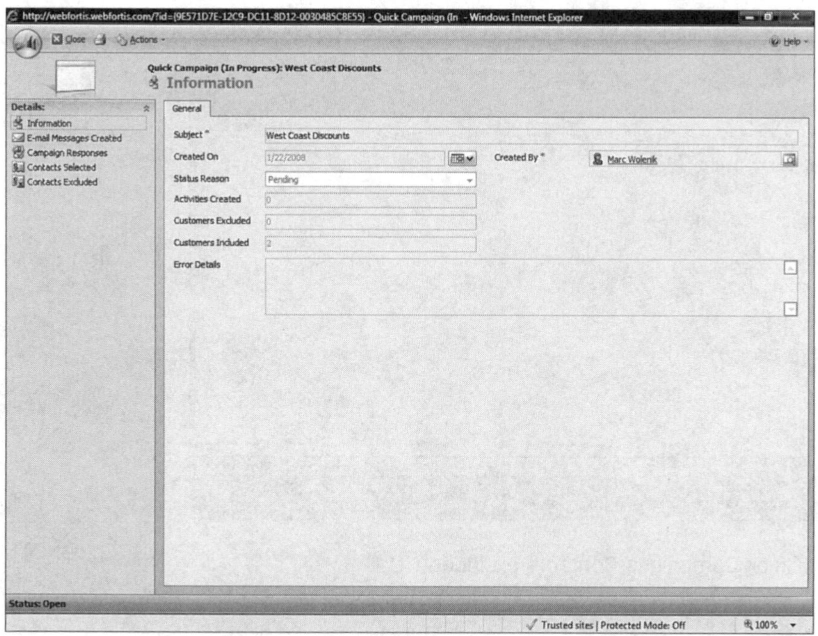

FIGURE 11.26 Quick Campaigns status.

In reviewing the form, you can easily see what the Quick Campaign was for and who received e-mail messages by selecting E-mail Messages Created from the near navigation. Additionally, you can track any responses to the Quick Campaign, just as you would for a regular Campaign. Finally, you can easily see which Contacts received the e-mail and which were excluded and why by examining the details found in each node. For the example shown, one of the Contacts did not have an e-mail, creating an exception (see Figure 11.27).

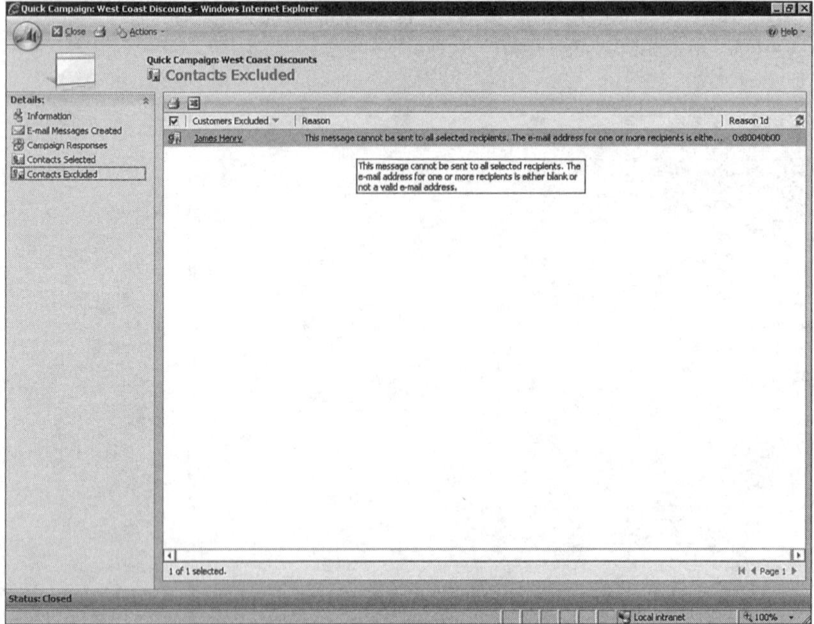

FIGURE 11.27 Quick Campaigns Contacts excluded.

Summary

In reviewing the Marketing options for Microsoft Dynamics CRM, it is easy to see that Microsoft Dynamics CRM offers a full set of marketing options and capabilities. From its powerful Campaign-management features to its quick-and-easy Quick Campaigns, you can easily market to existing and potential clients, report on results, and determine which marketing efforts worked.

CHAPTER 12

Working with Service

IN THIS CHAPTER

Service and Service Activities Explained

Services are the best way to manage resources such as time and materials within the organization. Resources can consist of users, resource groups, or teams; and materials are defined as facilities or equipment.

A Service is basically anything that involves resource time and materials. It is different than a product, for which you have to manage stock and quantities. With a Service, the critical considerations are the time allocated to the necessary resources and the stock of materials. For example, imagine that an IT company has two technicians who can repair computers. When one goes to a client to repair a computer, that technician might take 1 hour or more to perform the work and, depending on the service required, might need to use materials such as a new CD-ROM or computer part. You can schedule all these tasks in Microsoft Dynamics CRM via Service Activities. Although you can also schedule this Service as an appointment, the difference between them is that a Service Activity has an associated Service. You use appointments for meetings with clients that do not involve performing any service.

When Service Activities are scheduled, they appear on the user's CRM calendar (found in My Workspace), as well as appointments on the Outlook calendar.

TIP

When working with the Outlook client, there is full-featured functionality for Services, unless you are offline. When offline, the Service Calendar is unavailable; however, appointments can still be viewed on the Outlook calendar.

The Service Area of Microsoft CRM has the following options, by default:

- Service Calendar
- Cases
- Accounts
- Contacts
- Knowledge Base
- Contracts
- Products
- Services

You can customize these options from the Site Map entity, as explained in Chapter 19, "Customizing Entities."

The Accounts, Contacts, and Products options are specifically covered in Chapter 8, "Working with Customers," and Chapter 10, "Working with Sales," and therefore are not covered here.

Services

The Service Activities use Services to define and configure how time and resources will be managed when a user schedules a Service Activity. When Services are created, they can be reused or modified to fit your needs. For our example, we create a Service from scratch.

For example, consider an IT company that has a service called Network Installation that might take 3 hours to complete and that requires one of the three technicians to go to the customer's office.

To set up this service example, follow these steps:

1. Go to the Service area and click Services. Then click the New button. The New Service Information form appears (see Figure 12.1).

By default, each service has the following required fields:

- `Name`
- `Initial Status Reason`
- `Default Duration`
- `Start Activities Every`

To configure the resources needed to accomplish the service, navigate to the Required Resources tab (see Figure 12.2).

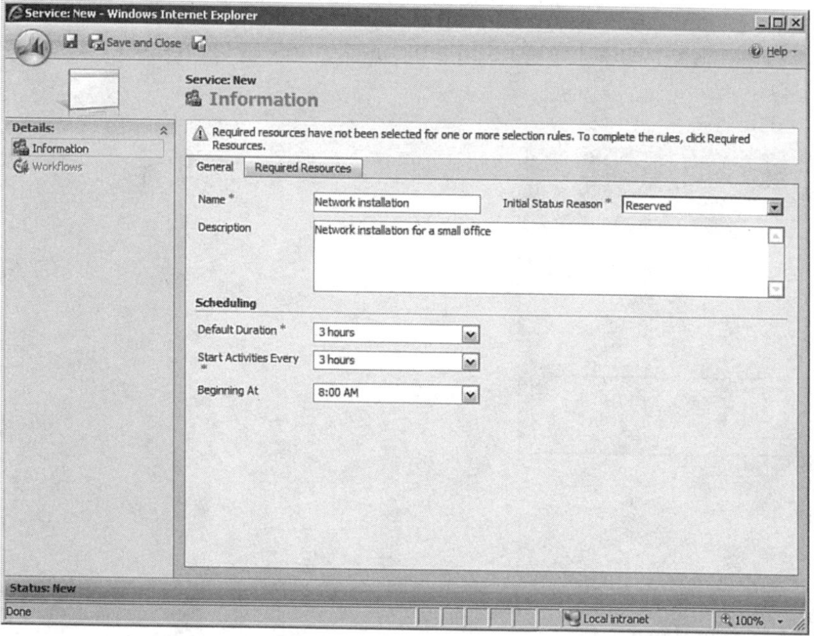

FIGURE 12.1 New Service window interface.

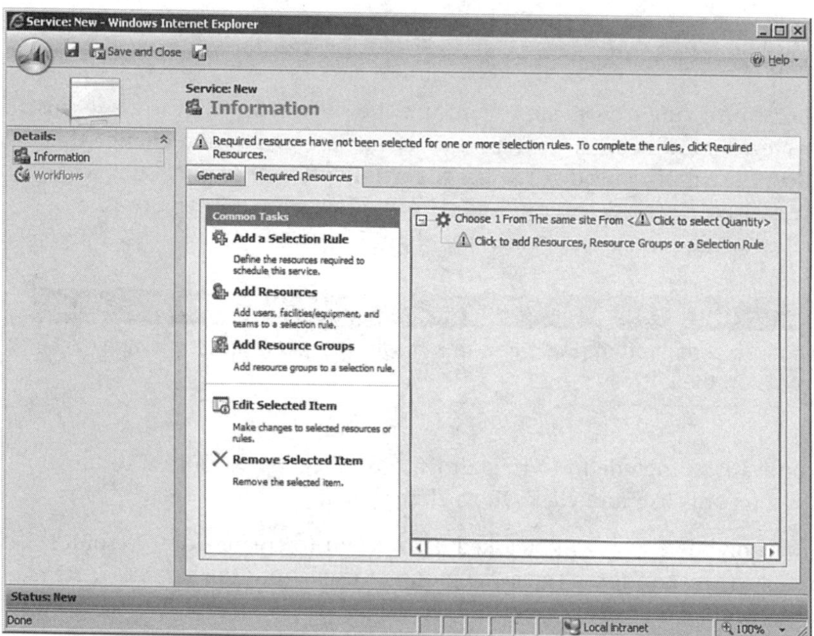

FIGURE 12.2 Configuring required resources.

Select the first option from the tree displayed on the right that says Choose 1 from the Same Site from <Click to Select Quantity>, and double-click it to display the window shown in Figure 12.3.

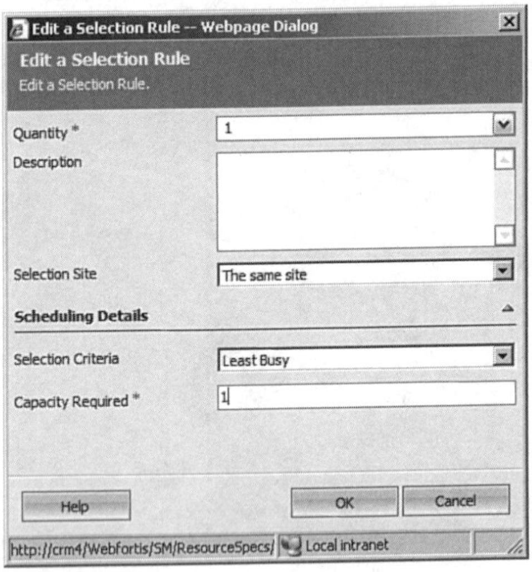

FIGURE 12.3 Editing a selection rule.

If you don't see the Scheduling Details fields, click on the arrow at the right of that title to expand the section.

This example requires only one technician to perform the service, so you can close this window. (If you were going to need more than one technician, you would change the values here to reflect the number needed.) Select the child option that says Click to Add Resources, Resources Groups, or a Selection Rule. The window shown in Figure 12.4 displays the available resources that you want to assign.

NOTE

Click the Search for Records button (the one with a magnifying glass icon) to display all available records on the left.

Select the users you want to include from the left list box, click the >> button to move them to the Selected records list, and click OK to close this dialog box.

If you add more than one user, you will be asked if you want to create a new Resource Group. This is useful, as you can reuse the same group of users on other services instead of selecting the users one by one (see Figure 12.5).

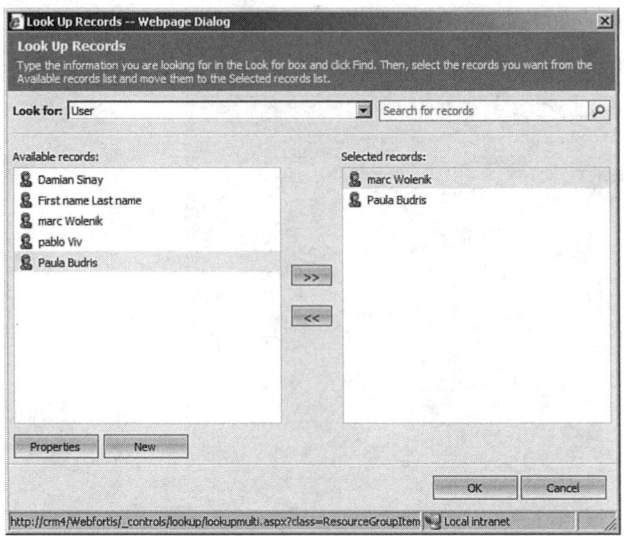

FIGURE 12.4 Adding resources to a selection rule.

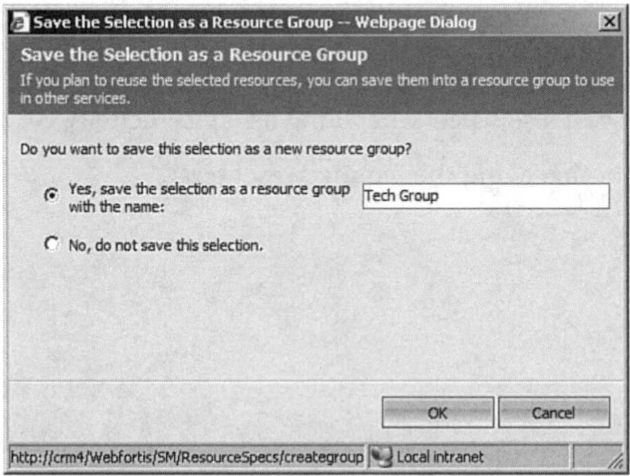

FIGURE 12.5 Saving the selection as a Resource Group.

To further work with Services, you might need to create Facility/Equipment and Resource Groups, if you haven't done so yet. You can do this by going to Settings, Business Management. Refer to Chapter 14, "Settings and Configuration," for detailed information about how to add and manage these kinds of entities.

After you select the required resources, you will see them, as shown in Figure 12.6.

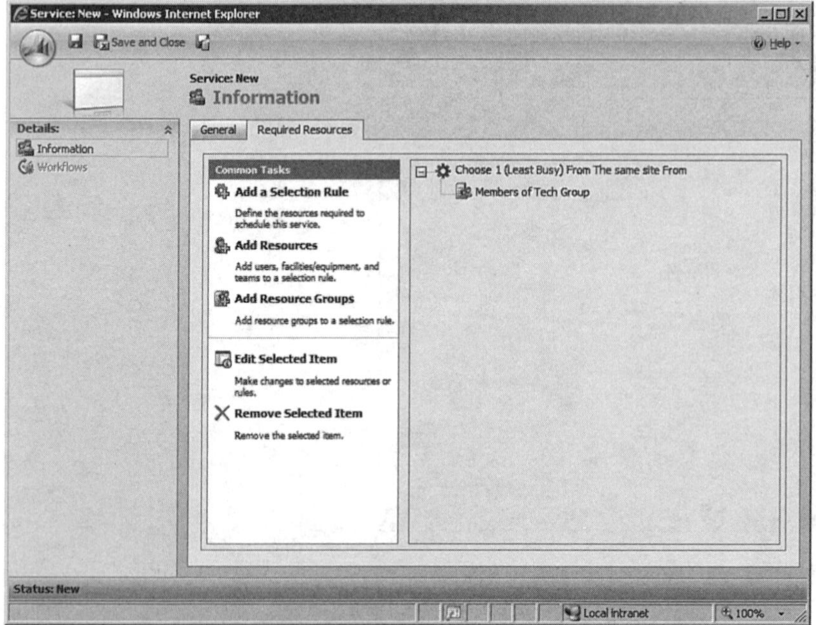

FIGURE 12.6 RequiredResources.

These resources are the ones the user must choose when scheduling a Service Activity.

You also can perform some Common Tasks managing the required resources:

- Add a Selection Rule
- Add Resources
- Add Resource Groups
- Edit Selected Item
- Remove Selected Item

NOTE

Unfortunately, the Service entity doesn't support customizations. If you want to customize it, consider adding a new custom attribute for your business services.

Click the Save and Close button to finish the new service creation.

Refer to the Microsoft website for more information and common scenarios on how to further use Services: www.microsoft.com/dynamics/crm/using/services/serviceactivitydiagram.mspx.

Service Calendar

The Service Calendar checks resource availability and schedules appointments for the resources. Figure 12.7 shows the Service Calendar interface. When a customer calls to request a service, you can easily manage a general agenda and reserve or request a time for a resource or equipment based on the requested service. Additionally, you can manage the existing schedules and make changes, if necessary.

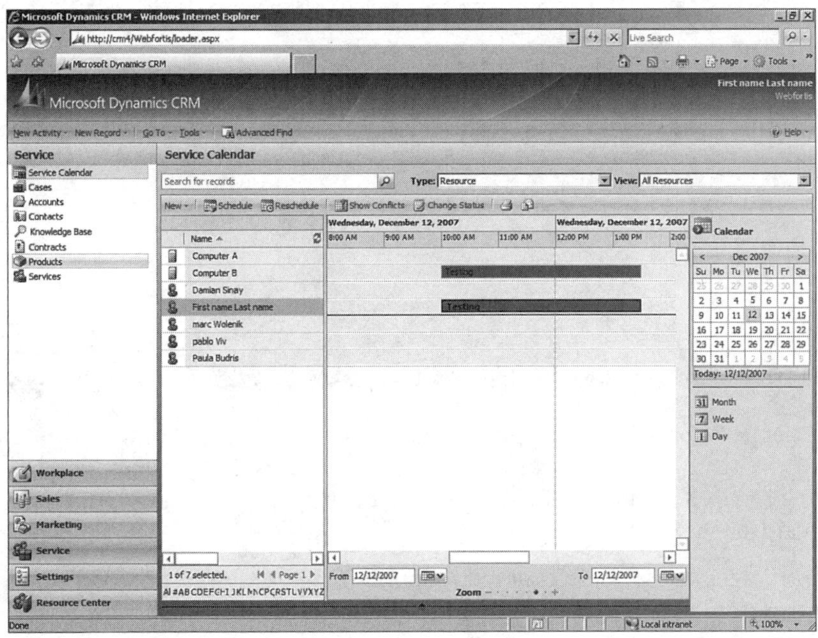

FIGURE 12.7 Main Service Area interface.

By default, the Service Calendar is displayed showing the time and usage allocation for facility/equipment, as well as the tasks scheduled for the users.

NOTE

The Service Calendar is available only to users with System Administrator or one of the Scheduler roles. If users do not have these roles, they see the time allocated on their personal calendars as appointments, which are accessed by going to Workspace, Calendar.

As you can see in Figure 12.8, each activity state has a different color so that you can easily recognize its status. To see this table from the CRM Web Application, go to Help, Contents and do a search of Legend of Colors and Statuses.

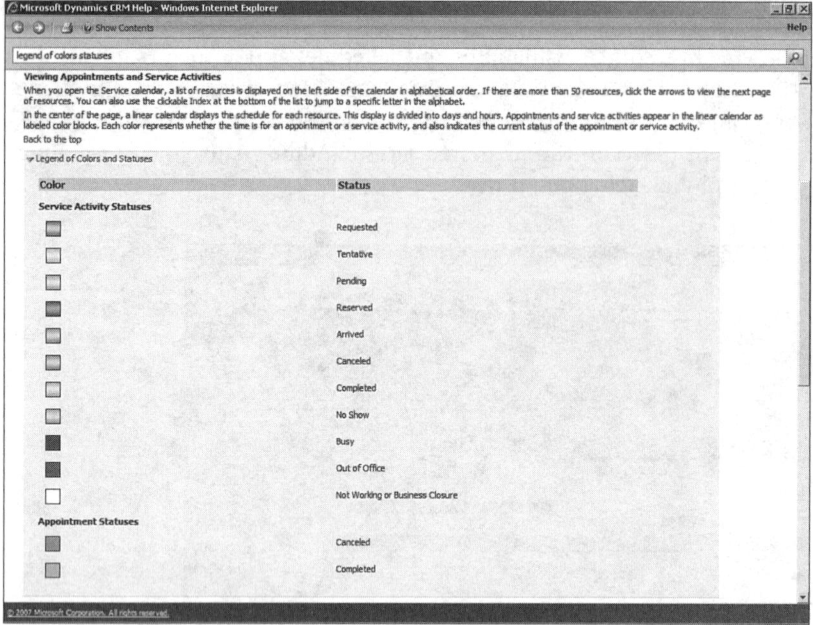

FIGURE 12.8 Color table for Service Activities status.

You can display the Service Calendar by month, week, or day, and you can also display it within a custom date range specified.

To view it by month, week, or day, select the View option in the lower-right portion of the interface. For a custom date range, navigate to the bottom of the calendar view and enter the date range.

TIP

You can use the calendars next to the date input fields to more easily select a date.

If you have many resources and equipment, you can easily locate a resource by using the search text box on the top by typing the first few letters of the resource name.

The Service Calendar shows the two types of activities you can create from this interface: the Service Activity and the Appointment activities.

Service Activity

A Service Activity helps you schedule appointments for resources associated with a Service. Before creating Service Activities, you must define and create your business services as covered in detail in the "Services" section of this chapter.

To create a new Service Activity from the Service Calendar interface, click New and select Service Activity (see Figure 12.9).

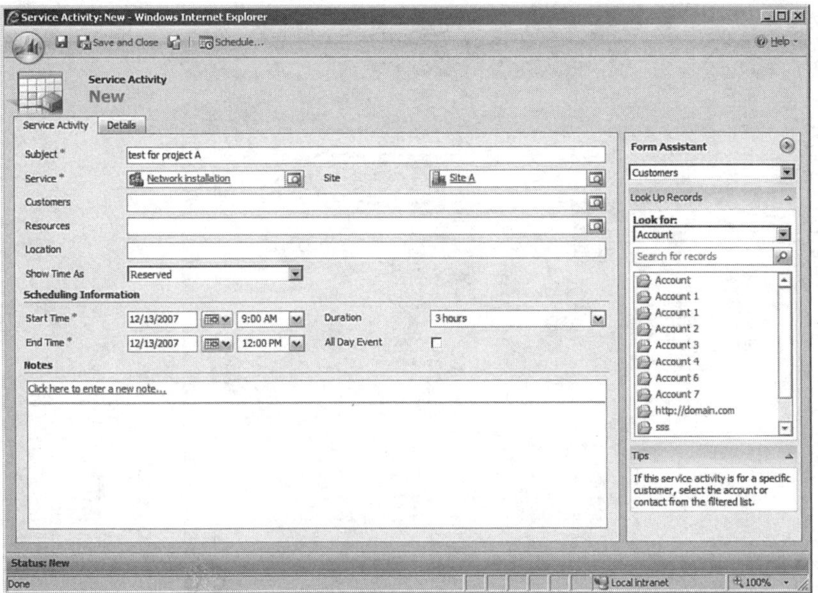

FIGURE 12.9 New Service Activity.

When creating a new Service Activity, you are required to enter a Subject, a Service, and the Time (start and end dates) for the activity. Depending on the service selected, you might also be required to select one or more resources or equipment. If so, after selecting the Service, click the Schedule button from the top menu bar.

A new window opens for scheduling a service. In this example (see Figure 12.10), the Form Assistant displays the resources that are available for completion in the `Resources` field. When the Resources field has the focus, you will see Service Rule options in the Form Assistant that must be selected. In this example, one of the displayed resources must be selected (see Figure 12.10).

You can select one of the resources from the Form Assistant or click the Find Available Times button to list all the available resources and times (see Figure 12.11).

NOTE

If you see errors when clicking on the Available Times button, that might be because the Resources don't have a Site specified. Be sure the Facilities and Users have one Site set.

Select the resource that matches your desired time availability and click the Schedule button. Notice that you might have to select more than one resource, depending on how the service was initially defined.

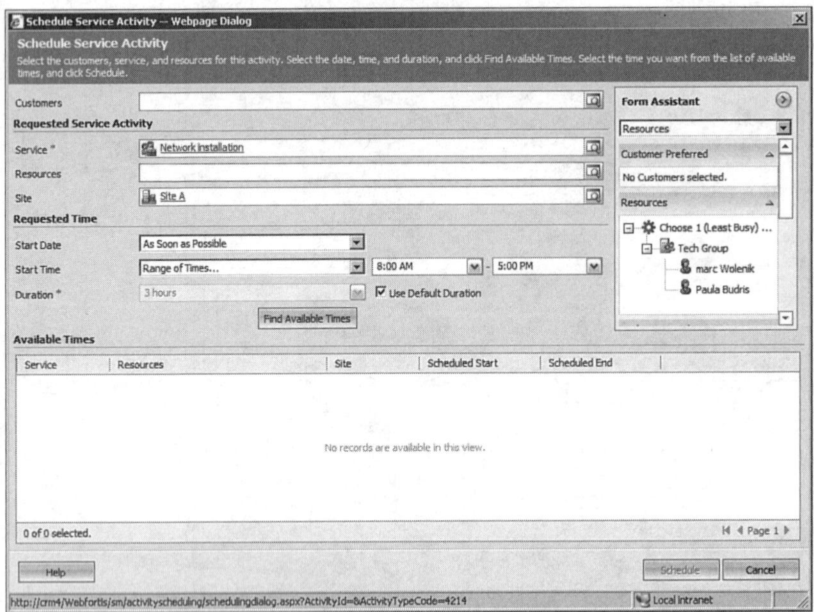

FIGURE 12.10 Scheduling a Service Activity.

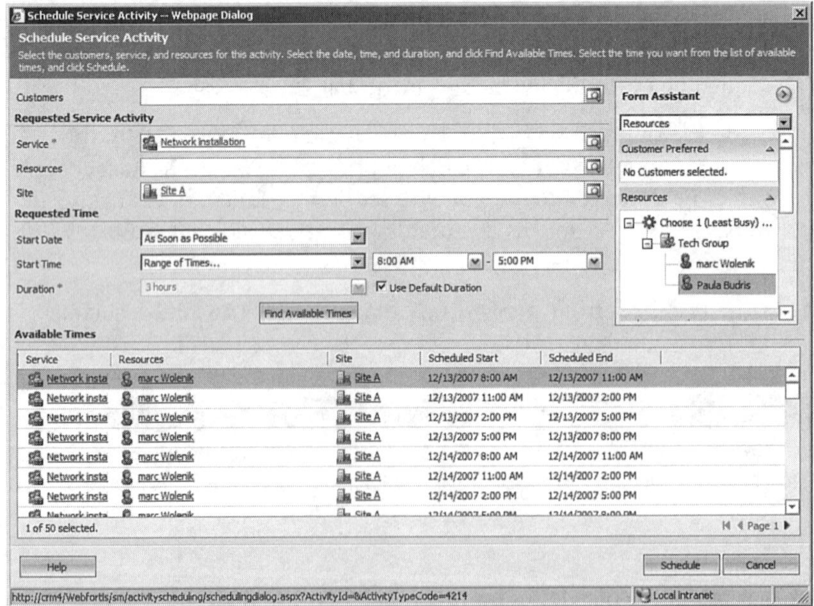

FIGURE 12.11 Selecting resources.

Finally, click Save and Close to finish the service activity. This closes the window, and you will see the scheduled activity on the Service Calendar. Each affected user sees the Service Activity on his or her calendar that is in the Workspace area (see Figure 12.12), as well as having the appointment on the Outlook calendar if using the Outlook client.

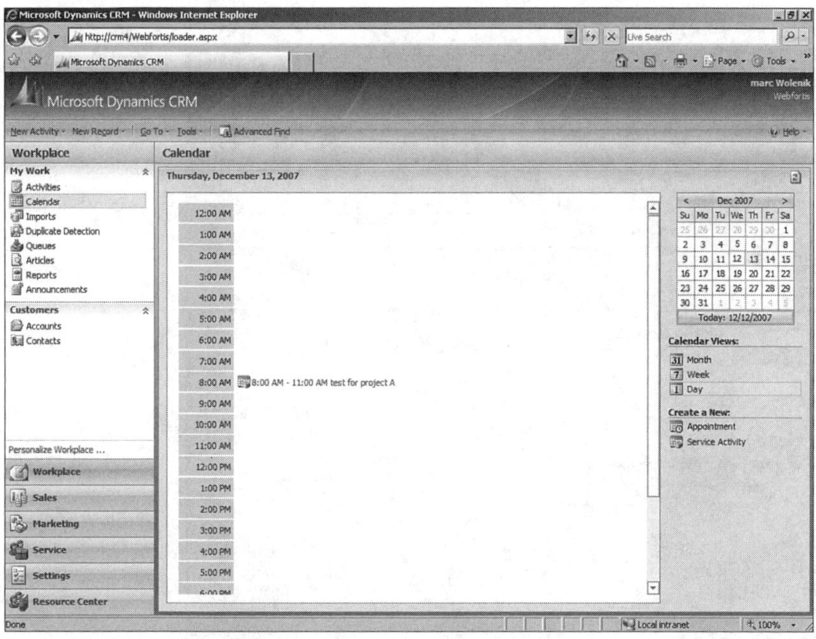

FIGURE 12.12 User workplace calendar.

TIP

Users are not notified via e-mail when you schedule a Service Activity for them by default. However, you could easily customize that by creating a custom workflow for the Service Activity entity. Refer to Chapter 20, "Workflow Development," for more details about how to create custom workflows.

You can easily reschedule Service Activities, if necessary. For example, suppose that a customer has to reschedule an appointment. The Customer Service Representative could easily do that by clicking the Reschedule button and checking the next available time, to verify availability of the resources to the Service to be rescheduled.

TE

Another hidden pane, at the bottom of the window, shows resources and facility details. If you click the black arrow located in the middle bottom of the main Service Calendar window, another panel displaying the selected resource details appears (see Figure 12.13).

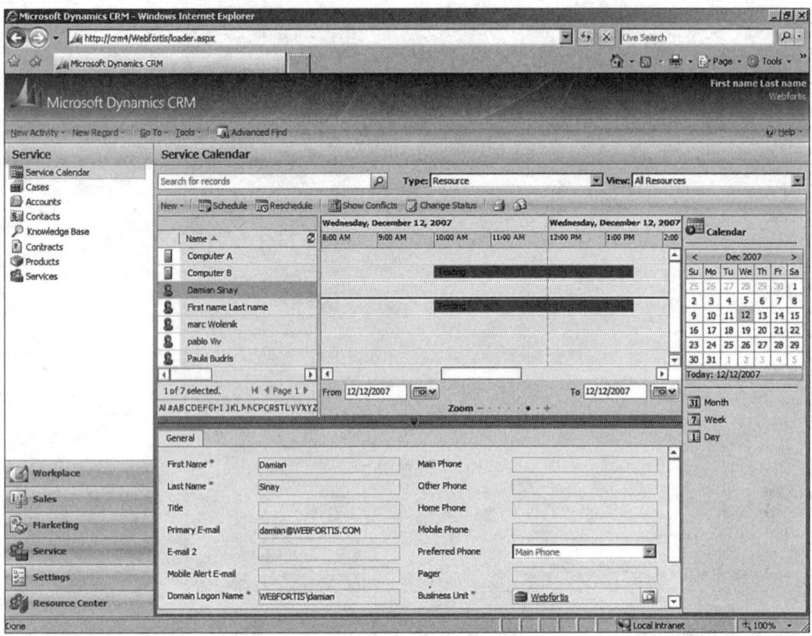

FIGURE 12.13 Resource details panel expanded.

Managing Users' Working Time

You can change the working hours for a user from the Service Calendar. You open a user's details by selecting and then double-clicking the user. Navigating then to the Work Hours tab from the Details section, you can see and configure the user's working times, as shown in Figure 12.14.

Suppose the user Damian is going on vacation from 10/22 to 10/27. You can easily set up these days as Time Off to prevent other users from scheduling appointments or services activities with him. From the Set Up menu that is inside the Monthly View tab, click Time Off to configure the holidays, as shown in Figure 12.15.

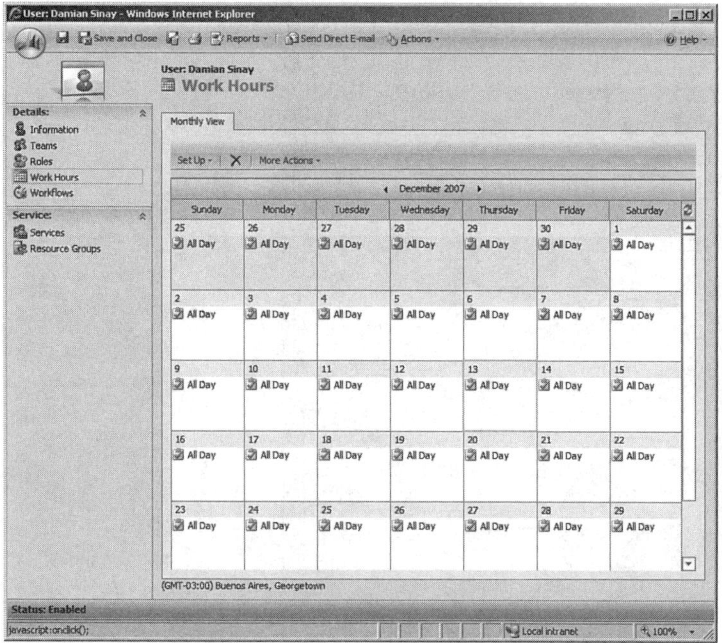

FIGURE 12.14 Work Hours tab for a user.

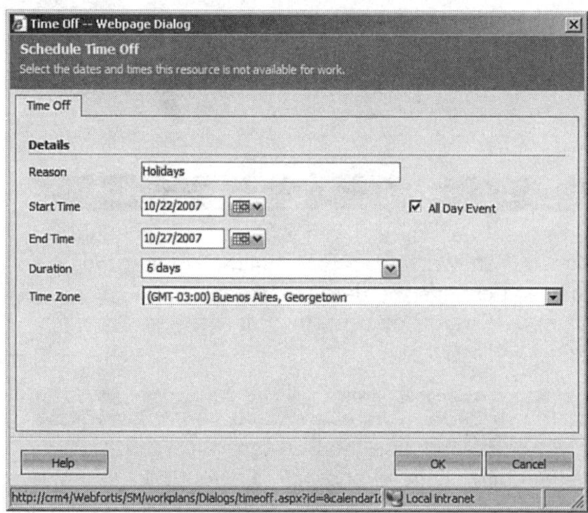

FIGURE 12.15 Configuring Time Off.

Figure 12.16 shows how the work hours are displayed after configuring Time Off.

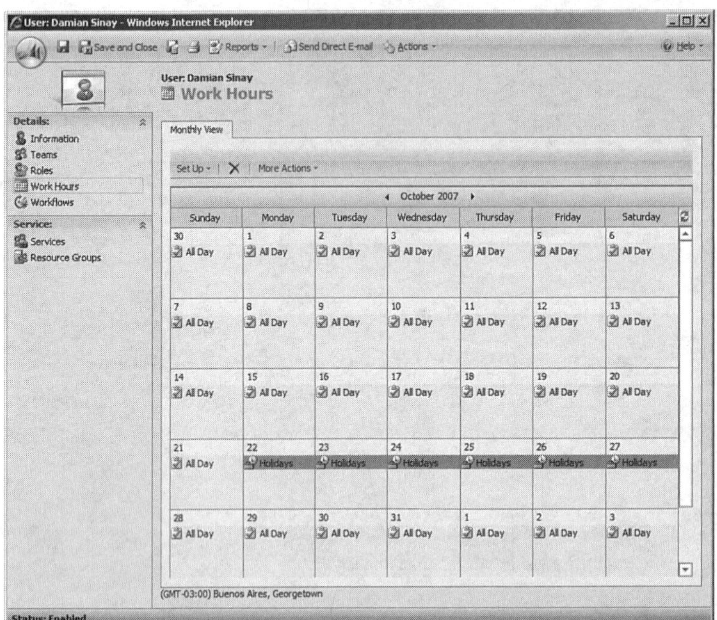

FIGURE 12.16 Work Hours with holidays.

You can use this same process to configure sick days, personal errands, or similar situations.

NOTE

Even though the work hours for the user are set as Time Off, other users can schedule activities for this user on those days. However, they receive an alert message that the user is scheduled for time off so that they can change the dates, if necessary.

TIP

For general holidays when the business will be closed, use the Business Closures calendar in the Settings, Business Management option, as shown in Figure 12.17.

Appointment

Appointments differ from Service Activities because they don't need to have a Service associated with them. To create a new appointment, go to the Service Area, Service Calendar, and click New, Appointment. Figure 12.18 illustrates the Appointment window.

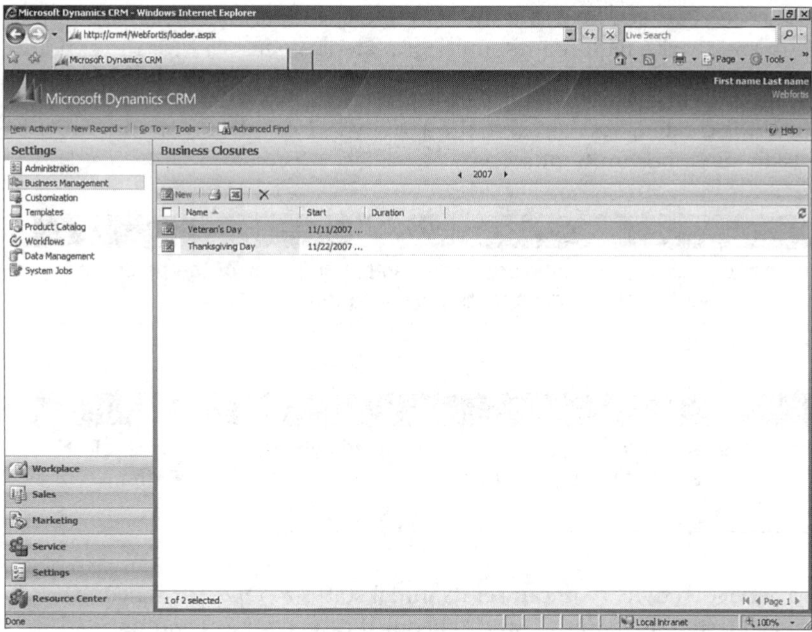

FIGURE 12.17 Business Closures interface.

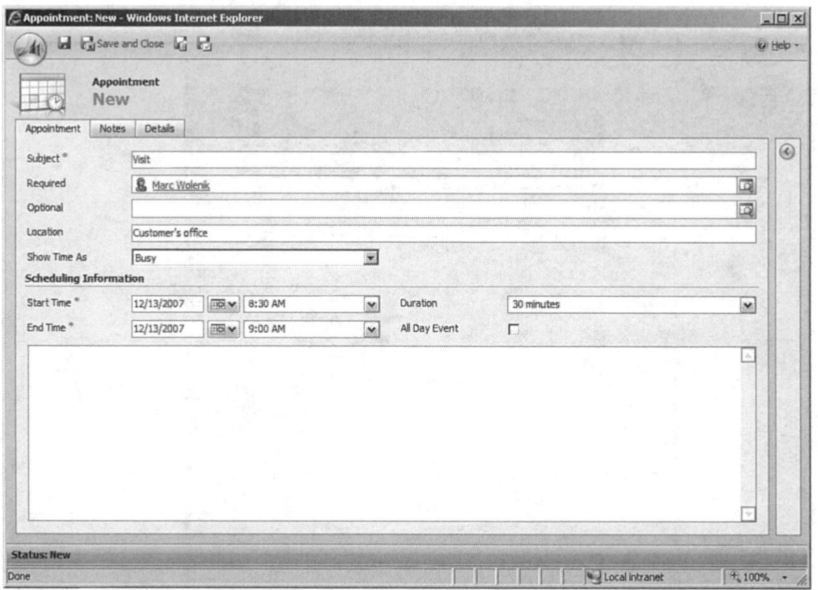

FIGURE 12.18 Creating a new appointment.

The required fields are the `Subject` field and the start and end times for the appointment. If you want, you can specify the required resources or materials necessary for the appointment and the optional resources.

After the appointment is created, you can save the activity as Completed, or you can convert the activity to an Opportunity or a Case.

NOTE

If you choose to save the activity as Completed, you can't change any of the properties for that activity, nor change the status back to its previous status.

TIP

Unlike Service Activities, appointments can't be rescheduled by using the Reschedule button. To reschedule an appointment, just open the appointment and change the dates.

When you create a Service Activity, you can set its initial status to Open or Scheduled. Open can be set as Requested or Tentative, and Scheduled can be set as Pending, Reserved, In Progress, or Arrived. To change the status of a Service Activity, select the activity first and then click on the Change Status Button (see Figure 12.19).

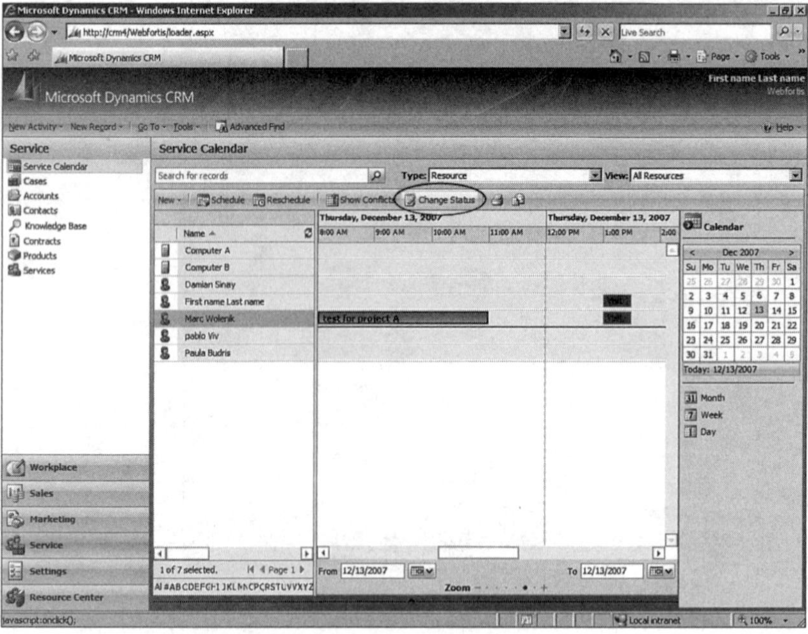

FIGURE 12.19 Changing Service Activity status.

After clicking the Change Status button, the dialog displayed in Figure 12.20 will appear, giving you the options to change the Service Activity status, close the activity, and complete it.

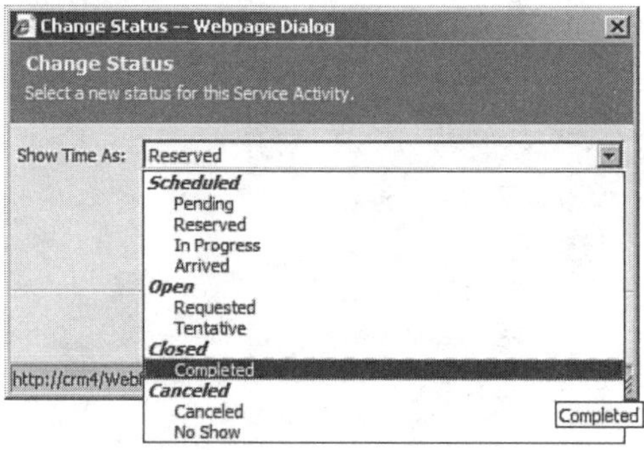

FIGURE 12.20 Changing Service Activity status to Completed.

Cases

Cases are usually used to track customer problems, questions, and issues (as shown in Figure 12.21). Each Case is assigned a unique identifier with a prefix of `CAS` by default that you can customize by going to Settings, Administration, Auto-numbering.

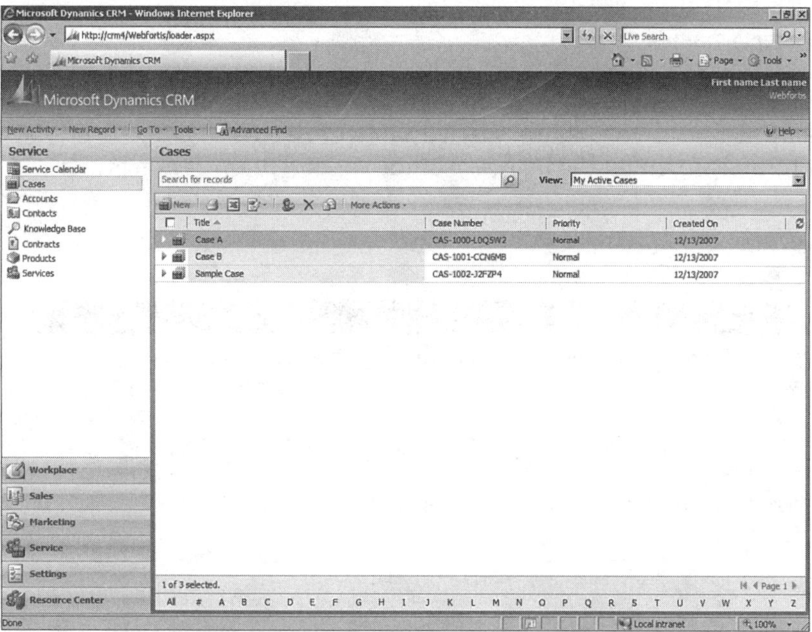

FIGURE 12.21 Cases interface.

Before starting to work with Cases, it is a good idea to prepare and define the Subjects for the Knowledge Base (KB), explained later in this chapter. The reason for this is that to create a new Case, you must enter a Title for the Case, the associated customer (which can be an Account or Contact), and a Subject, which is related to the Knowledge Base.

To create a new Case, click New (as shown in Figure 12.22).

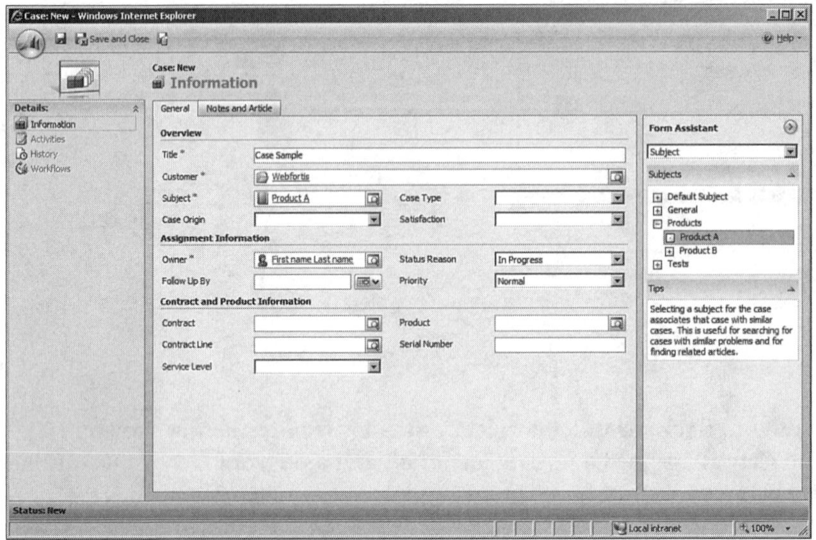

FIGURE 12.22 Creating a new Case.

After selecting the Subject, you can move to the Notes and Article tab and look up the Knowledge Base articles associated with the selected Subject (see Figure 12.23). You can do this by using the Form Assistant on the right side of the window or by opening the Article pop-up.

After entering the required values, click Save and Close to create the new Case.

TIP

You can also create a Case from an Activity by converting the Activity to a Case. This is useful when you need to open a Case that originated from an e-mail or a phone conversation.

After creating a Case, you can perform the following actions:

- Follow Up
- Delete Case
- Resolve Case
- Cancel Case

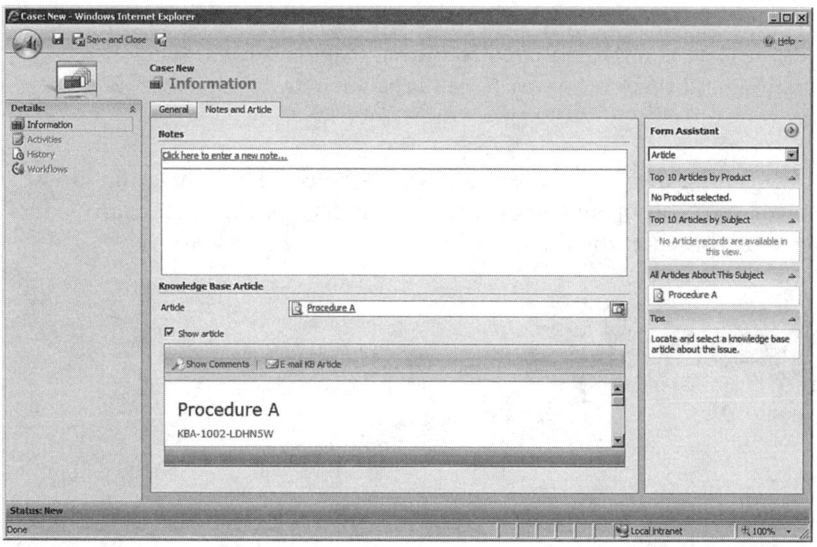

FIGURE 12.23 Associating a Knowledge Base article to a Case.

Follow Up

Follow Up switches the Form Assistant on the right side of the window to easily create an activity that will be associated with the Case, as shown in Figure 12.24. You can use this option, for example, to add a reminder to call the customer with the resolution at a specific date and time.

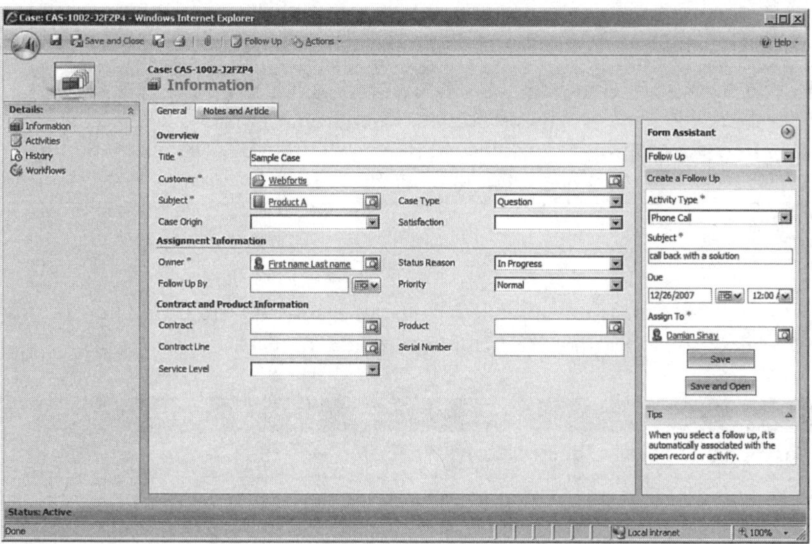

FIGURE 12.24 Follow Up.

Delete Case

This option deletes the Case and its associated records and activities. This operation requires a confirmation, and there is no way to roll it back.

Resolve Case

Resolve the Case by opening the Case and going to the Actions menu item at the top and selecting Resolve Case. This opens the Case resolution dialog box, as shown in Figure 12.25, where you can enter the resolution description and billable time.

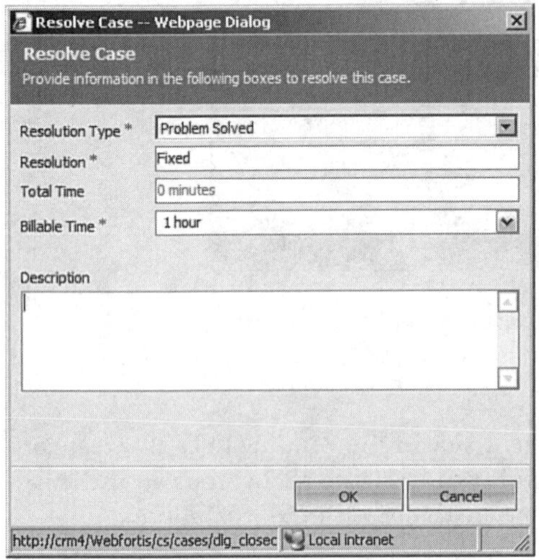

FIGURE 12.25 Case resolution dialog box.

TIP

After a Case is resolved, you can't edit its properties. If you want to make a change to a resolved Case, you must reactivate it by selecting Reactivate from the Actions menu, making your changes, and then resolving it again.

Cancel Case

This option changes the Case status to Cancelled. You can reactivate the Case later, if necessary. After you select this option, a confirmation dialog appears.

NOTE

To cancel a Case, you can't have an open activity associated with the Case.

Reports

There are some predefined reports built for Cases that you can run for the selected record or based on all records. To see these reports from the Cases interface, click the Report icon, as shown in Figure 12.26.

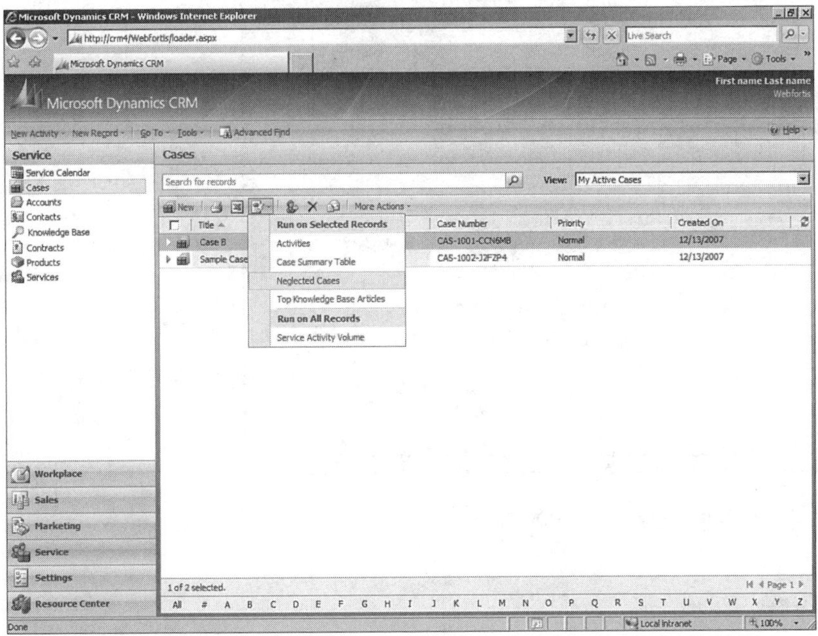

FIGURE 12.26 Case-related reports.

The available reports are

- Activities
- Case Summary Table
- Neglected Cases
- Top Knowledge Base Articles
- Service Activity Volume

Figure 12.27 shows a Cases Summary Table report.

TIP

If the predefined reports don't meet your needs, you can easily create custom reports using the new Report Wizard. For more information about working with reports, refer to Chapter 13, "Reporting."

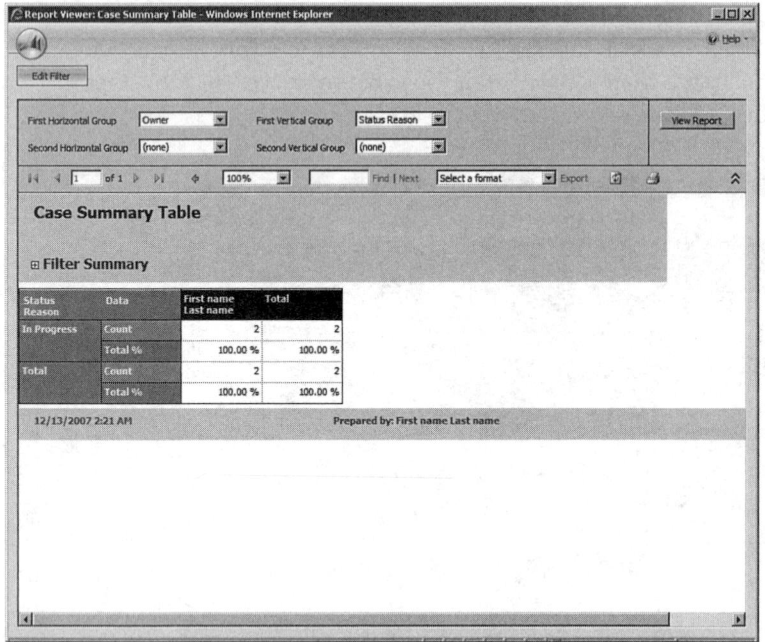

FIGURE 12.27 Cases Summary Table report.

Knowledge Base

As its name implies, the Knowledge Base (KB) is a common repository where users can share their experience and search for solutions for common issues and customers' questions.

The Knowledge Base has a small predefined workflow:

1. Anyone with the right permissions can create articles.
2. Articles are submitted for review.
3. A higher-level permissions user reviews articles and approves or disapproves them.
4. When approved, articles are published.

Figure 12.28 shows the steps involved in this workflow.

Before you start to write Knowledge Base articles, it is important to consider the following things:

- Be sure to prepare the right article Templates so you have a consistent Knowledge Base of articles. You can manage Templates by going to Settings, Templates, Articles Templates (see Figure 12.29).

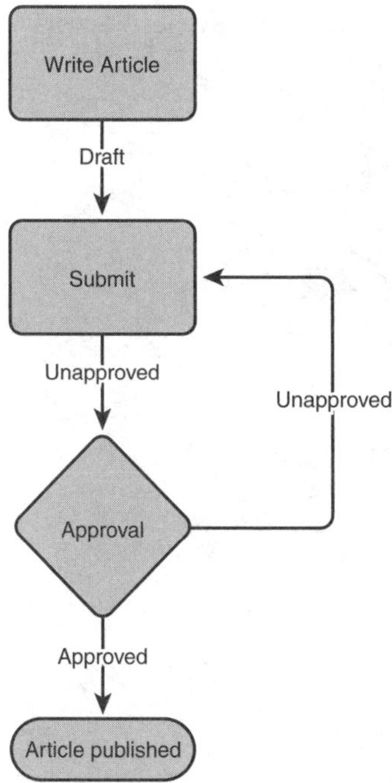

FIGURE 12.28 Knowledge Base workflow.

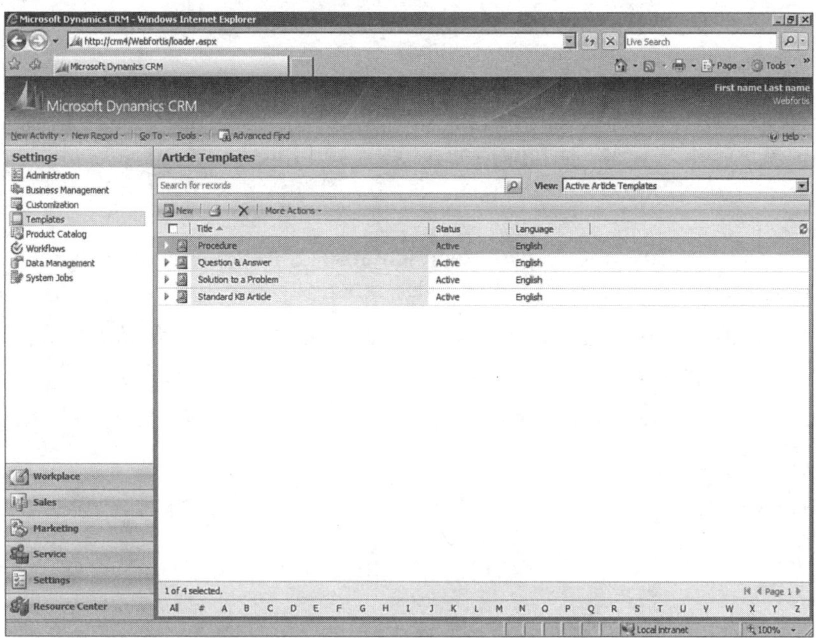

FIGURE 12.29 Managing Article Templates.

- Be sure to set up the topics where you want people to submit their articles so users can search for them more easily after they are published. You can do this by going to Settings, Business Management, Subjects (see Figure 12.30).

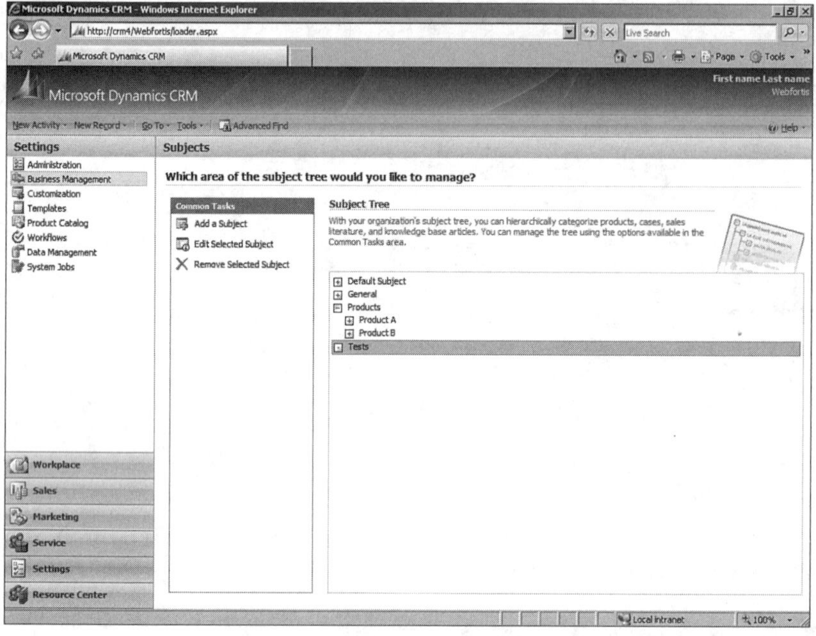

FIGURE 12.30 Configuring the subject tree.

- Be sure to set up the right permissions to the users who can write and submit articles, the users who can approve or reject the articles, and the users who can publish the articles.

By default, users with a CSR (Customer Service Representative) role can write and submit articles; CSR Managers can approve, reject, and publish articles.

Figure 12.31 shows the default interface when you access the Knowledge Base interface as Administrator.

This interface is divided into the following views:

- Article Queues
- Full Text Search
- Keyword Search
- Title Search
- Article Number Search
- Subject Browse

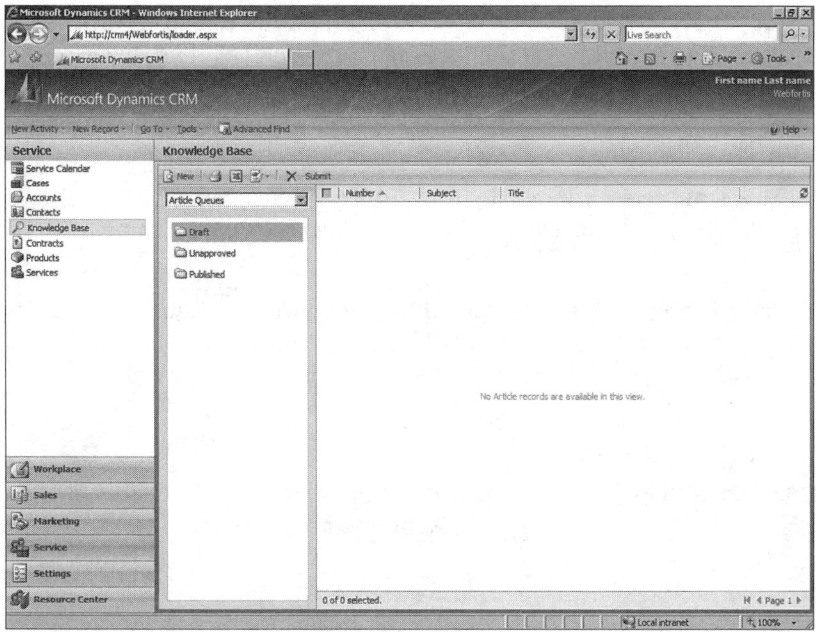

FIGURE 12.31 Knowledge Base interface.

No matter which view you are using, you can always create a new article. To create a new Knowledge Base Article, follow these steps:

1. Click the New button. You will see the window shown in Figure 12.32.

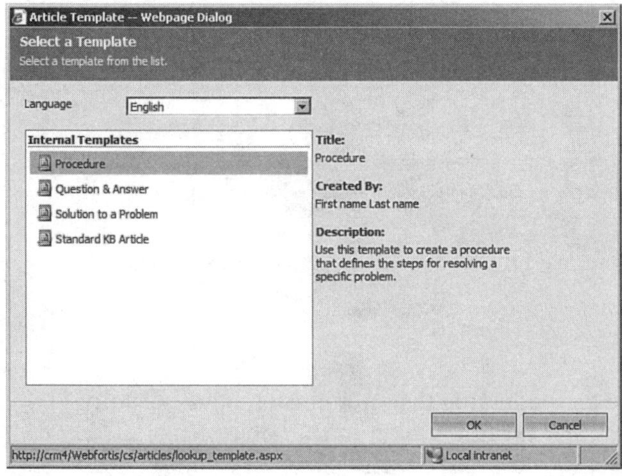

Figure 12.32 Selecting a Template.

A new feature of Microsoft Dynamics CRM 4.0 is that now you can create articles for different languages, depending on the language packs you have installed (see Chapter 14 for more information on Language Packs). You also can create an article for any specific language, or you can create an article for All Languages if you want to have the article available for everybody.

2. Select the Language and select a Template from the list. Notice that the Internal Templates vary depending on the language selected. Press the OK button to continue.
3. Enter the Title and Subject, which are required for any article (see Figures 12.33 and 12.34). The body format of the article depends on the selected Template. It is recommended that you enter keywords for a faster search and lookup of the articles.
4. Click Save and Close to continue.

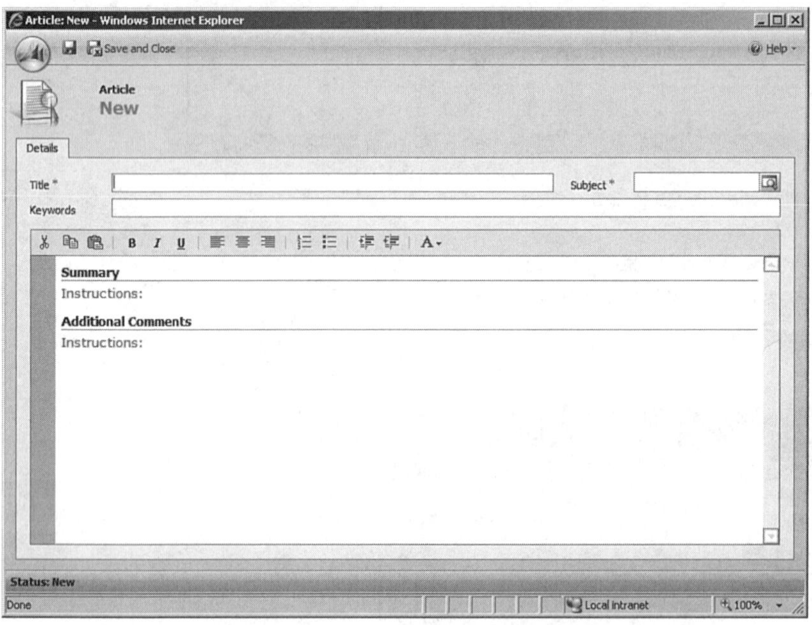

FIGURE 12.33 Writing a Knowledge Base article based on the Standard KB Article Template.

Subjects

To create new subjects, you must be logged in as System Administrator. Click Settings, Business Management, Subjects; click any existing subject in the Subject Tree, and click the Add a Subject link from the Common Tasks list box, as shown in Figure 12.35.

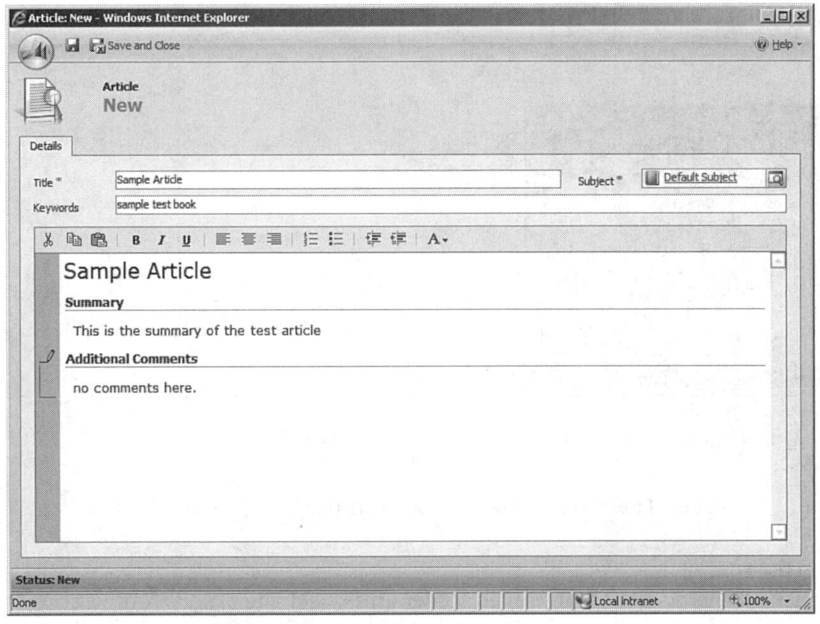

FIGURE 12.34 Writing a KB article.

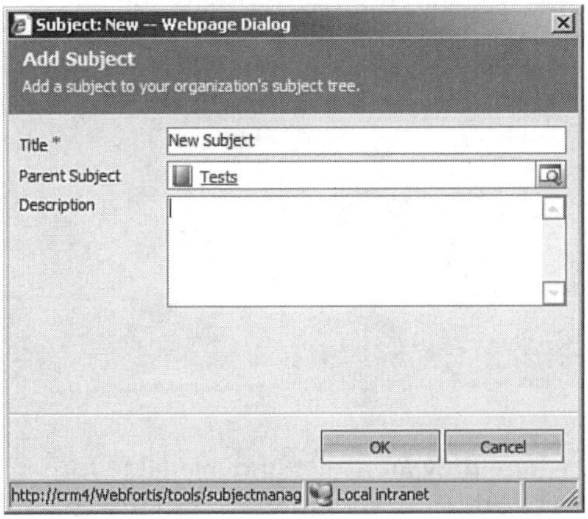

FIGURE 12.35 Subject Tree options.

All articles go directly to the Draft folder when created, which means that they aren't available to users until the article is published.

Submitting a KB Article

An article must be submitted before it can be approved or disapproved. To submit an article, you must move to the Draft folder, select the article you want to submit, and click the Submit button. You receive a dialog alert to confirm the operation, as shown in Figure 12.36.

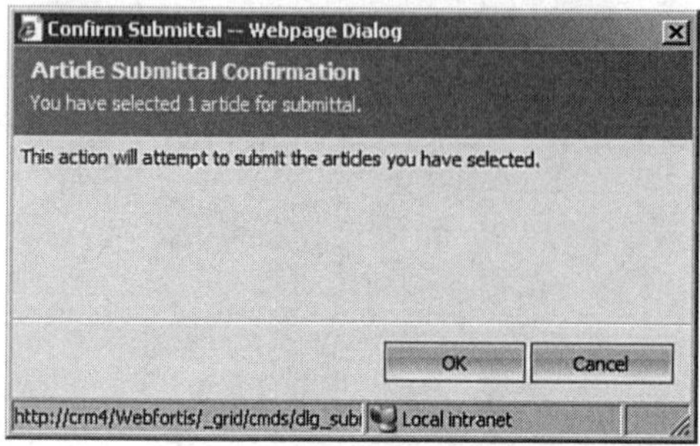

FIGURE 12.36 Article submission.

Click OK to submit the article. The article will be moved to the Unapproved folder.

Approving a KB Article

To approve an Article, move to the Unapproved folder and select the article you want to approve; then click the Approve button (see Figure 12.37).

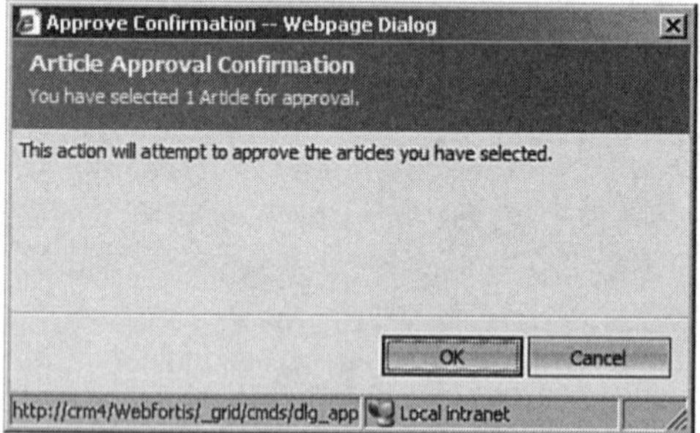

FIGURE 12.37 Article approval.

Approved articles move to the Published folder, where they are ready and available for other users. Once the Article is published, it can't be edited or modified. To modify an Article, it must be unpublished, which you do by opening a published Article and clicking Unpublish. That action will move the Article to the Unapproved folder where you will be able to edit it. Notice the Article will be unavailable to users during editing. After modifying the Article, it must be approved again to be available to users.

Rejecting a KB Article

To reject an article, open the article located in the Unapproved queue and click the Reject button (see Figure 12.38).

This enables you to enter the rejection reason (see Figure 12.39).

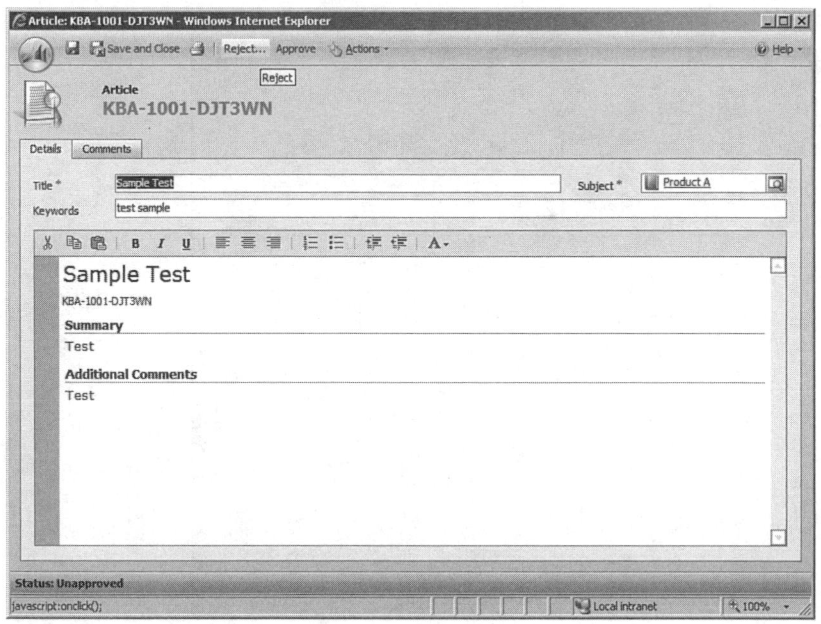

FIGURE 12.38 Article review for rejection.

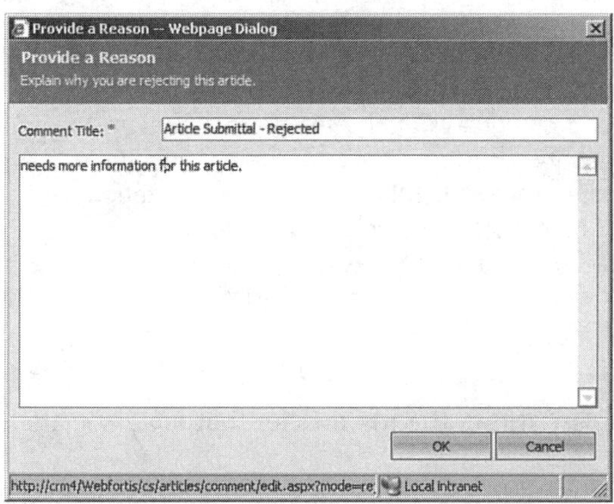

FIGURE 12.39 Article rejection.

After you click OK, the article moves back to the Draft queue. If the user who wrote the article wants to see the comments and reasons for the rejection, he will have to move to the Draft queue, select the article and double-click it, and move to the Comments tab (see Figure 12.40).

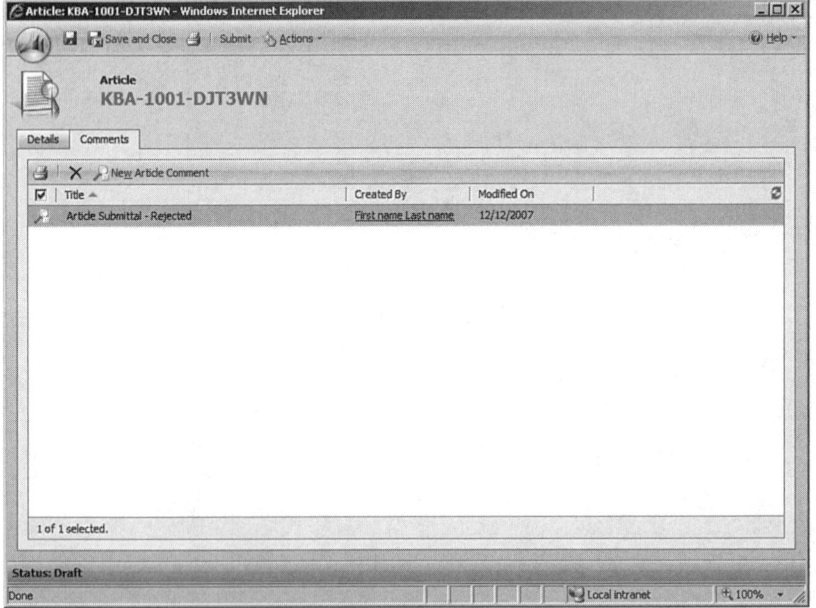

FIGURE 12.40 Article rejection reasons.

TIP

The Knowledge Base article default workflow doesn't send alerts when a user submits, approves, or rejects an article. A good practice would be to create a custom workflow for Article and/or Article Comment entities so that users can be notified via e-mail when an article is submitted, approved, or rejected. This is a nice customization that was not possible in previous versions of Microsoft Dynamics CRM. Refer to Chapter 20 for more details about how to create custom workflows.

Reports

A predefined report built for the Knowledge Base shows the top articles that are associated and used on Cases (see Figure 12.41).

NOTE

If the report option is empty, you must have at least one Case record associated with the Knowledge Base articles.

Knowledge Base Articles Security

The Knowledge Base is not available to all roles by default. For example, the Salesperson role doesn't have access to see KB articles, whereas a Customer Representative does. Of course, you can customize and change this configuration as necessary.

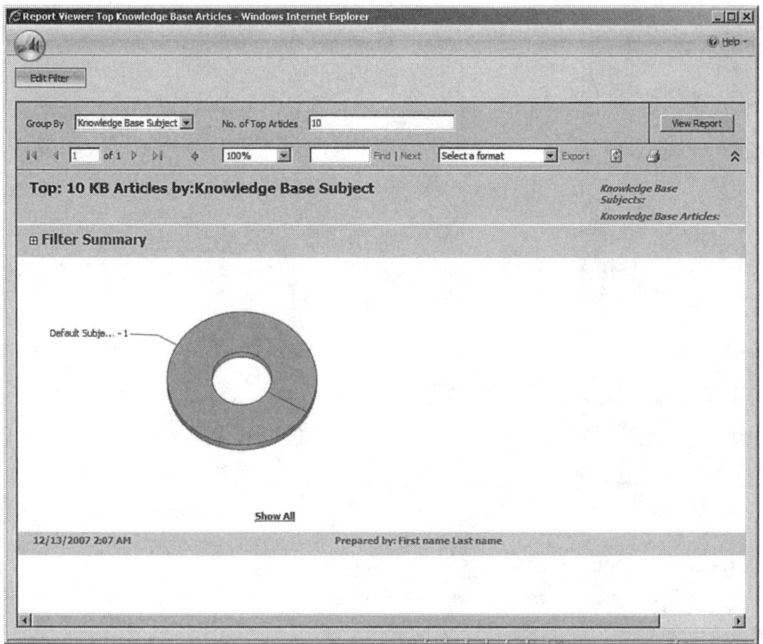

FIGURE 12.41 Top Knowledge Base Articles Report.

Contracts

Contracts are created from a Template that is defined by a language. A Contract is a group of services and products that you sell to a client during a period of time, and are very useful in managing service obligations. With a Contract, you define when you start providing services to a customer and when you finish; both dates are required when you create a Contract. Each Contract also has billing information associated with it, such as which client you will bill, to what address you will send invoices, and billing frequency (monthly, quarterly, annually, and so on). The products you sell are defined in Contract lines, where you can enter product details such as the quantity, the time you will include for support Cases, and the total price and discounts.

To create new Contracts, follow these steps:

1. Navigate to the Contracts section within the Service tab and click New.
2. Select a Template (see Figure 12.42). To create a new Template, go to Settings, Templates, and select the Contract Templates option (refer to Chapter 14 for more information on how to manage and create new Templates).
3. Enter the required fields `Customer Name`, `Customer`, `Contract Start Date`, `Contract End Date`, `Billing Information`, and `Currency` (see Figure 12.43). Click Save to continue.

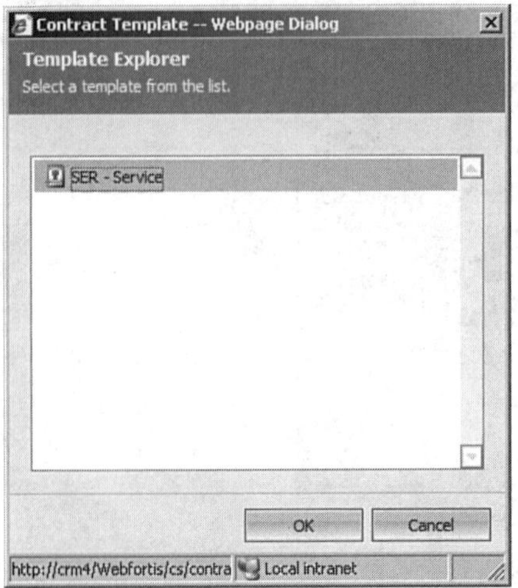

FIGURE 12.42 Selecting a Contract Template for a new Contract.

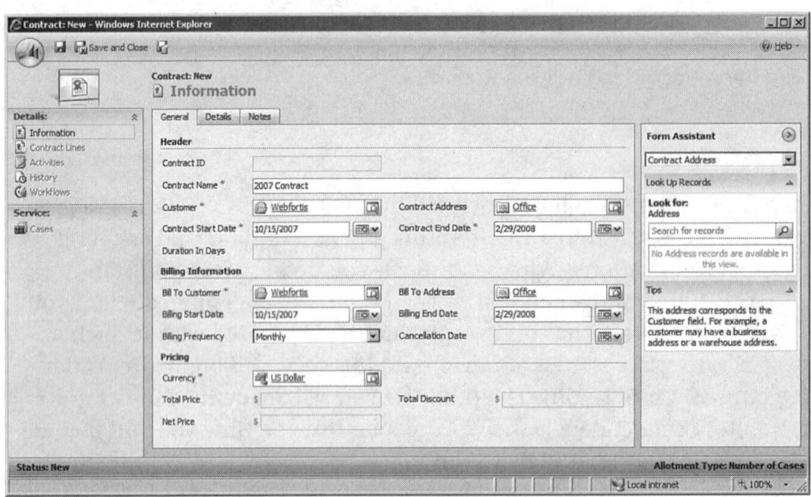

FIGURE 12.43 Creating a new Contract.

4. Go to the Contract Lines tab inside the Details section, and click the New Contract Line button.

5. Enter the required fields (see Figure 12.44).

6. Click Save and Close.

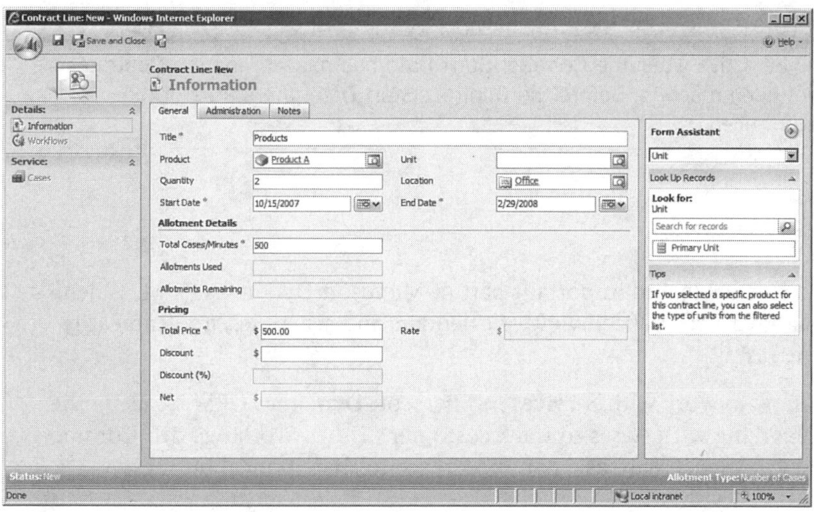

FIGURE 12.44 Creating a New Contract Line.

Each Contract also has a specific calendar associated with it. You can access it by clicking on the Calendar button on the top menu of the Contract form. This is useful for customer representatives to know whether the client should be supported 24×7 or only at regular times. You can use a check box to easily convert the calendar to 24×7 Support, as shown in Figure 12.45.

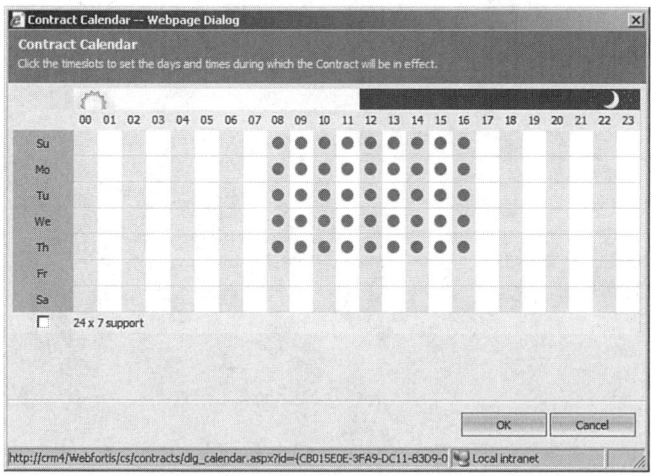

FIGURE 12.45 Contract Calendar.

After the Contract is created, its status is Draft. To make a Contract Active, you must open the Contract record, go to Actions from the top menu, and select the Invoice Contract option. Notice that to invoice a Contract, it must contain at least one Contract line.

NOTE

The Contract will be active when the Contract Start Date has passed and the Contract End Date has not been reached. Before the Contract Start Date, the status of the Contract will say Invoiced.

Summary

The Service area is a valuable and important part of Microsoft Dynamics CRM. When used correctly, you have a centralized view of calendars and schedules, and can easily perform scheduling tasks.

You have learned how to work with Services in Microsoft Dynamics CRM by using the Service Calendar, working with Cases to track customer's issues, working with Contracts, and managing the Knowledge Base as a common place to share typical business procedures.

CHAPTER 13
Reporting

IN THIS CHAPTER

- ▶ Reporting Defined
- ▶ Report Wizard
- ▶ Scheduled Reports
- ▶ Exporting
- ▶ Advanced Features

This version of Microsoft Dynamics CRM features improved reporting capabilities. Reports are more dynamic and flexible, and a Reporting Wizard is now included that enables Users to create basic reports on-the-fly and share them with the organization.

Reporting Defined

Microsoft Dynamics CRM handles all the reports with Microsoft SQL Server Reporting Services (SRS), which is a separate application that you can install on a different server than SQL Server or the Microsoft Dynamics CRM Server if desired. Microsoft Dynamics CRM then connects to SRS by using the Reporting Services URL, as specified during installation.

The Connector for Microsoft SQL SRS is not required during a normal, non-IFD installation. For IFD installations, or when you make modifications to the default setup, you must install the Connector for Microsoft SQL SRS, to avoid the error shown in Figure 13.1.

To install the Connector for Microsoft SQL Server, follow the steps outlined in Chapter 5, "Setting Up CRM 4.0."

After the Connector is installed, you can access reports in Microsoft Dynamics CRM from the main reporting interface, which is found in the Workplace area, or directly from various entities in the system (Accounts, Contacts, etc.) (see Figure 13.2). When viewing reports in the system, you can see all available reports; however, you may or may not be able to display the underlying data, depending on your permissions.

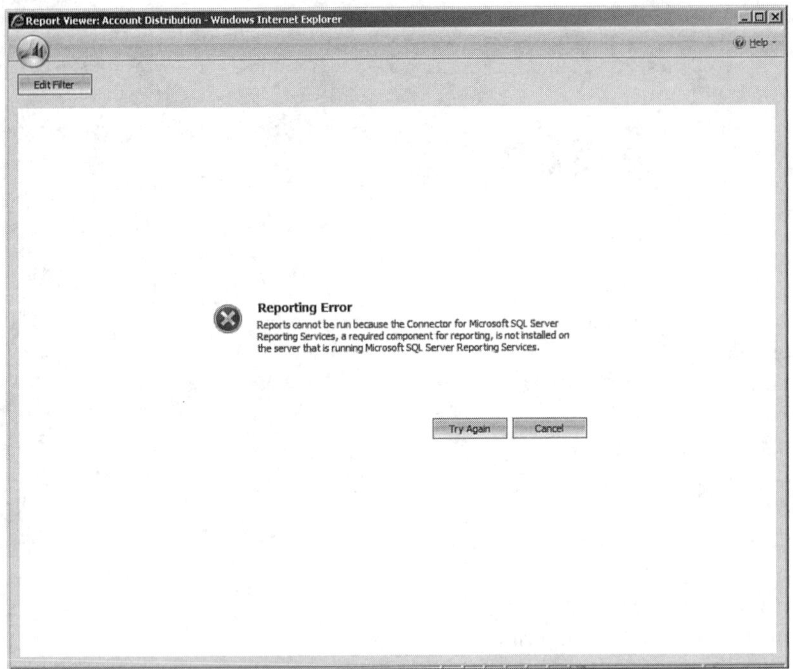

FIGURE 13.1 Reporting error.

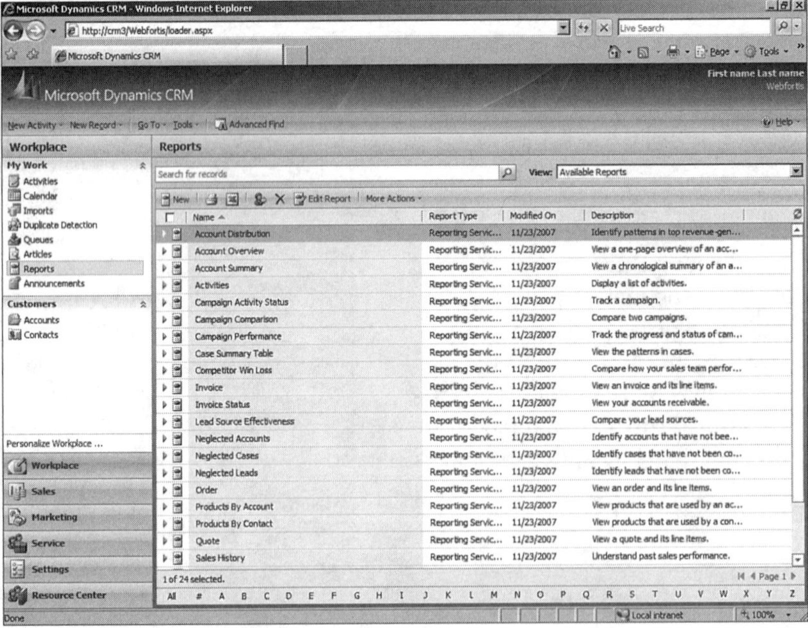

FIGURE 13.2 Reports in the Workplace.

When working with an entity record, such as Contacts shown in Figure 13.3, you can run specific entity reports without needing to access the main Reports area by accessing the Reports option on the top menu bar.

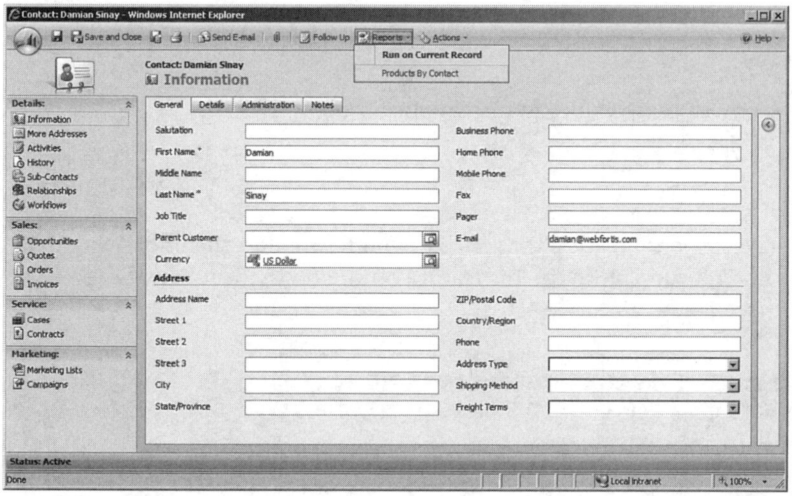

FIGURE 13.3 Reports from the Contact entity.

Although some reports are already configured to run directly from the entity, you can easily modify a report so that it is available as part of the entity. To do so, follow these steps:

1. Select a report from the Main Reports interface located in Workplace, Reports, by clicking it to select it, and select Edit Report from the toolbar.

2. When the report definition window opens, select Related Record Types from the Categorization section and then click the ... button. Adding one of the available values to the selected values enables you to run that report directly from the selected entity (see Figure 13.4).

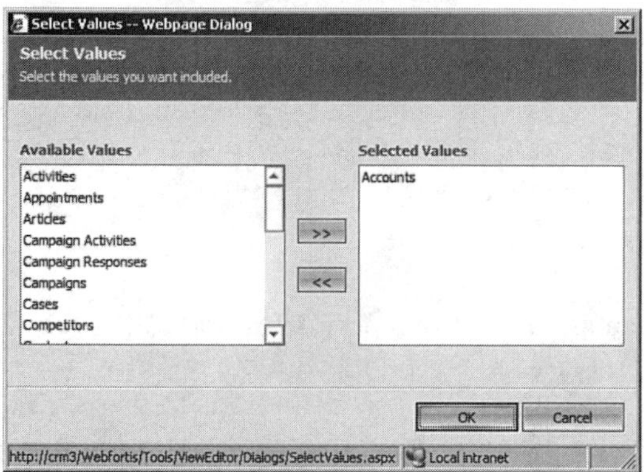

FIGURE 13.4 Related record types for reports.

3. You can also use the Display In option to configure where you want to have the reports available. You can set the following values for this property:

   - Forms for Related Record Types
   - Lists for Related Record Types
   - Reports Area

   You can choose any of these values to display the report.

Reports Filters

All reports in CRM have a special feature that enables you to prefilter the underlying data when you run a report. You can configure this feature on the first screen when you double-click a report (see Figure 13.5).

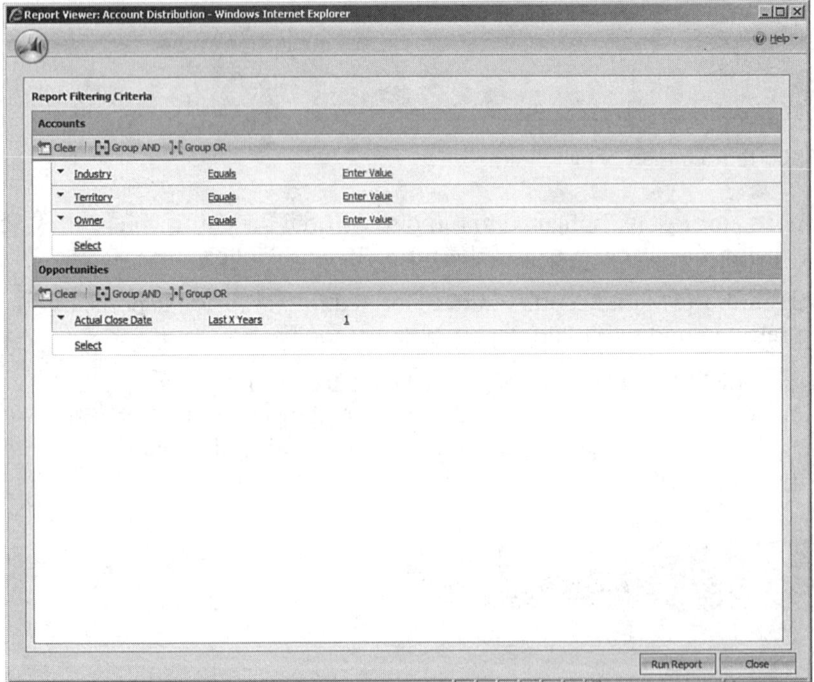

FIGURE 13.5 Report Filtering Criteria.

You will see the report criteria that are defined as part of the report definition. Although you can manually change these values and properties every time you run a report, you can also change the default filtering criteria by editing the report definition. To do so, go to the main Reports option located in Workplace, Reports, select the report you want to modify, and then select Edit Default Filter from the More Actions drop-down menu (see Figure 13.6).

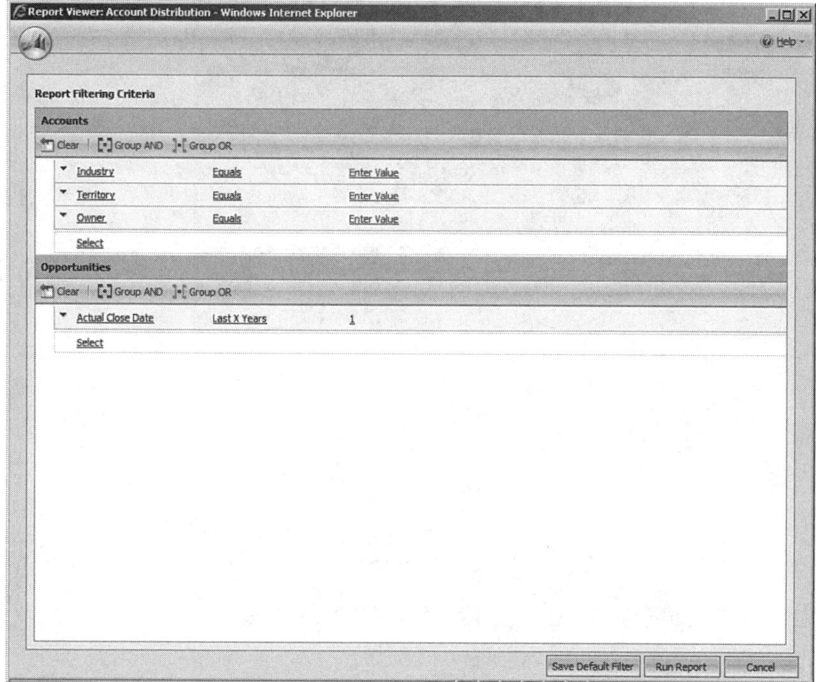

FIGURE 13.6 Modifying the default Report Filtering Criteria.

Make any necessary changes and then click the Save Default Filter button to save your changes. This change will affect all Users running the report.

Categories

Reports are divided into categories so that they can be easily found. This is especially useful when working with many custom reports in the organization.

By default, only the following four categories are created in the system, but you can easily create more as necessary:

- Administrative Reports
- Marketing Reports
- Sales Reports
- Service Reports

Each category has a predefined view to filter and is easily accessible, as shown in Figure 13.7.

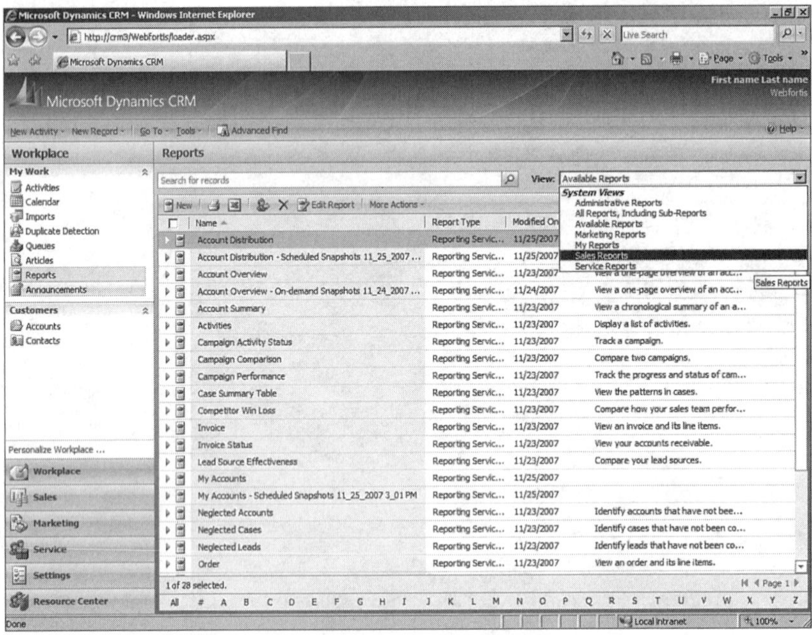

FIGURE 13.7 Report categories views.

To set a category on a report, select the report from the Reports interface and then click the Edit Report button. Click the ... button under the last section labeled Categorization, and then select the required categories for the report (see Figure 13.8).

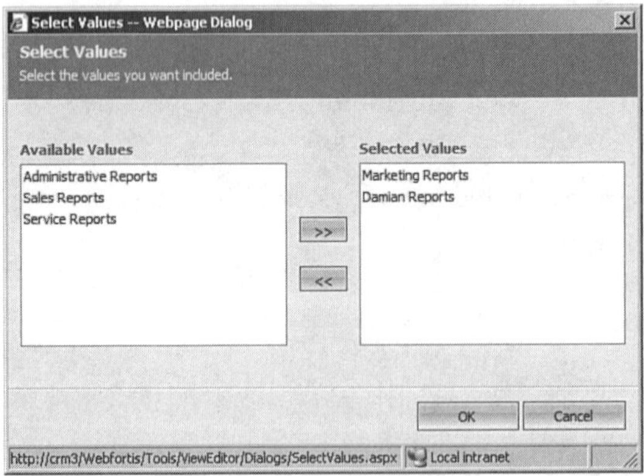

FIGURE 13.8 Associating report categories.

To create new report categories, navigate to the Administration area in Settings and click System Settings. Select the Reporting tab to edit the categories, as shown in Figure 13.9.

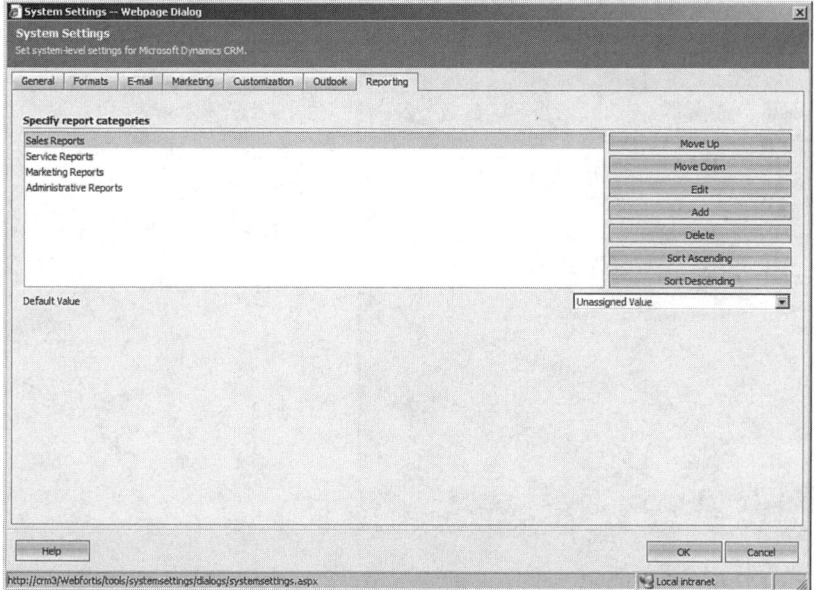

FIGURE 13.9 Managing reporting categories.

Click the Add button to create a new category and enter a label for the new category. Then click OK twice to close the dialog boxes.

NOTE

To use any newly created category, you must create the view manually.

Administration

When editing a report (by selecting a report and then Edit Report from the top menu), there are two tabs—General and Administration. The Administration option is used to configure the administrative options for the report. By using the options on the tab, you can set the owner of the report and whether the report should be viewed by the User or by the entire organization (see Figure 13.10).

TIP

You can also change the report owner by selecting Assign from the Actions drop-down menu.

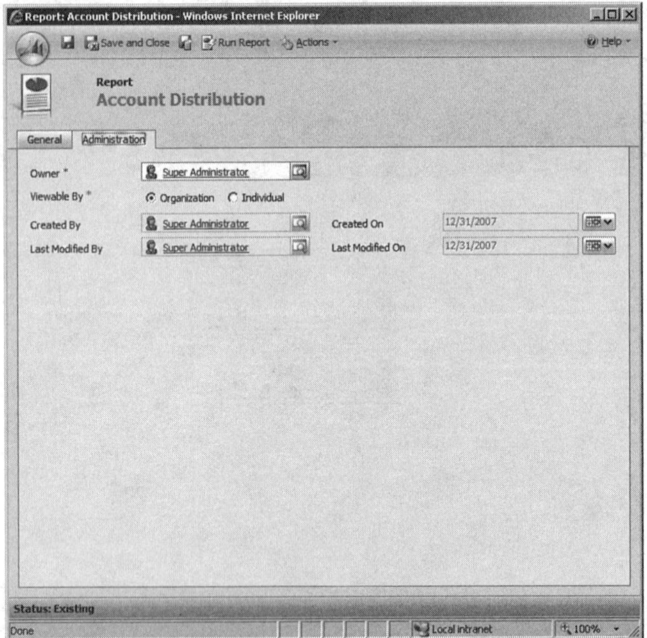

FIGURE 13.10 Report administration.

Report Wizard

The Report Wizard is a new feature with this version of Microsoft Dynamics CRM that enables Users to build basic reports without development knowledge. The Report Wizard gives Users an easy-to-use interface for building reports. Additionally, the final reports are actually Microsoft SQL SRS reports, or `.rdl` files, that you can further manipulate using a more advanced editing tool such as Visual Studio.

NOTE

As explained later, you can edit reports built with the Report Wizard using Visual Studio to increase performance, layout, and report complexity. However, after you have modified a report (or if it has been created in Visual Studio), it might be unavailable to be modified further with the Report Wizard due to the advanced editing nature of Visual Studio.

To use the Report Wizard, follow these steps:

1. Navigate to Workplace and then Reports. Select New, which opens the dialog box shown in Figure 13.11.

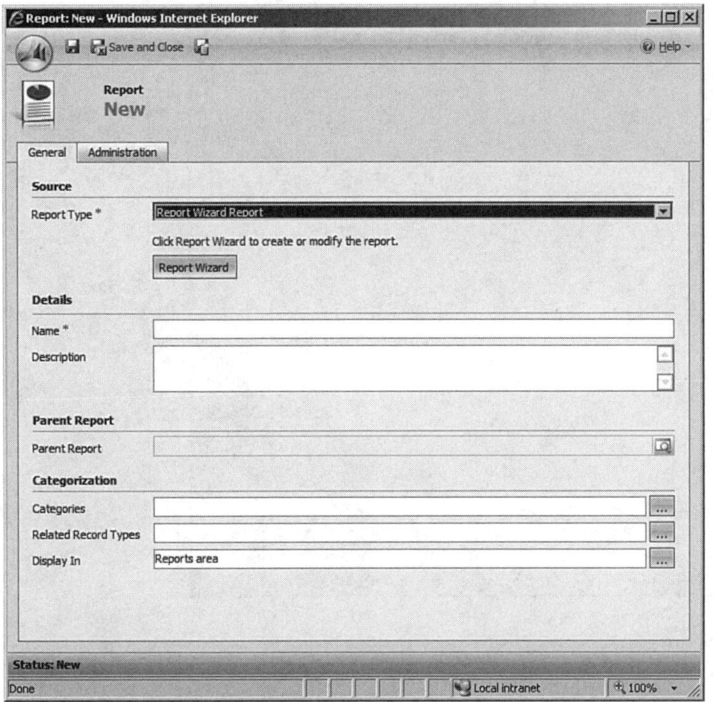

FIGURE 13.11 New report.

2. The Report Type option defaults to Report Wizard Report, which is the one used in this example. If you had created an external report, such as one using Visual Studio, you would select Existing File and upload the file directly. Link to a Web Page enables you to link to a web page that contains a report.

3. Click the Report Wizard button to start the wizard. After it starts, you have two options for creating a new report (see Figure 13.12):

   - Start a New Report
   - Start from an Existing Report

   The second option allows you to only create a new report from a report that was previously generated through this wizard, and it allows you to make edits to an existing report through the wizard. If you have other languages installed on the CRM server, you will also be able to select the report language on this step. In this example, you'll create a new report by selecting the first option and clicking Next to continue.

4. The Report Properties dialog box is displayed where you must enter a name for the report; you also must select the Primary Record Type (see Figure 13.13). The Primary Record Type will be one of the entities available in the system, such as Accounts, Contacts, and so on.

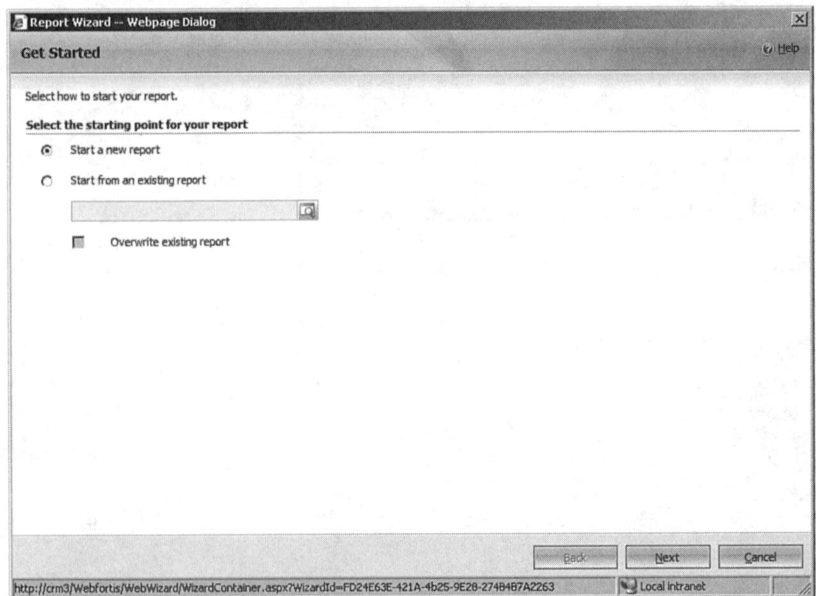

FIGURE 13.12 Report Wizard.

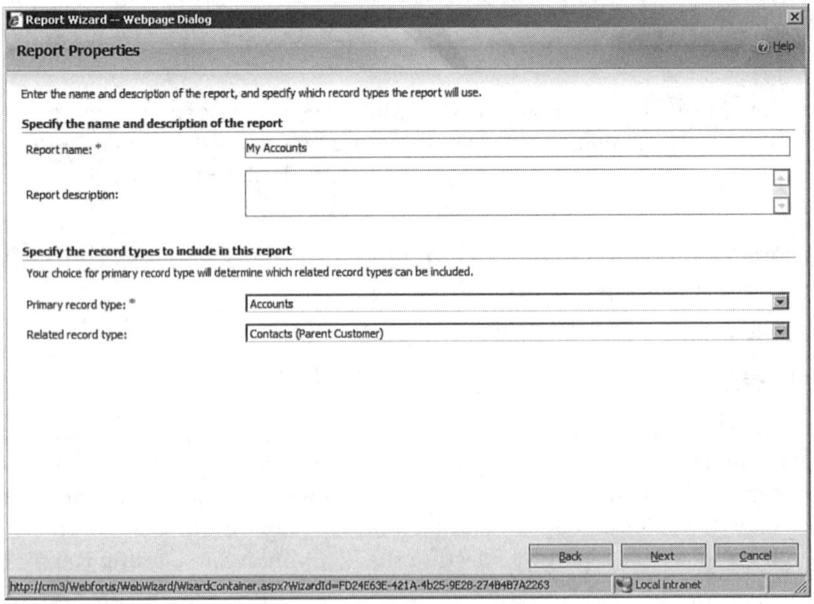

FIGURE 13.13 Report Properties.

NOTE

The Related Record Type option values depend on the entity you select on the Primary Record Type. It shows all the entities related to the primary entity selected. We will select Contacts as the Related Record Type so that we can create a report of the Contacts by Account, for example.

Click Next to continue.

5. Select the default report filters for the primary or related record types selected in the previous step (see Figure 13.14).

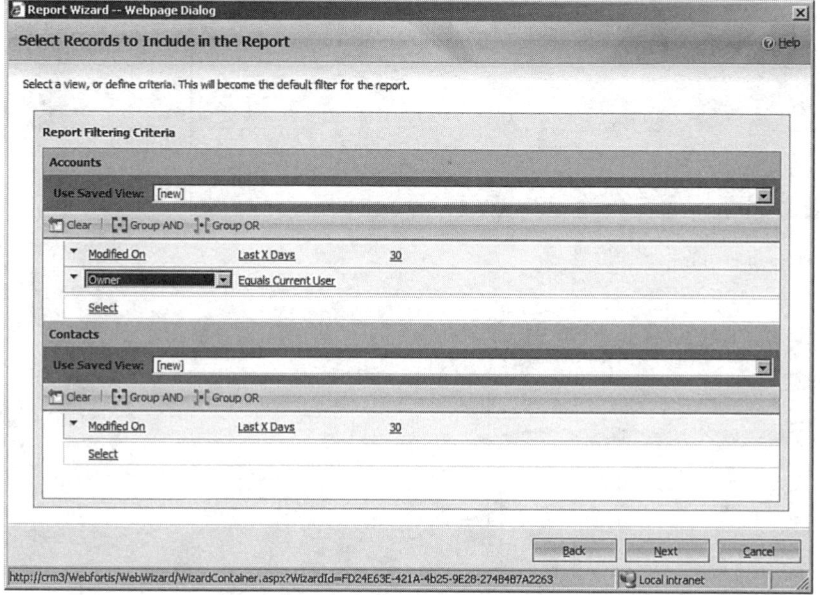

FIGURE 13.14 Report Wizard report filtering criteria.

You can use a previously used View or create a new one. To add a new filter, click on the Select link and select the property you want to use. In this example, we selected the property Owner with criteria of Equals Current User.

Click Next to continue.

6. The Lay Out Fields dialog box appears. You can define the properties you want to have displayed on the report (see Figure 13.15).
7. Select the main box labeled Click Here to Add a Column to add the fields you want to see in the report. As shown in Figure 13.16, you can choose the Record Type, which is limited to the entities you selected as Primary and Related Record Types in the previous steps.

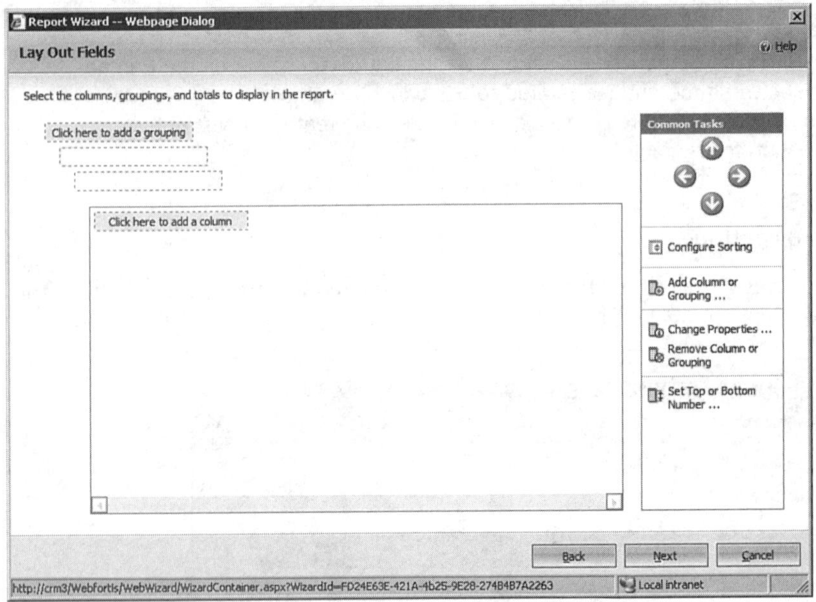

FIGURE 13.15 Lay Out Fields.

FIGURE 13.16 Adding columns to the report.

8. After selecting the Record Type, select the Column, which will be any of the properties of the Record Type you previously selected. The Data Type and Name are displayed only for informational purposes, and you can't change them from this interface. The only thing you can change is the Column Width in pixels.

The last option in the Add Column dialog box is called Summary Type. It is available for only some data types, such as money and numeric data types.

Figure 13.17 shows the available options that you can select for the Summary Type. (They are similar to SQL aggregate functions.)

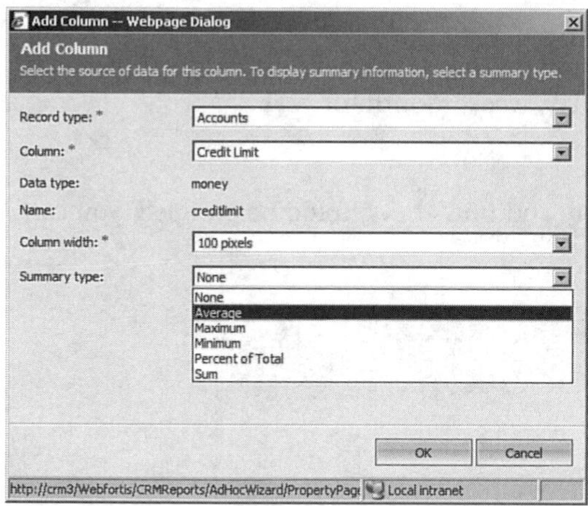

FIGURE 13.17 Summary Types.

9. If any of the Summary Types were used, it is a good idea to configure the grouping by selecting the box labeled Click Here to Add a Grouping. Figure 13.18 shows the grouping options.

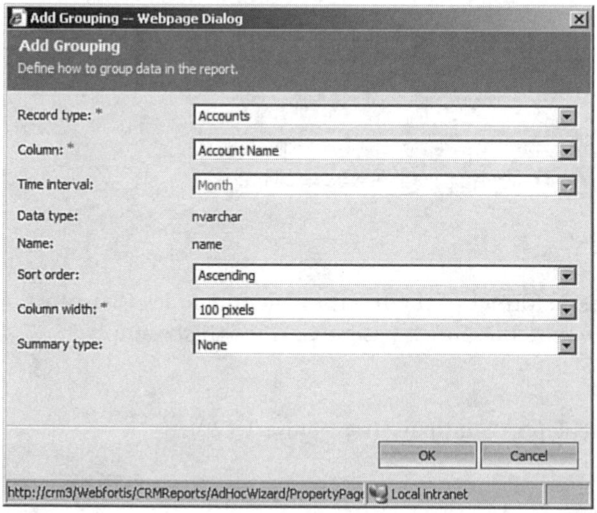

Add Grouping -- Webpage Dialog
Add Grouping
Define how to group data in the report.
Record type: * Accounts
Column: * Account Name
Time interval: Month
Data type: nvarchar
Name: name
Sort order: Ascending
Column width: * 100 pixels
Summary type: None
OK Cancel
http://crm3/Webfortis/CRMReports/AdHocWizard/PropertyPag Local intranet

FIGURE 13.18 Add a Grouping.

The columns that you can select in the grouping are based on any of the entities previously selected.

NOTE

You can create up to three different groupings that will be nested among them.

The Time Interval option is available only for fields that have `datetime` as their data type. The options enable grouping by day, week, month, or year.

Click Next to continue.

10. After defining which columns to display and how they should be grouped, you can specify their format (see Figure 13.19).

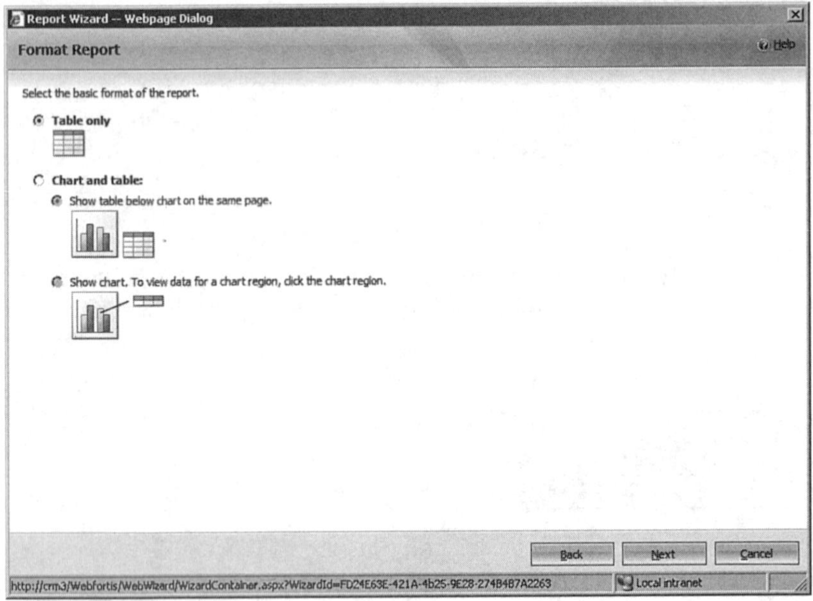

FIGURE 13.19 Format report.

From here, you can select the basic format of the report, which includes Charting. Select Table Only here because you're building a basic report for this example.

Click Next to continue.

11. The last step of the wizard is the Report Summary (see Figure 13.20).

Click Next to continue.

12. The report is generated and the results are displayed (see Figure 13.21). Note that there may be a delay while the report is generated.

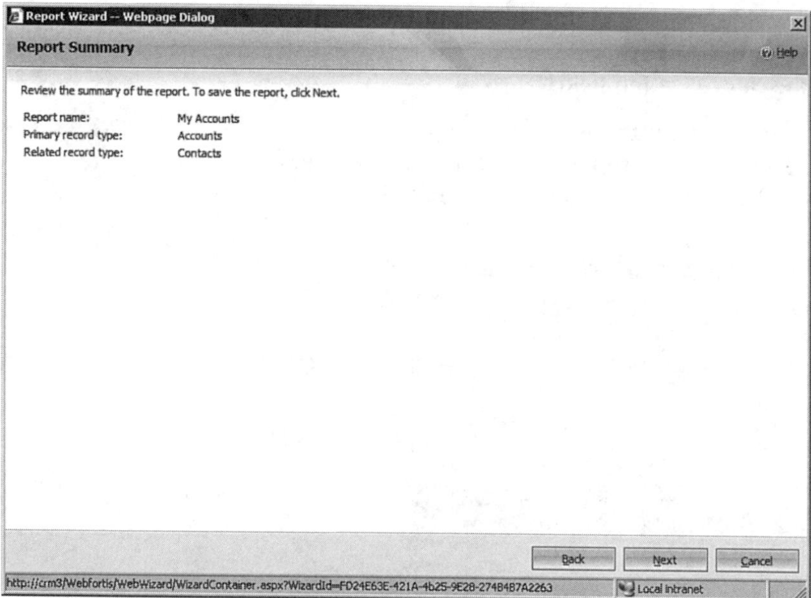

FIGURE 13.20 Report Summary.

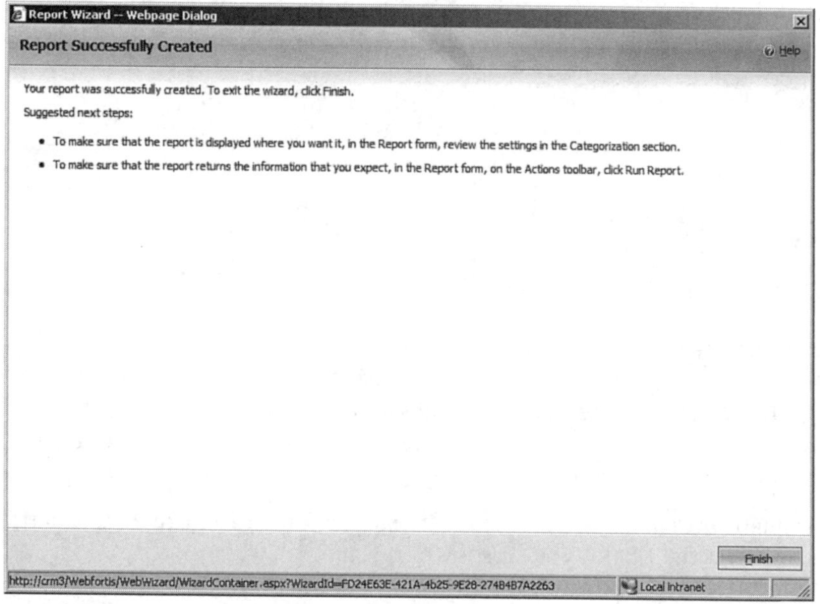

FIGURE 13.21 Report Successfully Created.

13

13. Click Finish to close the wizard. If necessary, you can now select and edit the properties of the report. Notice that the wizard has autopopulated the name of the report and the categorization fields.

14. To test the new report, select the report from the Reports interface and select either Run Report, located on the top menu of this dialog box or double-click the report name. Figure 13.22 shows the report after it has been run.

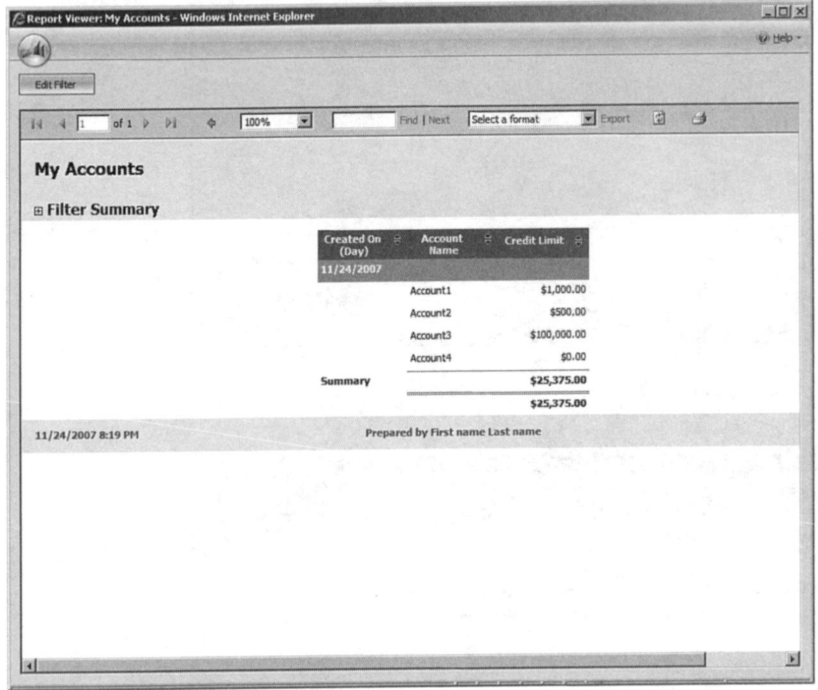

FIGURE 13.22 Running the report.

If you want to modify the report you just created, you can easily run the Report Wizard again. For example, suppose you want to change the selected format from a table to a graphical chart representation. If you select the Report Wizard button, the report will start with the starting point selected for this report, with the option to overwrite it, as shown in Figure 13.23.

Continue through the Report Wizard steps. Change the format from Table to Chart and Table, and select the Chart Type, as shown in Figure 13.24.

NOTE

The Pie Chart type might be disabled if you didn't select the Sum or Percent option in the Summary columns.

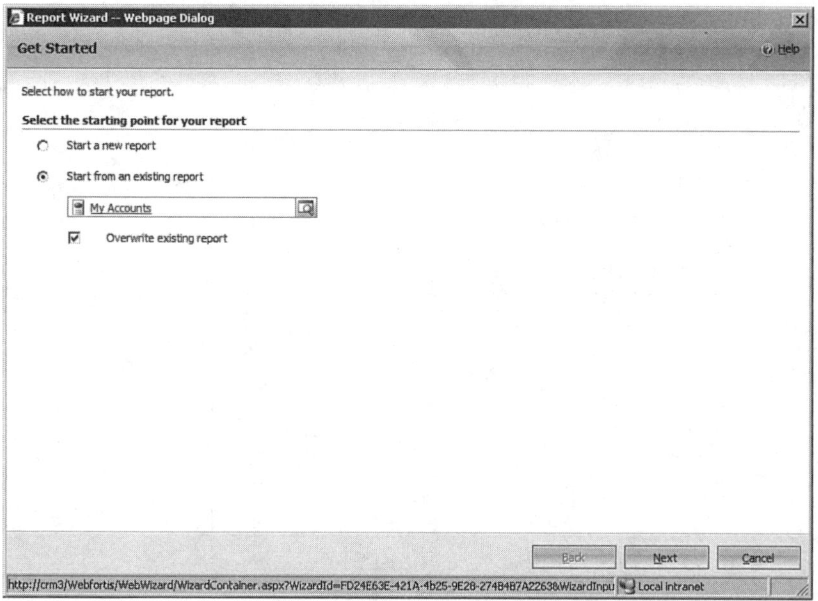

FIGURE 13.23 Modifying the report.

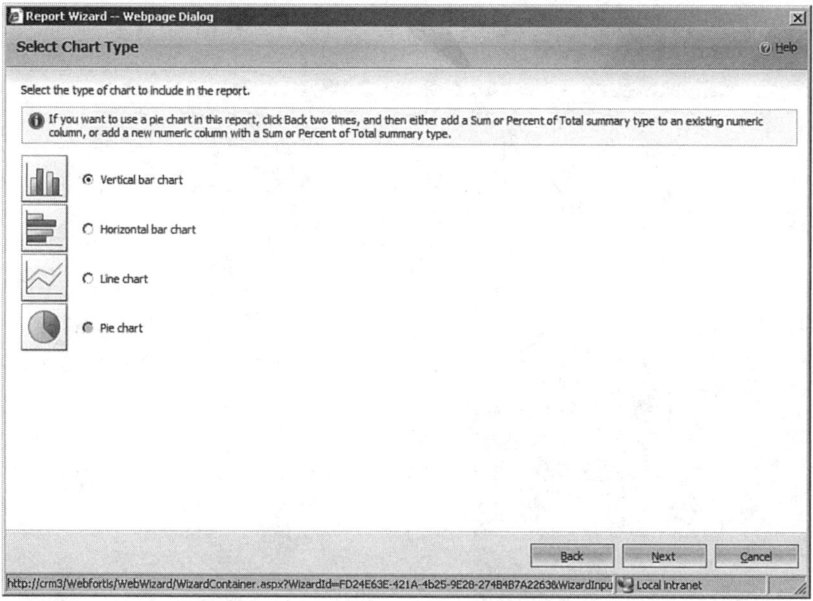

FIGURE 13.24 Select Chart Type.

Click Next to customize the Chart Format. You can select the labels of the x- and y-axis, as well as the fields for them, as shown in Figure 13.25.

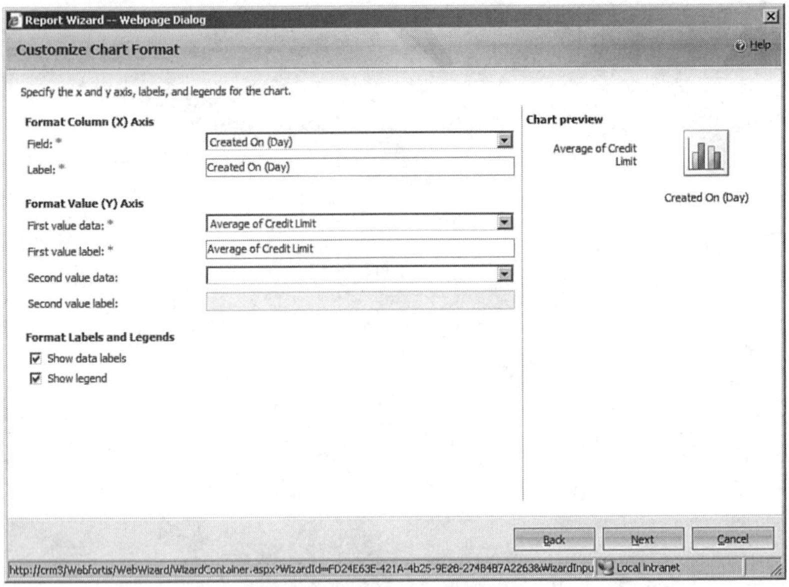

FIGURE 13.25 Customize Chart Format.

Click Next to go to the Summary screen for review, and then click Next to modify the report. Now if you run the report, it will appear as shown in Figure 13.26.

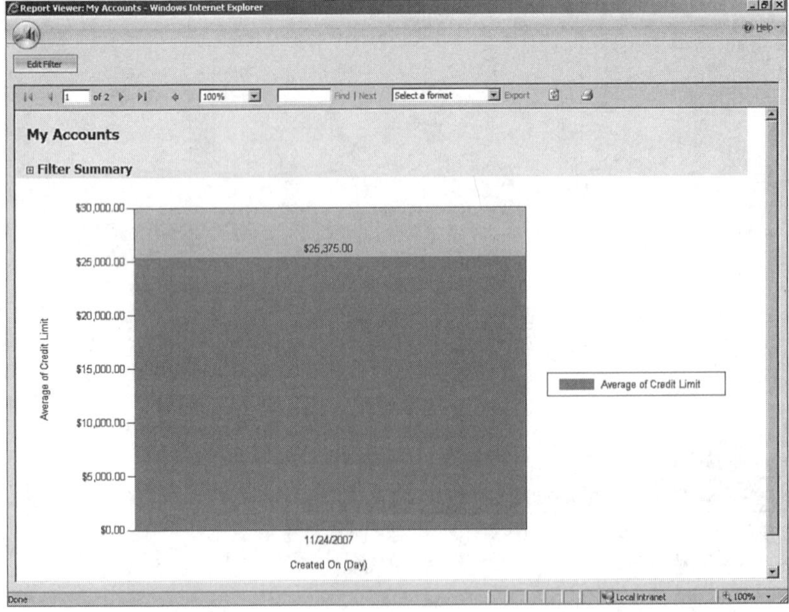

FIGURE 13.26 Running the report with the Chart format.

Scheduled Reports

SRS has many advanced features that are closely integrated in this version of Microsoft Dynamics CRM. For example, you can now schedule report execution.

To access this feature from the Reports interface, select a report and then select Schedule Report from the More Actions drop-down menu (see Figure 13.27).

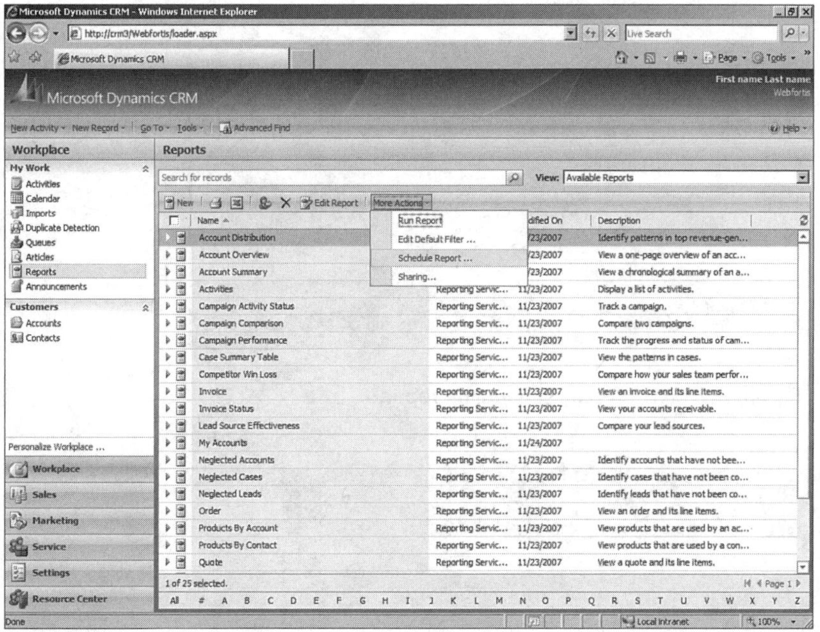

Figure 13.27 Schedule Report.

NOTE

By default, only administrators have access to this feature. To give this feature to a lower-privileged role, an administrator must grant permission in the Add Reporting Services Reports security option under Miscellaneous Privileges in the Core Records tab of the security role configuration interface. The interface can be accessed from the Settings Area, Administration Section by clicking Security Roles and then double-clicking the role you want to customize. Figure 13.28 shows this permission added to the Customer Service Representative role.

The Report Scheduling Wizard starts and presents two options (see Figure 13.29):

- On Demand
- On a Schedule

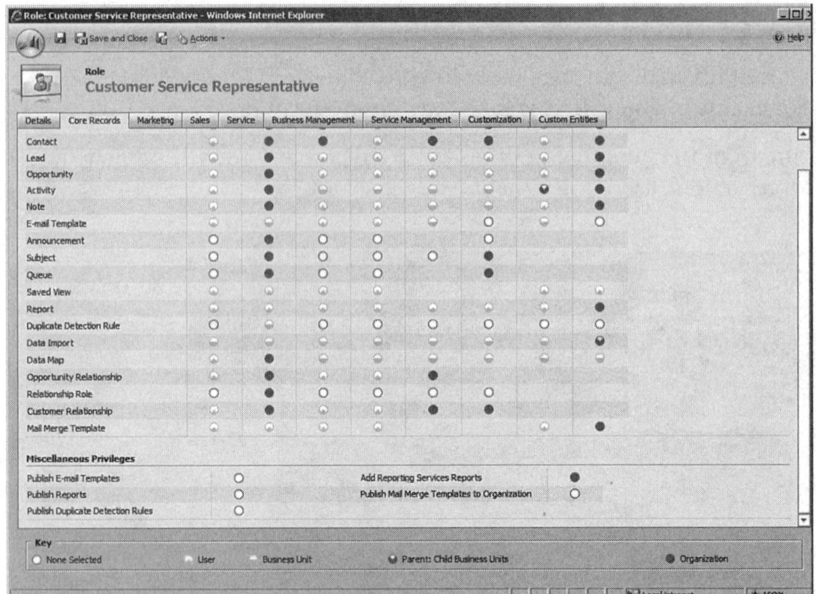

FIGURE 13.28 Setting permissions for scheduling reports.

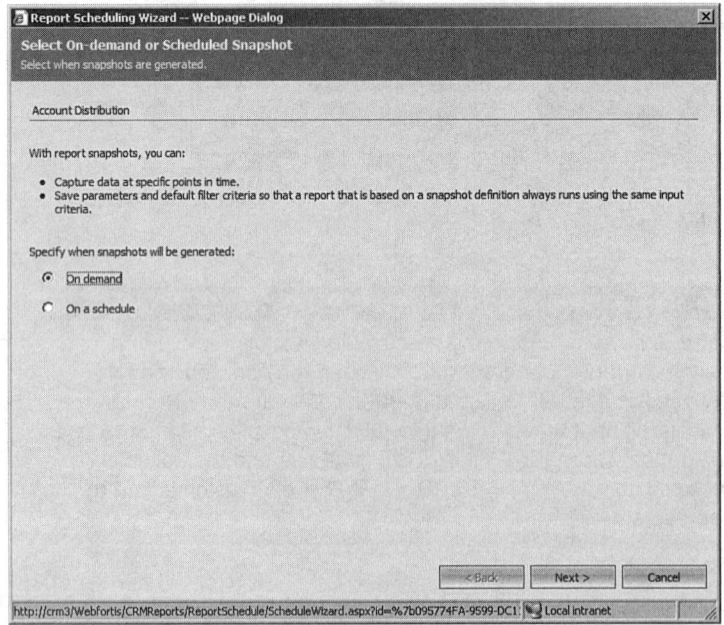

FIGURE 13.29 Report Scheduling Wizard.

On Demand

On-demand reports generate a snapshot report as soon as you finish the wizard.

Depending on the report selected, you must specify values for the report parameters, as shown in Figure 13.30.

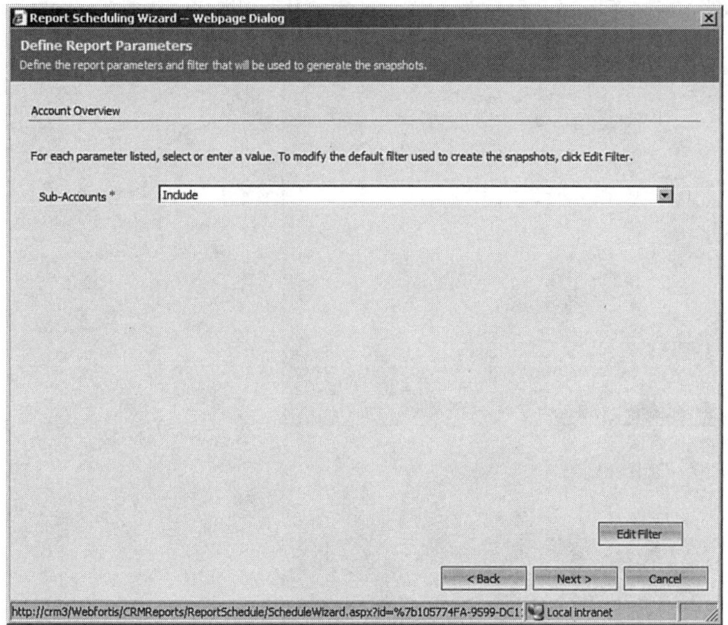

FIGURE 13.30 Define report parameters.

You can also edit the default filters by clicking the Edit Filter button (see Figure 13.31).

After you click Next, you can choose whether to generate the report snapshot now or just save the report snapshot definition for later use (see Figure 13.32).

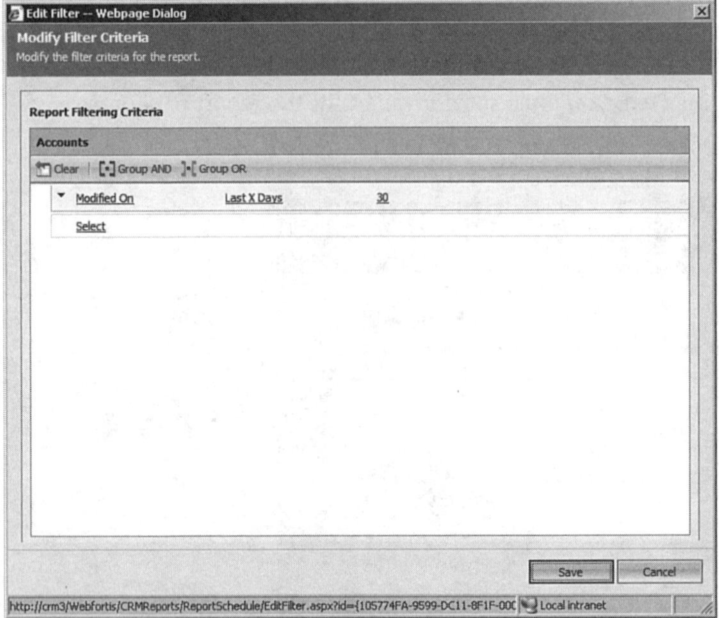

FIGURE 13.31 Modify Filter Criteria.

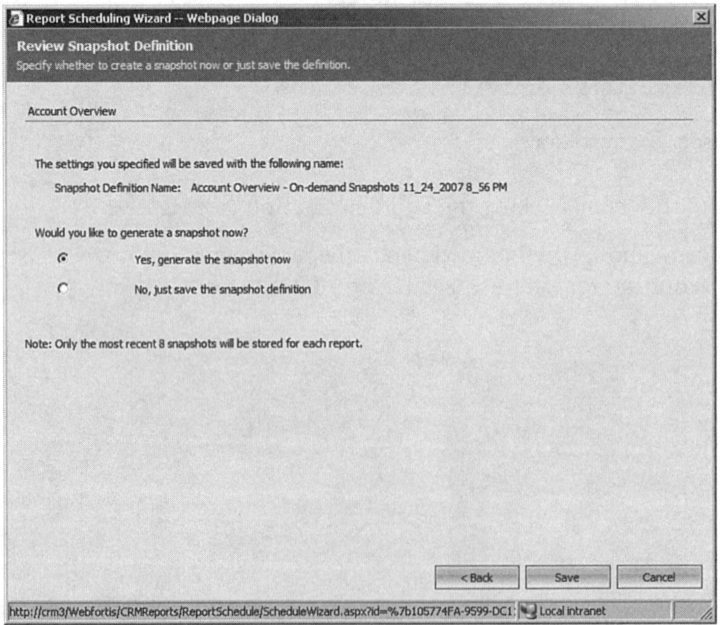

FIGURE 13.32 Review Snapshot Definition.

If you choose the first option and then select Save, the new snapshot report is generated and the overview is detailed, as shown in Figure 13.33.

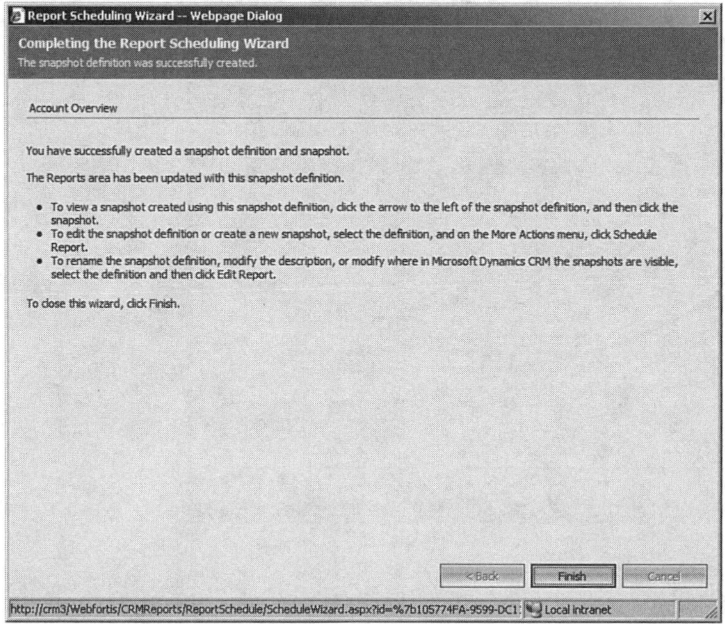

FIGURE 13.33 Completing the Report Scheduling Wizard.

This screen contains all the necessary instructions to access and view the snapshot report that was just created.

Click Finish to close the wizard. You will then see the snapshot shown in Figure 13.34.

On a Schedule

Selecting On a Schedule enables you to select the frequency of the report execution, as well as the time when you want the report to execute (see Figure 13.35). The available options for the frequency are as follows:

- Once
- Hourly
- Daily
- Weekly
- Monthly

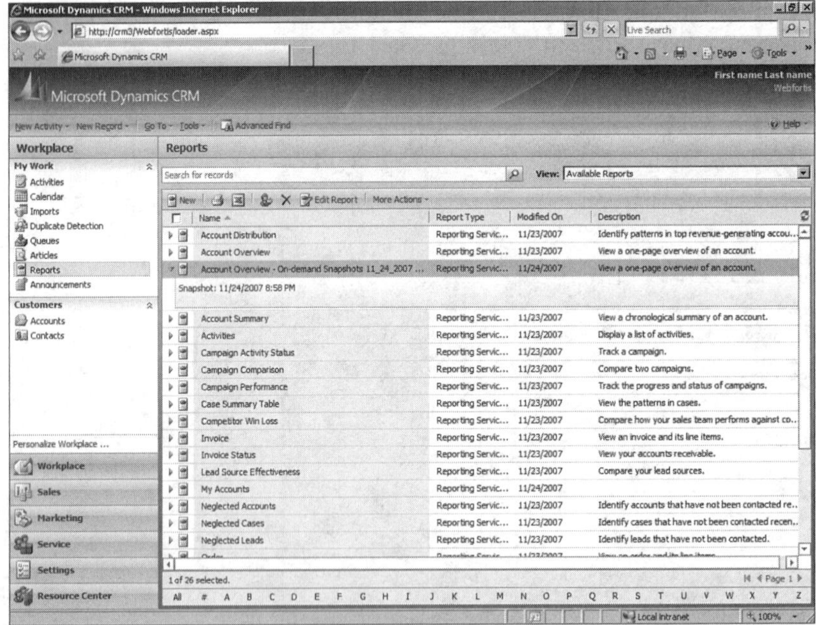

FIGURE 13.34 Snapshot report.

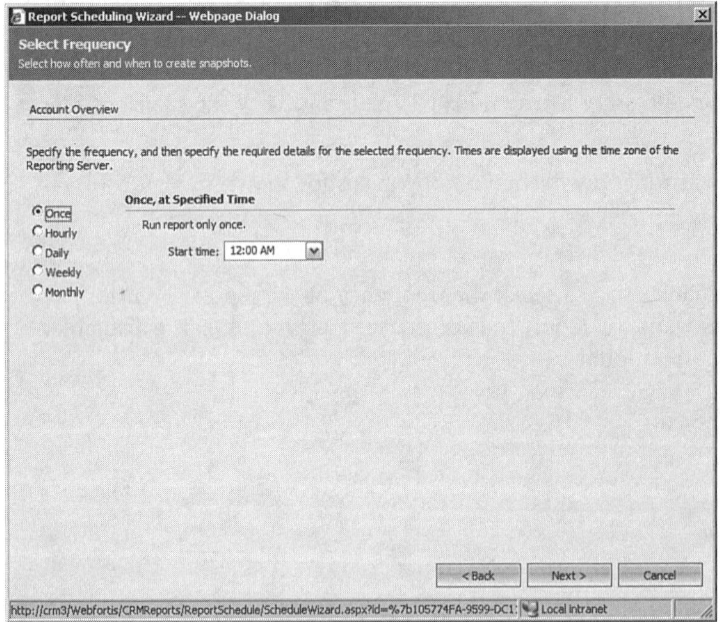

FIGURE 13.35 Select Frequency for Once option.

Depending on the desired frequency, different options are displayed. For example, if you select Once, you can select only the Start Time. But if you select Hourly, you can select the number of hours and minutes you want the report to be run (see Figure 13.36).

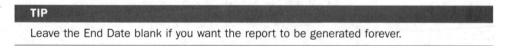

FIGURE 13.36 Select Frequency for Hourly option.

Similarly, the options change for Daily, Weekly, and Monthly.

Select the Start Date and the End Date for the report (see Figure 13.37).

TIP

Leave the End Date blank if you want the report to be generated forever.

After you set the starting and ending dates, you can define the report parameters and edit the default filters for the report. These interfaces are similar to the ones in the On Demand option, explained previously. When you have defined the parameters, click Next. The Overview is presented, so you can review the scheduling report settings (see Figure 13.38).

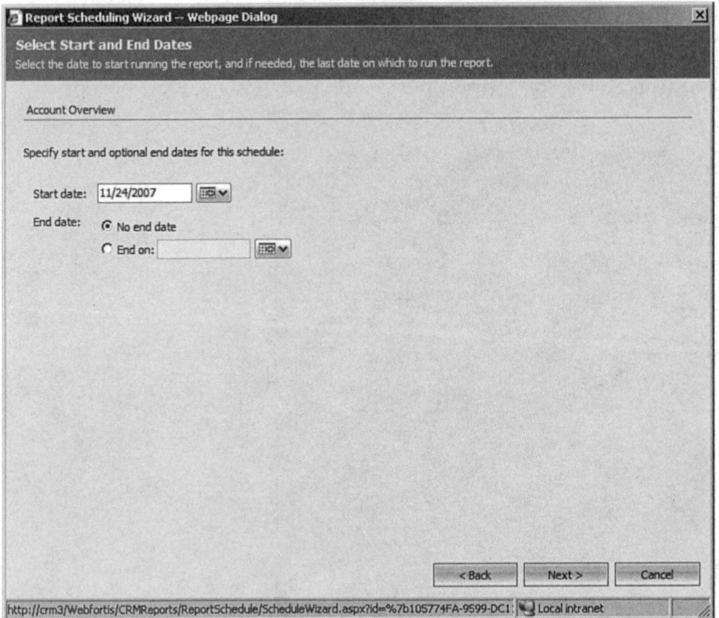

FIGURE 13.37 Select Start and End Dates.

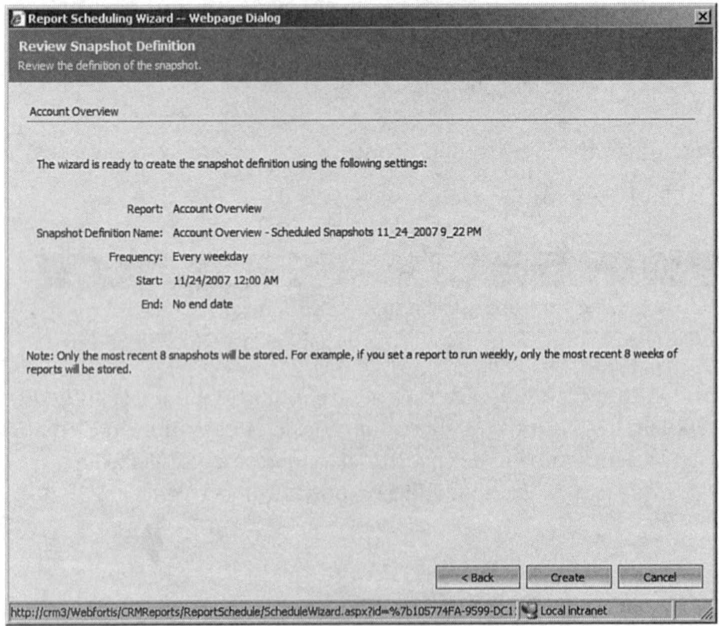

FIGURE 13.38 Review Snapshot Definition.

NOTE

If errors occur when you're trying to schedule a report, the SRS server most likely is not configured properly with a valid execution Account. To check or change this, start the Reporting Services Configuration Manager application that is inside the Microsoft SQL Server 2005 programs group (located on the server that has SQL Server loaded on it and inside the Configuration Tools (see Figure 13.39).

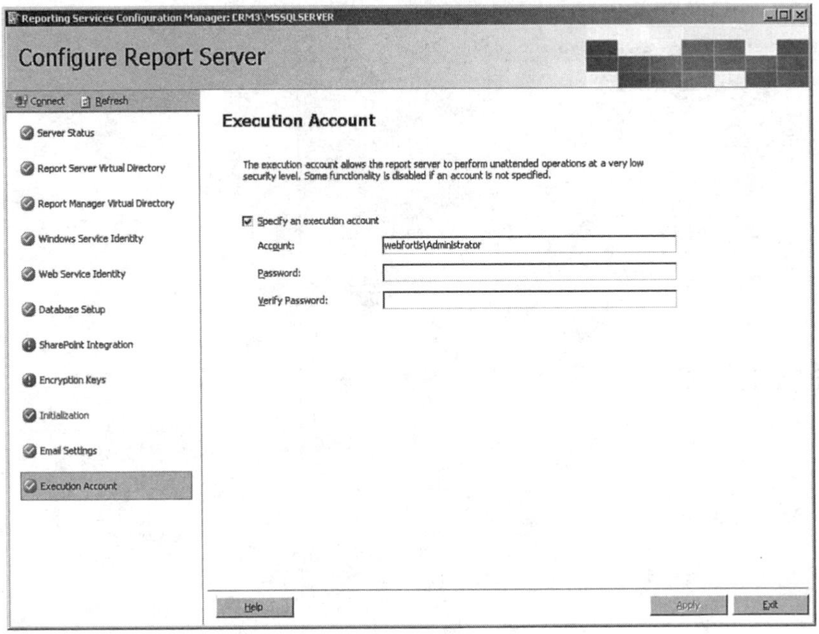

FIGURE 13.39 Execution Account configuration.

Exporting

You can export all Microsoft Dynamics CRM reports and report data in the following formats:

- XML
- CSV (comma-separated values)
- TIFF file (static images)
- Acrobat (PDF) file
- Web archive
- Excel

This option is available in the top navigation bar of any report as a drop-down menu near Export. It allows reports within Microsoft Dynamics CRM to be completely portable and enables you to easily manipulate the data.

To export the actual report (not just the report format or data), select the report you want to export from the Reports interface and select Edit Report from the top menu. When the report properties window appears, go to the Actions menu and select Download Report, as shown in Figure 13.40.

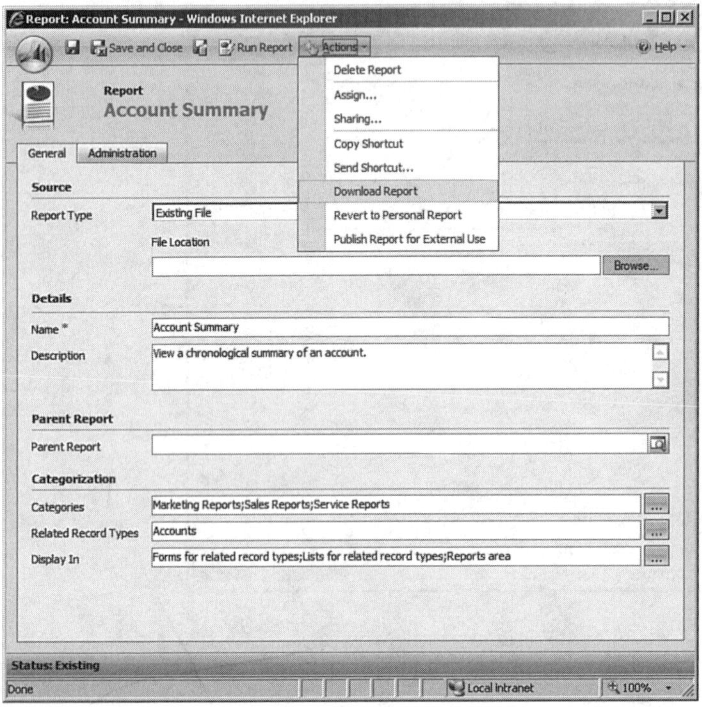

FIGURE 13.40 Download Report.

This option enables you to download the report in its Report Definition Language (RDL) format. This is the standard SRS extension based on XML that you can edit using an editor such as Visual Studio 2005, previously mentioned in this chapter.

Refer to the Chapter 18, "Advanced Reporting," for advanced reports customization.

When working with a multitenant environment (more than one organization), it is important to remember that each organization has its own set of reports. As such, you might want to make some custom reports available across all organizations. The only way to do that is to export the report definitions to your local machine or server and then move them to another organization or implementation.

NOTE

Previous versions of CRM included a command-line tool called `DownloadReports.exe` that downloaded all the reports from an organization. At press time, it was unavailable with this version of Microsoft Dynamics CRM.

Advanced Features

Apart from running, creating, editing, and/or downloading reports, there are other actions you can perform when working with reports.

Sharing Reports

Any reports that you create are available to you. If you want to share your custom report with a User who has lower privilege role levels, select the report from the Main Reports interface and select Sharing from the More Actions drop-down menu (see Figure 13.41).

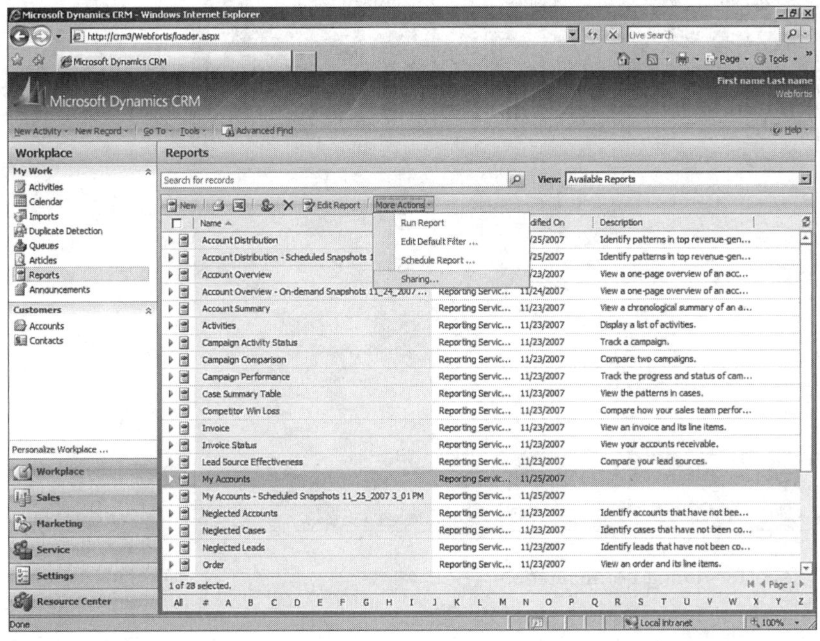

FIGURE 13.41 Sharing reports.

From this interface, you can give the following permissions to Users:

- **Read**—Enables the User to run the report.
- **Write**—Enables the User to modify the report definition and to change the properties and default filters.

- **Delete**—Enables the User to delete the report
- **Append**—Not applicable.
- **Assign**—Enables the User to change the owner of the report. This setting also gives write permission to the User for the report.
- **Share**—Enables the User to share the report with other Users.

NOTE

If you add only read permissions to a User, that User will be able to share the report with other Users even though you didn't select the Share option. This is because the default permissions are set to allow sharing between Users. Of course, the User can give only read permissions to the other Users, but carefully consider the implications of each permission before you set them. Figure 13.42 illustrates the sharing options available with reports.

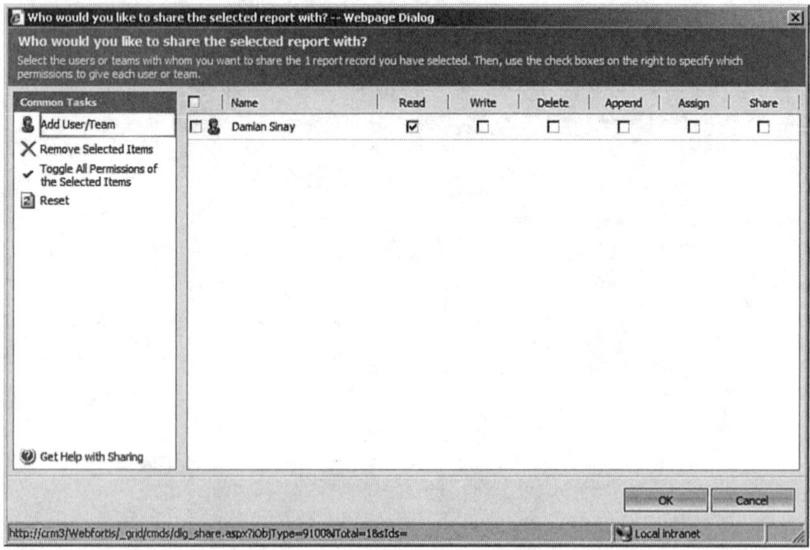

FIGURE 13.42 Reports-sharing permissions.

Exposing Reports to SRS

Unlike previous versions of Microsoft CRM, this version of Dynamics CRM doesn't expose every report in the SRS Manager application directly. If you want to use a report from another application, the reports must be published. For example, if you go to the Report Manager application of SRS, you will see a folder created for the organization; however, it looks empty (see Figure 13.43).

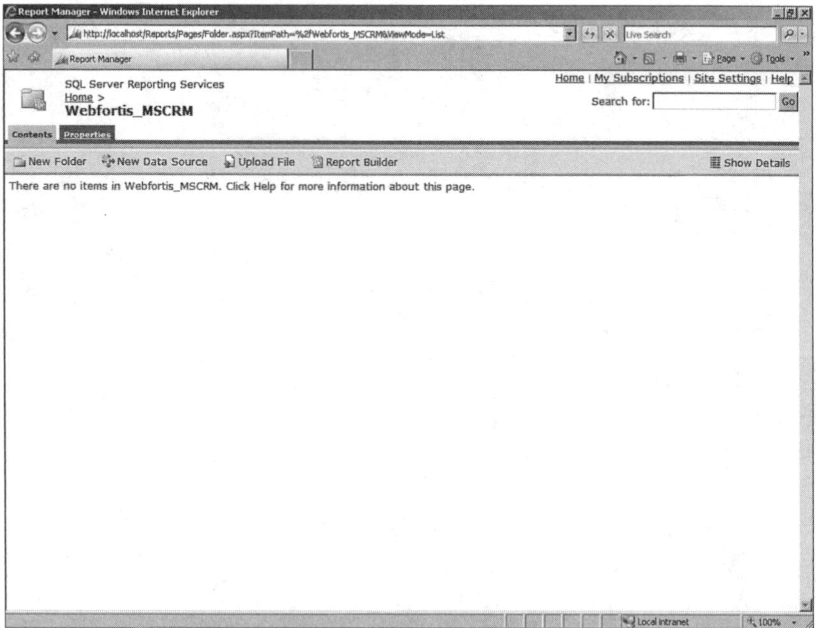

FIGURE 13.43 Report Manager.

The reports are there, but they are hidden. To unhide them, select Show Details. The reports then appear in the 4.0 subfolder (see Figure 13.44). These reports are hidden by default to prevent Users from manipulating them directly from this interface, as frequently Users modify them from this interface and change them in ways that make them incompatible from the CRM application.

If you need to use any of these reports or expose them to another application, you need to go to the CRM interface, select the report you want to expose, select Edit Report, and then select Publish Report for External Use from the Actions drop-down menu (see Figure 13.45).

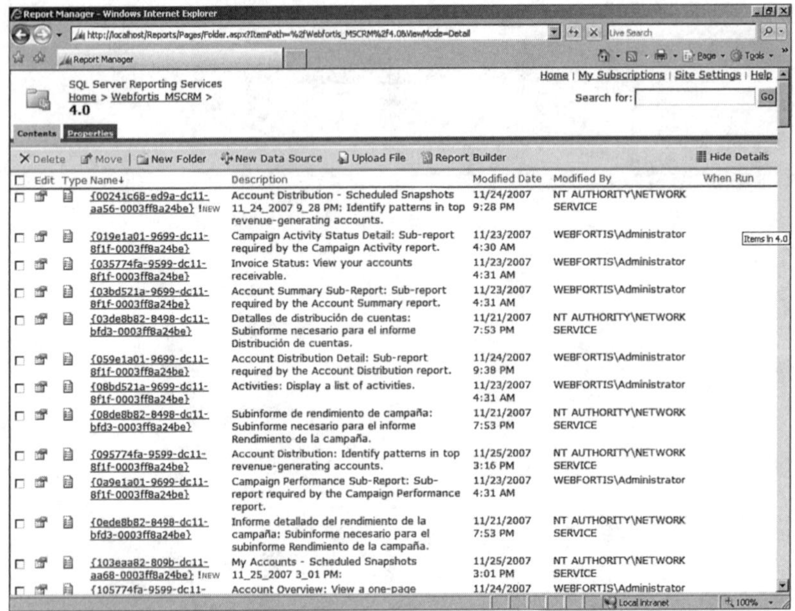

FIGURE 13.44 CRM 4.0 reports in Report Manager.

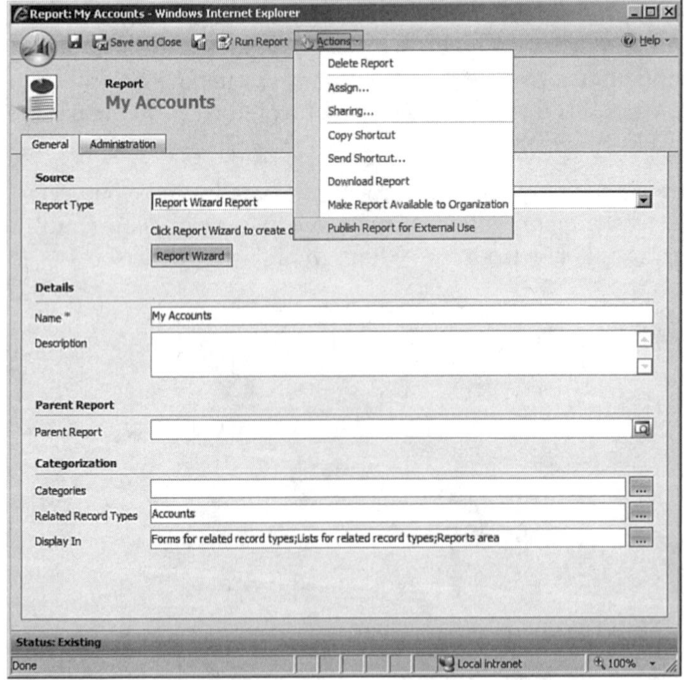

FIGURE 13.45 Publish Report for External Use.

After you select this option, no confirmation or message states that the operation was completed. In fact, the only way to verify that it was published is to go to the Report Manager web application and navigate to your CRM organization folder. You will see that the report is now available (see Figure 13.46).

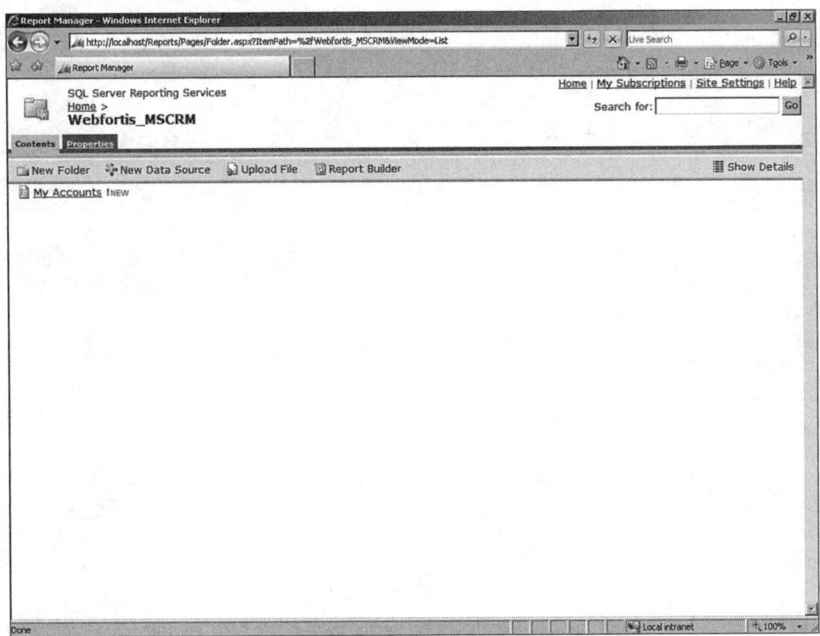

FIGURE 13.46 CRM report exposed in the Report Manager for external use.

Summary

This chapter described how Microsoft Dynamics CRM manages reports and how you can create new reports easily with the Report Wizard. We also reviewed the report scheduling feature and how to export the reports for backups or redeployment purposes. Finally, we reviewed the advanced features of the reports.

CHAPTER 14

Settings and Configuration

IN THIS CHAPTER

- Administration
- Business Management
- Customization
- Templates
- Product Catalog
- Workflows
- Data Management
- System Jobs

Proper setup and configuration of Microsoft Dynamics CRM is critical to a successful implementation.

As you have seen in the previous chapters, and as we make clear in this chapter, the Settings area drives most of the core functionality for Microsoft Dynamics CRM. From User setup, to template management, to language options and workflows, the Settings area quickly becomes *the* place to go for proper configuration and tuning of your business.

NOTE

The Settings area is a carefully controlled access point. In fact, previous versions of Microsoft CRM assumed that because only System Administrators would be accessing it, this area had to be accessed from the web client, and it wasn't even accessible from the Outlook client. That has changed in this version, and both clients have full functionality of the Settings area. However, if you want to remove access (aside from role membership, as you'll see later in this chapter), you can modify the site map so that it will not appear (refer to Chapter 19, "Customizing Entities," for more information about working with the site map).

Any good implementation should consist of at least two main components when considering Microsoft Dynamics CRM. The first component is the physical setup. This includes everything from loading the application on the server to configuring clients and ensuring that a proper backup strategy is in place. The second component is the configuration and customization of the application. Configuration and customization in this sense refers to how the application works in response to how you need it to work. As an example of this, Microsoft Dynamics CRM has no default workflows when it is first loaded. Your business might never need a workflow built, but most business that use Microsoft Dynamics CRM can really benefit from them (and we strongly recommend reviewing Chapter 20, "Workflow Development").

NOTE

Although there are no workflows included, Microsoft has included a basic form of Sales Force Automation (SFA) in the form of Lead conversion (refer to Chapter 10, "Working with Sales").

Additional considerations related to configuration include the previous components already mentioned: setting up Users, choosing which languages to deploy, selecting the Currency types, and so on.

Administration

The Administration page has the following options:

- Announcements
- Business Units
- System Settings
- Users
- Privacy Preferences (Partner Hosted or On Premise only)
- Auto-Numbering
- Security Roles
- Teams
- Languages
- Product Updates (Partner Hosted or On Premise only)
- Billing (CRM Online only)
- Organization Notifications and Status (CRM Online only)

Figure 14.1 shows the Administration screen from the Settings area with the Partner Hosted or On Premise options visible.

Announcements

Announcements enable you to easily communicate with your CRM Users by creating rich messages that display by default in the My Workspace, Announcements section of Microsoft Dynamics CRM (see Figure 14.2).

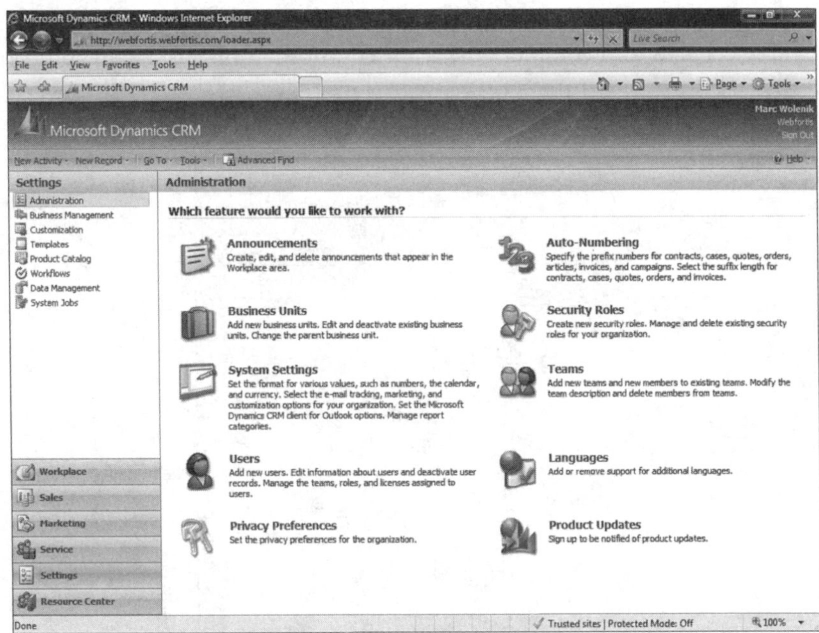

FIGURE 14.1 Settings, Administration screen.

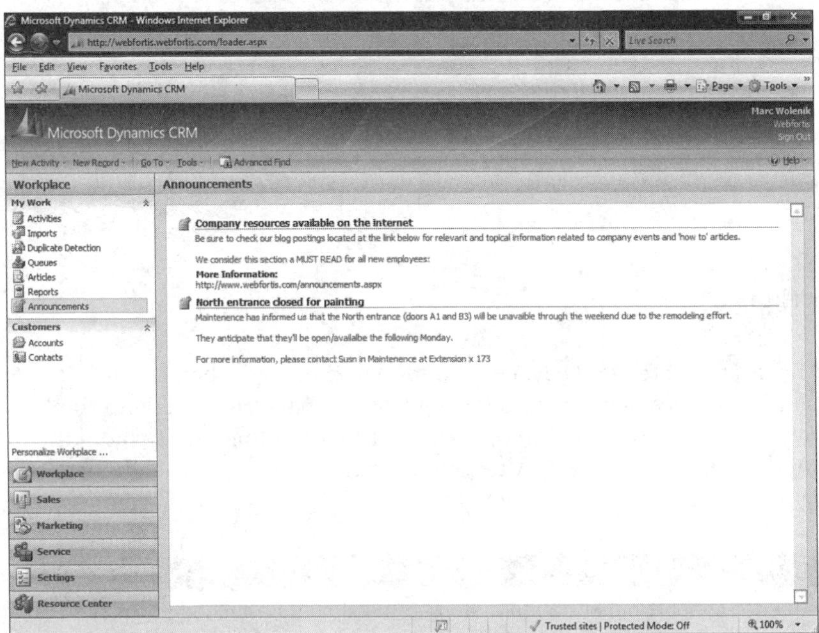

FIGURE 14.2 Announcements in My Workplace.

Announcements are listed by creation date, with the most recent at the top. When creating Announcements, select New and complete the required information (see Figure 14.3).

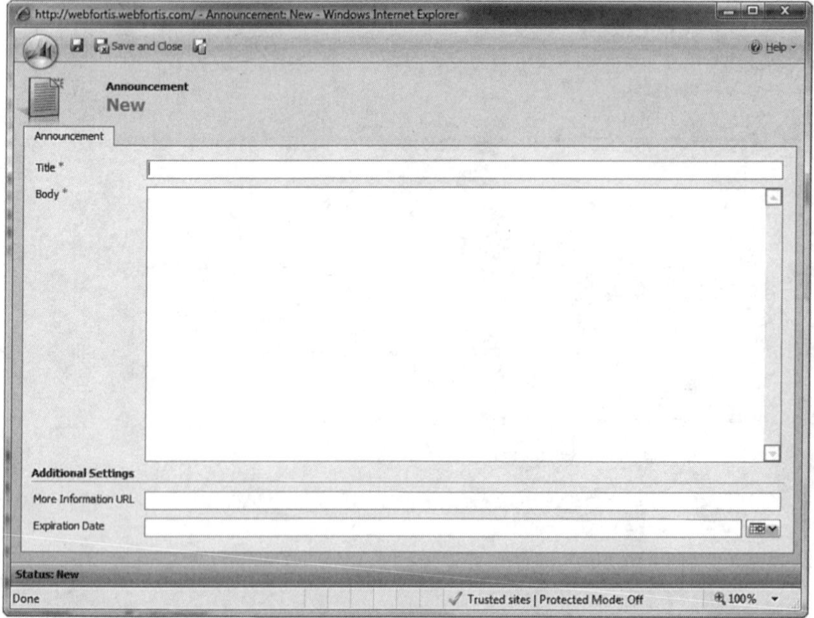

FIGURE 14.3 Creating new Announcements.

Announcements have four properties:

- `Title`
- `Body`
- `URL`
- `Expiration Date`

The two required fields are `Title` and `Body`. `URL` is optional; however, when entered, it displays on the main Announcements page, allowing Users to navigate directly to the entered URL. Finally, `Expiration Date` is an optional value that automatically hides the Announcement after the date has expired. After the Announcement has expired, there is no way to reactivate it—you must create a new one.

NOTE

Announcements do not support either rich formatting or documents attached to them. If you need to refer to external documents, consider placing them on a common web directory and inserting the URL into the documents.

Business Units

You control access to information across the organization with Business Units, Teams, and territories. With Microsoft Dynamics CRM, you can create multiple Child Business Units and assign Users that have access to only the information within their Business Unit, not their Parent Business Unit.

When Microsoft Dynamics CRM is first installed, you specify the Parent Business Unit as the Organization name during the installation. This is the default Business Unit that will derive any Child Business Units. If your organization is relatively small or has no separated Business Units (other than the organization itself), there is little reason to make any changes to the Business Units. As such, you end up with one Business Unit with the same name as your organization. However, if you have multiple Business Units, you will want to configure them here.

NOTE

You may have multiple Child Business Units (see Figure 14.4), but you cannot change or disable the Parent Business Unit (which is created during setup) or make it a Child Business Unit. If you need to change the Parent Business Unit for any reason (to correct a spelling error, because the wrong Business Unit was assigned as the Parent, and so on), you must uninstall and completely reinstall Microsoft Dynamics CRM with the correct Business Unit specified.

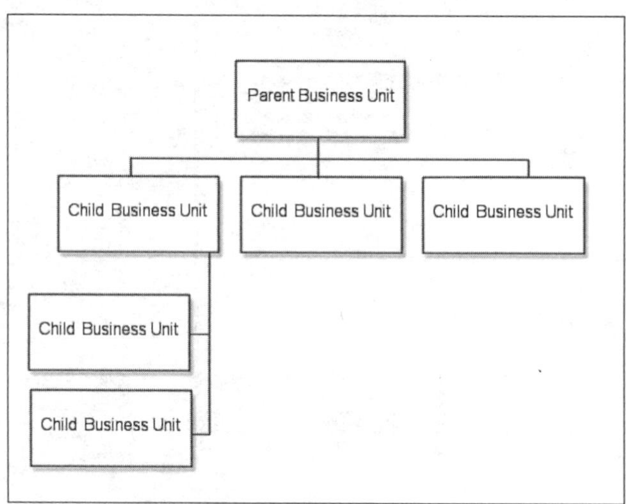

FIGURE 14.4 Parent and Child Business Units.

Because of the way the Security Roles work, it is important to consider setting up both Business Units and the Security Roles. (For more information about Security Roles, see the "Security Roles" section later in this chapter.) Additionally, because Users are assigned Business Units as a required field for their setup, when you disable a Business Unit, all

Users assigned to that Business Unit (and any Child Business Units) are deactivated and cannot log into the system until they are reassigned to an active Business Unit.

NOTE

Users are not deactivated or deleted if the Business Unit is deactivated. They remain valid/active Users in the system, but they cannot log in because their Business Unit is disabled. This is an important distinction because they continue to consume a Client Access License (CAL), even though they have no access to the system. A User can be moved to a different Business Unit after the original Business Unit is deactivated if necessary. (For more information about working with Users, see the "Users" section later in this chapter.)

By default, when viewing the Business Units from the Administration screen, the Active Business Units appear with their Parent Business Unit (see Figure 14.5).

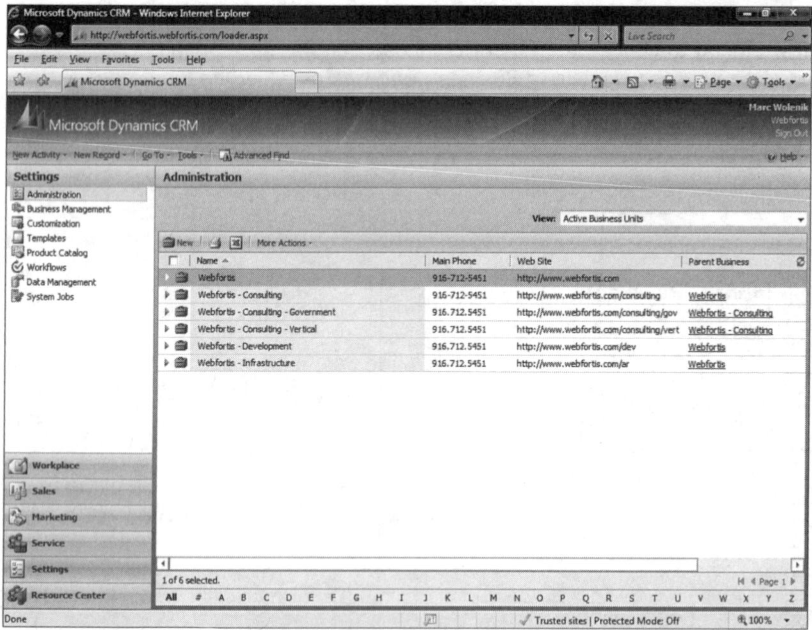

FIGURE 14.5 Business Unit view.

By selecting More Actions on this screen, you can enable a deactivated Business Unit, disable an active Business Unit, and change the Parent Business of a Child Business Unit.

To create a new Business Unit, select New on the main Business Unit Administration screen (see Figure 14.5).

The new Business Unit screen has two required fields that must be populated (see Figure 14.6). The first is the Name of the Business Unit, and the second is the Parent Business Unit.

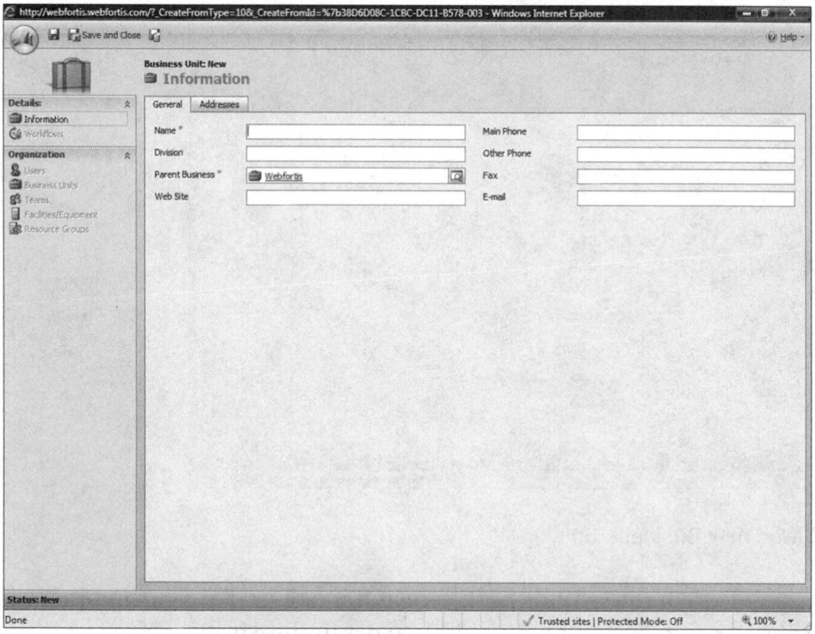

FIGURE 14.6 New Business Unit.

By default, the Parent Business Unit is populated with the Organization Business Unit (or Master Business Unit), but you can change this to a Child Business Unit if you want. As mentioned previously, you *must* have a Parent Business Unit for any new Business Units that are created.

NOTE

You can disable Business Units after creating them, but you *cannot* delete them.

After you enter the desired Name and select the Parent Business Unit, click Save to enter specific address information related to the Business Unit, as well as to begin to build out Organizational information specific to the Business Unit (see Figure 14.7).

TIP

You cannot change the Business Unit Name after saving it. Additionally, although the Parent Business Unit appears to be locked, you can easily change it by selecting Actions, Change Parent Business.

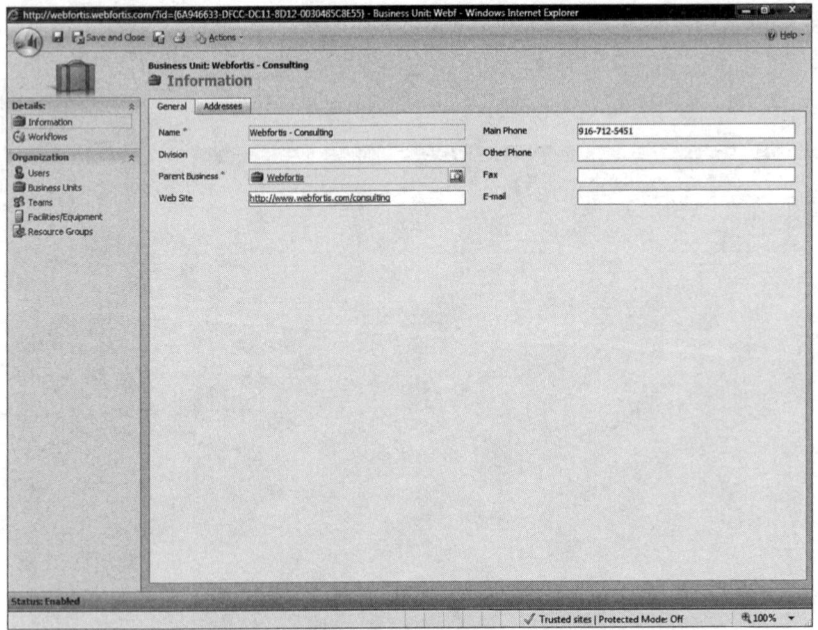

FIGURE 14.7 Saved new Business Unit.

Security Roles are specific to Business Units, with certain limitations. For more information on Security Roles, see the "Security Roles" section later in this chapter.

The Organizational information options are on the near navigation:

- Users
- Business Units
- Teams
- Facilities/Equipment
- Resource Groups

Users

Selecting Users shows you who is assigned to that Business Unit (see Figure 14.8).

User assignment to Business Units is explained in greater detail later in this chapter in the "Administration—Users" section. However, when adding Users, be aware of the following:

- Only Users who have *not* been added to the CRM can be added to newly created Business Units from the New Business Unit screen. If you want to assign Users to a newly created Business Unit who are already in the system, you must first navigate to the User (Settings, Users) and select Change Business Unit from the Actions or More Actions drop-down options.

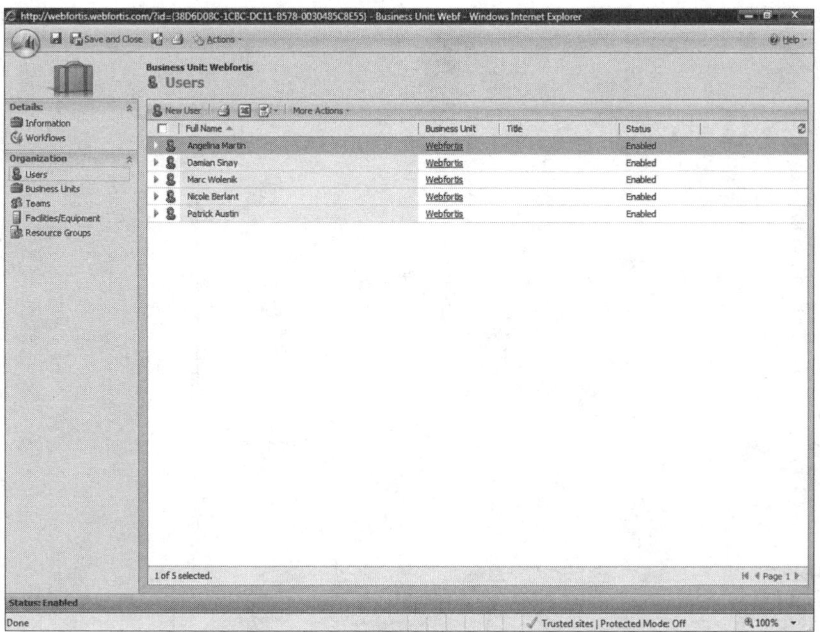

FIGURE 14.8 Business Unit Users.

- You cannot move the current User (that is, the User who is logged in) to a Business Unit. Instead, you must delegate access to another User and either request that the other User make the changes or log in as the other User and make the changes. (Be sure to grant the necessary Security Role of either System Administrator or System Customizer to the other User before you attempt to make this change.)
- Only Users who are assigned to the Business Unit you're working with appear on the Users screen. To see Users of Child Business Units, you must select the Child Business Units separately.
- When Users are moved from an existing Business Unit to a new Business Unit, all role information is removed, and it must be manually reassigned.

Business Units

Business Units displays the Child Business Units of the selected Business Unit (see Figure 14.9).

NOTE

Note that in the same way Subcontacts work on the Contacts form, only the *direct* Child Business Units display on the screen. To view Child Business Units that might exist, you must select the Child Business Unit and navigate to the Business Units section of the Child Business Unit.

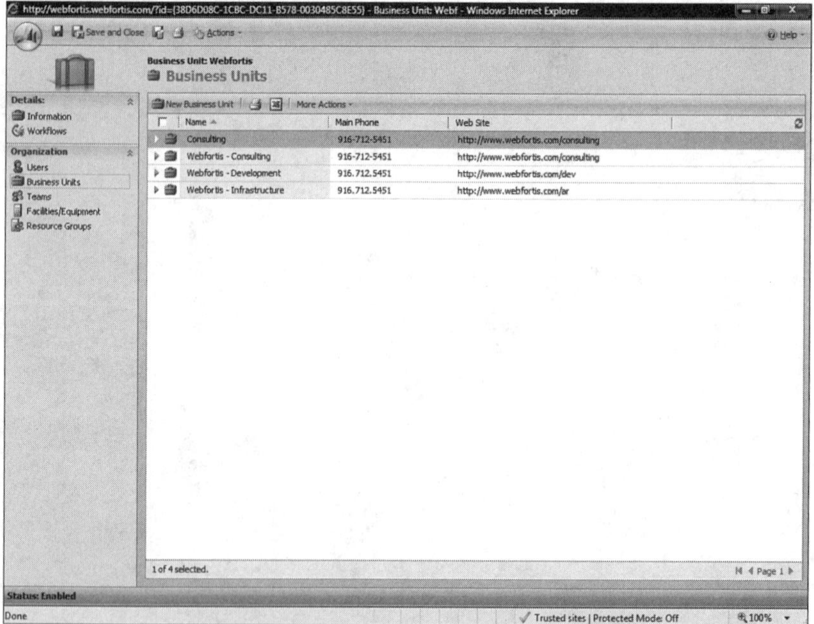

FIGURE 14.9 Business Units.

From here you can easily create a new Child Business Unit by selecting New Business Unit. You can also enable and disable any existing Business Units displayed.

Teams

Because Teams are specific to Business Units, selecting Teams shows you which Teams are assigned to that Business Unit (see Figure 14.10). Teams are explained in greater detail later in this chapter in the "Administration—Teams" section.

Facilities/Equipment

As with Teams, Facilities/Equipment is specific to Business Units. Selecting Facilities/ Equipment shows you what Facilities/Equipment is assigned to that Business Unit (see Figure 14.11). Facilities/Equipment is explained in greater detail later in this chapter in the section "Business Management—Facilities/Equipment."

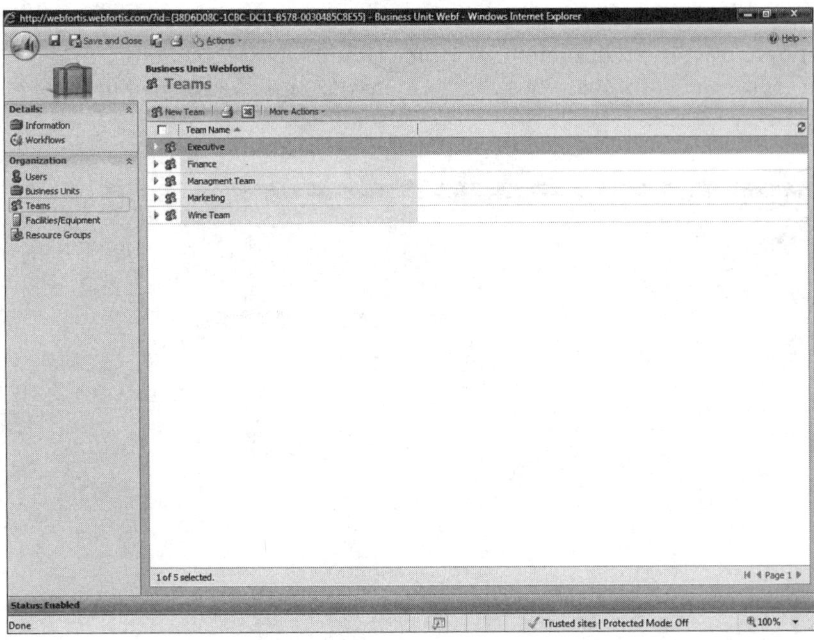

FIGURE 14.10 Business Unit Teams.

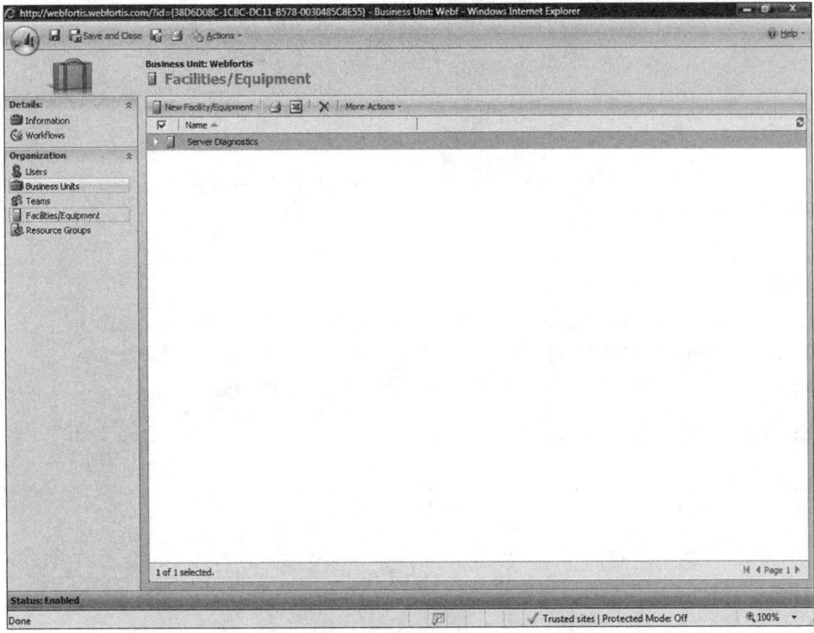

FIGURE 14.11 Business Unit Facilities/Equipment.

Resource Groups

As with both Teams and Facilities/Equipment, Resource Groups are specific to Business Units. Selecting Resource Groups shows you what Resource Groups are assigned to that Business Unit (see Figure 14.12).

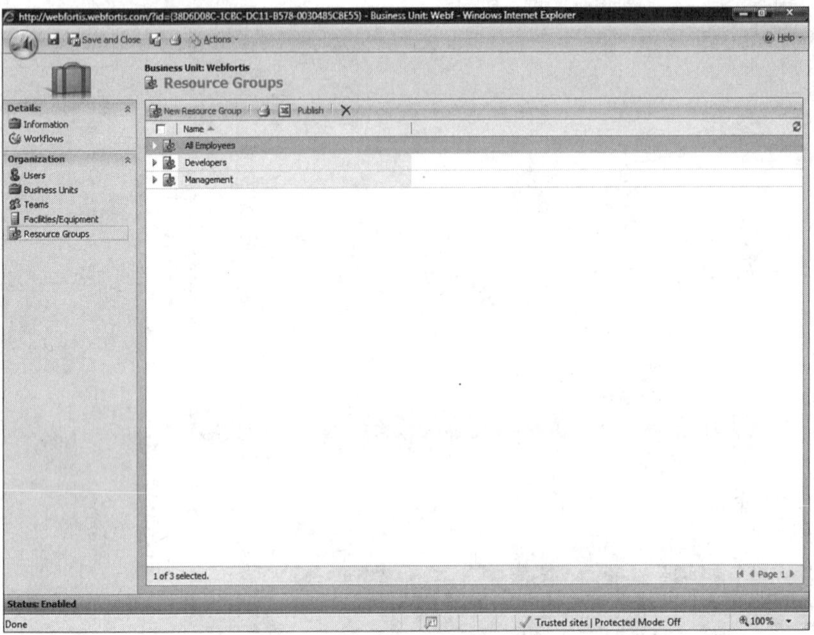

FIGURE 14.12 Business Unit Resource Groups.

Resource Groups are explained in greater detail later in this chapter in the section "Business Management—Resource Groups."

System Settings

Located on the main Administration page after selecting Settings, the System Settings interface is similar to (and often confused with) the User Options interface. Here you make systemwide settings that affect all Users (unlike the User Options).

The System Settings interface is divided into seven tabbed sections (see Figure 14.13).

The sections are as follows:

- General
- Formats
- E-mail
- Marketing
- Customization
- Outlook
- Reporting

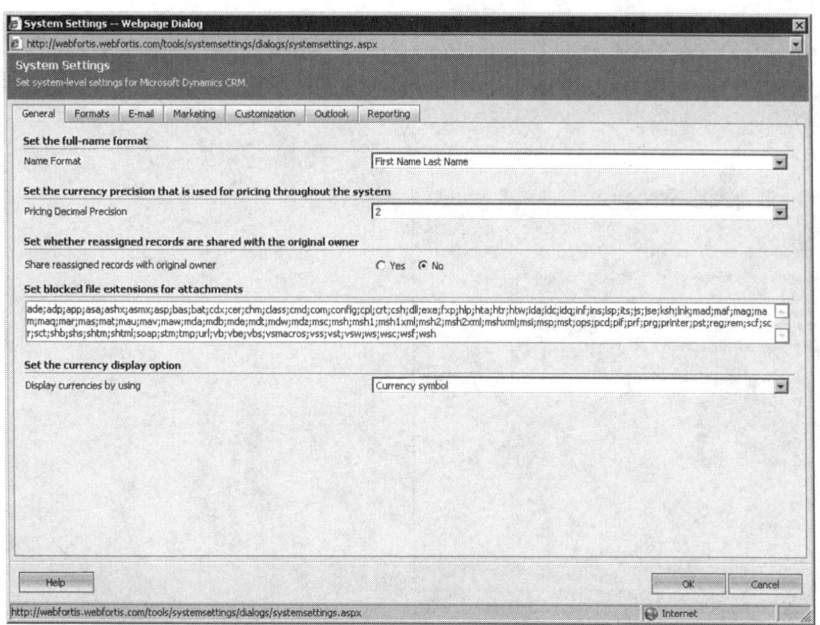

FIGURE 14.13 System Settings.

General

In the General section, you can set and change the following options:

- **Full-name format**—This is the default way the User and Customer names are displayed when using Microsoft Dynamics CRM.

> **NOTE**
>
> If you select to change the Full-name format, you will only be able to change the format on *new* records added to the system. All existing records will continue to display in the original format. Although it can take some effort, one way of correcting this for existing records is to export all of them, delete or deactivate them, and then re-import them. They will take on the new format during re-import. Be sure to carefully consider this prior to attempting, as it may be more trouble than it's worth.

- **Currency precision**—When working with Currency fields throughout Microsoft Dynamics CRM, you can set the level of precision (from 0 to 4) for the decimal.
- **Entity sharing**—This option enables you to specify whether an Entity is shared with the original owner by default when it is reassigned, or whether the new owner assumes complete ownership of the Entity. By default, this is set to No.

14

- **Blocked file extensions**—By default, the listed file extensions are blocked and prevented from being uploaded. Attempting to upload a document with one of the blocked file extensions listed will result in an error when trying to upload (see Figure 14.14).

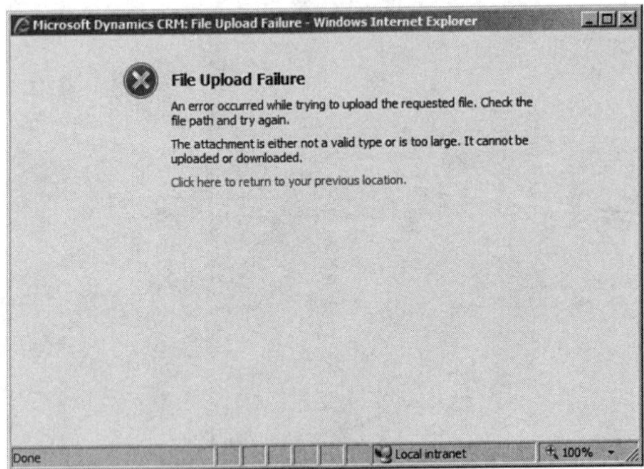

FIGURE 14.14 File upload error.

These are the recommended and default extensions designed to keep your system safe and prevent malicious files from being uploaded. However, you can edit this list as you see fit.

- **Currency display option**—You can choose to display either the Currency symbol (in the case of U.S. dollars and Euros, this would be $ and €, respectively) or the Currency code (again, in the case of U.S. dollars and Euros, this would be USD and EUR, respectively).

Formats

The Formats section enables you to customize how Microsoft Dynamics CRM formats data such as dates, times, and numbers (see Figure 14.15).

Selecting a value from the drop-down menu populates the default values for the selected region in the Format Preview, showing you how the information will be formatted. If you need to further edit them for regional, custom formats or other settings, select Customize (as shown on Figure 14.15) and make advanced configurations (see Figure 14.16).

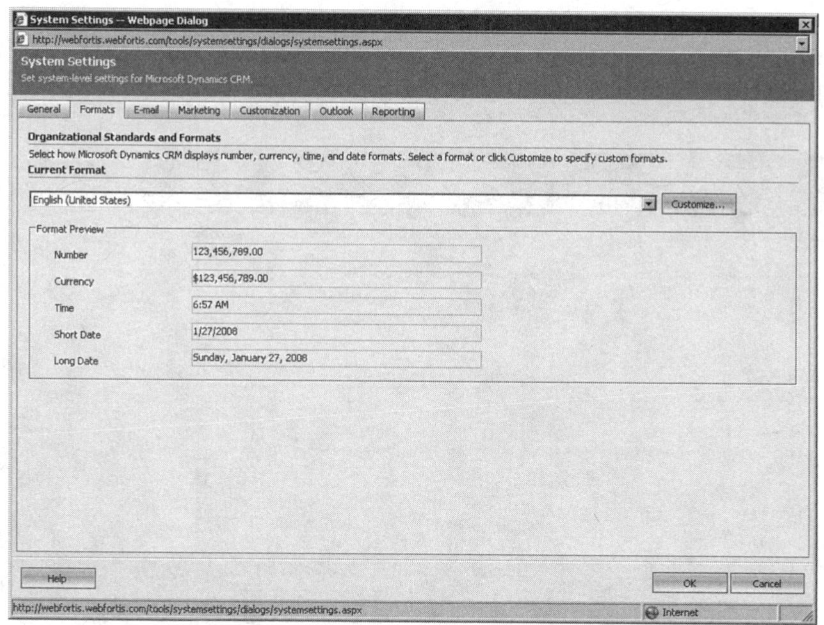

FIGURE 14.15 Format options.

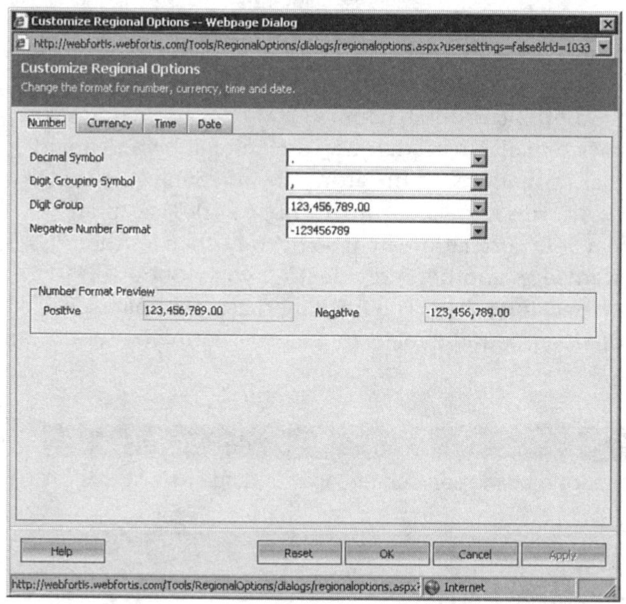

FIGURE 14.16 Customize Regional Options.

E-mail

The E-mail options involve configuration changes to how Microsoft Dynamics CRM works with e-mail (see Figure 14.17).

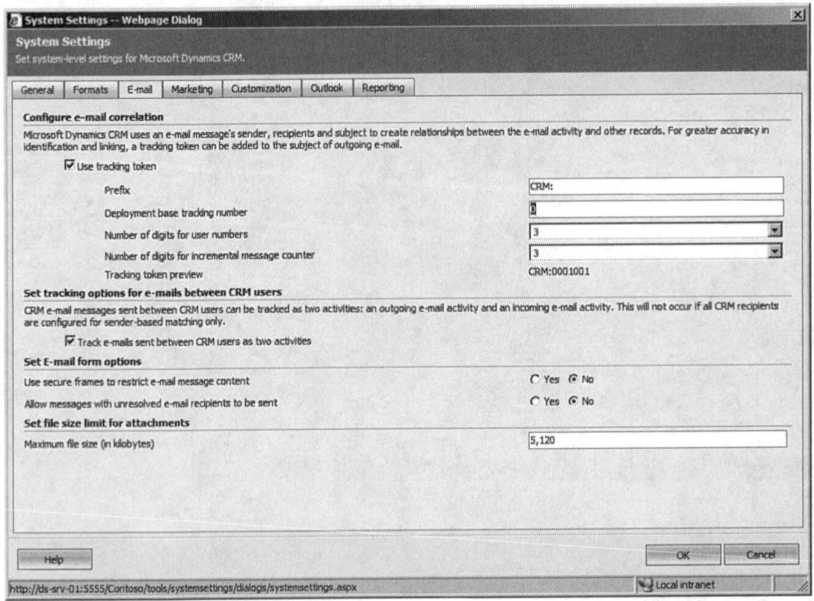

FIGURE 14.17 E-mail setting options.

- **E-mail correlation**—This version of Microsoft Dynamics CRM does not require you to use the tracking token to track e-mails. Instead, it uses a feature known as Smart Tracking that automatically tracks e-mails using the From, To, and Subject to match the e-mail. For a variety of reasons, this correlation might not be 100% accurate. (Common reasons why you may lose correlation are if somebody changes the Subject, or if the e-mail is forwarded to another individual.) If you require 100% correlation, you should use the tracking token. The tracking token automatically appends itself to the Subject of all outbound e-mails in whatever form you select on this tab (see Figure 14.18).

NOTE

The Prefix of the tracking token cannot be blank, can contain spaces, and has a maximum value of 20 characters.

Figure 14.19 shows how the tracking token is structured.

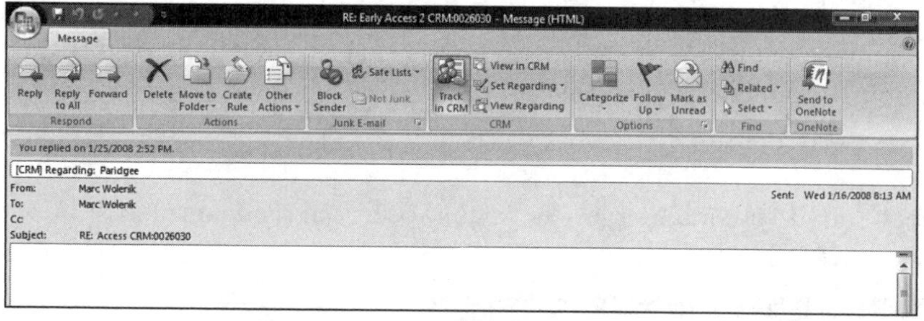

FIGURE 14.18 E-mail with tracking token in the Subject line.

Notice the "Track and CRM" button in Figure 14.18. This is used to promote an email received in Outlook into CRM and can be used to "untrack" an item if using Office 2007.

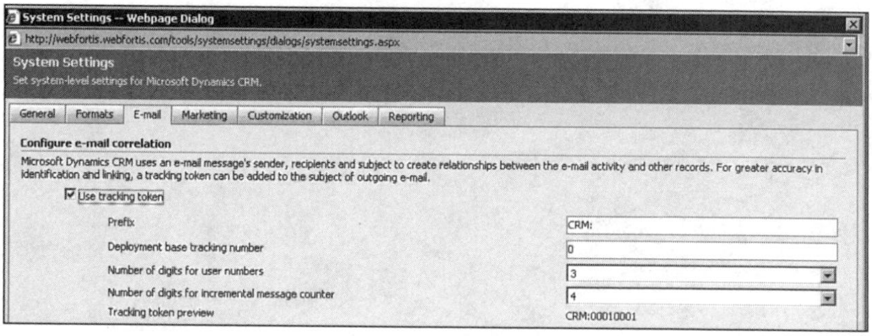

FIGURE 14.19 Tracking token explained.

- **CRM User tracking options**—By default, when a User sends a CRM e-mail to another CRM User, both e-mails are recorded as an Activity for the selected record (one Activity of `type = 'e-mail'` outgoing and one Activity of `type = 'e-mail'` incoming).
- **E-mail form options**—Select whether to restrict e-mail message content via secure frames and whether to allow messages with unresolved e-mail recipients. Secure frames are used to prevent malicious code execution that might exist when opening e-mails in CRM. Unresolved e-mail recipients are recipients that are not found in the Account, Contact, Lead or User e-mail address fields.
- **File size limitations**—Enter the file size allowed for uploading attachments to e-mails. The default is 5,120Kb (5MB) and the maximum value is 8,192Kb (8MB).

Marketing

The Marketing options allow for powerful and easy management related to Marketing when using Microsoft Dynamics CRM (see Figure 14.20).

FIGURE 14.20 Marketing settings.

- **Enable Direct E-mail via Mail Merge**—By default, Users can send e-mail as

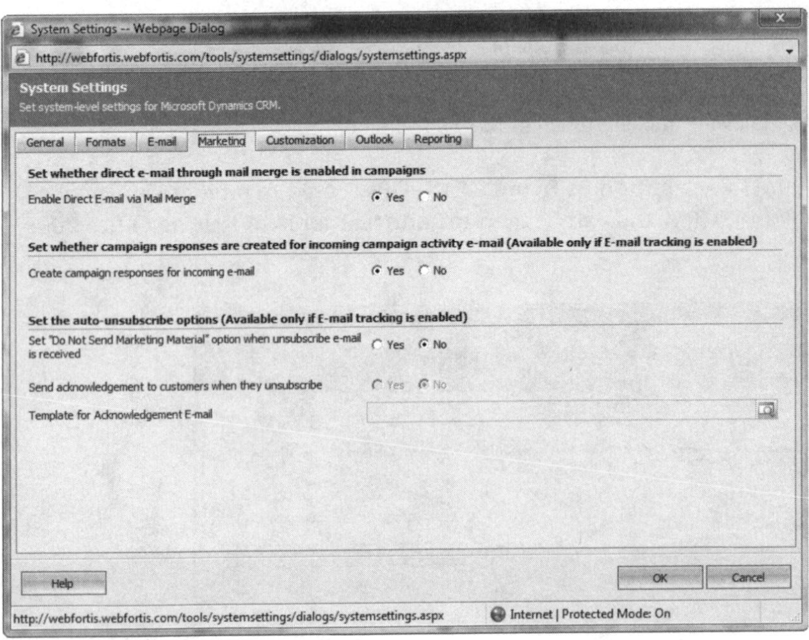

  Campaign Activities using the Mail Merge feature. If you want to prevent this functionality, change the value here.

- **Create Campaign Responses for Incoming E-mail**—If E-mail Tracking is enabled, you can configure Microsoft Dynamics CRM to automatically create a Campaign Response for incoming e-mail. This is enabled by default.

- **Auto-unsubscribe**—Again, if E-mail Tracking is enabled, you can configure Microsoft Dynamics CRM to change the value on the customer record of Do Not Send Marketing Material to True if an unsubscribe e-mail is received. Furthermore, you can configure whether the customer will receive an acknowledgment of the unsubscribe request and select a template for this acknowledgment.

The Unsubscribe option is available when preparing Marketing by inserting an option allowing Users to click a link that allows them to unsubscribe from future Marketing Campaigns (see Chapter 11, "Working with Marketing," for more information about working with this feature).

Customization

When making customizations to Microsoft Dynamics CRM, several options specific to customizations are set here initially (see Figure 14.21).

FIGURE 14.21 Customization options.

- **Custom entities and attributes prefix**—By default, the prefix `new` is used when creating new entities and attributes (see Figure 14.22).

  You can change this value to any eight-character value, provided that the first two characters start with letters. Additionally, the prefix cannot be `mscrm` because that prefix is reserved for system entities. Note that if this value is changed, it will only affect new customizations as existing customizations will retain the previous values.

- **Custom menus and toolbars**—When the `ISV.Config` file has been modified to show customer buttons or toolbars (see Chapter 23, "ISV Customizations," for more information about the `ISV.Config` file), you can select which client to show these options. The values are listed here:
  - Outlook
  - Outlook Offline
  - Web Application

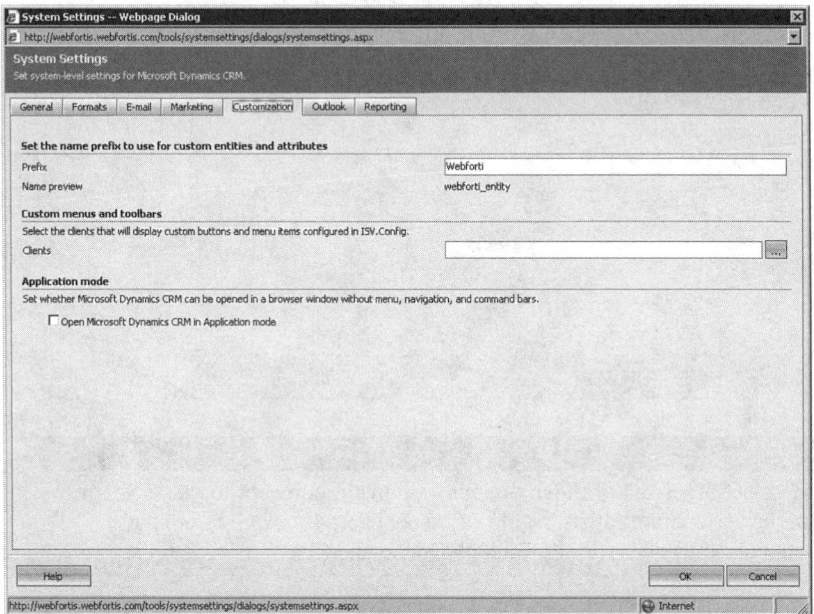

FIGURE 14.22 The `Name` value uses the prefix entered here.

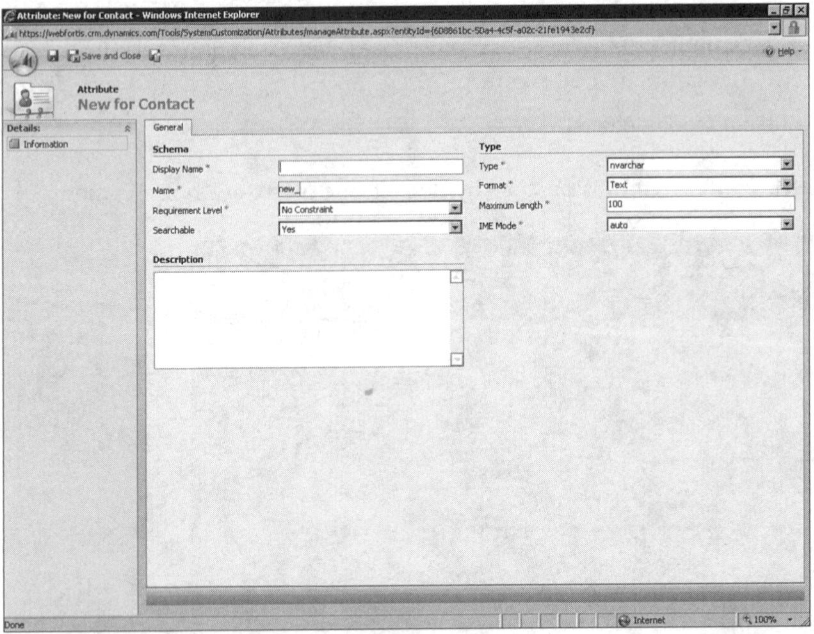

NOTE

Although you can select any or all of these options, you might not want to select them. For example, a particular customization might not be configured to work in offline mode, so it should not be available in the Outlook Offline client.

- **Application mode**—Converts Internet Explorer into a dedicated CRM application by removing the browser address, tabs, toolbars, and menu bars. Unlike previous versions, Microsoft Dynamics CRM does not operate in application mode by default (see Figures 14.23 and 14.24).

If you change the Application mode, you must close all instances of Microsoft Dynamics CRM and reopen Internet Explorer for them to take effect.

NOTE

While working with Application mode turned on, you might receive a message that says "The webpage you are viewing is trying to close the window. Do you want to close this window?" This is because, when you open Microsoft Dynamics CRM in Application mode, the system first opens a regular browser and then must open a new window to serve the application in Application mode. You must click Yes to open CRM. Additionally, be sure to disable any pop-up blockers that you might have because they will inhibit CRM from opening in a new window as well.

FIGURE 14.23 Microsoft CRM with Application mode turned off.

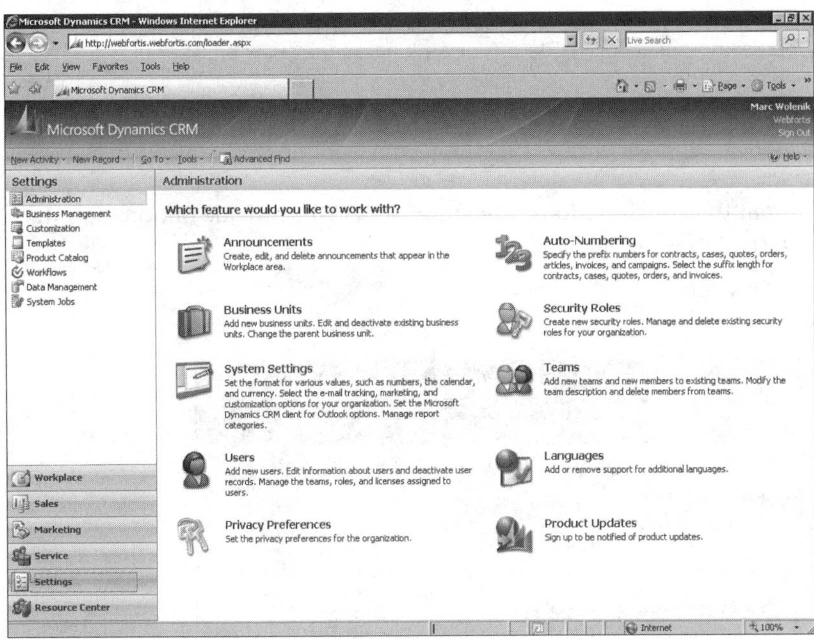

FIGURE 14.24 Microsoft CRM with Application mode turned on.

14

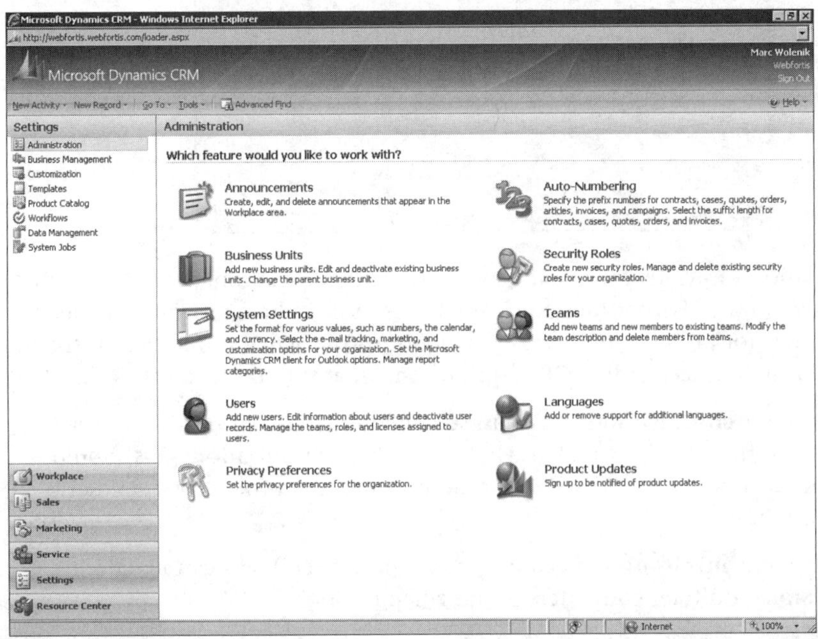

TIP

When working in Application mode, you can press Ctrl+N to open a new window. The application will open with Application mode off for as long as that new browser is opened.

Outlook

Distinctly separate from the e-mail options, the Outlook options provide options specifically designed for Outlook (see Figure 14.25).

FIGURE 14.25 Outlook options.

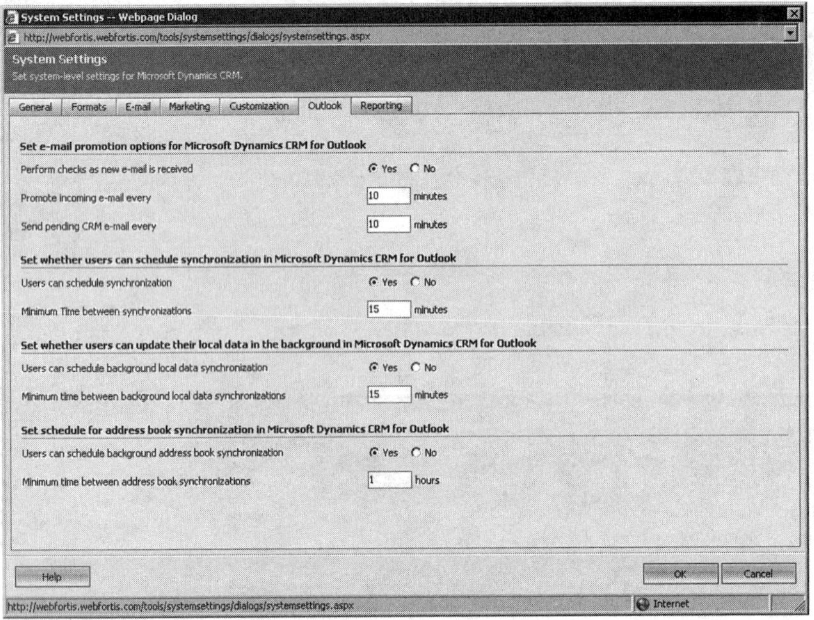

- **E-mail promotion options**—Incoming e-mail to Outlook is automatically promoted to CRM based on the User settings configured. The options here set whether the e-mail is eligible for promotion as it arrives, performs the actual promotion at specified intervals, and sends pending CRM specific e-mail at the specified interval.
- **User schedule synchronization**—You can set whether Users can manually schedule synchronization from Outlook and at what interval synchronizations this should occur. For optimal performance, set this to no less then than the recommended default of 15 minutes.
- **Local data synchronization**—You can set if and how often Users can update the data that is stored on their computers to use when offline.
- **Address book synchronization**—As with the User schedule synchronization, this enables Users to schedule background address book synchronization and set the

time interval between synchronizations.

Reporting

The Reporting options enable you to create and manage the categories that reports are grouped into (see Figure 14.26).

FIGURE 14.26 Reporting options.

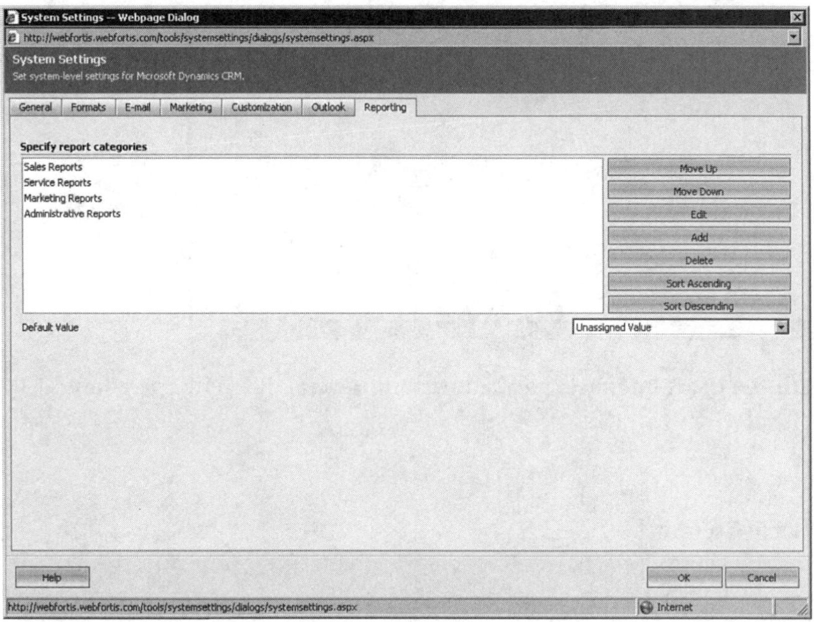

Reports can belong to none, one, or multiple categories, and allow for easy grouping of different kinds. When you edit an existing report or create a new report, you assign the categories listed here.

NOTE

If you add a new category here, you can assign it to new or existing reports; however, it is not an available option in the Report views until you create a View for the new category.

Users

Found on the Administration option from the Settings area, Microsoft Dynamics Users are created and managed in the Users section (see Figure 14.27).

FIGURE 14.27 Users.

14

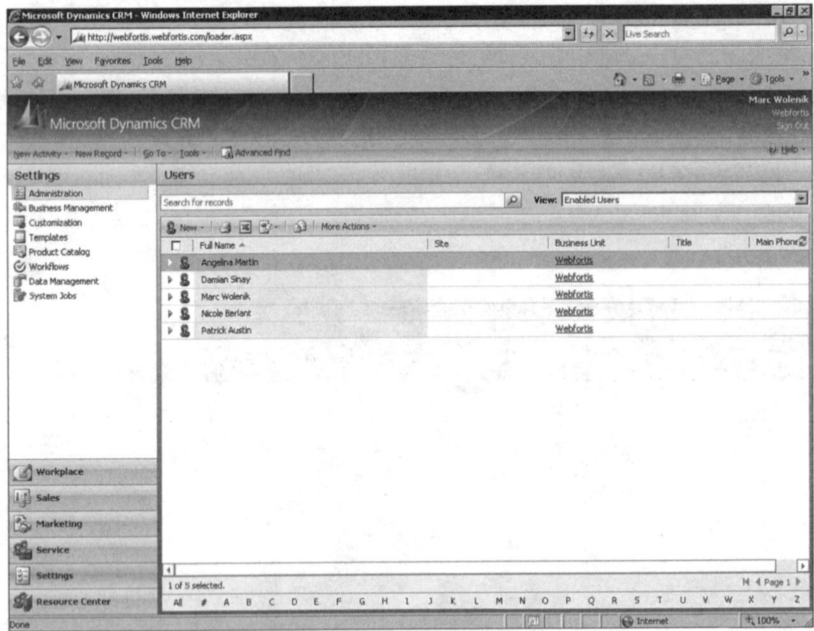

When working with the Users interface, you can perform several different operations:

- Add a new User
- Add multiple Users
- Enable or disable Users
- Manage User Roles
- Manage Quotas
- Change Business Units
- Change Managers
- Send Invitation (CRM Online only)
- View Users

These options and their locations are explained further in the following sections.

Add a New User

To add a new User, select the New option and then User, located in the upper-left corner. Figure 14.28 shows the new User form.

FIGURE 14.28 Create a new User (On Premise or Partner Hosted).

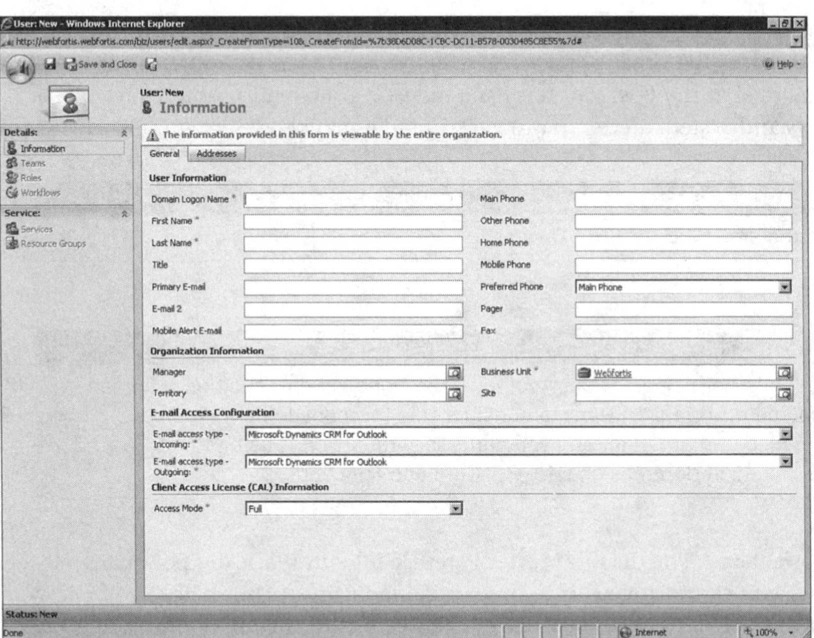

NOTE

If you do not have a New option here, you might not have sufficient rights or privileges to create new Users.

After you add Users to the CRM system, you can only deactivate them; you cannot delete them. For that reason, you can "add" a User only once. If you have already added a User and you don't see him or her, be sure to check the Disabled User's view to see if that User has already been added.

User Information Although it is not required, it is highly recommended that you complete the Domain Logon Name first. (This option is not available in CRM Online.) When you enter this information and move to the next field, automatic resolution is attempted on the entered value; assuming that it is fully qualified with a domain, the other two required fields, `First Name` and `Last Name`, are populated. If auto-population does not occur, be sure to enter the exact first and last name as well as the e-mail address for the User that exists in the AD. An example of this is `<domain>\<user name>`, where `<domain>` is the domain for your organization, and User is the domain User name.

NOTE

The Domain Logon Name is not required for CRM Online Users.

…ining fields in the User Information section are optional and allow for richer rep…g on Users across the organization. We usually recommend completing at least the primary e-mail so that the User can receive e-mails. If no e-mail is entered, events (such as workflows and system alerts) that need to send e-mails to Users will fail.

NOTE

The `E-Mail` is a required field for CRM Online.

TIP

If your organization is not using another tool for User management, such as a human resource management, you might want to consider this for management. You can customize it to include other fields, and you can easily report on it using the Advanced Find feature, explained in depth in Chapter 7, "Common Functions."

Organizational Information The default Master Parent Unit automatically populates Business Units, but you can change this to any available Business Unit before you click Save. After you save the record, you must select Change Business Unit from the Actions menu to change the Business Unit.

Similar to Business Units, you must set the Manager before you click Save: After you save the record, you must select Change Manager from the Actions menu to change or set the Manager.

`Territory` and `Site` are optional lookup fields. If you have not created any territories or sites in the system, you can leave these blank.

NOTE

Although not required, Service Activities can use sites. Refer to Chapter 12, "Working with Service," for more information about configuring Service Activities.

E-mail Access Configuration Here you set the two options for e-mail access type configuration (Incoming and Outgoing), with the default of Microsoft Dynamics CRM Client for Outlook. For more information about these values, refer to Chapter 15, "E-mail Configuration."

Client Access License You can set the Access Mode for Users to the following:

- Full
- Administrative
- Read-Only

NOTE

Both Administrative and Read-Only have significantly restricted access to the system.

TIP

Previous versions of Microsoft CRM included an option on the Users record for Restricted User Mode. This option has been replaced by either the Administrative or Read-Only modes.

Addresses You can add Mailing and Other Address information to the User record as well (see Figure 14.29).

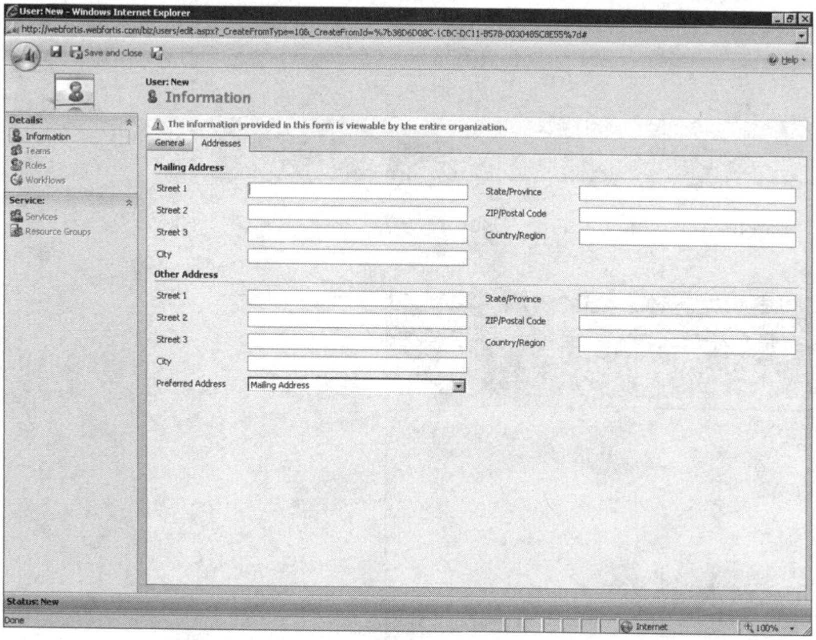

FIGURE 14.29 New User addresses.

Teams After you have successfully created and saved a User, that User can join existing Teams by selecting Teams from the near navigation (see Figure 14.30).

By default, Users have no Team membership.

To join a Team, select Join Teams. Select the lookup icon to view all available Teams (see Figure 14.31).

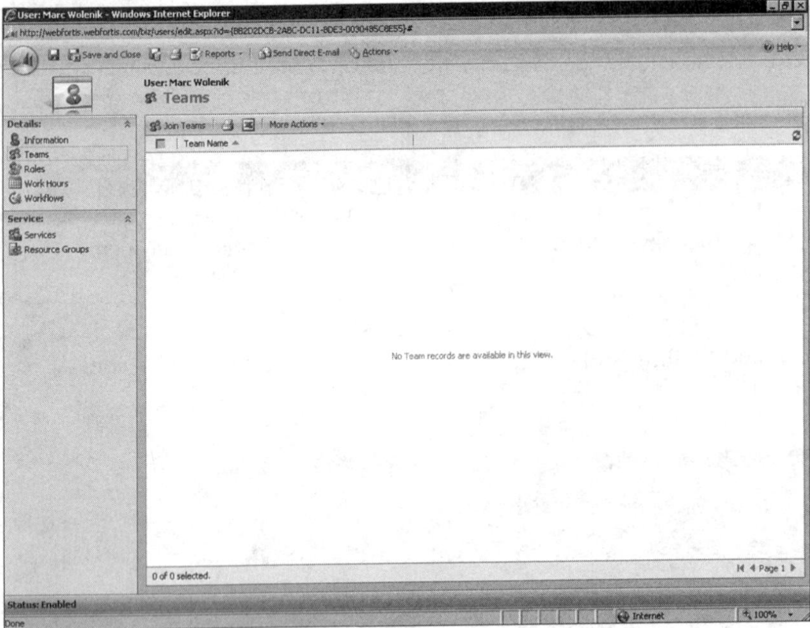

FIGURE 14.30 Team membership for a new User.

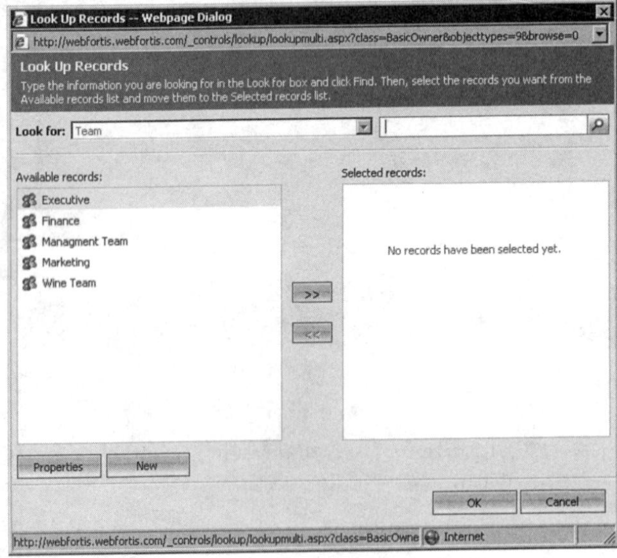

FIGURE 14.31 Joining Teams for a new User.

Users can belong to none, one, or many Teams. If they do belong to a Team, they benefit from Team record sharing.

For more information about Teams, see the "Teams" section later in this chapter.

Roles For Users to be able to do anything in Microsoft Dynamics CRM, they must be assigned a role. Roles are explained later in this chapter; however, after a User has been created, or if the User has had its Business Unit changed, that User has no roles and must be assigned one before he can use the system (see Figure 14.32).

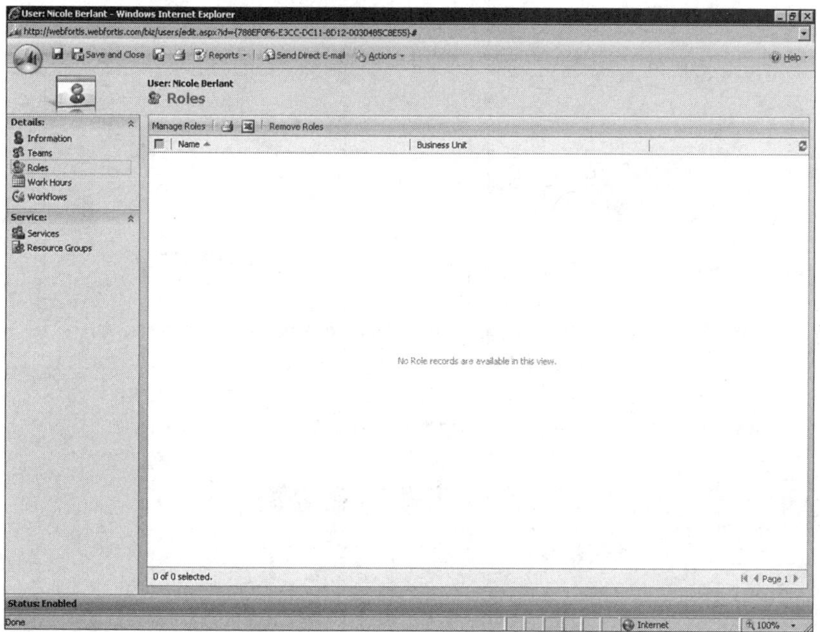

FIGURE 14.32 Role membership for a new User.

To grant them access to a role, select Manage Roles and select which roles you want the User to belong to (see Figure 14.33).

NOTE

Users must belong to at least one role, and their permissions are based on the highest role selected. If the User has both the restrictive Role of Customer Service Representative as well as the System Administrator Role, they will have System Administrator rights throughout the system. See the "Roles" section later in this chapter on creating new roles if you need to mix permissions between roles.

Workflows Here you can see any completed workflows that were run on the User entity. Because this is for a new User, you won't see any available here unless you have a workflow built for the Create event of the User entity when initially setting up your system.

For more information about workflows, refer to Chapter 20.

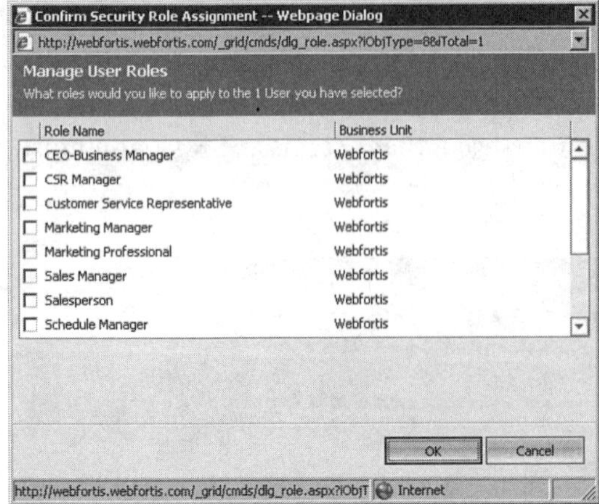

FIGURE 14.33 Role membership options.

Services When viewing an existing User record, any Service records associated with the User are available by selecting Services from the Service option on the near navigation (see Figure 14.34). A service is any work performed for a customer by a User and resources. By default, a new User will have no Services associated with them.

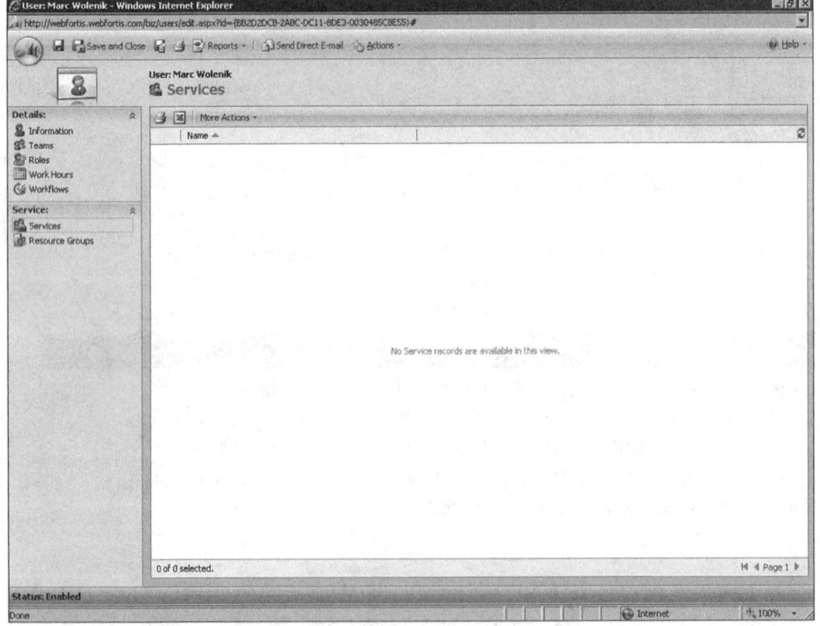

FIGURE 14.34 Services for the selected User.

For more information about creating and working with Services, refer to Chapter 12.

Resource Groups You can add Users to existing Resource Groups by selecting Resource Groups from the near navigation (see Figure 14.35). A Resource Group is a collection of Users, facilities, or equipment. The advantage to having them is that they can be scheduled interchangeably. For example, a Resource Group of everyone who works for you that is qualified to service a particular line of cars can be grouped. Then, when you need to schedule that service, you'll pick from that group instead of among individual employees.

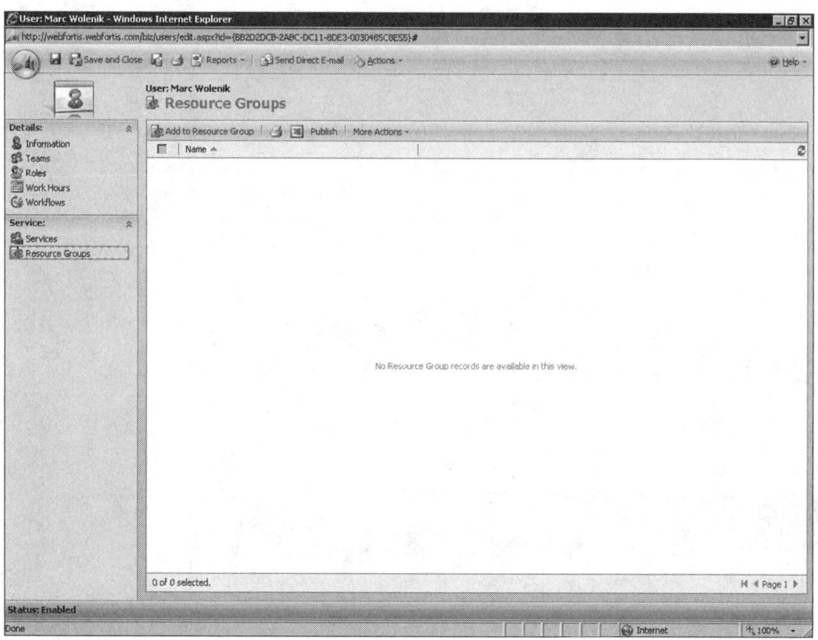

FIGURE 14.35 Resource Groups.

For more information about Resource Groups, refer to the "Resource Groups" section later in this chapter.

Adding Multiple Users

Unlike in previous versions, you can easily add multiple Users at one time. To do so, select the New option on the Users page and then select Multiple Users.

The Add Users Wizard opens (see Figure 14.36).

To complete the wizard, follow these steps:

1. Select the Business Unit and click Next to continue.
2. Select which Security Roles the Users will belong to (see Figure 14.37). As with individual Users, all Users must have at least one Security Role to be able to use the system. When setting the roles for multiple Users, *all* Users who will be added will receive the same Security Roles selected. Click Next to continue.

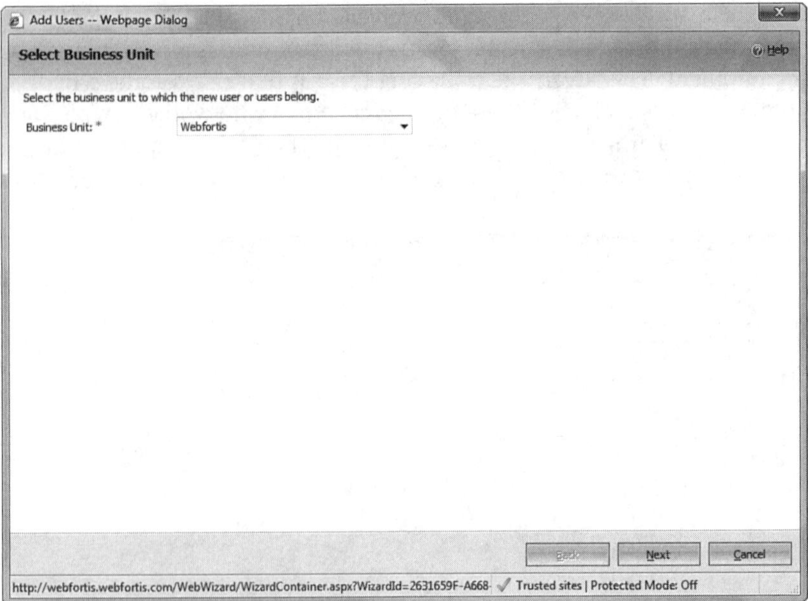

FIGURE 14.36 Add Users Wizard.

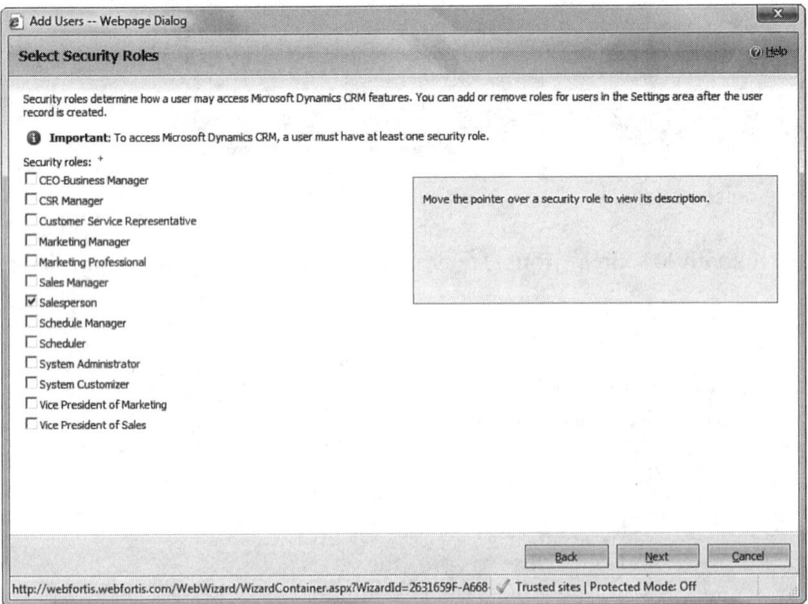

FIGURE 14.37 Selecting Security Roles with the Add Users Wizard.

NOTE

If you don't select Security Roles, the Users will still be created, but you will receive an alert after they have been added that you must assign at least one Security Role to the new Users. When you are adding many Users, this can be time consuming, so consider adding the role here.

3. Select the license type for each User (see Figure 14.38). The license type selected will apply to all Users to be added. However, because Administrative and Read-Only do not consume a CAL, you might want to select either of these first, and then go back and edit individual Users with Full license rights to ensure that you don't go over your limit of Full Users. Click Next to continue.

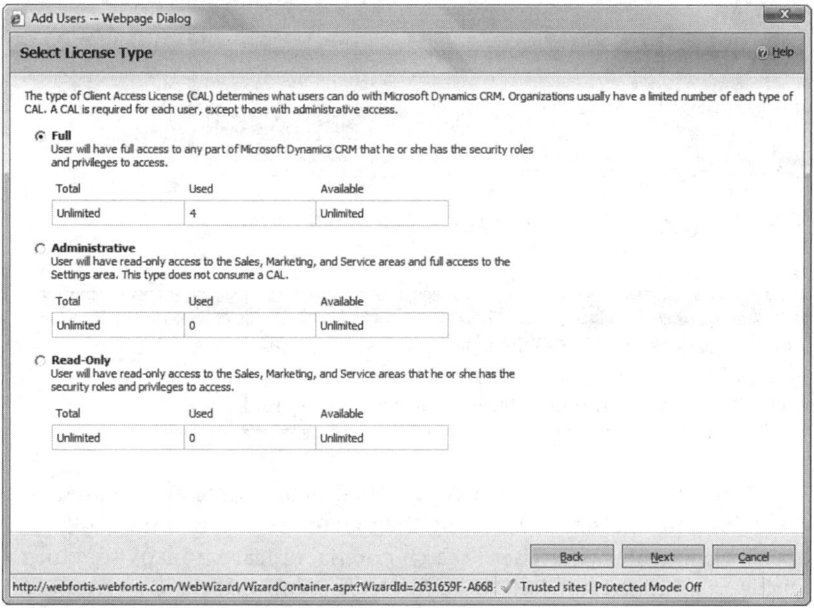

FIGURE 14.38 Selecting the license type with the Add Users Wizard.

4. If using On Premise or Partner Hosted, select the domain or group from the Active Directory that the Users belong to (see Figure 14.39). If Select Users from All Trusted Domains and Groups is selected, all available Users on the current trusted domain and/or groups are presented on the next screen. If Select Users from the Following Domain or Group is selected, the option to select the specific group is presented. Be sure the group node you select contains your Users; if a node is selected that does not have the Users, it will not show up on the next screen; you will have to navigate back to this screen to select an alternate node containing the Users. Click Next to continue.

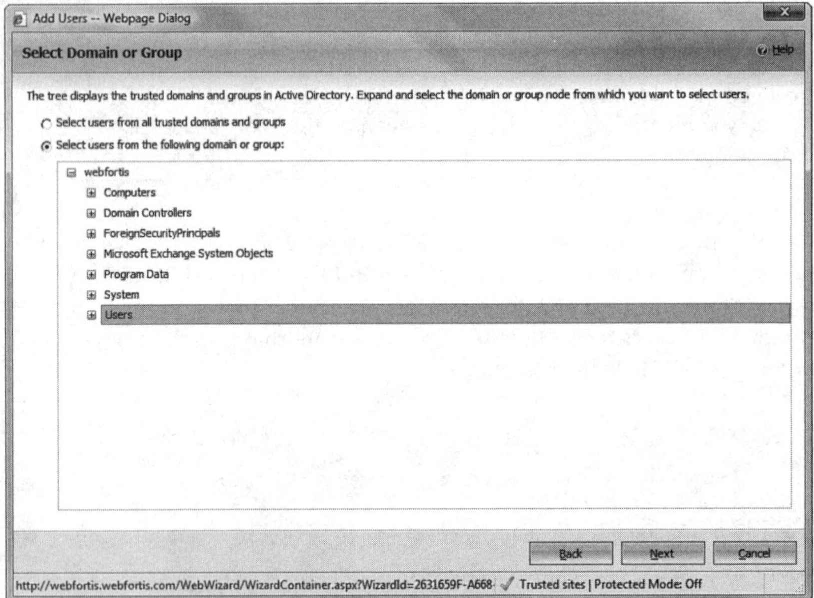

FIGURE 14.39 Selecting a domain or group with the Add Users Wizard.

NOTE

When adding multiple Users using CRM Online, the process is similar, except that you don't select the Users from the computer domain. Rather, the Users are added by adding their first and last name and their e-mail address (see Figure 14.40).

5. Select the Users you want to add by either typing their names separated by a semicolon, or by searching from them by selecting the lookup icon. When the lookup dialog box opens, either enter your Users' search criteria, or leave it blank to return all Users available to be added to CRM. After you have confirmed the Users to be added, they will be added to the textbox where you can remove individuals if necessary (see Figure 14.41).

   Only Users who have not been already added to Microsoft Dynamics CRM are available to be added. Click Create New Users to continue.

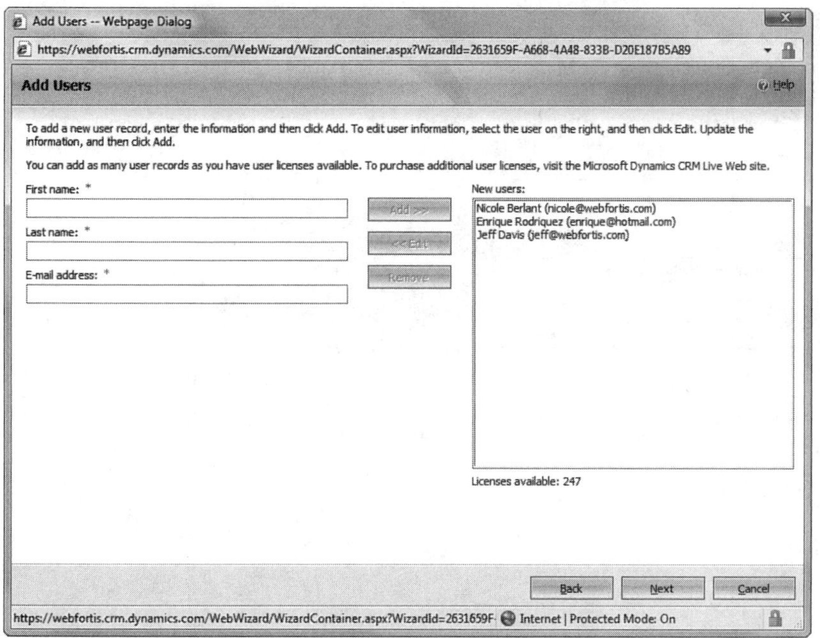

FIGURE 14.40 Selecting Users with the Add Users Wizard for CRM Online.

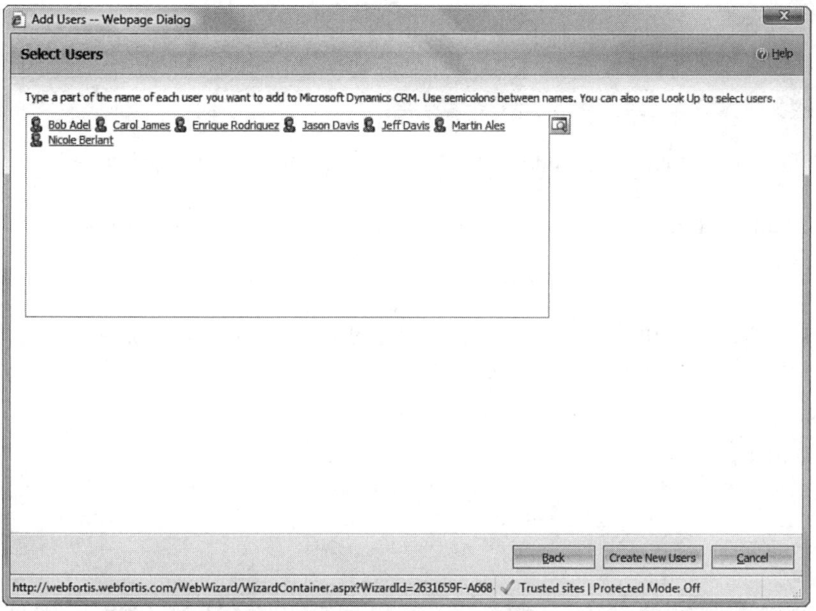

FIGURE 14.41 Selecting Users with the Add Users Wizard (On Premise or Partner Hosted).

NOTE

When adding multiple Users using CRM Online, you have the option to send e-mail invitations to the Users asking them to join. This is something that you do during setup (see Figure 14.42) or later by navigating to the User by selecting Settings, Administration and Users, Send Invitation.

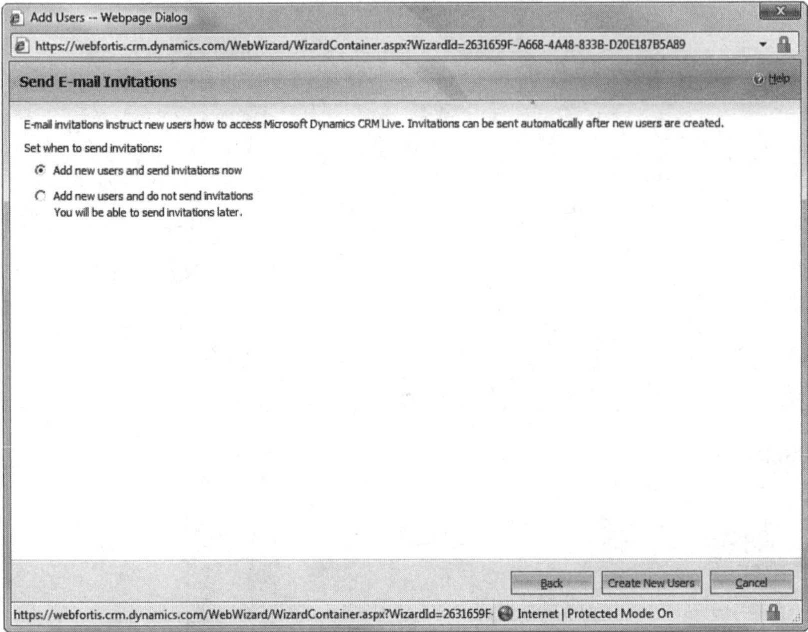

FIGURE 14.42 Send e-mail invitations during the Add Users Wizard for CRM Online.

6. The Users are added to Microsoft Dynamics CRM. This step might take several minutes.
7. When this is completed, you will see the Finish screen (see Figure 14.43). Any alerts or problems with the addition process display here. Select either Add More Users to add more Users or Close to complete the wizard.

Enable or Disable Users

From the More Actions drop-down menu, you can either enable or disable selected Users. By disabling a User, you remove her license, and you can add a new User to use that license if you want.

NOTE

Disabling Users may cause any existing workflows or System Jobs that the User has created or owns to fail.

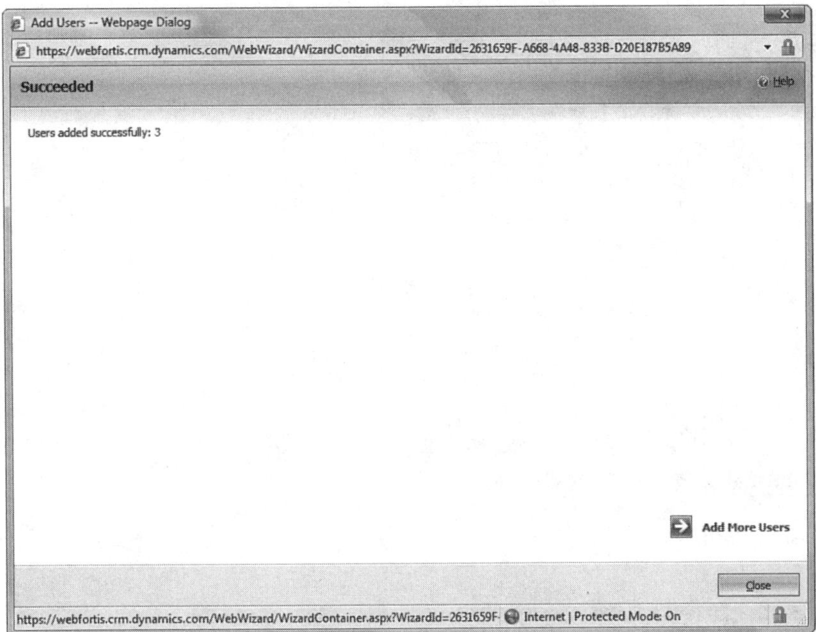

FIGURE 14.43 Finishing the Add Users Wizard.

Manage User Roles

From the More Actions drop-down menu, you can manage selected Users' Roles. Microsoft Dynamics CRM is role-based, which provides a powerful mechanism to manage Users. Because Users must belong to at least one role, but can belong to more, it is important to remember that the User will have the permissions from a higher role.

NOTE

You can select multiple Users at the same time, by holding down either Ctrl or Shift. Thus, if you select a single User, only the existing roles display. If you select multiple Users, no roles are selected, by default.

Manage Quotas

By default, this option is not available from the More Actions drop-down menu until the Fiscal Year has been set (see the "Fiscal Year Settings" section later in this chapter). After the Fiscal Year has been set, Quotas can be assigned to Users (see Figure 14.44).

You can set Sales Quotas for multiple Users by selecting multiple Users and then selecting Manage Quotas from the More Actions drop-down menu.

You can view Quotas by selecting Quotas from the Details option when viewing a Users record (see Figure 14.45). By default the Current Fiscal Year is displayed; however, you can display all Quota years by selecting the All Fiscal Years tab.

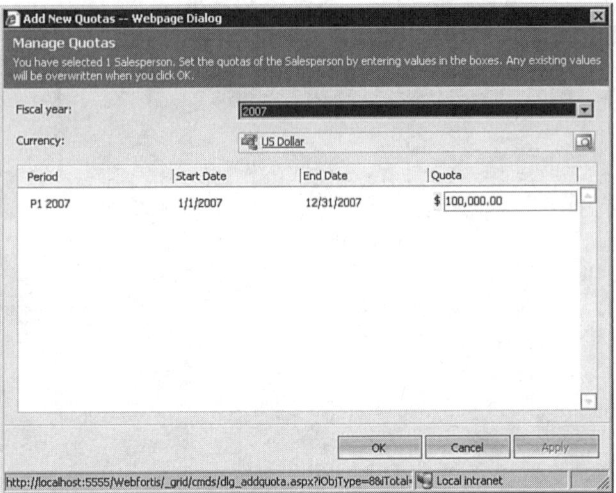

FIGURE 14.44 Set Quota.

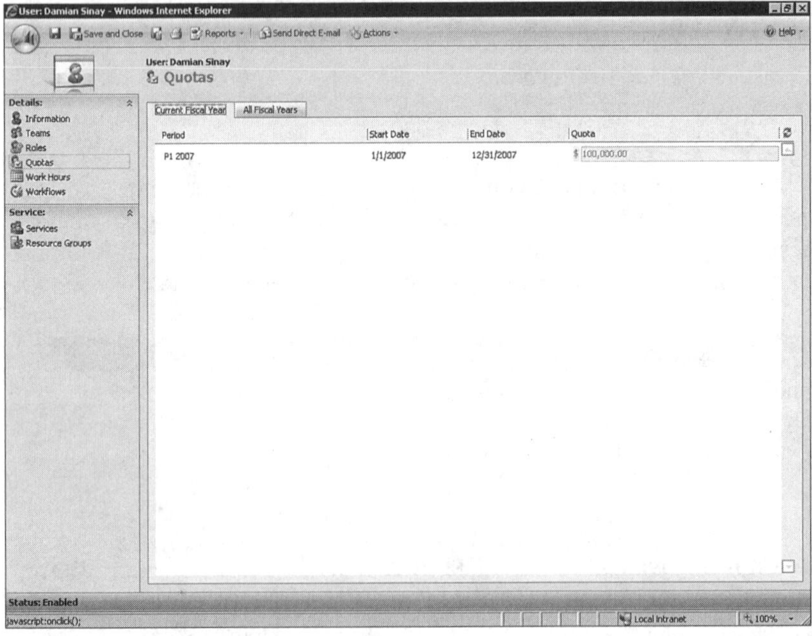

FIGURE 14.45 Quota details.

TIP

If Quotas are not displayed or available on the User's near navigation, check that the Fiscal Year has been set up and saved.

Change Business Units

Available as an option from the More Actions drop-down menu, you can change selected Users' Business Units (see Figure 14.46).

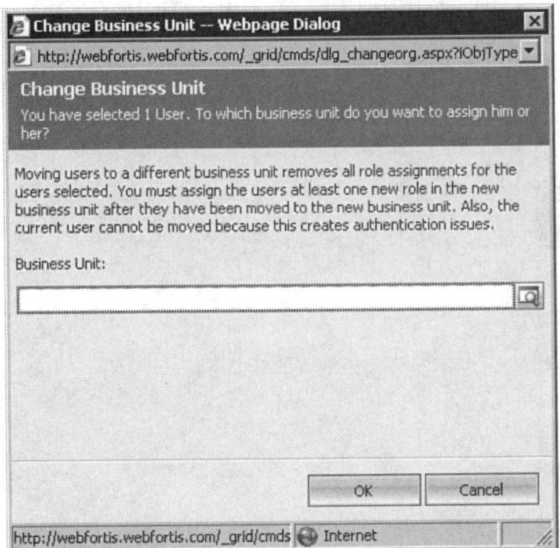

FIGURE 14.46 Changing a Business Unit.

For more information about Business Units and the effects of changing Users' assigned Business Units, refer to the previous section named "Business Units."

Change Managers

Available as an option from the More Actions drop-down menu, you can change the selected User Manager (see Figure 14.47).

FIGURE 14.47 Changing the Manager.

You can set another User as the Manager (provided that the selected User is not one previously selected as the Change Manager) as the Manager of the selected Users.

Send Invitation (CRM Online Only)

When adding new Users for CRM Online, the Users must accept the invitation and associate their login with a Passport account. During the setup process of Users for CRM Online, you have the option to send them an invitation. If they don't receive it or you need to re-send it for any reason, you can select Send Invitation from the Actions drop-down menu (see Figure 14.48).

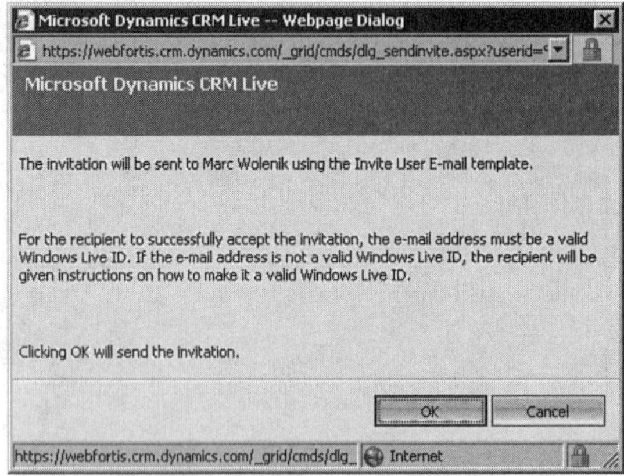

FIGURE 14.48 Send a CRM Online invitation to a User.

View Users

When working with the Main Users Interface, as shown in Figure 14.27, these are the default system views for a User:

- **Administrative Access Users**—Shows all enabled Users with administrative access permissions
- **Disabled Users**—Shows all Users who are disabled
- **Enabled Users**—Shows all Users who are active
- **Full Access Users**—Shows all enabled Users who have a Full Access CAL
- **Local Business Users**—Shows all enabled Users who report to the selected Business Unit Organization that the logged-in User is working with
- **My Direct Reports**—Shows all enabled Users who have the current User as their manager
- **Read-Only Access Users**—Shows all enabled Users who have a Read-Only Access CAL
- **Subsidiary Users**—Shows all enabled Users who report to Child Business Units

Privacy Preferences

Privacy Preferences enables you to specify whether your organization participates in the Customer Experience Improvement Program (CEIP) (see Figure 14.49).

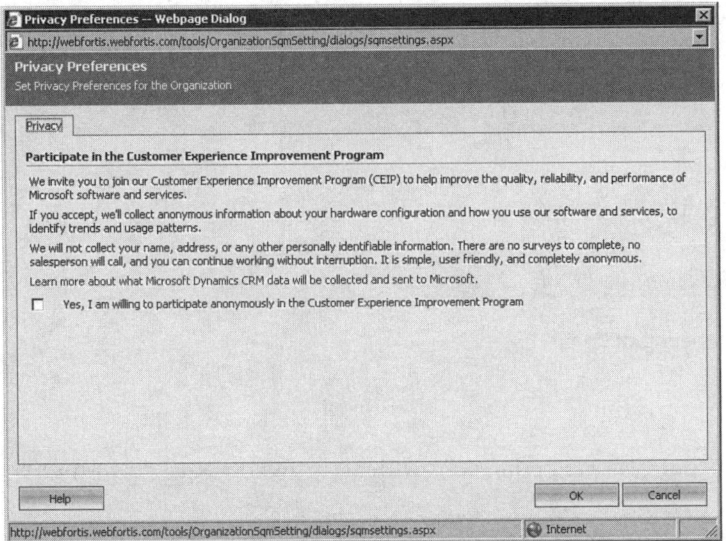

FIGURE 14.49 Privacy Preferences.

The default for this is established when Microsoft Dynamics CRM is installed, and we recommend participation because it will improve future products and releases.

Auto-Numbering

By default, Microsoft Dynamics CRM auto-numbers the following entities incrementally:

- Contracts
- Cases
- Articles
- Quotas
- Orders
- Invoices
- Campaigns

With the exception of Articles, you can adjust the suffix length (see Figure 14.50).

NOTE

Changing a prefix number to a new value applies to newly created records; it does not change existing records.

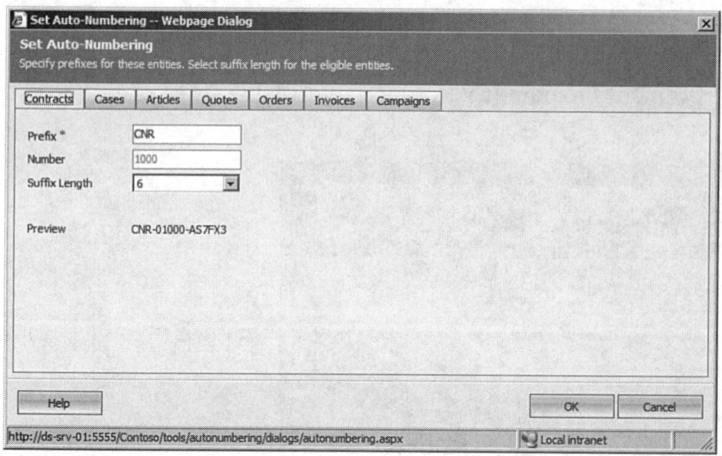

FIGURE 14.50 Auto-Numbering options.

Security Roles

Microsoft Dynamics CRM controls User permissions with Security Roles (see Figure 14.51).

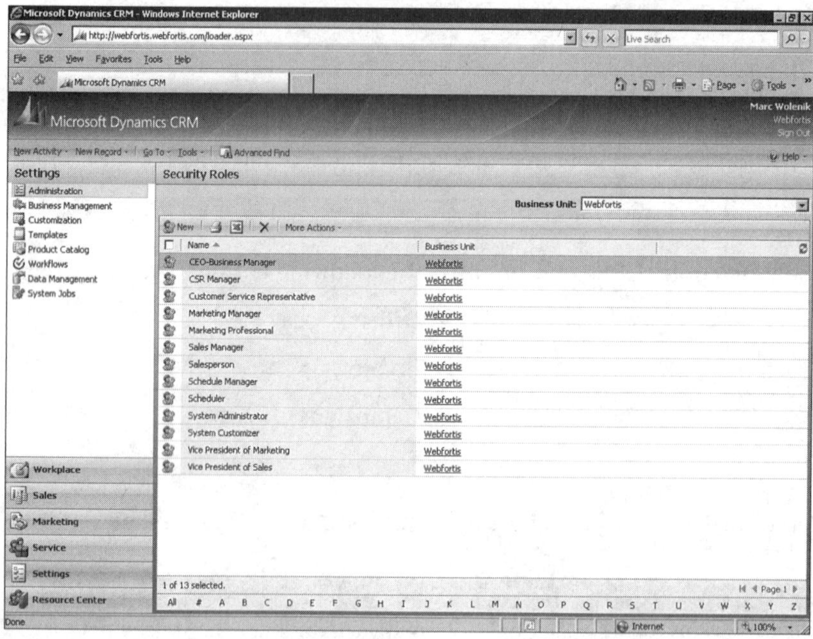

FIGURE 14.51 Security Roles.

NOTE

Although Microsoft Dynamics CRM integrates tightly with Active Directory to determine its User base, permissions established in Active Directory have no correlation with Users in Microsoft Dynamics CRM. As such, it is quite possible to have an Active Directory membership of Enterprise Administrator, but be in Read-Only User Mode or have a minimal role setting in Microsoft Dynamics CRM and vice versus.

By default, the following Security Roles are included with Microsoft Dynamics CRM 4.0:

- CEO-Business Manager
- CSR Manager
- Customer Service Representative
- Marketing Manager
- Marketing Professional
- Sales Manager
- Salesperson
- Schedule Manager
- Scheduler
- System Administrator
- System Customizer
- Vice President of Marketing
- Vice President of Sales

With Microsoft Dynamics CRM 4.0, Security Roles are flexible and easily created, and extend security to custom entities. By default, new Security Roles are created on the Organizational level and inherited by Child Business Units, regardless of which Business Unit is selected from the Security Roles Administration screen. Additionally, with regard to how Security Roles are inherited:

- New Security Roles are automatically created on the Master Business Unit and inherited to all Child Business Units.
- Copied Security Roles are created on the selected Business Unit, are available only on the selected Business Unit, and are inherited by all Child Business Units of the selected Business Unit (not any Parent Business Units).
- Inherited Security Roles cannot be modified or deleted. To make changes to inherited Security Roles, you must select the Business Unit that the Security Role is assigned to and then make changes there. All changes are inherited to Child Business Units.

Based on this, if a specific Security Role is required on a Child Business Unit, you must create a new Security Role, navigate to the Child Business Unit, and select Copy Role from the More Actions drop-down menu. After you copy the Security Role, you cannot modify it. The Security Role also will apply only to the Business Unit and any children where it was copied.

To view the specific access granted by any role, double-click the desired role to bring up the Role settings screen (see Figure 14.52).

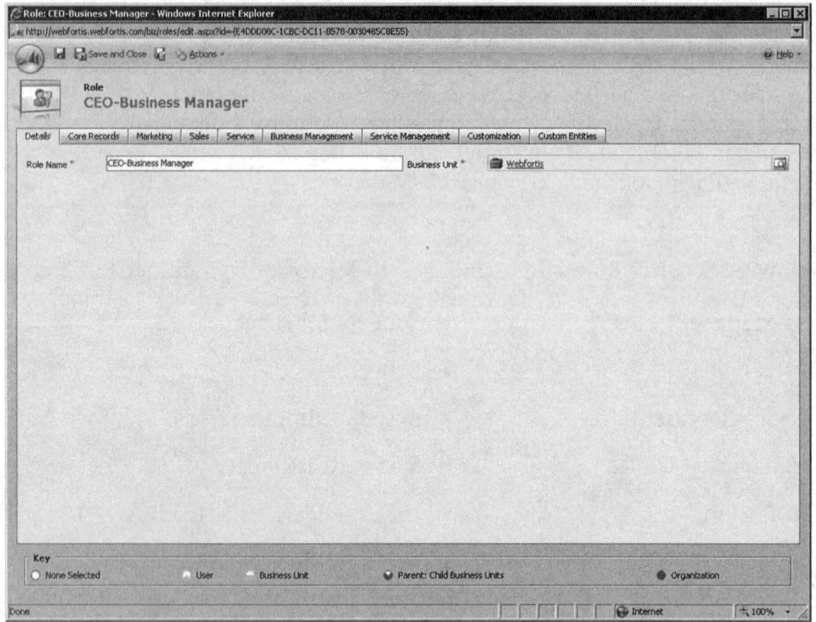

FIGURE 14.52 Role settings for CEO-Business Manager.

The tabs across break out the major access points within Microsoft Dynamics CRM 4.0:

- Details
- Core Records
- Marketing
- Sales
- Service
- Business Management
- Service Management
- Customization
- Custom Entities

Before we explain each of the sections, it is important to review the Key at the bottom of each form; it applies to all tabs except the Details tab (see Figure 14.53).

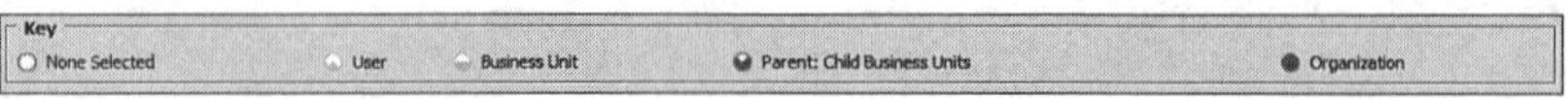

FIGURE 14.53 Security Role Key.

The symbols indicated are how permissions are granted on the records for the selected Security Role. Records within Microsoft Dynamics CRM 4.0 have either Organizational permissions or User permissions. When applying permissions, you select the Entity (for example, Account, Contact, or Lead) and then associate the action with the record (Create, Read, Write, and so on) and, finally, the level of access (as indicated on the Key).

The level of access is explained as follows:

- **None selected**—The User cannot perform the selected action.
- **User**—The User can perform the selected action only on the records that he or she owns.
- **Business Unit**—The User can perform the selected action on records owned by anyone in the Business Unit that this User belongs to, but not Child or Parent Business Units.
- **Parent: Child Business Units**—The User can perform the selected action on records within his or her Business Unit (same as Business Unit access), and perform the selected action on any Child Business Units of his or her Business Unit (but not the Parent Business Unit).
- **Organization**—The User can perform the selected action on any record within the organization.

NOTE

Some Entities either can't have permission levels set on them or have only limited options. In the first case, where there is no ability to set a permission level, this is usually because that functionality doesn't exist, so there is no reason to set permissions on it. An example of this is on the Business Management tab, for the Entity User and the action Delete. Because Users can't be deleted (only deactivated), there is no capability to set a permission level on it.

Carefully consider how you want to set permissions by selecting the level of access for the selected role; Users might have trouble accessing records without the correct permissions.

TIP

If you only want to share some records between Users, consider using Teams. Team membership is often used to allow access to records that Users normally don't have access to. For more information about Teams, see the "Teams" section later in this chapter.

You can set security levels across all Entities by clicking the action label at the top of the screen.

NOTE

When setting permissions for Security Roles, no option enables you to secure individual fields or individual records. Instead, the permissions selected apply to all records of the selected type. (For example, if Read permission for Account is granted to a role, the User will have the capability to read *all* Account records.)

TIP

You cannot update or modify the System Administrator Role. This ensures that permissions aren't accidentally denied within that role, preventing access to make corrections.

Details

The Details tab displays the Security Role name and the Business Unit that the role applies to (see Figure 14.54). If the Security Role is an inherited role (as previously described), you cannot change the Role name.

Core Records

As its name implies, permissions for general or "core" access to the system are set in Core Records. Access from everything to Accounts, Contacts, Leads, and so on is controlled on this screen (see Figure 14.54).

NOTE

Entities that you can't set on the core records are available on the other tabs. For example, the capability to set permissions on the Case entity is not available in the core records interface because Case is a Service Entity and, therefore, is found on the Service tab. If you don't find the entity you want to set, be sure to check all the tabs across the top.

The permission options are divided across the top, while the entities affected are listed in rows (see Figure 14.54). The permissions (or privilege) are as follows:

- **Create**—The ability to create a new record
- **Read**—The ability to open and read an existing record
- **Write**—The ability to make and save changes to an existing record, including deleting data from the record (however, not to delete the entire record)
- **Delete**—The ability to delete an existing record
- **Append**—The ability to append the current record to another record
- **Append To**—The ability to append a different record to the current record
- **Assign**—The ability to assign the record to another User
- **Share**—The ability to share the record with another User

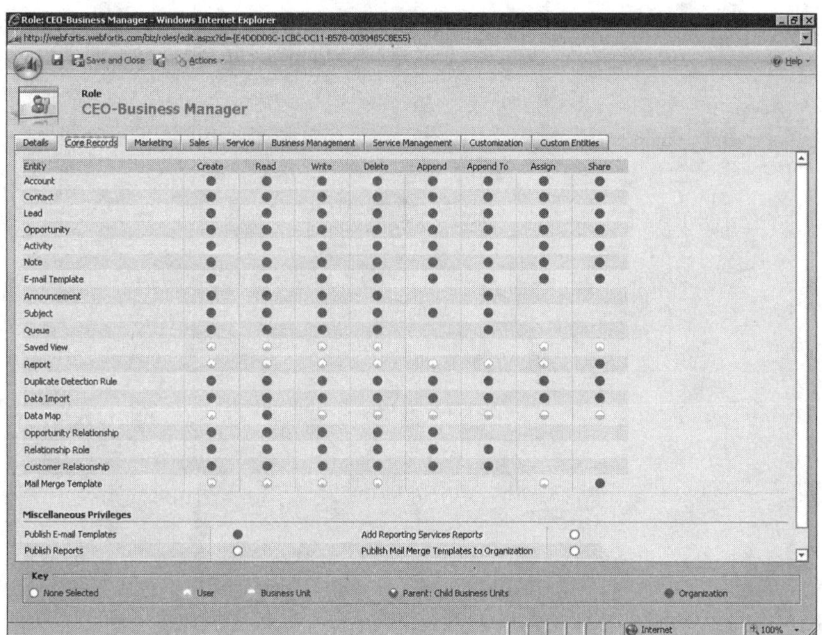

FIGURE 14.54 Security Role—Core Records.

NOTE

The difference between Append and Append To is that Append enables you to append the current record to another record, whereas Append To gives you the ability to append another record to this record.

Additional options include Miscellaneous Privileges, located at the bottom of the form, and include options such as the capability to publish various objects and add reports.

Marketing

Marketing has the same permission options listed in Core Records (see Figure 14.55).

The only Marketing miscellaneous privilege is Create Quick Campaign. Note that Quick Campaigns are different than Campaigns, and the only permission for a Quick Campaign is the ability to create one (see Chapter 11 for the differences between Campaigns and Quick Campaigns).

Sales

Sales has the same permission options listed in Core Records (see Figure 14.56).

The three miscellaneous privileges give a User with this role the ability to override pricing on the Quota, the invoice, or the order.

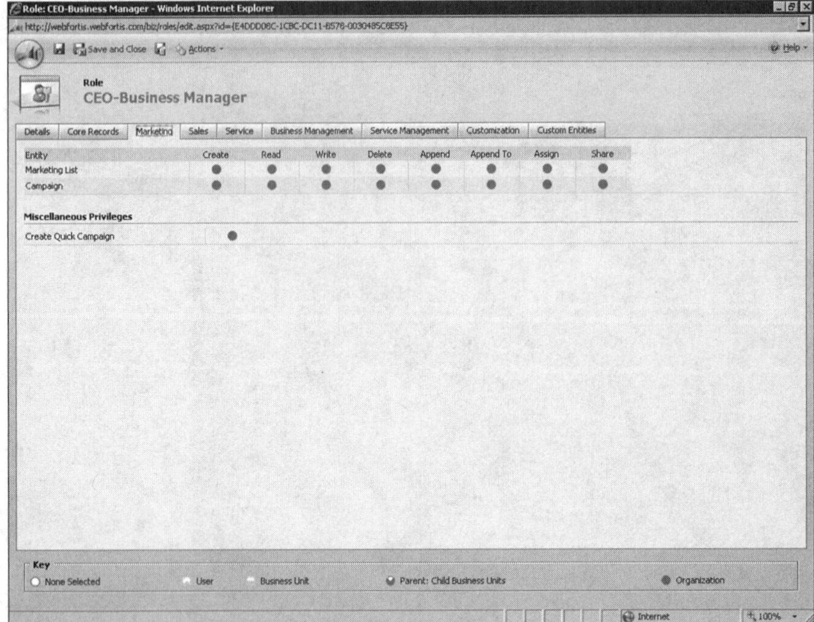

FIGURE 14.55 Security Role—Marketing Records.

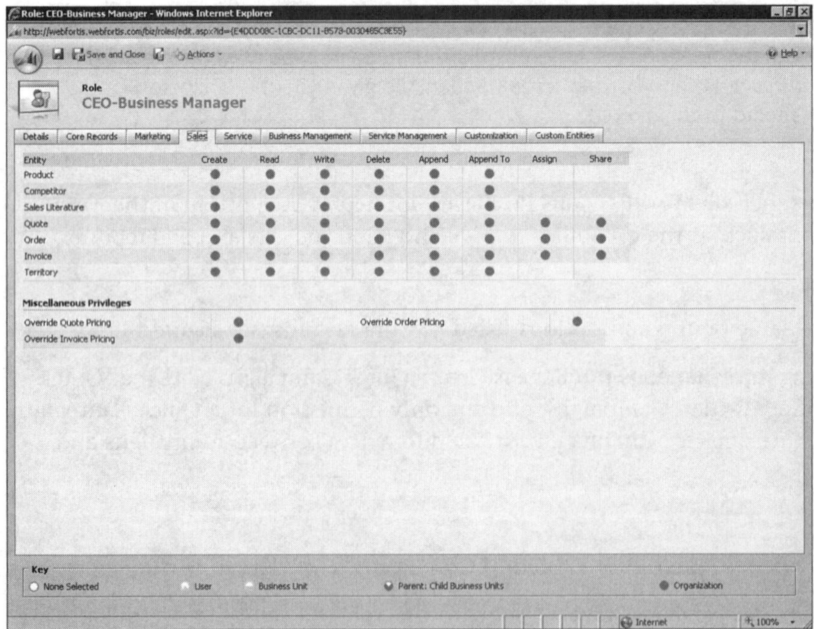

FIGURE 14.56 Security Role—Sales Records.

Service

Sales has the same permission options listed in Core Records (see Figure 14.57).

The ability to publish Articles is the only other miscellaneous privilege available on the Service tab.

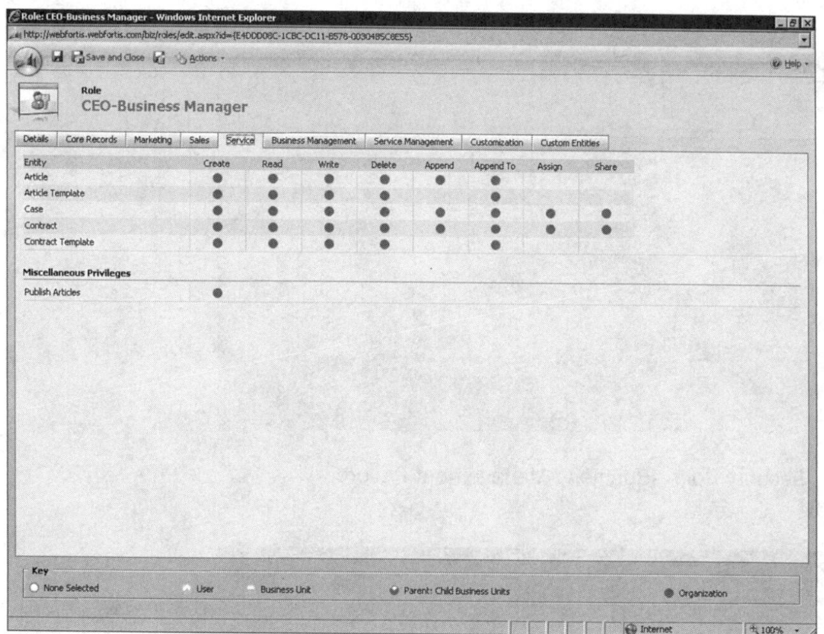

FIGURE 14.57 Security Role—Service Records.

Business Management

Business Management permissions are slightly different than those listed in Core Records. They include the options Reparent and Enable/Disable (see Figure 14.58):

- **Reparent**—The ability to assign a different parent to an existing record in the system
- **Enable/Disable**—The ability to literally enable or disable the object

The miscellaneous privileges associated with Business Management include several settings that can affect usage of CRM, such as the capabilities Go Offline and Export to Excel.

Service Management

Service Management has the same permission options listed in Core Records, with the exception of the capability Assign and Share (see Figure 14.59).

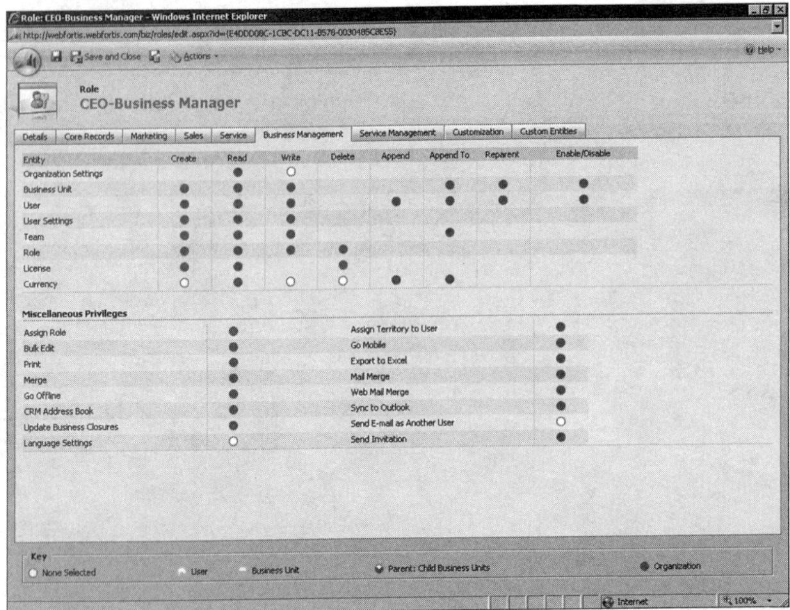

FIGURE 14.58 Security Role—Business Management Records.

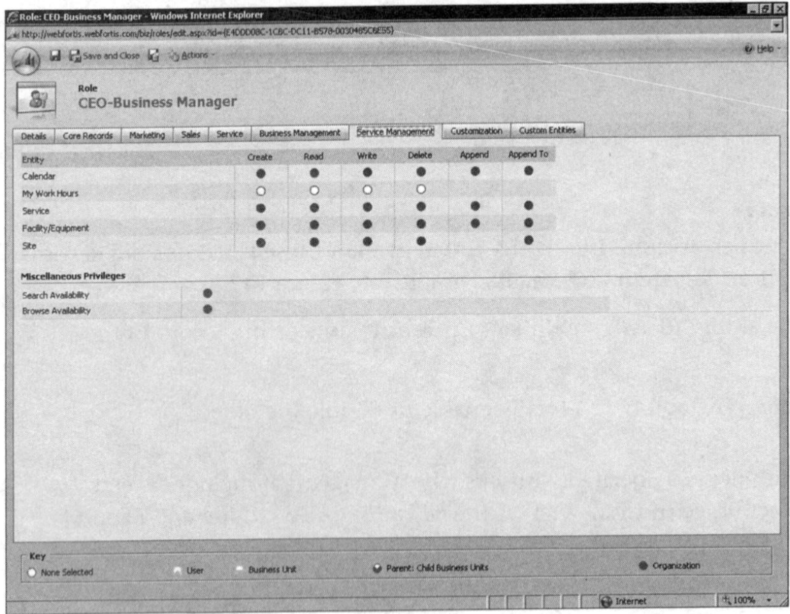

FIGURE 14.59 Security Role—Service Management Records.

The miscellaneous privileges enable the User to search and browse.

Customization

Customization has the same permission options listed in Core Records (see Figure 14.60).

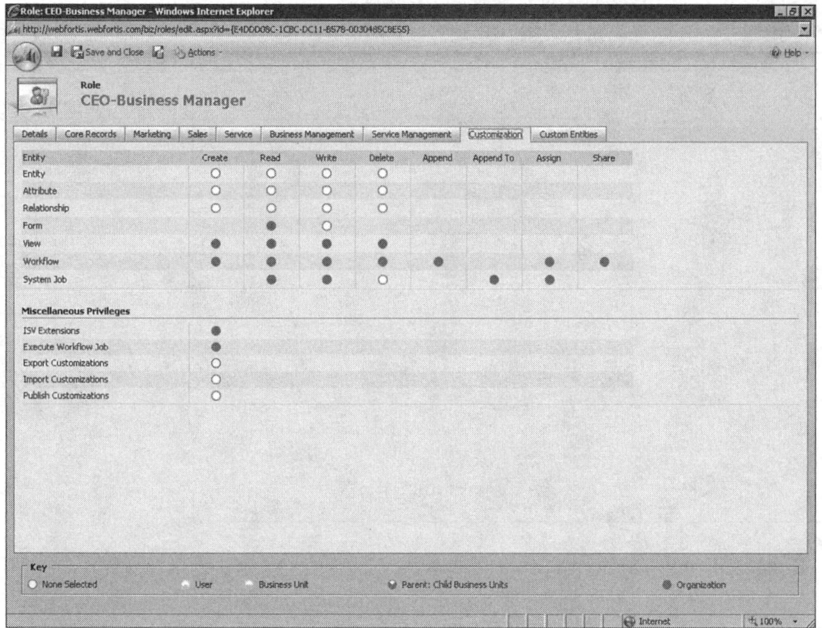

FIGURE 14.60 Security Role—Customization Records.

Miscellaneous privileges include the capability to work with ISV extensions, execute workflow jobs, and export, import, and publish customizations.

Custom Entities

By default, there are no custom entities. The Custom Entities tab gives the options to set permissions only if a Custom Entity exists (see Figure 14.61).

When an entity is created, permissions need to be established across the Security Roles and are the same as listed in the Core Records previously.

Teams

The concept of Teams in Microsoft Dynamics CRM is designed around the idea that members of a Team can share records that members wouldn't ordinarily have access to. An example of this is Users in different Business Units who belong to the same Team. These Users could view records across the business units by sharing them.

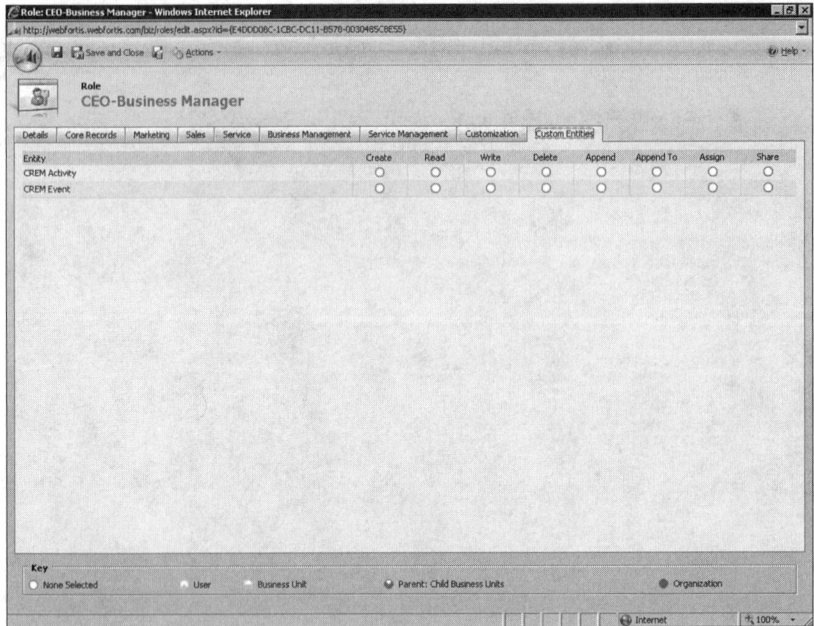

FIGURE 14.61 Security Role—Custom Entities Records.

TIP

After you create a Team, you cannot delete it. However, you can deactivate a Team by removing all Users from it. You can add Users to a Team at any time, so a deactivated Team becomes active again when Users are added back to it.

Figure 14.62 shows the Team interface found in Settings, Administration.

The process of creating and managing Teams in Microsoft Dynamics CRM is very straightforward. To create a new Team, follow these steps:

1. Navigate to Settings, Administration, Teams (see Figure 14.62). Select New.
2. Enter the Team name and select the Business Unit. By default, the root Business Unit is selected (see Figure 14.63). Click Save to enable the Members option on the near navigation.

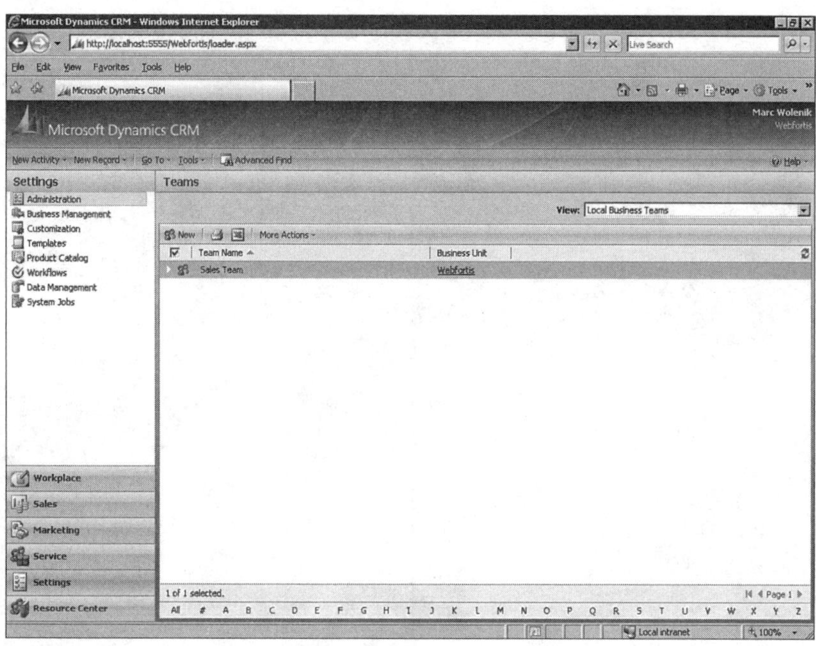

FIGURE 14.62 Teams in Microsoft Dynamics CRM.

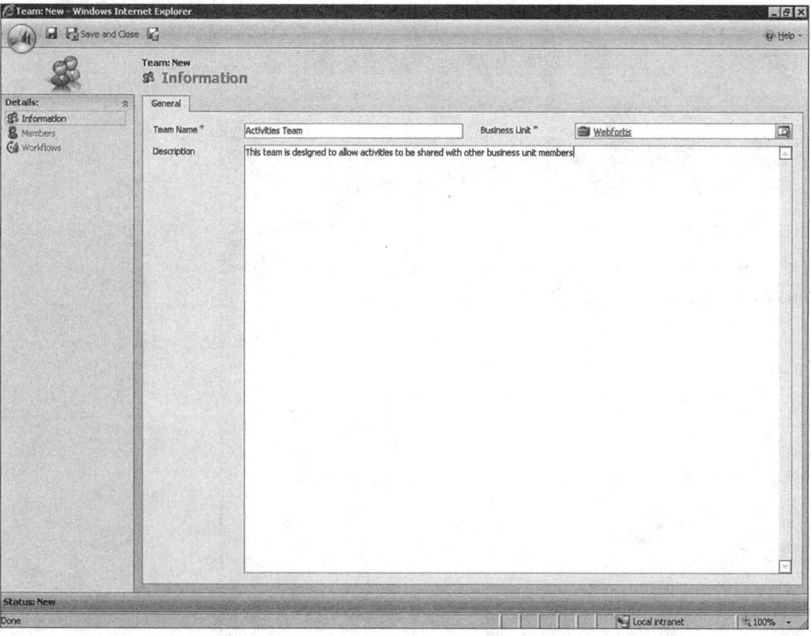

FIGURE 14.63 Creating a new Team in Microsoft Dynamics CRM.

3. Select the Users from the system who will be part of the Team by clicking Add Members (see Figure 14.64). Click Save and Close to continue.

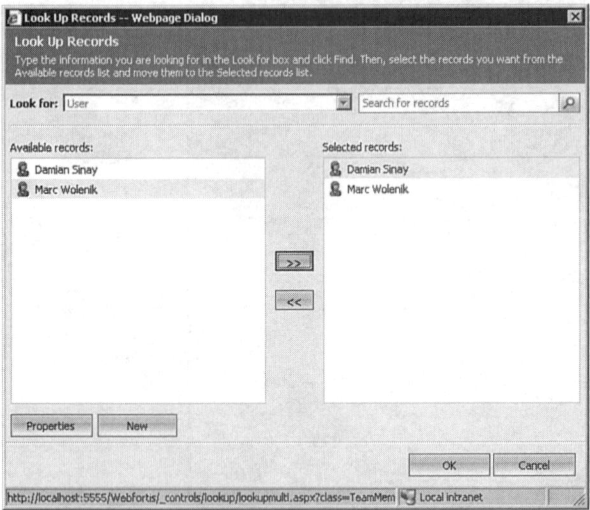

FIGURE 14.64 Adding members to a new Team in Microsoft Dynamics CRM.

4. The newly created Team is displayed on the Teams interface (see Figure 14.65).

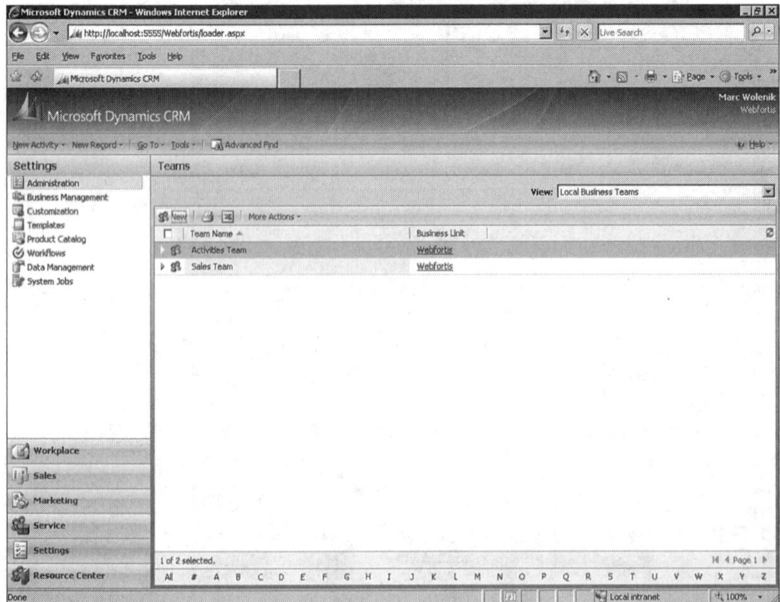

FIGURE 14.65 Newly created Teams in Microsoft Dynamics CRM.

Now that you have created your Team, sharing records with the Team is very simple. Follow these steps:

1. Navigate to a record. In this example, you'll navigate to a Lead in the system. Select Sharing from the More Actions drop-down menu (see Figure 14.66).

2. The sharing interface appears (see Figure 14.67). Select Add User/Team to continue.

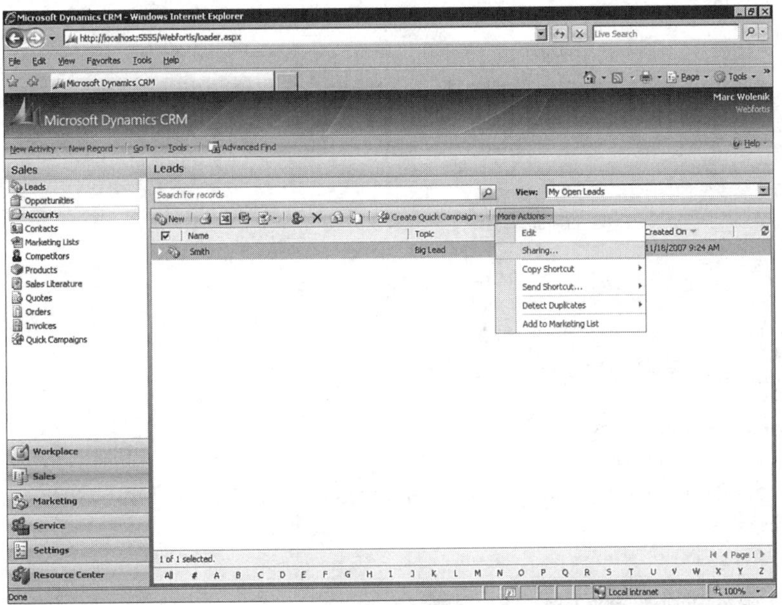

FIGURE 14.66 Sharing a Lead in Microsoft Dynamics CRM.

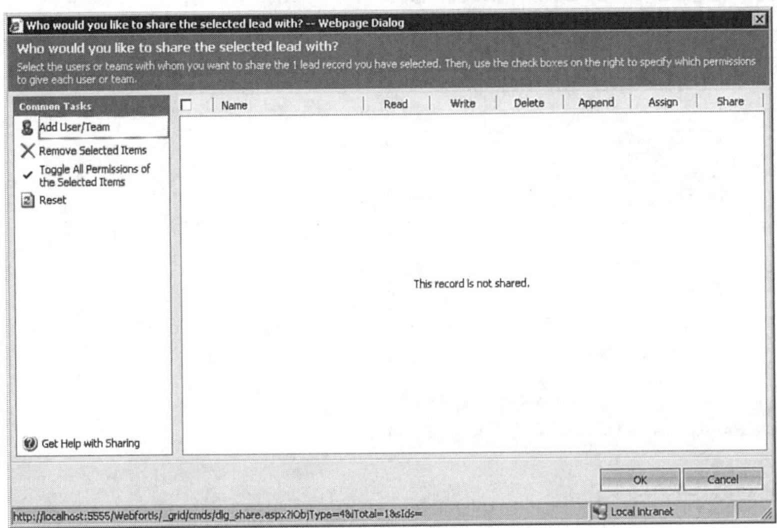

FIGURE 14.67 Sharing interface.

3. Select to share the record with either a User or a Team (see Figure 14.68).

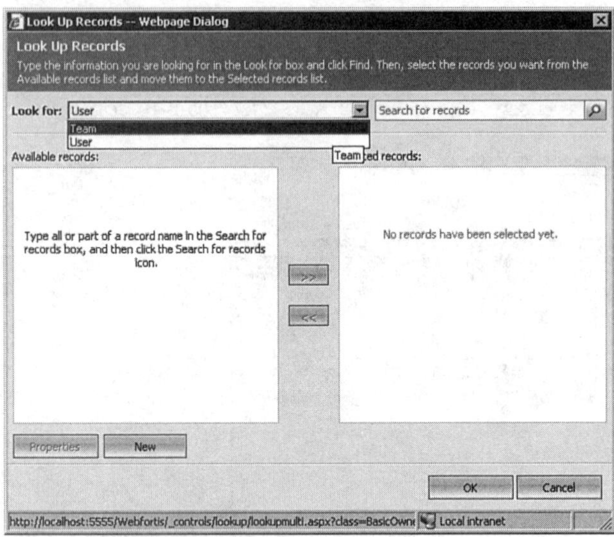

FIGURE 14.68 Look Up Records page.

4. Select from the available Teams, and click >> to add them (see Figure 14.69). Click OK to continue.

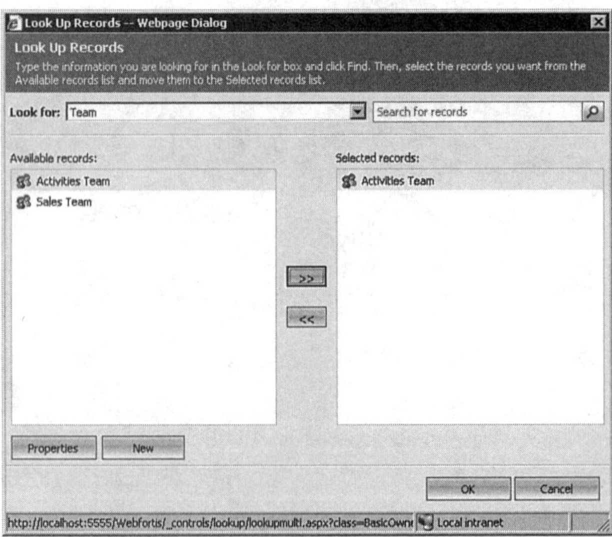

FIGURE 14.69 Selecting records.

5. The selected Team is now available on the sharing interface, and you can give it access for either Read, Write, Delete, Append, Assign, or Share (see Figure 14.70).

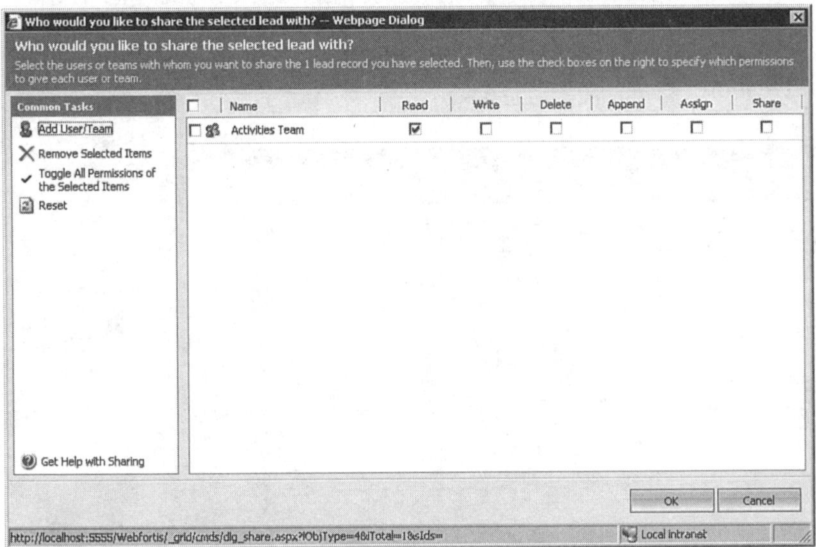

FIGURE 14.70 Sharing a record.

Languages

Microsoft Dynamics CRM is incredibly multilingual. It can serve as many languages are available via the Multilingual User Interface (MUI) packs. These MUI packs are available from Microsoft via download. When installed, they enable Users to select what language they want to work with. By default, Microsoft Dynamics CRM comes with no MUIs installed.

MUIs work by translating *most* of the labels within Microsoft Dynamics CRM to the selected MUI language. In rare cases when the MUIs are unavailable to translate, the translation falls back to the installed base language. Note that MUIs do not translate the data information contained within Microsoft Dynamics CRM.

TIP

When using right-to-left MUIs, such as Hebrew and Arabic, the language and the navigation pane displays from right to left as well. That is why the navigation pane in Microsoft Dynamics CRM is continually referred to as the "near navigation" instead of the "left navigation."

NOTE

Although customizations must be done in the base language, they can be translated so that they are viewed in the different language.

Follow these steps to install a MUI:

1. Navigate to the MUI file (when downloaded) on your computer. Typically, the format of the MUI file is `MUISetup_<language>_i386.msi`, where `<language>` is the Local ID code (LCID) to be installed. The LCID is a value defined by Microsoft that determines the language (that is, 1033=English, 3082=Spanish, etc.). Double-click to begin the installation (see Figure 14.71).

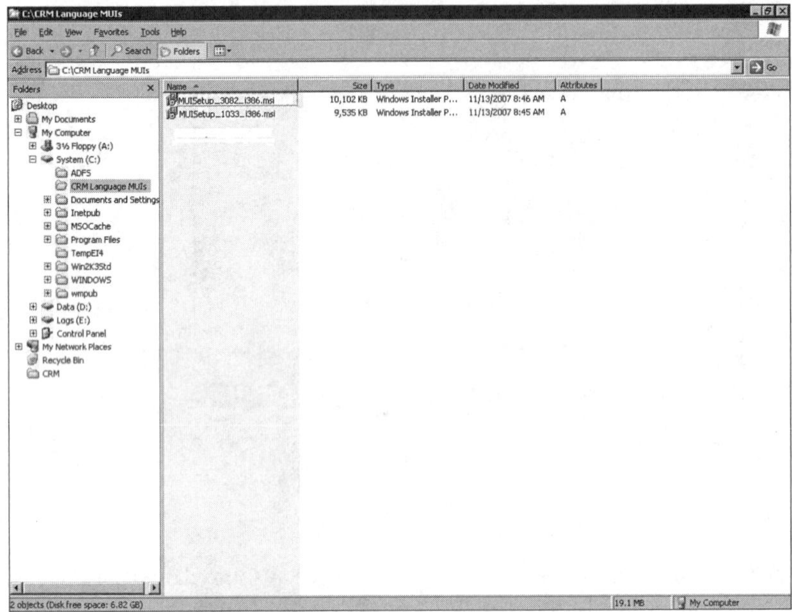

FIGURE 14.71 Sample Multilingual User Interface (MUI) packs.

2. Accept the license agreement and click Install to continue (see Figure 14.72).

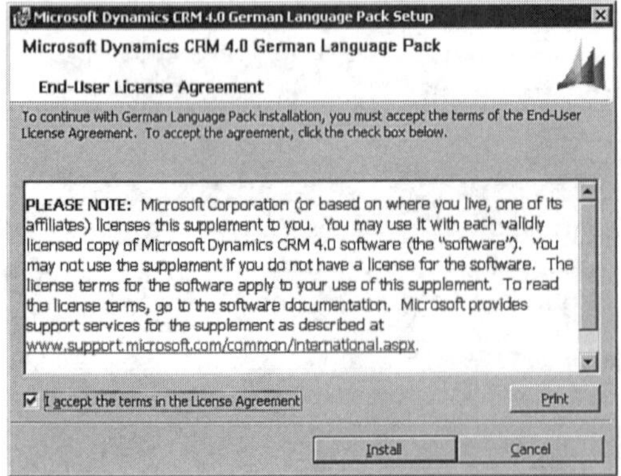

FIGURE 14.72 MUI license agreement.

3. The MUI installs and, when completed, returns a confirmation page that the MUI has been installed (see Figure 14.73).

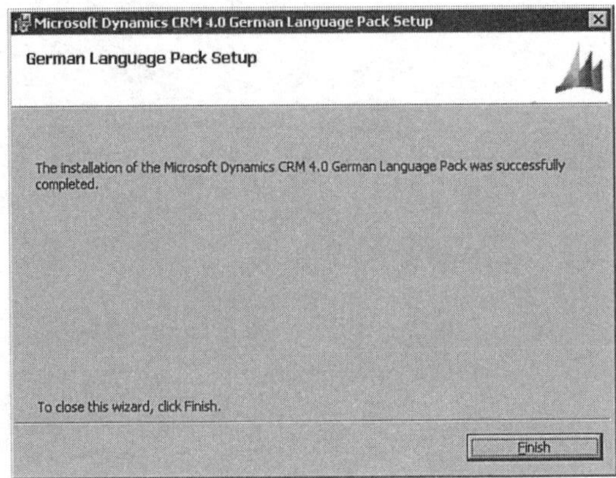

FIGURE 14.73 MUI installed.

When the MUI is installed, it is listed when Languages is selected from the Settings menu (see Figure 14.74).

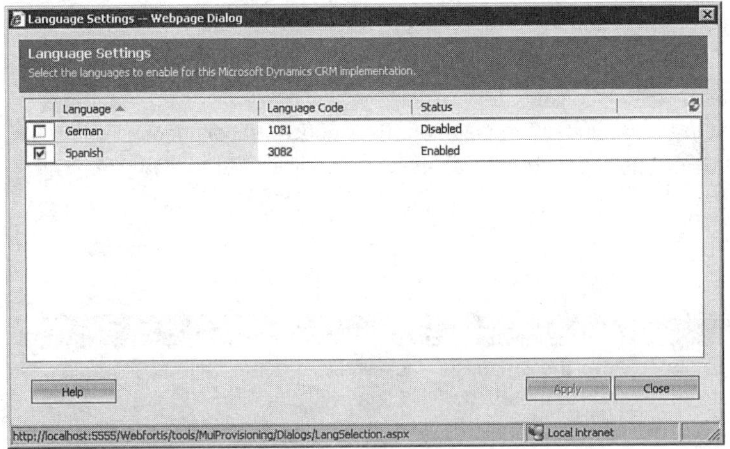

FIGURE 14.74 Installed languages.

By default, installed languages are disabled and must be enabled.

Users can now select which language they want to work with by navigating to Tools, Options, and selecting the Languages tab (see Figure 14.75).

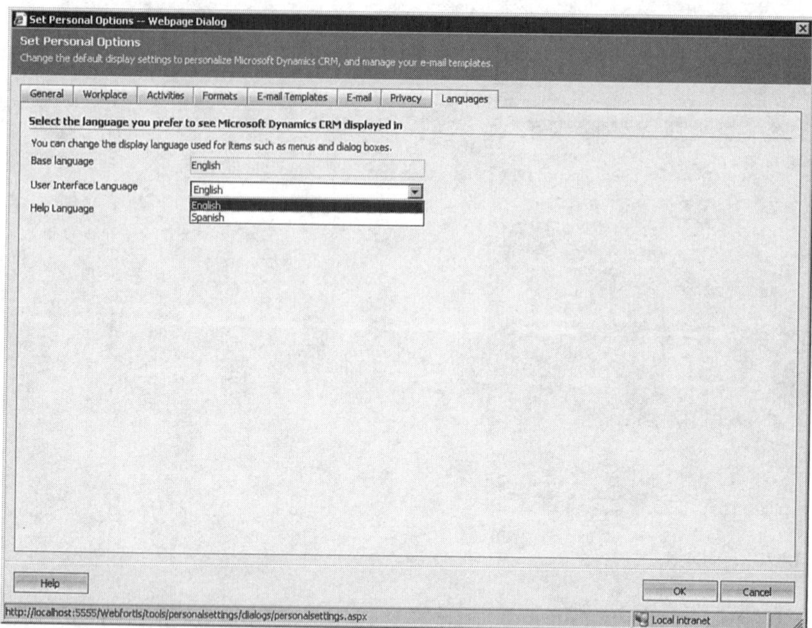

FIGURE 14.75 Installed languages available to Users.

Only the languages that have been enabled are available for Users to select.

NOTE

There is a special setting in the Business Management Role under Miscellaneous Privileges called Language Settings. It allows the enabling/disabling of MUI languages. If you're unable to perform MUI configuration changes, be sure to check your Role settings for this permission.

TIP

Check the Mail Merge Templates after the language packs have been installed. Several different ones are loaded with each MUI installed.

Product Updates (Partner Hosted or On Premise Only)

Product Updates enables you to sign up for the Microsoft Dynamics CRM Product Update newsletter (see Figure 14.76).

A Windows Live ID is required to complete the registration. When subscribed, Users can receive communications from Microsoft related to Microsoft Dynamics CRM Product Updates.

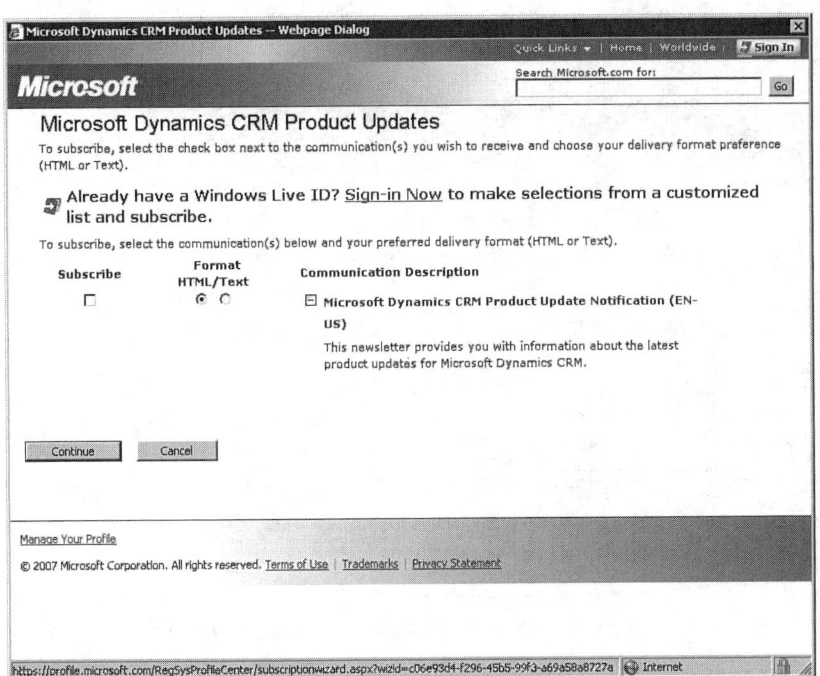

FIGURE 14.76 Product Updates.

A Windows Live ID is an account that is set up, verified, and administrated by Microsoft. With Windows Live, you can verify your identity by any system using the Live/Passport network.

NOTE

This is not the same as the Windows Server (Exchange, SQL, and so on) and Office updates that are a required part of good computer hygiene. As such, be sure to regularly check for required updates because they might not be included in the newsletter.

Billing (CRM Online Only)

Found only with CRM Online, the Settings/Administration area has a Billing option that allows CRM Online administrators to set payment and billing options (see Figure 14.77).

When you select the Billing option, a new window opens that verifies your Windows Live ID and then takes you to the billing and account management interface for your CRM Online account (see Figure 14.78).

From this interface, you can add account delegates, view your payment details, and see what services you are using.

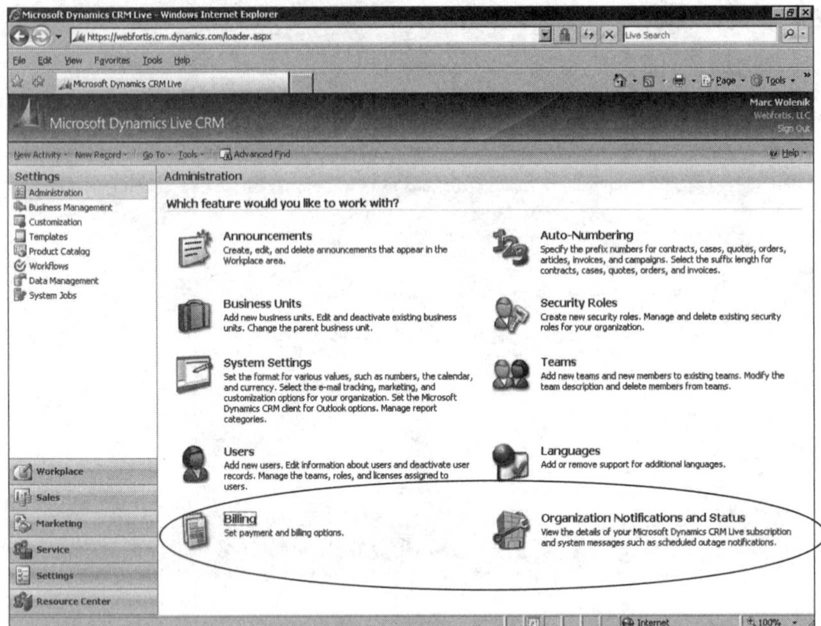

FIGURE 14.77 CRM Online options of Billing and Organization Notifications and Status.

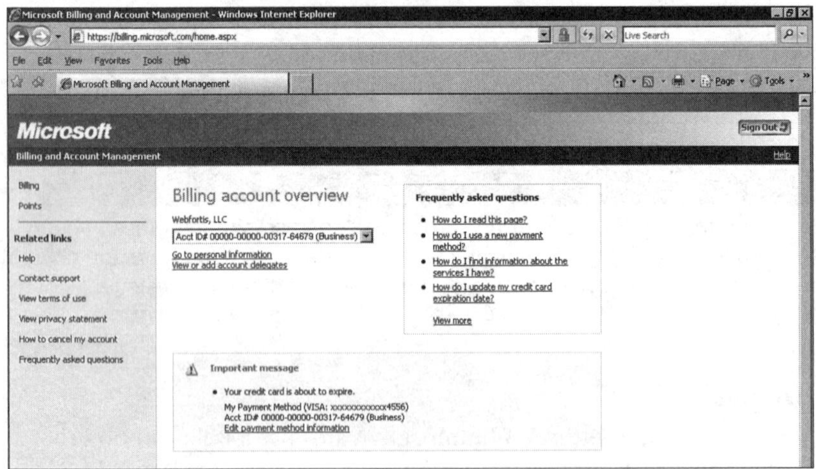

FIGURE 14.78 Billing and Account Management interface.

Organization Notifications and Status (CRM Online Only)

As with the Billing option explained previously, the Organization Notifications and Status options are found only with CRM Online in Settings, Administration (see Figure 14.77).

The Organization Notifications and Status screen is used to show information related to your CRM Online account such as the number of licenses you have available and your total storage available and used (see Figure 14.79). This information will be particular to your organization and the plan that you've purchased.

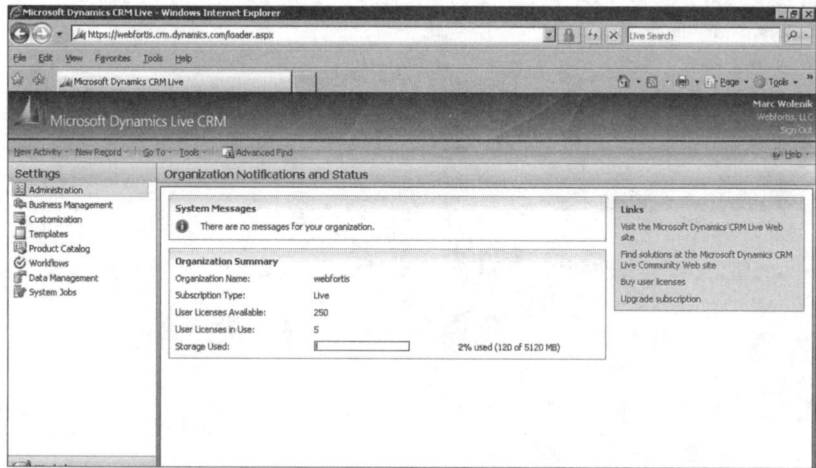

FIGURE 14.79 CRM Online Organization Notifications and Status.

For more information about the different plans and options available, refer to Chapter 3, "The Evolution of Microsoft Dynamics CRM 4.0," or check the CRM Online website for updated information.

Business Management

Located in the Settings area, the Business Management page has the following options:

- Fiscal Year Settings
- Facilities/Equipment
- Resource Groups
- Sales Territories
- Sites
- Currencies
- Business Closures
- Queues
- Salespeople with Quotas (Available only after setting the fiscal year)
- Services
- Subjects
- Relationship Roles

Figure 14.80 shows the Business Management interface.

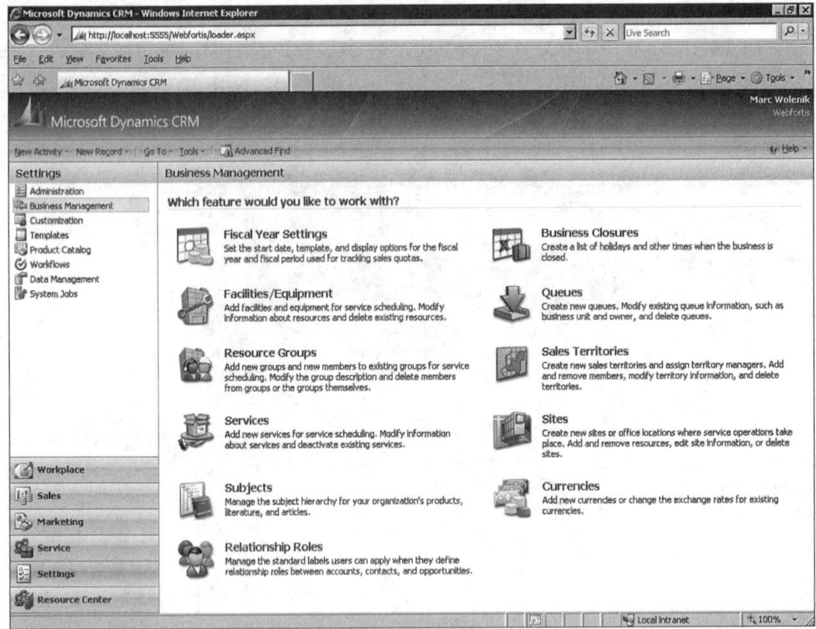

FIGURE 14.80 Settings, Business Management.

Fiscal Year Settings

To work with sales Quotas, you must set the Fiscal Year Settings. Be careful when setting the fiscal period; you cannot change it after it has been set (see Figure 14.81).

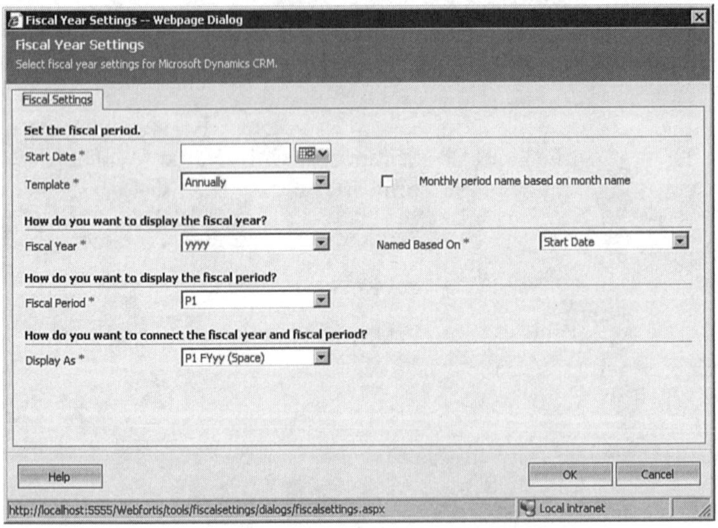

FIGURE 14.81 Fiscal Year Settings.

These are the required fields for the Fiscal Year Settings:

- **Start Date**—The year the fiscal year starts
- **Template**—The description of how the fiscal year is divided
- **Fiscal Year**—The fiscal year display options
- **Named Based On**—Whether the displayed name is based on the start or end of the fiscal year
- **Fiscal Period**—The fiscal period abbreviation
- **Display As**—How the fiscal year is displayed

TIP

As previously indicated, setting the Fiscal Year enables you to set Quotas on Users.

Facilities/Equipment

Services use Facilities/Equipment when scheduling resources (see Figure 14.82).

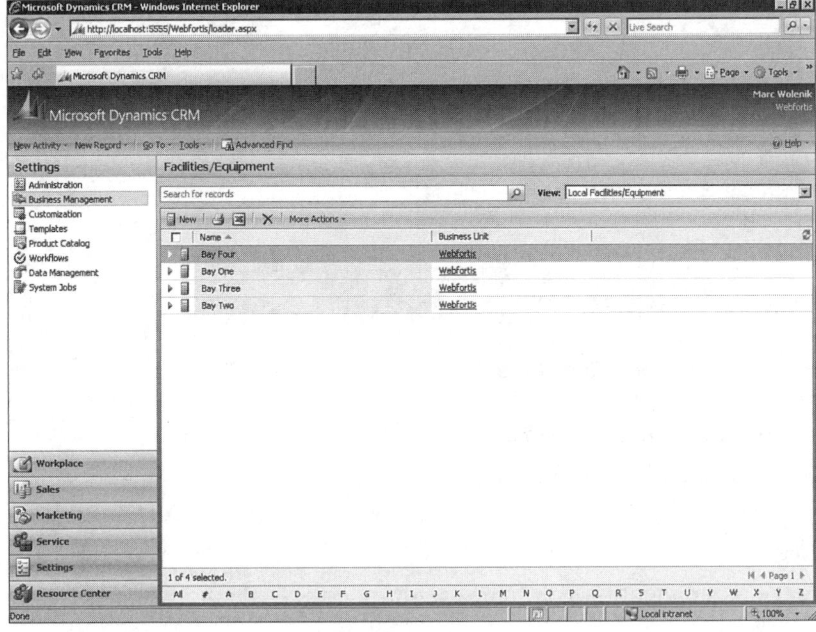

FIGURE 14.82 Facilities/Equipment.

Facilities/Equipment is necessary when performing scheduling because it makes up the Resources component. It differs from a business location because it makes up the necessary services component to complete a service Task. If a business location is needed, add a Site, as explained later in this chapter.

For more information on Service Scheduling, refer to Chapter 12.

Resource Groups

Resource Groups consist of a grouping of Users, Teams, Facility/Equipment, or other Resource Groups for the purposes of Service Scheduling.

To create a Resource Group, select New and enter the name of the Resource Group (see Figure 14.83).

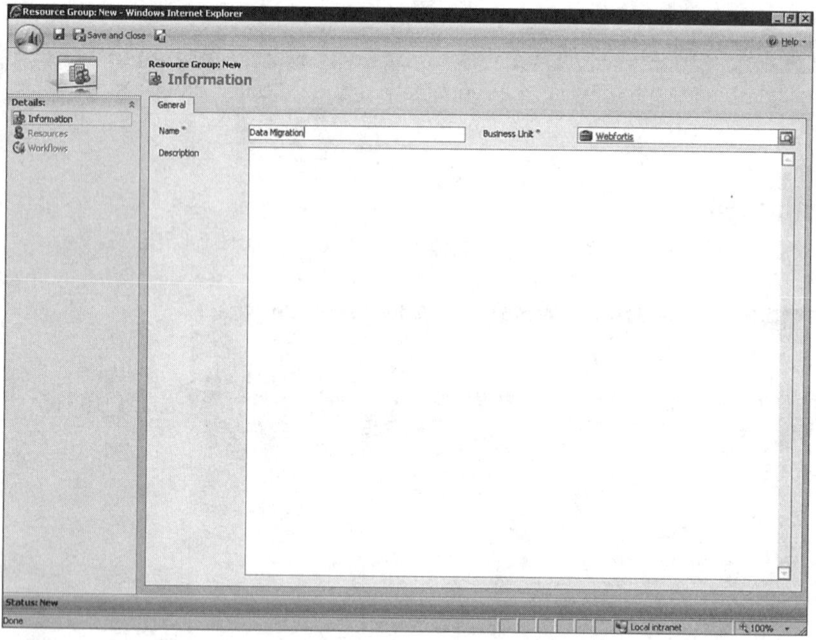

FIGURE 14.83 Creating a new Resource Group.

After you save the Resource Group, you can add resources (see Figure 14.84).

For more information on Service Scheduling, refer to Chapter 12.

Sales Territories

Sales territories are the grouping of Users into one territory, with a common manager specific to the territory.

NOTE

The territory manager is not necessarily the Users manager.

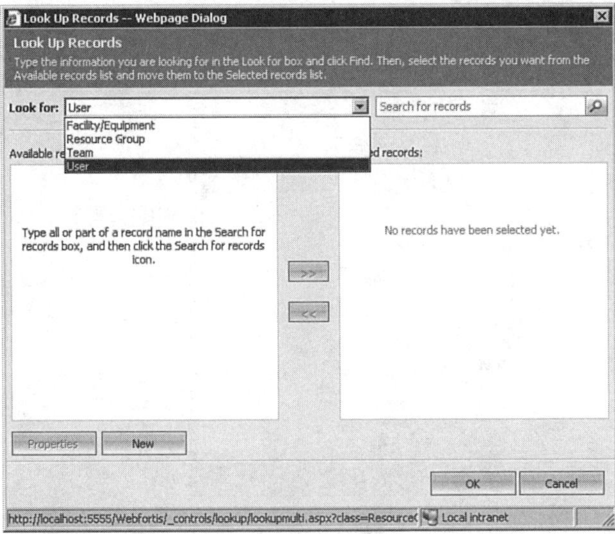

FIGURE 14.84 Adding resources to a Resource Group.

TIP

Because Users can be assigned to only one territory, if you want to assign a User to more than one of your existing territories, you must create a new territory that covers the existing ones and assign the User to that new territory.

To create a new territory, select New, and enter the territory name and, if applicable, the territory manager (see Figure 14.85). (Users in territories are either Users or a manager.)

Select Users to add to the territory. Because Users can be assigned to only single territory, they are removed from any previously assigned territories when assigned to the new one (see Figure 14.86).

Territories are very useful for summarizing data in Sales Reports, as well as obtaining various metrics data on Activities by territory.

The territory manager is used for reporting and/or workflow purposes.

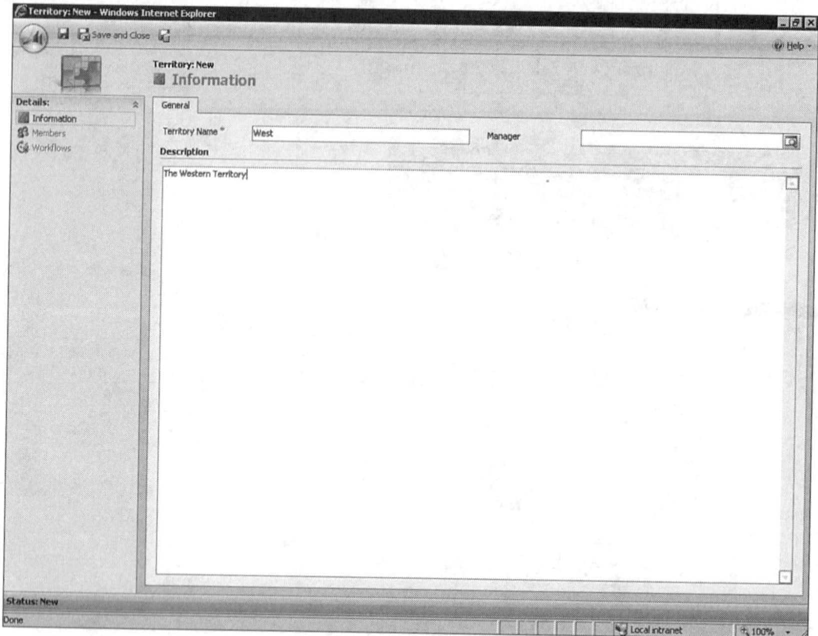

FIGURE 14.85 Creating a new territory.

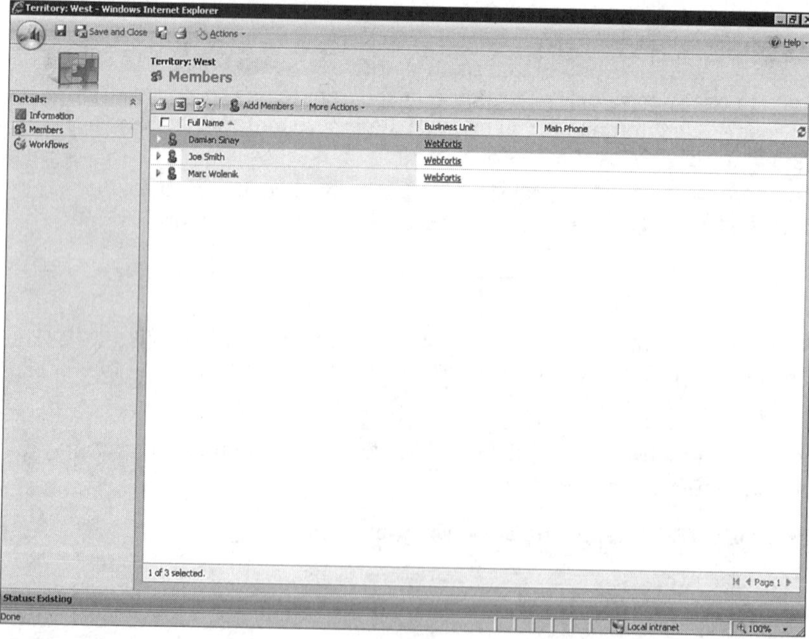

FIGURE 14.86 Assigning Users to a territory.

Sites

Sites are the physical location where work is done and resources are to be assigned in the service scheduling.

When creating a site, the only required information is the location name (see Figure 14.87).

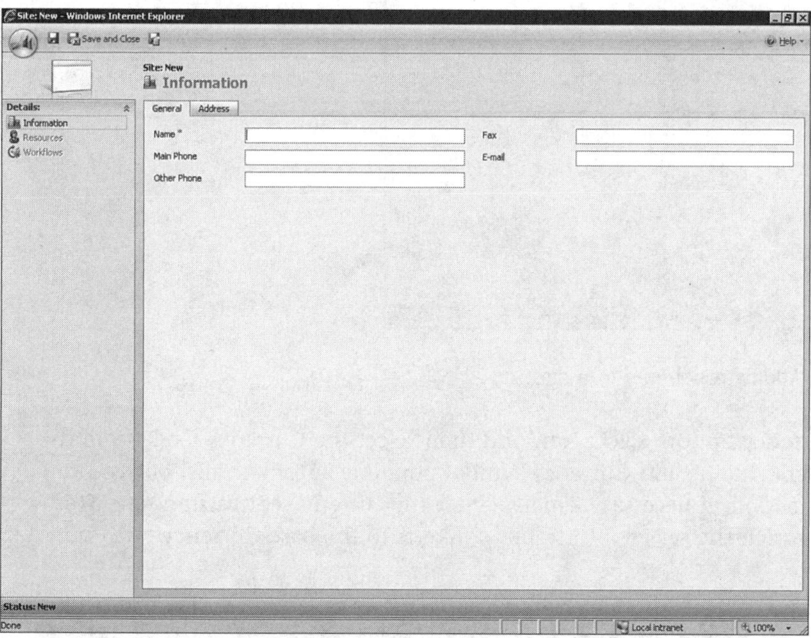

FIGURE 14.87 Creating a site.

After the site has been created, you can assign resources consisting of either Users or Facility/Equipment to it (see Figure 14.88).

For more information on Service Scheduling, refer to Chapter 12.

Currencies

As with languages, Currencies are added and managed from the Settings page. When they are added and active, they are available to the User. When a Currency other than the base Currency is used, the values associated with the record are converted (based on the conversion rate entered for that Currency) to the base Currency.

Although you cannot delete a Currency if it has been associated with a record, you can disable it, preventing it from being used on any new records.

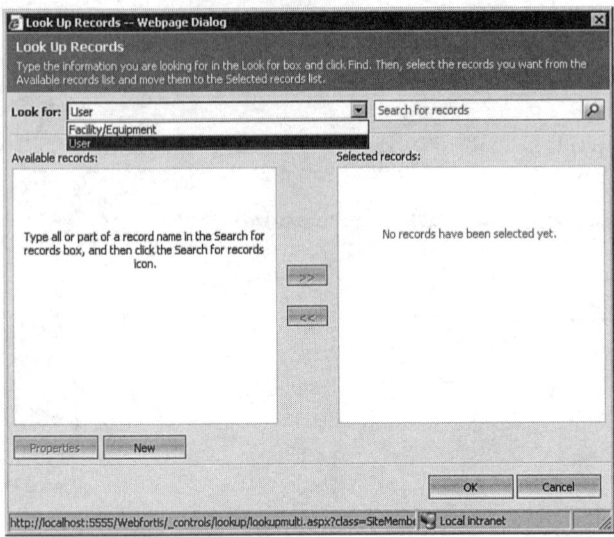

FIGURE 14.88 Adding resources to a site.

To add a new Currency option, select New and then select the Currency Code from the lookup. The Currency name and Currency symbol populate automatically, but you can change this information, if necessary. Finally, enter the currency conversion rate. This is the amount at which the selected Currency converts to the base Currency rate (see Figure 14.89).

NOTE

The conversion rate entered for a Currency remains at that rate until a System Administrator updates it. Potentially, inaccurate data can be reported if the conversion rate is not updated relatively frequently, based on the selected Currency conversion fluctuations. One consideration might be to extend the functionality of Microsoft Dynamics CRM by calling a Web Service to automatically calculate conversion on a monthly, weekly, daily, or even hourly rate. For more information on extending Microsoft Dynamics CRM, refer to Chapter 22, "Web Services."

After new currencies are created, different currencies can be assigned to transactions such as Quotas, Orders, Invoices, and Price Lists. When this happens, Microsoft Dynamics CRM converts the money fields to the base currency using the exchange rate entered for the selected currency.

It is important to understand when this conversion might happen, as transactions can happen over a period of time, during which exchange rates might have been changed. An example of this is a Quote that was created, but waited for approval for three months. During that time, the exchange rate could have been adjusted several times.

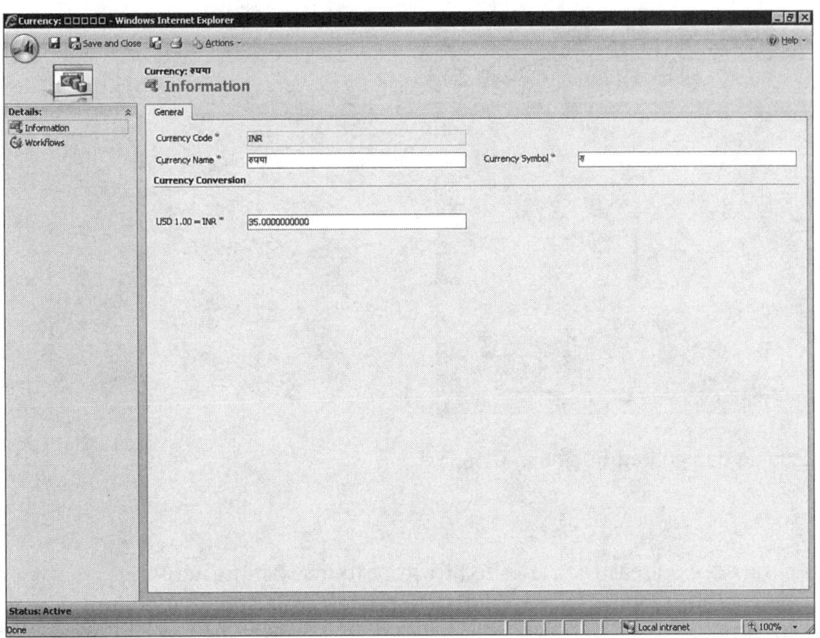

FIGURE 14.89 Creating a new Currency.

Exchange rates are updated when Quotes, Orders, Invoices, or Price Lists are created or when any field is updated that relates to currency. Additionally, if the state of the entity changes, exchange rates are recalculated.

NOTE

It is important to note that changing a currency rate will have no effect on any entity that is using that currency, unless one of the conditions previously mentioned (updated or has its state change) is met. Because of this, you may view a transaction that has an old exchange rate unless you explicitly update it by changing the values or changing the entity state.

Business Closures

Business Closures are useful for managing service Activities. A User cannot schedule Activities during a time when a Business Closure is designated unless the Do Not Observe option is selected.

When creating the Business Closure, you have the option to create it as a full-day, multiple-day, or part-of-the-day event (see Figure 14.90).

By default, Business Closures are managed on the current year. To create Business Closures for another year, select the year toggle near the top of the interface.

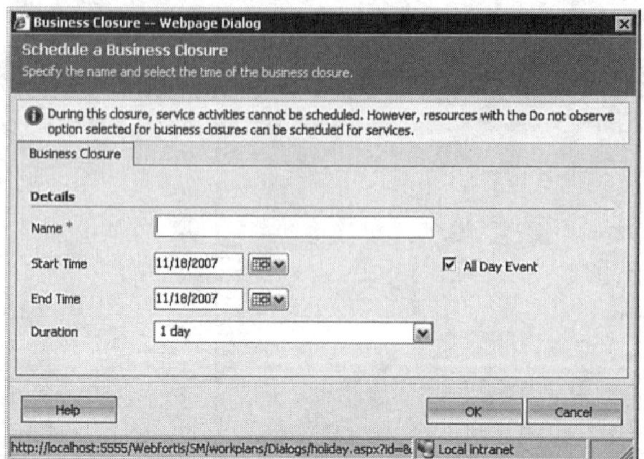

FIGURE 14.90 Adding designated Business Closures.

Queues

Queues serve as general access areas that are used to store items such as Activities or Cases. You can set up custom Queues to automatically process incoming e-mail and convert them to Activities.

Microsoft Dynamics CRM comes with two types of Queues:

- System queues are the two Queues located in My Workplace: Assigned and In Progress. The Assigned Queue has Activities and Cases that you have not accepted but that are assigned to you. When you've accepted the Activity or Case, it moves to your In Progress Queue. If you have been assigned a Case but believe it should be assigned to someone else, you must first accept it and then reassign it.
- Custom Queues are created from the Settings, Business Administration interface. After they are created, they are available in My Workplace under Queues. They can be used for any purpose and can be set up to automatically route e-mails as Activities.

To create a Queue, follow these steps:

1. Navigate to Settings, Business Management, Queues. Select New to create a new Queue.
2. Enter the Queue name, the Business Unit, and the owner.
3. Enter the e-mail address that the Queue will use to gather incoming e-mails and automatically convert them to Activities if desired (see Figure 14.91).

   You can enter only one e-mail address.
4. Select how Microsoft CRM should work with e-mails received by the e-mail address entered for the Queue. By default, the system processes all incoming e-mail messages and converts them to Activities. However, you can set from the drop-down

menu to process only incoming e-mails that are in response to other e-mails previously sent from CRM or only e-mails received that resolve to existing CRM Leads, Contacts, or Accounts.

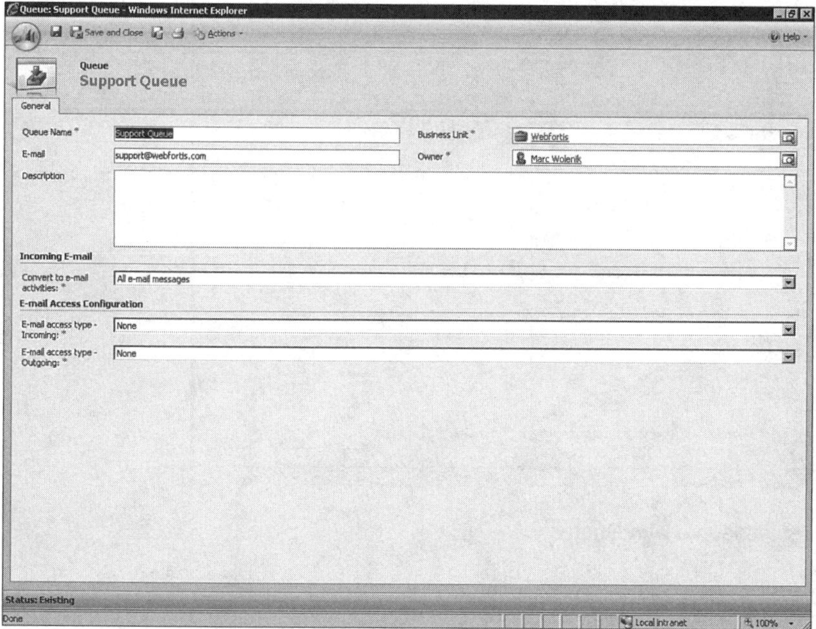

FIGURE 14.91 Queue setup.

5. Configure how e-mail access should work for both incoming and outgoing (for more information about configuring e-mail access, refer to Chapter 15).

Salespeople with Quotas

Available only after the fiscal year has been set and Quotas have been assigned to Users, the Salespeople with Quotas option is available from Settings, Business Management. It shows Users whom have Quotas assigned to them from this interface (see Figure 14.92).

NOTE

If you do not see the Salespeople with Quotas option on the Business Management interface, it is likely that you have either not set the fiscal year (found in Fiscal Year Settings on the same Business Management interface), or you have not assigned any Quotas to any Users. Additionally, you will be unable to assign any Quotas until the fiscal year has been set, so be sure to check there first.

Refer to the previous section "Managing Quotas" for more information about working with Quotas.

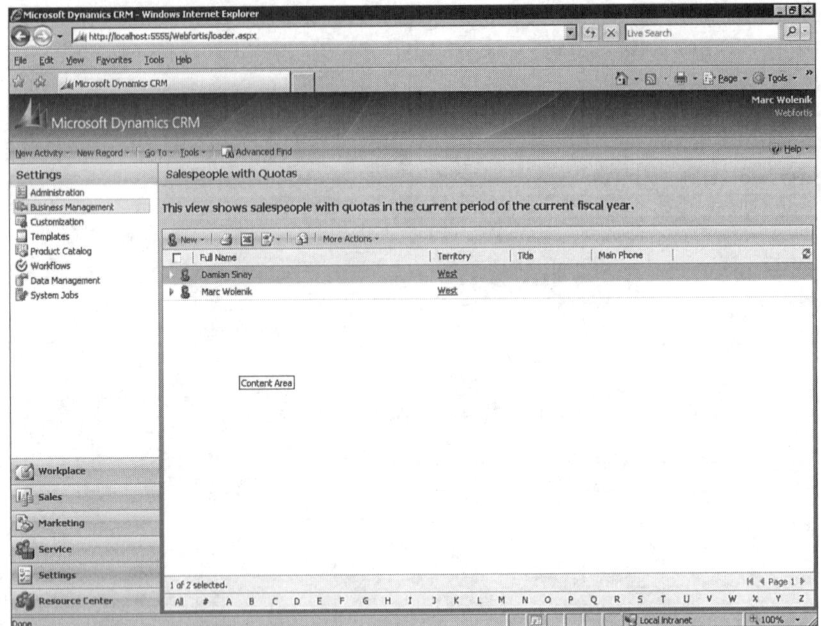

FIGURE 14.92 Salespeople with Quotas.

Services

Services are Activities performed by one or multiple resources that are scheduled using the Service Scheduling module.

For more information about working with Services, refer to Chapter 12.

Subjects

Subjects relate to the individual topics that make up your organization. They provide context and are a required relation when working with and creating the following entities:

- Cases
- Sales Literature
- Knowledge Base Articles
- Products

Generally, Subjects include information related to these entities and are hierarchal in nature (see Figure 14.93).

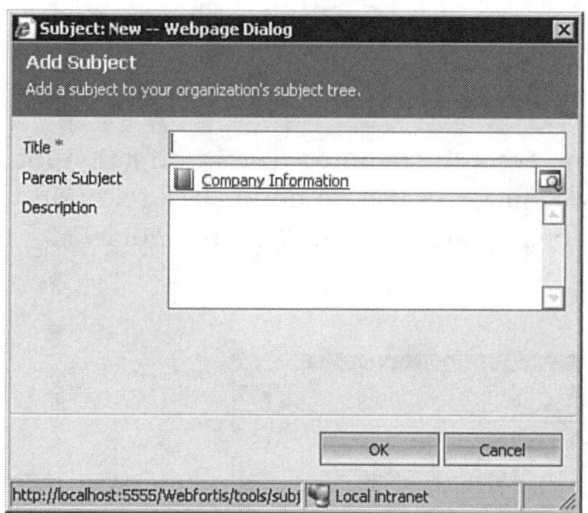

FIGURE 14.93 Sample company Subject hierarchy.

To create new Subjects, select the node that is the parent of the new Subject on the Subject Tree; then select Add a Subject. By default, the Add Subject Parent Subject populates with the Subject previously selected. Enter a value in the Title and any corresponding description (see Figure 14.93). Selecting OK adds the entered Subject to the Subject Tree, making it available for selection when working with the previous entities.

TIP

Carefully consider setting up the Subject Tree for your products. Although an association is not required, Subjects let you effectively categorize products for searching and reporting. When setting up the Subject Tree for Products, the Subjects will usually be at a more general level than the actual product. For example, a Subject might be Computers, and actual products associated might be Laptop, Desktop, and Handheld.

Relationship Roles

Relationship Roles are available only for Accounts, Contacts, and Opportunities. They are designed to enable Users to configure relationship types that might exist between records of these entities in the system. Relationship Roles can be used for any kind of relationship, including business, familiar, and social ones.

Earlier versions of Microsoft Dynamics CRM that did not have the current level of flexibility for entity relationships (specifically, the new option with Microsoft Dynamic CRM 4.0 allowing many-to-many relationships) and Relationship Roles were used extensively to manage relationships. Although it is still possible to do this, consider creating new, custom relationships directly for the entities listed earlier as an alternative to working with Relationship Roles (for more information about working with and adding customer relationships, refer to Chapter 19).

Creating specific Relationship Roles is not required. Furthermore, when making and adding Relationship Roles, it is not required to have a role for each side of the relationship.

To create a new Relationship Role, select New and enter the required field information for Role Name (see Figure 14.94). Although it is not required, if you do not make a selection for Account, Contact, or Opportunity, the Relationship Role will be active but not available to use on any entity.

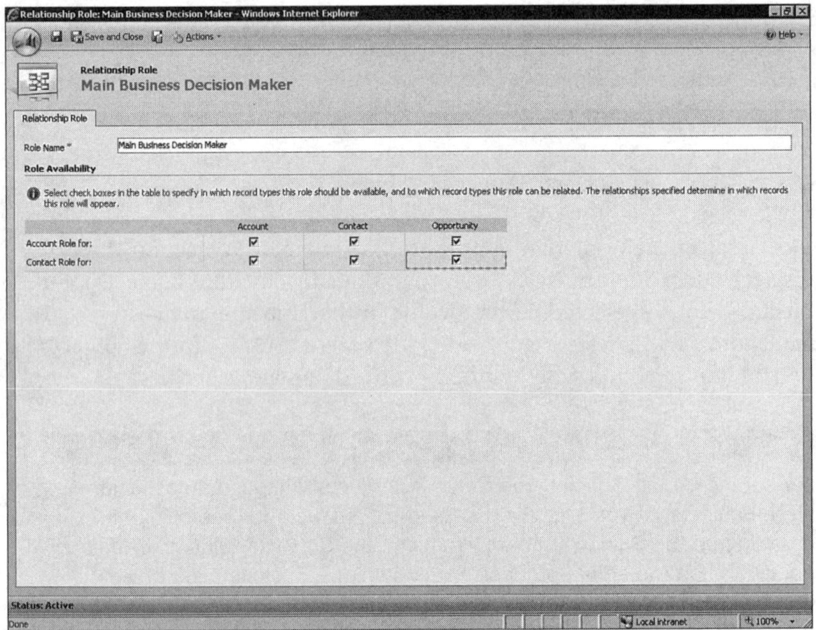

FIGURE 14.94 Creating a Relationship Role.

When creating the relationship, you can set the type of relationship based on the Relationship Roles that have been created. Because we've created only one Relationship Role in this example, called Main Business Decision Maker, we'll select it only for the sample Contact, not the sample Account shown (see Figure 14.95).

Navigating to the Relationships for the sample Contact, you can easily see the role (see Figure 14.96).

After setup, Users can easily query on any roles.

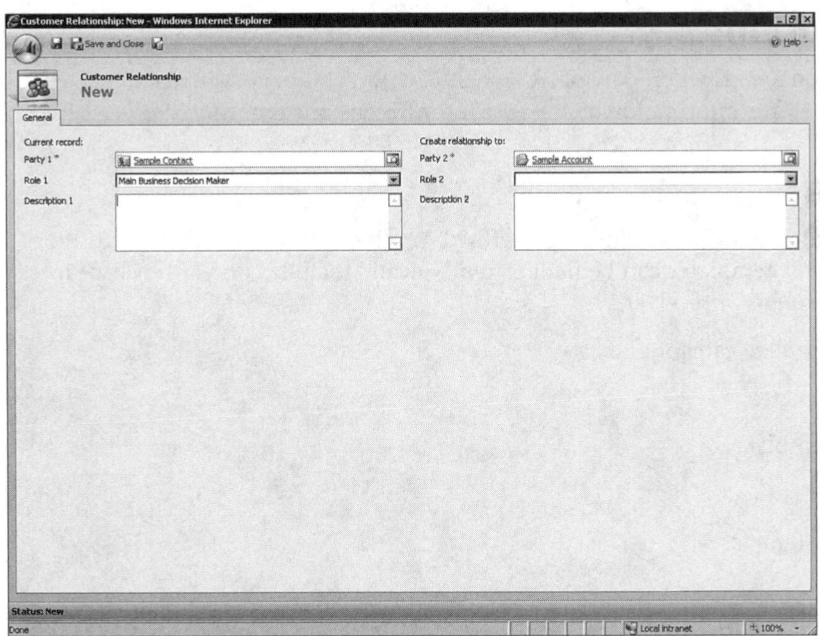

FIGURE 14.95 Sample Relationship Role.

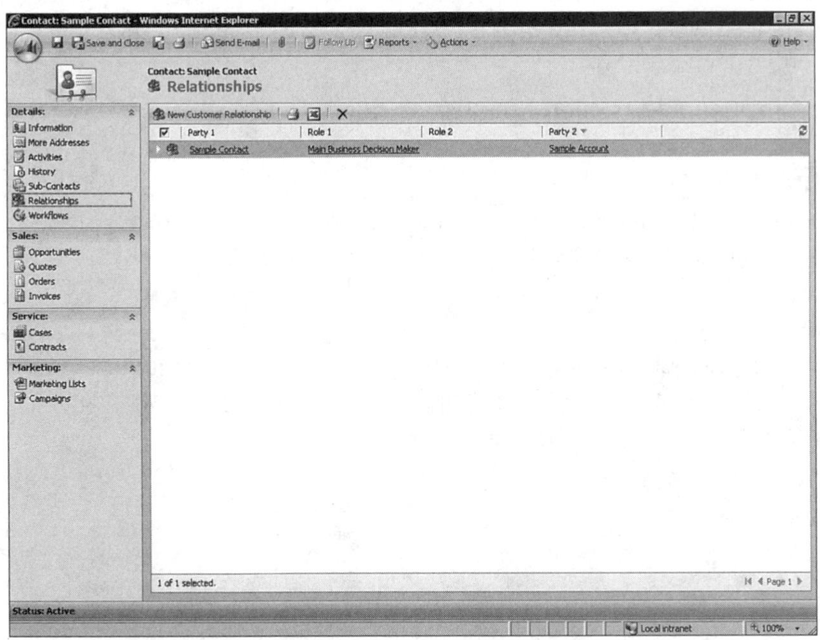

FIGURE 14.96 Relationship Roles.

Customization

The Customization area is where Microsoft Dynamics CRM can be modified extensively. Refer to Chapter 19 for information about working with customizations.

Templates

Templates facilitate the management of predefined Articles, Contracts, e-mails, and Word mail merges. E-mail Templates can be built to dynamically include context-sensitive information such as senders or receivers.

Four different Template categories exist:

- Article Templates
- Contract Templates
- E-mail Templates
- Mail Merge Templates

Templates can be active or inactive, and can be in any language that the System Administrator makes available.

Article Templates

Article Templates are used when working with the Knowledge Base (found in the Service section of Microsoft Dynamics CRM).

They can include formatted titles, sections, and section titles.

Contract Templates

Contract Templates are used to manage Contracts and include information such as the billing frequency and the service allotment.

E-mail Templates

E-mail Templates are the richest templates because they allow for specific customizations specific to the sender and receiver. E-mail Templates have several core properties that make up how they work:

- Template Type
- Viewable By
- Language

Template Type

The Template Type is selected when the template is first created (see Figure 14.97).

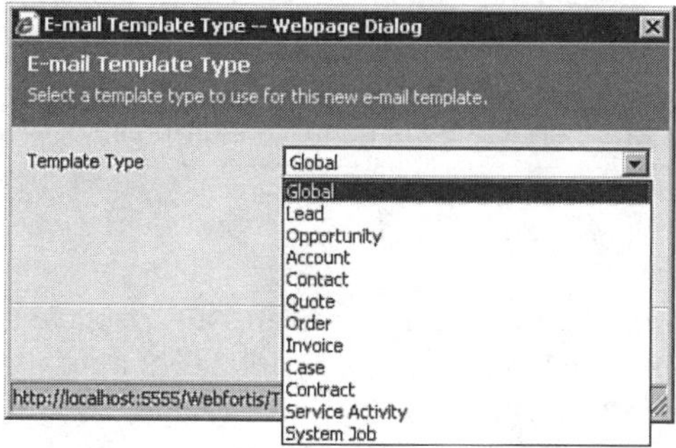

FIGURE 14.97 Template Type.

Selecting the template type determines what data fields are available to work with on the template. Table 14.1 describes which data fields are available with the template type.

TABLE 14.1 Template Type/Entity Data Fields Available Table

Template Type	Entity Data Fields Available
Global	User
Lead	User, Lead
Opportunity	User, Account, Contact, Opportunity
Account	User, Account, Contact
Contact	User, Account, Contact
Quota	User, Account, Contact, Quota
Order	User, Account, Contact, Order
Invoice	User, Account, Contact, Invoice
Case	User, Account, Contact, Case
Contract	User, Account, Contact, Contract
Service Activity	User, Account, Contact, Service Activity, Site, Service
System Job	User, System Job

Viewable By

Viewable By is a property that identifies where the E-mail Template is available. The entire organization can view and use Templates created in the Settings area (assuming that everyone has have adequate permission from the Security Role).

Users can create their own E-mail Templates from their personal options, and, by default, the permissions on their personal templates are set at Individual. You can promote these templates to an Organizational level and use them across the organization by selecting Make Template Available to Organization from the Actions drop-down menu. For more information about working with individual templates, see Chapter 9, "Working with the Workplace."

TIP

The User who owns the personal template or the administrator can promote it by navigating to All E-mail Templates and selecting it where Viewable By is equal to Individual.

Language

The language property is the language of the template. By default, templates are displayed in the view as All E-mail Templates and show only the base language templates. If a new template is created and another language is selected, it will not show in All E-mail Templates—you must select All Language E-mail Templates to see the templates that exist outside of the base template.

As with the rest of the system, the only language options are those that the System Administrator has loaded and made available in the Languages section of Settings.

When creating a Template, follow these steps:

1. Select New and select the template type (see Figure 14.97).
2. Select the language, the title, and, optionally, the description. These are specific to the template properties, and the recipient will not see them.
3. The recipient will see the Subject and the body, and these are available for dynamic content. To enter dynamic content, place the cursor in either the Subject or the body, and click the Insert/Update button at the top of the form. (If the cursor is in the title or the description, the dynamic fields will be placed in the body by default.) The Data Field Values interface then opens, enabling you to add data fields. Click Add to add a data field (see Figure 14.98).

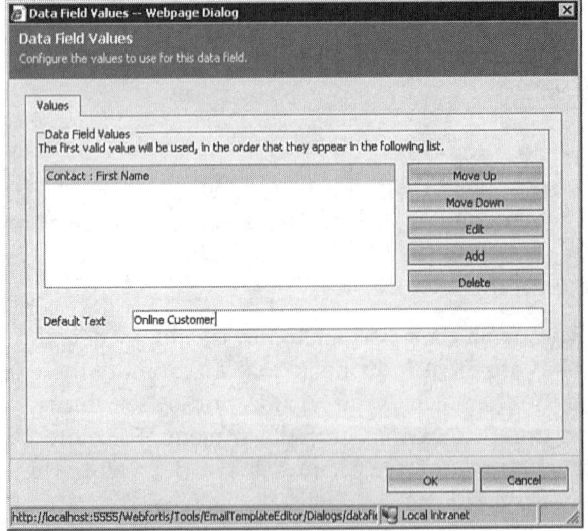

FIGURE 14.98 Insert/Update for a Template.

The Default Text option enables you to enter alternate text in cases when the selected data field is blank.

4. Select the record type to work with. By default, the User record information will always be available, along with content-specific information related to the template type (see previous discussion on template type).

5. Select the attribute from Record Type and add it to Data Field Values. Selecting more than one value causes Microsoft Dynamics CRM to add only one value from the list—whichever one it finds first. Additionally, each data field must be added uniquely. An example might be the name of the Contact. If you select First Name and then Last Name as part of the same data field, Microsoft Dynamics CRM uses the First Name (if available), not the Last Name. If the First Name is not available, it uses the Last Name. If neither is available, it uses the default text entered. If there was no default text, this will be blank. Format the text and/or dynamic areas as desired (see Figure 14.99).

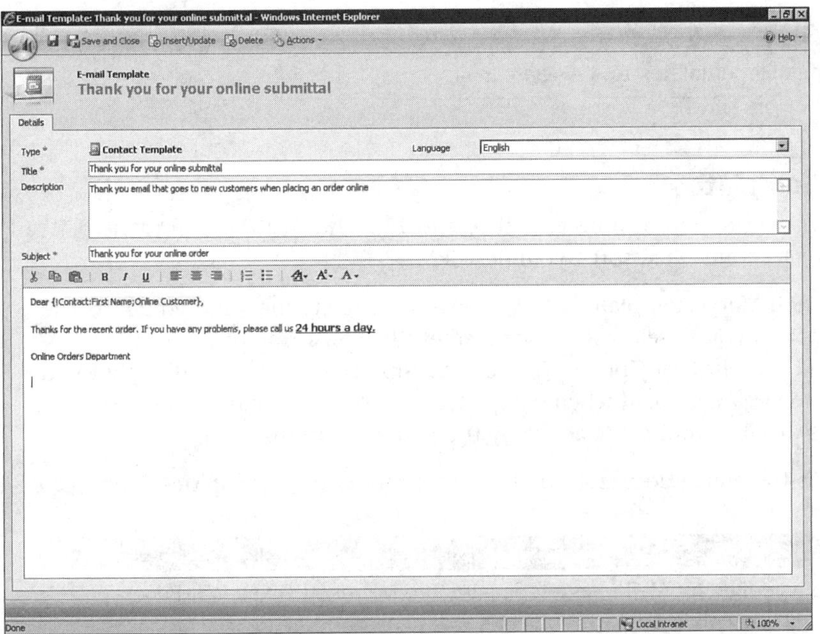

FIGURE 14.99 Formatted template.

NOTE

Templates cannot have attachments. If attachments are necessary, we recommend either including a URL to a public website where the attachment can be downloaded or including the attachment with the individual e-mail.

TIP

You can include images in templates, but they must be available on public websites. Navigate to the website, and copy and then paste the image directly into the body of the template.

Another use for templates is in the creation of an e-mail signature. To do this, create a template with Template Type equal to Global and add the desired signature values. When creating an e-mail, select the Insert Template option and insert the Signature template.

TIP

You can add multiple templates to a single e-mail.

Mail Merge Templates

Mail Merge Templates are powerful because they allow for the creation of formatted Word documents with data from Microsoft Dynamics CRM.

To create a new Mail Merge Template, select New and complete the required fields. The categorization enables you to select the associated entity, consisting of a Quote, Opportunity, Lead, Account, or Contact. The ownership defaults to Individual, but you can change that to Organizational when completed. Template language is limited to the language options installed and made active by the System Administrator.

File Attachment is the merge document that is associated with the Mail Merge Template.

NOTE

The only acceptable files for Mail Merge templates are Microsoft Office Word documents saved in Office XML format.

Figure 14.100 shows a new Mail Merge Template associated to the Contact entity.

Refer to Chapter 7 for details about creating Mail Merge Templates.

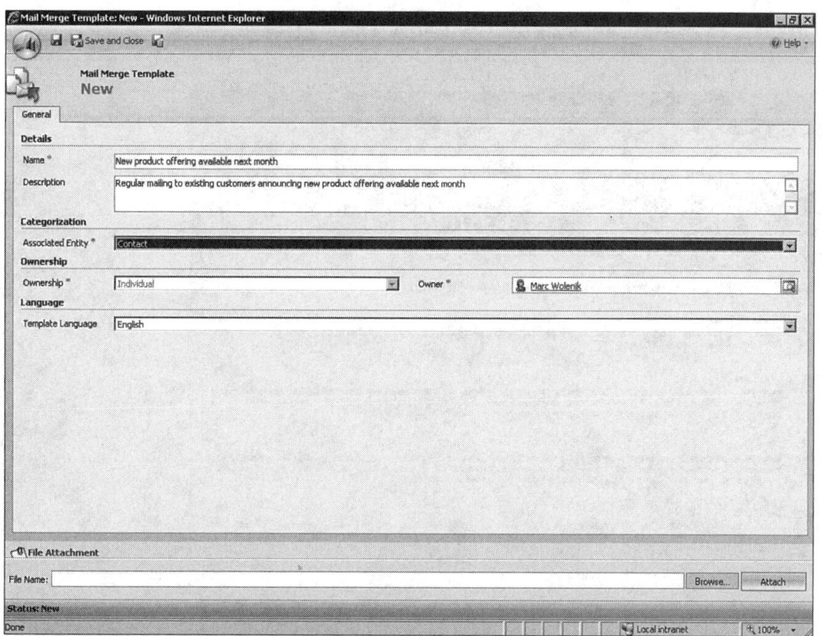

FIGURE 14.100 Mail Merge Template.

Product Catalog

Information about the products being sold is managed in the Product Catalog. You must set up four areas:

- Discount Lists
- Unit Groups
- Price Lists
- Products

To set up products, it is recommended that you set up the areas in the order listed, but you can edit them in any order.

TIP

Although they're not listed in the previous list, products associated with both Currencies are classified by Subject. If you're setting up a large Product List, it might make sense to build the Subject categories and add whatever Currencies you want to work with before you start working with products because editing each product later might be time consuming.

Figure 14.101 shows the Product Catalog and the four areas that must be set up.

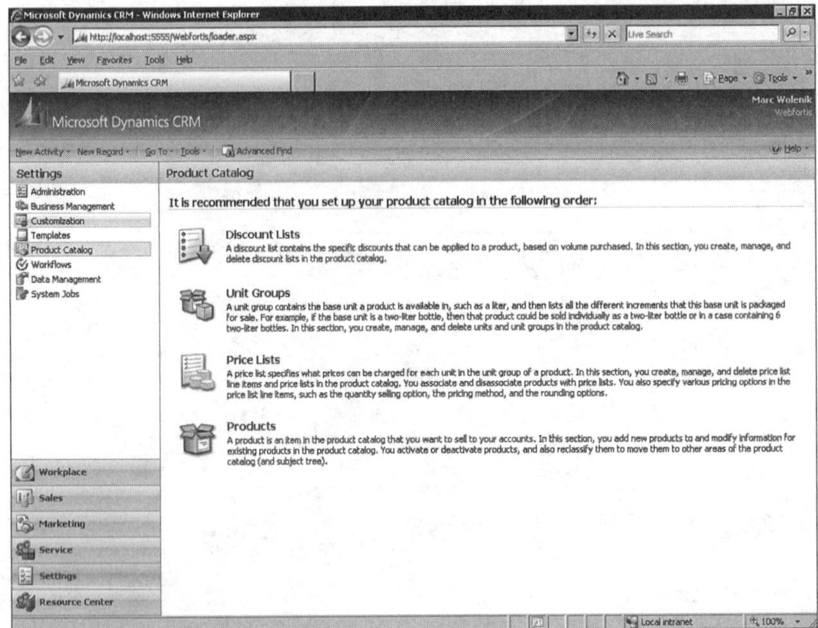

Figure 14.101 Product Catalog.

NOTE

Many Microsoft Dynamics CRM Users will undoubtedly be interested in having their Product Catalog managed by another application—typically, their accounting or ERP system. At press time, there was no out-of-the-box functionality to enable this, but it is highly anticipated that a series of “connectors” will be available to integrate with other Dynamics product. Additionally, this type of work is quite common with integration and implementation shops; because of the way Microsoft Dynamics CRM exposes itself via Web Services, it can be done programmatically for almost any type of ERP/accounting system. Be sure to check Chapter 26, “Third-Party Add-On Options,” for other third-party add-ons that enable this type of functionality.

Discount Lists

Commonly referred to as discount schedules, Discount Lists allow discounts to be given based on quantity. Discounts can be based on either percentage or amount of the quantity ordered within an entered range (see Figure 14.102).

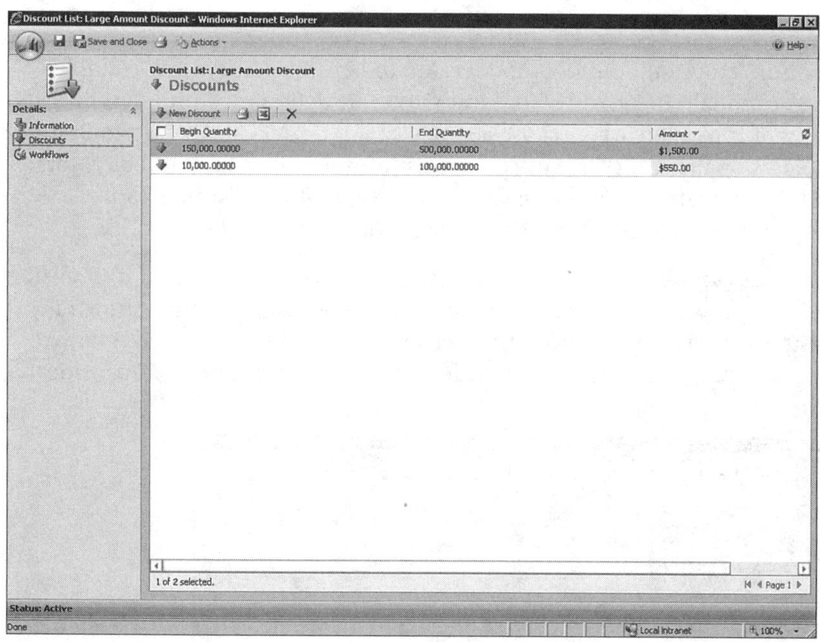

FIGURE 14.102 Discount List configured for varied quantities.

When thinking about setting up Discount Lists, consider how you want the discount to be applied. The following table shows an example of how a Discount List might work using percentages:

Beginning Quantity	Ending Quantity	Percentage Discount
1,000	5,000	3.50
5,001	25,000	5.00
25,001	100,000+	7.50

To setup a Discount List with amounts, this could work as follows:

Beginning Quantity	Ending Quantity	Amount Discount
1,000	5,000	$ 50.00
5,001	25,000	$ 150.00
25,001	100,000+	$ 500.00

In both cases, no discount will be applied if the quantity ordered is less than 1,000.

You can create as many Discount Lists as necessary and, although not required, associate them with different Price Lists and Price List Items (see the section "Price Lists," later in this chapter).

Unit Groups

Unit Groups determine groupings of how products are to be sold. The typical example of unit groups is a can of soda. The quantity (or Unit Group) is determined on how the soda is purchased because it is possible to purchase a single can, a 6-pack, and a case consisting of 12 or 24 cans. Additionally, Unit Groups can consist of minutes, hours, and days for services offered. Our explanation is by no means definitive, and Unit Groups can comprise any level of quantities for whatever products your company sells.

Each of these quantities consists of a primary unit, which is the lowest level of unit available and, in the case of services, could be at any level. The following example shown in Figure 14.103 illustrates a services company that sells its services by the second (granted, this is a somewhat far fetched scenario, but it clearly illustrates how to set up quantities).

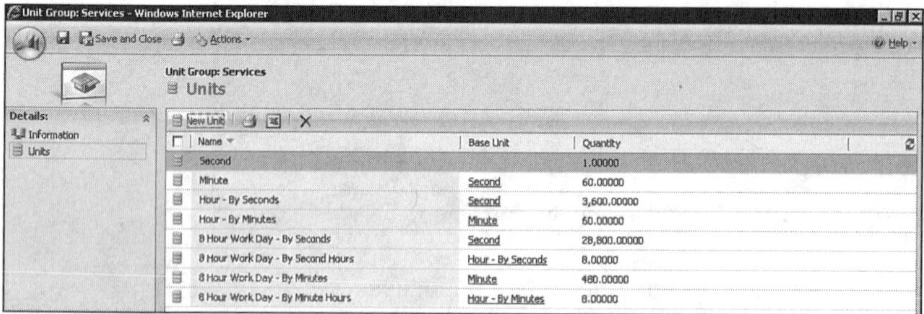

FIGURE 14.103 Unit Group for Services by the second.

Note that, in this example, the last four lines for "8 Hour Work Day" are all the same—they all charge 8 hours for the day, but they comprise different quantities of the base unit.

Unit Groups are associated with products, as well as the default unit for the product.

Price Lists

Price Lists make up groupings of products with associated pricing. If you don't have varied pricing for any reason, you could easily set up a single Price List (called Standard Price List, Default Price List, or similar) with all your products and their pricing on it. Additionally, it might be common to have only a small number of prices lists, such as Retail and Wholesale. However, no limit governs the number of available Price Lists—you can create multiple prices lists by customer, region, time of year, or other consideration.

TIP

Too many Price Lists can create confusion when your salespeople are attempting to build Quotes, Orders, or Invoices. If you use many Price Lists, be sure to use a comprehensive naming strategy to ensure that the right list is used.

Although you need to create Price Lists next in the hierarchy, they aren't completed until you add products to each list. Fortunately, you can do this in the final step when the products are built, and, if necessary, you can return to the Price List Items for each Price List to edit the items associated with them.

Price Lists consist of the Currency, name, and start/end date that the Price List is applicable for, as well as Price List Items (see Figure 14.104).

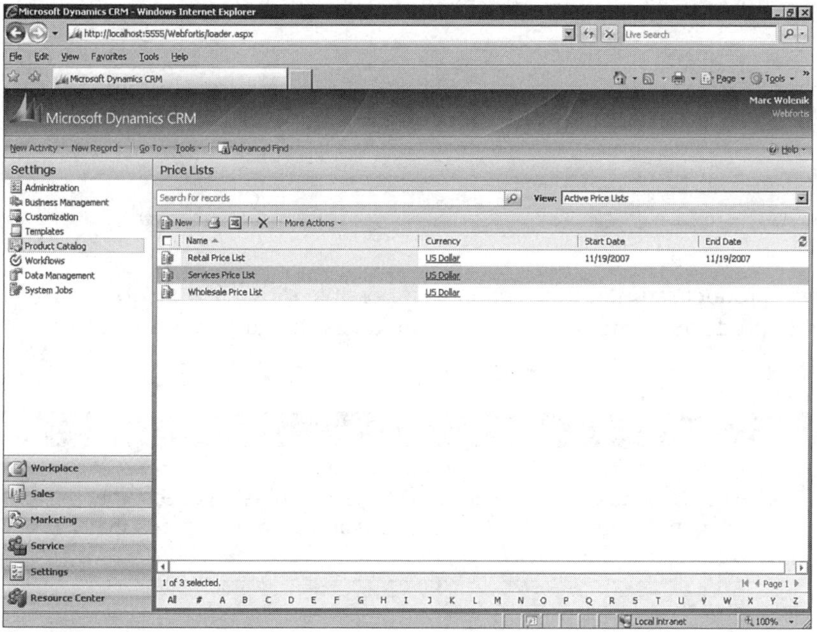

FIGURE 14.104 Price Lists.

NOTE

Although you can configure the Start and End dates for the Price List, they are not enforced, and Users can continue to use them after the date has passed. You must manually deactivate or delete them after the date has passed, to prevent them from being used.

TIP

You can easily set up Price Lists in conjunction with Discount Lists for promotional and seasonal pricing for specific products. To do this, create a new Discount List with the discount and quantity of discount. (For this scenario, in which the promotional pricing would apply to every item, regardless of quantity, the beginning quantity would be 1 and the ending quantity would be whatever maximum level you wanted to set.) Create a new Price List and add existing products and units, as well as the Discount List you previously set up. Be sure to name both the Price List and the Discount List accordingly so that you'll know what they are for.

Products

Products is where you set up and maintain the products you sell. Several aspects make up a product:

- Product Information
- Substitutes
- Price List Items
- Kit Products

Although we review product setup in this section, it is possible for your Users to create products as Write In products. Write In products are products that are not set up in the Product Catalog.

TIP

Be sure to monitor the use of Write In products by your salespersons. Frequently, salespeople will use Write In products to manipulate the system to sell products that *are* in the Product Catalog, to create product discounts or solve other limitations that aren't normally available.

Product Information

Product Information includes required information of ID, Name, Unit Group, Default Unit, and Decimals Supported (see Figure 14.105).

Additionally, it is important to set the Product Type. In the previous example, we selected Services, but you can set this to Sales Inventory, Miscellaneous Charges, or Flat Fees as well.

The Description tab enables you to enter vendor information as well as weight and volume information. This is helpful for automation and shipping routines that might be incorporated into the system related to e-commerce situations.

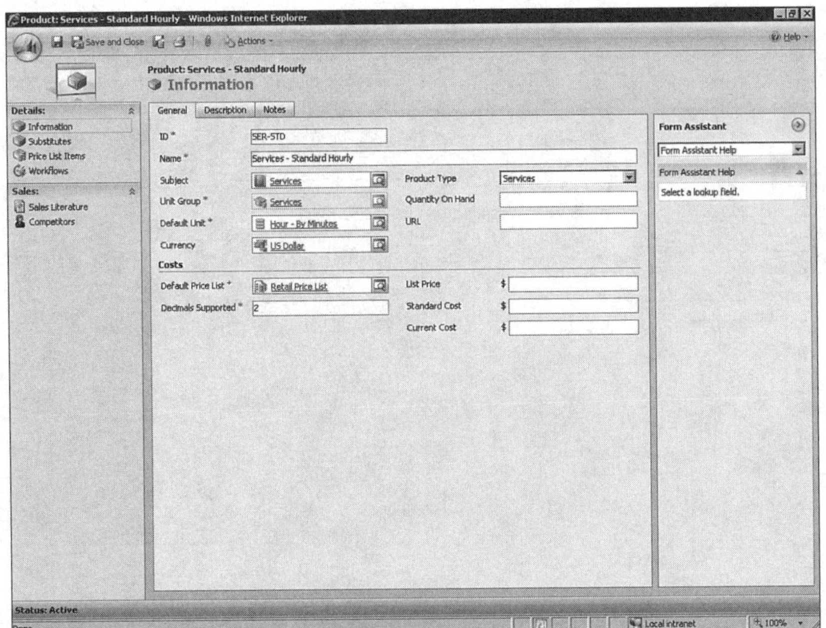

FIGURE 14.105 Product Information.

Substitutes

Substitutions are products from the Product Catalog that can be substituted for the product being created or edited. Substitutions are not the same as Write In products that can consist of any item; these are predefined substitutions for the product being edited.

Price List Items

The Price List Items are the product groupings applicable to the product, as well as their association to the actual product and units (see Figure 14.106).

Additional important options include Quantity Selling Option, which, in the example shown, enables you to sell in any fashion. This is good because we've selected hours as our product, and we want to invoice in only 15-minute increments, or ¼ quantity.

Kit Products

Kit Products are a number of products bundled as a "Kit" for purposes of selling as a group. A Kit Product has a single price that makes up each item in the Kit. To create a Kit Product, select the product and, from the More Actions menu, select Convert to Kit. (Similarly, if you want to demote a Kit Product to a regular product, select Convert to Product.) An example of a Kit Product might be a 1-hour service call on a computer that includes a new mouse and a new computer (see Figure 14.107).

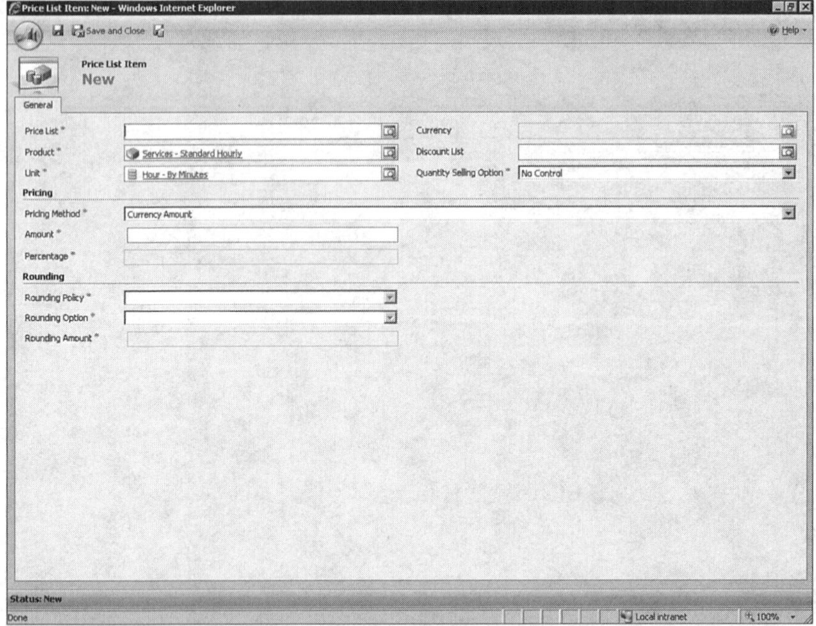

FIGURE 14.106 Product Price List information.

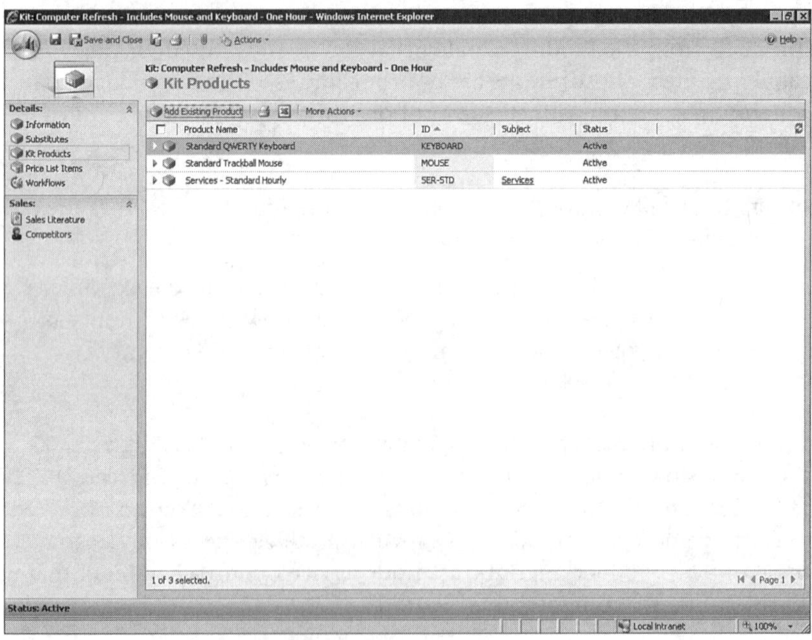

FIGURE 14.107 Kit Product example.

Workflows

You can create and manage workflows from this interface.

For more information on working with workflows, refer to Chapter 20.

Data Management

Data Management is designed to easily manage the following:

- Duplication Detection Settings
- Duplicate Detection Rules
- Duplicate Detection Jobs
- Bulk Record Deletion
- Data Maps
- Imports

For more information about working with Data Management, refer to Chapter 6, "Data Migration and Conversion"; see Chapter 20 for information about Duplicate Detection.

System Jobs

Just as every entity in Microsoft Dynamics CRM has a workflow entity association to it that displays any workflow used by that entity, the system itself has workflow. This workflow is referred to as a System Job, and it generally runs in the background. The System Jobs interface provides the capability to view the status of System Jobs and cancel, postpone, pause, or resume them by selecting these options from the More Actions dropdown menu.

By default, the interface displays the System Jobs and their status (see Figure 14.108).

You can open any of the displayed jobs by double-clicking them, and any errors are displayed here.

TIP

What's in a name? Generally, a lot of System Jobs are labeled as Matchcode Update Jobs. The term *Matchcode* refers to the Match conditions of the Base Record to the Matching Record in duplicate detection rules. The Matchcode conditions are limited to 450 characters.

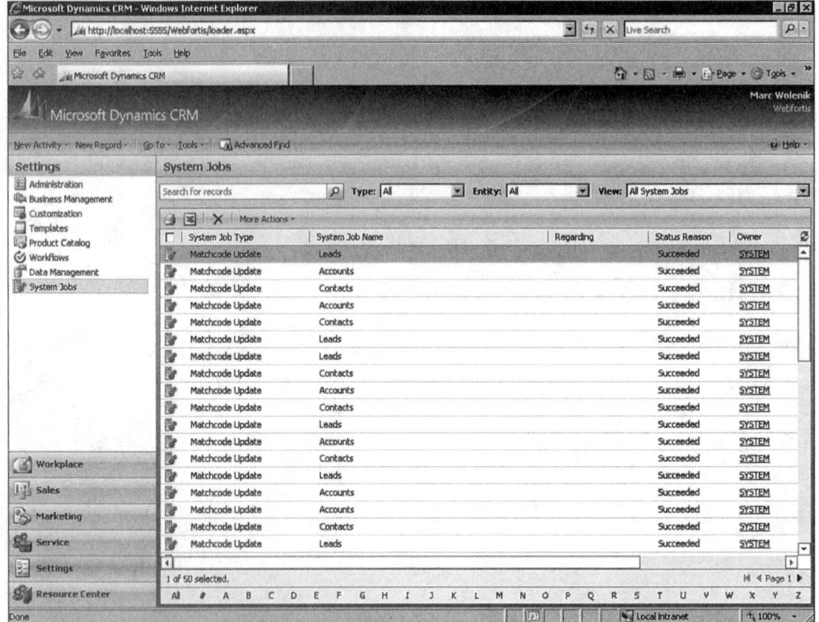

FIGURE 14.108 System Jobs.

Summary

This chapter reviewed the areas that make up the Settings area for CRM and discussed how they are important and relevant to setting up, maintaining, and managing your business. Additionally, this chapter detailed how to configure the security of CRM through the use of Roles and Business Units.

You will visit many aspects of the Settings area only occasionally, but others are dynamic (such as adding and removing Users and permissions, activating and deactivating Product Lists, and creating customizations for the system) and will be used often.

Hopefully, this chapter has illustrated the importance of becoming familiar with the different Settings areas because it will be a frequently accessed resource area for System Administrators.

CHAPTER 15

E-mail Configuration

IN THIS CHAPTER

- Configuring the E-mail Services
- The MS CRM E-mail Router Explained
- Rule Deployment Wizard
- Tracking Incoming E-mails
- Queues

Because configuring the e-mail services for either incoming or outgoing e-mails is not a simple task, we have taken extra effort in this chapter to explain how to make the necessary configurations. Depending on your Users and implementation needs, you can decide which configuration is best for your organization.

NOTE

The e-mail settings are not set up during server installation, to permit Users to configure their preferred configuration.

Configuring the E-mail Services

By default, Users must use the Microsoft Outlook client to be able to send and track incoming e-mails in Microsoft Dynamics CRM. If you don't install the Outlook client and you want to send a direct e-mail to a Contact using the web application, you will be surprised to find that the e-mails are not actually going out.

For example, you might want to send a direct e-mail to a Contact in the Microsoft CRM Web Application by opening a Contact record and clicking on the Send E-mail button, as shown in Figure 15.1.

Notice the tooltip in Figure 15.1 says Send an e-mail regarding this Contact. That is because the Contact is not only used in the `To` field but also in the `Regarding` field which is another field that is used by Microsoft Dynamics CRM to make the e-mail activity relate to the Contacts (see Figure 15.2). For example, you might change the To address and send the e-mail to another person, which would be also related to the first Contact, and you will see the e-mail in the history of both Contacts.

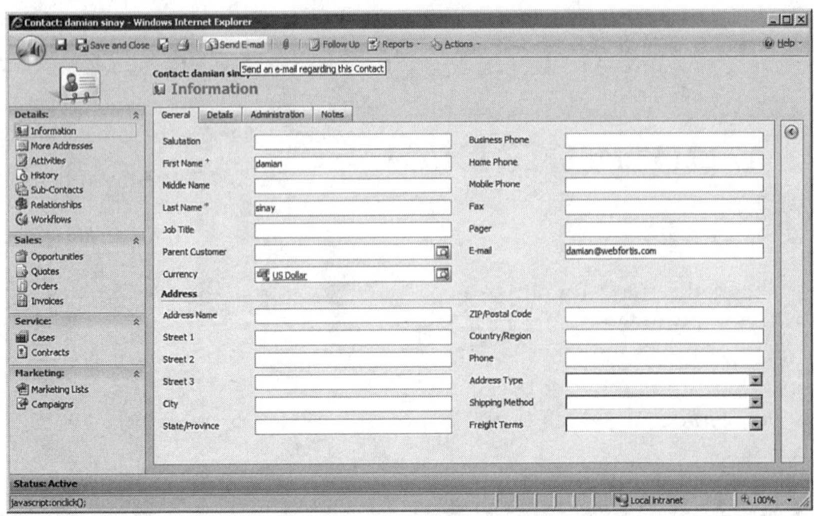

FIGURE 15.1 Sending direct e-mail to a Contact from Microsoft Dynamics CRM.

Figure 15.2 displays what happens when you select Send E-mail, allowing you to compose a new e-mail.

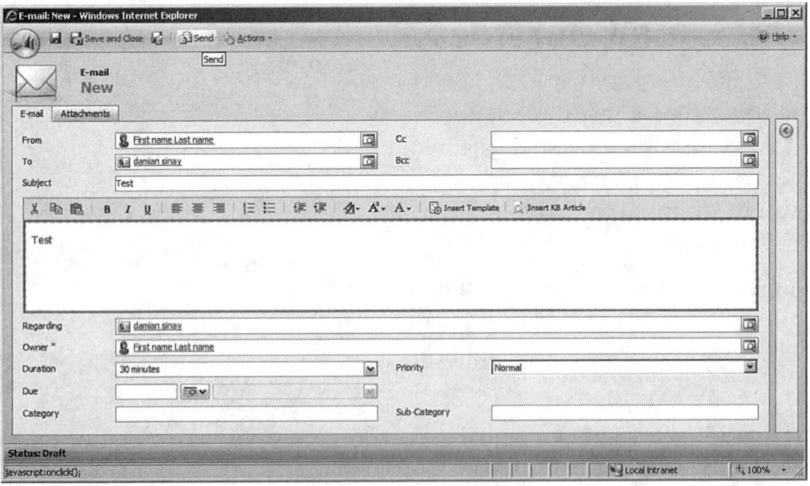

FIGURE 15.2 Composing an e-mail to a Contact.

However, after you compose the e-mail and click the Send button, the e-mail might not go out as expected. When you view the history for that Contact, you will see the e-mail is there. However, when you open the e-mail you just sent, you might see the yellow warning bar alerting you that the message has not been delivered, with a message such as "This message has not yet been submitted for delivery. For more information, see help" (see Figure 15.3).

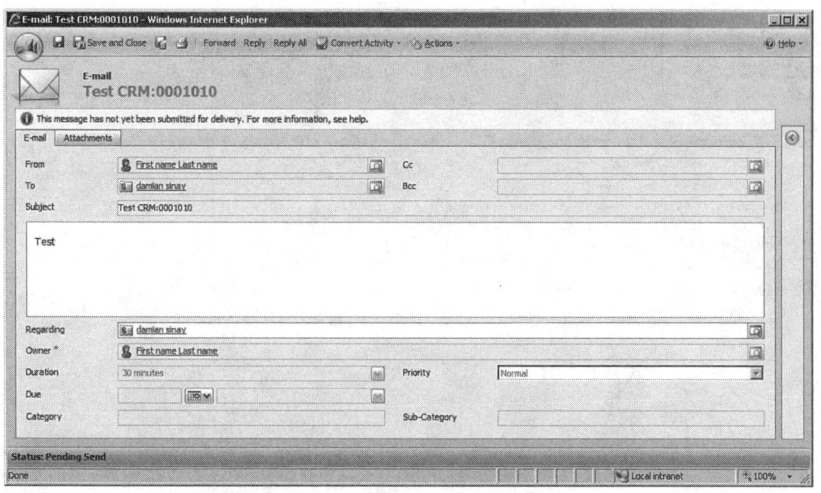

FIGURE 15.3 Warning message alert for undelivered e-mail.

If you do attempt to refer to Help for the error, you'll find little explanation regarding this specific error, and unless Users are sending e-mail using Outlook, it can be very confusing to troubleshoot.

The e-mails are not going out because the User's default configuration is to use Outlook as the Dynamics CRM client (instead of the IE web application) for outgoing e-mail. If you want to change this, you need to install the CRM Outlook client and change the configuration by going to the CRM menu option, selecting Options, and going to the E-mail tab, as shown in Figure 15.4. Checking the option Allow Microsoft Dynamics CRM to Send E-mail Using CRM for Outlook will permit the e-mails to go out using Outlook.

You need to consider a few factors when using the Outlook client to send e-mails. First, the e-mails are actually going out through Outlook. This happens when the User starts Outlook, and Outlook synchronizes with the CRM Server. If the User prepared several e-mails through the web application and didn't open the Outlook application for a long time (for example, a month), the e-mails won't be sent until the User opens Outlook. This can be a real problem, for obvious reasons.

Using Outlook as the e-mail gateway is the default configuration, and you must consider whether this configuration will work well with your business. If you want to have the e-mails composed through the web application sent out directly (not through Outlook), you must install and configure the CRM E-mail Router as described later in this chapter. Also, you will need to configure each User's preferences to use the E-mail Router, as shown in Figure 15.5. This is something that will have to be configured for every User as you might want to have some Users use the Outlook client only. To properly configure the E-mail Router for outbound e-mails, go to Settings, Administration, Users, Open the User you want to configure the E-mail Router, and change the drop-down that says E-mail Access type—Outgoing from Microsoft Dynamics CRM for Outlook to E-mail Router (remember, you must first install and configure the CRM E-mail Router).

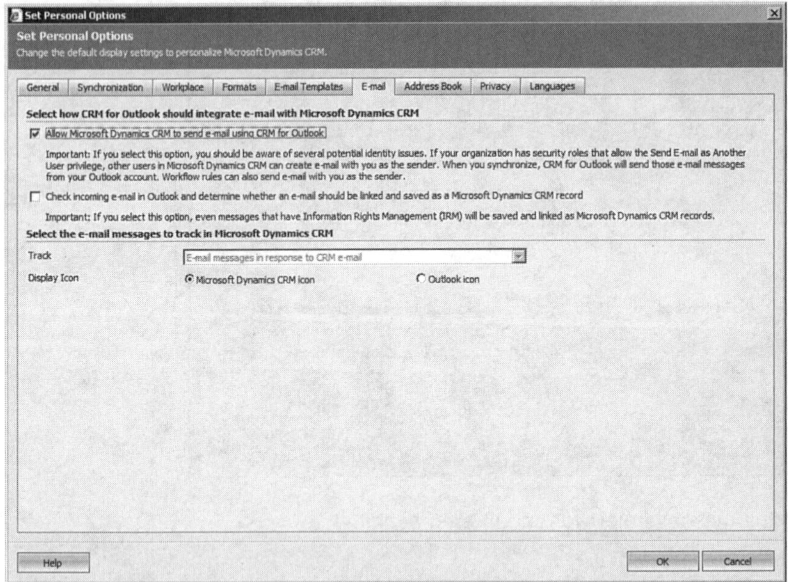

FIGURE 15.4 Outlook client e-mail options.

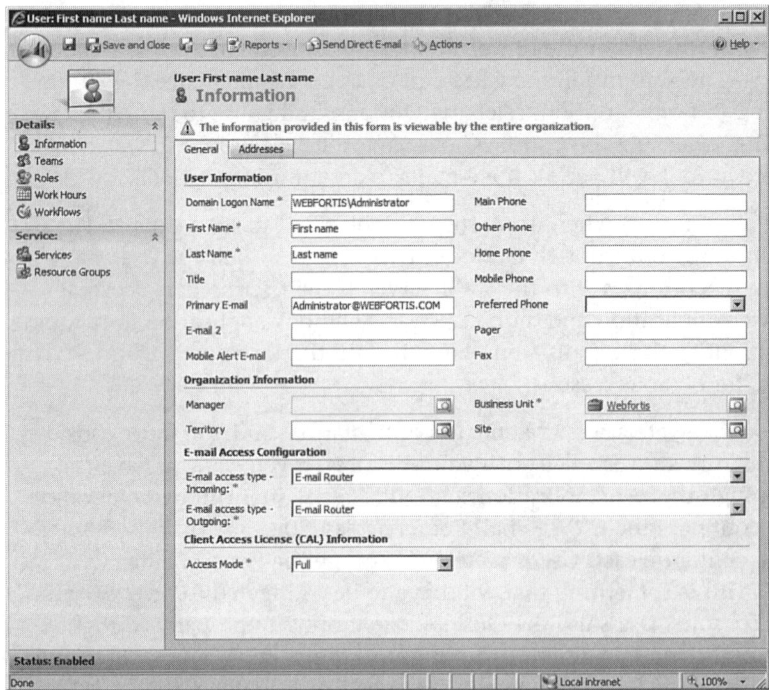

FIGURE 15.5 Configuring outgoing e-mail access type to use E-mail Router.

The MS CRM E-mail Router Explained

The CRM E-mail Router is a piece of software that receives messages from a service and forwards the messages to another service. In this case, the messages are received from the CRM Server, and they are forwarded to Microsoft Exchange or to the configured e-mail server.

The CRM E-mail Router comes as a separate installation file and must be installed after the CRM Server installation. The good thing is that you can install the CRM E-mail Router on a separate server; this doesn't need to be the same server where you have Microsoft Exchange Server installed or the same machine where you have the CRM Server installed. You can even install it on a separate server or computer running Windows XP Professional, Windows Vista Business, or Enterprise as those are the versions that can be joined to a domain. (The Windows XP Home and Windows Vista Home versions are not supported.) If you install the CRM E-mail Router on a separate server, be sure this computer is on and available all the time or the e-mails won't be sent when this computer is offline. Additionally, the server must be a member of the same domain of the CRM Server, and you might also be required to install the Microsoft Exchange Server MAPI Client and Collaboration Data Object component before installing the CRM E-mail Router. This can be downloaded from www.microsoft.com/downloads/details.aspx?FamilyID=e17e7f31-079a-43a9-bff2-0a110307611e&DisplayLang=en.

Unlike with the previous versions of Microsoft CRM, you are not obliged to use Microsoft Exchange Server as your primary e-mail server. You can use any e-mail server because the router works with the most popular e-mail protocols:

- Post Office Protocol 3 (POP3) for incoming e-mails
- Simple Mail Transport Protocol (SMTP) for outgoing e-mails

To install the CRM E-mail Router, follow these steps:

1. Use the `setupexchange.exe` file to start the setup process (see Figure 15.6). This file is located in the Exchange\i386 folder of the Microsoft Dynamics CRM 4.0 CD or can be downloaded from the Microsoft website at www.microsoft.com/downloads/details.aspx?FamilyID=e1358499-3fdb-45b8-adf0-7585f758277e&DisplayLang=en for the On-Premise and Hosted editions. The first screen enables you to check for available updates of the installation files before starting the installation.
2. Check for updated installation files that are downloaded and installed automatically after selecting Update Installation Files (Recommended).
3. Accept the license agreement (see Figure 15.7).

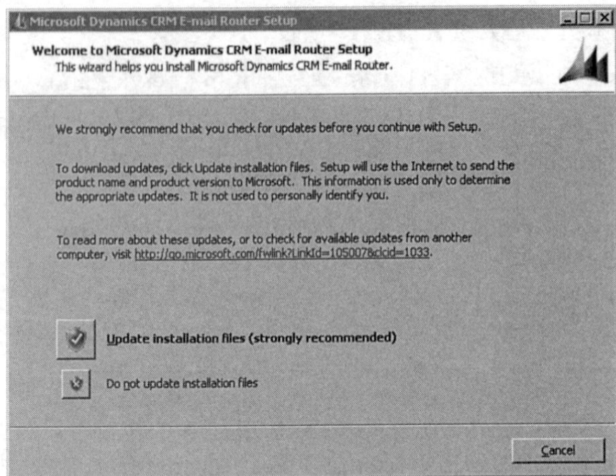

FIGURE 15.6 CRM E-mail Router setup.

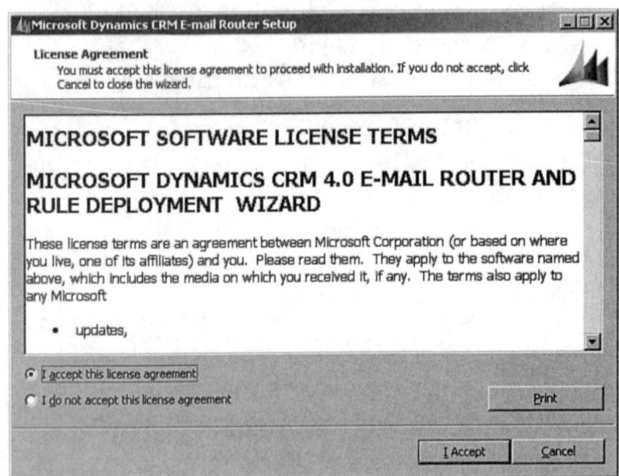

FIGURE 15.7 License agreement.

4. If any required components are missing, they appear in the list (see Figure 15.8). Select Install to download and install any missing components. Because the components might be downloaded from the Internet, ensure that you have an active Internet connection on the server.

   After the components are downloaded and installed, click Next to continue.

5. Select the router components you want to install and then click Next to continue (see Figure 15.9). If you are using Microsoft Exchange Server, you need the Rule Deployment Wizard (explained later in this chapter). If you will be using the POP3 protocol from another e-mail server, you can install the CRM E-mail Router component only.

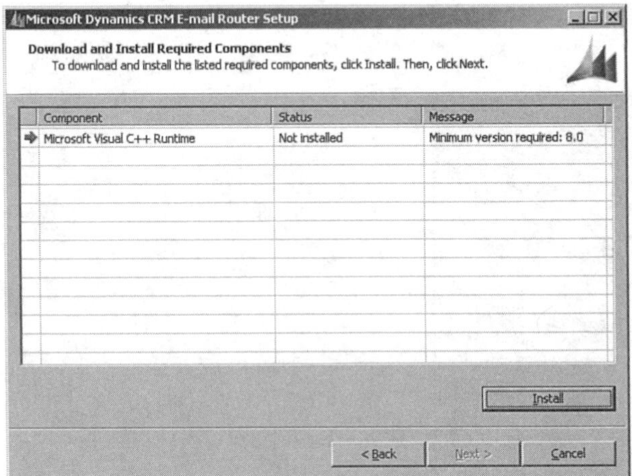

FIGURE 15.8 Downloading and installing required components.

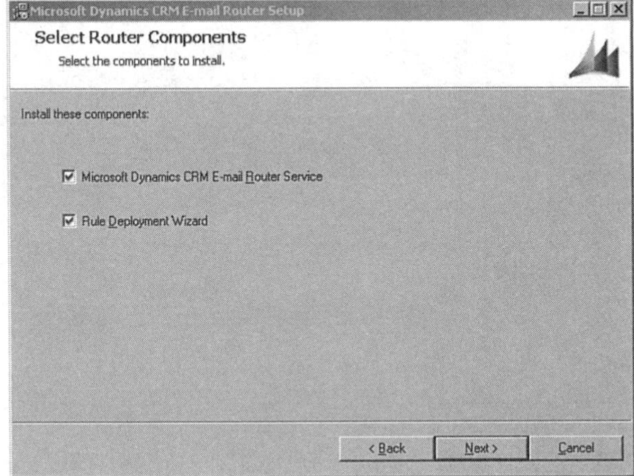

FIGURE 15.9 Select Router Components.

6. Select the installation directory and then click Next to continue.
7. Setup validates the system and checks for possible errors. If everything is okay, click Next to continue (see Figure 15.11).

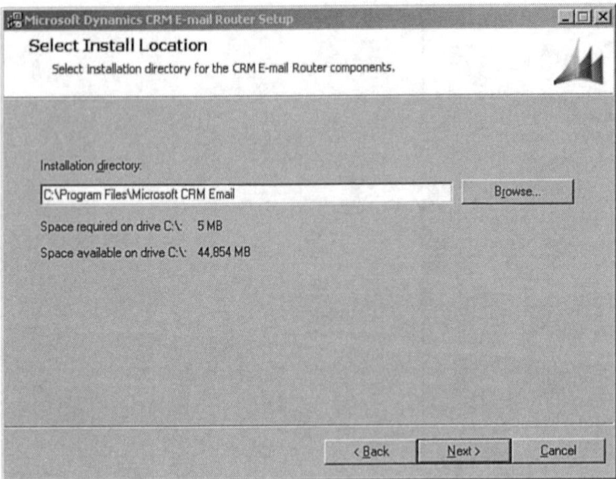

FIGURE 15.10 Select Installation Location.

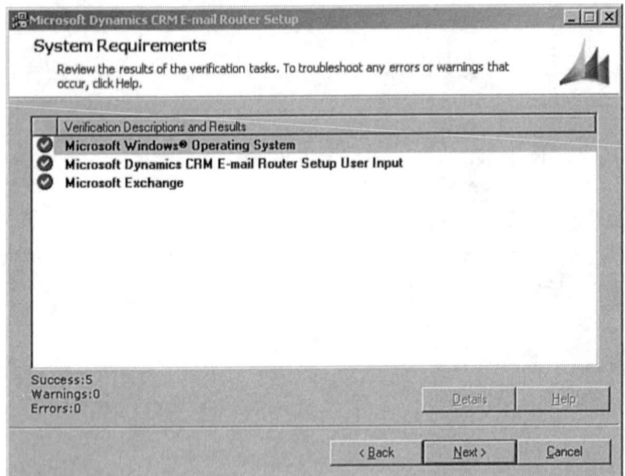

FIGURE 15.11 System requirements validation.

8. Verify that the check box Launch Configuration Manager after installation completes is marked and then click Install (see Figure 15.12).

9. When the installation has completed, you can use the E-mail Router Configuration Manager (see Figure 15.13). Refer to the next section for configuration options.

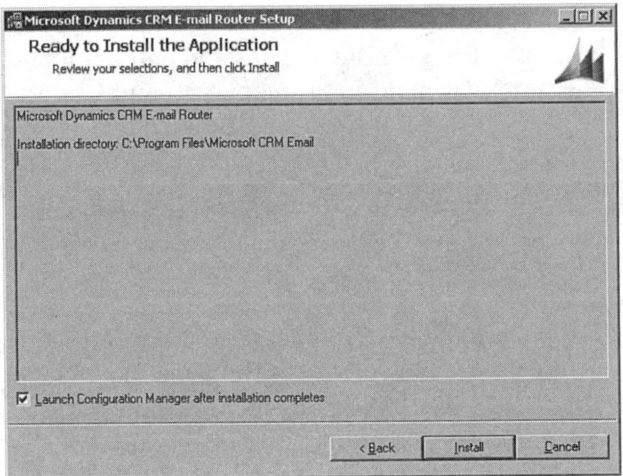

FIGURE 15.12 Ready to install the application.

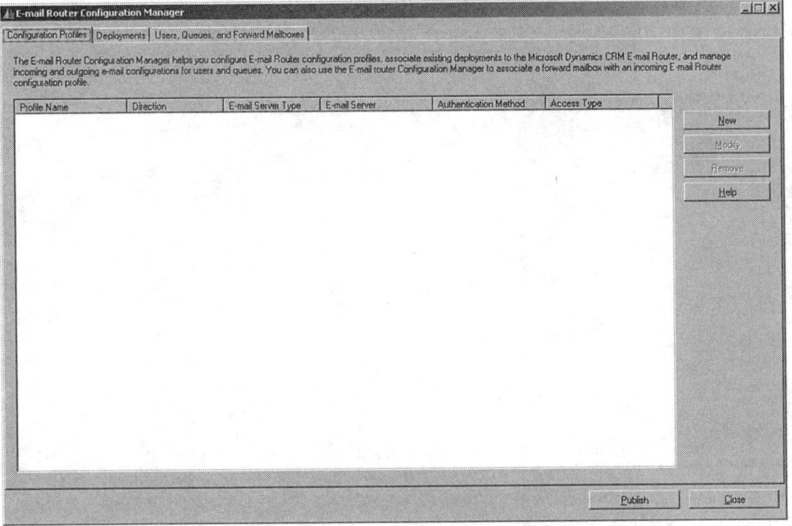

FIGURE 15.13 E-mail Router Configuration Manager.

Configuring the CRM E-mail Router

After you install the CRM E-mail Router, you must configure it.

As shown in Figure 15.13, the application is divided into three main areas:

- Configuration Profiles
- Deployments
- User, Queues, and Forward Mailboxes

Configuration Profiles

You must create at least one configuration profile for incoming e-mails and another for outgoing e-mails. The configuration profiles can be generic and can apply to multiple or all User configurations.

NOTE

You can create as many profiles as needed for the infrastructure of the company.

Creating the Outgoing Profile To create a new configuration profile, select New on the right side of the application and enter a name for the new profile in the E-mail Router Configuration Profile dialog box (see Figure 15.14). Select Outgoing for Direction, verify that SMTP is selected in E-mail Server Type, and then select your authentication type. Normally, Anonymous is selected as the authentication type unless your SMTP server requires authentication. Under Location, enter the name of the Exchange server or the SMTP server address. Finally, select Local System Account for the Access Credentials. This will be the only option available if Anonymous is selected as the authentication type. If Windows authentication is selected, you can select Other Specified, and you must enter the username and password for the User who will be connecting to the SMTP server.

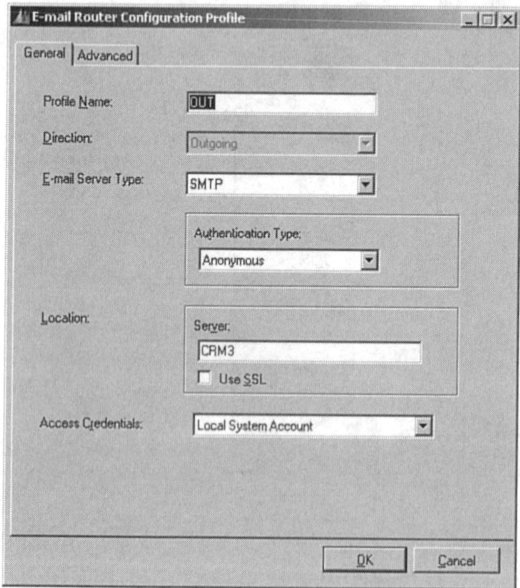

FIGURE 15.14 Configuring outgoing profile.

If you are using your local SMTP server, configure the relay restrictions property and have the reverse DNS records set for the server IP address. Also be sure that the domain is configured properly, to avoid being blacklisted for spam.

Creating the Incoming Profile To create another profile for the incoming e-mail, select New, located on the right of the application. Figure 15.15 shows a new profile using Microsoft Exchange Server.

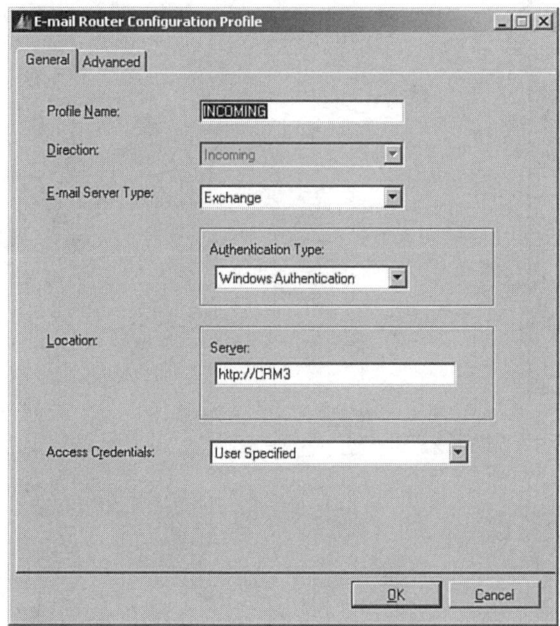

FIGURE 15.15 Configuring incoming profile for Exchange.

You also have the option to use the POP3 protocol for incoming e-mails if you don't use Microsoft Exchange Server (see Figure 15.16).

NOTE

If you want to use the POP3 protocol with Microsoft Exchange 2003, be aware that this service is disabled by default on Microsoft Exchange 2003. To enable it, go to Services (inside the Administrative tools in the Control Panel) and double-click the service with the name Microsoft Exchange POP3 to open the settings. Change the startup type to Automatic, click the Apply button, and then click the Start button (see Figure 15.17). This enables POP3 on Exchange.

The `Server` field under the Location area must be a valid URL with http:// or https:// for the Microsoft Exchange option or a valid address without the protocol for the POP3 option.

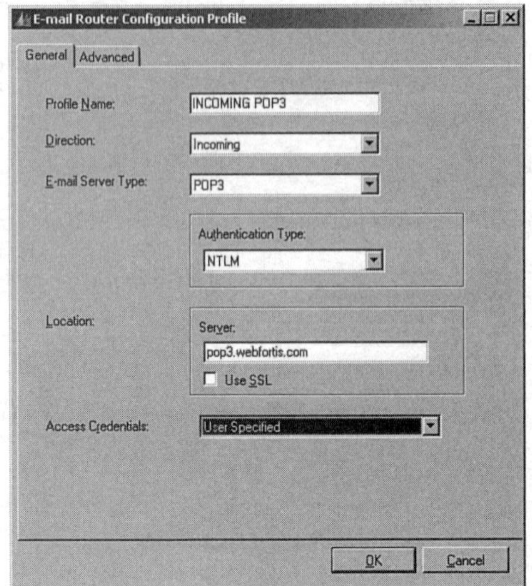

FIGURE 15.16 Configuring incoming profile for POP3 protocol.

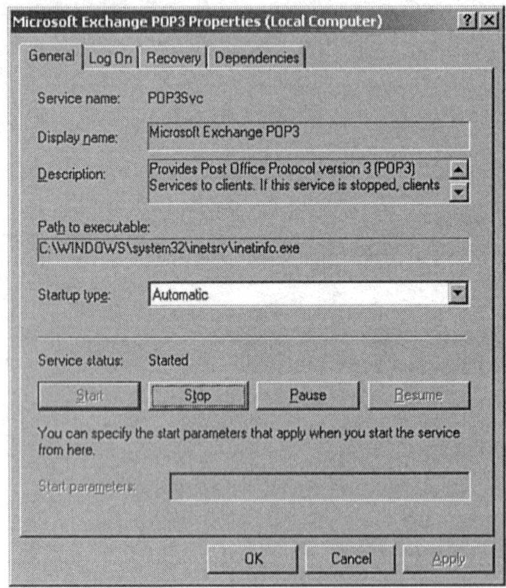

FIGURE 15.17 Enabling the POP3 protocol for Microsoft Exchange Server 2003.

The authentication type supported for Exchange can only be Windows Authentication.

The authentication types supported for POP3 are NTLM and Clear Text. If you are going to use the latter, it is recommended you use SSL to secure the User's credentials over the network. For the credentials, you have the option to have the User specify one (discussed in the next section "Deployments") or enter a fixed username and password when creating the incoming profile.

To test the POP3 or exchange info, you need to create an incoming profile. You can use the Microsoft Outlook application and create an account manually to be sure you have the right connection and credential information.

Deployments

After configuring the profiles, you need to create and set up a deployment where you want to use and apply the profiles. Notice you will be able to set the profiles for each User after configuring the deployment in the next section, "Users, Queues, and Forward Mailboxes."

You can configure two types of deployments:

- My Company
- An online service provider

NOTE

For Microsoft Dynamics CRM Online, you will have to download and install a different CRM E-mail Router specially designed for this version.

The first option, My Company, is used with On-Premise deployments (see Figure 15.18).

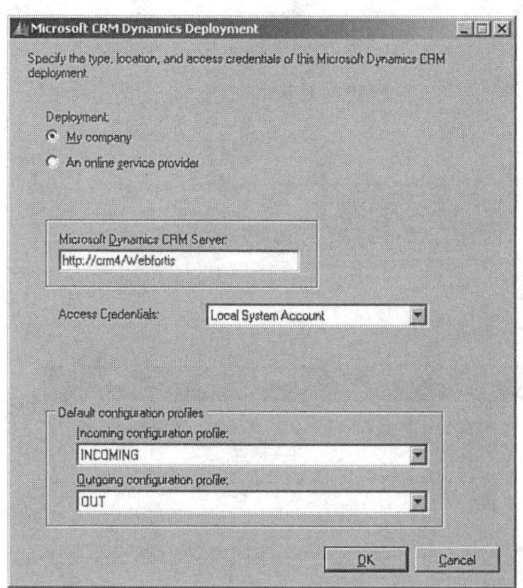

FIGURE 15.18 Configuring deployment for On-Premise CRM organizations.

The second option (an Online Service Provider) is used when IFD is enabled. (For more information about IFD, refer to Chapter 17, "Forms Authentication.")

Enter the appropriate values for the Microsoft Dynamics CRM Server (http://<servername>/<organization>). Notice the organization name is case-sensitive, so it must be entered in the same case as it was created when installing the CRM Server. Enter the Access Credentials and select the default configuration profiles. In this case, we selected our newly created profiles of `INCOMING` and `OUT` created in the previous section. The incoming and outgoing profiles selected here will be the default options for the Users and queues, but you can change these values for each User in the following section, if desired.

User, Queues, and Forward Mailboxes

Select the deployment from the top drop-down list and click Load Data to see the Users and Queues tab, shown on Figure 15.19.

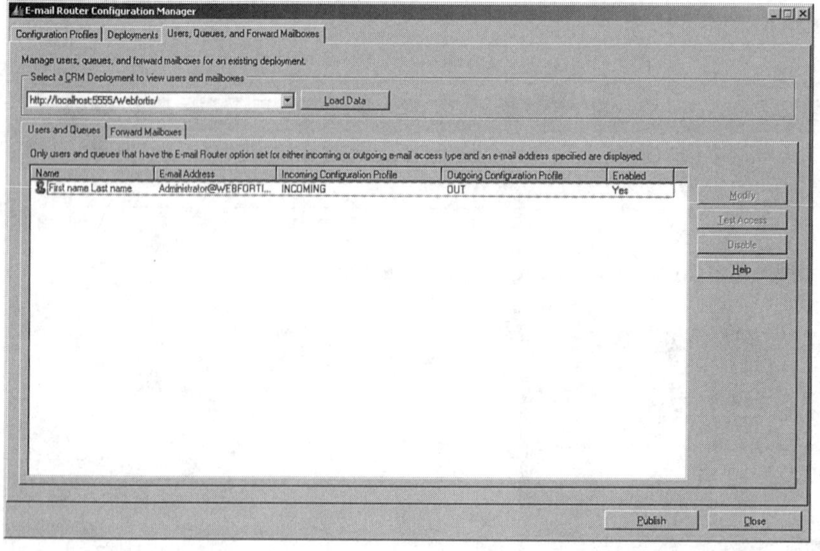

FIGURE 15.19 Users and Queues.

> **NOTE**
>
> Only the Users and queues that are configured to use the E-mail Router are shown here.

Click Test to verify that everything is configured properly. A successful test looks similar to Figure 15.20.

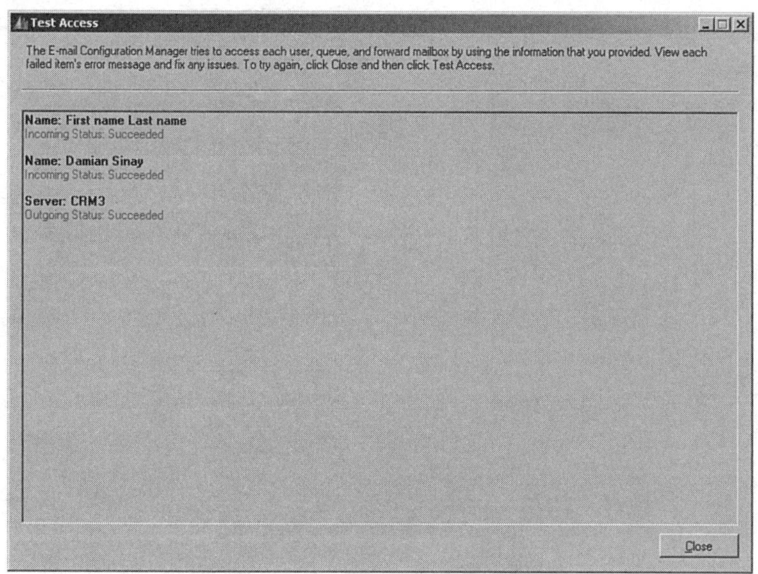

FIGURE 15.20 Testing E-mail Router configurations.

Forward Mailboxes

Forward Mailboxes are used to process incoming e-mails, and they require a dedicated mailbox to receive and forward them. There are a couple of reasons why you might want to use them. Primarily, you can use a single set of credentials for a single mailbox; however, there is a benefit in polling (only one mailbox is polled) as well as using taking advantage of Exchange forwarding rules.

Previous versions of Microsoft CRM used the Forward Mailboxes functionality to process incoming e-mails without using Microsoft Outlook. This option works only with Microsoft Exchange Server, and it requires having a dedicated mailbox to process the incoming e-mails. The Users or queues that want to use this option must have some rules deployed that you can create using the Rule Deployment Wizard, described later in this chapter.

The E-mail Router Configuration Manager Forward Mailboxes configuration is shown in Figure 15.21.

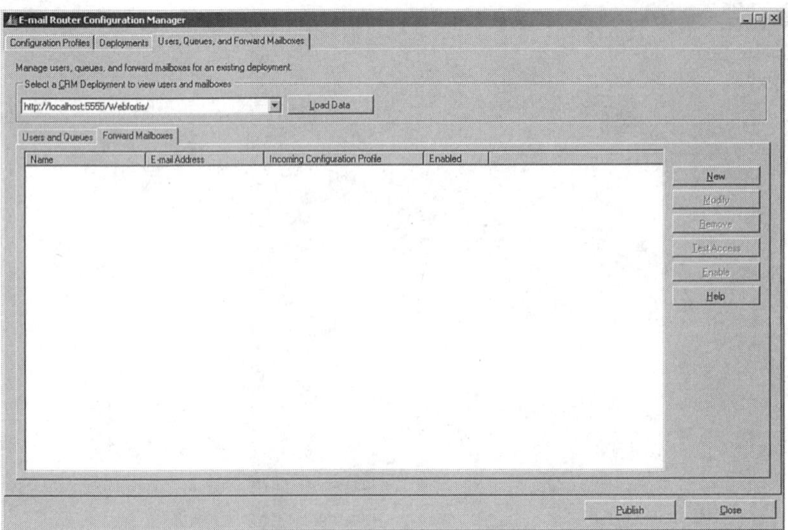

FIGURE 15.21 Forward Mailboxes.

Figure 15.22 shows the processing flow of an incoming e-mail for a User who utilizes Forward Mailboxes. The e-mail is first received by the User's mailbox and then is forwarded to the Router mailbox.

NOTE

Many Users can forward their e-mails to the same router mailbox.

The CRM E-mail Router Service polls the Router mailbox looking for incoming messages. When it finds an e-mail, it inserts the e-mail into CRM as a new E-mail activity for the User or queue that forwarded the e-mail. The e-mail is then deleted from the Router mailbox, depending on the configurations, as shown in Figure 15.23.

Microsoft recommends this technique if you are using Microsoft Exchange Server as your primary e-mail server. However, you don't actually need to set up a forward mailbox to receive e-mails. The incoming profile configured to use Exchange will be sufficient in most cases.

The outgoing e-mails are processed asynchronously, and the default polling is scheduled for every 1,000 seconds (about 15 minutes), so you must wait that time before the e-mails are actually sent.

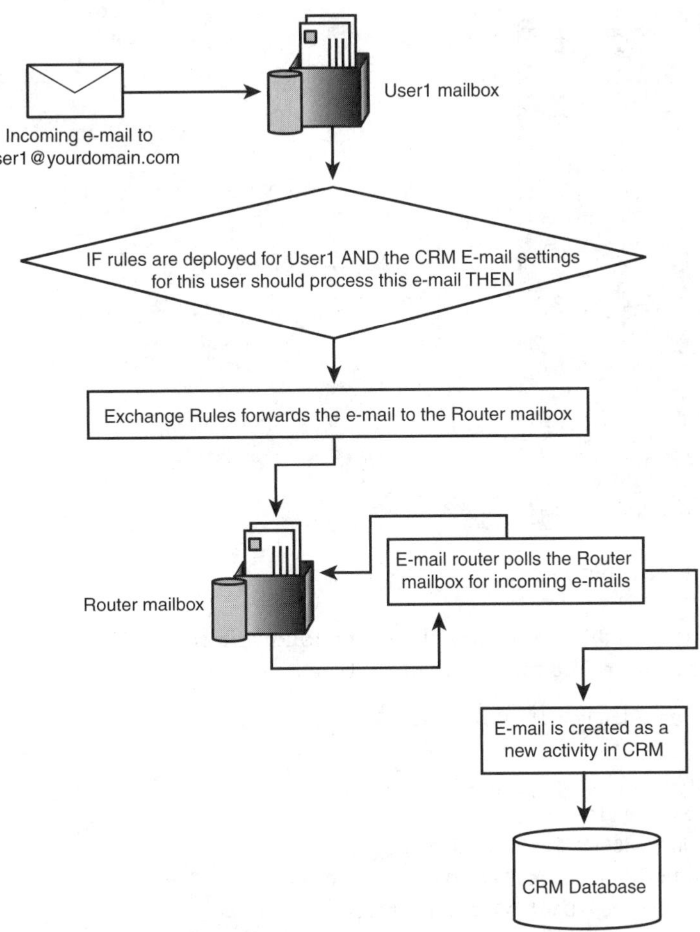

FIGURE 15.22 Forward Mailboxes processing flow.

TIP

To increase the speed at which outgoing e-mails are sent, you can edit the configuration file `Microsoft.Crm.Tools.EmailAgent.xml` (which is usually located at `C:\Program Files\Microsoft CRM Email\Service`) and find the `SchedulingPeriod` element. We recommend changing its default value to 10 seconds.

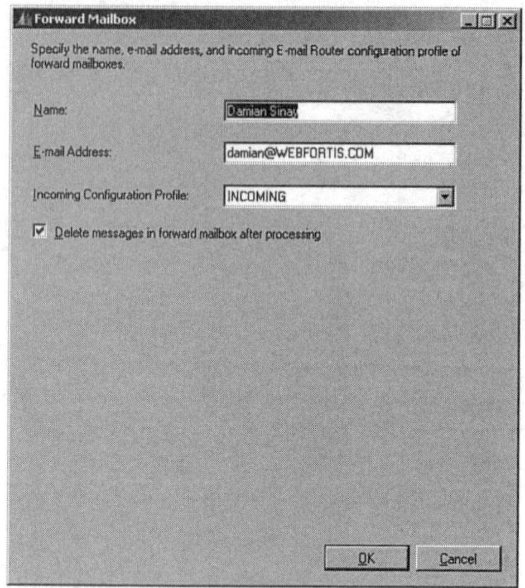

FIGURE 15.23 Forward Mailbox configuration.

To change the value at which e-mails are processed, use the following code and change the value within the `SchedulingPeriod` node of the `EmailAgent.xml`:

```
<?xml version="1.0" encoding="utf-8"?>
<Configuration>
 <SystemConfiguration>
  <MaxThreads>50</MaxThreads>
  <MaxThreadExecution>600000</MaxThreadExecution>
  <SchedulingPeriod>10</SchedulingPeriod>
  <ConfigRefreshPeriod>5000</ConfigRefreshPeriod>
  <ConfigUpdatePeriod>3600000</ConfigUpdatePeriod>
  <LogLevel>1</LogLevel>
 </SystemConfiguration>
```

Rule Deployment Wizard

The Rule Deployment Wizard is used for the Users or queues configured as forward mailboxes because they need server rules installed on Microsoft Exchange to forward e-mails to the Router mailbox (see Figure 15.22).

The Rule Deployment Wizard requires Microsoft Exchange Server 2003 SP2 or later, and it must be run for the Users or queues that will be processing their incoming e-mails with the Forward Mailboxes option.

To run the Rule Deployment Wizard, follow these steps:

1. Select Start, All Programs. Then go to the Microsoft Dynamics CRM E-mail Router programs group and click Run Deployment Wizard. The window shown in Figure 15.24 appears.

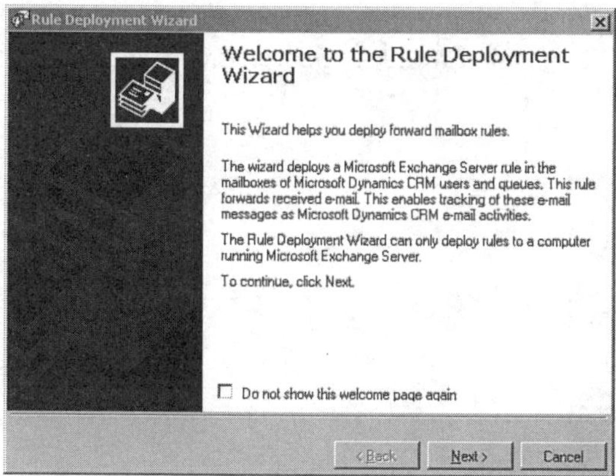

FIGURE 15.24 Rule Deployment Wizard.

The wizard can be configured to be installed on three deployment types:

- My Company (for On-Premise installations)
- An online service provider
- Remember that for Microsoft Dynamics CRM Online, you will have to download and install a different CRM E-mail Router specially designed for this version as explained earlier.

2. Installing on My Company requires entering the Microsoft CRM Server URL address with the organization name (for example http://<servername>/<organization>). Notice the organization name is case-sensitive, so it must be entered in the same case as it was created when installing the CRM Server. See Figure 15.25.

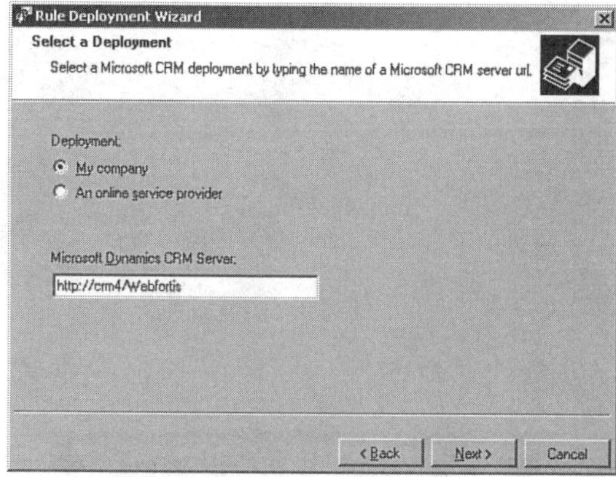

FIGURE 15.25 Select a Deployment.

3. You must create a mailbox in Exchange from which the router will monitor the forwarded e-mails. We've created a mailbox called router2@webfortis.com for this example (see Figure 15.26).

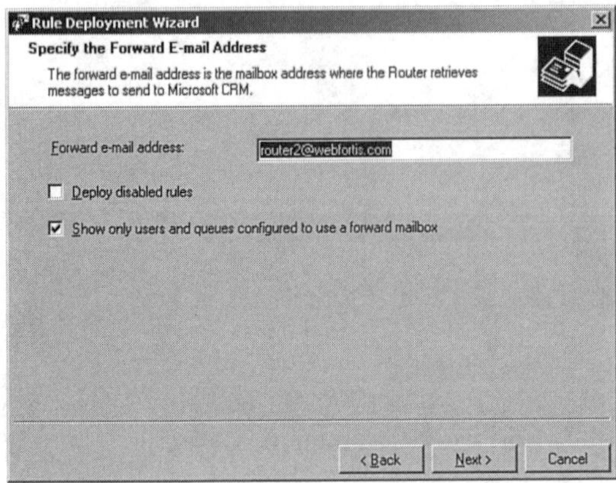

FIGURE 15.26 Specifying the Forward E-mail Address.

4. Verify that the check box Show Only Users and Queues Configured to Use a Forward Mailbox is checked and enter the Forward E-mail Address. Click Next to select the Users you want to apply the rules to (see Figure 15.27).

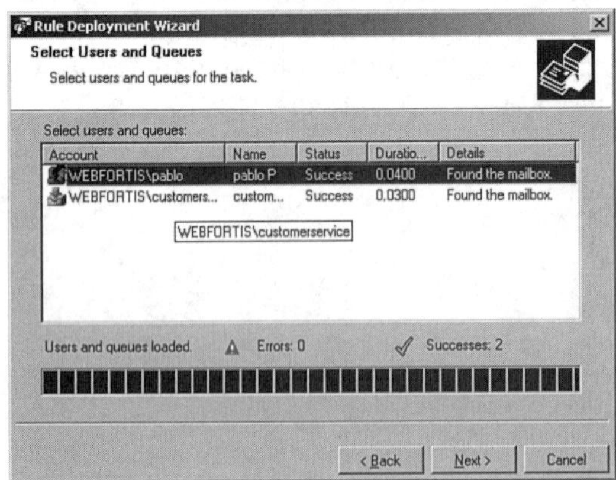

FIGURE 15.27 Select Users and Queues.

NOTE

If you don't see any User or queue here, then that must be because there are not any Users or queues configured to use a Forward Mailbox in the E-mail access type—incoming. You will have to go to the CRM web application and configure this on the User or queue options.

5. Click Next to continue. You can verify that the mailbox has the rules already installed by selecting the first option and then click Next, as shown in Figure 15.28.

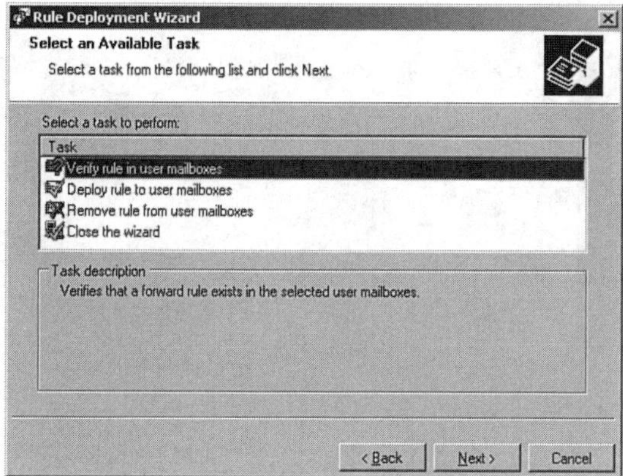

FIGURE 15.28 Select an Available Task.

6. If Users don't have rules installed for them, you will see the error shown in Figure 15.29.

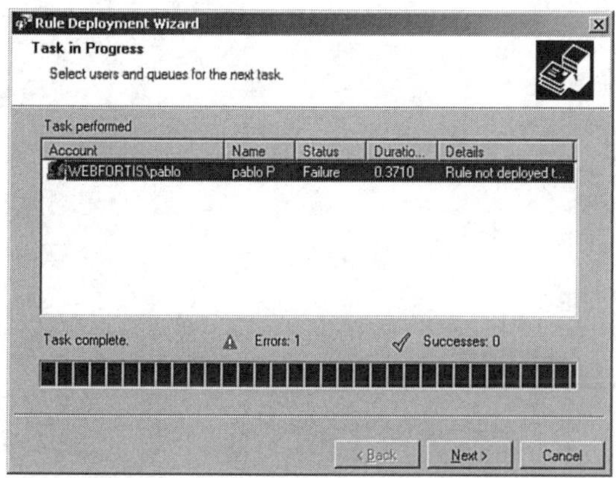

FIGURE 15.29 Rule Not Deployed error.

7. Click Next and then select Deploy Rule to User Mailboxes, as shown in Figure 15.30.

8. Click Next. The rules then are installed for the User mailbox. Figure 15.31 shows the results.

9. After deploying the rules, click Next to see the last step (see Figure 15.32).

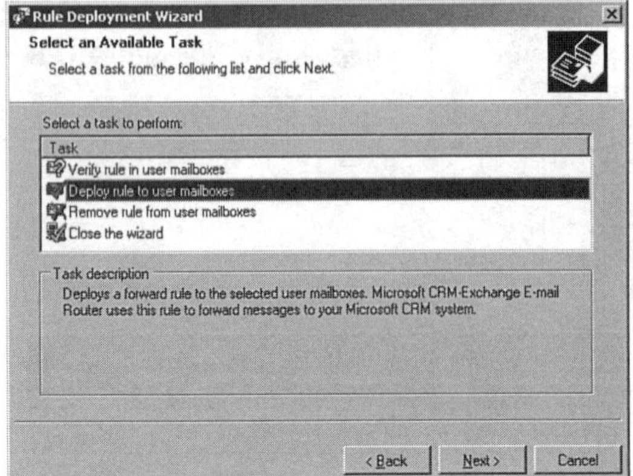

FIGURE 15.30 Deploying rules to User mailboxes.

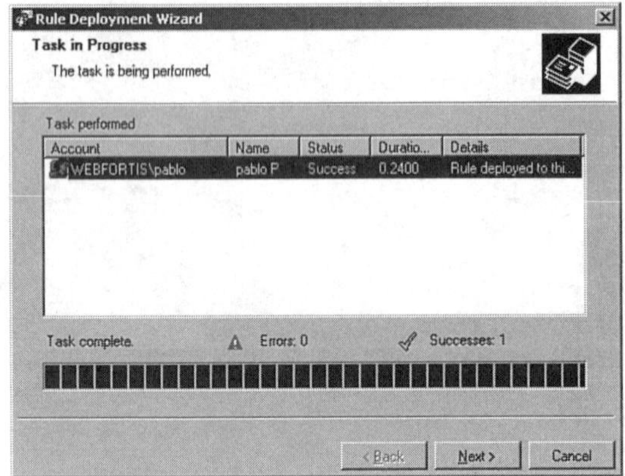

FIGURE 15.31 Rules deployed successfully.

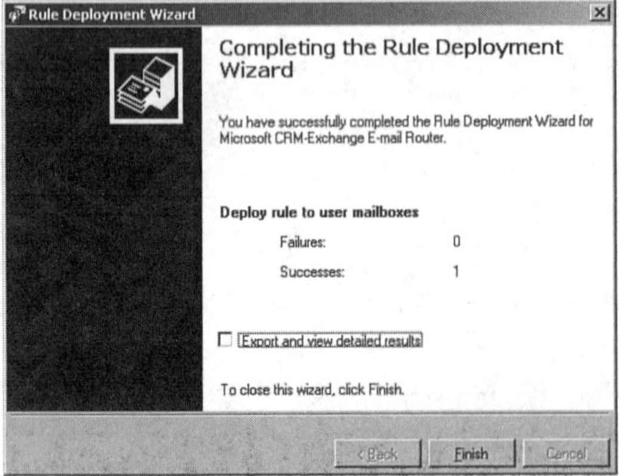

FIGURE 15.32 Wizard completed.

Tracking Incoming E-mails

You can track incoming e-mails in two ways:

- By using the CRM tracking token
- Through message filtering and correlation

The tokens work by appending a code in the subject of the e-mail with a form similar to `CRM:0001006`. You can configure this in the system options, as described in Chapter 14, "Settings and Configuration."

The filtering and correlation to track incoming e-mails involves a new method that doesn't require appending data on the e-mail's subject line. Instead, it uses an intelligent way to figure the thread of the e-mail using the e-mail's sender, the e-mail's recipient, the e-mail subject, and any CC. This method is not 100% effective, but you can use it if you don't want the CRM tracking tokens to alter the e-mails.

NOTE

By default, only incoming e-mails that are received as a response to an e-mail sent from Dynamics CRM are tracked. If you want CRM to track all incoming e-mails, you must change your personal settings from the web application by going to Tools, Options, and then going to the E-mail tab, as shown in Figure 15.33.

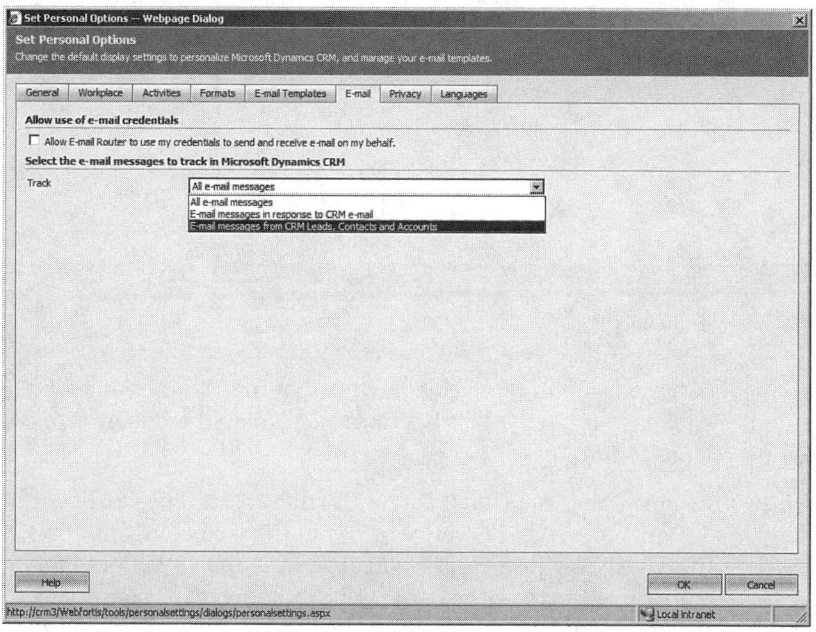

FIGURE 15.33 Tracking options for incoming e-mail.

15

You can select to track all e-mails, the e-mails that are responses to CRM e-mails, or the e-mail messages from CRM Leads, Contacts, and Accounts.

NOTE

The option that says Allow E-mail Router to Use My Credentials to Send and Receive E-mail on My Behalf is only available if your User is configured to receive or send e-mails through the CRM E-mail Router.

You can see all the incoming e-mails CRM tracks by going to the Workplace, then Activities, and then changing the type drop-down from All to E-mail (see Figure 15.34).

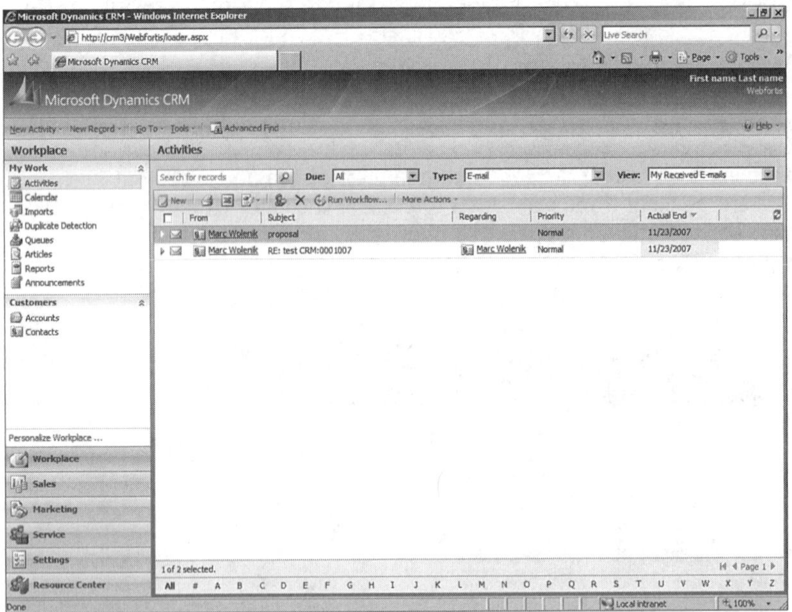

FIGURE 15.34 My received e-mails.

One of the most common issues related to received e-mails is that the "From" e-mail address sometimes can't be mapped properly. This is shown with an alert red icon with a question mark on it (see Figure 15.35).

This can happen for two reasons: Either the e-mail address doesn't match any existing e-mail address on any Lead, Contact, User, or Account record in the system organization, or more than one system record exists with the same e-mail address and CRM doesn't know which one it should be mapped to. In either case, the User must map the e-mail address manually by opening the e-mail and clicking the red e-mail address. The dialog box shown in Figure 15.36 illustrates how to allow the User to resolve the issue by selecting an existing record or by creating a new one.

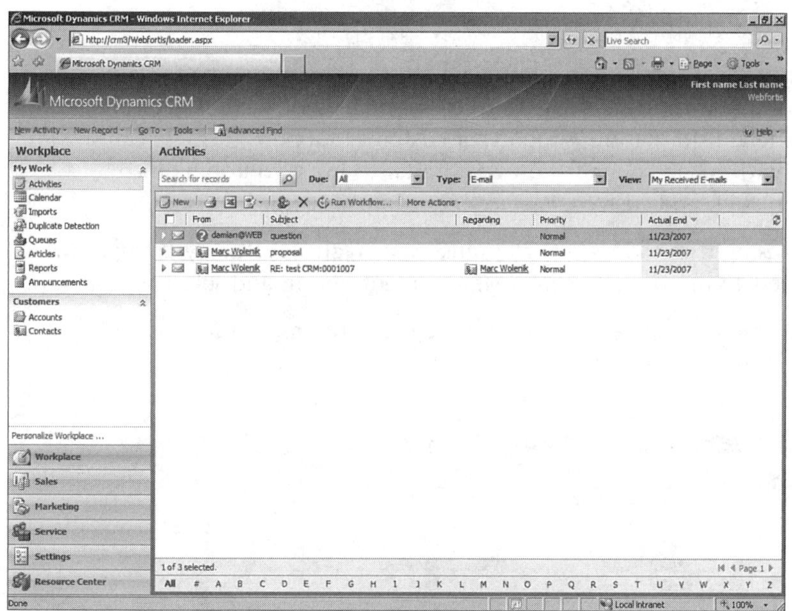

FIGURE 15.35 E-mail with an unmapped "From" address.

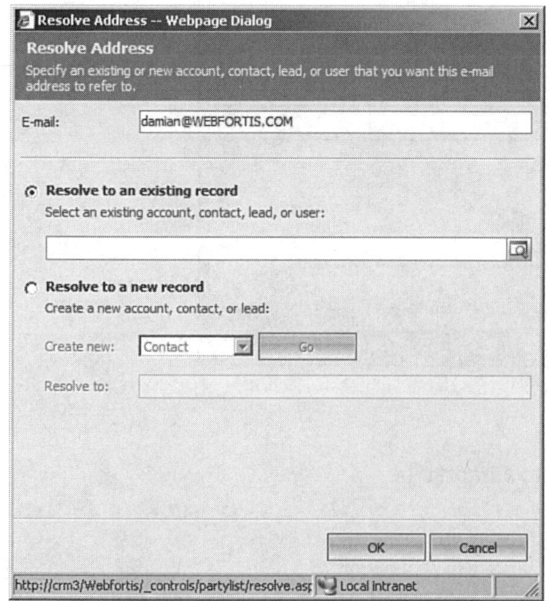

FIGURE 15.36 Resolving unmapped addresses.

For more information about setting and configuring tracking tokens, refer to Chapter 14.

Queues

Queues are primarily used for general incoming e-mails that are not related to a specific User. A common example is to use a queue to receive e-mails sent to your organization for queries related to general information, support, or customer support. In these cases, you could create queues with related e-mail addresses similar to info@yourdomain.com, support@yourdomain.com, and customerservice@yourdomain.com, for example.

To track the e-mails using these addresses, you must first create a queue by going to the Settings area, and then going to the Business Management option and selecting Queues.

Select New to create a new queue, and then set the e-mail options accordingly (see Figure 15.37).

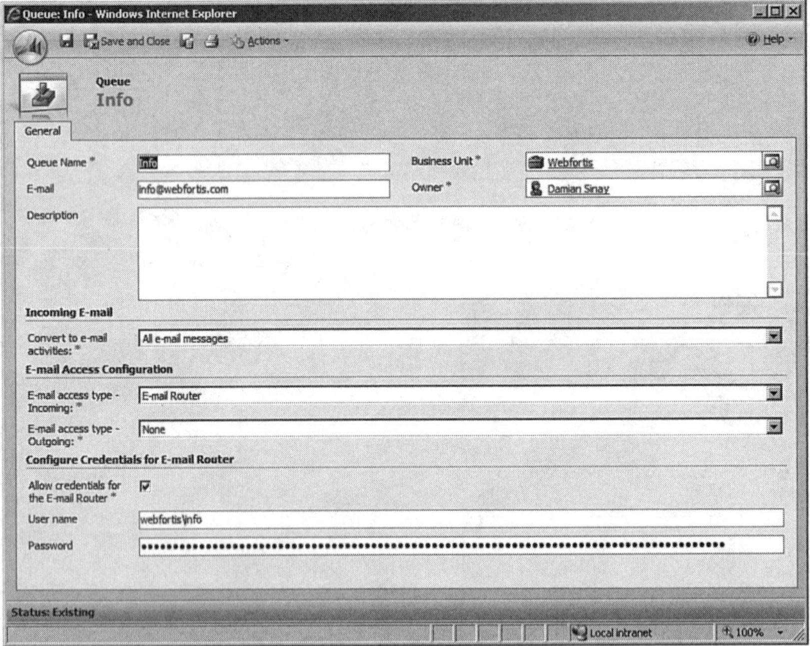

FIGURE 15.37 Creating a new queue for Info.

For more information about queues, refer to Chapter 14.

Summary

This chapter described how Microsoft CRM processes incoming and outgoing e-mails and covered available options for sending and receiving e-mails that will be tracked as activities in Dynamics CRM. It also described the different system configuration options to track the incoming e-mails by reviewing the E-mail Router Service, Microsoft Outlook Client, and Forward Mailbox E-mail configuration and their deployment rules.

CHAPTER 16

Configuration and Customization Tools

IN THIS CHAPTER

- .NET Framework
- Development Tools
- What CRM Is and What Can Be Customized
- Interacting with Microsoft Dynamics CRM

Throughout this book, we refer to a variety of development utilities that you can use to perform configuration and customizations. Although these are not necessarily centric to Microsoft Dynamics CRM, this chapter explains the foundations of these tools and technologies, to give you a better understanding of why and how things work.

Obviously, our focus is on what is commonly referred to as the Microsoft Stack. The Microsoft Stack is the unified and common family of Microsoft products, such as Windows servers, SQL Server, Exchange, and Office. Because Windows Server 2003, .NET (referred to as "dot net"), has been a core component unifying these applications through interoperability and Service Oriented Architecture (SOA) to become the standard in application development.

SOA is a principal wherein applications can be delivered and consumed as services, and are comprised of standard protocols and interfaces. In the case of Microsoft Dynamics CRM, data and business logic is delivered via Web Services that can be accessed and updated through any application that can consume Web Services.

For more information on working with Microsoft Dynamics CRM Web Services, refer to Chapter 22, "Web Services."

.NET Framework

Microsoft Windows servers use a common component set to execute and manage applications. This component set includes the Common Language Runtime (CLR), which manages the execution environment as well as the code libraries that make up the base language, and are together referred to as the .NET Framework. This framework was introduced in beta in late 2000 with Version 1.0, and several versions have been introduced since then. The major versions include the following, and their appropriate editing tools:

- .NET 1.0, Visual Studio 2002
- .NET 1.1, Visual Studio 2003 (this is the version CRM 3.0 uses)
- .NET 2.0, Visual Studio 2005 and 2008
- .NET 3.0, Visual Studio 2005 and 2008
- .NET 3.5, Visual Studio 2008

The 3.0 version of the .NET Framework consists of the following components that leverage the .NET 2.0 Framework (as such, .NET 3.0 requires .NET 2.0 to be installed as well):

- **Windows Workflow Foundation (WF)**—This allows for the creation of logical business and data workflow via a graphical designer (shown in Figure 16.1). It is a huge improvement for developers because the capability to leverage workflow for changing business environments prompts both rapid development and change.

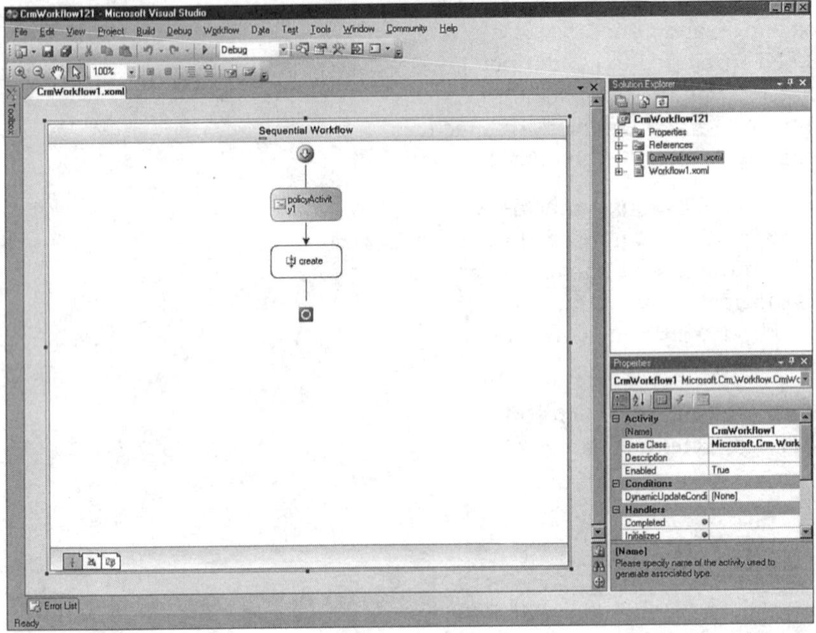

FIGURE 16.1 Workflow designer.

- **Windows Presentation Foundation (WPF)**—The WPF is a new way to write client interfaces and graphics based on XAML files that are an extension of XML files, but for applications.

- **Windows Communication Foundation (WCF)**—This service-oriented model allows for messaging between same and disparate applications.
- **CardSpace**—This provides digital identifiers via virtual cards.

.NET 3.5 introduced several new features, including Language Integrated Query (LINQ), which enables developers to create structured queries on the .NET classes in a similar language such as SQL language but with less effort and code writing. This version also has AJAX integrated directly within the framework. Previous versions required a separate download. AJAX is the technology commonly referred to as Web 2.0, and it avoids the common problem of forcing web pages to post–back to the server for page interactions in ASP.NET. Web 2.0 gives the user better functionality and experience with Web applications.

The .NET Framework has been included by default on all servers since Windows 2003. (Older versions of Windows can download and install the framework, for compatibility purposes.)

Microsoft Dynamics CRM 4.0 uses the .NET 3.0 Framework, which includes .NET 2.0, Ajax.NET, WF, WPF, and WCF.

Development Tools

As we've mentioned throughout this book, the preferred tool for development is Microsoft Visual Studio .NET. Visual Studio is the preferred Microsoft development environment for working with and creating .NET projects. The following versions are supported for developing applications for Microsoft Dynamics CRM:

- Visual Studio 2005 Professional Edition (including Team System)
- Visual Studio 2008 Professional Edition (including Team System)

Visual Studio Express and earlier versions of Visual Studio are not supported for development of Microsoft Dynamics CRM plug-ins, but they can be used to create objects that can consume Web services as well as websites, if desired.

Visual Studio is an integrated development environment with rich controls and features that allow for rapid development (see Figure 16.2).

When performing Microsoft Dynamics CRM customizations, Visual Studio provides benefits such as IntelliSense and debugging options. Additionally, all code can be compiled for quicker execution.

Visual Studio should be used to make/build the following objects in CRM:

- Reports
- Workflows
- Custom ASP.NET applications and web pages that can be embedded in an IFRAME
- Plug-ins, components (`.dlls`) that interact with external databases/systems

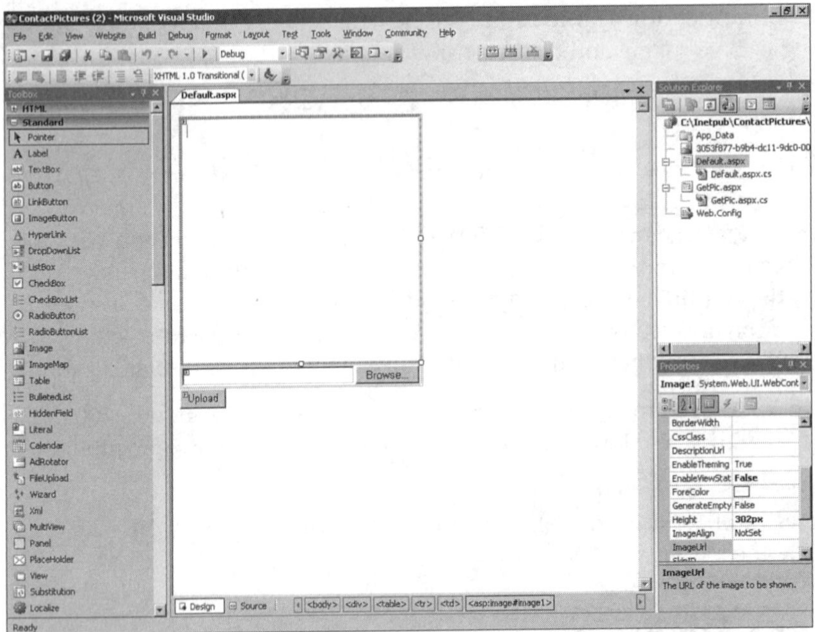

FIGURE 16.2 Visual Studio.

As always, when working with the Microsoft Dynamics CRM database, be sure to create your objects working in the context provided. For example, it might not be necessary to impersonate a Microsoft CRM administrator if you're just performing routine update Tasks, and this can potentially create a security risk. Additionally, when working with Visual Studio to create objects, frequently the objects become unavailable for editing in Microsoft Dynamics CRM. This is the case for custom reports that are created using the Microsoft Dynamics CRM Report Wizard. If you edit one of these reports with Visual Studio, they might not be able to be edited again through the Report Wizard.

For example, when invoking the CRM SDK Web Services, you can impersonate the User who is invoking the Web service as follows:

```
using System;
using System.Web.Services.Protocols;
using System.Text;
using System.Net;
using System.Xml;
using ConsoleApplication1.CRMSdk;

CrmAuthenticationToken token = new CrmAuthenticationToken();
token.AuthenticationType = 0; // Use Active Directory authentication.
token.OrganizationName = "webfortis";
```

```
CrmService crmService = new CrmService();
crmService.Url = "http://localhost/MSCRMServices/2007/CrmService.asmx";
crmService.CrmAuthenticationTokenValue = token;
crmService.Credentials =
new NetworkCredential("UserName","UserPassword","UserDomain");

// Create a new account owned by the impersonated user.
account account = new account();
account.name = "test account";
Guid accountid = crmService.Create(account);
```

The lines in bold mark the points you need to modify with the User you want to impersonate. Notice the following code won't work if IFD is enabled on the CRM Server. If that is the case, then you should use code as follows:

```
using System;
using System.Web.Services.Protocols;
using System.Text;
using System.Net;
using System.Xml;
using ConsoleApplication1.CRMSdk;
using ConsoleApplication1.CRMSdk.Discovery;

CrmService crmService = new CrmService();
crmService.Url = GetIFDConnection("OrganizationName",
"http:// OrganizationName.domain.com", "UserDomain", "UserName", "UserPassword",
crmService);

// Create a new account owned by the impersonated user.
account account = new account();
account.name = "test account";
Guid accountid = crmService.Create(account);

public string GetIFDConnection(string organization, string server,
        string domain, string username, string password, CrmService crmService)
        {
            //Remove any trailing forward slash from the end of the server URL.
            server = server.TrimEnd(new char[] { '/' });

            // Initialize an instance of the CrmDiscoveryService Web service proxy.
            CrmDiscoveryService disco = new CrmDiscoveryService();
            disco.Url = server +
            ➥"/MSCRMServices/2007/SPLA/CrmDiscoveryService.asmx";

            //Retrieve a list of available organizations.
            RetrieveOrganizationsRequest orgRequest =
```

16

```
            new RetrieveOrganizationsRequest();
        orgRequest.UserId = domain + "\\" + username;
        orgRequest.Password = password;
        RetrieveOrganizationsResponse orgResponse =
            (RetrieveOrganizationsResponse)disco.Execute(orgRequest);

        //Find the desired organization.
        foreach (OrganizationDetail orgdetail in orgResponse.
        ➥OrganizationDetails)
        {
            if (String.Compare(orgdetail.OrganizationName, organization,
            ➥true) == 0)
            {
                //Retrieve the ticket.
                RetrieveCrmTicketRequest ticketRequest =
                    new RetrieveCrmTicketRequest();
                ticketRequest.OrganizationName = organization;
                ticketRequest.UserId = domain + "\\" + username;
                ticketRequest.Password = password;
                RetrieveCrmTicketResponse ticketResponse =
                    (RetrieveCrmTicketResponse)disco.Execute(ticketRequest);

                //Create the CrmService Web service proxy.
                CrmSdk.CrmAuthenticationToken sdktoken =
                    new CrmSdk.CrmAuthenticationToken();
                sdktoken.AuthenticationType = 2; // Use IFD Authentication
                sdktoken.OrganizationName = organization;
                sdktoken.CrmTicket = ticketResponse.CrmTicket;
                crmService.CrmAuthenticationTokenValue = sdktoken;
                return orgdetail.CrmServiceUrl;
            }
        }
        return "";
    }
```

Because CRM Online uses Passport authentication, neither of the two previous code samples will work on CRM Online. To use the code to connect and impersonate a user on CRM Online, you will have to reference the `IdCrlWrapper.dll` in your project. This assembly is not built by default in the CRM SDK, and you will have to build it by opening the project `idcrlwrapper.csproj` that is located in the SDK\Server\Helpers\CS\IdCrlWrapper folder with Visual Studio 2005. You will also need to copy the `msidcrl40.dll` file that is on the SDK\bin to your solution bin folder.

The following code sample can be used on CRM Online:

```
using System;
using System.Web.Services.Protocols;
```

```
using System.Text;
using System.Net;
using System.Xml;
using ConsoleApplication1.CRMSdk;
using ConsoleApplication1.CRMSdk.Discovery;
using Microsoft.Crm.Passport.Sample;

static private string _partner = "crm.dynamics.com";
static private string _environment = "Production";
static private string _hostname = "dev.crm.dynamics.com";

static void Main(string[]args)
{
CrmService crmService = new CrmService();
crmService.Url = GetLiveConnection("OrganizationName",
_hostname , "passport@hotmail.com", "PassportPassword", crmService);

// Create a new account owned by the impersonated user.
account account = new account();
account.name = "test account";
Guid accountid = crmService.Create(account);
}
public static string GetLiveConnection(string organization, string server,
                         string username, string password, CrmService crmService)
        {

            //Remove any trailing forward slash from the end of the server URL.
            server = server.TrimEnd(new char[] { '/' });

            // Initialize an instance of the CrmDiscoveryService Web service proxy.
            CrmDiscoveryService disco = new CrmDiscoveryService();
            disco.Url = "https://"  + server +
"/MSCRMServices/2007/Passport/CrmDiscoveryService.asmx";

            // Retrieve a policy from the Web service.
            RetrievePolicyRequest policyRequest = new RetrievePolicyRequest();
            RetrievePolicyResponse policyResponse =
                (RetrievePolicyResponse)disco.Execute(policyRequest);

            // Retrieve a ticket from the Windows Live (Passport) service.
            LogonManager lm = new LogonManager();
            string passportTicket = lm.Logon(username, password, _partner,
                policyResponse.Policy, _environment);
            // Dispose of the LogonManager object to avoid a FileNotOpen exception.
            lm.Dispose();

            //Retrieve a list of available organizations.
```

16

```
        RetrieveOrganizationsRequest orgRequest =
            new RetrieveOrganizationsRequest();

        orgRequest.PassportTicket = passportTicket;


        RetrieveOrganizationsResponse orgResponse =
            (RetrieveOrganizationsResponse)disco.Execute(orgRequest);

        //Find the desired organization.
        foreach (OrganizationDetail orgdetail in
        ➥orgResponse.OrganizationDetails)
        {
            if (String.Compare(orgdetail.OrganizationName, organization,
➥true) == 0)
            {
                //Retrieve the ticket.
                RetrieveCrmTicketRequest ticketRequest =
                    new RetrieveCrmTicketRequest();
                ticketRequest.OrganizationName = organization;
                ticketRequest.PassportTicket = passportTicket;

                RetrieveCrmTicketResponse ticketResponse =
                    (RetrieveCrmTicketResponse)disco.Execute(ticketRequest);

                //Create the CrmService Web service proxy.
                CrmAuthenticationToken sdktoken =
                    new CrmAuthenticationToken();
                sdktoken.AuthenticationType = 1; // Use Passport Authentication
                sdktoken.OrganizationName = organization;
                sdktoken.CrmTicket = ticketResponse.CrmTicket;
                crmService.CrmAuthenticationTokenValue = sdktoken;
                return orgdetail.CrmServiceUrl;
            }
        }
        return "";
    }
```

What CRM Is and What Can Be Customized

With this release of Microsoft Dynamics CRM, you can customize almost any entity. When you're considering making customizations to Microsoft Dynamics CRM, generally the work falls into one of the following categories:

- **Reporting**—This includes creating new reports and modifying existing reports.
- **Forms**—Form customization is the most popular kind of customization. It can include adding and removing attributes or sections to forms, as well as modifying

attribute properties (such as changing the business required/recommended options). More advanced form customizations include developing custom applications via IFRAME integration that can work directly with the underlying form.

- **Business automation**—This includes developing workflows to monitor, task, or alert individuals or to change information based on predefined criteria. The capability to develop workflows is one of the most powerful features of Microsoft Dynamics CRM and allows for advanced automation.
- **Display of information**—Developing customized views enables you to display information in a custom manner for Users.
- **Integration with other applications**—The most complicated of customizations, extending functionality of Microsoft Dynamics CRM to integrate with other applications involves a deep understanding of both Microsoft Dynamics CRM and the other application. Some common examples of this include:
    - **Website integration**—You can extend Microsoft Dynamics CRM functionality to a customer website that displays information to your vendors, purchasers, or customers. The Microsoft Dynamics CRM Case functionality is a great example that can benefit your customers by letting them log into your corporate website and create a Case directly from the web page that, once submitted, is assigned to your Case resolution team. Allowing your customers to directly search your approved Knowledge Base articles from your website is another example of this type of functionality.
    - **ERP/Accounting integration**—Because Microsoft Dynamics CRM is not a point-of-sale or accounting system, and is designed to integrate with the ERP/Accounting system of your choice, this is a common customization. This integration can be performed with the use of Microsoft CRM Web Services and the ERP/Accounting system's Web Services (provided that it has Web Services). Alternatively, the ERP/Accounting system could be set up to read batch files created from the Microsoft Dynamics CRM Web Services.
    - **Third-party/ISV integration**—Extending functionality of Microsoft Dynamics CRM has become a model for several companies, and a host of actual products and add-ons interact with Microsoft Dynamics CRM data, business processes, and workflow. For more information about these companies, refer to Chapter 26, "Third-Party Add-On Options."

Interacting with Microsoft Dynamics CRM

When considering how to interact with Microsoft Dynamics CRM, you should consider several things:

- **Security limitations**—This is especially important when you are considering interacting with data across organizations and, to a lesser extent, across business units and User records. The filtered views that are inherent to Microsoft Dynamics CRM help to control a lot of what can be done, but the context of your changes is important.

- **Component development**—Because Microsoft Dynamics CRM can have objects developed and then integrated (such as reports and/or advanced workflows using Visual Studio, for example), you should consider what functionality to extend on the external application versus included/modified CRM forms.
- **Access to CRM forms**—Microsoft Dynamics CRM forms are URL-based, which means that you have direct access to the forms via a direct URL, as well as to the form with record data on it if you include the GUID of the record. This type of access is referred to as URL addressable. Table 16.1 illustrates the default URLs for several entities:

TABLE 16.1 Default URLs for Entities

Entity	**URL**
Account	http://<servername>/<organization>/SFA/accts/edit.aspx
Contact	http://<servername>/<organization>/SFA/conts/edit.aspx
Opportunity	http://<servername>/<organization>/SFA/opps/edit.aspx
Case	http://<servername>/<organization>/CS/cases/edit.aspx
Product	http://<servername>/<organization>/Products/product/edit.aspx
E-mail	http://<servername>/<organization>/Activities/email/edit.aspx
Task	http://<servername>/<organization>/Activities/task/edit.aspx
Campaigns	http://<servername>/<organization>/MA/camps/edit.aspx
Custom	http://<servername>/<organization>/UserDefined/edit.aspx?etc=<entity_code>

To open any blank form, select the entity and enter the URL. If you want to open the form with record data, include the GUID after the `?ID=` query string. For example, if you wanted to open the Contact form for a Contact with the object ID of `32026626-1CA4-DC11-BFF0-0030485C8E55`, you would enter the URL http://<servername>/<organization>/SFA/conts/edit.aspx?ID={32026626-1CA4-DC11-BFF0-0030485C8E55}.

Figure 16.3 illustrates the blank form with the URL of http://<servername>/<organization>/SFA/conts/edit.aspx entered.

Figure 16.4 illustrates the same form, but with the previous GUID entered into the URL as follows: http://<servername>/<organization>/SFA/conts/edit.aspx?ID={32026626-1CA4-DC11-BFF0-0030485C8E55}. As you can see, all the fields are populated with the Contact's detail information.

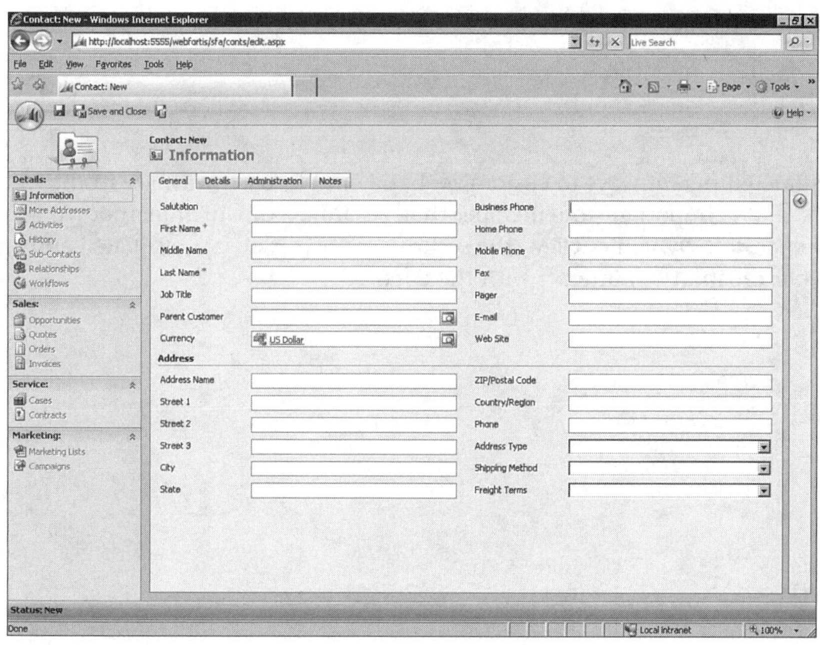

FIGURE 16.3 Blank Contact form.

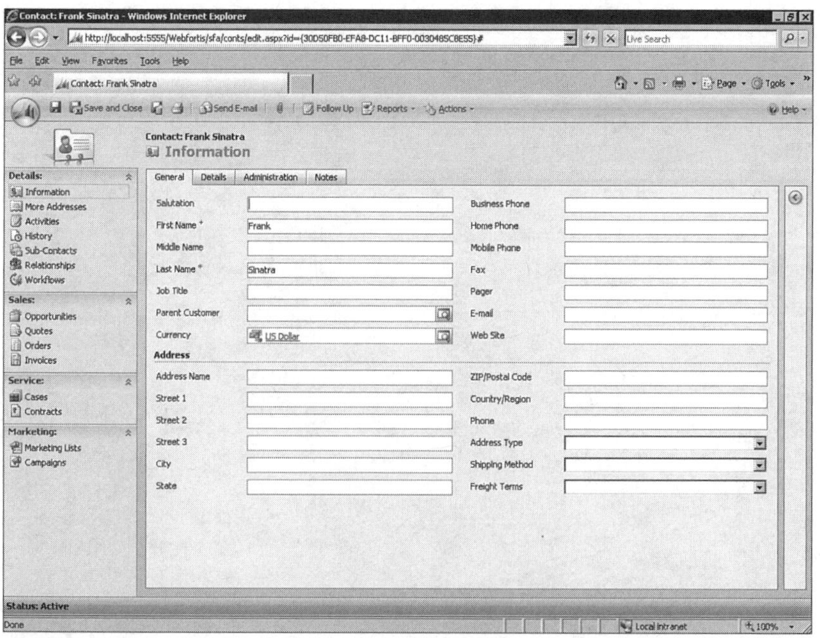

FIGURE 16.4 Populated Contact form.

Both of these forms were called directly from a web page, without first navigating to CRM.

Summary

This chapter illustrated different ways to customize, build, and interact with Microsoft Dynamics CRM data. It is important to remember that, regardless of which method you use to work with Microsoft Dynamics CRM, the security context is always evaluated and could influence your capability to interact with the data.

CHAPTER 17

Forms Authentication

IN THIS CHAPTER

- ▶ IFD Defined
- ▶ Forms Authentication
- ▶ Configuring IFD
- ▶ IFD Tool
- ▶ IFD Updates
- ▶ Working with IFD and Multiple Organizations

IFD Defined

Internet Facing Deployment (IFD) is a feature that enables Users to log on to Microsoft Dynamics CRM with a type of authentication known as Forms authentication. Forms authentication is a method of authentication that prompts Users with a web page interface instead of Integrated Windows Authentication. The default installation for Microsoft Dynamics CRM is Integrated Windows Authentication.

The advantage of Integrated Windows Authentication is that it is transparent for Users who access the Microsoft Dynamics CRM server from computers that belong to the domain. These computers do not require User information such as name and password to be entered because they are already authenticated by Active Directory when Users initially log on. If you access the Microsoft Dynamics CRM server from a computer that doesn't belong to the domain, you get the Windows authentication dialog box (see Figure 17.1).

TIP

The automated login for users that belong to the same domain happens because of a default setting in the Internet Explorer browser. If you want to use a different user, you should change this setting by going to the Tools menu of IE and selecting Internet Options. Move to the Security Tab, select the Local Intranet icon, and click Custom Level. Move to the last options and select Prompt for username and password, as shown in Figure 17.2. Click OK to close the dialog boxes.

FIGURE 17.1 Windows authentication dialog box.

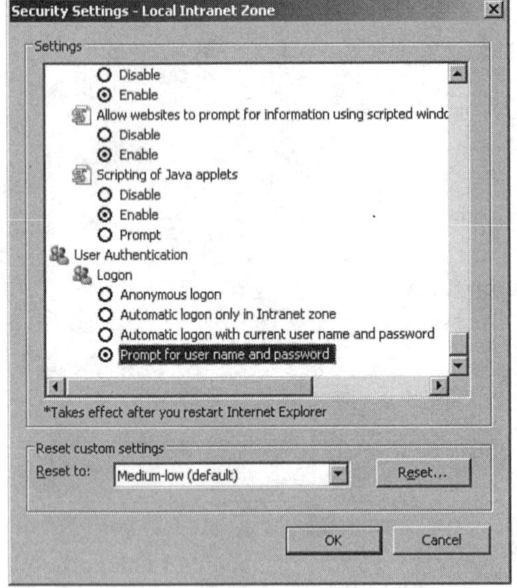

FIGURE 17.2 Changing automated Windows authentication to prompt the username and password.

If you want to access your CRM Server from the Internet or from computers that are outside the network using Forms authentication, you must implement the IFD feature.

Although IFD is intended to be used by Microsoft Dynamics CRM–hosted service providers to give their Users a customized login page, you can enable IFD for your own organization with an On-Premise installation if you want. On the other hand, CRM Online uses another type of authentication based on Passport authentication (see Figure 17.3).

When Microsoft Dynamics CRM is installed using the setup wizard, you cannot enable IFD using the setup wizard. Instead, you must manually configure IFD, as described in the next section.

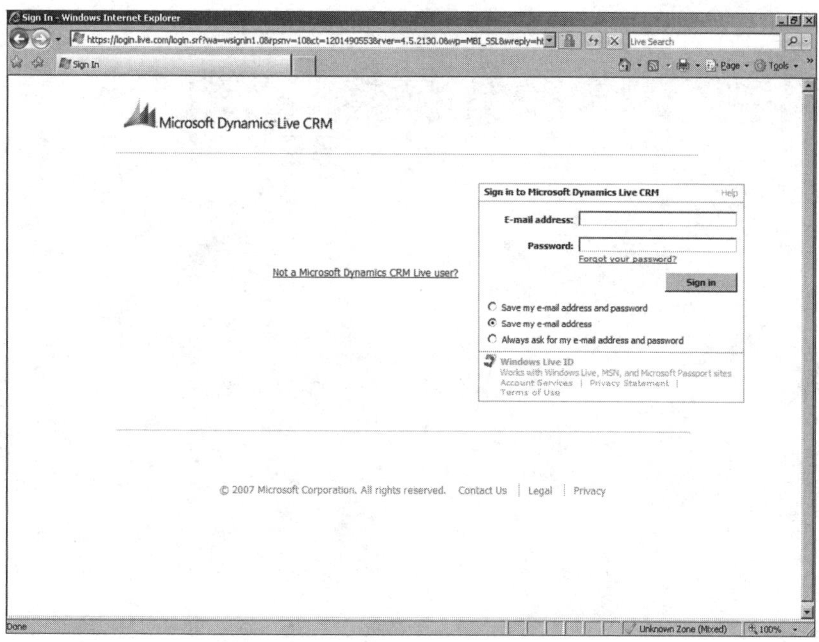

FIGURE 17.3 CRM Online with Passport authentication.

Forms Authentication

IFD comes with another type of authentication, called ServiceProviderLicenseAgreement, that uses Forms authentication. With this method, the User enters credentials (username and password) inside a form of a page instead of using the Windows authentication dialog box.

Figure 17.4 shows what happens when the User types the Microsoft Dynamics URL for an organization with IFD enabled in the browser.

Forms authentication sends the username and password in clear text by making a `POST` method of HTTP, so you should use SSL to protect this sensitive data, if desired.

Another configuration needed by Forms authentication is that you must set anonymous access in the Internet Information Services configuration. To check that, follow these steps:

1. Open the IIS manager application by clicking the Start window button in the taskbar and then selecting Administrative Tools, Internet Information Services (IIS) Manager (see Figure 17.5).

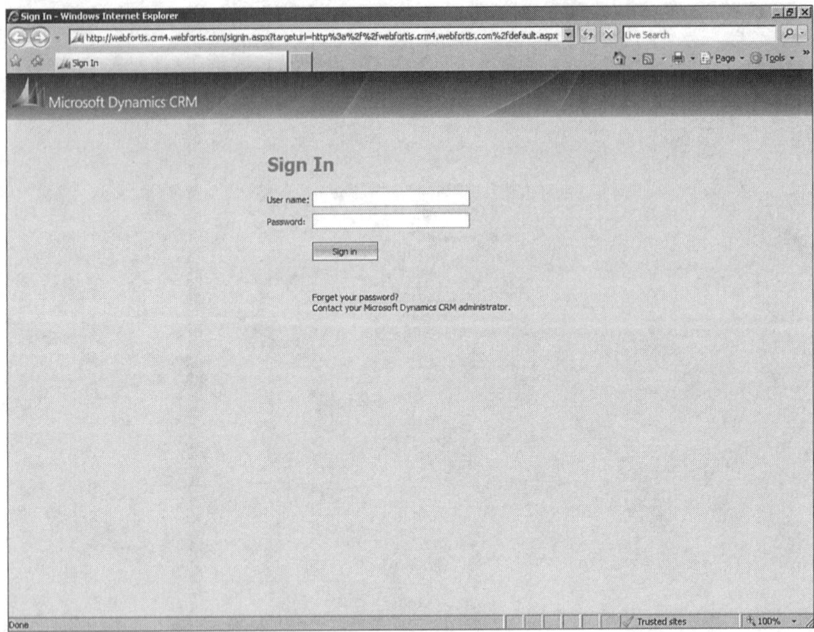

FIGURE 17.4 IFD with Forms authentication.

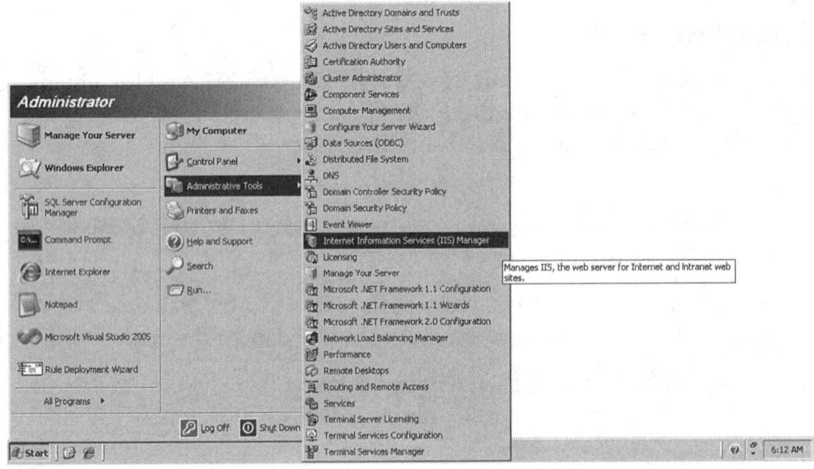

FIGURE 17.5 Opening the IIS Manager application.

2. Expand your server name node and then expand the websites; position the mouse on the link for the Microsoft Dynamics CRM website (see Figure 17.6).

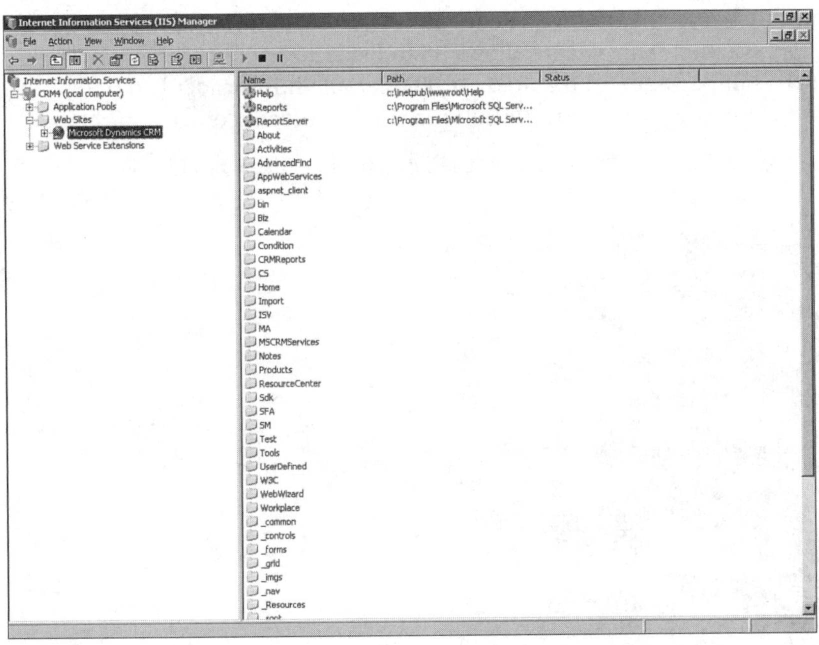

FIGURE 17.6 Microsoft Dynamics CRM website.

3. Right-click this site and select the Properties menu option. You will see the dialog box shown in Figure 17.7.

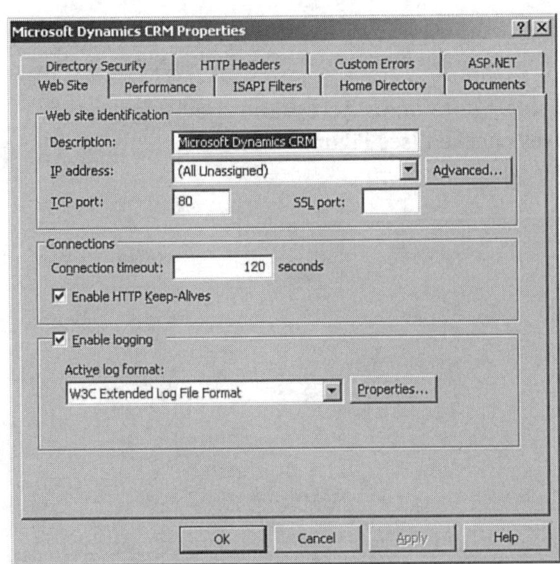

FIGURE 17.7 Microsoft Dynamics CRM website.

It is important to verify that the website identification section IP Address has a value of All Unassigned. This setting allows IIS to listen to requests for any host header, which is important and required for IFD. Sample host header URLs are http://crm4.webfortis.com and http://webfortis.crm4.webfortis.com.

4. Validate the security settings by selecting the Directory Security tab (see Figure 17.8).

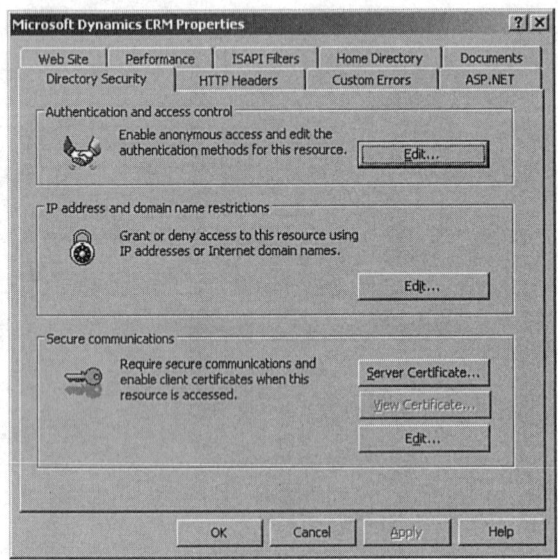

FIGURE 17.8 Directory Security tab.

5. Click the Edit button under the Authentication and Access Control area.

   It is important to have both the Enable Anonymous Access and the Integrated Windows Authentication check boxes checked (see Figure 17.9).

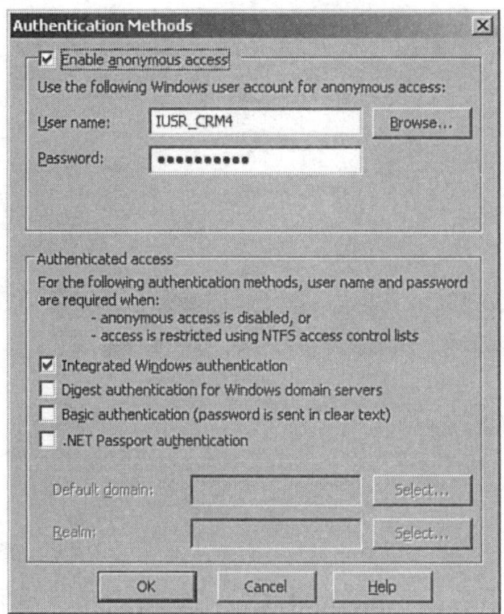

FIGURE 17.9 Authentication methods.

Configuring IFD

Before installing Microsoft Dynamics CRM, you must install it using a configuration file to enable IFD. The Microsoft Dynamics CRM setup file (`setupserver.exe`) accepts parameters that specify a configuration file to load.

You must still satisfy the requirements for an On-Premise installation of Microsoft Dynamics CRM (refer to Chapter 4, "Requirements for CRM 4.0," for more information and details on the requirements).

Additionally, you must install at least these components:

- Windows Active Directory
- SQL Server 2005 or SQL Server 2008
- SQL Server 2005 or 2008 Reporting Services
- .NET Framework 2.0 and 3.0
- Microsoft Exchange Server (optional)

NOTE

You can install these components on separate machines, if desired.

Additionally, you must have the following IFD components configured:

- SSL certificate (optional)
- DNS server configurations
- XML setup configuration file

NOTE

IFD can be configured on any of the On-Premise versions: Workgroup, Professional, and Enterprise.

The next sections explain these IFD components.

SSL Certificate

Because IFD uses Forms authentication as its authentication method which results in Users' credentials being posted to the server, you should encrypt the credentials with a Secure Socket Layer (SSL) certificate. SSL encrypts information using 128-bit encryption and is the same level of protection major banking and financial institutions use. SSL uses port 443, so this port must be set to allow traffic in your firewall, provided that you're using SSL.

You can obtain SSL certificates from a number of different certificate-issuing authorities, including www.verisign.com and www.thawte.com. Be sure to get a multiple-domain certificate or an unlimited subdomain (wildcard) certificate because you will need to use the certificate for at least two URL addresses, as explained in the "DNS Server Configurations" section. If you are not ready to get an SSL certificate and you want to try the IFD feature, you can omit the SSL configurations and install the server with `http` only. To do this, you must configure the XML configuration file in the `rootdomainscheme` element, as described later in this chapter. Then you can change the configurations to allow `https` when you get the certificate after installing the CRM Server.

DNS Server Configurations

A very important consideration when implementing IFD is to configure the Domain Name Service (DNS) properly. Setup doesn't do this—and without DNS properly configured, the forms authentication page might not work. The DNS service is used to map a domain name to an IP address. To explain further, domains are mapped to IP addresses—for example, `<www.domain name.com>` equals `123.123.12.3`. You can also add hosts below the domain as `www`, `ftp`, and so on, and map different IP addresses to them. An example of that might be `<ftp.domain name.com>` equals `123.123.12.4`.

You must complete some necessary DNS configurations, and, depending on the DNS server you are using, the configurations could be different.

These configurations are required for every organization you can set up in Microsoft Dynamics CRM. If you are installing the Enterprise version, which supports multitenancy, you must create a host entry in your DNS for each organization.

This is because the IFD uses an URL in this format:

> https://organizationName.CrmServerName.domainName.com.

If your domain name is webfortis.com, your server name is crm4, and your organization name is Webfortis, this URL will be used:

> https://webfortis.crm4.webfortis.com.

If you have another organization with the name Test on the same server, it will be accessed using this URL:

> https://test.crm4.webfortis.com.

You must configure your DNS so that crm4.webfortis.com, webfortis.crm4.webfortis.com, and test.crm4.webfortis.com all point to the same IP address.

TIP

To verify the IP address resolved by DNS from a client computer, you can use the `ping` command from a command prompt window, as shown in Figure 17.10.

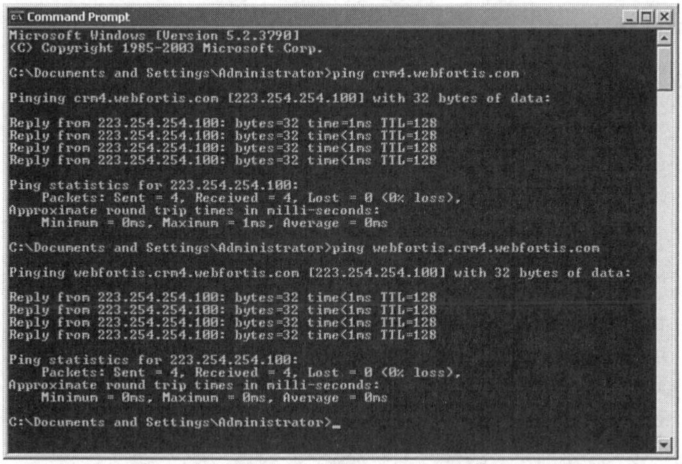

```
Command Prompt
Microsoft Windows [Version 5.2.3790]
(C) Copyright 1985-2003 Microsoft Corp.

C:\Documents and Settings\Administrator>ping crm4.webfortis.com

Pinging crm4.webfortis.com [223.254.254.100] with 32 bytes of data:

Reply from 223.254.254.100: bytes=32 time=1ms TTL=128
Reply from 223.254.254.100: bytes=32 time<1ms TTL=128
Reply from 223.254.254.100: bytes=32 time<1ms TTL=128
Reply from 223.254.254.100: bytes=32 time<1ms TTL=128

Ping statistics for 223.254.254.100:
    Packets: Sent = 4, Received = 4, Lost = 0 (0% loss),
Approximate round trip times in milli-seconds:
    Minimum = 0ms, Maximum = 1ms, Average = 0ms

C:\Documents and Settings\Administrator>ping webfortis.crm4.webfortis.com

Pinging webfortis.crm4.webfortis.com [223.254.254.100] with 32 bytes of data:

Reply from 223.254.254.100: bytes=32 time<1ms TTL=128
Reply from 223.254.254.100: bytes=32 time<1ms TTL=128
Reply from 223.254.254.100: bytes=32 time<1ms TTL=128
Reply from 223.254.254.100: bytes=32 time<1ms TTL=128

Ping statistics for 223.254.254.100:
    Packets: Sent = 4, Received = 4, Lost = 0 (0% loss),
Approximate round trip times in milli-seconds:
    Minimum = 0ms, Maximum = 0ms, Average = 0ms

C:\Documents and Settings\Administrator>_
```

FIGURE 17.10 Verifying hosts with the ping command.

NOTE

If you don't specify the organization name in the URL—for example, http://crm4.webfortis.com—the Microsoft Dynamics CRM server redirects Users to the default organization URL. In our example, this is https://webfortis.crm4.webfortis.com/, assuming that Webfortis is configured as the default organization.

XML Setup Configuration File

For the Microsoft Dynamics CRM to create your server as an IFD server, you must create a configuration file that will be passed as a parameter to the SetupServer.exe application. This configuration file is named `server.xml` and should be located in the same directory where you have the CRM installation files (where SetupServer.exe is located in your hard disk) during server setup.

The necessary settings are explained as follows:

- `LicenseKey`—With this element, you must enter your Microsoft Dynamics CRM license key. Alternatively, you can use the trial license from Microsoft that is available at www.microsoft.com/downloads/details.aspx?familyid=A9C110FD-AAC8-4D2A-B401-7801B1866E82&displaylang=en. The Microsoft Dynamics key is formatted similarly to `XXXXX-XXXXX-XXXXX-XXXXX-XXXXX`.
- `SqlServer`—Enter the SQL Server instance name, using the NetBIOS name. For example, this could be `CRMSQL` if you have SQL Server running on a different server, or `CRM4` if you have SQL server running on the same machine where you will install the CRM server, etc.
- `Reporting`—This value takes the SRS Report server URL address. It is usually http://servername/reportserver or similar. If you have SRS configured with SSL, you must enter the URL with `https` instead of `http` and change the `UseSSL` attribute to `true`.
- `Organization`—Enter the Organization name for your company. This value has a limit of 30 characters.
- `OU`—Enter the Active Directory Organization Unit. The AD OU is usually similar to `DC=WEBFORTIS,DC=COM` for a domain with the name webfortris.com. To find your OU value, you can open the regedit utility on the computer where you have Active Directory installed, and navigate to the key `HKEY_LOCAL_MACHINE\SYSTEM\CurrentControlSet\Services\NTDS\Parameters`.

  Then check the Root Domain parameter (see Figure 17.11).
- `internalnetworkaddress`—This element must have the CRM Server internal IP address followed by the network mask you will use to define your internal network and your external network. For example, if the internal server IP address is 223.254.254.26, the value `223.254.254.26-255.255.255.255` sets up all the other IP as external because the network mask is set to 255.255.255.255.

  With this configuration, all Users will get IFD with Forms authentication, not Windows authentication.

  If you want to treat all IP address as internal so that everybody get Windows authentication, you should use a value such as `223.254.254.26-0.0.0.0`.

  In a common scenario, you would have this value set similarly to `223.254.254.26-255.255.255.0`.

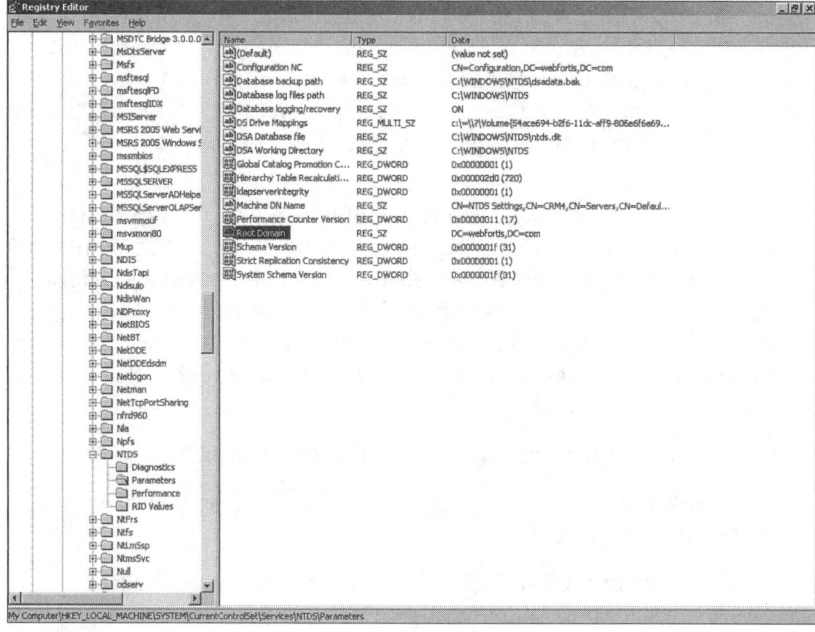

FIGURE 17.11 Finding the OU in the Registry.

This example treats any IP address in the range of `223.254.254.1` to `255` as internal and uses Windows authentication security integrated, not IFD. All the other IP addresses outside that range will use IFD Forms authentication.

- `rootdomainscheme`—This element specifies whether you will use `http` or `https`. As we explained previously, we recommend using `https` here.
- `sdkrootdomain`—For this element, you must have the fully qualified domain (FQDN) of your Microsoft Dynamics CRM server. For example, crm4.webfortis.com will be the URL to be used by the SDK.
- `webapplicationrootdomain`—This element requires a parameter similar to the one we just used in `sdkrootdomain`. This will be the URL that the web clients and Outlook clients will access.

17

TIP

If you don't want to use a long URL, you can just avoid using the server name in the `sdkrootdomain` and `webapplicationrootdomain` parameters and enter only the domain name there. For example, if you use webfortis.com, Users would access the CRM by going to http://webfortis.webfortis.com and http://test.webfortis.com instead of http://webfortis.crmserver.webfortis.com and http://test.crmserver.webfortis.com. This is mostly intended for use by domains with names such as crmhosted.com or mscrmsolutions.com, so the final URL for the organization will make more sense, as in http://webfortis.mscrmsolutions.com.

- `IncomingExchangeServer`—This optional value is the Exchange server name using the NetBIOS name—`EXCHSRV`, for example. This element is optional because Microsoft Dynamics CRM doesn't require Microsoft Exchange server, and you can use any POP3-compatible server to process the incoming e-mails. Refer to Chapter 15, "E-mail Configuration," for more details about e-mail server configurations.

Apart from the elements described previously, you can configure a few other optional elements. We have detailed only the minimum required elements that must be configured for an IFD installation. For a complete list of all the elements you can configure, refer to the `crm40sp deployment.pdf` document that is part of the Microsoft Dynamics CRM 4.0: Planning and Deployment Guidance for Service Providers, which you can download from www.microsoft.com/downloads/details.aspx?FamilyID=6e211231-30fe-4df2-9b81-15cfb87adcf1&DisplayLang=en.

To install Microsoft Dynamics CRM with this method, follow these steps:

1. Create the XML file with the name `server.xml` on the folder where you have extracted the CRM server setup files.
2. Enter the following content in the `server.xml` file. Be sure to change the text in bold:

```
<?xml version="1.0" encoding="utf-8"?>
<CRMSetup>
    <Server>
        <Patch update="false">\\crm4\share\patchfile.msp</Patch>
        <LicenseKey>XXXXX-XXXXX-XXXXX-XXXXX-XXXXX</LicenseKey>
        <SqlServer>CRM4</SqlServer>
        <Database create="true"/>
        <Reporting UseSSL="false" URL="http://crm4/ReportServer"/>
        <OrganizationCollation>Latin1_General_CI_AI</OrganizationCollation>
        <basecurrency isocurrencycode="USD" currencyname="US Dollar"
          ➥currencysymbol="$" />
        <Organization>Webfortis</Organization>
        <OrganizationUniqueName>Webfortis</OrganizationUniqueName>
        <OU>DC=WEBFORTIS,DC=COM</OU>
        <WebsiteUrl create="false">/LM/W3SVC/1</WebsiteUrl>
        <InstallDir>c:\Program Files\Microsoft CRM4</InstallDir>
        <ifdsettings enabled="true">
            <internalnetworkaddress>223.254.254.26-255.255.255.255
              ➥</internalnetworkaddress>
            <rootdomainscheme>https</rootdomainscheme>
            <sdkrootdomain>CRM4.WEBFORTIS.COM</sdkrootdomain>

<webapplicationrootdomain>CRM4.WEBFORTIS.COM</webapplicationrootdomain>
        </ifdsettings>
        <SQM optin="false"/>
        <Email>
```

```
            <IncomingExchangeServer name="crm4"/>
        </Email>
    </Server>
</CRMSetup>
```

3. Save and close the `server.xml` file.
4. Open a command prompt by going to the Windows Start button and clicking Run.
5. Enter **cmd** and click OK.
6. Move to the folder where you have extracted the CRM Server setup files with the `cd` command. If you have them in `C:\CRM Server 4.0 Setup`, use this command:

```
cd C:\CRM Server 4.0 Setup
```

7. Execute the CRM Server setup application with the following parameters:

```
SetupServer.exe /Q /QR /InstallAlways /L c:\crmlog.log /config server.xml
```

You use the `/Q` parameter here to specify that you'll be performing a quiet installation through a configuration file specified by the `/config` parameter. The `/Q` parameter also requires you to specify the file where the errors will be logged, which you do with the `/L` parameter. Finally, you can use the `/QR` switch to see the progress bars when setup is being executing.

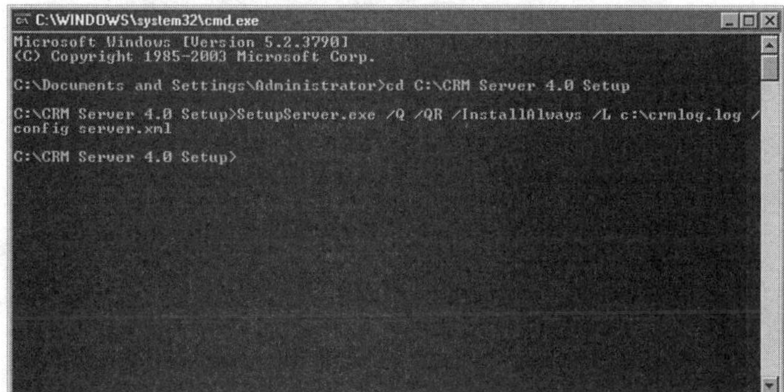

FIGURE 17.12 Installing Microsoft Dynamics CRM Server with IFD.

8. Notice that setup returns to the command prompt, but it runs in background. You will see the progress of setup, as shown in Figure 17.13.

NOTE

If you don't see the Microsoft Dynamics CRM server start to install, there might be an error. You can check the error file located at `C:\crmlog.log` with any text editor, such as Notepad, to review any errors that might exist.

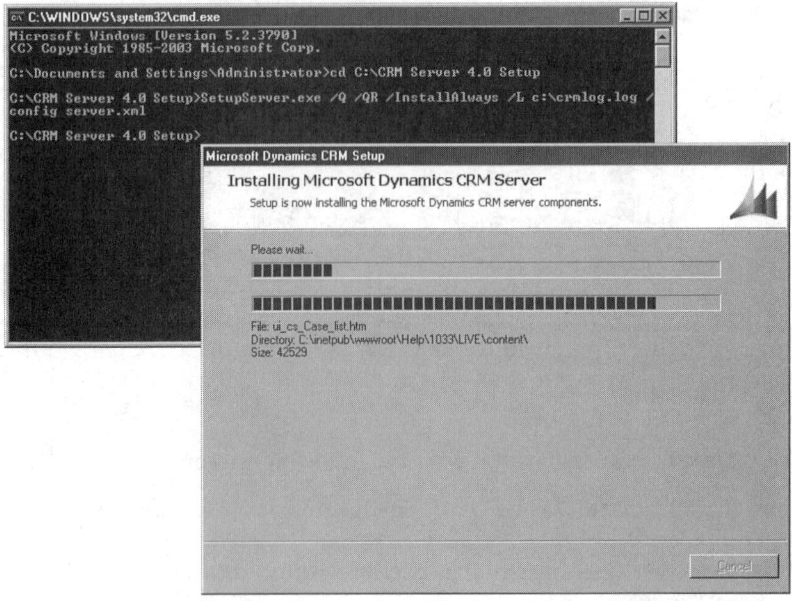

FIGURE 17.13 Installing Microsoft Dynamics CRM Server progress screen.

Setup takes several minutes to complete. When setup finishes, you see the screen shown in Figure 17.14, and you have to restart the computer.

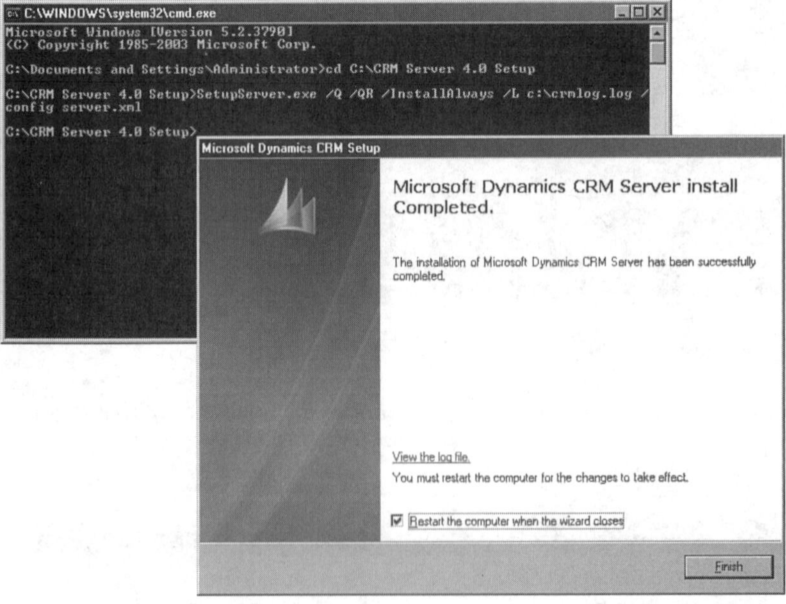

FIGURE 17.14 Microsoft Dynamics CRM Server installation completed.

NOTE

After installing Dynamics CRM with IFD enabled, you must install the SRS data connector to have the Reports work. The connector installation is not required if you don't have IFD enabled because it is not necessary on non-IFD installations. Chapter 5, "Setting Up CRM 4.0," explains the SRS Data connector setup.

IFD Tool

Microsoft has indicated that the release of a specific application called the IFD Tool may be made available in the future. This tool would be used to easily enable IFD features after installing Dynamics CRM using the setup wizard. This tool was unavailable at press time and, therefore, we haven't included it in this book.

IFD Updates

Switching Between `http` and `https`

After you have installed the Microsoft Dynamics CRM server with IFD using the XML configuration file explained previously, you can enable `https` or `http` using the deployment configuration tool. You can download this tool from www.microsoft.com/downloads/details.aspx?FamilyID=6e211231-30fe-4df2-9b81-15cfb87adcf1&DisplayLang=en.

This tool comes in two versions, one for 32 bits and another for 64 bits. When you download the executable file from the link, it extracts the tool `microsoft.crm.deploymentconfigtool.exe`.

17

Follow these steps to enable IFD on a current CRM installation:

1. Open a command prompt by going to the Windows Start button and clicking Run.
2. Enter **`cmd`** and click OK.
3. Using the `cd` command, move to the folder where you extracted the IFD tool. If you have them in `c:\IFD tool`, use this command:

   ```
   cd C:\IFD tool
   ```

4. Execute the `microsoft.crm.deploymentconfigtool.exe` console application with the following parameters (see Figure 17.15):

   ```
   microsoft.crm.deploymentconfigtool.exe ifdsettings
   ➥update -rootdomainscheme:https -sdkrootdomain:crm4.webfortis.com
   ➥-webapprootdomain:crm4.webfortis.com
   ```

NOTE

The parameters of this tool are similar to the elements used in the configuration file, described previously in this chapter.

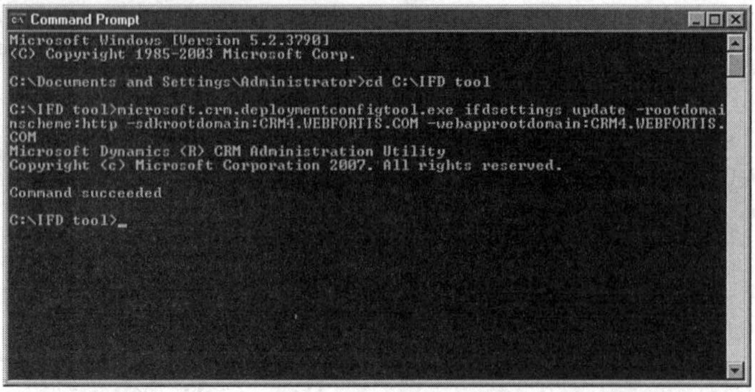

```
Command Prompt
Microsoft Windows [Version 5.2.3790]
(C) Copyright 1985-2003 Microsoft Corp.

C:\Documents and Settings\Administrator>cd C:\IFD tool

C:\IFD tool>microsoft.crm.deploymentconfigtool.exe ifdsettings update -rootdomai
nscheme:http -sdkrootdomain:CRM4.WEBFORTIS.COM -webapprootdomain:CRM4.WEBFORTIS.
COM
Microsoft Dynamics (R) CRM Administration Utility
Copyright (c) Microsoft Corporation 2007. All rights reserved.

Command succeeded

C:\IFD tool>_
```

FIGURE 17.15 Switching between `http` and `https`.

You can also use this tool to change the SDK root domain name, as well as the web application root domain name, if required.

Changing the External Address Scope

If you want to change the external address scope, or change the addresses that will receive IFD Forms authentication and determine which addresses will receive Windows authentication, you can do this. First update the `IfdInternalNetworkAddress` key in the Registry by using `regedit` at any time. You don't need to restart the server, and the CRM server automatically updates the change.

NOTE

Before you make *any* change to your Registry, be sure to make a backup of your complete registry. Incorrect registry changes can result in system instability or corruption.

Open the Registry editor by going to Start, Run, and enter **`Regedit`**. Navigate to the key `My Computer\HKEY_LOCAL_MACHINE\SOFTWARE\Microsoft\MSCRM`.

Find the key with the name `IfdInternalNetworkAddress` and enter the server local IP address followed by a `-` character and the network mask you want to allow access to.

For example, the value `223.254.254.26-255.255.255.255` will set Forms authentication for all addresses.

If you want to use Windows authentication access only for external addresses, you should use the setting (see Figure 17.16) 223.254.254.26-0.0.0.0.

To change the key value, double-click the `IfdInternalNetworkAddress` key and set the new value in the dialog box that appears (see Figure 17.17).

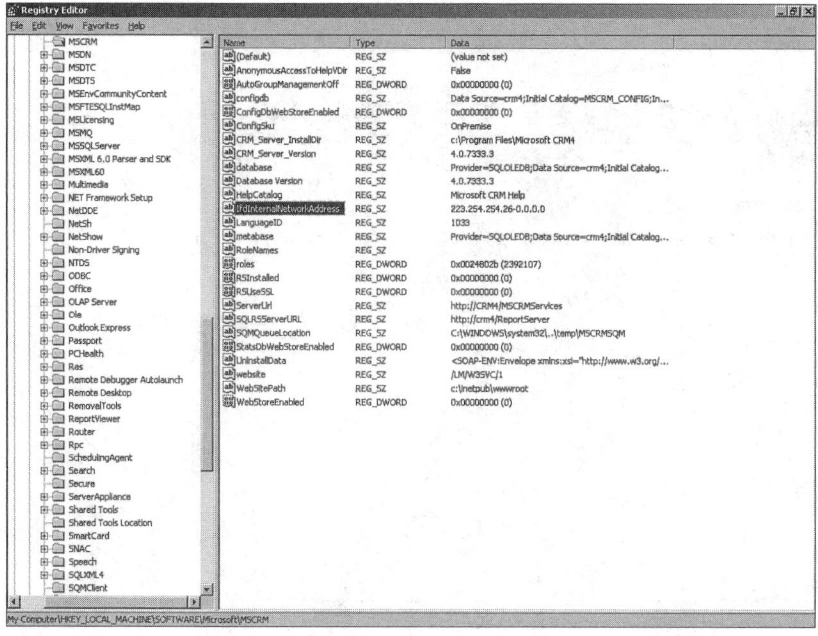

FIGURE 17.16 Configuring IFD external access with Regedit.

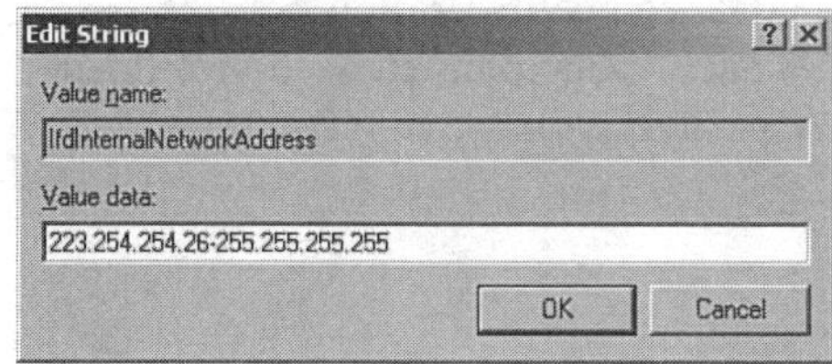

FIGURE 17.17 Changing IFD external access.

17

Working with IFD and Multiple Organizations

Only the Enterprise version of Microsoft Dynamics CRM supports multitenancy, or multiple organizations. Because of this, this is the version that service providers use. Users will be able to access each CRM organization's website via a unique URL.

For example, an organization with the name Brown would be able to access Microsoft Dynamics CRM at https://brown.crm4.webfortis.com, and the organization Webfortis would be able to access https://webfortis.crm4.webfortis.com from the same server.

The CRM web application is the same with or without IFD enabled. The only exception is that the User will see a Sign Out link below the organization name when IFD is enabled (see Figure 17.18).

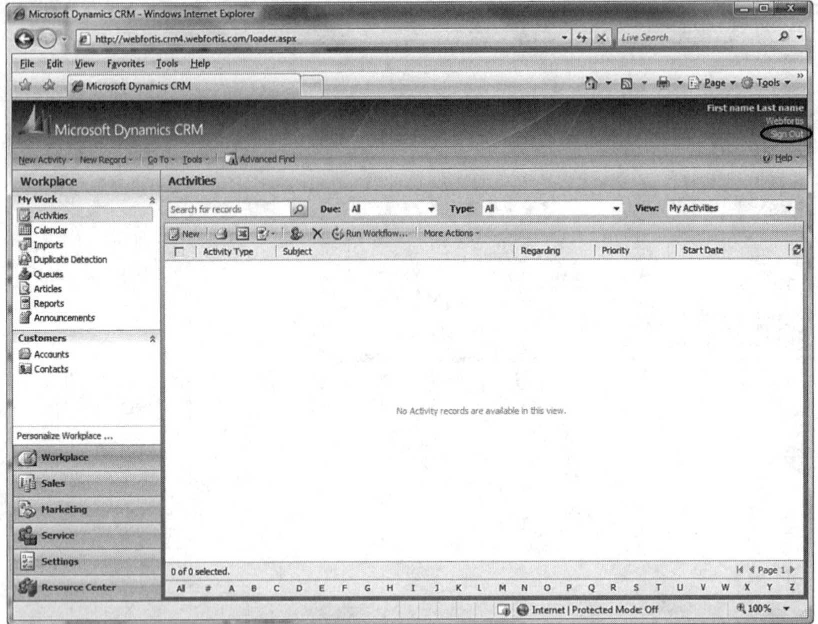

FIGURE 17.18 Sign Out link on IFD.

For more information about working with IFD and advanced configuration options, download the Microsoft Dynamics CRM 4.0 Internet Facing Deployment Scenarios document from www.microsoft.com/downloads/details.aspx?familyid=3861E56D-B5ED-4F7F-B2FD-5A53BC71DAFC&displaylang=en.

Summary

This chapter showed you how to expose a Dynamics CRM Server to the Internet by installing the IFD feature so that Users can authenticate via Forms authentication over the Internet. We reviewed all the required configurations necessary to set up this feature, as well as how to enable the IFD on a fresh Dynamics CRM installation.

CHAPTER 18

Advanced Reporting

IN THIS CHAPTER

Introduction to SRS

SRS, or Microsoft SQL Reporting Services, is a client/server reporting platform that is installed within Microsoft SQL Server. It is based on the Service Oriented Architecture (SOA), so it can be used as a service. SRS was introduced within Microsoft Dynamics CRM 3.0 using Microsoft SQL Server 2000 (previously, CRM used Crystal Reporting). Microsoft Dynamics CRM 4.0 uses SQL Server 2005 or SQL Server 2008 and either version of SRS.

NOTE

At press time, Microsoft SQL Server 2008 was still in beta and exact specifications related to Microsoft SQL Server 2008 were unavailable. The specifications provided here apply to Microsoft SQL Server 2005.

SRS consists of the following components:

- **Report Manager**—This is a web application that acts as a User interface application to manage and deploy the reports in the platform, as well as to manage the security access of each report. It is usually located from the server that has SRS loaded at via http://localhost/reports.
- **Report Server**—This is a service that provides a common interface and entry point for all applications (including the Report Manager mentioned previously, as well as Microsoft Dynamics CRM) to interact with the Report Server. It is usually located from the server that has SRS loaded via http://localhost/reportsserver

- **Report Database**—SRS uses a database stored in SQL Server as the repository of the deployed reports. It usually has the name of ReportServer.
- **SQL Reporting Services** (using the Microsoft SQL Server instance name)—This is a Windows service that is responsible for processing related functions, such as report scheduling.
- **Other components**—Configuration Tools, Visual Studio 2005 projects templates for reports authoring, .NET controls to render and display the reports in Windows, and custom web applications and API documentation for extensibility and development.

Separate from these components, SRS has the following features:

- Support for report snapshot creation.
- Support for scheduling of automated snapshot reports.
- Alerts so you can be notified via e-mail when a report is created.
- Capability for all reports to be exported in the following formats:
  - Microsoft Excel
  - Acrobat PDF
  - Web archive
  - TIFF images
  - CSV (comma delimited)
- Capability to build reports with the open standard Report Definition Language (RDL), which is based on XML standards. Reports then can be built not only with Visual Studio, but also with other third-party tools.
- Capability for each report to manage different data sources. This means that it is not necessarily tied to Microsoft SQL Server data. Reports can show data from any .NET-compatible data provider or from any OLEDB data provider.
- Capability to display data in either tabular, matrix, or graphical forms, as well as using expressions to format the data properly.

Microsoft Dynamics CRM handles all the reports through this system and takes advantage of all its benefits.

NOTE

CRM Online users' ability to fully interact with SRS is limited because Microsoft controls it.

SRS is a very complex platform, and the scope of detailing every aspect of SRS exceeds this publication. We recommend reviewing the online Microsoft SQL Server books for more detailed information about this product if required. To understand this chapter, you need only a basic understanding of SRS and SQL.

NOTE

Previous versions of Microsoft Dynamics CRM had a common problem with CRM and SRS communication, referred to as the double-hop Kerberos authentication, when both were installed on different servers causing authentication errors when trying to run and see reports from the CRM Web Application interface. Fortunately, this problem has been resolved in CRM 4.0 with an additional component called the SRS Data Connector, which must be installed separately on the CRM Server. (Refer to Chapter 5, "Setting up CRM 4.0," for detailed instructions about its setup.)

SRS controls are great to build reports with, but they do have some drawbacks. One of the most important is their inability to display HTML data properly. If you try to show data that was stored in HTML format, all formatting will be lost, and the HTML will be displayed with HTML tags. The only way we've found to deal with this issue has been to create a function in SQL to clean the HTML tags so the text can be easily read; however, all formatting is lost. This is an issue that Microsoft doesn't seem to have in its plans to fix with the next version of SQL (SQL Server 2008).

Custom Reports

Custom reports are reports written with an external tool such as Visual Studio 2005. As you learned in Chapter 13, "Reporting," you can easily build new basic custom reports with the Report Wizard in Microsoft Dynamics CRM; however, reports created are not so flexible. In some cases, you need to write more complex reports and have a more flexible page layout and design. With those cases, you need to use a tool such as Visual Studio to create and build your custom reports.

When Are Custom Reports Recommended?

Users can need custom reports for a variety of reasons. Some of these reasons are as follows:

- Special or custom designs such as those that have complex layouts that can't be done with the Report Wizard.
- When you need to have a report with mixed data from data sources other than Microsoft CRM. For example, you might control the inventory counts of your products on a separated system that uses an Oracle database, and you want to have one report that shows the CRM orders with their product details from Oracle and their inventory counts.

You can build custom reports with SRS or with any other report application, such as Crystal Reports, or even with a custom application built in ASP.NET. The scope and range of all the applications that can be used to build custom reports exceed the scope of this book.

Building Custom Reports with SRS

When you install Microsoft SQL Server 2005 Reporting Services tools, it installs Visual Studio 2005 and project templates that you can use to build SRS reports. You can find these project templates under the Business Intelligence Projects group (see Figure 18.1).

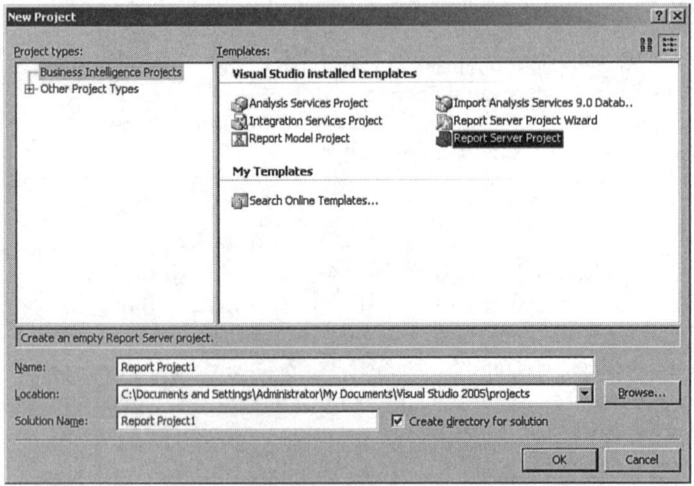

FIGURE 18.1 Business Intelligence Projects group in Visual Studio 2005.

NOTE

Notice that if you don't have Visual Studio installed, the SQL Server 2005 Setup will install a limited version of Visual Studio that can only be used to build Reports and use Business Intelligence projects; however, you won't be able to create Windows Forms applications or custom websites with this version.

The Microsoft Dynamics CRM SDK comes with very detailed documentation about custom reports development (refer to the Reporting Writers Guide in the SDK).

Even though you can create a new report in Visual Studio 2005 from scratch, we recommend using one of the existing reports that are preinstalled within CRM as a template. To do so, follow these steps:

1. Go to the Workplace and then click on Reports.
2. Select the report you want to use as a template. Generally, you want to select a report that is similar to the one you want to create. For example, if you want to create a custom sales report, select one of the existing sales reports. Click the Edit Report button.
3. Select the Actions menu from the top menu and select Download Report. For this example, use the Account Distribution report.

4. Save the report on your local machine.
5. Rename the file with the new name of the report you want to build. In this example, rename the report to `Contacts Report.rdl`.
6. Start Visual Studio 2005 from the Start Windows button. Then select All Programs, Microsoft Visual Studio 2005, Microsoft Visual Studio 2005.
7. Go to the File menu and select New, Project.
8. Click on Business Intelligence Projects in the project templates area and select the Report Server Project template.
9. In the solution explorer, right-click on the Reports folder and click on Add Existing Item.
10. Navigate to the folder where you stored the `Contacts Report.rdl` report in step 5, and click on the Add button.

Developing and Testing Reports in Visual Studio

After you create your report project and add the report in Visual Studio, as explained previously, you are ready to start modifying the report. To test the report quickly, you must fix the datasets connection strings to point to your CRM Server database. To do so, follow these steps:

1. Open the report you want to edit and go to the Data section of it by clicking the Data tab. You will see the error shown on Figure 18.2. This happens because, by default, the reports are defined to use another database that is replaced by the CRM when the reports are deployed.

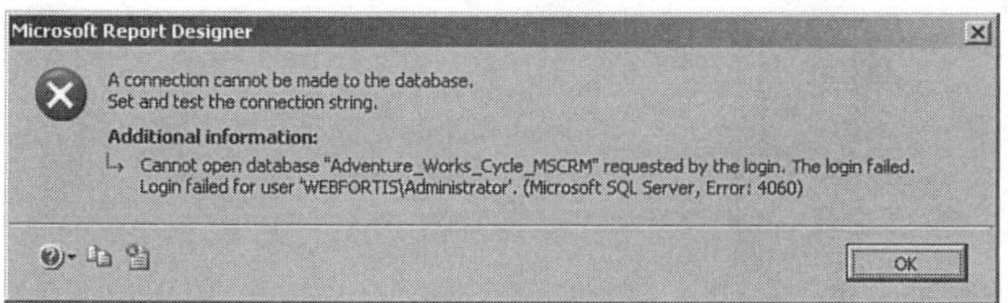

FIGURE 18.2 Creating a new shared data source.

2. Click the ... button near the drop-down menu containing the datasets, shown in Figure 18.3.
3. When the window shown in Figure 18.4 opens, click the ... button near the data source with the name of CRM.

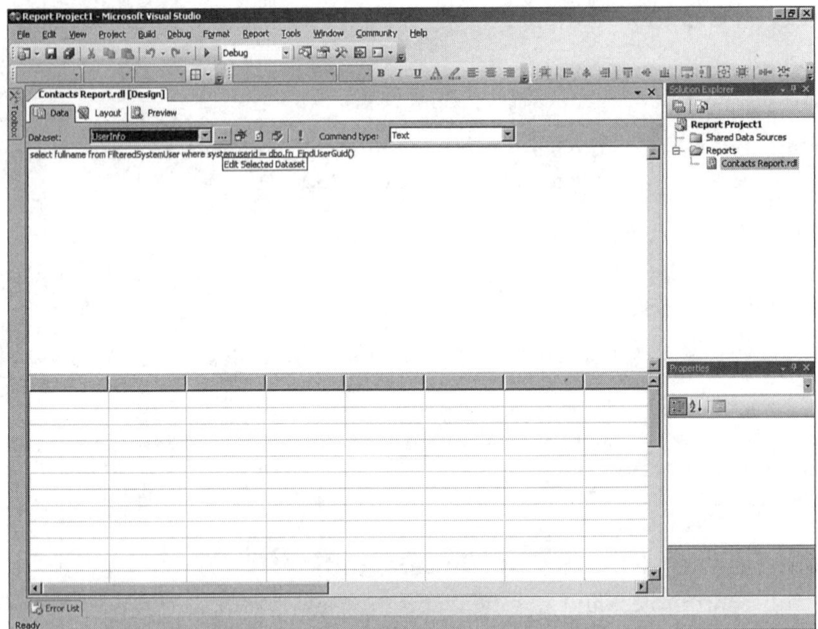

FIGURE 18.3 Editing the selected dataset.

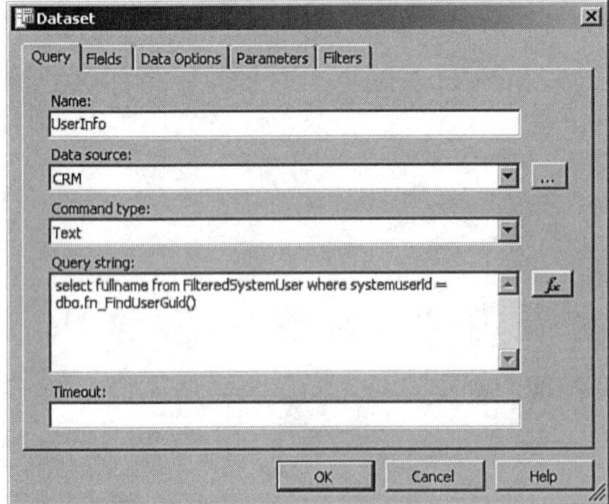

FIGURE 18.4 Modifying the data source.

4. Click the Edit button, near the `Connection String` field (see Figure 18.5).

5. Select your server name in the `Server Name` field and locate the CRM database that has the name of *`OrganizationName`*`_MSCRM` (see Figure 18.6).

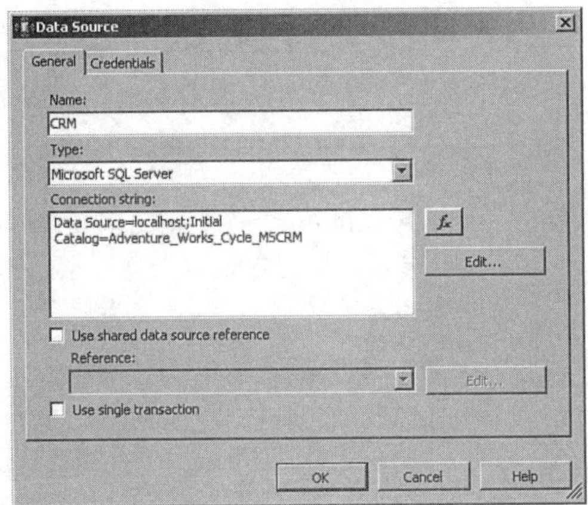

FIGURE 18.5 Creating a connection.

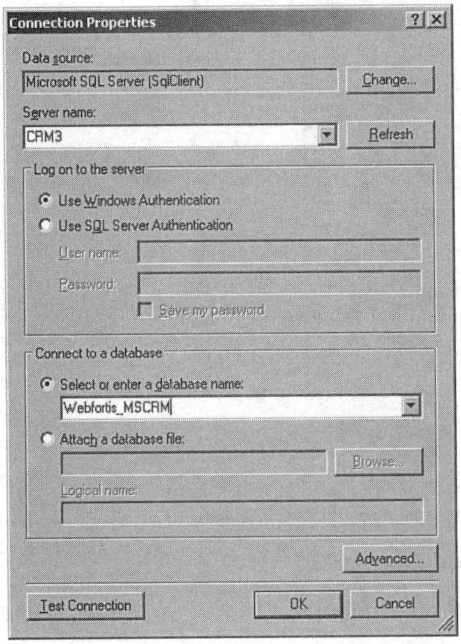

FIGURE 18.6 Configuring the connection.

6. Click the Test Connection button to be sure it connects successfully.
7. Click OK three times to close the dialog box.

TIP

The reports that are running on the SRS server use a shared data source, so you should not deploy this data source.

As shown in Figure 18.7, Microsoft Dynamics CRM has three different types of custom reports.

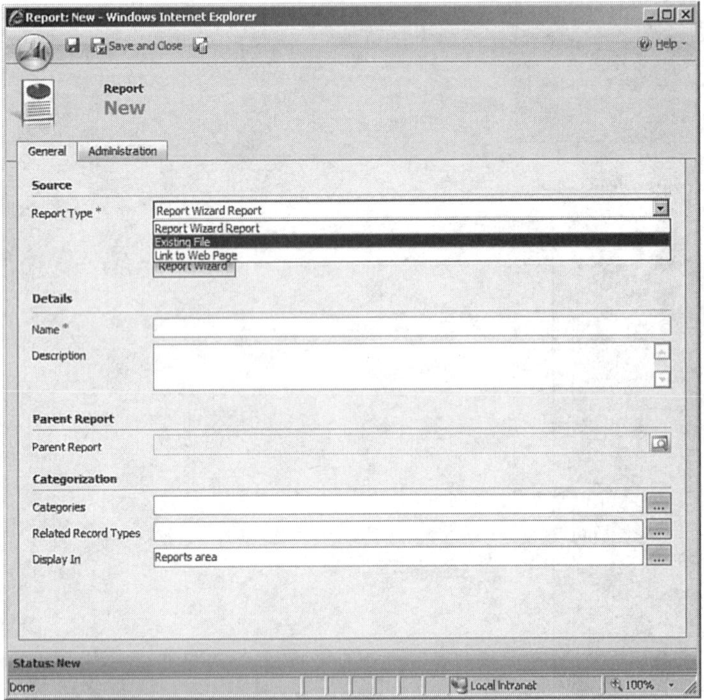

FIGURE 18.7 Custom report types.

- **Report Wizard Report**—Chapter 13 explained this option.
- **Existing File**—This option is described later in this chapter
- **Link to Web Page**—This option is used only to link to an existing web page. It is explained later in this chapter.

When writing custom reports in Visual Studio, remember to take advantage of the benefits of the CRM prefiltering feature. Prefiltering is explained next.

Filtered Views

Although you can build your SQL queries by using the tables directly from the CRM SQL Server dataset, this is not recommended. In the CRM SQL Server tables shown in Figure 18.8, you will notice that the Accounts entity has more than one table. The same is true for the other entities.

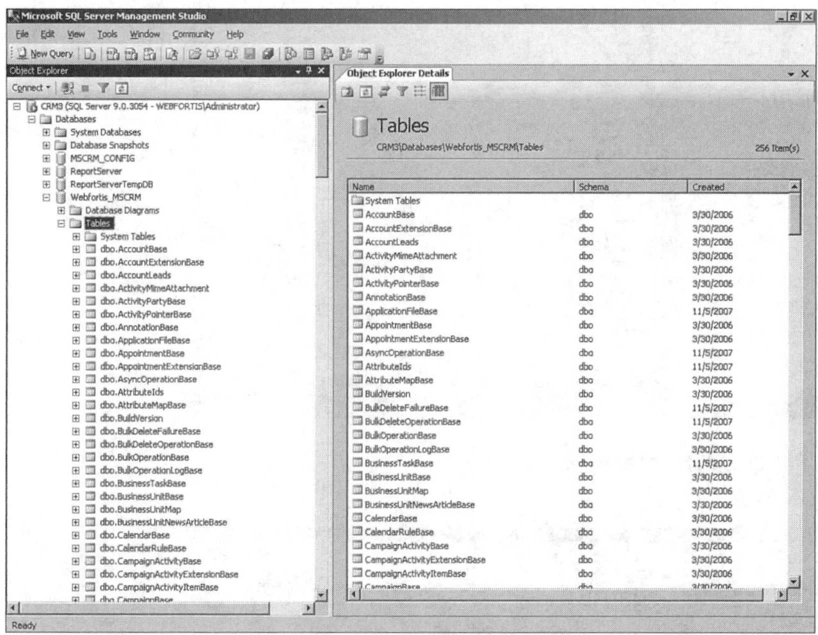

FIGURE 18.8 CRM SQL database tables.

Instead of using these tables for SQL queries, there are predefined views that make life a lot easier: You don't have to spend time trying to understand the complexity of the tables by studying the CRM ERD. The views shown in Figure 18.9 will match the CRM entity diagram by default.

A lot of views have names similar to the CRM entity names. The views you should use with your reports are the ones with the `Filtered` prefix, as shown in Figure 18.10.

If you want to create a report that shows all the Contact names, your underlying query should look similar to this:

```
select fullname from FilteredContact
```

One of the advantages of using these views is that they are updated every time you add a custom attribute to an entity from the CRM customizations interface. Additionally, when a custom entity is created in CRM, it automatically creates a filtered view for the new custom entity. In the previous example, the database view name would be dbo.FilteredContact.

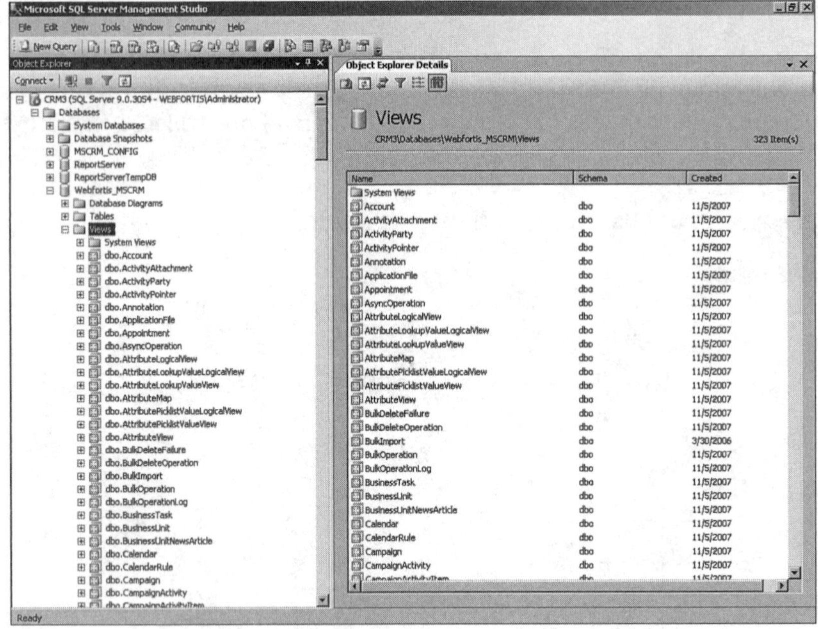

FIGURE 18.9 CRM SQL database views.

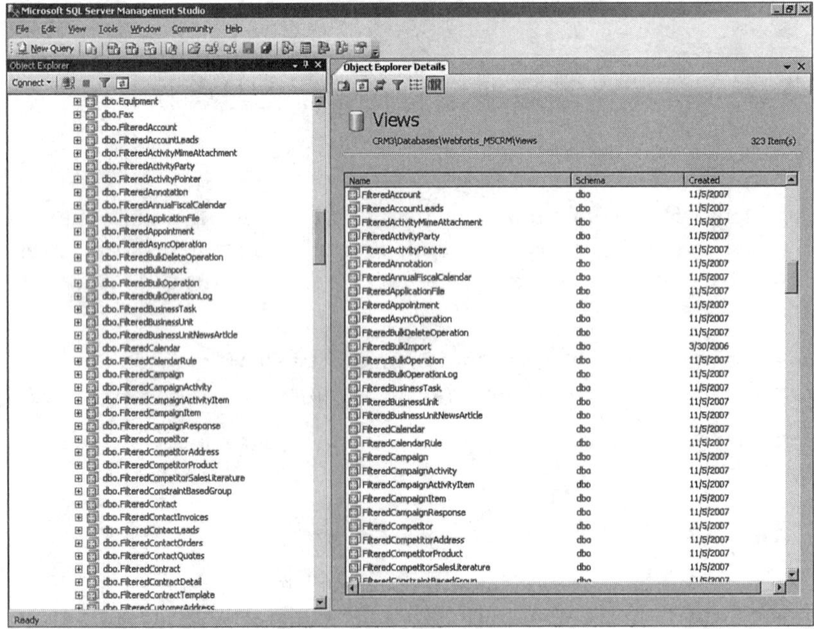

FIGURE 18.10 CRM SQL database filtered views.

Most important, filtered views provide security based on the User record permissions, so they show only the data that the User who is running the report has permissions to see.

NOTE

The custom properties and entities also have the prefix shown in the schema name. By default, this prefix is equal to `New` (but you can change that in System Settings—refer to Chapter 14, "Settings and Configuration"). If you create a custom entity with the name of Event, the filtered view created will be `dbo.FilteredNew_event` by default.

Deployment

To deploy a report in SRS, you normally use the Report Manager web application when not working with CRM. However, you should not use this option when working with custom CRM reports because you won't be able to see the report in CRM if you do.

To deploy a report for CRM, you must use the CRM client interface and follow these steps (notice that you can deploy reports from either the Web or Outlook client interfaces):

1. Go to the Reports area by going to the Workplace and then clicking Reports (as shown in Figure 18.11).

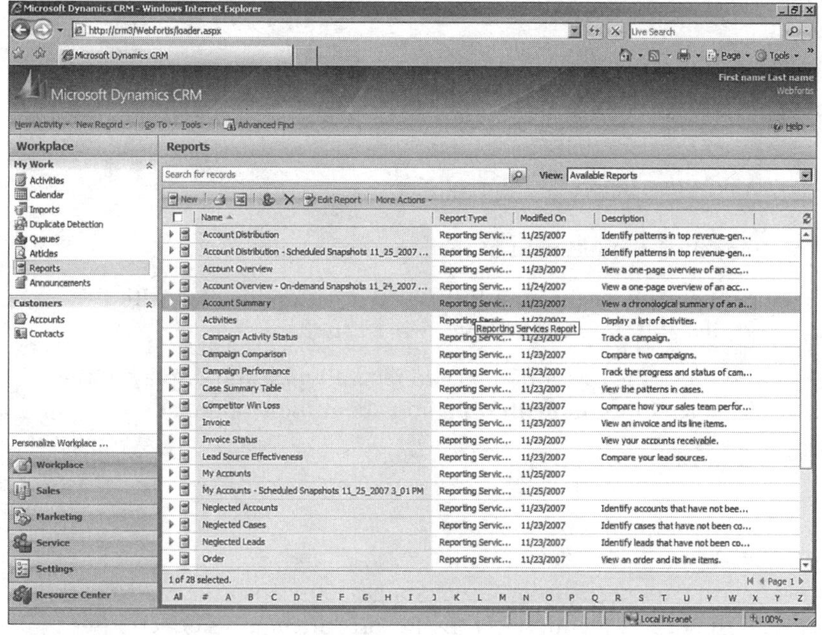

FIGURE 18.11 Reports area.

2. Click the New button.
3. Select Existing File in the Report Type property (see Figure 18.12).

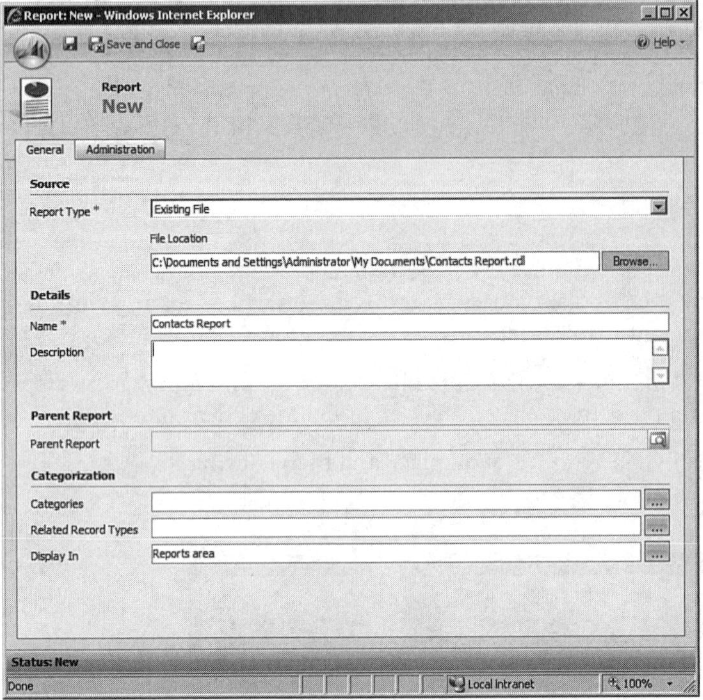

FIGURE 18.12 Deploying a new report.

4. Under File Location, enter the full path of the report you built.
5. Optionally, change the name of the report; this will be autopopulated with the name of the report file, and the two don't need to be the same.
6. Optionally, you can select the categories, related record types, and display in the options (refer to Chapter 13 for more information about these options).
7. Click the Save and Close button on the top menu.

Reports Parameters

To see the predefined report parameters from Visual Studio 2005, open the report you are authoring and, from the Report menu, select the Report Parameters submenu (see Figure 18.13).

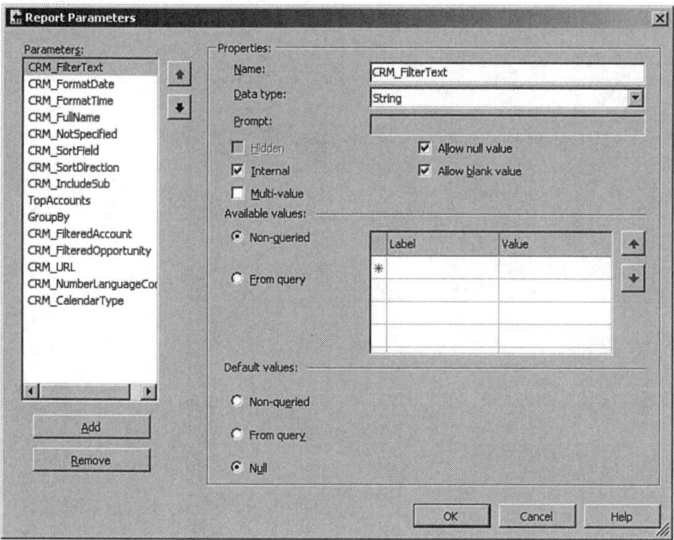

FIGURE 18.13 Report Parameters.

The parameters include the following:

- CRM_FilterText—This parameter is used to display the Filter Summary text box (located in the report header), which display the prefilters selected by the User. Figure 18.14 shows this parameter value as `Accounts: Account Name: Equals Webfortis`.
- CRM_URL—This parameter provides drill-through capabilities on the CRM reports. This supplies quick links to edit the entities instances that you display on your report, for example. Figure 18.15 shows an example of a report that displays the Contacts; it has the Contact names as links so that the User can edit the Contact or see more details by easily clicking the links.

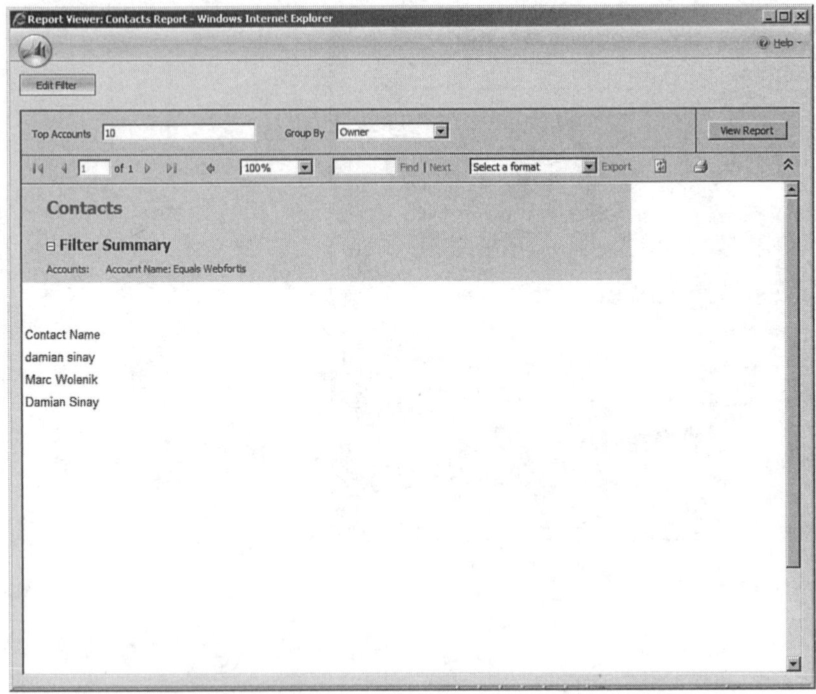

FIGURE 18.14 `CRM_FilterText` parameter.

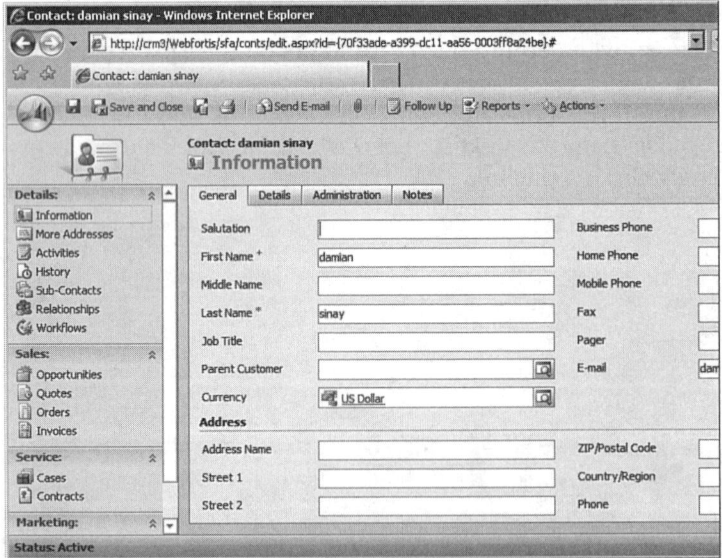

FIGURE 18.15 Drill-through with `CRM_URL` parameter.

- CRM_FilteredEntity—This parameter is used to set up the default prefilters on your reports. You can add as many parameters as you like on the same report; you might have parameters such as CRM_FilteredContact and CRM_FilteredAccount, for example. When you deploy and run your report, you will see the prefilters, as shown in Figure 18.16.

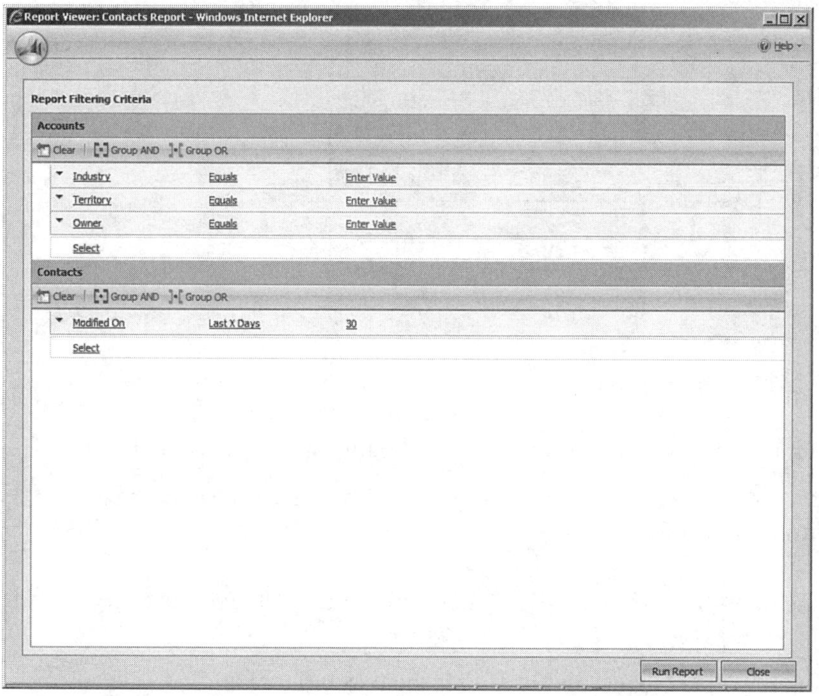

FIGURE 18.16 CRM_FilteredEntity parameters.

NOTE

If you don't have any of these parameters defined, the report will run automatically without having the User select the prefilters. Also, Users won't be able to add prefilters by modifying the default report filters from the CRM reports area through the Web or Outlook client interfaces.

- CRM_Locale—This parameter determines the language of the User running the report. It is useful for multilanguage report implementations. This parameter must have a default value from a query using the fn_GetFormatStrings() function and using the NumberLanguageCode for the Value field, as shown in Figure 18.17.

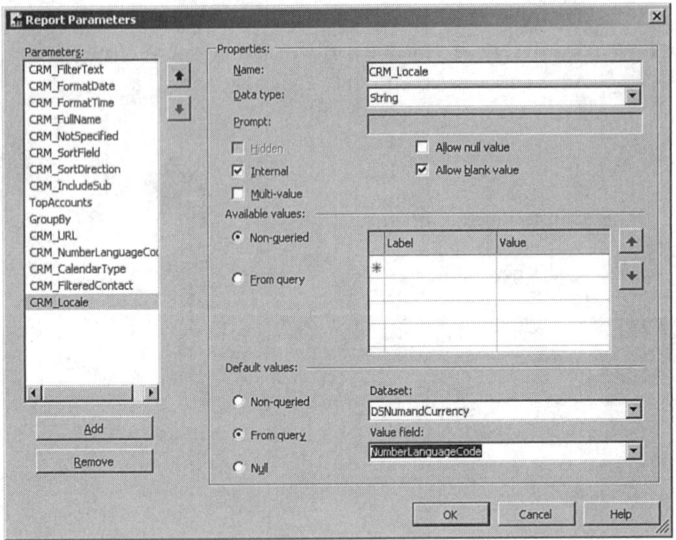

FIGURE 18.17 `CRM_Locale` parameter.

This function returns a value of `en-US` for English language in the United States.

- `CRM_SortField` and `CRM_SortDirection`—These parameters set the default sorting field and direction of the report.

Keep in mind these important considerations when using the `CRM_FilteredEntity` parameters:

- When adding these parameters, be sure to set them as internal and set a default value of `distinct` or `null`. This default value can be either a nonqueried value, or come from a query.
- Apart from adding the `CRM_FilteredEntity` parameters to the report, be sure to add the `CRMAF_FilteredEntity` alias to the filtered views you use in your queries of the datasets. For example, if your query is as follows, the report will always show all the Contacts, even though the User uses the prefilters:

  ```
  select fullname from FilteredContact
  ```

  To have the filters work properly, you must add the alias. Doing so affects our example as follows:

  ```
  DECLARE @SQL nvarchar(Max)
  SET @SQL = 'SELECT fullname FROM ('+@CRM_FilteredContact +') AS FC'
  EXEC (@SQL)
  ```

After you add this query to the dataset, click the Refresh button so you can start using the fields on your report, or you will get errors when you try to test and deploy it.

Another method in using the prefilters is to use the `CRMAF_FilteredEntity` alias to the filtered views. For example, you could build your query as follows:

```
select fullname from FilteredContact as CRMAF_FilteredContact
```

NOTE

Using them this way, you don't have to add the `CRM_FilteredEntity` parameter.

Building Custom Reports with ASP.NET

Another way to create a custom report is to create an ASP.NET web application that displays data and then use the Link to Web Page option to deploy it, as explained previously. Using this method doesn't enable you to use all the benefits inherent to SRS (including the capability to pass parameters to the reports and also use prefiltering). If you need to create a report using this method, you must handle the filtering options in your application manually.

NOTE

It is *always* recommended to use the filtering views. If you use Windows authentication in your application, the security will be in place.

This next example shows a custom report built in ASP.NET 3.5 that takes advantage of the LINQ language syntax. You will need to have Visual Studio 2008 installed to follow this sample:

1. Open Visual Studio 2008 and create a new project by going to File, New, Web Site, as shown in Figure 18.18.
2. Select ASP.NET Web Site project and enter the location address where your website will be located. For the language in this sample, use C# and the 3.5 Framework.
3. Click OK to create the website.
4. Under the Solution Explorer, right-click your website URL and select Add New Item.
5. Select LINQ to SQL Classes, as shown in Figure 18.19.
6. Click the Add button.
7. Click the Server Explorer to see the data connections.

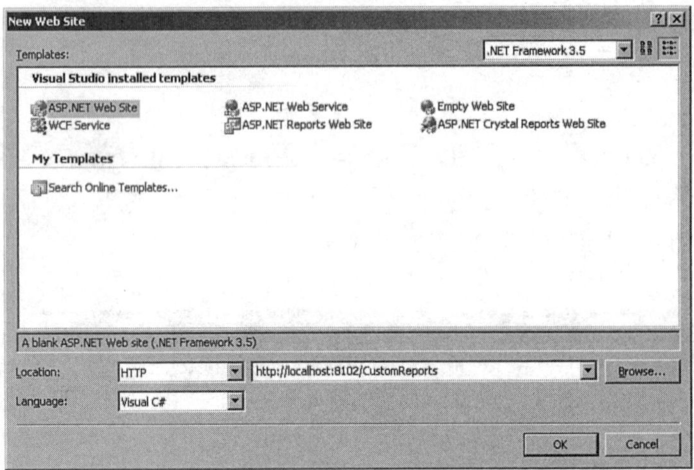

FIGURE 18.18 Creating a new website project.

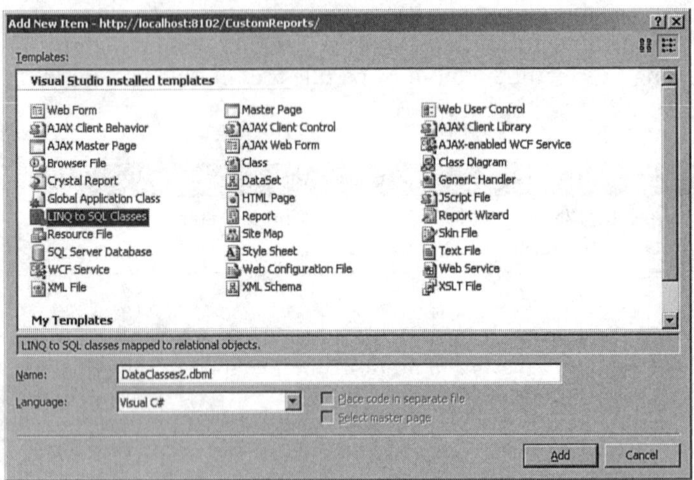

FIGURE 18.19 Adding LINQ to SQL classes.

8. Click the Add Connection button to add a new connection, as shown in Figure 18.20.
9. Select Microsoft SQL Server as the data source and click Continue (see Figure 18.21).

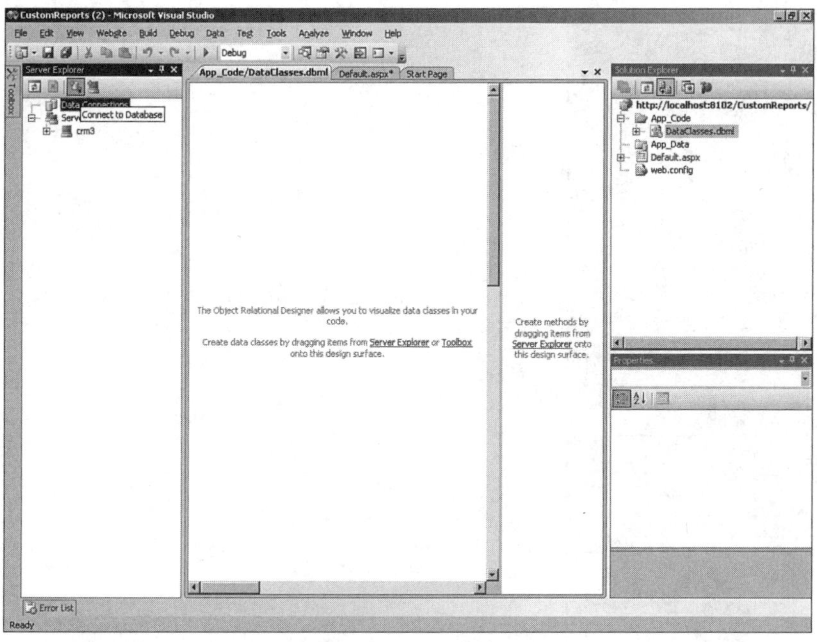

FIGURE 18.20 Adding the database connection.

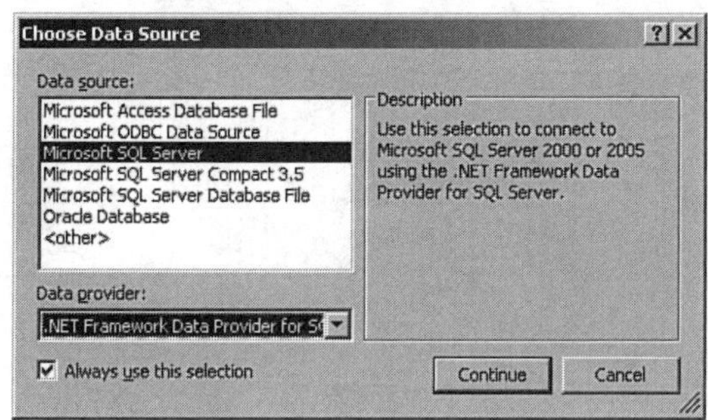

FIGURE 18.21 Selecting the data source.

10. Select your CRM database server and then your organization database name (see Figure 18.22).

11. Click Test Connection to be sure you have access and then click OK.

12. Expand the data connection you just created from the Server Explorer and expand the Views folder.

13. Locate the `FilteredContact` view, and drag and drop it into the Object Relational Designer, as shown in Figure 18.23.

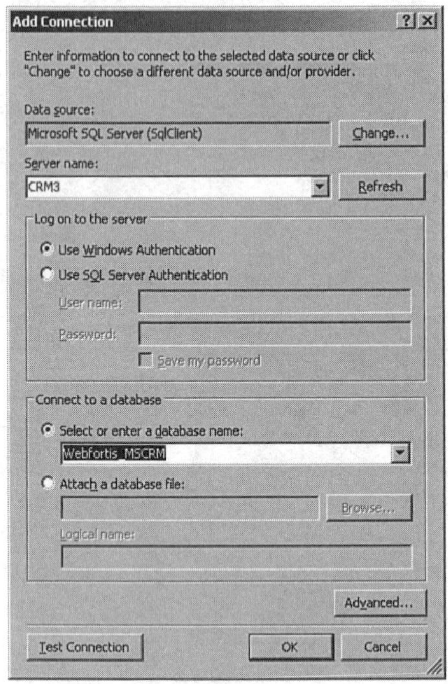

FIGURE 18.22 Selecting the data database.

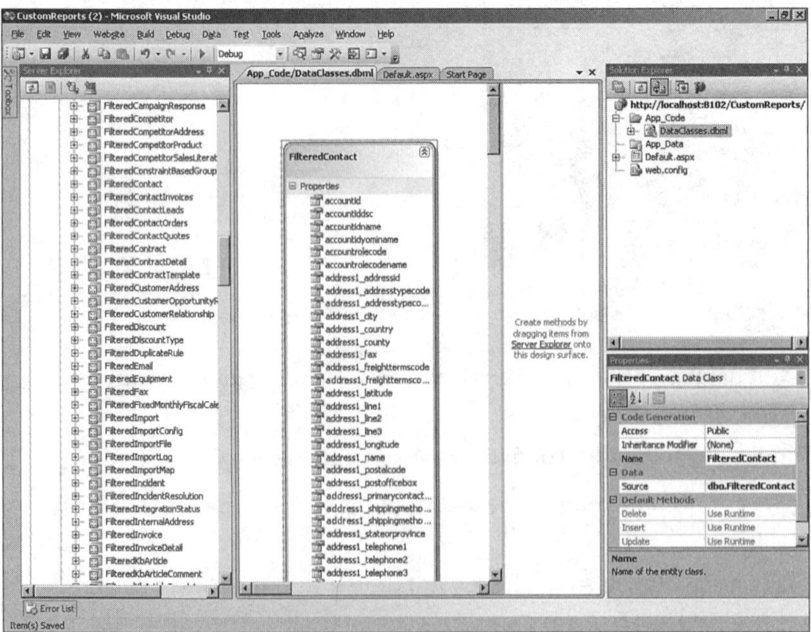

FIGURE 18.23 Adding FilteredContact to the Object Relational Designer.

14. Open the `Default.aspx` page, and drag and drop a `GridView` control from the toolbox, as shown in Figure 18.24.

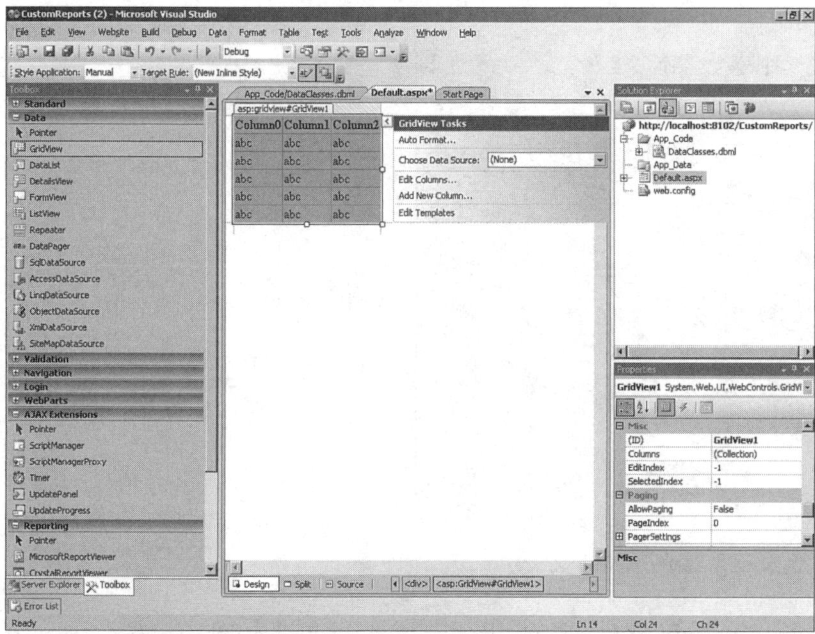

FIGURE 18.24 Adding a `DataView` control.

15. Under the GridView Tasks, choose a data source and select New Data Source.

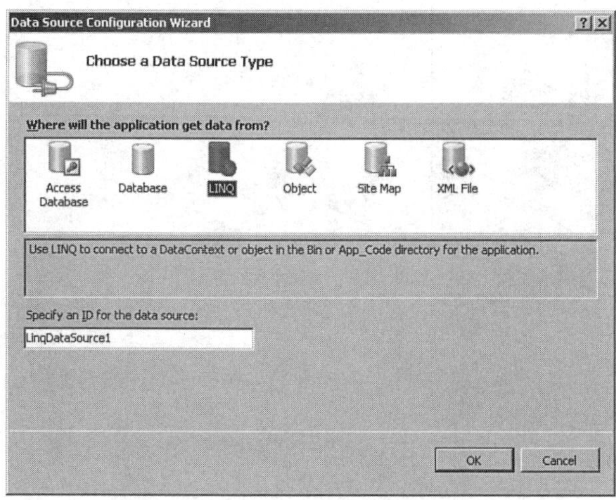

FIGURE 18.25 Adding a LINQ data source.

16. Select LINQ and click OK, as shown in Figure 18.25.
17. Leave the option that is displayed in the context object, as shown in Figure 18.26, and click Next.

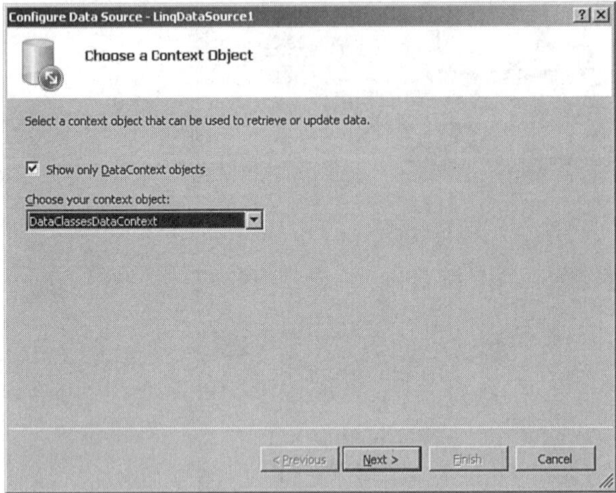

FIGURE 18.26 Choose a Context Object.

18. Select the fields you want to display in the `GridView` control. Here we select `fullname` and `jobtitle`, as shown in Figure 18.27.

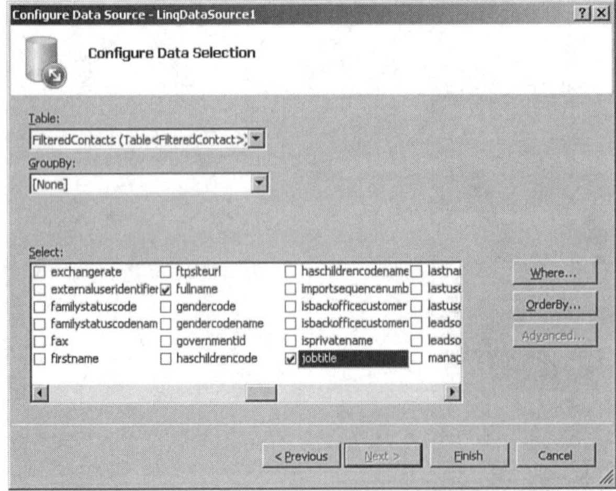

FIGURE 18.27 Configure Data Selection.

19. Click the Finish button.

To test the application you created, press Ctrl+F5. You should get a page similar to the one displayed in Figure 18.28.

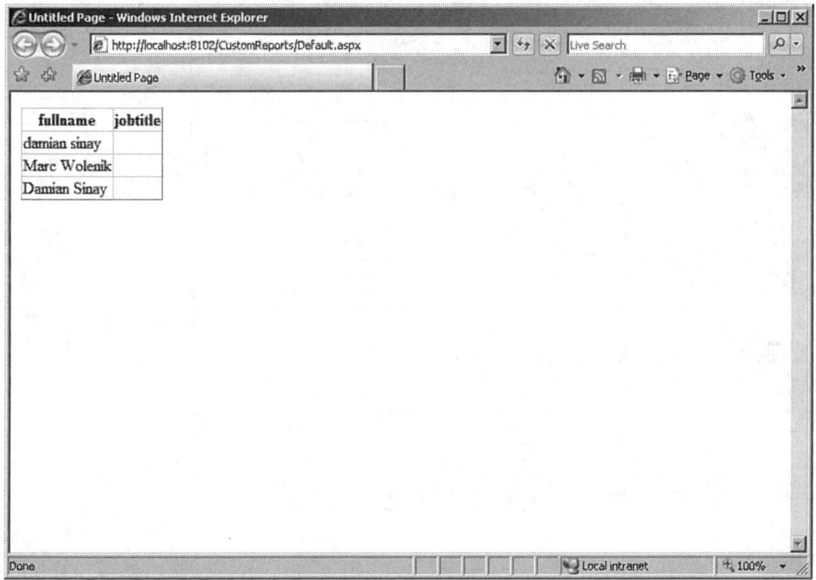

FIGURE 18.28 Testing the custom report.

Deployment

Similarly to what we explained previously, you must use the CRM client interface following these steps. (Notice that you can deploy reports from either the Web or Outlook client interfaces.)

1. Go to the Workplace and then click on Reports (see Figure 18.29).
2. Click the New button (see Figure 18.30).
3. Select Link to Web Page in the Report Type property.
4. Under Web Page URL, enter the URL of the custom application you built.
5. Enter a name for the report.
6. Optionally, you can select the Categories, Related Record Types, and Display In options.
7. Click the Save and Close button.

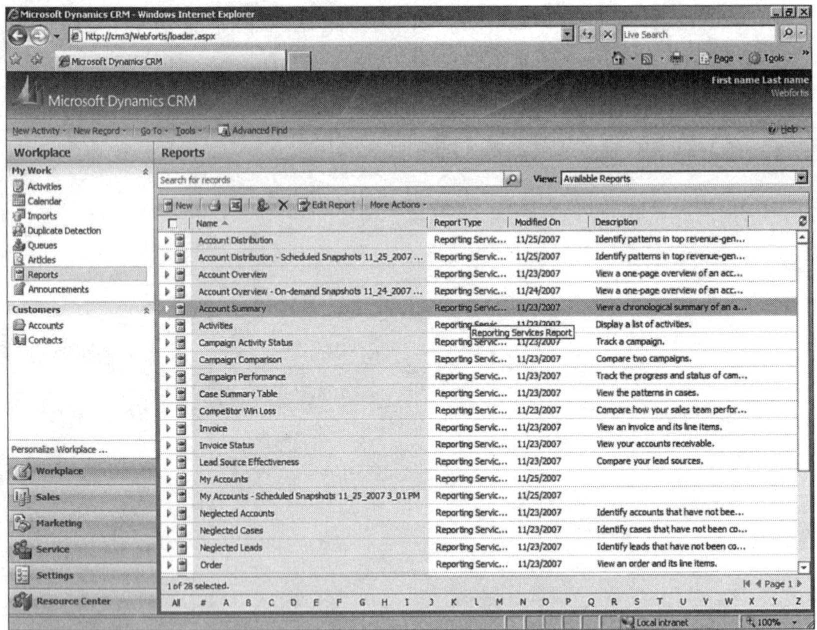

FIGURE 18.29 Reports area.

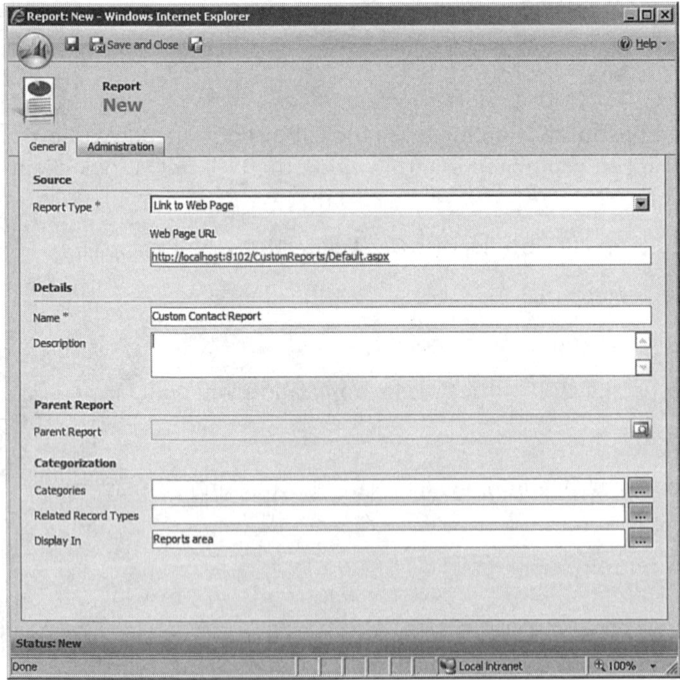

FIGURE 18.30 Deploying a new report.

Now you will see the report added in the reports area and shown in the list. When you double-click the report, a new IE window opens with the custom application page, as shown in Figure 18.31.

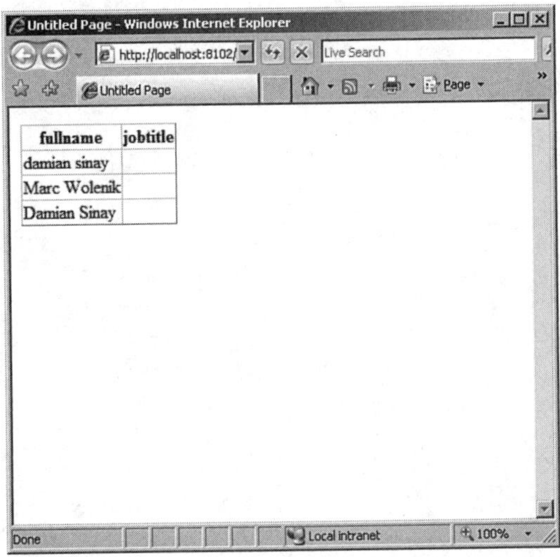

FIGURE 18.31 Testing the custom report in CRM.

Summary

This chapter covered SRS, described the components that are involved, such as the Report Manager and the Report Server, and discussed some of its features and benefits such as the creating and scheduling of automated reports. Finally, we looked at different options to build custom reports with SRS using Visual Studio and the Business Intelligence Projects or by a custom web application in ASP.NET 3.5 with Visual Studio.

CHAPTER 19

Customizing Entities

IN THIS CHAPTER

Customizing Entities

One of the most powerful features of Microsoft Dynamics CRM is that you can customize almost all entities, such as Accounts, Contacts, Opportunities, etc.

Navigate to the main entities customization screen by going to Settings and Customization, and you see that you can customize entities in several ways (see Figure 19.1).

You can customize existing entities or create new entities.

Customization Principles

Chapter 16, "Configuration and Customization Tools," discussed some basic principles related to customizations. The most basic principle is that Microsoft Dynamics CRM is built in an *n*-tier model with the user interface layers (web client and Outlook client) on the top, the application layer in the middle, and the database layer represented by the SQL Server on the bottom. Therefore, you should always make the customizations following the principles described in this chapter.

NOTE

If you are an expert SQL database administrator or developer, you might be tempted to create database triggers or stored procedures, or change the database schema; however, we *strongly* recommend that you *not* touch the database directly in any situation. Doing so is considered an unsupported customization and might cause the application to break or fail.

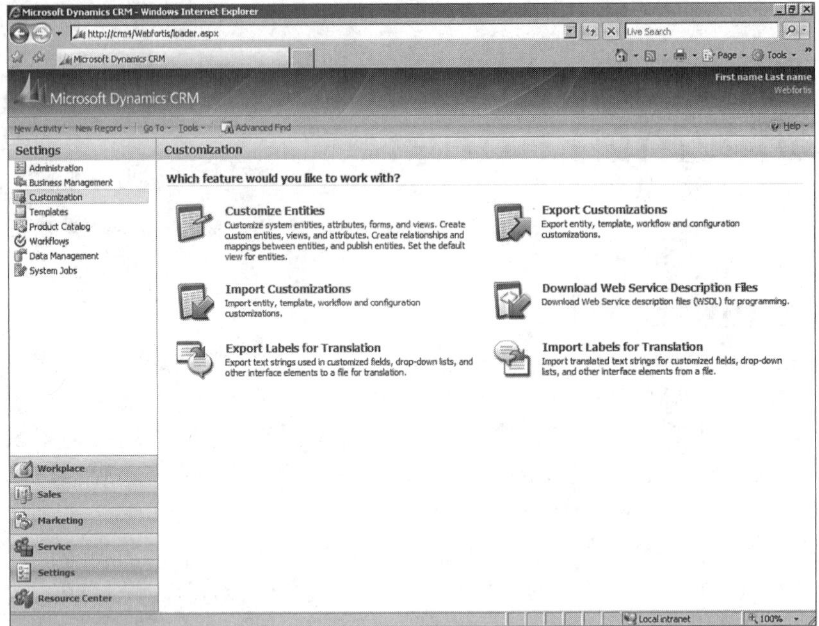

FIGURE 19.1 Customization interface.

NOTE

Two kinds of customization characteristics exist when working with Microsoft Dynamics CRM: supported and unsupported. We outline only supported customizations that follow Microsoft best practices and will generally not fail when the product is upgraded. Unsupported customizations might perform any function, but they fall outside the range of Microsoft's testing when considering upgrades, database schema changes, and support rollups. Unsupported customizations can have the following results:

- Service packs might fail, break, or not install.
- Upgrades to the product might cause unexpected results or fail entirely.
- The application or database might become unstable and fail to work.

MS CRM Entity Model

Similar to an XML document, all objects in Microsoft Dynamics CRM are treated as an entity or an attribute. Account, Contacts, Activities, and so on are all entities in the CRM system, and every entity has attributes, which are the fields related to the entity. An example of this is Account and Account Name. Account is an entity and Account Name is an attribute. We will review the Account entity, for example. From the Web Application, go to Settings, Customization, Customize Entities. Double-click Account and move to the Attributes tab (see Figure 19.2).

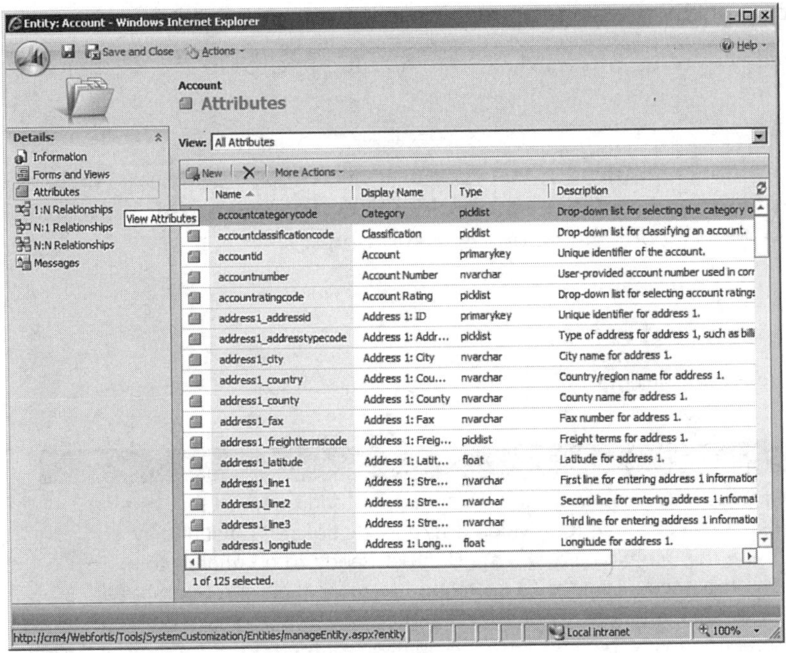

FIGURE 19.2 Attributes of the Account entity.

Attributes

Attributes can be of the following property types:

- `nvarchar`—Used for small texts or strings
- `picklist`—Used for drop-downs or combo boxes, with a limited set of fixed options

> **TIP**
>
> Because the picklist can display only simple, nondynamic options, you might want to use a new custom entity if you need something that is more dynamic or complex than the options provided and create a relationship between them.

- `bit`—Used for Boolean values such as `yes` or `no`
- `int`—Used for numbers
- `float`—Used for numbers with decimals (similar to float but with larger precision [up to 10])
- `money`—Used for amounts
- `ntext`—Used for large texts or strings
- `datetime`—Used for dates

Depending on which property type you use, they have different properties.

Entities are associated with other entities via a customization referred to as a Relationship.

Relationships

Relationships are now more user-friendly; you no longer need to be a database system administrator expert to use and configure relationships between entities. This version of Microsoft Dynamics CRM supports the following relationships:

- 1:*N* relationships (one to many)
- *N*:1 relationships (many to one)
- *N*:*N* relationships (many to many)

NOTE

The last relationship type (many to many) is a welcome new addition with this version of Microsoft Dynamics CRM because it provides a frequently desired functionality. For example, you could use this functionality when a Contact needs to be related to more than one Account and the Account needs to be related to more than one Contact at the same time. For example, suppose you have a contact who works for two different companies: The contact needs to belong to two companies as the parent Account and needs to be configured as primary or secondary Contact under the Account entity. With this case, you need to have more than one Contact associated with the Account side representing a many-to-many relationship.

Another new feature is the capability to add as many relationships as you want and to add more than one relationship to the same entity. For example, you can have a custom entity called Customer and add two fields called `Primary Contact` and `Secondary Contact`—both related to the `Contact` entity.

Finally, another feature to relationships is the ability to relate an entity to itself, which is referred to as self-referential. Using this type of relationship, you can use any type of relationship (1:N, N:1 or N:N) to relate an entity to itself.

1:*N* Relationships

Figure 19.3 displays the window where you can create a new 1:*N* relationship. With this type of relationship, the primary key is the entity you are customizing. For example, if you are working with the Account entity, you could use this type of relationship to specify the primary account for another entity, such as Contacts, for which the custom attribute defined by this relationship will contain only one Account.

N:1 Relationships

With this type of relationship (shown in Figure 19.4), the primary key is the entity you select. Therefore, the entity you are customizing is the foreign key. For example, if you wanted a Contact to have multiple Accounts associated with it, you would apply this relationship to the Account entity.

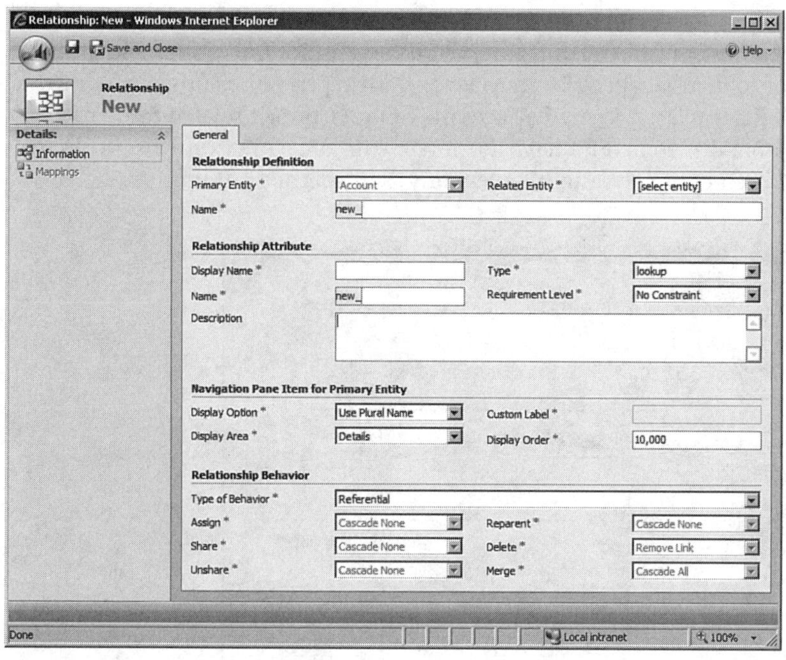

FIGURE 19.3 Creating a new 1:*N* relationship.

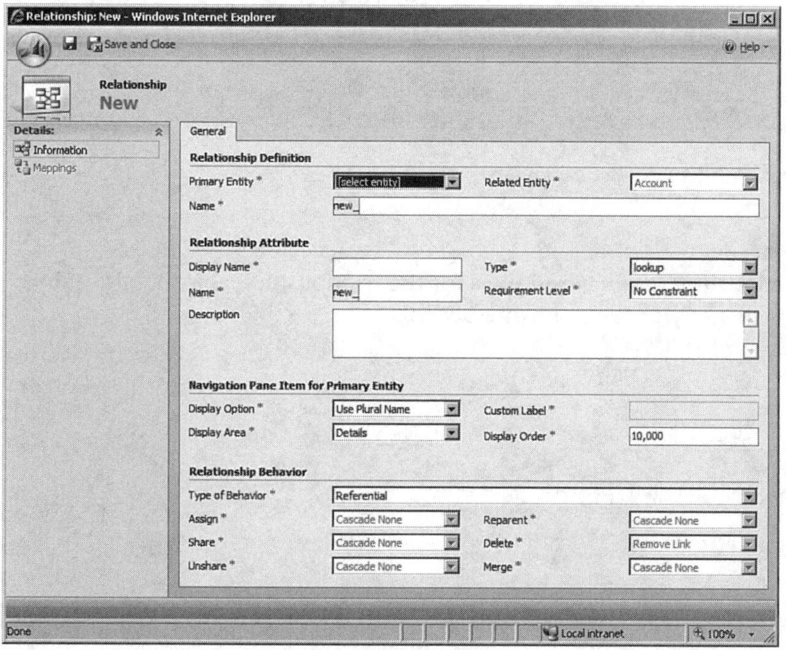

FIGURE 19.4 Creating a new *N*:1 relationship.

N:N Relationships

With this type of relationship (shown in Figure 19.5), there is not one primary key and another secondary or foreign key because they act as both types. For example, you might want to have one Contact related to many Accounts or one Contact related to many Contacts. In a real situation, you could have a Contact with a new person who works for two companies, and each company might have many Contacts apart from this one.

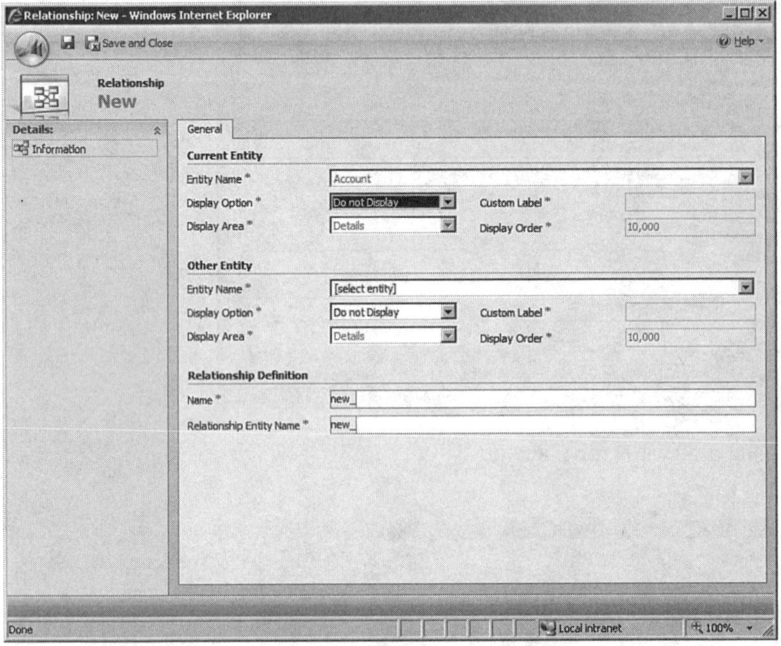

FIGURE 19.5 Creating a new *N:N* relationship.

Relationship Behavior

For N:1 and 1:N relationships, there are settings for the relationship behavior, also called Cascading Rules, which apply to the following operations:

- `Assign`
- `Share`
- `Unshare`
- `Reparent`
- `Delete`
- `Merge`

As shown in Figure 19.4, the Type of Behavior drop-down list contains four options:

- Parental
- Referential
- Referential, Restrict Delete
- Configurable Cascading

The first three options are templates, and the last option, Configurable Cascading, allows you to configure the cascading manually for each operation.

The first four operations (Assign, Share, Unshare, and Reparent) share these same cascading types:

- `Cascade All`—This option affects the current entity record and its related entity records, so the operation is performed on both entities.
- `Cascade Active`—This option affects the current entity record and its related entity records that have a status of Active.
- `Cascade User-Owned`—This option affects the current entity record and its related entity records that are owned by the user who is performing the operation only.
- `Cascade None`—This option only affects the current entity without affecting the related entity records.

The Delete operation has different cascading options as follows:

- `Cascade All`—This option is the same as explained for the other operations with the consideration that if you have a relationship 1:N between Account and Contact and you have one Account record with ten Contacts related, when you delete the Account, all ten Contacts will be also deleted.
- `Remove Link`—Using the preceding example, if you delete the Account record, the Contacts won't be deleted but the link between the Contacts to the Account will be removed.
- `Restrict`—Using the preceding example, you won't be able to delete the Account until you delete all the related Contacts manually first. Only when the Account doesn't have any related records can it be deleted.

The Merge operation will change between Cascade None and Cascade All depending on the primary entity selected and can't be modified.

Messages

Messages display information to the user based on a variety of actions. Users can customize these messages to display richer or different information, if desired, as shown in Figure 19.6.

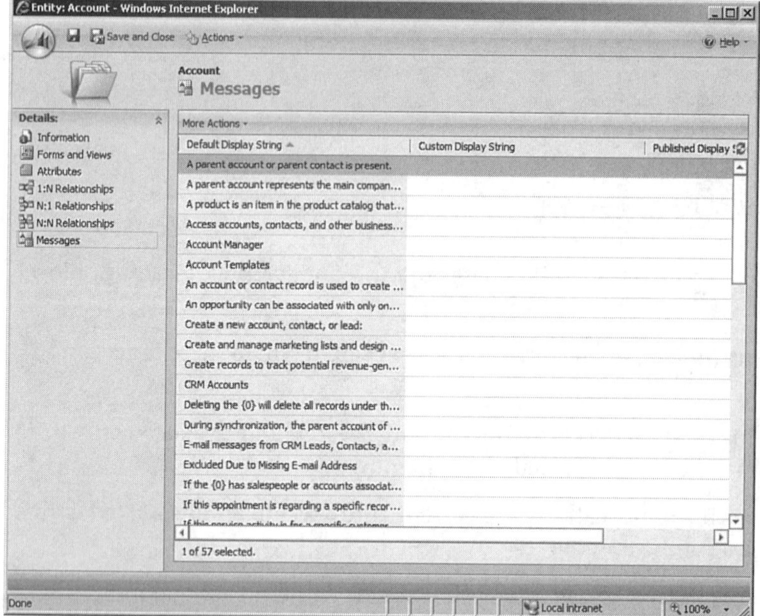

FIGURE 19.6 Messages customizations.

Basic Customizations

Basic customizations are customizations to Microsoft Dynamics CRM that don't require any knowledge of programming or database design and configuration. Basic customizations include showing and hiding controls on a Form, and hiding or showing columns in a View. To make this type of customization, open the entity record you want to customize and go to the Forms and Views tab in the left bar inside the Details section.

Form Customizations

Each entity supports only one Interface Form, and it can't be deleted. This means that you can't create another Form if you want to have different Forms for different Users, roles, or Business Units.

You can perform the following customizations to a Form (see Figure 19.7):

- Add, Remove, or Move Tabs
- Add, Remove, or Move Sections
- Add, Remove, or Move Fields
- Add, Remove, or Move IFRAMES
- Change Form Properties

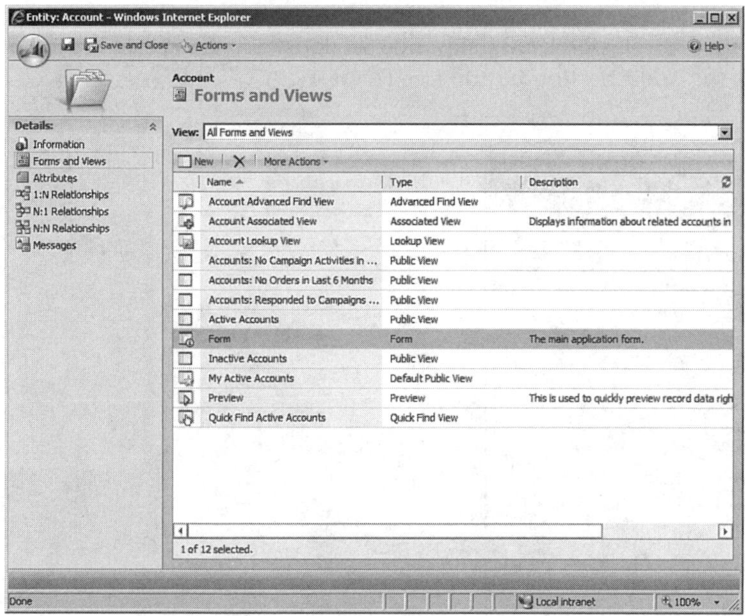

FIGURE 19.7 Forms and Views customizations.

Add, Remove, or Move Tabs

Each Form supports a maximum of eight tabs. Figure 19.8 shows a new tab with the label My Tab, added to the Form after you click the Add a Tab button.

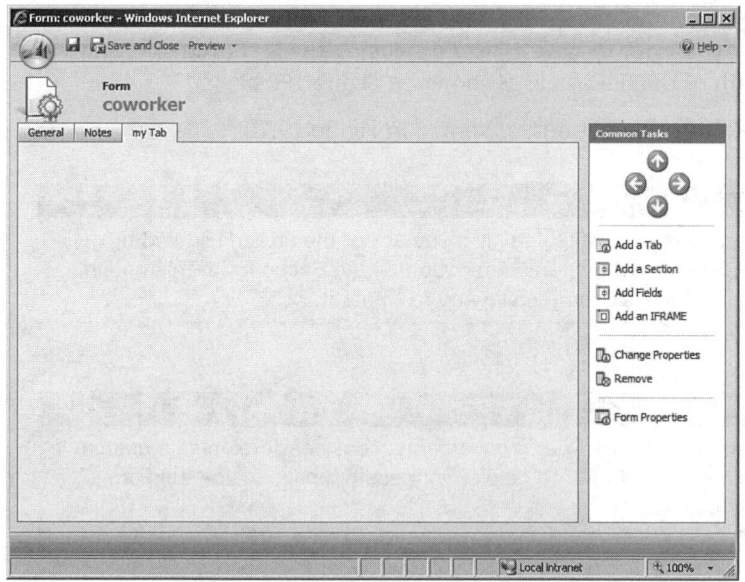

FIGURE 19.8 New custom tab added called My Tab.

Add, Remove, or Move Sections

Sections are used to group controls of related fields. The Sections must be within a tab. To add a new Section, click the Add a Section button (see Figure 19.9).

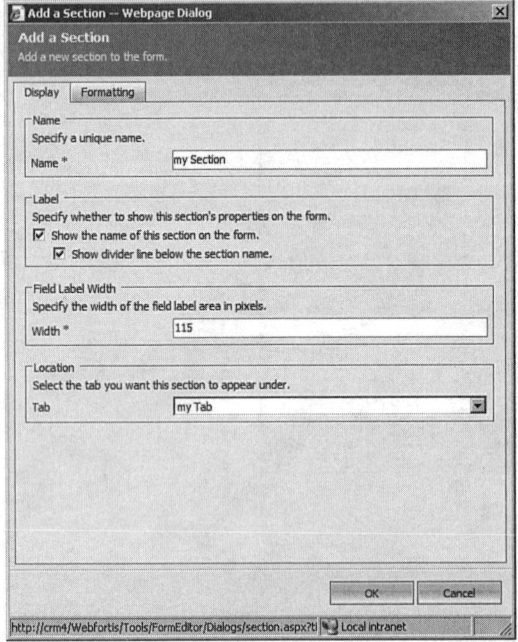

FIGURE 19.9 Adding a new Section to the tab.

You can choose whether you want to have a label displaying the Section name, and you can also specify the width of the field area, as shown in Figure 19.9.

You also have some limited layout options, as shown in Figure 19.10.

NOTE

The predefined layout options are available only if you select the Fixed Field Width option value for the Section layout property. After you add the Section with this option, you can't change the layout unless you remove and re-create it.

TIP

If the predefined layouts don't match your requirements, consider developing a custom page in ASP.NET and adding an IFRAME to display your custom page inside the Form, as detailed later in this chapter.

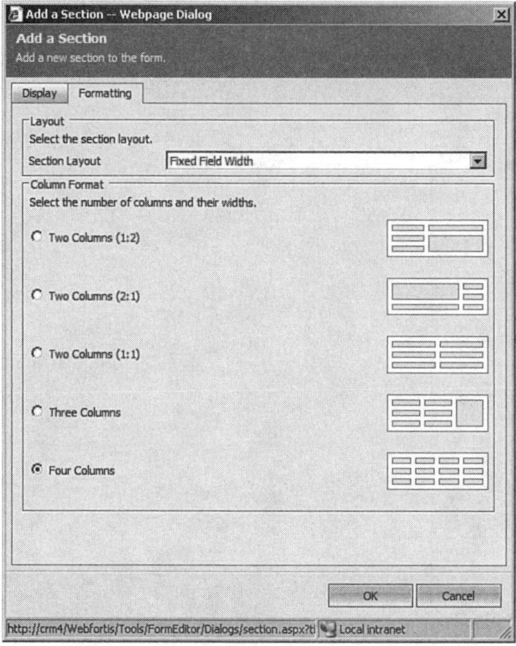

FIGURE 19.10 Selecting the layout.

Add, Remove, or Move Fields

Fields are used to display the entity attributes with input controls; if you created a new attribute, as described earlier in this chapter, you need to add a field for that attribute to have users enter values.

NOTE

To avoid adding duplicate fields, Figure 19.11 shows only the available fields that have not already been added to any tab in the Form.

TIP

You can use the arrows to move a field to the left, right, top, or bottom inside the Section, as shown in Figure 19.12. To change the field from one Section to another, click Change Properties and select the Section from the Section drop-down list.

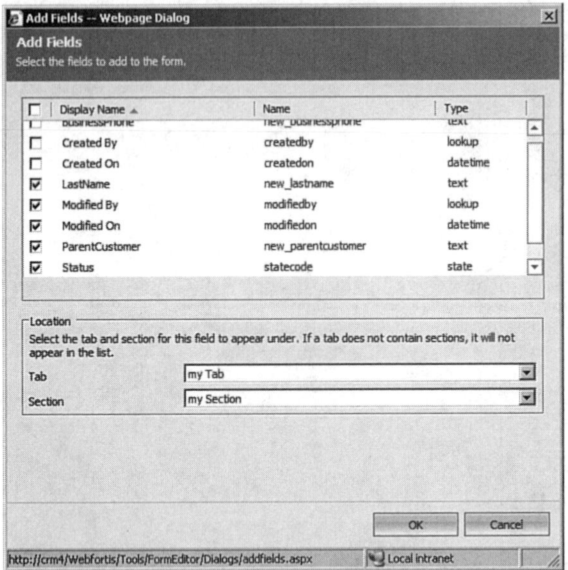

FIGURE 19.11 Selecting the fields to be displayed.

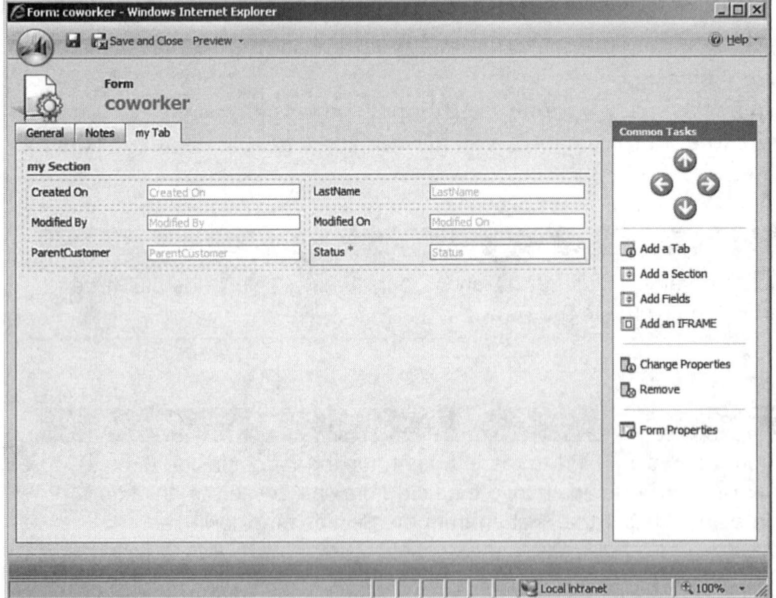

FIGURE 19.12 Fields added to the Section.

Add, Remove, or Move IFRAMES

You can use IFRAMES to display custom applications or pages inside the Form. This is extremely helpful when you need to put advanced input/output controls that are not included in the CRM controls toolset. Examples include a complex grid, a picture control, or a movie control integrated with Flash or Silverlight. When you click Add an IFRAME, you get the dialog box in Figure 19.13 that requires the name for the IFRAME as well as the URL of your application.

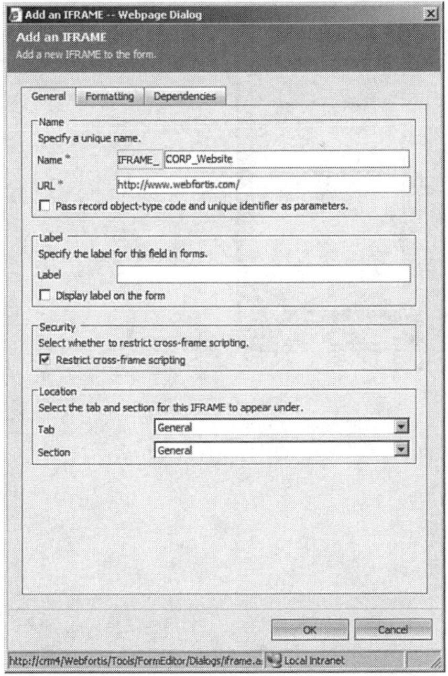

FIGURE 19.13 Adding an IFRAME.

For example, we are going to enter CORP Website in the Name property and http://www.webfortis.com in the URL property. When adding the IFRAME with the default values, you will see the IFRAME inserted in the Form, as shown in Figure 19.14.

Most of the time, you want the IFRAME to expand vertically to fill the entire Form. To do that, select the IFRAME and click on Change Properties; then move to the Formatting tab. Under the Row Layout Section of the dialog box, check the Automatically expand to use the available space check box (see Figure 19.15).

In the Scrolling section, you can choose whether you want to have the IFRAME show the scroll bars (Vertical and Horizontal) As Necessary (which is the default value), Always, or Never. Finally, you can specify if you want to show a border around the IFRAME by clicking the Display Border property inside the Border section.

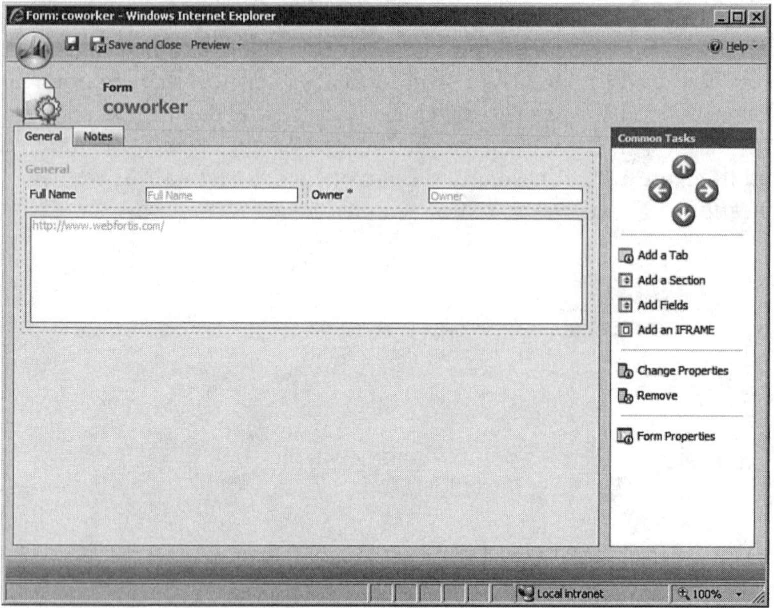

FIGURE 19.14 IFRAME added to the Form.

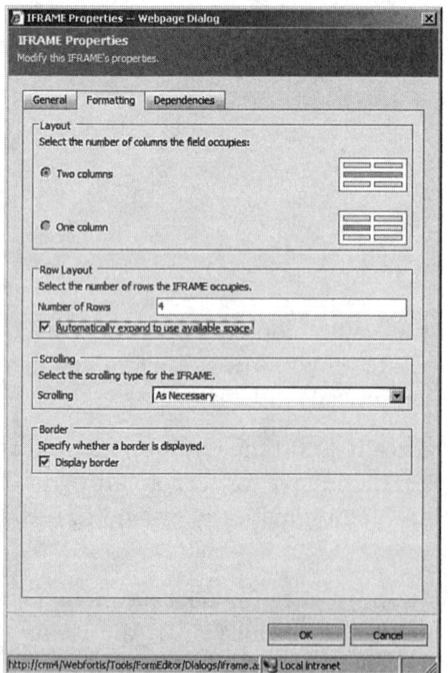

FIGURE 19.15 Making the IFRAME expand to use the available space.

Click the OK button to accept this change, and you see the IFRAME now expands on the Form (see Figure 19.16).

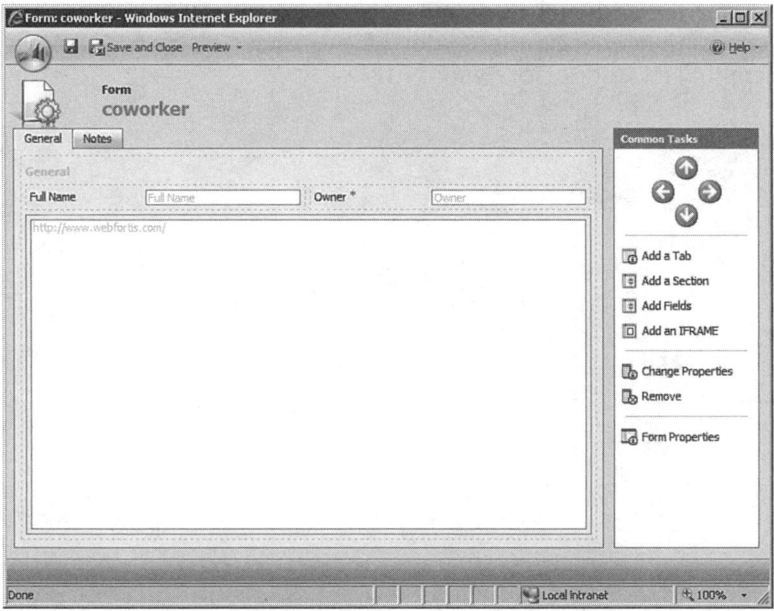

FIGURE 19.16 IFRAME expands to use the available space.

To test the Form with the IFRAME, click the Preview button on top of the window and select the Create Form menu option. We used our corporate URL www.webfortis.com for the IFRAME example that has both JavaScript ActiveX controls that we use to show Adobe Flash content. Because of that, we won't see the page render properly inside the IFRAME. Figure 19.17 shows the page with errors.

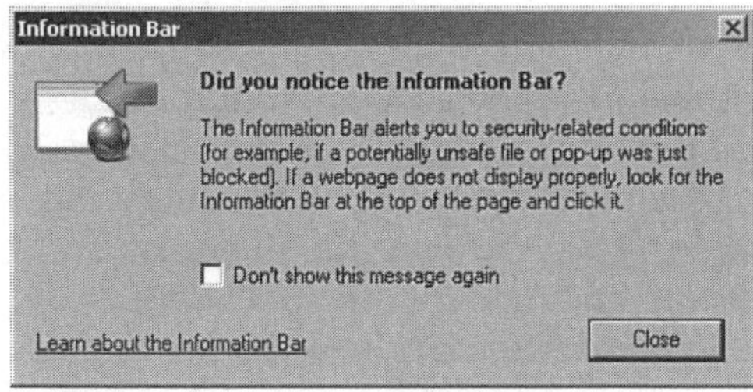

FIGURE 19.17 IFRAME test with errors.

This behavior is normal and it is the default behavior. The protection is set by default on the IFRAME properties to prevent the external pages from executing JavaScript codes or

ActiveX controls that might perform unintended operations on the CRM application, such as closing the Form unexpectedly without allowing CRM to control the window and saving the data properly. You can, however, change this security setting to have your page load correctly if you're sure there will not be a problem by selecting the IFRAME and clicking Change Properties. Under the Security section of the dialog box, uncheck the Restrict cross-frame scripting check box (see Figure 19.18).

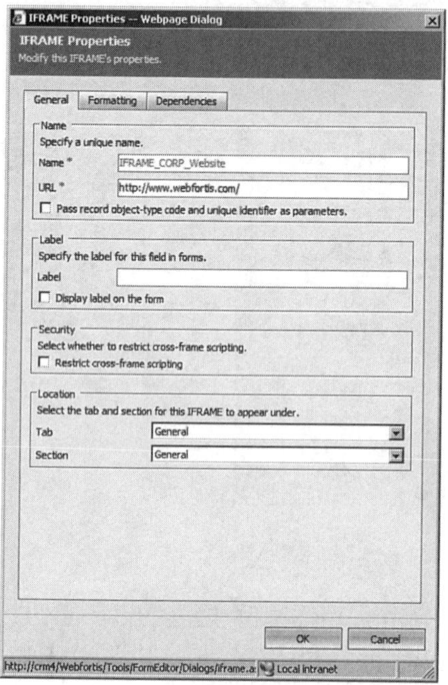

FIGURE 19.18 Removing the cross-frame scripting protection.

Click OK to close the dialog box, and test it using the Preview top menu and selecting Create Form. You will see the page loads properly without any warnings (see Figure 19.19).

For this sample, we used a webpage URL that will show the same content (our corporate web page), regardless of when and where in CRM it is shown. Most of the time, however, you will want to use the IFRAME to show different content depending on the entity and record instance being displayed. For example, you may want to show the company webpage in an IFRAME when working with Accounts, and then show an individual's picture in the IFRAME when working with Contacts. For those cases, you will need to create a custom ASP.NET application and read the GUID of the record that will be passed to the web application. This is accomplished by setting the check box that says Pass record object-type code and unique identifier as parameters. For a complete sample of how this works, refer to Chapter 24, "Interacting with Custom Web Applications."

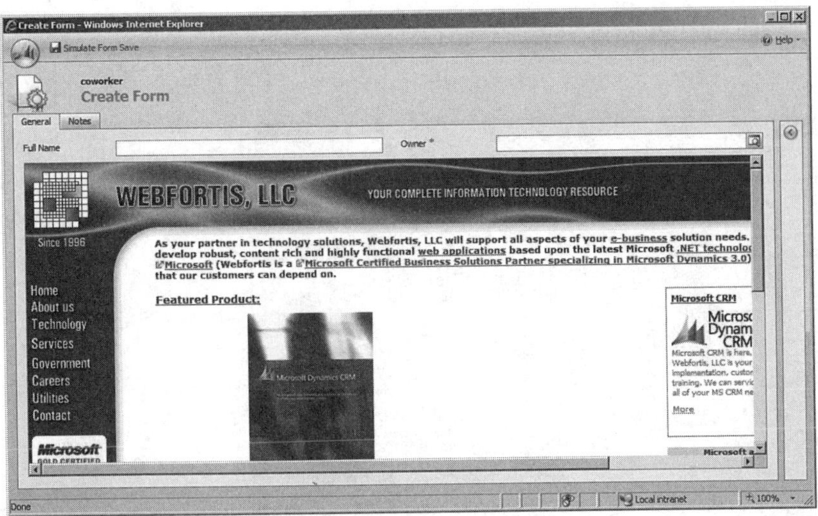

FIGURE 19.19 IFRAME test with active content displayed.

Change Properties of a Tab, Section, Field, or IFRAME

From this option, you can access the properties of the Section you are positioning. For example, if you select a tab, you have access to the tab properties. If you select a field, the properties are related to the field selected.

Change Form Properties

From this option, you have access to the general form properties. These properties are not visible to the user; they include such events as the form assistance integration, and the nonevent dependencies fields.

After you complete your customizations to the Form, you can easily preview them by clicking the Preview button and choosing one of the form mode options, such as Create Form, Update Form, or Read-Only Form (see Figure 19.20).

When you are done with the customizations, you can click Save and Close to save your work.

For the customizations to be visible and usable by users, they must be published. See the "Publishing Customizations" section later in this chapter on how to do this.

View Customizations

A View is a read-only representation of the entity's records. They show just a few of the entity's properties, and you can see them in the main screen of the entities in the Advanced Find results and in the Look Up Records results.

Several different types of Views are created by default for each entity, and you can easily create new Views. For each View, you can customize the fields to be displayed by adding, removing, or changing the display position of each column. You can also set the desired width in pixels for each column (see Figure 19.21). By default, the columns have a fixed width of 100 pixels.

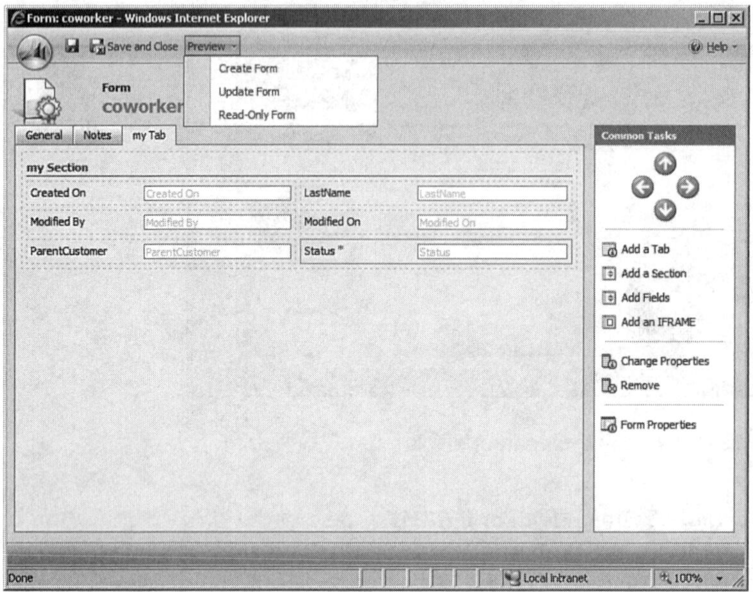

FIGURE 19.20 Preview Form menu items.

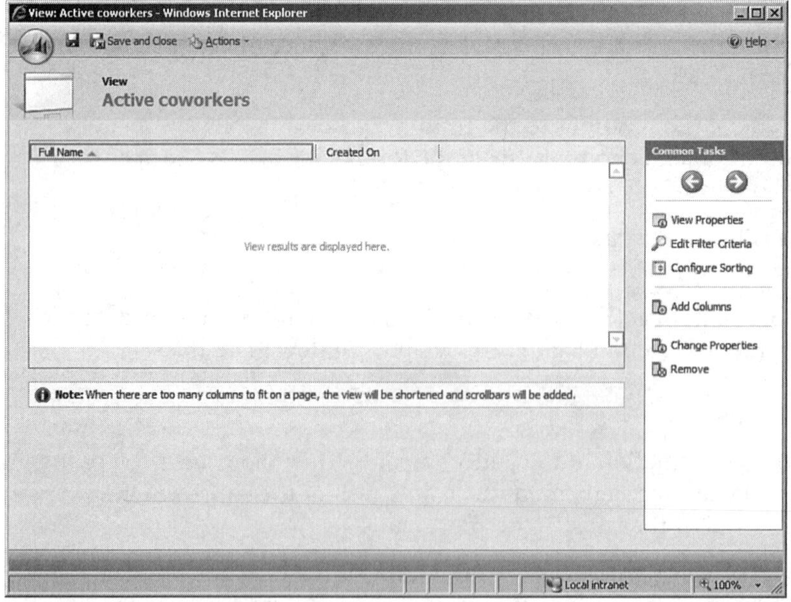

FIGURE 19.21 View customizations.

Publishing Customizations

When you have completed your desired changes to an entity, you must publish the Form so that users can see and use the changes. To publish it, select the entity you want to publish and click the Publish button. If you have changes to more than one entity, you can also quickly publish all the customizations by clicking the More Actions button and then selecting Publish All Customizations, as illustrated in Figure 19.22.

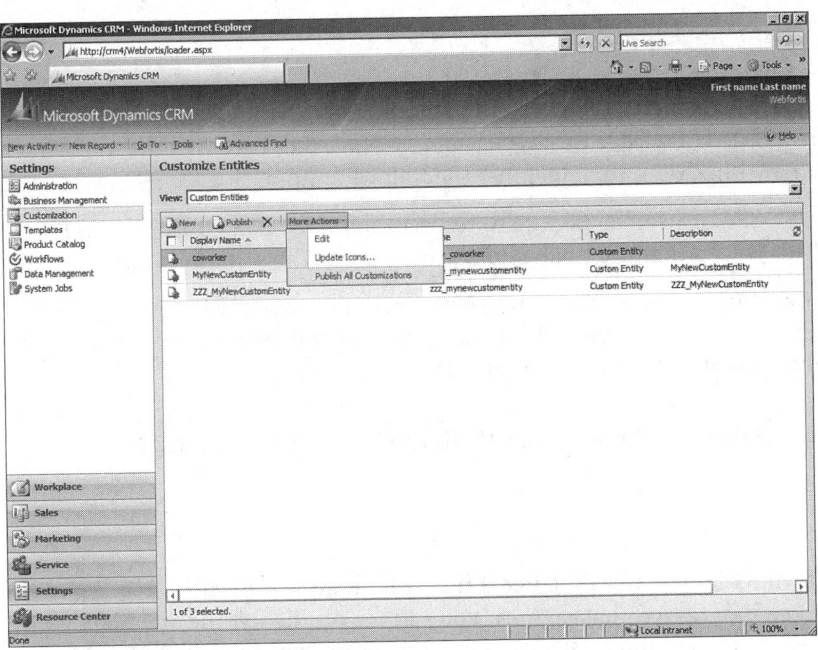

FIGURE 19.22 Publishing all customizations.

> **NOTE**
>
> If you delete an entity, you don't need to publish the customizations. It will be unavailable to users as soon as you delete it.

> **NOTE**
>
> After you make a customization to either Forms or Views, you must publish the entity for users to see the changes.

Menus and Controls Customizations

Menus are the options you can select from the top menu, such as New Activity, New Record, Go to Tools, and Advanced Find—these are always visible in the main Form.

Notice that every entity has its own menu items as well when you go to create or update a record.

Controls are the buttons shown in the top bar below the menu. These buttons vary depending on the entity you are positioned on. Examples of these controls are New, Print, and Export to Excel.

You can customize menus and controls in two ways:

- Site Map
- `ISV.Config`

Both ways require a little knowledge of how to manage XML files because both are XML files. When working with XML files, remember the following rules:

- XML files are case-sensitive, so be sure to respect each node name case to avoid problems. This means that the node name `<root>` is not the same as `<ROOT>`.
- Each node needs to be closed. For example, if you open a node with `<root>`, you need to later close it with `</root>`. If the node doesn't contain children nodes, you can open and close it in the same line—for example, `<root />`.

For more information about working with XML files and their specifications, visit www.w3.org.

Site Map

The Site Map is the file that describes the items that will be shown on each Area. For example, when you are in the Workplace Area, you can see on the left the Site Map options of Activities, Calendar, Imports, and so on. These options are quick links to the entities' administration that you can customize when you want to have another frequently used entity.

The Site Map is an XML file that needs to be exported first to be edited, and then it needs to be reimported to be updated. For more information, see the section "Exporting and Importing Entity Customizations," later this chapter, or go to Settings, Customizations, Export Customizations, and select the View Client Extensions, as shown in Figure 19.23.

The following code illustrates the Site Map main nodes structure:

```
<SiteMap>
    <SiteMap>
      <Area>
         <Group>
           <SubArea>
```

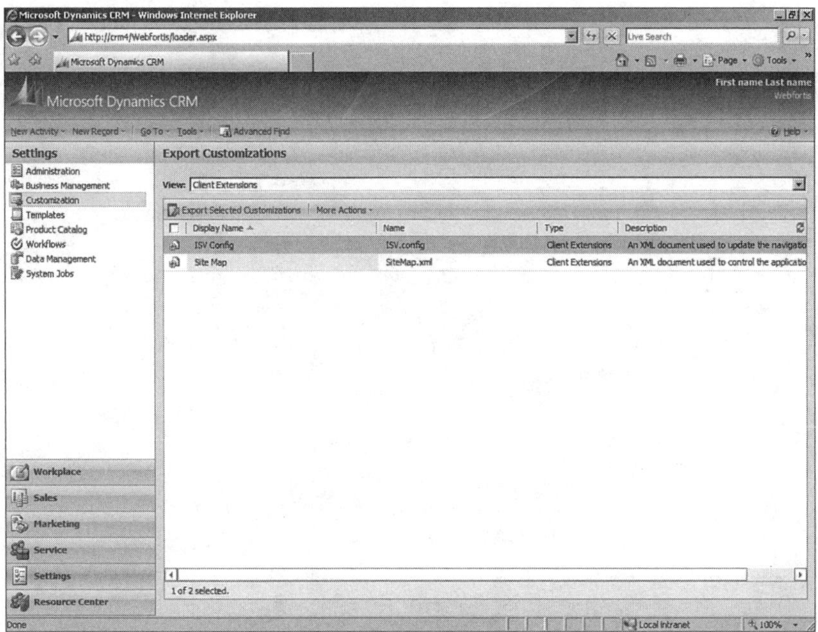

FIGURE 19.23 Locating the Site Map and `ISV.Config` customization by using the Client Extensions View.

Site Map Node

This is the main and root entry-level node. Inside this node should be another node with the same name, Site Map, which will contain all the Area nodes as children.

Area Node

Each area represents the main navigation buttons located on the near navigation that are displayed on the main interface. By default, the Site Map is configured with six main areas:

- Workplace
- Sales
- Marketing
- Service
- Settings
- Resource center

Figure 19.24 illustrates these navigation options or areas on the Web Application user interface.

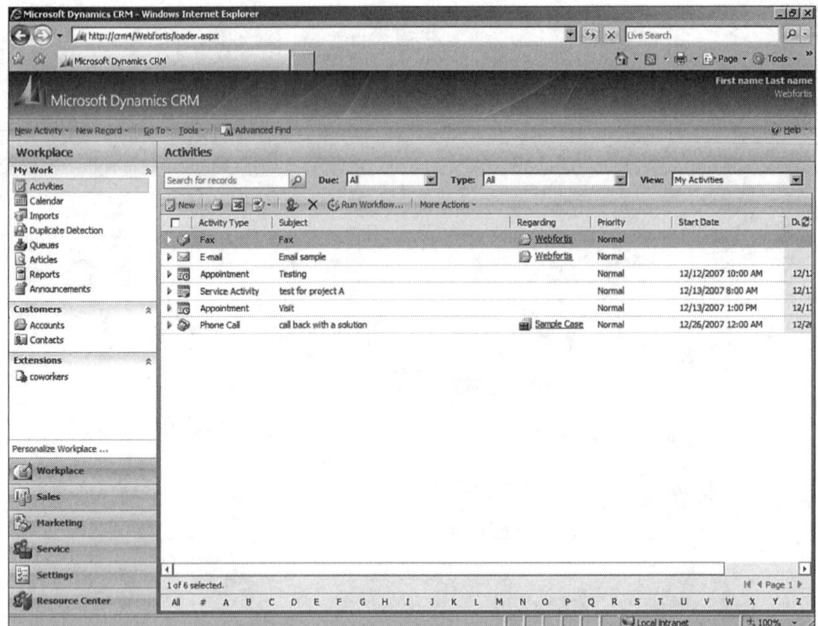

FIGURE 19.24 Areas displayed in the bottom-left corner of the screen.

The following code illustrates the area node with its default attributes for the Workplace area:

```
<Area Id="Workplace" ResourceId="Area_Workplace" ShowGroups="true"
➥Icon="/_imgs/workplace_24x24.gif" DescriptionResourceId="Workplace_Description">
```

These are the attributes of the Workplace Area code:

- `Id`—The unique identifier name for each Area
- `ResourceId`—The ResourceId.
- `ShowGroups`—This attribute is only necessary if the Area has more than one Group child nodes.
- `Icon`—The URL for the icon to be displayed near the Area title.
- `DescriptionResourceId`—This is for internal use only.

Group Node

This element is used to contain a group of subarea nodes. Each group will be displayed on the near navigation above the Area buttons with the capability to be collapsed or expanded.

Subarea Node

These nodes are used to provide the links to the pages or websites (configured by their URLs) inside the Group sections.

For example, suppose we want to add a new area to the Site Map called Webfortis to be used as a collection of links related to our organization and external application. We could add the following code into the Site Map file right after the last </Area> node and before the </SiteMap>.

TIP

While we can use any Text editor to make these changes, Visual Studio 2005 is the recommended option to edit the xml file of the Site Map.

```
<Area Id="WebfortisArea" Title="Webfortis" ShowGroups="true"
➥Icon="/_imgs/resourcecenter_24x24.gif" >
        <Group Id="Group1" Title="External">
                <SubArea Id="nav_subArea1" Title="Website"
➥Icon="/_imgs/ico_18_129.gif" Url="http://www.webfortis.com" />
                <SubArea Id="nav_subArea2"  Title="Microsoft"
➥Icon="/_imgs/ico_16_sales.gif" Url="http://www.microsoft.com"
➥AvailableOffline="false" />
        </Group>
        <Group Id="Group2" Title="Internal">
                <SubArea Id="nav_subArea11" Title="Intranet"
➥Icon="/_imgs/ico_18_129.gif" Url="http://www.webfortis.com/Internal"
➥AvailableOffline="false" />
                <SubArea Id="nav_subArea12" Title="Cost Control"
➥Icon="/_imgs/ico_16_sales.gif" Url="http://www.webfortis.com/CC"
➥AvailableOffline="false" />
        </Group>
</Area>
```

Save the changes and import the Site Map. For detailed instructions about importing Site Map customizations, see the "Exporting and Importing Entity Customizations" section later in this chapter, or go to Settings, Customizations, Import Customizations, upload the xml file you edited, and click the Import Selected Customizations button.

After importing this customization, you would see the result shown in Figure 19.25.

NOTE

Important considerations when adding new Areas, Groups, or Subareas: Be sure to use unique names for the `Id` attributes, and do not use the `ResourceId` and `DescriptionResourceID` attributes in your custom elements, as those are for internal use only. Use the `Title` Attribute to display the text instead.

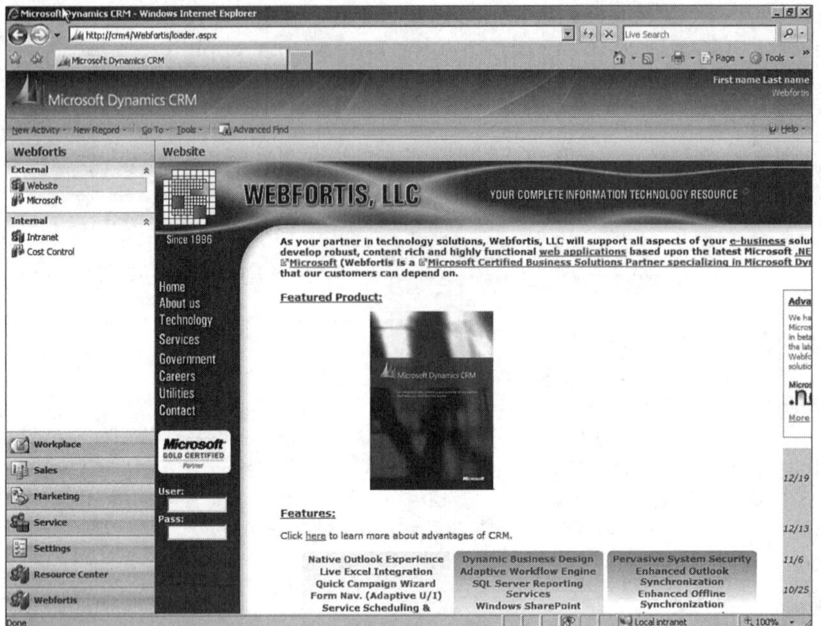

FIGURE 19.25 Customized Site Map.

ISV.Config

`ISV.Config` is an XML file used to add custom menu items and controls to the toolbars; it is intended to be used by Independent Software Vendors (ISVs) who want to add extra features to CRM. Although the Site Map is intended to be used as shortcuts to custom entities or web applications, when you want to add shortcuts on an entity Form to other web applications or interfaces that are not really CRM entities, you use the `ISV.Config` file.

In the same way that the `SiteMap.XML` is exported to be modified and then reimported to the system to be updated, the `ISV.Config` must also be exported and reimported.

The `ISV.Config` file is disabled by default, so changes you make to it aren't visible unless you configure it correctly. You can do this from Settings, Administration, System Settings, and then the Customization tab, as shown in Figure 19.26.

Under the Custom Menus and Toolbars section, click the ... button and select the client's applications interface where you want the `ISV.config` customizations to be enabled (see Figure 19.27).

System Settings -- Webpage Dialog
System Settings
Set system-level settings for Microsoft Dynamics CRM.
General | Formats | E-mail | Marketing | Customization | Outlook | Reporting
Set the name prefix to use for custom entities and attributes
Prefix: New
Name preview: new_entity
Custom menus and toolbars
Select the clients that will display custom buttons and menu items configured in ISV.Config.
Clients
Application mode
Set whether Microsoft Dynamics CRM can be opened in a browser window without menu, navigation, and command bars.
Open Microsoft Dynamics CRM in Application mode
Help | OK | Cancel
http://crm4/Webfortis/tools/systemsettings/dialogs/systemsettings.aspx | Local intranet

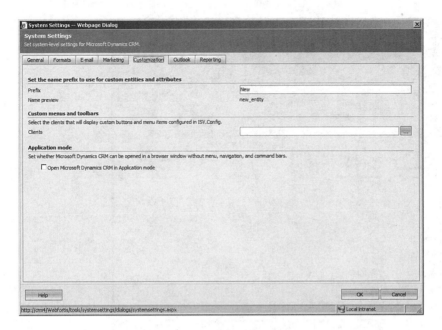

FIGURE 19.26 Custom Menus and Toolbars.

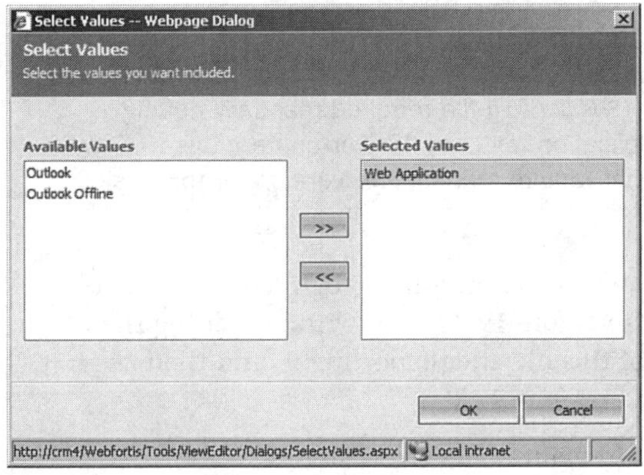

FIGURE 19.27 Enabling `ISV.Config` for the web application only.

19

After enabling the `ISV.Config file`, you see the new menus and toolbars, as shown in Figure 19.28.

NOTE

You might need to refresh the browser page by pressing the F5 key.

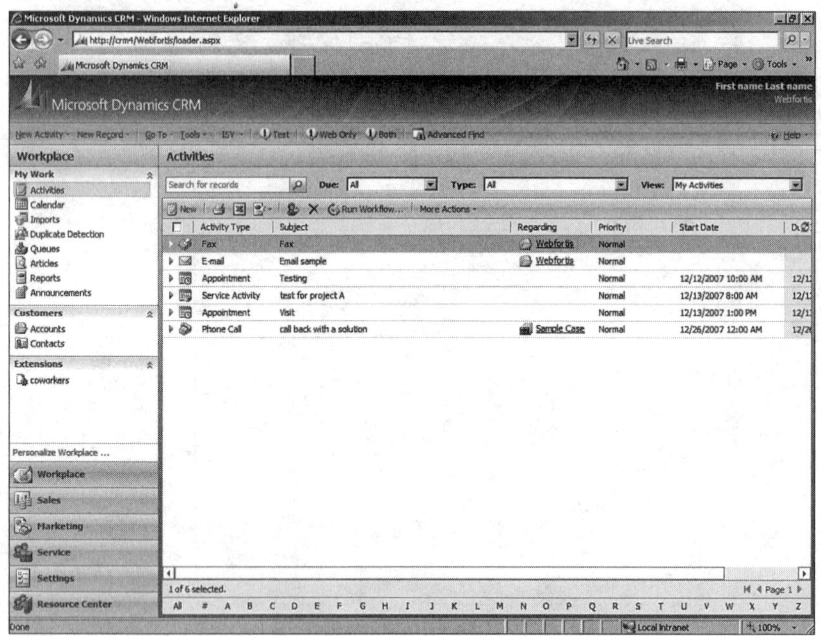

FIGURE 19.28 Default `ISV.Config` menus and toolbars.

NOTE

In previous versions of CRM, enabling the `ISV.Config` file required manually editing the `Web.Config` file located in the root application folder in IIS. Fortunately, this version of Microsoft Dynamics CRM does not require manual intervention for this task.

The `ISV.Config` comes with some testing menus and buttons predefined on it, so you will see the custom menus and buttons shown in Figure 19.28 even without editing the file. It is recommended that you make a backup of this file after exporting it, and then clean it up to add your custom menus and buttons.

The following code illustrates the `ISV.Config` main nodes structure:

```
<IsvConfig>
    <configuration>
        <Root>
        </Root>
        <Entities>
        </Entities>
        <ServiceManagement>
        </ServiceManagement>
    </configuration>
</IsvConfig>
```

IsvConfig Node

This is the main root node that should contain the `<configuration>` node only.

Configuration Node

This node configures the version number supported by this file for compatibility issues. An example of this follows:

```
<configuration version="3.0.0000.0">
```

Root Node

The root node defines the global application menus and toolbars. These items are located in the main and default user interfaces.

This node can contain any instances of the following nodes:

```
<Root>
    <MenuBar>
        <CustomMenus>
            <Menu>
            </Menu>
    </MenuBar>
    <ToolBar>
        <Button>
        </Button>
        <ToolBarSpacer />
    </ToolBar>
</Root>
```

Button Node

The button node defines a button, and it contains the following child nodes:

```
<Button>
    <Titles>
        <Title />
    </Titles>
    <ToolTips>
        <ToolTip />
    </ToolTips>
</Button>
```

The Button element node contains the following attributes:

- `AccessKey`—This attribute specifies the key used as a shortcut to fire the button command without having to click it with the mouse. This attribute accepts only one character for the access key, and it should be used in conjunction with the Alt key. An example is setting Alt+K to direct access to the button without having to use the mouse to click it.

- `Client`—This attribute specifies for which client application you want to have the button shown. You have two possibilities:
  - Web
  - Outlook

TIP

If this attribute is omitted, the button is displayed on both clients, so be sure to specify this value if you want the button displayed on only one client. The following code represents a button that will be displayed on only the web client:

```
<Button Client="Web">
```

- `AvailableOffline`—This property is used when the `Client` property is omitted or it has a value of `Outlook` to specify whether the button should be displayed in offline or online mode of the CRM Outlook client.
- `Icon`—This attribute specifies the icon to be displayed near the text inside the button. This parameter expects a URL for the icon, and icons are located in a predefined folder called _imgs. You can see files with the `ico` prefix followed by a number and, in some cases, by the language code—for example:

```
<Button Icon="/imgs/ico_18_debug.gif" >
```

NOTE

The icon file needs to be a GIF file with a resolution of 16×16 8-bit color (256 colors) for the web application; and 16×16, 32×32 4-bit color (16 colors) for Outlook.

- `JavaScript`—This attribute adds JavaScript code that will be executed after the button is clicked. For example, the following code displays a pop-up alert dialog box with the text of `test`:

```
<Button JavaScript="alert('test');" >
```

- `PassParams`—This attribute is used when the button is placed inside an entity element. It is omitted for the root element, and it indicates whether parameters are passed to the URL in the query string. This attribute is useful in conjunction with the `ValidForUpdate` attribute to pass the entity instance ID to the page to be displayed in the window. If you are calling a custom application, you can use a Web Service or the APIs to retrieve all the other necessary values with this method.
- `Url`—This attribute specifies the URL address where the user will be redirected when clicking the button. An example of this follows:

```
<Button Url="http://www.webfortis.com" >
```

NOTE

If both `JavaScript` and `Url` have values, this property is ignored.

- `ValidForCreate`—This attribute is used when the button is placed inside an entity element. It is omitted for the root element, and it indicates whether the button should be displayed when a new record of an entity will be created.
- `ValidForUpdate`—This attribute is also used when the button is placed inside an entity element. It is omitted for the root element, and it indicates whether the button should be displayed when an existing record of an entity will be updated.
- `WinMode`—This attribute has the following options:
  - `0` = Window (the default value if the attribute is omitted): This option opens a new instance of Internet Explorer (IE) containing the location of the URL address entered in the `Url` attribute.
  - 1 = Modal Dialog box: A modal dialog box is one that must be closed to go back and work with the opener window. This prevents users from working with the window behind until they close the dialog box that will be opened by the button.
  - 2 = Modeless dialog box: This option opens a dialog box, but, as opposed to the previous option, users can keep working with the windows behind without needing to close this dialog box.
- `WinParams`—With this attribute, you can specify the parameters to be passed when a modal or modeless dialog box option value is used in the previous attribute. For example, you can specify the dialog box position and size, as shown here:

```
<Button WinMode="1" WinParams="dialogLeft:0; dialogTop:0; dialogHeight:100px;
➥dialogWidth:100px">
```

Adding a new button to the toolbar that will take the user to Yahoo! is very easy. Just add the following lines of code inside the `<ToolBar>` node:

```
<Button Icon="/_imgs/ico_18_debug.gif"  Url="http://www.Yahoo.com"
➥Client="Web">
    <Titles>
        <Title LCID="1033" Text="Yahoo" />
    </Titles>
    <ToolTips>
        <ToolTip LCID="1033" Text="Yahoo website." />
    </ToolTips>
</Button>
```

19

Entities Node

Each entity has its own menu items and toolbar, so if you want to add a button or a menu item to be related to only one entity, such as the Account, you would add the button element inside the Entity node. To see an example of how to add a custom menu to the Account entity, follow these steps:

1. Export the `ISV.config` file to be edited. For detailed instructions, see the "Exporting and Importing Entity Customizations" section later in this chapter, or go to Settings, Customizations, Export Customizations, and select the View Client Extensions, as shown in Figure 19.23.
2. Open the file you exported with any text editor like Notepad or Visual Studio (recommended).
3. Do a find for `<Entity name="account">` and enter the highlighted code below inside the CustomMenus element.

```
<Entities>
     <Entity name="account">
      <MenuBar>
         <!-- Custom Menus that you may add -->
         <CustomMenus>
           <Menu>
             <Titles>
               <Title LCID="1033" Text="ISV.NEW" />
             </Titles>
             <MenuItem Url="http://www.microsoft.com" PassParams="0"
➥WinMode="1">
               <Titles>
                 <Title LCID="1033" Text="Coming Soon..." />
               </Titles>
             </MenuItem>
      </MenuBar>
     </Entity>
</Entities>
```

NOTE

The Titles element might contain several Title child nodes—one for each language—with their own LCID to identify the language where 1033 means English, for example.

Save the changes and import the `ISV.Config` back into CRM. For detailed instructions about importing `ISV.Config` customizations, see the "Exporting and Importing Entity Customizations" section later in this chapter, or go to Settings, Customizations, Import Customizations, upload the xml file you edited, and click the Import Selected Customizations button.

After importing the customizations, go to the Workplace, select Accounts, and open any Account or create a new Account. You see the new custom menu added, as shown in Figure 19.29.

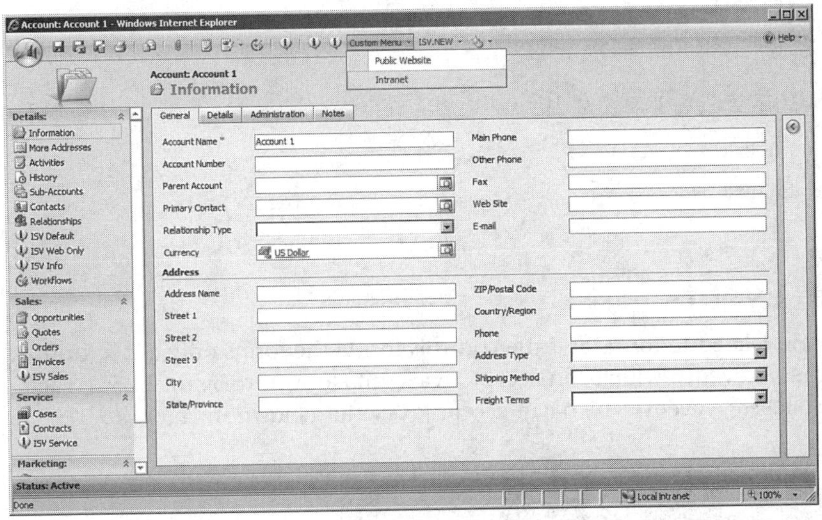

FIGURE 19.29 New Custom Menu added to the Account entity Form.

`ServiceManagement` Node

This element customizes the Service Calendar (refer to Chapter 12, "Working with Service," for more information about this section).

The `ServiceManagement` node only contains a child node named `AppointmentBook`. The `AppointmentBook` node can have one of these nodes:

- `SmoothScrollLimit`—This option sets the maximum number of blocks to be displayed by a service activity before autoscrolling the appointment when it is selected or displayed.
- `ValidationChunkSize`—This option is used to configure the amount of activities to be validated simultaneously by the server. The validation occurs in cases where more than one activity requires the same resource or materials.
- `TimeBlocks`—With each `TimeBlock` element, you can apply a different style to each status code of a Service Activity.

See this example:

```
<ServiceManagement>
   <AppointmentBook>
     <SmoothScrollLimit>2000</SmoothScrollLimit>
     <TimeBlocks>
```

```
        <!-- All CSS Class mapping for Service activities -->
        <TimeBlock EntityType="4214" StatusCode="1"
➥CssClass="ganttBlockServiceActivityStatus1" />
      </TimeBlocks>
    </AppointmentBook>
  </ServiceManagement>
```

The `EntityType` attribute can be one of the following values:

4214—Service activity

4201—Appointment

JavaScript Events

JavaScript events are related to forms and the controls inside the forms only. Each form has `OnLoad` and `OnSave` events, which can accept JavaScript (shown in Figure 19.30). Each field also has the `OnChange` event, which can accept JavaScript (shown in Figure 19.31).

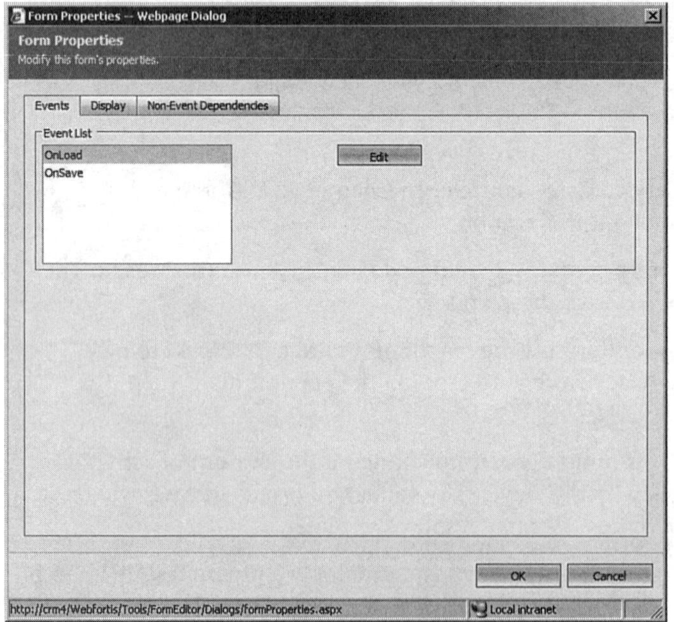

FIGURE 19.30 Form events that you can customize with JavaScript.

OnLoad

The `OnLoad` event occurs every time the window of an entity is open, either when you edit an existing record or when you create a new one.

OnSave

The OnSave event occurs every time the Save icon or the Save and Close button is pressed.

OnChange

The OnChange event is fired every time the value of the field is changed and after it loses the focus.

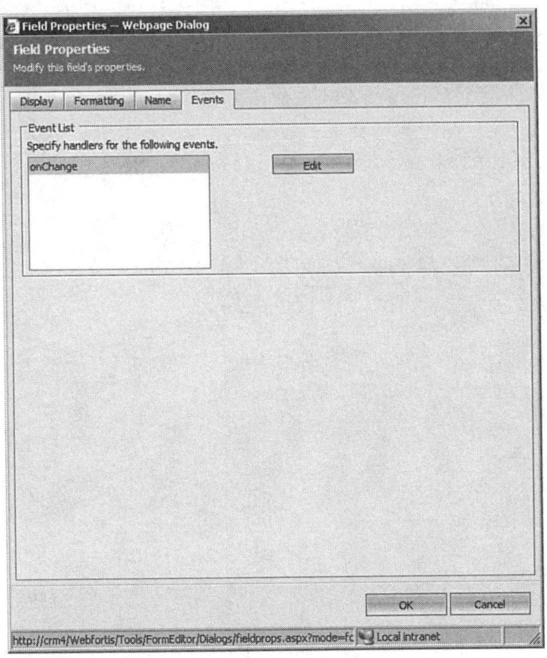

FIGURE 19.31 Form Fields events that you can customize with JavaScript.

Advanced Event-Handling Tips and Tricks

If you are familiar with JavaScript and HTML, you might be thinking, "How can I add JavaScript code for all the other events that any regular HTML INPUT control has, such as the onkeypress, onkeyup, or onkeydown events?" Although you can have Microsoft Dynamics CRM perform these types of actions, it requires a little more effort. Let's look at an example of how to add the onkeyup event.

Suppose that you have a custom entity called House to which you have added the following custom fields: width, height, and area. You want to have the area automatically calculated from the width and height without forcing the user to move the focus from one control to the other to see the changes. You could add the following piece of code in the OnLoad event to attach a field control to the standard onkeyup event:

```
crmForm.all.new_height.attachEvent ("onkeyup", doCalc);
crmForm.all.new_width.attachEvent ("onkeyup", doCalc);
function doCalc ()
{
crmForm.all.new_area.value = crmForm.all.new_height.value *
crmForm.all.new_width.value;
}
```

To see this sample working, follow these steps:

1. Go to Settings, Customizations, Customize Entities.
2. Click New to create a new entity.
3. Enter **House** in the `Display Name` field and **Houses** in the `Plural Name` field (see Figure 19.32).

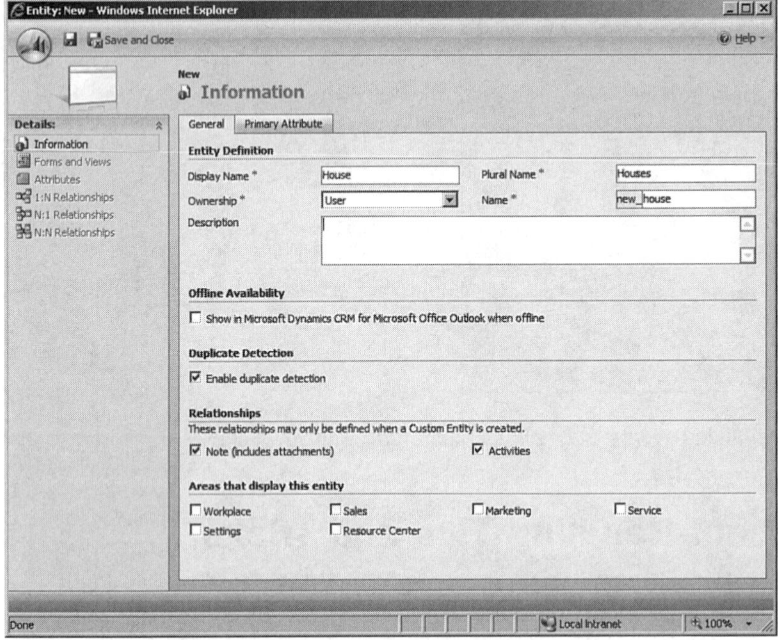

FIGURE 19.32 Creating the House custom entity.

4. Click Save (do not close the window).
5. Click Attributes from the left side options under the Details section (see Figure 19.33).
6. Click New to add the custom attribute.
7. Enter **Height** in `Display Name`, and select float in the `Type` field (see Figure 19.34).

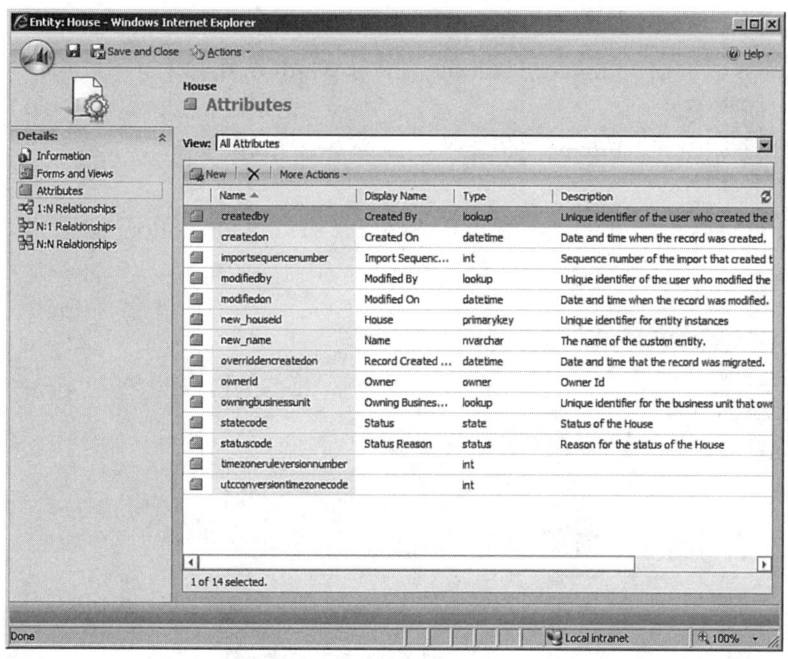

FIGURE 19.33 Attributes.

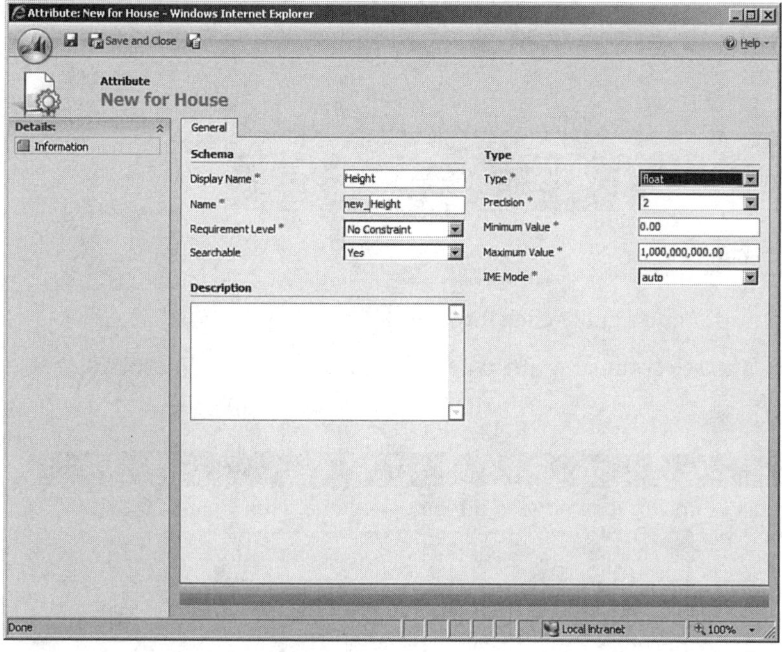

FIGURE 19.34 Adding Height attribute.

8. Click Save and Close to save the attribute.
9. Repeat steps 6 to 8 with the difference and then enter Width in the Display Name using the same float type.
10. Repeat steps 6 to 8 with the difference and then enter Area in the Display Name using the same float type.
11. Click Forms and Views from the left-side options under the Details section (see Figure 19.35).

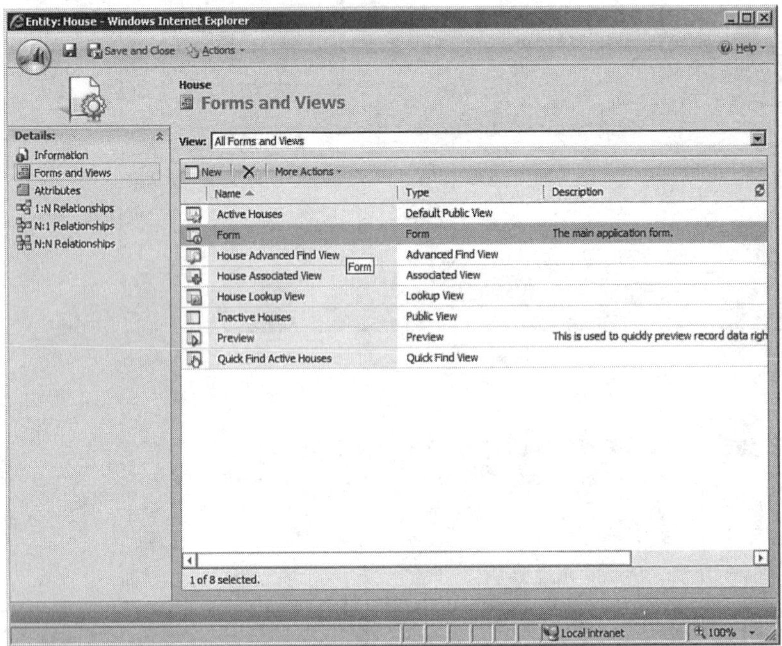

FIGURE 19.35 Forms and Views.

12. Select the Form record and double-click it to edit it.
13. Click Add Fields and select the new attributes we created (Height, Width, and Area) (see Figure 19.36).

TIP

Click the Name heading to easily locate these attributes together (see Figure 19.37).

14. Click OK to add the fields to the Form.

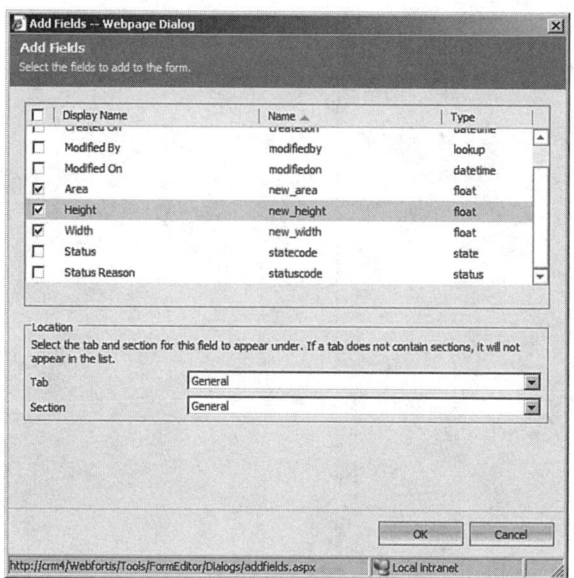

FIGURE 19.36 Adding Fields.

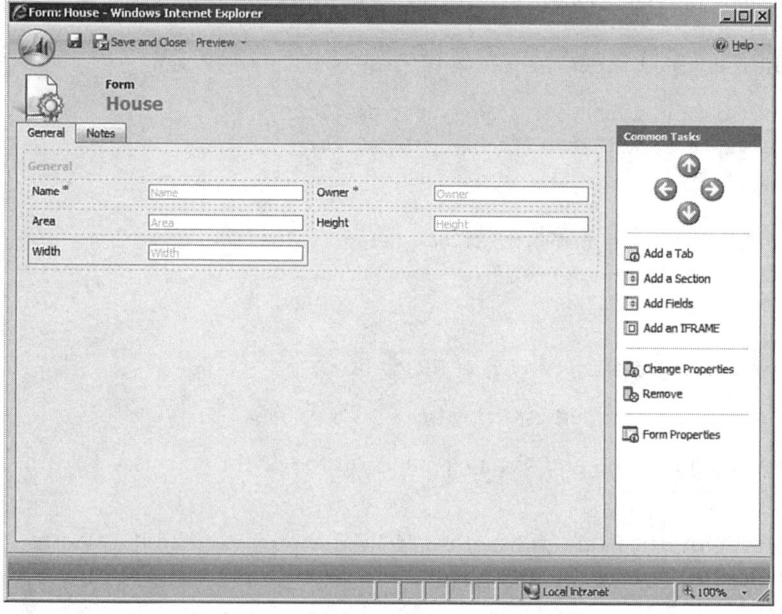

FIGURE 19.37 Custom fields added to the Form.

15. Click Form Properties.

16. Select the `OnLoad` event from the list and click Edit (see Figure 19.38).

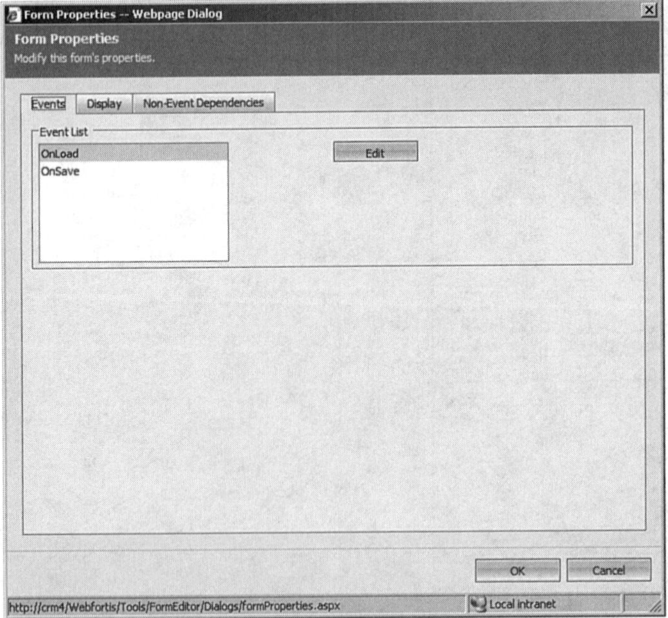

FIGURE 19.38 Selecting OnLoad event.

17. Check the Event is enabled; enter the following code (see Figure 19.39):

```
crmForm.all.new_height.attachEvent ("onkeyup", doCalc);
crmForm.all.new_width.attachEvent ("onkeyup", doCalc);
function doCalc ()
{
crmForm.all.new_area.value = crmForm.all.new_height.value *
crmForm.all.new_width.value;
}
```

18. Click OK to close the event detail properties dialog box.
19. Click OK to close the Form Properties dialog box.
20. Click the Preview menu button and select Create Form to test the code (see Figure 19.40).
21. Enter a value on the Height field (for example, 10) and enter a value to the Width Field (for example, 10). You see the Area Field is set automatically with the calculated result (100).

TIP

Check the MSDN library for full details of all the events supported in the HTML `INPUT` element.

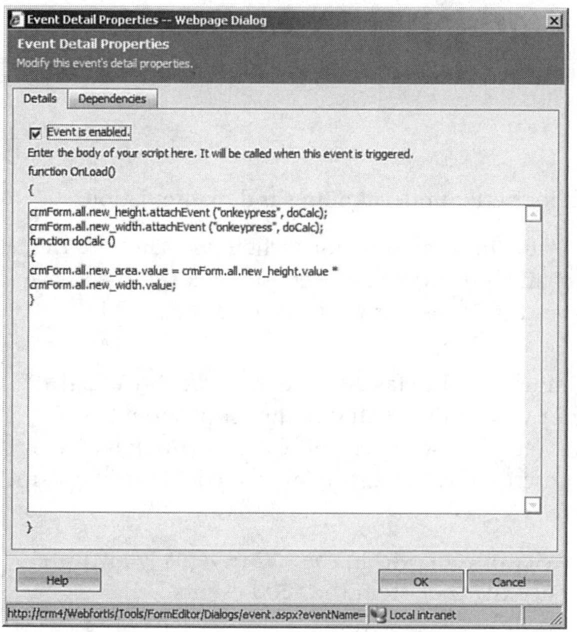

FIGURE 19.39 Adding code to the `OnLoad` event.

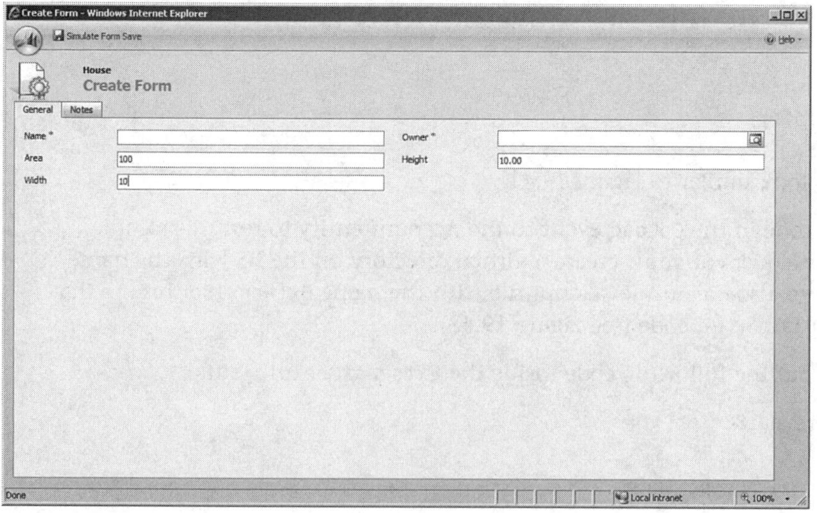

FIGURE 19.40 Testing the solution.

19

Tips and Tricks When Working with Events

When you work with JavaScript code, you encounter some disadvantages of using the regular web interface:

- The interface lacks IntelliSense.
- The JavaScript code is not colored for better understanding and manipulation.
- It is tedious to debug and correct errors in some situations when you can't use the preview feature to simulate your changes because you need to touch the code, save the changes, publish the updates, and then see if it works as expected.

To avoid all these disadvantages, you can use a richer JavaScript editor, such as Visual Studio. To be able to work with JavaScript within Visual Studio, the script should be located in the virtual folder of the same web server of Microsoft CRM. If you don't have access to that server (on CRM Online subscriptions, for example), you could put the script on a separate web server.

Basically, instead of developing with JavaScript code within the CRM events, you create the JavaScript externally and then reference the code from the CRM events.

The following code in the `OnLoad` event is an example of referencing an external JavaScript file:

```
var oXML = new XMLHttpRequest();
oXML.open('GET', "/ExternalScripts/ExternalScript.js", false);
oXML.send('');
eval(oXML.responseText);
CallExternalScript();
```

The code should look similar to Figure 19.41.

We will put this code in the `OnLoad` event to the Account entity to test this sample. Before testing this code, you must create a virtual directory on the IIS with the name ExternalScripts and also create a JavaScript file with the name `ExternalScript.js` that can contain your JavaScript code (see Figure 19.42).

For an easy test, put the following code inside the `ExternalScript.js` file:

```
function CallExternalScript()
{
    alert("external script works!");
}
```

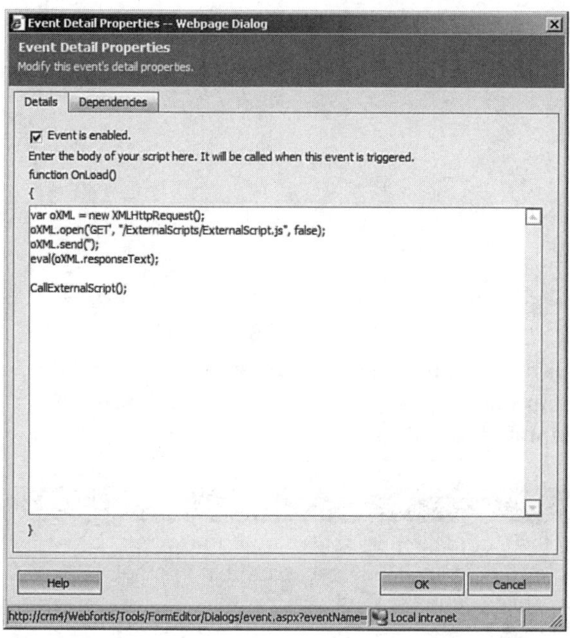

FIGURE 19.41 Code to call external JavaScript file.

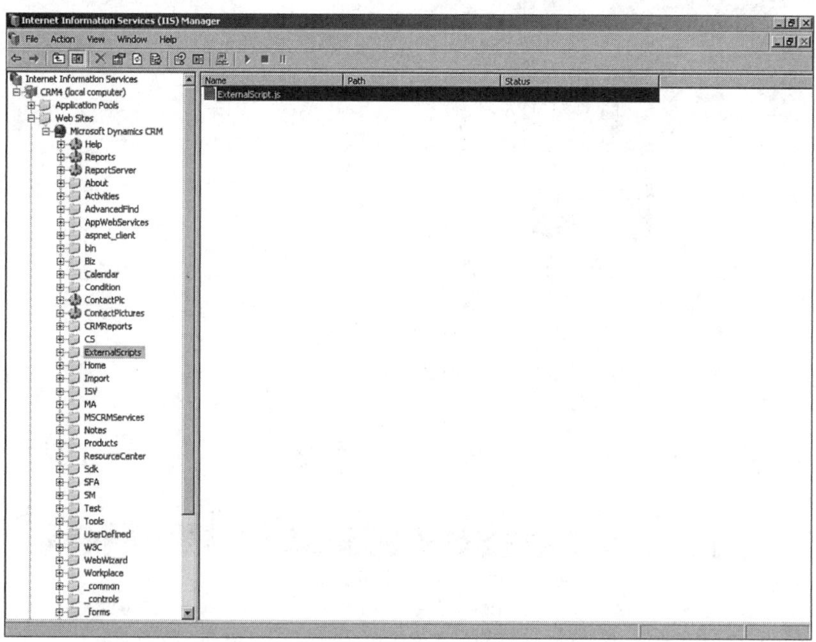

FIGURE 19.42 ExternalScripts location on IIS.

After publishing the customizations to the Account Entity Form, when you open or create a new Account, you will see the alert popup (see Figure 19.43).

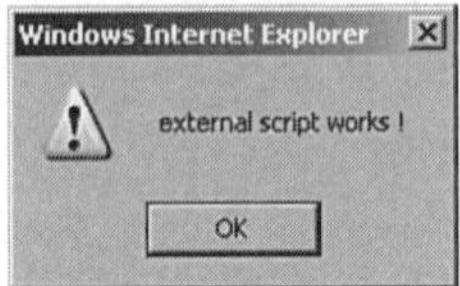

FIGURE 19.43 Testing the ExternalScripts.

To change that alert message or add your own custom code, you only need to edit the external file to make your changes without having to publish the entity customizations. This will be easier for debugging JavaScript codes.

TIP

Be sure to set the content expiration of the ExternalScripts folder in IIS to expire immediately, as shown on Figure 19.44, or the script will be cached within Internet Explorer and you won't see the changes while you make them.

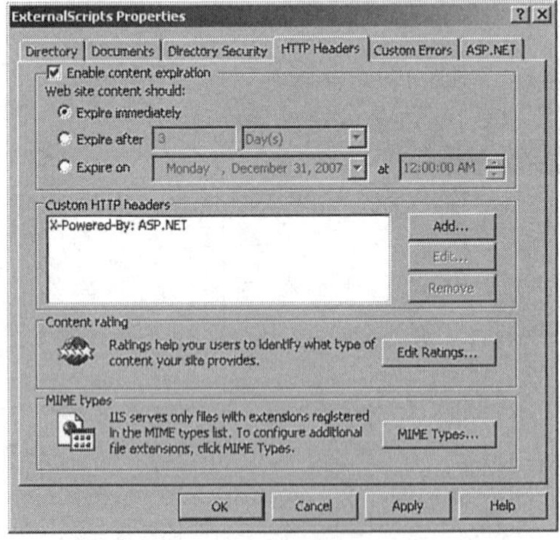

FIGURE 19.44 Enabling content expiration to expire immediately.

NOTE

Even though it is more comfortable to work within Visual Studio to edit and develop JavaScript codes, we recommended that you copy the external code to the event text box of the Form and delete the external reference after you have the script working and debugged. By doing this, you can export the code with the entity customizations for backup or transport it.

TIP

A good utility to work with JavaScript customizations is the Internet Explorer Developer Toolbar, which you can download from the Microsoft website at www.microsoft.com/downloads/details.aspx?FamilyId=E59C3964-672D-4511-BB3E-2D5E1DB91038&displaylang=en.

Exporting and Importing Entity Customizations

You can export all customizations made on any entity out of the CRM system to be used on other CRM implementations or for backup purposes.

Exporting Customizations

To export a customization, go to Settings, Customization, Export Customizations (see Figure 19.45).

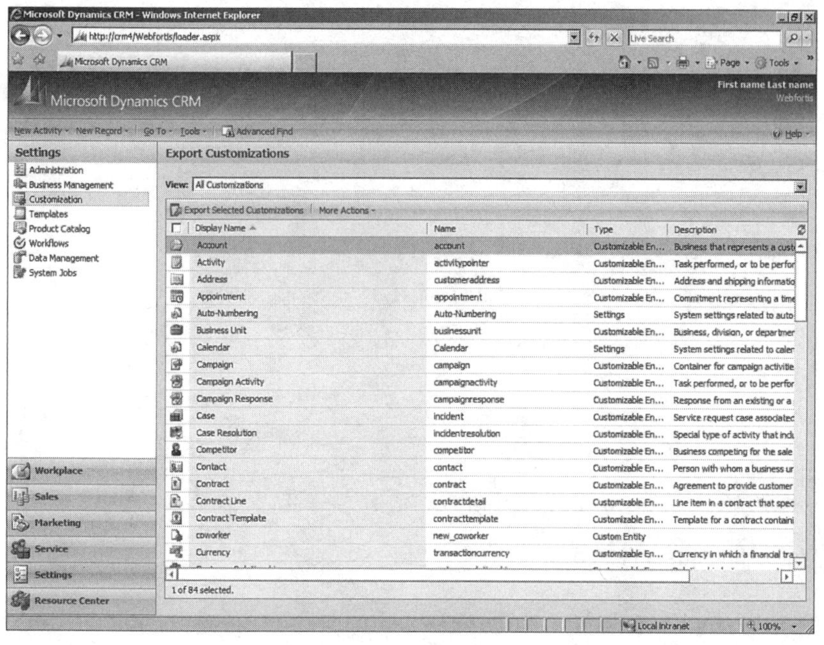

FIGURE 19.45 Exporting customizations.

You can export all customizations for all the entities by clicking More Actions, Export All Customizations, or you can export only a few customizations by selecting them from the Quickview (you can select more than one by holding the Ctrl key), by just clicking Export Selected Customizations.

This version of CRM has improved the export because the customizations are prepared for download as a compressed zip file that is light and useful for fast download, especially with low-bandwidth Internet connections.

When you look inside the downloaded compressed zip file, you will see an XML file with the name `customizations.xml`. (Notice that even when exporting more than one entity, the zip file contains only one XML file `customizations.xml`.) This XML file contains all the customized entities.

Importing Customizations

To import a customization, go to Settings, Customization, Import Customizations (see Figure 19.46).

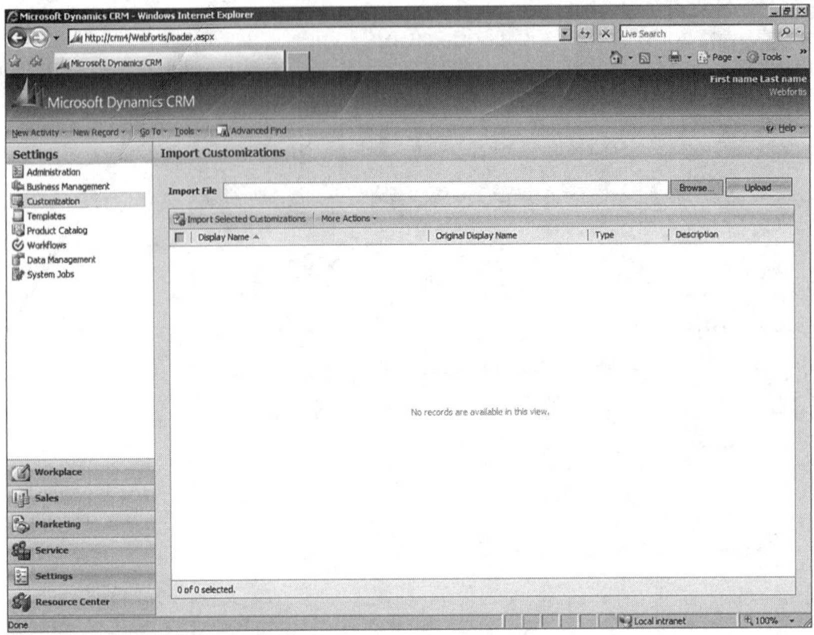

FIGURE 19.46 Importing customizations.

Enter the filename with the full path in the Import File text box. (This path should be no longer than 100 characters.) You can also click the Browse button to locate the file on your hard drive. After you click the Upload button, you see the customizations that are available to import, as shown in Figure 19.47.

You can upload the XML file or a zip file containing the `customizations.xml` file.

To import all the customizations on the uploaded file, you can click More Actions, Import All Customizations. If you don't want to import all the customizations, you can select the customizations you want (holding the Ctrl key to select more than one) and click Import

Selected Customizations. After clicking any of these buttons, you will be alerted to confirm the import operation as it cannot be canceled or reverted after it has started (see Figure 19.48).

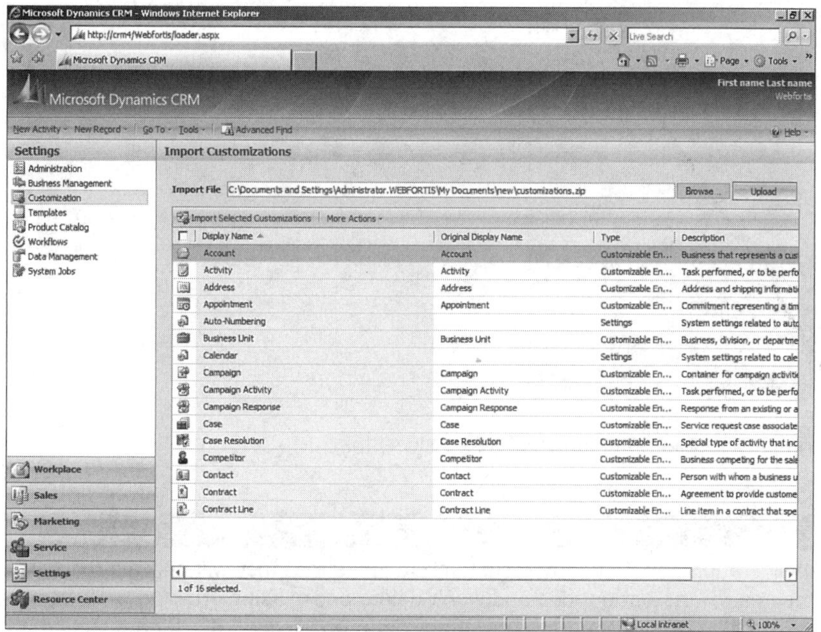

FIGURE 19.47 Selecting import customizations.

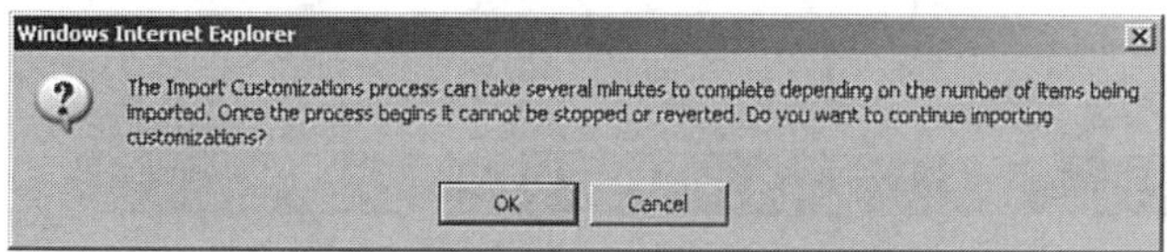

FIGURE 19.48 Import customizations alert.

Click OK to import the customizations. When the process finishes, you see the result with any detail about errors if there are any (see Figure 19.49).

NOTE

After the customizations are imported, you need to publish them to have them available to users.

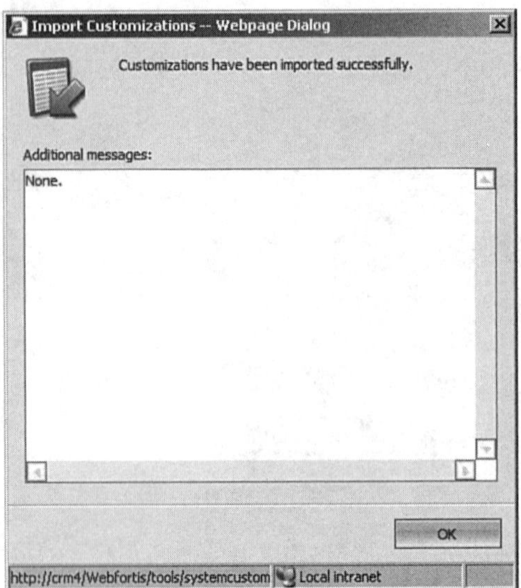

FIGURE 19.49 Import customizations completed successfully.

NOTE

An important consideration about importing customizations is that they will only add or append new attributes to existent entities and won't delete any missing attribute or data. So there is no risk of losing the data you or any other user added if you had previously added a new attribute and then imported an older version without that attribute. However, the new fields you might have added to the Form or to the Views will be deleted.

TIP

When importing customizations for the Site Map or the `ISV.config`, you might accidentally delete the Settings Area or import an errored file. This might break the web application and access to the Import Customization interface (see Figure 19.50), which would allow you to restore a backup which may not be possible. If that happens, you can use the following link to access the interface directly:

```
http://<servername>:<port>/<organizationname>/tools/
systemcustomization/systemcustomization.aspx
```

For example:

```
http://crm4/webfortis/tools/systemcustomization/
systemcustomization.aspx
```

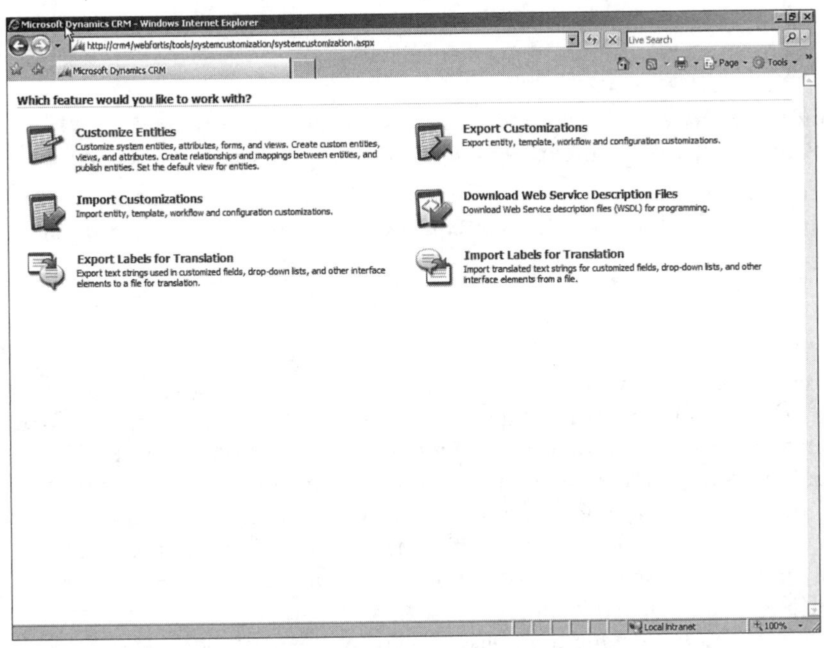

FIGURE 19.50 Customizations interface to recover a broken application.

Working with the SDK

The CRM software development kit (SDK) is a compound of help files, documentation, binary tools, and code samples that gives developers the capability to extend and understand advanced Microsoft Dynamics CRM customizations. By "advanced customizations," we refer to all customizations that can't be done through the standard CRM user interfaces, such as the ones you saw earlier on this chapter. To develop these advanced customizations, you need a tool such as Visual Studio 2005, along with a solid knowledge and understanding of .NET development and programming in languages such as C# or VB .NET.

The SDK doesn't usually come with the product media, so you must download it from Microsoft. The SDK can be found at www.microsoft.com/downloads/details.aspx?familyid=82E632A7-FAF9-41E0-8EC1-A2662AAE9DFB&displaylang=en or by searching for CRM 4.0 SDK at http://msdn2.microsoft.com/en-us/default.aspx.

Advanced customizations can include these:

- Server programming
    - **Advanced workflow development**—For details about workflow development, refer to Chapter 20, "Workflow Development."
    - **Plug-ins development**—For details about plug-ins development, refer to Chapter 21, "Plug-Ins."

19

- Client programming
- Reports development
    - Advanced report development with SQL Server Reporting Services (SSRS): For details about SRS development, refer to Chapter 18, "Advanced Reporting."

The main help file is the `CrmSdk4.chm` file; it contains detailed documentation about all these topics.

Summary

This chapter looked at the CRM entity model, the attribute types we can use to add new fields to the entity forms, and the relationships between the entities that can be 1:N , N:1, or N:N. We made some basic customizations adding tabs, sections, and controls to the forms. We used and reviewed the IFRAME control and also added menus and controls to the toolbar using the Site Map and the `ISV.Config` files. We explained how to use JavaScript events exposed by the forms controls, like the `OnLoad` and `OnSave` events to extend the Forms, and the `OnChange` event for the fields, and how to add other events manually, like the `onkeyup`. We made a sample about how to call an external script to easily debug our scripts without having to publish the entity customizations. Finally, we detailed how to import and export customizations and reviewed the SDK and its uses.

CHAPTER 20

Workflow Development

IN THIS CHAPTER

- ▶ Workflow Basics
- ▶ Duplicate Detection Rules
- ▶ Creating Workflows in Windows Workflow Foundation (WWF) with Visual Studio

Workflow Basics

Before digging into Workflow development, let's briefly review what Workflow means in IT terms.

A Workflow is basically a series of functions or methods called steps that are performed sequentially. The flow can change the processing direction of the sequential steps by using conditionals referred to as Conditional Branches. Figure 20.1 shows a simple sample conditional Workflow as it would appear on a flowchart.

Workflow is an excellent tool for managing both data and processes. With Workflow rules, you can easily ensure that certain steps are followed and that required business processes are executed.

One important consideration is that Workflows in Microsoft Dynamics CRM are executed asynchronously, and they use a Windows service to act as a Host application for the Workflow engine to work. This Windows service is called the Microsoft CRM Asynchronous Processing Service and must be running on the server or else the Workflows won't execute. Notice that if this service is not running, you won't see any of the Workflows you created throughout this chapter running properly. However, they will run as soon as you start this service because they are queued. So it is a good idea to verify the Windows service is running by going to Start, Control Panel, Administrative tools, Services and start the Microsoft CRM Asynchronous Processing Service if it is not running (as shown in Figure 20.2).

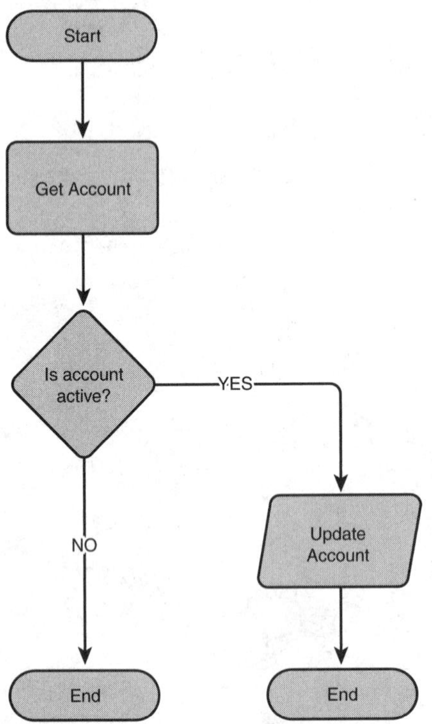

FIGURE 20.1 Workflow sample image.

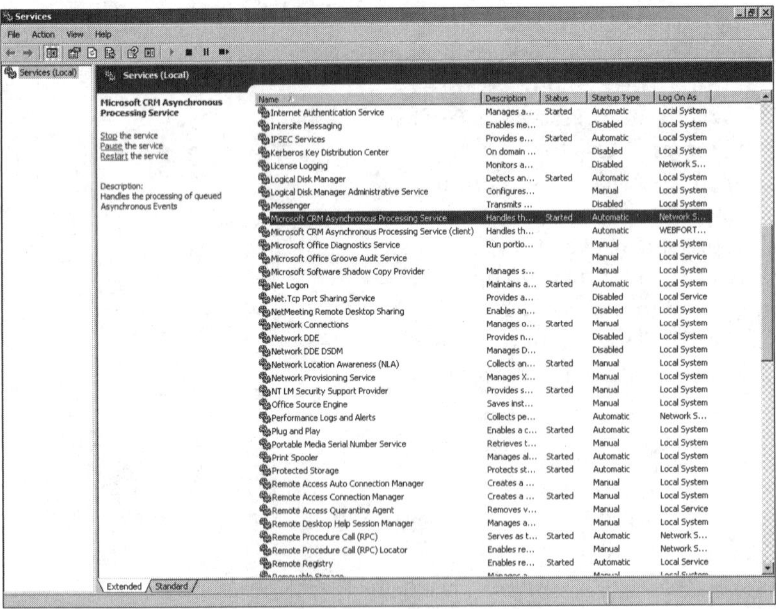

FIGURE 20.2 Checking if Microsoft CRM Asynchronous Processing Service is running.

Another consideration is that since Workflows are executed asynchronously, they don't run immediately, and, depending on the server overhead, they might take some seconds or minutes to complete. If you need a process to run immediately, it would be better for you to think about creating plug-ins that can be set to be executed synchronously. (See Chapter 21, "Plug-Ins," for detailed instructions about how to use and create plug-ins.)

Another new feature related to Workflows is that they are now treated as entities in CRM, so you can use the Advanced Find tool to look up Workflows, and you can also create reports based on them.

Creating Workflows with Microsoft Dynamics CRM

In Microsoft CRM Version 3.0, a Windows application called Workflow Manager had to be used when creating and setting up Workflows. This application required administrative privileges to use. (While other users could create Workflows using this application, their Workflows often failed when implemented due to permissions problems—often without any explanation.)

With Microsoft Dynamics CRM, the old Workflow Manager Windows application doesn't exist, and the new Workflow Manager is embedded directly into the web and Outlook client applications. Thus, you can easily create and manage Workflows.

By default, any valid CRM user can create Workflows; however, the permissions to create Workflows can be configured by roles, to prevent users from creating new Workflows that might corrupt the system data. Figure 20.3 shows where permissions are set in the Settings, Security Roles area for creating Workflows using the Salesperson Role as an example.

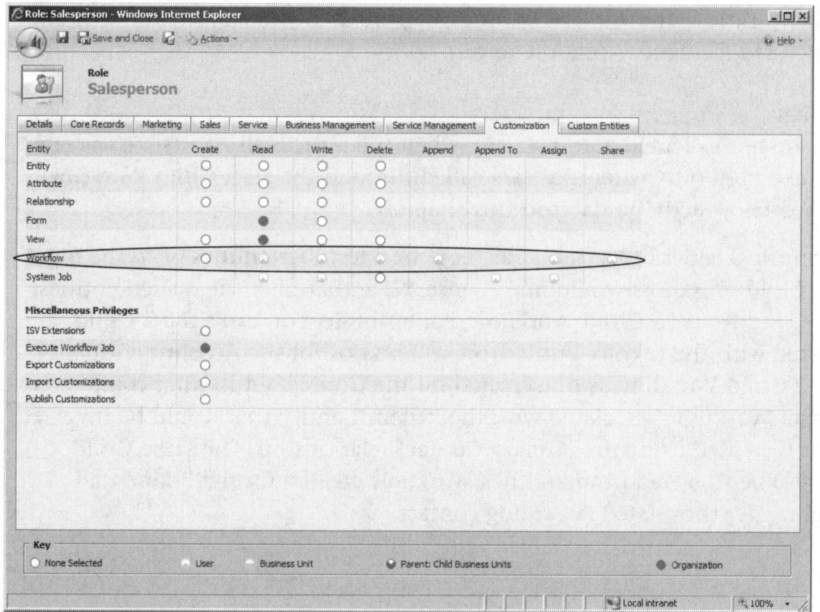

FIGURE 20.3 Workflow permissions configuration.

Refer to Chapter 14, "Settings and Configuration," for more information about setting permission levels.

Other improvements to the previous Workflow Manager include additional triggering events and run settings.

The events that trigger a Workflow are:

- Record is created
- Record status changes
- Record is assigned
- Record attributes change
- Record is deleted

Notice that Record attributes change has been included and allows you to reference any field on the underlying entity. This is a vast improvement from the previous version.

The details of each event are outlined later in this chapter.

The run settings are:

- On Demand
- As a Child Workflow

On Demand

If this option is specified, the Workflow can be triggered manually by going to the associated entity and clicking the Run Workflow button. Notice in Figure 20.4 that this button will be visible only if an On-Demand Workflow was created and published for that entity.

After clicking Run Workflow, the window shown in Figure 20.5 will appear, allowing the user to select which On-Demand Workflow to run.

As a Child Workflow

Child Workflows are not executed automatically when the associated events are triggered. Instead, they are executed only when they are called through the Start Child Workflow activity (see the Workflow activities later in this chapter).

If you need to perform a series of steps that are common to other entities or to the organization, using a Child Workflow would make sense. Note that only the related entities' Workflows can be used to call a Child Workflow. For example, you can't call a Child Workflow associated with the Invoice entity from a Workflow of the Account entity. A good example of a Child Workflow is one created for the Contact entity that could be called from another Workflow associated with the Account entity that would be triggered when an Account is created using the Primary Contact relationship. The same Child Workflow could also be triggered from another Workflow created for the Phone Call entity that would trigger the related Regarding contact.

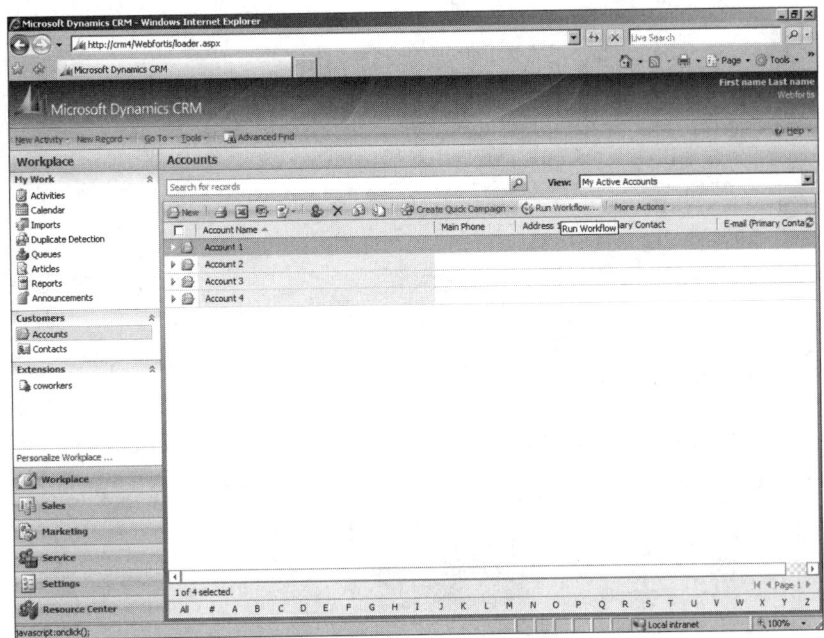

FIGURE 20.4 Run Workflow for the Account entity.

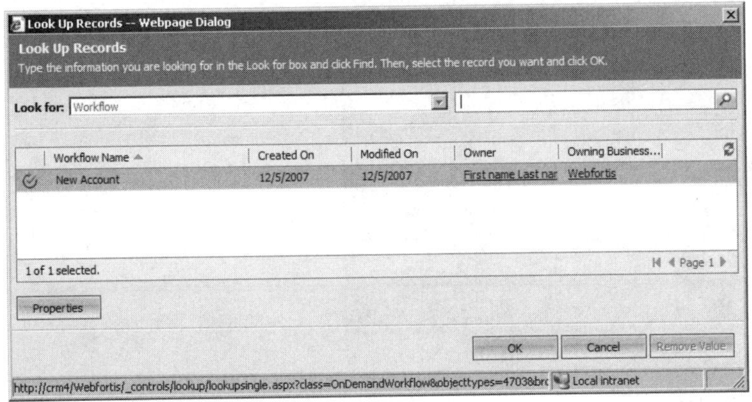

FIGURE 20.5 Running an On-Demand Workflow for the Account entity.

If neither On Demand nor As a Child Workflow is selected, the Workflow will run automatically when the triggering event is triggered.

To access the new Workflow Manager, follow these steps:

1. From the main interface, navigate to Go To, Settings, Workflows (as shown in Figure 20.6).

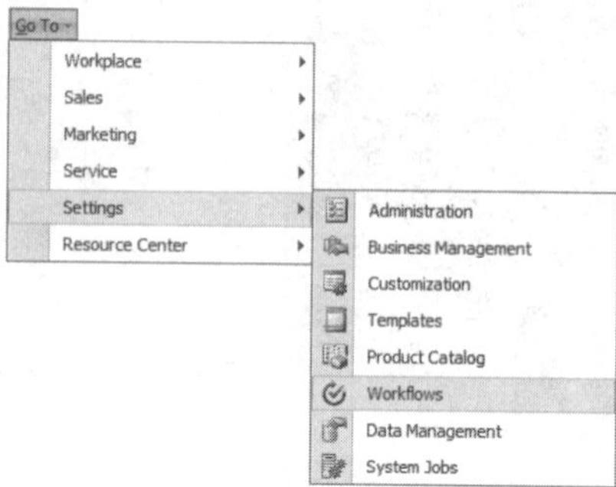

FIGURE 20.6 Settings, Workflows screen.

2. To create a new Workflow, click New and the Create Workflow dialog window will appear (see Figure 20.7).

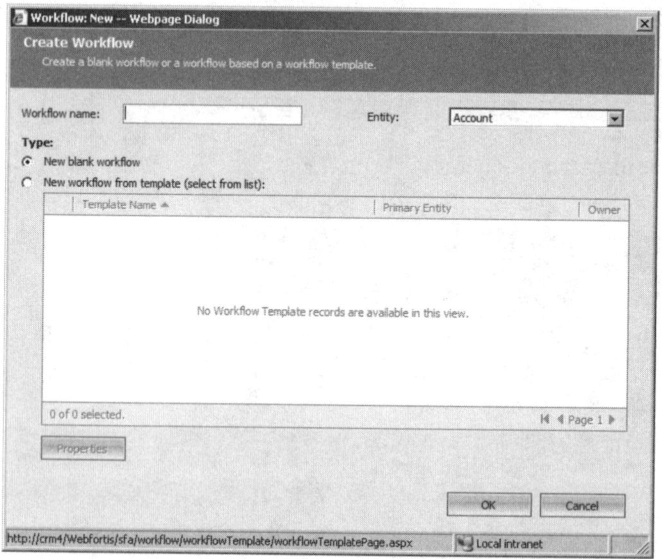

FIGURE 20.7 Create Workflow window.

There is an option to create either a blank Workflow or a New Workflow from a Template. For this example, we're going to create a blank Workflow; however, as explained later in this chapter, when working with the Workflow, it can either be saved as a regular Workflow or it can be saved as a Workflow Template. If saved as a Workflow Template, it can be referenced in this list for additional customization and/or other options.

Notice that when creating a new Workflow, you must associate it with a base entity. The entity is a drop-down option (found in Figure 20.7) and can be from any entity in the system.

3. Enter a name for the New Workflow, select an entity record type, select New Blank Workflow, and click OK (see Figure 20.8).

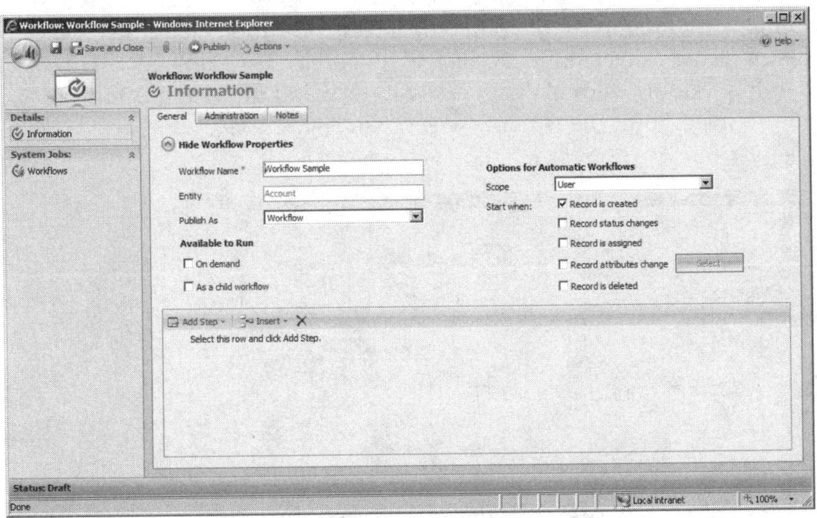

FIGURE 20.8 Workflow properties.

Now you are ready to start adding any of the following steps by clicking Add Step:

- Stage
- Check condition
- Wait condition
- Create record
- Update record
- Assign record
- Send E-mail

- ▶ Start Child Workflow
- ▶ Change status
- ▶ Stop Workflow

Stage

Although stages are used for grouping purposes (see Figure 20.9), they are also stored in the database, enabling you to report on the different stages and various stage metrics, such as the number of records affected for each stage. If you have a complex Workflow with several steps in it, grouping steps makes it easier to read and understand. You can collapse or expand the stages to fit the window screen (see Figure 20.9).

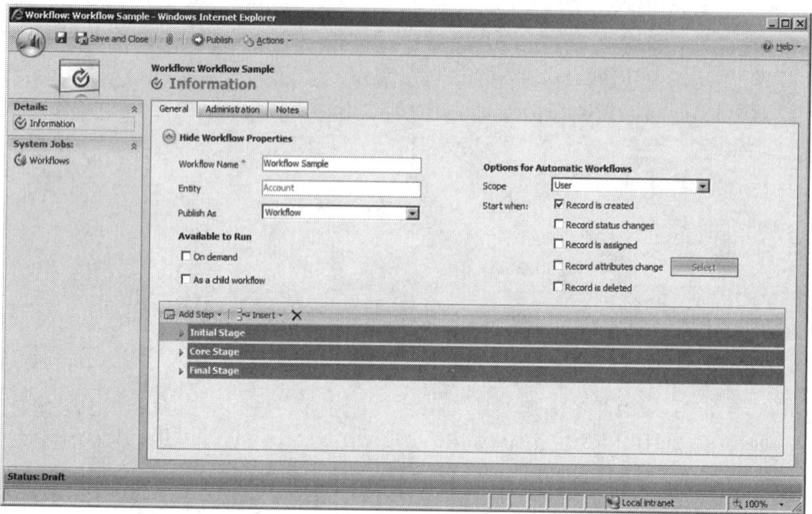

FIGURE 20.9 Workflow stages as shown on a 3 stage Workflow collapsed.

Check Condition

A check condition is a Boolean evaluation similar to the `if...then` conditional in programming. (For those unfamiliar with an `if…then` conditional, it is the way conditions are evaluated. For example if a=b, then c=d.). The condition to be evaluated can be either true or false.

The following sample is a Workflow that will use a check condition to see if a newly added Account name equals the value entered for its website. If so, it will send an e-mail alerting us that a new Account has been created.

1. Click Add step, then select Check Condition (see Figure 20.10).
2. Enter an optional description in the Type a Step Description Here box. The condition we're going to add is if the Account is equal to some value, then perform some action. To add this condition, click the link that says <condition> Click to Configure (see Figure 20.11).

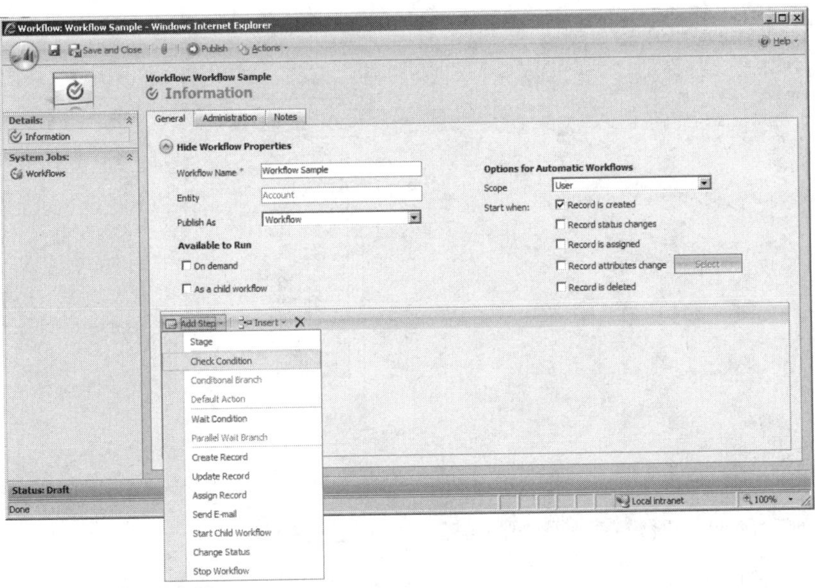

FIGURE 20.10 Adding a check condition.

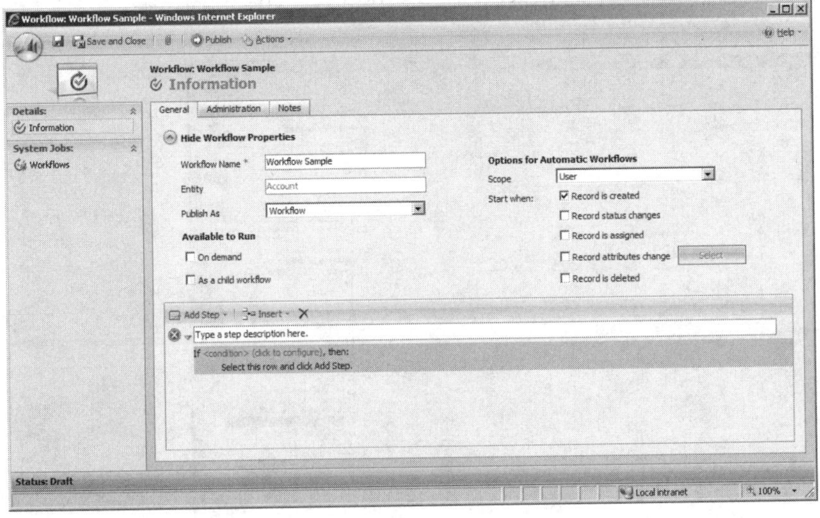

FIGURE 20.11 Using a check condition.

3. Select Account, Account Name, Equals to enter a fixed-value condition in the Specify Workflow Condition dialog box that opens (see Figure 20.12). For more information about working with this dialog screen, refer to Chapter 7, “Common Functions,” section “Advanced Find,” as it uses the same principals when selecting entities and conditions).

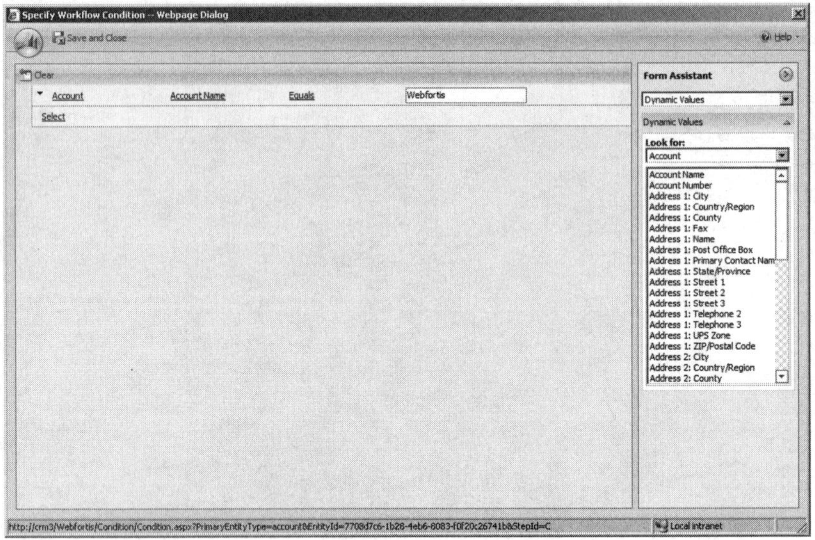

FIGURE 20.12 Configuring the evaluation expression based on a hard-coded value.

4. To set a dynamic value, select an entity from the drop-down list, and click the desired field in the list box below to set the condition (see Figure 20.13).

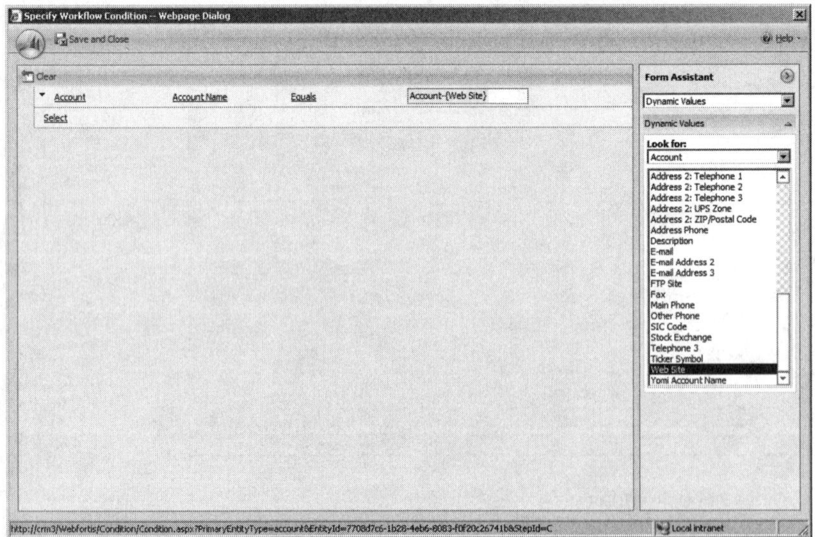

FIGURE 20.13 Configuring the evaluation expression based on an entity property.

5. Click Save and Close to continue.

6. Click Select This Row, Add Step, Send E-mail (see Figure 20.14).

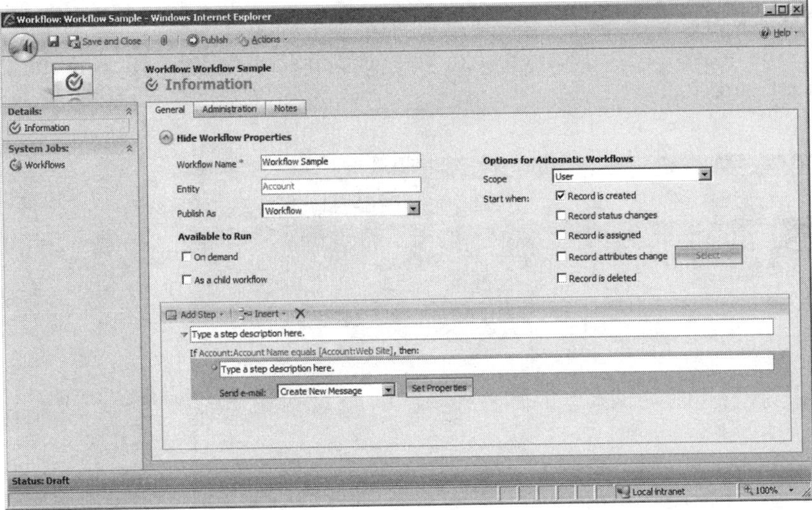

FIGURE 20.14 Creating an e-mail based on a conditional.

7. Click Set Properties to continue.
8. Enter a subject and body message for the new e-mail (see Figure 20.15).

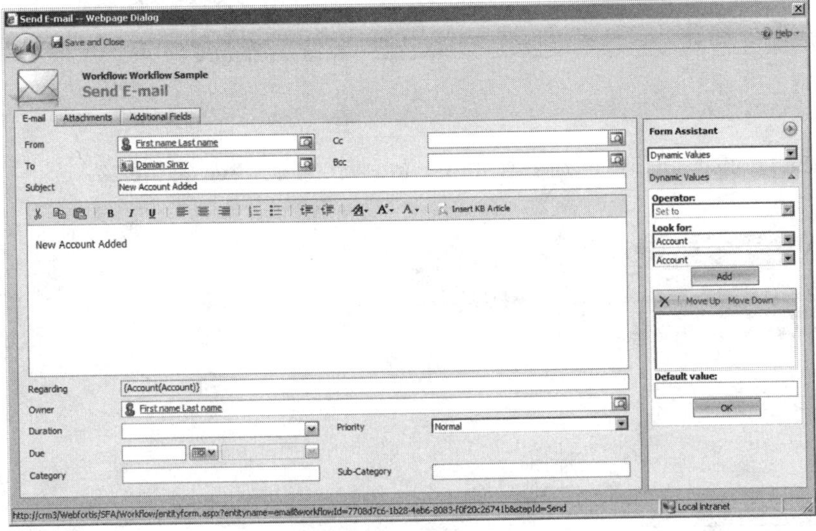

FIGURE 20.15 Configuring the e-mail properties.

9. Click Save and Close.

20

Workflow Activation

Before you can use the Workflow you just created, you need to activate it by clicking the Publish button (see Figure 20.16).

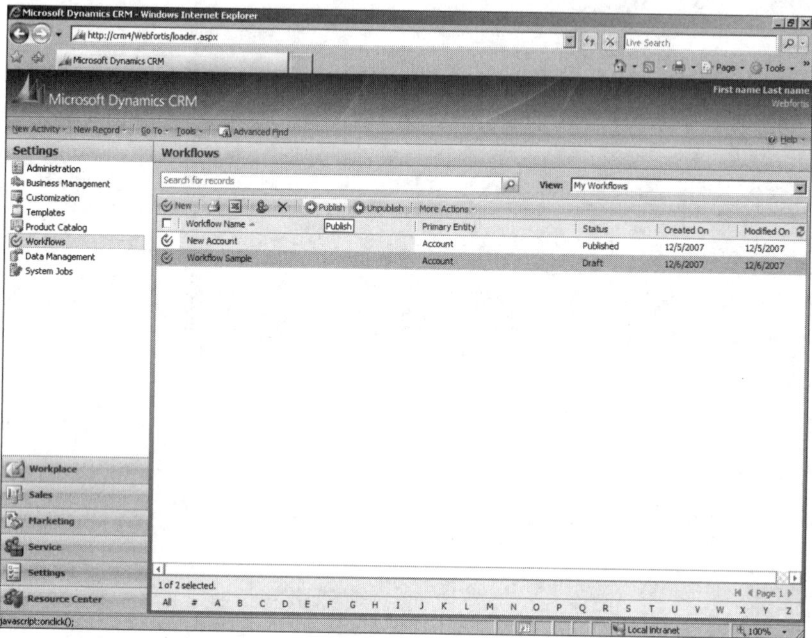

FIGURE 20.16 Publishing a Workflow.

When you click the Publish button, a confirmation window appears (see Figure 20.17).

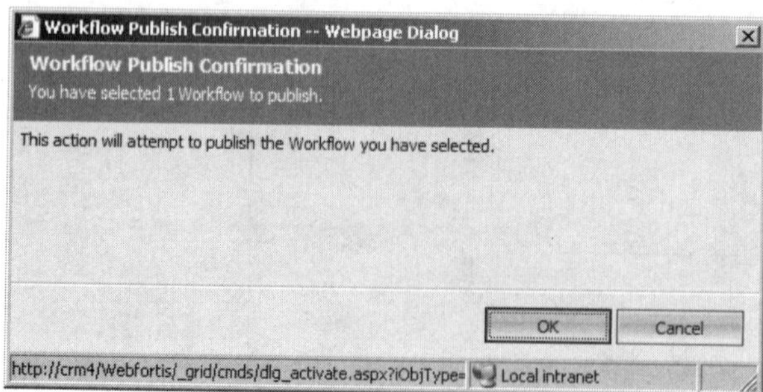

FIGURE 20.17 Workflow Publish Confirmation dialog box.

You can always deactivate the Workflow by clicking the Unpublish button (see Figure 20.18). If you need to make any change to a Workflow, you must unpublish it first because the capability to edit it is disabled if the Workflow is active and published.

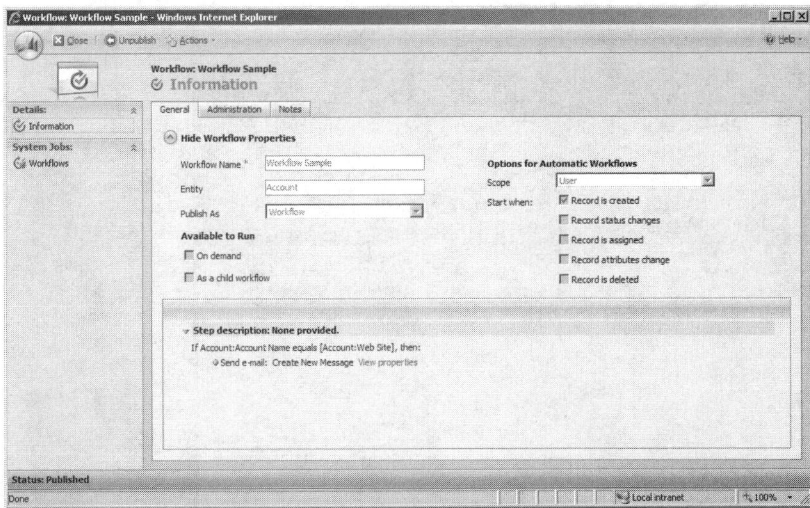

FIGURE 20.18 Viewing a published Workflow with the settings disabled.

Testing the Workflow

When a new Account is created, your Workflow sample is triggered. You can see the progress of a Workflow by looking at the Status Reason. To do that, from the top menu, click Go To, Settings, System Jobs, and change the Type to Workflow option to filter only the Workflows (see Figure 20.19).

When working with this screen, you have the option to select from the drop-downs at the top to filter the view. By default, they are selected to All System Jobs, All Types, and All Entities; however, if you select a value from the drop-down list (such as Type equal to Workflow), the result will filter to only those Types. You can also see the workflow progress from the Workflow tab in the near navigation of the entity. This is very useful in seeing both the executed workflow as well as the specific record instance workflow.

Note that the Workflow engine is asynchronous and the Workflow may not immediately be trigged when the Account is created. When the Workflow finishes, the new e-mail activity is created, and you can go to your Workplace and see the e-mail in the activities area.

Depending on your e-mail router configurations, the e-mail will be sent directly to the destination, or it will be queued as an activity (see Figure 20.20).

Notice you will have to change the Type drop-down list to E-mail to see the e-mails' activities as they are not shown by default if your e-mail router is configured to send the e-mails automatically. For more details about how to set up e-mails and use the e-mail router, refer to Chapter 15, "E-mail Configuration."

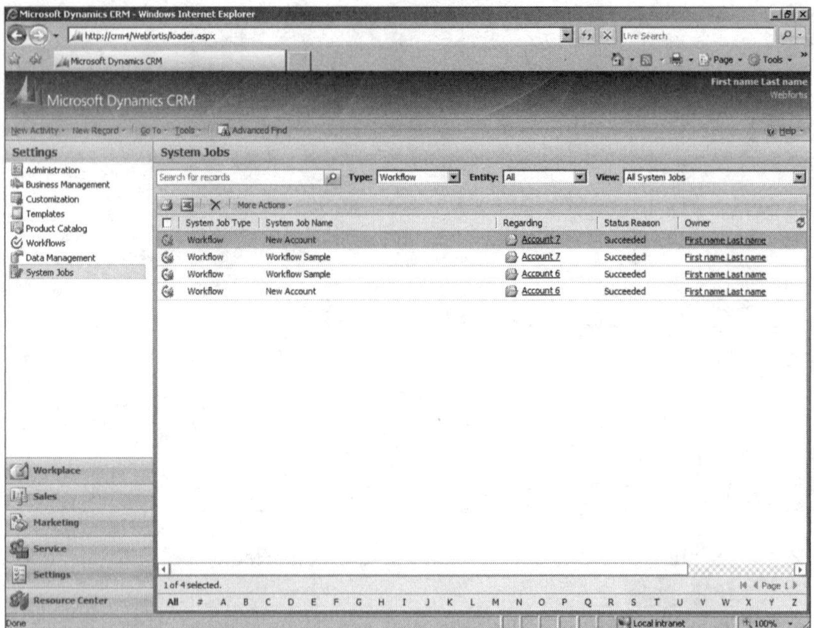

FIGURE 20.19 Monitoring Workflow progress.

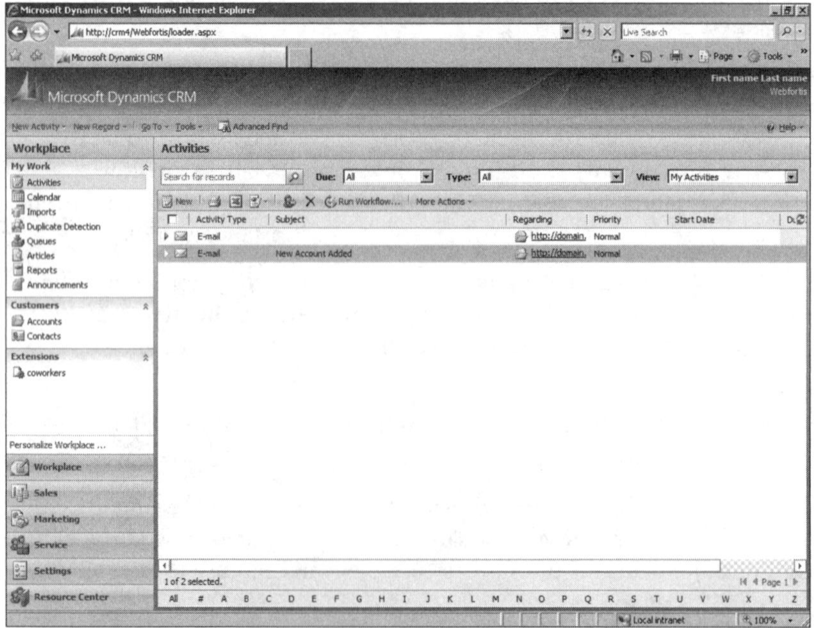

FIGURE 20.20 Workflow results with a new e-mail activity created for the new account.

The conditions described in the following sections are the conditions previously described during Workflow creation.

Wait Condition

The wait condition can put the Workflow to sleep until a condition changes, such as the property of the associated entity or after a period of time has elapsed. Notice that if you use this step, the workflow status will appear as In Progress during the wait time.

Create Record

Use this activity to create a new instance of any entity. The user can hardcode the properties or retrieve them from the associated entity.

Update Record

This activity updates an existing instance of an entity.

Assign Record

This activity assigns the associated entity to a user.

Send E-mail

This activity sends an e-mail by creating a new message or using a template.

You can create a new e-mail message or use a predefined template as a recommended option. For additional information about how to create e-mail templates, refer to Chapter 14.

Start Child Workflow

This activity calls a Child Workflow. As described earlier, a Child Workflow is one that needs to be created with the As a Child Workflow setting.

Change Status

This step changes the associated entity status. The status type varies by entity. Table 20.1 lists the different entities and statuses affected by Change Status.

TABLE 20.1 Entities and Statuses Affected by Change Status

Entity	Status
Accounts	Active, Inactive
Appointments	Canceled, Completed, Open, Scheduled
Article templates	Active, Inactive
Articles	Draft, Published, Unapproved
Campaign activities	Canceled, Closed, Open
Campaign responses	Canceled, Closed, Open
Campaign	Active
Cases	Active, Canceled, Resolved
Contacts	Active, Inactive
Contract lines	Canceled, Existing, Expired, Renewed
Contracts	Active, Canceled, Draft, Expired, Invoiced, On Hold

TABLE 20.1 Continued

Entity	Status
Currencies	Active, Inactive
Discount lists	Active, Inactive
Invoices	Active, Canceled, Closed (deprecated), Paid
Leads	Disqualified, Open, Qualified
Mail merge templates	Active, Inactive
Marketing lists	Active, Inactive
Opportunities	In Progress, On Hold, Won
Orders	Active, Canceled, Fulfilled, Invoiced, Submitted
Price lists	Active, Inactive
Products	Active, Inactive
Quotes	Active, Closed, Draft, Won
Service activities	Canceled, Closed, Open, Scheduled
Services	Active, Inactive
System jobs	Completed, Locked, Ready, Suspended
Users	Disabled, Enabled
Workflows	Draft, Published

Figure 20.21 shows the Change Status activity.

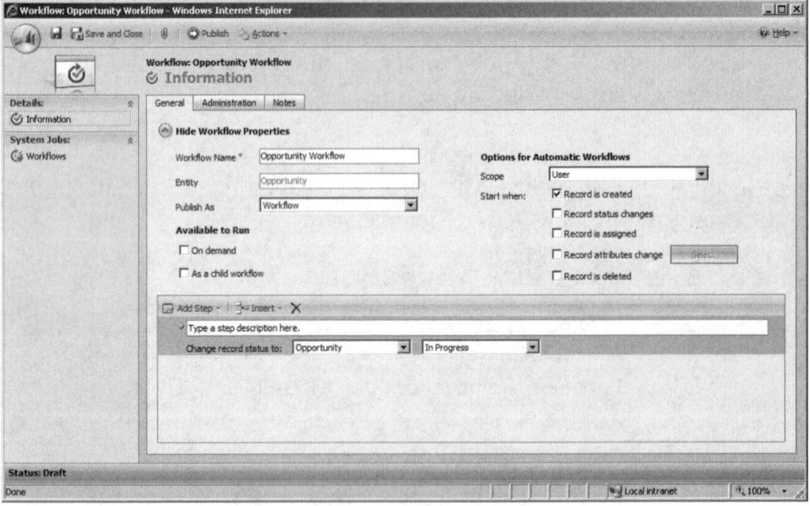

FIGURE 20.21 Change status step for an opportunity.

Stop Workflow

This step stops the execution of the current Workflow. You can change the result status of the Workflow from Succeed to Canceled.

Use this activity step inside a conditional to prevent the Workflow from continuing if a property doesn't meet the criteria you expect.

Workflow Events

Workflows can automatically execute when one or a combination of the following events are triggered. (Refer to Figure 20.21 under Options for Automatic Workflows):

- Record Is Created
- Record Status Changes
- Record Is Assigned
- Record Attributes Change
- Record Is Deleted

Record is Created

This event is triggered after a new record of the associated entity is created.

Record Status Changes

This event is triggered when a record of the associated entity status changes (see Table 20.1 for the various entity status), such as when a record of an Account is activated or deactivated, or when a record of an Opportunity entity status changes to Won.

Record Is Assigned

This event triggers when an instance of the associated entity is assigned to a user.

Record Attributes Change

This new event for Microsoft Dynamics CRM is useful because you can trigger a Workflow when any properties of a record from the associated entity change.

Record Is Deleted

This new event for Microsoft Dynamics CRM is triggered when a record of the associated entity is deleted.

Workflow Scope

Workflows created through this interface can be applied to the following areas:

- Users
- Business units
- Parent: Child business units
- Organization

These items are the various scope options—what the Workflow will apply to across the system. If you select User, this Workflow will work for only the user who owns the Workflow. If you want the Workflow to work on the entire business unit or on the organizational level, you should select the appropriate option. Note that only the user who owns the Workflow can see the tracking history.

Exporting and Importing Workflows

You can transfer Workflows from one organization to another by exporting them as compressed zip files and then importing them into the new system. This is extremely helpful if you have multiple organizations and want to reuse your Workflows, or for backup and restoration purposes.

Export

To export a Workflow, navigate to Settings, Customization, Export Customizations. Select Workflows from the View drop-down menu (see Figure 20.22).

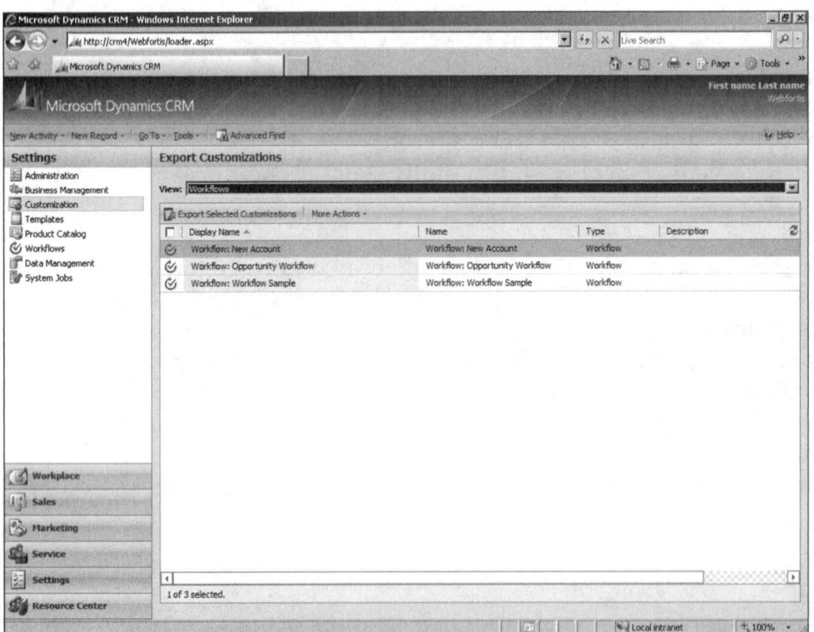

FIGURE 20.22 Exporting Workflows.

You can export all Workflows by clicking on More Actions and selecting Export All Customizations or export only the selected Workflows. To select more than one Workflow at a time, hold the Ctrl key by clicking in Export Selected Customizations (see Figure 20.23).

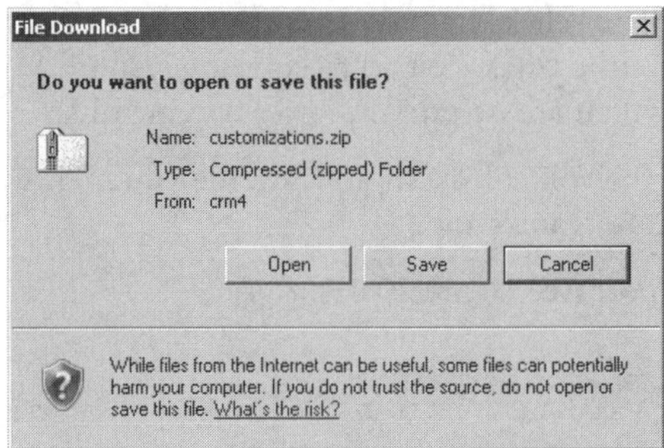

FIGURE 20.23 Downloading the customized Workflow.

The Workflow is downloaded as a compressed zip file. Inside the compressed zip file resides an XML file named `customizations.xml`.

Import

To import a Workflow, follow these steps:

1. Go to Settings, Customization, Import Customizations (see Figure 20.24).

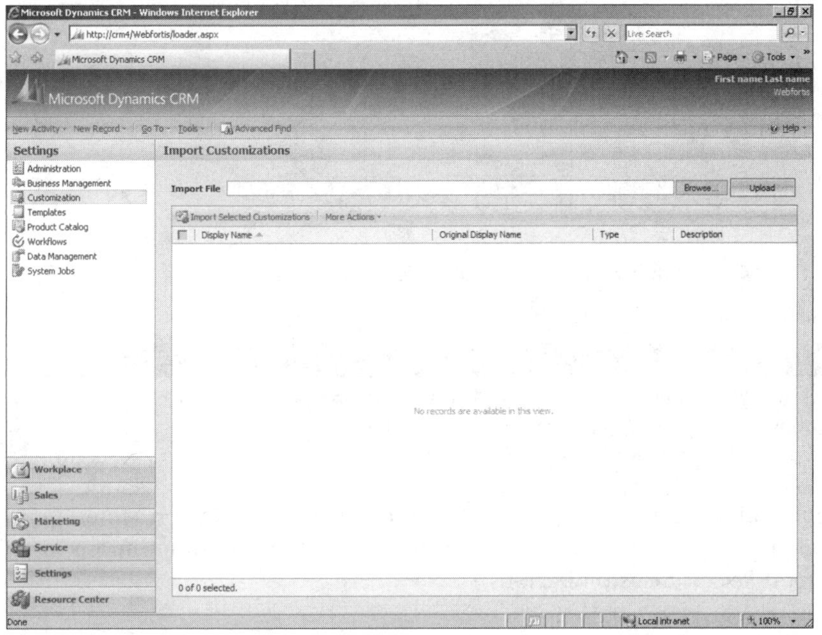

FIGURE 20.24 Importing Workflows.

2. Enter the local path of the customization file or click the Browse button to locate the customized Workflow file on your hard disk. Click Upload to continue. Note that you can upload compressed zip files, which are helpful on lower bandwidths.

   As indicated previously, the customization file will consist of an XML file you might have previously exported from another CRM organization.

3. Review the customizations you want to import (see Figure 20.25).

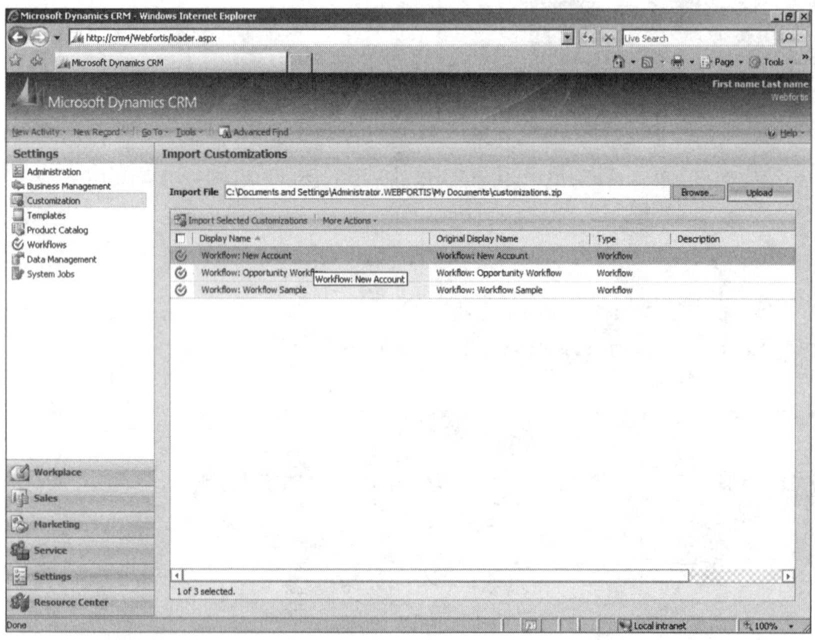

FIGURE 20.25 Reviewing Workflow customizations before importing.

NOTE

It is important to use descriptive texts on your Workflow names, as you won't be able to open them to review them internally before importing them.

4. You can import all customizations from the uploaded file by clicking on More Actions, Import All Customizations, or import only the selected customizations by selecting Import Selected Customizations.

Duplicate Detection Rules

Another new feature of Microsoft Dynamics CRM is the Duplicate Detection Rules. Previous versions required users to consider creating Workflows to detect duplicate records. Now you can use the Duplicate Detection Rule to manage duplicates. Duplicate records can be defined in any manner applicable to your organization and are flexible. The following example illustrates Contacts that have the same e-mail address; however, if your business rules require unique addresses, we could easily add a Duplicate Detection Rule on Address.

To access the Duplicate Detection Rule interface, follow these steps:

1. Click Settings, Data Management, Duplicate Detection Rules (see Figure 20.26).

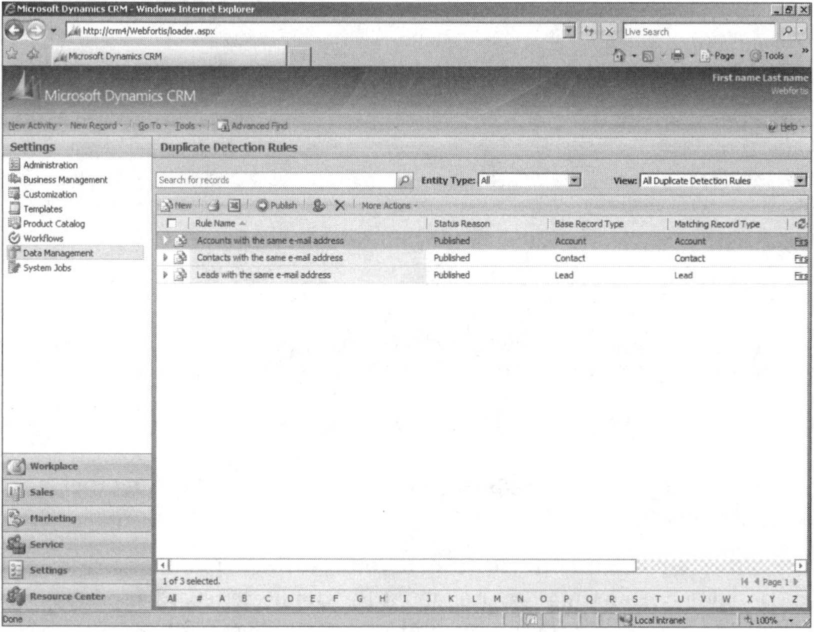

FIGURE 20.26 The Duplicate Detection Rules interface.

2. By default, three predefined rules exist:

   - Accounts with the same e-mail address
   - Contacts with the same e-mail address
   - Leads with the same e-mail address

These rules are active and running by default when Microsoft Dynamics CRM is loaded. If you don't want them, you should either unpublish them or delete them.

If you don't want to have duplicate Account names in the system, you can easily prevent that by creating a new rule by clicking New and entering the required information in which the Base record type and Matching record type are both Account. If you want to ensure that no duplicate Account and Contact names existed, change the Base or Matching record type appropriately (see Figure 20.27).

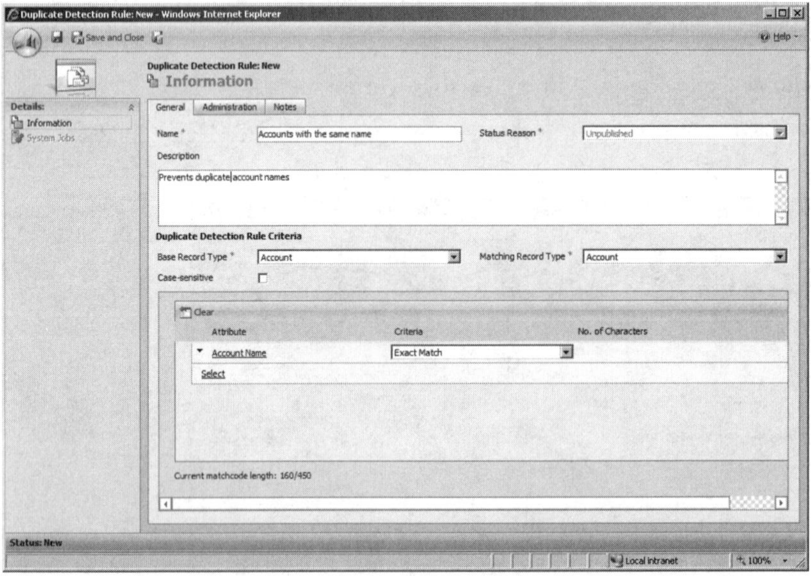

FIGURE 20.27 Creating a new rule to prevent duplicate Account names.

3. Similar to Workflows, the new rule needs to be published to work. Clicking the Publish button publishes the rule.

After this rule is published, if a user tries to create an account with a name that already exists in the system, a dialog box alerting the user about the duplicate record appears after either Save or Save and Close is clicked on the account record (see Figure 20.28).

Clicking Save Record inserts a duplicate record. However, if you click Cancel, the operation ends and the Account is not created.

These rules apply to the business unit in the system by default. However, you can change this setting by configuring the security under Settings, Security Roles, Data management of each CRM role in the system.

When viewing the System Jobs node for any Duplicate Detection Job, the history of the Job will be displayed (see Figure 20.29).

You should have no more than three to five Duplicate Detection Rules for each entity, or performance will start to decrease.

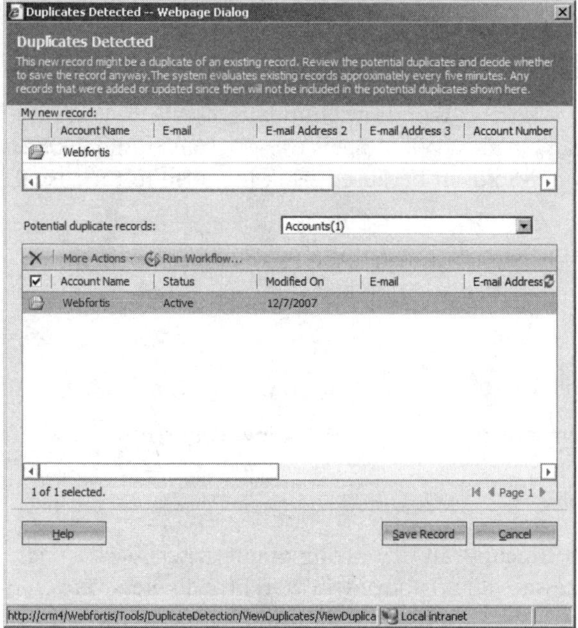

FIGURE 20.28 Duplicates detection dialog alert.

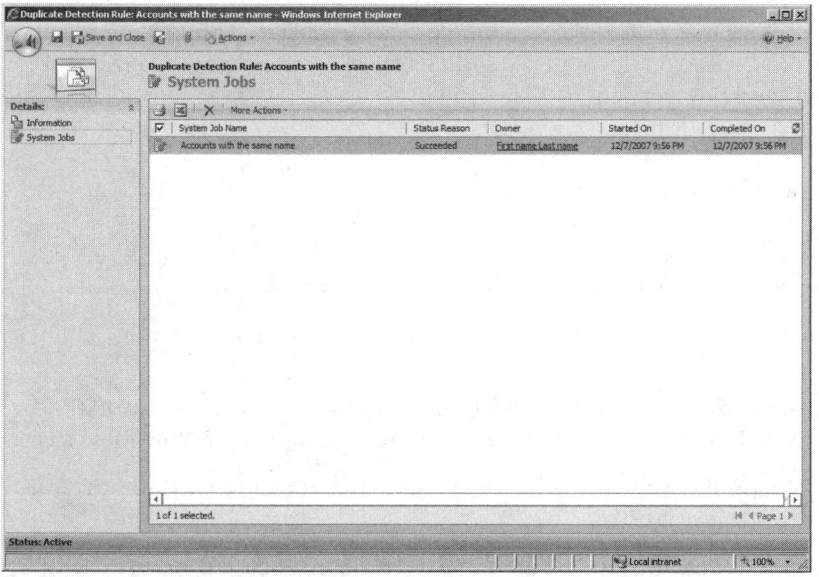

FIGURE 20.29 Duplicates detection rules jobs.

Creating Workflows in Windows Workflow Foundation (WWF) with Visual Studio

You also can create Workflows by using Windows Workflow Foundation (WWF). WWF is new to .NET Framework 3.0, and you can create WWF projects using Visual Studio 2005. However, you must download WWF from Microsoft because it isn't included in the Visual Studio 2005 setup.

To start developing Workflows with WWF, you must install the following components on the development machine:

- Visual Studio 2005
- .NET Framework 3.0 Redistributable Package
- Microsoft Visual Studio 2005 Extensions for Windows Workflow Foundation
- Microsoft CRM 4.0 SDK

Although the scope of this book does not include all these components, users need to be aware that only Visual Studio 2005 Professional and above will work; the Express version of Visual Studio is not supported. Chapter 19, "Customizing Entities," explains the Microsoft Dynamics CRM SDK in greater detail.

No-Code Workflow

The CRM 4.0 SDK comes with a new Visual Studio project template to build No-Code Workflows. These No-Code Workflows are Extensible Object Markup Language (XOML) files—they contain Workflow markup in XML format.

The advantages of No-Code Workflows include the following:

- Can be deployed without compiling
- Easier to develop
- Can be deployed on live CRM servers or on-premise servers
- Can share WWF activities by adding parallel tasks or `loop/while` conditions

Before being able to create a No-Code Workflow, you need to install the CRM Workflow project templates, which is not a trivial task. To install these templates, follow these steps:

1. Locate the solution file with the name `WorkflowConfigurationTool.sln` in the SDK folder\Tools (see Figure 20.30).
2. Open the solution file with Visual Studio 2005 (see Figure 20.31). (Don't try this with Visual Studio 2008 because it will fail after converting the codes.)

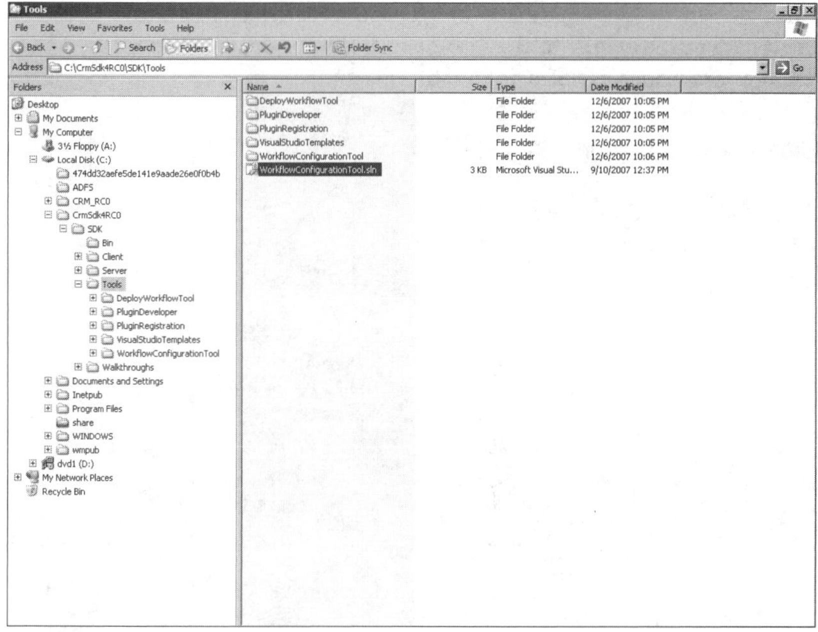

FIGURE 20.30 Locating `WorkflowConfigurationTool.sln` in the SDK.

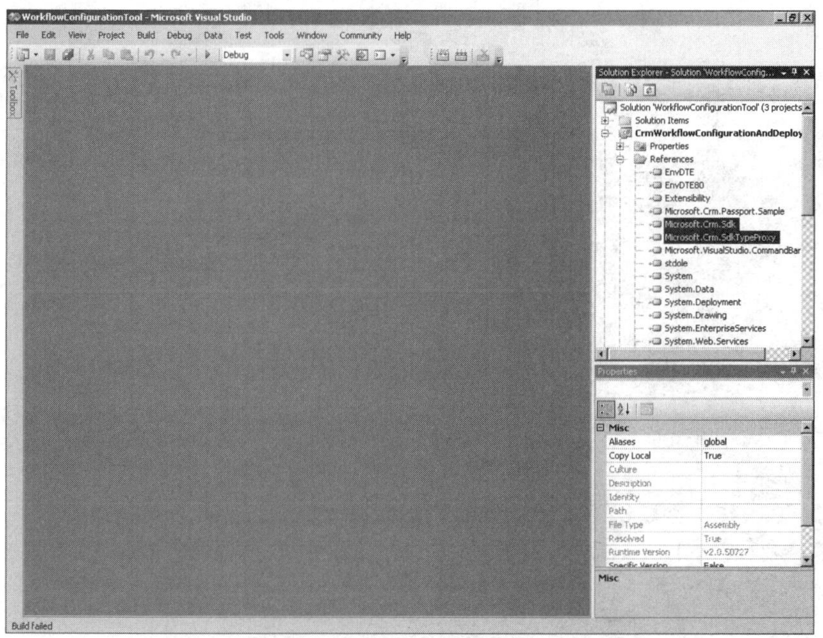

FIGURE 20.31 `WorkflowConfigurationTool.sln` in Visual Studio 2005.

3. Add the missing references (see Figure 20.32) `Microsoft.Crm.Sdk.dll` and `Microsoft.Crm.SdkTypeProxy.dll` to the `CrmWorkflowConfigurationAndDeployment` project. (These files are under the SDK folder\bin.)

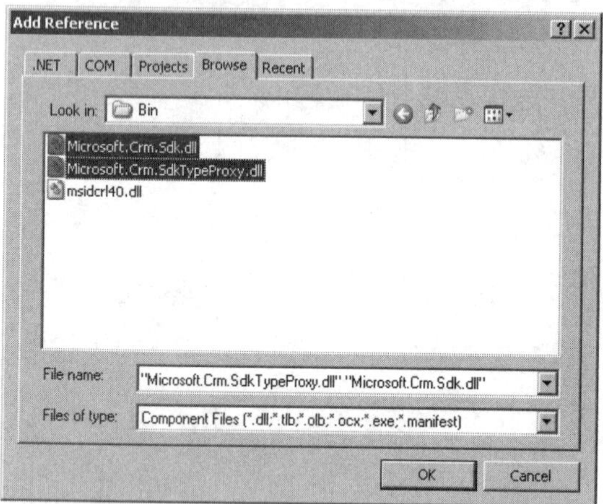

FIGURE 20.32 Adding missing references.

4. Update the web references for the two Web Services, as shown in Figure 20.33. Note that you might need to update the URLs if you are trying to compile the solution from another machine different than the server where the CRM is installed.

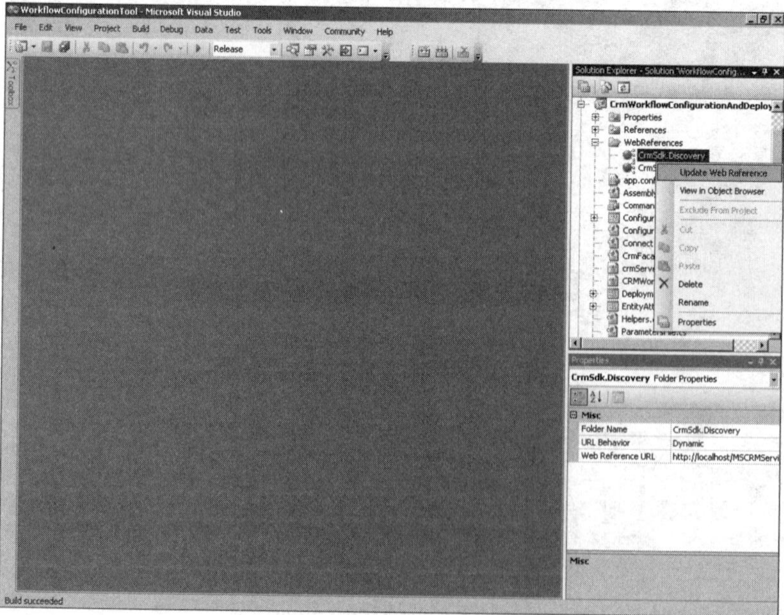

FIGURE 20.33 Updating web references.

5. Change the compilation mode to release (see Figure 20.34).

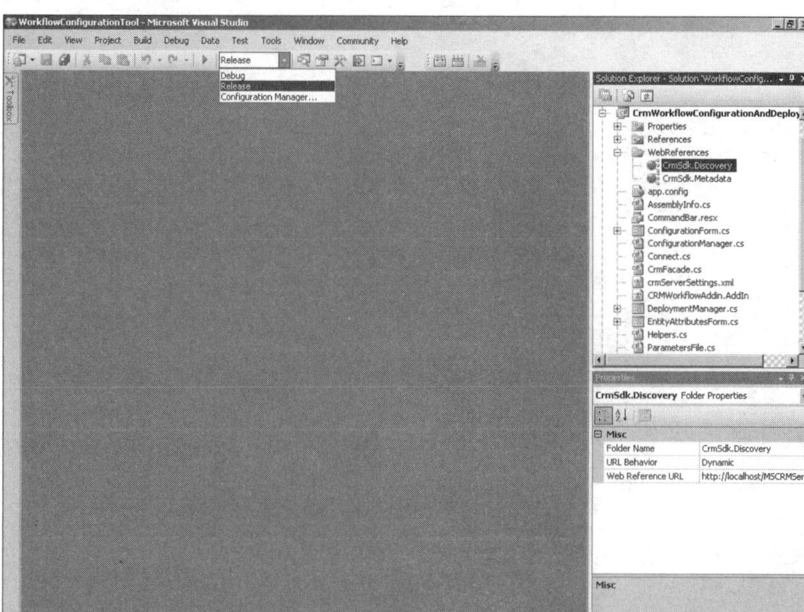

FIGURE 20.34 Changing compilation mode to release.

6. Build the entire solution.

7. Close Visual Studio, go to the SDK\Tools\DeployWorkflowTool\Release folder and execute the `setup.exe` file (see Figure 20.35).

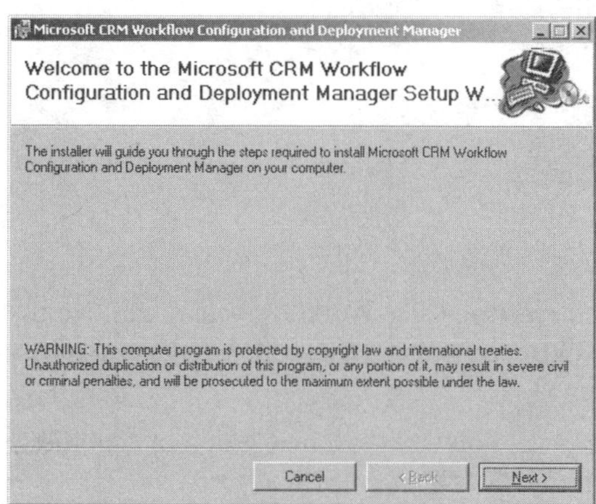

FIGURE 20.35 CRM Workflow Configuration and Deployment Manager Setup.

8. Click Next to confirm installation (see Figure 20.36).

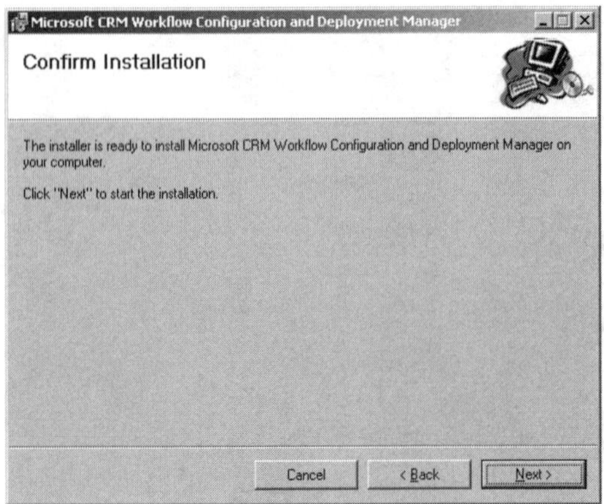

FIGURE 20.36 Confirm installation.

9. Click Next to continue (see Figure 20.37).

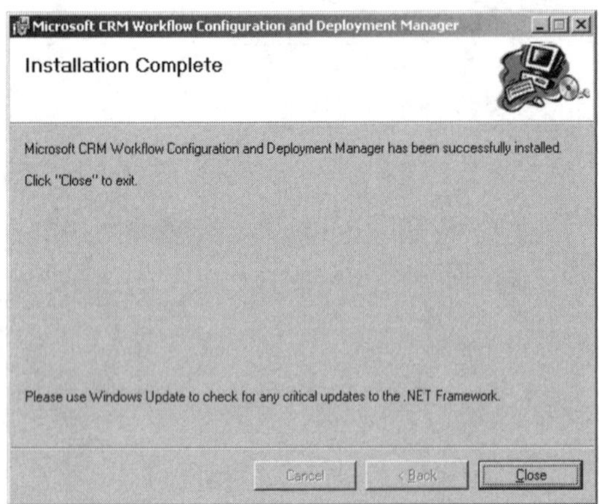

FIGURE 20.37 Installation complete.

Now you can start Visual Studio 2005 and start creating CRM Workflow assemblies. From Visual Studio, go to File, New, Project. Expand Visual C# node, click CRM node, and select CRM 4.0 Workflow (see Figure 20.38).

When you create a new project using this template, you will see a new group of activities specially designed to be used with CRM (see Figure 20.39).

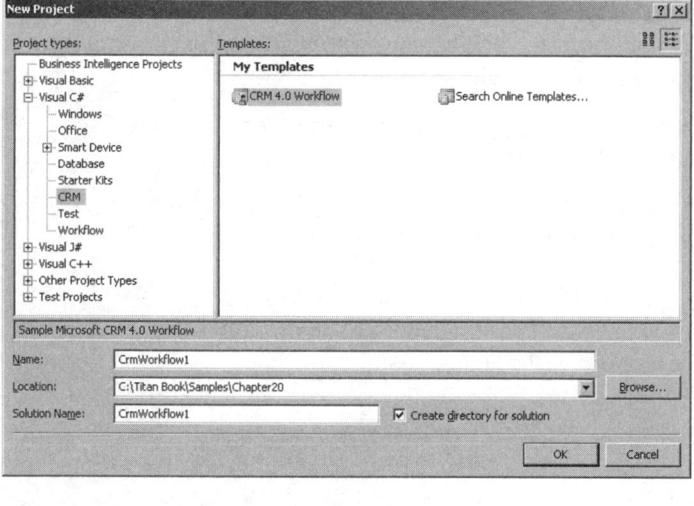

FIGURE 20.38 CRM 4.0 Workflow project template for Visual Studio 2005.

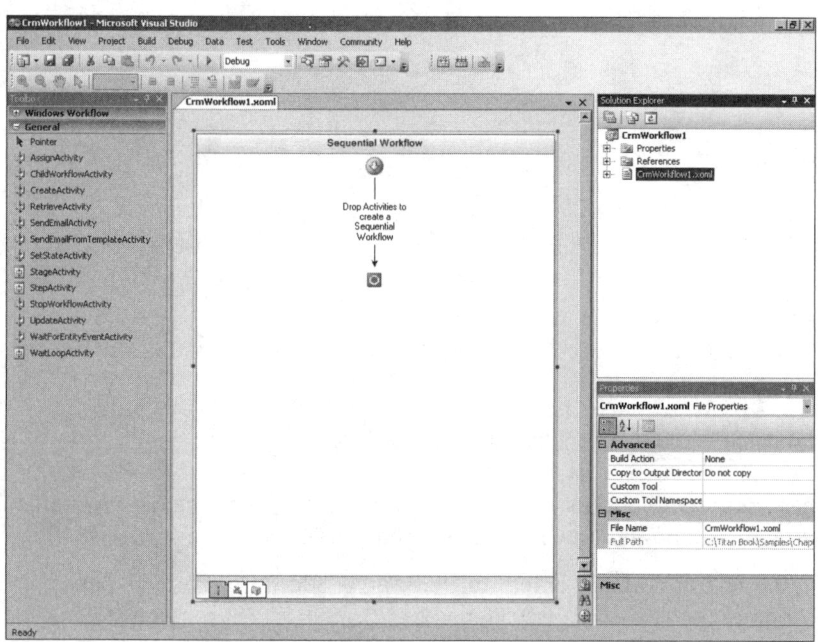

FIGURE 20.39 Workflow activities for CRM.

If you don't see these activities in the toolbox, right-click the General Tab and click the Choose Items menu option. Then browse and add the `Microsoft.Crm.Sdk.dll`, which is located in the SDK\bin folder.

To configure and deploy these Workflows, you must install a Visual Studio add-in that comes with the CRM SDK. The add-in installer filename is `DeployAddin.msi`. Install it by double-clicking the file and following the installation procedure.

The following example shows how to build a Workflow that will create a Phone Call activity for every new Contact added to CRM.

To create the sample, you first must perform the following configuration tasks. (These configurations need to be performed once for each CRM Workflow project.)

Configuration

1. Go to the Tools menu in Visual Studio and select the Microsoft Dynamics CRM menu option, Configure Workflow (see Figure 20.40).

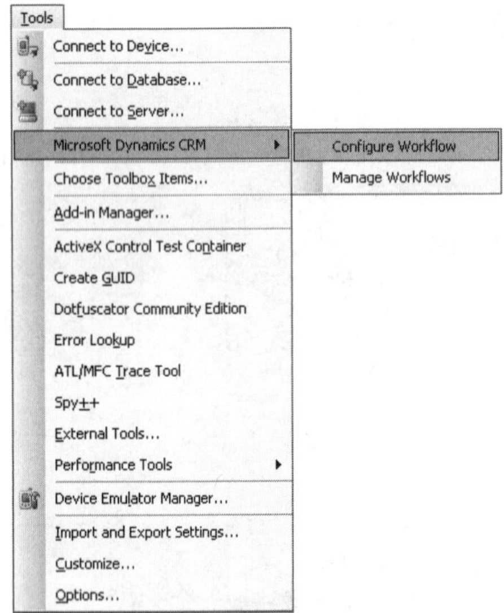

FIGURE 20.40 Workflow deployment configuration menu.

2. The first screen asks you to choose whether you want to configure the deployment for CRM Online or an on-premise CRM server (see Figure 20.41).
3. Select the On-Premise option and enter the CRM server address, username, password, and Windows domain name (see Figure 20.42).
4. Select the organization where you want to deploy the Workflow (see Figure 20.43).
5. Enter a name for the Workflow.

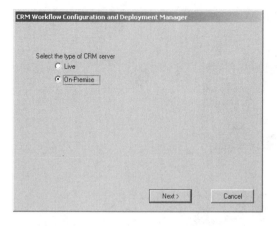

FIGURE 20.41 CRM deployment types.

FIGURE 20.42 CRM on-premise server configuration.

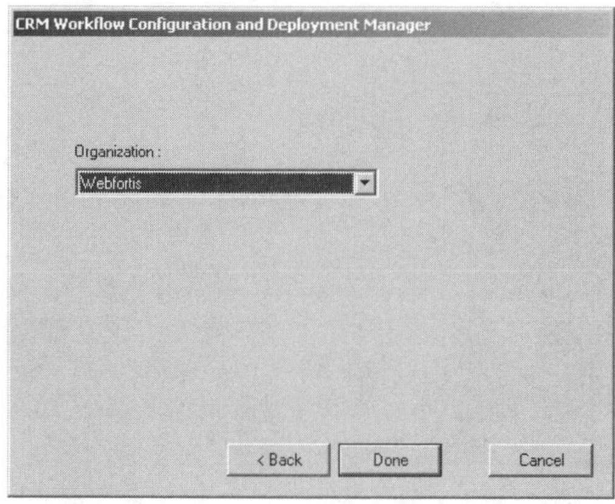

FIGURE 20.43 Organization selection.

6. In the General section, locate the XOML Workflow filename on your hard disk by clicking Browse (see Figure 20.44).

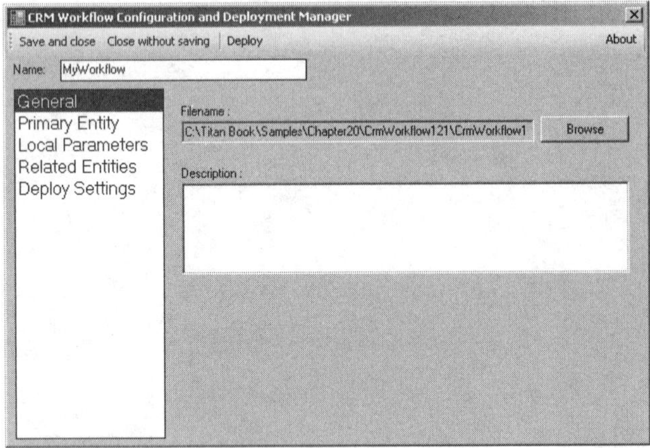

FIGURE 20.44 XOML file selection.

Notice this will be autopopulated by default with the Workflow from the project you just created.

7. Move to the Primary Entity selection in the list box.
8. Click Update List because all the entity types might not show by default.
9. Select the entity you want to associate the Workflow with. For this example, we use the Contact entity.
10. In SDK Events, check the Create option (see Figure 20.45).

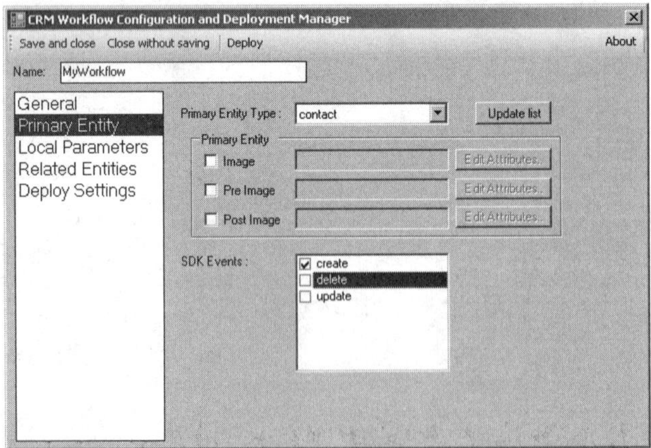

FIGURE 20.45 Primary entity and SDK events selection.

11. Move to the Local Parameters section.
12. Enter **`NewContactWelcomePhoneCall`** as the Parameter name and select the `Microsoft.Crm.Sdk.DynamicEntity` in the Type Name drop-down box. Then click Add (see Figure 20.46). You can create any properties you need here.

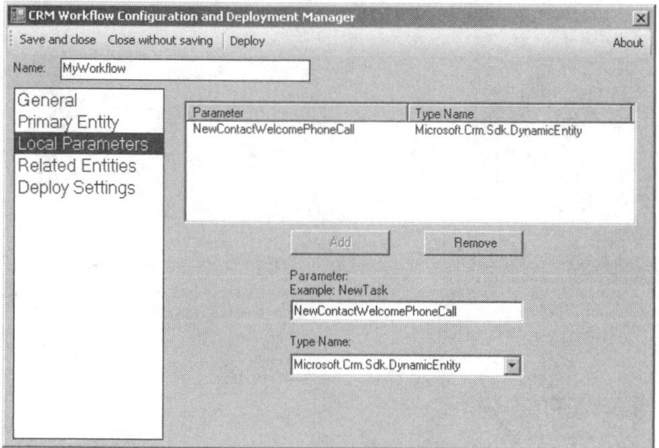

FIGURE 20.46 Parameters configuration.

13. Click Save and Close.

You have now performed the necessary configurations to start actual development.

Development

To start development on the Workflow, you first need to add a Policy activity (located in the Windows Workflow toolbox). When working with No-Code workflows, you can't use the code behind to enter code; therefore, the Policy activity is needed so you can create rules and add some coding as we see next. Then add a CRM Create activity below the first one. (The policy is used to set up the property you created in the configuration section.)

To develop the Workflow, follow these steps:

1. Select the Policy activity, which is under the Windows Workflow section in the toolbox, and drag it into the `CrmWorkflow1.xoml` file or double-click the item and it will be automatically added.
2. Go to the Properties window and select the `RuleSetReference` property; then click the ... button.
3. Click the New button (see Figure 20.47).
4. Click the Add Rule button.
5. In the Condition section, enter **`true`** (see Figure 20.48).

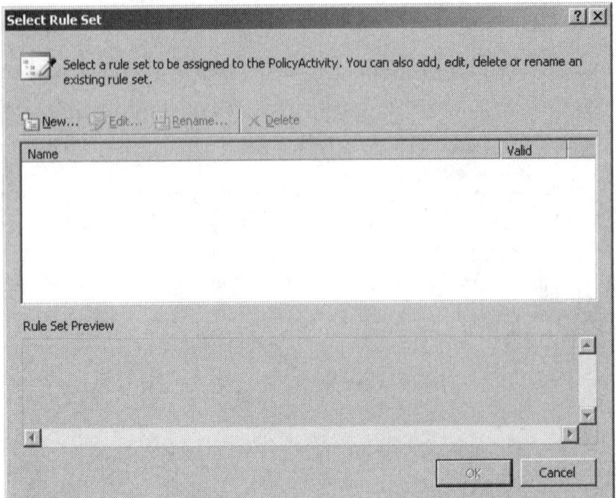

FIGURE 20.47 Select Rule Set.

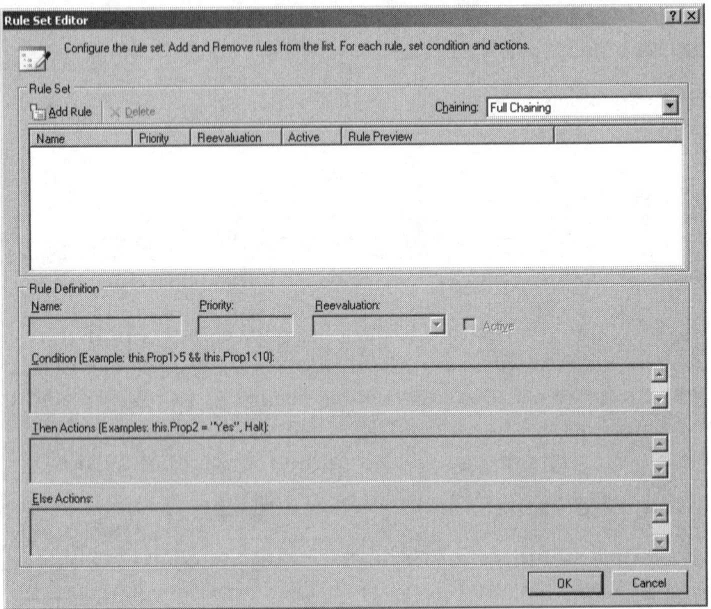

FIGURE 20.48 Rule Set Editor.

6. In the Then section, enter the following code:

```
this._NewContactWelcomePhoneCall =
Microsoft.Crm.Workflow.CrmWorkflow.CreateEntity("phonecall")
this._NewContactWelcomePhoneCall["subject"] = "Call this new contact"
```

7. Click OK to close the Rule Set Editor.

8. Click OK to close the RuleSetReference dialog box.

9. Select the CreateActivity item that is in the toolbox under the General group, drag this activity to the Workflow under the PolicyActivity you added in step 1 (see Figure 20.47), and go to the properties window.

   If you don't see these activities in the toolbox, right-click the General Tab and click the Choose Items menu option. Then browse and add the `Microsoft.Crm.Sdk.dll` which is located in the SDK\bin folder.

10. Select the Entity property and click on the ... button.

11. Select the `NewContactWelcomePhoneCall` property (see Figure 20.49).

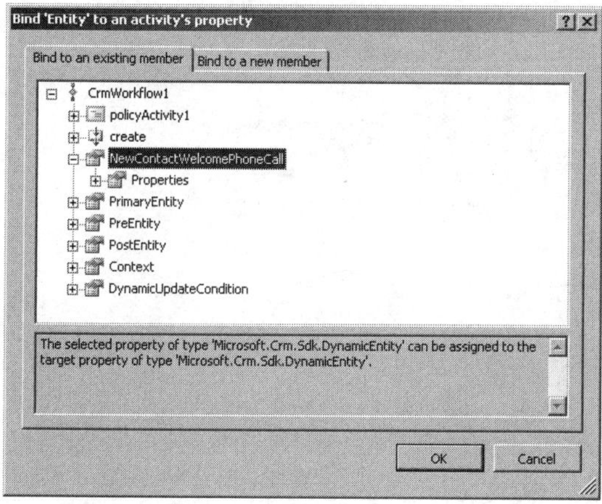

FIGURE 20.49 Property selection.

12. Click OK to continue.

13. Save the Workflow.

The resulting Workflow should look similar to Figure 20.50.

Deployment

1. Go to the Tools menu in Visual Studio and select the Microsoft Dynamics CRM menu option, followed by Configure Workflow.

2. Click the Deploy button (see Figure 20.51) and click Yes to continue.

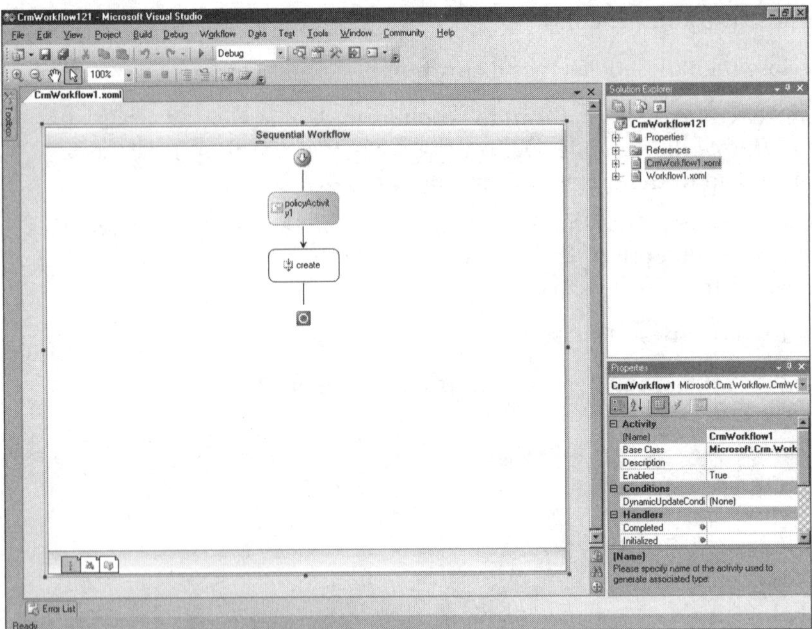

FIGURE 20.50 Final No-Code Workflow sample.

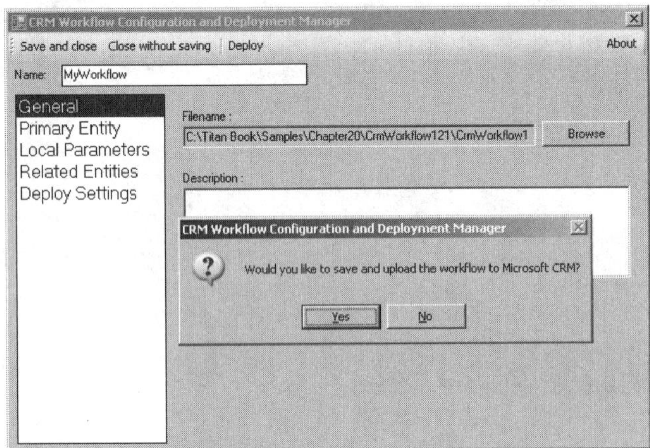

FIGURE 20.51 No-Code Workflow deployment.

3. To publish the Workflow click Yes (see Figure 20.52).
4. Click OK to continue (see Figure 20.53).
5. Click Save and Close.

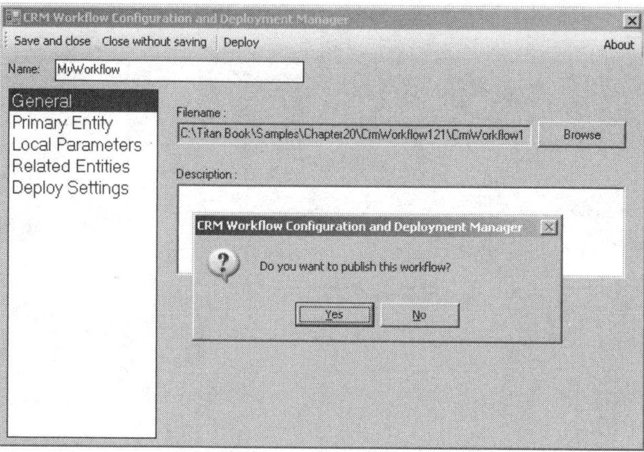

FIGURE 20.52 No-Code Workflow publication.

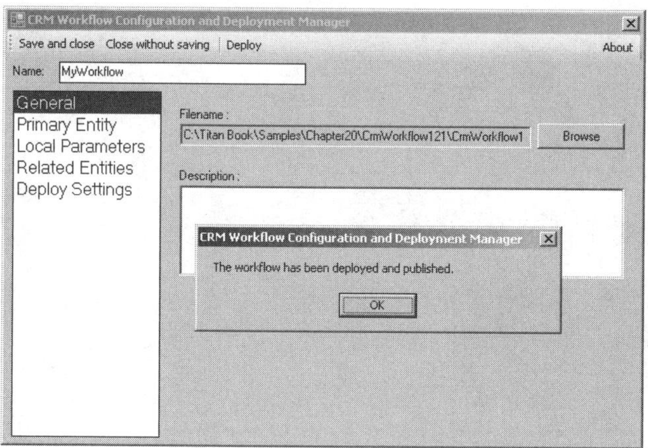

FIGURE 20.53 No-Code Workflow publish result dialog box.

To see the Workflow that was just deployed, open Internet Explorer and go to the CRM web interface. Go to Settings and then to Workflows (see Figure 20.54).

From this interface, you can publish and unpublish the Workflows in the same way as any regular Workflow.

You can also see the deployed Workflows and publish or unpublish them from Visual Studio. Go to the Tools menu, select the Microsoft Dynamics CRM menu option, and then select Manage Workflows (see Figure 20.55).

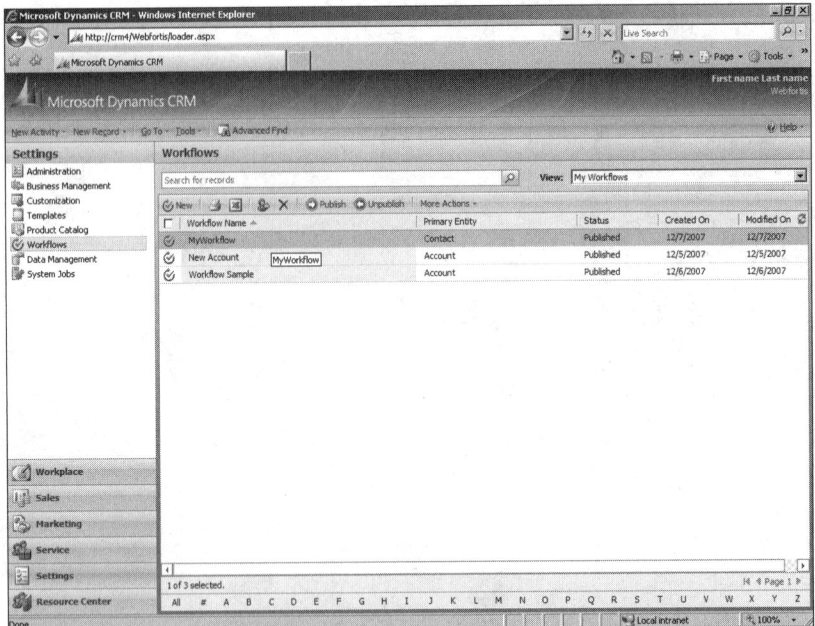

FIGURE 20.54 Reviewing No-Code Workflows.

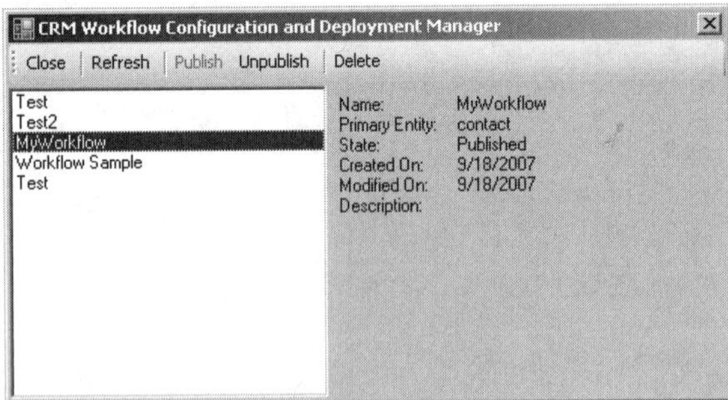

FIGURE 20.55 Reviewing No-Code Workflows with Visual Studio.

Custom Workflow Activities

Custom workflow activities are used to build workflow with code behind using WWF. The difference between them and No-Code workflows that we reviewed previously is that custom workflow activities are compiled in dynamic link libraries (DLL) and can be used from the Workflow interface found in either the Web or Outlook client applications as new steps. To create a custom workflow activity, open Visual Studio 2005 and create a new project using the Workflow Activity Library template that is inside the Visual C#, Workflow project types (see Figure 20.56).

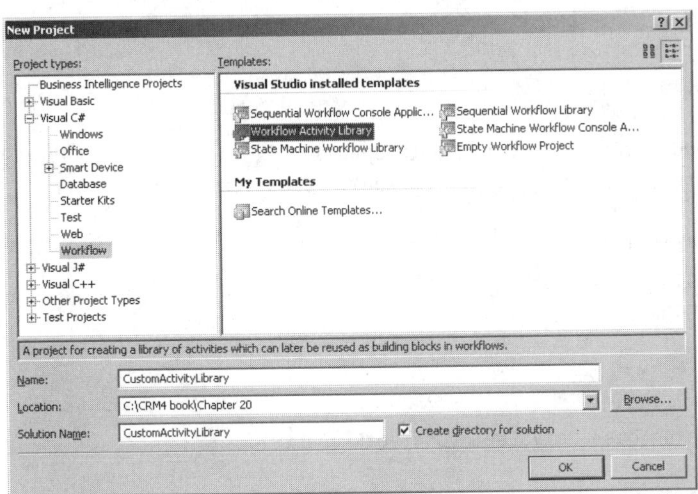

FIGURE 20.56 Creating a new Workflow Activity Library project in Visual Studio 2005.

After creating the project, you will have to add the references for microsoft.crm.sdk.dll and microsoft.crm.sdktypeproxy.dll.

With this project, you can add any workflow activity from the toolbox as well as add code in C# in the code behind if desired. For our example, we use the same sample we used for the No-Code workflow but this time with a custom activity. Go to see the code behind and replace any existing code with the following:

```
using System;
using System.ComponentModel;
using System.ComponentModel.Design;
using System.Collections;
using System.Drawing;
using System.Workflow.ComponentModel.Compiler;
using System.Workflow.ComponentModel.Serialization;
using System.Workflow.ComponentModel;
using System.Workflow.ComponentModel.Design;
using System.Workflow.Runtime;
using System.Workflow.Activities;
using System.Workflow.Activities.Rules;
using Microsoft.Crm.Workflow;
using Microsoft.Crm.Sdk;

namespace CustomActivityLibrary
{
    [CrmWorkflowActivity("Custom Activity", "Custom Activities Library")]
    public partial class CustomActivity : SequenceActivity
    {
```

```
        public CustomActivity()
        {
            InitializeComponent();
        }
        public static DependencyProperty myContactProperty =
DependencyProperty.Register("myContact", typeof(Lookup), typeof(CustomActivity));

        [CrmInput("My contact")]
        [CrmReferenceTarget("contact")]
        public Lookup myContact
        {
            get
            {
                return (Lookup)base.GetValue(myContactProperty);
            }
            set
            {
                base.SetValue(myContactProperty, value);
            }
        }
        protected override ActivityExecutionStatus Execute(
                                ActivityExecutionContext executionContext)
        {
            // Get the context service.
            IContextService contextService =
                (IContextService)executionContext.GetService(typeof(IContextSer-
vice));
            IWorkflowContext context = contextService.Context;

            // Use the context service to create an instance of CrmService.
            ICrmService crmService = context.CreateCrmService();

            // Creates the Phone Call activity for this conatct
            Microsoft.Crm.SdkTypeProxy.phonecall nyPhoneCall =
                        new Microsoft.Crm.SdkTypeProxy.phonecall();
            nyPhoneCall.subject = "Call this new contact";
            nyPhoneCall.regardingobjectid = myContact;
            crmService.Create(nyPhoneCall);
            return ActivityExecutionStatus.Closed;
        }
    }
}
```

Build the solution in debug mode to create the assembly.

To deploy the custom workflow activities, register the compiled assembly as a Plug-In using the same plugindeveloper tool we used in Chapter 21, with minor changes to the `register.xml` file. Here is an example of how the `register.xml` file should look for our sample:

```
<?xml version="1.0" encoding="utf-8" ?>
<Register
    LogFile = "Plug-in Registration Log.txt"
    Server  = "http://crm4"
    Org     = "Webfortis"
    Domain  = "Webfortis"
    UserName= "administrator" >

        <Solution SourceType="0" Assembly="C:\CRM4 book\Chapter 20\CustomActiv-
ityLibrary\CustomActivityLibrary\bin\Debug\CustomActivityLibrary.dll">
                <WorkflowTypes>
                        <WorkflowType TypeName="CustomActivityLibrary.CustomActiv-
ity" FriendlyName="Custom Activity"/>
                </WorkflowTypes>
        </Solution>
</Register>
```

NOTE

If you have problems finding and building the referenced plugindeveloper tool, refer to Chapter 21, in the "Plug-In Developer Tool" section.

After deploying the custom workflow activity, you can use it on any Workflow. To do this, go to Settings, Workflow, and click New. Enter a name for the workflow and select Contact in the Entity. Click OK to move to the next step. Then click Add Step and you will see the new group called Custom Activities Library with our Custom Activity inside (see Figure 20.57).

Add a step with the Custom Activity and click the Set Properties button.

You can set any custom property you added on the code. Our example sets the My Contact property we used to send the current contact where the workflow will be running (see Figure 20.58).

Click Save, Close to close the Set Custom Step Input Properties and then click Save to save the workflow. Click Publish to test this solution.

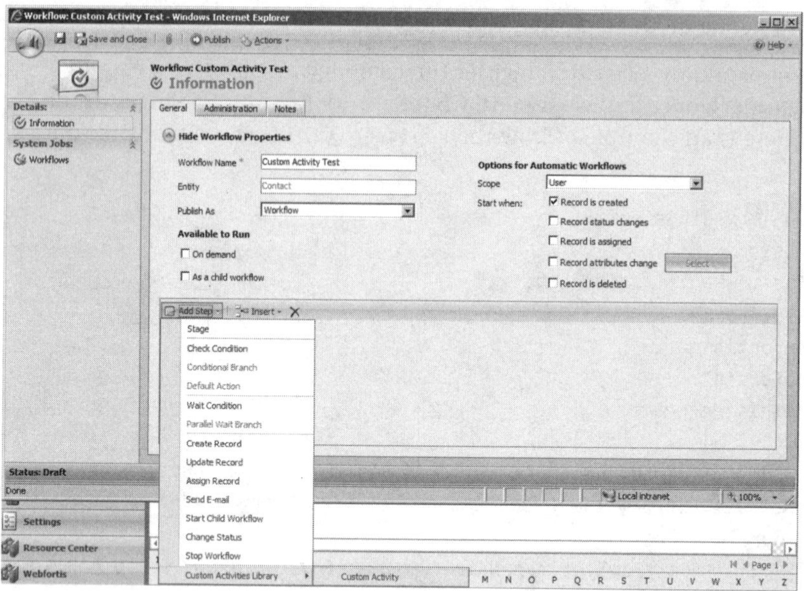

FIGURE 20.57 Using the Custom Activity on a Workflow.

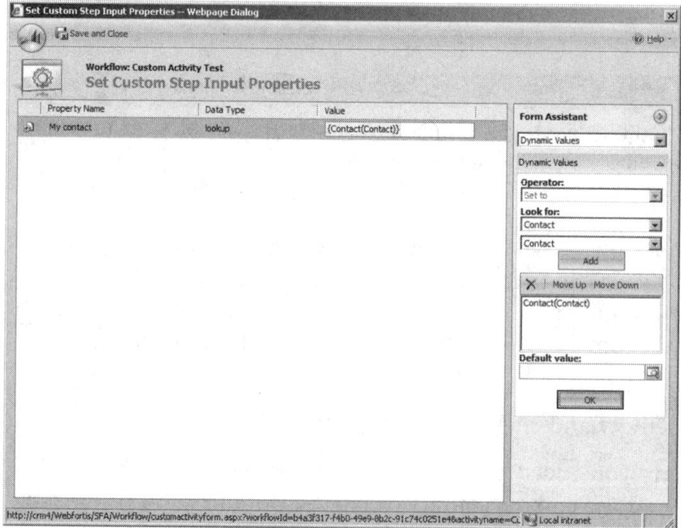

FIGURE 20.58 Setting properties to the Custom Activity.

NOTE

After any changes are made to the codes and the solution is recompiled, you will have to restart the Microsoft CRM Asynchronous Processing Service and in some situations, you might also need to restart IIS before redeploying the modified assembly.

You can install custom workflow activities on On-Premise servers only, because they are not supported by CRM Online servers. This is because they could potentially have malicious or poorly written code that might affect overall server performance. (Partner-Hosted CRM accounts might support custom workflow activities; however, check with your specific partner first.)

To learn more about .NET 3.0 and WWF development, go to www.netfx3.com.

Summary

This chapter illustrated how to use and work with Workflows in Microsoft Dynamics CRM. We created Workflows with the CRM application interfaces, as well as with Microsoft Visual Studio 2005. We learned that Workflows run asynchronously, and that they need a Windows service to run.

It is important to be aware that you must have the correct copy of Visual Studio (Visual Studio 2005 Professional or higher), and that thoroughly reviewing the Microsoft Dynamics CRM SDK available from Microsoft will supply many code samples and examples that will help you model your code.

The SDK for Microsoft Dynamics CRM 4.0 can be found by searching the Microsoft MSDN site for CRM SDK located at http://msdn2.microsoft.com/en-us/default.aspx.

CHAPTER 21

Plug-Ins

IN THIS CHAPTER

Plug-Ins

Plug-Ins in Microsoft Dynamics CRM 4.0 are what used to be referred to as Callouts in Microsoft Dynamics CRM 3.0. A Plug-In is a .NET assembly that can be used to intercept events generated from the CRM system to perform a variety of actions. An example of event interception is an entity that will be created, updated, or deleted; an action can be virtually anything. Some common Plug-In uses might include these:

- Performing a complicated update routine on CRM entities and/or attributes when it might be impractical to use JavaScript or Workflow
- Grabbing data from another system and updating CRM when an entity instance is created or updated
- Updating another system programmatically from CRM (such as an accounting system)

Using Plug-Ins, you can fire a custom action or event on an Account, for example, either before or after it has been created, updated, or deleted. Additionally, other events can be handled from a Plug-In, such as Assign, Merge, and Handle. Refer to the software development kit (SDK) for a complete list of events supported.

TIP

Not every event works in offline mode of the Microsoft CRM Outlook client. Although online mode supports all events, offline clients can manage only half of them. Refer to the CRM SDK for a complete list of events supported in offline mode.

Figure 21.1 shows the Event execution pipeline order in which the event and the Plug-In calls are executed.

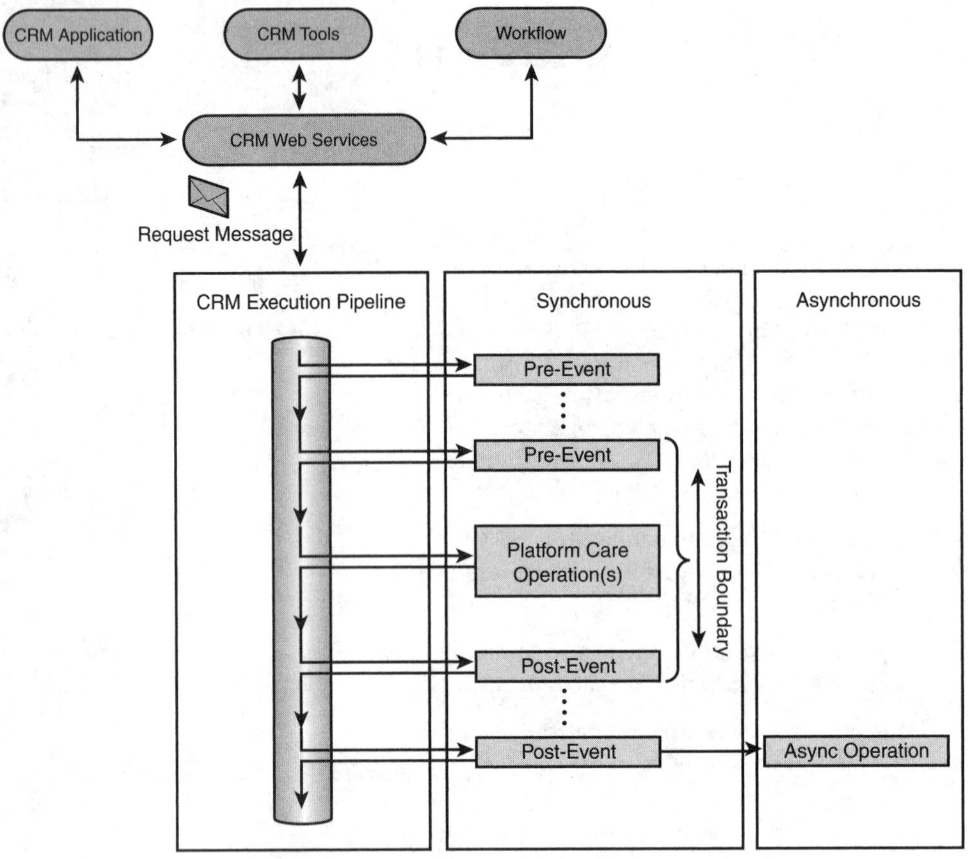

FIGURE 21.1 Event execution pipeline.

Unlike the previous version of Microsoft Dynamics CRM (and a welcome change), you don't need to restart the IIS when you register or unregister Plug-Ins.

NOTE

CRM Online currently does not support Plug-Ins, and CRM hosting providers may not support them as well for security reasons. Check with your hosting provider if you want to use a Plug-In before you attempt to install it.

When Is It Recommended to Use a Plug-In?

Use a Plug-In when you need to integrate Microsoft Dynamics CRM with another legacy system or when you want to extend or customize the original functionality or behaviors of Microsoft Dynamics CRM.

Further usage of Plug-Ins could be to enhance the existing Microsoft Dynamics CRM architecture by adding records and/or auditing for operations made on an entity (for example, who changed what property and when Workflow is inappropriate).

Modes

You can set up Plug-Ins in synchronous or asynchronous mode.

Synchronous mode starts the execution of the Plug-In when the event is fired and blocks the CRM application process until the executed method finishes. This option is not recommended if you perform a process that might take a long time to execute.

TIP

If you want to prevent a record from being created or updated, this should be the desired mode in conjunction with the Pre stage (see the next section for stages).

Asynchronous mode releases the application process, and the user can continue working while the code is executed.

NOTE

Asynchronous mode can't be combined with the Pre stage.

Stages

Plug-Ins can be set up in the Pre or Post stages:

The Pre stage sends control to the Plug-In before the real event is executed in the core system. As an example, you might attach a Plug-In to the `Create` event of the Account entity; your code would execute before the Account is actually created in the CRM system. With this method, you could prevent the Account or the entity record from being created, if desired.

The Post stage is executed after the real event has executed in the core system. So following the example just described, your code would be executed only after the Account record is created.

Deployment Types

There are three different ways to deploy a Plug-In:

- Server Only
- Outlook client
- Both

Server Only means that the Plug-In will execute on the server. Execution will occur when users use the Web client or the Outlook online client as well as when any workflow is executed.

With the Outlook client, the Plug-In executes on the client's user machine where Outlook is running. This is especially useful when running in offline mode.

The Both type executes the Plug-In on the server and in the Outlook client.

The deployment type you select depends on what you want to do. If you need to access data from an external system and need to have the user connected to the Internet or the network, you will want to have the Plug-In run only on the server side—the Outlook client will not have network access.

Plug-In Development

To develop a Plug-In, you must download the Microsoft Dynamics CRM 4.0 SDK from the Microsoft website. The SDK can be found at http://www.microsoft.com/downloads/details.aspx?familyid=82E632A7-FAF9-41E0-8EC1-A2662AAE9DFB&displaylang=en or by searching for CRM 4.0 at SDK at http://msdn2.microsoft.com/en-us/default.aspx.

Download the `CRMSdk4.exe` file, save it, and execute it to choose the folder where you want to decompress the files (see Figure 21.2).

To create a Plug-In, you must create a new Class Library project in Visual Studio 2005 by going to the File Menu, New, Project. Then select Visual C#/Windows in the project types on the left and Class Library on the right. Enter a name for the project and select the location and a Solution Name (see Figure 21.3).

NOTE

Microsoft Dynamics CRM 4.0 is based on the .NET Framework 2.0, so we need to use Visual Studio 2005 or 2008 to create class libraries. We can also create class libraries projects in a variety of languages such as Visual Basic .NET or C#. For the examples in this book, we use C#. The previous version of Dynamics CRM 3.0 was based on .NET framework 1.1, and all callout assemblies had to be created with Visual Studio 2003.

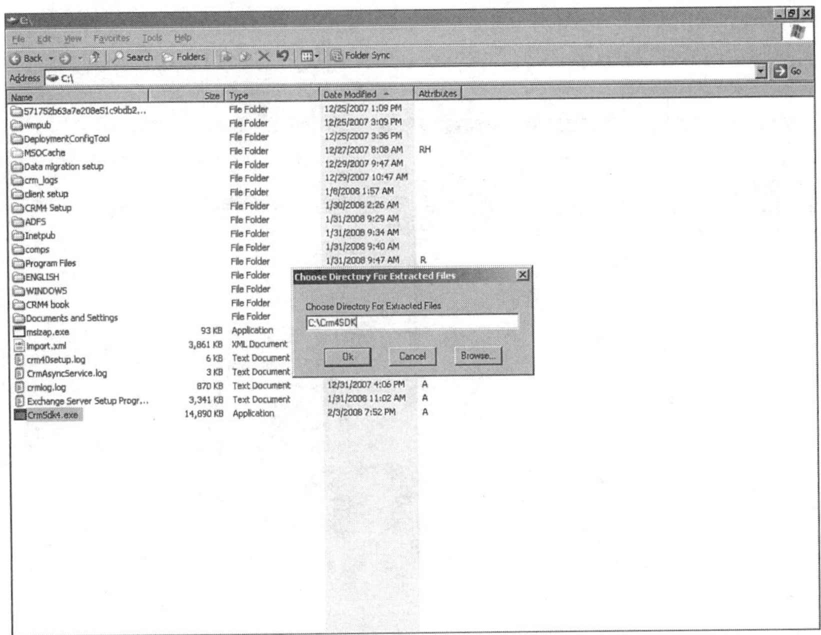

FIGURE 21.2 Extracting the SDK files.

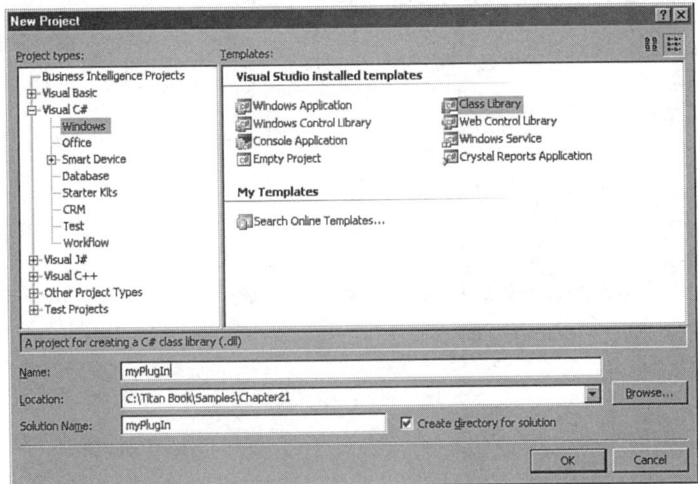

FIGURE 21.3 Creating a new Class Library project for a Plug-In.

The project template creates a new public class by default; after you create the project, you must add a reference to the `Microsoft.Crm.Sdk.dll` file to your project as well as add another reference to `Microsoft.Crm.SdkTypeProxy.dll`. These DLL files are located inside the SDK\Bin subfolder. To add these references follow these steps:

1. Go to the Solution Explorer and select the Solution name (the root node of the tree), right-click, and select the Add Reference menu option (see Figure 21.4).

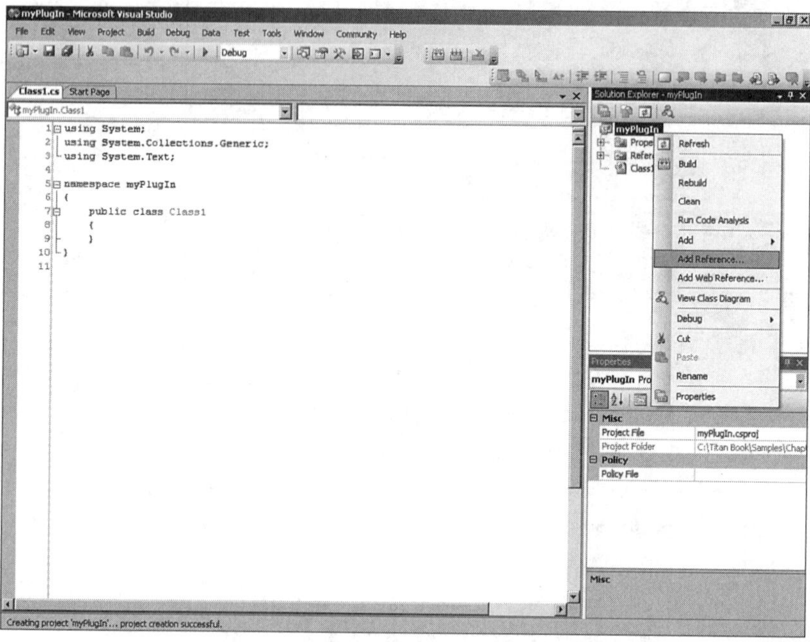

FIGURE 21.4 Adding references to the project.

2. Move to the Browse tab (see Figure 21.5).

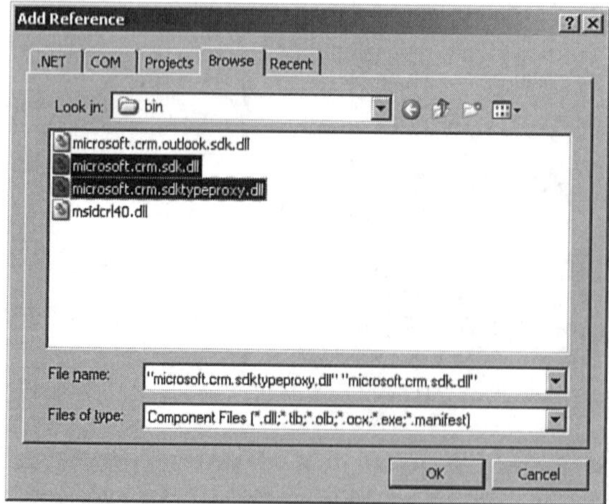

FIGURE 21.5 Browse tab to add new references.

3. Locate the SDK\Bin directory on your local drive and select both `Microsoft.Crm.Sdk.dll` and `Microsoft.Crm.SdkTypeProxy.dll` files. (To select more than one file hold the Ctrl key.)

4. Click OK to add the references to your project. You see these files inside the References folder of your project in the Solution Explorer (see Figure 21.6).

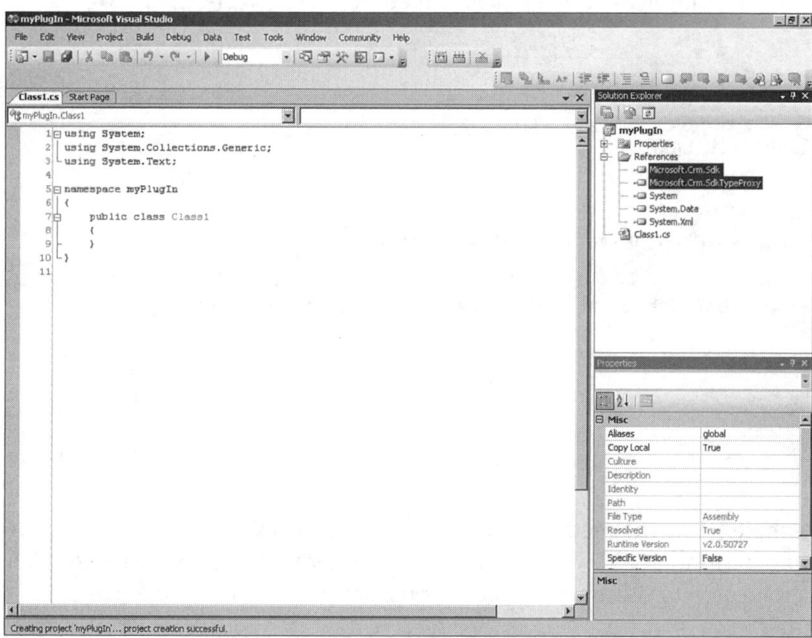

FIGURE 21.6 Checking new references added.

Finally, add the `using` sentence to the `Microsoft.Crm.Sdk` and `Microsoft.Crm.SdkTypeProxy` namespaces and implement the IPlugin interface as shown in the following code:

```
using System;
using System.Collections.Generic;
using System.Text;
using Microsoft.Crm.Sdk;
using Microsoft.Crm.SdkTypeProxy;

namespace myPlugIn
{
    public class Class1 : IPlugin
    {

    }
}
```

NOTE

You can implement more than one Plug-In on the same assembly using different classes, if you want to.

As with any other interface, you must explicitly implement methods. In the case of the IPlugin interface, you must implement the `Execute` method, as shown in the following code:

```
namespace myPlugIn
{
  public class Class1 :IPlugin
  {
    #region IPlugin Members
    public void Execute(IPluginExecutionContext context)
    {
      throw new Exception("The method or operation is not implemented.");
    }
    #endregion
  }

}
```

The previous code implements the method but it only acts to throw an exception. We update the Account description field with the unique identifier value that is assigned when the Account is created to illustrate a more useful example.

To perform this sample, delete the line that is inside the `Execute` method:

```
throw new Exception("The method or operation is not implemented.");
```

and enter the following code instead:

```
        DynamicEntity entity =
(DynamicEntity)context.InputParameters.Properties["Target"];
        if (entity.Name == EntityName.account.ToString())
        {
            Guid id = (Guid)context.OutputParameters.Properties["Id"];
            Key myKey = new Key(id);

            if (!entity.Properties.Contains("accountid"))
```

```
        {
        entity.Properties["accountid"] = myKey;
        }
        if (!entity.Properties.Contains("description"))
        {
        entity.Properties["description"] = "GUID = " +  id.ToString();
        ICrmService service = context.CreateCrmService(true);
        service.Update(entity);
        }
    }
```

TIP

For additional information about entity names and attributes, navigate to http://<servername>/sdk/list.aspx where `<servername>` is the name of the server where you have installed CRM. When working with entity attributes, you will find this link very useful as you can avoid having to go to Settings, Customization and opening each entity window to determine a property name.

Plug-In Deployment

Before explaining details about Plug-In development, it is a good idea to review deployment options so that you can easily follow the sample code that is included with the development section of this chapter.

The first step in Plug-In deployment involves registering your Plug-In and signing the assembly with a strong-key. A strong-key is necessary for security reasons so that the assembly can be trusted to execute external code, such as when invoking a web service. To sign your assemblies, follow these steps:

1. Go to Solution Explorer and select your project; right-click and select the Properties menu option (see Figure 21.7).
2. Go to the Signing tab and check the Sign the Assembly check box (see Figure 21.8).

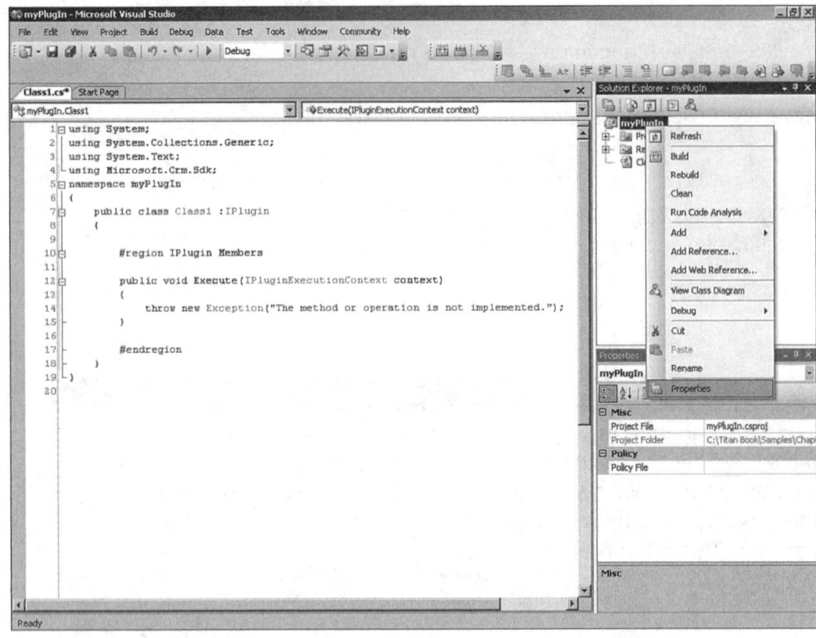

FIGURE 21.7 Properties menu item of the project.

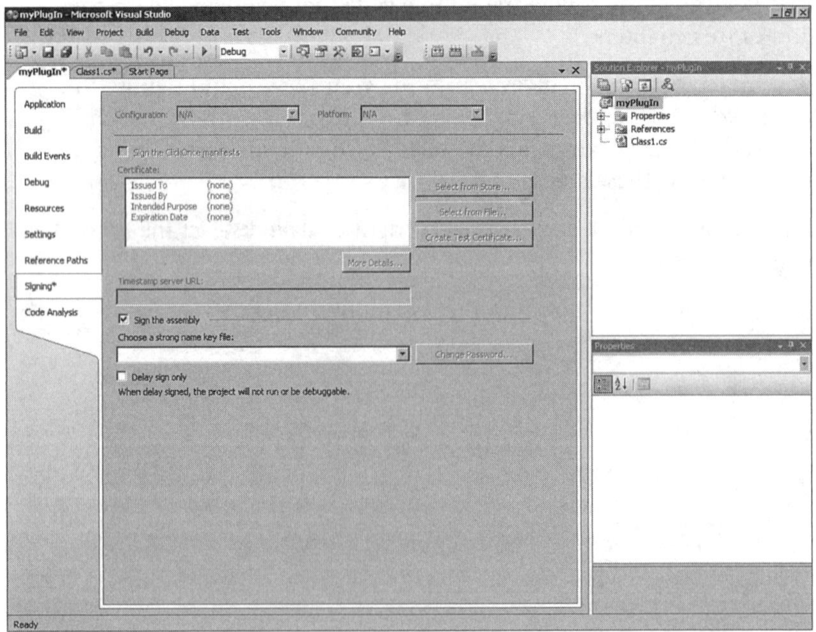

FIGURE 21.8 Signing tab.

3. Create a new string name key file by selecting New from the drop-down control (see Figure 21.9).

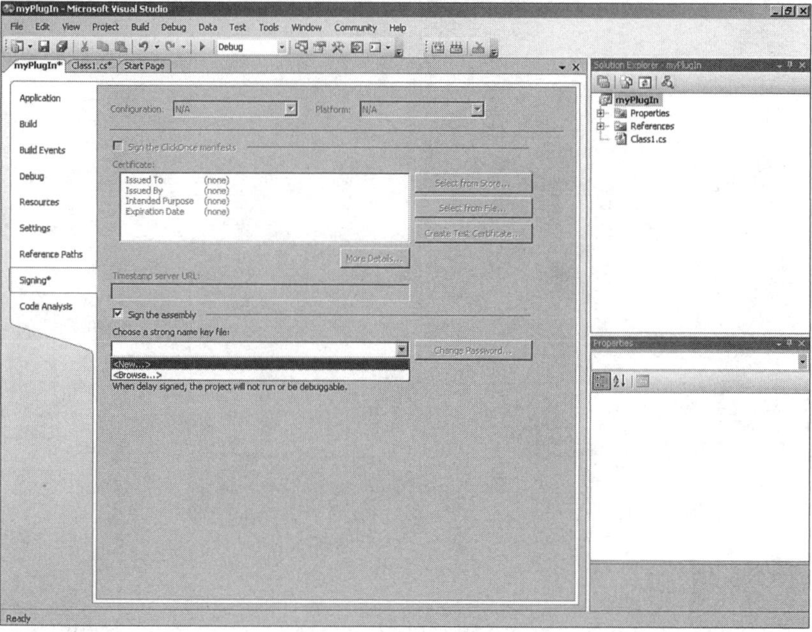

FIGURE 21.9 Selecting New strong name key file.

4. Enter a name for the Key file and, optionally (but recommended), enter a password to protect the strong-key (see Figure 21.10).

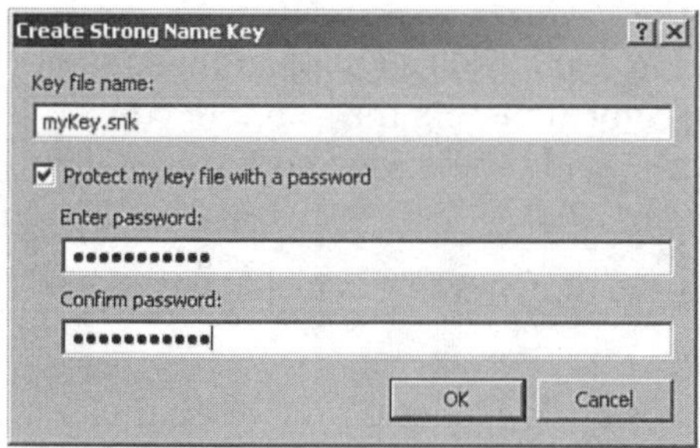

FIGURE 21.10 Creating a strong name key.

5. Click OK to close the dialog box, and you will see the new created strong name key will be added to your project in the Solution Explorer (see Figure 21.11).

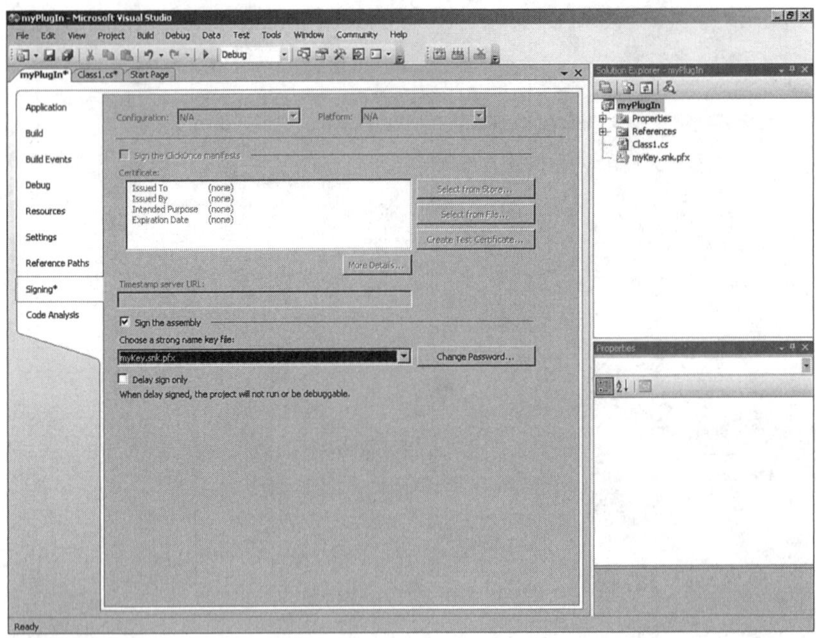

FIGURE 21.11 Signing the assembly.

Now you are ready to build the solution. You can build it by going to the Build menu and selecting the Build myPlugin menu option. (Notice that myPlugin is the name of the project so this name might be different on your solution.) You must deploy the Plug-In prior to testing it.

To deploy your Plug-In, you need to register it. You can do this programmatically or by using a tool that comes with the CRM SDK called PluginRegistration. PluginRegistration also comes with the source codes and is located in the CrmSdk4\SDK\Tools\PluginRegistration folder. You must have Visual Studio 2005 installed to open the `PluginRegistration.sln` file located in that folder. Before building the solution, you must add two missing web references to the solution. To add these web references, follow these steps:

1. In the Solution Explorer, right-click and select the Add Web Reference menu option (see Figure 21.12).
2. In the URL box, enter the address of your Microsoft Dynamics CRM. For example, enter http://<servername>/MSCRMServices/2007/CrmServiceWsdl.aspx and click Go (see Figure 21.13).

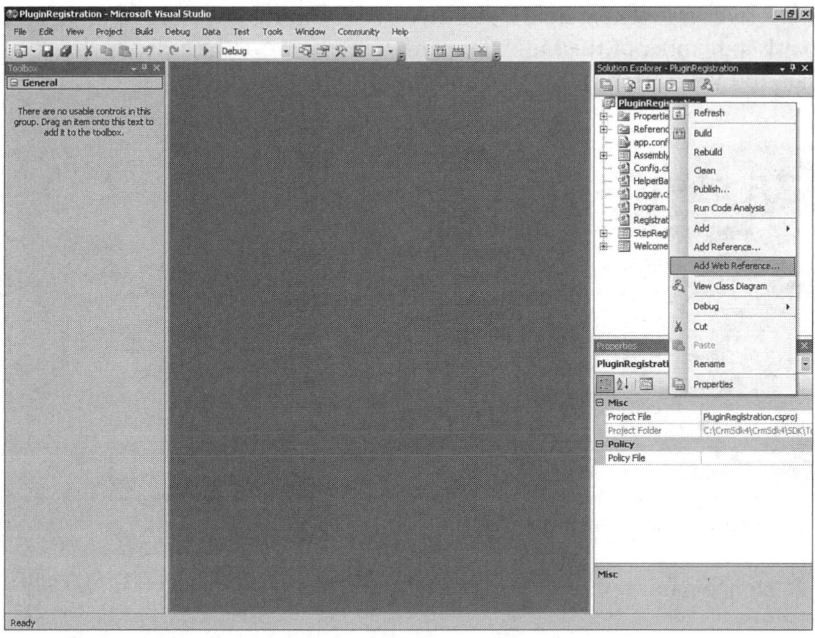

FIGURE 21.12 Adding Web References to the solution.

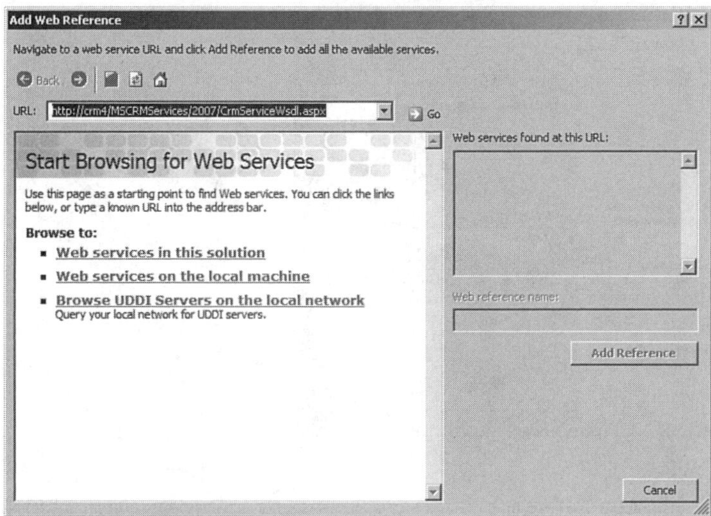

FIGURE 21.13 Adding CRM Web References to the solution.

3. If you are not working on a machine that is a member of the same domain where the CRM server is installed, you will be asked to enter your username and password. It must be a valid windows User account as well as a valid Microsoft CRM user with

Administrative privileges (see Figure 21.14). If you are running the solution from a computer that is a member of the same domain, then you won't be asked to enter the credentials and you can skip this step and move to the next step.

FIGURE 21.14 Entering web service credentials.

4. In the Web Reference name, enter CrmSdk (see Figure 21.15).

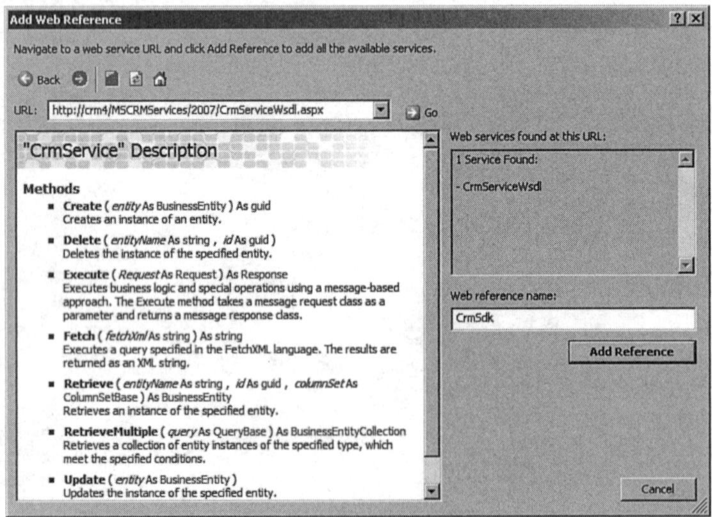

FIGURE 21.15 Adding CrmSdk Web Reference.

5. Click Add Reference. The Web Reference will be added to your Web References folder of the project. You can see it in the Solution Explorer (see Figure 21.16).

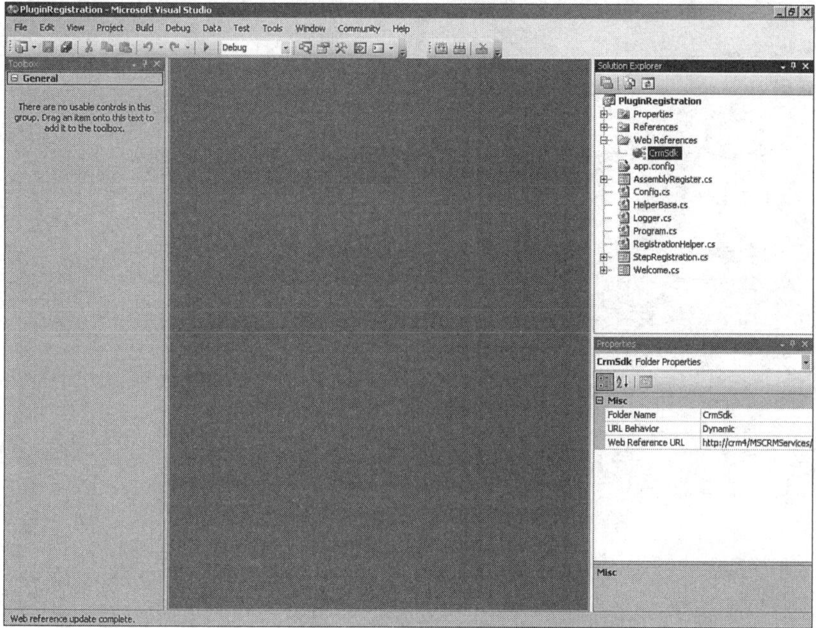

FIGURE 21.16 Reviewing CrmSdk Web Reference added to your project.

6. In the properties window, change the URL Behavior property to Static (see Figure 21.17).

7. Now you must add another Web Reference to the discovery service. To do that in the Solution Explorer, right-click and select the Add Web Reference menu option (see Figure 21.12).

8. In the URL box, enter the address of your Microsoft Dynamics CRM Discovery service. For example http://<servername>/MSCRMServices/2007/AD/CrmDiscoveryService.asmx, and click Go.

9. In the Web Reference name, enter CrmSdk.Discovery (see Figure 21.18).

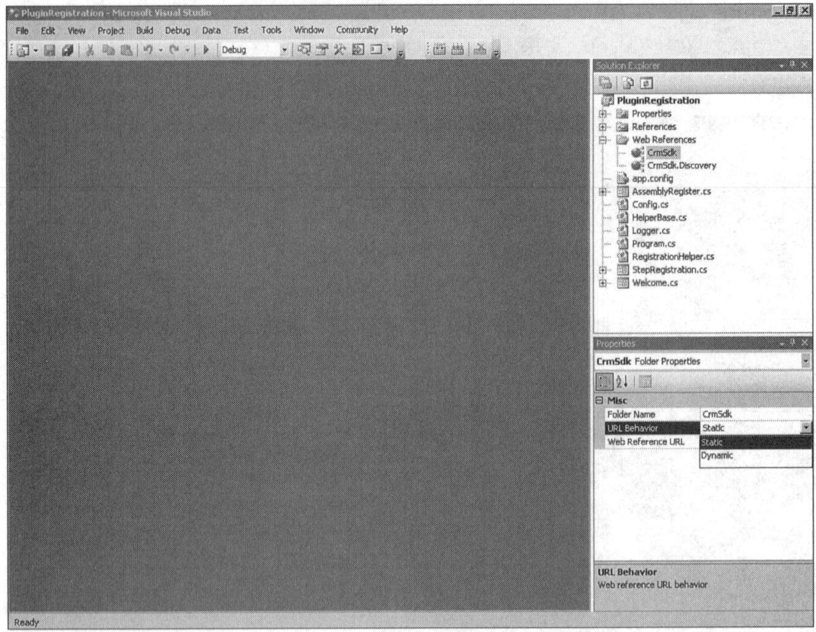

FIGURE 21.17 Changing the URL Behavior property to static.

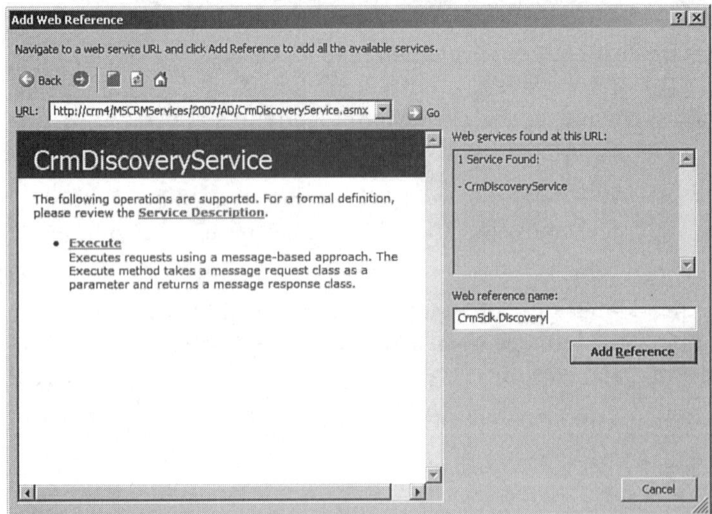

FIGURE 21.18 Adding CrmSdk web reference.

10. Click Add Reference. The Web Reference will be added to your Web References folder of the project. You can see it in the Solution Explorer (see Figure 21.19).

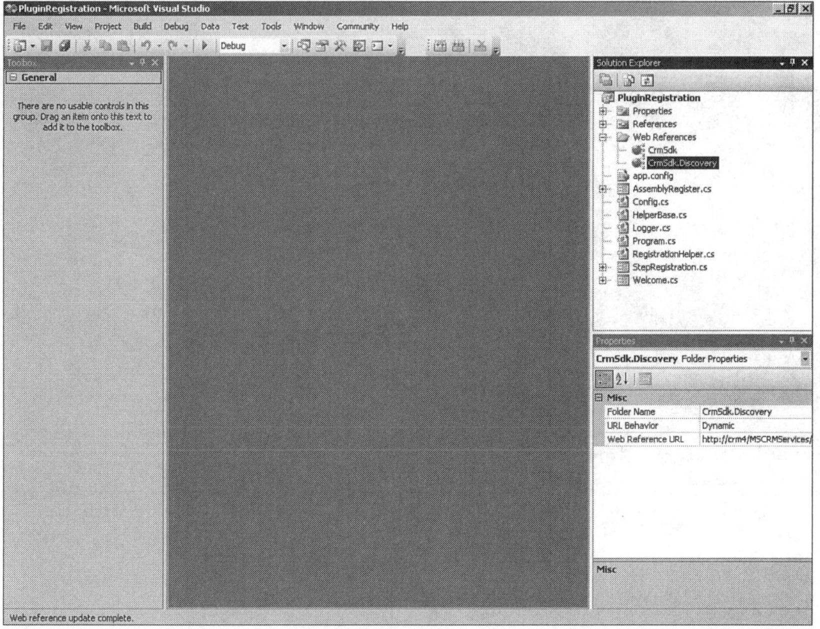

FIGURE 21.19 Reviewing CrmSdk.Discovery Web Reference added to your project.

11. In the properties window, change the URL Behavior property to Static.

12. Build the entire solution (see Figure 21.20).

After you successfully build the solution, you will find the application `PluginRegistration.exe` inside the CrmSdk4\SDK\Tools\PluginRegistration\bin\Debug folder. You can close the Visual Studio application and run this tool directly from this folder, or you can follow these steps to integrate this tool into the Visual Studio 2005 application as a recommended option:

1. From Visual Studio 2005, go to the Tools menu and click External Tools (see Figure 21.21).

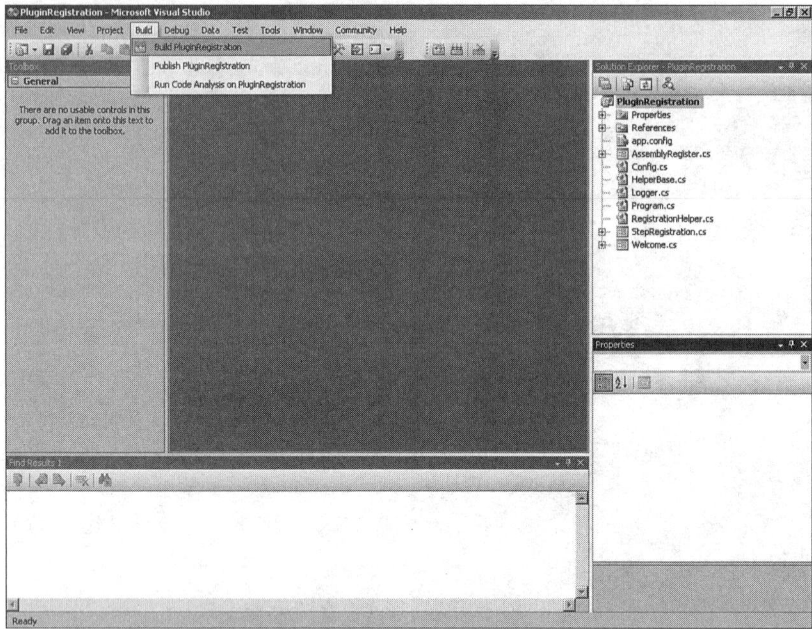

FIGURE 21.20 Building PluginRegistration.

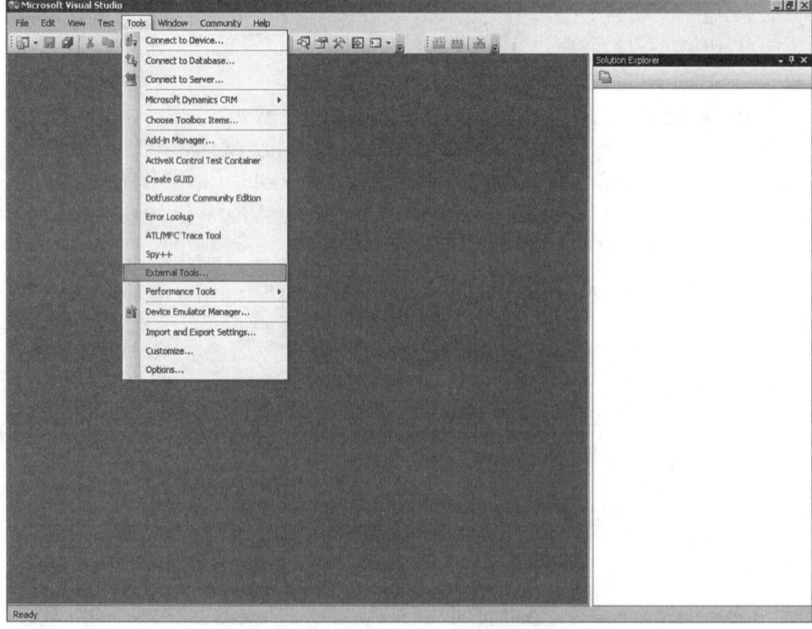

FIGURE 21.21 Visual Studio External Tools menu option.

2. You will get a dialog box as shown in Figure 21.22.

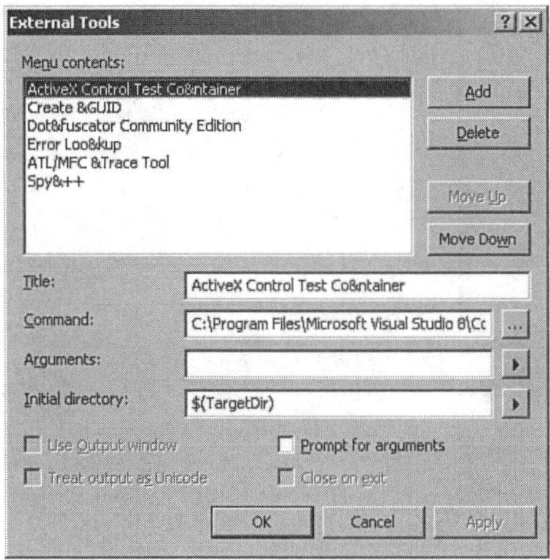

FIGURE 21.22 External Tools dialog box.

3. Click the Add button and change the Title to CRM Plug-In Registration (see Figure 21.23).

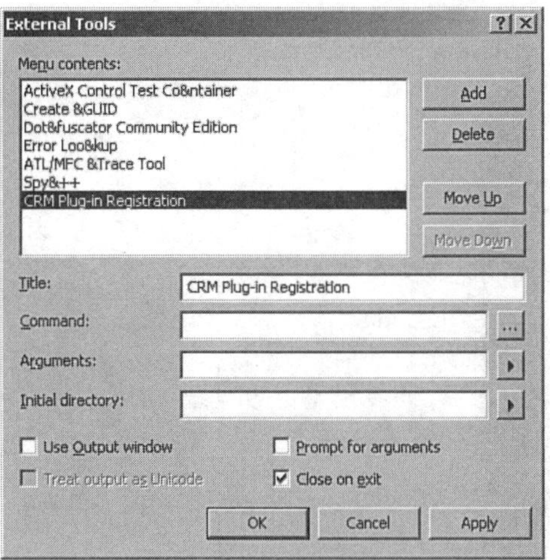

FIGURE 21.23 Adding CRM Plug-In Registration.

4. Click the ... button near the Command field and locate the `PluginRegistration.exe` application file that should be located in the CrmSdk4\SDK\Tools\PluginRegistration\bin\Debug folder (see Figure 21.24).

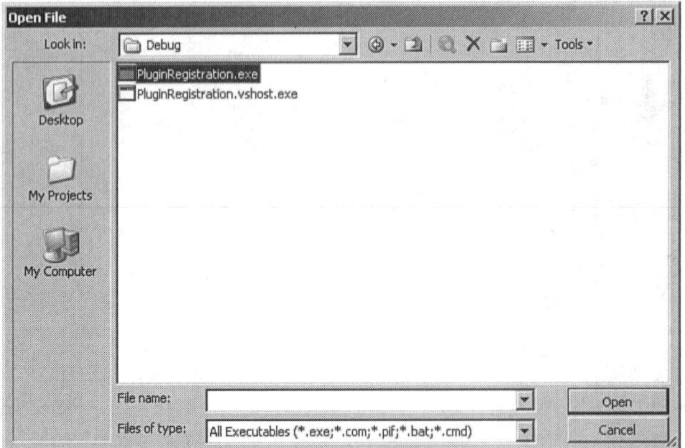

FIGURE 21.24 Locating `PluginRegistration.exe` application.

5. Click Open to close the dialog box, and click OK to close the External Tools dialog box.

This way you can run the PluginRegistration tool from Visual Studio 2005 application by going to the Tools menu, CRM Plug-In Registration (see Figure 21.25).

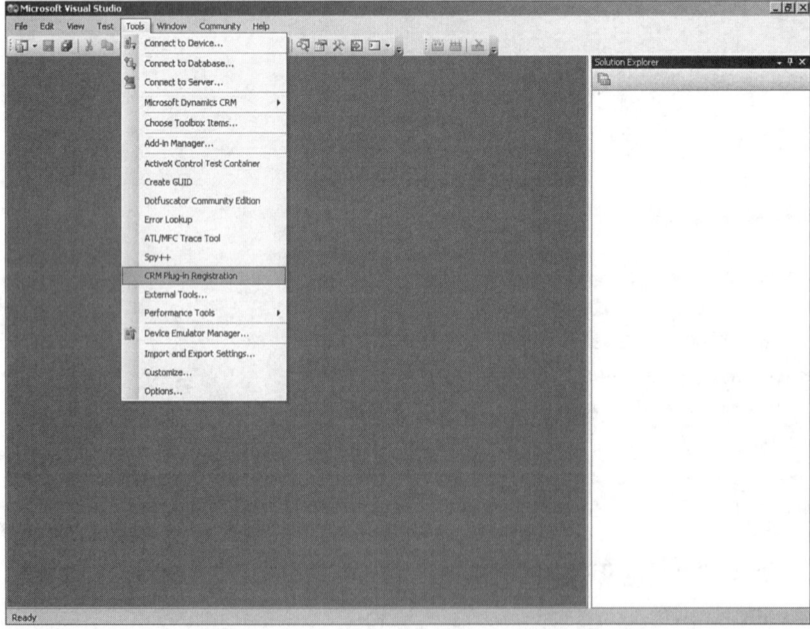

FIGURE 21.25 Accessing the PluginRegistration tool from Visual Studio.

Plug-In Registration

When you run this tool, you must enter information for Server Name, User Name, User Password, and Domain Name, as shown in Figure 21.26. The user name and password must be a valid windows account and also a valid Microsoft CRM user with Administrative roles assigned.

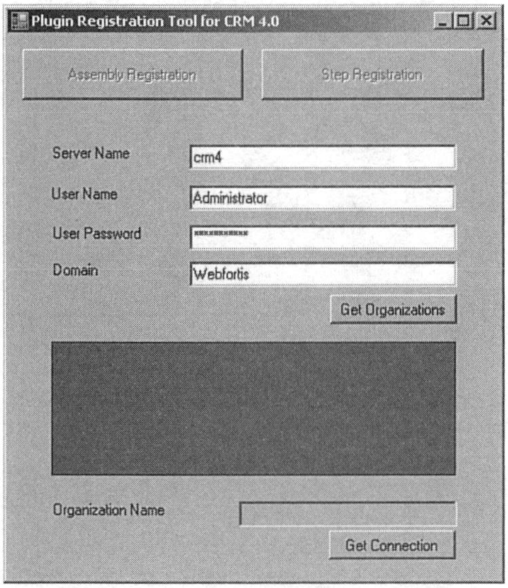

FIGURE 21.26 Registering the Plug-In.

TIP

Be sure to include the port number in the Server Name—for example, `Server:5555` if you're not using the dedicated server port of 80.

After you enter these values, you must click Get Organizations. The organizations are listed, as shown in Figure 21.27.

Select the organization where you want to deploy and register your Plug-In, and click Get Connection. If you are connected successfully to the CRM organization, you will receive the dialog box alert shown in Figure 21.28.

This operation enables the two main buttons on the top, Assembly Registration and Step Registration.

To register your assembly, click the Assembly Registration button. The window in Figure 21.29 opens.

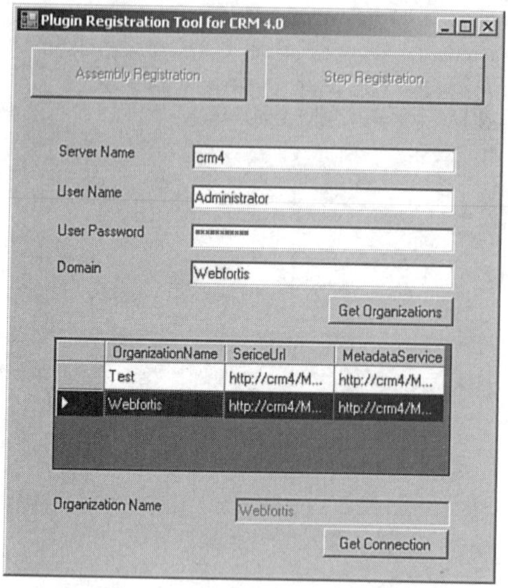

FIGURE 21.27 Selecting Organizations to register a Plug-In.

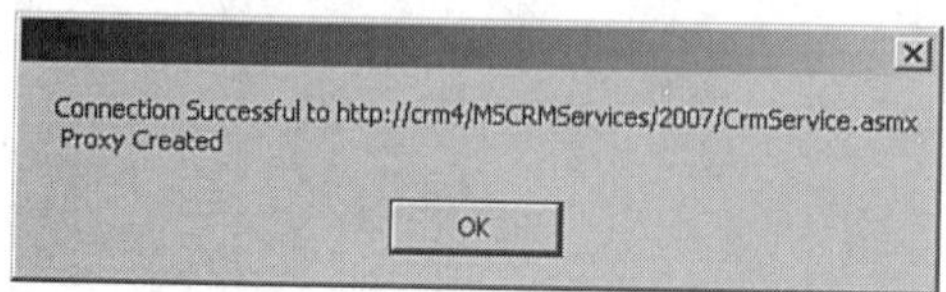

FIGURE 21.28 Successful Organization connection.

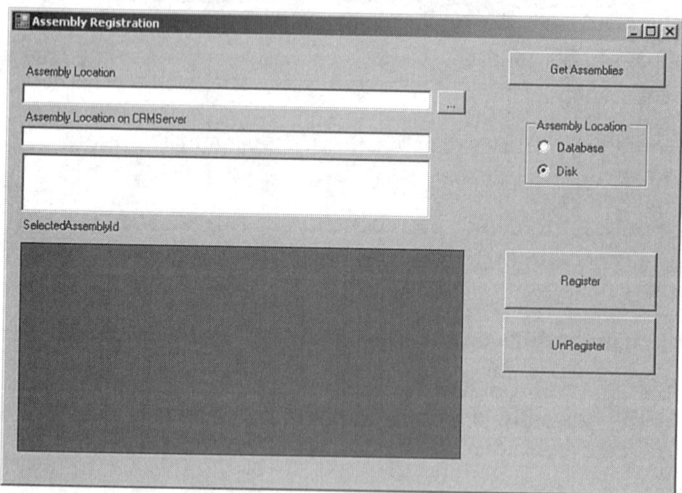

FIGURE 21.29 Assembly registration window.

Locate your assembly by clicking the ... button near the Assembly location text box and select the Database option under Assembly Location. Be sure to select the class you want to register that appears on the list. Then click the Register button. When the assembly is registered, it is assigned a unique identifier, as shown in Figure 21.30. You will be able to find the Plug-In by its Assembly name, so the GUID doesn't need to be recorded. (Note that your Assembly ID will differ from the one shown.)

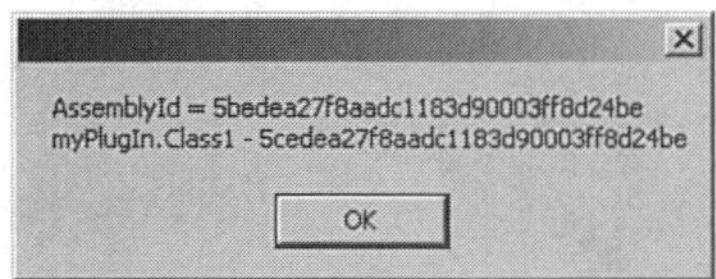

FIGURE 21.30 Registered Assembly unique identifier.

Now click the Get Assemblies button to review that your assembly was properly registered (see Figure 21.31).

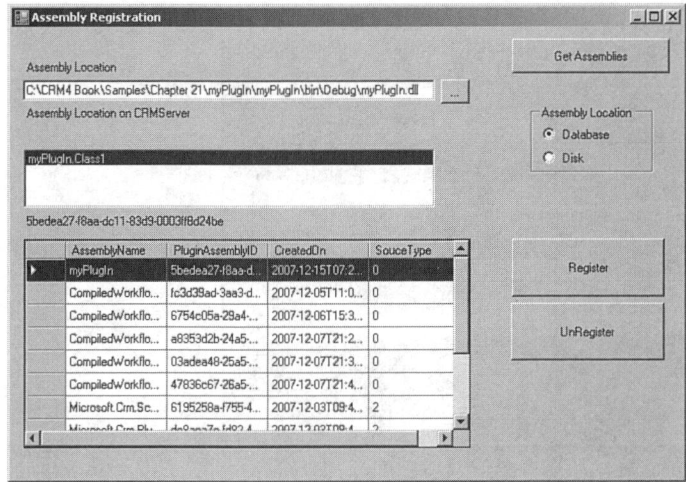

FIGURE 21.31 Reviewing assembly registration.

Close the Assembly Registration dialog box after registering the Plug-In. Now you must associate it with an entity and an event. To do that, click the Step Registration button that is on the Plug-In Registration tool for CRM 4.0 (see Figure 21.32).

Locate the Plug-In you just registered in the Steps registered for AssemblyName dropdown list, and click the Get Steps button. As you can see in Figure 21.33, the grid will show no steps.

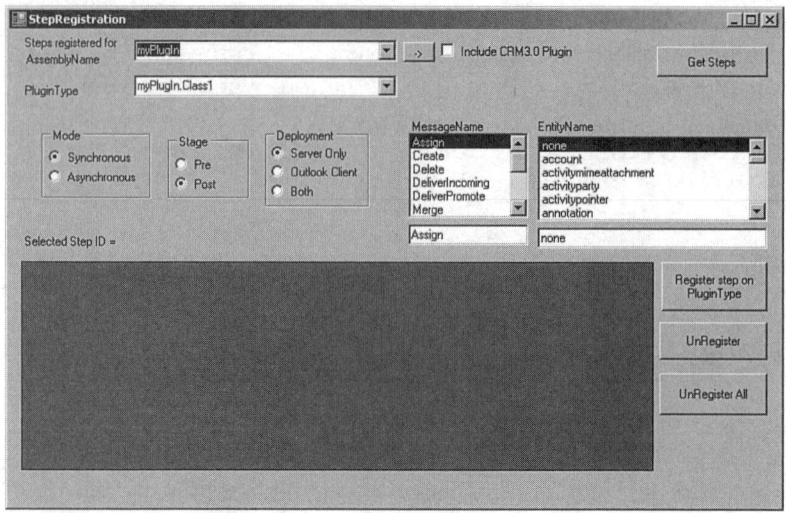

FIGURE 21.32 Step registrations dialog box.

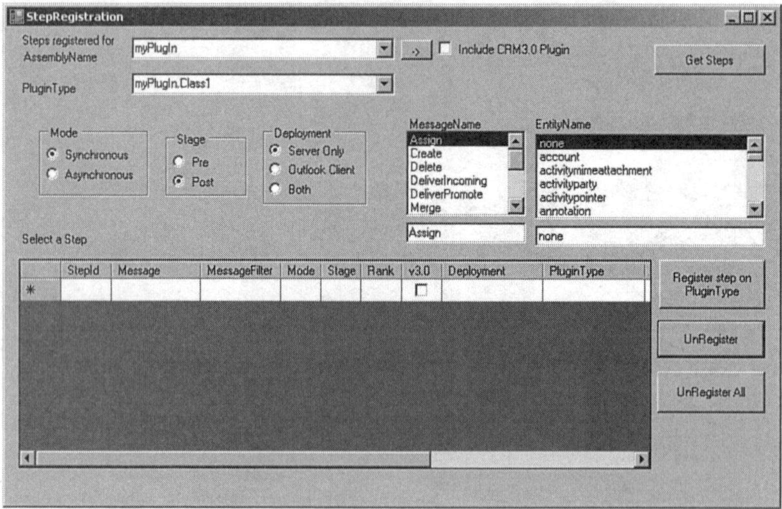

FIGURE 21.33 Getting steps.

To register a step, select a message from the MessageName list. In our example, we are going to select Create for the MessageName and Account from the EntityName list box (which, as is implied, is going to fire our Plug-In when an Account is created). Select the Register step on the PluginType button that will assign a GUID for the step ID, as shown in Figure 21.34. (Your GUID will differ from the one shown.)

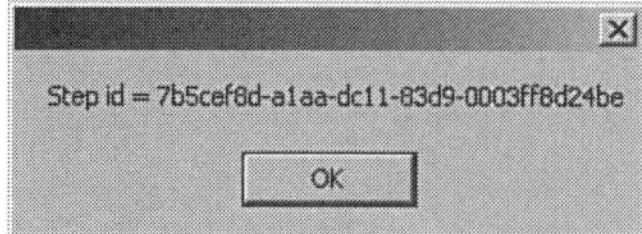

FIGURE 21.34 New GUID created for step registration.

Click OK to close this message box with the GUID and click the Get Steps button again. You see the new step registered (see Figure 21.35).

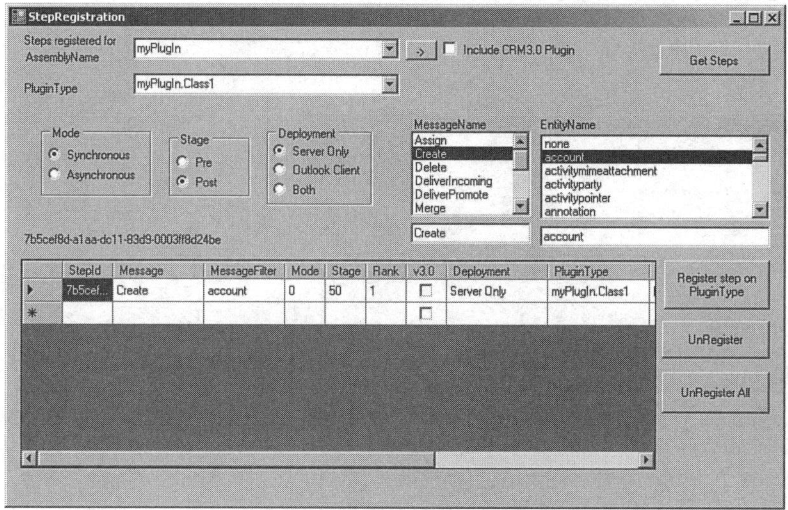

FIGURE 21.35 Step registrations review.

As you can see in Figure 21.29, you can deploy the assembly to either the local hard disk or the database server.

NOTE

Be sure to properly debug and test your Plug-In before implementing it to a production environment. If the Plug-In has an error, users cannot create accounts if you attached the Plug-In to the account `Create` event and the Pre stage (see Figure 21.36).

Plug-In Deregistration

To unregister your Plug-In, click the Get Assemblies button, which lists the installed Plug-Ins (see Figure 21.37).

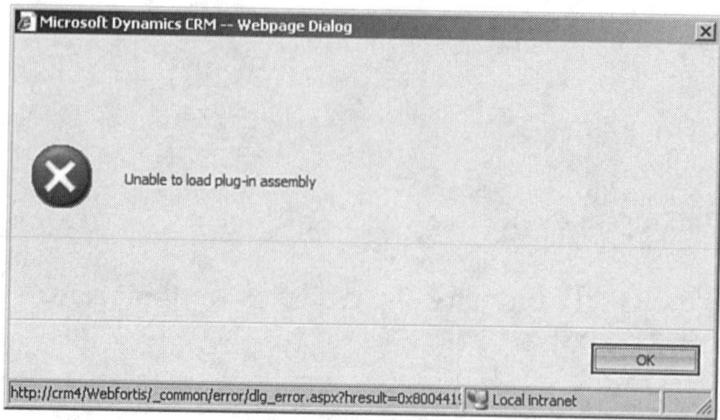

FIGURE 21.36 Plug-In errors prevent users from creating records.

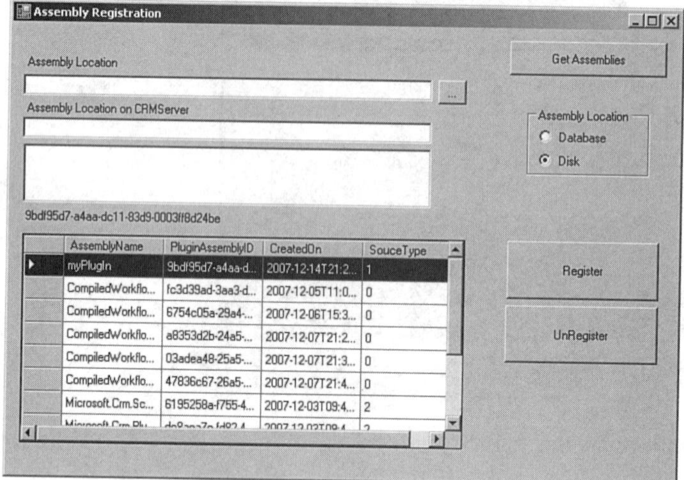

FIGURE 21.37 Assemblies installed on the system organization.

Select the Plug-In you want to delete and click the UnRegister button. Be sure to select the entire row, as shown in Figure 21.37, before clicking the UnRegister button.

FIGURE 21.38 Successful Plug-In unregistration.

Plug-In Debugging

There are two ways to debug your Plug-In. The first is attaching the debugger to the `w3p.exe` process, and the other is forcing the add-in to call the debugger. For either of these methods, it is recommended to try them on a testing environment as these methods use Visual Studio and will interrupt users jobs if attempted on a production environment.

Before trying any of these methods, you need to build your Plug-In with Debug mode and put the PDB (project data base) file generated by the compiler in the following directory (assuming you have the CRM server installed on C:\Program Files\Microsoft Dynamics CRM\):

```
C:\Program Files\Microsoft Dynamics CRM\Server\bin\assembly
```

Unfortunately, you must restart the IIS after copying the PDB file. This is something that can be done via the command prompt by running the following command at a command line prompt:

```
Iisreset
```

NOTE

You must copy the PDB file every time you rebuild the solution and restart the IIS.

Attaching the Debugger to the `w3wp.exe` Process

With this mode, you have to open your Plug-In solution in Visual Studio 2005 first and put in breakpoints where you want to stop and debug your code. To put a breakpoint, press F9 or go to the Debut menu and select the Toggle Breakpoint option (see Figure 21.39).

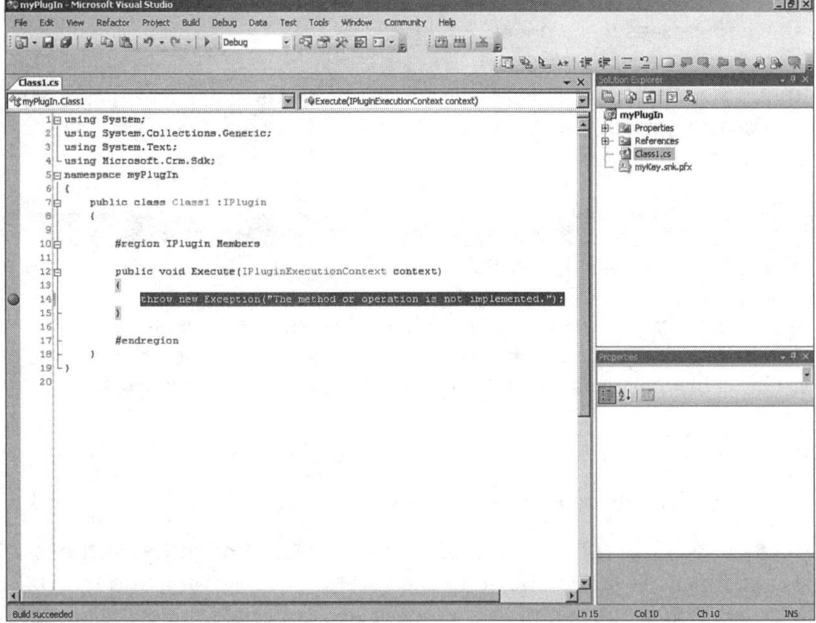

FIGURE 21.39 Setting breakpoints on your code.

You must start the debugger by attaching the Visual Studio debugger to the `w3wp.exe` process. To do that, go to the Debug menu and select the Attach to Process option (see Figure 21.40).

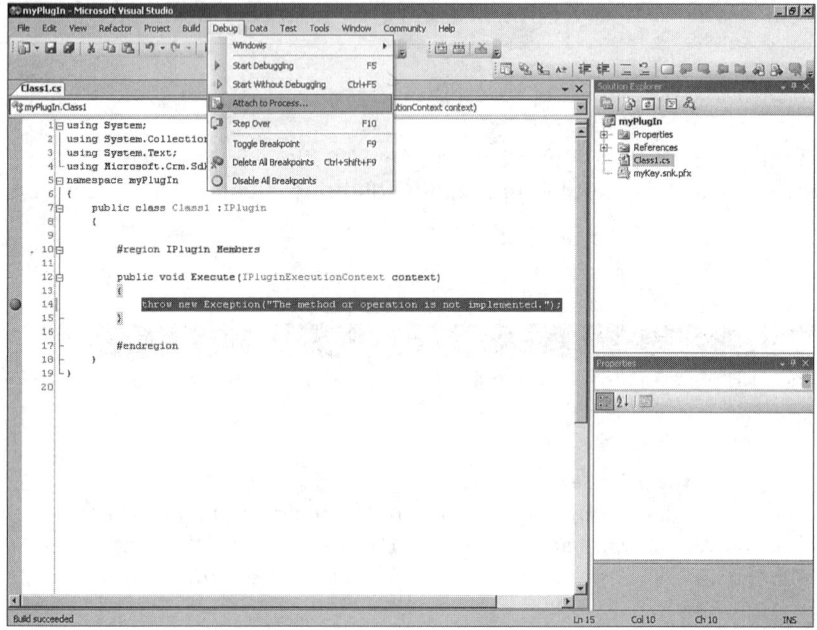

FIGURE 21.40 Attach to process menu option.

When the Attach to Process dialog box appears, be sure to check the check boxes that say Show Processes from All Users and Show Processes in All Sessions. Locate the `w3wp.exe` process, and select it (see Figure 21.41).

NOTE

If you don't find the `w3wp.exe` process, it is probably because you must first open an Internet Explorer window and browse to your CRM organization URL, so the IIS will load the application pool represented by the `w3wp.exe`. You might also see more than one instance of this process depending on the application pools configured in the server. To be sure you select all the instances you find, hold the CTRL key before pressing the Attach button.

Press the Attach button to start debugging the Plug-In.

Assuming you registered a Plug-In with a step associated to the Account entity on the Create event (as our example did), when you go to the CRM web application and try to create a new Account, you will be automatically switched to the Visual Studio 2005 application after you click Save or Save and Close on the Account Form (see Figure 21.42).

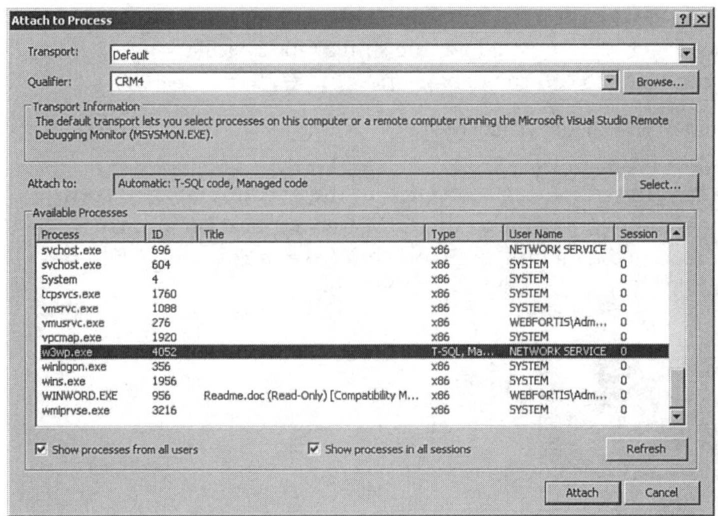

FIGURE 21.41 Attaching the debugger to the w3wp.exe process.

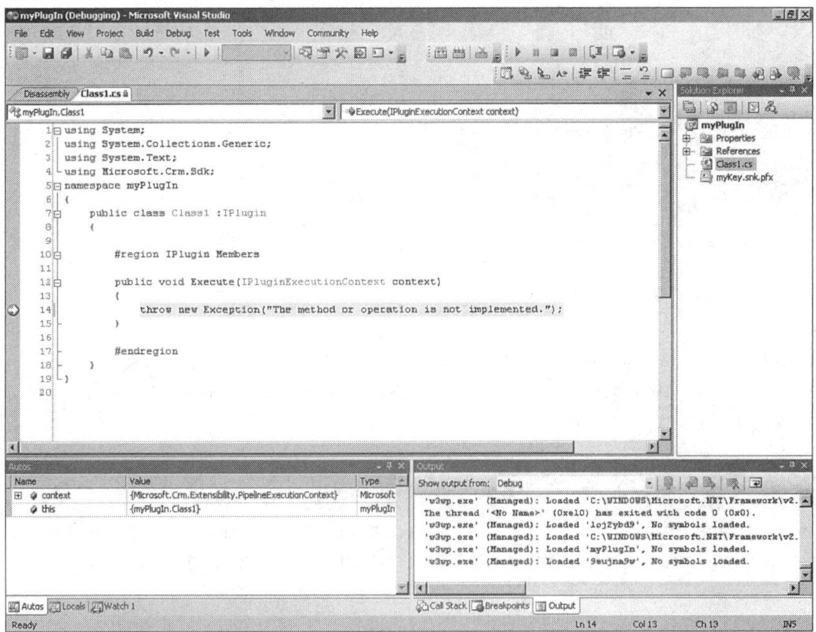

FIGURE 21.42 Debugging the Plug-In.

When you finish the debugging, you can stop the debugger by going to the Debug menu and clicking either the Stop Debugging or Detach All menu options.

Forcing the Add-In to Call the Debugger

To force CRM to call the debugger, you must add a line similar to the following in your add-in source code where you want to call the debugger:

```
System.Diagnostics.Debugger.Launch();
```

Assuming you registered a Plug-In with a step associated to the Account entity on the `Create` event (as our example did), when you go the CRM web application and try to create a new Account, you see the dialog box after you click Save or Save and Close on the Account form (see Figure 21.43).

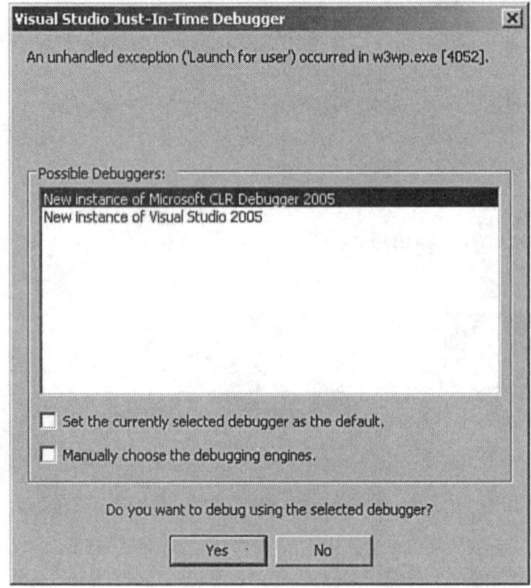

FIGURE 21.43 Visual Studio Just-In-Time Debugger.

Click Yes to open a new interface of Microsoft Visual CLR Debugger 2005, and you see that the code of your Plug-In stopped its execution right on the line of code we added to launch the debugger (see Figure 21.44).

TIP

It is recommended to select the New instance of Visual Studio 2005 option instead of the CLR debugger, as the first one will show the codes colored and the second one will not.

NOTE

If you try saving the Account from a machine different than the server, the dialog box shown in Figure 21.43 will be displayed on the server machine and not on the client machine.

Be sure to comment or remove all the lines where you put the `Debugger.Launch()` method after debugging and fixing your Plug-In before deploying it to production.

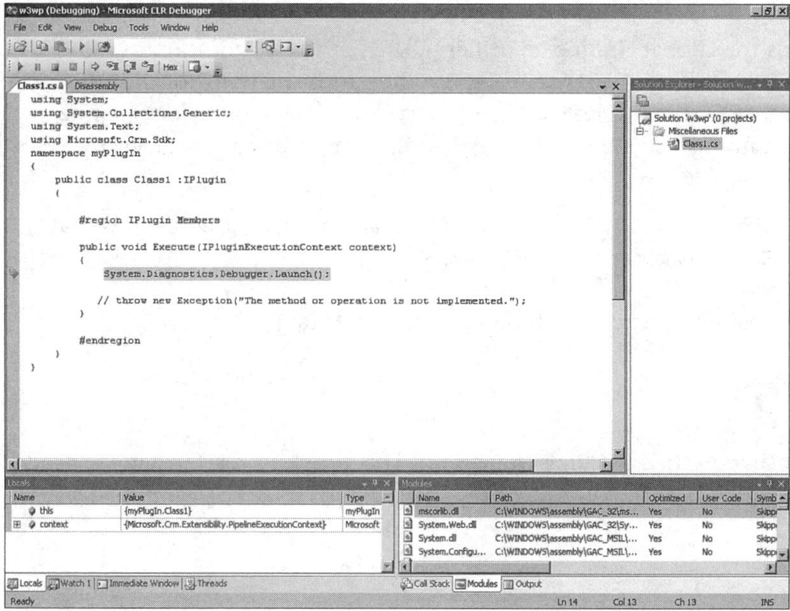

FIGURE 21.44 Plug-In debugging in Visual Studio.

IPluginExecutionContext

`IPluginExecutionContext` is the only parameter that the `Execute` method receives.

From this object, you can query all the property values associated with the entity and event context where the method is executed.

This class contains the following properties:

- `BusinessUnitId`
- `CallerOrigin`
- `CorrelationId`
- `CorrelationUpdatedTime`
- `Depth`
- `InputParameters`
- `InvocationSource`
- `IsExecutingInOfflineMode`
- `MessageName`
- `Mode`
- `OrganizationId`
- `OrganizationName`
- `OutputParameters`
- `ParentContext`
- `PostEntityImages`
- `PreEntityImages`
- `PrimaryEntityName`
- `SecondaryEntityName`
- `SharedVariables`
- `Stage`
- `UserId`
- `CreateCrmService`
- `CreateMetadataServices`

`BusinessUnitId`

This property returns the Global Unique Identifier (GUID) of the business unit of the entity. Notice that this is not the GUID of the entity. To return the GUID of the entity, you must cast the entity first and then use the primary key of the entity. For example, if you are working with Accounts, you should use the following code to get the entity record identifier:

```
DynamicEntity entity = (DynamicEntity)context.InputParameters.Properties["Target"];
if (entity.Name == EntityName.account.ToString())
{
    Guid id = (Guid)context.OutputParameters.Properties["Id"];
}
```

`CallerOrigin`

This property returns who called the Plug-In method. This property is an instance of the `CallerOrigin` class, which has the following properties:

- `Application`
- `AsyncService`
- `WebServiceApi`

The `Application` value means the web application is the caller originator of the event. `AsyncService` means the asynchronous service is the caller originator of the event. The `WebServiceApi` value means the originator was from a Web Service call.

You can use this property, for example, to detect whether the originator is the web application so that you can prevent a record from being updated or created from the Plug-In code:

```
if (context.CallerOrigin is ApplicationOrigin)
{
    throw new Exception("You are not allowed to updated this record from this [ccc]
interface.");
}
else if (context.CallerOrigin is AsyncServiceOrigin)
{
    // ok, do something
}
else if (context.CallerOrigin is WebServiceApiOrigin)
{
    // ok, do something
}
```

If you build a Plug-In using this code and register it to the `Update` event of the Account entity in the Pre stage, the users will get the error shown in Figure 21.45 when they try to save a change on an Account record using the web application.

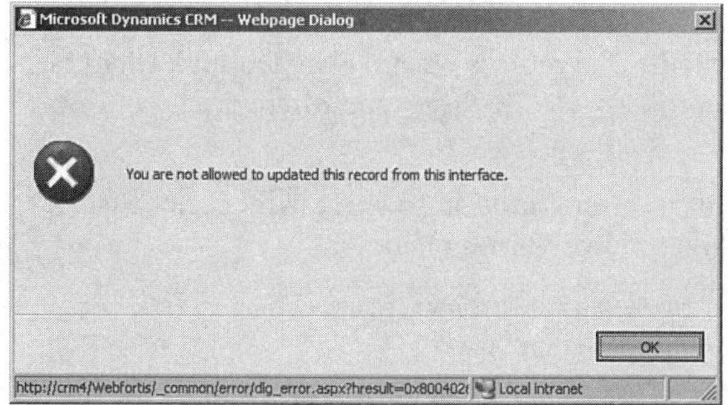

FIGURE 21.45 Showing errors to users from a Plug-In by throwing exceptions.

`CorrelationId`

This property returns the GUID of the Plug-In event instance. Every time the event fires, it generates a new GUID that can be read from this property.

You can use this property for tracking and login purposes, especially when you have more than one Plug-In attached to the same event to see if the codes execute for the same event pipeline.

`CorrelationUpdatedTime`

This property returns the date and time of the event execution. This property is a `CrmDateTime` class type.

`Depth`

This property returns the depth of the originated event. This property is of integer type and grows as the Plug-In execution goes deeper. This can happen if your Plug-In calls a Web Service to update another entity that also fires an event for another Plug-In execution code. There is a limitation of eight nested calls to avoid deadlocks in the current system, so if this value grows above `8`, an exception will be thrown.

`InputParameters`

This property retrieves the request parameters associated with the event, as illustrated in the code example used with the `BusinessUnitId` property. You can use this property to retrieve the entity of which the event is fired:

```
DynamicEntity entity = (DynamicEntity)context.InputParameters.Properties["Target"];
```

`InvocationSource`

This property is used to determine whether the Plug-In has been invoked by a parent or a child source in the event pipeline. This property is of integer type where the following is true:

`0` = Parent

`1` = Child

`IsExecutingInOfflineMode`

This property is used only for Outlook clients and returns whether the Outlook client is running in online or offline mode. This property is a Boolean type where `true` = offline mode.

Plug-Ins can be executed in online and/or in offline modes. To check which mode is executing at runtime, you can also use the following lines of codes:

```
CrmService myService = (CrmService)context.CreateCrmService(true);
if ( service.Url.StartsWith("http://localhost:2525") )
{
    // running in offline mode
}
else
{
    // running in online mode
}
```

`MessageName`

This property returns the event's name that invoked the Plug-In. It is a string—for example, `Update`, `Create`, `Delete`, and so on.

`Mode`

This property returns the mode in which the Plug-In is running. It can be synchronous or asynchronous. This parameter is an integer type where the following is true:

`0` = synchronous

`1` = asynchronous

`OrganizationId`

This property returns the organization GUID where the Plug-In is running.

Even though Plug-Ins are registered by organization ID, having this property helps if you have a generic Plug-In developed that will be installed in different organizations and you need to perform different tasks depending on the organization the Plug-In is running. This way, you can maintain only one Visual Studio Solution and source codes.

`OrganizationName`

Similar to `OrganizationId`, but this property returns the name of the organization instead of the GUID.

`OutputParameters`

This property is the collection of properties returned by the event. A common output parameter is the GUID returned when an entity is created. Be careful when adding parameters on Pre stages because they could be overwritten after the system processes the core event. As an example of this, imagine that you want to return the `accountid` property that is created when a Plug-In is attached to the `Create` event of the Account entity in the Post stage:

```
Guid myAccountID = (Guid)context.OutputParameters.Properties[ ParameterName.Id];
```

`ParentContext`

This property accesses the `IPluginExecutionContext` instance of the parent Plug-In when your Plug-In is executed as a child. This property returns a null object if you are executing from a parent Plug-In.

`PostEntityImages`

This property contains the collection of properties with the values after the system executes the core operation.

NOTE

You need to specify what properties you want to have on this collection when you register the Plug-In.

`PreEntityImages`

This property contains the collection of properties with the values before the system executes the core operation. This is very useful on Post stages to see what values the associated entity had before an update operation, for example.

NOTE

As with `PostEntityImages`, you also need to specify what properties you want to have with this collection when you register the Plug-In.

`PrimaryEntityName`

This property gets the related primary entity name you specified when you registered the Plug-In. This property is a type of string and returns the name of the associated entity—for example, Account, Contact, and so on.

`SecondaryEntityName`

This property gets the related secondary entity name if you specified one when registering the Plug-In. This entity is commonly used in the Parent Account or Contact of the Account entity. This property is a type of string and returns the string `none` if no secondary entity name is specified.

`SharedVariables`

This property is used as a common repository to store properties that Plug-Ins will share. It is useful when you need to pass a parameter value from one Plug-In to another that is executed in the same event pipeline.

`Stage`

This property returns the stage, which can be Pre or Post as an integer value. The following is true for this property:

`10` = Pre

`50` = Post

NOTE

The other stages (`20`, `30`, and `40`) are reserved for internal CRM events and cannot be used.

`UserId`

This property returns the GUID of the user who is invoking the operation.

The `IPluginExecutionContext` class contains the following methods:

- `CreateCrmService`
- `CreateMetadataService`

`CreateCrmService`

This method instantiates the CRM SDK Web Service. You could also have a Web Reference in your Plug-In to call and use this Web Service, but this method is optimized for better performance. Refer to Chapter 22, "Web Services," for more details about how to work with Web Services.

`CreateMetadataService`

This method instantiates the CRM metadata Web Service. You could also have a Web Reference in your Plug-In to call and use this Web Service, but this method is optimized for better performance. Refer to Chapter 22 for more details about how to work with Web Services.

Plug-In Developer Tool

When you are developing Plug-Ins, the task of registering and unregistering the Plug-In to debug and test your code using `PluginRegistration` tool becomes fairly tedious. Every time you make a change, you need to reregister the Plug-In and so on with the associated events. To make this task easier, the SDK includes a tool called PluginDeveloper that comes with the source codes, enabling you to customize it, if needed. This tool is located in the CrmSdk4\SDK\Tools\PluginDeveloper folder of the SDK and is not compiled by default when you install the SDK, so to start using it you must open the `PluginDeveloper.sln` solution file in Visual Studio 2005 and build the solution. In the same way we built the PluginRegistration tool, we must add the Web References first before building the solution. (See the necessary steps to add the CRM Web Services references detailed earlier in this chapter.)

This tool is a console application type that must be run from the command prompt.

To use this tool, you need to create and configure an XML file with the name `register.xml`. The SDK comes with a sample `register.xml` file you can use as a base to build your own files with a few modifications without having to create it from scratch. This sample file is located in the same directory of the PluginDeveloper project and is also part of the solution.

TIP

Be sure to enter the organization name on the `Org` attribute of the Register node in the correct case because it is case-sensitive.

A sample of this file content follows:

```
<?xml version="1.0" encoding="utf-8" ?>
<Register
        LogFile = "Plugin Registration Log.txt"
        Server = "http://crm4:5555"
        Org = "Webfortis"
        Domain=""
        UserName="administrator"
        >

    <Solution SourceType="0" Assembly="C:\crm4
➥Book\Samples\Chapter21\myPlugIn\myPlugIn\bin\Debug\myPlugIn.dll">
        <WorkflowTypes>
        </WorkflowTypes>

        <Steps>
            <Step
                CustomConfiguration = ""
                Description = "Plug-In which generates a context report"
                FilteringAttributes = "name,accountid"
                ImpersonatingUserId = ""
                InvocationSource = "0"
                MessageName = "Update"
                Mode = "0"
                PluginTypeFriendlyName = "Custom Plugin"
                PluginTypeName = "myPlugIn.Class1"
                PrimaryEntityName = "account"
                SecondaryEntityName = ""
                Stage = "50"
                SupportedDeployment = "0" >
            </Step>
```

```
        </Steps>
    </Solution>
</Register>
```

The highlighted lines are the minimum lines you must change with your Plug-In information. You might also want to change the `PrimaryEntityName` and the `MessageName` attributes of the Step node.

NOTE

If you intend to use this tool by running the solution from Visual Studio, be sure to edit the `register.xml` file that is inside the \CrmSdk4\SDK\Tools\PluginDeveloper\ folder and not the one in the CrmSdk4\SDK\Tools\PluginDeveloper\bin\Debug folder, as it will be overwritten when you build the solution.

After you configure and run the developer tool by pressing F5 in Visual Studio, a console application starts and you are prompted to enter the configured user's password because that is the only parameter that is not configured in the XML file (see Figure 21.46).

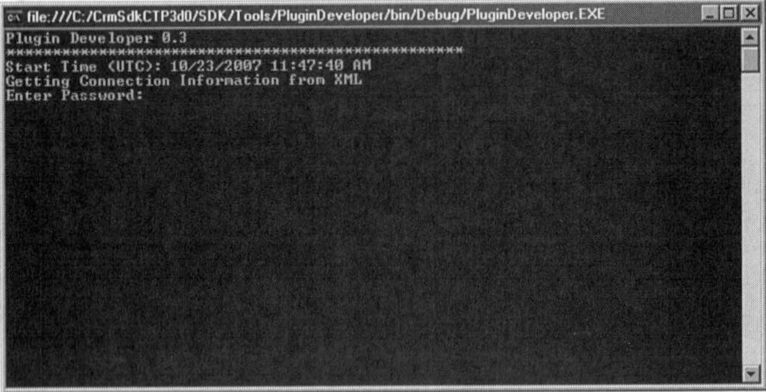

FIGURE 21.46 Entering the password on the developer tool.

After entering the password, your Plug-In automatically is registered or re-registered, and you will see the message status (see Figure 21.47).

TIP

Because this tool comes with the source codes, you can easily modify the tool so that it will not ask you to enter the password and use the credentials of the user running the tool. Refer to Chapter 22 for more on how to make these configurations when invoking Web Services in CRM. Additionally, this tool (as well as the Plugin Registration tool) are designed to be used with Windows authentication. If you need to use these tools with IFD or CRM Online, you should change the authentication methods in the source codes. (Refer to Chapter 16, "Configuration and Customization Tools," for sample code using different authentication methods.)

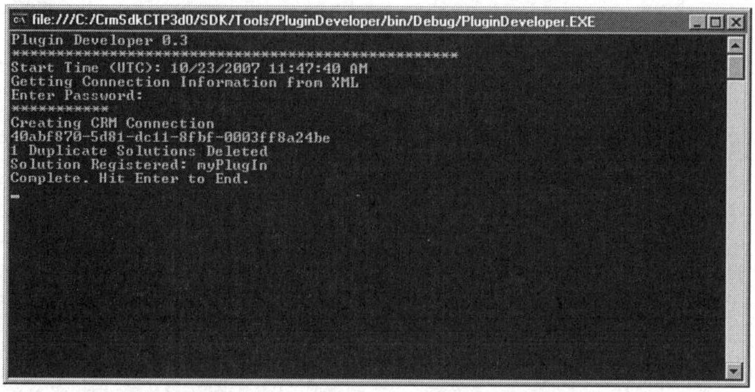

Figure 21.47 Plug-In registration with the developer tool.

Plug-In Samples

The SDK comes with some Plug-In samples; one is a post-invoice Plug-In that updates the parent invoice account after the invoice's state changes to Paid. Another sample is the PreAccount Plug-In, which creates a random account number when an account is created. You can find the code for these samples in VB .NET and in C# within the SDK in the sdk\server\fullsample folder.

Summary

In this chapter, you learned about Plug-Ins—what they are and when it is recommended to use them. You created a basic Plug-In and reviewed all the development properties and methods of the `IPluginExecutionContext` class. You learned how to deploy and register the Plug-Ins using different tools, such as PluginRegistration and the developer tool. Finally, you learned how to test and debug your Plug-In using different ways like attaching the debugger to the `w3wp.exe` process or by forcing the add-in to launch a new debugger instance.

CHAPTER 22
Web Services

IN THIS CHAPTER

Web Services Fundamentals

Microsoft Dynamics CRM uses the Service Oriented Architecture (SOA) concept, which implements a series of Web Services to provide extensibility support. By using these Web Services, we can integrate other applications and systems with Microsoft CRM, as well as extend its capabilities.

Web Services are based on Simple Object Access Protocol (SOAP) messages. This protocol uses Extended Markup Language (XML), which provides usability through Hypertext Transfer Protocol (HTTP) communication transports.

In simple terms, this gives applications and systems an easy way to communicate using standard protocols to interoperate and share functionalities.

Web Services are language- and platform-independent, so basically they can be consumed by an application written in Java, Visual Basic, or C#. They also can be used on a Microsoft Windows–based OS, as well as UNIX and Macintosh platforms.

The samples included in this chapter are written using C# with Visual Studio 2005. However, as shown with the last sample in this chapter, we could consume the Web Services using JavaScript.

The Microsoft CRM Web Services are divided and defined into three main groups:

- Discovery Web Service
- Main Data Web Service
- Metadata Web Service

To easily see these Web Services' definitions and get the URL addresses of the Web Services Description Language (WSDL) documents within Microsoft CRM, follow these steps:

1. Go to Settings, Customizations (see Figure 22.1).

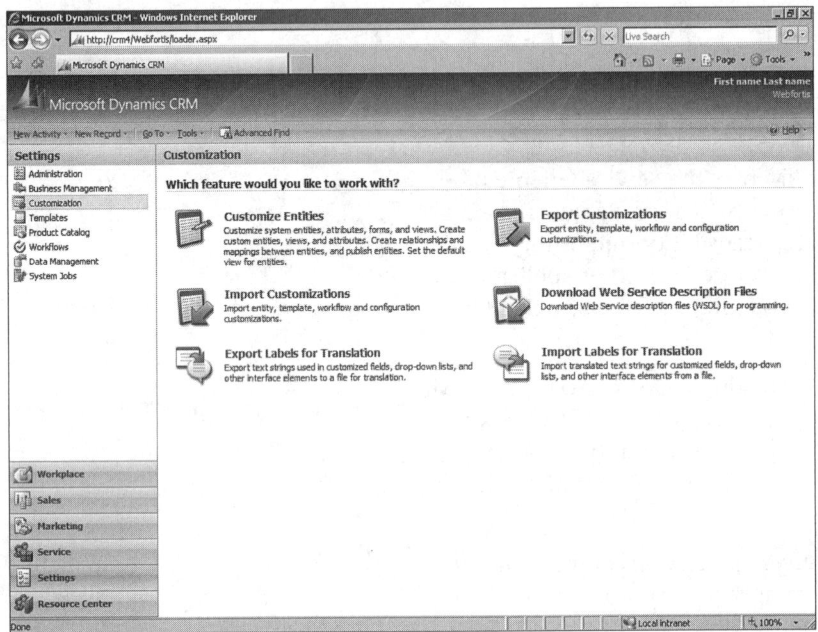

FIGURE 22.1 Navigating to Settings, Customization.

2. Select the option Download Web Services Description Files (see Figure 22.2).

As you can see in Figure 22.2, you can download the definitions for two main Web Services—the Main Data and the Metadata Web Services. The Discovery Web Service is not shown because it is not organization-dependent.

To understand how to use these Web Services, you need to create a new console application in C# to follow the examples of this chapter. To do so, open Visual Studio 2005 and go to File, New, Project. From the project types, go to Visual C#/Windows and select the Console Application on the right side where the templates are (see Figure 22.3).

The Web Services definition files are explained next.

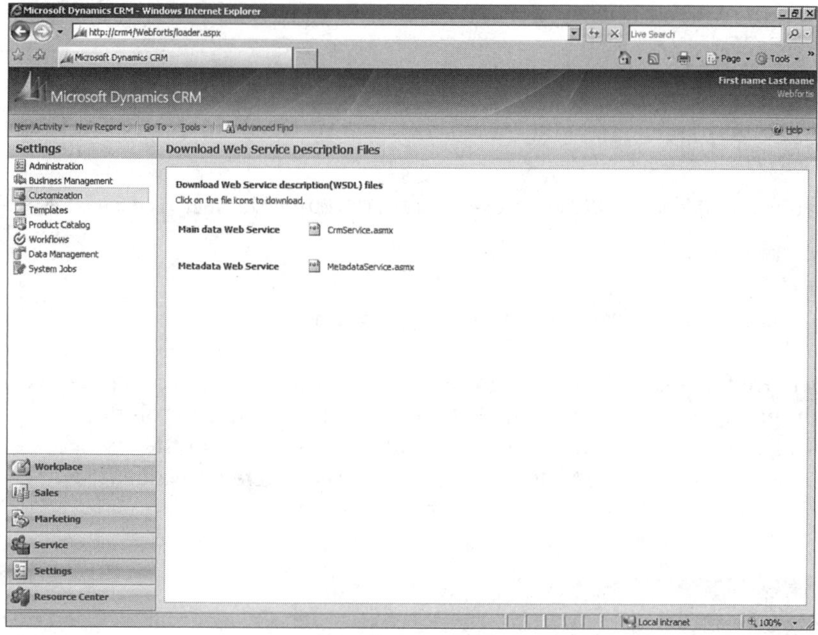

FIGURE 22.2 Downloading Web Services description files.

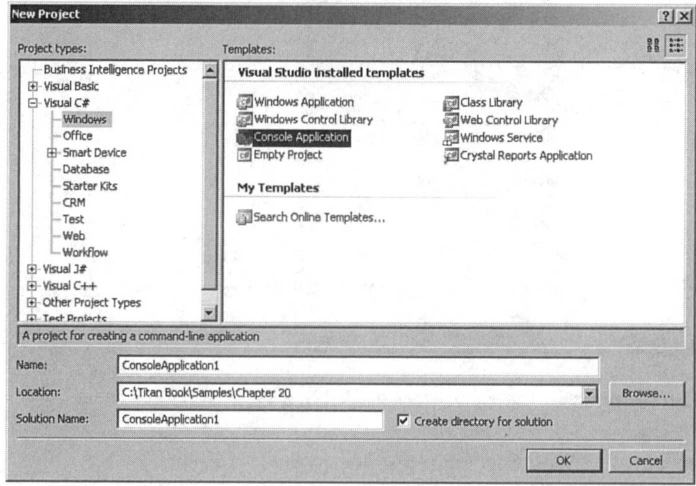

FIGURE 22.3 Creating a console application in Visual Studio 2005.

Discovery Web Service

As we explained previously, one of the new features of Microsoft CRM is the multi-tenancy capability, which is support for more than one organization on the same server.

In previous versions, the Microsoft CRM product was limited to only one Organization per server.

Because of that, you need to query a general Web Service called CRMDiscoveryService that will give you the right Web Service for the organization you want to work with. You can find the query by navigating here:

```
http://<servername>:<portnumber>/MSCRMServices/2007/AD/CrmDiscoveryService.asmx?WSDL
```

For example:

```
http://crm4:5555/MSCRMServices/2007/AD/CrmDiscoveryService.asmx?WSDL
```

To add a Web Reference for this Web Service, go to Visual Studio 2005, and using the new console application project you created, right-click the project name in the Solution Explorer and choose Add Web Reference from the menu. Enter the URL of the discovery service, click GO, and then enter **CrmSdk.Discovery** as the Web Reference Name (see Figure 22.4).

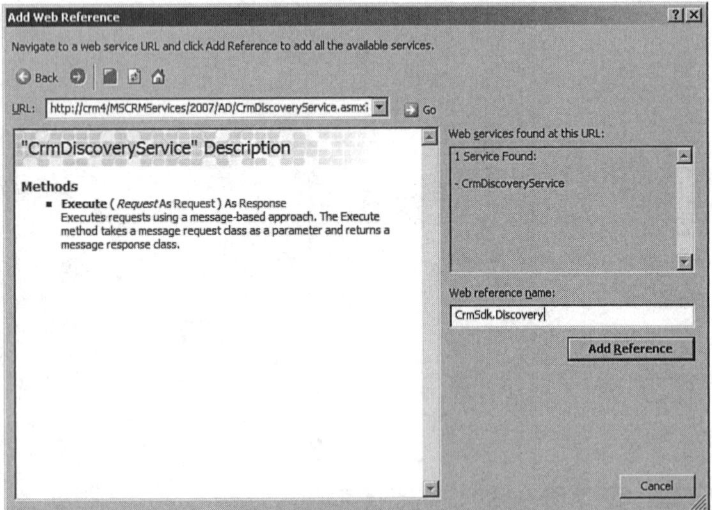

FIGURE 22.4 Adding a Web Reference to the CrmDiscoveryService Web Service.

Click Add Reference to finally add the Web Service reference to your project.

NOTE

Visual Studio must be run from a computer connected to the same domain and LAN as the CRM Server for all the samples in this chapter or you will be prompted to enter the Windows credentials when adding the Web Service reference. For different ways of authentication, such as for IFD and CRM Online scenarios, refer to Chapter 16, "Configuration and Customization Tools" in the "Development Tools" section.

By querying this Web Service, you can retrieve all the organizations that a specific user belongs to and get the right Web Service location. An example of this follows:

```
namespace ConsoleApplication1
{
    class Program
    {
        static void Main(string[] args)
        {
            Console.WriteLine(GetCrmServiceForOrganization("Webfortis"));
            Console.ReadKey();
        }

        private static string GetCrmServiceForOrganization(string organizationName)
        {
            string urlResult = "";
            CrmSdk.Discovery.CrmDiscoveryService myCrm = new ➥
            CrmSdk.Discovery.CrmDiscoveryService();
            myCrm.Credentials = ➥
            System.Net.CredentialCache.DefaultNetworkCredentials;
            CrmSdk.Discovery.RetrieveOrganizationsRequest myRequest = new ➥
            CrmSdk.Discovery.RetrieveOrganizationsRequest();
            CrmSdk.Discovery.RetrieveOrganizationsResponse myResponse = ➥
            (CrmSdk.Discovery.RetrieveOrganizationsResponse)myCrm.Execute ➥
            (myRequest); foreach (CrmSdk.Discovery.OrganizationDetail tDetail in ➥
            myResponse.OrganizationDetails)
            {
                Console.WriteLine("Organization = " + tDetail.OrganizationName);
                if (String.Compare(tDetail.OrganizationName, organizationName, ➥
                true) ==0)
                {
                    return tDetail.CrmServiceUrl;
                }
            }
            return urlResult;
        }
    }
}
```

This function illustrates how to get the correct Web Service address to use for the organization you want to work with.

Main Data Web Service

The other Web Service reference that is necessary for a custom application is the Main Data Web Service:

```
http://<servername>:<portnumber>/MSCRMServices/2007/CrmServiceWsdl.aspx
```

For example:

```
http://crm4:5555/MSCRMServices/2007/CrmServiceWsdl.aspx
```

To add a Web Reference for this Web Service, go to Visual Studio 2005 and using the new console application project you created earlier, right-click the project name in the Solution Explorer and choose Add Web Reference from the menu. Enter the URL of the Main Data Web Service and click GO. Then enter **`CrmSdk`** as the Web Reference Name (see Figure 22.5).

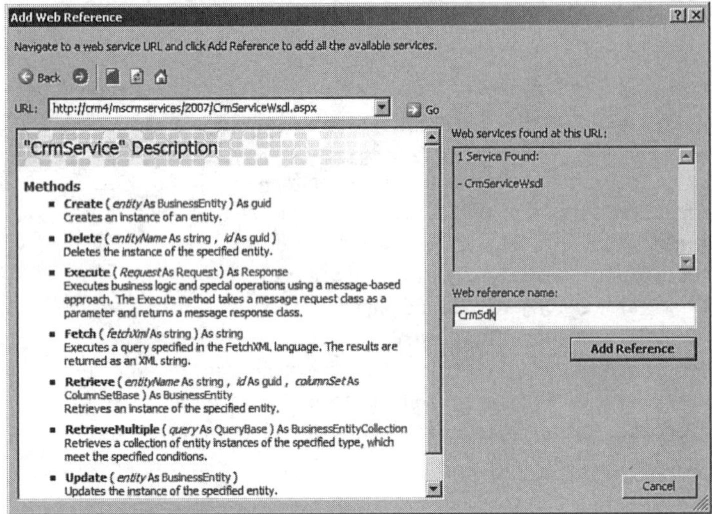

FIGURE 22.5 Adding a Web Reference for the Main Data Web Service.

Click Add Reference to add the Web Service reference to your project.

This Web Service has the following methods:

- `Create`
- `Retrieve`
- `RetrieveMultiple`
- `Delete`
- `Execute`
- `Fetch`
- `Update`

`Create` Method

This method is used to create new instances of an existing entity, such as a new Account or Contact.

This method has only one implementation: It returns a Global Unique Identifier (GUID), which is the unique identifier of the new entity record to be created; it accepts one parameter of type `BusinessEntity`. Because all entities in CRM inherit from the `BusinessEntity` base class, you can pass any entity class to this input parameter.

This is an example of how to create a new Account record programmatically in Visual Studio 2005 with C#:

```
private static string CreateAccount(string organizationName, string accountName)
{
    try
    {
        CrmSdk.CrmService myCrm = new CrmSdk.CrmService();
        myCrm.Url = GetCrmServiceForOrganization(organizationName);
        CrmSdk.CrmAuthenticationToken myToken = ➥
        new CrmSdk.CrmAuthenticationToken();
        myToken.AuthenticationType = 0;
        myToken.OrganizationName = organizationName;
        myCrm.CrmAuthenticationTokenValue = myToken;
        myCrm.Credentials = System.Net.CredentialCache.DefaultCredentials;
        CrmSdk.account newAccount = new CrmSdk.account();
        newAccount.name = accountName;
        Guid newAccountId = myCrm.Create(newAccount);
        return newAccountId.ToString();
    }
    catch (System.Web.Services.Protocols.SoapException soapEx)
    {
        Console.WriteLine("SOAP exception: " + soapEx.Detail.InnerText + "  " + ➥
        soapEx.ToString());
        return soapEx.Detail.InnerText + "  " + soapEx.ToString();
    }
    catch (Exception ex)
    {
        Console.WriteLine("General exception: " + ex.ToString());
        return "General exception: " + ex.ToString();
    }
}
```

To test this method, you need to pass the organization name and the name of the new Account you want to create to the method parameters, as follows:

```
Console.WriteLine("New Account GUID = " + CreateAccount("Webfortis", "New ➥
Account"));
```

You can put the line above inside the Main function of your program to test it so the Main function should look like this:

```
static void Main(string[] args)
{
    Console.WriteLine("New Account GUID = " + CreateAccount("Webfortis", "New ➥
    Account"));
    Console.ReadKey(); //added for debugging purposes only
}
```

When running this code (either by pressing F5 or by going to Debug), Start Debugging, you should see an output similar to Figure 22.6.

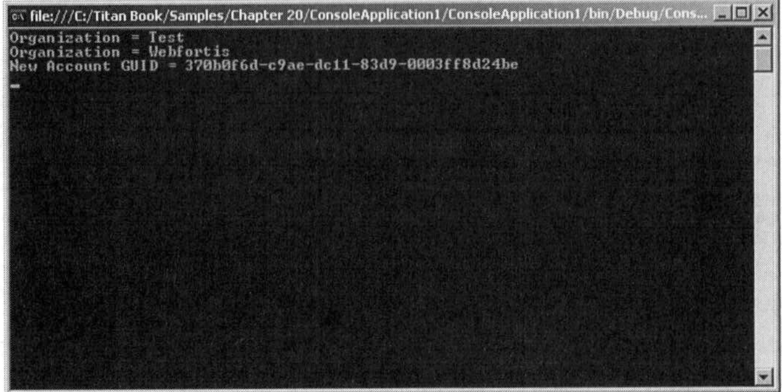

FIGURE 22.6 Creating an Account through the Main Data Web Service.

Now if you go to the CRM web client application, you will see the new Account (see Figure 22.7).

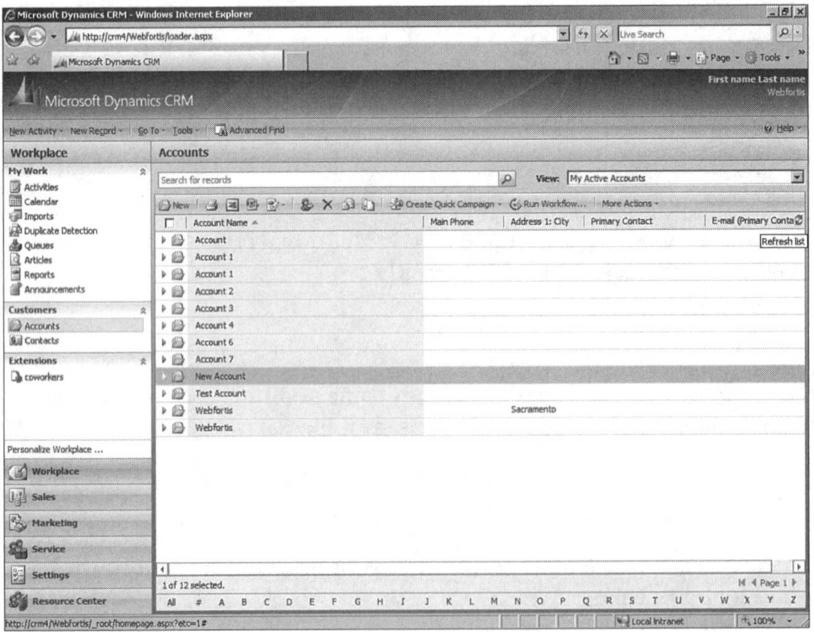

FIGURE 22.7 Reviewing the new Account created through the Main Data Web Service.

Be sure to assign *all* the Business Required fields for the entity you will create programmatically to avoid exceptions.

`Retrieve` Method

This method gets an instance of an entity object. To get more than one instance of an entity, use the `RetrieveMultiple` method (explained in the next section).

This method returns a class type of `BusinessEntity`, so it is necessary to cast the returned value to the entity you want to retrieve.

The input parameters are the string of the entity name, the GUID of the instance of the entity, and a set of columns or fields you want to retrieve.

It is important to define the columns you want to retrieve in the last parameter, or you will get null values even though the instance in the CRM system has values.

This is an example of the `Retrieve` method:

```
private static CrmSdk.account RetrieveAccount(string organizationName, ➥
        Guid accountId)
{
    try
    {
        CrmSdk.CrmService myCrm = new CrmSdk.CrmService();
        myCrm.Url = GetCrmServiceForOrganization(organizationName);
        CrmSdk.CrmAuthenticationToken myToken = ➥
        new CrmSdk.CrmAuthenticationToken();
        myToken.AuthenticationType = 0;
        myToken.OrganizationName = organizationName;
        myCrm.CrmAuthenticationTokenValue = myToken;
        myCrm.Credentials = System.Net.CredentialCache.DefaultCredentials;
        CrmSdk.ColumnSet columns = new CrmSdk.ColumnSet();
        // add more attributes if you want separated by coma below
        columns.Attributes = new string[] { "name" , "accountid"  };
        Guid myAccountId = accountId;
        CrmSdk.account myAccount =
        (CrmSdk.account)myCrm.Retrieve(CrmSdk.EntityName.account.ToString(),
                                       myAccountId, columns);
        return myAccount;
    }
    catch (System.Web.Services.Protocols.SoapException soapEx)
    {
        Console.WriteLine("SOAP exception: " + soapEx.Detail.InnerText
                      + "  " + soapEx.ToString());
        return null;
    }
    catch (Exception ex)
    {
        Console.WriteLine("General exception: " + ex.ToString());
        return null;
    }
}
```

NOTE

Remember to always replace Webfortis with your organization name.

As you can see from this sample method, you need to know the GUID of the account record (or of the entity we want to retrieve) to use this method. We can combine the CreateAccount method we created in the previous section to test this as follows:

```
static void Main(string[] args)
{
    string newAccountId = CreateAccount("Webfortis", "Test Account");
    Console.WriteLine("New Account GUID = " + newAccountId);
    Console.WriteLine ("Checking new account created = " +
            RetrieveAccount("Webfortis", new Guid(newAccountId)).name);
    Console.ReadKey(); //added for debugging purposes only
}
```

After running this test, you will see output similar to that shown in Figure 22.8.

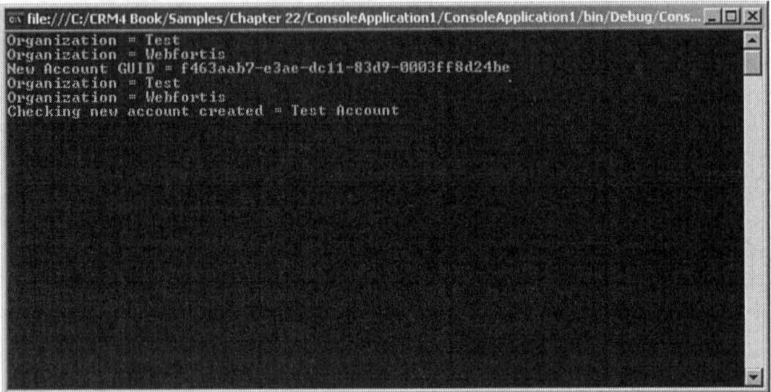

FIGURE 22.8 Testing the `Retrieve` method of the Main Data Web Service.

It is important to understand that you must know the GUID to use this code. This might not be practical when you know only the name and not the GUID. In these cases, you have to use the `RetrieveMultiple` method, as explained in the next section.

`RetrieveMultiple` Method

This method gets one or more than one instance of an entity.

For example, you can use this method to retrieve *all* the Accounts for an organization, as illustrated here:

```
private static void GetAllAccounts(string organizationName)
{
    try
    {
        CrmSdk.CrmService myCrm = new CrmSdk.CrmService();
        myCrm.Url = GetCrmServiceForOrganization(organizationName);
        CrmSdk.CrmAuthenticationToken myToken = ➥
        new CrmSdk.CrmAuthenticationToken();
        myToken.AuthenticationType = 0;
        myToken.OrganizationName = organizationName;
        myCrm.CrmAuthenticationTokenValue = myToken;
        myCrm.Credentials = System.Net.CredentialCache.DefaultCredentials;

        // Creates a column set holding the names of the columns to be retreived
        CrmSdk.ColumnSet colsPrincipal = new CrmSdk.ColumnSet();
        // Sets the Column Set's Properties
        colsPrincipal.Attributes = new string[] { "accountid", "name" };

        // Create the Query Expression
        CrmSdk.QueryExpression queryPrincipal = new CrmSdk.QueryExpression();

        // Set the QueryExpression's Properties
        queryPrincipal.EntityName = CrmSdk.EntityName.account.ToString();
        queryPrincipal.ColumnSet = colsPrincipal;

        /// Retrieve the accounts.
        CrmSdk.BusinessEntityCollection myAccounts = myCrm.RetrieveMultiple(
                                                  queryPrincipal);
        Console.WriteLine("\nGetAllAccounts found {0} accounts\n", ➥
                        myAccounts.BusinessEntities.Length);
        foreach (CrmSdk.BusinessEntity myEntity in myAccounts.BusinessEntities)
        {
            CrmSdk.account myAccount = (CrmSdk.account)myEntity;
            Console.WriteLine(myAccount.name);
        }
    }
    catch (System.Web.Services.Protocols.SoapException soapEx)
    {
        Console.WriteLine("SOAP exception: " + soapEx.Detail.InnerText + "  " + ➥
        soapEx.ToString());
    }
    catch (Exception ex)
    {
        Console.WriteLine("General exception: " + ex.ToString());
    }
}
```

22

NOTE

Remember to always replace Webfortis with your organization name.

To test this method, you need to pass the organization name to the method parameter. The Main function should be as follows:

```
static void Main(string[] args)
{
    GetAllAccounts("Webfortis");
    Console.ReadKey(); //added for debugging purposes only
}
```

When running this code, either by pressing F5 or by going to Debug, Start Debugging, you should see an output similar to Figure 22.9.

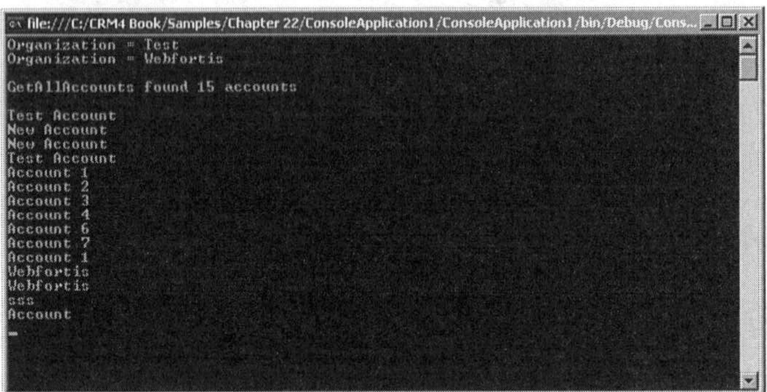

FIGURE 22.9 Testing the `RetrieveMultiple` method.

You can apply filters on the data you want, in addition to retrieving only the fields or properties you want to get.

For example, to retrieve all the Accounts whose names match or start with a selected first letter, use this code:

```
private static List<CrmSdk.account> GetAllAccountsByName(string organizationName,
        string accountName, CrmSdk.ConditionOperator conditionalOperator)
{
    List<CrmSdk.account> accounts = null;
    try
    {
        CrmSdk.CrmService myCrm = new CrmSdk.CrmService();
        myCrm.Url = GetCrmServiceForOrganization(organizationName);
        CrmSdk.CrmAuthenticationToken myToken = ➥
        new CrmSdk.CrmAuthenticationToken();
```

```
myToken.AuthenticationType = 0;
myToken.OrganizationName = organizationName;
myCrm.CrmAuthenticationTokenValue = myToken;
myCrm.Credentials = System.Net.CredentialCache.DefaultCredentials;

// Creates a column set holding the names of the columns to be retreived
CrmSdk.ColumnSet colsPrincipal = new CrmSdk.ColumnSet();
// Sets the Column Set's Properties
colsPrincipal.Attributes = new string[] { "accountid", "name" };

// Create a ConditionExpression
CrmSdk.ConditionExpression conditionPrincipal =
                        new CrmSdk.ConditionExpression();

// Sets the ConditionExpressions Properties so that the condition
// is true when the ownerid of the account Equals the principalId
conditionPrincipal.AttributeName = "name";
conditionPrincipal.Operator = conditionalOperator;
conditionPrincipal.Values = new object[1];
conditionPrincipal.Values[0] = accountName;

// Create the FilterExpression
CrmSdk.FilterExpression filterPrincipal = new CrmSdk.FilterExpression();

// Set the FilterExpression's Properties
filterPrincipal.FilterOperator = CrmSdk.LogicalOperator.And;
filterPrincipal.Conditions = new CrmSdk.ConditionExpression[] ➥
                           { conditionPrincipal };

// Create the Query Expression
CrmSdk.QueryExpression queryPrincipal = new CrmSdk.QueryExpression();

// Set the QueryExpression's Properties
queryPrincipal.EntityName = CrmSdk.EntityName.account.ToString();
queryPrincipal.ColumnSet = colsPrincipal;
queryPrincipal.Criteria = filterPrincipal;

/// Retrieve the accounts.
CrmSdk.BusinessEntityCollection myAccounts = myCrm.RetrieveMultiple ➥
                           (queryPrincipal);
accounts = new List<ConsoleApplication1.CrmSdk.account>();
Console.WriteLine("\nGetAllAccountsByName found {0} accounts\n", ➥
myAccounts.BusinessEntities.Length);
foreach (CrmSdk.BusinessEntity myEntity in myAccounts.BusinessEntities)
{
```

22

```
            CrmSdk.account myAccount = (CrmSdk.account)myEntity;
            accounts.Add(myAccount);
            Console.WriteLine(myAccount.name);
        }
        return accounts;
    }
    catch (System.Web.Services.Protocols.SoapException soapEx)
    {
        Console.WriteLine("SOAP exception: " + soapEx.Detail.InnerText
                        + "  " + soapEx.ToString());
        return null;
    }
    catch (Exception ex)
    {
        Console.WriteLine("General exception: " + ex.ToString());
        return null;
    }
}
```

NOTE

Remember to always replace Webfortis with your organization name.

To test this method, you need to pass the organization name to the method parameter. The Main function should be as follows:

```
static void Main(string[] args)
{
    List<CrmSdk.account> accounts;
    Console.WriteLine("Accounts that starts with the letter A");
    accounts = GetAllAccountsByName("Webfortis", "A%",
        ConsoleApplication1.CrmSdk.ConditionOperator.Like);
    if (accounts == null)
    {
        Console.WriteLine("No accounts found");
    }

    Console.WriteLine("Accounts equal to 'Test Account'");
    accounts = GetAllAccountsByName("Webfortis", "Test Account",
    ConsoleApplication1.CrmSdk.ConditionOperator.Equal);
    if (accounts == null)
    {
        Console.WriteLine("No accounts found");
    }
    Console.ReadKey(); //added for debugging purposes only
}
```

When running this code, either by pressing F5 or by going to Debug, Start Debugging, you should see an output similar to Figure 22.10.

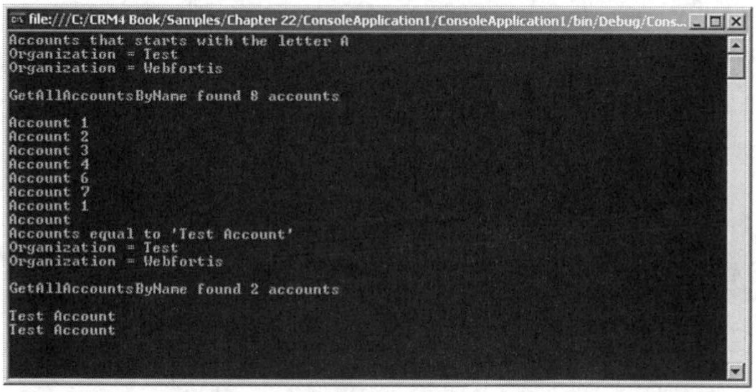

FIGURE 22.10 Matching Accounts.

`Delete` Method

This method deletes an existing instance of an entity. This method doesn't return any value and accepts two inputs parameters. The first parameter is a string containing the entity type (you can use the `EntityName` enumerator here), and the second parameter is the GUID of the instance of the entity you will delete.

This is an example of how to delete a new Account programmatically in Visual Studio 2005 with C#:

```
private static string DeleteAccount(string organizationName, Guid accountToDelete)
{
    try
    {
        CrmSdk.CrmService myCrm = new CrmSdk.CrmService();
        myCrm.Url = GetCrmServiceForOrganization(organizationName);
        CrmSdk.CrmAuthenticationToken myToken = ➥
        new CrmSdk.CrmAuthenticationToken();
        myToken.AuthenticationType = 0;
        myToken.OrganizationName = organizationName;
        myCrm.CrmAuthenticationTokenValue = myToken;
        myCrm.Credentials = System.Net.CredentialCache.DefaultCredentials;
        myCrm.Delete(CrmSdk.EntityName.account.ToString(), accountToDelete);
        return "Account successfully deleted";
    }
    catch (System.Web.Services.Protocols.SoapException soapEx)
    {
        Console.WriteLine("SOAP exception: " + soapEx.Detail.InnerText
                        + "  " + soapEx.ToString());
```

```
        return "SOAP exception: " + soapEx.Detail.InnerText
                    + "  " + soapEx.ToString();
    }
    catch (Exception ex)
    {
        Console.WriteLine("General exception: " + ex.ToString());
        return "General exception: " + ex.ToString();
    }
}
```

NOTE

Remember to always replace Webfortis with your organization name.

To test this method, you need to pass the organization name to the method parameter as well as the GUID of the account to be deleted. Because you might not know the GUID of the account but you might know the account name, we will combine the GetAllAccountsByName method we created previously. The Main function to delete all the accounts that matches with the name Test Account should be as follows:

```
static void Main(string[] args)
    List<CrmSdk.account> accounts;
    Console.WriteLine("Accounts equal to 'Test Account'");
    accounts = GetAllAccountsByName("Webfortis", "Test Account",
    ConsoleApplication1.CrmSdk.ConditionOperator.Equal);
    if (accounts == null)
    {
        Console.WriteLine("No accounts found");
    }
    else
    {
        foreach (CrmSdk.account myAccount in accounts)
        {
            Console.WriteLine(
                DeleteAccount("Webfortis", myAccount.accountid.Value));
        }
    }
    Console.ReadKey(); //added for debugging purposes only
}
```

When running this code, either by pressing F5 or by going to Debug, Start Debugging, you should see an output similar to Figure 22.11.

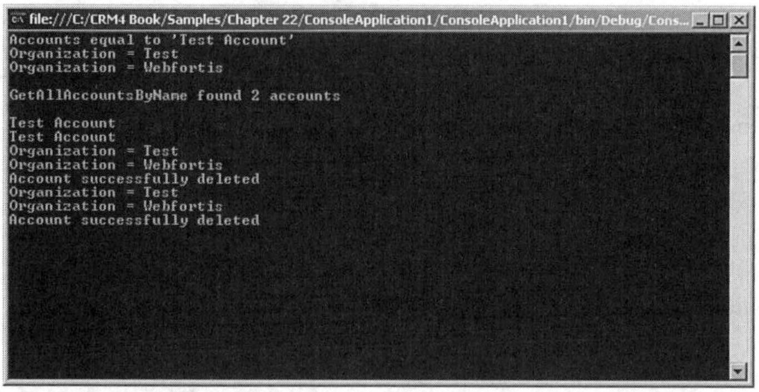

```
file:///C:/CRM4 Book/Samples/Chapter 22/ConsoleApplication1/ConsoleApplication1/bin/Debug/Cons...
Accounts equal to 'Test Account'
Organization = Test
Organization = Webfortis

GetAllAccountsByName found 2 accounts

Test Account
Test Account
Organization = Test
Organization = Webfortis
Account successfully deleted
Organization = Test
Organization = Webfortis
Account successfully deleted
```

FIGURE 22.11 Account deleted example.

`Execute` **Method**

This method executes business logic.

It returns a `Response` object and accepts a parameter as the input of the `Request` type.

You can use this method as a wildcard for all the other methods. This means that you can create an Account by using this method because the class called `CreateRequest` derives from `Request` and can be used as the input parameter; you receive a `CreateResponse` as the result. The same happens for `UpdateRequest`, `UpdateResponse`, `RetrieveRequest`, and `RetrieveResponse`.

NOTE

If you don't remember how to create a case, refer to Chapter 12, "Working with Service."

However, this method is usually used for things you can't do with the other methods. A good example is to use this method, close a CRM Case. Although the Case entity can be updated, you can't update the status by using the `Update` method. To close a Case, you need to use this method:

```
private static bool CloseCase(string organizationName, Guid caseId)
{
    try
    {
        CrmSdk.CrmService myCrm = new CrmSdk.CrmService();
        myCrm.Url = GetCrmServiceForOrganization(organizationName);
        CrmSdk.CrmAuthenticationToken myToken = ➥
        new CrmSdk.CrmAuthenticationToken();
        myToken.AuthenticationType = 0;
        myToken.OrganizationName = organizationName;
```

```
            myCrm.CrmAuthenticationTokenValue = myToken;
            myCrm.Credentials = System.Net.CredentialCache.DefaultCredentials;

            CrmSdk.incident myIncident = new CrmSdk.incident();
            myIncident.incidentid = new CrmSdk.Key();
            myIncident.incidentid.Value = caseId;

            CrmSdk.incidentresolution myIncidentResolution = ➥
            new CrmSdk.incidentresolution();
            myIncidentResolution.incidentid = new CrmSdk.Lookup();
            myIncidentResolution.incidentid.type = ➥
            CrmSdk.EntityName.incident.ToString();
            myIncidentResolution.incidentid.Value = myIncident.incidentid.Value;

            CrmSdk.CloseIncidentRequest closeIncident = ➥
            new CrmSdk.CloseIncidentRequest();
            closeIncident.IncidentResolution = myIncidentResolution;
            closeIncident.Status = -1;
            myCrm.Execute(closeIncident);
            Console.WriteLine("Case successfully closed ");
            return true;
        }
        catch (System.Web.Services.Protocols.SoapException soapEx)
        {
            Console.WriteLine("SOAP exception: " + soapEx.Detail.InnerText
                              + "  " + soapEx.ToString());
            return false;
        }
        catch (Exception ex)
        {
            Console.WriteLine("General exception: " + ex.ToString());
            return false;
        }
    }
```

Fetch **Method**

This method executes a query defined by the FetchXML language.

This method is similar to the `RetrieveMultiple` method, but it returns a string containing the XML representation of the entities result set.

A few points to remember about the `Fetch` method:

- `Fetch` does not support a Union join. To view all the tasks for an account by checking all the contacts of a Contact, you need to perform separate `Fetch` methods—one on the contact tasks and the one on the account contacts—and then merge the results.

- The result set of records depends on the user privilege that invokes the Web Service.
- Performance is lower than when using `Retrieve` or `RetrieveMultiple` methods.

The following code example shows how to use this method to retrieve all contacts with all their properties:

```
private static void GetAllContacts(string organizationName)
{
    try
    {
        CrmSdk.CrmService myCrm = new CrmSdk.CrmService();
        myCrm.Url = GetCrmServiceForOrganization(organizationName);
        CrmSdk.CrmAuthenticationToken myToken = new
CrmSdk.CrmAuthenticationToken();
        myToken.AuthenticationType = 0;
        myToken.OrganizationName = organizationName;
        myCrm.CrmAuthenticationTokenValue = myToken;
        myCrm.Credentials = System.Net.CredentialCache.DefaultCredentials;

        // Retrieve all Contacts.
        StringBuilder fetchStr = new StringBuilder();
        fetchStr.Append(@"<fetch mapping='logical'>");
        fetchStr.Append(@"<entity name='contact'><all-attributes/>");
        fetchStr.Append(@"</entity></fetch>");

        // Fetch the results.
        String resultXML = myCrm.Fetch(fetchStr.ToString());

        System.Xml.XmlDocument myXMLDoc = new System.Xml.XmlDocument();
        myXMLDoc.LoadXml(resultXML);
        System.Xml.XmlNodeList myNodeList = myXMLDoc.GetElementsByTagName➥
        ("fullname");
        Console.WriteLine("\nGetAllContacts found {0} ➥
        contacts\n", myNodeList.Count);
        foreach (System.Xml.XmlNode myNode in myNodeList)
        {
            Console.WriteLine("Contact fullname = {0}", myNode.InnerText);
        }
    }
    catch (System.Web.Services.Protocols.SoapException soapEx)
    {
        Console.WriteLine("SOAP exception: " + soapEx.Detail.InnerText
                          + "  " + soapEx.ToString());
    }
```

```
    catch (Exception ex)
    {
        Console.WriteLine("General exception: " + ex.ToString());
    }
}
```

Update Method

This method updates data related to an instance of an entity.

This method has only one implementation and doesn't return a value. In the same way as the `Create` method, it accepts one parameter of type `BusinessEntity`. Because all the entities in CRM inherit from the `BusinessEntity` base class, you can pass any entity class to this input parameter. To use this method, you must set at least the `ID` property of the entity to be updated. For example, you would set the `accountid` property if you wanted to update an account.

This is an example of how to update an existing Account programmatically in Visual Studio 2005 with C#:

```
private static string UpdateAccountName(string organizationName, ➥
        Guid accountId, string newName)
{
    try
    {
        CrmSdk.CrmService myCrm = new CrmSdk.CrmService();
        myCrm.Url = GetCrmServiceForOrganization(organizationName);
        CrmSdk.CrmAuthenticationToken myToken = ➥
        new CrmSdk.CrmAuthenticationToken();
        myToken.AuthenticationType = 0;
        myToken.OrganizationName = organizationName;
        myCrm.CrmAuthenticationTokenValue = myToken;
        myCrm.Credentials = System.Net.CredentialCache.DefaultCredentials;

        CrmSdk.account myAcoount = new CrmSdk.account();
        myAcoount.accountid = new CrmSdk.Key();
        myAcoount.accountid.Value = accountId;
        myAcoount.name = newName;
        myCrm.Update(myAcoount);
        return "Account successfully updated ";
    }
    catch (System.Web.Services.Protocols.SoapException soapEx)
    {
```

```
            Console.WriteLine("SOAP exception: " + soapEx.Detail.InnerText
                        + "  " + soapEx.ToString());
            return "SOAP exception: " + soapEx.Detail.InnerText
                        + "  " + soapEx.ToString();
        }
        catch (Exception ex)
        {
            Console.WriteLine("General exception: " + ex.ToString());
            return "General exception: " + ex.ToString();
        }
    }
```


Note that only the properties you set are updated. This means that, in the previous example, only the company name property will be changed and the other properties will keep their values. This happens even though they are not set and they have null values when sending them to the `Update` method.

Metadata Web Service

This Web Service is the one that provides access to the entire CRM metadata.

A new feature with this version of Microsoft CRM, the metadata can now be used to create, update, or delete entities, as well as create or delete relationships within entities. You can also use it to add, delete, or modify attributes to an existing entity programmatically.

This Web Service can be very useful for ISVs to look up entities on a setup installer to see if the product was already installed or to check whether any conflict exists with the entities of the CRM system on which a customization would be deployed.

The URL for this Web Service reference is

```
http://<servername>:<portnumber>/MSCrmServices/2007/MetadataService.asmx
```

For example:

```
http://crm4:5555/MSCrmServices/2007/MetadataService.asmx
```

To add a Web Reference for this Web Service, go to Visual Studio 2005 and, using the new console application project you created, right-click the project name in the Solution Explorer and choose Add Web Reference from the menu. Enter the URL of the metadata Web Service, click GO, and then enter **`CrmSdk.Metadata`** as the Web Reference Name (see Figure 22.12).

Click Add Reference to finally add the Web Service reference to your project.

This Web Service exposes only one method, the `Execute` method.

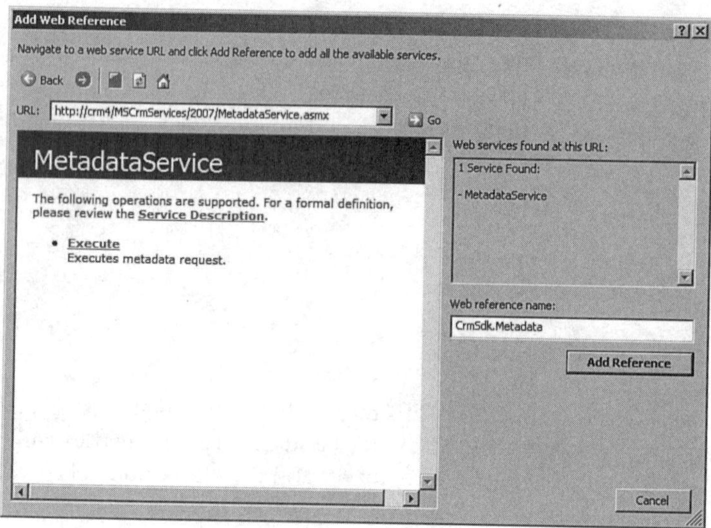

FIGURE 22.12 Adding a Web Reference to the Metadata Web Service.

`Execute` Method

This method accepts the following submethods:

- `CreateAttribute`
- `CreateEntity`
- `CreateManyToMany`
- `CreateOneToMany`
- `DeleteAttribute`
- `DeleteEntity`
- `DeleteOptionValue`
- `DeleteStatusValue`
- `DeleteRelationship`
- `InsertOptionValue`
- `InsertStatusValue`
- `OrderOption`
- `OrderStatus`
- `RetrieveAllEntities`
- `RetrieveAttribute`
- `RetrieveEntity`
- `RetrieveRelationship`
- `RetrieveTimestamp`
- `UpdateAttribute`
- `UpdateEntity`
- `UpdateOptionValue`
- `UpdateStatusValue`
- `UpdateRelationship`

Each of these submethods has its own `Request` and `Response` classes.

To use the `CreateAttribute` method, for example, you must create an instance of `CreateAttributeRequest`, and the `Execute` method would return an instance of `CreateAttributeResponse`.

For example, you might use the following code to find out whether the custom entity `new_MyNewCustomEntity` already exists in a CRM implementation. As with the Main Data Web Service, you will generate a common method to retrieve the Metadata Web Service URL for the organization by using the Discovery Web Service. You will use this method throughout the samples related to the Metadata Web Service.


```
private static string GetCrmMetadataServiceForOrganization(string organizationName)
    {
        string urlResult = "";
        try
        {
            CrmSdk.Discovery.CrmDiscoveryService myCrm = ➥
            new CrmSdk.Discovery.CrmDiscoveryService();
            myCrm.Credentials = ➥
            System.Net.CredentialCache.DefaultNetworkCredentials;
            CrmSdk.Discovery.RetrieveOrganizationsRequest myRequest = ➥
            new CrmSdk.Discovery.RetrieveOrganizationsRequest();
            CrmSdk.Discovery.RetrieveOrganizationsResponse myResponse = ➥
            (CrmSdk.Discovery.RetrieveOrganizationsResponse)myCrm.Execute ➥
            (myRequest);
            foreach (CrmSdk.Discovery.OrganizationDetail tDetail in ➥
            myResponse.OrganizationDetails)
            {
                Console.WriteLine("Organization = " + tDetail.OrganizationName);

                if (stringCompare(tDetail.OrganizationName, organizationName, ➥
                true) ==0)
                {
                    return tDetail.CrmMetadataServiceUrl;
                }
            }
        }
        catch (System.Web.Services.Protocols.SoapException soapEx)
        {
            Console.WriteLine("SOAP exception: " + soapEx.Detail.InnerText ➥
            + "  " + soapEx.ToString());
        }
        catch (Exception ex)
        {
            Console.WriteLine("General exception: " + ex.ToString());
        }
        return urlResult;
    }
```

Now you can add the code for the sample where it has two parameters, the organization name and the entity name.

```
private static bool CheckEntity(string organizationName, string entityName)
    {
        try
        {
            CrmSdk.Metadata.MetadataService myCrm = ➥
            new CrmSdk.Metadata.MetadataService();
            myCrm.Url = GetCrmMetadataServiceForOrganization(organizationName);
            CrmSdk.Metadata.CrmAuthenticationToken myToken = ➥
            new CrmSdk.Metadata.CrmAuthenticationToken();
            myToken.AuthenticationType = 0;
            myToken.OrganizationName = organizationName;
            myCrm.CrmAuthenticationTokenValue = myToken;
            myCrm.Credentials = System.Net.CredentialCache.DefaultCredentials;

            CrmSdk.Metadata.RetrieveEntityRequest myRequest = ➥
            new CrmSdk.Metadata.RetrieveEntityRequest();
            myRequest.LogicalName = entityName.ToLower();
            CrmSdk.Metadata.RetrieveEntityResponse myResponse;
            myResponse = (CrmSdk.Metadata.RetrieveEntityResponse)
            myCrm.Execute(myRequest);
            return true;
        }
        catch (System.Web.Services.Protocols.SoapException soapEx)
        {
            Console.WriteLine("SOAP exception: " + soapEx.Detail.InnerText ➥
            + "  " + soapEx.ToString());
            return false;
        }
        catch (Exception ex)
        {
            Console.WriteLine("General exception: " + ex.ToString());
            return false;
        }
    }
```

Now if you want to check if the Account or `new_MyNewCustomEntity` entities exist on the organization with the name Webfortis, you could use the following code:

```
static void Main(string[] args)
{
        Console.WriteLine("Account entity exists = " + ➥
        CheckEntity("Webfortis", "Account"));
        Console.WriteLine("new_MyNewCustomEntity entity exists = ➥
        " + CheckEntity("Webfortis", "new_MyNewCustomEntity"));

        Console.ReadKey();
}
```

That code should return `true` for the Account entity and `False` for the `new_MyNewCustomEntity` entity (assuming you have not created any custom entity with the name of `new_MyNewCustomEntity` on your CRM system).

The following code sample shows how to create a custom entity using this Web Service programmatically.


```
private static bool CreateCustomEntity(string organizationName, string entityName)
{
   try
   {

        CrmSdk.Metadata.MetadataService myCrm = ➥
        new CrmSdk.Metadata.MetadataService();
        myCrm.Url = GetCrmMetadataServiceForOrganization(organizationName);
        CrmSdk.Metadata.CrmAuthenticationToken myToken = ➥
        new CrmSdk.Metadata.CrmAuthenticationToken();
        myToken.AuthenticationType = 0;
        myToken.OrganizationName = organizationName;
        myCrm.CrmAuthenticationTokenValue = myToken;
        myCrm.Credentials = System.Net.CredentialCache.DefaultCredentials;

        // Creates new entity
        CrmSdk.Metadata.EntityMetadata myNewEntity = ➥
        new CrmSdk.Metadata.EntityMetadata();
        myNewEntity.Description = CreateLabel(entityName);
        myNewEntity.DisplayCollectionName = CreateLabel(entityName);
        myNewEntity.DisplayName = CreateLabel(entityName);

        myNewEntity.IsAvailableOffline = new CrmSdk.Metadata.CrmBoolean();
        myNewEntity.IsAvailableOffline.Value = true;
        myNewEntity.DuplicateDetection = new CrmSdk.Metadata.CrmBoolean();
        myNewEntity.DuplicateDetection.Value = true;
        myNewEntity.SchemaName = entityName;
        myNewEntity.LogicalName = entityName;
        myNewEntity.OwnershipType = new CrmSdk.Metadata.CrmOwnershipTypes();
        myNewEntity.OwnershipType.Value = CrmSdk.Metadata.OwnershipTypes.UserOwned;

        // creates primary attribute
        CrmSdk.Metadata.StringAttributeMetadata myPrimaryAttr = ➥
        new CrmSdk.Metadata.StringAttributeMetadata();
        myPrimaryAttr.DisplayName = CreateLabel("Name");
        myPrimaryAttr.Description = CreateLabel("this is the Name");
        myPrimaryAttr.AttributeType = new CrmSdk.Metadata.CrmAttributeType();
        myPrimaryAttr.AttributeType.Value = CrmSdk.Metadata.AttributeType.String;
        myPrimaryAttr.MaxLength = new CrmSdk.Metadata.CrmNumber();
```

```
        myPrimaryAttr.MaxLength.Value = 100;
        myPrimaryAttr.SchemaName = "new_Name";
        myPrimaryAttr.Format = new CrmSdk.Metadata.CrmStringFormat();
        myPrimaryAttr.Format.Value = CrmSdk.Metadata.StringFormat.Text;
        myPrimaryAttr.RequiredLevel = ➥
        new CrmSdk.Metadata.CrmAttributeRequiredLevel();
        myPrimaryAttr.RequiredLevel.Value = ➥
        CrmSdk.Metadata.AttributeRequiredLevel.Required;
        myPrimaryAttr.DisplayMask = new CrmSdk.Metadata.CrmDisplayMasks();
        myPrimaryAttr.DisplayMask.Value = CrmSdk.Metadata.DisplayMasks.PrimaryName;
        myPrimaryAttr.LogicalName = "new_name";

        // prepare request
        CrmSdk.Metadata.CreateEntityRequest myRequest = ➥
        new CrmSdk.Metadata.CreateEntityRequest();
        myRequest.Entity = myNewEntity;
        myRequest.HasActivities = true;
        myRequest.HasNotes = true;
        myRequest.PrimaryAttribute = myPrimaryAttr;

        CrmSdk.Metadata.CreateEntityResponse myResponse;
        myResponse = (CrmSdk.Metadata.CreateEntityResponse)myCrm.Execute(myRequest);
        return true;
    }
    catch (System.Web.Services.Protocols.SoapException soapEx)
    {
        Console.WriteLine("SOAP exception: " + soapEx.Detail.InnerText ➥
        + "  " + soapEx.ToString());
        return false;
    }
    catch (Exception ex)
    {
        Console.WriteLine("General exception: " + ex.ToString());
        return false;
    }
}
```

NOTE

The code uses a custom method called `CreateLabel` to simplify the code used to set up the labels; they must be managed in a collection because of the Multilanguage feature. This sample uses only the English language for the strings, but you can easily customize it to use other languages.

```
private static CrmSdk.Metadata.CrmLabel CreateLabel(string myString)
{
   CrmSdk.Metadata.CrmLabel myLabel = new CrmSdk.Metadata.CrmLabel();
   CrmSdk.Metadata.LocLabel[] myLabels = new CrmSdk.Metadata.LocLabel[1];
   myLabels[0] = new CrmSdk.Metadata.LocLabel();
   myLabels[0].Label = myString;
   myLabels[0].LanguageCode = new CrmSdk.Metadata.CrmNumber();
   myLabels[0].LanguageCode.Value = 1033; // English code
   myLabel.LocLabels = myLabels;
   return myLabel;
}
```

Now if you want to create a new entity with the name of `new_MyNewCustomEntity` on the organization with the name Webfortis, you could use the following code:

```
static void Main(string[] args)
{
        CreateCustomEntity("Webfortis", "new_MyNewCustomEntity");

        Console.ReadKey();
}
```

NOTE

Be sure the entity name doesn't already exist in the CRM system, or the `Execute` method will raise an exception. To be sure, you could use the `CheckEntity` method you created before and use a code as follows:

```
static void Main(string[] args)
{
   if (!CheckEntity("Webfortis", "new_MyNewCustomEntity"))
        {
              CreateCustomEntity("Webfortis", "new_MyNewCustomEntity");
        }
   Console.ReadKey();
}
```

In addition, you must set at least the primary attribute on the request, and this one must be required.

You can also use this Web Service if you want to show all the options from a Picklist attribute on another application.

As another example, imagine that you needed to retrieve all possible values for the `Shipping Method` property for `Accounts`. Because the `Shipping Method` is a Picklist, you would have to query the MetaData to get the values.

This method can be used as follows:

```
private static void GetShippingMethod(string organizationName)
{
    CrmSdk.Metadata.MetadataService myCrm = new CrmSdk.Metadata.MetadataService();
    myCrm.Url = GetCrmMetadataServiceForOrganization(organizationName);
    CrmSdk.Metadata.CrmAuthenticationToken myToken = ➥
    new CrmSdk.Metadata.CrmAuthenticationToken();
    myToken.AuthenticationType = 0;
    myToken.OrganizationName = organizationName;
    myCrm.CrmAuthenticationTokenValue = myToken;
    myCrm.Credentials = System.Net.CredentialCache.DefaultCredentials;

    CrmSdk.Metadata.RetrieveAttributeRequest myRequest = ➥
    new CrmSdk.Metadata.RetrieveAttributeRequest();
    myRequest.EntityLogicalName = CrmSdk.EntityName.account.ToString();
    myRequest.LogicalName = "address1_shippingmethodcode";

    CrmSdk.Metadata.RetrieveAttributeResponse myResponse;
    myResponse = (CrmSdk.Metadata.RetrieveAttributeResponse)
    myCrm.Execute(myRequest);
    foreach (CrmSdk.Metadata.Option myOption in ((CrmSdk.Metadata.➥
    PicklistAttributeMetadata)(myResponse.AttributeMetadata)).Options)
    {
        Console.WriteLine(myOption.Label.LocLabels[0].Label);
    }
}
```

Now if you want to test this method on the organization with the name Webfortis, you could use the following code:

```
static void Main(string[] args)
{
        GetShippingMethod("Webfortis");
        Console.ReadKey();
}
```

Samples

Because the Web Services are platform-independent, it is not strictly necessary to access the Web Services from a .NET assembly or a compiled application. You could access the Web Services using JavaScript, for example.

JavaScript

This is an example of how to get and set the Address from an Account using JavaScript by querying the CRM Main Data Web Service. This sets the Contact address when selecting an Account as the parent Customer field automatically (without requiring you to enter it again). So to have this sample work properly, you must select an Account with the address fields populated with some data. Also, notice that the following sample works only if you select a parent Account for a Contact and not a parent Contact; however, after reviewing this sample, you could easily modify it to work with parent Contacts if desired.

The purpose of this sample is to show how you can consume a Web Service without having to build a .NET application or component to make some of your business customizations. For more details about working with JavaScript customizations refer to Chapter 19, "Customizing Entities."

To create this sample, follow these steps:

1. Go to Settings, Customizations, Customize Entities, and select the Contact entity in Microsoft CRM (see Figure 22.13).

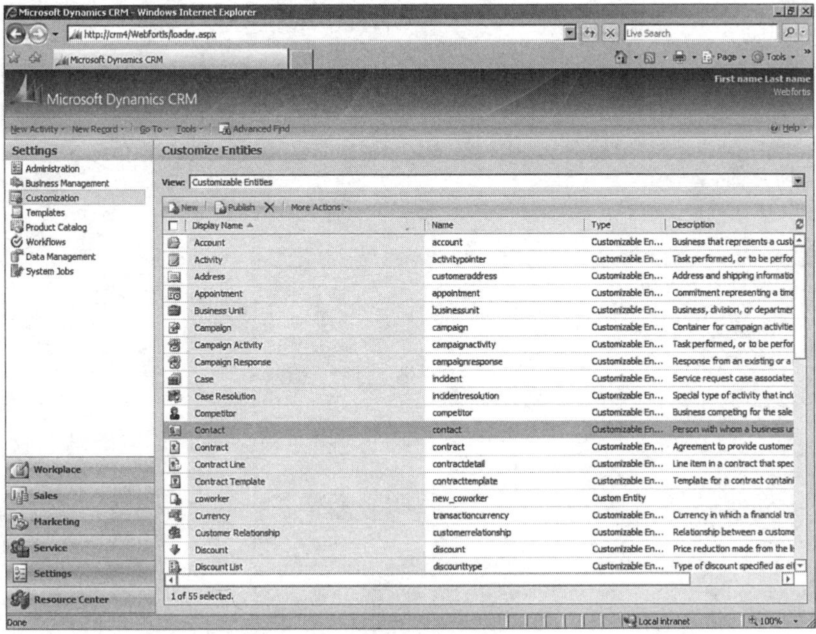

FIGURE 22.13 Contact customization.

2. Double-click Contact and go to Details, Forms and Views on the left side of the window (see Figure 22.14).

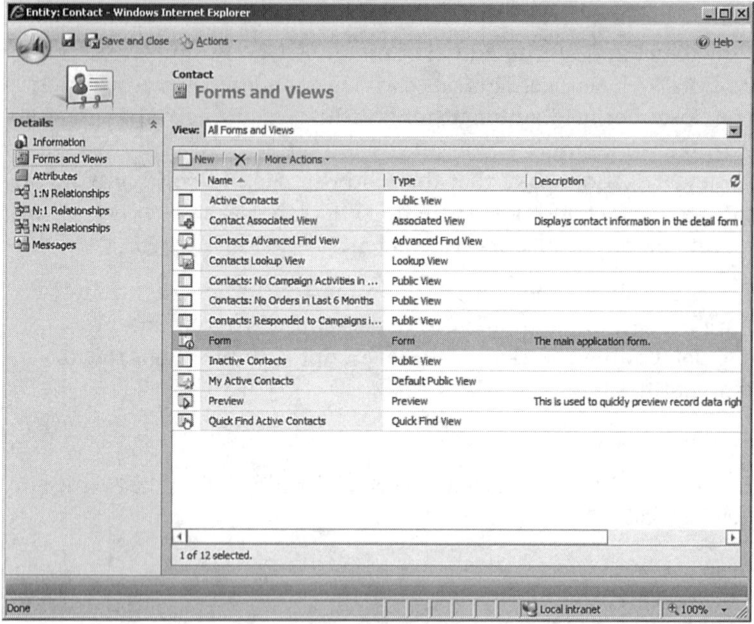

FIGURE 22.14 Forms and Views customization.

3. Double-click Form with The Main Application Form Description to open it (see Figure 22.15).

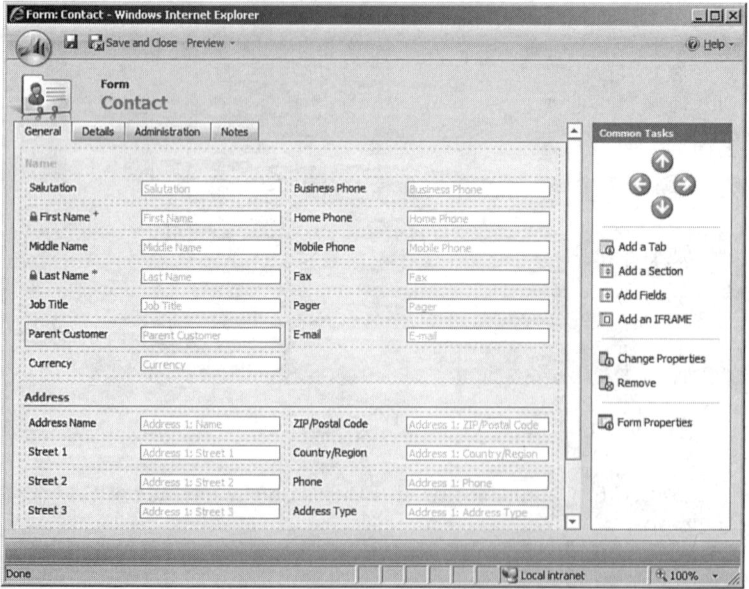

FIGURE 22.15 Main Form customization.

4. Click the `Parent Customer` field and click Change Properties (see Figure 22.16).

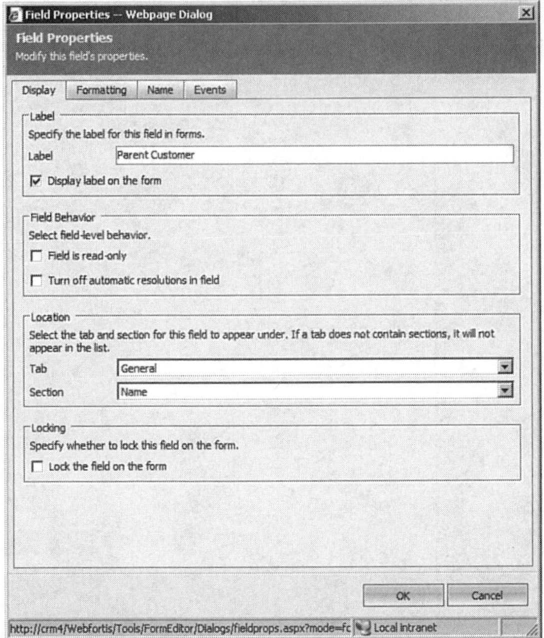

FIGURE 22.16 Parent Customer property page.

5. Select the Events tab (see Figure 22.17).

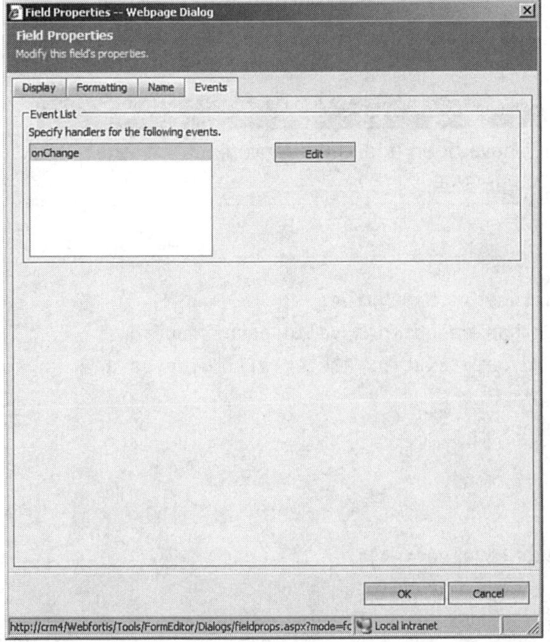

FIGURE 22.17 Events tab.

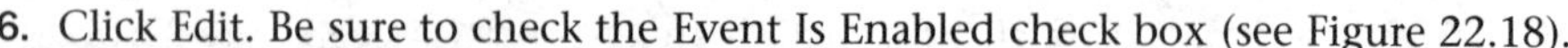

6. Click Edit. Be sure to check the Event Is Enabled check box (see Figure 22.18).

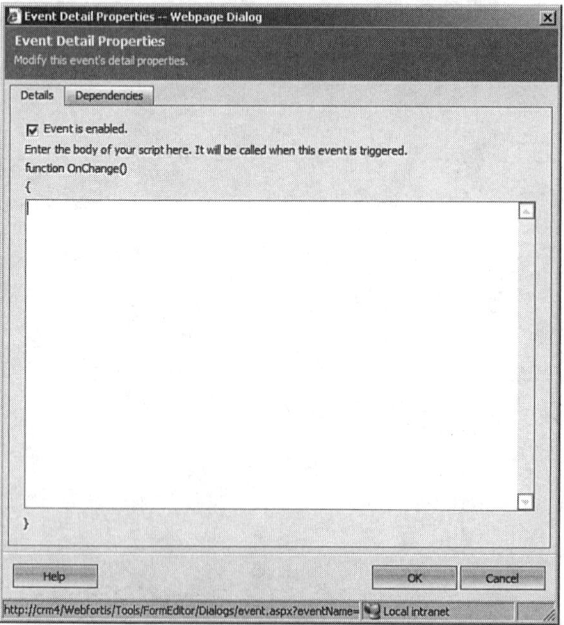

FIGURE 22.18 The `OnChange` event.

7. Insert the following code sample in the text box (see Figure 22.19). Be sure to change Webfortis with your organization name on line 19 of the WriteHeader method. (Check the comment line in bold.)

NOTE

The line numbers later in this code snippet have been added for convenient reference only. They should not be included in the actual code.

```
var CustomerID;
CustomerID = crmForm.all.parentcustomerid.DataValue;
// first of all checks if the user has selected a valid parent customer
// the crmForm.all.parentcustomerid.DataValue parameter will give us a ➥
vector with
// the GUID of the selected customer
if (CustomerID != null)
    {
        //Cleans the old address first
        crmForm.all.address1_name.DataValue = "";
        crmForm.all.address1_postalcode.DataValue = "";
        crmForm.all.address1_line1.DataValue = "";
```

```
        crmForm.all.address1_line2.DataValue = "";
        crmForm.all.address1_line3.DataValue = "";
        crmForm.all.address1_city.DataValue = "";
        crmForm.all.address1_stateorprovince.DataValue = "";
        crmForm.all.address1_addresstypecode.DataValue = "";
        crmForm.all.address1_country.DataValue = "";

        var strEnvelope ;
   // prepares the SOAP header message
        strEnvelope = WriteHeader();
   // prepares the SOAP message conditions
        strEnvelope+= WriteCondition( CustomerID[0].id );
   // prepares the SOAP message footer
        strEnvelope+= WriteFooter();
   // calls the web service
        CallCRMWebservice(strEnvelope);
    }
    else
    {
        alert("Select Parent Customer first!");
    }

// this function prepares the SOAP header message needed by the Web Service ➥
call
function WriteHeader()
{
    var strEnvelope ="<?xml version='1.0' encoding='utf-8'?>";
    // each SOAP message starts with the soap:Envelope node which contains
   // a Header and Body nodes
    strEnvelope += "<soap:Envelope ➥
xmlns:soap=\"http://schemas.xmlsoap.org/soap/envelope/\" ➥
xmlns:xsi=\"http://www.w3.org/2001/XMLSchema-instance\" ➥
xmlns:xsd=\"http://www.w3.org/2001/XMLSchema\">" ;
   // Soap:Header initialization here
    strEnvelope += "<soap:Header>";
    strEnvelope += "<CrmAuthenticationToken ➥
xmlns=\"http://schemas.microsoft.com/crm/2007/WebServices\">";
    strEnvelope += "<AuthenticationType ➥
xmlns=\"http://schemas.microsoft.com/crm/2007/CoreTypes\  ➥
">0</AuthenticationType>";
    // Change Webfortis for your Organization name here.
    strEnvelope += "<OrganizationName ➥
xmlns=\"http://schemas.microsoft.com/crm/2007/CoreTypes\➥
">Webfortis</OrganizationName>";
strEnvelope += "<CallerId ➥
```

```
xmlns=\"http://schemas.microsoft.com/crm/2007/CoreTypes\">➥
00000000-0000-0000-0000-000000000000</CallerId>";
    strEnvelope += "</CrmAuthenticationToken>";
    strEnvelope += "</soap:Header>";
   // Soap:Body initialization here
    strEnvelope += "<soap:Body>" ;
   // we'll call the RetrieveMultiple method to get the parent customer ➥
   address
    strEnvelope += "<RetrieveMultiple xmlns= ➥
    \"http://schemas.microsoft.com/crm/2007/WebServices\">"
    strEnvelope+= "<query ➥
   xmlns:q1='http://schemas.microsoft.com/crm/2006/Query' ➥
    xsi:type='q1:QueryExpression' >";
   // you will asume the parent customer is an account so you will only ➥
   retrieve the
   // if the user selected an account as the parent customer.
   // if the user selected a contact then this code won't work
    strEnvelope += " <q1:EntityName>account</q1:EntityName>" ;
    strEnvelope += "<q1:ColumnSet xsi:type=\"q1:ColumnSet\" >";
    strEnvelope += "<q1:Attributes>";
   // prepares the list of attributes you want to get back from the web ➥
   service call
    strEnvelope += "<q1:Attribute>address1_name</q1:Attribute>";
    strEnvelope += "<q1:Attribute>address1_postalcode</q1:Attribute>";
    strEnvelope += "<q1:Attribute>address1_line1</q1:Attribute>";
    strEnvelope += "<q1:Attribute>address1_line2</q1:Attribute>";
    strEnvelope += "<q1:Attribute>address1_line3</q1:Attribute>";
    strEnvelope += "<q1:Attribute>address1_city</q1:Attribute>";
    strEnvelope += "<q1:Attribute>address1_stateorprovince</q1:Attribute>";
    strEnvelope += "<q1:Attribute>address1_addresstypecode</q1:Attribute>";
    strEnvelope += "<q1:Attribute>address1_country</q1:Attribute>";
    strEnvelope += "</q1:Attributes>";
    strEnvelope += "</q1:ColumnSet>";
    // you don't want to retrieve dupplicated records so you set the ➥
    // Distinct option
    strEnvelope+= " <q1:Distinct >1</q1:Distinct>" ;
    strEnvelope+= " <q1:Criteria>" ;

    strEnvelope+= " <q1:FilterOperator >Or</q1:FilterOperator>" ;
    strEnvelope+= " <q1:Conditions >" ;
    return strEnvelope;
}
// this function prepares the SOAP message conditions receiving the accountid
// by parameter
function WriteCondition( accountid)
{
```

```
    var strEnvelope;
    strEnvelope = " <q1:Condition >" ;
    strEnvelope += " <q1:AttributeName >accountid</q1:AttributeName>" ;
    strEnvelope += " <q1:FilterOperator>Equal</q1:FilterOperator>" ;
    strEnvelope += " <q1:Values>" ;
    strEnvelope += " <q1:Value xsi:type='xsd:string'>" +  accountid  + ➥
    "</q1:Value>";
    strEnvelope += " </q1:Values>" ;
    strEnvelope += "</q1:Condition>" ;
    return strEnvelope;
}

// this function prepares the SOAP message footer needed to finish with the ➥
// whole SOAP
// message
function WriteFooter()
{
    var strEnvelope;
    strEnvelope = "</q1:Conditions>" ;
    strEnvelope += " </q1:Criteria>" ;
    strEnvelope += " </query>";
    strEnvelope += " </RetrieveMultiple>";
    strEnvelope += "</soap:Body>";
    strEnvelope += "</soap:Envelope>";
    return strEnvelope;
}

// this function calls the CRM Main Data web service
// function CallCRMWebservice(strEnvelope)
{
    // Creates the XML and HTTP object
    var xmlSubjectInfo = new ActiveXObject("Msxml2.DOMDocument");
    var oXml = new ActiveXObject("Microsoft.XMLDOM");
    var objHttp = new ActiveXObject("Msxml2.XMLHTTP");
    // here you setup the Main Data Web Service URL. Since you use a ➥
    // relative URL this code should work on any environment for any ➥
    // organization
    var url = '/MSCrmServices/2007/CrmService.asmx';

    // Sends the POST message to the Web Service
    objHttp.open("POST", url, false);

    objHttp.setRequestHeader("Content-Type", "text/xml; charset=utf-8");
    objHttp.setRequestHeader("SOAPAction", ➥
    "http://schemas.microsoft.com/crm/2007/WebServices/RetrieveMultiple");
    objHttp.setRequestHeader("Content-Length", strEnvelope.length);
```

22

```
    objHttp.send(strEnvelope);

    oXml.loadXML(objHttp.responseXML.xml);
    var nodeslst = oXml.selectNodes("//RetrieveMultipleResult");
    // Parses the result
    if(nodeslst.length>0)
    {
    for (var i=0; i < ➥
    nodeslst[0].childNodes[0].childNodes[0].childNodes.➥
    length; i++)
    {
    if (nodeslst[0].childNodes[0].childNodes[0].childNodes[i].nodeName == ➥
    "q1:address1_name")
            {
                crmForm.all.address1_name.DataValue =

nodeslst[0].childNodes[0].childNodes[0].childNodes[i].text;
            }
            else if (nodeslst[0].childNodes[0].childNodes[0].childNodes[i].➥
            nodeName == "q1:address1_postalcode")
            {
                crmForm.all.address1_postalcode.DataValue =

nodeslst[0].childNodes[0].childNodes[0].childNodes[i].text;
            }
            else if (nodeslst[0].childNodes[0].childNodes[0].childNodes[i].➥
            nodeName == "q1:address1_line1")
            {
                crmForm.all.address1_line1.DataValue =

nodeslst[0].childNodes[0].childNodes[0].childNodes[i].text;
            }
            else if (nodeslst[0].childNodes[0].childNodes[0].childNodes[i].➥
            nodeName == "q1:address1_line2")
            {
                crmForm.all.address1_line2.DataValue =

nodeslst[0].childNodes[0].childNodes[0].childNodes[i].text;
            }
            else if (nodeslst[0].childNodes[0].childNodes[0].childNodes[i].➥
            nodeName == "q1:address1_line3")
            {
                crmForm.all.address1_line3.DataValue =
```

```
nodeslst[0].childNodes[0].childNodes[0].childNodes[i].text;
            }
            else if (nodeslst[0].childNodes[0].childNodes[0].childNodes[i].➥
            nodeName == "q1:address1_city")
            {
                crmForm.all.address1_city.DataValue =
nodeslst[0].childNodes[0].childNodes[0].childNodes[i].text;
            }
            else if
(nodeslst[0].childNodes[0].childNodes[0].childNodes[i].nodeName == ➥
            "q1:address1_stateorprovince")
            {
                crmForm.all.address1_stateorprovince.DataValue =
nodeslst[0].childNodes[0].childNodes[0].childNodes[i].text;
            }
            else if (nodeslst[0].childNodes[0].childNodes[0].childNodes[i].➥
            nodeName == "q1:address1_addresstypecode")
            {
                crmForm.all.address1_addresstypecode.DataValue =
nodeslst[0].childNodes[0].childNodes[0].childNodes[i].text;
            }

            else if (nodeslst[0].childNodes[0].childNodes[0].childNodes[i].➥
            nodeName == "q1:address1_country")
            {
                crmForm.all.address1_country.DataValue =
nodeslst[0].childNodes[0].childNodes[0].childNodes[i].text;
            }
        }
    }
    return;
}
```

8. Click OK to close the dialog box.
9. Click OK again to close the Field Properties dialog box.
10. Click Save and Close to close the Contact Form window.
11. Click Save and Close to close the Entity Contact window.
12. Click the Publish button to publish the customization.

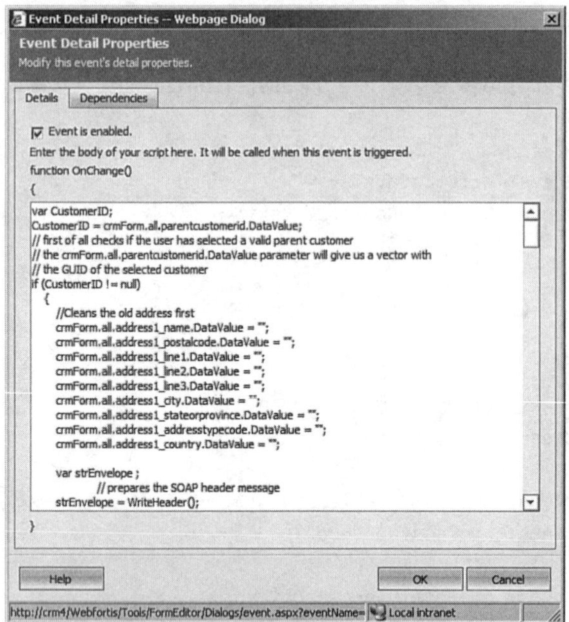

FIGURE 22.19 JavaScript code to call the CRM Web Services.

To test the solution, follow these steps:

1. Go to Workplace, Contacts.
2. Select a Contact and double-click it to open it or click New to create a new Contact (see Figure 22.20).

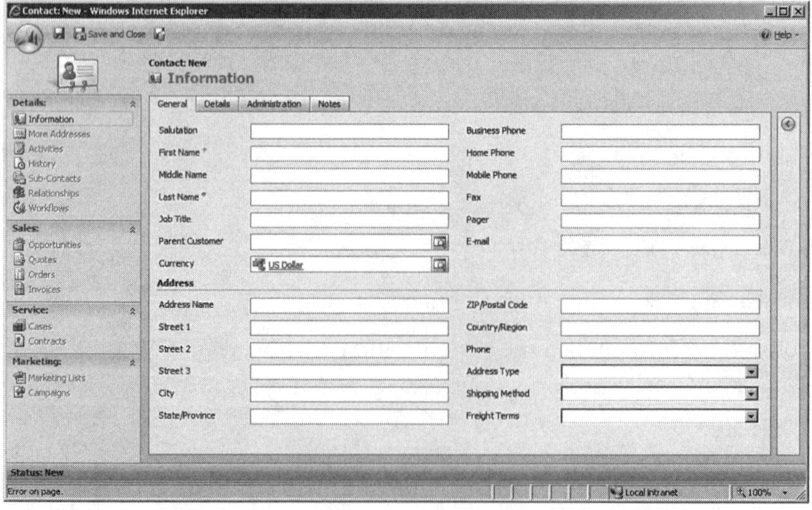

FIGURE 22.20 Creating a new Contact.

3. Click the icon button near Parent Customer to select an Account (see Figure 22.21).

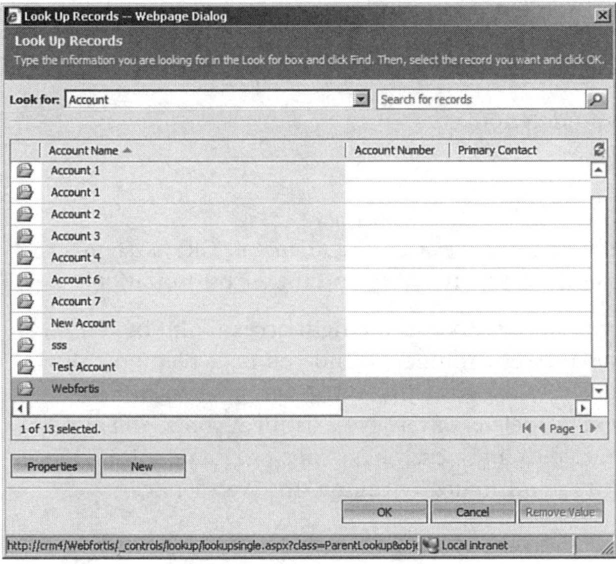

FIGURE 22.21 Select a Parent Account.

4. Click OK to close the dialog box. You will see the Contact address automatically filled in with the selected Account address (see Figure 22.22).

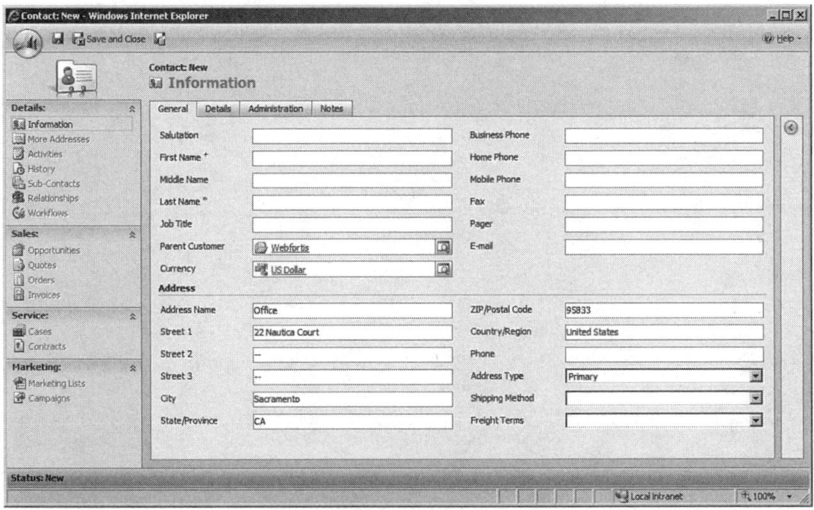

FIGURE 22.22 The new Contact address filled automatically with the selected Account address.

If you are not familiar with SOAP messages and want to implement similar customizations, we suggest making the customizations in a .NET solution using the Web Services and inspecting the Request messages. You can do this by using a network inspector tool such as Fiddler, which enables you to become familiar with what is contained in the Request message.

You can download Fiddler from www.fiddlertool.com.

Summary

In this chapter, you learned about the Web Services that the Microsoft CRM system exposes and how to use them to extend the functionality and make customizations.

You explored the Discovery service that is used to find the right access point of your organization especially useful for multitenancy environments, and you have seen how the Main Data Web Service manages the entity records with all the samples you will need to create new records for any entity, update, delete, or retrieve existing records. You also looked at the Metadata Web Service used to make customizations programmatically; for example, creating a new custom entity or attributes by calling this Web Service.

CHAPTER 23
ISV Customizations

IN THIS CHAPTER

- ISV Solutions
- Customizations for ISVs
- Online Help Customizations

If you're considering extending functionality of Microsoft Dynamics CRM, you might consider packaging your functionality as an "add-on" and then selling it. If you do that, you'll be considered an Independent Software Vendor (ISV). In this chapter, we look at some special code considerations that must be given by ISVs when coding an add-on for distribution.

ISV Solutions

ISVs are usually organizations that want to develop and sell add-ons for Microsoft Dynamics CRM. These add-ons either enable functionality that doesn't exist or augment existing functionality. Some considerations that ISVs need to have include these:

- The add-on must support different scenarios and implementations. It must run on implementations where customers have CRM, SQL, and SRS installed on the same server, or on different servers, with or without IFD enabled, for example.
- ISVs must provide an installer application. Users should be able to install the add-on by running a setup wizard that doesn't replace any system DLLs or components that might also require restarting the server after the installation.
- ISVs must provide a clean uninstaller application. If the user wants to uninstall the add-on, the uninstaller should clean any temporary folder or files created upon installation, and the uninstaller application must be available in Add/Remove Programs located in the Windows Control Panel.

- The add-on should have a user manual with detailed instructions about how to use and configure the add-on.
- The add-on product should provide serial key validations to protect licensed users. ISVs should develop logic to recognize which users are licensed with their own mechanism.
- ISVs might provide trial versions so that users can test the add-ons before buying them. It is recommended to provide trial versions so that users can test the add-on in a period of, for example, 15 or 30 days. After that period, code could block the add-on functionality without blocking any CRM native features.
- The add-on should be certified by VeriTest and follow its guidelines. Certifying a product makes it appear to be more reliable to customers. For more information about the requirements for certifying a product, go to www.veritest.com/certification/ms/msdynamics/.

TIP

If you don't already have a platform developed to provide serial key validations or trial versioning support, we recommend the shareware starter kit from Microsoft, located at http://msdn2.microsoft.com/en-us/vbasic/ms789080.aspx. It also provides PayPal integration for e-commerce integration to your add-on.

General Development Considerations for ISVs

If your add-on uses the Microsoft Dynamics CRM SDK Web Services, you should not assume any previous custom entity exists in the Web Service reference. Further, it is recommended that you reference the default WSDL that is shipped with the CRM server in its default installation. Then use the `DynamicEntity` class to reference the custom entities at runtime, as explained in the `DynamicEntity` section later in this chapter.

Additionally, you should handle all exceptions that might occur on your add-on using a global exception handler, and you should provide detailed logging and tracing so users can troubleshoot any problems. It is also recommended that you use the Windows event log to record any exceptions that your add-on might throw—this is where experienced servers administrators will expect to see any errors.

All the .NET assemblies must have strong names and must be also digitally signed. For more information about how to add a strong name to an assembly, refer to Chapter 21, "Plug-Ins." The Deployment section shows in detail how to add a strong-key to a Plug-In.

To digitally sign your assembly, you must use the .NET tool `Signcode.exe` and get a certificate from a third-party authority to prove that your assembly codes are safe.

Customizations for ISVs

ISVs should make only supported customizations and should guarantee that the CRM server system will work after uninstalling the add-on. The add-on should use its own data storage and configuration files and should not corrupt the CRM database or the CRM configuration files. However, your add-on can reference and use any of the published CRM Web Services that come with the SDK, as explained in Chapter 22, "Web Services."

Common ISV customizations can include any or all of the following:

- Capability to modify and enable the `ISV.Config` file
- Capability to create custom entities and relationships
- Custom application integration
- Plug-In development and registration
- Workflow development and registration
- Report development and installation

`ISV.Config` Considerations

If your add-on needs to modify the `ISV.Config` file, you should create a backup of the current `ISV.Config` file during the installation process and save the backup with a friendly name so users can use it when uninstalling, if necessary. You should prompt users to confirm that they want to restore the `ISV.Config` file to the backup made during the installation step; Users might have added or installed other add-ons after installing yours, and restoring the backup might break other add-on functionality.

Custom Entity Considerations

If your add-on needs to create custom entities, you should use a prefix other than the default prefix for the entity schema names, so users can easily differentiate your custom entities. For example, the default prefix for entities is `new_`, but users can change this value. So if you need to create a custom entity called `Event`, its schema name should not be `new_event`—it should use a different prefix, such as `web_event`.

You can check the default prefix by going to Settings, Administration and System Settings, and then navigating to the Customization tab, as shown in Figure 23.1.

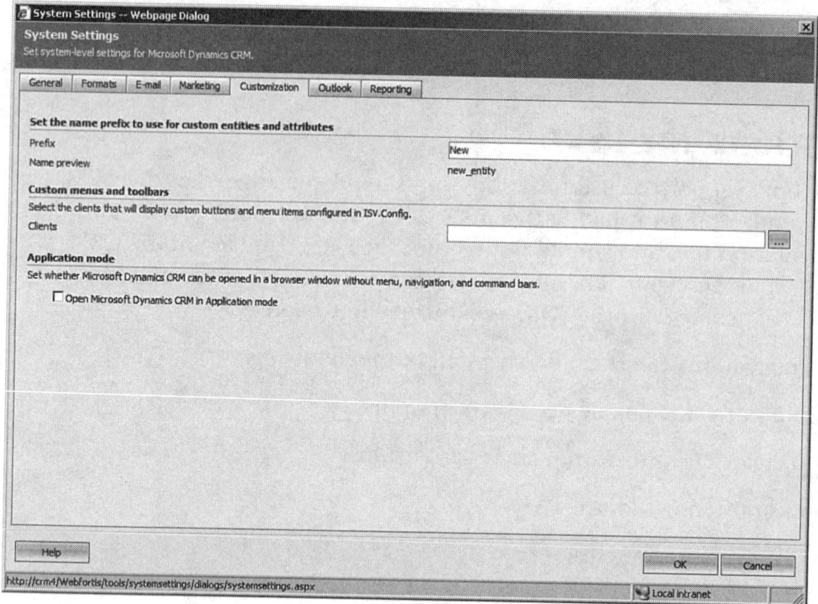

FIGURE 23.1 System settings for customizations.

Because you will probably be installing your add-on using an installer, you must get this prefix programmatically. You can do so by querying the `schemanameprefix` property of the `Organization` entity, as follows (this code uses functions defined and explained in Chapter 22):

```
private static string GetCustomizationsPrefix(string organizationName)
 {
     try
     {
         CrmSdk.CrmService myCrm = new CrmSdk.CrmService();
         myCrm.Url = GetCrmServiceForOrganization(organizationName);
         CrmSdk.CrmAuthenticationToken myToken =
                     new CrmSdk.CrmAuthenticationToken();
         myToken.AuthenticationType = 0;
         myToken.OrganizationName = organizationName;
         myCrm.CrmAuthenticationTokenValue = myToken;
         myCrm.Credentials = System.Net.CredentialCache.DefaultCredentials;

         // Creates a column set holding the names of the columns to be
            ➥retreived
         CrmSdk.ColumnSet colsPrincipal = new CrmSdk.ColumnSet();
         // Sets the Column Set's Properties
         colsPrincipal.Attributes = new string[] { "schemanameprefix" };
```

```
    // Create the Query Expression
    CrmSdk.QueryExpression queryPrincipal =
      ➥new CrmSdk.QueryExpression();


    // Create a ConditionExpression
    CrmSdk.ConditionExpression conditionPrincipal =
                            new CrmSdk.ConditionExpression();

    // Sets the ConditionExpressions Properties so that the condition
    // is true when the ownerid of the account Equals the principalId
    conditionPrincipal.AttributeName = "name";
    conditionPrincipal.Operator = CrmSdk.ConditionOperator.Equal;
    conditionPrincipal.Values = new object[1];
    conditionPrincipal.Values[0] = organizationName;

    // Create the FilterExpression
    CrmSdk.FilterExpression filterPrincipal =
      ➥new CrmSdk.FilterExpression();

    // Set the FilterExpression's Properties
    filterPrincipal.FilterOperator = CrmSdk.LogicalOperator.And;
    filterPrincipal.Conditions =
            new CrmSdk.ConditionExpression[] { conditionPrincipal };



    // Set the QueryExpression's Properties
    queryPrincipal.EntityName =
      ➥CrmSdk.EntityName.organization.ToString();
    queryPrincipal.ColumnSet = colsPrincipal;

    /// Retrieve the organization.
    CrmSdk.BusinessEntityCollection myOrgs =
                          myCrm.RetrieveMultiple(  queryPrincipal);
    foreach (CrmSdk.BusinessEntity myEntity in myOrgs.BusinessEntities)
    {
        CrmSdk.organization myOrg = (CrmSdk.organization)myEntity;
        Console.WriteLine(myOrg.schemanameprefix);
        return myOrg.schemanameprefix;
    }
}
catch (System.Web.Services.Protocols.SoapException soapEx)
{
    Console.WriteLine("SOAP exception: " + soapEx.Detail.InnerText
                      + "  " + soapEx.ToString());
```

23

```
        }
        catch (Exception ex)
        {
            Console.WriteLine("General exception: " + ex.ToString());
        }
        return "";
    }
```

Notice that in this example, the `schemanameprefix` property returns the prefix value without the _ character and also with capitalization. You should convert the string to lowercase and append the _ character for use with your custom entities.

DynamicEntity

Suppose that you create a new entity called `Event` whose schema name is `web_event` and that also has a custom attribute called `Name` that has a schema name of `web_name`. If you were not an ISV, you would reference the CRM Web Services after creating the custom entity, and you could create a record for it as follows:

```
private static string CreateEventRecord(string organizationName, string
  ➥eventName)
    {
        try
        {
            CrmSdk.CrmService myCrm = new CrmSdk.CrmService();
            myCrm.Url = GetCrmServiceForOrganization(organizationName);
            CrmSdk.CrmAuthenticationToken myToken =
              ➥new CrmSdk.CrmAuthenticationToken();
            myToken.AuthenticationType = 0;
            myToken.OrganizationName = organizationName;
            myCrm.CrmAuthenticationTokenValue = myToken;
            myCrm.Credentials = System.Net.CredentialCache.DefaultCredentials;
            CrmSdk.web_event newEvent = new CrmSdk.new_event();
            newEvent.web_name = eventName;

            Guid newEventId = myCrm.Create(newEvent);
            return newEventId.ToString();
        }
        catch (System.Web.Services.Protocols.SoapException soapEx)
        {
            Console.WriteLine("SOAP exception: " + soapEx.Detail.InnerText + "
              ➥" + soapEx.ToString());
            return soapEx.Detail.InnerText + "  " + soapEx.ToString();
        }
        catch (Exception ex)
        {
```

```
            Console.WriteLine("General exception: " + ex.ToString());
            return "General exception: " + ex.ToString();
        }
    }
```

The previous code is an example of something an ISV should not do because it must not assume that the Web service already has the entity created. You should use the `DynamicEntity` class instead, as follows (the lines in bold show the differences between the codes):

```
private static string CreateEventRecord(string organizationName, string
  ➥eventName)
  {
      try
      {
          CrmSdk.CrmService myCrm = new CrmSdk.CrmService();
          myCrm.Url = GetCrmServiceForOrganization(organizationName);
          CrmSdk.CrmAuthenticationToken myToken =
            ➥new CrmSdk.CrmAuthenticationToken();
          myToken.AuthenticationType = 0;
          myToken.OrganizationName = organizationName;
          myCrm.CrmAuthenticationTokenValue = myToken;
          myCrm.Credentials = System.Net.CredentialCache.DefaultCredentials;
          CrmSdk.DynamicEntity newEvent = new CrmSdk.DynamicEntity();
          newEvent.Name = "web_event";

          CrmSdk.StringProperty eventname = new CrmSdk.StringProperty();
          eventname.Name = " web_name";
          eventname.Value = eventName;
          newEvent.Properties = new CrmSdk.Property[] { eventname };
          Guid newEventId = myCrm.Create(newEvent);
          return newEventId.ToString();
      }
      catch (System.Web.Services.Protocols.SoapException soapEx)
      {
          Console.WriteLine("SOAP exception: " + soapEx.Detail.InnerText +
            ➥"  " + soapEx.ToString());
          return soapEx.Detail.InnerText + "  " + soapEx.ToString();
      }
      catch (Exception ex)
      {
          Console.WriteLine("General exception: " + ex.ToString());
          return "General exception: " + ex.ToString();
      }
  }
```

By using this code, you can work with any custom entity without needing to update the CRM SDK Web Service references in your project at compiling time. The `DynamicEntity` class will also be helpful if you allow users to create custom entities and attributes by using your add-on. Because you set the Name of the `DynamicEntity` class by using a string, you could have this string stored in a custom database for example.

Helper Classes

The SDK comes with many helper classes that you can use in your add-ons to follow the best-practice methods of accessing and using the CRM entities.

You can find these helper classes in the `sdk\server\helpers\cs\crmhelpers` folder. The helper classes are written in C#, and you can use them in your own codes.

Consider some examples of when you might use the helper classes:

- `queryexpressionhelper.cs`—When working with query expressions
- `filterexpressionhelper.cs`—When working with filter expressions
- `orderexpressioncollection.cs`—When working with sort expressions

Online Help Customizations

You can customize Online Help by adding new content to provide help support for your add-ons. The structure of the help is as follows:

```
CRM Web Site
    Help
        <language code> - 1033 for English
            LIVE (for Dynamics live)
                Content
                    images
            OP (for On premise deployments)
                Content
                    images
```

It is recommended that you put your help files in a separate folder so they won't be overwritten or lost when applying future CRM upgrades or service packs. This folder must be inside the Content folder (see Figure 23.2).

Inside the OP and LIVE folders is the `help_toc.xml` file, which is an XML file that contains the table of contents (TOC). You will want to modify this file to link your custom help files.

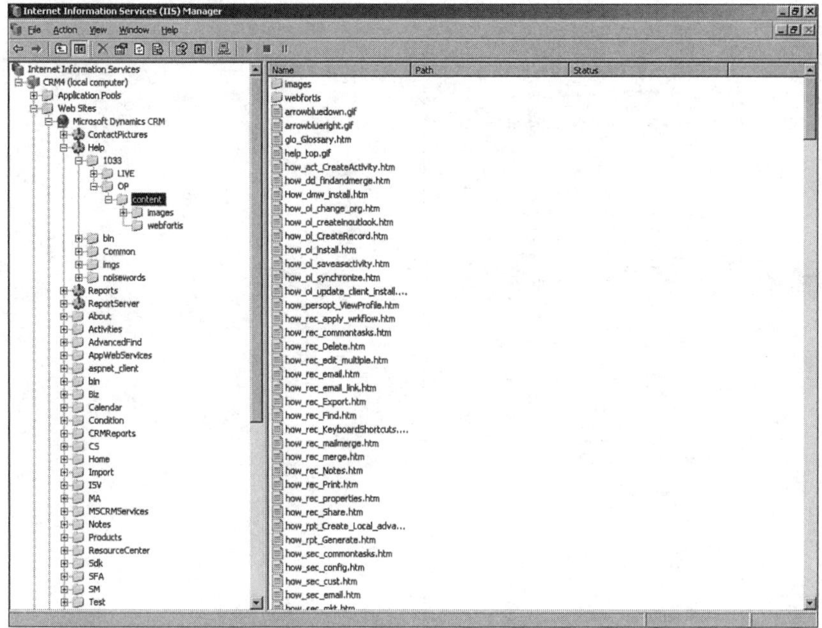

FIGURE 23.2 Help folders structure.

The `help_toc.xml` file contains several elements:

- `books`—This is the first element of the XML help file and must occur only once.
- `section`—This is nonclickable text that describes the title of the section.
- `volume`—This is clickable text that will be added with a book icon on the left that will contain the pages and links. It can be expanded and collapsed.
- `chapter`—This is similar to `volume`, but it must be inside the `volume` element to create subgroups of help pages.
- `page`—You can place this element inside the `volume` or `chapter` elements. It contains the actual links to your help pages. This element has an attribute called `topic` where you must put the filename without its extension. The filename must be an HTML static file with the `.htm` extension.

Figure 23.3 shows where these elements are placed.

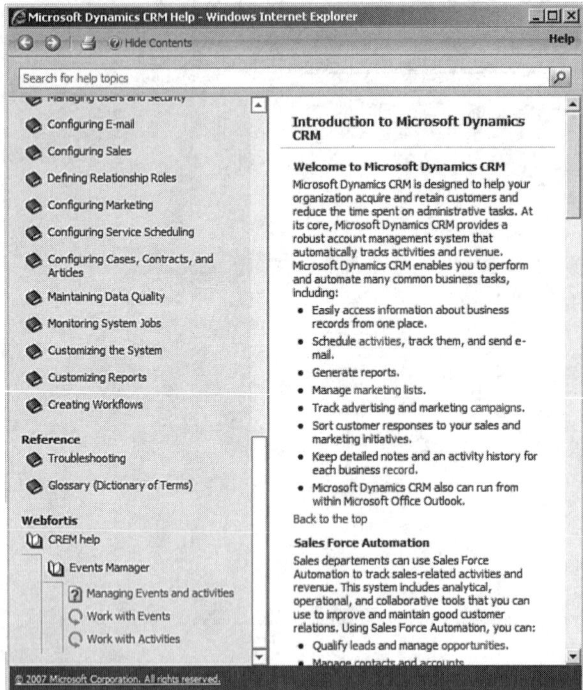

FIGURE 23.3 Elements shown in a help file.

The following code is an example of a customized topic.

```
<books>
    <section>Webfortis</section>
    <volume pro="true" sbe="true"
            code="crem_help"
            name="CREM Help">
        <chapter code="crem_help" name="Events Manager">
            <page
    topic="webfortis/crem_main">Managing Events and activities</page>
            <page procedure="true"
    topic="webfortis/crem_work_with_Events">Work with Events</page>
            <page procedure="true"
    topic="webfortis/crem_work_with_activities">Work with Activities</page>
        </chapter>
    </volume>
</books>
```

Notice we used a separate folder called webfortis that refers to our customized help files in the topic attribute. This folder must be created inside the \Help\1033\OP\content folder.

You must put the following tags inside the head element of your customized HTML help files so it will include all the necessary CRM references.

```
<head>
  <META http-equiv="Content-Type" content="text/html; charset=iso-8859-1">
  <title>Working Offline</title>
  <link rel="stylesheet" type="text/css" href="../phie17.css">
  <link rel="stylesheet" type="text/css" href="../msnuxa.css">
  <script language="javascript" src="../msnpanehelp_script.js">
  </script>
  <meta name="keywords" content="email,mail,messages">
  <link rel="stylesheet" type="text/css" href="/help/common/help.css">
  <script language="JavaScript" src="/help/common/help.js">
  </script>
</head>
```


You must also modify the body element of the page by adding the syncToc JavaScript function on the onload event, as follows:

```
<body onload="syncToc();">
```

Adding Context-Sensitive Help to the Customized Entity Lists and Forms

You can add context-sensitive help for your customized entities in two places. The first is on the custom event list page where users click the Help link and then Help on This Page (see Figure 23.4).

You can also add context-sensitive help in the new record entity form where users click Help and then Help on This Page (see Figure 23.5).

To add the context-sensitive help, you must edit the TOC file in the same way you did in the previous section and refer to the following comment:

```
<!-- CUSTOMIZATION: TOPICS FOR CUSTOMIZED ENTITIES -->
```

Then, just below that comment, add the following two lines:

```
<page pro="true" sbe="true" topic="webfortis/crem_work_with_Events"
➥filename="/_root/homepage.aspx?etc=10000">Events</page>
<page pro="true" sbe="true" topic="webfortis/crem_work_with_Events"
➥filename="/userdefined/edit.aspx?etc=10000#">Working with Events</page>
```

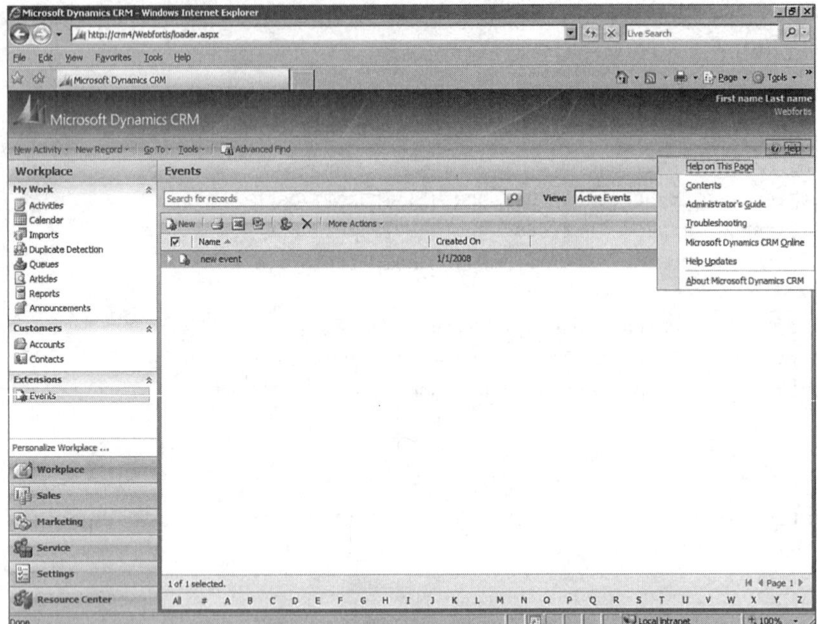

FIGURE 23.4 Context-sensitive help in the custom entity list page.

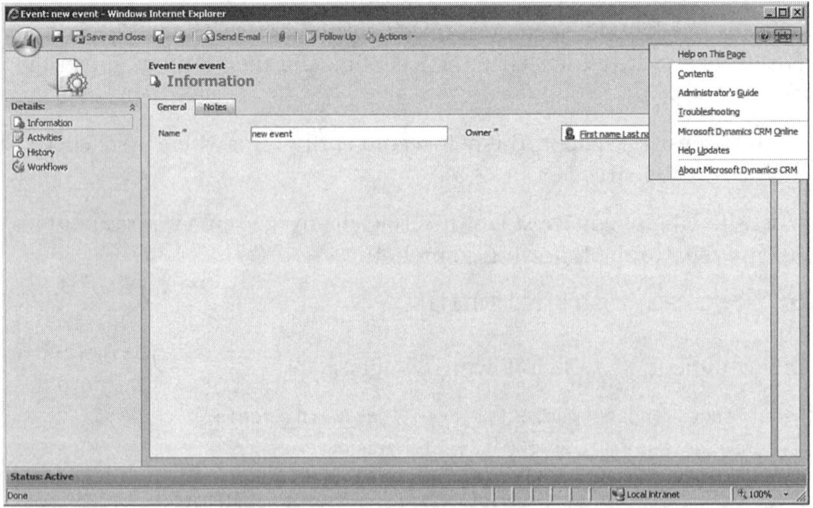

FIGURE 23.5 Context-sensitive help in the custom entity record form.

Note that you must replace the number `10000` with the type code of your custom entity. To determine the custom entity type code, you can edit a record of your custom entity and press F11 or Ctrl+N to open the form in a new window. You can then see the full URL, and you will see the type code in the `etc` parameter (see Figure 23.6).

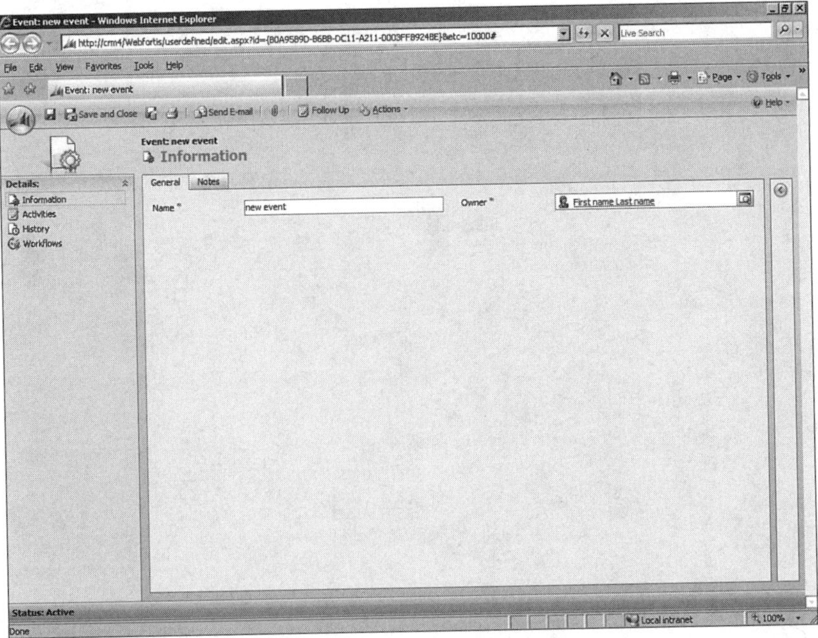

FIGURE 23.6 Seeing the entity type code in the `etc` parameter of the query string.

The first line assigns the context-sensitive help for the entity page list, and the second line is assigned to the form of the entity record. You must add the # next to the type code for the second line to work. You then must specify the help file in the topic attributes in the same way you did for the custom help files.

Summary

This chapter reviewed all requirements and considerations for ISVs when developing and distributing add-ons. ISVs must have considerations for custom applications and customizations that you make for not only your organization. ISVs also must be sure that their add-ons can work for a variety of scenarios. They cannot assume that any previous customizations are in place, and they must be sure to use the `DynamicEntity` class when consuming the CRM SDK Web Services. Finally, this chapter showed how to customize the Online Help for CRM to add context-sensitive help for the custom entities and its forms.

23

CHAPTER 24

Interacting with Custom Web Applications

IN THIS CHAPTER

Enhanced MS CRM Functionality with Custom ASP.NET Apps

You can enhance Microsoft Dynamics CRM functionality by creating custom Active Server Pages .NET (ASP.NET) web applications to interact with Microsoft Dynamics CRM interfaces and data in different ways:

- Using the Site Map
- Using the `ISV.Config` file
- Using IFRAMEs

Chapter 19, "Customizing Entities," thoroughly explains all uses of the Site Map and the `ISV.Config` file. Inline Frames (IFRAMEs) are usually the easiest and best solution to use for your custom web applications when you need to show or update data based on the entities' records.

You can create custom ASP.NET web application using Visual Studio 2005 or 2008. When you create a custom ASP.NET application, you have these options:

You can host and deploy the custom ASP.NET web application on the following:

- A different server than the CRM web server
- The same web server where the CRM web server is installed, but on a different website
- The same CRM web server and website, but inside a new virtual folder

Depending on where you host your custom ASP.NET application, each option has some advantages and some disadvantages.

For the first option, hosting the application on a different server than the CRM web server, you don't need to be worried about CRM website configurations. This is the best option when you're considering Microsoft Dynamics CRM Online implementations that don't allow you to host your applications on their servers.

The disadvantage is that you need another machine to host the custom application, and you are responsible for handling security properly.

If you host the custom ASP.NET web application on the same website as the CRM server, you must be aware of the following:

- Locate your application in a different folder than the CRM web folder. We do not recommend that you place your custom pages inside the CRM web folder.
- Use a different application pool than the CRM web server to provide isolation, as explained in the "ASP.NET Web Application Deployment" section later in this chapter. Isolation is important because if your custom code has a bug that can take the application offline, it will affect only your application, not the whole CRM website.

Query String Parameters

Microsoft Dynamics CRM uses Query String parameters to set values on pages. A Query String is a set of variables and variable values appended to the URL. A sample URL follows:

```
http://crm4/Webfortis/ContactPictures/Default.aspx?type=2&typename=contact&id={3053
➥F877-B9B4-DC11-9DC0-0003FF8924BE}&orgname=Webfortis&userlcid=1033&orglcid=1033
```

Everything after the `.aspx?` is the Query String.

These are the Query String parameters:

- `type`—Parameter that passes the entity code identifier. It is an integer value where `2` equals the Contact entity. For all type codes, see Table 24.1.
- `typename`—The schema name of the entity, such as `contact`.
- `id`—The unique identifier of the record instance of the entity. This is also referred to as the Global Unique Identifier (GUID). Note that this parameter is available only for existing records. If you are creating a new record, this parameter isn't available until after you save the record.
- `orgname`—The name of the organization.
- `userlcid`—The language code identifier for the User who is running the application. For example, `1033` represents the English language.
- `orglcid`—The organization language code identifier. This is the default organization base language. For example, `1033` represents the English language.

TABLE 24.1 Entities Type Code

Entity Name	Type Code
Account	1
Activity	4200
Address	1071
Appointment	4201
Business Unit	10
Campaign	4400
Campaign Activity	4402
Campaign Response	4401
Case	112
Case Resolution	4206
Competitor	123
Contact	2
Contract	1010
Contract Line	1011
Contract Template	2011
Currency	9105
Customer Relationship	4502
Discount	1013
E-mail	4202
E-mail Template	2010
Facility/Equipment	4000
Fax	4204
Invoice	1090
Invoice Product	1091
Lead	4
Letter	4207
Mail Merge Template	9106
Marketing List	4300
Opportunity	3
Opportunity Product	1083
Opportunity Relationship	4503
Order	1088
Order Product	1089
Phone Call	4210
Price List	1022
Price List Item	1026
Product	1024
Quick Campaign	4406
Quote	1084
Quote Product	1085

TABLE 24.1 Continued

Entity Name	Type Code
Report	9100
Report Related Category	9102
Resource Group	4007
Role	1036
Sales Literature	1038
Service Activity	4214
Subject	129
Task	4212
Team	9
Territory	2013
Unit	1055
Unit Group	1056
User	8

All customized entities type codes start from `10000`.

Sample IFRAME Customization

Chapter 19 illustrated a sample IFRAME customization using a URL that showed the same content for every record of the entity where we added the IFRAME. Most of the time you'll want to use the IFRAME to show different content, depending on the record instance of the form. For example, suppose you want to show a picture of your Contacts in the Contact form. This is a perfect scenario in which you would need to use an IFRAME in the Contact form, because Microsoft Dynamics CRM has no built-in functionality to do this. The following example illustrates how to perform a modification such as this one. You can easily modify or extend this example to work with other entities or application parameters.

Custom ASP.NET Web Application Development

First, you must build your custom ASP.NET application. To do so, follow these steps:

1. Open Visual Studio 2005 or Visual Studio 2008. In this example, you'll use Visual Studio 2005.
2. Go to New, Web Site (see Figure 24.1).
3. Select File System for location and select Visual C# for Language; then enter the path where you will place the application—for example, `C:\Inetpub\ContactPictures` (see Figure 24.2).

NOTE

The path must be different than the path where the CRM website is installed.

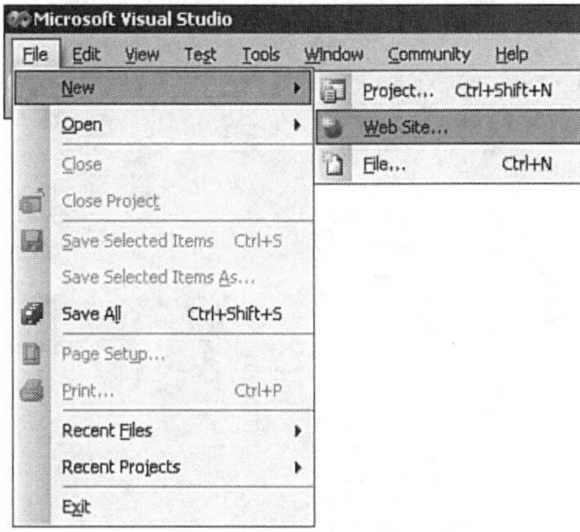

FIGURE 24.1 New Web Site menu.

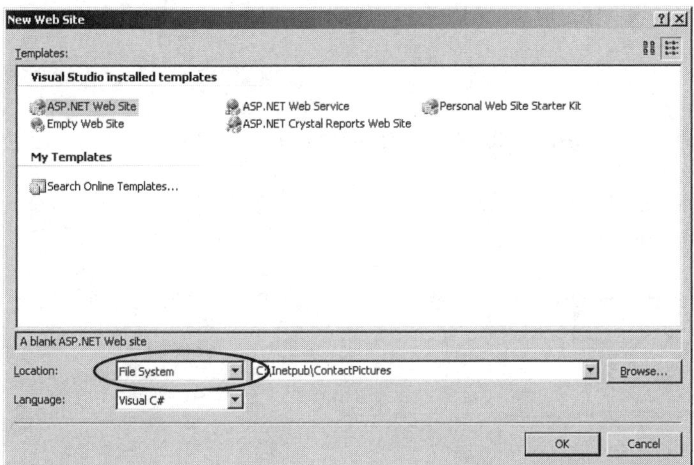

FIGURE 24.2 New Web Site properties.

4. Click OK.

5. In the `Default.aspx` page, replace the default code with the following code. This code adds an HTML table to the page, a picture control, a `FileUpload` control (so

Users can browse their local folders), and a `Button` control so Users can upload the selected image file:

```
<%@ Page Language="C#" AutoEventWireup="true"  CodeFile="Default.aspx.cs"
Inherits="_Default" %>
<!DOCTYPE html
PUBLIC "-//W3C//DTD XHTML 1.0 Transitional//EN"
"http://www.w3.org/TR/xhtml1/DTD/xhtml1-transitional.dtd">
<html xmlns="http://www.w3.org/1999/xhtml" >
<head runat="server">
    <title>Untitled Page</title>
</head>
<body>
    <form id="form1" runat="server">
    <div>
        <table>
            <tr>
                <td>
                    <asp:Image ID="Image1" runat="server"
                    Height="302px" Width="305px"
                    EnableViewState="False" /></td>
            </tr>
            <tr>
                <td>
                    <asp:FileUpload ID="FileUpload1"
                    runat="server"
                    Width="304px" /></td>
            </tr>
        </table>
        <asp:Button ID="Button1" runat="server"
            OnClick="Button1_Click"
            Text="Upload" />
    </div>
    </form>
</body>
</html>
```

6. Change to Design view. The page should look similar to Figure 24.3. Notice that the image control appears with a red X, to indicate a broken link. This is normal behavior because no image has been uploaded yet.

7. Edit the code behind by right-clicking the page `Default.aspx` file from the Solution Explorer and selecting View Code.

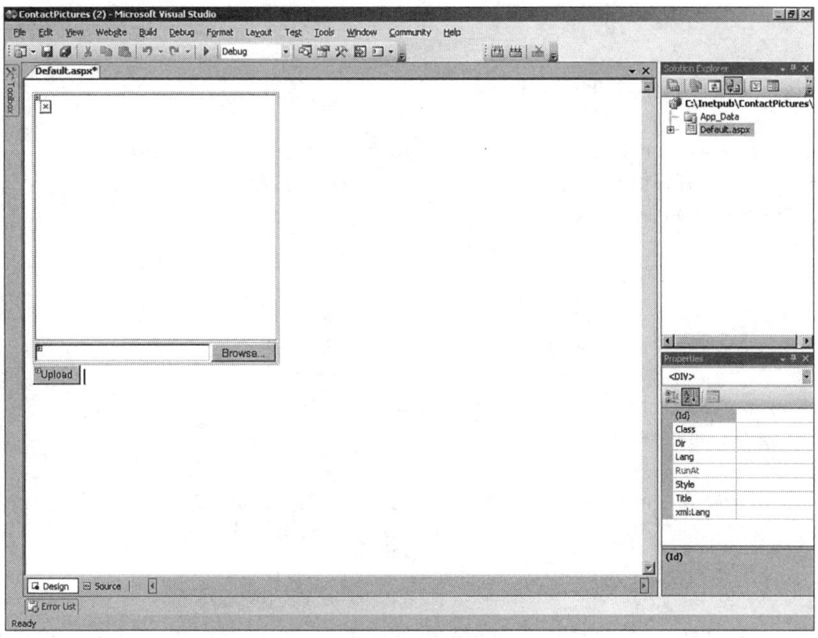

FIGURE 24.3 Default page in Design view.

8. Replace the code behind with the following code:

```
using System;
using System.Data;
using System.Configuration;
using System.Web;
using System.Web.Security;
using System.Web.UI;
using System.Web.UI.WebControls;
using System.Web.UI.WebControls.WebParts;
using System.Web.UI.HtmlControls;
using System.IO;

public partial class _Default : System.Web.UI.Page
{
    protected void Page_Load(object sender, EventArgs e)
    {
      if (Request.QueryString["id"] != null)
      {
        string contactId = new Guid(Request.QueryString["id"]).ToString();
        string pictureFilename = Path.Combine(Server.MapPath("/" +
"contactPictures"),
```

24

```
                contactId + ".jpg");

            if (File.Exists(pictureFilename))
            {
                string pictureURL = "../" + "contactPictures/GetPic.aspx?id="
                    + contactId + "&temp=" + Guid.NewGuid().ToString();
                Image1.ImageUrl = pictureURL;
            }
          }
        }
        protected void Button1_Click(object sender, EventArgs e)
        {
            string contactId = new Guid(Request.QueryString["id"]).ToString();
            if (FileUpload1.HasFile)
            {
                string pictureFilename = Path.Combine(Server.MapPath("/" +
    "contactPictures"),
                    contactId + ".jpg");

                FileUpload1.SaveAs(pictureFilename);

                string pictureURL = "../" + "contactPictures/GetPic.aspx?id="
                    + contactId + "&temp=" + Guid.NewGuid().ToString();
                Image1.ImageUrl = pictureURL;
            }

        }
    }
```

9. Create another page by right-clicking the project name in the Solution Explorer and selecting Add New Item.
10. Name the page **GetPic.aspx** and click the Add button (see Figure 24.4).
11. Clear all the code on the page except for the first line. The code should have only this line:

```
<%@ Page Language="C#" AutoEventWireup="true"
➥CodeFile="GetPic.aspx.cs" Inherits="GetPic" %>
```

12. Edit the code behind by right-clicking the page GetPic.aspx file from the Solution Explorer and selecting View Code.

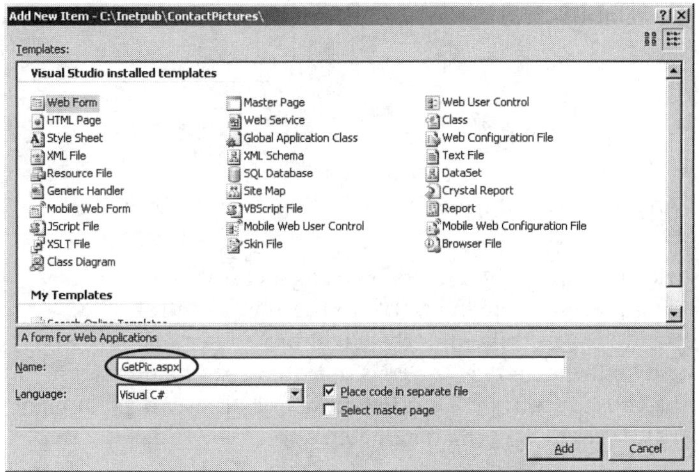

FIGURE 24.4 Adding a new page to the web project.

13. Replace the code behind with the following code:

```
using System;
using System.Data;
using System.Configuration;
using System.Collections;
using System.Web;
using System.Web.Security;
using System.Web.UI;
using System.Web.UI.WebControls;
using System.Web.UI.WebControls.WebParts;
using System.Web.UI.HtmlControls;
using System.IO;

public partial class GetPic : System.Web.UI.Page
{
    protected void Page_Load(object sender, EventArgs e)
    {
        string picid = Request.QueryString["id"];
        string pictureFilename = Path.Combine(
            Server.MapPath("/contactPictures"), picid + ".jpg");
        Response.Clear();
        Response.ClearHeaders();
        Response.AppendHeader("content-type", "image/jpeg");
```

```
            Response.WriteFile(pictureFilename);
            Response.Flush();
            Response.End();
        }
    }
```

14. Build the solution by going to the Build menu and selecting Build Web Site.

In this application, we use a trick to display the picture by using a custom page called `GetPic.aspx` that is responsible for sending the image file to the `Image` control. This approach avoids having the picture cached on either the client browser or the web server; the Users will see the image updated when a new image is uploaded. Alternatively, you can prevent this by altering the URL to always use a different query string. An example of this is to append a new GUID at the end of a `temp` parameter:

```
http://crm4/Webfortis/contactPictures/GetPic.aspx?id=3053f877-b9b4-dc11-9dc0-
➥0003ff8924be&temp=b4f18418-0d0d-401b-81c1-3196cf314a0d
```

ASP.NET Web Application Deployment

After you have built your custom web application and tested it, you are ready to deploy it. You must create the application virtual directory in Internet Information Services (IIS). Notice that, with this sample, you use the same web server as the CRM website. To deploy the web application, follow these steps:

1. Open the IIS Manager by going to Start, Control Panel, Administrative Tools, Internet Information Services (IIS) Manager.
2. Expand the server name (with this sample, it is CRM4) and select the Application Pools folder. You will create a new application pool for the application to isolate it and not affect the CRM website application pool. Right-click the Application Pools folder and select New, Application Pool (see Figure 24.5).

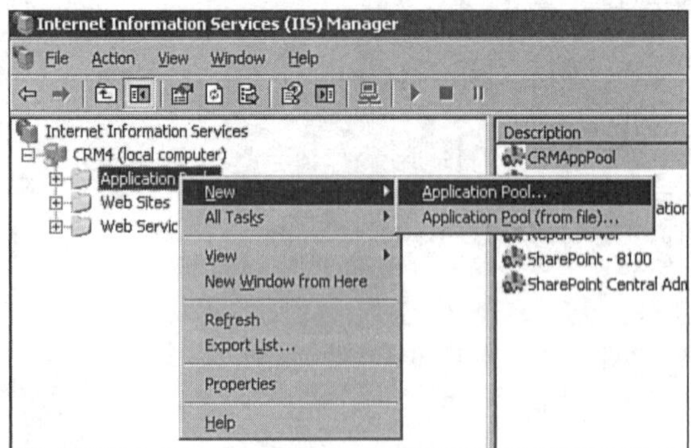

FIGURE 24.5 Creating a new application pool.

3. Enter **`ContactPictures`** in the Application Pool ID text box and click OK (see Figure 24.6).

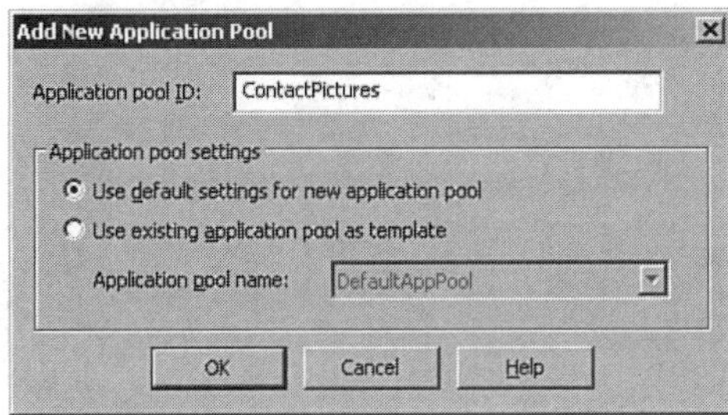

FIGURE 24.6 `ContactPictures` application pool.

4. Expand the Web Sites folder.

5. Locate the website for your CRM system (see Figure 24.7).

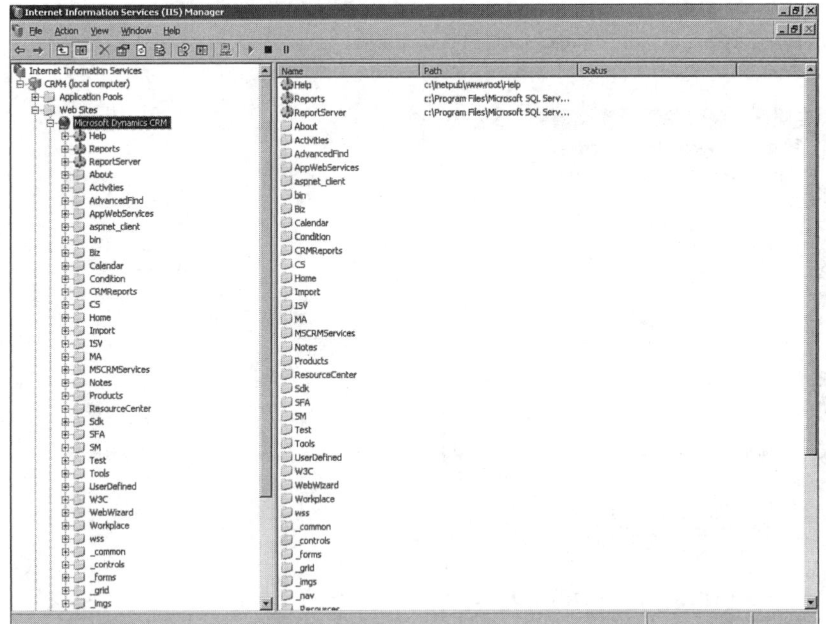

FIGURE 24.7 Microsoft Dynamics CRM website in IIS Manager.

6. Right-click the Microsoft Dynamics CRM website and select New, Virtual Directory (see Figure 24.8).

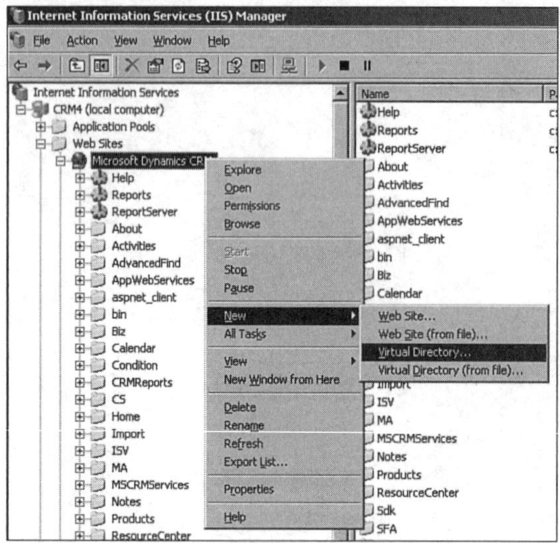

FIGURE 24.8 New Virtual Directory context menu.

7. When the wizard appears, click Next (see Figure 24.9).

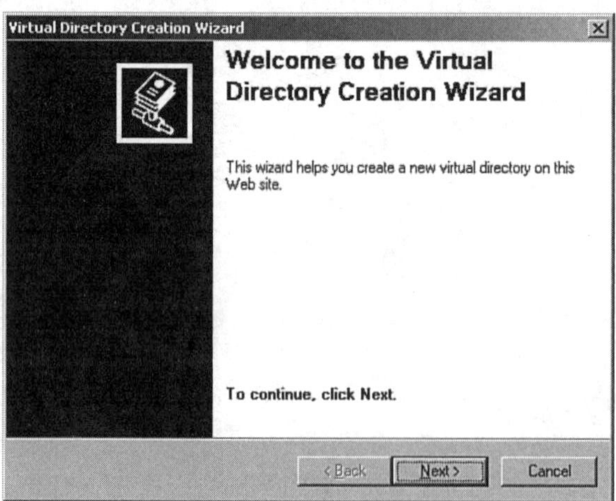

FIGURE 24.9 Virtual Directory Creation Wizard.

8. Enter **ContactPictures** in the Alias textbox and click Next (see Figure 24.10).

9. Enter the path where you created the website application in Visual Studio—for example, C:\Inetpub\ContactPictures—and click Next (see Figure 24.11).

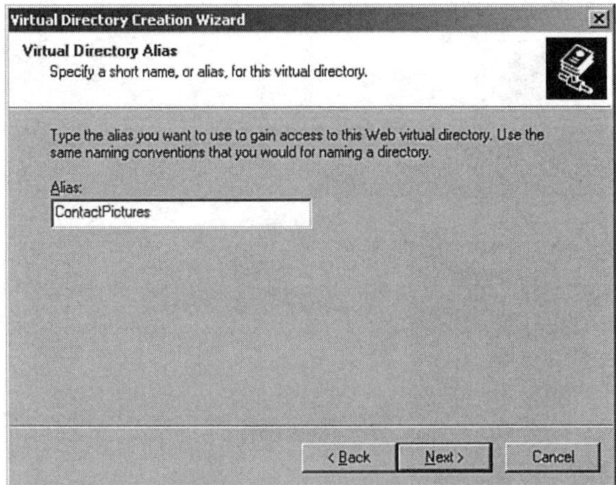

FIGURE 24.10 Virtual Directory Alias.

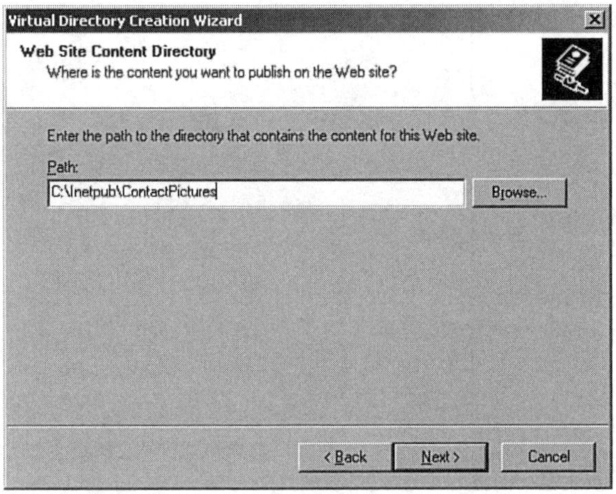

FIGURE 24.11 Website content directory.

10. Check Read and Run scripts (such as ASP) and click Next (see Figure 24.12).
11. Click Finish (see Figure 24.13).
12. Right-click the virtual directory you just created and select Properties.

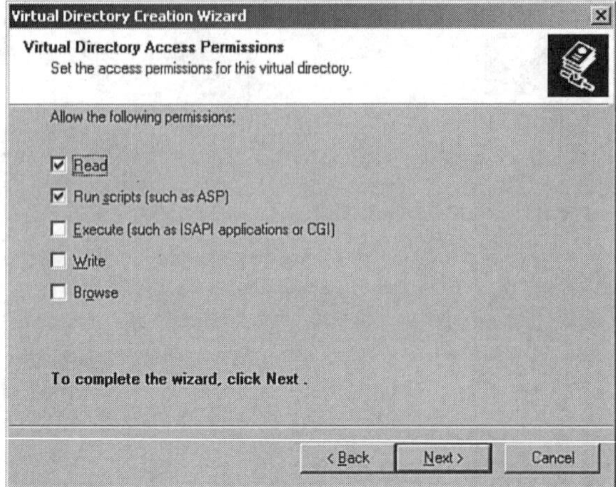

FIGURE 24.12 Virtual Directory Access Permissions.

FIGURE 24.13 Virtual Directory successfully created.

13. Change the application pool to the one you created in the step 3 with the name **`ContactPictures`** (see Figure 24.14). Also move to the ASP.NET tab to check that the ASP.NET version is set to 2.0.50727.

14. Click OK.

15. Close the Internet Information Services Manager.

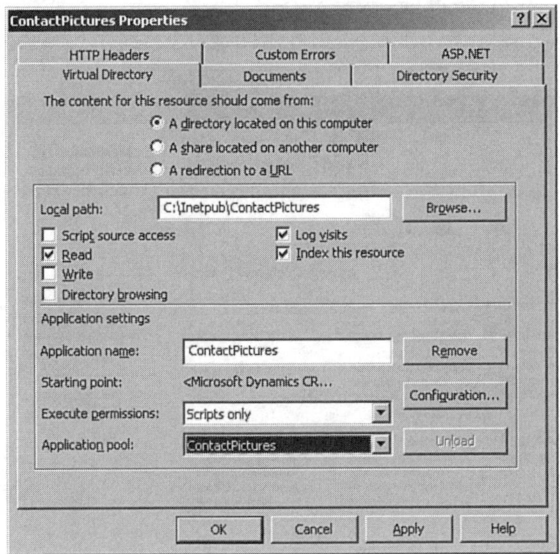

FIGURE 24.14 ContactPictures properties.

Contact Entity Customization

You are now ready to customize the Contact entity to show the application you've developed by creating a new tab and adding an IFRAME to it.

1. From the CRM web client application, go to Settings and then Customizations (see Figure 24.15).
2. Click Customize Entities and locate the Contact entity (see Figure 24.16).
3. Open the Contact entity by double-clicking it.
4. Then go to Forms and Views, and double-click the Form record.

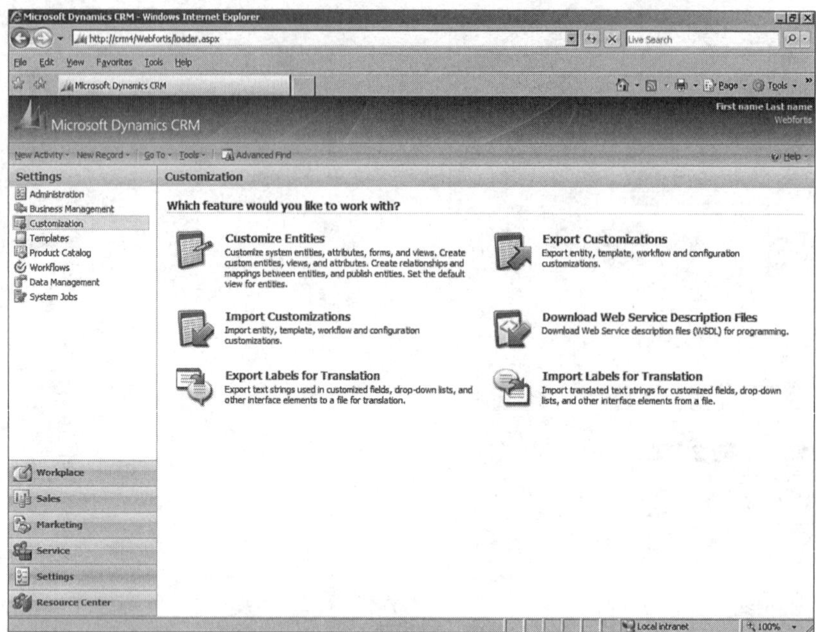

FIGURE 24.15 Customization interface.

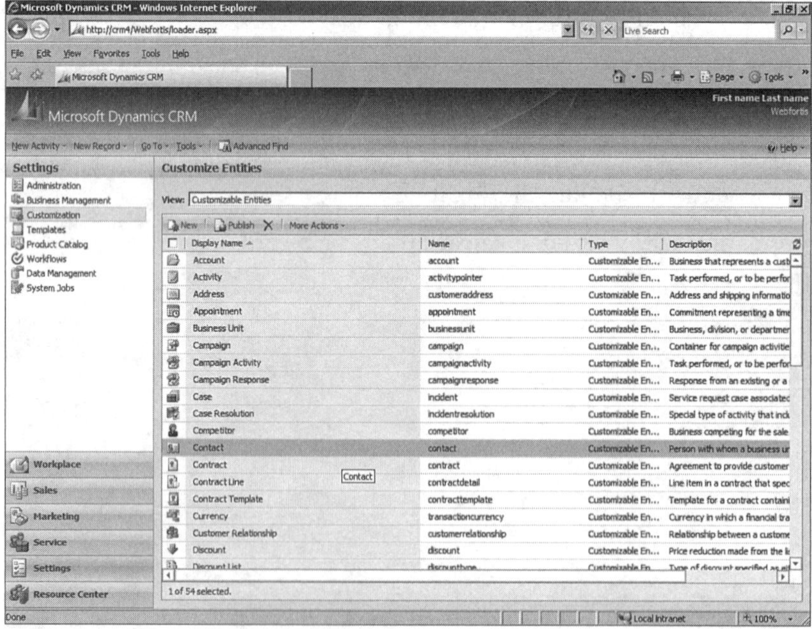

FIGURE 24.16 Contact entity.

5. Click Add a Tab and enter **`Picture`** for the Name; then click OK (see Figure 24.17).

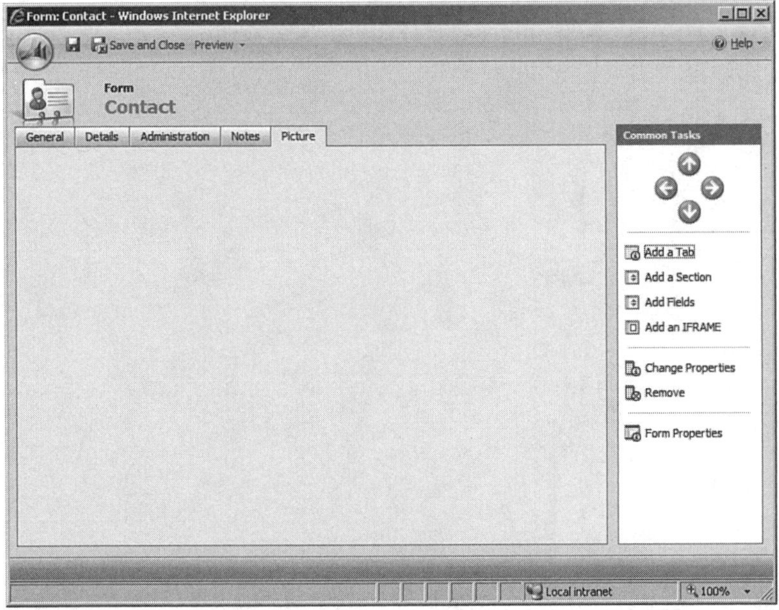

FIGURE 24.17 Adding a new tab for Picture.

6. Click Add a Section to add a section inside the tab (remember that you must add sections controls first to add an IFRAME or other controls to the form), name the section as **`Picture`**, and click OK.

7. Click Add an IFRAME to insert an IFRAME inside the section.

8. In the Add an IFRAME properties, enter **`Picture`** for the Name; enter **`../../ContactPictures/Default.aspx`** for the URL.

   Then check the box for Pass Record Object-Type Code and Unique Identifier as Parameters. This last property is the most important one for our purposes because it adds the GUID of the Contact in the Query String for the Contact you are editing, enabling you to uniquely identify each Contact. Uncheck the box for Restrict Cross-Frame Scripting (see Figure 24.18).

9. Move to the Formatting tab and check the Automatically Expand to Use Available Space box under Row Layout (see Figure 24.19).

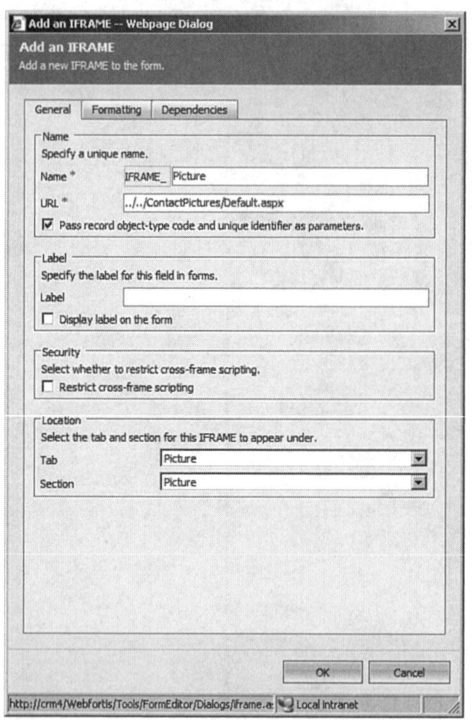

FIGURE 24.18 Adding a new IFRAME with the Pass Record Object-Type Code and Unique Identifier as Parameters option.

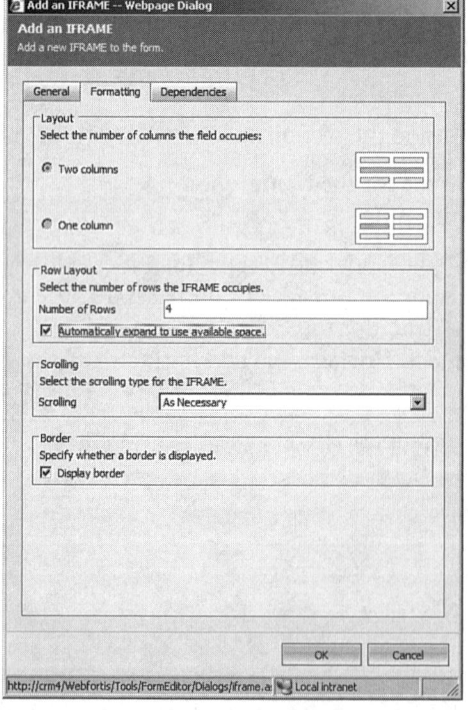

FIGURE 24.19 Automatically Expand to Use Available Space.

10. Click OK to close the Add an IFRAME properties dialog box. Your form should look similar to Figure 24.20.

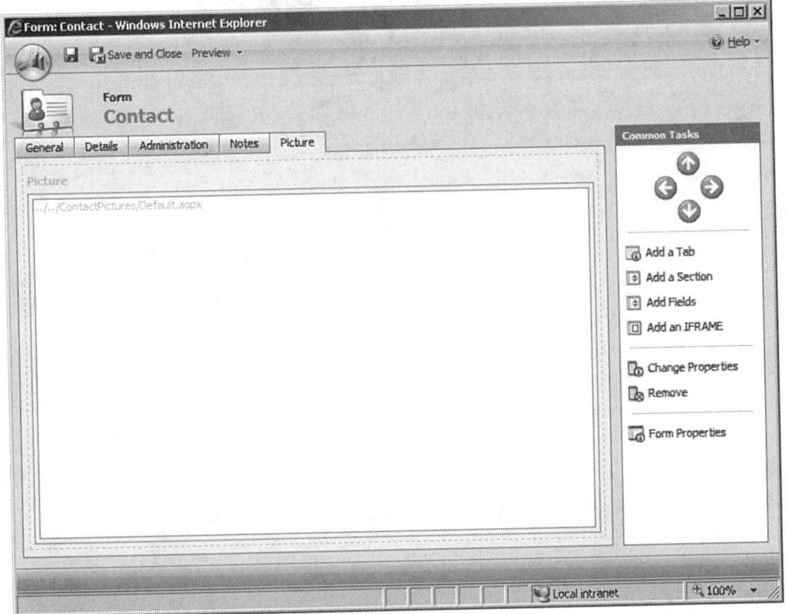

FIGURE 24.20 New IFRAME added to show the Contact picture.

11. Click Save and Close to save the form changes.
12. Click Save and Close to save the entity changes.
13. Click Publish to publish your changes.

Testing

You are ready to test the customization.

1. From the CRM web client, go to the Workplace and then select Contacts (see Figure 24.21).
2. Select a Contact and double-click to open it. Note that you must use an existing Contact to use this solution. If you are creating a new one, you must first save the record before uploading the picture, so the record will have a GUID that can be assigned to the picture. (We discuss ways of handling errors and similar situations later in the "Improvements" section.)
3. Move to the Picture tab.

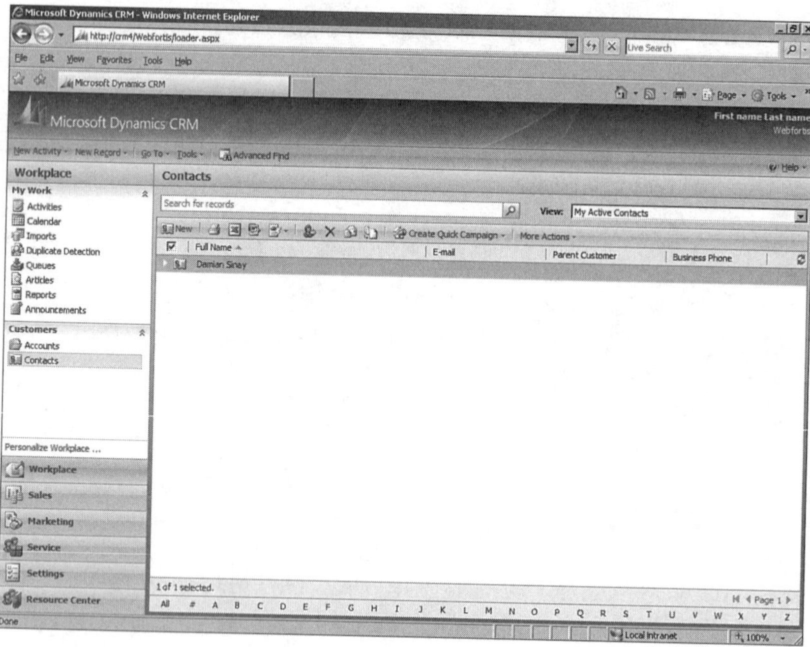

FIGURE 24.21 Contacts list.

4. Enter the full path of the image file you want to upload or click Browse to locate the file in your local disks (see Figure 24.22).

   Notice that the embedded application in the tab looks pretty rough. We address how to make it look more professional in the next section, "Improvements."

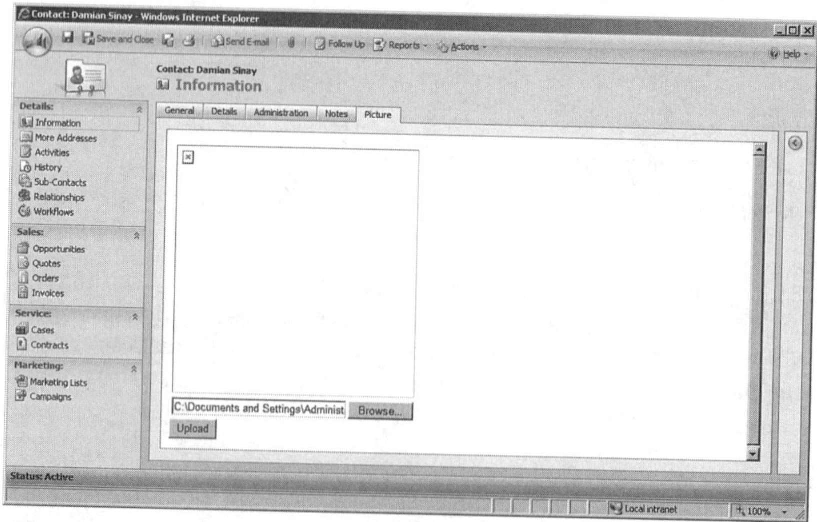

FIGURE 24.22 Uploading a picture to a Contact.

5. Click the Upload button.
6. You will see the uploaded image, as shown in Figure 24.23.

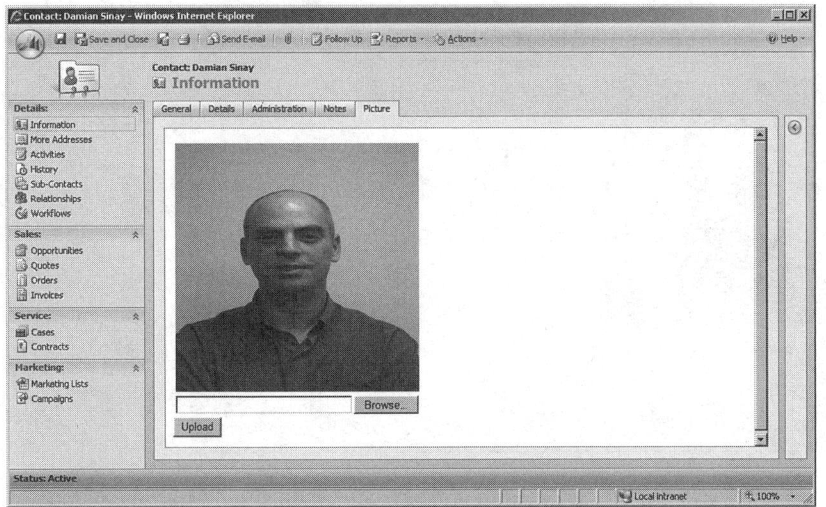

FIGURE 24.23 Contact with picture uploaded.

7. In this example, you don't need to save the record because the picture will be updated as soon it is uploaded. However, you could easily add more sophisticated functions and controls such as previewing, saving, etc.

Improvements

Because our example is fairly simple, you might want to add some of these improvements for this solution.

Adding CRM Styles

The application looks strange and unprofessional inside the IFRAME. You will probably want to make the application look more like Microsoft Dynamics CRM. You can do that easily by applying the CRM cascading style sheet (CSS) to your application. To do this, add the following line inside the `<Head>` element in the `Default.aspx` page:

```
<link rel="stylesheet" type="text/css"
href="../../_common/styles/global.css.aspx?lcid=1033" />
```

After you apply the styles, your application will look like Figure 24.24.

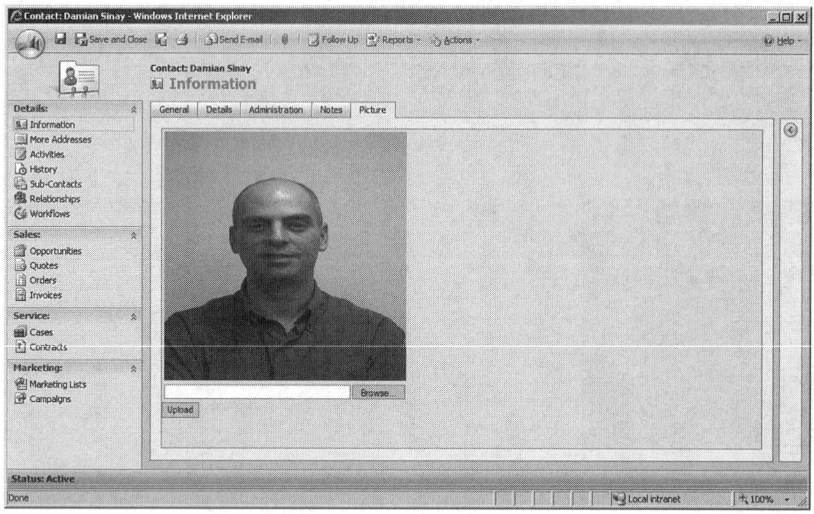

FIGURE 24.24 Contact with picture uploaded and Microsoft Dynamics CRM styles added.

Considerations for IFRAME in Offline Clients

When you implement IFRAMEs on the Microsoft Dynamics forms, they will not be accessible when the Outlook client is in offline mode. You can use the following code to detect whether the client is running in online or offline modes:

```
if ( Request.Url.ToString().StartsWith("http://localhost:2525") )
{
    // running in offline mode
}
else
{
    // running in online mode
}
```

Improving the Save Behavior

In the sample, the picture is updated automatically without the User having to save the record. We did that to simplify the code sample, but the User might expect to update the picture only when saving the record. To do that, you must create a new custom attribute for the Contact entity called `pictureid` (or similar), with a type of `nvarchar` and a length of 100, where you can store a unique identifier (for example a GUID) for the picture that is going to be uploaded. To do that, you use the CRM SDK Web Services to query the attribute value to show the right picture and then update the attribute in the `OnSave` event of the form. For more information about working with the CRM SDK Web Services, refer to Chapter 22, "Web Services."

You could use this same example to show companies' logos by applying a similar customization to the Account entity.

Summary

This chapter looked at how to integrate a custom ASP.NET web application with Microsoft Dynamics CRM using IFRAMEs. You learned how an entity form passes the parameters to an application so that you can determine which record, entity, and organization you are working on. Finally, you learned about some improvements, such as using cascading styles sheets (CSS) files, to give your application the Microsoft Dynamics CRM look.

CHAPTER 25

Migrating Data from Other Systems to Microsoft Dynamics CRM

IN THIS CHAPTER

- When to Work with the Microsoft Dynamics CRM Tools
- Considerations When Working with the Data
- Migration Options
- Third-Party Tools

Microsoft Dynamics CRM comes with some very powerful tools to migrate data. However, sometimes you might want to migrate the data manually, such as in these situations:

- The data comes from a custom source, such as a custom CRM system, or the data is disorganized.
- The CRM application is closed source and does not allow for easy data extraction.
- Multiple data sources exist.
- Attachments need to be migrated.

When performing data migrations, it is important to realize that data migration is not a one-time process. Typically, it is performed numerous times, with different types and amounts of data, and with validation and corrections occurring throughout the process. This is common even when working with the tools included with Microsoft Dynamics CRM.

Although we cannot review every data migration scenario, this chapter reviews the key consideration points when evaluating a data migration that the system does not support with its out-of-the-box tools or functionality.

When to Work with the Microsoft Dynamics CRM Tools

Chapter 6, "Data Migration and Conversion," covers these tools in greater detail, but we briefly review them here.

When considering a data migration for Microsoft Dynamics CRM, you'll likely be working with one of the following tools/methods:

- Data Migration Manager
- Import Data Wizard
- Manual
- Custom
- Tracing

Data Migration Manager

The Data Migration Manager is a powerful tool that can migrate data quickly and easily (see Figure 25.1).

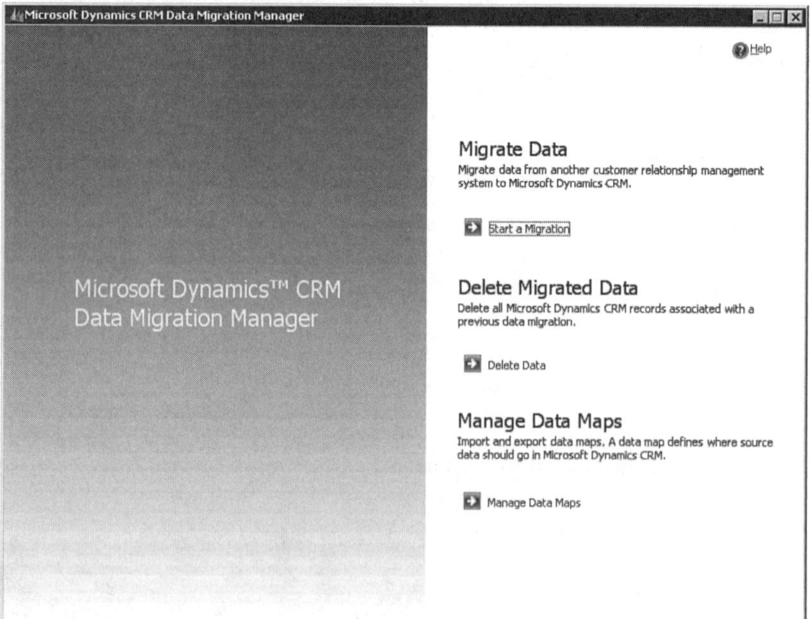

FIGURE 25.1 Data Migration Manager.

When working with the Data Migration Manager, you can create and work with Data Maps, and you can perform complex data transformations on the data. Other benefits of using the tool include the ability to do the following:

- Assign records to different Users
- Create custom record types and attributes
- Migrate data from multiple sources
- Upload files and attachments
- Perform complex data modifications

The Data Migration Manager cannot perform the following tasks:

- Update existing records
- Detect duplicates on either the existing records or the migrated records (see the Considerations When Working with the Data section for more information about data cleanup)

Although the Data Migration Manager can't handle updating records or detecting duplicates, you can use Microsoft Dynamics CRM to perform duplicate detection and record merges on the records after they are migrated. Functionality exists within the Data Migration Manager for migrating records and attachments. This is discussed later in this chapter in the section "Migration Options."

Import Data Wizard

You can find the Import Data Wizard by navigating to Tools, Import Data (see Figure 25.2).

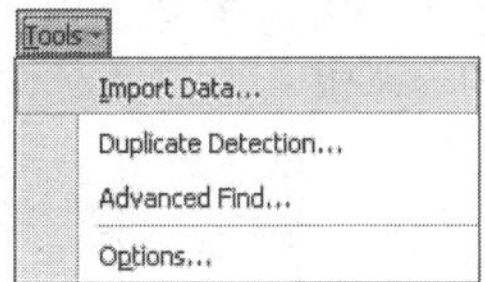

FIGURE 25.2 Import Data Wizard.

The Import Data Wizard is designed for relatively small and easy migrations requiring no complex data manipulation. (Because you can migrate only one file at a time, you need to perform every step for each table.) Working with the Import Data Wizard offers these advantages:

- Automatic mapping is performed based on the column headings in the source file.
- Duplicate detection is enabled.

The Import Data Wizard has these limitations:

- All imported records are assigned to one User.
- After completing the migration, you cannot easily roll it back.
- Complex data modification must be done before using the Import Data Wizard.
- Uploading files and attachments is not supported.

The next option should be considered only when working with smaller migrations.

Manual

Although both the Data Migration Manager and the Import Data Wizard perform a number of tasks that make data migration easier, a third option is often used when working with especially difficult, albeit smaller, data migrations: manually entering data into the system.

This option requires you to enter the data by hand into Microsoft Dynamics CRM. The underlying data can be in any form, but you should consider the scope this task might entail—for example, it might not be feasible when working with several thousand records. Additionally, you must consider errors that are inherent when working with data manually. Advantages to working with the data manually include these:

- You can perform any kind of data manipulation. Because the data is being entered for the first time, you can transform it during the entry.
- Regardless of the complexity of the data, if you have a relatively small data set, it might be cheaper to perform the migration manually.
- You can easily upload documents and attachments.

When performing a migration manually, be aware that large data sets are impractical with this type of migration because of the amount of time and resources required.

Custom

A more advanced option is to develop a custom tool that interacts with both the source data and the Microsoft Dynamics CRM Web Services. You could use Visual Studio to write the tool manually, and it would interact with both the source data and Microsoft Dynamics CRM based on whatever custom business rules you define. You might use this option when you can't export the source data for some reason (usually because it is proprietary or protected), and it is recommended only for experienced developers when none of the other migration options is feasible.

NOTE

When working with the Microsoft Dynamics CRM data, don't touch the database tables directly. Instead, use the exposed Web Services for Microsoft Dynamics CRM, as explained fully in Chapter 22, "Web Services."

Tracing

Microsoft Dynamics CRM has detailed migration logging that you can turn on or off. By default, tracing is turned off; however, you can turn it on by editing the Registry before you perform the migration.

> **NOTE**
>
> When working with the Registry, you can cause serious problems if you incorrectly modify the settings. We always recommend backing up your Registry before you perform any modifications.

To turn on tracing in Microsoft Dynamics CRM, follow these steps:

1. Open the Registry by navigating to Start, Run, and typing **`regedit`**.
2. Navigate to the following Key within the Registry: `HKEY_LOCAL_MACHINE\SOFWARE\Microsoft\Data Migration Wizard`.
3. Change the value in the `TraceEnabled` Key from `00000000` to `00000001` (see Figure 25.3).

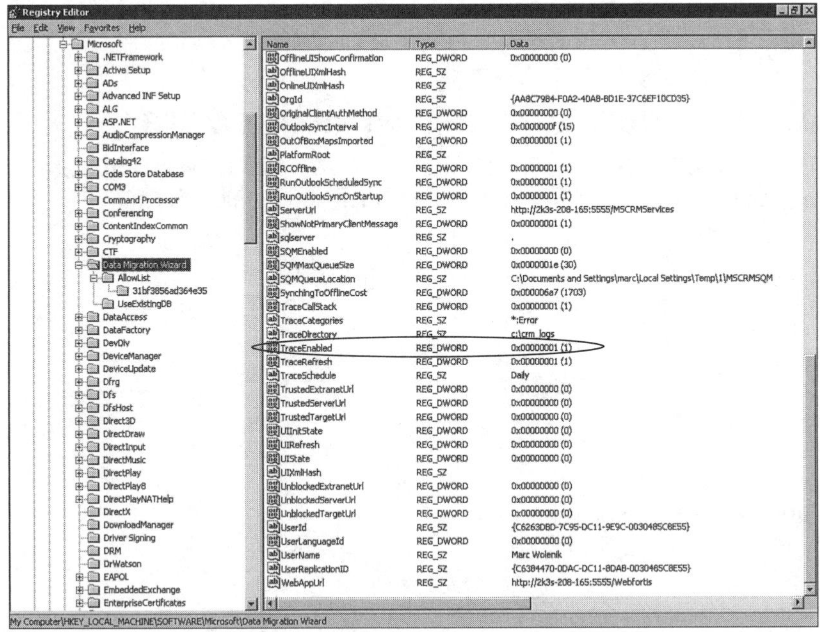

FIGURE 25.3 Registry settings with TraceEnabled.

4. Create a new String Value in the Registry called `TraceDirectory` where you want the trace logs to be created. In our example, we created one at `C:\crm_logs\`.

   These are the Registry values for tracing:

   - `TraceEnabled`—`DWORD, 1=on, 0=off`.
   - `TraceDirectory`—String, set to the full path where you want the log files to be created.
   - `TraceSchedule`—String, with `Daily`, `Hourly`, `Weekly`, and `Monthly` as values.
   - `TraceRefresh`—`DWORD, 1`. Tracing reloads when this number is incremented.
   - `TraceCallStack`—`DWORD, 1`. This value is set only if you want to see the call-stack information.
   - `TraceCategories`—String, with options of either * for verbose or the following: `Application`, `Application_Outlook`, `Exception`, `Platform`, `Platform_ImportExportPublish`, `Platform_Metadata`, `Platform_Sdk`, `Platform_Soap`, `Platform_Sql`, `Platform_Workflow`, `SchedulingEngine`, `Unmanaged_Outlook`, `Unmanaged_Platform`, `Unmanaged_Sql`, and `ObjectModel`.

Be sure to turn off tracing when you have finished troubleshooting, or you can easily create large trace logs.

Considerations When Working with the Data

When planning a migration, you must organize and prepare the data to be migrated, to ensure a valid mapping between the source system and Microsoft Dynamics CRM. Consider the following steps:

- Exporting the data from the source
- Cleaning up the data
- Preparing the data
- Mapping the data
- Importing
- Performing testing and validation
- Reimporting

It is important to make frequent backups of your source database files when working with files during the migration process. Additionally, you might want to make a backup of your Microsoft Dynamics CRM databases so that you can restore them later, if needed.

To back up your Microsoft Dynamics CRM databases, follow these steps:

1. Navigate to Start, All Programs, Microsoft SQL Server 2005, and select the SQL Server Management Studio for the version of SQL you're running. In our example, we're running SQL Server 2005.
2. You will see several databases within the Databases node when expanded (see Figure 25.4). Note that your configuration could differ from the example, depending on what applications are running on your SQL Server.

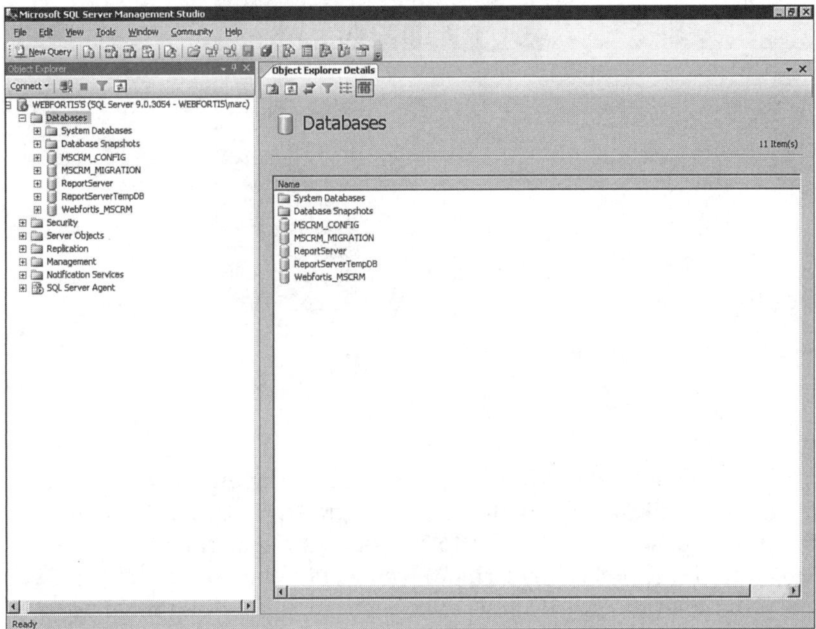

FIGURE 25.4 Databases with the Database node of SQL Server.

3. Select the database that houses your data. This is in the format of <organization>_MSCRM. In our example, the database is Webfortis_MSCRM. After selecting the database, right-click and select Tasks, Backup. The Back Up Database Wizard opens, and you can perform a full backup on the database (see Figure 25.5).

   We have only a single organization represented in our example. If you have several organizations, you must perform a backup on each of the organizations.
4. Repeat step 3 for the Microsoft Dynamics configuration database, which should be named MSCRM_CONFIG.

Store your backups on a separate server or drive, to avoid data loss.

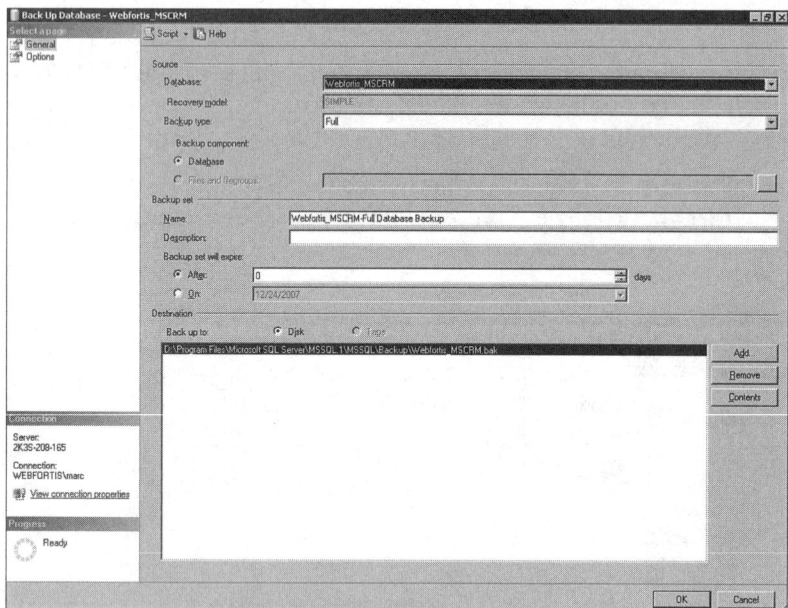

FIGURE 25.5 SQL Server Back Up Database Wizard.

Exporting the Data from the Source

When working with a data source, you must ensure that the application can export to a comma-separated value (CSV) file because both the Data Migration Manager and the Import Data Wizard require this format. It is safe to assume that if you can get the data out of the source application (in almost any fashion), you will be able to convert to a CSV file. You can make a CSV file from virtually any Office application by saving the file as a CSV file, or by importing the data into Excel and saving it as a CSV file from there.

The format of a CSV file is one that has a header row and values. An example CSV file with a header row and 2 rows of data follows:

```
Full Name,Last Name,Parent Customer,Business Phone
Damian Sinay, Sinay,,
Marc Wolenik, Wolenik,,
```

We cannot describe all data extraction and export options and techniques from the multitude of existing CRM applications. However, be sure that your application enables you to export your data easily by searching for an Export option within the application. More advanced options to extract data include connecting directly to the database of the source application, either by using connector tools (described later in this chapter in the section "Third-Party Tools") or by building an intermediary database to pull the data.

Because you'll be working with a CSV file, you might wonder how to import attachments. Because Microsoft Dynamics CRM maps all notes and attachments into the Notes of the entity, you can migrate attachments only to entities that support Notes. Figure 25.6 shows the Account entity and the availability of Notes.

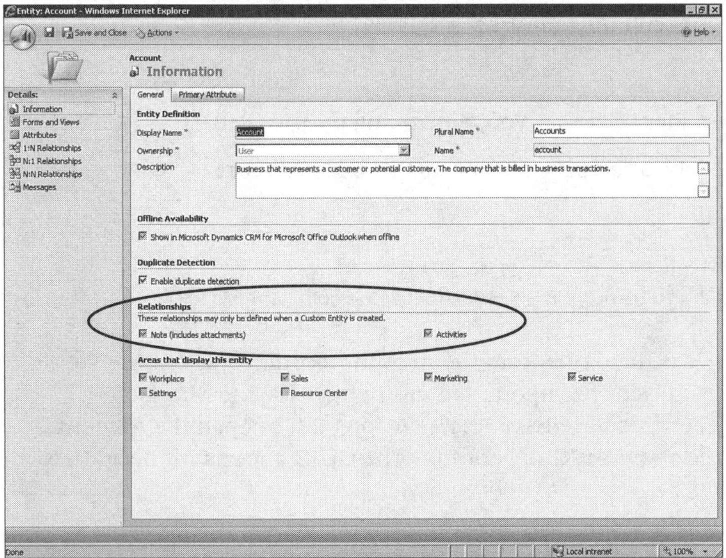

FIGURE 25.6 Notes supported in the Account entity.

Other entities, such as Sales Literature and Roles, do not support Notes and, therefore, will not support migrating attachments (see Figure 25.7).

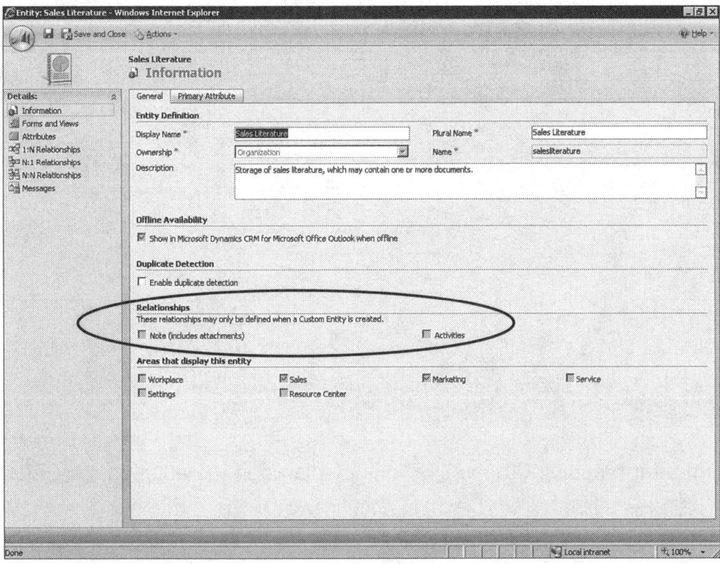

FIGURE 25.7 Notes not supported in the Sales Literature entity.

To import attachments, follow these steps:

1. Create a CSV file with three columns. In our example, we've created a file named `Notes.csv` with one row. If you were going to migrate multiple notes, you would have multiple rows. The columns must be as follows:

   - The document
   - The CRM record identifier that you're mapping to (the GUID)
   - The filename of the attachment—for example `contract.doc`

   A sample CSV file follows:

   ```
   Document Name,ID,File Name
   Contract.doc,32026626-1CA4-DC11-BFF0-0030485C8E55,contract.doc,
   ```

   The ID in this example is the GUID from the Account record. To determine the GUID for the record you want to import, you must either use the Microsoft Dynamics CRM Web Services to retrieve it (see Chapter 22) or open the Account from the web interface and press Ctrl+N or F11. The GUID appears in the address box URL (see Figure 25.8).

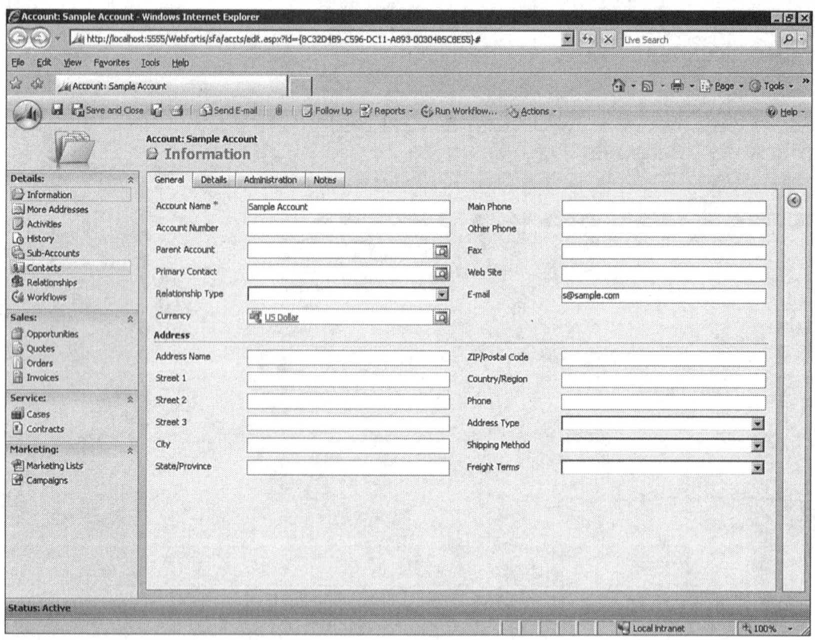

FIGURE 25.8 Account form after pressing Ctrl+N. The ID is displayed in the address bar URL.

2. Create a subfolder directly under the folder that has the `Notes.csv` file called either Documents or Attachments, and place the attachment in the folder (see Figure 25.9).

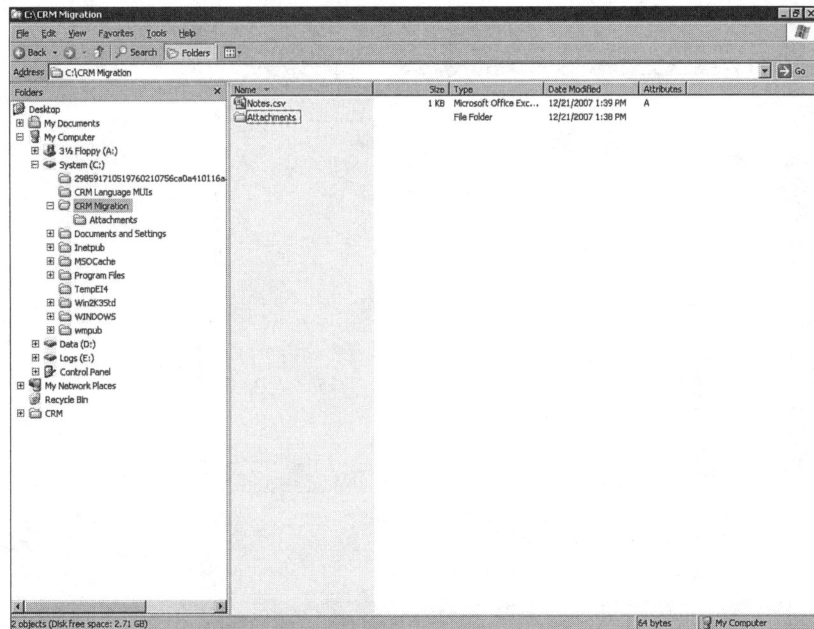

FIGURE 25.9 Directory structure for mapping attachments.

If you're working with attachments that exceed 32MB, you must modify the `web.config` file located in the Microsoft Dynamics CRM root as explained here: http://support.microsoft.com/kb/295626.

3. Start the Data Migration Manager, select Start a Migration from the Migrate Data options, and then select Start a New Migration on the next screen, followed by Start a Migration.

4. Click Next to get started, specify the migration name (optionally), click Next again, and add your file to the migration (see Figure 25.10). Click Next to continue.

5. The file parses and you should see a screen similar to Figure 25.11. Click Next to continue.

6. The Data Migration Manager validates the file and attempts to map it. Because it is a new mapping, it is unmapped. Select Next to continue.

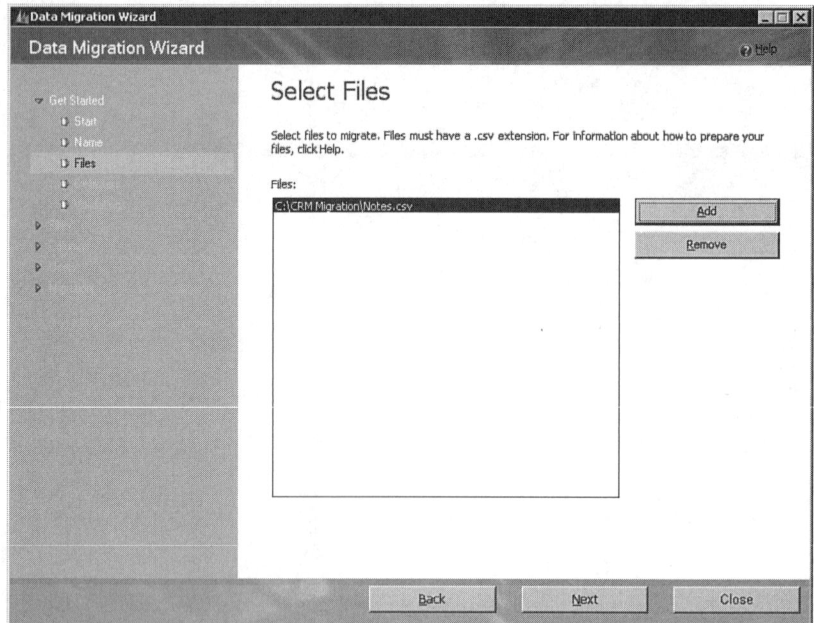

FIGURE 25.10 Add file to migration attachments.

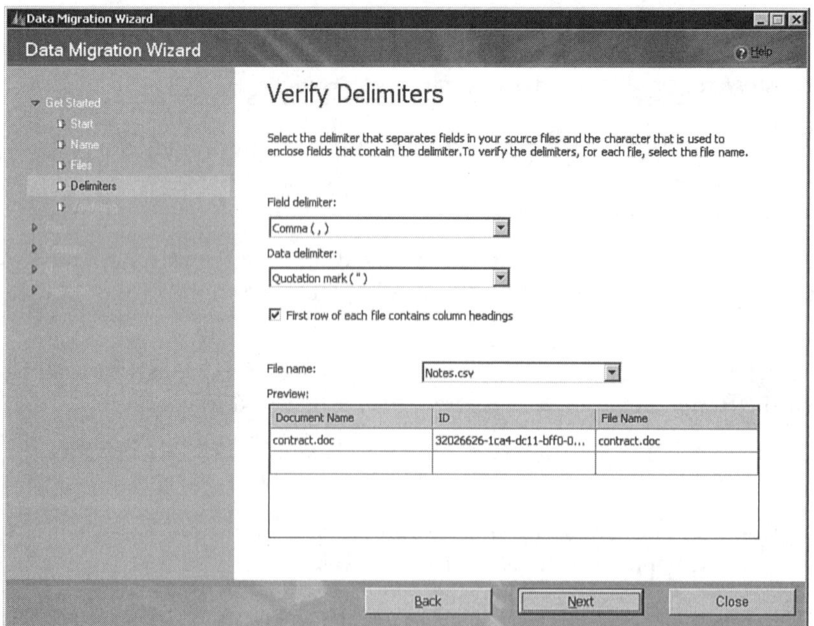

FIGURE 25.11 Data Migration Manager preview.

7. Select Map This File to an Existing Microsoft Dynamics CRM Entity and verify that Note is selected. Mark the Includes Attachments check box option, and click Next to continue (see Figure 25.12).

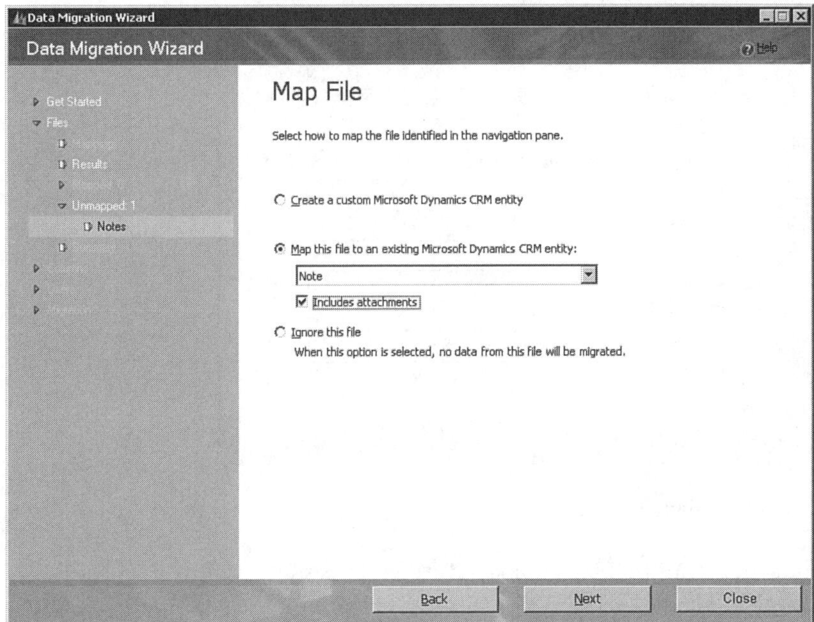

FIGURE 25.12 Data Migration Manager map file.

8. The file summary screen indicates that the files are manually mapped. Click Next to continue.

9. The column mapping results show the file with unmapped columns. Click Next to perform the mappings.

10. For the Document Name value on our CSV, the mapping should be to the `Document *` attribute. Click Next to continue.

11. For the ID value on the CSV, the mapping refers to the ID of the Account, so you need to select the Regarding attribute. Click Next to continue. Define the relationship by selecting Account and Account (Primary Key) (see Figure 25.13). Click Next to continue.

12. For the File Name value on the CSV, the mapping should be to the `File Name` attribute. Click Next three times and then click Migrate Data to perform the migration.

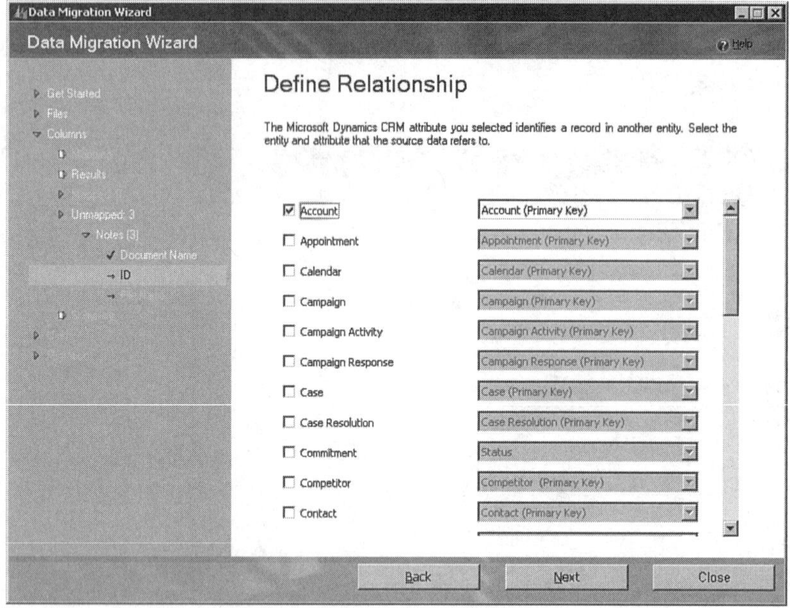

FIGURE 25.13 Data Migration Manager map file.

13. The data is migrated and the file is uploaded. When it is successful, you will see results, as shown in Figure 25.14.

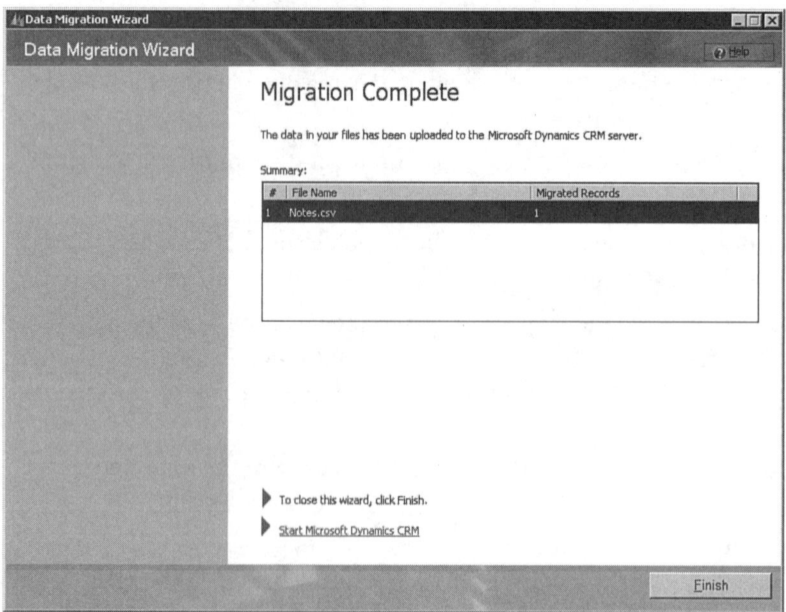

FIGURE 25.14 Data Migration Manager migration complete.

14. If you navigate to the Account entity specified by the ID in the migration and select Notes, you'll see the uploaded document (see Figure 25.15).

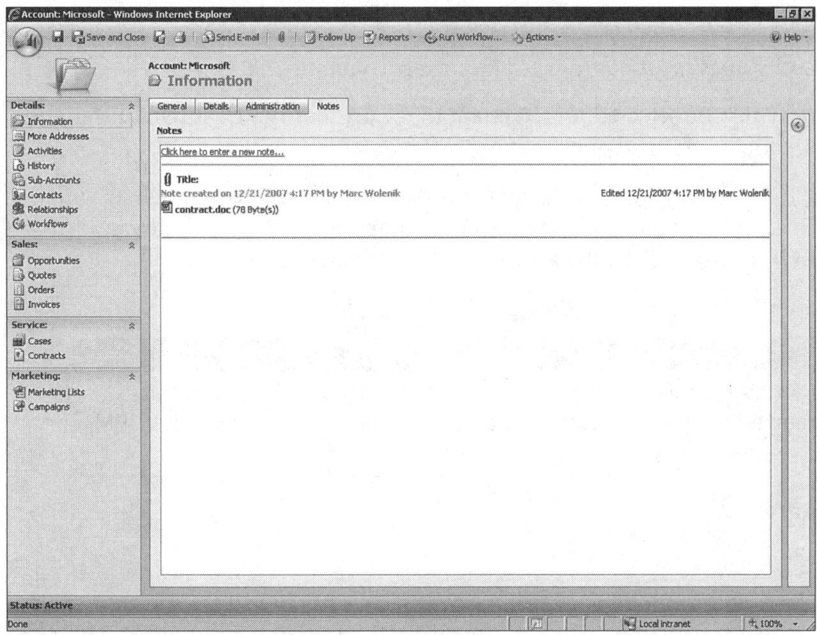

FIGURE 25.15 Notes field on our Account entity.

You can augment your CSV file to include other information, such as created dates and User information, for a richer upload.

Data Cleanup

When performing migrations, it is important to consider the old adage along the lines of "Garbage in—garbage out." Regardless of how well the data is extracted, if it was poorly structured or erred in any manner (misspellings, missing values, and so on), the same problems will exist in the new system after the migration.

Therefore, we always recommend doing data cleansing before you attempt a migration. Data cleansing can mean a number of things, but generally it involves one or more of the following:

- Checking for and removing duplicates
- Eliminating older and unnecessary data
- Validating and updating information
- Organizing your data structure

Data Preparation

After you extract and clean the data, you must prepare it for migration into Microsoft Dynamics CRM to conform to the structure and shape of the Microsoft Dynamics CRM database. These preparations include the following:

- Data types and values must conform to Microsoft Dynamics CRM.
- Proper entities must be selected for the mapping. Consider the existing entities and whether you should add new ones to handle the data.
- Conforming to the structure of CRM might require additional work, such as when source data has multiple addresses (Microsoft Dynamics CRM stores addresses in a separate entity), multiple list values, or varying data value lengths.

TIP

When preparing a CSV file for migration, consider leaving the source columns and adding extra columns that have the corrected data in them. Microsoft Dynamics CRM can ignore columns that are not specific to the migration.

Data Mapping

Data mapping enables you to move your data from the CSV file to the Microsoft Dynamics CRM entities and attribute values. The entity is the source point for the data in Microsoft Dynamics CRM. If you're moving a source data file that you've used previously to manage companies you've done business with, you'll probably be mapping the source file to the Accounts entity. If your source data file includes both individuals and the companies that they work for, consider performing two mappings: the first for the companies for the Accounts entity, and the second one for individuals for the Contacts entity. You'll want to reference the Accounts values as the Parent Account when you migrate the individuals to the Contacts entity, to preserve your relationships.

Microsoft Dynamics CRM ships with several Data Maps with predefined mappings for migration purposes, and Microsoft plans to make more available for download from the Microsoft website.

Chapter 6 explains Data Maps more fully.

Importing

When performing a data import, consider importing only a few records for each entity initially. These few records should include a good sample of the underlying data that will enable you to thoroughly test the records, including any relationships, data modifications, and values.

As part of the import process, be aware of any exceptions generated and develop a solution that you can apply to all the underlying values. It is important to consider relational issues as part of the exceptions that could occur that refer to nonexistent parent relations if the parent doesn't exist in the import set. An example of this is attempting to import Contacts that have a relation to a nonexistent Account. If you import a sample of the Account information first and then a sample of the Contacts, but some of the Contacts refer to Accounts that weren't part of the initial Account load, it will create an error. However, this is a known error and you could disregard it.

Testing and Validation

You should test and validate the migration several times during the migration process. This should include a thorough review of the entities, the attribute values, and any reports that might be related to the migrated data.

It is often helpful to create quantitative validation test scripts that you can compare to the expected results, especially when you're working with any kind of data transformations. An example of a validation test script might look something like this table.

Entity	Attribute	Source Value	Migrated Value	Transform
Account	Account Name	Joe's Oyl	Joe's Oil	✓
Account	Account Phone	8005551212	(800) 555-1212	✓
Account	Account Fax	N/A	N/A	
Account	Account Contact	Mike Smith	Mike Smith	Mike Smith (Contact)

In this example, you can compare the source values and the migrated values, and confirm that expected transformations have occurred (see the Account Name and the Account Phone source and migrated values). Additionally, you can confirm that the contact information is correct and relates as expected.

Additional steps for testing and validation might include having the actual Users work with the data samples to check whether they are seeing what they expect. This can often prove to be a valuable step for system validation because Users often report that although the data is there, it doesn't display as they expected it to (or how it used to). We recommend considering application customizations and enhancements or User training to solve these kinds of issues.

When undergoing User testing, be sure to test the following:

- The web client
- The Outlook client (both offline and online)
- The data from an internal perspective and with multiple levels of Users
- Any external requirements that might exist regarding the data

Finally, although we're considering only data testing and validation in this chapter, it is prudent to include system testing and validation considerations for Microsoft Dynamics CRM as well. Ensure that the following are true:

- Access restrictions or privileges are in place.
- The application performs as expected.
- External access is enabled (if required).

Reimporting

After the data has been tested and validated, and considered ready for migration, you will want to clean the database and perform the import for the final time.

If you don't properly clean your database before you perform the final migration, you could end up with duplicates or test data mixed with your good data. You can clean Microsoft CRM in a number of different ways, depending on how your migration is performed and the number of records. A simple way (depending on the entity migrated to) is to simply select the records and delete them. Alternatively, you can roll back the migration using the Data Migration Manager (see Figure 25.16).

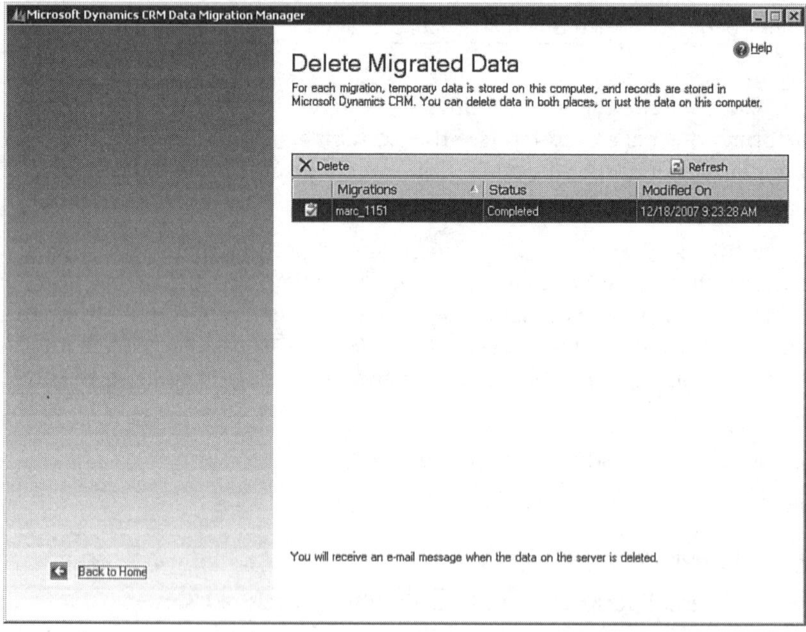

FIGURE 25.16 Data Migration Manager—deleting migrated data.

More complex methods include completely reinstalling Microsoft Dynamics CRM, or taking backups of your Microsoft Dynamics CRM SQL Server database tables before any migration testing and then restoring them to their original state when you're ready to perform the migration.

Custom

You might consider developing a custom migration tool if you can connect to your source database directly or via a database connection. Additionally, because you can interact directly with Microsoft Dynamics CRM via Web Services and filtered views, it might make sense to consider a custom data connector.

Refer to Chapter 22 for more information about working with Web Services and Microsoft Dynamics CRM, as well as the "Third-Party Tools" section later in this chapter for data connector options.

Migration Options

Unlike a new implementation, performing a migration from an existing application presents some complexities. Evaluate business processes that are centric to the old system when migrating to Microsoft Dynamics CRM. Additionally, regardless of how successful your data migration is, you must consider the following:

- **Migration challenges and options**—One of the most common considerations when evaluating the migration is how much effort to devote to migrating data. The options for migration are as follows (these options consider only the data, not business processes):
    - **Perform a complete migration of all data, including history and attachments, for full backward-compatibility and reporting**—Enables the older system to be archived. This is initially more expensive because of the effort required to migrate and test all the data, reports, and business processes.
    - **Migrate just a snapshot of the current data**—Migrates only the current active data. For example, Accounts and Contact data is migrated, but historical data is not. This allows for a rich base of data that builds from the start of the implementation. Historical data would need to be retrieved from the older system, which can remain running for just this purpose.
    - **Perform no data migration, and have the Users utilize the new system as if the organization is new**—Popular when the old system contains especially poor quality of data or will take more effort to clean than to simply leave and start fresh.
- **Decide whether the old system should continue to run in parallel with the new system for ongoing validation and backup purposes**—If this is the case, you must prepare for the additional workload of maintaining two systems. If this is an acceptable scenario, we recommend it because it provides the greatest amount of redundancy if an unforeseen problem occurs with the migration. Because the old system will still be live, you can use it if problems occur.

- **Consider phasing out the old system**—If you decide to continue using the old system, you'll definitely want to plan for when to discontinue use of it. Additionally, you'll want to consider how to deactivate the system, as well as where and how to store the system in case you need it later. Be sure to properly document common functions, reports, and, most important, login procedures.

NOTE

As mentioned, be sure to include the system administrator's login credentials when archiving an older system. Countless organizations have needed to use application hacks or back doors to get into an old system after disuse of only a few months.

Third-Party Tools

A Data Connector is a tool that enables you to connect to a database for a number of purposes. Usually these are used to read or edit data, and you can use them during migrations or as intermediary objects to pass data. Some of the more common connectors for Microsoft Dynamics include the following:

- BizTalk
- Scribe
- Custom

Because you can use these connectors to interface directly with the data, you can use them for both migrations as well as integrations with other applications.

BizTalk

BizTalk (or Microsoft BizTalk Server) is an application that enables disparate programs to communicate with each other through the use of Adapters that are built and designed around the data and necessary business processes.

Microsoft employed BizTalk to communicate between Microsoft Dynamics CRM and Microsoft Dynamics GP (Great Plains) with Microsoft Dynamic CRM Version 3.0. BizTalk was available as a free download for this type of integration, and it required simply hooking up the two systems to make them fully integrated.

Although tentative plans as of the date of publication include a similar option with Microsoft Dynamics CRM 4.0 (Microsoft has mentioned including NAV and SL connectors, in addition to the GP connector), no formal delivery dates or commitments to this solution have been made. As such, you might want to consider Scribe as an option.

You can find more information about BizTalk by visiting the Microsoft web page for BizTalk, located at www.microsoft.com/biztalk/default.mspx.

Scribe

Scribe (or Scribe Software) offers several solutions for Microsoft Dynamics CRM integration and migration. Using templates that are predefined or customized, Users can perform mapping functions between Microsoft Dynamics CRM and virtually any other system that supports either Scribe or Open Database Connectivity (ODBC) standard.

Scribe is an incredibly useful utility for not only performing Data Mappings and migrations, but also for integrating disparate systems with Microsoft Dynamics CRM.

NOTE

Working with the Scribe tools is not for the novice user. In fact, Scribe recommends users complete a series of courses and achieve Scribe Certification prior to attempting working with them.

Refer to Chapter 26, "Third-Party Add-On Options," for more information about working with the Scribe products.

Custom

Because of the way Microsoft Dynamics CRM works with filtered views and Web Services, it might be easier to simply write a custom adapter that lets you interface with your data directly. Be sure that you properly understand the data, as well as the recommended methods of interacting with it, by studying the samples outlined in this book and the SDK.

NOTE

Be sure to check the licensing requirements when working directly with the data. The Microsoft Dynamics CRM Data Connector is a license that is required when you want to interface with the Microsoft Dynamics CRM data in disparate applications.

See Chapter 21, "Plug-Ins," and Chapter 22 for information about directly working with the data as well as some samples.

Summary

This chapter reviewed the options when considering a migration from an older system. It is important to remember the value and effort related to both data migration and business processes that might have existed around an older system. Microsoft Dynamics CRM is extremely flexible, and you can adopt it to work with almost any data migration or business process; however, realize that business processes might have existed to handle shortcomings of older systems, and they should probably be evaluated as part of a new Microsoft Dynamics CRM implementation as well.

When deciding to perform a data migration of any kind, be sure to dedicate time, budget, and resources to the proper cleanup, mapping, and validation of the migration. Without this, the migration might result in a new Microsoft Dynamics CRM setup with the same problems that existed before the migration.

Finally, several tools are available for performing a data migration. We reviewed a few of them; however, the market for these types of tools is always changing, so evaluate your particular needs and integration options before you commit to any one choice.

CHAPTER 26

Third-Party Add-On Options

IN THIS CHAPTER

- Products for Microsoft Dynamics CRM
- Companies That Provide CRM Solutions
- Other Resources

Many companies have embraced Microsoft Dynamics CRM and are in the business of providing add-on solutions that can add value or bring necessary requirements to your installation. We have attempted to list and describe some of the products and companies that offer a variety of solutions for Microsoft Dynamics CRM. Many of the products and companies listed have existing solutions for Microsoft Dynamics CRM 3.0, and most have indicated that they're working to ensure that their products and services are compatible with Microsoft Dynamics CRM 4.0.

Neither the authors nor the publisher are making any attempt to vouch for the products, services, and companies listed here. We are including them in this book merely to highlight what other features are available for purchase for Microsoft Dynamics CRM. Before purchasing any, you should attempt to verify that the solutions and organizations listed in this chapter will meet your needs.

Products for Microsoft Dynamics CRM

This section outlines product solutions that you or your IT staff can implement for a variety of solutions. Before purchasing any product, thoroughly review the required functionality within Microsoft Dynamics CRM to be sure that a product is necessary.

Integration and Migration (Scribe Software)

Scribe Software provides configurable migration and integration software solutions for a variety of products, including Microsoft Dynamics CRM. Scribe Software is a

Microsoft Gold Partner and has a strong history and relationship with Microsoft and Microsoft Dynamics CRM.

The Scribe Software core product set for Microsoft Dynamics CRM consists of Scribe Insight, which uses Scribe Adapters and Scribe Templates to perform mappings to and from Microsoft Dynamics CRM.

There are three components to Scribe Insight:

- Scribe Workbench
- Scribe Console
- Scribe Integration Server

Scribe Workbench

The Scribe Workbench allows you to create template files via a graphical interface (see Figure 26.1). The template files define the source and target data connection and include options to perform the following:

- Rules to perform data cleaning, complex data mappings, transformation, and processing logic. The rules can include formulas for case conversion, field concatenation or decomposition, calculations, field parsing, field substitution, and conditional conversion.
- Capability to define complex data matching using multiple fields with Boolean logic and exact or fuzzy matching.
- Automatically branching to different steps based on User-defined conditions. The steps can perform data updates, insertion, or stop processing.

After the template files are created using the Scribe Workbench, they can be reused for additional or other migrations/mappings.

Scribe Console

The Scribe Console is used to create, control, and manage the data loading or integration via its User interface (see Figure 26.2).

The Scribe Console features:

- Event Management
- Alert Notifications
- Exception Handling
- Data Views

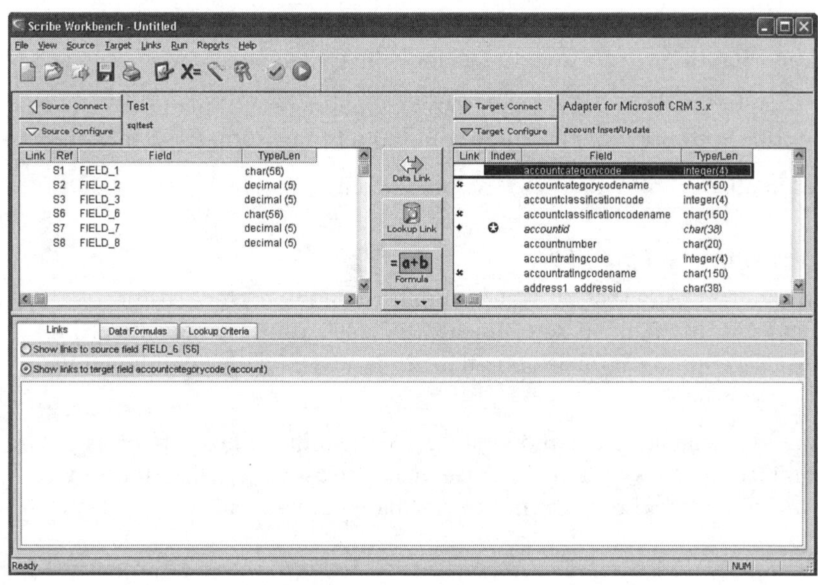

FIGURE 26.1 Scribe Workbench.

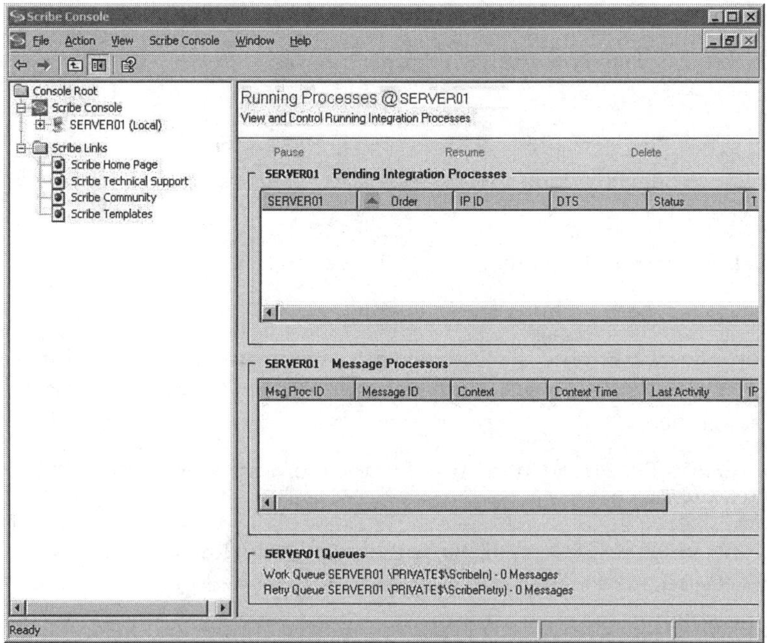

FIGURE 26.2 Scribe Console.

Scribe Integration Server

The Scribe Integration Server is what's used to facilitate the exchange of data.

As we outlined in Chapter 25, "Migrating Data from Other Systems to Microsoft Dynamics CRM," Scribe Software provides a powerful toolset to perform these migrations.

For more information about Scribe, visit www.scribesoft.com.

Enhanced Functionality (c360)

c360 is a CDC Software company that provides a number of add-on products for Microsoft Dynamics CRM. In 2005, Microsoft recognized c360 as its Partner Choice ISV (Independent Software Vendor). c360 has more than 25 products that extend functionality for Microsoft Dynamics CRM.

While some of its products are available individually, c360 bundles a majority of its products together in Productivity Packs. There are three main packs—Core, Sales, and Service, and the products included within each cannot be purchased individually.

A few of the company's solutions include these:

- Record editing of Microsoft Dynamics CRM directly from the grid view
- The ability to explore relationships visually
- Alert functionality for a number of Microsoft Dynamics CRM criteria
- Multiple CRM screens displayed on a single Console interface
- Address validation

c360 continues to develop products around the Microsoft Dynamics CRM platform that are easy to install and maintain.

The productivity packs for Microsoft Dynamics CRM 4.0 are as follows:

- Core Productivity Pack, which includes the following:
  - **c360 Explorer Search Engine**—Integrated with Microsoft Office SharePoint Server (MOSS), the Explorer provides near instant searching on all CRM data, including attachments.
  - **c360 Relationship Explorer/Charting**—A visual representation of the relationships that exist in the database (see Figure 26.3).
  - **Summary**—An integrated screen displaying all open and closed Activities, Notes, and CRM records.
  - **Multi Field Search**—Allows for search across multiple entities and fields.
  - **Console**—Allowing for a custom display of Microsoft Dynamics CRM, Console allows Users to display multiple CRM workspaces within a single window.

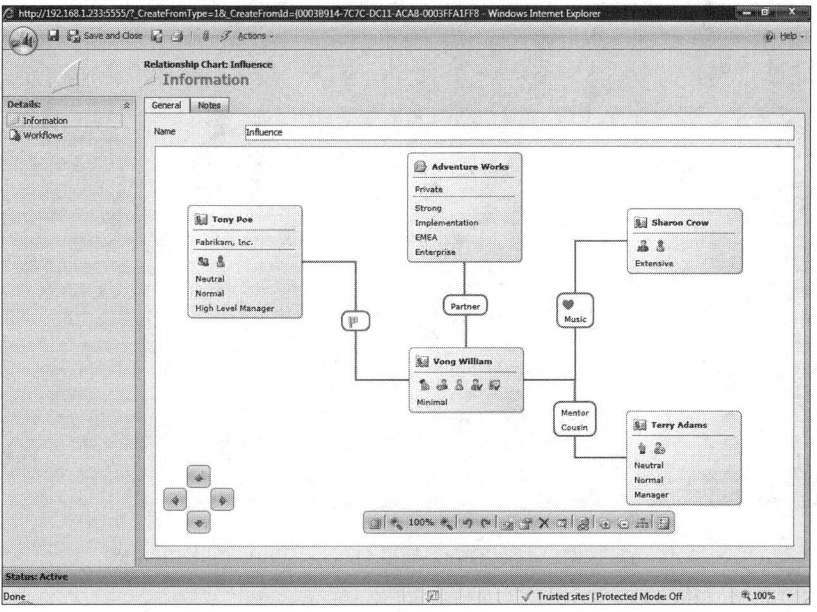

FIGURE 26.3 c360 Relationship Explorer interface.

- **CRM/SharePoint Integration**—Allows organizations to leverage Microsoft Office SharePoint capabilities and integrate them into Microsoft Dynamics CRM.
- **Record Editor**—Easy to use inline grid editor.
- **Alerts**

- **Audit**—A powerful and necessary tool for compliance purposes as well as viewing, tracking (Audit Tracker), and analyzing (Audit Analyzer) all changes made to CRM.
- **Field Level Security**—A very useful tool that allows for enhanced security by setting security by User role on the field level. With this tool, administrators have the ability to set permissions of disabled, forbidden, or hidden for individual fields within CRM (see Figure 26.4).
- **Customer Portal**—A useful tool for extending functionality of the Knowledge Base as well as Case management to external/customer facing websites. This tool is customizable and can integrate easily with virtually any website.
- **E-mail Marketing**—A hosted service provided through c360, c360 E-mail Marketing allows Users to deliver HTML e-mail campaigns with metrics such as click-rates.
- **BI Analytics**—A powerful Business Intelligence (BI) component, c360 BI Analytics provides powerful dashboards for analytics (see Figure 26.5).

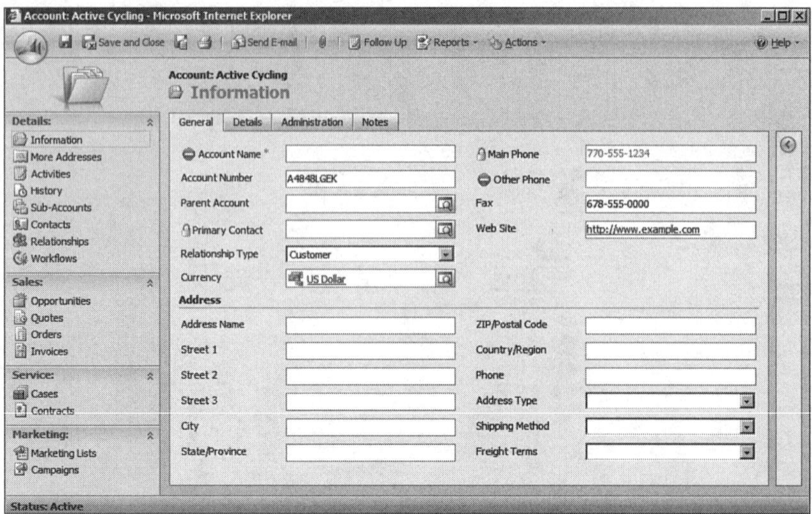

FIGURE 26.4 c360 Microsoft Dynamics CRM with Field Level Security implemented.

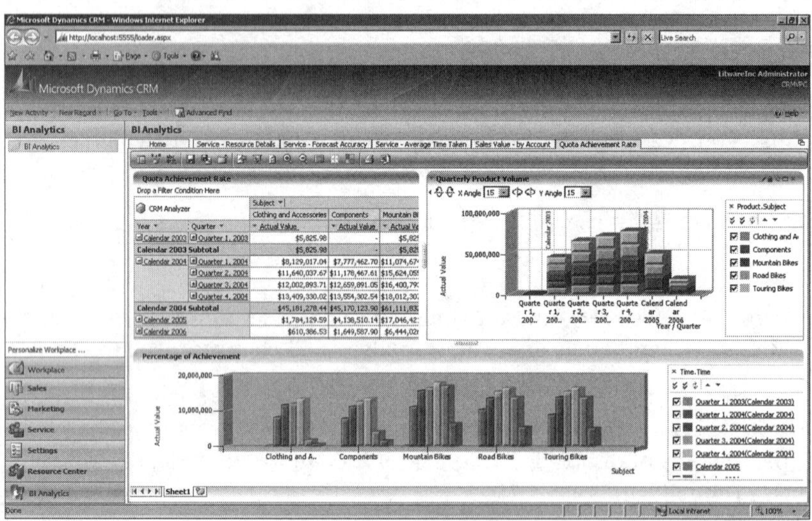

FIGURE 26.5 c360 BI Analytics Interface.

- **Group Calendar**—An enhancement that allows organizations to view calendars of other Users in their organization.

If you are an existing c360 customer, be sure to check with c360 prior to upgrading, as c360 products purchased for Microsoft Dynamics CRM 3.0 may be incompatible with Microsoft Dynamics CRM 4.0.

For more information about c360, visit www.c360.com.

CRM Scanning (IntellaScan)

IntellaScan is a scanning solution that enables you to scan your documents and then upload them directly to any Microsoft Dynamics CRM record in Portable Document Format (PDF). Intellascan is produced by Intellagent Solutions, which is a Microsoft Certified Partner.

For more information about IntellaScan and Intellagent Solutions, visit www.intellagentsolutions.com.

SMS Add-On (withCRM)

withCRM offers an integration component known as SMSforCRM that integrates with Microsoft Dynamics CRM, providing high-volume integrated Simple Messaging Service (SMS) messaging capabilities in several editions. The SMSforCRM can service up to 191 countries and features the following:

- Bulk SMS campaigns with Microsoft Dynamics CRM Marketing Lists
- Built-in gateway server to queue and deliver messages
- Support for multiple delivery attempts if the gateway is down, as well as support for delivery acknowledgments and notifications
- Capability for Users to see your company as the sender
- Capability to check the status of a message delivered from Microsoft Dynamics CRM

For more information about withCRM, visit www.withCRM.com.

Field Service Management (Astea)

For companies that specialize in field service management, Astea offers a solution called FieldCentrix. Astea is a Microsoft Gold Certified Partner and focuses on extending Microsoft Dynamics CRM to encompass supply chain and logistics functionality. FieldCentrix features the following:

- Contract management service histories
- Graphical scheduling and dispatch
- Work-order activity management
- Customer self-service portal
- Time, parts, and expense tracking

For more information about FieldCentrix, visit www.astea.com.

Business Intelligence (Strategy Companion)

Strategy Companion offers Business Intelligence for Microsoft Dynamics CRM in a product called BI Analytics. BI Analytics is a collection of 25 analytical reports that include interactive pie, column, bar, and pivot table charts. Additional functionality of BI analytics includes the following:

- Dashboard interface
- Drilldowns
- Alerts
- Visualization tools

For more information about BI Analyzer, visit www.strategycompanion.com.

Lotus Notes and GroupWise Integration (LinkPoint360)

LinkPoint360 offers solutions for Microsoft Dynamics CRM and native integration with Lotus Notes and GroupWise. The LinkPoint product for Microsoft Dynamics CRM also features the following:

- Logging of inbound and outbound e-mail and attachments in Microsoft Dynamics CRM activity history
- Recording of e-mail messages on Contact, Account, Opportunity, or Incident level
- Functionality when working with either Lotus Notes Connected or Island mode
- Functionality when working with Novel GroupWise Office, Cached, or Remote mode
- Synchronization of Microsoft Dynamics CRM calendar, contact, and task activities with Lotus Notes or Novell GroupWise

For more information about LinkPoint, visit www.linkpoint360.com.

Filtered Lookups (Stunnware)

To overcome some of the lookup limitations with lookups, Stunnware has released a tool called the Filtered Lookup for Microsoft Dynamics CRM 4.0. Originally designed as a way of showing filtered information (such as only products that are on the selected Price List for an Opportunity, rather than all products in the Product Catalog), it has been enhanced to include the following features:

- Easy to install, use, and customize
- Auto-complete functionality
- Support for multitenancy and multilanguage

The Filtered Lookup for Microsoft Dynamics CRM 4.0 tool is shown in Figure 26.6.

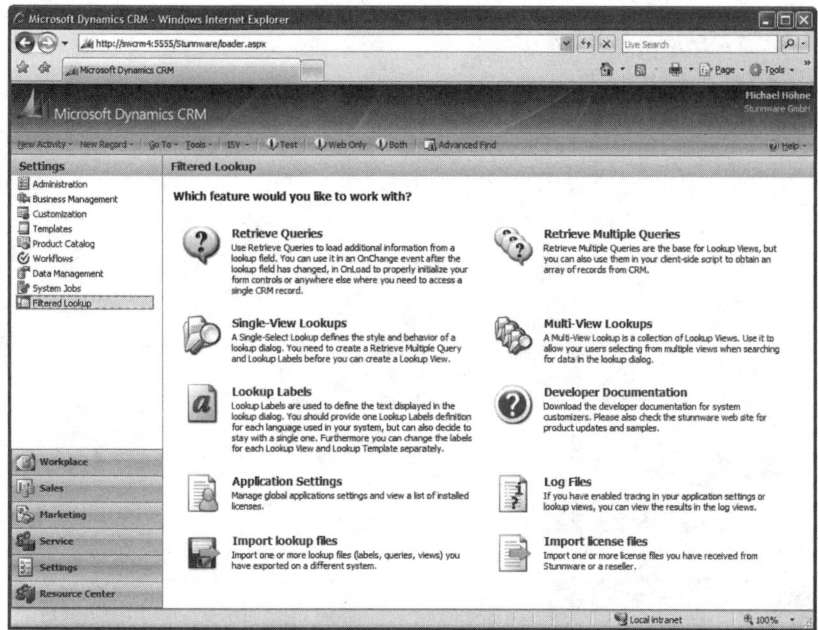

FIGURE 26.6 Stunnware's Filtered Lookup for Microsoft Dynamics CRM 4.0 tool.

For more information about Stunnware and the Filtered Lookup for Microsoft Dynamics CRM 4.0, visit www.stunnware.com/Products/FLD4/Default.htm.

Mobile Access for Windows (CWR Mobility)

CWR Mobility is a Microsoft Gold Certified Partner that delivers a full featured Microsoft Dynamics CRM client to Users of Windows mobile devices (see Figure 26.7).

Its client is completely customizable and allows Users to interact with Microsoft Dynamics CRM in real-time via their handheld devices. The client is built specifically for mobile devices and includes an intuitive and easy-to-use interface (see Figure 26.8).

Additional features of the product include:

- Rich integration with the mobile device including the capability to make phone calls from entered data and then record the call directly within CRM from the mobile device
- Create new records directly on the mobile device, with synchronization to the main CRM database
- Multilanguage support
- Multicurrency support

For more information about CWR Mobility, visit www.cwrmobility.com.

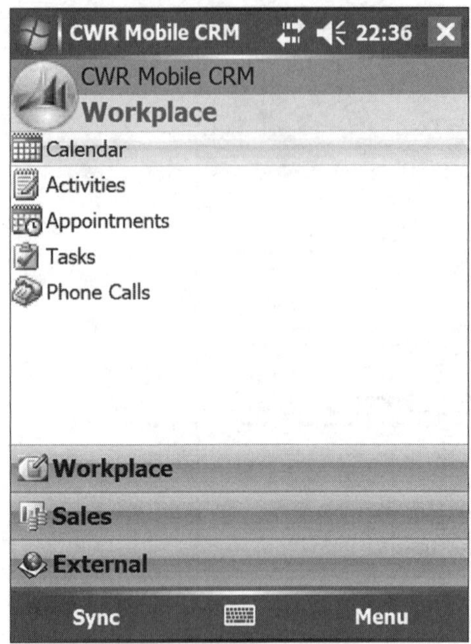

FIGURE 26.7 CWR Mobility Windows Mobile client for Microsoft Dynamics CRM 4.0.

FIGURE 26.8 Microsoft Dynamics CRM Account information on the CWR Mobility Mobile client.

Mobile Access for BlackBerry (TenDigits)

TenDigits, a Microsoft Gold Certified ISV Partner and Research In Motion (RIM) Preferred ISV Partner, provides a mobile version of Microsoft Dynamics CRM for both Windows Mobile and BlackBerry mobile devices called MobileAccess for Dynamics CRM (see Figure 26.9). MobileAccess for Dynamics CRM delivers its functionality through Event Driven Push, which updates devices instantly without User involvement.

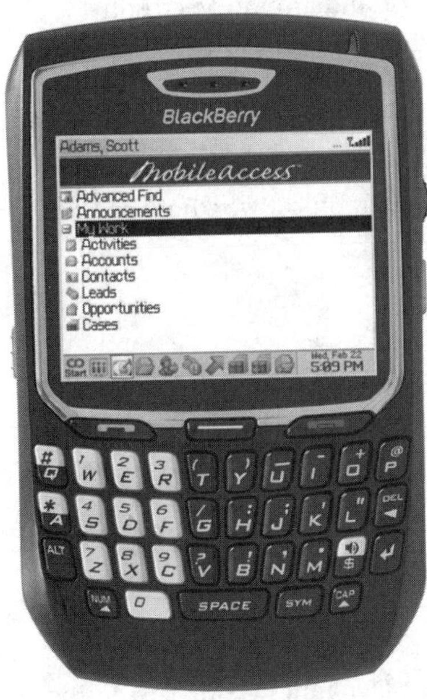

FIGURE 26.9 MobileAccess for Dynamics CRM from TenDigits.

Additional features of the product include the following:

- **Always-Available Wireless CRM**—Work anywhere with instant access to your data online and offline with full CRM functionality regardless of your location.
- **Multi-tasking, Graphical User Interface**—Navigate instantly between various records, lists, tasks, and applications without losing track of anything.
- **Strong Application Integration**—Dial phone numbers, browse websites, and compose e-mails directly from fields. Log e-mails and phone calls from your BlackBerry to account and contact history in CRM. Gain access to internal applications such as AX, GP, and SAP to find timely information relevant to your CRM records.
- **Alert Notifications**—Bring Users' attention to important events with proactive alerts for action.

- **Copy/Log to CRM**—Track handheld e-mails and phone calls using corresponding CRM activities with automatic, smart recipient linking.

For more information about TenDigits, visit www.TenDigits.com.

Companies That Provide CRM Solutions

Many companies offer services and solutions particularly for and around Microsoft Dynamics CRM. We have listed a few that offer both services and products.

Tenrox

Tenrox delivers an integrated Project Workforce Management Solution for Microsoft Dynamics CRM. This solution integrates the following via a graphical workflow engine:

- Time and expense tracking
- Cost and revenue accounting
- Workforce planning
- Project process management
- Analytics

For more information about Tenrox, visit www.tenrox.com.

SalesCentric

SalesCentric develops visual software products for Microsoft Dynamics CRM. These products are marketed via Microsoft CRM partners and provide quick visibility into your Accounts.

The key product, Relationship Carts, enables you to quickly understand the underlying basis of relationships that make up Accounts.

For more information about SalesCentric, visit www.salescentric.com.

GaleForce Solutions, Inc.

GaleForce Solutions offers a number of products for the financial services industry. Because of security and other requirements specific to the financial services industry, GaleForce Solutions has developed a suite of add-ons that provide an ideal feature set for financial services.

The product list includes the following:

- **Enhanced security**—Allows security permissions to be set at the field level and specifies which forms are visible to Users based on rules. Additionally, auditing is captured at the record and field levels, which includes the author and date of change.

- **Enhanced customer management**—Extends functionality of Mic
CRM to support the creation of custom call lists and call plans, with
call assignments and results.
- **Financial account management**—Provides real-time access to financial tra
tions by customer or account.
- **Relationship tree**—Includes an alert, deal management, and relationship view that includes a Windows-based tree structure within the CRM interface.

Webfortis, LLC

Webfortis, a Gold Certified Microsoft Partner, is a leading provider in Microsoft Dynamics CRM implementation, migration, and customization projects. It provides advanced integrated solutions such as event-management solutions and Microsoft Dynamics CRM integration with websites and disparate systems such as Accounting/ERP and other applications.

Webfortis delivers integration, migration, and custom development services, as well as the following:

- Complex data migration and integration from disparate systems
- Extension of Microsoft Dynamics CRM to customer and internal facing websites
- Online e-commerce options for Microsoft Dynamics CRM
- Custom reports, SharePoint integration, complex Workflows, Plug-Ins, and entities development

Since early versions of Microsoft Dynamics CRM, Webfortis has focused only on CRM and is a Gold Certified Microsoft Partner.

For more information about Webfortis, visit www.webfortis.com.

Other Resources

This section includes resources for Microsoft Dynamics CRM products and solutions that are available for customization or extension by you. You are expected to have experience developing or modifying code to use most of the products listed on these sites, and they come with varying levels of support. We urge you to thoroughly review the solutions and products, and consider trying them on a development or test instance of Microsoft Dynamics CRM before you load them on a production machine.

CodePlex

Previously known as Gotdotnet, CodePlex has become the official place for Microsoft Dynamics CRM developers to post a variety of add-on solutions. These solutions are open source, which enables you to modify them for your particular needs. Although Microsoft sponsors these solutions, they usually include no warranty or support (see Figure 26.10).

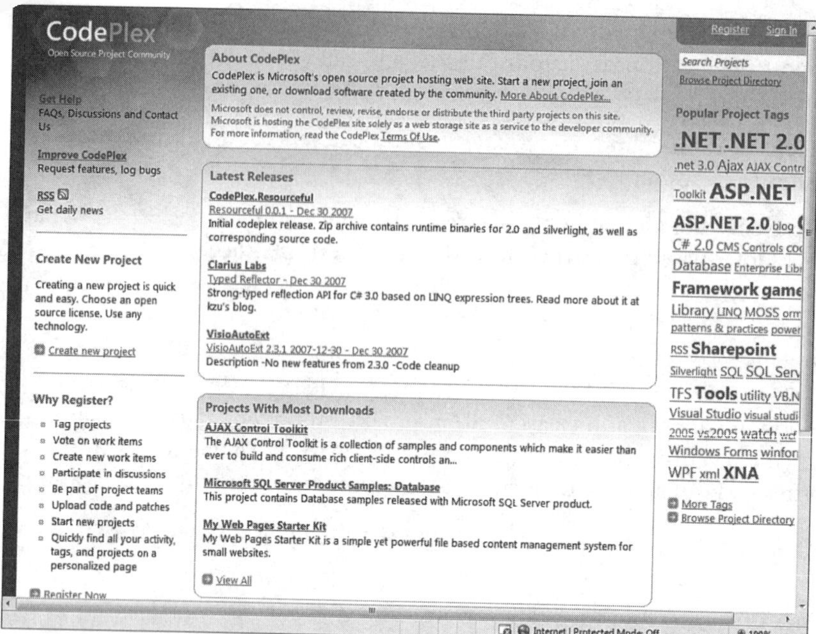

Figure 26.10 CodePlex website.

CodePlex has a number of projects that are in various states of development at any point in time, licensed under the Microsoft Permissive License (Ms-PL). To locate CRM projects on the CodePlex site, select Search the Project Directory from the top right and then add Microsoft CRM as the Search criteria. Most of the existing projects are available only for Microsoft Dynamics CRM 3.0, but look for them to be available for Microsoft Dynamics CRM 4.0 in the near future.

A few of the more popular projects for Microsoft Dynamics CRM are listed here:

- **CRM Mobile Express**—Currently available only for Microsoft Dynamics CRM 3.0, CRM Mobile Express enables Users to access features of Microsoft Dynamics CRM on their mobile device, including full sales, marketing, and customer service functionality.

- **Microsoft Dynamics Snap for Microsoft Dynamics CRM**—Snap is a Dynamics family product that extends functionality of Microsoft Dynamics CRM to Microsoft Office products.

- **Microsoft Dynamics CRM Analytics Foundation**—This provides a business intelligence solution that includes an Online Analytical Processing (OLAP) cube built on the Microsoft Dynamics CRM 3.0 schema. It leverages technologies such as SQL Server, SharePoint, Business Scorecard Manager, and Excel (each of which is available separately). Figure 26.11 shows a Service dashboard built on SharePoint.

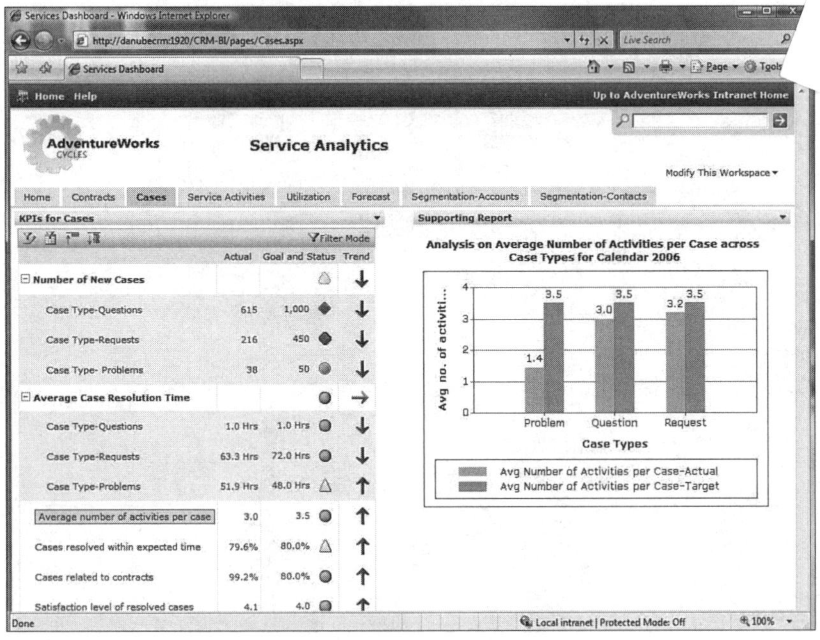

FIGURE 26.11 CRM Analytics.

- **LinqtoCRM**—LinqtoCRM provides a custom LINQ query provider for Microsoft Dynamics CRM.

For more information about CodePlex, visit www.codeplex.com.

The Code Project

The Code Project is an open source website that includes both projects and programming articles (see Figure 26.12).

To locate articles and solutions for Microsoft Dynamics, enter "Microsoft CRM" or "MS CRM" in the Search For text box and click Search. Multiple articles, samples, and products can be extended.

A few of the projects and articles include these:

- Microsoft CRM 3.0 file attachment to any CRM entity
- Microsoft Office SharePoint Server 2007 (MOSS) and Microsoft CRM Integration options
- Creation of a CRM Vista Sidebar Gadget

For more information about the Code Project, visit www.codeproject.com.

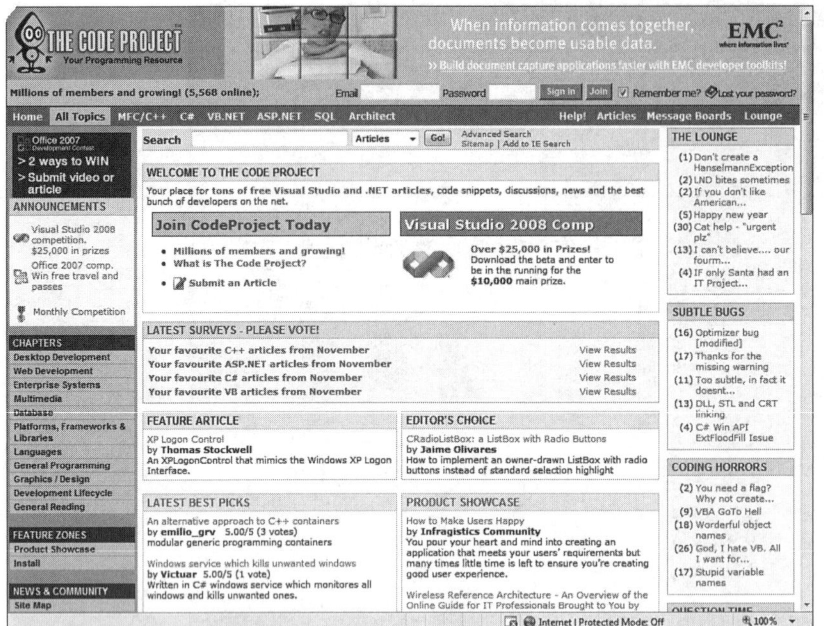

FIGURE 26.12 The Code Project website.

MicrosoftDynamicsAddons.com

MicrosoftDynamicsAddons.com is a leading online directory of Add-on products for the Dynamics family. Add-on vendors upload their Add-ons by Dynamics product and include product information such as availability, pricing, and contact information. Users are able to browse the site by product and category, as well as search by keyword, language, country, and CRM version. Although not affiliated with Microsoft, the community at large helps support the site by posting, rating products, and leaving comments about individual Add-ons (see Figure 26.13).

The site categories include:

- Manufacturing
- Professional Services
- Distribution
- Web/Integration
- Financial
- Reporting
- Other

For more information about MicrosoftDynamicsAddons.com, visit www.microsoftdynamicsaddons.com.

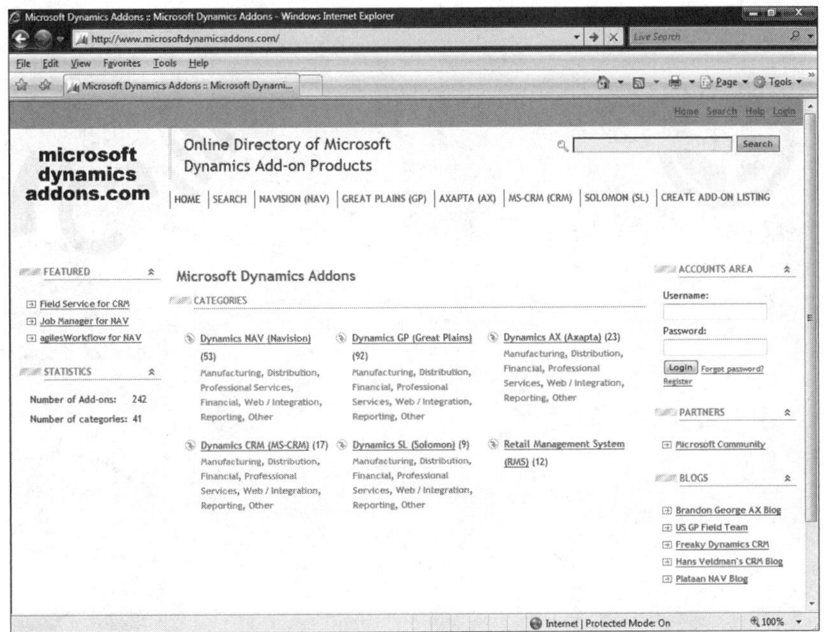

FIGURE 26.13 MicrosoftDynamicsAddons.com website.

Summary

Many products are available for Microsoft Dynamics CRM to extend its functionality. Be sure to check with Microsoft or your implementation partner before purchasing the products listed here, however, because the solution you need might already be available within Microsoft Dynamics CRM, just not fully understood.

Additionally, when possible, work with the companies and products to see if they offer a trial download of their product. If they do, implement the trial before you purchase, to see if it both meets your needs and scales to your organization.

CHAPTER 27

Other Microsoft Dynamics Products

IN THIS CHAPTER

- Great Plains (GP)
- Navision (NAV)
- Solomon (SL)
- Axapta (AX)
- Others
- Licensing

As mentioned in the beginning of the book, the Dynamics family now includes many enterprise applications besides Microsoft Dynamics CRM. Although these are currently somewhat disparate in nature, the future path points to a product that will have the benefits of each contained in one. Combine that with the power of SharePoint, and the options are endless.

It is important to remember that Microsoft Dynamics CRM includes some basic sales order accounting functionality, such as quoting, orders, and invoicing, but it is by no means a complete accounting system. Users implementing Microsoft Dynamics CRM should seriously consider which ERP and accounting package they want to use when considering the accounting features of quoting, orders, and invoicing. Because you can extend Microsoft Dynamics CRM so easily, you can consider virtually any backend system for business financials, provided that you're willing to both make and support the extensions to your systems. We generally recommend that customers consider a Dynamics solution for their backend system when considering Microsoft Dynamics CRM. This means that the customer should consider what the Dynamics family can offer its organization, both now and in the future. With the addition of Business Ready Licensing (BRL) that provides different options when obtaining products in the Dynamics family, significant cost reductions can be realized when considering an enterprise solution. Refer to Licensing at the end of this chapter for more information on BRL.

Although the applications listed in this chapter are sold separately, they all have a common backend and similar hardware and software requirements. Additionally, they are not third-party applications, and they offer full support from both Microsoft and its partners. Thus, when you commit to any of the applications in the Dynamics family, the incremental cost from a hardware, software, and support/customization standpoint are minimal because you're already supporting one of Dynamics products. Additionally, when you're comparing Dynamics with other third-party (non-Microsoft) applications, seriously consider what kind of support you will receive when you have problems. Frequently, customers who have switched to Dynamics GP or SL, for example, from other accounting packages complain that when they had a problem with their previous accounting packages, they had to call their original manufacturer and their support partner (if one existed), and finally, they were recommended to contact Microsoft because the manufacturer was blaming system incompatibilities. (Of course, it ran fine for two years before suddenly not working.) With a Dynamics solution, customers can be assured that one source can deliver the fix, and they won't likely suffer the runaround of blame on the system, then the application, and then back again.

As for the future, Microsoft has made it clear that it is striving toward a common application referred to as Dynamics. What this means exactly remains to be seen, but all indications are that the future Dynamics product will feature a SQL Server database on a SharePoint server with any or all of the features from any of the applications discussed in this chapter. The power and reliability of SQL Server; with the versioning, workflow, and searching of SharePoint; and any business functionality desired from the various ERP applications in the Dynamics family will truly be a marvel of modern technology.

Great Plains (GP)

Great Plains (GP) is the recommended Microsoft accounting package for smaller to midsize organizations. Microsoft acquired GP in 2001 from Great Plains Accounting, and it has a solid foundation and User base. GP was the first Microsoft product that integrated with Microsoft Dynamics CRM 3.0, and Microsoft has plans to integrate Microsoft Dynamics CRM 4.0 with the latest version of GP.

Figure 27.1 shows the GP application.

Some of the features of GP include the following:

- A familiar User interface
- Integration with SharePoint Server 2007
- Similar technology as other products in the Dynamics family, including Microsoft Office, Microsoft Internet Explorer, and SQL Server
- Workflow integration for business process management
- Flexible searching and reporting options
- Advanced business intelligence (BI)

GP works well for small to midsize organizations with general accounting needs that are looking for a complete financial package.

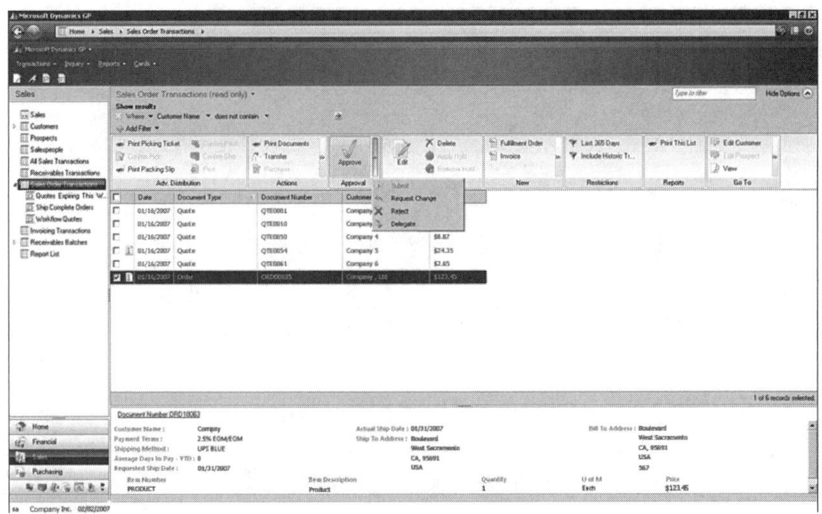

FIGURE 27.1 GP.

Navision (NAV)

At around the same time Microsoft purchased GP, it also acquired *Navision* (NAV). NAV is marketed similarly as GP, but it includes the capability to specialize based on industry or other specific needs. Its rich and easily customizable platform supports modifications from customers, partners, and industry-specific solutions. A multitude of industry-specific solutions surround NAV; just a few come from the retail, food and beverage, construction, manufacturing, and distribution industries.

Figure 27.2 shows the NAV application.

Some of the features of NAV include the following:

- A familiar User interface
- Similar technology as other products in the Dynamics family, including Microsoft Office, Microsoft Internet Explorer, and SQL Server
- Integration with multisite and international organizations
- Support for customization and add-ins
- Rich and powerful facilities for manufacturing, distribution, and sales and marketing

NAV is an ideal accounting package for small to midsize organizations with specific accounting or business process needs that are looking for a complete financial package.

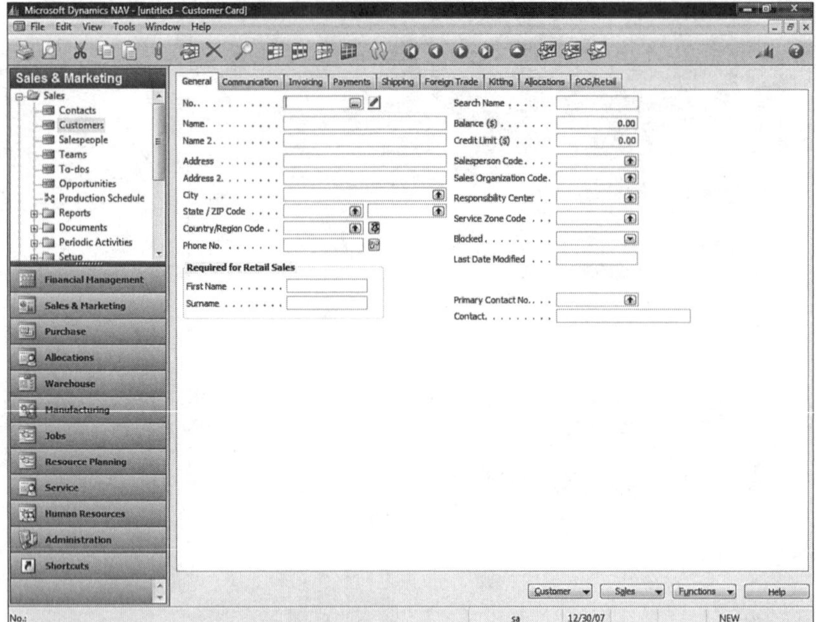

FIGURE 27.2 NAV.

Solomon (SL)

Similar in nature to GP, *Solomon* (SL) offers a complete accounting solution for small to midsize organizations. The main difference between SL and GP is that SL is more project-based and serves industries such as professional services, construction, and field operations with rich estimation and management tools.

Figure 27.3 shows the SL application.

Some of the features of SL include the following:

- A familiar User interface
- Similar technology as other products in the Dynamics family, including Microsoft Office, Microsoft Internet Explorer, and SQL Server
- Integration options with Microsoft Project 2003 or 2007, MapPoint, and RMS

SL works well for small to midsize organizations with project-based accounting or business process needs that are looking for a complete financial package.

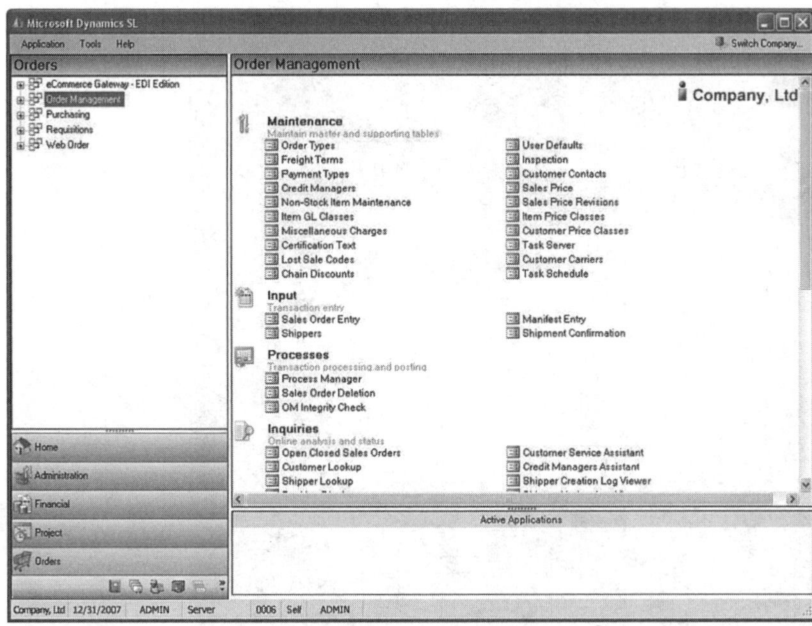

FIGURE 27.3 SL.

Axapta (AX)

Microsoft Axapta (AX) was originally developed in Denmark and is an ideal solution for midsize and larger organizations. Similar to NAV, it is designed and marketed by Microsoft as a comprehensive business-management package that can service large international organizations.

Figure 27.4 shows the AX application.

Some of the features of AX include the following:

- A familiar User interface
- Similar technology as other products in the Dynamics family, including Microsoft Office, Microsoft Internet Explorer, and SQL Server
- Integration with multisite and international organizations
- Support for customization and add-ins
- Rich and powerful facilities for manufacturing, distribution, and sales and marketing

AX is suited to midsize to large organizations with specific accounting or business process needs that are looking for a complete financial package.

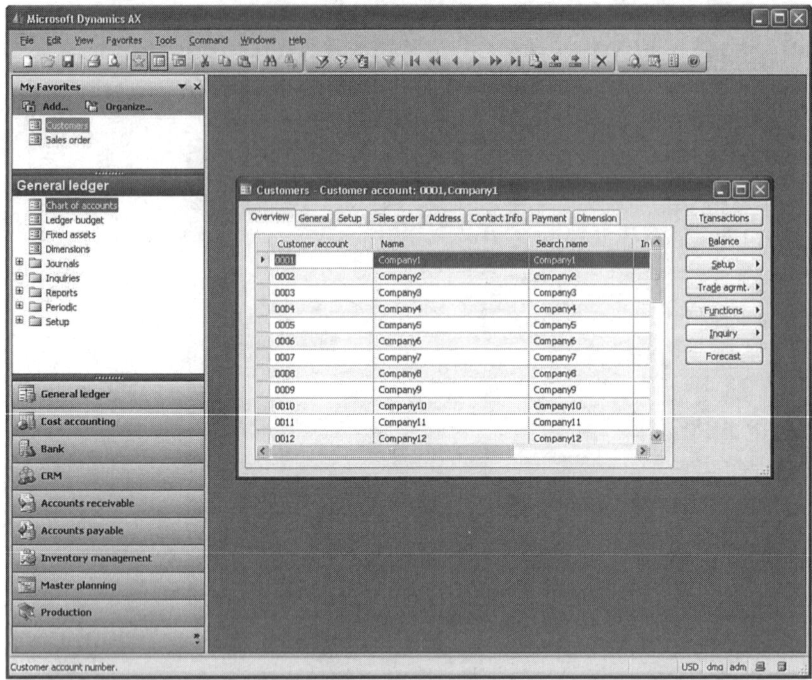

FIGURE 27.4 AX.

Others

In addition to the products previously mentioned (AX, NAV, SL, and GP), the Dynamics family includes other products that service a number of areas. Although complete integration among any of these products is currently still in the planning stage, customers who are interested in one or more of these solutions can take comfort in Microsoft's intent to deliver support and functionality across the entire Dynamics family.

The Dynamics family includes these additional products:

- **Point of Sale (POS)**—Point of Sale is specifically designed for small retail operations, generally limited to single stores. It includes Microsoft Office Accounting Professional 2007 for point of sale and financial management.
- **Retail Management System (RMS)**—Similar in nature to POS, RMS is designed for both small and midsize retailers that need a point-of-sale solution and is not limited to a single location. It has integration components for both GP and NAV, and it provides powerful centralized reporting and control.
- **Snap**—Featured by Microsoft as a "new breed of application called Office Business Applications (OBAs)," Snap extends Dynamics functionality from your Dynamics application to your Office applications. Snap examples include search capabilities

from CRM or AX into Outlook; data lookup from CRM or AX into Word, Excel, or Outlook; and report generation from CRM or AX into Excel.

- **Forecaster**—Designed to work with not just Dynamics accounting packages, Forecaster gives Users more control over their finances and costs by providing tools for budgeting and planning.
- **FRx**—FRx is a reporting tool that enables you to build customized financial management reports. Using FRx, you can view individual Dynamics transactions that comprise your financial statements.
- **Microsoft Office Accounting Professional**—Designed for very small organizations (less than 25), Microsoft Office Accounting Professional has full-featured financial management with the familiarity of Microsoft Office.
- **Microsoft Small Business Financials**—Designed for businesses that have outgrown either Microsoft Office Accounting Professional or similar packages (such as QuickBooks), Microsoft Small Business Financials includes a full suite of utilities, such as financial management, distribution, payroll, and inventory management.

Licensing

Licensing requirements vary depending on which Dynamics product you're considering. However, Microsoft announced a new licensing model in mid-2006 called Business Ready Licensing (BRL). BRL is offered for Microsoft Dynamics GP, Microsoft Dynamics AX, Microsoft Dynamics NAV, and Microsoft Dynamics SL in three different manners:

- Microsoft Dynamics Business Essentials
- Microsoft Dynamics Advanced Management
- Microsoft Dynamics Advanced Management Enterprise

The advantage to BRL licensing is that Users pay for licensing on a per-User basis rather than on a per-module basis. This gives Users full access to every module in the system.

For more and current information related to licensing Dynamics products, visit the Microsoft licensing web page at www.microsoft.com/dynamics/purchase/editionsandlicensing.mspx.

NOTE

Due to the complexity and frequent changes to the Microsoft licensing program, we recommend contacting a Microsoft Dynamics Partner to help you find the right license program for your needs. Microsoft Dynamics Partners can be found at www.microsoft.com/dynamics/solutionfinder.mspxp.

Summary

The Microsoft Dynamics family holds a number of powerful and feature-rich applications that can combine to deliver a winning solution for almost any organization.

Selecting the right system for your organization should be a thoughtful process, and we urge you to consider seeking advice from Microsoft Certified Partners who specialize in the packages you're considering.

APPENDIX

Default Values for Status and Status Reason Attributes

Use this list to determine whether any Status Reason values need to be customized and to identify default values needed for your organization. Status values are not customizable.

This list is also useful for planning whether workflow rules that need to be created as records are moved from one status to another, or when a particular Status Reason is defined.

In the Status Reason column, items in bold are default values.

Entity (Schema Name)	StateCode	Status (StateCodeName)	StatusCode	Status Reason (StatusCodeName)
Account				
(account)	0	Active	1	**Active**
	1	Inactive	2	**Inactive**
Activity				
(activitypointer)	0	Open	1	**Open**
	1	Completed	2	**Completed**
	2	Canceled	3	**Canceled**
	3	Scheduled	4	**Scheduled**
Appointment				
(appointment)	0	Open	1	**Free**
			2	Tentative
	1	Completed	3	**Completed**
	2	Canceled	4	**Canceled**
	3	Scheduled	5	**Busy**
			6	Out of Office

Entity (Schema Name)	StateCode	Status (StateCodeName)	StatusCode	Status Reason (StatusCodeName)
Article				
(kbarticle)	1	Draft	1	**Draft**
	2	Unapproved	2	**Unapproved**
	3	Published	3	**Published**
Campaign*				
(campaign)	0	Active	0	**Proposed**
			1	Ready To Launch
			2	Launched
			3	Completed
			4	Canceled
			5	Suspended
Campaign				
(campaignactivity)	0	Open	0	In Progress
			1	**Proposed**
			4	Pending
			5	System Aborted
			6	Completed
	1	Closed	2	**Closed**
	2	Canceled	3	**Canceled**
Campaign Response				
(campaignresponse)	0	Open	1	**Open**
	1	Closed	2	**Closed**
	2	Canceled	3	**Canceled**
Case				
(incident)	0	Active	1	**In Progress**
			2	On Hold
			3	Waiting for Details
			4	Researching
	1	Resolved	5	**Problem Solved**
	2	Canceled	6	**Canceled**
Case Resolution				
(incidentresolution)				
(not customizable)	0	Open	1	**Open**
	1	Completed	2	**Closed**
	2	Canceled	3	**Canceled**
Contact				
(contact)	0	Active	1	**Active**
	1	Inactive	2	**Inactive**

Entity (Schema Name)	StateCode	Status (StateCodeName)	StatusCode	Status Reason (StatusCodeName)
Contract (contract)	0	Draft	1	**Draft**
	1	Invoiced	2	**Invoiced**
	2	Active	3	**Active**
	3	On Hold	4	**On Hold**
	4	Canceled	5	**Canceled**
	5	Expired	6	**Expired**
Contract Line (contractdetail)	0	Existing	1	**New**
	1	Renewed	2	**Renewed**
	2	Canceled	3	**Canceled**
	3	Expired	4	**Expired**
Discount (discounttype)	0	Active	100001	**Active**
	1	Inactive	100002	**Inactive**
E-mail (email)	0	Open	1	**Draft**
	1	Completed	2	**Completed**
			3	Sent
			4	Received
	2	Canceled	5	**Canceled**
Fax (fax)	0	Open	1	**Open**
	1	Completed	2	**Completed**
			3	Sent
			4	Received
	2	Canceled	5	**Canceled**
Invoice (invoice)	0	Active	1	**New**
			2	Partially Shipped
			4	Billed
			5	Booked (applies to services)
			6	Installed (applies to services)
	1	Closed (deprecated)	3	**Canceled (deprecated)**
			7	Paid in Full (deprecated)
	2	Paid	100001	**Complete**
			100002	Partial
	3	Canceled	100003	**Canceled**

Entity (Schema Name)	StateCode	Status (StateCodeName)	StatusCode	Status Reason (StatusCodeName)
Lead				
(`lead`)	0	Open	1	**New**
			2	Contacted
	1	Qualified	3	**Qualified**
	2	Disqualified	4	**Lost**
			5	Cannot Contact
			6	No Longer Interested
			7	Canceled
Letter				
(`letter`)	0	Open	1	Open
			2	**Draft**
	1	Completed	3	Received
			4	**Sent**
	2	Canceled	5	**Canceled**
Marketing List				
(`list`)	0	Active	0	**Active**
	1	Inactive	1	**Inactive**
Opportunity				
(`opportunity`)	0	Open	1	**In Progress**
			2	On Hold
	1	Won	3	**Won**
	2	Lost	4	**Canceled**
			5	Out-Sold
Order				
(`salesorder`)	0	Active	1	**New**
			2	Pending
	1	Submitted	3	**In Progress**
	2	Canceled	4	**No Money**
	3	Fulfilled	100001	**Complete**
			100002	Partial
	4	Invoiced	100003	**Invoiced**
Phone Call				
(`phonecall`)	0	Open	1	**Open**
	1	Completed	2	**Sent**
			4	Received
	2	Canceled	3	**Canceled**
Product				
(`product`)	0	Active	1	**Active**
	1	Inactive	2	**Inactive**

Entity (Schema Name)	StateCode	Status (StateCodeName)	StatusCode	Status Reason (StatusCodeName)
Quote				
(`quote`)	0	Draft	1	**In Progress**
	1	Active	2	**In Progress**
			3	Open
	2	Won	4	**Won**
	3	Closed	5	Lost
			6	Canceled
			7	**Revised**
Service Activity				
(`serviceappointment`)	0	Open	1	**Requested**
			2	Tentative
	1	Closed	8	**Completed**
	2	Canceled	9	**Canceled**
			10	No Show
	3	Scheduled	3	**Pending**
			4	Reserved
			6	In Progress
			7	Arrived
Task				
(`task`)	0	Open	2	**Not Started**
			3	In Progress
			4	Waiting on Someone Else
			7	Deferred
	1	Completed	5	**Completed**
	2	Canceled	6	**Canceled**

**To set workflow rules for campaigns, use the Status Reason attribute rather than the Status attribute.*

A

B

C

How can we make this index more useful? Email us at indexes@samspublishing.com

How can we make this index more useful? Email us at indexes@samspublishing.com

D

F

G

J-K

L

M

N

O

P

Q

R

S

How can we make this index more useful? Email us at indexes@samspublishing.com

W-X-Y-Z